SEVENTH
EDITION

WORLD HISTORY

VOLUME II: SINCE 1500

WILLIAM J. DUIKER
The Pennsylvania State University

JACKSON J. SPIELVOGEL
The Pennsylvania State University

WADSWORTH
CENGAGE Learning™

Australia • Brazil • Japan • Korea • Mexico • Singapore • Spain • United Kingdom • United States

**World History, Seventh Edition,
Volume II: Since 1500**
William J. Duiker and Jackson J. Spielvogel

Senior Publisher: Suzanne Jeans

Acquisitions Editor: Brooke Barbier

Senior Development Editor:
  Margaret McAndrew Beasley

Assistant Editor: Lauren Floyd

Editorial Assistant: Katie Coaster

Managing Media Editor: Lisa Ciccolo

Media Editor: Kate MacLean

Marketing Manager: Cynthia Barnes

Marketing Coordinator: Lorreen Towle

Marketing Communications Manager:
  Glenn McGibbon

Content Project Manager: Anne Finley

Senior Art Director: Cate Rickard Barr

Production Technology Analyst: Jeff Joubert

Manufacturing Planner: Sandee Milewski

Rights Acquisition Specialist:
  Shalice Shah-Caldwell

Production Service: John Orr Book Services

Text Designer: Shawn Girsberger

Cover Designer: Walter Kopec

Cover Image: Rivera, Diego (1886–1957) © ARS,
  NY. The Well of Toledo (La fuente de Toledo).
  Location: Fundacion Dolores Olmedo,
  Mexico City, D.F., Mexico. Photo Credit:
  Schalkwijk/Art Resource, NY

Compositor: Cenveo Publisher Services

For product information and technology assistance, contact us at
Cengage Learning Customer & Sales Support, 1-800-354-9706

For permission to use material from this text or product,
submit all requests online at **www.cengage.com/permissions**.
Further permissions questions can be emailed to
permissionrequest@cengage.com.

Library of Congress Control Number: 2011932745

ISBN-13: 978-1-111-83167-7
ISBN-10: 1-111-83167-X

Wadsworth
20 Channel Center Street
Boston, MA 02210
USA

Cengage Learning is a leading provider of customized learning solutions with office locations around the globe, including Singapore, the United Kingdom, Australia, Mexico, Brazil and Japan. Locate your local office at **international.cengage.com/region**.

Cengage Learning products are represented in Canada by Nelson Education, Ltd.

For your course and learning solutions, visit **www.cengage.com**.

Purchase any of our products at your local college store or at our preferred online store **www.cengagebrain.com**.

Instructors: Please visit **login.cengage.com** and log in to access instructor-specific resources.

Printed in the United States of America
1 2 3 4 5 6 7 15 14 13 12 11

ABOUT THE AUTHORS

WILLIAM J. DUIKER is liberal arts professor emeritus of East Asian studies at The Pennsylvania State University. A former U.S. diplomat with service in Taiwan, South Vietnam, and Washington, D.C., he received his doctorate in Far Eastern history from Georgetown University in 1968, where his dissertation dealt with the Chinese educator and reformer Cai Yuanpei. At Penn State, he has written widely on the history of Vietnam and modern China, including the widely acclaimed *Communist Road to Power in Vietnam* (revised edition, Westview Press, 1996), which was selected for a Choice Outstanding Academic Book Award in 1982–1983 and 1996–1997. Other recent books are *China and Vietnam: The Roots of Conflict* (Berkeley, 1987), *Sacred War: Nationalism and Revolution in a Divided Vietnam* (McGraw-Hill, 1995), and *Ho Chi Minh* (Hyperion, 2000), which was nominated for a Pulitzer Prize in 2001. Although his research specialization is in the field of nationalism and Asian revolutions, his intellectual interests are considerably more diverse. He has traveled widely and has taught courses on the history of communism and non-Western civilizations at Penn State, where he was awarded a Faculty Scholar Medal for Outstanding Achievement in the spring of 1996.

TO YVONNE,
FOR ADDING SPARKLE TO THIS BOOK AND TO MY LIFE
W.J.D.

JACKSON J. SPIELVOGEL is associate professor emeritus of history at The Pennsylvania State University. He received his Ph.D. from The Ohio State University, where he specialized in Reformation history under Harold J. Grimm. His articles and reviews have appeared in such journals as *Moreana, Journal of General Education, Catholic Historical Review, Archiv für Reformationsgeschichte,* and *American Historical Review.* He has also contributed chapters or articles to *The Social History of the Reformation, The Holy Roman Empire: A Dictionary Handbook, Simon Wiesenthal Center Annual of Holocaust Studies,* and *Utopian Studies.* His work has been supported by fellowships from the Fulbright Foundation and the Foundation for Reformation Research. At Penn State, he helped inaugurate the Western civilization course as well as a popular course on Nazi Germany. His book *Hitler and Nazi Germany* was published in 1987 (sixth edition, 2010). He is the author of *Western Civilization,* published in 1991 (eighth edition, 2012). Professor Spielvogel has won five major university-wide teaching awards. During the year 1988–1989, he held the Penn State Teaching Fellowship, the university's most prestigious teaching award. In 1996, he won the Dean Arthur Ray Warnock Award for Outstanding Faculty Member and in 2000 received the Schreyer Honors College Excellence in Teaching Award.

TO DIANE,
WHOSE LOVE AND SUPPORT MADE IT ALL POSSIBLE
J.J.S.

BRIEF CONTENTS

DETAILED CONTENTS

MAPS

FEATURES

DOCUMENTS

FOR SEVERAL MILLION YEARS after primates first appeared on the surface of the earth, human beings lived in small communities, seeking to survive by hunting, fishing, and foraging in a frequently hostile environment. Then suddenly, in the space of a few thousand years, there was an abrupt change of direction as humans in a few widely scattered areas of the globe began to master the art of cultivating food crops. As food production increased, the population in those areas rose correspondingly, and people began to congregate in larger communities. Governments were formed to provide protection and other needed services to the local population. Cities appeared and became the focal point of cultural and religious development. Historians refer to this process as the beginnings of civilization.

For generations, historians in Europe and the United States pointed to the rise of such civilizations as marking the origins of the modern world. Courses on Western civilization conventionally began with a chapter or two on the emergence of advanced societies in Egypt and Mesopotamia and then proceeded to ancient Greece and the Roman Empire. From Greece and Rome, the road led directly to the rise of modern civilization in the West.

There is nothing inherently wrong with this approach. Important aspects of our world today can indeed be traced back to these early civilizations, and all human beings the world over owe a considerable debt to their achievements. But all too often this interpretation has been used to imply that the course of civilization has been linear, leading directly from the emergence of agricultural societies in ancient Mesopotamia to the rise of advanced industrial societies in Europe and North America. Until recently, most courses on world history taught in the United States routinely focused almost exclusively on the rise of the West, with only a passing glance at other parts of the world, such as Africa, India, and East Asia. The contributions made by those societies to the culture and technology of our own time were often passed over in silence.

Two major reasons have been advanced to justify this approach. Some people have argued that it is more important that young minds understand the roots of their own heritage than that of peoples elsewhere in the world. In many cases, however, the motivation for this Eurocentric approach has been the belief that since the time of Socrates and Aristotle, Western civilization has been the main driving force in the evolution of human society.

Such an interpretation, however, represents a serious distortion of the process. During most of the course of human history, the most advanced civilizations have been in East Asia or the Middle East, not in the West. A relatively brief period of European dominance culminated with the era of imperialism in the late nineteenth century, when the political, military, and economic power of the advanced nations of the West spanned the globe. During recent generations, however, that dominance has gradually eroded, partly as a result of changes taking place in Western societies and partly because new centers of development are emerging elsewhere on the globe—notably in Asia, with the growing economic strength of China and India and many of their neighbors.

World history, then, has been a complex process in which many branches of the human community have played an active part, and the dominance of any one area of the world has been a temporary rather than a permanent phenomenon. It will be our purpose in this book to present a balanced picture of this story, with all respect for the richness and diversity of the tapestry of the human experience. Due attention must be paid to the rise of the West, of course, since that has been the most dominant aspect of world history in recent centuries. But the contributions made by other peoples must be given adequate consideration as well, not only in the period prior to 1500, when the major centers of civilization were located in Asia, but also in our own day, where a multipolar picture of development is clearly beginning to emerge.

Anyone who wishes to teach or write about world history must decide whether to present the topic as an integrated whole or as a collection of different cultures. The world that we live in today, of course, is in many respects an interdependent one in terms of economics as well as culture and communications, a reality that is often expressed by the phrase "global village." The convergence of peoples across the surface of the earth into an integrated world system began in early times and intensified after the rise of capitalism in the early modern era. In recognition of this trend, historians trained in global history, as well as instructors in the growing number of world history courses, have now begun to speak and write of a "global approach" that gives less attention to the study of individual civilizations and focuses instead on the "big picture" or, as the world historian Fernand Braudel termed it, interpreting world history as a river with no banks.

On the whole, this development is to be welcomed as a means of bringing the common elements of the evolution of human society to our attention. But this approach also involves two problems. For the vast majority of their time on earth, human beings have lived in partial or virtually total isolation from each other. Differences in climate, location, and geographic features have created human societies very different from each other in culture and historical experience. Only in relatively recent times (the commonly accepted date has long been the beginning of the age of European exploration at the end of the fifteenth century, but some would now push it back to the era of the Mongol Empire or even earlier) have cultural interchanges begun to create a common "world system," in which events taking place in one part of the world are rapidly transmitted throughout the globe, often with momentous consequences. In recent generations, of course, the process of global interdependence has been proceeding even more rapidly. Nevertheless, even now the process is by no means complete, as ethnic and regional differences continue to exist and to shape the course of world history. The tenacity of these differences and sensitivities is reflected not only in the rise of internecine conflicts in such divergent areas as Africa, India, and eastern Europe but also in the emergence in recent years of such regional organizations as the African Union, the Association for the Southeast Asian Nations, and the European Union.

The second problem is a practical one. College students today often are not well informed about the distinctive character of civilizations such as China and India and, without sufficient exposure to the historical evolution of such societies, will assume all too readily that the peoples in these countries have had historical experiences similar to ours and will respond to various stimuli in a similar fashion to those living in western Europe or the United States. If it is a mistake to ignore those forces that link us together, it is equally a mistake to underestimate those factors that continue to divide us and to differentiate us into a world of diverse peoples.

Our response to this challenge has been to adopt a global approach to world history while at the same time attempting to do justice to the distinctive character and development of individual civilizations and regions of the world. The presentation of individual cultures is especially important in Parts I and II, which cover a time when it is generally agreed that the process of global integration was not yet far advanced. Later chapters adopt a more comparative and thematic approach, in deference to the greater number of connections that have been established among the world's peoples since the fifteenth and sixteenth centuries. Part V consists of a series of chapters that center on individual regions of the world while at the same time focusing on common problems related to the Cold War and the rise of global problems such as overproduction and environmental pollution.

We have sought balance in another way as well. Many textbooks tend to simplify the content of history courses by emphasizing an intellectual or political perspective or, most recently, a social perspective, often at the expense of sufficient details in a chronological framework. This approach is confusing to students whose high school social studies programs have often neglected a systematic study of world history. We have attempted to write a well-balanced work in which political, economic, social, religious, intellectual, cultural, and military history are integrated into a chronologically ordered synthesis.

Features of the Text

To enliven the past and let readers see for themselves the materials that historians use to create their pictures of the past, we have included **primary sources** (boxed documents) in each chapter that are keyed to the discussion in the text. The documents include examples of the religious, artistic, intellectual, social, economic, and political aspects of life in different societies and reveal in a vivid fashion what civilization meant to the individual men and women who shaped it by their actions. We have added questions to help guide students in analyzing the documents.

Each chapter has a **lengthy introduction and conclusion** to help maintain the continuity of the narrative and to provide a synthesis of important themes. Anecdotes in the chapter introductions dramatically convey the major theme or themes of each chapter. A **timeline** at the end of each chapter enables students to see the major developments of an era at a glance and within cross-cultural categories, while the more **detailed chronologies** reinforce the events discussed in the text. An **annotated bibliography** at the end of each chapter reviews the most recent literature on each period and also gives references to some of the older, "classic" works in each field.

Updated maps and extensive illustrations serve to deepen the reader's understanding of the text. **Map captions** are designed to enrich students' awareness of the importance of geography to history, and numerous **spot maps** enable students to see at a glance the region or subject being discussed in the text. Map captions also include a question to guide students' reading of the map. To facilitate understanding of cultural movements, illustrations of artistic works discussed in the text are placed near the discussions. **Chapter outlines and focus questions, including critical thinking questions,** at the beginning of each chapter give students a useful overview and guide them to the main subjects of each chapter. The focus questions are then repeated at the beginning of each major section in the chapter. A **glossary of important terms** (boldfaced in the text when they are introduced and defined) is provided at the back of the book to maximize reader comprehension. A **guide to pronunciation** is now provided in parentheses in the text, following the first mention of a complex name or term.

Comparative essays, keyed to the seven major themes of world history (see p. xxx), enable us to draw more concrete comparisons and contrasts across geographic, cultural, and chronological lines. **Comparative illustrations**, also keyed to the seven major themes of world history, continue to be a feature in each chapter. Both the comparative essays and the comparative illustrations conclude with focus questions to help students develop their analytical skills. We hope that the comparative essays and the comparative illustrations will assist instructors who wish to encourage their students to adopt a comparative approach to their understanding of the human experience.

The **Film & History feature**, now appearing in many chapters, presents a brief analysis of the plot as well as the historical significance, value, and accuracy of popular films. New features have been added on films such as *Gladiator*, *Marie Antoinette*, *The Young Victoria*, and *Persepolis*.

The **Opposing Viewpoints** feature, which was introduced in the sixth edition, presents a comparison of two or three primary sources to facilitate student analysis of historical documents. This feature has been expanded and now appears in almost every chapter. Focus questions are included to help students evaluate the documents.

New to This Edition

After reexamining the entire book and analyzing the comments and reviews of many colleagues who have found the book to be a useful instrument for introducing their students to world history, we have also made a number of other changes for the seventh edition.

We have continued to strengthen the global framework of the book, but not at the expense of reducing the attention assigned to individual regions of the world. New material has been added to most chapters to help students be aware of similar developments globally, including new comparative sections.

The enthusiastic response to the primary sources (boxed documents) led us to evaluate the content of each document carefully and add new documents throughout the text, including new comparative documents in the **Opposing Viewpoints** feature, which now appears in almost every chapter.

The **Suggested Reading** sections at the end of each chapter have been thoroughly updated and are organized under subheadings to make them more useful. New illustrations were added to every chapter. **Chapter Notes** have now been placed at the end of the book rather than at the end of each chapter.

A new format has been added to the end of each chapter. The **Chapter Summary** is illustrated with thumbnail images of chapter illustrations and combined with a **Chapter Timeline**. A **Chapter Review** has been added to assist students in studying the chapter. This review includes **Upon Reflection** essay questions and a list of **Key Terms** from the chapter.

Also new to the seventh edition are **historiographical subsections**, which examine how and why historians differ in their interpretation of specific topics. To keep up with the ever-growing body of historical scholarship, new or revised material has been added throughout the book on many topics (see specific notes below).

Chapter-by-Chapter Content Revisions

Chapter 1 New and revised material on early humans. New material on the following topics: gender roles in the Neolithic Age, Sargon of Akkad, democratization of the afterlife during the Middle Kingdom, the role of Kushite monarchs in Egypt, the early history of Israel, Hebrew monotheism, and Zoroastrianism. Two new historiographical subsections: "The Spread of Humans: Out of Africa or Multiregional?" and "Was There a United Kingdom of Israel?"

Chapter 2 New Opposing Viewpoints feature: "The Search for Truth." New historiographical subsection: "Who Were the Aryans?" Revised sections on Vedic religion and class and caste in India.

Chapter 3 Revised opening vignette and Map 3.1. New Opposing Viewpoints feature: "A Debate over Good and Evil." New material on the following: Shang religion, Qin politics, and cities in ancient China. New historiographical subsections: "The Shang Dynasty: China's Mother Culture?" and "Are All Hydraulic Societies Despotic?"

Chapter 4 New material on the following: the Persian Wars, Greek religion with special emphasis on the Olympic games, and the Greek impact on Roman civilization. New historiographical subsection: "The Legacy: Was Alexander Great?"

Chapter 5 New Film & History feature on *Gladiator*. New historiographical subsection: "What Caused the Fall of the Western Roman Empire?" New material on Han political, economic, and military policies. New section on "A Comparison of Rome and China." New document on Han China: "A Prescription for the Emperor."

Chapter 6 New material on the following: the Olmecs, including their use of chocolate, and Wari culture in South America. Revised chapter summary to include more comparisons with other ancient cultures. New historiographical subsections: "The Olmecs: Mother Culture or First Among Equals?" and "The Mystery of Mayan Decline."

Chapter 7 New document: "Winning Hearts and Minds in Murcia." New paragraph on the meaning of *jihad*. Expanded discussion of Arab scholarship. Revised opening vignette. New historiographical subsection: "Moorish Spain: An Era of 'Cultural Tolerance'?" New comparative illustration on medieval mapmaking.

Chapter 8 Two new documents: "Honoring the Sacred Tree God" and "The Nyanga Meet the Pygmies of Gabon." New historiographical subsection: "Africa: A Continent Without History?" New "Critical Thinking" question. Revised content on Axum, Kush, Bantu migrations, and Swahili culture. New information on the origins of agriculture in Africa.

Chapter 9 Revised chapter title and Map 9.1. New historiographical subsection: "When Did the Indians Become Hindus?" New material on early migrations to Southeast Asia and rice culture.

Chapter 10 Shortened opening section. New material on the following: civil service examinations, Tang land reforms, and the decline of noble families. Expanded discussions of women's roles and the role of the emperor and popular religion. New Opposing Viewpoints feature: "A Meeting of Two Worlds" (exchange of letters between Pope Innocent IV and the Mongols). Two new historiographical subsections: "The Mongols: A Reputation Undeserved?" and "Why Were the Voyages Abandoned?" (on the voyages of Zhenghe). New document: "Beautiful Women: The Scapegoats of Legend." New comparative illustration on "The Two Worlds of Tang China."

Chapter 11 New historiographical subsection: "Was Japan a Feudal Society?" New document: "How the Earth Was Formed."

Chapter 12 New material on the Germanic kingdoms. New section on the Iberian kingdoms. New Opposing Viewpoints feature: "Two Views of Trade and Merchants." New historiographical subsection: "What Were the Effects of the Crusades?"

Chapter 13 Clarified use of the terms *Later Roman Empire*, *Eastern Roman Empire*, and *Byzantine Empire*. New material on the following: the Byzantine capital of Constantinople as a "God-guarded city," court ritual in the Byzantine Empire, flagellants and anticlericalism, the English Peasants' Revolt of 1381, and conciliarism. New historiographical subsection: "Was There a Renaissance for Women?"

Chapter 14 Added material on Latin America from Chapter 18 including a Film & History feature on *The Mission*. New historiographical subsection: "Christopher Columbus: Hero or Villain?" Revised comparative essay on "The Columbian Exchange." New document: "The Price of Friendship" (on slavery). New material on Africa.

Chapter 15 New material on the following: religious piety on the eve of the Reformation, the impact of the Reformation on common people as seen in the Peasants' War, the Catholic Reformation, and court ritual at Versailles. New historiographical subsection: "Catholic Reformation or Counter-Reformation?" New material in the comparative illustration on Louis XIV and Kangxi.

Chapter 16 Reorganized section on the Mughals. New document: "Designing the Perfect Society" (on *Jalali's Ethics*). New historiographical subsection: "The Mughal Dynasty: A 'Gunpowder Empire'?"

Chapter 17 New material on seizure of Taiwan. New document: "Be My Brother, or I'll Bash Your Head In!" (on Japanese-Korean war). New historiographical subsection: "The Qing Economy: Ready for Takeoff?" Revised section on Korea.

Chapter 18 Moved discussion of Latin American society and the Film & History feature on *The Mission* to Chapter 14. New material on French colonization and the French monarchy on the eve of the French Revolution. New document: "British Victory in India." New Film & History feature: *Marie Antoinette*.

Chapter 19 New material on the following: Industrial Revolution in the United States, working laws, the emergence of a world economy, the role of violence in Marxism, and economic liberalism. New Film & History feature: *The Young Victoria*. Reduced material on Russia and nationalist movements in the Balkans. New historiographical subsection: "Did Industrialization Bring an Improved Standard of Living?"

Chapter 20 New material on the following: Zapata, the American Civil War, positive aspects of American society, and Octavia Hill.

Chapter 21 New comparative essay on "Imperialisms Old and New." New historiographical subsection: "Imperialism: the Balance Sheet." Revised material on Africa and traditional resistance.

Chapter 22 Revised sections on the Chinese economy, Japan's "closed country" policy, and Meiji reforms. Revised comparative essay on "Imperialism and the Global Environment." New Opposing Viewpoints feature: "The Wonders of Western Civilization: Two Views." New historiographical subsection: "What Explains Japanese Uniqueness?"

Chapter 23 New material on the following: the rush to war, the global nature of World War I, the use of tanks and airplanes, and the impact of Woodrow Wilson's rhetoric on self-determination on the colonial world. New historiographical subsection: "The Assassination of Francis Ferdinand: A 'Blank Check'?"

Chapter 24 Expanded section on Palestine between the wars. New section on the rise of nationalism in Egypt. New Opposing Viewpoints feature: "Islam in the Modern World: Two Views" (Atatürk and Iqbal). Added comparison of Latin America and Asian countries. New historiographical subsection: "Taisho Democracy: An Aberration?" New document: "A Pledge of Cooperation" (on the U.S. Good Neighbor policy).

Chapter 25 New material on the war in Asia and the Battle of Stalingrad. New section on "World War II and the European Colonies: Decolonization."

Chapter 26 Reorganized material on Dien Bien Phu and Taiwan. Revised and reduced material on denazification.

Chapter 27 New historiographical subsection: "Why Did the Soviet Union Collapse?" New document: "The Rights and Duties of Soviet Citizens." New Opposing Viewpoints feature: "Students Appeal for Democracy" (on Tiananmen Square demonstrations). Revised and updated section on China.

Chapter 28 New material on the following: France, Germany, Great Britain, Eastern Europe, Russia, the United States, Chile, Argentina, Brazil, the European Union and the euro, the West and Islam, and popular culture. New section on "Green Urban Planning," including a new comparative illustration on "Green Urbanism." New Opposing Viewpoints feature: "Islam and the West: Secularism in France."

Chapter 29 New reference to Muhammad Mossadegh. New comparative illustration on "Wealth and Poverty in the Middle East." New Film & History feature on *Persepolis*. New document: "Meeting the Challenges of Independence" (on speech of Tom Mboya). New historiographical subsection: "The Destiny of Africa: Unity or Diversity?" Updated material on the Middle East.

Chapter 30 Expanded section on Pakistan. New material on the following: Hindu-Muslim relations, caste and sexual relations, and Indian literature. New document: "A Marriage of Convenience." New document: "A Challenge for U.S. Diplomacy" (by President Zardari). New historiographical subsection: "What Is the Future of India?" Updated material on Indonesia. Revised sections on Japanese politics and society. New document: "The Emperor Is Not Divine" (on Emperor Hirohito).

Epilogue New material on global communications and new section, "The End of Excess," on the global economy and the financial crisis.

Because courses in world history at American and Canadian colleges and universities follow different chronological divisions, a one-volume comprehensive edition, a two-volume edition of this text, and a volume covering events to 1500 are being made available to fit the needs of instructors. Teaching and learning ancillaries include the following.

Instructor Resources

PowerLecture DVD with ExamView® and JoinIn® This dual platform, all-in-one multimedia resource includes the Instructor's Resource Manual; Test Bank, prepared by Robert Shannon Sumner (includes key term identification, multiple-choice, short answer, and essay questions); Microsoft® PowerPoint® slides of both lecture outlines and images and maps from the text that can be used as offered or customized by importing personal lecture slides or other material; and *JoinIn®* PowerPoint® slides with clicker content. Also included is ExamView, an easy-to-use assessment and tutorial system that allows instructors to create, deliver, and customize tests in minutes. Instructors can build tests with as many as 250 questions using up to twelve question types, and using ExamView's complete word-processing capabilities, they can enter an unlimited number of new questions or edit existing ones.

eInstructor's Resource Manual   Prepared by Richard Gianni of Purdue University Calumet, this manual has many features, including chapter outlines and summaries, lecture outlines, discussion questions for primary sources, video collections, suggested discussion and research topics, and suggested readings and resources. Available on the instructor's companion website.

WebTutor™ on Blackboard® or WebCT®   With the WebTutor's text-specific, preformatted content and total flexibility, instructors can easily create and manage their own custom course website. WebTutor's course management tool gives instructors the ability to provide virtual office hours, post syllabi, set up threaded discussions, track student progress with the quizzing material, and much more. For students, WebTutor offers real-time access to an interactive eBook and a full array of study tools, including animations and videos that bring the book's topics to life, plus chapter summaries, glossary flashcards (with audio), practice quizzes, web field trips, and web links.

CourseMate   Cengage Learning's History CourseMate brings course concepts to life with interactive learning, study tools, and exam preparation tools that support the printed textbook. Use Engagement Tracker to monitor student engagement in the course and watch student comprehension soar as your class works with the printed textbook and the textbook-specific website. An interactive eBook allows students to take notes, highlight, search, and interact with embedded media (such as quizzes, flashcards, and videos). Access to the History Resource Center, a "virtual reader," provides students with hundreds of primary sources. Learn more at www.cengage.com/coursemate.

Aplia™   This online interactive learning solution improves comprehension and outcomes by increasing student effort and engagement. Founded by a professor to enhance his own courses, Aplia provides automatically graded assignments, with detailed, immediate explanations on every question, and innovative teaching materials. Our easy-to-use system has been used by more than a million students at over 1,800 institutions. Features include "flipbook" navigation that allows students to easily scan the contents; chapter assignments, developed specifically for your textbook and customizable for your course, that are automatically graded and provide detailed responses to students; a course management system that allows you to post announcements, upload course materials, host student discussions, e-mail students, and manage your gradebook; and personalized support from a knowledgeable and friendly team. Our support team also offers assistance in customizing our assignments to your course schedule. To learn more, visit www.aplia.com.

Wadsworth World History Resource Center   Wadsworth's World History Resource Center gives your students access to a "virtual reader" with hundreds of primary sources including speeches, letters, legal documents and transcripts, poems, maps, simulations, timelines, and additional images that bring history to life, along with interactive assignable exercises. A map feature including Google Earth™ coordinates and exercises will aid in student comprehension of geography and use of maps. Students can compare the traditional textbook map with an aerial view

of the location today. It's an ideal resource for study, review, and research. In addition to this map feature, the resource center also provides blank maps for student review and testing.

CourseReader: World History   This is Cengage Learning's easy, affordable way to build your own online customizable reader. Through a partnership with Gale, *CourseReader: World History* searches thousands of primary and secondary sources, readings, and audio and video clips from multiple disciplines. Select exactly and only the material you want your students to work with. Each selection can be listened to (using the "Listen" button), to accommodate varied learning styles. Additionally, instructors can choose to add their own notes to readings to direct students' attention or ask questions about a particular passage. Each primary source is accompanied by an introduction and questions to help students understand the reading.

Student Resources

Companion Website   Prepared by Richard Gianni of Purdue University Calumet, this website provides a variety of resources to help you review for class. These study tools include a glossary, chapter summaries, fill-in-the-blank quizzes, interactive multiple-choice quizzes, essay questions, and web links.

WebTutor™ on Blackboard® or WebCT®   WebTutor™ offers real-time access to an interactive ebook and a full array of study tools, including animations and videos that bring the book's topics to life, plus chapter summaries, glossary flashcards (with audio), practice quizzes, web field trips, and web links.

CL eBook   This interactive multimedia ebook links out to rich media assets such as video and MP3 chapter summaries. Through this ebook, you can also access self-test quizzes, chapter outlines, focus questions, chronology and matching exercises, essay and critical thinking questions (for which the answers can be e-mailed to your instructor), primary source documents with critical thinking questions, and interactive (zoomable) maps. Available on iChapters.

iChapters   Save time and money by going to www.iChapters. com for choice in formats and savings and a better chance to succeed in class. iChapters.com, Cengage Learning's online store, is a single destination for more than 10,000 new textbooks, eTextbooks, eChapters, study tools, and audio supplements. You have the freedom to purchase à la carte exactly what you need when you need it. Save 50 percent on the electronic textbook, and pay as little as $1.99 for an individual eChapter.

CourseMate   The more you study, the better the results. Make the most of your study time by accessing everything you need to succeed in one place. Read your textbook, take notes, review flashcards, watch videos, download MP3s, review a pronunciation guide, and take practice quizzes—online with CourseMate. In addition you can access the History Resource Center, a "virtual reader" that provides you with hundreds of primary sources.

Aplia™ Aplia™ is an online interactive learning solution that helps you improve comprehension—and your grade—by integrating a variety of mediums and tools such as video, tutorials, practice tests, and an interactive ebook. Created by a professor to enhance his own courses, Aplia provides automatically graded assignments with detailed, immediate explanations on every question, as well as innovative teaching materials. More than a million students at over 1,800 institutions have used Aplia. Aplia™ should be purchased only when assigned by your instructor as part of your course.

CourseReader: World History This resource allows your instructor to build an affordable, online customizable reader for your course by searching thousands of primary and secondary sources, readings, and audio and video clips from multiple disciplines. Each selection can be listened to (using the "Listen" button), to accommodate different learning styles, and each primary source is accompanied by an introduction and questions to help you understand the reading.

Wadsworth World History Resource Center Wadsworth's World History Resource Center gives you access to a "virtual reader" with hundreds of primary sources including speeches, letters, legal documents and transcripts, poems, maps, simulations, timelines, and additional images that bring history to life, along with interactive assignable exercises. A map feature including Google Earth™ coordinates and exercises will aid in your comprehension of geography and use of maps. Students can compare the traditional textbook map with an aerial view of the location today. It's an ideal resource for study, review, and research. In addition to this map feature, the resource center also provides blank maps for student review and testing.

Rand McNally Historical Atlas of the World, 1e This valuable resource features more than seventy maps that portray the rich panoply of the world's history from preliterate times to the present. They show how cultures and civilization were linked and how they interacted. The maps make it clear that history is not static but rather is about change and movement across time. The maps show change by presenting the dynamics of expansion, cooperation, and conflict. This atlas includes maps that depict the world from the beginning of civilization; the political development of all major areas of the world; expanded coverage of Africa, Latin America, and the Middle East; the current Islamic world; and changes in the world's population from 1900 to 2000.

Writing for College History, 1e Prepared by Robert M. Frakes of Clarion University. This brief handbook for survey courses in American history, Western Civilization/European history, and world civilization guides students through the various types of writing assignments they will encounter in a history class. Providing examples of student writing and candid assessments of student work, this text focuses on the rules and conventions of writing for the college history course.

The History Handbook, 2e Prepared by Carol Berkin of Baruch College, City University of New York, and Betty Anderson of Boston University. This book teaches students both basic and history-specific study skills such as how to read primary sources, research historical topics, and correctly cite sources. Substantially less expensive than comparable skill-building texts, *The History Handbook* also offers tips for Internet research and evaluating online sources. Additionally, students can purchase and download the eAudio version of *The History Handbook* or any of its eighteen individual units at www.cengagebrain.com to listen to on the go.

Doing History: Research and Writing in the Digital Age, 1e Prepared by Michael J. Galgano, J. Chris Arndt, and Raymond M. Hyser of James Madison University. Whether you're starting down the path as a history major or simply looking for a straightforward and systematic guide to writing a successful paper, you'll find this text to be an indispensable handbook to historical research. This text's "soup to nuts" approach to researching and writing about history addresses every step of the process, from locating your sources and gathering information, to writing clearly and making proper use of various citation styles to avoid plagiarism. You'll also learn how to make the most of every tool available to you—especially the technology that helps you conduct research efficiently and effectively.

The Modern Researcher, 6e Prepared by Jacques Barzun and Henry F. Graff of Columbia University. This classic introduction to the techniques of research and the art of expression is used widely in history courses, but is also appropriate for writing and research methods courses in other departments. Barzun and Graff thoroughly cover every aspect of research, from the selection of a topic through the gathering, analysis, writing, revision, and publication of findings. They present the process not as a set of rules but through actual cases that put the subtleties of research in a useful context. Part One covers the principles and methods of research; Part Two covers writing, speaking, and getting one's work published.

Reader Program Cengage Learning publishes a number of readers, some containing exclusively primary sources, others a combination of primary and secondary sources, and some designed to guide students through the process of historical inquiry. Visit Cengage.com/history for a complete list of readers.

Document Exercise Workbook Prepared by Donna Van Raaphorst of Cuyahoga Community College. This collection of exercises is based around primary sources. Available in two volumes.

Custom Options

Nobody knows your students like you, so why not give them a text that is tailor-fit to their needs? Cengage Learning offers custom solutions for your course—whether it's making a small modification to *World History* to match your syllabus or combining multiple sources to create something truly unique. You can pick and choose chapters, include your own material, and add additional map exercises along with the *Rand McNally Atlas* to create a text that fits the way you teach. Ensure that your students get the most out of their textbook dollar by giving them exactly what they need. Contact your Cengage Learning representative to explore custom solutions for your course.

ACKNOWLEDGMENTS

BOTH AUTHORS GRATEFULLY acknowledge that without the generosity of many others, this project could not have been completed.

William Duiker would like to thank Kumkum Chatterjee and On-cho Ng for their helpful comments about issues related to the history of India and premodern China. His longtime colleague Cyril Griffith, now deceased, was a cherished friend and a constant source of information about modern Africa. Art Goldschmidt has been of invaluable assistance in reading several chapters of the manuscript, as well as in unraveling many of the mysteries of Middle Eastern civilization. Ian Bell, Carol Coffin, and Ruth Petzold have provided illustrations, and Dale Peterson has been an unending source of useful news items. Finally, he remains profoundly grateful to his wife, Yvonne V. Duiker, Ph.D. She has not only given her usual measure of love and support when this appeared to be an insuperable task, but she has also contributed her own time and expertise to enrich the sections on art and literature, thereby adding life and sparkle to this edition, as well as the earlier editions, of the book. To her, and to his daughters Laura and Claire, he will be forever thankful for bringing joy to his life.

Jackson Spielvogel would like to thank Art Goldschmidt, David Redles, and Christine Colin for their time and ideas. Daniel Haxall of Kutztown University provided valuable assistance with materials on postwar art, popular culture, Postmodern art and thought, and the digital age. He is especially grateful to Kathryn Spielvogel for her work as research associate. Above all, he thanks his family for their support. The gifts of love, laughter, and patience from his daughters, Jennifer and Kathryn; his sons, Eric and Christian; his daughters-in-law, Liz and Laurie; and his sons-in-law, Daniel and Eddie, were especially valuable. He also wishes to acknowledge his grandchildren, Devyn, Bryn, Drew, Elena, Sean, Emma, and Jackson, who bring great joy to his life. Diane, his wife and best friend, provided him with editorial assistance, wise counsel, and the loving support that made a project of this magnitude possible.

Thanks to Wadsworth's comprehensive review process, many historians were asked to evaluate our manuscript. We are grateful to the following for the innumerable suggestions that have greatly improved our work. Members of this edition's Editorial Review Board (asterisked) deserve our particular thanks.

Najia Aarim
  SUNY College at Fredonia

Jacob Abadi
  U.S. Air Force Academy

Henry Maurice Abramson
  Florida Atlantic University

Wayne Ackerson
  Salisbury University

Charles F. Ames Jr.
  Salem State College

Nancy Anderson
  Loyola University

J. Lee Annis
  Montgomery College

Monty Armstrong
  Cerritos High School

Gloria M. Aronson
  Normandale College

Charlotte Beahan
  Murray State University

Doris Bergen
  University of Vermont

Martin Berger
  Youngstown State University

Deborah Biffton
  University of Wisconsin—La Crosse

Charmarie Blaisdell
  Northeastern University

Brian Bonhomme
  Youngstown State University

Patricia J. Bradley
  Auburn University at Montgomery

Dewey Browder
  Austin Peay State University

Steve Bsharah
  Bakersfield College

Nancy Cade
  Pikeville College

Antonio Calabria
  University of Texas at San Antonio

Alice-Catherine Carls
  University of Tennessee—Martin

*Harry Carpenter
  Western Piedmont Community College

Yuan Ling Chao
  Middle Tennessee State University

Mark W. Chavalas
  University of Wisconsin

Hugh Clark
  Ursinus College

Joan Coffey
  Sam Houston State University

Eleanor A. Congdon
  Youngstown State University

Jason P. Coy
  College of Charleston

Edward R. Crowther
  Adams State College

John Davis
  Radford University

Ross Dunn
  San Diego State University

Lane Earn
  University of Wisconsin—Oshkosh

Roxanne Easley
  Central Washington University

C. T. Evans
  Northern Virginia Community College

Edward L. Farmer
  University of Minnesota

William W. Farris
  University of Tennessee

Nancy Fitch
  California State University, Fullerton

Kristine Frederickson
  Utah Valley University

Ronald Fritze
  Lamar University

Joe Fuhrmann
Murray State University

Robert Gerlich
Loyola University

Marc J. Gilbert
North Georgia College

William J. Gilmore-Lehne
Richard Stockton College of New Jersey

Richard M. Golden
University of North Texas

Candice Goucher
Washington State University—Vancouver

Joseph M. Gowaskie
Rider College

Jonathan Grant
Florida State University

Don Gustafson
Augsburg College

Deanna Haney
Lansing Community College

Jason Hardgrave
University of Southern Indiana

Jay Harmon
Catholic High School

Ed Haynes
Winthrop College

Robert Henry
Grossmont College

Marilynn Jo Hitchens
University of Colorado—Denver

Tamara L. Hunt
University of Southern Indiana

Linda Kerr
University of Alberta at Edmonton

David Koeller
North Park University

Zoltan Kramar
Central Washington University

Douglas Lea
Kutztown University

David Leinweber
Emory University

Thomas T. Lewis
Mount Senario College

Craig A. Lockard
University of Wisconsin—Green Bay

George Longenecker
Norwich University

Norman D. Love
El Paso Community College

Robert Luczak
Vincennes University

Aran MacKinnon
State University of West Georgia

*Matthew Maher
Metropolitan State College of Denver

Patrick Manning
Northeastern University

Eric Mayer
Victor Valley College

Dolores Nason McBroome
Humboldt State University

John McDonald
Northern Essex Community College

Andrea McElderry
University of Louisville

Jeff McEwen
Chattanooga State Technical Community College

Margaret McKee
Castilleja High School

Nancy McKnight
Stockton High School

Robert McMichael
Wayland Baptist University

David L. McMullen
University of North Carolina at Charlotte

John A. Mears
Southern Methodist University

Cristina Mehrtens
University of Massachusetts, Dartmouth

David A. Meier
Dickinson State University

Marc A. Meyer
Berry College

Stephen S. Michot
Mississippi County Community College

John Ashby Morton
Benedict College

William H. Mulligan
Murray State University

*Henry A. Myers
James Madison University

Marian P. Nelson
University of Nebraska at Omaha

Sandy Norman
Florida Atlantic University

Patrick M. O'Neill
Broome Community College

Roger Pauly
University of Central Arkansas

Norman G. Raiford
Greenville Technical College

Jane Rausch
University of Massachusetts—Amherst

Michael Redman
University of Louisville

Dianna K. Rhyan
Columbus State Community College

Merle Rife
Indiana University of Pennsylvania

Patrice C. Ross
Columbus State Community College

John Rossi
LaSalle University

Eric C. Rust
Baylor University

Maura M. Ryan
Springbrook High School

Jane Samson
University of Alberta

Keith Sandiford
University of Manitoba

Anthony R. Santoro
Christopher Newport University

Elizabeth Sarkinnen
Mount Hood Community College

Pamela Sayre
Henry Ford College

Bill Schell
Murray State University

*Linda Scherr
Mercer County Community College

Robert M. Seltzer
Hunter College

Patrick Shan
Grand Valley State University

David Shriver
Cuyahoga Community College

Brett Shufelt
Copiah-Lincoln Community College

David Simonelli
Youngstown State University

Amos E. Simpson
University of Southwestern Louisiana

Wendy Singer
Kenyon College

Christopher Sleeper
MiraCosta College

Marvin Slind
Washington State University

Paul Smith
Washington State University

John Snetsinger
California Polytechnic State University

Matthew Sneider
University of Massachusetts, Dartmouth

George Stow
LaSalle University

John C. Swanson
Utica College of Syracuse

Patrick Tabor
Chemeketa Community College

Anara Tabyshalieva
Marshall University

Tom Taylor
Seattle University

John G. Tuthill
University of Guam

Salli Vaegis
Georgia Perimeter College

Joanne Van Horn
Fairmont State College

Gilmar Visoni
Queensborough Community College

Peter von Sivers
University of Utah

Christopher J. Ward
Clayton College and State University

Walter Ward
   Georgia State University

Pat Weber
   University of Texas—El Paso

Douglas L. Wheeler
   University of New Hampshire

David L. White
   Appalachian State University

Elmira B. Wicker
   Southern University—Baton Rouge

Glee Wilson
   Kent State University

Laura Matysek Wood
   Tarrant County College

Harry Zee
   Cumberland County College

The authors are truly grateful to the people who have helped us to produce this book. We especially want to thank Clark Baxter, whose faith in our ability to do this project was inspiring. Margaret McAndrew Beasley thoughtfully, wisely, efficiently, and cheerfully guided the overall development of the seventh edition. We also thank Nancy Blaine for her suggestions and valuable insights. Pat Lewis was, as usual, an outstanding copyeditor. Abbie Baxter provided valuable assistance in suggesting illustrations and obtaining permissions for the illustrations. John Orr, of Orr Book Services, was as cooperative and cheerful as he was competent in matters of production management.

A NOTE TO STUDENTS ABOUT LANGUAGE AND THE DATING OF TIME

ONE OF THE MOST difficult challenges in studying world history is coming to grips with the multitude of names, words, and phrases in unfamiliar languages. Unfortunately, this problem has no easy solution. We have tried to alleviate the difficulty, where possible, by providing an English-language translation of foreign words or phrases, a glossary, and a pronunciation guide. The issue is especially complicated in the case of Chinese because two separate systems are commonly used to transliterate the spoken Chinese language into the Roman alphabet. The Wade-Giles system, invented in the nineteenth century, was the more frequently used until recent years, when the pinyin system was adopted by the People's Republic of China as its own official form of transliteration. We have opted to use the latter, as it appears to be gaining acceptance in the United States, but the initial use of a Chinese word is accompanied by its Wade-Giles equivalent in parentheses for the benefit of those who may encounter the term in their outside reading.

In our examination of world history, we also need to be aware of the dating of time. In recording the past, historians try to determine the exact time when events occurred. World War II in Europe, for example, began on September 1, 1939, when Adolf Hitler sent German troops into Poland, and ended on May 7, 1945, when Germany surrendered. By using dates, historians can place events in order and try to determine the development of patterns over periods of time.

If someone asked you when you were born, you would reply with a number, such as 1993. In the United States, we would all accept that number without question because it is part of the dating system followed in the Western world (Europe and the Western Hemisphere). In this system, events are dated by counting backward or forward from the birth of Jesus Christ (assumed to be the year 1). An event that took place 400 years before the birth of Christ would most commonly be dated 400 B.C. (before Christ). Dates after the birth of Christ are labeled as A.D. These letters stand for the Latin words *anno Domini*, which mean "in the year of the Lord" (the year since the birth of Christ). Thus, an event that took place 250 years after the birth of Christ is written A.D. 250. It can also be written as 250, just as you would not give your birth year as "A.D. 1993" but simply as "1993."

Many historians now prefer to use the abbreviations B.C.E. ("before the common era") and C.E. ("common era") instead of B.C. and A.D. This is especially true of world historians who prefer to use symbols that are not so Western or Christian oriented. The dates, of course, remain the same. Thus, 1950 B.C.E. and 1950 B.C. refer to the same year, as do A.D. 40 and 40 C.E. In keeping with the current usage by many world historians, this book uses the terms B.C.E. and C.E.

Historians also make use of other terms to refer to time. A decade is 10 years, a century is 100 years, and a millennium is 1,000 years. The phrase "fourth century B.C.E." refers to the fourth period of 100 years counting backward from 1, the assumed date of the birth of Christ. Since the first century B.C.E. would be the years 100 B.C.E. to 1 B.C.E., the fourth century B.C.E. would be the years 400 B.C.E. to 301 B.C.E. We could say, then, that an event in 350 B.C.E. took place in the fourth century B.C.E.

The phrase "fourth century C.E." refers to the fourth period of 100 years after the birth of Christ. Since the first period of 100 years would be the years 1 to 100, the fourth period or fourth century would be the years 301 to 400. We could say, then, for example, that an event in 350 took place in the fourth century. Likewise, the first millennium B.C.E. refers to the years 1000 B.C.E. to 1 B.C.E., and the second millennium C.E. refers to the years 1001 to 2000.

The dating of events can also vary from people to people. Most people in the Western world use the Western calendar, also known as the Gregorian calendar after Pope Gregory XIII, who refined it in 1582. The Hebrew calendar uses a different system in which the year 1 is the equivalent of the Western year 3760 B.C.E., once calculated to be the date of the creation of the world, according to the Old Testament. Thus, the Western year 2012 corresponds to the year 5772 on the Jewish calendar. The Islamic calendar begins year 1 on the day Muhammad fled from Mecca, which is the year 622 on the Western calendar.

THEMES FOR UNDERSTANDING WORLD HISTORY

AS THEY PURSUE their craft, historians often organize their material on the basis of themes that enable them to ask and try to answer basic questions about the past. Such is our intention here. In preparing the seventh edition of this book, we have selected several major themes that we believe are especially important in understanding the course of world history. These themes transcend the boundaries of time and space and have relevance to all cultures since the beginning of the human experience.

In the chapters that follow, we will refer to these themes frequently as we advance from the prehistoric era to the present. Where appropriate, we shall make comparisons across cultural boundaries or across different time periods. To facilitate this process, we have included a comparative essay in each chapter that focuses on a particular theme within the specific time period discussed in that section of the book. For example, the comparative essays in Chapters 1 and 6 deal with the human impact on the natural environment during the premodern era, while those in Chapters 22 and 30 discuss the issue during the age of imperialism and in the contemporary world. Each comparative essay is identified with a particular theme, although it should be noted that many essays deal with several themes at the same time.

We have sought to illustrate these themes through the use of comparative illustrations in each chapter. These illustrations are comparative in nature and seek to encourage the reader to think about thematic issues in cross-cultural terms, while not losing sight of the unique characteristics of individual societies. Our seven themes, each divided into two subtopics, are listed below.

 1. Politics and Government The study of politics seeks to answer certain basic questions that historians have about the structure of a society: How were people governed? What was the relationship between the ruler and the ruled? What people or groups of people (the political elites) held political power? What actions did people take to guarantee their security or change their form of government?

 2. Art and Ideas We cannot understand a society without looking at its culture, or the common ideas, beliefs, and patterns of behavior that are passed on from one generation to the next. Culture includes both high culture and popular culture. High culture consists of the writings of a society's thinkers and the works of its artists. A society's popular culture is the world of ideas and experiences of ordinary people. Today, the media have embraced the term *popular culture* to describe the current trends and fashionable styles.

 3. Religion and Philosophy Throughout history, people have sought to find a deeper meaning in human life. How have the world's great religions, such as Hinduism, Buddhism, Judaism, Christianity, and Islam, influenced people's lives? How have they spread to create new patterns of culture in other parts of the world?

 4. Family and Society The most basic social unit in human society has always been the family. From a study of family and social patterns, we learn about the different social classes that make up a society and their relationships with one another. We also learn about the role of gender in individual societies. What different roles did men and women play in their societies? How and why were those roles different?

 5. Science and Technology For thousands of years, people around the world have made scientific discoveries and technological innovations that have changed our world. From the creation of stone tools that made farming easier to advanced computers that guide our airplanes, science and technology have altered how humans have related to their world.

 6. Earth and the Environment Throughout history, peoples and societies have been affected by the physical world in which they live. Climatic changes alone have been an important factor in human history. Through their economic activities, peoples and societies, in turn, have also made an impact on their world. Human activities have affected the physical environment and even endangered the very existence of entire societies and species.

 7. Interaction and Exchange Many world historians believe that the exchange of ideas and innovations is the driving force behind the evolution of human societies. Knowledge of agriculture, writing and printing, metalworking, and navigational techniques, for example, spread gradually from one part of the world to other regions and eventually changed the face of the entire globe. The process of cultural and technological exchange took place in various ways, including trade, conquest, and the migration of peoples.

THE PEOPLES OF MESOPOTAMIA AND EGYPT, like the peoples of India and China, built the first civilizations. Blessed with an abundant environment in their fertile river valleys, beginning around 3000 B.C.E. they built technologically advanced societies, developed cities, and struggled with the problems of organized states. They developed writing to keep records and created literature. They constructed monumental architecture to please their gods, symbolize their power, and preserve their culture for all time. They developed new political, military, social, and religious structures to deal with the basic problems of human existence and organization. These first literate civilizations left detailed records that allow us to view how they grappled with three of the fundamental problems that humans have pondered: the nature of human relationships, the nature of the universe, and the role of divine forces in that cosmos. Although other peoples would provide different answers from those of the Mesopotamians and Egyptians, they posed the questions, gave answers, and wrote them down. Human memory begins with the creation of civilizations.

By the middle of the second millennium B.C.E., much of the creative impulse of the Mesopotamian and Egyptian civilizations was beginning to wane. Around 1200 B.C.E., the decline of the Hittites and Egyptians had created a power vacuum that allowed a number of small states to emerge and flourish temporarily. All of them were eventually overshadowed by the rise of the great empires of the Assyrians and Persians. The Assyrian Empire had been the first to unite almost all of the ancient Middle East. Even larger, however, was the empire of the Great Kings of Persia. The many years of peace that the Persian Empire brought to the Middle East facilitated trade and the general well-being of its peoples. It is no wonder that many peoples expressed their gratitude for being subjects of the Great Kings of Persia. Among these peoples were the Israelites, who created no empire but nevertheless left an important spiritual legacy. The evolution of monotheism created in Judaism one of the world's greatest religions; Judaism in turn influenced the development of both Christianity and Islam.

While the peoples of North Africa and the Middle East were actively building the first civilizations, a similar process was getting under way in India. The first civilization in India arose in the Indus River valley during the fourth millennium B.C.E. This Harappan civilization made significant political and social achievements for some two thousand years until the coming of the Aryans finally brought its end around 1500 B.C.E. The Aryans established political control throughout all of India and created a new Indian civilization. Two of the world's great religions, Hinduism and Buddhism, began in India. With its belief in reincarnation, Hinduism provided justification for the rigid class system of India. Buddhism was the product of one man, Siddhartha Gautama, whose simple message in the sixth century B.C.E. of achieving wisdom created a new spiritual philosophy that came to rival Hinduism.

With the rise of the Mauryan dynasty in the fourth century B.C.E., the distinctive features of a great civilization began to be clearly visible. It was extensive in its scope, embracing the entire Indian subcontinent and eventually, in the form of Buddhism and Hinduism, spreading to China and Southeast Asia. But the underlying ethnic, linguistic, and cultural diversity of the Indian people posed a constant challenge to the unity of the state. After the collapse of the Mauryas, the subcontinent would not come under a single authority again for several hundred years.

In the meantime, another great experiment was taking place far to the northeast, across the Himalaya Mountains. Like many other civilizations of antiquity, the first Chinese state was concentrated on a major river system. Beginning around 1600 B.C.E., the Shang dynasty created the first flourishing Chinese civilization. Under the Shang, China developed organized government, a system of writing, and advanced skills in the making of bronze vessels. During the Zhou dynasty, China began to adopt many of the features that characterized Chinese civilization for centuries. Especially important politically was the "mandate from Heaven," which, it was believed, gave kings a divine right to rule. The family, with its ideal of filial piety, also emerged as a powerful economic and social unit.

Once embarked on its own path toward the creation of a complex society, China achieved results that were in all respects the equal of its counterparts elsewhere. A new dynasty—the Han—then established a vast empire that lasted over four hundred years. During the glory years of the Han dynasty (202 B.C.E.–221 C.E.), China extended the boundaries of its empire far into the sands of central Asia and southward along the coast of the South China Sea into what is modern-day Vietnam. Chinese culture appeared to be unrivaled, and its scientific and technological achievements were unsurpassed.

Unlike the great centralized empires of the Persians and the Chinese, ancient Greece consisted of a larger number of small, independent city-states, most of which had populations of only a few thousand. Despite the small size of their city-states, these ancient Greeks created a civilization that was the fountainhead of Western culture. In classical Greece (c. 500–338 B.C.E.), Socrates, Plato, and Aristotle established the foundations of Western philosophy. Western literary forms are largely derived from Greek poetry and drama. Greek notions of harmony, proportion, and beauty have remained the touchstones for all subsequent Western art. A rational method of inquiry, so important to modern science, was conceived in ancient Greece. Many political terms are Greek in origin, and so too are concepts of the rights and duties of citizenship, especially as they were conceived in Athens, the first great democracy. The Greeks raised and debated the fundamental questions about the purpose of human existence, the structure of human society, and the nature of the universe that have concerned thinkers ever since.

For all of their brilliant accomplishments, however, the Greeks were unable to rise above the divisions and rivalries that caused them to fight each other and undermine their own civilization. Of course, their cultural contributions have outlived their political struggles. And the Hellenistic era, which emerged after the Greek city-states had lost their independence in 338 B.C.E. and Alexander the Great had defeated the Persian Empire and carved out a new kingdom in the Middle East, made possible the spread of Greek ideas to larger areas. New philosophical concepts captured the minds of many. Significant achievements were made in art, literature, and science. Greek culture spread throughout the Middle East and made an impact wherever it was carried. Although the Hellenistic world achieved a degree of political stability, by the late third century B.C.E. signs of decline were beginning to multiply, and the growing power of Rome would eventually endanger the Hellenistic world.

In the eighth and seventh centuries B.C.E., the Latin-speaking community of Rome emerged as an actual city. Between 509 and 264 B.C.E., the expansion of this city brought about the union of almost all of Italy under Rome's control. Even more dramatically, between 264 and 133 B.C.E., Rome expanded to the west and east and became master of the Mediterranean Sea and its surrounding territories, creating one of the largest empires in antiquity. Rome's republican institutions proved inadequate for the task of ruling an empire, however, and after a series of bloody civil wars, Octavian created a new order that would rule the empire in an orderly fashion. His successors established a Roman imperial state.

The Roman Empire experienced a lengthy period of peace and prosperity between 14 and 180 C.E. During this era, trade flourished and the provinces were governed efficiently. In the course of the third century, however, the Roman Empire came near to collapse due to invasions, civil wars, and economic decline. Although the emperors Diocletian and Constantine brought new life to the so-called Late Empire, their efforts shored up the empire only temporarily. In its last two hundred years, as Christianity, with its new ideals of spiritual equality and respect for human life, grew, a slow transformation of the Roman world took place. The Germanic invasions greatly accelerated this process. Beginning in 395, the empire divided into western and eastern parts, and in 476, the Roman Empire in the west came to an end.

Although the western Roman Empire lived on only as an idea, Roman achievements were bequeathed to the future. The Romance languages of today (French, Italian, Spanish, Portuguese, and Romanian) are based on Latin. Western practices of impartial justice and trial by jury owe much to Roman law. As great builders, the Romans left monuments to their skills throughout Europe, some of which, such as aqueducts and roads, are still in use today.

The fall of ancient empires did not mark the end of civilization. After 500 C.E., new societies eventually rose on the ashes of the ancient empires, while new civilizations were on the verge of creation across the oceans in the continents of North and South America. The Maya and Aztecs were especially successful in developing advanced and prosperous civilizations in Central America. Both cultures built elaborate cities with pyramids, temples, and palaces. Both were polytheistic and practiced human sacrifice as a major part of their religions. Mayan civilization collapsed in the ninth century, whereas the Aztecs fell to Spanish invaders in the sixteenth century. In the fifteenth century, another remarkable civilization—that of the Inka—flourished in South America. The Inkan Empire was carefully planned and regulated, which is especially evident in the extensive network of roads that connected all parts of the empire. However, the Inka, possessing none of the new weapons of the Spaniards, eventually fell to the foreign conquerors.

All of these societies in the Americas developed in apparently total isolation from their counterparts elsewhere in the world. This lack of contact with other human beings deprived them of access to developments taking place in Africa, Asia, and Europe. They did not know of the wheel, for example, and their written languages were not as sophisticated as those in other parts of the world. In other respects, however, their cultural achievements were the equal of those realized elsewhere. One development that the peoples of the Americas lacked was the knowledge of firearms. In a few short years, tiny bands of Spanish explorers were able to conquer the magnificent civilizations of the Americas and turn them into ruins.

After the collapse of Roman power in the west, the eastern Roman Empire, centered in Constantinople, continued in the eastern Mediterranean and eventually emerged as the unique Christian civilization known as the Byzantine Empire, which flourished for hundreds of years. One of the greatest challenges to the Byzantine Empire, however, came from a new force—Islam, a new religion that arose in the Arabian peninsula at the beginning of the seventh century C.E. and spread rapidly throughout the Middle East. It was the work of a man named Muhammad. After Muhammad's death, his successors organized the Arabs and set in motion a great expansion. Arab armies moved westward across North Africa and into Spain, as well as eastward into the Persian Empire, conquering Syria and Mesopotamia. Internal struggles, however, soon weakened the empire, although the Abbasid dynasty established an Arab empire in 750 that flourished for almost five hundred years.

Like other empires in the region, however, the Arab Empire did not last. Nevertheless, Islam brought a code of law and a written language to societies that had previously not had them. By creating a flourishing trade network stretching from West Africa to East Asia, Islam also brought untold wealth to thousands and a better life to millions. By the end of the thirteenth century, the Arab Empire was no more than a memory. But it left a powerful legacy in Islam, which remains one of the great religions of the world. In succeeding centuries, Islam began to penetrate into Africa and across the Indian Ocean into the islands of Southeast Asia.

The mastery of agriculture gave rise to three early civilizations in northern Africa: Egypt, Kush, and Axum. Later, new states emerged in different parts of Africa, some of them strongly influenced by the spread of Islam. Ghana, Mali, and Songhai were three prosperous trading states that flourished in West Africa between the twelfth and fifteenth centuries. Zimbabwe, which emerged around 1300, played an important role in the southern half of Africa. Africa was also an active participant in emerging regional and global trade with the Mediterranean world and across the Indian Ocean. Although the state-building process in sub-Saharan Africa was still in its early stages compared with the ancient civilizations of India, China, and Mesopotamia, in many respects the new African states were as impressive and sophisticated as their counterparts elsewhere in the world.

In the fifteenth century, a new factor came to affect Africa. Fleets from Portugal began to probe southward along the coast of West Africa. At first, their

sponsors were in search of gold and slaves, but when Portuguese ships rounded the southern coast of Africa by 1500, they began to seek to dominate the trade of the Indian Ocean as well. The new situation posed a challenge to the peoples of Africa, whose states would be severely tested by the demands of the Europeans.

The peoples of Africa were not the only ones to confront a new threat from Europe at the beginning of the sixteenth century. When the Portuguese sailed across the Indian Ocean, they sought to reach India, where a new empire capable of rivaling the great kingdom of the Mauryas was in the throes of creation. Between 500 and 1500, Indian civilization had faced a number of severe challenges. One was an ongoing threat from beyond the mountains in the northwest. This challenge, which began in the eleventh century, led to the takeover of all of northern India in the eleventh

century by Turkish warriors, who were Muslims. A second challenge came from the tradition of internal rivalry that had marked Indian civilization for hundreds of years and that continued almost without interruption down to the sixteenth century. The third challenge was the religious divisions between Hindus

and Buddhists, and later between Hindus and Muslims, that existed throughout much of this period.

During the same period that Indian civilization faced these challenges at home, it was having a profound impact on the emerging states of Southeast Asia. Situated at the crossroads between two oceans and two great civilizations, Southeast Asia has long served as a bridge linking peoples and cultures. When complex societies began to appear in the region, they were strongly influenced by the older civilizations of neighboring China and India. All the young states throughout the region—Vietnam, Angkor, Thailand, the Burmese kingdom of Pagan, and several states on the Malayan peninsula and Indonesian archipelago—were affected by foreign ideas and adopted them as a part of their own cultures. At the same time, the Southeast Asian peoples, like the Japanese, put their own unique stamp on the ideas that they adopted. The result was a region marked by cultural richness and diversity yet rooted in the local culture.

One of the civilizations that spread its shadow over the emerging societies of Southeast Asia was China. Between the sixth and fifteenth centuries, China was ruled by a series of strong dynasties and had advanced in many ways. The industrial and commercial sectors had grown considerably in size, complexity, and technological capacity. In the countryside, a flourishing agriculture bolstered China's economic prosperity. The civil service provided for a stable government bureaucracy and an avenue of upward mobility that was virtually unknown elsewhere in the world. China's achievements were unsurpassed throughout the world and made it a civilization that was the envy of its neighbors.

And yet some things had not changed. By 1500, China was still a predominantly agricultural society, with wealth based primarily on the ownership of land. Commercial activities flourished but remained under a high level of government regulation. China also remained a relatively centralized empire based on an official ideology that stressed the virtue of hard work, social conformity, and hierarchy. In foreign affairs, the long frontier struggle with the nomadic peoples along the northern and western frontiers continued unabated.

Along the fringes of Chinese civilization were a number of other agricultural societies that were beginning to follow a pattern of development similar to that of China, although somewhat later in time. All of these early agricultural societies were eventually influenced to some degree by their great neighbor. Vietnam remained under Chinese rule for a thousand years. Korea retained its separate existence but was long a tributary state of China and in many ways followed China's cultural example. Cut off from the mainland by 120 miles of ocean, the Japanese had little contact with the outside world during most of their early development. However, once the Japanese became acquainted with Chinese culture, they were quick to take advantage of the opportunity. In the space of a few decades, the young state adopted many features of Chinese society and culture and thereby introduced major changes into the Japanese way of life. Nevertheless, Japan was a society that was able to make use of ideas imported from beyond its borders without endangering its customs, beliefs, and institutions. Japan retained both its political independence and its cultural uniqueness.

After the collapse of the Roman Empire in the fifth century, a new European civilization slowly began to emerge in western Europe. The coronation of Charlemagne, the descendant of a Germanic tribe converted to Christianity, as Roman emperor in 800 symbolized the fusion of the three chief components of the new European civilization: the German tribes, the Roman legacy, and the Christian church. Charlemagne's Carolingian Empire fostered the idea of a distinct European identity. With the disintegration of that

empire, power fell into the hands of many different lords, who came to constitute a powerful group of nobles that dominated the political, economic, and social life of Europe. But quietly and surely, within this world of castles and private power, kings gradually began to extend their public power and laid the foundations for the European kingdoms that in one form or another have dominated European politics ever since.

European civilization began to flourish in the High Middle Ages (1000–1300). The revival of trade, the expansion of towns and cities, and the development of a money economy did not mean the end of a predominantly rural European society, but they did offer new opportunities for people to expand and enrich their lives. At the same time, the High Middle Ages also gave birth to an intellectual and spiritual revival that transformed European society. However, fourteenth-century Europe was challenged by an overwhelming number of disintegrative forces but proved remarkably resilient. Elements of recovery in the age of the Renaissance made the fifteenth century a period of significant artistic, intellectual, and political change in Europe. By the second half of the fifteenth century, the growth of strong, centralized monarchical states made possible the dramatic expansion of Europe into other parts of the world.

WORLD HISTORY

VOLUME II: SINCE 1500

The Emergence of New World Patterns (1500–1800)

HISTORIANS OFTEN REFER to the period from the sixteenth through eighteenth centuries as the early modern era. During these years, several factors were at work that created the conditions of our own time.

From a global perspective, perhaps the most noteworthy event of the period was the extension of the maritime trade network throughout the entire populated world. The Chinese had inaugurated the process with their groundbreaking voyages to East Africa in the early fifteenth century, but the primary instrument of that expansion was a resurgent Europe, which exploded onto the world scene with the initial explorations of the Portuguese and the Spanish at the end of the fifteenth century and then gradually came to dominate shipping on international trade routes during the next three centuries.

Some contemporary historians argue that it was this sudden burst of energy from Europe that created the first truly global economic network. According to Immanuel Wallerstein, one of the leading proponents of this theory, the Age of Exploration led to the creation of a new "world system" characterized by the emergence of global trade networks dominated by the rising force of European capitalism, which now began to scour the periphery of the system for access to markets and cheap raw materials.

Many historians, however, qualify Wallerstein's view and point to the Mongol expansion beginning in the thirteenth century or even to the rise of the Arab empire in the Middle East a few centuries earlier as signs of the creation of a global communications network enabling goods and ideas to travel from one end of the Eurasian supercontinent to the other.

Whatever the truth of this debate, there are still many reasons for considering the end of the fifteenth century to be a crucial date in world history. In the first place, it marked the end of the long isolation of the Western Hemisphere from the rest of the inhabited world. In so doing, it led to the creation of the first truly global network of ideas and commodities, which would introduce plants, ideas, and (unfortunately) new diseases to all humanity (see the comparative essay in Chapter 14). Second, the period gave birth to a stunning increase in trade and manufacturing that stimulated major economic changes not only in Europe but in other parts of the world as well.

The period from 1500 to 1800, then, was an incubation period for the modern world and the launching pad for an era of Western domination that would reach fruition in the nineteenth century. To understand why the West emerged as the leading force in the world at that time, it is necessary to grasp what factors were at work in Europe and why they were absent in other major civilizations around the globe.

Historians have identified improvements in navigation, shipbuilding, and weaponry that took place in Europe in the early modern era as essential elements in the Age of Exploration. As we have seen, many of these technological advances were based on earlier discoveries that had taken place elsewhere—in China, India, and the Middle East—and had then been brought to Europe on Muslim ships or along the trade routes through Central Asia. But it was the capacity and the desire of the Europeans to enhance their wealth and power by making practical use of the discoveries of others that was the significant factor in the equation and enabled them to dominate international sea lanes and create vast colonial empires in the Western Hemisphere.

European expansion was not fueled solely by economic considerations, however. As in the rise of Islam in the seventh and eighth centuries, religion played a major role in motivating the European Age of Exploration in the early modern era. Although Christianity was by no means a new faith in the sixteenth century (as Islam had been at the moment of Arab expansion), the world of Christendom was in the midst of a major period of conflict with the forces of Islam, a rivalry that had been exacerbated by the conquest of the Byzantine Empire by the Ottoman Turks in 1453.

Although the claims of Portuguese and Spanish adventurers that their activities were motivated primarily by a desire to bring the word of God to non-Christian peoples certainly included a considerable measure of self-delusion and hypocrisy, there seems no reason to doubt that religious motives played a meaningful part in the European Age of Exploration. Religious motives were perhaps less evident in the activities of the non-Catholic powers that entered the competition beginning in the seventeenth century. English and Dutch merchants and officials were more inclined to be motivated purely by the pursuit of economic profit.

Conditions in many areas of Asia were less conducive to these economic and political developments. In China, a centralized monarchy continued to rely on a prosperous agricultural sector as the economic foundation of the empire. In Japan, power was centralized under the powerful Tokugawa shogunate, and the era of peace and stability that ensued saw an increase in manufacturing and commercial activity. But Japanese elites, after initially expressing interest in the outside world, abruptly shut the door on European trade and ideas in an effort to protect the "land of the gods" from external contamination.

In the societies of India and the Middle East, commerce and manufacturing had played a vital role since the emergence of the Indian Ocean trade network in the first centuries C.E. But beginning in the eleventh century, the area had suffered through an extended period of political instability, marked by invasions by nomadic peoples from Central Asia. The violence of the period and the local rulers' lack of experience in promoting maritime commerce severely depressed urban manufacturing and trade.

In the early modern era, then, Europe was best placed to take advantage of the technological innovations that had become increasingly available. With its political stability, sources of capital, and a "modernizing elite," it was well equipped to wrest the greatest benefit from the new conditions. Whereas other regions were still beset by internal obstacles or had deliberately turned inward to seek their destiny, Europe now turned outward to seek a new and dominant position in the world. Nevertheless, significant changes were taking place in other parts of the world as well, and many of these changes had relatively little to do with the situation in the West. As we shall see, the impact of European expansion on the rest of the world was still limited at the end of the eighteenth century. Though European political authority was firmly established in a few key areas, such as the Spice Islands and Latin America, traditional societies remained relatively intact in most regions of Africa and Asia. And processes at work in these societies were often operating independently of events in Europe and would later give birth to forces that acted to restrict or shape the Western impact. One of these forces was the progressive emergence of centralized states, some of them built on the concept of ethnic unity. ◈

New Encounters: The Creation of a World Market

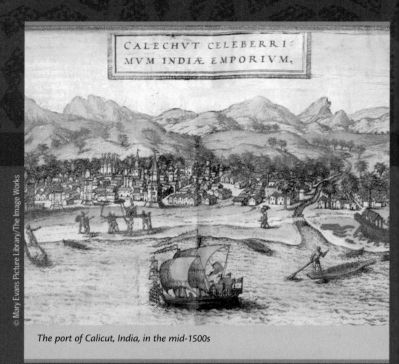

CALECHVT CELEBERRI:
MVM INDIÆ EMPORIVM.

The port of Calicut, India, in the mid-1500s

CHAPTER OUTLINE AND FOCUS QUESTIONS

An Age of Exploration and Expansion

Q How did Muslim merchants expand the world trade network at the end of the fifteenth century?

The Portuguese Maritime Empire

Q Why were the Portuguese so successful in taking over the spice trade?

The Conquest of the "New World"

Q How did Portugal and Spain acquire their empires in the Americas, and how did their methods of governing their colonies differ?

Africa in Transition

Q What were the main features of the African slave trade, and how did European participation in that trade affect traditional African practices?

Southeast Asia in the Era of the Spice Trade

Q What were the main characteristics of Southeast Asian societies, and how were they affected by the coming of Islam and the Europeans?

CRITICAL THINKING

Q Christopher Columbus has recently become a controversial figure in world history. Why do you think this is so, and how would you evaluate his contribution to the modern world?

WHEN THE PORTUGUESE FLEET arrived at the town of Calicut (KAL-ih-kuht) (now known as Kozhikode), on the western coast of India, in the spring of 1498, the fleet commander Vasco da Gama (VAHSH-koh dah GAHM-uh) ordered a landing party to go ashore to contact the local authorities. The first to greet them, a Muslim merchant from Tunisia, said, "May the Devil take thee! What brought thee hither?" "Christians and spices," replied the visitors. "A lucky venture, a lucky venture," replied the Muslim. "Plenty of rubies, plenty of emeralds! You owe great thanks to God, for having brought you to a country holding such riches!"[1]

Such words undoubtedly delighted the Portuguese, who sent a landing party ashore and concluded that the local population appeared to be Christians. Although it later turned out that they were mistaken—the local faith was a form of Hinduism—their spirits were probably not seriously dampened, for God was likely of less immediate importance than gold and glory to sailors who had gone through considerable hardship to become the first Europeans since the ancient Greeks to sail across the Indian Ocean. They left two months later with a cargo of spices and the determination to return soon with a second and larger fleet.

Vasco da Gama's maiden voyage to India inaugurated an extended period of European expansion into Asia, led by merchant adventurers and missionaries, that lasted several hundred years and had effects that are still felt today. Eventually, it resulted in a Western takeover of existing trade routes in the Indian Ocean and the establishment of colonies throughout Asia, Africa, and Latin America. In later years, Western historians would react to these events by describing the era as an "Age of Discovery" that significantly broadened the maritime trade network and set the stage for the emergence of the modern world.

In fact, however, the voyages of Vasco da Gama and his European successors were only the latest stage in a process that had begun generations earlier, at a time when European explorations were still restricted to the stormy waters of the North Atlantic Ocean. As we saw in Chapter 10, Chinese fleets under Zhenghe had roamed the Indian Ocean for several years during the early fifteenth century, linking China with societies as distant as the Middle East and the coast of East Africa. Although the voyages of Zhenghe were short in duration and had few lasting effects, the world of Islam was also expanding its reach as Muslim traders blazed new trails into Southeast Asia and across the Sahara to the civilizations that flourished along the banks of the Niger River. It was, after all, a Muslim from North Africa who greeted the Portuguese on their first appearance off the coast of India. In this chapter, we turn our attention to the stunning expansion in the scope and volume of commercial and cultural contacts that took place in the generations preceding and following Vasco da Gama's historic voyage to India, as well as to the factors that brought about this expansion.

An Age of Exploration and Expansion

Q FOCUS QUESTION: How did Muslim merchants expand the world trade network at the end of the fifteenth century?

Western historians have customarily regarded the voyage of Vasco da Gama as a crucial step in the opening of trade routes to the East. In the sense that the voyage was a harbinger of future European participation in the spice trade, this view undoubtedly has merit. In fact, however, as has been pointed out in earlier chapters, the Indian Ocean had been a busy thoroughfare for centuries. The spice trade had been carried on by sea in the region since the days of the legendary Queen of Sheba, and Chinese junks had sailed to the area in search of cloves and nutmeg since the Tang dynasty (see Chapter 10).

Islam and the Spice Trade

By the fourteenth century, a growing portion of the spice trade was being transported in Muslim ships sailing from ports in India or the Middle East. Muslims, either Arabs or Indian converts, had taken part in the Indian Ocean trade for centuries, and by the thirteenth century, Islam had established a presence in seaports on the islands of Sumatra and Java and was gradually moving inland. In 1292, the Venetian traveler Marco Polo observed that Muslims were engaging in missionary activity in northern Sumatra: "This kingdom is so much frequented by the Saracen merchants that they have converted the natives to the Law of Mahomet—I mean the townspeople only, for the hill people live for all the world

like beasts, and eat human flesh, as well as other kinds of flesh, clean or unclean."[2]

But the major impetus for the spread of Islam in Southeast Asia came in the early fifteenth century, with the foundation of a new sultanate at Malacca (muh-LAK-uh), on the strait that today bears the same name. The founder was Paramesvara (pahr-uh-muss-VAHR-uh), a vassal of the Hindu state of Majapahit (mah-jah-PAH-hit) on Java, whose original base of operations had been at Palembang (pah-lem-BAHNG), on the island of Sumatra. In 1390, he had moved his base to Tumasik (tuh-MAH-sik) (modern Singapore), at the tip of the Malay peninsula, hoping to enhance his ability to play a role in the commerce passing through the region. Under pressure from the expanding power of the Thai state of Ayuthaya (ah-yoo-TY-yuh) (see "Southeast Asia in the Era of the Spice Trade" later in this chapter) in the early fifteenth century, Paramesvara moved once again to Malacca. The latter's potential strategic importance was confirmed in the sixteenth century by a visitor from Portugal, who noted that Malacca "is a city that was made for commerce; . . . the trade

The Strait of Malacca

and commerce between the different nations for a thousand leagues on every hand must come to Malacca."[3]

Shortly after its founding, Malacca was visited by a Chinese fleet under the command of Admiral Zhenghe (see Chapter 10). To protect his patrimony from local rivals, Paramesvara agreed to become a tributary of the Chinese and cemented the new relationship by making an official visit to the Ming emperor in Beijing (see the box on p. 392). He also converted to Islam, undoubtedly with a view to enhancing Malacca's ability to participate in the trade that passed through the strait, much of which was dominated by Muslim merchants. Within a few years, Malacca had become the leading economic power in the region and helped promote the spread of Islam to trading ports throughout the islands of Southeast Asia, including Java, Borneo, Sulawesi (soo-lah-WAY-see), and the Philippines. Adoption of the Muslim faith was eased by the popularity of Sufism, a brand of Islam that expressed a marked tolerance for mysticism and local religious beliefs (see Chapter 7).

The Spread of Islam in West Africa

In the meantime, Muslim trade and religious influence continued to expand south of the Sahara into the Niger River valley in West Africa. The area had been penetrated by traders from across the Sahara since ancient times, and contacts undoubtedly increased after the establishment of Muslim control over the Mediterranean coastal regions. Muslim

A Chinese Description of Malacca

INTERACTION & EXCHANGE

Malacca, located on the west coast of the Malay peninsula, first emerged as a major trading port in the early fifteenth century, when its sultan, Paramesvara, avoided Thai rule with the aid of the emperor of China. This description of the area was written by a naval officer who served in one of the famous Chinese fleets that visited the city in the early fifteenth century.

Ma Huan, *Description of a Starry Raft*

This place did not formerly rank as a kingdom. It can be reached from Palembang on the monsoon in eight days. The coast is rocky and desolate, the population sparse. The country [used to pay] an annual tax of 40 taels of gold to Siam. The soil is infertile and yields [are] low. In the interior there is a mountain from [the slopes of] which a river takes its rise. The [local] folk pan the sands [of this river] to obtain tin, which they melt into ingots called *tou*. These weigh 1 kati 4 taels standard weight. [The inhabitants] also weave banana fiber into mats. Apart from tin, no other product enters into [foreign] trade. The climate is hot during the day but cool at night. [Both] sexes coil their hair into a knot. Their skin resembles black lacquer, but there are [some] white-complexioned folk among them who are of Chinese descent. The people esteem sincerity and honesty. They make a living by panning

tin and catching fish. Their houses are raised above the ground. [When constructing them,] they refrain from joining planks and restrict the building to the length of a [single] piece of timber. When they wish to retire, they spread their bedding side by side. They squat on their haunches when taking their meals. The kitchen and all its appurtenances is [also] raised [on stilts]. The goods [used in trading at Malacca] are blue and white porcelain, colored beads, colored taffetas, gold and silver. In the seventh year of Yung-lo [1409], the imperial envoy, the eunuch Cheng-Ho [Zhenghe], and his lieutenants conferred [on the ruler], by Imperial command, a pair of silver seals, and a headdress, girdle and robe. They also set up a tablet [stating that] Malacca had been raised to the rank of a kingdom, but at first Siam refused to recognize it. In the thirteenth year [of Yung-lo, 1415], the ruler [of Malacca, desirous of] showing his gratitude for the Imperial bounty, crossed the ocean and, accompanied by his consort and son, came to court with tribute. The Emperor rewarded him [appropriately], whereupon [the ruler of Malacca] returned to his [own] country.

 Why was Malacca such an important center of world trade?

---

traders—first Arabs and later African converts—crossed the desert carrying Islamic values, political culture, and legal traditions along with their goods. The early stage of state formation had culminated with the kingdom of Mali, symbolized by the renowned Mansa Musa, whose pilgrimage to Mecca in the fourteenth century had left an indelible impression on observers (see Chapter 8).

THE EMPIRE OF SONGHAI With the decline of Mali in the late fifteenth century, a new power eventually appeared: the empire of Songhai (song-GY). The founder of Songhai was Sonni Ali, a local chieftain who seized Timbuktu from its Berber overlords in 1468 and then sought to restore the formidable empire of his predecessors. Rumored to possess magical powers, Sonni Ali was criticized by Muslim scholars for supporting traditional religious practices, but under his rule, Songhai emerged as a major trading state in the region (see Map 14.1). When he died

MAP 14.1 The Songhai Empire. Songhai was the last of the great states to dominate the Niger River valley prior to the European takeover in the nineteenth century.

 What were the predecessors of the Songhai Empire in the region? Why is the area so important in African history?

The Great City of Timbuktu

INTERACTION & EXCHANGE

After its founding in the twelfth century, Timbuktu became a great center of Islamic learning and a fabled city of mystery and riches to Europeans. In the sixteenth century, Timbuktu was still a major commercial center on the trade route through the Sahara. This description of the city was written in 1526 by Leo Africanus, a Muslim from the Islamic state of Granada and one of the great travelers of his time.

Leo Africanus, *History and Description of Africa*

Here are many shops of artificers and merchants, and especially of such as weave linen and cotton cloth. And hither do the Barbary merchants bring cloth of Europe. All the women of this region, except the maid-servants, go with their faces covered, and sell all necessary victuals. The inhabitants, and especially strangers there residing, are exceeding rich, insomuch that the king that now is, married both his daughters to rich merchants. Here are many wells containing sweet water; and so often as the river Niger overfloweth, they convey the water thereof by certain sluices into the town. Corn, cattle, milk, and butter this region yieldeth in great abundance: but salt is very scarce here; for it is brought hither by land from Taghaza which is 500 miles distant. When I myself was here, I saw one camel's load of salt sold for 80 ducats. The rich king of Timbuktu hath many plates and scepters of gold, some whereof weigh 1,300 pounds: and he keeps a magnificent and well-furnished court. When he travelleth any whither he rideth upon a camel which is led by some of his noblemen; and so he doth likewise when he goeth forth to warfare, and all his soldiers ride upon horses. Whoever will speak unto this king must first fall down before his feet, and then taking up earth must first sprinkle it upon his own head and shoulders: which custom is ordinarily observed by . . . ambassadors from other princes. He hath always 3,000 horsemen, and a number of footmen that shoot poisoned arrows, attending upon him. They have often skirmishes with those that refuse to pay tribute, and so many as they take, they sell unto the merchants of Timbuktu. Here are very few horses bred, and the merchants and courtiers keep certain little nags which they use to travel upon: but their best horses are brought out of Barbary. . . . Here are great store of doctors, judges, priests, and other learned men, that are bountifully maintained at the king's cost and charges, and hither are brought divers manuscripts or written books out of Barbary, which are sold for more money than any other merchandise. The coin of Timbuktu is of gold without any stamp or superscription but in matters of small value they use certain shells brought hither out of the kingdom of Persia, 400 of which are worth a ducat: and $6\frac{2}{3}$ pieces of their gold coin weigh an ounce. The inhabitants are people of gentle and cheerful disposition, and spend a great part of the night singing and dancing through all the streets of the city.

 What role did the city of Timbuktu play in regional commerce, according to this author? What were the chief means of payment?

---

in 1492, his son ascended to the throne but was deposed shortly thereafter by one of his military commanders, who seized power as king under the name Askia Mohammed (r. 1493–1528).

Under the new ruler, a fervent Muslim, Songhai increasingly relied on Islamic institutions and ideology to strengthen national unity and centralize authority. Askia Mohammed himself embarked on a pilgrimage to Mecca and was recognized by the caliph of Cairo as the Muslim ruler of the Niger River valley. On his return from Mecca, he tried to revive Timbuktu as a major center of Islamic learning but had less success in converting his subjects. He did preside over a significant increase in trans-Saharan trade (notably in salt and gold), which provided a steady source of income to Songhai and other states in the region (see the box above). Despite the efforts of Askia Mohammed and his successors, however, centrifugal forces within Songhai eventually led to its breakup. The end came in 1591, when Moroccan forces armed with firearms conquered the city to gain control over the gold trade in the region.

A New Player: Europe

For almost a millennium, Catholic Europe had largely been confined to one area. Its one major attempt to expand beyond those frontiers, the Crusades, ultimately had failed. Of course, Europe had never completely lost contact with the outside world. In particular, with the revival of trade in the High Middle Ages, European merchants began to travel more frequently to Africa and Asia. Nevertheless, overall Europe's contacts with non-European civilizations remained limited until the fifteenth century, when Europeans began to embark on a remarkable series of overseas journeys. What caused European seafarers to undertake such dangerous voyages to the ends of the earth?

Europeans had long been attracted to the East. In the Middle Ages, myths and legends of an exotic land of great riches and magic were widespread. The most famous medieval travelers to the East were the Polos of Venice. In 1271, Nicolò and Maffeo, merchants from Venice, accompanied by Nicolò's son Marco, undertook the lengthy journey to the court of the great

Mongol ruler Khubilai Khan (see Chapter 10). As one of the Great Khan's ambassadors, Marco traveled to Japan as well and did not return to Italy until 1295. An account of his experiences, the *Travels*, proved to be the most informative of all the descriptions of Asia by medieval European travelers. Others, like the Franciscan friar John Plano Carpini, had preceded the Polos, but in the fourteenth century, the conquests of the Ottoman Turks and then the breakup of the Mongol Empire reduced Western traffic to the East. With the closing of the overland routes, a number of people in Europe became interested in the possibility of reaching Asia by sea. As noted in Chapter 10, Christopher Columbus himself possessed a copy of Marco Polo's *Travels*.

THE MOTIVES An economic motive thus looms large in Renaissance European expansion (see Chapter 13). The rise of capitalism in Europe was certainly a powerful spur to the process. Merchants, adventurers, and government officials had high hopes of finding precious metals and expanding the areas of trade, especially for the spices of the East. Spices continued to be transported to Europe via Arab intermediaries but were outrageously expensive. Adventurous Europeans did not hesitate to express their desire to share in the wealth. As one Spanish conquistador (kahn-KEESS-tuh-dor) explained, he and his kind went to the Americas to "serve God and His Majesty, to give light to those who were in darkness, and to grow rich, as all men desire to do."[4]

This statement expresses another major reason for the overseas voyages—religious zeal. A crusading mentality was particularly strong in Portugal and Spain, where the Muslims had largely been driven out in the Middle Ages. Contemporaries of Prince Henry the Navigator of Portugal, an outspoken advocate of European expansion, said that he was motivated by "his great desire to make increase in the faith of our Lord Jesus Christ and to bring him all the souls that should be saved." Although most scholars believe that the religious motive was secondary to economic considerations, it would be foolish to overlook the genuine desire on the part of both explorers and conquistadors, let alone missionaries, to convert the heathen to Christianity. Hernán Cortés (hayr-NAHN kor-TAYSS *or* kor-TEZ), the conqueror of Mexico, asked his Spanish rulers if it was not their duty to ensure that the native Mexicans were "introduced into and instructed in the holy Catholic faith."[5] Spiritual and secular affairs were closely intertwined in the sixteenth century. No doubt grandeur and glory, along with intellectual curiosity and a spirit of adventure, also played some role in European expansion.

THE MEANS If "God, glory, and gold" were the primary motives, what made the voyages possible? First of all, the expansion of Europe was a state enterprise, tied to the growth of centralized monarchies during the Renaissance. By the second half of the fifteenth century, European monarchies had increased both their authority and their resources and were in a position to turn their energies beyond their borders. For France, that meant the invasion of Italy, but for Portugal, a state not strong enough to pursue power in Europe, it meant going abroad. The Spanish scene was more complex, since the Spanish monarchy was strong enough by the sixteenth century to pursue power both on the Continent and beyond.

At the same time, by the end of the fifteenth century, European states had achieved a level of knowledge and technology that enabled them to conduct a regular series of voyages beyond Europe. Although the highly schematic and symbolic medieval maps were of little help to sailors, the *portolani* (pohr-tuh-LAH-nee), or detailed charts made by medieval navigators and mathematicians in the thirteenth and fourteenth centuries, were more useful. With details on coastal

© The Art Archive/Museo de la Torre del Oro, Seville/Gianni Dagli Orti

© The Art Archive/Marine Museum, Lisbon/Gianni Dagli Orti

European Warships During the Age of Exploration. Prior to the fifteenth century, most European ships were either small craft with triangular, lateen sails used in the Mediterranean or slow, unwieldy square-rigged vessels operating in the North Atlantic. By the sixteenth century, European naval architects began to build caravels (left), ships that combined the maneuverability and speed offered by lateen sails (widely used by sailors in the Indian Ocean) with the carrying capacity and seaworthiness of the square-riggers. For a century, caravels were the feared "raiders of the oceans." Eventually, as naval technology progressed, European warships developed in size and firepower, as the illustration of Portuguese carracks on the right shows.

contours, distances between ports, and compass readings, they proved of great value for voyages in European waters. But because the *portolani* were drawn on a flat surface and took no account of the curvature of the earth, they were of little use for longer overseas voyages. Only when seafarers began to venture beyond the coasts of Europe did they begin to accumulate information about the actual shape of the earth and how to measure it. By the end of the fifteenth century, cartography had developed to the point that Europeans possessed fairly accurate maps of the known world.

In addition, Europeans had developed remarkably seaworthy ships as well as new navigational techniques. European shipbuilders had mastered the use of the sternpost rudder (an import from China) and had learned how to combine the use of lateen sails with a square rig. With these innovations, they could construct **caravels** (KER-uh-velz), ships mobile enough to sail against the wind and engage in naval warfare

and also large enough to be armed with heavy cannons and carry a substantial amount of goods over long distances. Previously, sailors had used a quadrant and their knowledge of the position of the polestar to ascertain their latitude. Below the equator, however, this technique was useless. Only with the assistance of new navigational aids such as the compass (a Chinese invention) and the astrolabe, an astronomical instrument reportedly devised by Arab sailors (see Chapter 7), were they able to explore the high seas with confidence.

A final spur to exploration was the growing knowledge of the wind patterns in the Atlantic Ocean (see Map 14.2). The first European fleets sailing southward along the coast of West Africa had found their efforts to return hindered by the strong winds that blew steadily from the north along the coast. By the late fifteenth century, however, sailors had learned to tack out into the ocean, where they were able to catch westerly winds in the vicinity of the Azores that

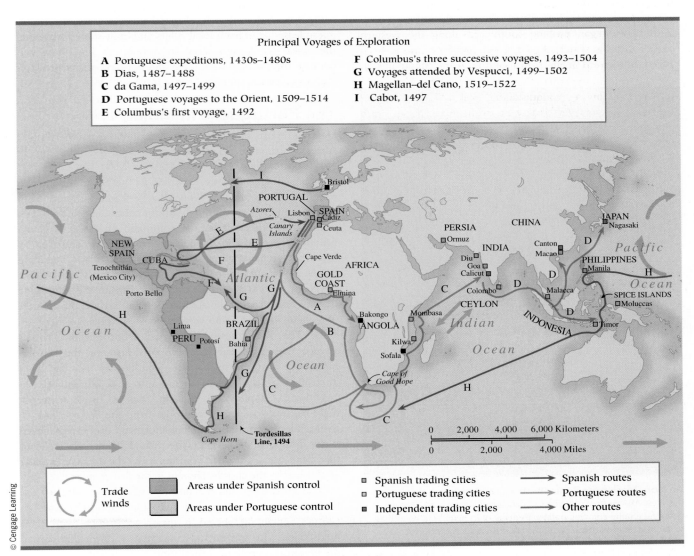

MAP 14.2 **European Voyages and Possessions in the Sixteenth and Seventeenth Centuries.** This map indicates the most important voyages launched by Europeans during their momentous Age of Exploration in the sixteenth and seventeenth centuries.

Q *Why did Vasco da Gama sail so far into the South Atlantic on his voyage to Asia?*

brought them back to the coast of western Europe. Christopher Columbus used this technique in his voyages to the Americas, and others relied on their new knowledge of the winds to round the continent of Africa in search of spices.

The Portuguese Maritime Empire

Q FOCUS QUESTION: Why were the Portuguese so successful in taking over the spice trade?

Portugal took the lead when it began exploring the coast of Africa under the sponsorship of Prince Henry the Navigator (1394–1460). Henry had three objectives: finding a Christian kingdom with which to ally against the Muslims, acquiring new trade opportunities for Portugal, and extending Christianity. In 1419, he founded a school for navigators on the southwestern coast of Portugal. Shortly thereafter, Portuguese fleets began probing southward along the western coast of Africa in search of gold, which had for centuries been carried northward from south of the Atlas Mountains in central Morocco. In 1441, Portuguese ships reached the Senegal River, just north of Cape Verde. They found no gold but brought home a cargo of black Africans, most of whom were sold as slaves to wealthy buyers elsewhere in Europe. Within a few years, about a thousand slaves a year were shipped from the area back to Lisbon. Although obtaining slaves had not been one of their original motives for exploring the west coast of Africa, the Portuguese had inadvertently found a way to circumvent the traditional trans-Saharan slave route from Central Africa to the Mediterranean.

Continuing southward, in 1471 the Portuguese discovered a new source of gold along the southern coast of the hump of West Africa (an area that would henceforth be known to Europeans as the Gold Coast). A few years later, they established contact with the state of Kongo, near the mouth of the Congo River in Central Africa, and with the inland state of Benin, north of the Gold Coast. To facilitate trade in gold, ivory, and slaves (not all slaves were brought back to Lisbon; some were bartered to local merchants for gold), the Portuguese leased land from local rulers and built stone forts along the coast. Trade was slow to develop at first, however, because the Portuguese initially did not have many products that appealed to potential African buyers.

The Portuguese in India

Hearing reports of a route to India around the southern tip of Africa, Portuguese sea captains continued their probing. In 1487, Bartolomeu Dias (bar-toh-loh-MAY-oo DEE-uhs) took advantage of westerly winds in the South Atlantic to round the Cape of Good Hope, but he feared a mutiny from his crew and returned home without continuing further. Ten years later, a fleet under the command of Vasco da Gama rounded the cape and stopped at several ports controlled by Muslim merchants along the coast of East Africa, including Sofala, Kilwa, and Mombasa. Then, having located a Muslim navigator who was familiar with seafaring in the region, da Gama's fleet crossed the Arabian Sea and arrived off the port of Calicut, on the southwestern coast of India, on May 18, 1498. The Portuguese crown had sponsored da Gama's voyage with the clear objective of destroying the Muslim monopoly over the spice trade, a monopoly that had been intensified by the Ottoman conquest of Constantinople in 1453 (see Chapter 16). Calicut was a major entrepôt (ON-truh-poh) on the long route from the Spice Islands to the Mediterranean Sea, but the ill-informed Europeans believed it was the source of the spices themselves. They had also heard that there was a Christian community in the area, supposedly established by the apostle Thomas in the first century C.E.

The Portuguese did not find any Christians, but they did find spices. Although he lost two ships along the way, da Gama's remaining vessels returned to Europe with their holds filled with ginger and cinnamon, a cargo that earned the investors a profit of several thousand percent.

The Search for Spices

During the next years, the Portuguese set out to gain control of the spice trade. In 1510, Admiral Afonso de Albuquerque

An Ivory Mask from Benin. By the end of the fifteenth century, the West African state of Benin had developed into an extensive and powerful empire enjoying trade with many of its neighbors, as well as with the state of Portugal. With the latter it traded ivory, forest products, and slaves in exchange for textiles and other European manufactured goods. This life-size ivory mask was probably intended to be worn by the king of Benin as a belt ornament in a gesture of gratitude to his mother, who had allegedly used her magical powers to help defeat his enemies. On the crest of the crown are carvings of Portuguese figures, providing one of the first examples in African art of the new trade relationship between that continent and Europe.

(ah-FAHN-soh day AL-buh-kur-kee) established his headquarters at Goa (GOH-uh), on the western coast of India south of present-day Mumbai (Bombay). From there, the Portuguese raided Arab shippers, provoking the following comment from an Arab source: "[The Portuguese] took about seven vessels, killing those on board and making some prisoner. This was their first action, may God curse them."[6] In 1511, Albuquerque attacked Malacca itself.

For Albuquerque, control of Malacca would serve two purposes. It could help destroy the Arab spice trade network by blocking passage through the Strait of Malacca, and it could also provide the Portuguese with a way station en route to the Spice Islands (known today as the Moluccas) and other points east. After a short but bloody battle, the Portuguese seized the city and put the local Arab population to the sword. They then proceeded to erect the normal accoutrements of the day—a fort, a "factory" (warehouse), and a church.

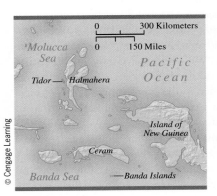

The Spice Islands

From Malacca, the Portuguese launched expeditions farther east, to China in 1514 and the Moluccas (muh-LUHK-uhz). There they signed a treaty with a local sultan for the purchase and export of cloves to the European market. Within a few years, they had managed to seize control of the spice trade from Muslim traders and had garnered substantial profits for the Portuguese monarchy.

Why were the Portuguese so successful? Basically, it was a matter of guns and seamanship. The first Portuguese fleet to arrive in Indian waters was relatively modest in size. It consisted of three ships and twenty guns, a force sufficient for self-defense and intimidation but not for serious military operations. Sixteenth-century Portuguese fleets were more heavily armed and were capable of inflicting severe defeats if necessary on local naval and land forces. The Portuguese by no means possessed a monopoly on the use of firearms and explosives, but their highly maneuverable, light ships enabled them to maintain their distance while bombarding the enemy with their powerful cannons. Such tactics gave them a military superiority over lightly armed rivals that they were able to exploit until the arrival of other European forces several decades later.

New Rivals Enter the Scene

Portugal's efforts to dominate the trade of the Indian Ocean were never totally successful, however. The Portuguese lacked both the numbers and the wealth to overcome local resistance and colonize the Asian regions. Moreover, their massive investments in ships and laborers for their empire (hundreds of ships and hundreds of thousands of workers in shipyards and overseas bases) proved very costly. Disease, shipwrecks, and battles took a heavy toll. The empire was simply too large and Portugal too small to maintain it, and by the end of the sixteenth century, the Portuguese were being severely challenged by rivals.

THE SPANISH First came the Spanish. Queen Isabella of Spain had already signaled her intent to enter the competition in 1492 when she sponsored the voyage of Christopher Columbus into the Atlantic Ocean in search of a westward route to the Indies. Two years later, in an effort to head off potential conflict between the two countries, the Treaty of Tordesillas (tor-day-SEE-yass) divided the newly discovered world into separate Portuguese and Spanish spheres of influence. Thereafter, the route east around the Cape of Good Hope was reserved for the Portuguese, while the route across the Atlantic (except for the eastern hump of South America) was assigned to Spain (see Map 14.2 on p. 395).

Columbus's later voyages eventually convinced influential figures at the Spanish court that the lands he had reached were not the Indies but an unknown land that possessed its own attractions. Still seeking a route to the Spice Islands, in 1519 Spain dispatched a fleet under the command of the Portuguese sea caption Ferdinand Magellan that sailed around the southern tip of South America, proceeded across the Pacific Ocean, and landed on the island of Cebu in the Philippine Islands. Although Magellan and some forty of his crew were killed in a skirmish with the local population, one of the two remaining ships sailed on to Tidor, in the Moluccas, and thence around the world via the Cape of Good Hope. In the words of a contemporary historian, they arrived in Cádiz

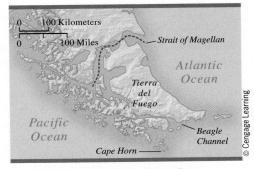

Cape Horn and the Strait of Magellan

"with precious cargo and fifteen men surviving out of a fleet of five sail."[7]

As it turned out, the Spanish could not follow up on Magellan's accomplishment, and in 1529, they sold their rights in Tidor to the Portuguese. But Magellan's voyage was not a total loss. In the absence of concerted resistance from the local population, the Spanish managed to consolidate their control over the Philippines, which eventually became a major Spanish base in the carrying trade across the Pacific. Spanish galleons carried silk and other luxury goods to Acapulco in exchange for silver from the mines of Mexico.

THE ENGLISH AND THE DUTCH The primary threat to the Portuguese toehold in Southeast Asia, however, came from the English and the Dutch. In 1591, the first English expedition to the Indies through the Indian Ocean arrived in

London with a cargo of pepper. Nine years later, a private joint-stock company, the East India Company, was founded to provide a stable source of capital for future voyages. In 1608, an English fleet landed at Surat (SOOR-et), on the northwestern coast of India. Trade with Southeast Asia soon followed.

The Dutch were quick to follow suit, and the first Dutch fleet arrived in India in 1595. In 1602, the Dutch East India Company was established under government sponsorship and was soon actively competing with the English and the Portuguese in the region. In 1641, the Dutch seized the entrepôt of Malacca, one of the linchpins of Portugal's trading empire in Asia.

The Conquest of the "New World"

 FOCUS QUESTION: How did Portugal and Spain acquire their empires in the Americas, and how did their methods of governing their colonies differ?

While the Portuguese were seeking access to the spice trade by sailing eastward through the Indian Ocean, the Spanish attempted to reach the same destination by sailing westward across the Atlantic. Although the Spanish came to overseas discovery and exploration later than the Portuguese, their greater resources enabled them to establish a far grander overseas empire.

The Voyages

An important figure in the history of Spanish exploration was an Italian from Genoa, Christopher Columbus (1451–1506). Knowledgeable Europeans were aware that the world was round but had little understanding of its size or the extent of the continent of Asia. Convinced that the circumference of the earth was smaller than contemporaries believed and that Asia was larger, Columbus believed that Asia could be reached by sailing due west instead of eastward around Africa. After being rejected by the Portuguese, he persuaded Queen Isabella of Spain to finance his exploratory expedition, which reached the Americas in October 1492 and explored the coastline of Cuba and the northern shores of the neighboring island of Hispaniola (his-puhn-YOH-luh or ees-pahn-YAH-luh). Columbus believed that he had reached Asia and in three subsequent voyages (1493, 1498, and 1502) sought in vain to find a route through the outer islands to the Asian mainland. In his four voyages, Columbus reached all the major islands of the Caribbean, which he called the Indies, as well as Honduras in Central America.

Although Columbus clung for the rest of his life to his belief that he had reached Asia, other navigators realized that he had discovered a new frontier altogether. State-sponsored explorers joined the race to what Europeans began to call the "New World." A Venetian seafarer, John Cabot, explored the New England coastline of the Americas under a license from King Henry VII of England. The continent of South America was discovered accidentally by the Portuguese sea captain Pedro Cabral (PAY-droh kuh-BRAHL) in 1500. Amerigo Vespucci (ahm-ay-REE-goh vess-POO-chee), a Florentine, accompanied several voyages and wrote a series of letters describing the geography of the lands he observed. The publication of these letters led to the use of the name "America" (after Amerigo) for the new lands.

The Conquests

The newly discovered territories that Europeans referred to as the New World actually contained flourishing civilizations populated by millions of people. But the Americas were new to the Europeans, who quickly saw opportunities for conquest and exploitation. With Portugal clearly in the lead in the race to exploit the riches of the Indies, the importance of these lands was magnified in the minds of the Spanish, especially these who saw a chance to win fame and fortune for themselves and their families.

The Spanish **conquistadors**, as they were called, were a hardy lot of mostly upper-class individuals motivated by a typical sixteenth-century blend of glory, greed, and religious crusading zeal. Although sanctioned by the Castilian crown, these groups were financed and outfitted privately, not by the government.

Their superior weapons, organizational skills, and determination brought the conquistadors incredible success. In 1519, a Spanish expedition under the command of Hernán Cortés landed at Veracruz, on the Gulf of Mexico. Marching to Tenochtitlán (teh-nahch-teet-LAHN) at the head of a small contingent of troops, Cortés received a friendly welcome from the Aztec monarch Moctezuma Xocoyotzin (mahk-tuh-ZOO-muh shoh-koh-YAHT-seen) (often called Montezuma), who initially believed his visitor was a representative of Quetzalcoatl (KWET-sul-koh-AHT-ul), the legendary and godlike "feathered serpent." The king and his subjects

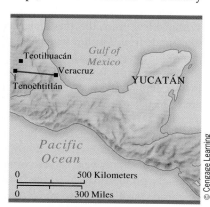

The Arrival of Hernán Cortés in Mexico

were astounded to see men on horseback, for the horse had disappeared from the Americas at least ten thousand years earlier.

But tensions soon erupted between the Spaniards and the Aztecs, provoked in part by demands by Cortés that the Aztecs renounce their native beliefs and accept Christianity. When the Spanish took Moctezuma hostage and began to destroy Aztec religious shrines, the local population revolted and drove the invaders from the city. Receiving assistance from the state of Tlaxcallan (tuh-lah-SKAH-lahn), Cortés managed to fight his way back into the city. Meanwhile, the Aztecs were beginning to suffer the first effects of the diseases

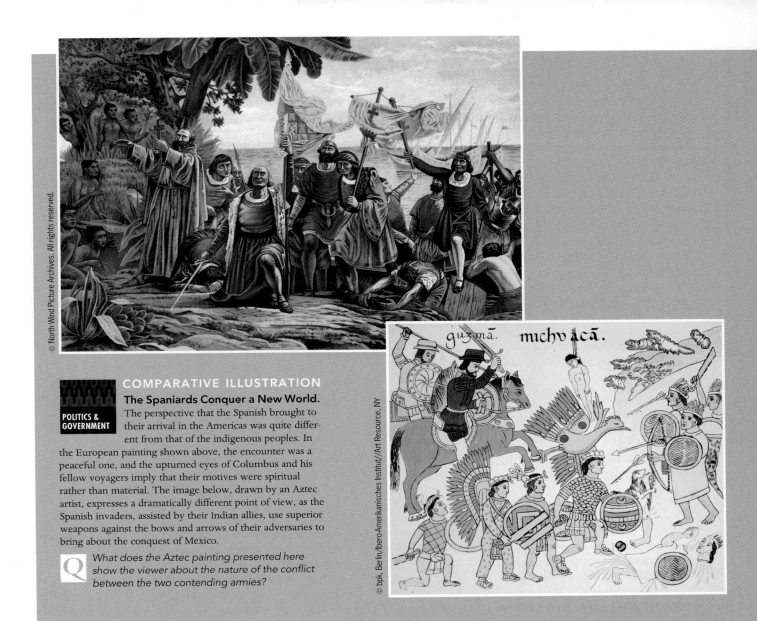

COMPARATIVE ILLUSTRATION

POLITICS & GOVERNMENT

The Spaniards Conquer a New World.
The perspective that the Spanish brought to their arrival in the Americas was quite different from that of the indigenous peoples. In the European painting shown above, the encounter was a peaceful one, and the upturned eyes of Columbus and his fellow voyagers imply that their motives were spiritual rather than material. The image below, drawn by an Aztec artist, expresses a dramatically different point of view, as the Spanish invaders, assisted by their Indian allies, use superior weapons against the bows and arrows of their adversaries to bring about the conquest of Mexico.

Q *What does the Aztec painting presented here show the viewer about the nature of the conflict between the two contending armies?*

brought by the Europeans, which would eventually wipe out the majority of the local population. In a battle that to many Aztecs must have seemed to symbolize the dying of the legendary fifth sun, the Aztecs were finally vanquished (see the comparative illustration above). Within months, their magnificent city and its temples, believed by the conquerors to be the work of Satan, had been destroyed (see the box on p. 400).

A similar fate awaited the powerful Inka Empire in South America. Between 1531 and 1536, another expedition, led by a hardened and somewhat corrupt soldier, Francisco Pizarro (frahn-CHESS-koh puh-ZAHR-oh) (1470–1541), destroyed Inka power high in the Peruvian Andes. The Spanish conquests were undoubtedly facilitated by the previous arrival of European diseases, which had decimated the local population. Although it took another three decades before the western

part of Latin America was brought under Spanish control (the Portuguese took over Brazil), already by 1535, the Spanish had created a system of colonial administration that made the New World an extension of the old—at least in European eyes.

THE PORTUGUESE IN BRAZIL Although the Spanish had taken the lead in planting their flag in the Western Hemisphere, they were not alone. In 1500, a Portuguese fleet inadvertently discovered the eastern coast of Latin America while en route to the Indies, and the Portuguese crown established the colony of Brazil in the area, basing its claim on the Treaty of Tordesillas, which had allocated that territory to the Portuguese sphere of influence. Like their Spanish rivals, the Portuguese initally saw their new colony as a source of gold and silver, but they soon discovered that profits could be made in

An Aztec's Lament

INTERACTION & EXCHANGE

The Spanish conquest of Mexico had an indelible impact on the vanquished local population. Aztec memoirs of the battle were collected by the Spanish a few years after the seizure of Tenochtitlán and were later translated from the original Nahuatl (NAH-waht-ul), the Aztec language, into Spanish or other European languages. In this passage, an Aztec observer describes the enormous sense of sorrow he felt at the tragedy that had befallen his compatriots. Note that the writer concludes that the defeat was ordained by the "Giver of Life" because of his displeasure with the Aztec people.

Flowers and Songs of Sorrow

Nothing but flowers and songs of sorrow
are left in Mexico and Tlatelolco,
where once we saw warriors and wise men.

We know it is true
that we must perish,
for we are mortal men.

You, the Giver of Life,
you have ordained it.

We wander here and there
in our desolate poverty.
We are mortal men.
We have seen bloodshed and pain
where once we saw beauty and valor.

We are crushed to the ground;
we lie in ruins.
There is nothing but grief and suffering
in Mexico and Tlatelolco,
where once we saw beauty and valor.

Have you grown weary of your servants?
Are you angry with your servants,
O Giver of Life?

 How did the author of this selection respond to the destruction of Aztec culture? Does he appear to be angry or resigned? What role did Aztec religion play in shaping his response?

---

other ways as well. A formal administrative system was instituted in Brazil in 1549, and Portuguese migrants arrived to establish plantations to produce sugar, coffee, and other tropical products for export to Europe.

Governing the Empires

In the sixteenth century, while Portugal came to dominate Brazil, Spain established a colonial empire that included Central America, most of South America, and parts of North America. Within the lands of Central and South America, a new civilization arose that we have come to call Latin America (see Map 14.3).

CHRONOLOGY	Spanish and Portuguese Activities in the Americas
Christopher Columbus's first voyage to the Americas	1492
Portuguese fleet arrives in Brazil	1500
Columbus's last voyages	1502–1504
Spanish conquest of Mexico	1519–1522
Francisco Pizarro's conquest of the Inkas	1531–1536
Viceroyalty of New Spain established	1535
Formal colonial administrative system established in Brazil	1549

Latin America rapidly became a multiracial society. Already by 1501, Spanish rulers allowed intermarriage between Europeans and the inhabitants of the Americas, whom the Europeans called Indians. Their offspring became known as **mestizos** (mess-TEE-zohz). In addition, over a period of three centuries, possibly as many as 8 million African slaves were brought to Spanish and Portuguese America to work the plantations that were established (see "The Slave Trade" later in this chapter). **Mulattoes** (muh-LAH-tohz)—the offspring of Africans and whites—joined mestizos and descendants of whites, Africans, and local Indians to produce a unique multiracial society in Latin America.

THE STATE AND THE CHURCH IN COLONIAL LATIN AMERICA Although the colonial empires of Portuguese Brazil and Spanish America lasted more than three hundred years, the difficulties of communication and travel between the Americas and Europe made it virtually impossible for the home-country monarchs to provide close regulation of their empires. This left colonial officials in Latin America with much autonomy in implementing imperial policies. Nevertheless, the Iberians tried to keep the most important posts of colonial government in the hands of Europeans.

At the head of the administrative system that the Portuguese established for Brazil in the mid-sixteenth century was the position of governor-general. The governor-general (later called a **viceroy**) developed a bureaucracy but had at best

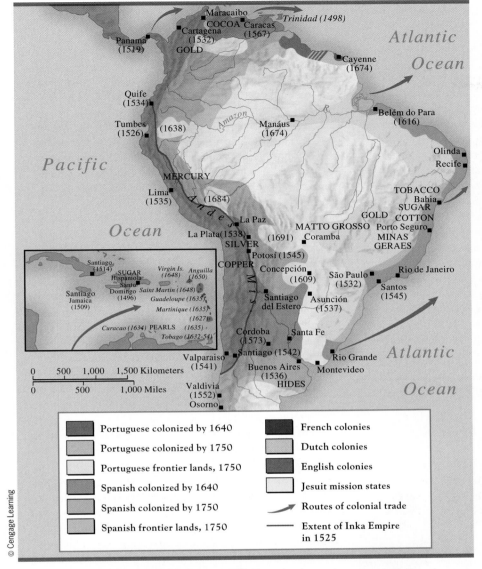

MAP 14.3 **Latin America from c. 1500 to 1750.** From the sixteenth century, Latin America was largely the colonial preserve of the Spanish, although Portugal dominated Brazil. The Latin American colonies supplied the Spanish and Portuguese with gold, silver, sugar, tobacco, cotton, and animal hides.

Q *How do you explain the ability of Europeans to dominate such large areas of Latin America?*

Map legend:

- Portuguese colonized by 1640
- Portuguese colonized by 1750
- Portuguese frontier lands, 1750
- Spanish colonized by 1640
- Spanish colonized by 1750
- Spanish frontier lands, 1750
- French colonies
- Dutch colonies
- English colonies
- Jesuit mission states
- Routes of colonial trade
- Extent of Inka Empire in 1525

© Cengage Learning

only loose control over the captains-general, who were responsible for governing the districts into which Brazil was divided.

To rule his American empire, the king of Spain appointed viceroys, the first of which was established for New Spain (Mexico) in 1535. Another viceroy was appointed for Peru in 1543. Much later, in the eighteenth century, two additional viceroyalties—New Granada and La Plata—were added. Viceroyalties were in turn subdivided into smaller units. All of the major government positions were held by Spaniards. For **creoles**—American-born descendants of Europeans—the chief opportunity to hold a government post was in city councils.

From the beginning of their conquest of lands in the Western Hemisphere, Spanish and Portuguese rulers were determined to convert the indigenous peoples to Christianity.

This policy gave the Catholic Church an important role to play in the Americas—a role that added considerably to church power. Catholic missionaries fanned out to different parts of the Spanish Empire. To facilitate their efforts, missionaries brought Indians together into villages where they could be converted, taught trades, and encouraged to grow crops (see the Film & History feature on p. 402). The missions also enabled the missionaries to control the lives of the Indians and keep them docile.

The Catholic Church built hospitals, orphanages, and schools that instructed Indian students in the rudiments of reading, writing, and arithmetic. The church also provided outlets for women other than marriage. Nunneries were places of prayer and quiet contemplation, but women in religious orders, many of them of aristocratic background, often lived well and operated outside their establishments by running schools and hospitals. Indeed, one of these nuns, Sor Juana Inés de la Cruz (SAWR HWAH-nuh ee-NAYSS day lah KROOZ) (1651–1695), became one of seventeenth-century Latin America's best-known literary figures. She wrote poetry and prose and urged that women be educated.

EXPLOITING THE RICHES OF THE AMERICAS As we noted earlier, both the Portuguese and the Spanish sought to profit economically from their colonies in Latin America. One source of wealth came from the abundant supplies of gold and silver. Wherever they went in the Americas, Europeans sought gold and silver. One Aztec observer commented that the Spanish conquerors "longed and lusted for gold. Their bodies swelled with greed, and their hunger was ravenous; they hungered like pigs for that gold."[8] Rich silver deposits were found and exploited in Mexico and southern Peru (modern Bolivia). When the mines at Potosí (poh-toh-SEE) in Peru were opened in 1545, the value of precious metals imported into Europe quadrupled. It has been estimated that between 1503 and 1650, some 16 million kilograms (17,500 tons) of silver and 185,000 kilograms (200 tons) of gold entered the port of Seville in Spain.

Although the pursuit of gold and silver offered prospects of fantastic financial rewards, agriculture proved to be a more abiding and more rewarding source of prosperity for Latin

The Mission (1986)

Directed by Roland Joffé, *The Mission* examines religion, politics, and colonialism in Europe and South America in the mid-eighteenth century. The movie begins with a flashback as Cardinal Altamirano (Ray McAnally) is dictating a letter to the pope to discuss the fate of the Jesuit missions in Paraguay. (The Jesuits were members of the Society of Jesus, a Roman Catholic religious order that was founded in the sixteenth century.) He begins by describing the establishment of a new Jesuit mission (San Carlos) in Spanish territory in the borderlands of Paraguay and Brazil. Father Gabriel (Jeremy Irons) has been able to win over the Guaraní Indians and create a community based on communal livelihood and property (private property has been abolished). The mission includes dwellings for the Guaraní and a church where they can practice their new faith by learning the Gospel and singing hymns. This small band of Jesuits is joined by Rodrigo Mendozo (Robert De Niro), who has been a slave trader dealing in Indians and now seeks to atone for killing his brother

in a fit of jealous rage by joining the community at San Carlos. Won over to Father Gabriel's perspective, he also becomes a member of the Jesuit order.

Cardinal Altamirano now travels to South America, sent by a pope anxious to appease the Portuguese monarch over the activities of the Jesuits. Portuguese settlers in Brazil are eager to use the local people as slaves and to confiscate their communal lands and property. In 1750, when Spain agrees to turn over the Guaraní territory in Paraguay to Portugal, the settlers seize their opportunity. Although the cardinal visits a number of missions, including San Carlos, and obviously approves of their accomplishments, his hands are tied by the Portuguese king, who is threatening to disband the Jesuit order if the missions are not closed. The cardinal acquiesces, and Portuguese troops are sent to take over the missions. Although Rodrigo and the other Jesuits join the Guaraní in fighting the Portuguese while Father Gabriel remains nonviolent, all are massacred. The cardinal returns to Europe, dismayed by the murderous activities of the Portuguese but hopeful that the Jesuit order will be spared. All is in vain, however, as the Catholic monarchs of Europe expel the Jesuits from their countries and pressure Pope Clement XIV into disbanding the Jesuit order in 1773.

In its approach to the destruction of the Jesuit missions, *The Mission* clearly exalts the dedication of the Jesuit order and praises its devotion to the welfare of the Indians. The movie ends with a small group of Guaraní children, now all orphans, picking up a few remnants of debris in their destroyed mission and moving off down the river back into the wilderness to escape enslavement. The final words on the screen illuminate the movie's message about the activities of the Europeans who destroyed the local civilizations in their conquest of the Americas: "The Indians of South America are still engaged in a struggle to defend their land and their culture. Many of the priests who, inspired by faith and love, continue to support the rights of the Indians, do so with their lives," a reference to the ongoing struggle in Latin America against the regimes that continue to oppress the landless masses.

The Jesuit missionary Father Gabriel (Jeremy Irons) with the Guaraní Indians of Paraguay before their slaughter by Portuguese troops

© Warner Brothers/Courtesy Everett Collection

America. The American colonies became sources of raw materials for Spain and Portugal as sugar, tobacco, chocolate, precious woods, animal hides, and a number of other natural products made their way to Europe. In turn, the mother countries supplied their colonists with manufactured goods (see Map 14.4). Both Spain and Portugal closely regulated the trade of their American colonies to keep others out, but the English and the French eventually became too powerful to be excluded from this lucrative Latin American market.

To produce these goods, colonial authorities initially tried to rely on local sources of human labor. Spanish policy

toward the Indians was a combination of confusion, misguided paternalism, and cruel exploitation. Confusion arose over the nature of the Indians. Queen Isabella declared the Indians to be subjects of Castile and instituted the **encomienda system**, under which European settlers received grants of land and could collect tribute from the indigenous peoples and use them as laborers. In return, the holders of an **encomienda** (en-koh-MYEN-duh) were supposed to protect the Indians and supervise their spiritual and material needs. In practice, this meant that the settlers were free to implement the system as they pleased. Three thousand miles from

© Cengage Learning

MAP 14.4 Patterns of World Trade Between 1500 and 1800. This map shows the major products that were traded by European merchants throughout the world during the era of European exploration.

Q *What were the primary sources of gold and silver, so sought after by Columbus and his successors?*

Spain, Spanish settlers largely ignored their government and brutally used the Indians to pursue their own economic interests. Indians were put to work on sugar plantations and in the lucrative gold and silver mines.

Forced labor, starvation, and especially disease took a fearful toll on Indian lives. With little or no natural resistance to European diseases, the Indians were ravaged by smallpox, measles, and typhus brought by the explorers and the conquistadors (see the comparative essay on p. 405). Although scholarly estimates vary drastically, a reasonable guess is that at least half of the local population in some areas died of European diseases. On Hispaniola alone, out of an initial population of 100,000 when Columbus arrived in 1493, only 300 Indians survived by 1570. In 1542, largely in response to the publications of Bartolomé de Las Casas (bahr-toh-loh-MAY day lahs KAH-sahs), a Dominican monk who championed the Indians, the government abolished the *encomienda* system and provided more protection for the Indians (see the box on p. 404). By then, however, the indigenous population had been decimated by disease, causing the Spanish—and eventually the Portuguese as well—to import African slaves to replace the Indians in the sugar fields.

The Competition Intensifies

The success of the Spanish and the Portuguese in exploiting the riches of the Americas soon attracted competition from other European trading states. The Dutch formed the Dutch West India Company in 1621 to compete with Spanish and Portuguese interests in the Americas. But although it made some inroads in Brazil (briefly taking control of the sugar plantations around the port city of Bahia from the Portuguese) and the Caribbean (see Map 14.3), the company's profits were never large enough to cover its expenditures. Dutch settlements were also established on the North American continent. The mainland colony of New Netherland stretched from the mouth of the Hudson River as far north as present-day Albany, New York.

In the second half of the seventeenth century, however, rivalry and years of warfare with the English and the French (who had also become active in North America, establishing colonies in the Caribbean and in Louisiana at the mouth of the Mississippi River) brought the decline of the Dutch commercial empire in the Americas. In 1664, the English seized the colony of New Netherland and renamed it New York, and the Dutch West India Company soon went bankrupt. In

Las Casas and the Spanish Treatment of the American Indians

INTERACTION & EXCHANGE

Bartolomé de Las Casas (1474–1566) was a Dominican monk who participated in the conquest of Cuba and received land and Indians in return for his efforts. But in 1514, he underwent a radical transformation that led him to believe that the Indians had been cruelly mistreated by his fellow Spaniards. He spent the remaining years of his life (he lived to the age of ninety-two) fighting for the Indians. This selection is taken from his most influential work, *Brevísima Relación de la Destrucción de las Indias*, known to English readers as *The Tears of the Indians*. This work was largely responsible for the reputation of the Spanish as inherently "cruel and murderous fanatics." Many scholars today feel that Las Casas may have exaggerated his account to shock his contemporaries into action.

Bartolomé de Las Casas, *The Tears of the Indians*

There is nothing more detestable or more cruel than the tyranny which the Spaniards use toward the Indians for the getting of pearl. Surely the infernal torments cannot much exceed the anguish that they endure, by reason of that way of cruelty; for they put them under water some four or five ells deep, where they are forced without any liberty of respiration, to gather up the shells wherein the Pearls are; sometimes they come up again with nets full of shells to take breath, but if they stay any while to rest themselves, immediately comes a hangman row'd in a little boat, who as soon as he hath well beaten them, drags them again to their labor. Their food is nothing but filth, and the very same that

contains the Pearl, with small portion of that bread which that Country affords; in the first whereof there is little nourishment; and as for the latter, it is made with great difficulty, besides that they have not enough of that neither for sustenance; they lie upon the ground in fetters, lest they should run away; and many times they are drown'd in this labor, and are never seen again till they swim upon the top of the waves; oftentimes they also are devoured by certain sea monsters, that are frequent in those seas. Consider whether this hard usage of the poor creatures be consistent with the precepts which God commands concerning charity to our neighbor, by those that cast them so undeservedly into the dangers of a cruel death, causing them to perish without any remorse or pity, or allowing them the benefit of the Sacraments, or the knowledge of Religion; it being impossible for them to live any time under the water; and this death is so much the more painful, by reason that by the coarctation of the breast, while the lungs strive to do their office, the vital parts are so afflicted that they die vomiting the blood out of their mouths. Their hair also, which is by nature black, is hereby changed and made of the same color with that of the sea Wolves; their bodies are also so besprinkled with the froth of the sea, that they appear rather like monsters than men.

What forms of cruelty did Las Casas mention in this account? Compare the treatment of the Indians described here with the treatment of African slaves described in the selection on p. 410.

1663, Canada became the property of the French crown and was administered as a French province. But the French failed to provide adequate men or money, allowing their continental wars to take precedence over the conquest of the North American continent. By the early eighteenth century, the French began to cede some of their American possessions to their English rival.

The English, meanwhile, had proceeded to create a colonial empire in the Western Hemisphere along the Atlantic seaboard of North America. Early efforts to establish English settlements near Cape Hatteras and the Chesapeake Bay made it evident that colonizing American lands was not necessarily conducive to quick profits. But the desire to escape from religious oppression combined with economic interests did make successful colonization possible, as the Massachusetts Bay Company demonstrated. The Massachusetts colony had only 4,000 settlers in its early years, but by 1660, their numbers had swelled to 40,000. Although the

English had established control over most of the eastern seaboard by the end of the seventeenth century, the North American colonies still remained of minor significance to the English economy.

Christopher Columbus: Hero or Villain?

For centuries, the explorer Christopher Columbus has been viewed throughout the world in a positive light. By discovering the Western Hemisphere, he opened up the world and laid the foundations for the modern global economy. Recently, however, some historians have begun to challenge the prevailing image of Columbus as a heroic figure in world history and view him instead as a symbol of European colonial repression and a prime mover in the virtual extinction of the peoples and cultures of the Americas (see the comparative essay "The Columbian Exchange" on p. 405).

The Columbian Exchange

INTERACTION & EXCHANGE

In the Western world, the discovery of the Americas has traditionally been viewed in a largely positive sense, as the first step in a process that expanded the global trade network and eventually led to increased economic well-being and the spread of civilization throughout the world. In recent years, however, that view has come under sharp attack from some observers, who point out that for the peoples of the Americas, the primary legacy of the European conquest was not improved living standards but harsh colonial exploitation and the spread of pestilential diseases that devastated local populations.

There is no doubt that the record of the European conquistadors in the Western Hemisphere leaves much to be desired, and certainly the voyages of Columbus were not of universal benefit to his contemporaries or to later generations. They not only resulted in the destruction of vibrant civilizations that were evolving in the Americas but also led ultimately to the enslavement of millions of Africans, who were separated from their families and shipped to a far-off world in deplorable, inhuman conditions.

But to focus solely on the evils committed in the name of exploration and civilization misses a larger point and obscures the long-term ramifications of the Age of Exploration. The age of European expansion that began with Prince Henry the Navigator and Christopher Columbus was only the latest in a series of population movements that included the spread of nomadic peoples across Central Asia and the expansion of Islam out of the Middle East after the death of the prophet Muhammad. In fact, the migration of peoples in search of survival and a better livelihood has been a central theme in the evolution of the human race since the dawn of prehistory. Virtually all of the migrations involved acts of unimaginable cruelty and the forcible displacement of peoples and societies.

In retrospect, it seems clear that the consequences of such broad population movements are too complex to be summed up in moral or ideological simplifications. The Mongol invasions and the expansion of Islam are two examples of movements that brought benefits as well as costs for the peoples who were affected. By the same token, the European conquest of the Americas not only brought the destruction of cultures and dangerous new diseases but also initiated the exchange of plant and animal species that have ultimately been of widespread benefit to peoples throughout the globe. The introduction of the horse, the cow, and various grain crops vastly increased food production in the Americas. The cultivation of corn, manioc, and the potato, all of them products of the Western Hemisphere,

Collections of the Library of Congress, Washington, DC

Massacre of the Indians. This sixteenth-century engraving is an imaginative treatment of what was probably an all-too-common occurrence as the Spanish attempted to enslave the American peoples and convert them to Christianity.

has had the same effect in Asia, Africa, and Europe. The **Columbian Exchange**, as it is sometimes labeled, has had far-reaching consequences that transcend facile moral judgments.

The opening of the Americas had other long-term ramifications as well. The importation of vast amounts of gold and silver fueled a price revolution that for years distorted the Spanish economy. At the same time, the increase in liquid capital due to this expansion was a crucial factor in the growth of commercial capitalism that set the stage for the global economy of the modern era. Some have even suggested that the precious metals that flowed into the treasuries of major European trading states may have helped finance the Industrial Revolution (see Chapter 19) that is now spreading rapidly throughout the modern world.

Viewed in that context, the Columbian Exchange, whatever its moral failings, ultimately brought benefits to peoples throughout the world. For some, the costs were high, and it can be argued that the indigenous peoples of the Americas might have better managed the transformation on their own. But the "iron law" of history operates at its own speed and does not wait for laggards. For good or ill, the Columbian Exchange marks a major stage in the transition between the traditional and the modern world.

How can the costs and benefits of the Columbian Exchange be measured? What standards would you apply in attempting to measure them?

Certainly, they have a point. As we have seen, the immediate consequences of Columbus's voyages were tragic for countless peoples in what Europeans innocently called the "New World." And as historical studies have shown, Columbus himself was not an entirely sympathetic figure. He viewed the indigenous peoples that he encountered with condescension, describing them to his sponsors as naïve innocents who could be exploited for the purpose of bringing wealth and power to Spain. As a consequence, the treatment of the local population by his men was frequently brutal.

But is it fair to blame Columbus for possessing many of the character traits and prejudices common to his era? To do so is to demand that an individual transcend the limitations of his time and adopt the values of another generation several hundred years into the future—something that few, if any, would be able to achieve. Perhaps it is better to note simply that Columbus and his contemporaries showed relatively little understanding and sympathy for the cultural values of peoples who lived beyond the borders of their own civilization, a limitation that would probably apply to one degree or another to all generations, including our own. Whether Columbus was a hero or a villain will remain a matter of debate. That he and his contemporaries played a key role in the emergence of the modern world is a matter on which there can be no doubt.

Africa in Transition

 FOCUS QUESTION: What were the main features of the African slave trade, and how did European participation in that trade affect traditional African practices?

Although the primary objective of the Portuguese in rounding the Cape of Good Hope was to find a sea route to the Spice Islands, they soon discovered that profits were to be made en route, along the eastern coast of Africa.

The Portuguese in Africa

In the early sixteenth century, a Portuguese fleet commanded by Francisco de Almeida (frahn-CHESS-koh duh ahl-MAY-duh) seized a number of East African port cities, including Kilwa, Sofala, and Mombasa, and built forts along the coast in an effort to control the trade in the area. Above all, the Portuguese wanted to monopolize the trade in gold, which was mined in the hills along the upper Zambezi River and then shipped to Sofala on the coast (see Map 14.4 on p. 403 and Chapter 8). For centuries, the gold trade had been monopolized by local Bantu-speaking Shona peoples at Zimbabwe. In the fifteenth century, it had come under the control of a Shona dynasty known as the Mwene Mutapa (MWAY-nay moo-TAH-puh).

The Mwene Mutapa had originally controlled the region south of the Zambezi River and may have been the builders of the impressive city known today as Great Zimbabwe, but sometime in the fifteenth century, they moved northeastward to the valley of the Zambezi. Here they encountered the arriving Portuguese, who had begun to move inland to gain access to the lucrative gold trade and had established ports on the Zambezi River. The Portuguese opened treaty relations with the Mwene Mutapa, and Jesuit priests were eventually posted to the court in 1561. At first, the Mwene Mutapa found the Europeans useful as an ally against local rivals, but by the end of the sixteenth century, the Portuguese had established a protectorate and forced the local ruler to grant title to large tracts of land to European officials and private individuals living in the area. Eventually, those lands would be integrated into the colony of Mozambique. The Portuguese, however, lacked the personnel, the capital, and the expertise to dominate local trade, and in the late seventeenth century, a vassal of the Mwene Mutapa succeeded in driving them from the plateau; his descendants maintained control of the area for the next two hundred years.

North of the Zambezi River, Bantu-speaking peoples were coming under pressure not only from the Portuguese but also from pastoralists migrating southward from the southern Sudan. The latter were frequently aggressive and began to occupy the rift valley and parts of the lake district that had previously been controlled by Bantu-speaking farmers. In some cases, the conflict between farmers and pastoralists was fairly clear-cut. In Rwanda and Burundi, immediately west of Lake Victoria, farming Hutu peoples defended their hilltop communities against roving Tutsi pastoralists occupying the surrounding lowlands.

The Dutch in South Africa

The first Europeans to settle in southern Africa were the Dutch. After an unsuccessful attempt to seize the Portuguese settlement on the island of Mozambique off the East African coast, in 1652 the Dutch set up a way station at the Cape of Good Hope to serve as a base for their fleets en route to the East Indies. At first, the new settlement was intended simply to provide food and other provisions to Dutch ships, but eventually it developed into a permanent colony. Dutch farmers, known as **Boers** and speaking a Dutch dialect that evolved into Afrikaans, began to settle in the sparsely occupied areas outside the city of Cape Town. The temperate climate and the absence of tropical diseases made the territory near the cape almost the only land south of the Sahara that the Europeans found suitable for habitation.

The Dutch, like their chief rivals, the English and the French, also took advantage of the decline of the Songhai Empire to become active in the West African trade in the mid-sixteenth century, encroaching particularly on the Portuguese spheres of influence. During the mid-seventeenth century, the Dutch seized a number of Portuguese forts along the West African coast while at the same time taking over the bulk of the Portuguese trade across the Indian Ocean.

The Slave Trade

The European exploration of the African coastline had little apparent significance for most peoples living in the interior of the continent, except for a few who engaged in direct or indirect trade with the foreigners. But for peoples living on or near the coast, the impact was often great indeed. As the trade in slaves increased during the sixteenth, seventeenth, and eighteenth centuries, thousands and then millions of men, women, and even children were removed from their homes and forcibly exported to plantations in the Western Hemisphere.

THE ARRIVAL OF THE EUROPEANS As we saw in Chapter 8, there were different forms of slavery in Africa before the arrival of the Europeans For centuries, slaves—often captives seized in battle or in raids between neighboring villages—had been used in many African societies as agricultural laborers or as household servants. Many served as domestic servants or as wageless workers for the local ruler, and some were permitted to purchase their freedom under certain conditions. After the expansion of Islam south of the Sahara in the eighth century, a vigorous traffic in slaves developed, as Arab merchants traded for slaves along routes snaking across the Sahara or up the Nile River valley. Once transported to the Middle East, most such captives were used as domestic servants or as workers on plantations throughout the region. Slavery also existed in many European countries, where a few slaves from Africa or Slavic-speaking peoples captured in war in the regions near the Black Sea (the English word *slave* derives from "Slav") were used for domestic purposes or as agricultural workers in the lands adjacent to the Mediterranean.

With the arrival of the Europeans in Africa in the fifteenth century, the African slave trade changed dramatically, although the change did not occur immediately. At first, the Portuguese simply replaced European slaves with African ones. During the second half of the fifteenth century, about a thousand slaves were taken to Portugal each year; the vast majority were apparently destined to serve as domestic servants for affluent families throughout Europe. But the discovery of the Americas in the 1490s and the subsequent planting of sugarcane in South America and on the islands of the Caribbean changed the situation. Cane sugar was native to Indonesia and had first been introduced to Europeans from the Middle East during the Crusades. By the fifteenth century, it was grown (often by slaves from Africa or the region of the Black Sea) in modest amounts on Cyprus, Sicily, and southern regions of the Iberian peninsula. But when the Ottoman Empire seized much of the eastern Mediterranean (see Chapter 16), the Europeans needed to seek out new areas suitable for cultivation. In 1490, the Portuguese established sugar plantations worked by African laborers at São Tomé, an island off the central coast of Africa. Demand increased as sugar gradually replaced honey as a sweetener, especially in northern Europe.

But the primary impetus to the sugar industry came from the colonization of the Americas. During the sixteenth century, plantations were established along the eastern coast of Brazil and on several islands in the Caribbean. Because the cultivation of cane sugar is an arduous process demanding both skill and large quantities of labor, the new plantations required more workers than could be provided by the Indian population in the Americas, many of whom had died of diseases imported from Europe and Africa. Since the climate and soil of much of West Africa were not especially conducive to the cultivation of sugar, African slaves began to be shipped to Brazil and the Caribbean to work on the plantations. The first were sent from Portugal, but in 1518, a Spanish ship carried the first boatload of African slaves directly from Africa to the Americas.

A Sugar Plantation. As a result of the growing popularity of sugar in Europe in the sixteenth century, sugar plantations were established in suitable areas throughout the tropical regions of South America and the Caribbean islands. Shown here is a plantation established by the French on the island of Hispaniola. The back-breaking nature of the work is clearly evident, as slaves imported from Africa cut the sugarcane and bring it to the mill for crushing and transformation into raw sugar. The inset shows a contemporary sugar plantation on the island of St. Kitts. Sugar is still grown on a number of islands in the Caribbean, although profit margins are low because of the volatility of the price of sugar.

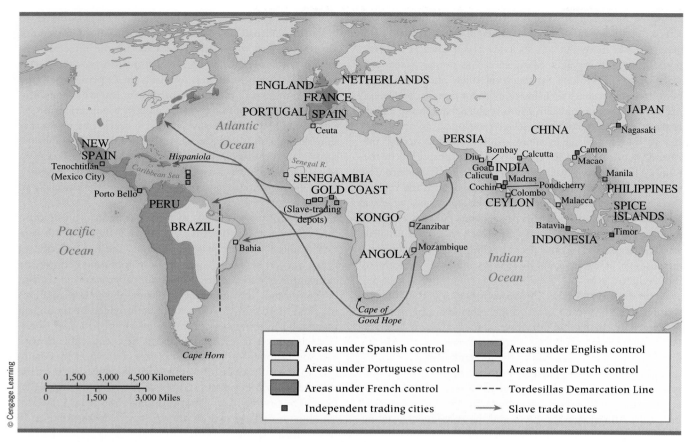

MAP 14.5 **The Slave Trade.** Beginning in the sixteenth century, the trade in African slaves to the Americas became a major source of profit to European merchants. This map traces the routes taken by slave-trading ships, as well as the territories and ports of call of European powers in the seventeenth century.

Q *What were the major destinations for the slave trade?*

GROWTH OF THE SLAVE TRADE During the next two centuries, the trade in slaves increased by massive proportions (see Map 14.5). An estimated 275,000 enslaved Africans were exported to other countries during the sixteenth century, more than two-thirds of them to the Americas. The total climbed beyond a million in the seventeenth century and jumped to 6 million in the eighteenth century, when the trade spread from West and Central Africa to East Africa. Even during the nineteenth century, when Great Britain and a number of other European countries attempted to end the slave trade, nearly 2 million humans were exported. It has been estimated that altogether as many as 10 million African slaves were transported to the Americas between the early sixteenth and the late nineteenth centuries. As many as 2 million were exported to other areas during the same period.

THE MIDDLE PASSAGE One reason for these astonishing numbers, of course, was the tragically high death rate. In what is often called the **Middle Passage**, the arduous voyage from Africa to the Americas, losses were frequently appalling. Although figures on the number of slaves who died on the journey are almost entirely speculative, during the first shipments, up to one-third of the human cargo may have died of disease or malnourishment. Even among crew members, mortality rates were sometimes as high as one in four. Later merchants became more efficient and reduced losses to about 10 percent. Still, the future slaves were treated inhumanely, chained together in the holds of ships reeking with the stench of human waste and diseases carried by vermin.

Ironically, African slaves who survived the brutal voyage fared somewhat better than whites after their arrival. Mortality rates for Europeans in the West Indies were ten to twenty times higher than in Europe, and death rates for those newly arrived in the islands averaged more than 125 per 1,000 annually. But the figure for Africans, many of whom had developed at least a partial immunity to yellow fever, was only about 30 per 1,000.

The reason for the staggering death rates was clearly more than maltreatment, although that was certainly a factor. As we have seen, the transmission of diseases from one continent to another brought high death rates among those lacking immunity. African slaves were somewhat less susceptible to European diseases than the American Indian populations. Indeed, they seem to have possessed a degree of immunity, perhaps because their ancestors had developed antibodies to diseases common to the Old World from the centuries of contact via the trans-Saharan trade. The Africans would not have had immunity to native American diseases, however.

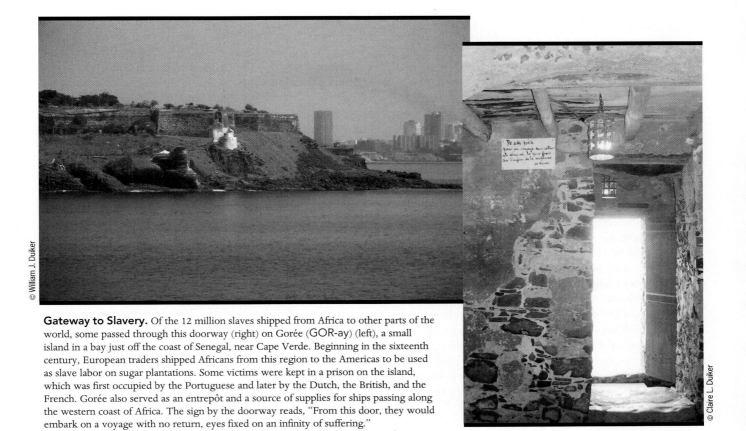

Gateway to Slavery. Of the 12 million slaves shipped from Africa to other parts of the world, some passed through this doorway (right) on Gorée (GOR-ay) (left), a small island in a bay just off the coast of Senegal, near Cape Verde. Beginning in the sixteenth century, European traders shipped Africans from this region to the Americas to be used as slave labor on sugar plantations. Some victims were kept in a prison on the island, which was first occupied by the Portuguese and later by the Dutch, the British, and the French. Gorée also served as an entrepôt and a source of supplies for ships passing along the western coast of Africa. The sign by the doorway reads, "From this door, they would embark on a voyage with no return, eyes fixed on an infinity of suffering."

The mortality rates were higher for immigrants than for individuals born in the Americas, who as children gradually developed at least a partial immunity to many diseases. Death rates for native-born slaves tended to be significantly lower than for recent arrivals, which raises the question of why the slave population did not begin to rise after the initial impact of settlement had worn off. The answer appears to be a matter of economics. In the first place, only half as many women were enslaved as men, birthrates for women living in slavery were low, and infant mortality was high. In the second place, as long as the price of slaves was low, many slave owners in the West Indies apparently believed that purchasing a new slave was less expensive than raising a child from birth to working age at adolescence. After the price of slaves began to rise during the eighteenth century, plantation owners started to devote more efforts to replenishing the supply of workers by natural methods.

SOURCES OF SLAVES Slaves were obtained by traditional means. As mentioned earlier, before the coming of the Europeans, most slaves in Africa were prisoners or war captives or had inherited their status. When Europeans first began to take part in the slave trade, they would normally purchase slaves from local African merchants at the infamous slave markets in exchange for gold, guns, or other European manufactured goods such as textiles or copper or iron utensils (see the box on p. 410). At first, local slave traders obtained their supply from nearby regions, but as demand increased, they had to move further inland to find their victims. In a few

cases, local rulers became concerned about the impact of the slave trade on the political and social well-being of their societies (see the box on p. 411). As a general rule, however, the local monarchs viewed the slave trade as a source of income, and many launched forays against defenseless villages in search of unsuspecting victims.

Historians once thought that Europeans controlled the terms of the slave trade and were able to obtain victims at bargain prices. Recently, however, it has become clear that African intermediaries—private merchants, local elites, and trading state monopolies—were very active in the process and were often able to dictate the price, volume, and availability of slaves to European purchasers. The majority of the slaves sold to European buyers were males; females, who were in great demand in Africa and on the trans-Saharan trade, tended to be reserved for those markets. The slave merchants were often paid in various types of imported goods, including East Asian textiles (highly desired for their bright colors and durability), furniture, and other manufactured products. Until the end of the seventeenth century, the Portuguese preferred gold to slaves and would sometimes pay for the gold by selling slaves to African kingdoms that were short of labor. In fact, not until the beginning of the eighteenth century did slaves surpass gold and ivory as the continent's leading exports.

THE EFFECTS OF THE SLAVE TRADE The effects of the slave trade varied from area to area. It might be assumed that apart from the tragic effects on the lives of individual victims and

A Slave Market in Africa

FAMILY & SOCIETY

Traffic in slaves had been carried on in Africa since the kingdom of the pharaohs in ancient Egypt. But the slave trade increased dramatically after the arrival of European ships off the coast of West Africa. The following passage by a Dutch observer describes a slave market in Africa and the conditions on the ships that carried the slaves to the Americas.

Slavery in Africa: A Firsthand Report

Not a few in our country fondly imagine that parents here sell their children, men their wives, and one brother the other. But those who think so deceive themselves, for this never happens on any other account but that of necessity, or some great crime; most of the slaves that are offered to us are prisoners of war, who are sold by the victors as their booty.

When these slaves come to Fida, they are put in prison all together; and when we treat concerning buying them, they are brought out into a large plain. There, by our surgeons, whose province it is, they are thoroughly examined, even to the smallest member, and that naked too, both men and women, without the least distinction or modesty. Those that are approved as good are set on one side; and the lame or faulty are set by as invalids. . . .

The invalids and the maimed being thrown out, . . . the remainder are numbered, and it is entered who delivered them. In the meanwhile, a burning iron, with the arms or name of the companies, lies in the fire, with which ours are marked on the breast. This is done that we may distinguish them from the slaves of the English, French, or others (which are also marked with their mark), and to prevent the Negroes exchanging them for worse, at which they have a good hand.

I doubt not but this trade seems very barbarous to you, but since it is followed by mere necessity, it must go on; but we take all possible care that they are not burned too hard, especially the women, who are more tender than the men.

When we have agreed with the owners of the slaves, they are returned to their prison. There from that time forward they are kept at our charge, costing us two pence a day a slave; which serves to subsist them, like our criminals, on bread and water. To save charges, we send them on board our ships at the very first opportunity, before which their masters strip them of all they have on their backs so that they come aboard stark naked, women as well as men. In this condition they are obliged to continue, if the master of the ship is not so charitable (which he commonly is) as to bestow something on them to cover their nakedness.

You would really wonder to see how these slaves live on board, for though their number sometimes amounts to six or seven hundred, yet by the careful management of our masters of ships, they are so regulated that it seems incredible. And in this particular our nation exceeds all other Europeans, for the French, Portuguese and English slave ships are always foul and stinking; on the contrary, ours are for the most part clean and neat.

The slaves are fed three times a day with indifferent good victuals, and much better than they eat in their own country. Their lodging place is divided into two parts, one of which is appointed for the men, the other for the women, each sex being kept apart. Here they lie as close together as it is possible for them to be crowded.

We are sometimes sufficiently plagued with a parcel of slaves which come from a far inland country who very innocently persuade one another that we buy them only to fatten and afterward eat them as a delicacy. When we are so unhappy as to be pestered with many of this sort, they resolve and agree together (and bring over the rest to their party) to run away from the ship, kill the Europeans, and set the vessel ashore, by which means they design to free themselves from being our food.

I have twice met with this misfortune; and the first time proved very unlucky to me, I not in the least suspecting it, but the uproar was quashed by the master of the ship and myself by causing the abettor to be shot through the head, after which all was quiet.

What is the author's overall point of view toward the institution of slavery? Does he justify the practice? How does he compare Dutch behavior with that of other European countries involved in the slave trade?

their families, the practice would have led to the depopulation of vast areas of the continent. This did occur in some areas, notably in modern Angola, south of the mouth of the Congo River, and in thinly populated regions in East Africa, but it was less true in West Africa. There high birthrates were often able to counterbalance the loss of able-bodied adults, and the introduction of new crops from the Americas, such as maize, peanuts, and manioc (see the photo on p. 412), led to an increase in food production that made it possible to support a larger population. One of the many cruel ironies of history is that while the institution of slavery was a tragedy for many, it benefited others.

Still, there is no denying the reality that from a moral point of view, the slave trade represented a tragic loss for

The Price of Friendship

INTERACTION & EXCHANGE

King Afonso I of the state of Kongo was one of Portugal's chief African allies during the early sixteenth century. A convert to Christianity, he used his relationship with the Portuguese to extend the territory of his kingdom at the expense of neighboring states in the region. Captives obtained during his military campaigns were sold to merchants and then exported abroad as slaves. As the demand for slaves increased, however, traders began to trap and enslave Afonso's own subjects, while flooding the country with goods from abroad that undermined his royal authority.

In this letter, written in 1526, Afonso appealed to his "brother" sovereign, Dom João III, king of Portugal, to prevent such unscrupulous merchants from seizing his subjects and selling them as slaves to European sea captains. The letter is a vivid testimonial to how the slave trade destabilized African societies on or near the coast during the sixteenth and seventeenth centuries.

A Letter to King João

[1526] Sir, your Highness [of Portugal] should know how our Kingdom is being lost in so many ways that it is convenient to provide for the necessary remedy, since this is caused by the excessive freedom given by your factors and officials to the men and merchants who are allowed to come to this Kingdom to set up shops with goods and many things which have been prohibited by us, and which they spread throughout our Kingdoms and Domains in such an abundance that many of our vassals, whom we had in obedience, do not comply because they have the things in greater abundance than we ourselves; and it was with these things that we had them content and subjected under our vassalage and jurisdiction, so it is doing a great harm not only to the service of God, but the security and peace of our Kingdoms and State as well.

And we cannot reckon how great the damage is, since the mentioned merchants are taking every day our natives, sons of the land and the sons of our noblemen and vassals and our relatives, because the thieves and men of bad conscience grab them wishing to have the things and wares of this Kingdom which they are ambitious of; they grab them and get them to be sold; and so great, Sir, is the corruption and licentiousness that our country is being completely depopulated, and Your Highness should not agree with this nor accept it as in your service. And to avoid it we need from those [your] Kingdoms no more than some priests and a few people to teach in schools, and no other goods except wine and flour for the holy sacrament. That is why we beg of Your Highness to help and assist us in this matter, commanding your factors that they should not send here either merchants or wares, because it is *our will that in these Kingdoms there should not be any trade of slaves nor outlet for them.* Concerning what is referred above, again we beg of Your Highness to agree with it, since otherwise we cannot remedy such an obvious damage. Pray Our Lord in His mercy to have Your Highness under His guard and let you do for ever the things of His service. I kiss your hand many times.

At our town of Congo, written on the sixth day of July.
João Teixeira did it in 1526.
The King, Dom Afonso.

[On the back of this letter the following can be read: To the most powerful and excellent prince Dom João, King our Brother.]

 In what ways were the European merchants destabilizing the kingdom of Kongo? What remedy did Afonso propose?

---

millions of Africans, not only for the individual victims but also for their families. One of the more poignant aspects of the trade is that as many as 20 percent of those sold to European slavers were children, a statistic that may be partly explained by the fact that many European countries enacted regulations that permitted more children than adults to be transported aboard the ships.

Beyond the effects on individual Africans and their families, the slave trade also had a corrosive impact on the structure of society as a whole. Another consequence of the arrival of the Europeans was the introduction of firearms into the African continent. As the European demand for slaves steadily increased, African slave traders began to use their newly purchased guns to raid neighboring villages in search of captives, initiating a chain of violence that rapidly extended into the interior and created a climate of fear and insecurity throughout the region. Old polities were undermined, and new regimes ruled by rapacious "merchant princes" began to proliferate on the coast.

How did Europeans justify cruelty of such epidemic proportions? In some cases, they rationalized that slave traders were only carrying on a tradition that had existed for centuries throughout the Mediterranean and African world. In others, they eased their consciences by noting that slaves brought from Africa would now be exposed to the Christian faith and would be able to replace American Indian workers, many of whom were considered too physically fragile for the heavy human labor involved in cutting sugarcane.

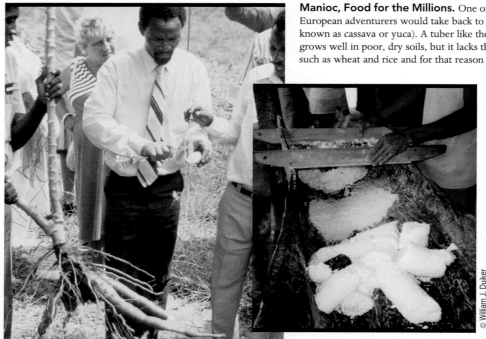

Manioc, Food for the Millions. One of the plants native to the Americas that European adventurers would take back to the Old World was manioc (also known as cassava or yuca). A tuber like the potato, manioc is a prolific crop that grows well in poor, dry soils, but it lacks the high nutrient value of grain crops such as wheat and rice and for that reason never became popular in Europe (except as a source of tapioca). It was introduced to Africa in the seventeenth century. Because it flourishes in dry climates and can be preserved easily for consumption at a later date, it eventually became a staple food for up to one-third of the population of that continent. Shown at the left is a manioc plant growing in East Africa. On the right, a Brazilian farmer on the Amazon River sifts peeled lengths of manioc into fine grains that will be dried into flour.

Political and Social Structures in a Changing Continent

Of course, the Western economic penetration of Africa had other dislocating effects. As in other parts of the non-Western world, the importation of manufactured goods from Europe undermined the foundations of local cottage industries and impoverished countless families. The demand for slaves and the introduction of firearms intensified political instability and civil strife. At the same time, the impact of the Europeans should not be exaggerated. Only in a few isolated areas, such as South Africa and Mozambique, were permanent European settlements established. Elsewhere, at the insistence of African rulers and merchants, European influence generally did not penetrate beyond the coastal regions.

Nevertheless, inland areas were often affected by events taking place elsewhere. In the western Sahara, for example, the diversion of trade routes toward the coast led to the weakening of the old Songhai trading empire and its eventual conquest by a vigorous new Moroccan dynasty in the late sixteenth century. Morocco had long hoped to expand its influence into the Sahara in order to seize control over the

commerce in gold and salt, and in 1590, Moroccan forces defeated Songhai's army at Gao, on the Niger River, and then occupied the great caravan center of Timbuktu. Even after the departure of the invaders, Songhai was beyond recovery, and the next two centuries were marked by ongoing strife between divergent states and intense competition between Muslims in the cities and towns and adherents of traditional African religions in rural areas.

European influence had a more direct impact along the coast of West Africa, especially in the vicinity of European forts such as Dakar and Sierra Leone, but no European colonies were established there before 1800. Most of the numerous African states in the area from Cape Verde to the delta of the Niger River were sufficiently strong to resist Western encroachments, and they often allied with each other to force European purchasers to respect their monopoly over trading operations. Some, like the powerful Ashanti kingdom, established in 1680 on the Gold Coast, profited substantially from the rise in seaborne commerce. Some states, particularly along the so-called Slave Coast, in what is now Benin and Togo, or in the densely populated Niger River delta, took an active part in the slave trade. The demands of slavery and the temptations of economic profit, however, also contributed to the increase in conflict among the states in the area.

This was especially true in the region of the Congo River, where Portuguese activities eventually led to the splintering of the state of Kongo and two centuries of rivalry and internal strife among the successor states in the area. A similar pattern developed in East Africa, where Portuguese activities led to the decline and eventual collapse of the Mwene Mutapa. Northward along the coast, in present-day Kenya and Tanzania, African rulers, assisted by Arab forces from Oman and Muscat in the Arabian peninsula, expelled the Portuguese from Mombasa in 1698. Swahili culture now regained some of the dynamism it had possessed before the arrival of Vasco da Gama and his

CHRONOLOGY	The Penetration of Africa
Life of Prince Henry the Navigator	1394–1460
Portuguese ships reach the Senegal River	1441
Bartolomeu Dias sails around the tip of Africa	1487
First boatload of slaves to the Americas	1518
Dutch way station established at the Cape of Good Hope	1652
Ashanti kingdom established in West Africa	1680
Portuguese expelled from Mombasa	1698

Fort Jesus at Mombasa. Mombasa, a port city on the eastern coast of Africa, was a jumping-off point for the Portuguese as they explored the lands bordering the Indian Ocean. Erected in the early sixteenth century atop a bluff overlooking the harbor, Fort Jesus remained an imposing symbol of European power until 1698, when the Portuguese were expelled by the Arabs. They returned briefly in 1728 but were forced to evacuate a few months later.

successors. But with much shipping now diverted southward to the route around the Cape of Good Hope, the commerce of the area never completely recovered and was increasingly dependent on the export of slaves and ivory obtained through contacts with African states in the interior.

Southeast Asia in the Era of the Spice Trade

Q FOCUS QUESTION: What were the main characteristics of Southeast Asian societies, and how were they affected by the coming of Islam and the Europeans?

As we noted earlier, Southeast Asia would be affected in various ways by the expansion of the global trade network that began to accelerate in the early fifteenth century with the arrival of Chinese fleets under the command of Admiral Zhenghe. Although the Chinese threat soon receded, the Muslim faith, introduced by merchants from the Middle East, now began to make inroads on the Malay peninsula and in the Indonesian archipelago. The seizure of Malacca by a Portuguese fleet in 1511 inaugurated a period of intense conflict among various European competitors for control of the regional spice trade. At first, the rulers of most of the local states were able to fend off these challenges from abroad and maintain their independence. As we shall see in a later chapter, however, the reprieve was only temporary.

The Arrival of the West

As we have seen, the Spanish followed the Portuguese into Southeast Asia. By the seventeenth century, the Dutch,

English, and French had begun to join the scramble for rights to the lucrative spice trade.

Within a short time, the Dutch, through the aggressive and well-financed Dutch East India Company (Vereenigde Oost-Indische Compagnie, or VOC), which possessed ten times the capital of the English East India Company, had not only succeeded in elbowing their rivals out of the spice trade but had also begun to consolidate their political and military control over the area. On the island of Java, where they established a fort at Batavia (today's Jakarta) in 1619 (see the illustration on p. 389), the Dutch found that it was necessary to bring the inland regions under their control to protect their position on the coast. Rather than establishing a formal colony, however, they tried to rule as much as possible through the local landed aristocracy. On Java and the neighboring island of Sumatra, the VOC established pepper plantations, which soon produced massive profits for Dutch merchants in Amsterdam. Elsewhere they attempted to monopolize the clove trade by limiting cultivation of the crop to one island. By the end of the eighteenth century, the Dutch had succeeded in bringing almost the entire Indonesian archipelago under their control.

Competition among the European naval powers for territory and influence continued to intensify throughout the region, however, and prospects for the future were ominous. In the countless island groups scattered throughout the Pacific Ocean, local rulers were already finding it difficult to resist the growing European presence. The results were sometimes tragic, as indigenous cultures were quickly overwhelmed under the impact of Western material civilization, often leaving a sense of rootlessness and psychic stress in their wake (see the box on p. 414).

CHRONOLOGY The Spice Trade	
Vasco da Gama lands at Calicut in southwestern India	1498
Albuquerque establishes base at Goa	1510
Portuguese seize Malacca	1511
Portuguese ships land in southern China	1514
Magellan's voyage around the world	1519–1522
English East India Company established	1600
Dutch East India Company established	1602
English arrive at Surat in northwestern India	1608
Dutch fort established at Batavia	1619
Dutch seize Malacca from the Portuguese	1641
Burmese sack of Ayuthaya	1767

The March of Civilization

INTERACTION & EXCHANGE

As Europeans began to explore new parts of the world in the fifteenth century, they were convinced that it was their duty to introduce civilized ways to the heathen peoples of Asia, Africa, and the Americas. Such was the message of Spanish captain Vasco Núñez de Balboa (BAHS-koh NOON-yez day bal-BOH-uh) one September morning in 1513, when from a hill on the Isthmus of Panama he first laid eyes on the Pacific Ocean. Two centuries later, however, the intrepid British explorer James Cook, during his last visit to the island of Tahiti in 1777, expressed in his private journal his growing doubts that Europeans had brought lasting benefits to the Polynesian islanders. Such disagreements over the alleged benefits of Western civilization to non-Western peoples would continue to spark debate during the centuries that followed and remain with us today (see "Imperialism: The Balance Sheet" in Chapter 21).

Maori Tiki god, South Pacific.

Gonzalo Fernández de Ovieda, *Historia General y Natural de las Indias*

On Tuesday, the twenty-fifth of September of the year 1513, at ten o'clock in the morning, Captain Vasco Núñez, having gone ahead of his company, climbed a hill with a bare summit, and from the top of this hill saw the South Sea. Of all the Christians in his company, he was the first to see it. He turned back toward his people, full of joy, lifting his hands and his eyes to Heaven, praising Jesus Christ and his glorious Mother the Virgin, Our Lady. Then he fell upon his knees on the ground and gave great thanks to God for the mercy He had shown him, in allowing him to discover that sea, and thereby to render so great a service to God and to the most serene Catholic Kings of Castile, our sovereigns. . . .

And he told all the people with him to kneel also, to give the same thanks to God, and to beg Him fervently to allow them to see and discover the secrets and great riches of that sea and coast, for the greater glory and increase of the Christian faith, for the conversion of the Indians, natives of those southern regions, and for the fame and prosperity of the royal throne of Castile and of its sovereigns present and to come. All the people cheerfully and willingly did as they were bidden; and the Captain made them fell a big tree and make from it a tall cross, which they erected in that same place, at the top of the hill from which the South Sea had first been seen. And they all sang together the hymn of the glorious holy fathers of the Church, Ambrose and Augustine, led by a devout priest Andrés de Vera, who was with them, saying with tears of joyful devotion *Te Deum laudamus, Te Dominum confitemur*.

Journal of Captain James Cook

I cannot avoid expressing it as my real opinion that it would have been far better for these poor people never to have known our superiority in the accommodations and arts that make life comfortable, than after once knowing it, to be again left and abandoned in their original incapacity of improvement. Indeed they cannot be restored to that happy mediocrity in which they lived before we discovered them, if the intercourse between us should be discontinued. It seems to me that it has become, in a manner, incumbent on the Europeans to visit them once in three or four years, in order to supply them with those conveniences which we have introduced among them, and have given them a predilection for. The want of such occasional supplies will, probably, be felt very heavily by them, when it may be too late to go back to their old, less perfect, contrivances, which they now despise, and have discontinued since the introduction of ours. For, by the time that the iron tools, of which they are now possessed, are worn out, they will have almost lost the knowledge of their own. A stone hatchet is, at present, as rare a thing amongst them, as an iron one was eight years ago, and a chisel of bone or stone is not to be seen.

 Why did James Cook express regret that the peoples of Tahiti had been exposed to European influence? How might Captain Núñez de Balboa have responded?

© William J. Duiker

The arrival of the Europeans had somewhat less impact on mainland Southeast Asia, where cohesive monarchies in Burma (modern Myanmar), Thailand, and Vietnam resisted foreign encroachment. In addition, the coveted spices did not thrive on the mainland, so the Europeans' efforts there were far less determined than in the islands. The Portuguese did establish limited trade relations with several mainland states, including the Thai kingdom at Ayuthaya, Burma, Vietnam, and the remnants of the old Angkor kingdom in Cambodia. By the early seventeenth century, other nations had followed and had begun to compete actively for trade and missionary privileges. As was the case elsewhere, the Europeans soon became involved in local factional disputes as a means of obtaining political and economic advantages. In Burma, the English and the French supported rival groups in the internal struggles of the monarchy until a new dynasty emerged and threw the foreigners out. A similar process took place at Ayuthaya, which was eventually destroyed by a Burmese army in 1767.

In Vietnam, the arrival of Western merchants and missionaries coincided with a period of internal conflict among ruling groups in the country. After their arrival in the mid-seventeenth century, the European powers characteristically began to intervene in local politics, with the Portuguese and the Dutch supporting rival factions. By the end of the century, when it became clear that economic opportunities were limited, most European states abandoned their trading stations in the area. French missionaries attempted to remain, but their efforts were hampered by the local authorities, who viewed the Catholic insistence that converts give their primary loyalty to the pope as a threat to the legal status and prestige of the Vietnamese emperor (see the box on p. 416).

State and Society in Precolonial Southeast Asia

Between 1500 and 1800, Southeast Asia experienced the last flowering of traditional culture before the advent of European rule in the nineteenth century. Although the coming of the Europeans had an immediate and direct impact in some areas, notably the Philippines and parts of the Malay world, in most areas Western influence was still relatively limited. Europeans occasionally dabbled in local politics and modified regional trade patterns, but they generally were not a decisive factor in the evolution of local political or social systems.

Nevertheless, Southeast Asian societies were changing in several subtle ways—in their trade patterns, their means of livelihood, and their religious beliefs. In some ways, these changes accentuated the differences between individual states in the region. Yet beneath these differences was an underlying commonality of life for most people. Despite the diversity of cultures and religious beliefs in the area, Southeast Asians were in most respects closer to each other than they were to peoples outside the region. For the most part, the states and peoples of Southeast Asia were still in control of their own destiny.

RELIGION AND KINGSHIP During the early modern era, both Buddhism and Islam became well established in South-east Asia, although Christianity began to attract some converts, especially in port cities directly occupied by Europeans, such as Malacca and Batavia, and in the Philippines (see the comparative illustration on p. 417). Buddhism was dominant in lowland areas on the mainland, from Burma to Vietnam. At first, Muslim influence was felt mainly on the Malay peninsula and along the northern coasts of Java and Sumatra, where local merchants encountered their Muslim counterparts from foreign lands on a regular basis. At the same time, traditional religious beliefs continued to survive, especially in inland areas, where the local populations either ignored the new doctrines or integrated them into their traditional forms of spirit worship. Buddhists in rural Burma and Thailand, for example, might also believe in nature spirits. On Java and Sumatra, where Islam was slow to penetrate into the interior, the result was a division between devout Muslims in the cities and essentially animist peasants in the rural villages.

Both Buddhism and Islam brought other changes in their train—temple education for Buddhists and schools for Islamic scholars and new religious and moral restrictions on human behavior such as refraining from eating pork and drinking wine for Muslims (though some foreign Muslims complained that the latter rule was not always followed). Because Islam discouraged the traditional tattooing of the body, Muslim converts turned to the technique of decorating textiles called *batik* (buh-TEEK).

Buddhism and Islam also helped shape Southeast Asian political institutions. As the political systems began to mature, they evolved into four main types: Buddhist kings, Javanese kings, Islamic sultans, and Vietnamese emperors (for Vietnam, which was strongly influenced by China, see Chapter 11). In each case, institutions and concepts imported from abroad were adapted to local circumstances.

The Buddhist style of kingship took shape between the eleventh and the fifteenth centuries as Theravada Buddhism spread throughout the area. It became the predominant political system in the Buddhist states of mainland Southeast Asia—Burma, Ayuthaya, Laos, and Cambodia. Perhaps the most prominent feature of the Buddhist model was the god-like character of the monarch, who was considered by virtue of his *karma* to be innately superior to other human beings and served as a link between human society and the cosmos. Court rituals stressed the sacred nature of the monarch, and even the palace was modeled after the symbolic design of the Hindu universe. In its center was an architectural rendering of sacred Mount Meru, the legendary home of the gods.

The Javanese model was a blend of Buddhist and Islamic political traditions. Like their mainland counterparts, Javanese monarchs possessed a sacred quality and maintained the balance between the sacred and the material world, but as Islam penetrated the Indonesian islands in the fifteenth and sixteenth centuries, the monarchs began to lose their semidivine quality.

The Islamic model was found mainly on the Malay peninsula and along the coast of the Indonesian archipelago. In this pattern, the head of state was a sultan, who was viewed as a mortal, although he still possessed some magical qualities. The sultan served as a defender of the faith and staffed his

An Exchange of Royal Correspondence

INTERACTION & EXCHANGE

In 1681, King Louis XIV of France wrote a letter to the "king of Tonkin" (the Trinh family head, who was serving as viceroy to the Vietnamese ruler) requesting permission for Christian missionaries to proselytize in Vietnam. The latter politely declined the request on the grounds that such activity was prohibited by ancient custom. In fact, Christian missionaries had been active in Vietnam for years, and their intervention in local politics had aroused the anger of the court in Hanoi.

A Letter to the King of Tonkin from Louis XIV

Most high, most excellent, most mighty, and most magnanimous Prince, our very dear and good friend, may it please God to increase your greatness with a happy end!

We hear from our subjects who were in your Realm what protection you accorded them. We appreciate this all the more since we have for you all the esteem that one can have for a prince as illustrious through his military valor as he is commendable for the justice which he exercises in his Realm. We have even been informed that you have not been satisfied to extend this general protection to our subjects but, in particular, that you gave effective proofs of it to Messrs. Deydier and de Bourges. We would have wished that they might have been able to recognize all the favors they received from you by having presents worthy of you offered you; but since the war which we have had for several years, in which all of Europe had banded together against us, prevented our vessels from going to the Indies, at the present time, when we are at peace after having gained many victories and expanded our Realm through the conquest of several important places, we have immediately given orders to the Royal Company to establish itself in your kingdom as soon as possible, and have commanded Messrs. Deydier and de Bourges to remain with you in order to maintain a good relationship between our subjects and yours, also to warn us on occasions that might present themselves when we might be able to give you proofs of our esteem and of our wish to concur with your satisfaction as well as with your best interests.

By way of initial proof, we have given orders to have brought to you some presents which we believe might be agreeable to you. But the one thing in the world which we desire most, both for you and for your Realm, would be to obtain for your subjects who have already embraced the law of the only true God of heaven and earth, the freedom to profess it, since this law is the highest, the noblest, the most sacred, and especially the most suitable to have kings reign absolutely over the people.

We are even quite convinced that, if you knew the truths and the maxims which it teaches, you would give first of all to your subjects the glorious example of embracing it. We wish you this incomparable blessing together with a long and happy reign, and we pray God that it may please Him to augment your greatness with the happiest of endings.

Written at Saint-Germain-en-Laye, the 10th day of January, 1681,

Your very dear and good friend,
Louis

Answer from the King of Tonkin to Louis XIV

The King of Tonkin sends to the King of France a letter to express to him his best sentiments, saying that he was happy to learn that fidelity is a durable good of man and that justice is the most important of things. Consequently practicing of fidelity and justice cannot but yield good results. Indeed, though France and our Kingdom differ as to mountains, rivers, and boundaries, if fidelity and justice reign among our villages, our conduct will express all of our good feelings and contain precious gifts. Your communication, which comes from a country which is a thousand leagues away, and which proceeds from the heart as a testimony of your sincerity, merits repeated consideration and infinite praise. Politeness toward strangers is nothing unusual in our country. There is not a stranger who is not well received by us. How then could we refuse a man from France, which is the most celebrated among the kingdoms of the world and which for love of us wishes to frequent us and bring us merchandise? These feelings of fidelity and justice are truly worthy to be applauded. As regards your wish that we should cooperate in propagating your religion, we do not dare to permit it, for there is an ancient custom, introduced by edicts, which formally forbids it. Now, edicts are promulgated only to be carried out faithfully; without fidelity nothing is stable. How could we disdain a well-established custom to satisfy a private friendship? . . .

We beg you to understand well that this is our communication concerning our mutual acquaintance. This then is my letter. We send you herewith a modest gift, which we offer you with a glad heart.

This letter was written at the beginning of winter and on a beautiful day.

How does the king of Tonkin's response to Louis XIV's request compare with the answer given to the pope by the Mongol emperor Kuyuk Khan in 1244 on p. 284? Which response do you think was more conciliatory? Why?

© William J. Duiker

© William J. Duiker

COMPARATIVE ILLUSTRATION

The Face of Christianity in America and Asia. As European colonial officials and missionaries began to spread through the Americas and Asia in the sixteenth and seventeenth centuries, the churches that they built reflected the styles that had become popular in their own countries. The photograph on the left shows a baroque cathedral in Mexico City, the headquarters of Spanish rule in Central America. It was erected on the site of the Aztec temple to the sun god at Tenochtitlán, using materials from the dismantled Aztec pyramids.

The Dutch preferred a less ornate approach, as seen in the rose-colored church in Malacca shown at the right, erected after their takeover of that trading port in 1641.

Q *How did the spread of Christianity in America and Asia in the sixteenth and seventeenth centuries compare with the expansion of Islam in earlier times?*

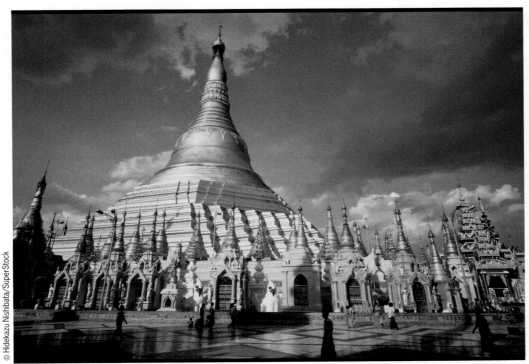

© Hidekazu Nishibata/SuperStock

In a Buddhist Wonderland. The Shwedagon Pagoda is the most sacred site in Myanmar (Burma). Located on a hill in today's capital of Yangon (formerly Rangoon), the pagoda was originally erected on the site of an earlier Buddhist structure sometime in the late first millennium C.E. Its centerpiece is a magnificent stupa covered in gold leaf that stands more than 320 feet high. The platform at the base of the stupa contains a multitude of smaller shrines and stupas covered with marble carvings and fragments of cut glass. It is no surprise that for centuries, the Buddhist faithful have visited the site, and the funds they have donated have made the Shwedagon stupa one of the wonders of the world.

bureaucracy mainly with aristocrats, but he also frequently relied on the Muslim community of scholars—the *ulama*—and was expected, at least in theory, to rule according to the *Shari'a*.

THE ECONOMY During the early period of European penetration, the economy of most Southeast Asian societies was based on agriculture, as it had been for thousands of years. Still, by the sixteenth century, commerce was beginning to affect daily life, especially in the cities that were beginning to proliferate along the coasts or on navigable rivers. In part, this was because agriculture itself was becoming more commercialized as cash crops like sugar and spices replaced subsistence farming of rice or other cereals in some areas.

Regional and interregional trade were already expanding before the coming of the Europeans. The central geographic location of Southeast Asia enabled it to become a focal point in a widespread trading network. Spices, of course, were the mainstay of the interregional trade, but other products were exchanged as well. The region exported tin (mined in Malaya

since the tenth century), copper, gold, tropical fruits and other agricultural products, cloth, gems, and luxury goods in exchange for manufactured goods, ceramics, and high-quality textiles such as silk from China (see the comparative illustration below). Although on balance the region was an importer of manufactured goods, it produced some high-quality goods of its own. The ceramics of Vietnam and Thailand, though not made with the high-temperature firing techniques used in China, were still of good quality. The Portuguese traveler Duarte Barbosa (DWAR-tay bar-BOH-suh) observed that the Javanese were skilled cabinetmakers, weapons manufacturers, shipbuilders, and locksmiths. The royal courts were both the main producers and the primary consumers of luxury goods, most of which were produced by highly skilled slaves in the employ of the court.

In general, Southeast Asians probably enjoyed a somewhat higher living standard than their contemporaries elsewhere in Asia. Although most of the population was poor by modern Western standards, hunger was not a widespread problem. Several factors help explain this relative prosperity. In the first

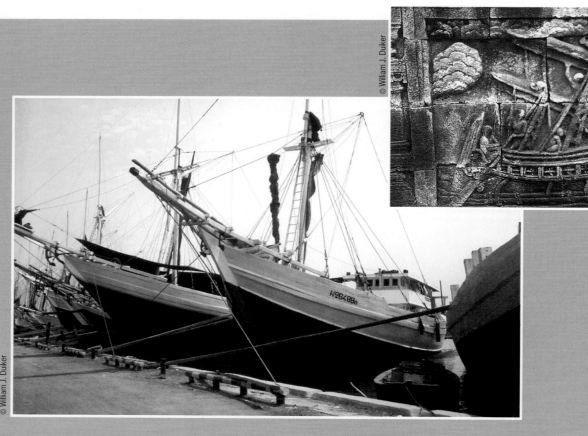

COMPARATIVE ILLUSTRATION

Bringing Lumber to Java. Long before the Europeans arrived, a brisk trade was taking place throughout the Indonesian islands and the South China Sea. Many of the goods that were transported through the area were carried on sturdy boats—called *pinisi*—that were manned by the Bugi (BOO-gih), a trading people who lived mainly in the eastern islands. The trade continues today as these cargo ships in the harbor of Jakarta attest. The Bugi were also widely feared as pirates, giving rise to the once-familiar parental admonition to children, "Don't let the bogyman get you!" The bas relief in the inset, from the temple of Borobudur, is a rare example of a sailing vessel in the ninth century C.E.

Q *What role did Southeast Asia play in the global trade network?*

place, most of Southeast Asia has been blessed with a salubrious climate. The uniformly high temperatures and the abundant rainfall enable two or even three crops to be grown each year. Second, although the soil in some areas is poor, the alluvial deltas on the mainland are fertile, and the volcanoes of Indonesia periodically spew forth rich volcanic ash that renews the mineral resources of the soil of Sumatra and Java. Finally, with some exceptions, most of Southeast Asia was relatively thinly populated. According to one estimate, the population of the entire region in 1600 was about 20 million, or about 14 persons per square mile, well below levels elsewhere in Asia. Only in a few areas such as the Red River delta in northern Vietnam was overpopulation a serious problem.

SOCIETY Social institutions tended to be fairly homogeneous throughout Southeast Asia. Compared with China and India, there was little social stratification, and the nuclear family predominated. In general, women fared better in the region than anywhere else in Asia. Daughters often had the same inheritance rights as sons, and family property was held jointly between husband and wife. Wives were often permitted to divorce their husbands, and monogamy was the rule rather than the exception. In some cases, the family of the groom provided the dowry in marriage, and married couples often went to live in the wife's village. Although women were usually restricted to specialized work, such as making ceramics, weaving, or transplanting the rice seedlings into the main paddy fields, and rarely possessed legal rights equal to those of men, they enjoyed a comparatively high degree of freedom and status in most societies in the region and, as we saw in Chapter 9, were sometimes involved in commerce. In the Indonesian islands, for example, women apparently devised a simple fourteen-character alphabet based on the Indian script to record their business transactions. This written language was often passed on to their daughters, while their sons were trained to read sacred works in religious schools.

CHAPTER SUMMARY

During the fifteenth century, the pace of international commerce increased dramatically. Chinese fleets visited the Indian Ocean while Muslim traders extended their activities into the Spice Islands and sub-Saharan West Africa. Then the Europeans burst onto the world scene. Beginning with the seemingly modest ventures of the Portuguese ships that sailed southward along the West African coast, the process accelerated with the epoch-making voyages of Christopher Columbus to the Americas and Vasco da Gama to the Indian Ocean in the 1490s. Soon a number of other European states had entered the fray, and by the end of the eighteenth century, they had created a global trade network dominated by Western ships and Western power that distributed foodstuffs, textiles, spices, and precious minerals from one end of the globe to the other.

In less than three hundred years, the expansion of the global trade network changed the face of the world. In some areas, such as the Americas and the Spice Islands, it led to the destruction of indigenous civilizations and the establishment of European colonies. In others, as in Africa, South Asia, and mainland Southeast Asia, it left native regimes intact but had a strong impact on local societies and regional trade patterns. In some areas, it led to an irreversible decline in traditional institutions and values, setting in motion a corrosive process that has not been reversed to this day.

At the time, many European observers viewed the process in a favorable light. Not only did it expand world trade and foster the exchange of new crops and discoveries between the Old and New Worlds, but it also introduced Christianity to "heathen peoples" around the globe. Many modern historians have been much more critical, concluding that European activities during the sixteenth and seventeenth centuries created a "tributary mode of production" based on European profits from unequal terms of trade that foreshadowed the exploitative relationship characteristic of the later colonial period. Other scholars have questioned that contention, however, and argue that although Western commercial operations had a significant impact on global trade patterns, they did not—at least not before the nineteenth century—usher in an era of Western dominance over the rest of the world. Muslim merchants were long able to evade European efforts to eliminate them from the spice trade, and the trans-Saharan caravan trade was relatively unaffected by European merchant shipping along the West African coast.

In the meantime, powerful empires continued to hold sway over the lands washed by the Muslim faith. Beyond the Himalayas, Chinese emperors in their new northern capital of Beijing retained proud dominion over all the vast territory of continental East Asia. We shall deal with these regions, and how they confronted the challenges of a changing world, in Chapters 16 and 17.

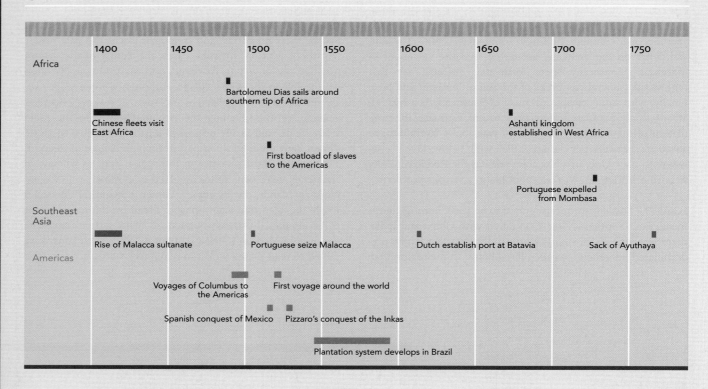

Timeline with rows for Africa, Southeast Asia, and Americas spanning dates 1400 to 1750.

- Chinese fleets visit East Africa (~1400)
- Bartolomeu Dias sails around southern tip of Africa (~1490)
- First boatload of slaves to the Americas (~1500)
- Ashanti kingdom established in West Africa (~1650)
- Portuguese expelled from Mombasa (~1700)
- Rise of Malacca sultanate (~1400)
- Portuguese seize Malacca (~1510)
- Dutch establish port at Batavia (~1620)
- Sack of Ayuthaya (~1750)
- Voyages of Columbus to the Americas (~1490)
- First voyage around the world (~1520)
- Spanish conquest of Mexico (~1520)
- Pizzaro's conquest of the Inkas (~1530)
- Plantation system develops in Brazil (~1550)

CHAPTER REVIEW

Upon Reflection

Q What were some of the key features of the Columbian Exchange, and what effects did they have on the world trade network?

Q How did the expansion of European power during the Age of Exploration compare with the expansion of the Islamic empires in the Middle East a few centuries earlier?

Q Why were the Spanish conquistadors able to complete their conquest of Latin America so quickly when their contemporaries failed to do so in Africa and Southeast Asia?

Key Terms

portolani (p. 394)
caravels (p. 395)
conquistadors (p. 398)
mestizos (p. 400)
mulattoes (p. 400)
viceroy (p. 400)
creoles (p. 401)
encomienda **system** (p. 402)
encomienda (p. 402)
Columbian Exchange (p. 405)
Boers (p. 406)
Middle Passage (p. 408)

Suggested Reading

EUROPEAN EXPANSION On the technological aspects of European expansion, see **F. Fernandez-Armesto, ed.,** *The Times Atlas of World Exploration* (New York, 1991), and **R. C. Smith,** *Vanguard of Empire: Ships of Exploration in the Age of Columbus* (Oxford, 1993). Also see **A. Pagden,** *Lords of All the World: Ideologies of Empire in Spain, Britain, and France, c. 1500–c. 1800* (New Haven, Conn., 1995). For an overview of the advances in map making that accompanied the Age of Exploration, see **T. Lester,** *The Fourth Part of the World: The Race to the Ends of the Earth, and the Epic Story of the Map That Gave America Its Name* (New York, 2009). Also see **A. Gurney,** *Compass: A Story of Exploration and Innovation* (New York, 2004), and **W. Bernstein's** impressive *A Splendid Exchange: How Trade Shaped the World* (New York, 2008).

COUNTRY-SPECIFIC STUDIES A gripping work on the conquistadors is **H. Thomas,** *Conquest: Montezuma, Cortés, and the Fall of Old Mexico* (New York, 1993).

On the Dutch, see **J. I. Israel,** *Dutch Primacy in World Trade, 1585–1740* (Oxford, 1989). British activities are chronicled in **S. Sen,** *Empire of Free Trade: The East India Company and the Making of the Colonial Marketplace* (Philadelphia, 1998), and **Anthony Wild's** elegant work *The East India Company: Trade and Conquest from 1600* (New York, 2000).

THE SPICE TRADE The effects of European trade in Southeast Asia are discussed in **A. Reid,** *Southeast Asia in the Age of Commerce, 1450–1680* (New Haven, Conn., 1989). On the spice trade, see **A. Dalby,**

Dangerous Tastes: The Story of Spices (Berkeley, Calif., 2000), and **J. Turner,** *Spice: The History of a Temptation* (New York, 2004).

THE SLAVE TRADE   On the African slave trade, see **P. E. Lovejoy,** *Transformations in Slavery: A History of Slavery in Africa* (Cambridge, 1983), and **P. Manning,** *Slavery and African Life* (Cambridge, 1990). **H. Thomas,** *The Slave Trade* (New York, 1997), provides a useful overview.

WOMEN   For a brief introduction to women's experiences during the Age of Exploration and global trade, see **S. Hughes** and **B. Hughes,** *Women in World History,* vol. 2 (Armonk, N.Y., 1997). The native American female experience with the European encounter is presented in

R. Gutierrez, *When Jesus Came the Corn Mothers Went Away: Marriage, Sexuality, and Power in New Mexico, 1500–1846* (Stanford, Calif., 1991).

Go to the CourseMate website at **www.cengagebrain.com** for additional study tools and review materials— including audio and video clips—for this chapter.

A nineteenth-century engraving showing Luther before the Diet of Worms

Europe Transformed: Reform and State Building

CHAPTER OUTLINE AND FOCUS QUESTIONS

The Reformation of the Sixteenth Century

Q What were the main tenets of Lutheranism, Calvinism, and Anabaptism, and how did they differ from each other and from Catholicism?

Europe in Crisis, 1560–1650

Q Why is the period between 1560 and 1650 in Europe considered an age of crisis, and how did the turmoil contribute to the artistic developments of the period?

Response to Crisis: The Practice of Absolutism

Q What was absolutism, and what were the main characteristics of the absolute monarchies that emerged in France, Prussia, Austria, and Russia?

England and Limited Monarchy

Q How and why did England avoid the path of absolutism?

The Flourishing of European Culture

Q How did the artistic and literary achievements of this era reflect the political and economic developments of the period?

CRITICAL THINKING

Q What was the relationship between European overseas expansion (as traced in Chapter 14) and political, economic, and social developments in Europe?

ON APRIL 18, 1521, A LOWLY MONK stood before the emperor and princes of Germany in the city of Worms (VAWRMZ). He had been called before this august diet (a deliberating council) to answer charges of heresy, charges that could threaten his very life. The monk was confronted with a pile of his books and asked if he wished to defend them all or reject a part. Courageously, Martin Luther defended them all and asked to be shown where any part was in error on the basis of "Scripture and plain reason." The emperor was outraged by Luther's response and made his own position clear the next day: "Not only I, but you of this noble German nation, would be forever disgraced if by our negligence not only heresy but the very suspicion of heresy were to survive. After having heard yesterday the obstinate defense of Luther, I regret that I have so long delayed in proceeding against him and his false teaching. I will have no more to do with him." Luther's appearance at Worms set the stage for a serious challenge to the authority of the Catholic Church. This was by no means the first crisis in the church's 1,500-year history, but its consequences were more far-reaching than anyone at Worms in 1521 could have imagined.

After the disintegrative patterns of the fourteenth century, Europe began a remarkable recovery that encompassed a revival of arts and letters in the fifteenth century, known as the Renaissance, and a religious renaissance in the sixteenth century, known as the Reformation. The resulting religious division of Europe (Catholics versus Protestants) was instrumental in triggering a series of wars that dominated much of European history from 1560 to 1650 and exacerbated the economic and social crises that were besetting the region.

One of the responses to the crises of the seventeenth century was a search for order. The most general trend was an extension of monarchical power as a stabilizing force. This development, which historians have called **absolutism** or *absolute monarchy*, was most evident in France during the flamboyant reign of Louis XIV, regarded by some as the perfect embodiment of an absolute monarch.

But absolutism was not the only response to the search for order in the seventeenth century. Other states, such as England, reacted very differently to domestic crisis, and yet another system emerged in which monarchs were limited by the power of their representative assemblies. Absolute and limited monarchy were the two poles of seventeenth-century state building.

The Reformation of the Sixteenth Century

Q FOCUS QUESTION: What were the main tenets of Lutheranism, Calvinism, and Anabaptism, and how did they differ from each other and from Catholicism?

The **Protestant Reformation** is the name given to the religious reform movement that divided the western Christian church into Catholic and Protestant groups. Although the Reformation began with Martin Luther in the early sixteenth century, several earlier developments had set the stage for religious change.

Background to the Reformation

Changes in the fifteenth century—the age of the Renaissance—helped prepare the way for the dramatic upheavals in sixteenth-century Europe.

THE GROWTH OF STATE POWER In the first half of the fifteenth century, European states had continued the disintegrative patterns of the previous century. In the second half of that century, however, recovery had set in, and attempts had been made to reestablish the centralized power of monarchical governments. To characterize the results, some historians have used the label "Renaissance states"; others have spoken of the "**new monarchies**," especially those of France, England, and Spain at the end of the fifteenth century (see Chapter 13).

What was new about these Renaissance monarchs was their concentration of royal authority, their attempts to suppress the nobility, their efforts to control the church in their lands, and their desire to obtain new sources of revenue in order to increase royal power and enhance the military forces at their disposal. Like the rulers of fifteenth-century Italian states, the Renaissance monarchs were often crafty men obsessed with the acquisition and expansion of political power. Of course, none of these characteristics was entirely new; a number of medieval monarchs, especially in the thirteenth century, had exhibited them. Nevertheless, the Renaissance period marks a significant expansion of centralized royal authority.

No one gave better expression to the Renaissance preoccupation with political power than Niccolò Machiavelli (nee-koh-LOH mahk-ee-uh-VEL-ee) (1469–1527), an Italian who wrote *The Prince* (1513), one of the most influential works on political power in the Western world. Machiavelli's major concerns in *The Prince* were the acquisition, maintenance, and expansion of political power as the means to restore and maintain order. In the Middle Ages, many political theorists stressed the ethical side of a prince's activity—how a ruler ought to behave based on Christian moral principles. Machiavelli bluntly contradicted this approach: "For the gap between how people actually behave and how they ought to behave is so great that anyone who ignores everyday reality in order to live up to an ideal will soon discover he had been taught how to destroy himself, not how to preserve himself."[1] Machiavelli considered his approach far more realistic than that of his medieval forebears. Political activity, therefore, could not be restricted by moral considerations. The prince acts on behalf of the state and for the sake of the state must be willing to let his conscience sleep. Machiavelli was among the first Western thinkers to abandon morality as the basis for the analysis of political activity. The same emphasis on the ends justifying the means, or on achieving results regardless of the methods employed, had in fact been expressed a thousand years earlier by a court official in India named Kautilya (kow-TIL-yuh) in his treatise on politics, the *Arthasastra* (ar-thuh-SAS-truh) (see Chapter 2).

SOCIAL CHANGES IN THE RENAISSANCE Social changes in the fifteenth century also helped to create an environment in which the Reformation of the sixteenth century could occur. After the severe economic reversals and social upheavals of the fourteenth century, the European economy gradually recovered as manufacturing and trade increased in volume. The Italians and especially the Venetians expanded their wealthy commercial empire, rivaled only by the increasingly powerful Hanseatic (han-see-AT-ik) League, a commercial and military alliance of north German coastal towns. Not until the sixteenth century, when overseas discoveries gave new importance to the states facing the Atlantic, did the Italian city-states begin to suffer from the competitive advantages of the more powerful national territorial states.

As noted in Chapter 12, society in the Middle Ages was divided into three estates: the clergy, or First Estate, whose preeminence was grounded in the belief that people should be guided to spiritual ends; the nobility, or Second Estate, whose privileges rested on the principle that nobles provided security and justice for society; and the peasants and inhabitants of the towns and cities, the Third Estate. Although this social order continued into the Renaissance, some changes also became evident.

Throughout much of Europe, the landholding nobles faced declining real incomes during most of the fourteenth and fifteenth centuries. Many members of the old nobility survived, however, and new blood also infused their ranks. In 1500, the nobles, old and new, who constituted between 2 and 3 percent of the population in most countries, still dominated society, as they had in the Middle Ages, holding important political posts and serving as advisers to the king.

Harbor Scene at Hamburg. Hamburg was a founding member of the Hanseatic League. This illustration from a fifteenth-century treatise on the laws of the city shows a busy port with ships of all sizes. At the left, a crane is used to unload barrels. In the building at the right, customs officials collect their dues. Merchants and townspeople are shown talking at dockside.

industry, and banking enabled them to dominate their urban communities economically, socially, and politically. Below them were the petty burghers—the shopkeepers, artisans, guild-masters, and guildsmen—who were largely concerned with providing goods and services for local consumption. Below these two groups were the propertyless workers earning pitiful wages and the unemployed, living squalid and miserable lives. These poor city-dwellers made up 30 to 40 percent of the urban population. The pitiful conditions of the lower groups in urban society often led them to support calls for radical religious reform in the sixteenth century.

THE IMPACT OF PRINTING The Renaissance witnessed the development of printing, which made an immediate impact on European intellectual life and thought. Printing from hand-carved wooden blocks had been done in the West since the twelfth century and in China even before that. What was new in the fifteenth century in Europe was multiple printing with movable metal type. The development of printing from movable type was a gradual process that culminated sometime between 1445 and 1450; Johannes Gutenberg (yoh-HAH-nuss GOO-ten-bayrk) of Mainz (MYNTS) played an important role in bringing the process to completion. Gutenberg's Bible, completed in 1455 or 1456, was the first true book produced from movable type.

By 1500, there were more than a thousand printers in Europe, who collectively had published almost 40,000 titles (between 8 million and 10 million copies). Probably half of these books were religious—Bibles and biblical commentaries, books of devotion, and sermons. Next in importance were the Latin and Greek classics, medieval grammars, legal handbooks, and works on philosophy.

The printing of books encouraged scholarly research and the desire to attain knowledge. Printing also stimulated the development of an ever-expanding lay reading public, a development that had an enormous impact on European society. Indeed, without the printing press, the new religious ideas of the Reformation would not have spread as rapidly as they did in the sixteenth century. Moreover, printing allowed European civilization to compete for the first time with the civilization of China.

Except in the heavily urban areas of northern Italy and Flanders, peasants made up the overwhelming mass of the Third Estate—they constituted 85 to 90 percent of the total European population. Serfdom had decreased as the manorial system continued its decline. Increasingly, the labor dues owed by peasants to their lord were converted into rents paid in money. By 1500, especially in western Europe, more and more peasants were becoming legally free. At the same time, peasants in many areas resented their social superiors and sought to keep a greater share of the benefits from their labor. In the sixteenth century, the grievances of peasants, especially in Germany, led many of them to support religious reform movements.

Inhabitants of towns and cities, originally merchants and artisans, constituted the remainder of the Third Estate. But by the fifteenth century, the Renaissance town or city had become more complex. At the top of urban society were the patricians, whose wealth from capitalistic enterprises in trade,

PRELUDE TO REFORMATION During the second half of the fifteenth century, the new Classical learning of the Italian Renaissance spread to the European countries north of the Alps and spawned a movement called **Christian humanism** or **northern Renaissance humanism**, whose major goal was the reform of Christianity. The Christian humanists believed in the ability of human beings to reason and improve themselves and thought that through education in the sources of Classical, and especially Christian, antiquity, they could instill an inner piety or an inward religious feeling that would bring about a reform of the church and society. To change society, they must first change the human beings who compose it.

The most influential of all the Christian humanists was Desiderius Erasmus (dez-i-DEER-ee-uss i-RAZZ-mus) (1466–1536), who formulated and popularized the reform program of Christian humanism. He called his conception of religion "the philosophy of Christ," by which he meant that Christianity should be a guiding philosophy for the direction of daily life rather than the system of dogmatic beliefs and practices that the medieval church seemed to stress. In other words, he emphasized inner piety and de-emphasized the external forms of religion (such as the sacraments, pilgrimages, fasts, and relics). To Erasmus, the reform of the church meant spreading an understanding of the philosophy of Jesus, providing enlightened education in the sources of early Christianity, and criticizing the abuses in the church. No doubt his work helped prepare the way for the Reformation; as contemporaries proclaimed, "Erasmus laid the egg that Luther hatched."

CHURCH AND RELIGION ON THE EVE OF THE REFORMATION Corruption in the Catholic Church was another factor that led people to want reform. Between 1450 and 1520, a series of popes—called the Renaissance popes—failed to meet the church's spiritual needs. The popes were supposed to be the spiritual leaders of the Catholic Church, but as rulers of the Papal States, they were all too often involved in worldly concerns. Julius II (1503–1513), the fiery "warrior-pope," personally led armies against his enemies, much to the disgust of pious Christians, who thought the pope's role was to serve as a spiritual leader. As one intellectual wrote, "How, O bishop standing in the room of the Apostles, dare you teach the people the things that pertain to war?" Many high church officials were also concerned with accumulating wealth and used their church offices as opportunities to advance their careers and their fortunes, and many ordinary parish priests seemed ignorant of their spiritual duties.

While the leaders of the church were failing to meet their responsibilities, ordinary people were clamoring for meaningful religious expression and certainty of salvation. As a result, for some the process of salvation became almost mechanical. As more and more people sought certainty of salvation through veneration of relics (bones or other objects intimately associated with the saints), collections of **relics** grew. Frederick the Wise, elector (one of the seven German princes who chose the Holy Roman Emperor) of Saxony and Martin Luther's prince, had amassed nearly 19,000 relics to which were attached **indulgences** that could reduce a person's time in purgatory by nearly 2 million years. (An indulgence is a remission, after death, of all or part of the punishment due to sin.) Other people sought certainty of salvation in more spiritual terms by participating in the popular mystical movement known as the Modern Devotion, which downplayed religious dogma and stressed the need to follow the teachings of Jesus.

What is striking about the revival of religious piety in the fifteenth century—whether expressed through such external forces as the veneration of relics and the buying of indulgences or the mystical path—was its adherence to the orthodox beliefs and practices of the Catholic Church. The agitation for certainty of salvation and spiritual peace occurred within the framework of the "holy mother Church." But disillusionment grew as the devout experienced the clergy's inability to live up to their expectations. The deepening of religious life, especially in the second half of the fifteenth century, found little echo among the worldly-wise clergy, and this environment helps explain the tremendous and immediate impact of Luther's ideas.

Martin Luther and the Reformation in Germany

Martin Luther (1483–1546) was a monk and a professor at the University of Wittenberg (VIT-ten-bayrk), where he lectured on the Bible. Probably sometime between 1513 and 1516, through his study of the Bible, he arrived at an answer to a problem—the assurance of salvation—that had disturbed him since his entry into the monastery.

Catholic doctrine had emphasized that both faith and good works were required for a Christian to achieve personal salvation. In Luther's eyes, human beings, weak and powerless in the sight of an almighty God, could never do enough good works to merit salvation. Through his study of the Bible, Luther came to believe that humans are saved not through their good works but through faith in the promises of God, made possible by the sacrifice of Jesus on the cross. This doctrine of salvation, or justification by grace through faith alone, became the primary doctrine of the Protestant Reformation (**justification by faith** is the act by which a person is made deserving of salvation). Because Luther had arrived at this doctrine from his study of the Bible, the Bible became for Luther, as for all other Protestants, the chief guide to religious truth.

Luther did not see himself as a rebel, but he was greatly upset by the widespread selling of indulgences. Especially offensive in his eyes was the monk Johann Tetzel, who hawked indulgences with the slogan "As soon as the coin in the coffer [money box] rings, the soul from purgatory springs." Greatly angered, in 1517 he issued a stunning indictment of the abuses in the sale of indulgences, known as the Ninety-Five Theses (see the box on p. 426). Thousands of copies were printed and quickly spread to all parts of Germany.

By 1520, Luther had begun to move toward a more definite break with the Catholic Church and called on the German princes to overthrow the papacy in Germany and establish a reformed German church. Through all his calls for change, Luther expounded more and more on his new doctrine of salvation. It is faith alone, he said, not good works, that justifies and brings salvation through Christ.

Unable to accept Luther's ideas, the church excommunicated him in January 1521. He was also summoned to appear before the Reichstag (RYKHSS-tahk) (imperial diet) of the Holy Roman Empire, convened by the newly elected

Luther and the Ninety-Five Theses

RELIGION & PHILOSOPHY

To most historians, the publication of Luther's Ninety-Five Theses marks the beginning of the Reformation. To Luther, they were simply a response to what he considered blatant abuses committed by sellers of indulgences. Although written in Latin, the theses were soon translated into German and disseminated widely across Germany. They made an immense impression on Germans already dissatisfied with the ecclesiastical and financial policies of the papacy.

Martin Luther, Selections from the Ninety-Five Theses

5. The Pope has neither the will nor the power to remit any penalties beyond those he has imposed either at his own discretion or by canon law.

20. Therefore the Pope, by his plenary remission of all penalties, does not mean "all" in the absolute sense, but only those imposed by himself.

21. Hence those preachers of Indulgences are wrong when they say that a man is absolved and saved from every penalty by the Pope's Indulgences.

27. It is mere human talk to preach that the soul flies out [of purgatory] immediately [when] the money clinks in the collection box.

28. It is certainly possible that when the money clinks in the collection box greed and avarice can increase; but the intercession of the Church depends on the will of God alone.

50. Christians should be taught that if the Pope knew the exactions of the preachers of Indulgences, he would rather have the basilica of St. Peter reduced to ashes than built with the skin, flesh, and bones of his sheep

[the indulgences that so distressed Luther were being sold to raise money for the construction of the new St. Peter's Basilica in Rome].

81. This wanton preaching of pardons makes it difficult even for learned men to redeem respect due to the Pope from the slanders or at least the shrewd questionings of the laity.

82. For example: "Why does not the Pope empty purgatory for the sake of most holy love and the supreme need of souls? This would be the most righteous of reasons, if he can redeem innumerable souls for sordid money with which to build a basilica, the most trivial of reasons."

86. Again: "Since the Pope's wealth is larger than that of the crassest Crassi of our time, why does he not build this one basilica of St. Peter with his own money, rather than with that of the faithful poor?"

90. To suppress these most conscientious questionings of the laity by authority only, instead of refuting them by reason, is to expose the Church and the Pope to the ridicule of their enemies, and to make Christian people unhappy.

94. Christians should be exhorted to seek earnestly to follow Christ, their Head, through penalties, deaths, and hells.

95. And let them thus be more confident of entering heaven through many tribulations rather than through a false assurance of peace.

 What were the major ideas of Luther's Ninety-Five Theses? Why did they have such a strong appeal in Germany?

Emperor Charles V (1519–1556). Ordered to recant the heresies he had espoused, Luther refused and made the famous reply that became the battle cry of the Reformation:

> Unless I am convicted by Scripture and plain reason—I do not accept the authority of popes and councils, for they have contradicted each other—my conscience is captive to the Word of God. I cannot and I will not recant anything, for to go against conscience is neither right nor safe. Here I stand, I cannot do otherwise. God help me. Amen.[2]

Members of the Reichstag were outraged and demanded that Luther be arrested and delivered to the emperor. But Luther's ruler, Elector Frederick of Saxony, stepped in and protected him.

During the next few years, Luther's movement began to grow and spread. As it made an impact on the common people, it also created new challenges. This was especially true of

the Peasants' War that erupted in 1524. Social discontent created by their pitiful conditions became entangled with religious revolt as the German peasants looked to Martin Luther for support. But when the peasants took up arms and revolted against their landlords, Luther turned against them and called on the German princes, who in Luther's eyes were ordained by God to maintain peace and order, to crush the rebels. By May 1525, the German princes had ruthlessly suppressed the peasant hordes. By this time, Luther found himself dependent on the state authorities for the growth of his reformed church.

Luther now succeeded in gaining the support of many of the rulers of the three hundred or so German states that made up the Holy Roman Empire. These rulers quickly took control of the churches in their territories. The Lutheran churches in Germany (and later in Scandinavia) became territorial or state churches in which the state supervised the affairs of the church. As part of the development of these state-

A Reformation Woodcut. In the 1520s, after Luther's return to Wittenberg, his teachings began to spread rapidly, ending ultimately in a reform movement supported by state authorities. Pamphlets containing picturesque woodcuts were important in the spread of Luther's ideas. In the woodcut shown here, the crucified Jesus attends Luther's service on the left, while on the right the pope is at a table selling indulgences.

dominated churches, Luther also instituted new religious services to replace the Catholic Mass. These focused on reading the Bible, preaching the word of God, and singing hymns. Following his own denunciation of clerical celibacy, Luther married a former nun, Katherina von Bora, in 1525. His union provided a model of married and family life for the new Protestant minister.

POLITICS AND RELIGION IN THE GERMAN REFORMATION
From its very beginning, the fate of Luther's movement was closely tied to political affairs. In 1519, Charles I, king of Spain and the grandson of Emperor Maximilian, was elected Holy Roman Emperor as Charles V. Charles V ruled over an immense empire, consisting of Spain and its overseas possessions, the traditional Austrian Habsburg lands, Bohemia, Hungary, the Low Countries, and the kingdom of Naples in southern Italy. Politically, Charles wanted to maintain his enormous empire; religiously, he hoped to preserve the unity of his empire in the Catholic faith. A number of problems, however, kept him preoccupied and cost him both his dream and his health.

Moreover, the internal political situation in the Holy Roman Empire was not in Charles's favor. Although all the German states owed loyalty to the emperor, during the Middle Ages these states had become quite independent of imperial authority. By the time Charles V was able to bring military forces to Germany in 1546, Lutheranism had become well established and the Lutheran princes were well organized. Unable to defeat them, Charles was forced to negotiate a truce. An end to religious warfare in Germany came in 1555 with the Peace of Augsburg (OUKS-boork). The division of Christianity was formally acknowledged; Lutheran states were to have the

same legal rights as Catholic states. Although the German states were now free to choose between Catholicism and Lutheranism, the peace settlement did not recognize the principle of religious toleration for individuals. The right of each German ruler to determine the religion of his subjects was accepted, but not the right of the subjects to choose their own religion. With the Peace of Augsburg, what had at first been merely feared was now certain: the ideal of Christian unity was forever lost. The rapid spread of new Protestant groups made this a certainty.

The Spread of the Protestant Reformation

Switzerland was home to two major Reformation movements. Zwinglianism and Calvinism. Ulrich Zwingli (OOL-rikh TSFING-lee) (1484–1531) was ordained a priest in 1506 and accepted an appointment as a cathedral priest in the Great Minster of Zürich (ZOOR-ik or TSIH-rikh) in 1518. Zwingli's preaching of the Gospel caused such unrest that in 1523 the city council held a public disputation (debate) in the town hall. Zwingli's party was accorded the victory, and over the next two years, evangelical reforms were promulgated in Zürich by a city council strongly influenced by Zwingli. Relics and images were abolished; all paintings and decorations were removed from the churches and replaced by whitewashed walls. The Mass was replaced by a new liturgy consisting of Scripture reading, prayer, and sermons. Monasticism, pilgrimages, the veneration of saints, clerical celibacy, and the pope's authority were all abolished as remnants of papal Christianity.

OPPOSING < VIEWPOINTS

A Reformation Debate: Conflict at Marburg

RELIGION & PHILOSOPHY

Debates played a crucial role in the Reformation period. They were a primary instrument for introducing the Reformation in innumerable cities as well as a means of resolving differences among like-minded Protestant groups. This selection contains an excerpt from the vivacious and often brutal debate between Luther and Zwingli over the sacrament of the Lord's Supper at Marburg in 1529. The two protagonists failed to reach agreement.

The Marburg Colloquy, 1529

THE HESSIAN CHANCELLOR FEIGE: My gracious prince and lord [Landgrave Philip of Hesse] has summoned you for the express and urgent purpose of settling the dispute over the sacrament of the Lord's Supper. . . . Let everyone on both sides present his arguments in a spirit of moderation, as becomes such matters. . . . Now then, Doctor Luther, you may proceed.

LUTHER: Noble prince, gracious lord! Undoubtedly the colloquy is well intentioned. . . . Although I have no intention of changing my mind, which is firmly made up, I will nevertheless present the grounds of my belief and show where the others are in error. . . . Your basic contentions are these: In the last analysis you wish to prove that a body cannot be in two places at once, and you produce arguments about the unlimited body which are based on natural reason. I do not question how Christ can be God and man and how the two natures can be joined. For God is more powerful than all our ideas, and we must submit to his word.

Prove that Christ's body is not there where the Scripture says, "This is my body!" Rational proofs I will not listen to. . . . God is beyond all mathematics and the words of God are to be revered and carried out in awe. It is God who commands, "Take, eat, this is my body." I request, therefore, valid scriptural proof to the contrary.

Luther writes on the table in chalk, "This is my body," and covers the words with a velvet cloth.

OECOLAMPADIUS [leader of the reform movement in Basel and a Zwinglian partisan]: The sixth chapter of John clarifies the other scriptural passages. Christ is not speaking there about a local presence. "The flesh is of no avail," he says. It is not my intention to employ rational, or geometrical, arguments—neither am I denying the power of God—but as long as I have the complete faith I will speak from that.

For Christ is risen; he sits at the right hand of God; and so he cannot be present in the bread. Our view is neither new nor sacrilegious, but is based on faith and Scripture. . . .

ZWINGLI: I insist that the words of the Lord's Supper must be figurative. This is ever apparent, and even required by the article of faith: "taken up into heaven, seated at the right hand of the Father." Otherwise, it would be absurd to look for him in the Lord's Supper at the same time that Christ is telling us that he is in heaven. One and the same body cannot possibly be in different places. . . .

LUTHER: I call upon you as before: your basic contentions are shaky. Give way, and give glory to God!

ZWINGLI: And we call upon you to give glory to God and to quit begging the question! The issue at stake is this: Where is the proof of your position? I am willing to consider your words carefully—no harm meant! You're trying to outwit me. I stand by this passage in the sixth chapter of John, verse 63, and shall not be shaken from it. You'll have to sing another tune.

LUTHER: You're being obnoxious.

ZWINGLI: *(excitedly)* Don't you believe that Christ was attempting in John 6 to help those who did not understand?

LUTHER: You're trying to dominate things! You insist on passing judgment! Leave that to someone else! . . . It is your point that must be proved, not mine. But let us stop this sort of thing. It serves no purpose.

ZWINGLI: It certainly does! It is for you to prove that the passage in John 6 speaks of a physical repast.

LUTHER: You express yourself poorly and make about as much progress as a cane standing in a corner. You're going nowhere.

ZWINGLI: No, no, no! This is the passage that will break your neck!

LUTHER: Don't be so sure of yourself. Necks don't break this way. You're in Hesse, not Switzerland.

 How did the positions of Zwingli and Luther on the sacrament of the Lord's Supper differ? What was the purpose of this debate? Based on this example, why did many Reformation debates led to further hostility rather than compromise and unity between religious and sectarian opponents? What implications did this have for the future of the Protestant Reformation?

As his movement began to spread to other cities in Switzerland, Zwingli sought an alliance with Martin Luther and the German reformers. Although both the German and the Swiss reformers realized the need for unity to defend against the opposition of the Catholic authorities, they were unable to agree on the interpretation of the Lord's Supper, the sacrament of Communion (see the box above). Zwingli believed that the scriptural words "This is my body, this is my blood" should be taken figuratively, not literally, and refused to accept Luther's insistence on the real presence of the body and blood of Jesus "in, with, and under the bread and wine." In October 1531, war erupted between the Swiss Protestant and Catholic states.

Zürich's army was routed, and Zwingli was found wounded on the battlefield. His enemies killed him, cut up his body, burned the pieces, and scattered the ashes. The leadership of Swiss Protestantism now passed to John Calvin, the systematic theologian and organizer of the Protestant movement.

CALVIN AND CALVINISM John Calvin (1509–1564) was educated in his native France, but after converting to Protestantism, he was forced to flee to the safety of Switzerland. In 1536, he published the first edition of the *Institutes of the Christian Religion*, a masterful synthesis of Protestant thought that immediately secured his reputation as one of the new leaders of Protestantism.

On most important doctrines, Calvin stood very close to Luther. He adhered to the doctrine of justification by faith alone to explain how humans achieved salvation. But Calvin also placed much emphasis on the absolute sovereignty or all-powerful nature of God—what Calvin called the "power, grace, and glory of God." One of the ideas derived from his emphasis on the absolute sovereignty of God—**predestination**—gave a unique cast to Calvin's teachings. This "eternal decree," as Calvin called it, meant that God had predestined some people to be saved (the elect) and others to be damned

John Calvin. After a conversion experience, John Calvin abandoned his life as a humanist and became a reformer. In 1536, Calvin began working to reform the city of Geneva, where he remained until his death in 1564. This sixteenth-century portrait of Calvin shows him near the end of his life.

(the reprobate). According to Calvin, "He has once for all determined, both whom He would admit to salvation, and whom He would condemn to destruction."[3] Although Calvin stressed that there could be no absolute certainty of salvation, his followers did not always make this distinction. The practical psychological effect of predestination was to give later Calvinists an unshakable conviction that they were doing God's work on earth, making Calvinism a dynamic and activist faith.

In 1536, Calvin began working to reform the city of Geneva. He was able to fashion a tightly organized church order that employed both clergy and laymen in the service of the church. The Consistory, a special body for enforcing moral discipline, functioned as a court to oversee the moral life, daily behavior, and doctrinal orthodoxy of Genevans and to admonish and correct deviants. Citizens in Geneva were punished for such varied "crimes" as dancing, singing obscene songs, drunkenness, swearing, and playing cards.

Calvin's success in Geneva enabled the city to become a vibrant center of Protestantism. Following Calvin's lead, missionaries trained in Geneva were sent to all parts of Europe. Calvinism became established in France, the Netherlands, Scotland, and central and eastern Europe, and by the mid-sixteenth century, Calvin's Geneva stood as the fortress of the Reformation.

THE ENGLISH REFORMATION The English Reformation was rooted in politics, not religion. King Henry VIII (1509–1547) had a strong desire to divorce his first wife, Catherine of Aragon, with whom he had a daughter, Mary, but no male heir. The king wanted to marry Anne Boleyn (BUH-lin *or* buh-LIN), with whom he had fallen in love. Impatient with the pope's unwillingness to grant him an annulment of his marriage, Henry turned to England's own church courts. As archbishop of Canterbury and head of the highest church court in England, Thomas Cranmer ruled in May 1533 that the king's marriage to Catherine was "absolutely void." At the beginning of June, Anne was crowned queen, and three months later, a child was born; much to the king's disappointment, the baby was a girl (the future Queen Elizabeth I).

In 1534, at Henry's request, Parliament moved to finalize the break of the Church of England with Rome. The Act of Supremacy of 1534 declared that the king was "the only supreme head on earth of the Church of England," a position that gave him control of doctrine, clerical appointments, and discipline. Although Henry VIII had broken with the papacy, little change occurred in matters of doctrine, theology, and ceremony. Some of his supporters, including Archbishop Cranmer, sought a religious reformation as well as an administrative one, but Henry was unyielding. But he died in 1547 and was succeeded by his son, the underage and sickly Edward VI (1547–1553), and during Edward's reign, Cranmer and others inclined toward Protestant doctrines were able to move the Church of England (or Anglican Church) in a more Protestant direction. New acts of Parliament gave the clergy the right to marry and created a new Protestant church service.

Edward VI was succeeded by Mary (1553–1558), a Catholic who attempted to return England to Catholicism. Her actions aroused much anger, however, especially when "bloody Mary" burned more than three hundred Protestant heretics. By the end of Mary's reign, England was more Protestant than it had been at the beginning.

THE ANABAPTISTS The Anabaptists were the radical reformers of the Protestant Reformation. To Anabaptists, the true Christian church was a voluntary association of believers who had undergone spiritual rebirth and had then been baptized into the church. Anabaptists advocated adult rather than infant baptism. They also wanted to return to the practices and spirit of early Christianity and considered all believers to be equal. Each church chose its own minister, who might be any member of the community since all Christians were considered priests (though women were often excluded).

Finally, unlike the Catholics and other Protestants, most Anabaptists believed in the complete separation of church and state. Government was to be excluded from the realm of religion and could not exercise political jurisdiction over real Christians. Anabaptists refused to hold political office or bear arms because many took the commandment "Thou shall not kill" literally. Their political beliefs as much as their religious beliefs caused the Anabaptists to be regarded as dangerous radicals who threatened the very fabric of sixteenth-century society. Indeed, the chief thing Protestants and Catholics could agree on was the need to persecute Anabaptists.

The Social Impact of the Protestant Reformation

The Protestants were especially important in developing a new view of the family. Because Protestantism had eliminated any idea of special holiness for celibacy and had abolished both monasticism and a celibate clergy, the family could be placed at the center of human life, and a new stress on "mutual love between man and wife" could be extolled (see the comparative essay "Marriage in the Early Modern World" on p. 431).

But were doctrine and reality the same? Most often, reality reflected the traditional roles of husband as the ruler and wife as the obedient servant whose chief duty was to please her husband. Luther stated it clearly:

> The rule remains with the husband, and the wife is compelled to obey him by God's command. He rules the home and the state, wages war, defends his possessions, tills the soil, builds, plants, etc. The woman on the other hand is like a nail driven into the wall . . . so the wife should stay at home and look after the affairs of the household, as one who has been deprived of the ability of administering those affairs that are outside and that concern the state. She does not go beyond her most personal duties.[4]

Obedience to her husband was not a wife's only role; her other important duty was to bear children. To Calvin and Luther, this function of women was part of the divine plan, and for most Protestant women, family life was their only destiny (see the box on p. 433). Overall, the Protestant Reformation did not noticeably alter women's subordinate place in society.

The Catholic Reformation

By the mid-sixteenth century, Lutheranism had become established in Germany and Scandinavia and Calvinism in Scotland,

Switzerland, France, the Netherlands, and eastern Europe. In England, the split from Rome had resulted in the creation of a national church. The situation in Europe did not look particularly favorable for the Roman Catholic Church (see Map 15.1).

CATHOLIC REFORMATION OR COUNTER-REFORMATION? There is no doubt that the Catholic Church underwent a revitalization in the sixteenth century. But was this reformation a **Catholic Reformation** or a Counter-Reformation? Some historians prefer the term *Counter-Reformation* to focus on the aspects that were a direct reaction against the Protestant movement. Historians who prefer the term *Catholic Reformation* point out that elements of reform were already present in the Catholic Church at the end of the fifteenth century and the beginning of the sixteenth century. Especially noticeable were the calls for reform from the religious orders of the Franciscans, Dominicans, and Augustinians. Members of these groups put particular emphasis on preaching to laypeople. Another example was the Oratory of Divine Love, first organized in Italy in 1497 as an informal group of clergy and laymen who worked to foster reform by emphasizing personal spiritual development and outward acts of charity. The Oratory's members included a Spanish archbishop, Cardinal Ximenes (khee-MAY-ness), who was especially active in using Christian humanism to reform the church in Spain.

No doubt, both positions on the nature of the reformation of the Catholic Church contain elements of truth. The Catholic Reformation revived the best features of medieval Catholicism and then adjusted them to meet new conditions, as is most apparent in the emergence of a new mysticism, closely tied to the traditions of Catholic piety, and the revival of monasticism through the regeneration of older religious orders and the founding of new orders.

THE SOCIETY OF JESUS Of all the new religious orders, the most important was the Society of Jesus, known as the Jesuits,

Ignatius of Loyola. The Jesuits became the most important new religious order of the Catholic Reformation. Shown here in a sixteenth-century painting by an unknown artist is Ignatius of Loyola, founder of the Society of Jesus. Loyola is seen kneeling before Pope Paul III, who officially recognized the Jesuits in 1540.

COMPARATIVE ESSAY

Marriage in the Early Modern World

FAMILY & SOCIETY

Marriage is an ancient institution. In China, myths about the beginnings of Chinese civilization maintained that the rite of marriage began with the primordial couple Fuxi and Nugun and that marriage actually preceded such discoveries as fire, farming, and medicine. In the early modern world, family and marriage were inseparable and were at the center of all civilizations.

In the early modern period, the family was still at the heart of Europe's social organization. For the most part, people viewed the family in traditional terms, as a patriarchal institution in which the husband dominated his wife and children. The upper classes in particular thought of the family as a "house," an association whose collective interests were more important than those of its individual members. Parents (especially the fathers) generally selected marriage partners for their children, based on the interests of the family. When the son of a French noble asked about his upcoming marriage, his father responded, "Mind your own business." Details were worked out well in advance, sometimes when children were only two or three years old, and were set out in a legally binding contract. An important negotiating point was the size of the dowry, money presented by the bride's family to the groom upon marriage. The dowry could be a large sum, and all families were expected to provide dowries for their daughters.

Arranged marriages were not unique to Europe but were common throughout the world. In China, marriages were normally arranged for the benefit of the family, often by a go-between, and the groom and bride were usually not consulted. Frequently, they did not meet until the marriage ceremony. Love was obviously not a reason for marriage and in fact was often viewed as a detriment because it could distract the married couple from their responsibility to the larger family unit. In Japan too, marriages were arranged, often by the heads of dominant families in rural areas, and the new wife moved in with the family of her husband. In India, not only were marriages arranged, but it was not uncommon for women to be married before the age of ten. In colonial Latin America, parents selected marriage partners for their children and often chose a dwelling for the couple as well. In many areas, before members of the lower classes could marry, they had to offer gifts to the powerful noble landowners in the region and obtain their permission. These nobles often refused to allow women to marry in order to keep them as servants.

Arranged marriages were the logical result of a social system in which men dominated and women's primary role was

Marriage Ceremonies. At the left is a detail of a marriage ceremony in Italy from a fresco painted by Dominico di Bartolo in 1443. At the right is a seventeenth-century Mughal painting showing Shah Jahan, the Mughal emperor (with halo). He is riding to the wedding celebration of his son, who rides before him.

© The Art Archive/Santa Maria della Scala Hospital, Siena/Alfredo Dagli Orti

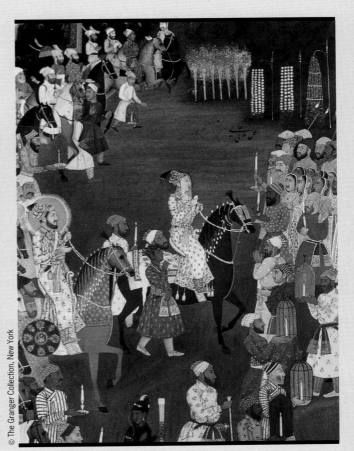

© The Granger Collection, New York

(continued)

(Comparative Essay continued)

to bear children, manage the household, and work in the field. Not until the nineteenth century did a feminist movement emerge in Europe to improve the rights of women. By the beginning of the twentieth century, that movement had spread to other parts of the world. The New Culture Movement in China, for example, advocated the free choice of spouses. Although the trend throughout the world is toward allowing people to choose their mates, in some areas, especially in rural communities, families remain active in choosing marriage partners.

 In what ways were marriage practices similar in the West and the East during the early modern period? Were there any significant differences?

founded by a Spanish nobleman, Ignatius of Loyola (ig-NAY-shuss of loi-OH-luh) (1491–1556). Loyola brought together a small group of individuals who were recognized as a reli-gious order by the pope in 1540. The new order was grounded on the principles of absolute obedience to the papacy, a strict hierarchical order for the society, the use of education to achieve its goals, and a dedication to engage in "conflict for God." A special vow of absolute obedience to the pope made the Jesuits an important instru-ment for papal policy. Jesuit missionaries proved singularly successful in restoring Catholicism to parts of Germany and eastern Europe.

Another prominent Jesuit activity was the propagation of the Catholic faith among non-Christians. Francis Xavier (ZAY-vee-ur) (1506–1552), one of the original members of the Society of Jesus, carried the message of Catholic Chris-tianity to the East. After attracting tens of thou-sands of converts in India, he traveled to Malacca and the Moluccas before finally reaching Japan in 1549. He spoke highly of the Japanese: "They are a people of excellent morals—good in general and not malicious."[5] Thousands of Japanese, espe-cially in the southernmost islands, became Chris-tians. In 1552, Xavier set out for China but died of fever before he reached the mainland.

Although conversion efforts in Japan proved short-lived, Jesuit activity in China, especially that of the Italian Matteo Ricci (ma-TAY-oh REE-chee), was more long-lasting. Recognizing the Chinese pride in their own culture, the Jesu-its attempted to draw parallels between Chris-tian and Confucian concepts and to show the similarities between Christian morality and Con-fucian ethics. For their part, the missionaries were much impressed with many aspects of Chi-nese civilization, and reports of their experiences heightened European curiosity about this great society on the other side of the world.

A REFORMED PAPACY A reformed papacy was another important factor in the develop-ment of the Catholic Reformation. The involve-ment of Renaissance popes in dubious finances and Italian political and military affairs had cre-ated numerous sources of corruption. It took the jolt of the Protestant Reformation to bring about serious reform. Pope Paul III (1534–1549) perceived the need for change and took the au-dacious step of appointing a reform commission

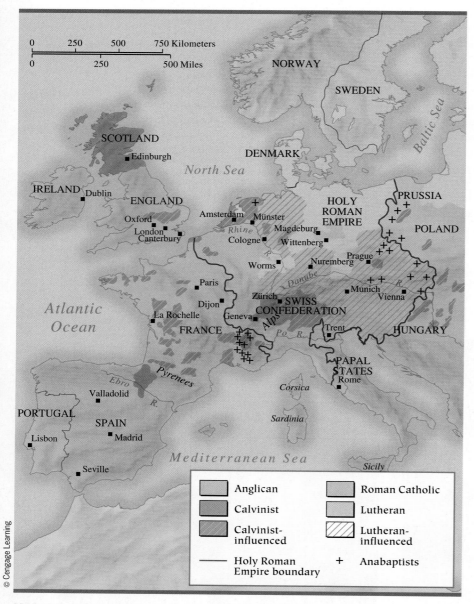

MAP 15.1 **Catholics and Protestants in Europe by 1560.** The Reformation continued to evolve beyond the basic split of the Lutherans from the Catholics. Several Protestant sects broke away from the teachings of Martin Luther, each with a separate creed and different ways of worship. In England, Henry VIII broke with the Catholic Church for political and dynastic reasons.

Q *Which areas of Europe were solidly Catholic, which were solidly Lutheran, and which were neither?*

© Cengage Learning

A Protestant Woman

FAMILY & SOCIETY

In the initial zeal of the Protestant Reformation, women were frequently allowed to play untraditional roles. Catherine Zell of Germany (c. 1497–1562) first preached beside her husband in 1527. After the death of her two children, she devoted the rest of her life to helping her husband and their Anabaptist faith. This selection is taken from one of her letters to a young Lutheran minister who had criticized her activities.

A Letter from Catherine Zell to Ludwig Rabus of Memmingen

I, Catherine Zell, wife of the late lamented Mathew Zell, who served in Strasbourg, where I was born and reared and still live, wish you peace and enhancement in God's grace. . . .

From my earliest years I turned to the Lord, who taught and guided me, and I have at all times, in accordance with my understanding and His grace, embraced the interests of His church and earnestly sought Jesus. Even in youth this brought me the regard and affection of clergymen and others much concerned with the church, which is why the pious Mathew Zell wanted me as a companion in marriage; and I, in turn, to serve the glory of Christ, gave devotion and help to my husband, both in his ministry and in keeping his house. . . . Ever since I was ten years old I have been a student and a sort of church mother, much given to attending sermons. I have loved and frequented the company of learned men, and I conversed much with them, not about dancing, masquerades, and worldly pleasures but about the kingdom of God. . . .

Consider the poor Anabaptists, who are so furiously and ferociously persecuted. Must the authorities everywhere be incited against them, as the hunter drives his dog against wild animals? Against those who acknowledge Christ the Lord in very much the same way we do and over which we broke with the papacy? Just because they cannot agree with us on lesser things, is this any reason to persecute them and in them Christ, in whom they fervently believe and have often professed in misery, in prison, and under the torments of fire and water?

Governments may punish criminals, but they should not force and govern belief, which is a matter for the heart and conscience not for temporal authorities. . . . When the authorities pursue one, they soon bring forth tears, and towns and villages are emptied.

 What new ideas did Catherine Zell bring to the Reformation? Why did people react so strongly against them?

---

to ascertain the church's ills. The commission's report in 1537 blamed the church's problems on the corrupt policies of popes and cardinals. Paul III also formally recognized the Jesuits and summoned the Council of Trent.

THE COUNCIL OF TRENT In March 1545, a group of high church officials met in the city of Trent on the border between Germany and Italy and initiated the Council of Trent, which met intermittently from 1545 to 1563 in three major sessions. The final decrees of the Council of Trent reaffirmed traditional Catholic teachings in opposition to Protestant beliefs. Scripture and tradition were affirmed as equal authorities in religious matters; only the church could interpret Scripture. Both faith and good works were declared necessary for salvation. Belief in purgatory and in the use of indulgences was strengthened, although the selling of indulgences was prohibited.

After the Council of Trent, the Roman Catholic Church possessed a clear body of doctrine and a unified structure under the acknowledged supremacy of the popes. Although the Roman Catholic Church had become one Christian denomination among many, the church entered a new phase of its history with a spirit of confidence.

Europe in Crisis, 1560–1650

 FOCUS QUESTION: Why is the period between 1560 and 1650 in Europe considered an age of crisis, and how did the turmoil contribute to the artistic developments of the period?

Between 1560 and 1650, Europe experienced religious wars, revolutions and constitutional crises, economic and social disintegration, and a witchcraft craze. It was truly an age of crisis.

CHRONOLOGY	Key Events of the Reformation Era
Luther's Ninety-Five Theses	1517
Excommunication of Luther	1521
Act of Supremacy in England	1534
Pontificate of Paul III	1534–1549
John Calvin's *Institutes of the Christian Religion*	1536
Society of Jesus (Jesuits) recognized as a religious order	1540
Council of Trent	1545–1563
Peace of Augsburg	1555

Politics and the Wars of Religion in the Sixteenth Century

By 1560, Calvinism and Catholicism had become activist religions dedicated to spreading the word of God as they interpreted it. Although their struggle for the minds and hearts of Europeans was at the heart of the religious wars of the sixteenth century, economic, social, and political forces also played important roles in these conflicts.

THE FRENCH WARS OF RELIGION (1562–1598) Religion was central to the French civil wars of the sixteenth century. The growth of Calvinism had led to persecution by the French kings, but the latter did little to stop the spread of Calvinism. Huguenots (HYOO-guh-nots), as the French Calvinists were called, constituted only about 7 percent of the population, but 40 to 50 percent of the French nobility became Huguenots, including the house of Bourbon (boor-BOHN), which stood next to the Valois (val-WAH) in the royal line of succession. The conversion of so many nobles made the Huguenots a potentially dangerous political threat to monarchical power. Still, the Calvinist minority was greatly outnumbered by the Catholic majority, and the Valois monarchy was staunchly Catholic.

The religious issue was not the only factor that contributed to the French civil wars. Towns and provinces, which had long resisted the growing power of monarchical centralization, were only too willing to join a revolt against the monarchy. So were the nobles, and the fact that so many of them were Calvinists created an important base of opposition to the crown.

For thirty years, battles raged in France between Catholic and Calvinist parties. Finally, in 1589, Henry of Navarre, the political leader of the Huguenots and a member of the Bourbon dynasty, succeeded to the throne as Henry IV (1589–1610). Realizing, however, that he would never be accepted by Catholic France, Henry converted to Catholicism. With his coronation in 1594, the Wars of Religion had finally come to an end. The Edict of Nantes (NAHNT) in 1598 solved the religious problem by acknowledging Catholicism as the official religion of France while guaranteeing the Huguenots the right to worship and to enjoy all political privileges, including the holding of public offices.

PHILIP II AND MILITANT CATHOLICISM The greatest advocate of militant Catholicism in the second half of the sixteenth century was King Philip II of Spain (1556–1598), the son and heir of Charles V. Philip's reign ushered in an age of Spanish greatness, both politically and culturally. Philip had inherited from his father Spain, the Netherlands, and possessions in Italy and the Americas. To strengthen his control, Philip insisted on strict conformity to Catholicism and strong monarchical authority. Achieving the latter was not an easy task, because each of the lands of his empire had its own structure of government.

The Catholic faith was crucial to the Spanish people and their ruler. Driven by a heritage of crusading fervor, Spain saw itself as a nation of people chosen by God to save Catholic Christianity from the Protestant heretics. Philip II, the "most Catholic king," became the champion of Catholicism throughout Europe. Spain's leadership of a "holy league" against Turkish encroachments in the Mediterranean resulted in a stunning victory over the Turkish fleet in the Battle of Lepanto (LEH-pahn-toh *or* LIH-pan-toh) in 1571. But Philip's problems with the Netherlands and the English Queen Elizabeth led to his greatest misfortunes.

Philip's attempt to strengthen his control in the Spanish Netherlands, which consisted of seventeen provinces (modern Netherlands and Belgium), soon led to a revolt. The nobles, who stood to lose the most politically, strongly opposed Philip's efforts. Religion also became a major catalyst for rebellion when Philip attempted to crush Calvinism. Violence erupted in 1566, and the revolt became organized, especially in the northern provinces, where the Dutch, under the leadership of William of Nassau, the prince of Orange, offered growing resistance. The struggle dragged on for decades until 1609, when a twelve-year truce ended the war, virtually recognizing the independence of the northern provinces. These seven northern provinces, which called themselves the United Provinces of the Netherlands, became the core of the modern Dutch state.

To most Europeans at the beginning of the seventeenth century, Spain still seemed the greatest power of the age, but the reality was quite different. The Spanish treasury was empty, the armed forces were obsolescent, and the government was inefficient. Spain continued to play the role of a great power, but real power had shifted to England.

THE ENGLAND OF ELIZABETH When Elizabeth Tudor, the daughter of Henry VIII and Anne Boleyn, ascended the throne in 1558, England was home to fewer than 4 million people. Yet during her reign (1558–1603), the small island kingdom became the leader of the Protestant nations of Europe and laid the foundations for a world empire.

Intelligent, cautious, and self-confident, Elizabeth moved quickly to solve the difficult religious problem she inherited from her half-sister, Queen Mary. Elizabeth's religious policy was based on moderation and compromise. She repealed the Catholic laws of Mary's reign, and a new Act of Supremacy designated Elizabeth as "the only supreme governor" of both church and state. The Church of England under Elizabeth was basically Protestant, but it was of a moderate bent that kept most people satisfied.

Caution and moderation also dictated Elizabeth's foreign policy. Nevertheless, Elizabeth was gradually drawn into conflict with Spain. Having resisted for years the idea of invading England as too impractical, Philip II of Spain was finally persuaded to do so by advisers who assured him that the people of England would rise against their queen when the Spaniards arrived. A successful invasion of England would mean the overthrow of heresy and the return of England to Catholicism. Philip ordered preparations for a fleet of warships, the *armada*, to spearhead the invasion of England.

The armada was a disaster. The Spanish fleet that finally set sail had neither the ships nor the manpower that Philip had planned to send. Battered by a number of encounters with the English, the Spanish fleet sailed back to Spain by a northward route around Scotland and Ireland, where it was further pounded by storms. Although the English and Spanish

Procession of Queen Elizabeth I. Intelligent and learned, Elizabeth Tudor was familiar with Latin and Greek and spoke several European languages. Served by able administrators, Elizabeth ruled for nearly forty-five years and generally avoided open military action against any major power. This picture, painted near the end of her reign, shows the queen in a ceremonial procession.

would continue their war for another sixteen years, the defeat of the armada guaranteed for the time being that England would remain a Protestant country.

Economic and Social Crises

The period of European history from 1560 to 1650 witnessed severe economic and social crises as well as political upheaval. Economic contraction began to be evident in some parts of Europe by the 1620s. In the 1630s and 1640s, as imports of silver from the Americas declined, economic recession intensified, especially in the Mediterranean area. Once the industrial and financial center of Europe in the age of the Renaissance, Italy was now becoming an economic backwater.

POPULATION DECLINE Population trends of the sixteenth and seventeenth centuries also reveal Europe's worsening conditions. The population of Europe increased from 60 million in 1500 to 85 million by 1600, the first major recovery of the European population since the devastation of the Black Death in the mid-fourteenth century. By 1650, however, records indicate that the population had declined, especially in central and southern Europe. Europe's longtime adversaries—war, famine, and plague—continued to affect population levels. After the middle of the sixteenth century, another "little ice age," when average temperatures fell, reduced harvests and led to food shortages. Europe's problems created social

tensions, some of which became manifested in an obsession with witches.

WITCHCRAFT MANIA Hysteria over witchcraft affected the lives of many Europeans in the sixteenth and seventeenth centuries. Perhaps more than 100,000 people were prosecuted throughout Europe on charges of witchcraft. As more and more people were brought to trial, the fear of witches, as well as the fear of being accused of witchcraft, escalated to frightening levels (see the box on p. 436).

Common people—usually those who were poor and without property—were more likely to be accused of witchcraft. Indeed, where lists are available, those mentioned most often are milkmaids, peasant women, and servant girls. In the witchcraft trials of the sixteenth and seventeenth centuries, more than 75 percent of the accused were women, most of them single or widowed and many over fifty years old.

That women should be the chief victims of witchcraft trials was hardly accidental. Nicholas Rémy (nee-koh-LAH ray-MEE), a witchcraft judge in France in the 1590s, found it "not unreasonable that this scum of humanity, i.e., witches, should be drawn chiefly from the feminine sex." To another judge, it came as no surprise that witches would confess to sexual experiences with Satan: "The Devil uses them so, because he knows that women love carnal pleasures, and he means to bind them to his allegiance by such agreeable provocations."[6]

A Witchcraft Trial in France

FAMILY & SOCIETY

Persecutions for witchcraft reached their high point in the sixteenth and seventeenth centuries, when tens of thousands of people were brought to trial. In this excerpt from the minutes of a trial in France in 1652, we can see why the accused witch stood little chance of exonerating herself.

The Trial of Suzanne Gaudry

28 May, 1652. . . . Interrogation of Suzanne Gaudry, prisoner at the court of Rieux. . . . During interrogations on May 28 and May 29, the prisoner confessed to a number of activities involving the devil.

Deliberation of the Court—June 3, 1652

The undersigned advocates of the Court have seen these interrogations and answers. They say that the aforementioned Suzanne Gaudry confesses that she is a witch, that she had given herself to the devil, that she had renounced God, Lent, and baptism, that she has been marked on the shoulder, that she has cohabited with the devil and that she has been to the dances, confessing only to have cast a spell upon and caused to die a beast of Philippe Cornié. . . .

Third Interrogation, June 27

This prisoner being led into the chamber, she was examined to know if things were not as she had said and confessed at the beginning of her imprisonment.

—Answers no, and that what she has said was done so by force.

Pressed to say the truth, that otherwise she would be subjected to torture, having pointed out to her that her aunt was burned for this same subject.

—Answers that she is not a witch. . . .

She was placed in the hands of the officer in charge of torture, throwing herself on her knees, struggling to cry, uttering several exclamations, without being able, nevertheless, to shed a tear. Saying at every moment that she is not a witch.

The Torture

On this same day, being at the place of torture.

This prisoner, before being strapped down, was admonished to maintain herself in her first confessions and to renounce her lover.

—Says that she denies everything she has said, and that she has no lover. Feeling herself being strapped down, says that she is not a witch, while struggling to cry . . . and upon being asked why she confessed to being one, said that she was forced to say it.

Told that she was not forced, that on the contrary she declared herself to be a witch without any threat.

—Says that she confessed it and that she is not a witch, and being a little stretched [on the rack] screams ceaselessly that she is not a witch.

Asked if she did not confess that she had been a witch for twenty-six years.

—Says that she said it, that she retracts it, crying that she is not a witch.

Asked if she did not make Philippe Cornié's horse die, as she confessed.

—Answers no, crying Jesus-Maria, that she is not a witch.

The mark having been probed by the officer, in the presence of Doctor Bouchain, it was adjudged by the aforesaid doctor and officer truly to be the mark of the devil.

Being more tightly stretched upon the torture rack, urged to maintain her confessions.

—Said that it was true that she is a witch and that she would maintain what she had said.

Asked how long she has been in subjugation to the devil.

—Answers that it was twenty years ago that the devil appeared to her, being in her lodgings in the form of a man dressed in a little cowhide and black breeches. . . .

Verdict

July 9, 1652. In the light of the interrogations, answers, and investigations made into the charge against Suzanne Gaudry, . . . seeing by her own confessions that she is said to have made a pact with the devil, received the mark from him, . . . and that following this, she had renounced God, Lent, and baptism and had let herself be known carnally by him, in which she received satisfaction. Also, seeing that she is said to have been a part of nocturnal carols and dances.

For expiation of which the advice of the undersigned is that the office of Rieux can legitimately condemn the aforesaid Suzanne Gaudry to death, tying her to a gallows, and strangling her to death, then burning her body and burying it here in the environs of the woods.

 Why were women, particularly older women, especially vulnerable to accusations of witchcraft? What "proofs" are offered here that Suzanne Gaudry had consorted with the devil? What does this account tell us about the spread of witchcraft persecutions in the seventeenth century?

By the mid-seventeenth century, the witchcraft hysteria had begun to subside. As governments grew stronger, fewer magistrates were willing to accept the unsettling and divisive conditions generated by the trials of witches. Moreover, by the end of the seventeenth century and the beginning of the eighteenth, more and more people were questioning their old attitudes toward religion and found it especially contrary to reason to believe in the old view of a world haunted by evil spirits.

ECONOMIC TRENDS IN THE SEVENTEENTH CENTURY In the course of the seventeenth century, new economic trends also emerged. **Mercantilism** is the name historians apply to the economic practices of the seventeenth century. According to the mercantilists, the prosperity of a nation depended on a plentiful supply of bullion (gold and silver). For this reason, it was desirable to achieve a favorable balance of trade in which goods exported were of greater value than those imported, promoting an influx of gold and silver payments that would increase the quantity of bullion. Furthermore, to encourage exports, governments should stimulate and protect export industries and trade by granting trade monopolies, encouraging investment in new industries through subsidies, importing foreign artisans, and improving transportation systems by building roads, bridges, and canals. By imposing high tariffs on foreign goods, they could reduce imports and prevent them from competing with domestic industries. Colonies were also deemed valuable as sources of raw materials and markets for finished goods.

Mercantilist theory on the role of colonies was matched in practice by Europe's overseas expansion. With the development of colonies and trading posts in the Americas and the East, Europeans embarked on an adventure in international commerce in the seventeenth century. Although some historians speak of a nascent world economy, we should remember that local, regional, and intra-European trade still predominated. At the end of the seventeenth century, for example, English imports totaled 360,000 tons, but only 5,000 tons came from the East Indies. What made the transoceanic trade rewarding, however, was not the volume but the value of its goods. Dutch, English, and French merchants were bringing back products that were still consumed largely by the wealthy but were beginning to make their way into the lives of artisans and merchants. Pepper and spices from the Indies, West Indian and Brazilian sugar, and Asian coffee and tea were becoming more readily available to European consumers.

The commercial expansion of the sixteenth and seventeenth centuries was made easier by new forms of commercial organization, especially the **joint-stock company**. Individuals bought shares in a company and received dividends on their investment while a board of directors ran the company and made the important business decisions. The return on investments could be spectacular. During its first ten years, investors received 30 percent annually on their money from the Dutch East India Company, which opened the Spice Islands and Southeast Asia to Dutch activity. The joint-stock company made it easier to raise large amounts of capital for world trading ventures.

Despite the growth of commercial capitalism, most of the European economy still depended on an agricultural system that had experienced few changes since the thirteenth century. At least 80 percent of Europeans still worked on the land. Almost all of the peasants in western Europe were free of serfdom, although many still owed a variety of feudal dues

to the nobility. Despite the expanding markets and rising prices, European peasants saw little or no improvement in their lot as they faced increased rents and fees and higher taxes imposed by the state.

Seventeenth-Century Crises: Revolution and War

During the first half of the seventeenth century, a series of rebellions and civil wars rocked the domestic stability of many European governments. A devastating war that affected much of Europe also added to the sense of crisis.

THE THIRTY YEARS' WAR (1618–1648) The Thirty Years' War began in 1618 in the Germanic lands of the Holy Roman Empire as a struggle between Catholic forces, led by the Habsburg Holy Roman Emperors, and Protestant—primarily Calvinist—nobles in Bohemia who rebelled against Habsburg authority (see Map 15.2). What began as a struggle over religious issues soon became a wider conflict perpetuated by political motivations as both minor and major European powers—Denmark, Sweden, France, and Spain—entered the war. The competition for European leadership between the Bourbon dynasty of France and the Habsburg dynasties of Spain and the Holy Roman Empire was an especially important factor. Nevertheless, most of the battles were fought on German soil (see the box on p. 439).

The war in Germany was officially ended in 1648 by the Peace of Westphalia, which proclaimed that all German states, including the Calvinist ones, were free to determine their own religion. The major contenders gained new territories, and France emerged as the dominant nation in Europe. The more than three hundred entities that made up the Holy Roman Empire were recognized as independent states, and each was given the power to conduct its own foreign policy; this brought an end to the Holy Roman Empire and ensured German disunity for another two hundred years. The Peace of Westphalia made it clear that political motives, not religious convictions, had become the guiding force in public affairs.

A MILITARY REVOLUTION? By the seventeenth century, war was playing an increasingly important role in European affairs. Military power was considered essential to a ruler's reputation and power; thus, the pressure to build an effective

CHRONOLOGY	Europe in Crisis, 1560–1650: Key Events
Reign of Philip II	1556–1598
French Wars of Religion	1562–1598
Outbreak of revolt in the Netherlands	1566
Defeat of the Spanish armada	1588
Edict of Nantes	1598
Truce between Spain and the Netherlands	1609–1621
Thirty Years' War	1618–1648
Peace of Westphalia	1648

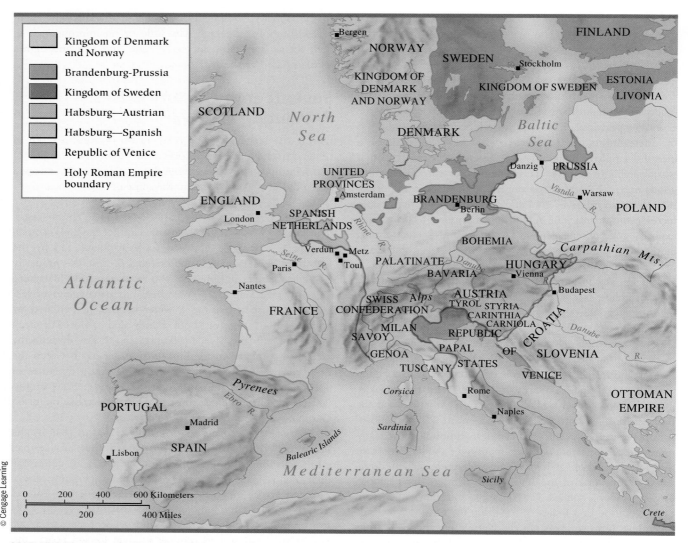

MAP 15.2 Europe in the Seventeenth Century. This map shows Europe at the time of the Thirty Years' War (1618–1648). Although the struggle began in Bohemia and much of the fighting took place in the Germanic lands of the Holy Roman Empire, the conflict became a Europe-wide struggle. Compare this map with Map 15.1.

Q *Which countries engaged in the war were predominantly Protestant, which were Catholic, and which were mixed?*

military machine was intense. Some historians believe that the changes that occurred in the science of warfare between 1560 and 1650 constituted a military revolution.

Medieval warfare, with its mounted knights and supplementary archers, had been transformed in the Renaissance by the employment of infantry armed with pikes and halberds and arranged in massed rectangles known as squadrons or battalions. The use of firearms required adjustments to the size and shape of the massed infantry and made the cavalry less effective.

It was Gustavus Adolphus (goo-STAY-vus uh-DAHL-fuss), the king of Sweden (1611–1632), who developed the first standing army of conscripts, notable for the flexibility of its tactics. The infantry brigades of Gustavus's army were composed of equal numbers of musketeers and pikemen, standing six men deep. They employed the salvo, in which all rows of the infantry fired at once instead of row by row. These salvos of fire, which cut up the massed ranks of the

opposing infantry squadrons, were followed by a pike charge, giving the infantry a primarily offensive deployment. Gustavus also used the cavalry in a more mobile fashion. After shooting a pistol volley, they charged the enemy with their swords. Additional flexibility was obtained by using lighter artillery pieces that were more easily moved during battle. All of these innovations required coordination, careful training, and better discipline, forcing rulers to move away from undisciplined mercenary forces.

Some historians have questioned the use of the phrase "military revolution" to describe the military changes from 1560 to 1660, arguing instead that military developments were gradual. In any case, for the rest of the seventeenth century, warfare continued to change. Standing armies, based partly on conscription, grew ever larger and more expensive. Standing armies necessitated better-disciplined and better-trained soldiers and led to the education of officers in military schools. Armies also introduced the use of linear rather than

The Face of War in the Seventeenth Century

POLITICS & GOVERNMENT

We have a firsthand account of the face of war in Germany from a picaresque novel called *Simplicius Simplicissimus,* written by Jakob von Grimmelshausen (YAH-kop fun GRIM-ulz-how-zun). The author's experiences as a soldier in the Thirty Years' War give his descriptions of the effect of the war on ordinary people a certain vividness and reality. This selection describes the fate of a peasant farm, an experience all too familiar to thousands of German peasants between 1618 and 1648.

Jakob von Grimmelshausen, *Simplicius Simplicissimus*

The first thing these horsemen did in the nice back rooms of the house was to put in their horses. Then everyone took up a special job, one having to do with death and destruction. Although some began butchering, heating water, and rendering lard, as if to prepare for a banquet, others raced through the house, ransacking upstairs and down; not even the privy chamber was safe, as if the golden fleece of Jason might be hidden there. Still others bundled up big packs of cloth, household goods, and clothes, as if they wanted to hold a rummage sale somewhere. What they did not intend to take along they broke and spoiled. Some ran their swords into the hay and straw, as if there hadn't been hogs enough to stick. Some shook the feathers out of beds and put bacon slabs, hams, and other stuff in the ticking, as if they might sleep better on these. Others knocked down the hearth and broke the windows, as if announcing an everlasting summer. They flattened out copper and pewter dishes and baled the ruined goods. They burned up bedsteads, tables, chairs, and benches, though there were yards and yards of dry firewood outside the kitchen. Jars and crocks, pots and casseroles all were broken, either because they preferred their meat broiled or because they thought they'd eat only one meal with us. In the barn, the hired girl was handled so roughly that she was unable to walk away, I am ashamed to report. They stretched the hired man out flat on the ground, stuck a wooden wedge

in his mouth to keep it open, and emptied a milk bucket full of stinking manure drippings down his throat; they called it a Swedish cocktail. He didn't relish it and made a very wry face. By this means they forced him to take a raiding party to some other place where they carried off men and cattle and brought them to our farm. Among those were my father, mother, and [sister] Ursula.

Then they used thumbscrews, which they cleverly made out of their pistols, to torture the peasants, as if they wanted to burn witches. Though he had confessed to nothing as yet, they put one of the captured hayseeds in the bake-oven and lighted a fire in it. They put a rope around someone else's head and tightened it like a tourniquet until blood came out of his mouth, nose, and ears. In short, every soldier had his favorite method of making life miserable for peasants, and every peasant had his own misery. My father was, as I thought, particularly lucky because he confessed with a laugh what others were forced to say in pain and martyrdom. No doubt because he was the head of the household, he was shown special consideration; they put him close to a fire, tied him by his hands and legs, and rubbed damp salt on the bottoms of his feet. Our old nanny goat had to lick it off and this so tickled my father that he could have burst laughing. This seemed so clever and entertaining to me—I had never seen or heard my father laugh so long—that I joined him in laughter, to keep him company or perhaps to cover up my ignorance. In the midst of such glee he told them the whereabouts of hidden treasure much richer in gold, pearls, and jewelry than might have been expected on a farm.

I can't say much about the captured wives, hired girls, and daughters because the soldiers didn't let me watch their doings. But I do remember hearing pitiful screams from various dark corners and I guess that my mother and our Ursula had it no better than the rest.

 What does this document reveal about the effect of war on ordinary Europeans?

---

square formations to provide greater flexibility and mobility in tactics. The use of firearms also increased as the musket with attached bayonet increasingly replaced the pike in the ranks of the infantry. A naval arms race in the seventeenth century led to more and bigger warships or capital ships known as "ships of the line."

Larger armies and navies could be maintained only by levying heavier taxes, making war a greater economic burden and an ever more important part of the early modern European state. The creation of large bureaucracies to supervise the military resources of the state led to growth in the power of state governments.

Response to Crisis: The Practice of Absolutism

 FOCUS QUESTION: What was absolutism, and what were the main characteristics of the absolute monarchies that emerged in France, Prussia, Austria, and Russia?

Many people responded to the crises of the seventeenth century by searching for order. An increase in monarchical power became an obvious means for achieving stability.

The result was what historians have called absolutism or absolute monarchy, in which the sovereign power or ultimate authority in the state rested in the hands of a king who claimed to rule by divine right—the idea that kings received their power from God and were responsible to no one but God. Late-sixteenth-century political theorists believed that sovereign power consisted of the authority to make laws, levy taxes, administer justice, control the state's administrative system, and determine foreign policy.

France Under Louis XIV

France during the reign of Louis XIV (1643–1715) has traditionally been regarded as the best example of the practice of absolute or **divine-right monarchy** in the seventeenth century. French culture, language, and manners reached into all levels of European society. French diplomacy and wars overwhelmed the political affairs of western and central Europe. The court of Louis XIV seemed to be imitated everywhere in Europe (see the comparative illustration on p. 441).

POLITICAL INSTITUTIONS One of the keys to Louis's power was his control of the central policy-making machinery of government because it was part of his own court and household. The royal court, located in the magnificent palace at Versailles (vayr-SY), outside Paris, served three purposes simultaneously: it was the personal household of the king, the location of central governmental machinery, and the place where powerful subjects came to find favors and offices for themselves and their clients. The greatest danger to Louis's personal rule came from the very high nobles and princes of the blood (the royal princes), who considered it their natural function to assert the policy-making role of royal ministers. Louis eliminated this threat by removing them from the royal council, the chief administrative body of the king, and enticing them to his court, where he could keep them preoccupied with court life and out of politics. Instead of the high nobility and royal princes, Louis relied for his ministers on nobles who came from relatively new aristocratic families. His ministers were expected to be subservient: "I had no intention of sharing my authority with them," Louis said.

Court life at Versailles itself became highly ritualized with Louis at the center of it all. The king had little privacy; only when he visited his wife or mother or mistress was he free of the noble courtiers who swarmed about the palace. Most daily ceremonies were carefully staged, including those attending Louis's rising from bed, dining, praying, attending Mass, and going to bed. A mob of nobles aspired to assist the king in carrying out these solemn activities. It was considered a great honor for a noble to be chosen to hand the king his shirt while dressing. Court etiquette was also a complex matter. Nobles and royal princes were arranged in an elaborate order of seniority and expected to follow certain rules of precedence. Who could sit down and on what kind of chair was a subject of much debate.

Louis's domination of his ministers and secretaries gave him control of the central policy-making machinery of government and thus authority over the traditional areas of monarchical power: the formulation of foreign policy, the making of war and peace, the assertion of the secular power of the crown against any religious authority, and the ability to levy taxes to fulfill these functions. Louis had considerably less success with the internal administration of the kingdom, however. The traditional groups and institutions of French society—the nobles, officials, town councils, guilds, and representative estates in some provinces—were simply too powerful for the king to have direct control over the lives of his subjects. As a result, control of the provinces and the people was achieved largely by bribing the individuals responsible for carrying out the king's policies.

THE ECONOMY AND THE MILITARY The cost of building palaces, maintaining his court, and pursuing his wars made

Chateaux de Versailles et de Trianon, Versailles//© Réunion des Musées Nationaux/Art Resource, NY

Interior of Versailles: The Hall of Mirrors. Pictured here is the exquisite Hall of Mirrors at Versailles. Located on the second floor, the hall overlooks the park below. Three hundred and fifty-seven mirrors were placed on the wall opposite the windows in order to create an illusion of even greater width. Careful planning went into every detail of the interior decoration. Even the doorknobs were specially designed to reflect the magnificence of Versailles. This photo shows the Hall of Mirrors after the restoration work that was completed in June 2007, a project that took three years, cost 12 million euros (more than $16 million), and included the restoration of the Bohemian crystal chandeliers.

COMPARATIVE ILLUSTRATION

Sun Kings, West and East. At the end of the seventeenth century, two powerful rulers held sway in kingdoms that dominated the affairs of the regions around them. Both rulers saw themselves as favored by divine authority—Louis XIV of France as a divine-right monarch and Kangxi (GANG-zhee) of China as possessing the mandate of Heaven. Thus, both rulers saw themselves not as divine beings but as divinely ordained beings whose job was to govern organized societies. On the left, Louis, who ruled France from 1643 to 1715, is seen in a portrait by Hyacinthe Rigaud (ee-ah-SANT ree-GOH) that captures the king's sense of royal dignity and grandeur. One person at court said of the king: "Louis XIV's vanity was without limit or restraint." On the right, Kangxi, who ruled China from 1661 to 1722, is seen in a portrait that shows him seated in majesty on his imperial throne. A dedicated ruler, Kangxi once wrote, "One act of negligence may cause sorrow all through the country, and one moment of negligence may result in trouble for hundreds and thousands of generations."

Q *Although these rulers practiced very different religions, why did they justify their powers in such a similar fashion?*

POLITICS & GOVERNMENT

finances a crucial issue for Louis XIV. He was most fortunate in having the services of Jean-Baptiste Colbert (ZHAHN-bap-TEEST kohl-BAYR) (1619–1683) as his controller general of finances. Colbert sought to increase the wealth and power of France through general adherence to mercantilism, which advocated government intervention in economic activities for the benefit of the state. To decrease imports and increase exports, Colbert granted subsidies to individuals who established new industries. To improve communications and the transportation of goods internally, he built roads and canals. To decrease imports directly, Colbert raised tariffs on foreign goods.

The increase in royal power that Louis pursued led the king to develop a professional army numbering 100,000 men in peacetime and 400,000 in time of war. To achieve the prestige and military glory befitting an absolute king as well as to

ensure the domination of his Bourbon dynasty over European affairs, Louis waged four wars between 1667 and 1713. His ambitions roused much of Europe to form coalitions against him to prevent the certain destruction of the European balance of power by Bourbon hegemony. Although Louis added some territory to France's northeastern frontier and established a member of his own Bourbon dynasty on the throne of Spain, he also left France impoverished and surrounded by enemies.

Absolutism in Central and Eastern Europe

During the seventeenth century, a development of great importance for the modern Western world took place with the appearance in central and eastern Europe of three new powers: Prussia, Austria, and Russia.

PRUSSIA Frederick William the Great Elector (1640–1688) laid the foundation for the Prussian state. Realizing that the land he had inherited, known as Brandenburg-Prussia, was a small, open territory with no natural frontiers for defense, Frederick William built an army of 40,000 men, making it the fourth largest in Europe. To sustain the army, Frederick William established the General War Commissariat to levy taxes for the army and oversee its growth. The Commissariat soon evolved into an agency for civil government as well. The new bureaucratic machine became the elector's chief instrument to govern the state. Many of its officials were members of the Prussian landed aristocracy, the Junkers (YOONG-kers), who also served as officers in the all-important army.

In 1701, Frederick William's son Frederick officially gained the title of king. Elector Frederick III became King Frederick I, and Brandenburg-Prussia simply Prussia. In the eighteenth century, Prussia emerged as a great power in Europe.

AUSTRIA The Austrian Habsburgs had long played a significant role in European politics as Holy Roman Emperors. By the end of the Thirty Years' War, the Habsburg hopes of creating an empire in Germany had been dashed. In the seventeenth century, the house of Austria created a new empire in eastern and southeastern Europe.

The nucleus of the new Austrian Empire remained the traditional Austrian hereditary possessions: Lower and Upper Austria, Carinthia, Carniola, Styria, and Tyrol. To these had been added the kingdom of Bohemia and parts of northwestern Hungary. After the defeat of the Turks in 1687 (see Chapter 16), Austria took control of all of Hungary, Transylvania, Croatia, and Slovenia, thus establishing the Austrian Empire in southeastern Europe. By the beginning of the eighteenth century, the house of Austria had assembled an empire of considerable size.

The Austrian monarchy, however, never became a highly centralized, absolutist state, primarily because it contained so many different national groups. The Austrian Empire remained a collection of territories held together by the Habsburg emperor, who was archduke of Austria, king of Bohemia, and king of Hungary. Each of these regions, however, had its own laws and political life.

FROM MUSCOVY TO RUSSIA A new Russian state had emerged in the fifteenth century under the leadership of the principality of Muscovy and its grand dukes. In the sixteenth century, Ivan IV (1533–1584) became the first ruler to take the title of *tsar* (the Russian word for "Caesar"). Ivan expanded the territories of Russia eastward and crushed the power of the Russian nobility. He was known as Ivan the Terrible because of his ruthless deeds, among them stabbing his son to death in a heated argument. When Ivan's dynasty came to an end in 1598, fifteen years of anarchy ensued until the Zemsky Sobor (ZEM-skee suh-BOR), or national assembly, chose Michael Romanov (ROH-muh-nahf) as the new tsar, establishing a dynasty that lasted more than four hundred years. One of its most prominent members was Peter the Great.

Peter the Great (1689–1725) was an unusual character. A strong man towering 6 feet 9 inches tall, Peter enjoyed low humor—belching contests and crude jokes—and vicious punishments, including floggings, impalings, and roastings (see the box on p. 443). Peter got a firsthand view of the West when he made a trip there in 1697–1698 and returned to Russia with a firm determination to westernize Russia. He was especially eager to borrow European technology in order to create the army and navy he needed to make Russia a great power.

As could be expected, one of his first priorities was the reorganization of the army and the creation of a navy. Employing both Russians and Europeans as officers, he conscripted peasants for twenty-five-year stints of service to build a standing army of 210,000 men and at the same time formed the first navy Russia had ever had.

To impose the rule of the central government more effectively throughout the land, Peter divided Russia into provinces. Although he hoped to create a "police state," by which he meant a well-ordered community governed in accordance with law, few of his bureaucrats shared his concept of loyalty to the state. Peter hoped to evoke a sense of civic duty among his people, but his own forceful personality created an atmosphere of fear that prevented any such sentiment.

The object of Peter's domestic reforms was to make Russia into a great state and military power. His primary goal was to "open a window to the west," meaning an ice-free port easily accessible to Europe. This could only be achieved on the Baltic, but at that time, the Baltic coast was controlled by Sweden, the most important power in northern Europe. A long and hard-fought war with Sweden won Peter the lands he sought. In 1703, Peter began the construction of a new city, Saint Petersburg, his window to the west and a symbol that Russia was looking westward to Europe. By the time Peter died in 1725, Russia had become a great military power and an important European state.

England and Limited Monarchy

 FOCUS QUESTION: How and why did England avoid the path of absolutism?

Not all states were absolutist in the seventeenth century. One of the most prominent examples of resistance to absolute monarchy came in England, where king and Parliament struggled to determine the roles each should play in governing England.

Conflict Between King and Parliament

With the death of the childless Queen Elizabeth I in 1603, the Tudor dynasty became extinct, and the Stuart line of rulers was inaugurated with the accession to the throne of Elizabeth's cousin, King James VI of Scotland, who became James I (1603–1625) of England. James espoused the divine right of kings, a viewpoint that alienated Parliament, which had grown accustomed under the Tudors to act on the premise that monarch and Parliament together ruled England as a "balanced polity." Then, too, the **Puritans**—Protestants

Peter the Great Deals with a Rebellion

POLITICS & GOVERNMENT

During his first visit to the West in 1697–1698, Peter received word that the Streltsy, an elite military unit stationed in Moscow, had revolted against his authority. Peter hurried home and crushed the revolt in a very savage fashion. This selection is taken from an Austrian account of how Peter dealt with the rebels.

Peter and the Streltsy

How sharp was the pain, how great the indignation, to which the tsar's Majesty was mightily moved, when he knew of the rebellion of the Streltsy, betraying openly a mind panting for vengeance! He was still tarrying at Vienna, quite full of the desire of setting out for Italy; but, fervid as was his curiosity of rambling abroad, it was, nevertheless, speedily extinguished on the announcement of the troubles that had broken out in the bowels of his realm. Going immediately to Lefort [one of his generals] . . . , he thus indignantly broke out: "Tell me, Francis, how I can reach Moscow by the shortest way, in a brief space, so that I may wreak vengeance on this great perfidy of my people, with punishments worthy of their abominable crime. Not one of them shall escape with impunity. Around my royal city, which, with their impious efforts, they planned to destroy, I will have gibbets and gallows set upon the walls and ramparts, and each and every one of them will I put to a direful death." Nor did he long delay the plan for his justly excited wrath; he took the quick post, as his ambassador suggested, and in four weeks' time he had got over about three hundred miles without accident, and arrived the 4th of September, 1698—a monarch for the well disposed, but an avenger for the wicked.

His first anxiety after his arrival was about the rebellion—in what it consisted, what the insurgents meant, who dared to instigate such a crime. And as nobody could answer accurately upon all points, and some pleaded their own ignorance, others the obstinacy of the Streltsy, he began to have suspicions of everybody's loyalty. . . . No day, holy or profane, were the inquisitors idle; every day was deemed fit and lawful for torturing. There were as many scourges as there were accused, and every inquisitor was a butcher. . . . The whole month of October was spent in lacerating the backs of culprits with the knout [flogging whip] and with flames; no day were those that were left alive exempt from scourging or scorching; or else they were broken upon the wheel, or driven to the gibbet, or slain with the ax. . . .

To prove to all people how holy and inviolable are those walls of the city which the Streltsy rashly meditated scaling in a sudden assault, beams were run out from all the embrasures in the walls near the gates, in each of which two rebels were hanged. This day beheld about two hundred and fifty die that death. There are few cities fortified with as many palisades as Moscow has given gibbets to her guardian Streltsy.

 How did Peter the Great deal with the revolt of the Streltsy? What does his approach to this problem tell us about the tsar?

---

within the Anglican Church who, inspired by Calvinist theology, wished to eliminate every trace of Roman Catholicism from the Church of England—were alienated by the king's strong defense of the Anglican Church. Many of England's gentry, mostly well-to-do landowners, had become Puritans and formed an important and substantial part of the House of Commons, the lower house of Parliament. It was not wise to alienate these men.

The conflict that had begun during the reign of James came to a head during the reign of his son Charles I (1625–1649). Like his father, Charles believed in divine-right monarchy, and religious differences also added to the hostility between Charles I and Parliament. The king's attempt to impose more ritual on the Anglican Church struck the Puritans as a return to Catholic practices. When Charles tried to force the Puritans to accept his religious policies, thousands of them went off to the "howling wildernesses" of America.

Civil War and Commonwealth

Grievances mounted until England finally slipped into a civil war (1642–1648) won by the parliamentary forces, due largely to the New Model Army of Oliver Cromwell, the only real military genius of the war. The New Model Army was composed primarily of more extreme Puritans known as the Independents, who, in typical Calvinist fashion, believed they were doing battle for God. As Cromwell wrote in one of his military reports, "Sir, this is none other but the hand of God; and to Him alone belongs the glory." We might give some credit to Cromwell; his soldiers were well trained in the new military tactics of the seventeenth century.

After the execution of Charles I on January 30, 1649, Parliament abolished the monarchy and the House of Lords and

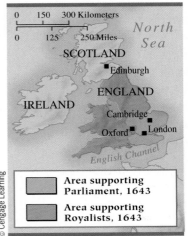

© Cengage Learning

Area supporting Parliament, 1643

Area supporting Royalists, 1643

Civil War in England

Oliver Cromwell. Oliver Cromwell was a dedicated Puritan who helped form the New Model Army that defeated the forces supporting King Charles I. The monarchy was abolished and replaced by a republic with Cromwell at its head. Cromwell proved unable to work with Parliament, however, and came to rely on force to rule England as a military dictatorship until his death in 1658. Cromwell is pictured here in 1649, preparing for battle.

CHRONOLOGY	Absolute and Limited Monarchy
France	
Louis XIV	1643–1715
Brandenburg-Prussia	
Frederick William the Great Elector	1640–1688
Elector Frederick III (King Frederick I)	1688–1713
Russia	
Ivan IV the Terrible	1533–1584
Peter the Great	1689–1725
First trip to the West	1697–1698
Construction of Saint Petersburg begins	1703
England	
Civil wars	1642–1648
Commonwealth	1649–1653
Charles II	1660–1685
Declaration of Indulgence	1672
James II	1685–1688
Glorious Revolution	1688
Bill of Rights	1689

proclaimed England a republic or commonwealth. But Cromwell and his army, unable to work effectively with Parliament, dispersed it by force and established a military dictatorship. After Cromwell's death in 1658, the army decided that military rule was no longer feasible and restored the monarchy in the person of Charles II, the son of Charles I.

Restoration and a Glorious Revolution

Charles was sympathetic to Catholicism, and Parliament's suspicions were aroused in 1672 when Charles took the audacious step of issuing the Declaration of Indulgence, which suspended the laws that Parliament had passed against Catholics and Puritans after the restoration of the monarchy. Parliament forced the king to suspend the declaration.

The accession of James II (1685–1688) to the crown virtually guaranteed a new constitutional crisis for England. An open and devout Catholic, his attempt to further Catholic interests made religion once more a primary cause of conflict between king and Parliament. James named Catholics to high positions in the government, army, navy, and universities. Parliamentary outcries against James's policies stopped short of rebellion because members knew that he was an old man and that his successors were his Protestant daughters Mary and Anne, born to his first wife. But on June 10, 1688, a son was born to James II's second wife, also a Catholic. Suddenly, the specter of a Catholic hereditary monarchy loomed large. A group of prominent English noblemen invited the Dutch chief executive, William of Orange, husband of James's daughter Mary, to invade England. William and Mary raised an army and invaded England while James, his wife, and their infant son fled to France. With little bloodshed, England had undergone its "Glorious Revolution."

In January 1689, Parliament offered the throne to William and Mary, who accepted it along with the provisions of a bill of rights (see the box on p. 445). The Bill of Rights affirmed Parliament's right to make laws and levy taxes. The rights of citizens to keep arms and have a jury trial were also confirmed. By deposing one king and establishing another, Parliament had destroyed the divine-right theory of kingship (William was, after all, king by grace of Parliament, not God) and asserted its right to participate in the government. Parliament did not have complete control of the government, but it now had the right to participate in affairs of state. Over the next century, it would gradually prove to be the real authority in the English system of **limited (constitutional) monarchy**.

The Flourishing of European Culture

 FOCUS QUESTION: How did the artistic and literary achievements of this era reflect the political and economic developments of the period?

Despite religious wars and the growth of absolutism, European culture continued to flourish. The era was blessed with a number of prominent artists and writers.

The Bill of Rights

POLITICS & GOVERNMENT

In 1688, the English experienced a bloodless revolution in which the Stuart king, James II, was replaced by Mary, James's daughter, and her husband, William of Orange. After William and Mary had assumed power, Parliament passed the Bill of Rights, which set out the rights of Parliament and laid the foundation for a constitutional monarchy.

The Bill of Rights

Whereas the said late King James II having abdicated the government, and the throne being thereby vacant, his Highness the prince of Orange (whom it hath pleased Almighty God to make the glorious instrument of delivering this kingdom from popery and arbitrary power) did (by the device of the lords spiritual and temporal, and diverse principal persons of the Commons) cause letters to be written to the lords spiritual and temporal, being Protestants, and other letters to the several counties, cities, universities, boroughs, and Cinque Ports, for the choosing of such persons to represent them, as were of right to be sent to parliament, to meet and sit at Westminster upon the two and twentieth day of January, in this year 1689, in order to such an establishment as that their religion, laws, and liberties might not again be in danger of being subverted; upon which letters elections have been accordingly made.

And thereupon the said lords spiritual and temporal and Commons, pursuant to their respective letters and elections, being now assembled in a full and free representation of this nation, taking into their most serious consideration the best means for attaining the ends aforesaid, do in the first place (as their ancestors in like case have usually done), for the vindication and assertion of their ancient rights and liberties, declare:

1. That the pretended power of suspending laws, or the execution of laws, by regal authority, without consent of parliament is illegal.
2. That the pretended power of dispensing with the laws, or the execution of law by regal authority, as it hath been assumed and exercised of late, is illegal.
3. That the commission for erecting the late court of commissioners for ecclesiastical causes, and all other commissions and courts of like nature, are illegal and pernicious.
4. That levying money for or to the use of the crown by pretense of prerogative, without grant of parliament, for longer time or in other manner than the same is or shall be granted, is illegal.
5. That it is the right of the subjects to petition the king, and all commitments and prosecutions for such petitioning are illegal.
6. That the raising or keeping a standing army within the kingdom in time of peace, unless it be with consent of parliament, is against law.
7. That the subjects which are Protestants may have arms for their defense suitable to their conditions, and as allowed by law.
8. That election of members of parliament ought to be free.
9. That the freedom of speech, and debates or proceedings in parliament, ought not to be impeached or questioned in any court or place out of parliament.
10. That excessive bail ought not to be required, nor excessive fines imposed, nor cruel and unusual punishments inflicted.
11. That jurors ought to be duly impaneled and returned, and jurors which pass upon men in trials for high treason ought to be freeholders.
12. That all grants and promises of fines and forfeitures of particular persons before conviction are illegal and void.
13. And that for redress of all grievances, and for the amending, strengthening, and preserving of the laws, parliament ought to be held frequently.

 How did the Bill of Rights lay the foundation for a constitutional monarchy in England?

Art: The Baroque

The artistic movement known as the **Baroque** (buh-ROHK) dominated the Western artistic world for a century and a half. The Baroque began in Italy in the last quarter of the sixteenth century and spread to the rest of Europe and Latin America. Baroque artists sought to harmonize the Classical ideals of Renaissance art with the spiritual feelings of the sixteenth-century religious revival. In large part, Baroque art and architecture reflected the search for power that was characteristic of much of the seventeenth century. Baroque churches and palaces featured richly ornamented facades, sweeping staircases, and an overall splendor meant to impress people. Kings and princes wanted not only their subjects but also other kings and princes to be in awe of their power.

Baroque painting was known for its use of dramatic effects to arouse the emotions. This style was especially evident in the works of Peter Paul Rubens (1577–1640) of Flanders, a prolific artist and an important figure in the

Louvre, Paris//© Réunion des Musées Nationaux/Art Resource, NY

Peter Paul Rubens, ***The Landing of Marie de' Medici at Marseilles.*** The Flemish painter Peter Paul Rubens played a key role in spreading the Baroque style from Italy to other parts of Europe. In *The Landing of Marie de' Medici at Marseilles*, Rubens made a dramatic use of light and color, bodies in motion, and luxurious nudes to heighten the emotional intensity of the scene. This was one of a cycle of twenty-one paintings dedicated to the queen mother of France.

Cornaro Chapel, Santa Maria della Vittoria, Rome//© Scala/Art Resource, NY

Gian Lorenzo Bernini, ***Ecstasy of Saint Theresa.*** One of the great artists of the Baroque period was the Italian sculptor and architect Gian Lorenzo Bernini. The *Ecstasy of Saint Theresa*, created for the Cornaro Chapel in the Church of Santa Maria della Vittoria in Rome, was one of Bernini's most famous sculptures. Bernini sought to convey visually Theresa's mystical experience when, according to her description, an angel pierced her heart repeatedly with a golden arrow.

spread of the Baroque from Italy to other parts of Europe. In his artistic masterpieces, bodies in violent motion, heavily fleshed nudes, a dramatic use of light and shadow, and rich sensuous pigments converge to express highly intense emotions.

Perhaps the greatest figure of the Baroque was the Italian architect and sculptor Gian Lorenzo Bernini (JAHN loh-RENT-zoh bur-NEE-nee) (1598–1680), who completed Saint Peter's Basilica at the Vatican and designed the vast colonnade enclosing the piazza in front of it. Action, exuberance, profusion, and dramatic effects mark the work of Bernini in the interior of Saint Peter's, where his *Throne of Saint Peter* hovers in midair, held by the hands of the four great doctors of the Catholic Church. Above the chair, rays of golden light drive a mass of clouds and angels toward the spectator. In his most striking sculptural work, the *Ecstasy of Saint Theresa*, Bernini depicts a moment of mystical experience in the life of the sixteenth-century Spanish saint. The elegant draperies and the expression on her face create a sensuously real portrayal of physical ecstasy.

Art: Dutch Realism

The supremacy of Dutch commerce in the seventeenth century was paralleled by a brilliant flowering of Dutch painting. Wealthy patricians and burghers of Dutch urban society commissioned works of art for their guild halls, town halls, and private dwellings. The interests of this bourgeois society were reflected in the subject matter of many Dutch paintings: portraits of themselves, group portraits of their military companies and guilds, landscapes, seascapes, genre scenes, still lifes, and the interiors of their residences. Unlike Baroque artists, Dutch painters were primarily interested in the realistic portrayal of secular everyday life.

This interest in painting scenes of everyday life is evident in the work of Judith Leyster (LESS-tur) (c. 1609–1660), who established her own independent painting career, a remarkable achievement for a woman in seventeenth-century Europe. Leyster became the first female member of the painters' Guild of Saint Luke in Haarlem, which enabled her to set up her own workshop and take on three male pupils. Musicians playing their instruments, women sewing, children laughing while playing games, and actors performing all form the subject matter of Leyster's portrayals of everyday Dutch life.

446 ❧ **CHAPTER 15** Europe Transformed: Reform and State Building

William Shakespeare: In Praise of England

ART & IDEAS

William Shakespeare is one of the most famous playwrights of the Western world. He was a universal genius, outclassing all others in his psychological insights, depth of characterization, imaginative skills, and versatility. His historical plays reflected the patriotic enthusiasm of the English in the Elizabethan era, as this excerpt from *Richard II* illustrates.

William Shakespeare, *Richard II*

This royal throne of kings, this sceptred isle,
This earth of majesty, this seat of Mars,
This other Eden, demi-Paradise,
This fortress built by Nature for herself
Against infection and the hand of war,
This happy breed of men, this little world,
This precious stone set in the silver sea,
Which serves it in the office of a wall
Or as a moat defensive to a house
Against the envy of less happier lands—
This blessed plot, this earth, this realm, this England,
This nurse, this teeming womb of royal kings,
Feared by their breed and famous by their birth,
Renowned for their deeds as far from home,

For Christian service and true chivalry,
As is the sepulcher in stubborn Jewry [the Holy
    Sepulcher in Jerusalem and the enduring Jewish
    community there]
Of the world's ransom, blessed Mary's Son—
This land of such dear souls, this dear dear land,
Dear for her reputation through the world,
Is now leased out, I die pronouncing it,
Like a tenement or pelting farm.
England, bound in with the triumphant sea,
Whose rocky shore beats back the envious siege
Of watery Neptune, is now bound in with shame,
With inky blots and rotten parchment bonds.
That England, that was wont to conquer others,
Hath made a shameful conquest of itself.
Ah, would the scandal vanish with my life,
How happy then were my ensuing death!

Why is William Shakespeare aptly described as not merely a playwright but a "complete man of the theater"? Which countries might Shakespeare have meant by the phrase "the envy of less happier lands"?

A Golden Age of Literature in England

In England, writing for the stage reached new heights between 1580 and 1640. The golden age of English literature is often called the Elizabethan era because much of the English cultural flowering occurred during Elizabeth's reign. Elizabethan literature exhibits the exuberance and pride associated with English exploits at the time (see the box above). Of all the forms of Elizabethan literature, none expressed the energy and intellectual versatility of the era better than drama. And no dramatist is more famous or more accomplished than William Shakespeare (1564–1614).

Shakespeare was a "complete man of the theater." Although best known for writing plays, he was also an actor and a shareholder in the chief acting company of the time, the Lord Chamberlain's Company, which played in various London theaters. Shakespeare is to this day hailed as a genius. A master of the English language, he imbued its words with power and majesty. And his technical proficiency was matched by incredible insight into human psychology.

Whether writing tragedies or comedies, Shakespeare exhibited a remarkable understanding of the human condition.

© Noortman, Maastricht, Netherlands//The Bridgeman Art Library

Judith Leyster, *Laughing Children with a Cat.* Although Judith Leyster was a well-known artist to her Dutch contemporaries, her fame diminished soon after her death. In the late nineteenth century, a Dutch art historian rediscovered her work. In *Laughing Children with a Cat*, painted in 1629, she shows two children laughing as one tickles the other, a scene repeated throughout history.

CHAPTER SUMMARY

In the last chapter, we observed how the movement of Europeans beyond Europe began to change the shape of world history. But what had made this development possible? After all, the Reformation of the sixteenth century, initially begun by Martin Luther, had brought about the religious division of Europe into Protestant and Catholic camps. By the middle of the sixteenth century, it was apparent that the religious passions of the Reformation era had brought an end to the religious unity of medieval Europe. The religious division (Catholics versus Protestant) was instrumental in beginning a series of religious wars that were complicated by economic, social, and political forces that also played a role.

The crises of the sixteenth and seventeenth centuries soon led to a search for a stable, secular order of politics and made

possible the emergence of a system of nation-states in which power politics took on increasing significance. Within those states, there slowly emerged some of the machinery that made possible a growing centralization of power. In those states called absolutist, strong monarchs with the assistance of their aristocracies took the lead in providing the leadership for greater centralization. In this so-called age of absolutism,

Louis XIV, the Sun King of France, was the model for other rulers. Strong monarchy also prevailed in central and eastern Europe, where three new powers made their appearance: Prussia, Austria, and Russia.

But not all European states followed the pattern of absolute monarchy. Especially important were developments in England, where a series of struggles between the king and Parliament took place in the seventeenth century. In the long run, the landed aristocracy gained power at the expense of the monarchs, thereby laying the foundations for a constitutional government in which Parliament provided the focus for the institutions of centralized power.

In all the major European states, a growing concern for power and dynamic expansion led to larger armies and greater conflict, stronger economies, and more powerful governments. From a global point of view, Europeans—with their strong governments, prosperous economies, and strengthened military forces—were beginning to dominate other parts of the world, leading to a growing belief in the superiority of their civilization.

Yet despite Europeans' increasing domination of global trade markets, they had not achieved their goal of diminishing the power of Islam, first pursued during the Crusades. In fact, as we shall see in the next chapter, in the midst of European expansion and exploration, three new and powerful Muslim empires were taking shape in the Middle East and South Asia.

CHAPTER TIMELINE

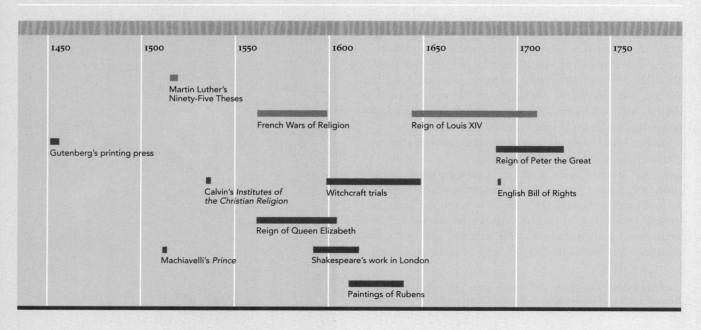

| 1450 | 1500 | 1550 | 1600 | 1650 | 1700 | 1750 |

Martin Luther's Ninety-Five Theses

French Wars of Religion

Reign of Louis XIV

Gutenberg's printing press

Reign of Peter the Great

Calvin's *Institutes of the Christian Religion*

Witchcraft trials

English Bill of Rights

Reign of Queen Elizabeth

Machiavelli's *Prince*

Shakespeare's work in London

Paintings of Rubens

CHAPTER REVIEW

Upon Reflection

Q What role did politics play in the success of the Protestant Reformation?

Q What did Louis XIV hope to accomplish through his domestic and foreign policies? To what extent did he succeed?

Q What role did the gentry play in seventeenth-century England?

Key Terms

absolutism (p. 423)
Protestant Reformation (p. 423)
new monarchies (p. 423)
Christian humanism (Northern Renaissance humanism) (p. 424)
relics (p. 425)
indulgences (p. 425)
justification by faith (p. 425)
predestination (p. 429)
Catholic Reformation (p. 430)
mercantilism (p. 437)
joint-stock company (p. 437)
divine-right monarchy (p. 440)
Puritans (p. 442)
limited (constitutional) monarchy (p. 444)
Baroque (p. 445)

Suggested Reading

THE REFORMATION: GENERAL WORKS Basic surveys of the Reformation period include **J. D. Tracy,** *Europe's Reformations, 1450–1650* (Oxford, 1999), and **D. MacCulloch,** *The Reformation* (New York, 2003). Also see the brief work by **U. Rublack,** *Reformation Europe* (Cambridge, 2005).

THE PROTESTANT AND CATHOLIC REFORMATIONS On Martin Luther's life, see **H. A. Oberman,** *Luther: Man Between God and the Devil* (New York, 1992). See also the brief biography by **M. Marty,** *Martin Luther* (New York, 2004). The most comprehensive account of the various groups and individuals who are called Anabaptist is **G. H. Williams,** *The Radical Reformation,* 2nd ed. (Kirksville, Mo., 1992). A good survey of the English Reformation is **A. G. Dickens,** *The English Reformation,* 2nd ed. (New York, 1989). On John Calvin, see **W. G. Naphy,** *Calvin and the Consolidation of the Genevan Reformation* (Philadelphia, 2003). A good introduction to the Catholic Reformation can be found in **R. P. Hsia,** *The World of Catholic Renewal, 1540–1770* (Cambridge, 1998).

EUROPE IN CRISIS, 1560–1650 On the French Wars of Religion, see **R. J. Knecht,** *The French Wars of Religion, 1559–1598,* 2nd ed. (New York, 1996). The fundamental study of the Thirty Years' War is now **P. H. Wilson,** *The Thirty Years War: Europe's Tragedy* (Cambridge, Mass., 2009). Witchcraft hysteria can be examined in **R. Briggs,** *Witches and Neighbours: The Social and Cultural Context of European Witchcraft,* 2nd ed. (Oxford, 2002).

ABSOLUTE AND LIMITED MONARCHY A solid and very readable biography of Louis XIV is **J. Levi,** *Louis XIV* (New York, 2004). On the creation of the Austrian state, see **P. S. Fichtner,** *The Habsburg Monarchy, 1490–1848* (New York, 2003). See **P. H. Wilson,** *Absolutism in Central Europe* (New York, 2000), on both Prussia and Austria. On Peter the Great, see **P. Bushkovitz,** *Peter the Great* (Oxford, 2001). On the English Civil War, see **M. A. Kishlansky,** *A Monarchy Transformed* (London, 1996), and **D. Purkiss,** *The English Civil War* (New York, 2006).

EUROPEAN CULTURE For a general survey of Baroque culture, see **F. C. Marchetti et al.,** *Baroque, 1600–1770* (New York, 2005). The literature on Shakespeare is enormous. For a biography, see **A. L. Rowse,** *The Life of Shakespeare* (New York, 1963).

Go to the CourseMate website at **www.cengagebrain.com** for additional study tools and review materials—including audio and video clips—for this chapter.

CHAPTER

16

The Muslim Empires

Turks fight Christians at the Battle of Mohács

CHAPTER OUTLINE AND FOCUS QUESTIONS

The Ottoman Empire

Q What was the ethnic composition of the Ottoman Empire, and how did the government of the sultan administer such a diverse population? How did Ottoman policy in this regard compare with the policies applied in Europe and Asia?

The Safavids

Q What problems did the Safavid Empire face, and how did its rulers attempt to solve them? How did their approaches compare with those in the other Muslim empires?

The Grandeur of the Mughals

Q What role did Islam play in the Mughal Empire, and how did the Mughals' approach to religion compare with that of the Ottomans and the Safavids? What might explain the similarities and differences?

CRITICAL THINKING

Q What were the main characteristics of each of the Muslim empires, and in what ways did they resemble each other? How were they distinct from their European counterparts?

THE OTTOMAN ARMY, led by Sultan Suleyman the Magnificent, arrived at Mohács, on the plains of Hungary, on an August morning in 1526. The Turkish force numbered about 100,000 men, and its weapons included three hundred new long-range cannons. Facing them was a somewhat larger European force, clothed in heavy armor but armed with only one hundred older cannons.

The battle began at noon and was over in two hours. The flower of the Hungarian cavalry had been destroyed, and 20,000 foot soldiers had drowned in a nearby swamp. The Ottomans had lost fewer than two hundred men. Two weeks later, they seized the Hungarian capital at Buda and prepared to lay siege to the nearby Austrian city of Vienna. Europe was in a panic, but Mohács was to be the high point of Turkish expansion in Europe.

In launching their Age of Exploration, European rulers had hoped that by controlling global markets, they could cripple the power of Islam and reduce its threat to the security of Europe. But the dream of Christian nations to expand their influence around the globe at the expense of their great Muslim rival had not entirely been achieved. On the contrary, the Muslim world, which seemed to have entered a period of decline with the collapse of the Abbasid caliphate during the era of the Mongols, managed to revive in the shadow of Europe's Age of Exploration, a period that witnessed the rise of three great Muslim empires. These powerful Muslim states—of the Ottomans, the Safavids, and the Mughals—dominated the Middle East and the South Asian subcontinent and brought a measure of stability to a region that had been in turmoil for centuries. One of them—the Ottoman Empire—managed to impose its rule over much of eastern Europe and achieve a dominant position in the Mediterranean world.

This stability, however, was not long-lived. By the end of the eighteenth century, much of India and the Middle East had come under severe European pressure and had returned to a state of anarchy, and the Ottoman Empire had entered a period of gradual decline. But that decline was due more to internal factors than to the challenge posed by a resurgent Europe.

The Ottoman Empire

Q FOCUS QUESTIONS: What was the ethnic composition of the Ottoman Empire, and how did the government of the sultan administer such a diverse population? How did Ottoman policy in this regard compare with the policies applied in Europe and Asia?

The Ottoman Turks were among the Turkic-speaking nomadic peoples who had spread westward from Central Asia in the ninth, tenth, and eleventh centuries. The first to appear were the Seljuk Turks, who initially attempted to revive the declining Abbasid caliphate in Baghdad. Later they established themselves in the Anatolian peninsula as the successors to the Byzantine Empire. Turks served as warriors or administrators, while the peasants who tilled the farmland were mainly Greek.

The Rise of the Ottoman Turks

In the late thirteenth century, a new group of Turks under the tribal leader Osman (os-MAHN) (1280–1326) began to consolidate power in the northwestern corner of the Anatolian peninsula. That land had been given to them by the Seljuk rulers as a reward for helping drive out the Mongols in the late thirteenth century. At first, the Osman Turks were relatively peaceful and engaged in pastoral pursuits, but as the Seljuk empire began to crumble in the early fourteenth century, the Osman Turks began to expand and founded the Osmanli (os-MAHN-lee) dynasty, with its capital at Bursa (BURR-suh). The Osmanlis later came to be known as the Ottomans.

A key advantage for the Ottomans was their location in the northwestern corner of the peninsula. From there they were able to expand westward and eventually take over the Bosporus and the Dardanelles, between the Mediterranean and the Black Seas. The Byzantine Empire, of course, had controlled the area for centuries, serving as a buffer between the Muslim Middle East and the Latin West. The Byzantines, however, had been severely weakened by the sack of Constantinople in the Fourth Crusade in 1204 and the occupation of much of the empire by western Europeans for the next half century. In 1345, Ottoman forces under their leader Orkhan (or-KHAHN) I (1326–1360) crossed the Bosporus for the first time to support a usurper against the Byzantine emperor in Constantinople. Setting up their first European base at Gallipoli (gah-LIP-poh-lee) at the Mediterranean entrance to the Dardanelles, Turkish forces expanded gradually into the Balkans and allied with fractious Serbian and Bulgar forces

against the Byzantines. In these unstable conditions, the Ottomans gradually established permanent settlements throughout the area, where Turkish provincial governors, called **beys** (BAYS) (from the Turkish *beg*, "knight"), collected taxes from the local Slavic peasants after driving out the previous landlords. The Ottoman leader now began to claim the title of **sultan** (SUL-tun) or sovereign of his domain.

In 1360, Orkhan was succeeded by his son Murad (moo-RAHD) I, who consolidated Ottoman power in the Balkans, set up a capital at Edirne (eh-DEER-nay) (see Map 16.1), and gradually reduced the Byzantine emperor to a vassal. Murad did not initially attempt to conquer Constantinople because his forces were composed mostly of the traditional Turkish cavalry and lacked the ability to breach the strong walls of the city. Instead, he began to build up a strong military administration based on the recruitment of Christians into an elite guard. Called **Janissaries** (JAN-nih-say-reez) (from the Turkish *yeni cheri*, "new troops"), they were recruited from the local Christian population in the Balkans and then converted to Islam and trained as foot soldiers or administrators. One of the major advantages of the Janissaries was that they were directly subordinated to the sultanate and therefore owed their loyalty to the person of the sultan. Other military forces were organized by the beys and were thus loyal to their local tribal leaders.

The Janissary corps also represented a response to changes in warfare. As the knowledge of firearms spread in the late fourteenth century, the Turks began to master the new technology, including siege cannons and muskets (see the comparative essay "The Changing Face of War" on p. 453). The traditional nomadic cavalry charge was now outmoded and was superseded by infantry forces armed with muskets. Thus, the Janissaries provided a well-armed infantry that served both as an elite guard to protect the palace and as a means of extending Turkish control in the Balkans. With his new forces, Murad defeated the Serbs at the famous Battle of Kosovo (KAWSS-suh-voh) in 1389 and ended Serbian hegemony in the area.

Expansion of the Empire

Under Murad's successor, Bayazid (by-uh-ZEED) I (1389–1402), the Ottomans advanced northward, annexed Bulgaria, and slaughtered the French cavalry at a major battle on the Danube. A defeat at Ankara (AN-kuh-ruh) at the hands of the Mongol warrior Tamerlane (see Chapter 9) in 1402 proved to be only a temporary setback. When Mehmet (meh-MET) II (1451–1481) succeeded to the throne, he was determined to capture Constantinople. Already in control of the Dardanelles, he ordered the construction of a major fortress on the Bosporus just north of the city, which put the Turks in a position to strangle the Byzantines.

THE FALL OF CONSTANTINOPLE The last Byzantine emperor desperately called for help from the Europeans, but only the Genoese came to his defense. With 80,000 troops ranged against only 6,000 to 8,000 defenders, Mehmet laid siege to Constantinople in 1453. In their attack on the city,

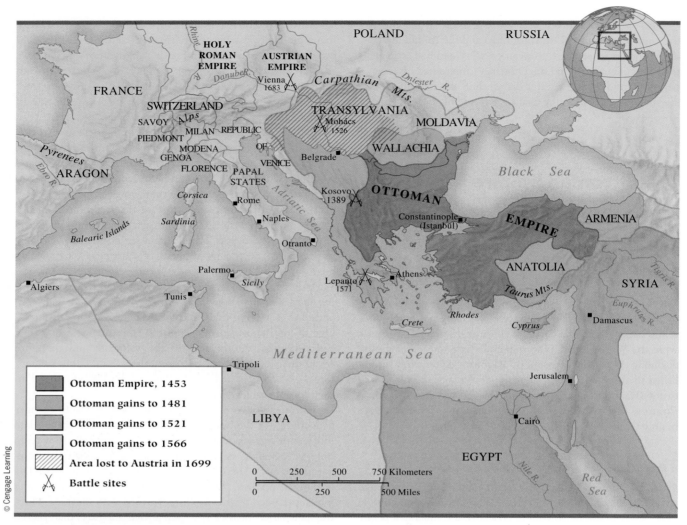

MAP 16.1 The Ottoman Empire. This map shows the territorial growth of the Ottoman Empire from the eve of the conquest of Constantinople in 1453 to the end of the seventeenth century, when a defeat at the hands of Austria led to the loss of a substantial portion of central Europe.

Q *Where did the Ottomans come from?*

the Turks made use of massive cannons with 26-foot barrels that could launch stone balls weighing up to 1,200 pounds each. The Byzantines stretched heavy chains across the Golden Horn, the inlet that forms the city's harbor, to prevent a naval attack from the north and prepared to make their final stand behind the 13-mile-long wall along the western edge of the city. But Mehmet's forces seized the tip of the peninsula north of the Golden Horn and then dragged their ships overland across the peninsula from the Bosporus and put them into the water behind the chains. Finally, the walls were breached; the Byzantine emperor died in the final battle (see the box on p. 373 in Chapter 13). Mehmet II, standing before the palace of the emperor, paused to reflect on the passing nature of human glory. But it was not long before he and the Ottomans were again on the march.

THE ADVANCE INTO WESTERN ASIA AND AFRICA With their new capital at Constantinople, renamed Istanbul, the

Ottoman Turks had become a dominant force in the Balkans and the Anatolian peninsula. They now began to advance to the east against the Shi'ite kingdom of the Safavids (sah-FAH-weeds) in Persia (see "The Safavids" later in this chapter), which had been promoting rebellion among the Anatolian tribal population and disrupting Turkish trade through the Middle East. After defeating the Safavids at a major battle in 1514, Emperor Selim (seh-LEEM) I (1512–1520) consolidated Turkish control over Mesopotamia and then turned his attention to the Mamluks (MAM-looks) in Egypt, who had failed to support the Ottomans in their struggle against the Safavids. The Mamluks were defeated in Syria in 1516; Cairo fell a year later. Now controlling several of the holy cities of Islam, including Jerusalem, Mecca, and Medina, Selim declared himself the new caliph, or successor to Muhammad. During the next few years, Turkish armies and fleets advanced westward along the African coast, occupying Tripoli, Tunis, and Algeria and eventually penetrating almost to the Strait of

COMPARATIVE ESSAY

The Changing Face of War

"War," as the renowned French historian Fernand Braudel once observed, "has always been a matter of arms and techniques. Improved techniques can radically alter the course of events." Braudel's remark was directed to the situation in the Mediterranean region during the sixteenth century, when the adoption of artillery changed the face of warfare and gave enormous advantages to the countries that stood at the head of the new technological revolution. But it could as easily have been applied to the present day, when potential adversaries possess weapons capable of reaching across oceans and continents.

One crucial aspect of military superiority, of course, lies in the nature of weaponry. From the invention of the bow and arrow to the advent of the atomic era, the possession of superior instruments of war has provided a distinct advantage against a poorly armed enemy. It was at least partly the possession of bronze weapons, for example, that enabled the invading Hyksos to conquer Egypt during the second millennium B.C.E.

Mobility is another factor of vital importance. During the second millennium B.C.E., horse-drawn chariots revolutionized the art of war from the Mediterranean Sea to the Yellow River valley in northern China. Later, the invention of the stirrup enabled mounted warriors to shoot arrows from horseback, a technique applied with great effect by the Mongols as they devastated civilizations across the Eurasian supercontinent.

To protect themselves from marauding warriors, settled societies began to erect massive walls around their cities and fortresses. That in turn led to the invention of siege weapons like the catapult and the battering ram. The Mongols allegedly even came up with an early form of chemical warfare, hurling human bodies infected with the plague into the bastions of their enemies.

The invention of explosives launched the next great revolution in warfare. First used as a weapon of war by the Tang

© William J. Duiker

Roman troops defeating Celtic warriors; from the Great Altar of Pergamum.

dynasty in China, explosives were brought to the West by the Turks, who used them with great effectiveness in the fifteenth century against the Byzantine Empire. But the Europeans quickly mastered the new technology and took it to new heights, inventing handheld firearms and mounting iron cannons on their warships. The latter represented a significant advantage to European fleets as they began to compete with rivals for control of the Indian and Pacific Oceans.

The twentieth century saw revolutionary new developments in the art of warfare, from armed vehicles to airplanes to nuclear arms. But as weapons grow ever more fearsome, they are more dangerous to use, resulting in the paradox of the Vietnam War, when lightly armed Viet Cong guerrilla units were able to fight the world's mightiest army to a virtual standstill. As the Chinese military strategist Sun Tzu had long ago observed, victory in war often goes to the smartest, not the strongest.

 Why were the Europeans, rather than other peoples, able to make effective use of firearms to expand their influence throughout the world?

Gibraltar (see Map 16.1). In their advance, the invaders had taken advantage of the progressive disintegration of the Nasrid (NAS-rid) dynasty in Morocco, which had been in decline for decades and had lost its last foothold on the European continent when Granada fell to Spain in 1492.

The impact of Turkish rule on the peoples of North Africa was relatively light. Like their predecessors, the Turks were Muslims, and they preferred where possible to administer their conquered regions through local rulers. The central government utilized appointed **pashas** (PAH-shuz) who were directly responsible to Istanbul; the pashas collected taxes, paying a fixed percentage as tribute to the central government, and maintained law and order. The Turks ruled from coastal cities such as Algiers, Tunis, and Tripoli and made no attempt to control the interior beyond maintaining the trade routes through the Sahara to the

© Bibliothèque Nationale, Paris/The Bridgeman Art Library

The Turkish Conquest of Constantinople. Mehmet II put a stranglehold on the Byzantine capital of Constantinople with a surprise attack by Turkish ships, which were dragged overland and placed in the water behind the enemy's defense lines. In addition, the Turks made use of massive cannons that could launch stone balls weighing up to 1,200 pounds each. The heavy bombardment of the city walls presaged a new kind of warfare in Europe. Notice the fanciful Gothic interpretation of the city in this contemporary French miniature of the siege.

commercial centers along the Niger River. Meanwhile, local pirates along the Barbary Coast—the northern coast of Africa from Egypt to the Atlantic Ocean—competed with their Christian rivals in raiding the shipping that passed through the Mediterranean.

By the seventeenth century, the links between the imperial court in Istanbul and its appointed representatives in the Turkish regencies in North Africa had begun to weaken. Some of the pashas were dethroned by local elites, while others, such as the bey of Tunis, became hereditary rulers. Even Egypt, whose agricultural wealth and control over the route to the Red Sea made it the most important country in the area to the Turks, gradually became autonomous under a new official class of Janissaries. Many of them became wealthy landowners by exploiting their official positions and collecting tax revenues far in excess of what they had to remit to Istanbul. In the early eighteenth century, the Mamluks returned to power, although the Turkish government

managed to retain some control by means of a viceroy appointed from Istanbul.

TURKISH EXPANSION IN EUROPE After their conquest of Constantinople in 1453, the Ottoman Turks tried to complete their conquest of the Balkans, where they had been established since the fourteenth century. Although they were successful in taking the Romanian territory of Wallachia (wah-LAY-kee-uh) in 1476, the resistance of the Hungarians initially kept the Turks from advancing up the Danube valley. From 1480 to 1520, internal problems and the need to consolidate their eastern frontiers kept the Turks from any further attacks on Europe.

Suleyman (SOO-lay-mahn) I the Magnificent (1520–1566), however, brought the Turks back to Europe's attention (see the box on p. 455). Advancing up the Danube, the Turks seized Belgrade in 1521 and won a major victory over the Hungarians at the Battle of Mohács (MOH-hach) on the Danube in 1526. Subsequently, the Turks overran most of Hungary, moved into Austria, and advanced as far as Vienna, where they were finally repulsed in 1529. At the same time, they extended their power into the western Mediterranean and threatened to turn it into a Turkish lake until a large Turkish fleet was destroyed by the Spanish at Lepanto in 1571. Despite the defeat, the Turks continued to hold nominal suzerainty over the southern shores of the Mediterranean. One year after Lepanto, the Turks reconstituted their fleet and seized the island of Cyprus. Responding to the joy expressed in Europe over the naval victory, the **grand vizier** (veh-ZEER) (Turkish *vezir*), or chief minister, in Constantinople remarked to the Venetian ambassador, "There is a big difference between our loss and yours. In taking Cyprus, we have cut off one of your arms. In sinking our fleet you only shaved our beard. A lost arm cannot be replaced, but a shorn beard grows back quickly to its prior magnificence."[1]

Although Christians in Europe frequently called for new Crusades against the "infidel" Turks, by the beginning of the seventeenth century the Ottoman Empire was being treated like any other European power by European rulers seeking alliances and trade concessions. During the first half of the seventeenth century, the Ottoman Empire was viewed as a "sleeping giant." Involved in domestic bloodletting and heavily threatened by a challenge from Persia, the Ottomans were content with the status quo in eastern Europe. But under a new line of grand viziers in the second half of the seventeenth century, the Ottoman Empire again took the offensive. By mid-1683, the Ottomans had marched through the Hungarian plain and laid siege to Vienna. Repulsed by a mixed army of Austrians, Poles, Bavarians, and Saxons, the Turks retreated and were pushed out of Hungary by a new European coalition. Although they retained the core of their empire, the Ottoman Turks would never again be a threat to Europe. The Turkish empire held together for the rest of the seventeenth and the eighteenth centuries, but it faced new challenges from the ever-growing Austrian Empire in southeastern Europe and the new Russian giant to the north.

A Portrait of Suleyman the Magnificent

POLITICS & GOVERNMENT

Suleyman I was perhaps the greatest of all Ottoman sultans. Like King Louis XIV of France and Emperor Kangxi of China, he presided over his domain at the peak of its military and cultural achievement. This description of him was written by Ghislain de Busbecq (GEE-lan duh booz-BEK), the Habsburg ambassador to Constantinople. Busbecq observed Suleyman at first hand and, as this selection indicates, was highly impressed by the Turkish ruler.

Ghislain de Busbecq, *The Turkish Letters*

The Sultan was seated on a rather low sofa, no more than a foot from the ground and spread with many costly coverlets and cushions embroidered with exquisite work. Near him were his bow and arrows. His expression, as I have said, is anything but smiling, and has a sternness which, though sad, is full of majesty. On our arrival we were introduced into his presence by his chamberlains, who held our arms—a practice which has always been observed since a Croatian sought an interview and murdered the Sultan Amurath in a revenge for the slaughter of his master, Marcus the Despot of Serbia. After going through the pretense of kissing his hand, we were led to the wall facing him backwards, so as not to turn our backs or any part of them toward him. He then listened to the recital of my message, but, as it did not correspond [to] his expectations (for the demands of my imperial master [the Habsburg emperor Ferdinand I] were full of dignity and independence, and, therefore, far from acceptable to one who thought that his slightest wishes ought to be obeyed), he assumed an expression of disdain, and merely answered *"Giusel, giusel,"* that is, "Well, well." We were then dismissed to our lodging. . . .

You will probably wish me to describe the impression which Suleyman made upon me. He is beginning to feel the weight of years, but his dignity of demeanor and his general physical appearance are worthy of the ruler of so vast an empire. He has always been frugal and temperate, and was so even in his youth, when he might have erred without incurring blame in the eyes of the Turks. Even in his earlier years he did not indulge in wine or in those unnatural vices to which the Turks are often addicted. Even his bitterest critics can find nothing more serious to allege against him than his undue submission to his wife and its result in his somewhat precipitate action in putting Mustapha [his firstborn son, by another wife] to death, which is generally imputed to her employment of love potions and incantations. It is generally agreed that ever since he promoted her to the rank of his lawful wife, he has possessed no concubines, although there is no law to prevent his doing so. He is a strict guardian of his religion and its ceremonies, being not less desirous of upholding his faith than of extending his dominions. For his age—he has almost reached his sixtieth year—he enjoys quite good health, though his bad complexion may be due to some hidden malady; and indeed it is generally believed that he has an incurable ulcer or gangrene on his leg. This defect of complexion he remedies by painting his face with a coating of red powder, when he wishes departing ambassadors to take with them a strong impression of his good health; for he fancies that it contributes to inspire greater fear in foreign potentates if they think that he is well and strong. I noticed a clear indication of this practice on the present occasion; for his appearance when he received me in the final audience was very different from that which he presented when he gave me an interview on my arrival.

What were the main achievements of Suleyman that caused him to be called "the Magnificent"? Is this description the work of an admirer or a critic? Why do you think so?

The Nature of Turkish Rule

Like other Muslim empires in Persia and India, the Ottoman political system was the result of the evolution of tribal institutions into a sedentary empire. At the apex of the Ottoman system was the sultan, who was the supreme authority in both a political and a military sense. The origins of this system can be traced back to the bey, who was only a tribal leader, a first among equals, who could claim loyalty from his chiefs so long as he could provide booty and grazing lands for his subordinates. Disputes were settled by tribal law; Muslim law was secondary. Tribal leaders collected taxes—or booty—from areas under their control and sent one-fifth on to the bey. Both administrative and military power were centralized under the bey, and the capital was wherever the bey and his administration happened to be.

THE ROLE OF THE SULTAN But the rise of empire brought about changes and an adaptation to Byzantine traditions of rule much as Abbasid political practices had been affected by Persian monarchical tradition at an earlier time in Baghdad. The status and prestige of the sultan now increased relative to the subordinate tribal leaders, and the position took on the trappings of imperial rule. Court rituals were inherited from the Byzantines and Persians, and a centralized administrative system was adopted that increasingly isolated the sultan in his palace. The position of the sultan was hereditary, with a son, although not necessarily the eldest, always succeeding the father. This practice led to chronic succession struggles upon the death of individual sultans, and the losers were often executed (strangled with a silk bowstring) or later imprisoned. Potential heirs to the throne were assigned as provincial governors to provide them with experience.

THE HAREM The heart of the sultan's power was in the Topkapi (tahp-KAH-pee) Palace in the center of Istanbul. Topkapi (meaning "cannon gate") was constructed in 1459 by Mehmet II and served as an administrative center as well as the private residence of the sultan and his family. Eventually, it had a staff of 20,000 employees. The private domain of the sultan was called the **harem** ("sacred place"). Here he resided with his concubines. Normally, a sultan did not marry but chose several concubines as his favorites; they were accorded this status after they gave birth to sons. When a son became a sultan, his mother became known as the queen mother and served as adviser to the throne. This tradition, initiated by the influential wife of Suleyman the Magnificent, often resulted in considerable authority for the queen mother in affairs of state.

Like the Janissaries, members of the harem were often of slave origin and formed an elite element in Ottoman society. Since the enslavement of Muslims was forbidden, slaves were taken among non-Islamic peoples. Some concubines were prisoners selected for the position, while others were purchased or offered to the sultan as gifts. They were then trained and educated like the Janissaries in a system called *devshirme* (dev-SHEER-may) ("collection"). *Devshirme* had originated in the practice of requiring local clan leaders to provide prisoners to the sultan as part of their tax obligation. Talented males were given special training for eventual placement in military or administrative positions, while their female counterparts were trained for service in the harem, with instruction in reading, the Qur'an, sewing and embroidery, and musical performance. They were ranked according to their status, and some were permitted to leave the harem to marry officials. If they were later divorced, they were sometimes allowed to return to the harem.

Unique to the Ottoman Empire from the fifteenth century onward was the exclusive use of slaves to reproduce its royal heirs. Contrary to myth, few of the women of the imperial harem were used for sexual purposes, as the majority were relatives of the sultan's extended family—sisters, daughters, widowed mothers, and in-laws, with their own personal slaves and entourages. Contemporary European observers compared the atmosphere in the Topkapi harem to a Christian nunnery, with its hierarchical organization, enforced chastity, and rule of silence.

Because of their proximity to the sultan, the women of the harem often wielded so much political power that the era has been called the "sultanate of women." Queen mothers administered the imperial household and engaged in diplomatic relations with other countries while controlling the marital alliances of their daughters with senior civilian and

© Topkapi Palace Museum, Istanbul/The Bridgeman Art Library

Recruitment of the Children. The Ottoman Empire, like its Chinese counterpart, sought to recruit its officials on the basis of merit. Through the system called *devshirme* ("collection"), youthful candidates were selected from the non-Muslim population in villages throughout the empire. In this painting, an imperial officer is counting coins to pay for the children's travel expenses to Istanbul, where they will undergo extensive academic and military training. Note the concern of two of the mothers and a priest as they question the official, who undoubtedly underwent the process himself as a child. As they leave their family and friends, the children carry their worldly possessions in bags slung over their shoulders.

military officials or members of other royal families in the region. One princess was married seven separate times from the age of two after her previous husbands died either in battle or by execution.

ADMINISTRATION OF THE GOVERNMENT The sultan ruled through an imperial council that met four days a week and was chaired by the grand vizier. The sultan often attended behind a screen, whence he could privately indicate his desires to the grand vizier. The latter presided over the imperial bureaucracy. Like the palace guard, the bureaucrats were not an exclusive group but were chosen at least partly by merit from a palace school for training officials. Most officials were Muslims by birth, but some talented Janissaries became senior members of the bureaucracy, and almost all the later grand viziers came from the *devshirme* system.

Local administration during the imperial period was a product of Turkish tribal tradition and was similar in some respects to fief-holding in Europe. The empire was divided into provinces and districts governed by officials who, like their tribal predecessors, combined both civil and military functions. They were assisted by bureaucrats trained in the palace school in Istanbul. Senior officials were assigned land in fief by the sultan and were then responsible for collecting taxes and supplying armies to the empire. These lands were then farmed out to the local cavalry elite called the *sipahis* (suh-PAH-heez), who obtained their salaries by exacting a tax from all peasants in their fiefdoms. These local officials were not hereditary aristocrats, but sons often inherited their fathers' landholdings, and the vast majority were descendants of the beys who had formed the tribal elites before the imperial period.

Religion and Society in the Ottoman World

Like most Turkic-speaking peoples in the Anatolian peninsula and throughout the Middle East, the Ottoman ruling elites were Sunni Muslims. Ottoman sultans had claimed the title of caliph ("defender of the faith") since the early sixteenth century and thus were theoretically responsible for guiding the flock and maintaining Islamic law, the *Shari'a*. In practice, the sultan assigned these duties to a supreme religious authority, who administered the law and maintained a system of schools for educating Muslims.

Islamic law and customs were applied to all Muslims in the empire. Although most Turkic-speaking people were Sunni Muslims, some communities were attracted to Sufism (see Chapter 7) or other heterodox doctrines. The government tolerated such activities as long as their practitioners remained loyal to the empire, but in the early sixteenth century, unrest among these groups—some of whom converted to the Shi'ite version of Islam—outraged the conservative *ulama* and eventually led to war against the Safavids (see "The Safavids" later in this chapter).

THE TREATMENT OF MINORITIES Non-Muslims—mostly Orthodox Christians (Greeks and Slavs), Jews, and Armenian Christians—formed a significant minority within the empire, which treated them with relative tolerance. Non-Muslims were compelled to pay a head tax (as compensation for their exemption from military service), and they were permitted to practice their religion or convert to Islam (people who were already Muslim were prohibited from adopting another faith). Most of the population in European areas of the empire remained Christian, but in some places, such as the Balkan territory now known as Bosnia and Herzegovina, substantial numbers converted to Islam.

Each religious group within the empire was organized as an administrative unit called a *millet* (mi-LET) ("nation" or "community"). Each group, including the Muslims themselves, had its own patriarch, priest, or grand rabbi

CHRONOLOGY   The Ottoman Empire

Reign of Osman I	1280–1326
Ottoman Turks cross the Bosporus	1345
Murad I consolidates Turkish power in the Balkans	1360
Ottomans defeat the Serbian army at Kosovo	1389
Tamerlane defeats the Ottoman army at Ankara	1402
Reign of Mehmet II the Conqueror	1451–1481
Turkish conquest of Constantinople	1453
Turks defeat the Mamluks in Syria and seize Cairo	1516–1517
Reign of Suleyman I the Magnificent	1520–1566
Defeat of the Hungarians at Battle of Mohács	1526
Defeat of the Turks at Vienna	1529
Battle of Lepanto	1571
Second siege of Vienna	1683

who dealt as an intermediary with the government and administered the community according to its own laws. The leaders of the individual *millets* were responsible to the sultan and his officials for the behavior of the subjects under their care and collected taxes for transmission to the government. Each *millet* established its own system of justice, set its own educational policies, and provided welfare for the needy.

Nomadic peoples were placed in a separate *millet* and were subject to their own regulations and laws. They were divided into the traditional nomadic classifications of tribes, clans, and "tents" (individual families) and were governed by their hereditary chiefs, the beys. As we have seen, the beys were responsible for administration and for collecting taxes for the state.

SOCIAL CLASSES The subjects of the Ottoman Empire were also divided by occupation and place of residence. In addition to the ruling class, there were four main occupational groups: peasants, artisans, merchants, and pastoral peoples. The first three were classified as "urban" residents. Peasants tilled land that was leased to them by the state (ultimate ownership of all land resided with the sultan), but the land was deeded to them, so they were able to pass it on to their heirs. They were not allowed to sell the land and thus in practice were forced to remain on the soil. Taxes were based on the amount of land the peasants possessed and were paid to the local *sipahis*, who held the district in fief.

Artisans were organized according to craft guilds. Each guild, headed by a council of elders, was responsible not only for dealing with the governmental authorities but also for providing financial services, social security, and training for its members. Outside the ruling elite, merchants were the most privileged class in Ottoman society. They were largely exempt from government regulations and taxes and were therefore able in many cases to amass large fortunes.

Charging interest was technically illegal under Islamic law, but the rules were often ignored in practice. In the absence of regulations, merchants often established monopolies and charged high prices, which caused them to be bitterly resented by other subjects of the empire.

THE POSITION OF WOMEN Technically, women in the Ottoman Empire were subject to the same restrictions that afflicted their counterparts in other Muslim societies, but their position was ameliorated to some degree by a variety of factors. In the first place, non-Muslims were subject to the laws and customs of their own religions; thus, Orthodox Christian, Armenian Christian, and Jewish women were spared some of the restrictions applied to their Muslim sisters. In the second place, Islamic laws as applied in the Ottoman Empire defined the legal position of women comparatively tolerantly. Women were permitted to own and inherit property, including their dowries. They could not be forced into marriage and in certain cases were permitted to seek a divorce. As we have seen, women often exercised considerable influence in the palace and in a few instances even served as senior officials, such as governors of provinces. The relatively tolerant attitude toward women in Ottoman-held territories has been ascribed by some to Turkish tribal traditions, which took a more egalitarian view of gender roles than the sedentary societies of the region did.

The Ottomans in Decline

The Ottoman Empire reached its zenith under Suleyman the Magnificent, often known as Suleyman Kanuni, or "the lawgiver," who launched the conquest of Hungary. But Suleyman also sowed the seeds of the empire's eventual decline. He executed his two most able sons on suspicion of factionalism and was succeeded by Selim II (the Sot, or "the drunken sultan"), the only surviving son.

By the seventeenth century, signs of internal rot had begun to appear, although the first loss of imperial territory did not occur until 1699, at the Treaty of Karlowitz (KARL-oh-vits). Apparently, a number of factors were involved. In the first place, the administrative system inherited from the tribal period began to break down. Although the *devshirme* system of training officials continued to function, *devshirme* graduates were now permitted to marry and inherit property and to enroll their sons in the palace corps. Thus, they were gradually transformed from a meritocratic administrative elite into a privileged and often degenerate hereditary caste. Local administrators were corrupted and taxes rose as the central bureaucracy lost its links with rural areas. The imperial treasury was depleted by constant wars, and transport and communications were neglected. Interest in science and technology, once a hallmark of the Arab empire, was in decline. In addition, the empire was increasingly beset by economic difficulties, caused by the diversion of trade routes away from the eastern Mediterranean and the price inflation brought about by the influx of cheap American silver.

Another sign of change within the empire was the increasing degree of material affluence and the impact of Western ideas and customs. Sophisticated officials and merchants began to mimic the habits and lifestyles of their European counterparts, dressing in the European fashion, purchasing Western furniture and art objects, and ignoring Muslim strictures against the consumption of alcohol and sexual activities outside marriage. During the sixteenth and early seventeenth centuries, coffee and tobacco were introduced into polite Ottoman society, and cafés for the consumption of both began to appear in the major cities (see the box on p. 459). One sultan in the early seventeenth century issued a decree prohibiting the consumption of both coffee and tobacco, arguing (correctly, no doubt) that many cafés were nests of antigovernment intrigue. He even began to wander incognito through the streets of Istanbul at night. Any of his subjects detected in immoral or illegal acts were summarily executed and their bodies left on the streets as an example to others.

There were also signs of a decline in competence within the ruling family. Whereas the first sultans reigned twenty-seven years on average, later ones averaged only thirteen years. The throne now went to the oldest surviving male, while his rivals were kept secluded in a latticed cage and thus had no governmental experience if they succeeded to rule. Later sultans also became less involved in government, and more power flowed to the office of the grand vizier, called the **Sublime Porte** (PORT), or to eunuchs and members of the harem. Palace intrigue increased as a result.

Ottoman Art

The Ottoman sultans were enthusiastic patrons of the arts and maintained large ateliers of artisans and artists, primarily at the Topkapi Palace in Istanbul but also in other important cities of the vast empire. The period from Mehmet II in the fifteenth century to the early eighteenth century witnessed a flourishing of pottery, rugs, silk and other textiles, jewelry, arms and armor, and calligraphy. All adorned the palaces of the new rulers, testifying to their opulence and exquisite taste. The artists came from all parts of the realm and beyond. Besides Turks, there were Persians, Greeks, Armenians, Hungarians, and Italians, all vying for the esteem and generous rewards of the sultans and fearing that losing favor might mean losing their heads! In the second half of the sixteenth century, Istanbul alone listed more than 150 craft guilds, ample proof of the artistic activity of the era.

ARCHITECTURE By far the greatest contribution of the Ottoman Empire to world art was its architecture, especially the magnificent mosques of the second half of the sixteenth century. Traditionally, prayer halls in mosques were subdivided by numerous pillars that supported small individual domes, creating a private, forestlike atmosphere. The Turks, however, modeled their new mosques on the open floor plan of the Byzantine church of Hagia Sophia (completed in 537), which had been turned into a mosque by Mehmet II, and

A Turkish Discourse on Coffee

INTERACTION & EXCHANGE

Coffee was introduced to Turkey from the Arabian peninsula in the mid-sixteenth century and reportedly came to Europe during the Turkish siege of Vienna in 1527. The following account was written by Katib Chelebi (kah-TEEB CHEL-uh-bee), a seventeenth-century Turkish author who compiled an extensive encyclopedia and bibliography. In *The Balance of Truth*, he described how coffee entered the empire and the problems it caused for public morality. In the Muslim world, as in Europe and later in colonial America, rebellious elements often met in coffeehouses to promote antigovernment activities. Chelebi died in Istanbul in 1657, reportedly while drinking a cup of coffee.

Katib Chelebi, *The Balance of Truth*

[Coffee] originated in Yemen and has spread, like tobacco, over the world. Certain sheikhs, who lived with their dervishes [ascetic followers] in the mountains of Yemen, used to crush and eat the berries . . . of a certain tree. Some would roast them and drink their water. Coffee is a cold dry food, suited to the ascetic life and sedative of lust. . . .

It came to Asia Minor by sea, about 1543, and met with a hostile reception, *fetwas* [decrees] being delivered against it. For they said, Apart from its being roasted, the fact that it is drunk in gatherings, passed from hand to hand, is suggestive of loose living. It is related of Abul-Suud Efendi that he had holes bored in the ships that brought it, plunging their cargoes of coffee into the sea. But these strictures and prohibitions availed nothing. . . . One coffeehouse was opened after another, and men would gather together, with great eagerness and enthusiasm, to drink. Drug addicts in particular, finding it a life-giving thing, which increased their pleasure, were willing to die for a cup.

Storytellers and musicians diverted the people from their employments, and working for one's living fell into disfavor. Moreover the people, from prince to beggar, amused themselves with knifing one another. Toward the end of 1633, the late Ghazi Gultan Murad, becoming aware of the situation, promulgated an edict, out of regard and compassion for the people, to this effect: Coffeehouses throughout the Guarded Domains shall be dismantled and not opened hereafter. Since then, the coffeehouses of the capital have been as desolate as the heart of the ignorant. . . . But in cities and towns outside Istanbul, they are opened just as before. As has been said above, such things do not admit of a perpetual ban.

Why did coffee come to be regarded as a dangerous substance in the Ottoman Empire? Were the authorities successful in suppressing its consumption?

---

began to push the pillars toward the outer wall to create a prayer hall with an uninterrupted central area under one large dome. With this plan, large numbers of believers could worship in unison in accordance with Muslim preference. By the mid-sixteenth century, the greatest of all Ottoman architects, Sinan (si-NAHN), began erecting the first of his eighty-one mosques with an uncluttered prayer area. Each was topped by an imposing dome, and often, as at Edirne, the entire building was framed with four towering narrow minarets. By emphasizing its vertical lines, the minarets camouflaged the massive stone bulk of the structure and gave it a feeling of incredible lightness. These four graceful minarets would find new expression sixty years later in India's white marble Taj Mahal (see "Mughal Culture" later in this chapter).

The lightness of the exterior was reinforced in the mosque's interior by the soaring height of the dome and the numerous windows. Added to this were delicate plasterwork and tile decoration that transformed the mosque into a monumental oasis of spirituality, opulence, and power. Sinan's masterpieces, such as the Suleymaniye (soo-lay-MAHN-ee-eh) and the Blue Mosque of Istanbul, were always part of a large socioreligious compound that included a library, school, hospital, mausoleums, and even bazaars, all of equally magnificent construction.

Earlier, the thirteenth-century Seljuk Turks of Anatolia had created beautiful tile decorations with two-color mosaics. Now Ottoman artists invented a new glazed tile art with painted flowers and geometrical designs in brilliant blue, green, yellow, and their own secret "tomato red." Entire walls, both interior and exterior, were covered with the painted tiles, which adorned palaces as well as mosques. Produced at Iznik (the old Nicaea), the distinctive tiles and pottery were in great demand; the city's ateliers boasted more than three hundred artisans in the late sixteenth century.

TEXTILES The sixteenth century also witnessed the flourishing of textiles and rugs. The Byzantine emperor Justinian had introduced the cultivation of silkworms to the West in the

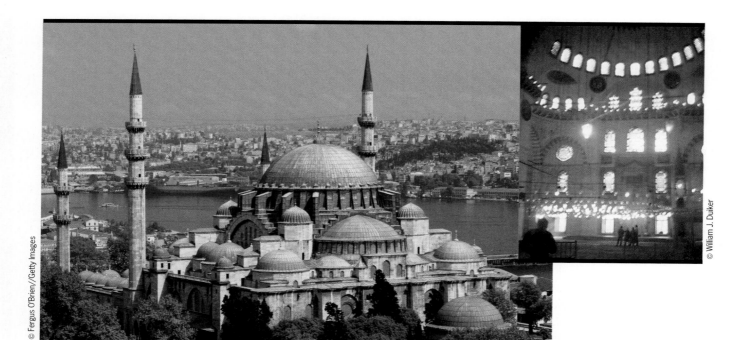

© Fergus O'Brien//Getty Images

© William J. Duiker

The Suleymaniye Mosque, Istanbul. The magnificent mosques built under the patronage of Suleyman the Magnificent are a great legacy of the Ottoman Empire and a fitting supplement to Hagia Sophia, the cathedral built by the Byzantine emperor Justinian in the sixth century C.E. Towering under a central dome, these mosques seem to defy gravity and, like European Gothic cathedrals, convey a sense of weightlessness. The Suleymaniye Mosque is one of the most impressive and most graceful in Istanbul. A far cry from the seventh-century desert mosques constructed of palm trunks, the Ottoman mosques stand among the architectural wonders of the world. Under the massive dome, the interior of the Suleymaniye Mosque offers a quiet refuge for prayer and reflection, bathed in muted sunlight and the warmth of plush carpets, as shown in the inset photo.

sixth century, and the silk industry resurfaced under the Ottomans. Its capital was at Bursa, where factories produced silks for wall hangings, soft covers, and especially court costumes. Perhaps even more famous than Turkish silk are the rugs.

But whereas silks were produced under the patronage of the sultans, rugs were a peasant industry. Each village boasted its own distinctive design and color scheme for the rugs it produced.

© William J. Duiker

Clothes Make the Man. Having traveled westward from China over the Silk Road, the production of silk got under way in the Ottoman Empire, from which it spread to Europe and Imperial Russia. In the sixteenth and seventeenth centuries, stunning silk caftans such as those shown here radiated Ottoman splendor and power. Their voluminous size, vibrant colors, intricate designs, and sumptuous fabrics aggrandized the wearer—usually a courtier—in both physical and political stature. Magnificent bolts of silk were offered by sultans as diplomatic gifts to solidify political alliances, as well as to reward high officials for their loyalty to the dynasty. To show respect and allegiance during court rituals, officials had to kiss the hem of the sultan's caftan.

The Safavids

 FOCUS QUESTIONS: What problems did the Safavid Empire face, and how did its rulers attempt to solve them? How did their approaches compare with those in the other Muslim empires?

After the collapse of the empire of Tamerlane in the early fifteenth century, the area extending from Persia into Central Asia lapsed into anarchy. The Uzbeks (ooz-BEKS), Turkic-speaking peoples from Central Asia, were the chief political and military force in the area. From their capital at Bokhara (boh-KAHR-uh *or* boo-KAH-ruh), they maintained a semblance of control over the fluid tribal alignments until the emergence of the Safavid dynasty in Persia at the beginning of the sixteenth century.

The Rise of the Safavids

The Safavid dynasty was founded by Shah Ismail (IS-mah-eel) (1487–1524), a descendant of Sheikh Safi al-Din (SAH-fee ul-DIN) (hence the name *Safavid*), who traced his origins to Ali, the fourth *imam* of the Muslim faith. In the early fourteenth century, Safi had been the leader of a community of Turkic-speaking people in Azerbaijan, near the Caspian Sea. Safi's community was one of many Sufi mystical religious groups throughout the area. In time, the doctrine spread among nomadic groups throughout the Middle East and was transformed into the more activist Shi'ite faith. Its adherents were known as "red heads" because of their distinctive red cap with twelve folds, meant to symbolize allegiance to the twelve *imams* of the Shi'ite faith.

In 1501, Ismail seized much of the lands of modern Iran and Iraq and proclaimed himself shah of a new Persian state. Baghdad was subdued in 1508, as were the Uzbeks in Bokhara shortly thereafter. Ismail now sent Shi'ite preachers into Anatolia to proselytize and promote rebellion among Turkish tribal peoples in the Ottoman Empire. In retaliation, the Ottoman sultan, Selim I, advanced against the Safavids in Persia and won a major battle near Tabriz (tah-BREEZ) in 1514. But Selim could not maintain control of the area, and Ismail regained Tabriz a few years later.

The Ottomans returned to the attack in the 1580s and forced the new Safavid shah, Abbas (uh-BAHS) I (1587–1629), to sign a punitive peace in which he acceded to the loss of much territory. The capital was subsequently moved from Tabriz in the northwest to Isfahan (is-fah-HAHN) in the south. Still, it was under Shah Abbas that the Safavids reached the zenith of their glory. He established a system similar to the Janissaries in Turkey to train administrators to replace the traditional warrior elite. He also used the period of peace to strengthen his army, now armed with modern weapons, and in the early seventeenth century, he attempted to regain the lost territories. Although he had some initial success, war resumed in the 1620s, and a lasting peace was not achieved until 1638 (see Map 16.2).

Collapse of the Dynasty

Abbas the Great had managed to strengthen the dynasty significantly, and for a time after his death in 1629, it remained stable and vigorous. But succession conflicts plagued the dynasty. Partly as a result, the power of the more militant Shi'ites began to increase at court and in Safavid society at large. The intellectual freedom that had characterized the empire at its height was curtailed under the pressure of religious orthodoxy, and Iranian women, who had enjoyed considerable freedom and influence during the early empire, were forced to withdraw into seclusion and behind the veil. Meanwhile, attempts to suppress the religious beliefs of minorities led to increased popular unrest. In the early eighteenth century, Afghan warriors took advantage of local revolts to seize the capital of Isfahan, forcing the remnants of the Safavid ruling family to retreat to Azerbaijan, their original homeland. As the Ottomans seized territories along the western border, the empire finally collapsed in 1723. Eventually, order was restored by the military adventurer Nadir Shah Afshar (NAH-der shah ahf-SHAR), who launched an extended series of campaigns that restored the country's borders and even occupied the Mughal capital of Delhi (see "The Shadows Lengthen" later in this chapter). After his death, the Zand dynasty ruled until the end of the eighteenth century.

Safavid Politics and Society

Like the Ottoman Empire, Persia under the Safavids was a mixed society. The Safavids had come to power with the support of nomadic Turkic-speaking tribal groups, and leading elements from those groups retained considerable influence within the empire. But the majority of the population were Iranian, descendants of migrating peoples who had arrived in the area in the first millennium B.C.E.; most of them were farmers or townspeople, with attitudes inherited from the relatively sophisticated and urbanized culture of pre-Safavid Iran. Faced with the problem of integrating unruly Turkic-speaking tribal peoples with the sedentary Persian-speaking population of the urban areas, the Safavids used the Shi'ite faith as a unifying force (see the box on p. 463). The shah himself acquired an almost divine quality and claimed to be the spiritual leader of all Islam. Shi'ism was declared the state religion.

Although there was a landed aristocracy, aristocratic power and influence were firmly controlled by strong-minded shahs, who confiscated aristocratic estates when possible and brought them under the control of the crown. Appointment to senior positions in the bureaucracy was by merit rather than birth. To avoid encouraging competition between Turkish and

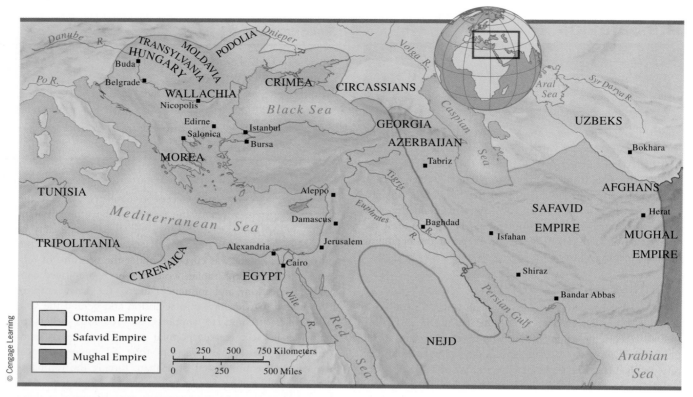

MAP 16.2 The Ottoman and Safavid Empires, c. 1683. During the seventeenth century, the Ottoman and Safavid Empires contested vigorously for hegemony in the eastern Mediterranean and the Middle East. This map shows the territories controlled by each state in the late seventeenth century.

Q *Which states shared control over the ancient lands in the Tigris and Euphrates valleys? In what modern-day countries are those territories?*

non-Turkish elements, Shah Abbas I hired a number of foreigners from neighboring countries for positions in his government.

The Safavid shahs took a direct interest in the economy and actively engaged in commercial and manufacturing activities, although there was also a large and affluent urban bourgeoisie. Like the Ottoman sultan, one shah regularly traveled the city streets incognito to check on the honesty of his subjects. When he discovered that a baker and a butcher were overcharging for their products, he had the baker cooked in his own oven and the butcher roasted on a spit. Although the road system was said to be quite poor, most goods traveled by caravan. The government provided accommodations for weary travelers and, at least in times of strong rulers, kept the roads relatively clear of thieves and bandits.

At its height, Safavid Iran was a worthy successor of the great Persian empires of the past, although it was probably not as wealthy as its neighbors to the east and west, the Mughals and the Ottomans. Hemmed in by the seapower of the Europeans to the south and by the land power of the Ottomans to the west, the Safavids had no navy and were forced to divert overland trade with Europe through southern Russia to avoid an Ottoman blockade. Still, the brocades, carpets, and leather goods of Persia were highly prized throughout the world. A school of philosophy that sought truth in a fusion of rationalist and intuitive methods flourished in the sixteenth and seventeenth

centuries, and Safavid science, medicine, and mathematics were the equal of other societies in the region.

Safavid Art and Literature

Persia witnessed an extraordinary flowering of the arts during the reign of Shah Abbas I. His new capital, Isfahan, was a grandiose planned city with wide visual perspectives and a sense of order almost unique in the region. Shah Abbas ordered his architects to position his palaces, mosques, and bazaars around a massive rectangular polo ground. Much of the original city is still in good condition and remains the gem of modern Iran. The immense mosques are richly decorated with elaborate blue tiles. The palaces are delicate structures with unusual slender wooden columns. These architectural wonders of Isfahan epitomize the grandeur, delicacy, and color that defined the Safavid golden age. To adorn the splendid buildings, Safavid artisans created imaginative metalwork, tile decorations, and original and delicate glass vessels. The ceramics of the period, imitating Chinese prototypes of celadon or blue-and-white Ming design, largely ignored traditional Persian designs.

The greatest area of productivity, however, was in textiles. Silk weaving based on new techniques became a national industry. The silks depicted birds, animals, and flowers in a brilliant mass of color with silver and gold threads. Above all,

The Religious Zeal of Shah Abbas the Great

RELIGION & PHILOSOPHY

Shah Abbas I, probably the greatest of the Safavid rulers, expanded the borders of his empire into areas of the southern Caucasus inhabited by Christians and other non-Muslim peoples. After Persian control was assured, he instructed that the local peoples be urged to convert to Islam for their own protection and the glory of God. In this passage, his biographer, the Persian historian Eskander Beg Monshi (es-KAHN-der bayg MAHN-shee), recounts the story of that effort.

Eskander Beg Monshi, "The Conversion of a Number of Christians to Islam"

This year the Shah decreed that those Armenians and other Christians who had been settled in [the southern Caucasus] and had been given agricultural land there should be invited to become Muslims. Life in this world is fraught with vicissitudes, and the Shah was concerned [that] in a period when the authority of the central government was weak, these Christians . . . might be subjected to attack by the neighboring Lor tribes (who are naturally given to causing injury and mischief), and their women and children carried off into captivity. In the areas in which these Christian groups resided, it was the Shah's purpose that the places of worship which they had built should become mosques, and the muezzin's call should be heard in them, so that these Christians might assume the guise of Muslims, and their future status accordingly be assured. . . .

Some of the Christians, guided by God's grace, embraced Islam voluntarily; others found it difficult to abandon their Christian faith and felt revulsion at the idea. They were encouraged by their monks and priests to remain steadfast in their faith. After a little pressure had been applied to the monks and priests, however, they desisted, and these Christians saw no alternative but to embrace Islam, though they did so with reluctance. The women and children embraced Islam with great enthusiasm, vying with one another in their eagerness to abandon their Christian faith and declare their belief in the unity of God. Some five thousand people embraced Islam. As each group made the Muslim declaration of faith, it received instruction in the Koran and the principles of the religious law of Islam, and all bibles and other Christian devotional material were collected and taken away from the priests.

In the same way, all the Armenian Christians who had been moved to [the area] were also forcibly converted to Islam. . . . Most people embraced Islam with sincerity, but some felt an aversion to making the Muslim profession of faith. True knowledge lies with God! May God reward the Shah for his action with long life and prosperity!

How do Shah Abbas's efforts to convert nonbelievers to Islam compare with similar programs by Muslim rulers in India, as described in Chapter 9? What did the author of this selection think about the conversions?

---

carpet weaving flourished, stimulated by the great demand for Persian carpets in the West. Still highly prized all over the world, these seventeenth-century carpets reflect the grandeur and artistry of the Safavid dynasty.

The long tradition of Persian painting continued into the Safavid era, but changed dramatically in two ways during the second half of the sixteenth century. First, taking advantage of the growing official toleration of portraiture, painters

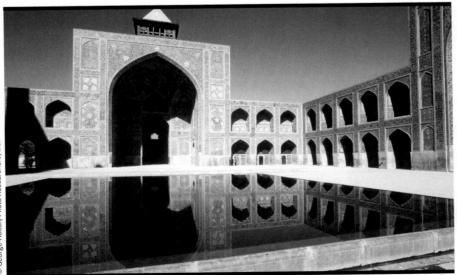

The Royal Academy of Isfahan. Along with institutions such as libraries and hospitals, theological schools were often included in the mosque compound. One of the most sumptuous was the Royal Academy of Isfahan, built by the shah of Persia in the early eighteenth century. This view shows the large courtyard surrounded by arcades of student rooms, reminiscent of the arrangement of monks' cells in European cloisters.

Hunters in a Landscape. Riza-i-Abbasi (ree-ZAH-yah-BAH-see) (1565–1635), the most renowned painter of the Safavid era, first won praise for his exquisite portraits of courtiers and lovers. Later, however, he switched to flowing line drawings of naturalistic subjects, such as this delicate rendering of three hunters in an enchanted setting. His style influenced later artists, who adapted it to other media, such as dazzling silk fabrics and the Persian carpets still much sought after in European markets. Especially popular were his colorful tile wall decorations depicting scenes of elegant peoples in flowing robes and turbans.

began to highlight the inner character of their subjects. Secondly, since royal patronage was not always forthcoming, artists sought to attract a larger audience by producing individual paintings that promoted their own distinctive styles and proudly bore their own signature.

The Grandeur of the Mughals

Q **FOCUS QUESTIONS:** What role did Islam play in the Mughal Empire, and how did the Mughals' approach to religion compare with that of the Ottomans and the Safavids? What might explain the similarities and differences?

In retrospect, the period from the sixteenth to eighteenth centuries can be viewed both as a high point of traditional culture in India and as the first stage of perhaps its biggest challenge. The era began with the creation of one of the subcontinent's greatest empires, that of the Mughals (MOO-guls). Mughal rulers, although foreigners and Muslims like many of their immediate predecessors, nevertheless brought India to a peak of political power and cultural achievement. For the first time since the Mauryan dynasty, the entire subcontinent was united under a single government, with a common culture that inspired admiration and envy throughout the region.

Babur: Founder of the Mughal Dynasty

When the Portuguese fleet led by Vasco da Gama arrived at the port of Calicut in the spring of 1498 (see Chapter 14), the Indian subcontinent was still divided into a number of Hindu and Muslim kingdoms. But it was on the verge of a new era of unity that would be brought about by a foreign dynasty called the Mughals. Like so many other rulers of northern India, the founders of the Mughal Empire were not natives of India but came from the mountainous region north of the Ganges River. The founder of the dynasty, known to history as Babur (BAH-burr) (1483–1530), had an illustrious pedigree. His father was descended from the great Asian conqueror Tamerlane, his mother from the Mongol conqueror Genghis Khan.

Babur had inherited a fragment of Tamerlane's empire in an upland valley of the Syr Darya (SEER DAHR-yuh) River (see Map 16.2). Driven south by the rising power of the Uzbeks and then the Safavid dynasty in Persia, Babur and his warriors seized Kabul in 1504 and, thirteen years later, crossed the Khyber Pass into India.

Following a pattern that we have seen before, Babur began his rise to power by offering to help an ailing dynasty against its opponents. Although his own forces were far less numerous than those of his adversaries, he possessed advanced weapons, including artillery, and used them to great effect. His use of mobile cavalry was particularly successful against his enemy's massed forces supplemented by mounted elephants. In 1526, with only 12,000 troops against an enemy force nearly ten times that size, Babur captured Delhi (DEL-ee) and established his power in the plains of northern India (see the box on p. 465). Over the next several years, he continued his conquests in northern India until his death in 1530 at the age of forty-seven.

Babur's success was due in part to his vigor and his charismatic personality, which earned him the undying loyalty of his followers. His son and successor, Humayun (hoo-MY-yoon) (1530–1556), was, in the words of one British historian, "intelligent but lazy." Whether or not this is a fair characterization, Humayun clearly lacked the will to consolidate his father's conquests and the personality to inspire loyalty among his subjects. In 1540, he was forced to flee to Persia, where he lived in exile for sixteen years. Finally, with the aid of the Safavid shah of Persia, he returned to India and reconquered Delhi in 1555 but died the following year in a household accident, reportedly from injuries suffered in a fall after smoking a pipeful of opium.

The Mughal Conquest of Northern India

POLITICS & GOVERNMENT

Babur, the founder of the great Mughal dynasty, began his career by allying with one Indian prince against another and then turned on his ally to put himself in power, a tactic that had been used by the Ottomans and the Mongols before him (see Chapter 10). In this excerpt from his memoirs, Babur describes his triumph over the powerful army of his Indian enemy, the Sultan Ibrâhim.

Babur, *Memoirs*

They made one or two very poor charges on our right and left divisions. My troops making use of their bows, plied them with arrows, and drove them in upon their center. The troops on the right and the left of their center, being huddled together in one place, such confusion ensued, that the enemy, while totally unable to advance, found also no road by which they could flee. The sun had mounted spear-high when the onset of battle began, and the combat lasted till midday, when the enemy were completely broken and routed, and my friends victorious and exulting. By the grace and mercy of Almighty God, this arduous undertaking was rendered easy for me, and this mighty army, in the space of half a day, laid in the dust. Five or six thousand men were discovered lying slain, in one spot, near Ibrâhim. We reckoned that the number lying slain, in different parts of this field of battle, amounted to fifteen or sixteen thousand men. On reaching Agra, we found, from the accounts of the natives of Hindustân, that forty or fifty thousand men had fallen in this field. After routing the enemy, we continued the pursuit, slaughtering, and making them prisoners. . . .

It was now afternoon prayers when Tahir Taberi, the younger brother of Khalîfeh, having found Ibrâhim lying dead amidst a number of slain, cut off his head, and brought it in. . . .

In consideration of my confidence in Divine aid, the Most High God did not suffer the distress and hardships that I had undergone to be thrown away, but defeated my formidable enemy, and made me the conqueror of the noble country of Hindustân. This success I do not ascribe to my own strength, nor did this good fortune flow from my own efforts, but from the fountain of the favor and mercy of God.

What did the Mughals' military tactics have in common with those used by the Ottomans and the Mongols as they expanded their empires? Why were these tactics successful?

Humayun was succeeded by his son Akbar (AK-bar) (1556–1605). Born while his father was living in exile, Akbar was only fourteen when he mounted the throne. Illiterate but highly intelligent and industrious, Akbar set out to extend his domain, then limited to the Punjab (puhn-JAHB) and the upper Ganges River valley. "A monarch," he remarked, "should be ever intent on conquest, otherwise his neighbors rise in arms against him. The army should be exercised in warfare, lest from want of training they become self-indulgent."[2] By the end of his life, he had brought Mughal rule to most of the subcontinent, from the Himalaya Mountains to the Godavari (goh-DAH-vuh-ree) River in central India and from Kashmir to the mouths of the Brahmaputra (brah-muh-POO-truh) and the Ganges. In so doing, Akbar had created the greatest Indian empire since the Mauryan dynasty nearly two thousand years earlier (see Map 16.3).

Akbar and Indo-Muslim Civilization

Although Akbar was probably the greatest of the conquering Mughal monarchs, like his famous predecessor Ashoka, he is best known for the humane character of his rule. Above all, he accepted the diversity of Indian society and took steps to reconcile his Muslim and Hindu subjects.

RELIGION AND THE STATE   Though raised an orthodox Muslim, Akbar had been exposed to other beliefs during his childhood and had little patience with the pedantic views of Muslim scholars at court. As emperor, he displayed a keen interest in other religions, not only tolerating Hindu practices in his own domains but also welcoming the expression of Christian views by his Jesuit advisers. Akbar put his policy of religious tolerance into practice by taking a Hindu princess as one of his wives, and the success of this marriage may well have had an effect on his religious convictions. He patronized classical Indian arts and architecture and abolished many of the restrictions faced by Hindus in a Muslim-dominated society.

During his later years, Akbar became steadily more hostile to Islam. To the dismay of many Muslims at court, he sponsored a new form of worship called the Divine Faith (*Din-i-Ilahi*), which combined characteristics of several religions with a central belief in the infallibility of all decisions reached by the emperor (see the box on p. 467). Some historians have maintained that Akbar totally abandoned Islam and adopted a Persian model of imperial divinity. But others have pointed out that the emperor was claiming only divine guidance, not divine status, and suggest that the new ideology was designed to cement the loyalty of officials to the person of the monarch. Whatever the case, the new faith aroused deep hostility in Muslim circles and vanished rapidly after his death.

MAP 16.3 The Mughal Empire. This map shows the expansion of the Mughal Empire from the death of Akbar in 1605 to the reign of Aurangzeb at the end of the seventeenth century.

Q *In which cities on the map were European settlements located? When did each group of Europeans arrive, and how did the settlements spread?*

ADMINISTRATIVE REFORMS Akbar also extended his innovations to the imperial administration. The empire was divided into provinces, and the administration of each province was modeled after the central government, with separate departments for military, financial, commercial, and legal affairs. Senior officials in each department reported directly to their counterparts in the capital city.

Although the upper ranks of the government continued to be dominated by nonnative Muslims, a substantial proportion of lower-ranking officials were Hindus, and a few Hindus were appointed to positions of importance. At first, most officials were paid salaries, but later they were ordinarily assigned sections of agricultural land for their temporary use; they kept a portion of the taxes paid by the local peasants in lieu of a salary. These local officials, known as *zamindars* (zuh-meen-DAHRZ), were expected to forward the rest of the taxes from the lands under their control to the central government, which also derived much of its revenue from the exploitation of substantial crown lands. *Zamindars* often recruited a number of military and civilian retainers and accumulated considerable power in their localities.

The same tolerance that marked Akbar's attitude toward religion and administration extended to the Mughal legal system. While Muslims were subject to the Islamic codes (the *Shari'a*), Hindu law (the *Dharmashastra*) applied to areas settled by Hindus, who after 1579 were no longer required to pay the unpopular *jizya* (JIZ-yuh), or poll tax on non-Muslims. Punishments for crime were relatively mild, at least by the standards of the day, and justice was administered in a relatively impartial and efficient manner.

A HARMONIOUS SOCIETY A key element in Akbar's vision of the ideal social order was the concept of harmony, meaning that each individual and group within the empire would play their assigned role and contribute to the welfare of society as a whole. This concept of social harmony was based in part on his vision of a world shaped by the laws of Islam as transmitted by Muhammad (*Shari'a*), but it also corresponded to the deep-seated indigenous belief in the importance of class hierarchy, as expressed in the Indian class and caste system (see the box on p. 468). In its overall conception, it bears a clear resemblance to the social structure adopted by the Mughals'contemporaries to the west, the Ottoman Empire.

Overall, Akbar's reign was a time of peace and prosperity. Although all Indian peasants were required to pay about one-third of their annual harvest to the state through the *zamindars*, in general the system was applied fairly, and when drought struck in the 1590s, the taxes were reduced or even suspended altogether. Thanks to a long period of relative peace and political stability, commerce and manufacturing flourished. Foreign trade, in particular, thrived as Indian goods, notably textiles, tropical food products, spices, and precious stones, were exported in exchange for gold and silver. Tariffs on imports were low. Much of the foreign commerce was handled by Arab traders, since the Indians, like their Mughal rulers, did not care for travel by sea. Internal trade, however, was dominated by large merchant castes, which also were active in banking and handicrafts.

Akbar's Successors

Akbar died in 1605 and was succeeded by his son Jahangir (juh-HAHN-geer) (1605–1628). During the early years of his reign, Jahangir continued to strengthen central control over the vast empire. Eventually, however, his grip began to

A Religion Fit for a King

RELIGION & PHILOSOPHY

Emperor Akbar's attempt to create a new form of religion, known as the Divine Faith, was partly a product of his inquisitive mind. But it was also influenced by Akbar's long friendship with Abu'l Fazl Allami (uh-BUL FAYZ-ul ahl-LAHM-mee), a courtier who introduced the young emperor to the Shi'ite tradition that each generation produces an individual (*imam*) who possesses a "divine light" capable of interpreting the holy scriptures. One of the sources of this Muslim concept was the Greek philosopher Plato's idea of a "philosopher king," who in his wisdom could provide humanity with an infallible guide in affairs of religion, morality, and statecraft. Akbar, of course, found the idea appealing, as it provided support for his efforts to reform religious practices in the empire. Abu'l Fazl, however, made many enemies with his advice and was assassinated at the order of Akbar's son, Jahangir, in 1602. In the following selection, Abu'l Fazl discusses the qualities of an individual who possesses the divine light.

Abu'l Fazl, *Institutes of Akbar*

Royalty is a light emanating from God, and a ray from the sun, the illuminator of the universe, the argument of the book of perfection, the receptacle of all virtues. Modern language calls this light the divine light, and the tongue of antiquity called it the sublime halo. It is communicated by God to kings without the intermediate assistance of anyone, and men, in the presence of it, bend the forehead of praise toward the ground of submission.

Again, many excellent qualities flow from the possession of this light:

1. *A paternal love toward the subjects.* Thousands find rest in the love of the king, and sectarian differences do not raise the dust of strife. In his wisdom, the king will understand the spirit of the age, and shape his plans accordingly.
2. *A large heart.* The sight of anything disagreeable does not unsettle him, nor is want of discrimination for him a source of disappointment. His courage steps in. His divine firmness gives him the power of requittal, nor does the high position of an offender interfere with it. The wishes of great and small are attended to, and their claims meet with no delay at his hands.
3. *A daily increasing trust in God.* When he performs an action, he considers God as the real doer of it [and himself as the medium] so that a conflict of motives can produce no disturbance.
4. *Prayer and devotion.* The success of his plans will not lead him to neglect, nor will adversity cause him to forget God and madly trust in man. He puts the reins of desire into the hands of reason; in the wide field of his desires he does not permit himself to be trodden down by restlessness; neither will he waste his precious time in seeking after that which is improper. He makes wrath, the tyrant, pay homage to wisdom, so that blind rage may not get the upper hand, and inconsiderateness overstep the proper limits. . . . He is forever searching after those who speak the truth and is not displeased with words that seem bitter but are, in reality, sweet. He considers the nature of the words and the rank of the speaker. He is not content with not committing violence, but he must see that no injustice is done within his realm.

 According to Abu'l Fazl, what role should the Mughal emperor play in promoting public morality? What tactics should he use to ensure that his efforts will be successful?

---

weaken (according to his memoirs, he "only wanted a bottle of wine and a piece of meat to make merry"), and the court fell under the influence of one of his wives, the Persian-born Nur Jahan (NOOR juh-HAHN) (see the box on p. 469). The empress took advantage of her position to enrich her own family and arranged for her niece Mumtaz Mahal (MOOM-tahz muh-HAHL) to marry her husband's third son and ultimate successor, Shah Jahan (1628–1657). When Shah Jahan succeeded to the throne, he quickly demonstrated the single-minded quality of his grandfather (albeit in a much more brutal manner), ordering the assassination of all of his rivals in order to secure his position.

THE REIGN OF SHAH JAHAN During a reign of three decades, Shah Jahan maintained the system established by his predecessors while expanding the boundaries of the empire by successful campaigns in the Deccan Plateau and against Samarkand, north of the Hindu Kush. But Shah Jahan's rule was marred by his failure to deal with the growing domestic problems. He had inherited a nearly empty treasury because of Empress Nur Jahan's penchant for luxury and ambitious charity projects. Though the majority of his subjects lived in grinding poverty, Shah Jahan's frequent military campaigns and expensive building projects put a heavy strain on the imperial finances and compelled him to raise taxes. At the same

Designing the Perfect Society

POLITICS & GOVERNMENT

In the late fifteenth century, the Persian author Muhammad ibn Asad Jalal ud-din al-Dawwani (al-da-WAH-nee) (1427–1501) wrote an essay on the ideal society entitled *Jalali's Ethics*. The work later attracted favorable notice at the Mughal court in India and eventually was paraphrased by Emperor Akbar's famous adviser Abu'l Fazl. It thus provides insight into the political and social views of key officials in Mughal India during the reign of its most famous ruler.

Jalali's Ethics

In order to preserve this political equipoise, there is a correspondence to be maintained between the various classes. Like as the equipoise of bodily temperament is affected by intermixture and correspondence of four elements, the equipoise of the political temperament is to be sought for in the correspondence of four classes.

1. *Men of the pen*, such as lawyers, divines, judges, bookmen, statisticians, geometricians, astronomers, physicians, poets. In these and their exertions in the use of their delightful pens, the subsistence of the faith and of the world itself is vested and bound up. They occupy the place in politics that water does among the elements. Indeed, to persons of ready understanding, the similarity of knowledge and water is as clear as water itself, and as evident as the sun that makes it so.

2. *Men of the sword*, such as soldiers, fighting zealots, guards of forts and passes, etc.; without whose exercise of the impetuous and vindictive sword, no arrangement of the age's interests could be effected; without the havoc of whose tempest-like energies, the materials of corruption, in the shape of rebellious and disaffected persons, could never be dissolved and dissipated. These then occupy the place of fire, their resemblance to it is too plain to require demonstration; no rational person need call in the aid of fire to discover it.

3. *Men of business*, such as merchants, capitalists, artisans, and craftsmen by whom the means of emolument and all other interests are adjusted; and through whom the remotest extremes enjoy the advantage and safeguard of each other's most peculiar commodities. The resemblance of these to air—the auxiliary of growth and increase in vegetables—the reviver of spirit in animal life—the medium of the undulation and movement of which all sorts of rare and precious things traverse the hearing to arrive at the headquarters of human nature—is exceedingly manifest.

4. *Husbandmen*, such as seedsmen, bailiffs, and agriculturists—the superintendents of vegetation and preparers of provender; without whose exertions the continuance of the human kind must be cut short. These are, in fact, the only producers of what had no previous existence; the other classes adding nothing whatever to subsisting products, but only transferring what subsists already from person to person, from place to place, and from form to form. How close these come to the soil and surface of the earth—the point to which all the heavenly circles refer—the scope to which all the luminaries of the purer world direct their rays—the stage on which wonders are displayed—the limit to which mysteries are confined—must be universally apparent.

In like manner then as in the composite organizations the passing of any element beyond its proper measure occasions the loss of equipoise, and is followed by dissolution and ruin, in political coalition, no less, the prevalence of any one class over the other three overturns the adjustment and dissolves the junction. Next attention is to be directed to the condition of the individuals composing them, and the place of every one determined according to his right.

 How does the social class system described here compare with the traditional division of classes in premodern India?

---

time, the government did little to improve rural conditions. In a country where transport was primitive (it often took three months to travel the 600 miles between Patna, in the middle of the Ganges River valley, and Delhi) and drought conditions frequent, the dynasty made few efforts to increase agricultural efficiency or to improve the roads or the irrigation network, although a grand trunk road was eventually constructed between the capital Agra (AH-gruh) and Lahore (luh-HOHR), a growing city several hundred miles to the northwest. A Dutch merchant in Gujarat (goo-juh-RAHT) described conditions during a famine in the mid-seventeenth century:

As the famine increased, men abandoned towns and villages and wandered helplessly. It was easy to recognize their condition: eyes sunk deep in head, lips pale and covered with slime, the skin hard, with the bones showing through, the belly nothing but a pouch hanging down empty, knuckles and kneecaps showing

The Power Behind the Throne

During his reign as Mughal emperor, Jahangir (1605–1628) was addicted to alcohol and opium. Because of his weakened condition, his Persian wife, Nur Jahan, began to rule on his behalf. She also groomed his young son Khurram to rule as the future emperor Shah Jahan and arranged for him to marry her own niece, Mumtaz Mahal, thereby cementing her influence over two successive Mughal rulers. During this period, Nur Jahan was the de facto ruler of India, exerting her influence in both internal and foreign affairs during an era of peace and prosperity. Although the extent of her influence was often criticized at court, her performance impressed many European observers, as these remarks by an English visitor attest.

Nur Jahan, Empress of Mughal India

If anyone with a request to make at Court obtains an audience or is allowed to speak, the King hears him indeed, but will give no definite answer of Yes or No, referring him promptly to Asaf Khan, who in the same way will dispose of no important matter without communicating with his sister, the Queen, and who regulates his attitude in such a way that the authority of neither of them may be diminished. Anyone then who obtains a favour must thank them for it, and not the King. . . .

Her abilities were uncommon; for she rendered herself absolute, in a government in which women are thought incapable of bearing any part. Their power, it is true, is sometimes exerted in the harem; but, like the virtues of the magnet, it is silent and unperceived. Nur Jahan stood forth in public; she broke through all restraint and custom, and acquired power by her own address, more than by the weakness of Jahangir. . . .

Her former and present supporters have been well rewarded, so that now most of the men who are near the King owe their promotion to her, and are consequently under . . . obligations to her. . . . Many misunderstandings result, for the King's orders or grants of appointments, etc., are not certainties, being of no value until they have been approved by the Queen.

 Based on this description, how does the position that Nur Jahan occupied in Mughul government compare with the roles played by other female political figures in China, Africa, and Europe? What do all of these women have in common?

---

prominently. One would cry and howl for hunger, while another lay stretched on the ground dying in misery; wherever you went, you saw nothing but corpses.[3]

In 1648, Shah Jahan moved his capital from Agra to Delhi and built the famous Red Fort in his new capital city. But he is best known for the Taj Mahal (tahj muh-HAHL) in Agra, widely considered to be the most beautiful building in India, if not in the entire world (see the comparative illustration on p. 476). The story is a romantic one—that the Taj was built by the emperor in memory of his wife Mumtaz Mahal, who had died giving birth to her thirteenth child at the age of thirty-nine. But the reality has a less attractive side: the expense of the building, which employed 20,000 masons over twenty years, forced the government to raise agricultural taxes, further impoverishing many Indian peasants.

THE RULE OF AURANGZEB Succession struggles returned to haunt the dynasty in the mid-1650s when Shah Jahan's illness led to a struggle for power between his sons Dara Shikoh (DA-ruh SHIH-koh) and Aurangzeb (ow-rang-ZEB). Dara Shikoh was described by his contemporaries as progressive and humane, although possessed of a violent temper and a strong sense of mysticism. But he apparently lacked political acumen and was outmaneuvered by Aurangzeb (1658–1707), who had Dara Shikoh put to death and then imprisoned his father in the fort at Agra.

Aurangzeb is one of the most controversial individuals in the history of India. A man of high principle, he attempted to eliminate many of what he considered India's social evils, prohibiting the immolation of widows on their husband's funeral pyre (*sati*), the castration of eunuchs, and the exaction of illegal taxes. With less success, he tried to forbid gambling, drinking, and prostitution. But Aurangzeb, a devout and somewhat doctrinaire Muslim, also adopted a number of measures that reversed the policies of religious tolerance established by his predecessors. The building of new Hindu temples was prohibited, and the Hindu poll tax was restored. Forced conversions to Islam were resumed, and non-Muslims were driven from the court. Aurangzeb's heavy-handed religious policies led to considerable domestic unrest and to a revival of Hindu fervor during the last years of his reign. A number of revolts also broke out against imperial authority.

THE SHADOWS LENGTHEN During the eighteenth century, Mughal power was threatened from both within and without. Fueled by the growing power and autonomy of the local gentry and merchants, rebellious groups in provinces throughout the empire, from the Deccan to the Punjab, began to reassert local authority and reduce the power of the Mughal emperor to that of a "tinsel sovereign." Increasingly divided, India was vulnerable to attack from abroad. In 1739, Delhi was sacked by the Persians, who left it in ashes and carried off its splendid Peacock Throne.

A number of obvious reasons for the virtual collapse of the Mughal Empire can be identified, including the draining of the imperial treasury and the decline in competence of the Mughal rulers. By 1700, the Europeans, who at first were no more than an irritant, had begun to seize control of regional trade routes and to meddle in the internal politics of the subcontinent (see "The Impact of European Power in India" later in the chapter).

It should be noted, however, that even at its height under Akbar, the empire was less a centralized state than a loosely knit collection of heterogeneous principalities held together by the authority of the throne, which tried to combine Persian concepts of kingship with the Indian tradition of decentralized power. Decline set in when centrifugal forces gradually began to predominate over centripetal ones.

Ironically, one element in this process was the very success of the system, which led to the rapid expansion of wealth and autonomous power at the local level. As local elites increased their wealth and influence, they became less willing to accept the authority and financial demands from Delhi. The reassertion of Muslim orthodoxy under Aurangzeb and his successors simply exacerbated the problem. This process was hastened by the growing European military and economic presence along the periphery of the empire.

The Impact of European Power in India

As we have seen, the first Europeans to arrive were the Portuguese. Although they established a virtual monopoly over regional trade in the Indian Ocean, they did not seek to penetrate the interior of the subcontinent but focused on establishing way stations en route to China and the Spice Islands. The situation changed at the end of the sixteenth century when the English and the Dutch entered the scene. Soon both powers were in active competition with Portugal and with each other for trading privileges in the region (see the box on p. 471).

Penetration of the new market was not easy for the Europeans because they initially had little to offer their hosts, who had been conducting a thriving trade with peoples throughout the Indian Ocean regional market for centuries. As a result, European merchants focused on taking part in the carrying trade between one Asian port and another. They paid for goods such as textiles and spices with gold and silver bullion, which was now being mined in increasing quantities in Latin America.

The experience of the English was a prime example. When the first English fleet arrived at Surat (SOOR-et), a thriving port on the northwestern coast of India, in 1608, the English request for trading privileges was rejected by Emperor Jahangir, at the suggestion of the Portuguese advisers already in residence at the imperial court. Needing lightweight Indian cloth to trade for spices in the East Indies, the English persisted, and in 1616, they were finally permitted to

Jahangir the Magnificent. In 1615, the English ambassador to the Mughal court presented an official portrait of King James I to Shah Jahangir, who returned the favor with a portrait of himself. Thus was established a long tradition of exchanging paintings between the two empires. As it turned out, the practice altered the style of Mughal portraiture, which had previously shown the emperor in action, hunting, participating at official functions, or engaging in battle. Henceforth, portraits of the ruler followed European practice by focusing on the opulence and spiritual power of the empire. In this painting, Jahangir has chosen spiritual over earthly power by offering a book to a sheikh while ignoring the Ottoman sultan, King James I, and the Hindu artist who painted the picture. Even the cherubs, a European artifice, are dazzled by the shah's divine character, which is further demonstrated by an enormous halo.

install their own ambassador at the imperial court in Agra. Three years later, the first English factory, or warehouse, was established at Surat.

During the next several decades, the English presence in India steadily increased as Mughal power waned. By midcentury, additional English factories had been established at Fort William (now the great city of Calcutta, recently renamed Kolkata) on the Hoogly River near the Bay of Bengal and, in 1639, at Madras (muh-DRAS *or* muh-DRAHS) (now Chennai) on the southeastern coast. From there, English ships carried Indian-made cotton goods to the East Indies, where they were bartered for spices, which were shipped back to England. Tensions between local authorities and the English over the payment of taxes led to a short war in 1686. The English were briefly expelled, but after differences were patched up, Aurangzeb permitted them to return.

The Capture of Port Hoogly

INTERACTION & EXCHANGE

In 1632, the Mughal ruler, Shah Jahan, ordered an attack on the city of Hoogly (HOOG-lee), a fortified Portuguese trading post on the northeastern coast of India. For the Portuguese, who had profited from half a century of triangular trade between India, China, and various countries in the Middle East and Southeast Asia, the loss of Hoogly at the hands of the Mughals hastened the decline of their influence in the region. Presented here are two contemporary versions of the battle. The first, from the *Padshahnama* (pad-shah-NAHM-uh) (*Book of Kings*), relates the course of events from the Mughal point of view. The second account is by John Cabral, a Jesuit missionary who was resident in Hoogly at the time.

The *Padshahnama*

During the reign of the Bengalis, a group of Frankish [European] merchants . . . settled in a place one *kos* from Satgaon . . . and, on the pretext that they needed a place for trading, they received permission from the Bengalis to construct a few edifices. Over time, due to the indifference of the governors of Bengal, many Franks gathered there and built dwellings of the utmost splendor and strength, fortified with cannons, guns, and other instruments of war. It was not long before it became a large settlement and was named Hoogly. . . . The Franks' ships trafficked at this port, and commerce was established, causing the market at the port of Satgaon to slump. . . . Of the peasants of those places, they converted some to Christianity by force and others through greed and sent them off to Europe in their ships. . . .

Since the improper actions of the Christians of Hoogly Port toward the Muslims was accurately reflected in the mirror of the mind of the Emperor before his accession to the throne, when the imperial banners cast their shadows over Bengal, and inasmuch as he was always inclined to propagate the true religion and eliminate infidelity, it was decided that when he gained control over this region he would eradicate the corruption of these abominators from the realm.

John Cabral, *Travels of Sebastian Manrique, 1629–1649*

Hugli continued at peace all the time of the great King Jahangir. For, as this Prince, by what he showed, was more attached to Christ than to Mohammad and was a Moor in name and dress only. . . . Sultan Khurram was in everything unlike his father, especially as regards the latter's leaning towards Christianity. . . . He declared himself the mortal enemy of the Christian name and the restorer of the law of Mohammad. . . . He sent a *firman* [order] to the Viceroy of Bengal, commanding him without reply or delay, to march upon the Bandel of Hugli and put it to fire and the sword. He added that, in doing so, he would render a signal service to God, to Mohammad, and to him. . . .

Consequently, on a Friday, September 24, 1632, . . . all the people [the Portuguese] embarked with the utmost secrecy. . . . Learning what was going on, and wishing to be able to boast that they had taken Hugli by storm, they [the imperialists] made a general attack on the Bandel by Saturday noon. They began by setting fire to a mine, but lost in it more men than we. Finally, however, they were masters of the Bandel.

 How do these two accounts of the Battle of Hoogly differ? Is there any way to reconcile the two into a single narrative?

English success in India attracted rivals, including the Dutch and the French. The Dutch abandoned their interests in India to concentrate on the spice trade in the middle of the seventeenth century, but the French were more persistent and briefly seized Madras in 1746. For a brief period, under the ambitious empire builder Joseph François Dupleix (zho-ZEF frahnh-SWAH doo-PLAY), the French competed successfully with the British. But the military genius of Sir Robert Clive (CLYV), an aggressive British administrator and empire builder who eventually became the chief representative of the East India Company in the subcontinent, and the refusal of the French government to provide financial support for Dupleix's efforts eventually left the French with only their fort at Pondicherry (pon-dir-CHEH-ree) and a handful of tiny enclaves on the southeastern coast.

In the meantime, Clive began to consolidate British control in Bengal (ben-GAHL), where the local ruler had attacked Fort William and imprisoned the local British population in the infamous Black Hole of Calcutta (an underground prison for holding the prisoners, many of whom died in captivity). In 1757, a small British force numbering about three thousand defeated a Mughal-led army over ten times that size in the Battle of Plassey (PLASS-ee). As part of the spoils of victory, the British East India Company exacted from the now-decrepit Mughal court the authority to collect taxes from extensive lands in the area surrounding Calcutta. Less than ten years later, British forces seized the reigning Mughal emperor in a skirmish at Buxar (buk-SAHR), and the British began to consolidate their economic and administrative control over Indian territory through the

A Pepper Plantation. During the Age of Exploration, pepper was one of the spices most sought by European adventurers. Unlike cloves and nutmeg, it was found in other areas in Asia besides the Indonesian archipelago. Shown here is a French pepper plantation in southern India. Eventually, the French were driven out of the Indian subcontinent by the British and retained only a few tiny enclaves along the coast.

MAP 16.4 India in 1805. By the early nineteenth century, much of the Indian subcontinent had fallen under British domination.

Q *Where was the capital of the Mughal Empire located?*

surrogate power of the now power-less Mughal court (see Map 16.4).

To officials of the East India Company, the expansion of their authority into the interior of the sub-continent probably seemed like a simple commercial decision, a move designed to seek guaranteed revenues to pay for the increasingly expensive military operations in India. To historians, it marks a major step in the gradual transfer of all of the Indian subcontinent to the British East India Company and later, in 1858, to the British crown. The process was more haphazard than deliberate. Under a new governor general, Warren Hastings, the British attempted to consolidate areas under their control and defeat such rivals as the rising Hindu Marathas (muh-RAH-tuhz), who exploited the decline of the Mughals to expand their own territories in Maharashtra (mah-huh-RAHSH-truh).

ECONOMIC DIFFICULTIES The company's takeover of vast landholdings, notably in the eastern Indian states of Orissa (uh-RIH-suh) and Bengal, may have been a windfall for enter-prising British officials, but it was a disaster for the Indian economy. In the first place, it resulted in the transfer of capital from the local Indian aristocracy to company officials, most of whom sent their profits back to Britain. Second, it hastened the destruction of once healthy local industries, because British goods such as machine-made textiles were imported duty-free into India to compete against local goods, many of which were produced on hand looms in Indian villages. Finally, British expansion hurt the peasants. As the British took over the administration of the land tax, they also applied British law, which allowed the lands of those unable to pay the tax to be confiscated. In the 1770s, a series of famines led to the death of an estimated one-third of the population in the areas under company administration. The British government attempted to resolve the problem by assigning tax lands to the local revenue collectors (*zamindars*) in the hope of transforming them into English-style rural gentry, but many collectors themselves fell into bankruptcy and sold their lands to absentee bankers while the now landless peasants remained in abject poverty. It was hardly an auspicious beginning to "civilized" British rule.

RESISTANCE TO THE BRITISH As a result of such conditions, Britain's rise to power in India did not go unchallenged. Although Mughal authority was by now virtually moribund, local forces took matters into their own hands. Astute Indian commanders avoided pitched battles with the well-armed British troops but harassed and ambushed them in the manner of guerrillas in our time. Said Haidar Ali (HY-dur AH-lee), one of Britain's primary rivals for control in southern India:

> You will in time understand my mode of warfare. Shall I risk my cavalry which cost a thousand rupees each horse, against your cannon ball which cost two pice? No! I will march your troops until their legs swell to the size of their bodies. You shall not have a blade of grass, nor a drop of water. I will hear of you every time your drum beats, but you shall not know where I am once a month. I will give your army battle, but it must be when I please, and not when you choose.[4]

Unfortunately for India, not all its commanders were as astute as Haidar Ali. In the last years of the eighteenth century, when the East India Company's authority came into the capable hands of Lord Cornwallis and his successor, Lord Mornington, the future marquess of Wellesley, the stage was set for the final consolidation of British rule over the subcontinent.

The Mughal Dynasty: A "Gunpowder Empire"?

To some recent historians, the success of the Mughals, like that of the Ottomans and the Safavids, was due to their mastery of the techniques of modern warfare, especially the use of firearms. In this view, firearms played a central role in the ability of all three empires to overcome their rivals and rise to regional hegemony. Accordingly, some scholars have labeled them "gunpowder empires." Although technical prowess in the art of warfare was undoubtedly a key element in their success, we should not forget that other factors, such as dynamic leadership, political acumen, and the possession

of an ardent following motivated by religious zeal, were at least equally important in their drive to power and ability to retain it.

In the case of the Mughals, the "gunpowder empire" thesis has been challenged by historian Douglas Streusand, who argues that the Mughals used "the carrot and the stick" to extend their authority, relying not just on heavy artillery but also on other forms of siege warfare and the offer of negotiations. Once in power, the Mughals created an empire that appeared highly centralized from the outside but was actually a collection of semiautonomous principalities ruled by provincial elites and linked together by the overarching majesty of the Mughal emperor—and not simply by the barrel of a gun. Even today, many Indians regard Akbar as the country's greatest ruler, a tribute not only to his military success but also to the humane policies adopted during his reign.

Society Under the Mughals: A Synthesis of Cultures

The Mughals were the last of the great traditional Indian dynasties. Like so many of their predecessors since the fall of the Guptas nearly a thousand years before, the Mughals were Muslims. But like the Ottoman Turks, the best Mughal rulers did not simply impose Islamic institutions and beliefs on the predominantly Hindu population; they combined Muslim with Hindu and even Persian concepts and cultural values in a unique social and cultural synthesis that even today seems to epitomize the greatness of Indian civilization. The new faith of Sikhism, founded in the early sixteenth century in an effort to blend both faiths (see Chapter 9), undoubtedly benefited from the mood of syncretism promoted by the Mughal court.

To be sure, Hindus sometimes attempted to defend themselves and their religious practices against the efforts of some Mughal monarchs to impose the Islamic religion and Islamic

CHRONOLOGY	The Mughal Era	
Arrival of Vasco da Gama at Calicut	1498	
Babur seizes Delhi	1526	
Death of Babur	1530	
Humayun recovers throne in Delhi	1555	
Death of Humayun and accession of Akbar	1556	
Death of Akbar and accession of Jahangir	1605	
Arrival of English at Surat	1608	
English embassy to Agra	1616	
Reign of Emperor Shah Jahan	1628–1657	
Foundation of English factory at Madras	1639	
Aurangzeb succeeds to the throne	1658	
Death of Aurangzeb	1707	
Sack of Delhi by the Persians	1739	
French capture Madras	1746	
Battle of Plassey	1757	

mores on the indigenous population. In some cases, despite official prohibitions, Hindu men forcibly married Muslim women and then converted them to the native faith, while converts to Islam normally lost all of their inheritance rights within the Indian family. Government orders to destroy Hindu temples were often ignored by local officials, sometimes as the result of bribery or intimidation. Although the founding emperor Babur expressed little admiration for the country he had subjected to his rule, ultimately Indian practices had an influence on the Mughal elites, as many Mughal chieftains married Indian women and adopted Indian forms of dress.

In some areas, Emperor Akbar's tireless effort to bring about a blend of Middle Eastern and South Asian religious and cultural values paid rich dividends, as substantial numbers of Indians decided to convert to the Muslim faith during the centuries of Mughal rule. Some were undoubtedly attracted to the egalitarian characteristics of Islam, but others found that the mystical and devotional qualities promoted by Sufi missionaries corresponded to similiar traditions among the local population. This was especially true in Bengal, on the eastern edge of the Indian subcontinent, where Hindu practices were not as well established and where forms of religious devotionalism had long been popular among the population.

THE ECONOMY Although much of the local population in the subcontinent lived in the grip of grinding poverty, punctuated by occasional periods of widespread famine, the first centuries of Mughal rule were in some respects a period of relative prosperity for the region. India was a leading participant in the growing foreign trade that crisscrossed the Indian Ocean from the Red Sea and the Persian Gulf to the Strait of Malacca and the Indonesian archipelago. High-quality cloth from India was especially prized, and the country's textile industry made it, in the words of one historian, "the industrial workshop of the world."

Long-term stability led to increasing commercialization and the spread of wealth to new groups within Indian society. The Mughal era saw the emergence of an affluent landed gentry and a prosperous merchant class. Members of prestigious castes from the pre-Mughal period reaped many of the benefits of the increasing wealth, but some of these changes transcended caste boundaries and led to the emergence of new groups who achieved status and wealth on the basis of economic achievement rather than traditional kinship ties. During the late eighteenth century, this economic prosperity was shaken by the decline of the Mughal Empire and the increasing European presence. But many prominent Indians reacted by establishing commercial relationships with the foreigners. For a time, such relationships often worked to the Indians' benefit. Later, as we shall see, they would have cause to regret the arrangement.

THE POSITION OF WOMEN Deciding whether Mughal rule had much effect on the lives of ordinary Indians is somewhat problematic. The treatment of women is a good example. Women had traditionally played an active role in Mongol tribal society—many actually fought on the battlefield alongside the men—and Babur and his successors often relied on the women in their families for political advice. Women from aristocratic families were often awarded honorific titles, received salaries, and were permitted to own land and engage in business. Women at court sometimes received an education, and Emperor Akbar reportedly established a girls' school at Fatehpur Sikri (fah-tay-POOR SIK-ree) to provide teachers for his own daughters. Aristocratic women often expressed their creative talents by writing poetry, painting, or playing music. Women of all castes were adept at spinning thread, either for their own use or to sell to weavers to augment the family income. Weaving was carried out in the home by all members of the families of the weaving subcaste. They sold simple cloth to local villages and fine cotton, silk, and wool to the Mughal court. By Akbar's reign, the textile manufacturing was of such high quality and so well established that India sold cloth to much of the world: Arabia, the coast of East Africa, Egypt, Southeast Asia, and Europe.

The Palace of the Winds at Jaipur. Built by the maharaja of Jaipur (JY-poor) in 1799, this imposing building, part of a palace complex, is today actually only a facade. Behind the intricate pink sandstone window screens, the women of the palace were able to observe city life while at the same time remaining invisible to prying eyes. The palace, like most of the buildings in the city of Jaipur, was constructed of sandstone, a product of the nearby desert of Rajasthan (RAH-juh-stahn).

To a certain degree, these Mughal attitudes toward women may have had an impact on Indian society. Women were allowed to inherit land, and some even possessed *zamindar* rights. Women from mercantile castes sometimes took an active role in business activities. At the same time, however, as Muslims, the Mughals subjected women to certain restrictions under Islamic law. On the whole, these Mughal practices coincided with and even accentuated existing tendencies in Indian society. The Muslim practice of isolating women and preventing them from associating with men outside the home (*purdah*) was adopted by many upper-class Hindus as a means of enhancing their status or protecting their women from unwelcome advances by Muslims in positions of authority. In other ways, Hindu practices were unaffected. The custom of *sati* continued to be practiced despite efforts by the Mughals to abolish it, and child marriage (most women were betrothed before the age of ten) remained common. Women were still instructed to obey their husbands without question and to remain chaste.

Mughal Culture

The era of the Mughals was one of synthesis in culture as well as in politics and religion. The Mughals combined Islamic themes with Persian and indigenous motifs to produce a unique style that enriched and embellished Indian art and culture. The Mughal emperors were zealous patrons of the arts and enticed painters, poets, and artisans from as far away as the Mediterranean. Apparently, the generosity of the Mughals made it difficult to refuse a trip to India. It was said that they would reward a poet with his weight in gold.

ARCHITECTURE Undoubtedly, the Mughals' most visible achievement was in architecture. Here they integrated Persian and Indian styles in a new and sometimes breathtakingly beautiful form best symbolized by the Taj Mahal, built by the emperor Shah Jahan in the mid-seventeenth century. Although the human and economic cost of the Taj tarnishes the romantic legend of its construction, there is no denying the beauty of the building. It had evolved from a style that originated several decades earlier with the tomb of Humayun, which was built by his widow in Agra in 1565 during the reign of Akbar.

Humayun's mausoleum had combined Persian and Islamic motifs in a square building finished in red sandstone and topped with a dome. The style was repeated in a number of other buildings erected throughout the empire, but the Taj brought the style to perfection. Working with a model created by his Persian architect, Shah Jahan raised the dome and replaced the red sandstone with brilliant white marble. The entire exterior and interior surface is decorated with cut-stone geometric patterns, delicate black stone tracery, or intricate inlay of colored precious stones in floral and Qur'anic arabesques (see the comparative illustration on p. 476). The technique of creating dazzling floral mosaics of lapis lazuli, malachite, carnelian, turquoise, and mother-of-pearl may have been introduced by Italian artists at the Mughal court. Shah Jahan had intended to erect a similar building in black marble across the river for his own remains, but the plans were abandoned after he was deposed by his son Aurangzeb. Shah Jahan spent his last years imprisoned in a room in the Red Fort at Agra; from his windows, he could see the beautiful memorial to his beloved wife.

The Taj was by no means the only magnificent building erected during the Mughal era. Akbar, who, in the words of a contemporary, "dresses the work of his mind and heart in the garment of stone and clay," was the first of the great Mughal builders. His first palace at Agra, the Red Fort, was begun in 1565. A few years later, he ordered the construction of a new palace at Fatehpur Sikri, 26 miles to the west. The new palace was built in honor of a Sufi mystic who had correctly forecast the birth of a son to the emperor. In gratitude, Akbar decided to build a new capital city and palace on the site of the mystic's home. Over a period of fifteen years, from 1571 to 1586, a magnificent new city in red sandstone was constructed. Although the city was abandoned before completion and now stands almost untouched, it is a popular destination for tourists and pilgrims.

PAINTING The other major artistic achievement of the Mughal period was painting. Painting had never been one of the great attainments of Indian culture due in part to a technological difficulty. Paper was not introduced to India from Persia until the latter part of the fourteenth century, so traditionally painting had been done on palm leaves, which had severely hampered artistic creativity. By the fifteenth century, Indian painting had made the transition from palm leaf to paper, and the new medium eventually stimulated a burst of creativity, particularly in the genre of miniatures, or book illustrations.

As in so many other areas of endeavor, painting in Mughal India resulted from the blending of two cultures. While living in exile, Emperor Humayun had learned to admire Persian miniatures. On his return to India in 1555, he invited two Persian masters to live in his palace and introduce the technique. His successor, Akbar, appreciated the new style and popularized it with his patronage. He established a state workshop at Fatehpur Sikri for two hundred artists, mostly Hindus, who worked under the guidance of the Persian masters to create the Mughal school of painting.

The "Akbar style" combined Persian with Indian motifs, such as the use of extended space and the portrayal of humans engaged in physical action, characteristics not usually seen in Persian art. Akbar also apparently encouraged the imitation of European art forms, including the portrayal of Christian subjects, the use of perspective, lifelike portraits, and the shading of colors in the Renaissance style. The depiction of the human figure in Mughal painting outraged orthodox Muslims at court, but Akbar argued that the painter, "in sketching anything that has life . . . must come to feel that he cannot bestow individuality upon his work, and is thus forced to think of God, the Giver of Life, and will thus increase in knowledge."[5]

ART & IDEAS

COMPARATIVE ILLUSTRATION

The Taj Mahal: Symbol of the Exotic East. The Taj Mahal, completed in 1653, was built by the Mughal emperor Shah Jahan as a tomb to glorify the memory of his beloved wife, Mumtaz Mahal. Raised on a marble platform above the Jumna River, the Taj is dramatically framed by contrasting twin red sandstone mosques, magnificent gardens, and a long reflecting pool that mirrors and magnifies its beauty. The effect is one of monumental size, near blinding brilliance, and delicate lightness, a startling contrast to the heavier and more masculine Baroque style then popular in Europe. The inset at the upper right shows an example of the exquisite inlay of precious stones that adorn the facade. The Taj Mahal inspired many imitations around the world, including the Royal Pavilion at Brighton, England (inset at lower right), constructed in 1815 to commemorate the British victory over Napoleon at Waterloo.

Q *How does Mughal architecture, as exemplified by the Taj Mahal, compare with the mosques erected by architects such as Sinan in the Ottoman Empire?*

Painting during Akbar's reign followed the trend toward realism and historical narrative that had originated in the Ottoman Empire. For example, Akbar had the illustrated *Book of Akbar* made to record his military exploits and court activities. Many of the paintings of Akbar's life portray him in action in the real world. After his death, his son and grandson continued the patronage of the arts.

LITERATURE The development of Indian literature was held back by the absence of printing, which was not introduced until the end of the Mughal era. Literary works were inscribed by calligraphers, and one historian has estimated that the library of Agra contained more than 24,000 volumes. Poetry, in particular, flourished under the Mughals, who established poets laureate at court. Poems were written in the Persian style and in the Persian language. In fact, Persian became the official language of the court until the sack of Delhi in 1739. At the time, the Indians' anger at their conquerors led them to adopt Urdu as the new language for

the court and for poetry. By that time, Indian verse on the Persian model had already lost its original vitality and simplicity and had become more artificial in the manner of court literature everywhere.

Another aspect of the long Mughal reign was a Hindu revival of devotional literature, much of it dedicated to Krishna and Rama. The retelling of the Ramayana in the vernacular, beginning in the southern Tamil languages in the eleventh century and spreading slowly northward, culminated in the sixteenth-century Hindi version by the great poet Tulsidas (tool-see-DAHSS) (1532–1623). His *Ramcaritmanas* (RAM-kah-rit-MAH-nuz) presents the devotional story with a deified Rama and Sita. Tulsidas's genius was in combining the conflicting cults of Vishnu and Shiva into a unified and overwhelming love for the divine, which he expressed in some of the most moving of all Indian poetry. The *Ramcaritmanas* has eclipsed its two-thousand-year-old Sanskrit ancestor in popularity and even became the basis of an Indian television series in the late 1980s.

CHAPTER SUMMARY

The three empires discussed in this chapter exhibited a number of striking similarities. First of all, they were Muslim in their religious affiliation, although the Safavids were Shi'ite rather than Sunni, a distinction that often led to mutual tensions and conflict. More important, perhaps, they were all of nomadic origin, and the political and social institutions that they adopted carried the imprint of their preimperial past. Once they achieved imperial power, however, all three ruling dynasties displayed an impressive capacity to administer a large empire and brought a degree of stability to peoples who had all too often lived in conditions of internal division and war.

The rise of these powerful Muslim states coincided with the opening period of European expansion at the end of the

fifteenth century and the beginning of the sixteenth. The military and political talents of these empires helped protect much of the Muslim world from the resurgent forces of Christianity. In fact, the Ottoman Turks carried their empire into the heart of Christian Europe and briefly reached the gates of the great city of Vienna. By the end of the eighteenth century, however, the Safavid dynasty had imploded, and the powerful Mughal Empire was in a state of virtual collapse. Only the Ottoman Empire was still functioning. Yet it too had lost much of its early expansionistic vigor and was showing signs of internal decay.

The reasons for the decline of these empires have inspired considerable debate among historians. One factor was undoubtedly the expansion of European power into the Indian Ocean and the Middle East. But internal causes were probably more important in the long run. All three empires experienced growing factionalism within the

ruling elite, incompetent leadership, and the emergence of divisive forces in the empire at large—factors that have marked the passing of traditional empires since early times. Climate change (the region was reportedly hotter and drier after the beginning of the seventeenth century) may have been a contributing factor. Paradoxically, one of the greatest strengths of these empires—their mastery of gunpowder—may have simultaneously been a serious weakness in that it allowed them to develop a complacent sense of security. With little incentive to turn their attention to new developments in science and technology, they were increasingly vulnerable to attack by the advanced nations of the West.

The Muslim empires, however, were not the only states in the Old World that were able to resist the first outward thrust of European expansion. Farther to the east, the mature civilizations in China and Japan faced down a similar challenge from Western merchants and missionaries. Unlike their counterparts in South Asia and the Middle East, as the nineteenth century dawned, they continued to thrive.

CHAPTER TIMELINE

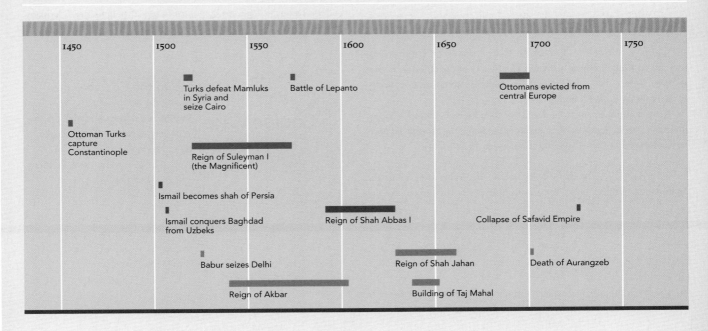

| 1450 | 1500 | 1550 | 1600 | 1650 | 1700 | 1750 |

Turks defeat Mamluks in Syria and seize Cairo

Battle of Lepanto

Ottomans evicted from central Europe

Ottoman Turks capture Constantinople

Reign of Suleyman I (the Magnificent)

Ismail becomes shah of Persia

Ismail conquers Baghdad from Uzbeks

Reign of Shah Abbas I

Collapse of Safavid Empire

Babur seizes Delhi

Reign of Shah Jahan

Death of Aurangzeb

Reign of Akbar

Building of Taj Mahal

Upon Reflection

Q How did the social policies adopted by the Ottomans compare with those of the Mughals? What similarities and differences do you detect, and what might account for them?

Q What is meant by the phrase "gunpowder empires," and to what degree did the Muslim states discussed here conform to this description?

Q What role did women play in the Ottoman, Safavid, and Mughal Empires? What might explain the similarities and differences? How did the treatment of women in these states compare with their treatment in other parts of the world?

Key Terms

bey (p. 451)
sultan (p. 451)
Janissaries (p. 451)
pashas (p. 453)
grand vizier (p. 454)
harem (p. 456)
devshirme (p. 456)
sipahis (p. 457)
millet (p. 457)
Sublime Porte (p. 458)
zamindars (p. 466)

Suggested Reading

CONSTANTINOPLE   A dramatic recent account of the Muslim takeover of Constantinople is provided by **R. Crowley** in *1453: The Holy War for Constantinople and the Clash of Islam and the West* (New York, 2005). Crowley acknowledges his debt to the classic by **S. Runciman,** *The Fall of Constantinople, 1453* (Cambridge, 1965).

OTTOMAN EMPIRE   Two useful general surveys of Ottoman history are **C. Finkel,** *Osman's Dream: The History of the Ottoman Empire* (Jackson, Tenn., 2006), and **J. Goodwin,** *Lords of the Horizons: A History of the Ottoman Empire* (London, 2002).

For the argument that the decline of the Ottoman Empire was not inevitable, see **E. Karsh et al.,** *Empires of the Sand: The Struggle for Mastery in the Middle East, 1789–1923* (Cambridge, Mass., 2001).

THE SAFAVIDS   On the Safavids, see **R. M. Savory,** *Iran Under the Safavids* (Cambridge, 1980). For a thoughtful if scholarly account of the reasons for the rise of the Safavid Empire, see **R. J. Abisaab,** *Converting Persia: Shia Islam and the Safavid Empire, 1501–1736* (London, 2004).

THE MUGHALS   For an elegant overview of the Mughal Empire and its cultural achievements, see **A. Schimmel,** *The Empire of the Great Mughals: History, Art and Culture,* trans. **C. Attwood** (London, 2004). The Mughal Empire is analyzed in a broad Central Asian context in **R. C. Foltz,** *Mughal India and Central Asia* (Karachi, 1998).

There are a number of specialized works on various aspects of the period. The concept of "gunpowder empires" is persuasively analyzed in **D. E. Streusand,** *The Formation of the Mughal Empire* (Delhi, 1989). Economic issues predominate in much recent scholarship. For example, see **O. Prakash,** *European Commercial Enterprise in Pre-Colonial India* (Cambridge, 1998). Finally, **K. N. Chaudhuri,** *Trade and Civilization in the Indian Ocean: An Economic History from the Rise of Islam to 1750* (Cambridge, 1985), views Indian commerce in the perspective of the regional trade network throughout the Indian Ocean.

For treatments of all three Muslim empires in a comparative context, see **J. J. Kissling et al.,** *The Last Great Muslim Empires* (Princeton, N.J., 1996). On the impact of Islam in the subcontinent, see **R. Eaton, ed.,** *Essay on Islam and Indian History* (New Delhi, 2000).

WOMEN OF THE OTTOMAN AND MUGHAL EMPIRES   For a detailed presentation of women in the imperial harem, consult **L. P. Peirce,** *The Imperial Harem: Women and Sovereignty in the Ottoman Empire* (Oxford, 1993). The fascinating story of the royal woman who played an important role behind the scenes is found in **E. B. Findly,** *Nur Jahan: Empress of Mughal India* (Oxford, 1993).

ART AND ARCHITECTURE   On the art of this era, see **R. C. Craven,** *Indian Art: A Concise History,* rev. ed. (New York, 1997); **J. Bloom** and **S. Blair,** *Islamic Arts* (London, 1997); **M. C. Beach** and **E. Koch,** *King of the World: The Padshahnama* (London, 1997); and **M. Hattstein** and **P. Delius,** *Islam: Art and Architecture* (Königswinter, Germany, 2004).

Go to the CourseMate website at **www.cengagebrain.com** for additional study tools and review materials— including audio and video clips—for this chapter.

© Hu Weibiao/Panorama/The Image Works

Emperor Kangxi

The East Asian World

CHAPTER OUTLINE
AND FOCUS QUESTIONS

China at Its Apex

Q Why were the Manchus so successful at establishing a foreign dynasty in China, and what were the main characteristics of Manchu rule?

Changing China

Q How did the economy and society change during the Ming and Qing eras, and to what degree did these changes seem to be leading toward an industrial revolution on the European model?

Tokugawa Japan

Q How did the society and economy of Japan change during the Tokugawa era, and how did Japanese culture reflect those changes?

Korea and Vietnam

Q To what degree did developments in Korea during this period reflect conditions in China and Japan? What were the unique aspects of Vietnamese civilization?

CRITICAL THINKING

Q How did China and Japan respond to the coming of the Europeans, and what explains the differences? What impact did European contacts have on these two East Asian civilizations through the end of the eighteenth century?

IN DECEMBER 1717, Emperor Kangxi (KANG-shee) returned from a hunting trip north of the Great Wall and began to suffer from dizzy spells. Conscious of his approaching date with mortality—he was now nearly seventy years of age—the emperor called together his sons and leading government officials in the imperial palace and issued an edict summing up his ideas on the art of statecraft. Rulers, he declared, should sincerely revere Heaven's laws as their fundamental strategy for governing the country. Among other things, those laws required that the ruler show concern for the welfare of the people, practice diligence, protect the state from its enemies, choose able advisers, and strike a careful balance between leniency and strictness, principle and expedience. That, he concluded, was all there was to it.[1]

Any potential successor to the throne in Beijing would have been well advised to attend to the emperor's advice. Kangxi was not only one of the longest reigning of all Chinese rulers but also one of the wisest. His era was one of peace and prosperity, and after half a century of rule, the empire was now at the zenith of its power and influence. As his life approached its end, Heaven must indeed have been pleased at the quality of his stewardship.

As for the emperor's edict, it clearly reflected the genius of Confucian teachings at their best and, with its emphasis on prudence, compassion, and tolerance, has a timeless quality that applies to our age as well as to the golden age of the Qing dynasty.

Kangxi reigned during one of the most glorious eras in the long history of China. Under the Ming (MING) and the early Qing (CHING) dynasties, the empire expanded its borders to a degree not seen since the Han and the Tang. Chinese culture was the envy of its neighbors and earned the admiration of many European visitors, including Jesuit priests and Enlightenment philosophes (see Chapter 18).

On the surface, China appeared to be an unchanging society patterned after the Confucian vision of a "golden age" in the remote past. This was indeed the image presented by China's rulers, who referred constantly to tradition as a model for imperial institutions and cultural values. Although few observers could have been aware of it at the time, however, China was changing—and rather rapidly.

A similar process was under way in neighboring Japan. A vigorous new shogunate (SHOH-gun-ut *or* SHOH-gun-ayt) called the Tokugawa (toh-koo-GAH-wah) rose to power in the early seventeenth century and managed to revitalize the traditional system in a somewhat more centralized form that enabled it to survive for another 250 years. But major structural changes were taking place in Japanese society, and by the nineteenth century, tensions were growing as the gap between theory and reality widened.

One of the many factors contributing to the quickening pace of change in both countries was contact with the West, which began with the arrival of Portuguese ships in Chinese and Japanese ports in the first half of the sixteenth century. The Ming and the Tokugawa initially opened their doors to European trade and missionary activity. Later, however, Chinese and Japanese rulers became concerned about the corrosive effects of Western ideas and practices and attempted to protect their traditional societies from external intrusion. But neither could forever resist the importunities of Western trading nations, nor were they able to inhibit the societal shifts that were taking place within their borders. When the doors to the West were finally reopened in the mid-nineteenth century, both societies were ripe for radical change.

China at Its Apex

Q **FOCUS QUESTION:** Why were the Manchus so successful at establishing a foreign dynasty in China, and what were the main characteristics of Manchu rule?

In 1514, a Portuguese fleet dropped anchor off the coast of China, just south of the Pearl River estuary and present-day Hong Kong. It was the first direct contact between the Chinese Empire and the West since the arrival of the Venetian adventurer Marco Polo two centuries earlier, and it opened an era that would eventually change the face of China and, indeed, all the world.

From the Ming to the Qing

Marco Polo had reported on the magnificence of China after visiting Beijing (bay-ZHING) during the reign of Khubilai Khan, the great Mongol ruler. By the time the Portuguese fleet arrived off the coast of China, of course, the Mongol Empire had long since disappeared. It had gradually

weakened after the death of Khubilai Khan and was finally overthrown in 1368 by a massive peasant rebellion under the leadership of Zhu Yuanzhang (JOO yoo-wen-JAHNG), who had declared himself the founding emperor of a new Ming (Bright) dynasty (1369–1644).

As we have seen, the Ming inaugurated a period of territorial expansion westward into Central Asia and southward into Vietnam while consolidating control over China's vast heartland. At the same time, starting in 1405, Admiral Zhenghe (JEHNG-huh) led a series of voyages that spread Chinese influence far into the Indian Ocean. Then, suddenly, after 1433 the voyages were discontinued, and the dynasty turned its attention to domestic concerns (see Chapter 10).

FIRST CONTACTS WITH THE WEST Despite the Ming's retreat from active participation in maritime trade, when the Portuguese arrived in 1514, China was in command of a vast empire that stretched from the steppes of Central Asia to the China Sea, from the Gobi Desert to the tropical rain forests of Southeast Asia. From the lofty perspective of the imperial throne in Beijing, the Europeans could only have seemed like an unusually exotic form of barbarian to be placed within the familiar framework of the tributary system, the hierarchical arrangement in which rulers of all other countries were regarded as "younger brothers" of the Son of Heaven. Indeed, the bellicose and uncultured behavior of the Portuguese so outraged Chinese officials that they expelled the Europeans, but after further negotiations, the Portuguese were permitted to occupy the tiny territory of Macao (muh-KOW), a foothold they would retain until the end of the twentieth century.

Initially, the arrival of the Europeans did not have much impact on Chinese society. Direct trade between Europe and China was limited, and Portuguese ships became involved in the regional trade network, carrying silk from China to Japan in return for Japanese silver. Eventually, the Spanish also began to participate, using the Philippines as an anchor in the galleon trade between China and the great silver mines in the Americas.

More influential than trade, perhaps, were the ideas introduced by Christian missionaries, who first received permission to reside in China in the last quarter of the sixteenth century. Among the most active and the most effective were highly educated Jesuits, who were familiar with European philosophical and scientific developments. Court officials were particularly impressed by the visitors' ability to predict the exact time of a solar eclipse, an event that the Chinese viewed with extreme reverence.

Recognizing the Chinese pride in their own culture, the Jesuits attempted to draw parallels between Christian and Confucian concepts (for example, they identified the Western concept of God with the Chinese character for Heaven) and to show the similarities between Christian morality and Confucian ethics. European inventions such as the clock, the prism, and various astronomical and musical instruments impressed Chinese officials, hitherto deeply imbued with a sense of the superiority of Chinese civilization, and helped

The Art of Printing

ART & IDEAS

Europeans obtained much of their early information about China from the Jesuits who served at the Ming court in the sixteenth and seventeenth centuries. The Italian Jesuit Matteo Ricci (ma-TAY-oh REE-chee) (1552–1610), who arrived in China in 1601, found much to admire in Chinese civilization. Here Ricci expresses a keen interest in Chinese printing methods, which at that time were well in advance of the techniques used in the West. Later Christian missionaries expressed strong interest in Confucian philosophy and Chinese ideas of statecraft.

Matteo Ricci, *The Diary of Matthew Ricci*

The art of printing was practiced in China at a date somewhat earlier than that assigned to the beginning of printing in Europe, which was about 1405. It is quite certain that the Chinese knew the art of printing at least five centuries ago, and some of them assert that printing was known to their people before the beginning of the Christian era, about 50 B.C.E. Their method of printing differs widely from that employed in Europe, and our method would be quite impracticable for them because of the exceedingly large number of Chinese characters and symbols. . . .

Their method of making printed books is quite ingenious. The text is written in ink, with a brush made of very fine hair, on a sheet of paper which is inverted and pasted on a wooden tablet. When the paper has become thoroughly dry, its surface is scraped off quickly and with great skill, until nothing but a fine tissue bearing the characters remains on the wooden tablet. Then, with a steel graver, the workman cuts away the surface following the outlines of the characters until these alone stand out in low relief. From such a block a skilled printer can make copies with incredible speed, turning out as many as fifteen hundred copies in a single day. . . . This scheme of engraving wooden blocks is well adapted for the large and complex nature of the Chinese characters, but I do not think it would lend itself very aptly to our European type, which could hardly be engraved upon wood because of its small dimensions.

Their method of printing has one decided advantage, namely, that once these tablets are made, they can be preserved and used for making changes in the text as often as one wishes. Additions and subtractions can also be made as the tablets can be readily patched. . . . We have derived great benefit from this method of Chinese printing, as we employ the domestic help in our homes to strike off copies of the books on religious and scientific subjects which we translate into Chinese from the languages in which they were written originally. In truth, the whole method is so simple that one is tempted to try it for himself after once having watched the process. The simplicity of Chinese printing is what accounts for the exceedingly large numbers of books in circulation here and the ridiculously low prices at which they are sold.

Q *How did the Chinese method of printing differ from that used in Europe at that time? What were the advantages of the Chinese system?*

Western ideas win acceptance at court. An elderly Chinese scholar expressed his wonder at the miracle of eyeglasses:

> *White glass from across the Western Seas*
> *Is imported through Macao:*
> *Fashioned into lenses big as coins,*
> *They encompass the eyes in a double frame.*
> *I put them on—it suddenly becomes clear;*
> *I can see the very tips of things!*
> *And read fine print by the dim-lit window*
> *Just like in my youth.*[2]

For their part, the missionaries were much impressed with many aspects of Chinese civilization, and reports of their experiences heightened European curiosity about this great society on the other side of the world (see the box above). By the late seventeenth century, European philosophers and political thinkers had begun to praise Chinese civilization and to hold up Confucian institutions and values as a mirror to criticize their counterparts in the West.

THE MING BROUGHT TO EARTH During the late sixteenth century, the Ming began to decline as a series of weak rulers led to an era of corruption, concentration of land ownership, and ultimately peasant rebellions and tribal unrest along the northern frontier. The inflow of vast amounts of foreign silver to pay for Chinese goods led to an alarming increase in inflation. Then the arrival of the English and the Dutch, whose ships preyed on the Spanish galleon trade between Asia and the Americas, disrupted the silver trade; silver imports plummeted, severely straining the Chinese economy by raising the value of the metal relative to that of copper. Crop yields declined due to harsh weather—linked to the "little ice age" of the early seventeenth century—and the resulting scarcity made it difficult for the government to provide food in times of imminent starvation. High taxes, necessitated in part because corrupt officials siphoned off revenues, led to rural unrest and violent protests among urban workers. A folk song of the period, addressed to the "Lord of Heaven," complained:

> *Old skymaster,*
> *You're getting on, your ears are deaf, your eyes are gone.*
> *Can't see people, can't hear words.*
> *Glory for those who kill and burn;*
> *For those who fast and read the scriptures,*

Starvation.

Fall down, old master sky, how can you be so high?

How can you be so high? Come down to earth.[3]

As always, internal problems were accompanied by disturbances along the northern frontier. Following long precedent, the Ming had attempted to pacify the frontier tribes by forging alliances with them, arranging marriages between them and the local aristocracy, and granting trade privileges. One of the alliances was with the Manchus (man-CHOOZ)—also known as the Jurchen (roor-ZHEN)—the descendants of a people who had briefly established a kingdom in northern China during the early thirteenth century. The Manchus, a mixed agricultural and hunting people, lived northeast of the Great Wall in the area known today as Manchuria (man-CHUR-ee-uh).

At first, the Manchus were satisfied with consolidating their territory and made little effort to extend their rule south of the Great Wall. But during the first decades of the seventeenth century, the problems of the Ming dynasty began to come to a head. A major epidemic devastated the population in many areas of the country. The suffering brought on by the epidemic helped spark a vast peasant revolt led by Li Zicheng (Li Tzu-ch'eng) (1604–1651). Li Zicheng (lee zuh-CHENG) was a postal worker in central China who had been dismissed from his job as part of a cost-saving measure by the imperial court, now increasingly preoccupied by tribal attacks along the frontier (see Map 17.1). In the 1630s, Li managed to extend the revolt throughout the country, and his forces finally occupied the capital, Beijing, in 1644. The last Ming emperor committed suicide by hanging himself from a tree in the palace gardens.

But Li was unable to hold his conquest. The overthrow of the Ming dynasty presented a great temptation to the Manchus. With the assistance of many military commanders who had deserted from the Ming, the Manchus seized Beijing. Li Zicheng's army disintegrated, and the Manchus declared a new dynasty: the Qing (Ch'ing, or Pure), which lasted from 1644 until 1911. Once again, China was under foreign rule.

The Greatness of the Qing

The accession of the Manchus to power in Beijing was not universally applauded. Their ruthless policies and insensitivity to Chinese customs soon provoked resistance. Some Ming loyalists fled to Southeast Asia, but others maintained their resistance to the new rulers from inside the country. One especially famous Ming loyalist, popularly known as Koxinga (gok-SHING-uh), took refuge on the island of Taiwan with many of his followers. Qing forces occupied the island in 1683 and incorporated it into the empire.

To make it easier to identify rebels, the government ordered all Chinese to adopt Manchu dress and hairstyles. All Chinese males were to shave their foreheads and braid their hair into a queue (KYOO); those who refused were to be executed. As a popular saying put it, "Lose your hair or lose your head."[4]

But the Manchus eventually proved to be more adept at adapting to Chinese conditions than their predecessors, the Mongols. Unlike the latter, who had tried to impose their own methods of ruling, the Manchus adopted the Chinese political system (although, as we shall see, they retained their distinct position within it) and were gradually accepted by most Chinese as the legitimate rulers of the country.

Like all of China's great dynasties, the Qing was blessed with a series of strong early rulers who pacified the country, rectified many of the most obvious social and economic inequities, and restored peace and prosperity. For the Ming dynasty, these strong emperors had been Zhu Yuanzhang and Yongle (YOONG-luh); under the Qing, they would be Kangxi (K'ang Hsi) and Qianlong (CHAN-loong) (Ch'ien Lung). The

© Cengage Learning

MAP 17.1 China and Its Enemies During the Late Ming Era. During the seventeenth century, the Ming dynasty faced challenges on two fronts: from China's traditional adversaries, nomadic groups north of the Great Wall, and from new arrivals, European merchants who had begun to press for trading privileges along the southern coast.

Q *How did these threats differ from those faced by previous dynasties in China?*

two Qing monarchs ruled China for well over a century, from the middle of the seventeenth century to the end of the eighteenth, and were responsible for much of the greatness of Manchu China.

THE REIGN OF KANGXI Kangxi (r. 1661–1722) was arguably the greatest ruler in Chinese history. Ascending to the throne at the age of seven, he was blessed with diligence, political astuteness, and a strong character and began to take charge of Qing administration while still an adolescent. During the six decades of his reign, Kangxi not only stabilized imperial rule by pacifying the restive peoples along the northern and western frontiers but also managed to make the dynasty acceptable to the general population. As an active patron of arts and letters, he cultivated the support of scholars through a number of major projects.

During Kangxi's reign, the activities of the Western missionaries, Dominicans and Franciscans as well as Jesuits, reached their height. An intellectually curious ruler like the Mughal emperor Akbar, Kangxi was quite tolerant of the Christians, and several Jesuit missionaries became influential at court. Several hundred court officials converted to Christianity, as did an estimated 300,000 ordinary Chinese. But the Christian effort was ultimately undermined by squabbling among the Western religious orders over the Jesuit policy of accommodating local beliefs and practices in order to facilitate conversion. The Jesuits had acquiesced to the emperor's insistence that traditional Confucian rituals such as ancestor veneration were civil ceremonies and thus could be undertaken by Christian converts. Jealous Dominicans and Franciscans complained to the pope, who issued an edict ordering all missionaries and converts to conform to the official orthodoxy set forth in Europe. At first, Kangxi attempted to resolve the problem by appealing directly to the Vatican, but the pope was uncompromising. After Kangxi's death, his successor began to suppress Christian activities throughout China.

THE REIGN OF QIANLONG Kangxi's achievements were carried on by his successors, Yongzheng (YOONG-jehng) (Yung Cheng, r. 1722–1736) and Qianlong (r. 1736–1795). Like Kangxi, Qianlong was known for his diligence, tolerance, and intellectual curiosity, and he too combined vigorous military action against the unruly tribes along the frontier with active efforts to promote economic prosperity, administrative efficiency, and scholarship and artistic excellence. The result was continued growth for the Manchu Empire throughout much of the eighteenth century.

But it was also under Qianlong that the first signs of the internal decay of the Manchu dynasty began to appear. The clues were familiar ones. Qing military campaigns along the frontier were expensive and placed heavy demands on the imperial treasury. As the emperor aged, he became less astute in selecting his subordinates and fell under the influence of corrupt elements at court, including the notorious Manchu official Heshen (HEH-shen) (Ho Shen). Funds officially destined for military or other official use were increasingly siphoned off by Heshen or his favorites, arousing resentment among military and civilian officials.

Corruption at the center led inevitably to unrest in rural areas, where higher taxes, bureaucratic venality, and rising pressure on the land because of the growing population had produced economic hardship. In central China, discontented peasants who had recently been resettled on infertile land launched a revolt known as the White Lotus Rebellion (1796–1804). The revolt was eventually suppressed at great expense.

QING POLITICS One reason for the success of the Manchus was their ability to adapt to their new environment. They retained the Ming political system with relatively few changes. They also tried to establish their legitimacy as China's rightful rulers by stressing their devotion to the principles of Confucianism. Emperor Kangxi ostentatiously studied the Confucian classics and issued a "sacred edict" that proclaimed to the entire empire the importance of the moral values established by "the Master" (see the box on p. 484).

Still, the Manchus, like the Mongols, were ethnically, linguistically, and culturally different from their subject population. The Qing attempted to cope with this reality by adopting a two-pronged strategy. One part of this strategy was aimed at protecting their distinct identity within an alien society. The Manchus, representing less than 2 percent of the entire population, were legally defined as distinct from everyone else in China. The Manchu nobles retained their aristocratic privileges, while their economic base was protected by extensive landholdings and revenues provided from the state treasury. Other Manchus were assigned farmland and organized into eight military units, called **banners**, which were stationed as separate units in various strategic positions throughout China. These "bannermen" were the primary fighting force of the empire. Ethnic Chinese were prohibited from settling in Manchuria and were still compelled to wear their hair in a queue as a sign of submission to the ruling dynasty.

At the same time that the Qing attempted to preserve their identity, they recognized the need to bring ethnic Chinese into the top ranks of imperial administration. Their solution was to create a system, known as **dyarchy** (DY-ahr-kee), in which all important administrative positions were shared equally by Chinese and Manchus. Of the six members of the grand secretariat, three were Manchu and three were Chinese. Each of the six ministries had an equal number of Chinese and Manchu members, and Manchus and Chinese also shared responsibilities at the provincial level. Below the provinces, Chinese were dominant. Although the system did not work perfectly, the Manchus' willingness to share power did win the allegiance of many Chinese. Meanwhile, the Manchus themselves, despite official efforts to preserve their separate language and culture, were increasingly assimilated into Chinese civilization.

The new rulers also tinkered with the civil service examination system. In an effort to make it more equitable, quotas were established for each major ethnic group and each province to prevent the positions from being monopolized by candidates from certain provinces in central China that had traditionally produced large numbers of officials. In practice,

Sixteen Confucian Commandments

POLITICS & GOVERNMENT

Although the Qing dynasty was of foreign origin, its rulers found Confucian maxims convenient for maintaining the social order. In 1670, the great emperor Kangxi issued the Sacred Edict to popularize Confucian values among the common people. The edict was read publicly at periodic intervals in every village in the country and set the standard for behavior throughout the empire. Note the similarities and differences between Kangxi's edict and the Japanese decree on p. 499.

Kangxi's Sacred Edict

1. Esteem most highly filial piety and brotherly submission, in order to give due importance to the social relations.
2. Behave with generosity toward your kindred, in order to illustrate harmony and benignity.
3. Cultivate peace and concord in your neighborhoods, in order to prevent quarrels and litigations.
4. Recognize the importance of husbandry and the culture of the mulberry tree, in order to ensure a sufficiency of clothing and food.
5. Show that you prize moderation and economy, in order to prevent the lavish waste of your means.
6. Give weight to colleges and schools, in order to make correct the practice of the scholar.
7. Extirpate strange principles, in order to exalt the correct doctrine.
8. Lecture on the laws, in order to warn the ignorant and obstinate.
9. Elucidate propriety and yielding courtesy, in order to make manners and customs good.
10. Labor diligently at your proper callings, in order to stabilize the will of the people.
11. Instruct sons and younger brothers, in order to prevent them from doing what is wrong.
12. Put a stop to false accusations, in order to preserve the honest and good.
13. Warn against sheltering deserters, in order to avoid being involved in their punishment.
14. Fully remit your taxes, in order to avoid being pressed for payment.
15. Unite in hundreds and tithing, in order to put an end to thefts and robbery.
16. Remove enmity and anger, in order to show the importance due to the person and life.

In what ways does this set of commandments conform to the principles of State Confucianism? How do these standards compare with those applied in Japan in the same era?

---

however, the examination system probably became less equitable during the Manchu era because increasingly positions were assigned to candidates who had purchased their degree instead of competing through the system. Moreover, positions were becoming harder to obtain because their number did not rise fast enough to match the unprecedented increase in population under Qing rule.

CHINA ON THE EVE OF THE WESTERN ONSLAUGHT In some ways, China was at the height of its power and glory in the mid-eighteenth century. But as we have seen, it was also during this period that the first signs of the decay of the Qing dynasty began to appear.

Unfortunately for China, the decline of the Qing occurred just as China's modest relationship with the West was about to give way to a new era of military confrontation and increased pressure for trade. The first problems came in the north, where Russian traders seeking skins and furs began to penetrate the region between Siberian Russia and Manchuria. Earlier the Ming dynasty had attempted to deal with the Russians by the traditional method of placing them in a tributary relationship and playing them off against other non-Chinese groups in the area. But the tsar refused to play by Chinese rules. His envoys to Beijing ignored the tribute system and refused to perform the **kowtow** (the ritual of prostration and touching the forehead to the ground), the classical symbol of

CHRONOLOGY	China During the Early Modern Era
Rise of the Ming dynasty	1369
Voyages of Zhenghe	1405–1433
Portuguese arrive in southern China	1514
Matteo Ricci arrives in China	1601
Li Zicheng occupies Beijing	1644
Manchus seize China	1644
Reign of Kangxi	1661–1722
Treaty of Nerchinsk	1689
First English trading post at Canton	1699
Reign of Qianlong	1736–1795
Lord Macartney's mission to China	1793
White Lotus Rebellion	1796–1804

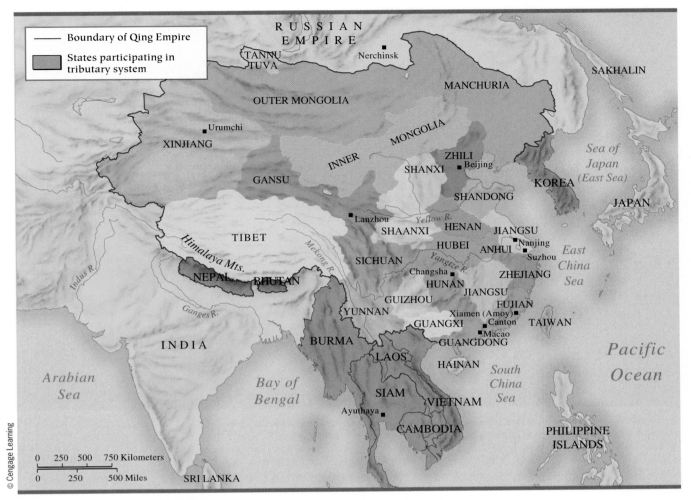

MAP 17.2 The Qing Empire in the Eighteenth Century. The boundaries of the Chinese Empire at the height of the Qing dynasty in the eighteenth century are shown on this map.

Q *What areas were linked in tributary status to the Chinese Empire, and how did they benefit the empire?*

fealty demanded of all foreign ambassadors to the Chinese court. Formal diplomatic relations were finally established in 1689, when the Treaty of Nerchinsk (ner-CHINSK), negotiated with the aid of Jesuit missionaries resident at the Qing court, settled the boundary dispute and provided for regular trade between the two countries. Through such arrangements, the Manchus were able not only to pacify the northern frontier but also to extend their rule over Xinjiang (SHIN-jyahng) and Tibet to the west and southwest (see Map 17.2). In the meantime, tributary relations were established with such neighboring countries as Korea, Burma, Vietnam, and Ayuthaya.

Dealing with the foreigners who arrived by sea was more difficult. By the end of the seventeenth century, the English had replaced the Portuguese as the dominant force in European trade. Operating through the East India Company, which served as both a trading unit and the administrator of English territories in Asia, the English established their first trading post at Canton (KAN-tun) in 1699. Over the next decades, trade with China, notably the export of tea and silk to England, increased rapidly. To limit contact between Chinese

and Europeans, the Qing licensed Chinese trading firms at Canton to be the exclusive conduit for trade with the West. Eventually, the Qing confined the Europeans to a small island just outside the city walls and permitted them to reside there only from October through March.

Canton in the Eighteenth Century

For a while, the British tolerated this system, which brought considerable profit to the East India Company and its shareholders. But by the end of the eighteenth century, the British had begun to demand that they be allowed access to other cities along the Chinese coast and that the country be opened to British manufactured goods. The British government and traders alike were restive at the uneven balance

© The Art Archive/Marine Museum, Stockholm/Gianni Dagli Orti

European Warehouses at Canton. Aggravated by the growing presence of foreigners in the eighteenth century, the Chinese court severely restricted the movement of European traders in China. They were permitted to live only in a compound near Canton during the seven months of the trading season and could go into the city only three times a month. In this painting, foreign flags (including, from the left, those of the United States, Sweden, Great Britain, and Holland) fly over the warehouses and residences of the foreign community while Chinese sampans and junks sit anchored in the river.

of trade between the two countries, which forced the British to ship vast amounts of silver bullion to China in exchange for its silk, porcelain, and tea. In 1793, a mission under Lord Macartney visited Beijing to press for liberalization of trade restrictions. A compromise was reached on the kowtow (Macartney was permitted to bend on one knee, as was the British custom), but Qianlong expressed no interest in British manufactured products (see the box on p. 487). An exasperated Macartney compared the Chinese Empire to "an old, crazy, first-rate man-of-war" that had once awed its neighbors "merely by her bulk and appearance" but was now destined under incompetent leadership to be "dashed to pieces on the shore."[5] With his contemptuous dismissal of the British request, the emperor had inadvertently sowed the seeds for a century of humiliation.

Changing China

FOCUS QUESTION: How did the economy and society change during the Ming and Qing eras, and to what degree did these changes seem to be leading toward an industrial revolution on the European model?

During the Ming and Qing dynasties, China remained a predominantly agricultural society; nearly 85 percent of its people were farmers. But although most Chinese still lived in rural villages, the economy was undergoing a number of changes that have led some historians to suggest that China, under other circumstances, might have experienced an industrial revolution as in the West. In this view, the arrival of Western imperialism in the nineteenth century not only failed to stimulate economic change but may actually have hindered it.

The Population Explosion

In the first place, the center of gravity was continuing to shift steadily from the north to the south. In the early centuries of Chinese civilization, the bulk of the population had been located along the Yellow River. Smaller settlements were located along the Yangtze and in the mountainous regions of the south, but the administrative and economic center of gravity was clearly in the north. By the Song period, however, that emphasis had begun to shift drastically as a result of climatic changes, deforestation, and continuing pressure from nomads in the Gobi Desert. By the early Qing, the economic breadbasket of China was located along the Yangtze River or in the mountains to the south. One concrete indication of this shift occurred during the Ming dynasty, when Emperor Yongle ordered the renovation of the Grand Canal to facilitate the shipment of rice from the Yangtze delta to the food-starved north.

The Tribute System in Action

INTERACTION & EXCHANGE

In 1793, the British emissary Lord Macartney visited the Qing Empire to request the opening of formal diplomatic and trading relations between his country and China. Emperor Qianlong's reply, addressed to King George III of Britain, illustrates how the imperial court in Beijing viewed the world. King George could not have been pleased. The document provides a good example of the complacency with which the Celestial Empire viewed the world beyond its borders.

A Decree of Emperor Qianlong

An Imperial Edict to the King of England: You, O King, are so inclined toward our civilization that you have sent a special envoy across the seas to bring to our Court your memorial of congratulations on the occasion of my birthday and to present your native products as an expression of your thoughtfulness. On perusing your memorial, so simply worded and sincerely conceived, I am impressed by your genuine respectfulness and friendliness and greatly pleased.

As to the request made in your memorial, O King, to send one of your nationals to stay at the Celestial Court to take care of your country's trade with China, this is not in harmony with the state system of our dynasty and will definitely not be permitted. Traditionally people of the European nations who wished to render some service under the Celestial Court have been permitted to come to the capital. But after their arrival they are obliged to wear Chinese court costumes, are placed in a certain residence, and are never allowed to return to their own countries. This is the established rule of the Celestial Dynasty with which presumably you, O King, are familiar. Now you, O King, wish to send one of your nationals to live in the capital, but he is not like the Europeans who come to Peking [Beijing] as Chinese employees, live there, and never return home again, nor can

he be allowed to go and come and maintain any correspondence. This is indeed a useless undertaking.

Moreover the territory under the control of the Celestial Court is very large and wide. There are well-established regulations governing tributary envoys from the outer states to Peking, giving them provisions [of food and traveling expenses] by our post-houses and limiting their going and coming. There has never been a precedent for letting them do whatever they like. Now if you, O King, wish to have a representative in Peking, his language will be unintelligible and his dress different from the regulations; there is no place to accommodate him. . . .

The Celestial Court has pacified and possessed the territory within the four seas. Its sole aim is to do its utmost to achieve good government and to manage political affairs, attaching no value to strange jewels and precious objects. The various articles presented by you, O King, this time are accepted by my special order to the office in charge of such functions in consideration of the offerings having come from a long distance with sincere good wishes. As a matter of fact, the virtue and prestige of the Celestial Dynasty having spread far and wide, the kings of the myriad nations come by land and sea with all sorts of precious things. Consequently there is nothing we lack, as your principal envoy and others have themselves observed. We have never set much store on strange or ingenious objects, nor do we need any more of your country's manufactures.

What reasons did the emperor give for refusing Macartney's request to have a permanent British ambassador in Beijing? How did the tribute system differ from the principles of international relations as practiced in the West?

Moreover, the population was beginning to increase rapidly. For centuries, China's population had remained within a range of 50 to 100 million, rising in times of peace and prosperity and falling in periods of foreign invasion and internal anarchy. During the Ming and the early Qing, however, the population increased from an estimated 70 to 80 million in 1390 to more than 300 million at the end of the eighteenth century. There were probably several reasons for this population increase: the relatively long period of peace and stability under the early Qing; the introduction of new crops from the Americas, including peanuts, sweet potatoes, and maize; and the planting of a new species of faster-growing rice from Southeast Asia (see the comparative essay "Population Explosion" on p. 488).

Of course, this population increase meant much greater pressure on the land, smaller farms, and a razor-thin margin of safety in the event of a natural disaster. The imperial court attempted to deal with the problem through various means, most notably by preventing the concentration of land in the hands of wealthy landowners. Nevertheless, by the eighteenth century, almost all the land that could be irrigated was already under cultivation, and the problems of rural hunger and landlessness were becoming increasingly serious.

Seeds of Industrialization

Another change that took place during the early modern period in China was the steady growth of manufacturing and

COMPARATIVE ESSAY

Population Explosion

EARTH & ENVIRONMENT

Between 1700 and 1800, Europe, China, and to a lesser degree India and the Ottoman Empire experienced a dramatic growth in population. In Europe, the population grew from 120 million people to almost 200 million by 1800; in China, from less than 200 million to more than 300 million during the same period.

Four developments in particular contributed to this population explosion. First, better growing conditions, made possible by an improvement in climate, affected wide areas of the world and enabled people to produce more food. Both China and Europe experienced warmer summers beginning in the early eighteenth century. Second, by the eighteenth century, people had begun to develop immunities to the epidemic diseases that had caused widespread loss of life between 1500 and 1700. The increase in travel by ship after 1500 had led to devastating epidemics. For example, the arrival of Europeans in Mexico introduced smallpox, measles, and chickenpox to a native population that had no immunities to European diseases. In 1500, between 11 and 20 million people lived in the area of Mexico; by 1650, only 1.5 million remained. Gradually, however, people developed resistance to these diseases.

A third factor in the population increase was the introduction of

© British Museum, London/The Bridgeman Art Library

Festival of the Yam. The spread of a few major food crops made possible new sources of nutrition to feed more people. The importance of the yam to the Ashanti people of West Africa is evident in this celebration of a yam festival at harvest time in 1817.

new foods. As a result of the Columbian Exchange (see the comparative essay on p. 405 in Chapter 14), American food crops, such as corn, potatoes, and sweet potatoes, were transported to other parts of the world, where they became important food sources. China imported a new species of rice from Southeast Asia that had a shorter harvest cycle than existing varieties. These new foods provided additional sources of nutrition that enabled more people to live for a longer time. At the same time, land development and canal building in the eighteenth century enabled government authorities to move food supplies to areas threatened with crop failure and famine.

Finally, the use of new weapons based on gunpowder allowed states to control larger territories and ensure a new degree of order. The early rulers of the Qing dynasty, for example, pacified the Chinese Empire and ensured a long period of peace and stability. Absolute monarchs achieved similar goals in a number of European states. Less violence resulted in fewer deaths at the same time that an increase in food supplies and a decrease in deaths from diseases were occurring, thus making possible in the eighteenth century the beginning of the world population explosion that persists to this day.

 What were the main reasons for the dramatic expansion in the world population during the early modern era?

---

commerce. Taking advantage of the long era of peace and prosperity, merchants and manufacturers began to expand their operations beyond their immediate provinces. Commercial networks began to operate on a regional and sometimes even a national basis as trade in silk, metal and wood products, porcelain, cotton goods, and cash crops like cotton and tobacco developed rapidly. Foreign trade also expanded as Chinese merchants set up extensive contacts with countries in Southeast Asia. As Chinese tea, silk, and porcelain became ever more popular in other parts of the world, the trade surplus grew as the country's exports greatly outnumbered its imports.

THE QING ECONOMY: READY FOR TAKEOFF? In recent years, a number of historians have suggested that because of

these impressive advances, by the end of the eighteenth century China was poised to make the transition from an agricultural to a predominantly manufacturing and commercial economy—a transition that began to take place in western Europe with the onset of the Industrial Revolution in the late eighteenth century (see Chapter 19).

Certainly, in most respects the Chinese economy in the mid-Qing era was as advanced as any of its counterparts around the world. China's achievements in technology over the past centuries were unsurpassed, and a perceptive observer at the time might well have concluded that the Manchu Empire would be highly competitive with the most advanced nations around the world for the indefinite future.

Nevertheless, a number of factors made it unlikely that China would advance rapidly into the industrial age. In the

Haggling Over the Price of Tea. An important item in the China trade of the eighteenth and early nineteenth centuries was tea, which had become extremely popular in Great Britain. The painting depicts the various stages of growing, processing, and marketing tea leaves. In the background, workers are removing tender young leaves from the bushes. In the foreground, British and Chinese merchants bargain over the price. After being dried, the leaves are packed into chests and loaded on vessels for shipment abroad.

first place, the mercantile class was not as independent in China as in some European societies. Trade and manufacturing in China remained under the firm control of the state. In addition, political and social prejudices against commercial activity remained strong. Reflecting an ancient preference for agriculture over manufacturing and trade, the state levied heavy taxes on manufacturing and commerce while attempting to keep agricultural taxes low.

To a considerable degree, these views were shared by the population at large, as the scholar-gentry continued to dominate intellectual fashions in China throughout the early Qing period. Chinese elites in general had little interest in the natural sciences or economic activities and often viewed them as a threat to their own dominant status within Chinese society as a whole. The commercial middle class, lacking social status and an independent position in society, had little say in intellectual matters.

At the root of such attitudes was the lingering influence of Neo-Confucianism, which remained the official state doctrine in China down to the end of the Qing dynasty. Although the founding fathers of Neo-Confucianism had originally focused on the "investigation of things," as time passed its practitioners tended to emphasize the elucidation of moral principles rather than the expansion of scientific knowledge. Though the Chinese economy was gradually being transformed from an agricultural to a commercial and industrial giant, scholars tended to look back to antiquity, rather than to empirical science, as the prime source for knowledge of the natural world and human events. The result was an intellectual environment that valued continuity over change and tradition over innovation.

The Chinese reaction to European clock-making techniques provides an example. In the early seventeenth century, the Jesuit priest Matteo Ricci introduced advanced European clocks driven by weights or springs. The emperor was fascinated and found the clocks more reliable than Chinese timekeepers. Over the next decades, European timepieces became a popular novelty at court, but the Chinese expressed little curiosity about the technology involved, provoking one European observer to remark that playthings like cuckoo clocks "will be received here with much greater interest than scientific instruments or *objets d'art*."[6]

Daily Life in Qing China

Despite the changes in the economy, daily life in China under the Ming and early Qing dynasties continued to follow traditional patterns.

THE FAMILY Chinese society continued to be organized around the family. As in earlier periods, the ideal family unit in Qing China was the joint family, in which three or four generations lived under the same roof. When sons married, they brought their wives to live with them in the family homestead. Prosperous families would add a separate section to the house to accommodate the new family unit. Unmarried daughters would also remain in the house. Aging parents and grandparents remained under the same roof until they died and were cared for by younger members of the household. This ideal did not always correspond to reality, however, since many families did not possess sufficient land to support a large household. One historian has estimated that only about 40 percent of Chinese families actually lived in joint families.

Still, the family retained its importance in early Qing times for the same reasons as in earlier times. As a labor-intensive society based primarily on the cultivation of rice, China needed large families to help with the harvest and to provide security for parents too old to work in the fields. Sons were especially prized, not only because they had strong backs but also because they would raise their own families under the parental roof. With few opportunities for employment

A Last Will and Testament

FAMILY & SOCIETY

The Ming dynasty official Yang Jisheng (YAHNG jee-SHENG) is remembered by historians of China primarily for his admirable courage in speaking out against the corruption of powerful forces at the imperial court. The reward for his courage was torture and eventual execution. On learning of his fate, Yang wrote from prison to his family on how to comport themselves in a proper Confucian manner. His "Final Instructions" were widely circulated during the late Ming and early Qing dynasties as a model for managing family affairs.

First, he pleaded with his wife not to commit suicide after his execution; in his day, widows often did so to proclaim their fidelity and chastity—a poignant parallel with the tradition of *sati* in India. Unfortunately, on the day of his execution, she hanged herself in the town marketplace. Second, he advised his two sons to devote themselves to studying for the civil service examination in preparation for a prestigious official career. Following the common practice of his day, he counseled them to focus on memorizing the text rather than on absorbing the inner message of the classics, a widely followed tendency that reduced the essential teachings of Confucius and his followers to a dry scholasticism.

Yang Jisheng, "Final Instructions"

To the Wife

My only regret will be that my two sons are both young. In studying they have both made progress, and in the future they will both succeed. I only fear that [my death will] adversely affect their [future]. My one daughter is not yet married; without someone to teach, guide, and take care of her, I am afraid she will be ridiculed. If I should happen to die, I leave you behind to teach and guide my sons and daughter into adulthood. If each is able to complete their household and establish their objectives, then it will be as if I am still alive. . . .

[My concubine] Erzhen is still young and moreover has no children. After I have died, see that she marries someone else. Give her an allotment of clothing and jewelry. . . . You must not have her stay at home and maintain widowhood. . . .

As for second elder sister and fourth elder sister, I'd like you always to look after them. As for fifth elder sister and sixth elder sister, when our father's concubine dies you should also become close to them. . . . The remaining household affairs I am sure you will deal with well.

To the Sons

You two are young in years. I fear that if you come to the notice of slick, sleazy people, they will try to tempt and defraud you. Some will ask you to dinner, some will tempt you to gamble, some will present you with objects you desire, some will tempt you with beautiful women. As soon as you enter their snare, you will suffer losses to them. Not only will the patrimony be completely dissipated, they'll also keep you from becoming a proper person. . . .

Preparing for the examinations is simply a matter of memorizing a great deal and composing a great deal. From the basic classics of the Four Books, memorize one thousand selections and read one hundred essays, one hundred policy inquiries, fifty declarations, and eighty judgments. If you have extra energy, read one hundred selections from the Five Classics and one hundred sections of better ancient prose. Every day compose one section of text, and every month write three essays and two policy inquiries. It is crucial to remember that you must not pass a single day without a teacher. If you have no teacher, then you have no strictness and no fear. . . . If you pass the local examinations or become a *jinshi* [obtain a doctorate], considering my bitter [experiences] it is best if you do not become an official. If you do become an official, you must be upright and honest, loyal and trustworthy, wholeheartedly serving the country to the best of your ability.

How did Yang Jisheng advise his sons to prepare for a career in the bureaucracy? How did he use his own official career as an example of proper behavior?

---

outside the family, sons had little choice but to remain with their parents and help on the land. Within the family, the oldest male was in charge, and theoretically, his wishes had to be obeyed by all family members (see the box above). These values were reiterated in Emperor Kangxi's Sacred Edict, which listed filial piety and loyalty to the family as its first two maxims.

For many Chinese, the effects of these values were most apparent in the choice of a marriage partner. Arranged marriages were the norm, and the primary consideration in selecting a spouse was whether the union would benefit the family unit as whole. The couple themselves usually had no say in the matter and might not even meet until the marriage ceremony. Not only was love considered unimportant in marriage, but it was often viewed as undesirable because it would draw the attention of the husband and wife away from their primary responsibility to the larger family unit.

Although this emphasis on filial piety might seem to represent a blatant disregard for individual rights, the obligations were not all on the side of the children. The father was expected to provide support for his wife and children and, like the ruler, was supposed to treat those in his care with respect and compassion. All too often, however, the male head of the family was able to exact his privileges without performing his responsibilities in return.

Beyond the joint family was the clan. Sometimes called a lineage, a clan was an extended kinship unit consisting of dozens or even hundreds of joint and nuclear families linked by a clan council of elders and a variety of other common social and religious functions. The clan served a number of useful purposes. Some clans possessed lands that could be rented out to poorer families, or richer families within the clan might provide land for the poor. Since there was no general state-supported educational system, sons of poor families might be invited to study in a school established in the home of a more prosperous relative. If the young man succeeded in becoming an official, he would be expected to provide favors and prestige for the clan as a whole.

Like joint families, clans were not universal, and millions of Chinese had none. The clans apparently originated in the great landed families of the Tang period and managed to survive despite periodic efforts by the imperial court to weaken and destroy them. In many cases, clan solidarity was weakened by intralineage conflicts or differing levels of status and economic achievement. Nevertheless, in the early modern period, they were still an influential force at the local level and were particularly prevalent in the south.

THE ROLE OF WOMEN In traditional China, the role of women had always been inferior to that of men. A sixteenth-century Spanish visitor to South China observed that Chinese women were "very secluded and virtuous, and it was a very rare thing for us to see a woman in the cities and large towns, unless it was an old crone."[7] Women were more visible, he said, in rural areas, where they frequently could be seen working in the fields.

The concept of female inferiority had deep roots in Chinese history. This view was embodied in the belief that only a male could carry on sacred family rituals and that men alone had the talent to govern others. Only males could aspire to a career in government or scholarship. Within the family system, the wife was clearly subordinated to the husband. Legally, she could not divorce her husband or inherit property. The husband, however, could divorce his wife if she did not produce male heirs, or he could take a second wife as well as a concubine for his pleasure. Life was especially difficult for a widow: she had to raise her children on a single income or fight off her dead husband's greedy relatives, who would try to coerce her to remarry because, by law, they would then inherit all of her previous property and her original dowry.

Female children were less desirable because of their limited physical strength and because their parents would have to pay a dowry to the parents of their future husbands. Female children normally did not receive an education, and in times when food was in short supply, daughters might even be put to death.

Though women were clearly inferior to men in theory, this was not always the case in practice. Capable women often compensated for their legal inferiority by playing a strong role within the family. Women were often in charge of educating the children and handling the family budget. Some privileged women also received training in the Confucian classics, although their schooling was generally for a shorter time and less rigorous than that of their male counterparts. A few produced significant works of art and poetry.

All in all, however, life for women in traditional China was undoubtedly difficult. In Chinese novels, women were treated as scullery maids or love objects. They were frequently under the domination of both their husband and their mother-in-law, and in some cases the bullying was so brutal that suicide seemed to be the only way out.

Cultural Developments

During the late Ming and early Qing dynasties, traditional culture in China reached new heights of achievement. With the rise of a wealthy urban class, the demand for art, porcelain, textiles, and literature increased dramatically.

THE RISE OF THE CHINESE NOVEL During the Ming dynasty, a new form of literature arose that eventually evolved into the modern Chinese novel. Although considered less respectable than poetry and nonfiction prose, these groundbreaking works (often written anonymously or under pseudonyms) were enormously popular, especially among well-to-do urban dwellers.

Written in a colloquial but realistic style, the new fiction produced vivid portraits of Chinese society. Many of the stories sympathized with society's downtrodden—often helpless maidens—and dealt with such crucial issues as love, money, marriage, and power. Adding to the realism were sexually explicit passages that depicted the private side of Chinese life. Readers delighted in sensuous tales that, no matter how pornographic, always professed a moral lesson; the villains were punished and the virtuous rewarded. During the more puritanical Qing era, a number of the more erotic works were censored or banned and found refuge in Japan, where several have recently been rediscovered by scholars.

Gold Vase Plum, known in English translation as *The Golden Lotus*, presents a cutting exposé of the decadent aspects of late Ming society. Considered by many the first realistic social novel—preceding its European counterparts by two centuries—*The Golden Lotus* depicts the depraved life of a wealthy landlord who cruelly manipulates those around him for sex, money, and power. In a rare exception in Chinese fiction, the villain is not punished for his evil ways; justice is served instead by the misfortunes that befall his descendants.

The Dream of the Red Chamber is generally considered China's most distinguished popular novel. Published in 1791, some 150 years after *The Golden Lotus*, it tells of the tragic love of two young people caught in the financial and moral disintegration of a powerful Chinese clan. The hero and the heroine, both sensitive and spoiled, represent the inevitable decline of the Chia family and come to an equally inevitable tragic end, she in death and he in an unhappy marriage to another.

THE ART OF THE MING AND THE QING During the Ming and the early Qing, China produced its last outpouring of traditional artistic brilliance. Although most of the creative work was modeled on past examples, the art of this period is impressive for its technical perfection and breathtaking quantity.

In architecture, the most outstanding example is the Imperial City in Beijing. Building on the remnants of the palace of the Yuan dynasty, the Ming emperor Yongle ordered renovations when he returned the capital to Beijing in 1421. Succeeding emperors continued to add to the palace, but the basic design has not changed since the Ming era. Surrounded by high walls, the immense compound is divided into a maze of private apartments and offices and an imposing ceremonial quadrangle with a series of stately halls for imperial audiences and banquets. The grandiose scale, richly carved marble, spacious gardens, and graceful upturned roofs also contribute to the splendor of the "Forbidden City."

Beijing Under the Ming and the Manchus, 1400–1911

The decorative arts flourished in this period, especially intricately carved lacquerware and boldly shaped and colored cloisonné (kloi-zuh-NAY *or* KLWAH-zuh-nay), a type of enamelwork in which thin metal bands separate areas of colored enamel. Silk production reached its zenith, and the best-quality silks were highly prized in Europe, where chinoiserie (sheen-wah-zuh-REE *or* shee-nwahz-REE), as Chinese art of all kinds was called, was in vogue. Perhaps the most famous of all the achievements of the Ming era was the blue-and-white porcelain, still prized by collectors throughout the world. Of unsurpassed luminosity, this porcelain was used by Ming emperors to promote the prestige of their opulent and powerful empire. One variety caused such a sensation in the Netherlands that the Dutch began to manufacture their own blue-and-white porcelain at a new factory set up in Delft.

During the Qing dynasty, artists produced great quantities of paintings, mostly for home consumption. The wealthy city of Yangzhou (YAHNG-Joh) on the Grand Canal emerged as an active artistic center. Inside the Forbidden City in Beijing, court painters worked alongside Jesuit artists and experimented with Western techniques. European art, however, did not greatly influence Chinese painting at this time; some Chinese artists dismissed it as mere "craftsmanship." Scholarly painters and the literati totally rejected foreign techniques and became obsessed with traditional Chinese styles. As a result, Qing painting became progressively more repetitive and stale. Ironically, the Qing dynasty thus represents both the apogee of traditional Chinese art and the beginning of its decline.

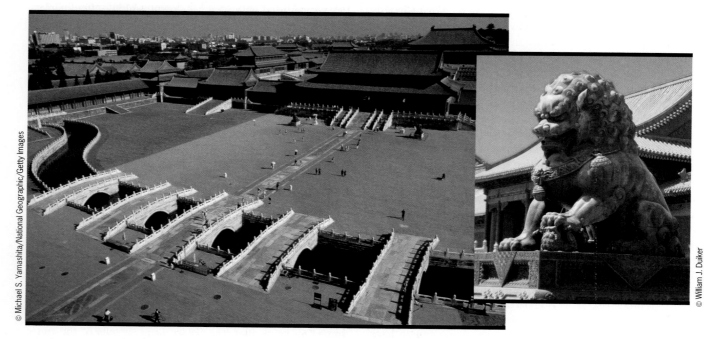

The Imperial City in Beijing. During the fifteenth century, the Ming dynasty erected an immense imperial city on the remnants of the palace of Khubilai Khan in Beijing. Surrounded by 6½ miles of walls, the enclosed compound is divided into a maze of private apartments and offices; it also includes an imposing ceremonial quadrangle with stately halls for imperial audiences and banquets. Because it was off-limits to commoners, the compound was known as the Forbidden City. The fearsome lion shown in the inset, representing the omnipotence of the Chinese Empire, guards the entrance to the private apartments of the palace.

© William J. Duiker

World-Class China Ware. Ming porcelain was desired throughout the world for its delicate blue-and-white floral decorations. The blue coloring was produced with cobalt that had originally been brought from the Middle East along the Silk Road and was known in China as "Mohammedan blue." In the early seventeenth century, the first Ming porcelain arrived in the Netherlands, where it was called *kraak* because it had been loaded on two Portuguese ships known as carracks seized by the Dutch fleet. It took Dutch artisans more than a century to learn how to produce a porcelain as fine as the examples brought from China.

Tokugawa Japan

Q FOCUS QUESTION: How did the society and economy of Japan change during the Tokugawa era, and how did Japanese culture reflect those changes?

At the end of the fifteenth century, the traditional Japanese system was at a point of near anarchy. With the decline in the authority of the Ashikaga (ah-shee-KAH-guh) shogunate at Kyoto (KYOH-toh), clan rivalries had exploded into an era of warring states similar to the period of the same name in Zhou dynasty China. Even at the local level, power was frequently diffuse. For a typical daimyo (DYM-yoh) (great lord), the domain had become little more than a coalition of fief-holders held together by a loose allegiance to the manor lord. Prince Shotoku's dream of a united Japan seemed only a distant memory (see Chapter 11). In actuality, Japan was on the verge of an extended era of national unification and peace under the rule of its greatest shogunate, the Tokugawa.

The Three Great Unifiers

The process began in the mid-sixteenth century with the emergence of three very powerful political figures: Oda Nobunaga (1568–1582), Toyotomi Hideyoshi (1582–1598), and Tokugawa Ieyasu (1598–1616). In 1568, Oda Nobunaga (OH-dah noh-buh-NAH-guh), the son of a samurai (SAM-uh-ry) and a

military commander under the Ashikaga shogunate, seized the imperial capital of Kyoto and placed the reigning shogun under his domination. During the next few years, the brutal and ambitious Nobunaga attempted to consolidate his rule throughout the central plains by defeating his rivals and suppressing the power of the Buddhist estates, but he was killed by one of his generals in 1582 before the process was complete. He was succeeded by Toyotomi Hideyoshi (toh-yoh-TOH-mee hee-day-YOH-shee), a farmer's son who had worked his way up through the ranks to become a military commander. Originally lacking a family name of his own, he eventually adopted the name Toyotomi ("abundant provider") to embellish his reputation for improving the material standards of his domain. Hideyoshi located his capital at Osaka (oh-SAH-kuh), where he built a castle to accommodate his headquarters, and gradually extended his power outward to the southern islands of Shikoku (shee-KOH-koo) and Kyushu (KYOO-shoo) (see Map 17.3). By 1590, he had persuaded most of the daimyo on the Japanese islands to accept his authority and created a national currency. Then he invaded Korea in an abortive effort to export his rule to the Asian mainland (see "Korea: In a Dangerous Neighborhood" later in this chapter).

Despite their efforts, however, neither Nobunaga nor Hideyoshi was able to eliminate the power of the local daimyo. Both were compelled to form alliances with some daimyo in order to destroy other more powerful rivals. At the conclusion of his conquests in 1590, Toyotomi Hideyoshi could claim to be the supreme proprietor of all registered lands in areas under his authority. But he then reassigned those lands as fiefs to the local daimyo, who declared their allegiance to him. The daimyo in turn began to pacify the countryside, carrying out extensive "sword hunts" to disarm the population and attracting samurai to their service. The Japanese tradition of decentralized rule had not yet been overcome.

After Hideyoshi's death in 1598, Tokugawa Ieyasu (toh-koo-GAH-wah ee-yeh-YAH-soo), the powerful daimyo of Edo (EH-doh)—modern Tokyo—moved to fill the vacuum. Neither Hideyoshi nor Oda Nobunaga had claimed the title of shogun (SHOH-gun), but Ieyasu named himself shogun in 1603, initiating the most powerful and long-lasting of all Japanese shogunates. The Tokugawa rulers completed the restoration of central authority begun by Nobunaga and Hideyoshi and remained in power until 1868, when a war dismantled the entire system. As a contemporary phrased it, "Oda pounds the national rice cake, Hideyoshi kneads it, and in the end Ieyasu sits down and eats it."[8]

Opening to the West

The unification of Japan took place almost simultaneously with the coming of the Europeans. Portuguese traders sailing in a Chinese junk that may have been blown off course by a typhoon had landed on the islands in 1543. Within a few years, Portuguese ships were stopping at Japanese ports on a

© Cengage Learning

MAP 17.3 Tokugawa Japan. This map shows the Japanese islands during the long era of the Tokugawa shogunate. Key cities, including the shogun's capital of Edo (Tokyo), are shown.

Q *Where was the imperial court located?*

regular basis to take part in the regional trade between Japan, China, and Southeast Asia. The first Jesuit missionary, Francis Xavier (ZAY-vee-ur), arrived in 1549.

Initially, the visitors were welcomed. The curious Japanese (the Japanese were "very desirous of knowledge," said Francis Xavier) were fascinated by tobacco, clocks, spectacles, and other European goods, and local daimyo were interested in purchasing all types of European weapons and armaments (see the box on p. 495). Oda Nobunaga and Toyotomi Hideyoshi found the new firearms helpful in defeating their enemies and unifying the islands. The effect on Japanese military architecture was particularly striking as local lords began to erect castles on the European model. Many of these castles, such as Hideyoshi's castle at Osaka, still exist today.

The missionaries also had some success. Though confused by misleading translations of sacred concepts in both cultures (Francis Xavier was notoriously poor at learning foreign languages), they converted a number of local daimyo, some of whom may have been motivated in part by the desire for commercial profits. By the end of the sixteenth century, thousands of Japanese in the southernmost islands of Kyushu and Shikoku had become Christians. One converted daimyo ceded the superb natural harbor of the modern city of Nagasaki (nah-gah-SAH-kee) to the Society of Jesus, which proceeded to use the new settlement for both missionary and trading purposes. But papal claims to the loyalty of all Japanese Christians and the European habit of intervening in local politics soon began to arouse suspicion in official circles. Missionaries added to the problem by deliberately destroying local idols and shrines and turning some temples into Christian schools or churches.

Musée des Arts Asiatiques–Guimet, Paris,//© Réunion des Musées Nationaux/ Art Resource, NY

Arrival of the Portuguese at Nagasaki. Portuguese traders, dressed in billowing pantaloons and broad-brimmed hats, landed in Japan by accident in 1543. In a few years, they were arriving regularly, taking part in a regional trade network involving Japan, China, and Southeast Asia. In these panels done in black lacquer and gold leaf, we see a late-sixteenth-century Japanese interpretation of the landing of Portuguese merchants at Nagasaki. Normally, Japanese screens are read from right to left, but this one is read left to right. Having arrived by ship, the Portuguese proceed in splendor to the Jesuit priests waiting in a church on the right.

A Present for Lord Tokitaka

SCIENCE & TECHNOLOGY

The Portuguese introduced firearms to Japan in the sixteenth century, and Japanese warriors were quick to explore the possibilities of these new weapons. In this passage, the daimyo of a small island off the southern tip of Japan receives an explanation of how to use the new weapons and is fascinated by the results. Note how Lord Tokitaka (toh-kuh-TAH-kuh) attempts to understand the procedures in terms of traditional Daoist beliefs.

The Japanese Discover Firearms

"There are two leaders among the traders, the one called Murashusa, and the other Christian Mota. In their hands they carried something two or three feet long, straight on the outside with a passage inside, and made of a heavy substance. The inner passage runs through it although it is closed at the end. At its side there is an aperture which is the passageway for fire. Its shape defies comparison with anything I know. To use it, fill it with powder and small lead pellets. Set up a small . . . target on a bank. Grip the object in your hand, compose your body, and closing one eye, apply fire to the aperture. Then the pellet hits the target squarely. The explosion is like lightning and the report like thunder. Bystanders must cover their ears. . . . This thing with one blow can smash a mountain of silver and a wall of iron. If one sought to do mischief in another man's domain and he was touched by it, he would lose his life instantly. Needless to say this is also true for the deer and stag that ravage the plants in the fields."

Lord Tokitaka saw it and thought it was the wonder of wonders. He did not know its name at first nor the details of its use. Then someone called it "iron-arms," although it was not known whether the Chinese called it so, or whether it was so called only on our island. Thus, one day, Tokitaka spoke to the two alien leaders through an interpreter: "Incapable though I am, I should like to learn about it." Whereupon, the chiefs answered, also through an interpreter: "If you wish to learn about it, we shall teach you its mysteries." Tokitaka then asked, "What is its secret?" The chief replied: "The secret is to put your mind aright and close one eye." Tokitaka said: "The ancient sages have often taught how to set one's mind aright, and I have learned something of it. If the mind is not set aright, there will be no logic for what we say or do. Thus, I understand what you say about setting our minds aright. However, will it not impair our vision for objects at a distance if we close an eye? Why should we close an eye?" To which the chiefs replied: "That is because concentration is important in everything. When one concentrates, a broad vision is not necessary. To close an eye is not to dim one's eyesight but rather to project one's concentration farther. You should know this." Delighted, Tokitaka said: "That corresponds to what Lao Tzu has said, 'Good sight means seeing what is very small.'"

That year the festival day of the Ninth Month fell on the day of the Metal and the Boar. Thus, one fine morning the weapon was filled with powder and lead pellets, a target was set up more than a hundred paces away, and fire was applied to the weapon. At first the people were astonished; then they became frightened. But in the end they all said in unison: "We should like to learn!" Disregarding the high price of the arms, Tokitaka purchased from the aliens two pieces of the firearms for his family treasure. As for the art of grinding, sifting, and mixing of the powder, Tokitaka let his retainer, Shinokawa Shoshiro, learn it. Tokitaka occupied himself, morning and night, and without rest in handling the arms. As a result, he was able to convert the misses of his early experiments into hits—a hundred hits in a hundred attempts.

How did Lord Tokitaka use Daoist concepts to explain something unfamiliar to him? What impact did the introduction of firearms have on Japanese society at the time?

EXPULSION OF THE CHRISTIANS Inevitably, the local authorities reacted. In 1587, Toyotomi Hideyoshi issued an edict prohibiting further Christian activities within his domains. Japan, he declared, was "the land of the Gods," and the destruction of shrines by the foreigners was "something unheard of in previous ages." To "corrupt and stir up the lower classes" to commit such sacrileges, he declared, was "outrageous."[9] The parties responsible (the Jesuits) were ordered to leave the country within twenty days. Hideyoshi was careful to distinguish missionary from trading activities, however, and merchants were permitted to continue their operations (see the box on p. 496).

The Jesuits protested the expulsion, and eventually Hideyoshi relented, permitting them to continue proselytizing as long as they were discreet. But he refused to repeal the edicts, and when the aggressive activities of newly arrived Spanish Franciscans aroused his ire, he ordered the execution of nine missionaries and a number of their Japanese converts. When the missionaries continued to interfere in local politics (some even tried to incite the daimyo in the southern islands against the shogunate government in Edo), Tokugawa Ieyasu completed the process by ordering the eviction of all missionaries in 1612. The persecution of Japanese Christians intensified,

Toyotomi Hideyoshi Expels the Missionaries

RELIGION & PHILOSOPHY

When Christian missionaries in sixteenth-century Japan began to interfere in local politics and criticize traditional religious practices, Toyotomi Hideyoshi issued an edict calling for their expulsion. In this letter to the Portuguese viceroy in Asia, Hideyoshi explains his decision. Note his conviction that the followers of the Buddha, Confucius, and Shinto all believe in the same God and his criticism of Christianity for rejecting all other faiths.

Toyotomi Hideyoshi, Letter to the Viceroy of the Indies

Ours is the land of the Gods, and God is mind. Everything in nature comes into existence because of mind. Without God there can be no spirituality. Without God there can be no way. God rules in times of prosperity as in times of decline. God is positive and negative and unfathomable. Thus, God is the root and source of all existence. This God is spoken of by Buddhism in India, Confucianism in China, and Shinto in Japan. To know Shinto is to know Buddhism as well as Confucianism.

As long as man lives in this world, Humanity will be a basic principle. Were it not for Humanity and Righteousness, the sovereign would not be a sovereign, nor a minister of a state a minister. It is through the practice of Humanity and Righteousness that the foundations of our relationships between sovereign and minister, parent and child, and husband and wife are established. If you are interested in the profound philosophy of God and Buddha, request an explanation and it will be given to you. In your land one doctrine is taught to the exclusion of others, and you are not yet informed of the [Confucian] philosophy of Humanity and Righteousness. Thus, there is no respect for God and Buddha and no distinction between sovereign and ministers. Through heresies you intend to destroy the righteous law. Hereafter, do not expound, in ignorance of right and wrong, unreasonable and wanton doctrines. A few years ago the so-called Fathers came to my country seeking to bewitch our men and women, both of the laity and clergy. At that time punishment was administered to them, and it will be repeated if they should return to our domain to propagate their faith. It will not matter what sect or denomination they represent—they shall be destroyed. It will then be too late to repent. If you entertain any desire of establishing amity with this land, the seas have been rid of the pirate menace, and merchants are permitted to come and go. Remember this.

 What reason did Hideyoshi give for prohibiting the practice of Christianity in Japan? How did his religious beliefs, as expressed in this document, differ from those of other religions like Christianity and Islam?

---

leading to an abortive revolt by Christian peasants on the island of Kyushu in 1637, which was bloodily suppressed.

At first, Japanese authorities hoped to maintain commercial relations with European countries even while suppressing the Western religion, but eventually they decided to regulate foreign trade more closely and closed the two major foreign factories on the island of Hirado (heh-RAH-doh) and at Nagasaki. The sole remaining opening to the West was at the island of Deshima (deh-SHEE-muh *or* deh-JEE-muh) in Nagasaki harbor, where in 1609 a small Dutch community was permitted to engage in limited trade with Japan (the Dutch, unlike the Portuguese and the Spanish, had not allowed missionary activities to interfere with their commercial interests). Dutch ships were permitted to dock at Nagasaki harbor only once a year and, after close inspection, were allowed to remain for two or three months. Conditions on the island of Deshima itself were quite confining: the Dutch physician Engelbert Kaempfer complained that the Dutch lived in "almost perpetual imprisonment."[10] Nor were the Japanese free to engage in foreign trade, as the *bakufu* (buh-KOO-foo *or* bah-KOO-fuh)—the central government—sought to restrict the ability of local authorities to carry out commercial transactions with foreign merchants. A small amount of commerce took place with China and other parts of Asia, but Japanese subjects of the shogunate were forbidden to leave the country on penalty of death.

The Tokugawa "Great Peace"

Once in power, the Tokugawa attempted to strengthen the system that had governed Japan for more than three hundred years. They followed precedent in ruling through the *bakufu*, composed now of a coalition of daimyo, and a council of elders. But the system was more centralized than it had been previously. Now the shogunate government played a dual role. It set national policy on behalf of the emperor in Kyoto while simultaneously governing the shogun's own domain, which included about one-quarter of the national territory as well as the three great cities of Edo, Kyoto, and Osaka. As before, the state was divided into separate territories, called domains (*han*), which were ruled by a total of about 250 individual daimyo lords. The daimyo themselves were divided into two types: the *fudai* (FOO-dy) **daimyo** (inside daimyo), who were mostly small daimyo that were directly subordinate to the shogunate, and the *tozama* (toh-ZAH-mah) **daimyo** (outside daimyo), who were larger, more independent lords that were usually more distant from the center of shogunate power in Edo.

DAIMYO AND SAMURAI In theory, the daimyo were essentially autonomous, since they were able to support themselves from taxes on their lands (the shogunate received its own revenues from its extensive landholdings). In actuality, the shogunate was able to guarantee daimyo loyalties by compelling daimyo lords to maintain two residences, one in their own domains and the other at Edo, and to leave their families in Edo as hostages for the daimyo's good behavior. Keeping up two residences also placed the Japanese nobility in a difficult economic position. Some were able to defray the high costs by concentrating on cash crops such as sugar, fish, and forestry products, but most were rice producers, and their revenues remained roughly the same throughout the period. The daimyo were also able to protect their economic interests by depriving their samurai retainers of their proprietary rights over the land and transforming them into salaried officials. The fief thus became a stipend, and the personal relationship between the daimyo and his retainers gradually gave way to a bureaucratic authority.

The Tokugawa also tinkered with the social system by limiting the size of the samurai class and reclassifying samurai who supported themselves by tilling the land as commoners. In fact, with the long period of peace brought about by Tokugawa rule, the samurai gradually ceased to be a warrior class and were required to live in the castle towns. As a gesture to their glorious past, samurai were still permitted to wear their two swords, and a rigid separation was maintained between persons of samurai status and the nonaristocratic segment of the population. The Jesuit missionary Francis Xavier observed that "on no account would a poverty-stricken gentleman marry with someone outside the gentry, even if he were given great sums to do so."[11]

SEEDS OF CAPITALISM The long period of peace under the Tokugawa shogunate made possible a dramatic rise in commerce and manufacturing, especially in the growing cities. By the mid-eighteenth century, Edo, with a population of more than one million, was one of the largest cities in the world. The growth of trade and industry was stimulated by a rising standard of living—driven in part by technological advances in agriculture and an expansion of arable land—and the voracious appetites of the aristocrats for new products. The daimyo's need for income also contributed as many of them began to promote the sale of local goods from their domains, such as textiles, forestry products, sugar, and sake (SAH-kee) (fermented rice wine).

Most of this commercial expansion took place in the major cities and the castle towns, where the merchants and artisans lived along with the samurai, who were clustered in neighborhoods surrounding the daimyo's castle. Banking flourished, and paper money became the normal medium of exchange in commercial transactions. Merchants formed guilds not only to control market conditions but also to facilitate government oversight and the collection of taxes. Under the benign, if somewhat contemptuous, supervision of

Japan's noble rulers, a Japanese merchant class gradually began to emerge from the shadows to play a significant role in the life of the Japanese nation. Some historians view the Tokugawa era as the first stage in the rise of an indigenous form of capitalism, based loosely on the Western model.

Eventually, the increased pace of industrial activity spread beyond the cities into rural areas. As in Great Britain, cotton was a major factor. Cotton had been introduced to China during the Song dynasty and had spread to Korea and Japan shortly thereafter. Traditionally, however, cotton cloth had been too expensive for the common people, who instead wore clothing made of hemp. Imports increased during the sixteenth century, however, when cotton cloth began to be used for uniforms, matchlock fuses, and sails. Eventually, technological advances reduced the cost, and specialized communities for producing cotton cloth began to appear in the countryside and were gradually transformed into towns. By the eighteenth century, cotton had firmly replaced hemp as the cloth of choice for most Japanese.

Not everyone benefited from the economic changes of the seventeenth and eighteenth centuries, however, notably the samurai, who were barred by tradition and prejudice from commercial activities. Although some profited from their transformation into a managerial class on the daimyo domains, most still relied on their revenues from rice lands, which were often insufficient to cover their rising expenses; consequently, they fell heavily into debt. Others were released from servitude to their lord and became "masterless samurai." Occasionally, these unemployed warriors—known as *ronin* (ROH-nihn), or "wave men"—revolted or plotted against the local authorities. In one episode, made famous in song and story as "The Forty-Seven *Ronin*," the masterless samurai of a local lord who had been forced to commit suicide by a shogunate official later assassinated the official in revenge. Although their act received wide popular acclaim, the *ronin* were later forced to take their own lives.

CHRONOLOGY	Japan and Korea During the Early Modern Era
First phonetic alphabet in Korea	Fifteenth century
Portuguese merchants arrive in Japan	1543
Francis Xavier arrives in Japan	1549
Rule of Oda Nobunaga	1568–1582
Seizure of Kyoto	1568
Rule of Toyotomi Hideyoshi	1582–1598
Edict prohibiting Christianity in Japan	1587
Japan invades Korea	1592
Death of Hideyoshi and withdrawal of the Japanese army from Korea	1598
Rule of Tokugawa Ieyasu	1598–1616
Creation of Tokugawa shogunate	1603
Dutch granted permission to trade at Nagasaki	1609
Order evicting Christian missionaries	1612
Yi dynasty of Korea declares fealty to China	1630s

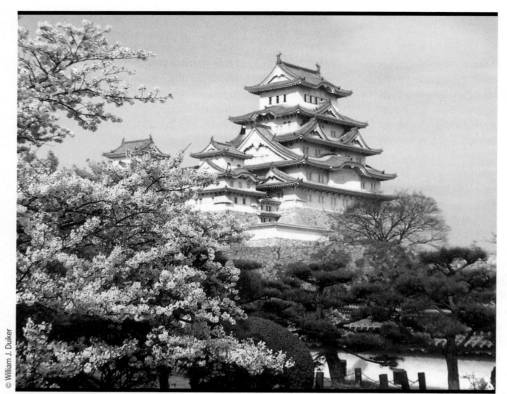

A Japanese Castle. In imitation of European castle architecture, the Japanese perfected a new type of fortress-palace in the early seventeenth century. Strategically placed high on a hilltop, constructed of heavy stone with tiny windows, and fortified by numerous watchtowers and massive walls, these strongholds were impregnable to arrows and catapults. They served as a residence for the local daimyo, while the castle compound also housed his army and contained the seat of local government. Himeji (HEE-meh-jee) Castle, shown here, is one of the most beautiful in Japan.

although the population doubled in the seventeenth century, a relatively low rate for the time period, so did the amount of cultivable land, while agricultural technology made significant advances.

The relatively low rate of population growth probably meant that Japanese peasants were spared the kind of land hunger that many of their counterparts in China faced. Recent evidence indicates that the primary reasons for the relatively low rate of population growth were late marriage, abortion, and infanticide. Honda Toshiaki (HAHN-duh toh-SHEE-ah-kee), a late-eighteenth-century demographer, described the situation:

> Aware that if they have many children they will not have any property to leave them, [husbands and wives] confer and decide that rather than rear children who in later years will have great difficulty in making a decent living, it is better to take precautions before they are born and not add another mouth to feed. If they do have a child, they secretly destroy it, calling the process by the euphemism of "thinning out."[12]

LAND PROBLEMS The effects of economic developments on the rural population during the Tokugawa era are harder to estimate. Some farm families benefited by exploiting the growing demand for cash crops. But not all prospered. Most peasants continued to rely on rice cultivation and were whipsawed between declining profits and rising costs and taxes (as daimyo expenses increased, land taxes often took up to 50 percent of the annual harvest). Many were forced to become tenants or to work as wage laborers on the farms of wealthy neighbors or in village industries. When rural conditions in some areas became desperate, peasant revolts erupted. According to one estimate, nearly seven thousand disturbances took place during the Tokugawa era. In general, though, the rural unrest was probably motivated less by a decline in the standard of living than by local factors and a new sense of peasant assertiveness. Peasant disturbances became a more or less routine means of protesting against rising taxes and official corruption or of demanding "benevolence" from the manor lord in times of natural disaster.

Some Japanese historians, influenced by a Marxist view of history, have interpreted such evidence as an indication that the Tokugawa economic system was exploitative, with feudal aristocrats oppressing powerless peasants. Recent scholars, however, have tended to adopt a more balanced view, maintaining that both agriculture and manufacturing and commerce experienced extensive growth. Some point out that

Life in the Village

The changes that took place during the Tokugawa era had a major impact on the lives of ordinary Japanese. In some respects, the result was an increase in the power of the central government at the village level. The shogunate increasingly relied on Confucian maxims advocating obedience and hierarchy to enhance its authority with the general population. Decrees from the *bakufu* instructed the peasants on all aspects of their lives, including their eating habits and their behavior (see the box on p. 499). At the same time, the increased power of the government led to more autonomy from the local daimyo for the peasants. Villages now had more control over their local affairs and were responsible to the central government as much as to the nearby manor lord, although land taxes were still paid to the daimyo.

At the same time, the Tokugawa era saw the emergence of the nuclear family (*ie*) as the basic unit in Japanese society. In previous times, Japanese peasants had few legal rights. Most were too poor to keep their conjugal family unit intact or to pass property on to their children. Many lived at the manorial residence or worked as servants in the households of more affluent villagers. Now, with farm income on the rise,

Keeping to the Straight and Narrow in Tokugawa Japan

POLITICS & GOVERNMENT

Like the Qing dynasty in China, the Tokugawa shoguns attempted to keep their subjects in line with decrees that carefully prescribed all kinds of behavior. As this decree, which was circulated in all Japanese villages, shows, the *bakufu* sought to be the moral instructor as well as the guardian and protector of the Japanese people.

Maxims for Peasant Behavior

1. Young people are forbidden to congregate in great numbers.
2. Entertainments unsuited to peasants, such as playing the samisen or reciting ballad dramas, are forbidden.
3. Staging sumo matches is forbidden for the next five years.
4. The edict on frugality issued by the *han* at the end of last year must be observed.
5. Social relations in the village must be conducted harmoniously.
6. If a person has to leave the village for business or pleasure, that person must return by ten at night.
7. Father and son are forbidden to stay overnight at another person's house. An exception is to be made if it is to nurse a sick person.
8. Corvée [obligatory labor] assigned by the *han* must be performed faithfully.
9. Children who practice filial piety must be rewarded.
10. One must never get drunk and cause trouble for others.
11. Peasants who farm especially diligently must be rewarded.
12. Peasants who neglect farm work and cultivate their paddies and upland fields in a slovenly and careless fashion must be punished.
13. The boundary lines of paddy and upland fields must not be changed arbitrarily.
14. Recognition must be accorded to peasants who contribute greatly to village political affairs.
15. Fights and quarrels are forbidden in the village.
16. The deteriorating customs and morals of the village must be rectified.
17. Peasants who are suffering from poverty must be identified and helped.
18. This village has a proud history compared to other villages, but in recent years bad times have come upon us. Everyone must rise at six in the morning, cut grass, and work hard to revitalize the village.
19. The punishments to be meted out to violators of the village code and gifts to be awarded the deserving are to be decided during the last assembly meeting of the year.

 Compare these maxims with the commandments issued by Emperor Kangxi in China, presented earlier in this chapter (see the box on p. 484). What do they indicate about the nature of politics in Tokugawa Japan?

---

the nuclear family took on the same form as in China, although without the joint family concept. The Japanese system of inheritance was based on primogeniture (pry-moh-JEN-ih-chur). Family property was passed on to the eldest son, although younger sons often received land from their parents to set up their own families after marriage.

THE ROLE OF WOMEN Another result of the changes under the Tokugawa was that women were somewhat more restricted than they had been previously. The rights of females were especially restricted in the samurai class, where Confucian values were highly influential. Male heads of households had broad authority over property, marriage, and divorce; wives were expected to obey their husbands on pain of death. Males often took concubines or homosexual partners, while females were expected to remain chaste. The male offspring of samurai parents studied the Confucian classics in schools established by the daimyo, while females were reared at home, where only the fortu-

nate might receive a rudimentary training in reading and writing Chinese characters. Some women, however, became accomplished poets and painters since, in aristocratic circles, female literacy was prized for enhancing the refinement, social graces, and moral virtue of the home. Under the Tokugawa, it was the obligation of the wife in elite families to reflect her husband's rank and status through a strict code of comportment and dress.

Women were similarly at a disadvantage among the common people. Marriages were arranged, and as in China, the new wife moved in with the family of her husband. A wife who did not meet the expectations of her spouse or his family was likely to be divorced. Still, gender relations were more egalitarian than among the nobility. Women were generally valued as childbearers and homemakers, and both sexes worked in the fields. Coeducational schools were established in villages and market towns, and about one-quarter of the students were female. Poor families, however, often put infant daughters to death or sold them into prostitution and

Evening Bell at the Clock. As woodblock prints became a popular form of pictorial expression in Tokugawa Japan, the painter Suzuki Harunobu (SOO-ZOO-kee hah-ROO-noh-boo) (ca. 1725–1770) used the technique to portray scenes of daily life in the homes of ordinary Japanese. In the print above, a Japanese woman dries herself with a towel, while her companion looks up at a chiming clock on the dresser.

the "floating world" of entertainment (see "The Literature of the New Middle Class" later in this chapter). During the late Tokugawa era, peasant women became more outspoken and active in social protests and in some cases played a major role in provoking demonstrations against government exactions or exploitation by landlords or merchants.

Such attitudes toward women operated within the context of the increasingly rigid stratification of Japanese society. Deeply conservative in their social policies, the Tokugawa rulers established strict legal distinctions between the four main classes in Japan (warriors, artisans, peasants, and merchants). Intermarriage between classes was forbidden in theory, although sometimes the prohibitions were ignored in practice. Below these classes were Japan's outcasts, the *eta* (AY-tuh). Formerly, they were permitted to escape their status, at least in theory. The Tokugawa made their status hereditary and enacted severe discriminatory laws against them, regulating their place of residence, their dress, and even their hairstyles.

Tokugawa Culture

Under the Tokugawa, the tensions between the old society and the emerging new one were starkly reflected in the arena of culture. On the one hand, the classical culture, influenced by Confucian themes, Buddhist quietism, and the samurai warrior tradition, continued to flourish under the patronage of the shogunate. On the other, a vital new set of cultural values began to appear, especially in the cities. This innovative era witnessed the rise of popular literature written by and for the townspeople. With the development of woodblock printing in the early seventeenth century, literature became available to the common people, literacy levels rose, and lending libraries increased the accessibility of printed works. In contrast to the previous mood of doom and gloom, the new prose was cheerful and even frivolous, its primary aim being to divert and amuse.

THE LITERATURE OF THE NEW MIDDLE CLASS The best examples of this new urban fiction are the works of Saikaku (SY-kah-koo) (1642–1693), considered one of Japan's finest novelists. Saikaku's greatest novel, *Five Women Who Loved Love*, relates the amorous exploits of five women of the merchant class. Based partly on real-life experiences, it broke from the Confucian ethic that stressed a wife's fidelity to her husband and portrayed women who were willing to die for love—and all but one eventually did. Despite the tragic circumstances, the tone of the novel is upbeat and sometimes comic, and the author's wry comments prevent the reader from becoming emotionally involved with the heroines' misfortunes. In addition to heterosexual novels for the merchant class, Saikaku also wrote of homosexual liaisons among the samurai.

In the theater, the rise of Kabuki (kuh-BOO-kee) threatened the long dominance of the *No* (NOH) play, replacing the somewhat restrained and elegant thematic and stylistic approach of the classical drama with a new emphasis on violence, music, and dramatic gestures. Significantly, the new drama emerged not from the rarefied world of the court but from the new world of entertainment and amusement (see the comparative illustration on p. 501). Its very commercial success, however, led to difficulties with the government, which periodically attempted to restrict or even suppress it. Early Kabuki was often performed by prostitutes, and shogunate officials, fearing that such activities could have a corrupting effect on the nation's morals, prohibited women from appearing on the stage; at the same time, they attempted to create a new professional class of male actors to impersonate female characters on stage. The decree had a mixed effect, however, because it encouraged homosexual activities, which had been popular among the samurai and in Buddhist monasteries since medieval times. Yet the use of male actors also promoted a greater emphasis on physical activities such as acrobatics and swordplay and furthered the evolution of Kabuki into a mature dramatic art.

In contrast to the popular literature of the Tokugawa period, poetry persevered in its more serious tradition. Although linked verse, so popular in the fourteenth and fifteenth centuries, found a more lighthearted expression in the sixteenth century, the most exquisite poetry was produced in the seventeenth century by the greatest of all Japanese poets, Basho (BAH-shoh) (1644–1694). He was concerned with the

COMPARATIVE ILLUSTRATION

FAMILY & SOCIETY

Popular Culture: East and West. By the seventeenth century, a popular culture distinct from the elite culture of the nobility was beginning to emerge in the urban worlds of both the East and the West. At the top is a festival scene from the pleasure district of Kyoto known as the Gion. Spectators on a balcony are enjoying a colorful parade of floats and costumed performers. The festival originated as a celebration of the passing of a deadly epidemic in medieval Japan. On the right below is a scene from the celebration of Carnival on the Piazza Sante Croce in Florence, Italy. Carnival was a period of festivities before Lent, celebrated primarily in Roman Catholic countries. It became an occasion for indulgence in food, drink, games, and practical jokes as a prelude to the austerity of the forty-day Lenten season from Ash Wednesday to Easter.

 Do festivals such as these still exist in our own day? What purpose might they serve?

---

search for the meaning of existence and the poetic expression of his experience. Basho's genius lies in his sudden juxtaposition of a general or eternal condition with an immediate perception, a spark that instantly reveals a moment of truth. Thanks to his love of Daoism and Zen Buddhism, Basho found answers to his quest for the meaning of life in nature, and his poems are grounded in seasonal imagery. The following are among his most famous poems:

> *The ancient pond*
> *A frog leaps in*
> *The sound of the water.*

> *On the withered branch*
> *A crow has alighted—*
> *The end of autumn.*

His last poem, dictated to a disciple only three days before his death, succinctly expressed his frustration with the unfinished business of life:

> *On a journey, ailing—*
> *my dreams roam about*
> *on a withered moor.*

Like all great artists, Basho made his poems seem effortless and simple. He speaks directly to everyone, everywhere.

TOKUGAWA ART Art also reflected the dynamism and changes in Japanese culture under the Tokugawa regime. The shogun's order that all daimyo and their families live every other year in Edo set off a burst of building as provincial rulers competed to erect the most magnificent mansion.

One of the *Fifty-Three Stations of the Tokaido Road*. This block print by the famous Japanese artist Ando Hiroshige shows the movement of goods along the main trunk road stretching along the east coast from Kyoto to Edo in mid-nineteenth-century Japan. With gentle humor, in a series of color prints Hiroshige portrayed the customs of travelers passing through various post stations along the road. These romantic and somewhat fanciful scenes, very popular at the time, evoke an idyllic past, filling today's viewer with nostalgia for the old Japan.

Furthermore, the shoguns themselves constructed splendid castles adorned with sumptuous, almost ostentatious decor and furnishings. And the prosperity of the newly rising merchant class added fuel to the fire. Japanese paintings, architecture, textiles, and ceramics all flourished during this affluent era.

Court painters filled magnificent multipaneled screens with gold foil, which was also used to cover walls and even ceilings. This lavish use of gold foil mirrored the grandeur of the new Japanese rulers but also served a practical purpose: it reflected light in the dark castle rooms, where windows were kept small for defensive purposes. In contrast to the almost gaudy splendors of court painting, however, some Japanese artists of the late sixteenth century returned to the tradition of black ink wash. No longer copying the Chinese, these masterpieces expressed Japanese themes and techniques. In *Pine Forest* by Tohaku (toh-HAH-koo), a pair of six-panel screens depicting pine trees, 85 percent of the paper is left blank, suggesting mist and the quiet of an autumn dawn.

Although Japan was isolated from the Western world during much of the Tokugawa era, Japanese art was enriched by ideas from other cultures. Japanese pottery makers borrowed both techniques and designs from Korea to produce handsome ceramics. The passion for "Dutch learning" inspired Japanese to study Western medicine, astronomy, and languages and also led to experimentation with oil painting and Western ideas of perspective and the interplay of light and dark. Some painters depicted the "southern barbarians," with

their strange ships and costumes, large noses, and plumed hats. Europeans desired Japanese lacquerware and metalwork, inlaid with ivory and mother-of-pearl, and especially the ceramics, which were now as highly prized as those of the Chinese.

Perhaps the most famous of all Japanese art of the Tokugawa era is the woodblock print. Genre painting, or representations of daily life, began in the sixteenth century and found its new mass-produced form in the eighteenth-century woodblock print. The now literate mercantile class was eager for illustrated texts of the amusing and bawdy tales that had circulated in oral tradition. At first, these prints were done in black and white, but later they included vibrant colors. The self-confidence of the age is dramatically captured in these prints, which represent a collective self-portrait of the late Tokugawa urban classes. Some prints depict entire city blocks filled with people, trades, and festivals, while others show the interiors of houses; thus, they provide us with excellent visual documentation of the times. Others portray the "floating world" of the entertainment quarter, with scenes of carefree revelers enjoying the pleasures of life.

One of the most renowned of the numerous block-print artists was Utamaro (OO-tah-mah-roh) (1754–1806), who painted erotic and sardonic women in everyday poses, such as walking down the street, cooking, or drying their bodies after a bath. Hokusai (HOH-kuh-sy) (1760–1849) was famous for *Thirty-Six Views of Mount Fuji*, a new and bold interpretation of the Japanese landscape. Finally, Ando Hiroshige

(AHN-doh hee-roh-SHEE-gay) (1797–1858) developed the genre of the travelogue print in his *Fifty-Three Stations of the Tokaido Road*, which presented ordinary scenes of daily life, both in the country and in the cities, all enveloped in a lyrical, quiet mood.

Why did a new popular culture begin to appear in Tokugawa Japan while traditional values continued to prevail in neighboring China? One factor was the rapid growth of the cities as the main point of convergence for all the dynamic forces taking place in Japanese society. But other factors may have been at work as well. Despite the patent efforts of the Tokugawa rulers to promote traditional Confucian values, Confucian doctrine had historically occupied a relatively weak position in Japanese society. In China, the scholar-gentry class served as the defenders and propagators of traditional orthodoxy, but the samurai, who were steeped in warrior values and had little exposure to Confucian learning, did not play a similar role in Japan. Tokugawa policies also contributed. Whereas the scholar-gentry class in Qing China continued to reside in the villages, serving as members of the local council or as instructors in local schools, the samurai class in Japan was deliberately isolated from the remainder of the population by government fiat and class privilege. The result was an ideological and cultural vacuum that would eventually be filled by the growing population of merchants and artisans in the major cities.

Korea and Vietnam

 FOCUS QUESTION: To what degree did developments in Korea during this period reflect conditions in China and Japan? What were the unique aspects of Vietnamese civilization?

On the fringes of the East Asian mainland, two of China's close neighbors sought to preserve their fragile independence from the expansionistic tendencies of the powerful Ming and Qing dynasties.

Korea: In a Dangerous Neighborhood

While Japan under the Tokugawa shogunate moved steadily out from the shadows of the Chinese Empire by creating a unique society with its own special characteristics, the Yi (YEE) dynasty in Korea continued to pattern itself, at least on the surface, after the Chinese model. The dynasty had been founded by the military commander Yi Song Gye (YEE song yee) in the late fourteenth century and immediately set out to establish close political and cultural relations with the Ming dynasty. From their new capital at Seoul (SOHL), located on the Han (HAHN) River in the center of the peninsula, the Yi rulers accepted a tributary relationship with their powerful neighbor and engaged in the wholesale adoption of Chinese institutions and values. As in China, the civil service examinations tested candidates on their knowledge of the Confucian classics, and success was viewed as an essential step toward upward mobility.

There were differences, however. As in Japan, the dynasty continued to restrict entry into the bureaucracy to members of the aristocratic class, known in Korea as the **yangban** (YAHNG-ban) (or "two groups," civilian and military). At the same time, the peasantry remained in serflike conditions, working on government estates or on the manor holdings of the landed elite. A class of slaves, called **chonmin** (CHAWN-min), labored on government plantations or served in certain occupations, such as butchers and entertainers, considered beneath the dignity of other groups in the population.

Eventually, Korean society began to show signs of independence from Chinese orthodoxy. In the fifteenth century, a phonetic alphabet for writing the Korean spoken language (*hangul*) was devised. Although it was initially held in contempt by the elites and used primarily as a teaching device, eventually it became the medium for private correspondence and the publishing of fiction for a popular audience. At the same time, changes were taking place in the economy, where rising agricultural production contributed to a population increase and the appearance of a small urban industrial and commercial sector, and in society, where the long domination of the *yangban* class began to weaken. As their numbers increased and their power and influence declined, some *yangban* became merchants or even moved into the ranks of the peasantry, further blurring the distinction between the aristocratic class and the common people.

Meanwhile, the Yi dynasty faced continual challenges to its independence from its neighbors. Throughout much of the sixteenth century, the main threat came from the north, where Manchu forces harassed Korean lands just south of the Yalu (YAH-loo) River (see Map 17.3 on p. 494). By the 1580s, however, the larger threat came from the east in the form of a newly united Japan. During much of the sixteenth century, leading Japanese daimyo had been involved in a protracted civil war, as Oda Nobunaga, Toyotomi Hideyoshi, and Tokugawa Ieyasu strove to solidify their control over the islands. Of the three, only Hideyoshi lusted for an empire beyond the seas. Although born to a commoner family, he harbored visions of grandeur and in the late 1580s announced plans to attack the Ming Empire (see the box on p. 504). When the Korean king Sonjo (SOHN-joe) (1567–1608) refused Hideyoshi's offer of an alliance, in 1592 the latter launched an invasion of the Korean peninsula.

At first the campaign went well, and Japanese forces, wreaking death and devastation throughout the countryside, advanced as far as the Korean capital at Seoul. But eventually the Koreans, under the inspired leadership of the military commander Yi Sunshin (YEE-soon-SHIN) (1545–1598), who designed fast but heavily armed ships that could destroy the more cumbersome landing craft of the invading forces, managed to repel the attack and safeguard their independence. The respite was brief, however. By the 1630s, a new threat from the Manchus had emerged from across the northern border. A Manchu force invaded northern Korea in the 1630s and eventually compelled the Yi dynasty to promise allegiance to the new imperial government in Beijing. Korea was relatively untouched by the arrival of European merchants and missionaries, although information about Christianity

Be My Brother, or I'll Bash Your Head In!

INTERACTION & EXCHANGE

In 1590, Toyotomi Hideyoshi defeated the last of his enemies and brought the islands of Japan under his rule. Shortly thereafter, an emissary from the Yi dynasty in Korea presented him with a letter congratulating him on his success. In his reply, presented here, Hideyoshi disclosed his plan to conquer the Chinese mainland and bring all of East Asia under his control. In a thinly veiled warning, which disclosed his megalomaniacal ambition, he demanded that the Yi ruler support his forthcoming attack on China. If not, he declared, Japan would exact terrible revenge. But the Korean king was more fearful of his powerful neighbor to the west and rejected Hideyoshi's demand for an alliance with Japan. Thereupon Hideyoshi attacked Korea in the so-called Imjin (IM-jin) War (1592–1598), which caused tremendous hardship throughout the peninsula.

Hideyoshi, Imperial Regent of Japan, to His Excellency the King of Korea

I read your epistle from afar with pleasure, opening and closing the scroll again and again to savor the aroma of your distinguished presence.

Now, then: This empire is composed of more than sixty provinces, but for years the country was divided, the polity disturbed, civility abandoned, and the realm unresponsive to imperial rule. Unable to stifle my indignation at this, I subjugated the rebels and struck down the bandits within the span of three or four years. As far away as foreign regions and distant islands, all is now in my grasp.

As I privately consider the facts of my background, I recognize it to be that of a rustic and unrefined minor retainer. Nevertheless: As I was about to be conceived, my dear mother dreamt that the wheel of the sun had entered her womb. The diviner declared, "As far as the sun shines, so will the brilliance of his rule extend. When he reaches his prime, the Eight Directions will be enlightened through his benevolence and the Four Seas replete with the glory of his name. How could anyone doubt this?" As a result of this miracle, anyone who turned against me was automatically crushed. Whomever I fought, I never failed to conquer. Now that the realm has been thoroughly pacified, I caress and nourish the people, solacing the orphaned and the desolate. Hence my subjects live in plenty and the revenue produced by the land has increased ten-thousand-fold over the past. Since this empire originated, never has the imperial court seen such prosperity or the capital city such grandeur as now.

Man born on this earth, though he live to a ripe old age, will as a rule not reach a hundred years. Why should I rest, then, grumbling in frustration, where I am? Disregarding the distance of the sea and mountain reaches that lie in between, I shall in one fell swoop invade Great Ming. I have in mind to introduce Japanese customs and values to the four hundred and more provinces of that country and bestow upon it the benefits of imperial rule and culture for the coming hundred million years.

Your esteemed country has done well to make haste in attending on our court. Where there is farsightedness, grief does not come near. Those who lag behind [in offering homage], however, will not be granted pardon, even if this is a distant land of little islands lying in the sea. When the day comes for my invasion of Great Ming and I lead my troops to the staging area, that will be the time to make our neighborly relations flourish all the more. I have no other desire but to spread my fame throughout the Three Countries, this and no more.

I have received your regional products as itemized. Stay healthy and take care.

Hideyoshi
Imperial Regent of Japan

 How did Hideyoshi justify his ambitious plan to bring all of eastern Asia under his control?

---

was brought to the peninsula by Koreans returning from tribute missions to China, and a small Catholic community was established there in the late eighteenth century.

Vietnam: The Perils of Empire

Vietnam—or Dai Viet (dy VEE-et), as it was known at the time—managed to avoid the fate of many of its neighbors during the seventeenth and eighteenth centuries. Isolated from the major maritime routes that passed through the region, the country was only peripherally involved in the spice trade with the West and did not suffer the humiliation of losing territory to European colonial powers. In fact, Dai Viet had followed an imperialist path of its own, defeating the trading state of Champa to the south in 1471 and imposing its suzerainty over the rump of the old Angkor empire—today known as Cambodia. The state of Dai Viet then extended from the Chinese border to the shores of the Gulf of Siam.

But expansion undermined the cultural integrity of traditional Vietnamese society, as those migrants who settled in the marshy Mekong River delta developed a "frontier spirit" far removed from the communal values long practiced in the old national heartland of the Red River valley. By the

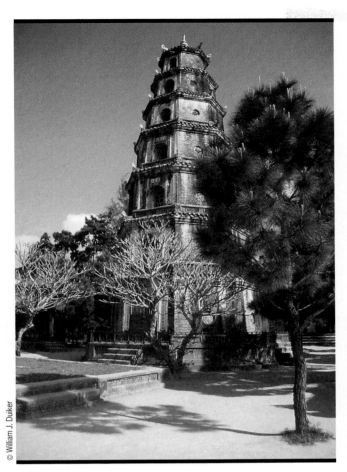

© William J. Duiker

seventeenth century, a civil war had split Dai Viet into two squabbling territories in the north and south, providing European powers with the opportunity to meddle in the country's internal affairs to their own benefit. In 1802, with the assistance of a French adventurer long active in the region, a member of the southern royal family managed to reunite the country under the new Nguyen (NGWEN) dynasty, which lasted until 1945.

To placate China, the country was renamed Vietnam (South Viet), and the new imperial capital was placed in the city of Hué (HWAY), a small river port roughly equidistant from the two rich river valleys that provided the country with its chief sustenance, wet rice. The founder of the new dynasty, who took the reign title of Gia Long, fended off French efforts to promote Christianity among his subjects and sought to promote traditional Confucian values among an increasingly diverse population.

The Thien Mu Pagoda in Hué. When the Nguyen dynasty came to power in Vietnam in 1802, it sought to bolster its legitimacy among the population by adhering to a highly traditional form of Confucian orthodoxy. The most visible manifestation of this policy was the new imperial palace at Hué, modeled after its counterpart in Beijing. In 1968, the palace complex was heavily damaged by the fighting between U.S. and North Vietnamese forces during the Tet offensive. It is now being restored as a national landmark. Adjacent to the palace is the beautiful Thien Mu pagoda, on the banks of the Perfume River. Shown here, the pagoda attests to the continuing influence of Buddhist beliefs in Vietnamese society.

CHAPTER SUMMARY

When Christopher Columbus sailed from southern Spain in his three ships in August 1492, he was seeking a route to China and Japan. He did not find it, but others eventually did. In 1514, Portuguese ships arrived on the coast of southern China. Thirty years later, a small contingent of Portuguese merchants became the first Europeans to set foot on the islands of Japan.

At first, the new arrivals were welcomed, if only as curiosities. Eventually, several European nations established trade relations with China and Japan, and Christian missionaries of various religious orders were active in both countries and in Korea as well. But their success was short-lived. Europeans eventually began to be perceived as detrimental to law and order, and during the seventeenth century, the majority of the foreign merchants and missionaries were

evicted from all three countries. From that time until the middle of the nineteenth century, China, Japan, and Korea were relatively little affected by events taking place beyond their borders.

That fact led many observers to assume that the societies of East Asia were essentially stagnant, characterized by agrarian institutions and values reminiscent of those of the feudal era in Europe. As we have seen, however, that picture is misleading, for all three countries were evolving and by the early nineteenth century were quite different from what they had been three centuries earlier.

Ironically, these changes were especially marked in Tokugawa Japan, a seemingly "closed" country, but one where traditional classes and institutions were under increasing strain, not only from the emergence of a new merchant class but also from the centralizing tendencies of the powerful Tokugawa shogunate. On the mainland as well, the popular image in the West of a "changeless China" was increasingly divorced from reality, as social and economic conditions were marked by a growing complexity, giving birth to tensions that by the middle of the nineteenth century would strain the Qing dynasty to its very core.

By the beginning of the nineteenth century, then, powerful tensions, reflecting a growing gap between the ideal and reality, were at work in Chinese and Japanese society. Under these conditions, both countries were soon forced to face a new challenge from the aggressive power of an industrializing Europe.

CHAPTER TIMELINE

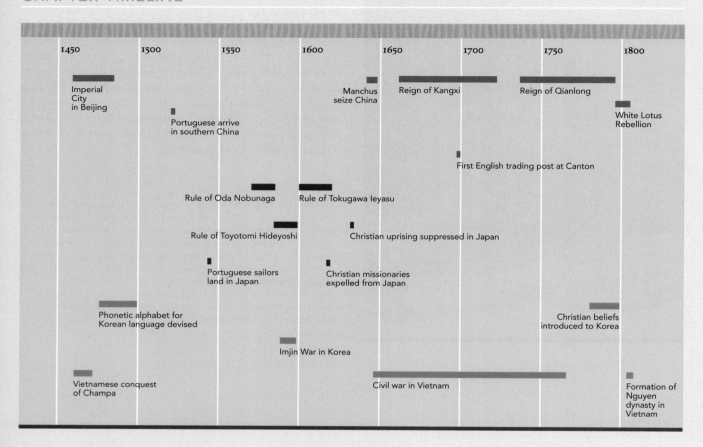

CHAPTER REVIEW

Upon Reflection

Q What factors at the end of the eighteenth century might have served to promote or to impede China's transition to an advanced industrial and market economy? Which factors do you think were the most important? Why?

Q Some historians have declared that during the Tokugawa era the Japanese government essentially sought to close the country to all forms of outside influence. Is that claim justified? Why or why not?

Q What was the nature of Sino-Korean relations during the early modern era? How did they compare with Chinese policies toward Vietnam?

Key Terms

banners (p. 483)
dyarchy (p. 483)

kowtow (p. 484)
fudai **daimyo** (p. 496)
tozama **daimyo** (p. 496)
ronin (p. 497)
yangban (p. 503)
chonmin (p. 503)

Suggested Reading

CHINA UNDER THE MING AND QING DYNASTIES Reliable surveys with a readable text are **T. Brook**, *The Troubled Empire: China in the Yuan and Ming Dynasties* (Cambridge, Mass., 2010), and **W. Rowe**, *China's Last Empire: Great Qing* (Cambridge, Mass., 2009). For fascinating vignettes of Chinese social conditions, see **J. Spence**, *Return to Dragon Mountain: Memories of a Late Ming Man* (New York, 2007) and *Treason by the Book* (New York, 2001).

L. Brockey, *Journey to the East: The Jesuit Mission to China, 1579–1724* (Cambridge, Mass., 2007), is an account of China's first encounter with Europe. For a defense of Chinese science, see **B. Elman**, *On Their*

Own Terms: Science in China, 1550–1900 (Cambridge, Mass., 2005). **J. E. Wills Jr.**, *Mountains of Fame: Portraits in Chinese History* (Princeton, N.J., 1994), is an interesting collection of biographies from across the gamut of Chinese history.

CHINESE LITERATURE AND ART   The best surveys of Chinese literature are **S. Owen**, *An Anthology of Chinese Literature: Beginnings to 1911* (New York, 1996), and **V. Mair**, *The Columbia Anthology of Traditional Chinese Literature* (New York, 1994). For a comprehensive introduction to the Chinese art of this period, see **M. Sullivan**, *The Arts of China*, 4th ed. (Berkeley, Calif., 1999), and **C. Clunas**, *Art in China* (Oxford, 1997). For the best introduction to the painting of this era, see **J. Cahill**, *Chinese Painting* (New York, 1977).

JAPAN AND KOREA   **C. Totman**, *A History of Japan,* 2nd ed. (Cambridge, Mass., 2005), is a reliable survey of Japanese history. For a more detailed analysis, see **J. W. Hall, ed.,** *The Cambridge History of Japan,* vol. 4 (Cambridge, 1991). Social issues are explored in **W. Farris,** *Japan's Medieval Population* (Honolulu, 2006). **B. Bodart-Baily,** *Kaempfer's Japan: Tokugawa Culture Observed* (Honolulu, 1999), is a first-hand account by a Western visitor to Tokugawa Japan. On Korea, see **M. Seth,** *A Concise History of Korea: From the Neolithic Period Through the Nineteenth Century* (Lanham, Md., 2006).

WOMEN IN CHINA AND JAPAN   For a brief introduction to women in the Ming and Qing dynasties as well as the Tokugawa era, see

S. Hughes and **B. Hughes,** *Women in World History,* vol. 2 (Armonk, N.Y., 1997), and **S. Mann** and **Y. Cheng, eds.,** *Under Confucian Eyes: Writings on Gender in Chinese History* (Berkeley, Calif., 2001). Also see **D. Ko, J. K. Haboush,** and **J. R. Piggott, eds.,** *Women and Confucian Culture in Premodern China, Korea, and Japan* (Berkeley, Calif., 2003). On women's literacy in seventeenth-century China, see **D. Ko,** *Teachers of the Inner Chambers: Women and Culture in Seventeenth-Century China* (Stanford, Calif., 1994). Most valuable is the collection of articles edited by **G. L. Bernstein,** *Re-Creating Japanese Women, 1600–1945* (Berkeley, Calif., 1991).

JAPANESE LITERATURE AND ART   Of specific interest on Japanese literature of the Tokugawa era is **D. Keene,** *World Within Walls: Japanese Literature of the Pre-Modern Era, 1600–1867* (New York, 1976). For the most comprehensive and accessible overview of Japanese art, see **P. Mason,** *Japanese Art* (New York, 1993).

CourseMate

Go to the CourseMate website at **www.cengagebrain.com** for additional study tools and review materials—including audio and video clips—for this chapter.

CHAPTER
18

The West on the Eve of a New World Order

The storming of the Bastille

© The Art Archive/Marc Charmet

CHAPTER OUTLINE
AND FOCUS QUESTIONS

Toward a New Heaven and a New Earth: An Intellectual Revolution in the West

Q   Who were the leading figures of the Scientific Revolution and the Enlightenment, and what were their main contributions?

Economic Changes and the Social Order

Q   What changes occurred in the European economy in the eighteenth century, and to what degree were these changes reflected in social patterns?

Colonial Empires and Revolution in the Americas

Q   What colonies did the British and French establish in the Americas, and how did their methods of administering their colonies differ?

Toward a New Political Order and Global Conflict

Q   What do historians mean by the term *enlightened absolutism*, and to what degree did eighteenth-century Prussia, Austria, and Russia exhibit its characteristics?

The French Revolution

Q   What were the causes, the main events, and the results of the French Revolution?

The Age of Napoleon

Q   Which aspects of the French Revolution did Napoleon preserve, and which did he destroy?

CRITICAL THINKING

Q   In what ways were the American Revolution, the French Revolution, and the seventeenth-century English revolutions alike? In what ways were they different?

IN PARIS ON THE MORNING of July 14, 1789, a mob of eight thousand men and women in search of weapons streamed toward the Bastille (bass-STEEL), a royal armory filled with arms and ammunition. The Bastille was also a state prison, and although it held only seven prisoners at the time, in the eyes of these angry Parisians, it was a glaring symbol of the government's despotic policies. The armory was defended by the marquis de Launay (mar-KEE duh loh-NAY) and a small garrison of 114 men. The attack began in earnest in the early afternoon, and after three hours of fighting, de Launay and the garrison surrendered. Angered by the loss of ninety-eight of their members, the victorious mob beat de Launay to death, cut off his head, and carried it aloft in triumph through the streets. When King Louis XVI was told the news of the fall of the Bastille by the duc de La Rochefoucauld-Liancourt (dook duh lah-RUSH-foo-koh-lee-ahn-KOOR), he exclaimed, "Why, this is a revolt." "No, Sire," replied the duc. "It is a revolution."

The French Revolution of 1789 was a key factor in the emergence of a new world order. Historians have often considered the eighteenth century the final phase of an old Europe that would be forever changed by the violent upheaval and reordering of society associated with the French Revolution. Before the Revolution, the old order—still largely agrarian, dominated by kings and landed aristocrats, and grounded in privileges for nobles, clergy, towns, and provinces—seemed content to continue a basic pattern that had prevailed since medieval times. As the century drew to a close, however, a new intellectual ethos based on rationalism and secularism emerged, and demographic, economic, social, and political patterns were beginning to change in ways that proclaimed the arrival of a new and more modern order.

The French Revolution demolished the institutions of the old regime and established a new order based on individual rights, representative institutions, and a concept of loyalty to the nation rather than to the monarch. The revolutionary upheavals of the era, especially in France, gave rise to new liberal and national political ideals, summarized in the French revolutionary slogan "Liberty! Equality! Fraternity!" that transformed France and then spread to other European countries and the rest of the world.

Toward a New Heaven and a New Earth: An Intellectual Revolution in the West

Q FOCUS QUESTION: Who were the leading figures of the Scientific Revolution and the Enlightenment, and what were their main contributions?

In the seventeenth century, a group of scientists set the Western world on a new path known as the **Scientific Revolution**, which brought to Europeans a new way of viewing the universe and their place in it. The Scientific Revolution affected only a small number of Europe's educated elite. But in the eighteenth century, this changed dramatically as a group of intellectuals popularized the ideas of the Scientific Revolution and used them to undertake a dramatic reexamination of all aspects of life. The widespread impact of these ideas on their society has caused historians ever since to call the eighteenth century in Europe the Age of Enlightenment.

The Scientific Revolution

The Scientific Revolution ultimately challenged conceptions and beliefs about the nature of the external world that had become dominant by the Late Middle Ages.

TOWARD A NEW HEAVEN: A REVOLUTION IN ASTRONOMY
The philosophers of the Middle Ages had used the ideas of Aristotle, Ptolemy (the greatest astronomer of antiquity, who lived in the second century C.E.), and Christianity to form the Ptolemaic (tahl-uh-MAY-ik) or **geocentric theory** of the universe. In this conception, the universe was seen as a series of concentric spheres with a fixed or motionless earth at its center. Composed of material substance, the earth was imperfect and constantly changing. The spheres that surrounded the earth were made of a crystalline, transparent substance and moved in circular orbits around the earth. The heavenly bodies, which in 1500 were believed to number ten, were

pure orbs of light, embedded in the moving, concentric spheres. Working outward from the earth, the first eight spheres contained the moon, Mercury, Venus, the sun, Mars, Jupiter, Saturn, and the fixed stars. The ninth sphere imparted to the eighth sphere of the fixed stars its daily motion, while the tenth sphere was frequently described as the prime mover that moved itself and imparted motion to the other spheres. Beyond the tenth sphere was the Empyrean Heaven—the location of God and all the saved souls. Thus, God and the saved souls were at one end of the universe, and humans were at the center. They had power over the earth, but their real purpose was to achieve salvation.

Nicolaus Copernicus (NEE-koh-lowss kuh-PURR-nuh-kuss) (1473–1543), a native of Poland, was a mathematician who felt that Ptolemy's geocentric system failed to accord with the observed motions of the heavenly bodies and hoped that his **heliocentric** (sun-centered) **theory** would offer a more accurate explanation. Copernicus argued that the sun was motionless at the center of the universe. The planets revolved around the sun in the order of Mercury, Venus, the earth, Mars, Jupiter, and Saturn. The moon, however, revolved around the earth. Moreover, what appeared to be the movement of the sun around the earth was really explained by the daily rotation of the earth on its axis and the journey of the earth around the sun each year. But Copernicus did not reject the idea that the heavenly spheres moved in circular orbits.

The next step in destroying the geocentric conception and supporting the Copernican system was taken by Johannes Kepler (yoh-HAHN-us KEP-lur) (1571–1630). A brilliant German mathematician and astronomer, Kepler arrived at laws of planetary motion that confirmed Copernicus's heliocentric theory. In his first law, however, he contradicted Copernicus by showing that the orbits of the planets around the sun were not circular but elliptical, with the sun at one focus of the ellipse rather than at the center.

Kepler's work destroyed the basic structure of the Ptolemaic system. People could now think in new terms of the actual paths of planets revolving around the sun in elliptical orbits. But important questions remained unanswered. For example, what were the planets made of? An Italian scientist achieved the next important breakthrough to a new cosmology by answering that question.

Galileo Galilei (gal-li-LAY-oh GAL-li-lay) (1564–1642) taught mathematics and was the first European to make systematic observations of the heavens by means of a telescope, inaugurating a new age in astronomy. Galileo turned his telescope to the skies and made a remarkable series of discoveries: mountains on the moon, four moons revolving around Jupiter, and sunspots. Galileo's observations seemed to destroy yet another aspect of the traditional cosmology in that the universe seemed to be composed of material similar to that of earth rather than a perfect and unchanging substance.

Galileo's revelations, published in *The Starry Messenger* in 1610, made Europeans aware of a new picture of the universe. But the Catholic Church condemned Copernicanism and ordered Galileo to abandon the Copernican thesis. The church attacked the Copernican system because it threatened

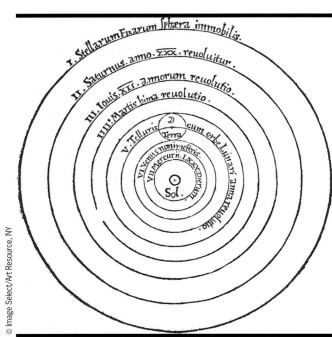

Medieval Conception of the Universe. As this sixteenth-century illustration shows, the medieval cosmological view placed the earth at the center of the universe, surrounded by a series of concentric spheres. The earth was imperfect and constantly changing, whereas the heavenly bodies that surrounded it were perfect and incorruptible. Beyond the tenth and final sphere was heaven, where God and all the saved souls were located. (The circles read, from the center outward: 1. Moon, 2. Mercury, 3. Venus, 4. Sun, 5. Mars, 6. Jupiter, 7. Saturn, 8. Firmament (of the Stars), 9. Crystalline Sphere, 10. Prime Mover; and around the outside, Empyrean Heaven—Home of God and All the Elect, that is, saved souls.)

The Copernican System. The Copernican system was presented in *On the Revolutions of the Heavenly Spheres*, published shortly before Copernicus's death. As shown in this illustration from the first edition of the book, Copernicus maintained that the sun was the center of the universe and that the planets, including the earth, revolved around it. Moreover, the earth rotated daily on its axis. (The circles read, from the center outward: Sun; VII. Mercury, orbit of 80 days; VI. Venus; V. Earth, with the moon, orbit of one year; IIII. Mars, orbit of 2 years; III. Jupiter, orbit of 12 years; II. Saturn, orbit of 30 years; I. Immobile Sphere of the Fixed Stars.)

not only Scripture but also an entire conception of the universe. The heavens were no longer a spiritual world but a world of matter.

By the 1630s and 1640s, most astronomers had come to accept the new heliocentric conception of the universe. Nevertheless, no one yet had explained motion in the universe and tied together the ideas of Copernicus, Galileo, and Kepler. This would be the work of an Englishman who has long been considered the greatest genius of the Scientific Revolution.

Isaac Newton (1642–1727) taught at Cambridge University, where he wrote his major work, *Mathematical Principles of Natural Philosophy*, known simply as the *Principia* (prin-SIP-ee-uh) by the first word of its Latin title. In the first book of the *Principia*, Newton defined the three laws of motion that govern the planetary bodies, as well as objects on earth. Crucial to his whole argument was the universal law of gravitation, which explained why the planetary bodies did not go off in straight lines but continued in elliptical orbits about the sun. In mathematical terms, Newton explained that every object in the universe is attracted to every other object by a force called gravity.

Newton had demonstrated that one mathematically proven universal law could explain all motion in the universe. At the same time, the Newtonian synthesis created a new cosmology in which the universe was seen as one huge, regulated machine that operated according to natural laws in absolute time, space, and motion. Newton's **world-machine** concept dominated the modern worldview until the twentieth century, when Albert Einstein's concept of relativity created a new picture of the universe.

TOWARD A NEW EARTH: DESCARTES AND RATIONALISM
The new conception of the universe contained in the cosmological revolution of the sixteenth and seventeenth centuries inevitably had an impact on the Western view of humankind. Nowhere is this more evident than in the work of the French philosopher René Descartes (ruh-NAY day-KART) (1596–1650). The starting point for Descartes's new system was doubt. As Descartes explained at the beginning of his most famous work, *Discourse on Method*, written in 1637, he decided to set aside all that he had learned and begin again. One fact seemed to Descartes beyond doubt—his own existence:

> I immediately became aware that while I was thus disposed to think that all was false, it was absolutely necessary that I who thus thought should be something; and noting that this truth *I think, therefore I am,* was so steadfast and so assured that the suppositions of the skeptics, to whatever extreme they might all be carried, could not avail to shake it, I concluded that I might without scruple accept it as being the first principle of the philosophy I was seeking.[1]

With this emphasis on the mind, Descartes asserted that he would accept only things that his reason said were true.

From his first postulate, Descartes deduced an additional principle, the separation of mind and matter. Descartes argued that since "the mind cannot be doubted but the body and material world can, the two must be radically different." From this came an absolute dualism between mind and matter, or what has also been called **Cartesian dualism**. Using mind or human reason and its best instrument, mathematics, humans can understand the material world because it is pure mechanism, a machine that is governed by its own physical laws because it was created by God—the great geometrician.

Descartes's separation of mind and matter allowed scientists to view matter as dead or inert, as something that was totally separate from themselves and could be investigated independently by reason. The split between mind and body led Westerners to equate their identity with mind and reason rather than with the whole organism. Descartes has rightly been called the father of modern **rationalism**.

EUROPE, CHINA, AND SCIENTIFIC REVOLUTIONS An interesting question that arises is why the Scientific Revolution occurred in Europe and not in China. In the Middle Ages, China had been the most technologically advanced civilization in the world. After 1500, that distinction passed to the West (see the comparative essay "The Scientific Revolution" on p. 512). Historians are not sure why. Some have contrasted the sense of order in Chinese society with the competitive spirit existing in Europe. Others have emphasized China's ideological viewpoint that favored living in harmony with nature rather than trying to dominate it. One historian has even suggested that China's civil service system drew the "best and the brightest" into government service, to the detriment of other occupations.

Background to the Enlightenment

The impetus for political and social change in the eighteenth century stemmed in part from the **Enlightenment**. The Enlightenment was a movement of intellectuals who were greatly impressed with the accomplishments of the Scientific Revolution. When they used the word *reason*—one of their favorite words—they were advocating the application of the **scientific method** to the understanding of all life. All institutions and all systems of thought were subject to the rational, scientific way of thinking if people would only free themselves from the shackles of past, worthless traditions, especially religious ones. If Isaac Newton could discover the natural laws regulating the world of nature, they too, by using reason, could find the laws that governed human society. This belief in turn led them to hope that they could make progress toward a better society than the one they had inherited. *Reason, natural law, hope, progress*—these were the buzzwords in the heady atmosphere of eighteenth-century Europe.

Major sources of inspiration for the Enlightenment were Isaac Newton and his fellow Englishman John Locke (1632–1704). Newton had contended that the world and everything in it worked like a giant machine. Enchanted by the grand design of this world-machine, the intellectuals of the Enlightenment were convinced that by following Newton's rules of reasoning, they could discover the natural laws that governed politics, economics, justice, and religion.

John Locke's theory of knowledge also made a great impact. In his *Essay Concerning Human Understanding*, written in 1690, Locke denied the existence of innate ideas and argued instead that every person was born with a *tabula rasa* (TAB-yuh-luh RAH-suh), a blank mind:

> Let us then suppose the mind to be, as we say, white paper, void of all characters, without any ideas. How comes it to be furnished? Whence comes it by that vast store which the busy and boundless fancy of man has painted on it with an almost endless variety? Whence has it all the materials of reason and knowledge? To this I answer, in one word, from experience. . . . Our observation, employed either about external sensible objects or about the internal operations of our minds perceived and reflected on by ourselves, is that which supplies our understanding with all the materials of thinking.[2]

By denying innate ideas, Locke's philosophy implied that people were molded by their environment, by whatever they perceived through their senses from their surrounding world. By changing the environment and subjecting people to proper influences, they could be changed and a new society created. And how should the environment be changed? Newton had paved the way: reason enabled enlightened people to discover the natural laws to which all institutions should conform.

The Philosophes and Their Ideas

The intellectuals of the Enlightenment were known by the French term *philosophes* (fee-loh-ZAHFS), although they were not all French and few were philosophers in the strict sense of the term. The **philosophes** were literary people, professors, journalists, economists, political scientists, and, above all, social reformers. They came from both the nobility and the middle class, and a few even stemmed from lower-middle-class origins. Although it was a truly international and cosmopolitan movement, the Enlightenment also enhanced the dominant role being played by French culture; Paris was its recognized capital. Most of the leaders of the Enlightenment were French. The French philosophes, in turn, affected intellectuals elsewhere and created a movement that touched the entire Western world, including the British and Spanish colonies in America (see Map 18.1). (The terms *British* and *Great Britain* came to be be used after 1707 when the United Kingdom of Great Britain came into existence, uniting the governments of England and Scotland, as well as Wales, which had been joined to England previously.)

To the philosophes, the role of philosophy was not just to discuss the world but to change it. To the philosophes, reason was a scientific method, and it relied on an appeal to facts. A spirit of rational criticism was to be applied to everything, including religion and politics. Spanning almost a century, the Enlightenment evolved with each succeeding generation,

COMPARATIVE ESSAY

The Scientific Revolution

SCIENCE & TECHNOLOGY

When Catholic missionaries arrived in China in the sixteenth century, they marveled at the sophistication of Chinese civilization and its many accomplishments, including woodblock printing and the civil service examination system. In turn, their hosts were impressed with European inventions such as the spring-driven clock and eyeglasses.

It is not surprising that visitors from the West were impressed with what they saw in China, for that country had long been at the forefront of human achievement. After the sixteenth century, however, Europe would take the lead in the advance of science and technology, a phenomenon that would ultimately bring about the Industrial Revolution and set in motion a transformation of human society.

Why did Europe suddenly become the engine for rapid change in the seventeenth and eighteenth centuries? One factor was the change in the European worldview, the shift from a meta-physical to a materialist perspective and the growing inclination among European intellectuals to question first principles. In contrast to China, where, for example, the "investigation of things" proposed by Song dynasty thinkers had been used to analyze and confirm principles first established by Confucius and his contemporaries, empirical scientists in early modern Europe rejected received religious ideas, developed a new

The telescope—a European invention.

© Iberfoto/The Image Works

conception of the universe, and sought ways to improve material conditions around them.

Why were European thinkers more interested in practical applications of their discoveries than their counterparts else-where? No doubt the literate mercantile and propertied elites of Europe were attracted to the new science because it offered new ways to exploit resources for profit. Some of the early scientists made it easier for these groups to accept the new ideas by show-ing how they could be applied directly to specific industrial and technological needs. Galileo, for example, consciously sought an alliance between science and the material interests of the educated elite when he assured his listeners that the science of mechanics would be quite useful "when it becomes necessary to build bridges or other structures over water, something occurring mainly in affairs of great importance."

Finally, the political changes that were beginning to take place in Europe during this period may also have con-tributed. Many European states enlarged their bureaucratic machinery and consolidated their governments in order to collect the revenues and amass the armies needed to compete militarily with rivals. Political leaders desperately sought ways to enhance their wealth and power and grasped eagerly at whatever tools were available to guarantee their survival and prosperity.

 Why did the Scientific Revolution emerge in Europe and not in China?

becoming more radical as new thinkers built on the contributions of their predecessors. A few individuals, however, dominated the landscape so completely that we can gain insight into the core ideas of the philosophes by focusing on the three French giants—Montesquieu, Voltaire, and Diderot.

MONTESQUIEU Charles de Secondat (SHARL duh suh-KAHN-da), the baron de Montesquieu (MOHN-tess-kyoo) (1689–1755), came from the French nobility. His most famous work, *The Spirit of the Laws*, was published in 1748. In this comparative study of governments, Montesquieu attempted to apply the scientific method to the social and political arena to ascertain the "natural laws" governing the social and political relationships of human beings. Montesquieu distinguished three basic kinds of governments: republic, monarchy, and despotism.

Montesquieu used England as an example of monarchy, and it was his analysis of England's constitution that led to his most lasting contribution to political thought—the impor-tance of checks and balances achieved by means of a **separa-tion of powers**. He believed that England's system, with its separate executive, legislative, and judicial branches that served to limit and control each other, provided the greatest freedom and security for a state. The translation of his work into English two years after publication ensured that it would be read by American political leaders, who eventually incor-porated its principles into the U.S. Constitution.

VOLTAIRE The greatest figure of the Enlightenment was François-Marie Arouet (frahn-SWAH-ma-REE ahr-WEH), known simply as Voltaire (vohl-TAYR) (1694–1778). Son of a prosperous middle-class family from Paris, he studied law,

Legend:
- ☀ Palaces modeled after Versailles
- 📖 Publication of scientific or philosophical journals
- ⌂ Important universities
- ⚲ Location of observatories
- ● Famous European academic centers

MAP 18.1 The Enlightenment in Europe. "Have the courage to use your own intelligence!" The words of the German philosopher Immanuel Kant (i-MAHN-yoo-el KAHNT) epitomize the role of the individual in using reason to understand all aspects of life—the natural world and the sphere of human nature, behavior, and institutions.

 Which countries or regions were at the center of the Enlightenment, and what reasons could account for peripheral regions being less involved?

although he achieved his first success as a playwright. Voltaire was a prolific author and wrote an almost endless stream of pamphlets, novels, plays, letters, philosophical essays, and histories.

Voltaire was especially well known for his criticism of traditional religion and his strong attachment to the ideal of religious toleration (see the box on p. 514). As he grew older, Voltaire became ever more strident in his denunciations. "Crush the infamous thing," he thundered repeatedly—the infamous thing being religious fanaticism, intolerance, and superstition.

Throughout his life, Voltaire championed not only religious tolerance but also **deism**, a religious outlook shared by most other philosophes. Deism was built on the Newtonian world-machine, which implied the existence of a mechanic (God) who had created the universe. To Voltaire and most other philosophes, the universe was like a clock, and God was the clockmaker who had created it, set it in motion, and allowed it to run according to its own natural laws.

DIDEROT Denis Diderot (duh-NEE dee-DROH) (1713–1784) was the son of a skilled craftsman from eastern France who became a writer so that he could be free to study and read in many subjects and languages. One of Diderot's favorite topics was Christianity, which he condemned as fanatical and unreasonable. Of all religions, Christianity, he averred, was the worst, "the most absurd and the most atrocious in its dogma."

The Attack on Religious Intolerance

Although Voltaire's ideas on religion were not original, his lucid prose, biting satire, and clever wit caused his works to be widely read and all the more influential. These two selections present different sides of Voltaire's attack on religious intolerance. The first is from his straightforward treatise *The Ignorant Philosopher*, and the second is from his only real literary masterpiece, the novel *Candide*, where he used humor to make the same fundamental point about religious intolerance.

Voltaire, *The Ignorant Philosopher*

The contagion of fanaticism then still subsists. . . . The author of the Treatise upon Toleration has not mentioned the shocking executions wherein so many unhappy victims perished in the valleys of Piedmont. He has passed over in silence the massacre of six hundred inhabitants of Valtelina, men, women, and children, who were murdered by the Catholics in the month of September, 1620. I will not say it was with the consent and assistance of the archbishop of Milan, Charles Borome, who was made a saint. Some passionate writers have averred this fact, which I am very far from believing; but I say, there is scarce any city or borough in Europe where blood has not been spilt for religious quarrels; I say, that the human species has been perceptibly diminished because women and girls were massacred as well as men; I say, that Europe would have had a third larger population if there had been no theological disputes. In fine, I say, that so far from forgetting these abominable times, we should frequently take a view of them, to inspire an eternal horror for them; and that it is for our age to make reparation by toleration, for this long collection of crimes, which has taken place through the want of toleration, during sixteen barbarous centuries.

Let it not then be said, that there are no traces left of that shocking fanaticism, of the want of toleration; they are still everywhere to be met with, even in those countries that are esteemed the most humane. The Lutheran and Calvinist preachers, were they masters, would, perhaps, be as little inclined to pity, as obdurate, as insolent as they upbraid their antagonists with being.

Voltaire, *Candide*

At last [Candide] approached a man who had just been addressing a big audience for a whole hour on the subject of charity. The orator peered at him and said:

"What is your business here? Do you support the Good Old Cause?"

"There is no effect without a cause," replied Candide modestly. "All things are necessarily connected and arranged for the best. It was my fate to be driven from Lady Cunégonde's presence and made to run the gauntlet, and now I have to beg my bread until I can earn it. Things could not have happened otherwise."

"Do you believe that the Pope is Antichrist, my friend?" said the minister.

"I have never heard anyone say so," replied Candide; "but whether he is or he isn't, I want some food."

"You don't deserve to eat," said the other. "Be off with you, you villain, you wretch! Don't come near me again or you'll suffer for it."

The minister's wife looked out of the window at that moment, and seeing a man who was not sure that the Pope was Antichrist, emptied over his head a chamber pot, which shows to what lengths ladies are driven by religious zeal.

 Compare the two approaches that Voltaire uses to address the problem of religious intolerance. Which do you think is more effective? Why?

Diderot's most famous contribution to the Enlightenment was the *Encyclopedia, or Classified Dictionary of the Sciences, Arts, and Trades,* a twenty-eight-volume compendium of knowledge that he edited and referred to as the "great work of his life." Its purpose, according to Diderot, was to "change the general way of thinking." It did precisely that in becoming a major weapon of the philosophes' crusade against the old French society. The contributors included many philosophes who attacked religious intolerance and advocated a program for social, legal, and political improvements that would lead to a society that was more cosmopolitan, more tolerant, more humane, and more reasonable. The *Encyclopedia* was sold to doctors, clergymen, teachers, lawyers, and even military officers, thus spreading the ideas of the Enlightenment.

TOWARD A NEW "SCIENCE OF MAN" The Enlightenment belief that Newton's scientific methods could be used to discover the natural laws underlying all areas of human life led to the emergence in the eighteenth century of what the philosophes called a "science of man," or what we would call the social sciences. In a number of areas, such as economics, politics, and education, the philosophes arrived at natural laws that they believed governed human actions.

Adam Smith (1723–1790) has been viewed as one of the founders of the modern discipline of economics. Smith believed that individuals should be free to pursue their own economic self-interest. Through the actions of these individuals, all society would ultimately benefit. Consequently, the state should in no way interrupt the free play of natural

A London Coffeehouse. Coffeehouses first appeared in the major cities of the Ottoman Empire in the sixteenth century, where they were often associated with antigovernment activity. They spread quickly throughout Europe and by the beginning of the eighteenth century had become a means for spreading Enlightenment ideas. In addition to drinking coffee, patrons of coffeehouses could read magazines and newspapers, exchange ideas, play chess, smoke, and even engage in business transactions. In this scene from a London coffeehouse around 1705, well-attired gentlemen make bids on commodities.

economic forces by government regulations on the economy but should leave it alone, a doctrine that subsequently became known as *laissez-faire* (less-ay-FAYR) (French for "leave it alone").

Smith allotted government only three basic functions: to protect society from invasion (via an army), defend its citizens from injustice (by means of a police force), and keep up certain public works, such as roads and canals, that private individuals could not afford.

THE LATER ENLIGHTENMENT By the late 1760s, a new generation of philosophes who had grown up with the worldview of the Enlightenment began to move beyond their predecessors' beliefs. Most famous was Jean-Jacques Rousseau (ZHAHNH-ZHAHK roo-SOH) (1712–1778), whose political beliefs were presented in two major works. In his *Discourse on the Origins of the Inequality of Mankind*, Rousseau argued that people had adopted laws and governors in order to preserve their private property. In the process, they had become enslaved by government. What, then, should people do to regain their freedom? In his celebrated treatise *The Social Contract*, published in 1762, Rousseau found an answer in the concept of the social contract, whereby an entire society agreed to be governed by its general will. Each individual might have a particular will contrary to the general will, but if the individual put his particular will (self-interest) above the general will, he should be forced to abide by the general will.

"This means nothing less than that he will be forced to be free," said Rousseau, because the general will, being ethical and not just political, represented what the entire community ought to do.

Another influential treatise by Rousseau was his novel *Émile*, one of the Enlightenment's most important works on education. Rousseau's fundamental concern was that education should foster, rather than restrict, children's natural instincts. Rousseau's own experiences had shown him the importance of the emotions. What he sought was a balance between heart and mind, between emotion and reason.

But Rousseau did not necessarily practice what he preached. His own children were sent to orphanages, where many children died at a young age. Rousseau also viewed women as "naturally different" from men. In *Émile*, Sophie, Émile's intended wife, was educated for her role as wife and mother by learning obedience and the nurturing skills that would enable her to provide loving care for her husband and children. Not everyone in the eighteenth century agreed with Rousseau, however.

THE "WOMAN QUESTION" IN THE ENLIGHTENMENT For centuries, many male intellectuals had argued that the nature of women made them inferior to men and made male domination of women necessary and right. In the Scientific Revolution, however, some women had made notable contributions. Maria Winkelmann (VINK-ul-mahn) in Germany, for example, was an outstanding practicing astronomer. Nevertheless, when she applied for a position as assistant astronomer at the Berlin Academy, for which she was highly qualified, she was denied the post by the academy's members, who feared that hiring a woman would set a bad precedent ("mouths would gape"). Winkelmann's difficulties with the Berlin Academy were typical of the obstacles women faced in being accepted in scientific work, which was considered a male preserve.

Female thinkers in the eighteenth century disagreed with this attitude and offered suggestions for improving conditions for women. The strongest statement for the rights of women was advanced by the English writer Mary Wollstonecraft (WULL-stun-kraft) (1759–1797), viewed by many as the founder of modern European **feminism**.

In her *Vindication of the Rights of Woman*, written in 1792, Wollstonecraft pointed out two contradictions in the views of women held by such Enlightenment thinkers as Rousseau. To argue that women must obey men, she said, was contrary to the beliefs of the same individuals that a system based on the arbitrary power of monarchs over their subjects or slave owners over their slaves was wrong. The subjection of women to men was equally wrong. In addition, she argued, the Enlightenment was based on an ideal of reason innate in all human beings. If women have reason, then they should

The Rights of Women

Mary Wollstonecraft responded to an unhappy childhood in a large family by seeking to lead an independent life. Few occupations were available for middle-class women in her day, but she survived by working as a teacher, chaperone, and governess to aristocratic children. All the while, she wrote and developed her ideas on the rights of women. This selection is taken from her *Vindication of the Rights of Woman*, written in 1792. This work led to her reputation as the foremost British feminist thinker of the eighteenth century.

Mary Wollstonecraft, *Vindication of the Rights of Woman*

It is a melancholy truth—yet such is the blessed effect of civilization—the most respectable women are the most oppressed; and, unless they have understandings far superior to the common run of understandings, taking in both sexes, they must, from being treated like contemptible beings, become contemptible. How many women thus waste life away the prey of discontent, who might have practiced as physicians, regulated a farm, managed a shop, and stood erect, supported by their own industry, instead of hanging their heads surcharged with the dew of sensibility, that consumes the beauty to which it at first gave luster. . . .

Proud of their weakness, however, [women] must always be protected, guarded from care, and all the rough toils that dignify the mind. If this be the fiat of fate, if they will make themselves insignificant and contemptible, sweetly to waste "life away," let them not expect to be valued when their beauty fades, for it is the fate of the fairest flowers to be admired and pulled to pieces by the careless hand that plucked them. In how many ways do I wish, from the purest benevolence, to impress this truth on my sex; yet I fear that they will not listen to a truth that dear-bought experience has brought home to many an agitated bosom, nor willingly resign the privileges of rank and sex for the privileges of humanity, to which those have no claim who do not discharge its duties. . . .

Would men but generously snap our chains, and be content with rational fellowship instead of slavish obedience, they would find us more observant daughters, more affectionate sisters, more faithful wives, and more reasonable mothers—in a word, better citizens. We should then love them with true affection, because we should learn to respect ourselves; and the peace of mind of a worthy man would not be interrupted by the idle vanity of his wife.

 What picture did Wollstonecraft paint of the women of her day? Why were they in such a deplorable state? Why did Wollstonecraft suggest that both women and men were at fault for the "slavish" situation of females?

---

have the same rights as men to obtain an education and engage in economic and political life (see the box above).

Culture in an Enlightened Age

Although the Baroque style that had dominated the seventeenth century continued to be popular, by the 1730s, a new style affecting decoration and architecture known as **Rococo** (ruh-KOH-koh) had spread throughout Europe. Unlike the Baroque, which stressed power, grandeur, and movement, Rococo emphasized grace, charm, and gentle action. Rococo rejected strict geometrical patterns and had a fondness for curves; it liked to follow the wandering lines of natural objects, such as seashells and flowers. It made much use of interlaced designs colored in gold with delicate contours and graceful arcs. Highly secular, its lightness and charm spoke of the pursuit of pleasure, happiness, and love.

Some of Rococo's appeal is evident in the work of Antoine Watteau (AHN-twahn wah-TOH) (1684–1721), whose lyrical views of aristocratic life, refined, sensual, and civilized, with gentlemen and ladies in elegant dress, revealed a world of upper-class pleasure and joy. Underneath that exterior, however, was an element of sadness as the artist revealed the fragility and transitory nature of pleasure, love, and life.

Another aspect of Rococo was that its decorative work could easily be paired with Baroque architecture. The palace at Versailles had made an enormous impact on Europe. "Keeping up with the Bourbons" became important as European rulers built grandiose palaces. While imitating Versailles in size, they were not so much modeled after the French classical style as they were after the seventeenth-century Italian Baroque, as modified by a series of brilliant German and Austrian sculptor-architects. This Baroque-Rococo architectural style typified eighteenth-century palaces and church buildings, and often the same architects designed both. This is evident in the work of one of the greatest architects of the eighteenth century, Johann Balthasar Neumann (yoh-HAHN BAHL-tuh-zahr NOI-mahn) (1687–1753). One of Neumann's masterpieces was the pilgrimage church known as the Vierzehnheiligen (feer-tsayn-HY-li-gen) (Fourteen Saints) in southern Germany. Secular and spiritual merge in its lavish

Antoine Watteau, *Return from Cythera*. Antoine Watteau was one of the most gifted painters in eighteenth-century France. His portrayal of aristocratic life reveals a world of elegance, wealth, and pleasure. In this painting, which is considered his masterpiece, Watteau depicts a group of aristocratic lovers about to depart from the island of Cythera, where they have paid homage to Venus, the goddess of love. Luxuriously dressed, they move from the woodlands to a golden barge that is waiting to take them from the island.

Vierzehnheiligen. Pictured here is the interior of the Vierzehnheiligen, the famous pilgrimage church in Bad Staffelstein, Bavaria, designed by Johann Balthasar Neumann. Elaborate detail, blazing light, rich colors, and opulent decoration were brought together to create a work of stunning beauty. The pilgrim in search of holiness is struck by an incredible richness of detail. Persuaded by joy rather than fear, the believer is lifted toward heaven on a cloud of rapture.

and fanciful ornamentation; light, bright colors; and elaborate, rich detail.

HIGH CULTURE Historians have grown accustomed to distinguishing between a civilization's high culture and its popular culture. **High culture** is the literary and artistic culture of the educated and wealthy ruling classes; **popular culture** is the written and unwritten culture of the masses, most of which has traditionally been passed down orally.

By the eighteenth century, the two forms were beginning to blend, owing to the expansion of both the reading public and publishing. Whereas French publishers issued 300 titles in 1750, about 1,600 were being published yearly in the 1780s. Although many of these titles were still intended for small groups of the educated elite, many were also directed to the new reading public of the middle classes, which included women and even urban artisans.

An important aspect of the growth of publishing and reading in the eighteenth century was the development of magazines for the general public. Great Britain saw 25 different periodicals published in 1700, 103 in 1760, and 158 in 1780. Along with magazines came daily newspapers. The first was printed in London in 1702, but by 1780, thirty-seven other English towns had their own newspapers.

POPULAR CULTURE   The distinguishing characteristic of popular culture is its collective nature. Group activity was especially common in the *festival*, a broad name used to cover a variety of celebrations: community festivals in Catholic Europe that celebrated the feast day of the local patron saint; annual festivals, such as Christmas and Easter, that went back to medieval Christianity; and the ultimate festival, Carnival, which was celebrated in the Mediterranean world of Spain, Italy, and France as well as in Germany and Austria.

Carnival began after Christmas and lasted until the start of Lent, the forty-day period of fasting and purification leading up to Easter. Because people were expected to abstain from meat, sex, and most recreations during Lent, Carnival was a time of great indulgence, when heavy consumption of food and drink was the norm. It was a time of intense sexual activity as well. Songs with double meanings that would ordinarily be considered offensive could be sung publicly at this time of year. A float of Florentine "keymakers," for example, sang this ditty to the ladies: "Our tools are fine, new and useful. We always carry them with us. They are good for anything. If you want to touch them, you can."[3]

Economic Changes and the Social Order

 FOCUS QUESTION: What changes occurred in the European economy in the eighteenth century, and to what degree were these changes reflected in social patterns?

The eighteenth century in Europe witnessed the beginning of economic changes that ultimately had a strong impact on the rest of the world.

New Economic Patterns

Europe's population began to grow around 1750 and continued to increase steadily. The total European population was probably around 120 million in 1700, 140 million in 1750, and 190 million in 1790. A falling death rate was perhaps the most important reason for this population growth. Of great significance in lowering death rates was the disappearance of bubonic plague, but so was diet. More plentiful food and better transportation of food supplies led to improved nutrition and relief from devastating famines.

More plentiful food was in part a result of improvements in agricultural practices and methods in the eighteenth century, especially in Britain, parts of France, and the Low Countries. Food production increased as more land was farmed, yields per acre increased, and climate improved. Climatologists believe that the "little ice age" of the seventeenth century waned in the eighteenth, especially evident in moderate

summers that provided more ideal growing conditions. Also important to the increased yields was the cultivation of new vegetables, including two important American crops, the potato and maize (Indian corn). Both had been brought to Europe from the Americas in the sixteenth century.

Textiles were the most important product of European industry in the eighteenth century. Most were still produced by master artisans in guild workshops, but in many areas, textile production was beginning to shift to the countryside where the "putting-out" or "domestic" system was used. A merchant-capitalist entrepreneur bought the raw materials, mostly wool and flax, and "put them out" to rural workers who spun the raw material into yarn and then wove it into cloth on simple looms. The capitalist entrepreneurs sold the finished product, made a profit, and used it to purchase materials to manufacture more. This system became known as the **cottage industry** because the spinners and weavers worked at spinning wheels and looms in the cottages where they lived.

In the eighteenth century, overseas trade boomed. Some historians speak of the emergence of a true global economy, pointing to the patterns of trade that interlocked Europe, Africa, the East, and the Americas (see Map 18.2). In one trade pattern, gold and silver flowed into Spain from its colonial American empire. Much of this gold and silver made its way to Britain, France, and the Netherlands in return for manufactured goods. The British, French, and Dutch merchants then used their profits to buy tea, spices, silk, and cotton goods from China and India to sell in Europe. The plantations of the Western Hemisphere were another important source of trading activity. The plantations produced coffee, tobacco, sugar, and cotton, which were shipped to Europe. In a third pattern of trade, British merchant ships carried British manufactured goods to Africa, where they were traded for cargoes of slaves, which were then shipped to Virginia and paid for with tobacco, which was in turn shipped back to Britain, where it was processed and then sold in Germany for cash.

Commercial capitalism resulted in enormous prosperity for some European countries. By 1700, Spain, Portugal, and the Dutch Republic, which had earlier monopolized overseas trade, found themselves increasingly overshadowed by France and England, which built hugely profitable colonial empires in the course of the eighteenth century. After the French lost the Seven Years' War in 1763, Britain emerged as the world's strongest overseas trading nation, and London became the world's greatest port.

European Society in the Eighteenth Century

The patterns of Europe's social organization, first established in the Middle Ages, continued well into the eighteenth century. Society was still divided into the traditional orders or estates determined by heredity.

Because society was still mostly rural in the eighteenth century, the peasantry constituted the largest social group, about 85 percent of Europe's population. There were rather wide differences within this group, however, especially

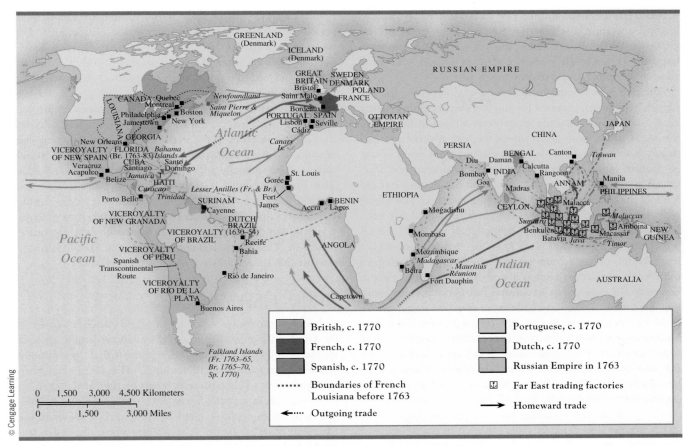

MAP 18.2 **Global Trade Patterns of the European States in the Eighteenth Century.** New patterns of trade interlocked Europe, Africa, the East, and the Americas. Dutch, English, French, Spanish, and Portuguese colonies had been established in North and South America, and the ships of these nations followed the trade routes across the Atlantic, Pacific, and Indian Oceans.

Q *With what regions did Britain conduct most of its trade?*

The Aristocratic Way of Life. The desire among British aristocrats for both elegance and greater privacy was fulfilled by the eighteenth-century country house. The painting on the right, by Richard Wilson, shows a typical English country house of the eighteenth century, surrounded by a simple and serene landscape. Thomas Gainsborough's *Conversation in the Park*, shown at the left, captures the relaxed life of two aristocrats in the park of their country estate.

between free peasants and serfs. In eastern Germany, eastern Europe, and Russia, serfs remained tied to the lands of their noble landlords. In contrast, peasants in Britain, northern Italy, the Low Countries, Spain, most of France, and some areas of western Germany were largely free.

The nobles, who constituted only 2 to 3 percent of the European population, played a dominating role in society. Being born a noble automatically guaranteed a place at the top of the social order, with all its attendant special privileges and rights. Nobles, for example, were exempt from many forms of taxation. Since medieval times, landed aristocrats had functioned as military officers, and eighteenth-century nobles held most of the important offices in the administrative machinery of state and controlled much of the life of their local districts.

Townspeople were still a distinct minority of the total population except in the Dutch Republic, Britain, and parts of Italy. At the end of the eighteenth century, about one-sixth of the French population lived in towns of two thousand people or more. The biggest city in Europe was London, with a million inhabitants; Paris was a little more than half that size.

Many cities in western and even central Europe had a long tradition of **patrician** oligarchies that continued to control their communities by dominating town and city councils. Just below the patricians stood an upper crust of the middle classes: nonnoble officeholders, financiers and bankers, merchants, wealthy *rentiers* (rahn-TYAYS) who lived off their investments, and important professionals, including lawyers. Another large urban group was the lower middle class, made up of master artisans, shopkeepers, and small traders. Below them were the laborers or working classes and a large group of unskilled workers who served as servants, maids, and cooks at pitifully low wages.

Colonial Empires and Revolution in the Americas

 FOCUS QUESTION: What colonies did the British and French establish in the Americas, and how did their methods of administering their colonies differ?

In the sixteenth century, Spain and Portugal had established large colonial empires in the Americas (see Chapter 14). Portugal continued to profit from its empire in Brazil. The Spanish also maintained an enormous South American empire, but Spain's importance as a commercial power declined rapidly in the seventeenth century because of a drop in the output of the silver mines and the poverty of the Spanish monarchy. By the beginning of the seventeenth century, both Portugal and Spain found themselves facing new challenges to their American empires from the Dutch, English, and French, who increasingly sought to create their own colonial empires in the Western Hemisphere, both within the West Indies and on the North American continent.

The West Indies

Both the French and British colonial empires in the Americas ultimately included large parts of the West Indies. The British held Barbados, Jamaica, and Bermuda, and the French possessed Saint-Dominique, Martinique, and Guadeloupe. On these tropical islands, both the British and the French developed plantations, worked by African slaves, which produced tobacco, cotton, coffee, and sugar, all products increasingly in demand in Europe.

The "sugar factories," as the sugar plantations in the Caribbean were called, played an especially prominent role. By the last two decades of the eighteenth century, Jamaica, one of Britain's most important colonies, was producing 50,000 tons of sugar annually with the slave labor of 200,000 blacks. The French colony of Saint-Dominique (later Haiti) had 500,000 slaves working on three thousand plantations during the same period. This colony produced 100,000 tons of sugar a year, but at the expense of a high death rate from the brutal treatment of the slaves. It is not surprising that Saint-Dominique saw the first successful slave uprising in 1793.

British North America

Although Spain had claimed all of North America as part of its American overseas empire, other nations largely ignored its claim, following the English argument that "prescription without possession availeth nothing." The Dutch had been among the first to establish settlements on the North American continent. Their activities began after 1609 when Henry Hudson, an English explorer hired by the Dutch, discovered the river that bears his name. Within a few years, the Dutch had established the mainland colony of New Netherland, which stretched from the mouth of the Hudson River as far north as Albany, New York. Present-day names such as Staten Island and Harlem remind us that it was the Dutch who initially settled the Hudson River valley. In the second half of the seventeenth century, competition from the English and French and years of warfare with those rivals led to the decline of the Dutch commercial empire. In 1664, the English seized the colony of New Netherland and renamed it New York.

In the meantime, the English had begun to establish their own colonies in North America. The first permanent English settlement in America was Jamestown, founded in 1607 in what is now Virginia. The settlers barely survived, making it clear that colonizing American lands was not necessarily conducive to quick profits. But the desire to practice one's own religion, combined with economic interests, could lead to successful colonization, as the Massachusetts Bay Company demonstrated. The Massachusetts colony had 4,000 settlers in its early years, but by 1660 their numbers had swelled to 40,000. By the end of the seventeenth century, the English had established control over most of the eastern seaboard of the present United States.

British North America came to consist of thirteen colonies. They were thickly populated, containing about 1.5 million people by 1750, and were also prosperous. Supposedly run by the British Board of Trade, the Royal Council, and Parliament, these thirteen colonies had legislatures that tended to act independently. Merchants in such port cities as Boston, Philadelphia, New York, and Charleston resented and resisted regulation from the British government.

A Sugar Mill in the West Indies. Cane sugar was one of the most valuable products produced in the West Indies. By 1700, sugar was replacing honey as a sweetener for increasing numbers of Europeans. This seventeenth-century French illustration shows the operation of a sugar mill in the French West Indies.

Both the North American and the West Indian colonies of Britain were assigned roles in keeping with mercantilist theory. They provided raw materials for the mother country while buying the latter's manufactured goods. Navigation acts regulated what could be taken from and sold to the colonies. Theoretically, the system was supposed to provide a balance of trade favorable to the mother country.

French North America

The French also established a colonial empire in North America. In 1534, the French explorer Jacques Cartier (ZHAHK kar-TYAY) had discovered the Saint Lawrence River and laid claim to Canada as a French possession. Not until Samuel de Champlain (sa-my-ELL duh shahm-PLAN *or* SHAM-playn) established a settlement at Quebec in 1608, however, did the French began to take a serious interest in Canada as a colony. In 1663, Canada was made the property of the French crown and administered by a French governor like a French province.

French North America was run autocratically as a vast trading area, where valuable furs, leather, fish, and timber were acquired. The inability of the French state to persuade its people to emigrate to its Canadian possessions, however, left the territory thinly populated. In the mid-eighteenth century, there were only about 15,000 French Canadians, most of whom were hunters, trappers, missionaries, or explorers. The French also failed to provide adequate men or money for the venture, allowing their wars in Europe to take precedence over the conquest of the North American continent. Already in 1713, by the Treaty of Utrecht, the French began to cede some of their American possessions to their British rival. As a result of the Seven Years' War, they surrendered the rest of their Canadian lands to Britain in 1763 (see "Changing Patterns of War: Global Confrontation" later in this chapter).

The American Revolution

By the mid-eighteenth century, increasing trade and industry had led to a growing middle class in Britain that favored expansion of trade and world empire. These people found a spokesman in William Pitt the Elder (1708–1778), who became prime minister in 1757 and began to expand the British Empire. In North America, after the end of the Seven Years' War in 1763, Britain controlled Canada and the lands east of the Mississippi.

The Americans and the British had different conceptions of how the empire should be governed, however. In eighteenth-century Britain, the king or queen and Parliament shared power, with Parliament gradually gaining the upper hand. The monarch chose ministers who were responsible to the crown and who set policy and guided Parliament. Parliament had the power to make laws, levy taxes, pass budgets, and indirectly influence the monarch's ministers. The British envisioned that Parliament would be the supreme authority performing these functions throughout the empire. But the Americans had their own representative assemblies. They believed that neither king nor Parliament should interfere in their internal affairs and that no tax could be levied without the consent of their own assemblies. After the Seven Years' War, when British policymakers sought to obtain new revenues from the colonies to pay for British army expenses in defending the colonies, the colonists resisted. An attempt to levy new taxes by the Stamp Act of 1765 led to riots and the law's quick repeal.

Crisis followed crisis in the 1770s until 1776, when the colonists decided to declare their independence from the British Empire. On July 4, 1776, the Second Continental Congress approved a declaration of independence written by Thomas Jefferson (1743–1826). A stirring political document, the

Declaration of Independence affirmed the Enlightenment's natural rights of "life, liberty, and the pursuit of happiness" and declared the colonies to be "free and independent states absolved from all allegiance to the British crown." The war for American independence had formally begun.

Of great importance to the colonies' cause was the support of foreign countries that were eager to gain revenge for earlier defeats at the hands of the British. French officers and soldiers served in the American Continental Army under George Washington (1732–1799), the commander in chief. When the British army of General Cornwallis was forced to surrender to a combined American and French army and French fleet under Washington at Yorktown in 1781, the British decided to call it quits. The Treaty of Paris, signed in 1783, recognized the independence of the American colonies and granted the Americans control of the territory from the Appalachians to the Mississippi River.

BIRTH OF A NEW NATION The thirteen American colonies had gained their independence, but a fear of concentrated power and concern for their own interests caused them to have little enthusiasm for establishing a united nation with a strong central government, and so the Articles of Confederation, ratified in 1781, did not create one. A movement for a different form of national government soon arose. In the summer of 1787, fifty-five delegates attended a convention in Philadelphia to revise the Articles of Confederation. The convention's delegates—wealthy, politically experienced, and well educated—rejected revision and decided instead to devise a new constitution.

The proposed United States Constitution established a central government distinct from and superior to the governments of the individual states. The central or federal government was divided into three branches, each with some power to check the functioning of the others. A president would serve as the chief executive with the power to execute laws, veto the legislature's acts, supervise foreign affairs, and direct military forces. Legislative power was vested in the second branch of government, a bicameral legislature composed of the Senate, elected by the state legislatures, and the House of Representatives, elected directly by the people. A supreme court and other courts "as deemed necessary" by Congress provided the third branch of government. They would enforce the Constitution as the "supreme law of the land."

The Constitution was approved by the states—by a slim margin. Important to its success was a promise to add a bill of rights to the Constitution as the new government's first piece of business. Accordingly, in March 1789, the new Congress enacted the first ten amendments to the Constitution, known ever since as the Bill of Rights. These guaranteed freedom of religion, speech, press, petition, and assembly, as well as the right to bear arms, protection against unreasonable searches and arrests, trial by jury, due process of law, and protection of property rights. Many of these rights were derived from the **natural rights** philosophy of the eighteenth-century philosophes and the American colonists. Is it any wonder that many European intellectuals saw the American Revolution as the embodiment of the Enlightenment's political dreams?

Toward a New Political Order and Global Conflict

 FOCUS QUESTION: What do historians mean by the term *enlightened absolutism*, and to what degree did eighteenth-century Prussia, Austria, and Russia exhibit its characteristics?

There is no doubt that Enlightenment thought had some impact on the political development of European states in the eighteenth century. The philosophes believed in natural rights, which were thought to be privileges that ought not to be withheld from any person. These natural rights included equality before the law, freedom of religious worship, freedom of speech and press, and the right to assemble, hold property, and seek happiness.

But how were these natural rights to be established and preserved? Most philosophes believed that people needed to be ruled by an enlightened ruler. What made rulers enlightened? They must allow religious toleration, freedom of speech and press, and the rights of private property. They must foster the arts, sciences, and education. Above all, they must obey the laws and enforce them fairly for all subjects. Only strong monarchs seemed capable of overcoming vested interests and effecting the reforms society needed. Reforms then should come from above (from absolute rulers) rather than from below (from the people).

Many historians once assumed that a new type of monarchy emerged in the later eighteenth century, which they called *enlightened despotism* or **enlightened absolutism**. Monarchs such as Frederick II of Prussia, Catherine the Great of Russia, and Joseph II of Austria supposedly followed the advice of the philosophes and ruled by enlightened principles. Recently, however, scholars have questioned the usefulness of the concept of enlightened absolutism. We can determine the extent to which it can be applied by examining the major "enlightened absolutists" of the late eighteenth century.

Prussia: The Army and the Bureaucracy

Frederick II, known as Frederick the Great (1740–1786), was one of the best-educated and most cultured monarchs of the eighteenth century. He was well versed in Enlightenment thought and even invited Voltaire to live at his court for several years. A believer in the king as the "first servant of the state," Frederick the Great was a conscientious ruler who enlarged the Prussian army (to 200,000 men) and kept a strict watch over the bureaucracy. The Prussian army, because of its size and excellent reputation, was the most important institution in the state. Its officers, who were members of the nobility or landed aristocracy, had a strong sense of service to the king or state. As Prussian nobles, they believed in duty, obedience, and sacrifice. The bureaucracy also had its own code in which the supreme values were obedience, honor, and service to the king as the highest duty.

For a time, Frederick seemed quite willing to make enlightened reforms. He abolished the use of torture except in treason and murder cases and also granted limited freedom of speech and press, as well as complete religious toleration. At the same time, however, he kept Prussia's rigid social structure and serfdom intact and avoided any additional reforms.

The Austrian Empire of the Habsburgs

The Austrian Empire had become one of the great European states by the beginning of the eighteenth century. Yet it was difficult to rule because it was a sprawling conglomerate of nationalities, languages, religions, and cultures (see Map 18.3). Empress Maria Theresa (1740–1780) managed to make administrative reforms that helped centralize the Austrian Empire, but they were done for practical reasons—to strengthen the power of the Habsburg state—and were accompanied by an enlargement and modernization of the armed forces. Maria Theresa remained staunchly conservative and was not open to the wider reform calls of the philosophes. But her successor was.

Joseph II (1780–1790) believed in the need to sweep away anything standing in the path of reason. As he said, "I have made Philosophy the lawmaker of my empire; her logical applications are going to transform Austria." Joseph's reform program was far-reaching. He abolished serfdom, abrogated the death penalty, and established the principle of equality of all before the law. Joseph carried out drastic religious reforms as well, including complete religious toleration.

Joseph's reform program proved overwhelming for Austria, however. He alienated the nobility by freeing the serfs and alienated the church by his attacks on the monastic establishment. Joseph realized his failure when he wrote the epitaph for his own gravestone: "Here lies Joseph II, who was unfortunate in everything that he undertook." His successors undid many of his reforms.

Russia Under Catherine the Great

Catherine II the Great (1762–1796) was an intelligent woman who was familiar with the works of the philosophes and seemed to favor enlightened reforms. She invited the French philosophe Diderot to Russia and, when he arrived, urged

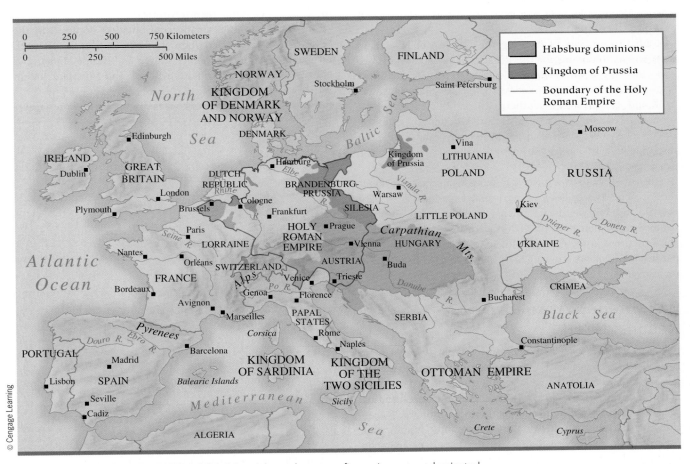

MAP 18.3 Europe in 1763. By the middle of the eighteenth century, five major powers dominated Europe—Prussia, Austria, Russia, Britain, and France. Each sought to enhance its power both domestically, through a bureaucracy that collected taxes and ran the military, and internationally, by capturing territory or preventing other powers from capturing territory.

Q *Given the distribution of Prussian and Habsburg holdings, in what areas of Europe were they most likely to compete for land and power?*

him to speak frankly "as man to man." He did, outlining a far-reaching program of political and financial reform. But Catherine was skeptical about impractical theories, which, she said, "would have turned everything in my kingdom upside down." She did consider the idea of a new law code that would recognize the principle of the equality of all people in the eyes of the law. But in the end she did nothing, knowing that her success depended on the support of the Russian nobility. In 1785, she gave the nobles a charter that exempted them from taxes.

Catherine's policy of favoring the landed nobility led to even worse conditions for the Russian peasants and a rebellion. Incited by an illiterate Cossack, Emelyan Pugachev (yim-yil-YAHN poo-guh-CHAHF), the rebellion began in 1773 and spread across southern Russia. But the rebellion soon faltered. Pugachev was captured, tortured, and executed. The rebellion collapsed completely, and Catherine responded with even stronger measures against the peasantry.

Above all, Catherine proved a worthy successor to Peter the Great in her policies of territorial expansion westward into Poland and southward to the Black Sea. Russia spread southward by defeating the Turks. Russian expansion westward occurred at the expense of neighboring Poland. In three partitions of Poland, Russia gained about 50 percent of Polish territory.

Enlightened Absolutism Reconsidered

Of the rulers we have discussed, only Joseph II sought truly radical changes based on Enlightenment ideas. Both Frederick II and Catherine II liked to talk about enlightened reforms, and they even attempted some. But the policies of neither seemed seriously affected by Enlightenment thought. Necessities of state and maintenance of the existing system took precedence over reform. Indeed, many historians maintain that Joseph, Frederick, and Catherine were all primarily guided by a concern for the power and well-being of their states. In the final analysis, heightened state power was used to create armies and wage wars to gain more power.

It would be foolish, however, to overlook the fact that the ability of enlightened rulers to make reforms was also limited by political and social realities. Everywhere in Europe, the hereditary aristocracy was still the most powerful class in society. Enlightened reforms were often limited to administrative and judicial measures that did not seriously undermine the powerful interests of the European nobility. As the chief beneficiaries of a system based on traditional rights and privileges for their class, they were not willing to support a political ideology that trumpeted the principle of equal rights for all. The first serious challenge to their supremacy would come in the French Revolution, an event that blew open the door to the modern world of politics.

Changing Patterns of War: Global Confrontation

The philosophes condemned war as a foolish waste of life and resources in stupid quarrels of no value to humankind. Despite their words, the rivalry among states that led to costly struggles remained unchanged in the European world of the eighteenth century. Europe consisted of a number of self-governing, individual states that were largely guided by the self-interest of the ruler. And as Frederick the Great of Prussia said, "The fundamental rule of governments is the principle of extending their territories."

By far the most dramatic confrontation occurred in the Seven Years' War. Although it began in Europe, it soon turned into a global conflict fought in Europe, India, and North America. In Europe, the British and Prussians fought

British Library, London//© Erich Lessing/Art Resource, NY

Robert Clive in India. Robert Clive was the leader of the army of the British East India Company. He had been commanded to fight the ruler of Bengal in order to gain trading privileges. After the Battle of Plassey in 1757, Clive and the East India Company took control of Bengal. In this painting by Edward Penny, Clive is shown receiving a grant of money for his injured soldiers from the local nabob or governor of Bengal.

British Victory in India

POLITICS & GOVERNMENT

The success of the British against the French in India was due to Robert Clive, who, in this excerpt from one of his letters, describes his famous victory at Plassey, north of Calcutta, on June 23, 1757. This battle demonstrated the inability of native Indian soldiers to compete with Europeans and signified the beginning of British control in Bengal. Clive claimed to have a thousand Europeans, two thousand sepoys (local soldiers), and eight cannons available for this battle.

Robert Clive's Account of His Victory at Plassey

At daybreak we discovered the [governor's army] moving toward us, consisting, as we since found, of about fifteen thousand horse and thirty-five thousand foot, with upwards of forty pieces of cannon. They approached apace, and by six began to attack with a number of heavy cannon, supported by the whole army, and continued to play on us very briskly for several hours, during which our situation was of the utmost service to us, being lodged in a large grove with good mud banks. To succeed in an attempt on their cannon was next to impossible, as they were planted in a manner round us and at considerable distances from each other. We therefore remained quiet in our post, in expectation of a successful attack upon their camp at night. About noon the enemy drew off their artillery and retired to their camp. . . .

On finding them make no great effort to dislodge us, we proceeded to take possession of one or two more eminences

lying very near an angle of their camp, from whence, and an adjacent eminence in their possession, they kept a smart fire of musketry upon us. They made several attempts to bring out their cannon, but our advanced fieldpieces played so warmly and so well upon them that they were always driven back. Their horse exposing themselves a good deal on this occasion, many of them were killed, and among the rest four or five officers of the first distinction; by which the whole army being visibly dispirited and thrown into some confusion, we were encouraged to storm both the eminence and the angle of their camp, which were carried at the same instant, with little or no loss; though the latter was defended (exclusively of blacks) by forty French and two pieces of cannon; and the former by a large body of blacks, both horse and foot. On this a general rout ensued, and we pursued the enemy six miles, passing upwards of forty pieces of cannon they had abandoned, with an infinite number of carts and carriages filled with baggage of all kinds. . . . It is computed there are killed of the enemy about five hundred.

Our loss amounted to only twenty-two killed and fifty wounded, and those chiefly blacks.

 In what ways, if any, would Clive's account likely have been different if the Battle of Plassey had occurred in Europe? According to the letter, what role did native Indians seemingly play in the battle? Why does Clive give them such little mention?

the Austrians, Russians, and French. With his superb army and military skill, Frederick the Great of Prussia was able for some time to defeat the Austrian, French, and Russian armies. Eventually, however, his forces were gradually worn down and faced utter defeat until a new Russian tsar withdrew Russian troops from the conflict. A stalemate ensued, ending the European conflict in 1763.

The struggle between Britain and France in the rest of the world had more decisive results. In India, local rulers allied with British and French troops fought a number of battles. Ultimately, the British under Robert Clive won out, not because they had better forces but because they were more persistent (see the box above). By the Treaty of Paris in 1763, the French withdrew and left India to the British.

The greatest conflicts of the Seven Years' War took place in North America, where it was known as the French and Indian War. British and French rivalry led to a number of confrontations. The French had more troops in North America but less naval support. The defeat of French fleets in 1759 left the French unable to reinforce their garrisons. That year, British forces under General Wolfe defeated the French under

General Montcalm on the Plains of Abraham, outside Quebec. The British went on to seize Montreal, the Great Lakes area, and the Ohio valley. The French were forced to make peace. In the Treaty of Paris, they ceded Canada and the lands east of the Mississippi to Britain. Their ally Spain transferred Spanish Florida to British control; in return, the French gave their Louisiana territory to the Spanish. By 1763, Great Britain had become the world's greatest colonial power. The loss of France's empire was soon followed by an even greater internal upheaval.

The French Revolution

 FOCUS QUESTION: What were the causes, the main events, and the results of the French Revolution?

The year 1789 witnessed two far-reaching events, the beginning of a new United States of America under its revamped constitution and the eruption of the French Revolution. Compared to the American Revolution a decade earlier, the

French Revolution was more complex, more violent, and far more radical in its attempt to reconstruct both a new political order and a new social order.

Background to the French Revolution

The root causes of the French Revolution must be sought in the condition of French society. Before the Revolution, France was a society grounded in privilege and inequality. Its population of 27 million was divided, as it had been since the Middle Ages, into three orders or estates.

SOCIAL STRUCTURE OF THE OLD REGIME The First Estate consisted of the clergy and numbered about 130,000 people who owned approximately 10 percent of the land. Clergy were exempt from the *taille* (TY), France's chief tax. Clergy were also radically divided: the higher clergy, stemming from aristocratic families, shared the interests of the nobility, while the parish priests were often poor and from the class of commoners.

The Second Estate consisted of the nobility, composed of about 350,000 people who owned about 25 to 30 percent of the land. The nobility had continued to play an important and even crucial role in French society in the eighteenth century, holding many of the leading positions in the government, the military, the law courts, and the higher church offices. The nobles sought to expand their power at the expense of the monarchy and to maintain their control over positions in the military, church, and government. Moreover, the possession of privileges remained a hallmark of the nobility. Common to all nobles were tax exemptions, especially from the *taille*.

The Third Estate, or the commoners of society, constituted the overwhelming majority of the French population. They were divided by vast differences in occupation, level of education, and wealth. The peasants, who constituted 75 to 80 percent of the total population, were by far the largest segment of the Third Estate. They owned 35 to 40 percent of the land, although their landholdings varied from area to area and more than half had little or no land on which to survive. Serfdom no longer existed on any large scale in France, but French peasants still had obligations to their local landlords that they deeply resented. These "relics of feudalism," or aristocratic privileges, had survived from an earlier age and included the payment of fees for the use of village facilities, such as the flour mill, community oven, and winepress.

Another part of the Third Estate consisted of skilled crafts-people, shopkeepers, and other wage earners in the cities. In the eighteenth century, these urban groups suffered a noticeable decline in purchasing power as consumer prices rose faster than wages. Their daily struggle for survival led many of these people to play an important role in the Revolution, especially in Paris.

About 8 percent of the population, or 2.3 million people, constituted the bourgeoisie or middle class, who owned about 20 to 25 percent of the land. This group included merchants, industrialists, and bankers who controlled the resources of trade, manufacturing, and finance and benefited from the economic prosperity after 1730. The bourgeoisie also included professional people—lawyers, holders of public offices, doctors, and writers. Many members of the bourgeoisie had their own set of grievances because they were often excluded from the social and political privileges monopolized by nobles.

Moreover, the new political ideas of the Enlightenment proved attractive to both the aristocracy and the bourgeoisie. Both elites, long accustomed to a new socioeconomic reality based on wealth and economic achievement, were increasingly frustrated by a monarchical system resting on privileges and on an old and rigid social order based on the concept of estates. The opposition of these elites to the **old order** led them ultimately to take drastic action against the monarchical **old regime**. In a real sense, the Revolution had its origins in political grievances.

OTHER PROBLEMS FACING THE FRENCH MONARCHY Although France had enjoyed fifty years of economic expansion in the first half of the eighteenth century, in the late 1780s bad harvests in 1787 and 1788 and the beginnings of a manufacturing depression had resulted in food shortages, rising prices for food and other goods, and unemployment in the cities. The number of poor, estimated at almost one-third of the population, reached crisis proportions on the eve of the Revolution.

The French monarchy seemed incapable of dealing with the new social realities. Louis XVI (1774–1792) had become king in 1774 at the age of twenty; he knew little about the operations of the French government and lacked the energy to deal decisively with state affairs. His wife, Marie Antoinette (ma-REE ahn-twahn-NET), was a spoiled Austrian princess who devoted much of her time to court intrigues (see the Film & History feature on p. 527). As France's crises worsened, neither Louis nor his queen seemed able to fathom the depths of despair and discontent that soon led to violent revolution.

The immediate cause of the French Revolution was the near collapse of government finances. Costly wars and royal extravagance drove French governmental expenditures ever higher. On the verge of a complete financial collapse, the government of Louis XVI was finally forced to call a meeting of the Estates-General, the French parliamentary body that had not met since 1614. The Estates-General consisted of representatives from the three orders of French society. In the elections for the Estates-General, the government had ruled that the Third Estate should get double representation (it did, after all, constitute 97 percent of the population). Consequently, while both the First Estate (the clergy) and the Second Estate (the nobility) had about three hundred delegates each, the Third Estate had almost six hundred representatives, most of whom were lawyers from French towns.

From Estates-General to National Assembly

The Estates-General opened at Versailles on May 5, 1789. It was troubled from the start with the question of whether voting should be by order or by head (each delegate having one

FILM & HISTORY

Marie Antoinette (2006)

The film *Marie Antoinette* (2006), directed by Sofia Coppola, is based on Antonia Fraser's interpretation of the early life of Marie Antoinette in her book, *Marie Antoinette: A Journey* (2001). The film begins with the marriage of Marie Antoinette (Kirsten Dunst), the daughter of Empress Maria Theresa of Austria (Marianne Faithful), to the dauphin Louis (Jason Schwartzman), the heir to the French throne. Four years later, in 1774, Marie Antoinette became queen of France; in 1793, she went to the guillotine. Although the Revolution and financial troubles of the monarchy briefly enter the film toward the end, the majority of the film focuses on the experiences of a young woman thrust into the court of Versailles where she faces increasing suspicion, frustration, and isolation.

Columbia/American Zoetrope/Sony/The Kobal Collection

Marie Antoinette (Kirsten Dunst) at Versailles.

Perhaps the best part of the film is the portrayal of court life at Versailles. The film depicts days filled with courtly ceremonies, daily mass, and attendance of the public at meals. Under intense scrutiny due to her Austrian heritage and unfamiliar with the protocol of life at Versailles, Marie Antoinette makes several early missteps. She refuses to speak to Louis XV's mistress, the comtesse du Barry (Asia Argento), because the comtesse threatens Marie Antoinette's position as the highest-ranking woman at court. Ignoring the king's mistress, however, places the young dauphine in the precarious position of appearing to insult the king.

In addition to her troubles at court, Marie Antoinette faces an even greater challenge: the need to secure her place by producing an heir to the French throne. But her young husband, whose interests include hunting, lock making, and reading, creates problems for the young couple. Their marriage is not consummated for seven years. During these years, Marie Antoinette faces increasing pressure from her mother, who has produced sixteen children while ruling the Austrian Empire. Bored but aware that she must remain chaste, the young dauphine turns to frivolous pursuits including games, plays, outings in Paris, decorating, gambling, and, above all, purchasing clothes. Marie Antoinette's desire for elaborate gowns is encouraged by her role as the taste maker for the French court. In 1782, she commissions ninety-three gowns made of silk and other expensive fabrics. The scene of Marie Antoinette's twenty-first birthday is particularly effective in conveying how her frustration and boredom have led her to a life of frivolity and luxury. Sitting in her finery, she plays cards and eats sweets until the early hours of the morning.

After the birth of her children, the first in 1777, Marie Antoinette begins to withdraw from the scrutiny of the court. In 1783, she is given the keys to the Petit Trianon, a small palace on the grounds of Versailles, where she spends most of her days. Although she is spending more time with her children and less on the frivolity of her earlier days at Versailles, her increasing estrangement from the court only worsens her reputation with the French public.

Filmed at Versailles, the film captures the grandeur and splendor of eighteenth-century royal life. But the movie did not receive favorable reviews when it opened in France, in part because of its use of contemporary music by artists such as The Cure and The Strokes and the inclusion of modern products such as Converse sneakers. Although the flurry of costumes and music can be distracting, they also convey the rebelliousness of a young woman, frustrated and bored, isolated, and yet always on display.

---

vote). Traditionally, each order would vote as a group and have one vote. That meant that the First and Second Estates could outvote the Third Estate two to one. The Third Estate demanded that each deputy have one vote. With the assistance of liberal nobles and clerics, that would give the Third Estate a majority. When the First Estate declared in favor of voting by order, the Third Estate responded dramatically. On June 17, 1789, the Third Estate declared itself the "National Assembly" and decided to draw up a constitution. This was the first step in the French Revolution because the Third Estate had no legal right to act as the National Assembly. But this audacious act was soon in jeopardy, as the king sided with the First Estate and threatened to dissolve the Estates-General. Louis XVI now prepared to use force.

COMPARATIVE ILLUS-TRATION

POLITICS & GOVERNMENT

Revolution and Revolt in France and China. Both France and China experienced revolutionary upheaval at the end of the eighteenth century and well into the nineteenth. In both countries, common people often played an important role. At the right is a scene from the storming of the Bastille in Paris in 1789. This early action by the people of Paris ultimately led to the overthrow of the French monarchy. At the top is a scene from one of the struggles during the Taiping Rebellion, a major peasant revolt in the mid-nineteenth century in China. An imperial Chinese army is shown recapturing the city of Nanjing from Taiping rebels in 1864.

 What role did common people play in revolutionary upheavals in France and China in the eighteenth and nineteenth centuries?

The common people, however, saved the Third Estate from the king's forces. On July 14, a mob of Parisians stormed the Bastille, a royal armory, and proceeded to dismantle it, brick by brick. Louis XVI was soon informed that the royal troops were unreliable. Louis's acceptance of that reality signaled the collapse of royal authority; the king could no longer enforce his will.

At the same time, popular revolts broke out throughout France, both in the cities and in the countryside (see the comparative illustration above). Behind the popular uprising was a growing resentment of the entire landholding system, with its fees and obligations. The fall of the Bastille and the king's apparent capitulation to the demands of the Third Estate now led peasants to take matters into their own hands. The peasant rebellions that occurred throughout France had a great impact on the National Assembly meeting at Versailles.

Destruction of the Old Regime

One of the first acts of the National Assembly was to abolish the rights of landlords and the fiscal exemptions of nobles, clergy, towns, and provinces. Three weeks later, the National Assembly adopted the Declaration of the Rights of Man and the Citizen (see the box on p. 529). This charter of basic liberties proclaimed freedom and equal rights for all men and access to public office based on talent. All citizens were to have the right to take part in the legislative process. Freedom of speech and the press were coupled with the outlawing of arbitrary arrests.

The declaration also raised another important issue. Did its ideal of equal rights for "all men" also include women? Many deputies insisted that it did, provided that, as one said, "women do not hope to exercise political rights and functions." Olympe de Gouges (oh-LAMP duh GOOZH), a playwright, refused to accept this exclusion of women from political rights. Echoing the words of the official declaration, she penned the Declaration of the Rights of Woman and the Female Citizen, in which she insisted that women should have all the same rights as men (see the box on p. 529). The National Assembly ignored her demands.

Because the Catholic Church was seen as an important pillar of the old order, it too was reformed. Most of the lands of the church were seized. The new Civil Constitution of the Clergy was put into effect in 1790. Both bishops and priests

The Natural Rights of the French People: Two Views

POLITICS & GOVERNMENT

One of the important documents of the French Revolution, the Declaration of the Rights of Man and the Citizen was adopted on August 26, 1789, by the National Assembly. The declaration affirmed that "men are born and remain free and equal in rights," that government must protect these natural rights, and that political power is derived from the people.

Olympe de Gouges (the pen name used by Marie Gouze) was a butcher's daughter who wrote plays and pamphlets. She argued that the Declaration of the Rights of Man and the Citizen did not apply to women and composed her own Declaration of the Rights of Woman and the Female Citizen in 1791.

Declaration of the Rights of Man and the Citizen

1. Men are born and remain free and equal in rights. Social distinctions can only be founded upon the general good.

2. The aim of all political association is the preservation of the natural and imprescriptible rights of man. These rights are liberty, property, security, and resistance to oppression.

3. The principle of all sovereignty resides essentially in the nation. No body or individual may exercise any authority which does not proceed directly from the nation.

4. Liberty consists in being able to do everything which injures no one else. . . .

6. Law is the expression of the general will. Every citizen has a right to participate personally or through his representative in its formation. It must be the same for all, whether it protects or punishes. All citizens being equal in the eyes of the law are equally eligible to all dignities and to all public positions and occupations according to their abilities and without distinction except that of their virtues and talents.

7. No person shall be accused, arrested, or imprisoned except in the cases and according to the forms prescribed by law. . . .

10. No one shall be disturbed on account of his opinions, including his religious views, provided their manifestation does not disturb the public order established by law.

11. The free communication of ideas and opinions is one of the most precious of the rights of man. Every citizen may, accordingly, speak, write and print with freedom, being responsible, however, for such abuses of this freedom as shall be defined by law.

12. The security of the rights of man and of the citizen requires public military force. These forces are, therefore,

established for the good of all and not for the personal advantage of those to whom they shall be entrusted.

14. All the citizens have a right to decide either personally or by their representatives as to the necessity of the public contribution, to grant this freely, to know to what uses it is put, and to fix the proportion, the mode of assessment, and of collection, and the duration of the taxes.

15. Society has the right to require of every public agent an account of his administration.

16. A society in which the observance of the law is not assured nor the separation of powers defined has no constitution at all.

17. Property being an inviolable and sacred right, no one shall be deprived thereof except where public necessity, legally determined, shall clearly demand it, and then only on condition that the owner shall have been previously and equitably indemnified.

Declaration of the Rights of Woman and the Female Citizen

Mothers, daughters, sisters and representatives of the nation demand to be constituted into a national assembly. Believing that ignorance, omission, or scorn for the rights of woman are the only causes of public misfortunes and of the corruption of governments, the women have resolved to set forth in a solemn declaration the natural, inalienable, and sacred rights of woman in order that this declaration, constantly exposed before all the members of the society, will ceaselessly remind them of their rights and duties. . . .

Consequently, the sex that is as superior in beauty as it is in courage during the sufferings of maternity recognizes and declares in the presence and under the auspices of the Supreme Being, the following Rights of Woman and of Female Citizens.

1. Woman is born free and lives equal to man in her rights. Social distinctions can be based only on the common utility.

2. The purpose of any political association is the conservation of the natural and imprescriptible rights of woman and man; these rights are liberty, property, security, and especially resistance to oppression.

3. The principle of all sovereignty rests essentially with the nation, which is nothing but the union of woman and man; no body and no individual can exercise any authority which does not come expressly from [the nation].

4. Liberty and justice consist of restoring all that belongs to others; thus, the only limits on the exercise of the natural

(continued)

rights of woman are perpetual male tyranny; these limits are to be reformed by the laws of nature and reason. . . .

6. The law must be the expression of the general will; all female and male citizens must contribute either personally or through their representatives to its formation; it must be the same for all: male and female citizens, being equal in the eyes of the law, must be equally admitted to all honors, positions, and public employment according to their capacity and without other distinctions besides those of their virtues and talents.

7. No woman is an exception; she is accused, arrested, and detained in cases determined by law. Women, like men, obey this rigorous law. . . .

10. No one is to be disquieted for his very basic opinions; woman has the right to mount the scaffold; she must equally have the right to mount the rostrum, provided that her demonstrations do not disturb the legally established public order.

11. The free communication of thought and opinions is one of the most precious rights of woman, since that liberty assured the recognition of children by their fathers. . . .

12. The guarantee of the rights of woman and the female citizen implies a major benefit; this guarantee must be instituted for the advantage of all, and not for the particular benefit of those to whom it is entrusted. . . .

14. Female and male citizens have the right to verify, either by themselves or through their representatives, the neces-

sity of the public contribution. This can only apply to women if they are granted an equal share, not only of wealth, but also of public administration, and in the determination of the proportion, the base, the collection, and the duration of the tax.

15. The collectivity of women, joined for tax purposes to the aggregate of men, has the right to demand an accounting of his administration from any public agent.

16. No society has a constitution without the guarantee of rights and the separation of powers; the constitution is null if the majority of individuals comprising the nation have not cooperated in drafting it.

17. Property belongs to both sexes whether united or separate; for each it is an inviolable and sacred right; no one can be deprived of it, since it is the true patrimony of nature, unless the legally determined public need obviously dictates it, and then only with a just and prior indemnity.

 What "natural rights" does the first document proclaim? To what extent was this document influenced by the writings of the philosophes? What rights for women does the second document enunciate? Given the nature and scope of the arguments in favor of natural rights and women's rights in these two documents, what key effects on European society would you attribute to the French Revolution?

---

were to be elected by the people and paid by the state. The Catholic Church, still an important institution in the life of the French people, now became an enemy of the Revolution.

By 1791, the National Assembly had completed a new constitution that established a limited constitutional monarchy. There was still a monarch (now called "king of the French"), but the new Legislative Assembly was to make the laws. The Legislative Assembly, in which sovereign power was vested, was to sit for two years and consist of 745 representatives, or deputies, chosen by an indirect system of election that preserved power in the hands of the more affluent members of society. A small group of 50,000 electors chose the deputies.

By 1791, the old order had been destroyed. The new order, however, had many opponents—Catholic priests, nobles, lower classes hurt by a rise in the cost of living, peasants who remained opposed to dues that had still not been abandoned, and political clubs like the Jacobins (JAK-uh-binz) that offered more radical solutions to France's problems. The king also made things difficult for the new government when he sought to flee France in June 1791 and almost succeeded before being recognized, captured, and brought back to Paris. In this unsettled situation, under a discredited and seemingly disloyal monarch, the new Legislative Assembly held its first session in October 1791. France's relations with the rest of Europe soon led to Louis's downfall.

On August 27, 1791, the monarchs of Austria and Prussia, fearing that revolution would spread to their countries, invited other European monarchs to use force to reestablish monarchical authority in France. The French fared badly in the initial fighting in the spring of 1792, and a frantic search for scapegoats began. As one observer noted, "Everywhere you hear the cry that the king is betraying us, the generals are betraying us, that nobody is to be trusted; . . . that Paris will be taken in six weeks by the Austrians. . . . We are on a volcano ready to spout flames."[4] Defeats in war coupled with economic shortages in the spring led to renewed political demonstrations, especially against the king. In August 1792, radical political groups in Paris attacked the royal palace, took the king captive, and forced the Legislative Assembly to suspend the monarchy and call for a national convention, chosen on the basis of universal male suffrage, to decide on the future form of government. The French Revolution was about to enter a more radical stage.

The Radical Revolution

In September 1792, the newly elected National Convention began its sessions. Dominated by lawyers and other professionals, two-thirds of its deputies were under the age of forty-five, and almost all had gained political experience as a result of the Revolution. Almost all distrusted the king. As a result, the convention's first step on September 21 was to abolish the monarchy and establish a republic. On January 21, 1793, the king was executed, and the destruction of the old regime was complete. But the execution of the king created new enemies for the Revolution both at home and abroad.

In Paris, the local government, known as the Commune, whose leaders came from the working classes, favored radical change and put constant pressure on the convention, pushing it to ever more radical positions. Meanwhile, peasants in the west and inhabitants of the major provincial cities refused to accept the authority of the convention.

A foreign crisis also loomed large. By the beginning of 1793, after the king had been put to death, most of Europe— an informal coalition of Austria, Prussia, Spain, Portugal, Britain, the Dutch Republic, and even Russia—aligned militarily against France. Grossly overextended, the French armies began to experience reverses, and by late spring, France was threatened with invasion.

A NATION IN ARMS To meet these crises, the convention gave broad powers to an executive committee of twelve known as the Committee of Public Safety, which came to be dominated by Maximilien Robespierre (mak-see-meel-YENH ROHBZ-pyayr). For a twelve-month period, from 1793 to 1794, the Committee of Public Safety took control of France. To save the Republic from its foreign foes, the committee decreed a universal mobilization of the nation on August 23, 1793:

> Young men will fight, young men are called to conquer. Married men will forge arms, transport military baggage and guns and will prepare food supplies. Women, who at long last are to take their rightful place in the revolution and follow their true destiny, will forget their futile tasks: their delicate hands will work at making clothes for soldiers; they will make tents and they will extend their tender care to shelters where the defenders of the *Patrie* [nation] will receive the help that their wounds require. Children will make lint of old cloth. It is for them that we are fighting: children, those beings destined to gather all the fruits of the revolution, will raise their pure hands toward the skies. And old men, performing their missions again, as of yore, will be guided to the public squares of the cities where they will kindle the courage of young warriors and preach the doctrines of hate for kings and the unity of the Republic.[5]

In less than a year, the French revolutionary government had raised an army of 650,000 and by 1795 had pushed the allies back across the Rhine and even conquered the Austrian Netherlands.

The French revolutionary army was an important step in the creation of modern **nationalism**. Previously, wars had been fought between governments or ruling dynasties by relatively small armies of professional soldiers. The new French army was the creation of a "people's" government; its wars were now "people's" wars. The entire nation was to be involved in the war. But when dynastic wars became people's wars, warfare increased in ferocity and lack of restraint. The wars of the French revolutionary era opened the door to the total war of the modern world.

REIGN OF TERROR To meet the domestic crisis, the National Convention and the Committee of Public Safety launched the "Reign of Terror." Revolutionary courts were instituted to protect the Republic from its internal enemies. In the course of nine months, 16,000 people were officially killed under the blade of the guillotine—a revolutionary device designed for the quick and efficient separation of heads from bodies (see the box on p. 532).

Revolutionary armies were set up to bring recalcitrant cities and districts back under the control of the National Convention. The Committee of Public Safety decided to make an example of Lyons (LYOHNH), which had defied the authority of the National Convention. By April 1794, some

Citizens in the New French Army. To save the Republic from its foreign enemies, the National Convention created a revolutionary army of unprecedented size. This illustration, from a book of paintings on the French Revolution by the Lesueur brothers, shows three citizens learning to drill, while a young volunteer is being armed and outfitted by his family.

Justice in the Reign of Terror

POLITICS & GOVERNMENT

The Reign of Terror created a repressive environment in which revolutionary courts often acted quickly to condemn traitors to the revolutionary cause. In this account, an English visitor describes the court, the procession to the scene of execution, and the final execution procedure.

J. G. Milligen, *The Revolutionary Tribunal* (Paris, October 1793)

In the center of the hall, under a statue of Justice, holding scales in one hand, and a sword in the other, sat Dumas, the President, with the other judges. Under them were seated the public accuser, Fourquier-Tinville, and his scribes. . . . To the right were benches on which the accused were placed in several rows, and gendarmes with carbines and fixed bayonets by their sides. To the left was the jury.

Never can I forget the mournful appearance of these funereal processions to the place of execution. The march was opened by a detachment of mounted gendarmes—the carts followed; they were the same carts as those that are used in Paris for carrying wood; four boards were placed across them for seats, and on each board sat two, and sometimes three victims; their hands were tied behind their backs, and the constant jostling of the cart made them nod their heads up and down, to the great amusement of the spectators. On the front of the cart stood Samson, the executioner, or one of his sons or assistants; gendarmes on foot marched by the side; then followed a hackney, in which was the reporting clerk, whose duty it was to witness the execution, and then return to the public accuser's office to report the execution of what they called the law.

The process of execution was also a sad and heart-rending spectacle. In the middle of the Place de la Revolution was erected a guillotine, in front of a colossal statue of Liberty, represented seated on a rock, a cap on her head, a spear in her hand, the other reposing on a shield. On one side of the scaffold were drawn out a sufficient number of carts, with large baskets painted red, to receive the heads and bodies of the victims. Those bearing the condemned moved on slowly to the foot of the guillotine; the culprits were led out in turn, and if necessary, supported by two of the executioner's assistants, but their assistance was rarely required. Most of these unfortunates ascended the scaffold with a determined step—many of them looked up firmly on the menacing instrument of death, beholding for the last time the rays of the glorious sun, beaming on the polished axe: and I have seen some young men actually dance a few steps before they went up to be strapped to the perpendicular plane, which was then tilted to a horizontal plane in a moment, and ran on the grooves until the neck was secured and closed in by a moving board, when the head passed through what was called, in derision, "the republican toilet seat"; the weighty knife was then dropped with a heavy fall; and, with incredible dexterity and rapidity, two executioners tossed the body into the basket, while another threw the head after it.

How were the condemned taken to the executioner? How did this serve to inflame the crowds? How were people executed? Why?

1,880 citizens of Lyons had been executed. When the guillotine proved too slow, cannon fire was used to blow condemned men into open graves. A German observed:

> Whole ranges of houses, always the most handsome, burnt. The churches, convents, and all the dwellings of the former patricians were in ruins. When I came to the guillotine, the blood of those who had been executed a few hours beforehand was still running in the street. . . . I said to a group of [radicals] that it would be decent to clear away all this human blood. Why should it be cleared? one of them said to me. It's the blood of aristocrats and rebels. The dogs should lick it up.[6]

EQUALITY AND SLAVERY: REVOLUTION IN HAITI Early in the French Revolution, the desire for equality led to a discussion of what to do about slavery. A club called Friends of the Blacks advocated the abolition of slavery, which was achieved in France in September 1791. However, French planters in the West Indies, who profited greatly from the use of slaves on their sugar plantations, opposed the abolition of slavery in the French colonies. When the National Convention came to power, the issue was revisited, and on February 4, 1794, guided by ideals of equality, the government abolished slavery in the colonies.

In one French colony, slaves had already rebelled for their freedom. In 1791, black slaves in the French sugar colony of Saint-Domingue (san doh-MAYNG) (the western third of the island of Hispaniola), inspired by the ideals of the revolution occurring in France, revolted against French plantation owners. Slaves attacked, killing plantation owners and their families and burning their buildings. White planters retaliated with equal

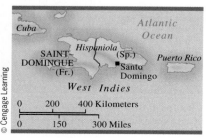

Revolt in Saint-Domingue

brutality. One wealthy French settler reported, "How can we stay in a country where slaves have raised their hands against their masters?"

Eventually, leadership of the revolt was taken over by Toussaint L'Ouverture (too-SANH loo-vayr-TOOR) (1746–1803), a son of African slaves, who seized control of all of Hispaniola by 1801. Although Napoleon, the French leader, had accepted the revolutionary ideal of equality, he did not reject the reports of white planters that the massacres of white planters by slaves demonstrated the savage nature of blacks. In 1802, he reinstated slavery in the French West Indian colonies and sent an army that captured L'Ouverture, who died in a French dungeon within a year. But the French soldiers, weakened by disease, soon succumbed to the slave forces. On January 1, 1804, the western part of Hispaniola, now called Haiti, announced its freedom and became the first state in Latin America to win its independence. Despite Napoleon's efforts to the contrary, one of the French revolutionary ideals had triumphed abroad.

Reaction and the Directory

By the summer of 1794, the French had been successful on the battlefield against their foreign foes, making the Reign of Terror less necessary. But the Terror continued because Robespierre, who had become a figure of power and authority, became obsessed with purifying the body politic of all the corrupt. Many deputies in the National Convention were fearful, however, that they were not safe while Robespierre was free to act and gathered enough votes to condemn him. Robespierre was sent to the guillotine on July 28, 1794.

After the death of Robespierre, a reaction set in as more moderate middle-class leaders took control. The Reign of Terror came to a halt, and the National Convention reduced the power of the Committee of Public Safety. In addition, in August 1795 a new constitution was drafted that reflected the desire for a stability that did not sacrifice the ideals of 1789. Five directors—known as the Directory—acted as the executive authority.

Government under the Directory (1795–1799) was characterized by stagnation and corruption. The Directory faced political enemies on both the left and the right. On the right, royalists who wanted to restore the monarchy continued their agitation. On the left, radical hopes of power were revived by continuing economic problems. Battered from both sides, unable to solve the country's economic problems, and still carrying on the wars inherited from the Committee of Public Safety, the Directory increasingly relied on the military to maintain its power. This led to a coup d'état in 1799 in which a popular military general, Napoleon Bonaparte (1769–1821), seized power.

The Age of Napoleon

 FOCUS QUESTION: Which aspects of the French Revolution did Napoleon preserve, and which did he destroy?

Napoleon dominated both French and European history from 1799 to 1815. The coup that brought him to power occurred exactly ten years after the outbreak of the French Revolution. In

CHRONOLOGY	The French Revolution
Meeting of the Estates-General	May 5, 1789
Formation of the National Assembly	June 17, 1789
Fall of the Bastille	July 14, 1789
Declaration of the Rights of Man and the Citizen	August 26, 1789
Civil Constitution of the Clergy	July 12, 1790
Flight of the king	June 20–21, 1791
Attack on the royal palace	August 10, 1792
Abolition of the monarchy	September 21, 1792
Execution of the king	January 21, 1793
Universal mobilization	August 23, 1793
Execution of Robespierre	July 28, 1794
Adoption of the Constitution of 1795 and the Directory	August 22, 1795

a sense, Napoleon brought the Revolution to an end, but he was also its child; he even called himself the Son of the Revolution. The French Revolution had made possible his rise first in the military and then to supreme power in France. Even beyond this, Napoleon had once said, "I am the Revolution," and he never ceased to remind the French that they owed to him the preservation of all that was beneficial in the revolutionary program.

The Rise of Napoleon

Napoleon was born in Corsica in 1769, only a few months after France had annexed the island. The son of an Italian lawyer whose family stemmed from the Florentine nobility, Napoleone Buonaparte (his birth name) grew up in the countryside of Corsica, a willful and demanding child who nevertheless developed discipline, thriftiness, and loyalty to his family. His father's connections in France enabled him to study first at a school in the French town of Autun, where he learned to speak French, and then to obtain a royal scholarship to study at a military school. At that time, he changed his first name to the more French-sounding Napoleon (he did not change his last name to Bonaparte until 1796).

Napoleon's military education led to his commission as a lieutenant in 1785, although he was not well liked by his fellow officers because he was short, spoke with an Italian accent, and had little money. For the next seven years, Napoleon spent much of his time reading the works of the philosophes, especially Rousseau, and educating himself in military matters by studying the campaigns of great military leaders from the past, including Alexander the Great, Charlemagne, and Frederick the Great. The French Revolution and the European war that followed broadened his sights and presented him with new opportunities.

Napoleon rose quickly through the ranks. In 1794, at the age of only twenty-five, he was made a brigadier general by the Committee of Public Safety. Two years later, he commanded the French armies in Italy, where he won a series of victories and returned to France as a conquering hero (see

Napoleon and Psychological Warfare

POLITICS & GOVERNMENT

In 1796, at the age of twenty-seven, Napoleon Bonaparte was given command of the French army in Italy, where he won a series of stunning victories. His use of speed, deception, and surprise to overwhelm his opponents is well known. In this selection from a proclamation to his troops in Italy, Napoleon also appears as a master of psychological warfare.

Napoleon Bonaparte, Proclamation to French Troops in Italy (April 26, 1796)

Soldiers:

In a fortnight you have won six victories, taken twenty-one standards [flags of military units], fifty-five pieces of artillery, several strong positions, and conquered the richest part of Piedmont [in northern Italy]; you have captured 15,000 prisoners and killed or wounded more than 10,000 men. . . . You have won battles without cannon, crossed rivers without bridges, made forced marches without shoes, camped without brandy and often without bread. Soldiers of liberty, only republican troops could have endured what you have endured. Soldiers, you have our thanks! The grateful *Patrie* [nation] will owe its prosperity to you. . . .

The two armies which but recently attacked you with audacity are fleeing before you in terror; the wicked men who laughed at your misery and rejoiced at the thought of the triumphs of your enemies are confounded and trembling.

But, soldiers, as yet you have done nothing compared with what remains to be done. . . . Undoubtedly the greatest obstacles have been overcome; but you still have battles to fight, cities to capture, rivers to cross. Is there one among you whose courage is abating? No. . . . All of you are consumed with a desire to extend the glory of the French people; all of you long to humiliate those arrogant kings who dare to contemplate placing us in fetters; all of you desire to dictate a glorious peace, one which will indemnify the *Patrie* for the immense sacrifices it has made; all of you wish to be able to say with pride as you return to your villages, "I was with the victorious army of Italy!"

 What themes did Napoleon use to play on the emotions of his troops and inspire them to greater efforts? Do you think Napoleon believed these words? Why or why not?

---

the box above). After a disastrous expedition to Egypt, Napoleon returned to Paris, where he participated in the coup that gave him control of France. He was only thirty years old.

After the coup of 1799, a new form of the Republic, called the Consulate, was proclaimed in which Napoleon, as first consul, controlled the entire executive authority of government. He had overwhelming influence over the legislature, appointed members of the administrative bureaucracy, commanded the army, and conducted foreign affairs. In 1802, Napoleon was made consul for life, and in 1804, he returned France to monarchy when he crowned himself Emperor Napoleon I.

Domestic Policies

One of Napoleon's first domestic policies was to establish peace with the oldest and most implacable enemy of the Revolution, the Catholic Church. In 1801, Napoleon arranged a concordat with the pope that recognized Catholicism as the religion of a majority of the French people. In return, the pope agreed not to raise the question of the church lands confiscated in the Revolution. As a result of the concordat, the Catholic Church was no longer an enemy of the French government, and Frenchmen who had acquired church lands during the Revolution were assured that they would not be stripped of them, an assurance that made them supporters of the Napoleonic regime.

Napoleon's most enduring domestic achievement was his codification of the laws. Before the Revolution, France had some three hundred local legal systems. During the Revolution, efforts were made to prepare a single code of laws for the entire nation, but it remained for Napoleon to bring the work to completion in the famous Civil Code. This preserved most of the revolutionary gains by recognizing the principle of the equality of all citizens before the law, the abolition of serfdom and feudalism, and religious toleration. Property rights were also protected.

At the same time, the Civil Code strictly curtailed the rights of some people. During the radical phase of the French Revolution, new laws had made divorce an easy process for both husbands and wives and allowed sons and daughters to inherit property equally. Napoleon's Civil Code undid these laws. Divorce was still allowed but was made more difficult for women to obtain. Women were now "less equal than men" in other ways as well. When they married, their property came under the control of their husbands.

Napoleon also developed a powerful, centralized administrative machine and worked hard to develop a bureaucracy of capable officials. Early on, the regime showed that it cared little whether the expertise of officials had been acquired in royal or revolutionary bureaucracies. Promotion, whether in civil or military offices, was to be based not on rank or birth but on ability only. This principle of a government career

The Coronation of Napoleon. In 1804, Napoleon restored monarchy to France when he crowned himself emperor. In the coronation scene painted by Jacques-Louis David, Napoleon is shown crowning his wife, the empress Josephine, while the pope looks on. The painting shows Napoleon's mother seated in the box in the background, even though she was not at the ceremony.

open to talent was, of course, what many bourgeois had wanted before the Revolution.

In his domestic policies, then, Napoleon both destroyed and preserved aspects of the Revolution. Although equality and the opening of careers to talent were retained in the law code, the creation of a new aristocracy, the strong protection accorded to property rights, and the use of conscription for the military make it clear that much equality had been lost. Liberty had been replaced by an initially benevolent despotism that grew increasingly arbitrary. Napoleon shut down sixty of France's seventy-three newspapers and insisted that all manuscripts be subjected to government scrutiny before they were published. Even the mail was opened by government police.

Napoleon's Empire

When Napoleon became consul in 1799, France was at war with a second European coalition of Russia, Great Britain, and Austria. Napoleon realized the need for a pause and made a peace treaty in 1802. But war was renewed in 1803 with Britain, which was soon joined by Austria, Russia, and Prussia in the Third Coalition. In a series of battles from 1805 to 1807, Napoleon's Grand Army defeated the Austrian, Prussian, and Russian armies, giving Napoleon the opportunity to create a new European order.

THE GRAND EMPIRE From 1807 to 1812, Napoleon was the master of Europe. His Grand Empire was composed of three major parts: the French Empire, dependent states, and allied states (see Map 18.4). Dependent states were kingdoms under the rule of Napoleon's relatives; these came to include Spain, the Netherlands, the kingdom of Italy, the Swiss Republic, the Grand Duchy of Warsaw, and the Confederation of the Rhine (a union of all German states except Austria and Prussia). Allied states were those defeated by Napoleon and forced to join his struggle against Britain; these included Prussia, Austria, Russia, and Sweden.

Within his empire, Napoleon sought acceptance of certain revolutionary principles, including legal equality, religious toleration, and economic freedom. In the inner core and dependent states of his Grand Empire, Napoleon tried to destroy the old order. Nobility and clergy everywhere in these states lost their special privileges. He decreed equality of opportunity with offices open to talent, equality before the law, and religious toleration. This spread of French revolutionary principles was an important factor in the development of liberal traditions in these countries.

Napoleon hoped that his Grand Empire would last for centuries; it collapsed almost as rapidly as it had been formed. As long as Britain ruled the waves, it was not subject to military attack. Napoleon hoped to invade Britain, but he could not overcome the British navy's decisive defeat of a combined

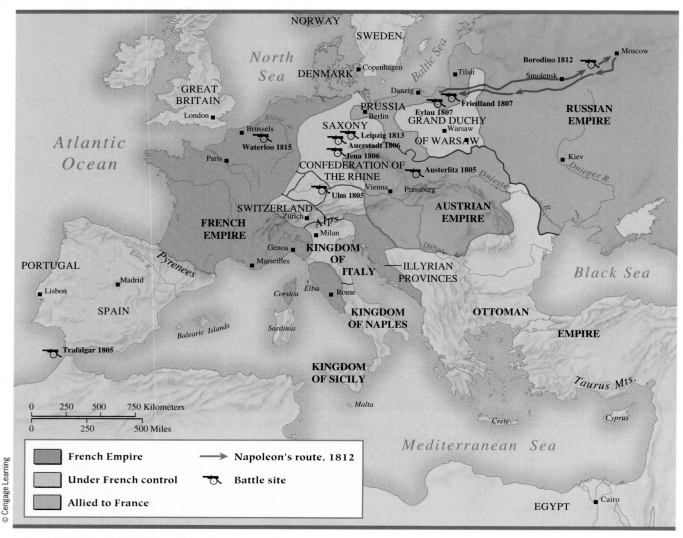

MAP 18.4 Napoleon's Grand Empire. Napoleon's Grand Army won a series of victories against Austria, Prussia, and Russia that gave the French emperor full or partial control over much of Europe by 1807.

Q *On the Continent, what is the overall relationship between distance from France and degree of French control, and how can you account for this?*

French-Spanish fleet at Trafalgar in 1805. To defeat Britain, Napoleon turned to his **Continental system**. An alliance put into effect between 1806 and 1808, it attempted to prevent British goods from reaching the European continent in order to weaken Britain economically and destroy its capacity to wage war. But the Continental system failed. Allied states resented it; some began to cheat and others to resist.

Napoleon also encountered new sources of opposition. His conquests made the French hated oppressors and aroused the patriotism of the conquered peoples. A Spanish uprising against Napoleon's rule, with British support, kept a French force of 200,000 pinned down for years.

THE FALL OF NAPOLEON The beginning of Napoleon's downfall came in 1812 with his invasion of Russia. The refusal of the Russians to remain in the Continental system left Napoleon with little choice. Although aware of the risks in invading such a huge country, he also knew that if the

Russians were allowed to challenge the Continental system unopposed, others would soon follow suit. In June 1812, he led his Grand Army of more than 600,000 men into Russia. Napoleon's hopes for victory depended on quickly defeating the Russian armies, but the Russian forces retreated and refused to give battle, torching their own villages and countryside to keep Napoleon's army from finding food. When the Russians did stop to fight at Borodino, Napoleon's forces won an indecisive and costly victory. When the remaining troops of the Grand Army arrived in Moscow, they found the city ablaze. Lacking food and supplies, Napoleon abandoned Moscow late in October and made a retreat across Russia in terrible winter conditions. Only 40,000 of the original 600,000 men managed to arrive back in Poland in January 1813.

This military disaster led other European states to rise up and attack the crippled French army. Paris was captured in March 1814, and Napoleon was sent into exile on the island of Elba, off the coast of Italy. Meanwhile, the Bourbon monarchy was restored in the person of Louis XVIII, the count of Provence, brother of the executed king. (Louis XVII, son of Louis XVI, had died in prison at age ten.) Napoleon, bored on Elba, slipped back into France. When troops were sent to capture him, Napoleon opened his coat and addressed them: "Soldiers of the 5th regiment, I am your Emperor. . . . If there is a man among you would kill his Emperor, here I am!" No one fired a shot. Shouting "Vive l'Empereur! Vive l'Empereur!" the troops went over to his side, and Napoleon entered Paris in triumph on March 20, 1815.

The powers that had defeated him pledged once more to fight him. Having decided to strike first at his enemies, Napoleon raised yet another army and moved to attack the allied forces stationed in what is now Belgium. At Waterloo on June 18, Napoleon met a combined British and Prussian army under the duke of Wellington and suffered a bloody defeat. This time, the victorious allies exiled him to Saint Helena, a small, forsaken island in the South Atlantic. Only Napoleon's memory continued to haunt French political life.

CHAPTER SUMMARY

In the Scientific Revolution, the Western world overthrew the medieval, Ptolemaic worldview and arrived at a new conception of the universe: the sun at the center, the planets as material bodies revolving around the sun in elliptical orbits, and an infinite rather than finite world. With the changes in the conception of "heaven" came changes in the conception of "earth." The work of Descartes left Europeans with the separation of mind and matter and the belief that by using only reason they could, in fact, understand and dominate the world of nature.

Highly influenced by the new worldview created by the Scientific Revolution, the philosophes of the eighteenth century hoped that they could create a new society by using reason to discover the natural laws that governed it. They believed that education could create better human beings and a better human society. They attacked traditional religion as the enemy and created the new "sciences of man" in economics, politics, and education. Together, the Scientific Revolution of the seventeenth century and the Enlightenment of the eighteenth century constituted an intellectual revolution that laid the foundations for a modern worldview based on rationalism and secularism.

Everywhere in Europe at the beginning of the eighteenth century, the old order remained strong. Nobles, clerics, towns, and provinces all had privileges. Everywhere in the eighteenth century, monarchs sought to enlarge their bureaucracies to raise taxes to support large standing armies. The existence of these armies led to wars on a worldwide scale. Indeed, the Seven Years' War could be viewed as the

first world war. Although the wars resulted in few changes in Europe, British victories enabled Great Britain to emerge as the world's greatest naval and colonial power. Meanwhile, in Europe increased demands for taxes to support these wars led to attacks on the old order and a desire for change not met by the ruling

monarchs. At the same time, a growing population as well as changes in finance, trade, and industry created tensions that undermined the foundations of the old order. Its inability to deal with these changes led to a revolutionary outburst at the end of the eighteenth century that marked the beginning of the end for the old order.

The revolutionary era of the late eighteenth century was a time of dramatic political transformations. Revolutionary upheavals, beginning in North America and continuing in France, spurred movements for political liberty and equality. The documents promulgated by these revolutions, the Declaration of Independence and the Declaration of the Rights of Man and the Citi-

zen, embodied the fundamental ideas of the Enlightenment and created a liberal political agenda based on a belief in popular sovereignty—the people as the source of political power—and the principles of liberty and equality. Liberty meant, in theory, freedom from arbitrary power as well as the freedom to think, write, and worship as one chose. Equality meant equality in rights, although it did not include equality between men and women.

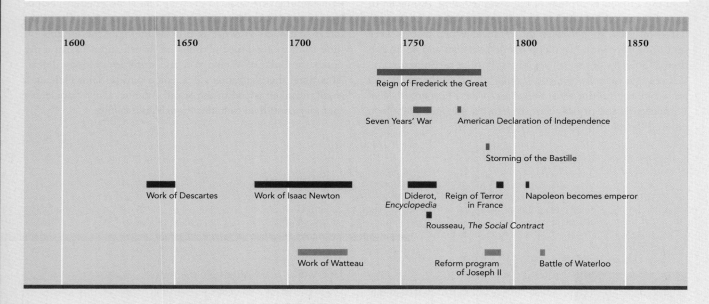

1600   1650   1700   1750   1800   1850

Reign of Frederick the Great

Seven Years' War   American Declaration of Independence

Storming of the Bastille

Work of Descartes   Work of Isaac Newton   Diderot, *Encyclopedia*   Reign of Terror in France   Napoleon becomes emperor

Rousseau, *The Social Contract*

Work of Watteau   Reform program of Joseph II   Battle of Waterloo

CHAPTER REVIEW

Upon Reflection

Q What was the impact of the intellectual revolution of the seventeenth and eighteenth centuries on European society?

Q How was France changed by the revolutionary events between 1789 and 1799, and who benefited the most from these changes?

Q In what ways did Napoleon's policies reject the accomplishments of the French Revolution? In what ways did his policies strengthen those accomplishments?

Key Terms

Scientific Revolution (p. 509)
geocentric theory (p. 509)
heliocentric theory (p. 509)
world-machine (p. 510)
Cartesian dualism (p. 511)
rationalism (p. 511)
Enlightenment (p. 511)
scientific method (p. 511)
philosophes (p. 511)
separation of powers (p. 512)
deism (p. 513)
laissez-faire (p. 515)
feminism (p. 515)
Rococo (p. 516)
high culture (p. 517)
popular culture (p. 517)
cottage industry (p. 518)
patrician (p. 520)
rentiers (p. 520)

natural rights (p. 522)
enlightened absolutism (p. 522)
old order (p. 526)
old regime (p. 526)
nationalism (p. 531)
Continental system (p. 536)

Suggested Reading

INTELLECTUAL REVOLUTION IN THE WEST Two general surveys of the Scientific Revolution are **J. R. Jacob,** *The Scientific Revolution: Aspirations and Achievements, 1500–1700* (Atlantic Highlands, N.J., 1998), and **J. Henry,** *The Scientific Revolution and the Origins of Modern Science,* 2nd ed. (New York, 2002). Good introductions to the Enlightenment can be found in **U. Im Hof,** *The Enlightenment* (Oxford, 1994), and **D. Outram,** *The Enlightenment,* 2nd ed. (Cambridge, 2005). See also **P. H. Reill** and **E. J. Wilson, eds.,** *Encyclopedia of the Enlightenment,* rev. ed. (New York, 2004). On women in the eighteenth century, see **M. E. Wiesner-Hanks,** *Women and Gender in Early Modern Europe* (Cambridge, 2000).

THE SOCIAL ORDER On the European nobility in the eighteenth century, see **J. Dewald,** *The European Nobility, 1400–1800,* 2nd ed. (Cambridge, 2004).

ENLIGHTENED ABSOLUTISM AND GLOBAL CONFLICT On enlightened absolutism, see **D. Beales,** *Enlightenment and Reform in Eighteenth-Century Europe* (New York, 2005).

THE FRENCH REVOLUTION A well-written, up-to-date introduction to the French Revolution can be found in **W. Doyle,** *The Oxford History of the French Revolution,* 2nd ed. (Oxford, 2003). On the entire revolutionary and Napoleonic eras, see **O. Connelly,** *The French Revolution and Napoleonic Era,* 3rd ed. (Fort Worth, Tex., 2000). For interesting insight into Louis XVI and French society, see **T. Tackett,** *When the King Took Flight* (Cambridge, Mass., 2003). An important work on the radical stage of the French Revolution is **D. Andress,** *The Terror: The Merciless War for Freedom in Revolutionary France* (New York, 2005). The importance of the revolutionary wars in the radical stage of the Revolution is underscored in **T. C. W. Blanning,** *The French Revolutionary Wars, 1787–1802* (New York, 1996).

THE AGE OF NAPOLEON The best biography of Napoleon is **S. Englund,** *Napoleon: A Political Life* (New York, 2004). See **A. I. Grab,** *Napoleon and the Transformation of Europe* (New York, 2003), on Napoleon's Grand Empire. On Napoleon's wars, see **D. A. Bell,** *The First Total War: Napoleon's Europe and the Birth of Warfare as We Know It* (Boston, 2007).

Go to the CourseMate website at **www.cengagebrain.com** for additional study tools and review materials— including audio and video clips—for this chapter.

THE PERIOD OF WORLD HISTORY from 1800 to 1945 was characterized by three major developments: the growth of industrialization, Western domination of the world, and the rise of nationalism. The three developments were, of course, interconnected. The Industrial Revolution became one of the major forces of change in the nineteenth century as it led Western civilization into the industrial era that has characterized the modern world. Beginning in Britain, it spread to the Continent and the Western Hemisphere in the course of the nineteenth century. At the same time, the Industrial Revolution created the technological means, including new weapons, by which the West achieved domination over much of the rest of the world by the end of the nineteenth century. Moreover, the existence of competitive European nation-states after 1870 was undoubtedly a major determinant in leading European states to embark on their intense scramble for overseas territory.

The advent of the industrial age had a number of lasting consequences for the world at large. On the one hand, the material wealth of the nations that successfully passed through the process increased significantly. In many cases, the creation of advanced industrial societies strengthened democratic institutions and led to a higher standard of living for the majority of the population. On the other hand, not all the consequences of the Industrial Revolution were beneficial. In the industrializing societies themselves, rapid economic change often led to widening disparities in the distribution of wealth and, with the decline in the pervasiveness of religious belief, a sense of rootlessness and alienation among much of the population.

A second development that had a major impact on the era was the rise of nationalism. Like the Industrial Revolution, the idea of nationalism originated in eighteenth-century Europe, where it was a product of the secularization of the age and the experience of the French revolutionary and Napoleonic eras. Although the concept provided the basis for a new sense of community and the rise of the modern nation-state, it also gave birth to ethnic tensions and hatreds that resulted in bitter disputes and civil strife and contributed to the competition that eventually erupted into world war.

Industrialization and the rise of national consciousness also transformed the nature of war itself. New weapons of mass destruction created the potential for a new kind of warfare that reached beyond the battlefield into the very heartland of the enemy's territory, while the concept of nationalism transformed war from the sport of kings to a matter of national honor and commitment. Since the French Revolution, governments had relied on mass conscription to defend the national cause, while their engines of destruction reached far into enemy territory to destroy the industrial base and undermine the will to fight. This trend was amply demonstrated in the two world wars of the twentieth century.

In the end, then, industrial power and the driving force of nationalism, the very factors that had created the conditions for European global dominance, contained the seeds for the decline of that dominance. These seeds germinated during the 1930s, when the Great Depression sharpened international competition and mutual antagonism, and then sprouted in the ensuing conflict, which for the first time spanned the entire globe. By the time World War II came to an end, the once powerful countries of Europe were exhausted, leaving the door ajar for the emergence of two new global superpowers, the United States and the Soviet Union, and for the collapse of the Europeans' colonial empires.

Europeans had begun to explore the world in the fifteenth century, but even as late as 1870, they had not yet completely penetrated North America, South America, Australia, or most of Africa. In Asia and Africa, with few exceptions, the Western presence was limited to trading posts. Between 1870 and 1914, Western civilization expanded into the rest of the Americas and Australia, while the bulk of Africa and Asia was divided into European colonies or spheres of influence. Two major events explain this remarkable expansion: the migration of many Europeans to other parts of the world due to population growth and the revival of imperialism, which was made possible by the West's technological advances. Beginning in the 1880s, European states began an intense scramble for overseas territory. This revival of imperialism—the "new imperialism," some have called it—led Europeans to carve up Asia and Africa.

What was the overall economic effect of imperialism on the subject peoples? For most of the population in colonial areas, Western domination was rarely beneficial and often destructive. Although a limited number of merchants, large landowners, and traditional hereditary elites undoubtedly prospered under the umbrella of the expanding imperialistic economic order, the majority of colonial peoples, urban and rural alike, probably suffered considerable hardship as a result of the policies adopted by their foreign rulers.

Some historians point out, however, that for all the inequities of the colonial system, there was a positive side to the experience as well. The expansion of markets and the beginnings of a modern transportation and communications network, while bringing few immediate benefits to the colonial peoples, offered considerable promise for future economic growth. At the same time, colonial peoples soon learned the power of nationalism, and in the twentieth century, nationalism would become a powerful force in the rest of the world as nationalist revolutions moved through Asia, Africa, and the Middle East. Moreover, the exhaustive struggles of two world wars sapped the power of the European states, and the colonial powers no longer had the energy or the wealth to maintain their colonial empires after World War II. ◆

The Beginnings of Modernization: Industrialization and Nationalism in the Nineteenth Century

Museo del Risorgimento, Milan//© Scala/Art Resource, NY

A meeting of the Congress of Vienna

CHAPTER OUTLINE AND FOCUS QUESTIONS

The Industrial Revolution and Its Impact

 What were the basic features of the new industrial system created by the Industrial Revolution, and what effects did the new system have on urban life, social classes, family life, and standards of living?

The Growth of Industrial Prosperity

 What was the Second Industrial Revolution, and what effects did it have on economic and social life? What were the main ideas of Karl Marx, and what role did they play in politics and the union movement in the late nineteenth and early twentieth centuries?

Reaction and Revolution: The Growth of Nationalism

 What were the major ideas associated with conservatism, liberalism, and nationalism, and what role did each ideology play in Europe between 1800 and 1870? What were the causes of the revolutions of 1848, and why did these revolutions fail?

National Unification and the National State, 1848–1871

 What actions did Cavour and Bismarck take to bring about unification in Italy and Germany, respectively, and what role did war play in their efforts?

The European State, 1871–1914

 What general political trends were evident in the nations of western Europe in the late nineteenth and early twentieth centuries, and to what degree were those trends also apparent in the nations of central and eastern Europe? How did the growth of nationalism affect international affairs during the same period?

CRITICAL THINKING

 In what ways was the development of industrialization related to the growth of nationalism?

IN SEPTEMBER 1814, hundreds of foreigners began to converge on Vienna, the capital city of the Austrian Empire. Many were members of European royalty—kings, archdukes, princes, and their wives—accompanied by their diplomatic advisers and scores of servants. Their congenial host was the Austrian emperor, Francis I, who never tired of regaling Vienna's guests with concerts, glittering balls, sumptuous feasts, and innumerable hunting parties. One participant remembered, "Eating, fireworks, public illuminations. For eight or ten days, I haven't been able to work at all. What a life!" Of course, not every waking hour was spent in pleasure during this gathering of notables, known to history as the Congress of Vienna. These people were also representatives of all the states that had fought Napoleon, and their real business was to arrange a final peace settlement after almost a decade of war. On June 8, 1815, they finally completed their task.

The forces of upheaval unleashed during the French revolutionary and Napoleonic wars were temporarily quieted in 1815 as rulers sought to restore stability by reestablishing much of the old order in a Europe ravaged by war. But the Western world had been changed, and it would not readily go back to the old system. New ideologies of change, especially liberalism and nationalism, products of the upheaval initiated in France, had become too powerful to be contained. The forces of change called forth revolts that periodically shook the West and culminated in a spate of revolutions in 1848. Some of the revolutions and revolutionaries were successful; most were not. And yet by 1870, many of the goals sought by the liberals and nationalists during the first half of the nineteenth century seemed to have been achieved. National unity became a reality in Italy and Germany, and many Western states developed parliamentary features.

During the late eighteenth and early nineteenth centuries, another revolution—an industrial one—transformed the economic and social structure of Europe and spawned the industrial era that has characterized modern world history.

The Industrial Revolution and Its Impact

Q FOCUS QUESTION: What were the basic features of the new industrial system created by the Industrial Revolution, and what effects did the new system have on urban life, social classes, family life, and standards of living?

The Industrial Revolution triggered an enormous leap in industrial production. Coal and steam replaced wind and water as new sources of energy and power to drive laborsaving machines. In turn, these machines required new ways of organizing human labor as factories replaced workshops and home workrooms. During the Industrial Revolution, Europe shifted from an economy based on agriculture and handicrafts to an economy based on manufacturing by machines and automated factories.

Although the Industrial Revolution took decades to spread, it was truly revolutionary in the way it fundamentally changed the world. Large numbers of people moved from the countryside to cities to work in the new factories. The creation of a wealthy industrial middle class and a huge industrial working class substantially transformed traditional social relationships. Finally, the Industrial Revolution altered how people related to nature, ultimately creating an environmental crisis that in the twentieth century was finally recognized as a danger to human existence itself.

The Industrial Revolution in Great Britain

Although the Industrial Revolution evolved over a period of time, historians generally agree that it began in Britain sometime after 1750.

ORIGINS A number of factors or conditions coalesced in Britain to produce the Industrial Revolution. Improvements in agricultural practices in the eighteenth century led to a significant increase in food production. British agriculture could now feed more people at lower prices with less labor; even

ordinary British families no longer had to use most of their income to buy food, giving them the wherewithal to purchase manufactured goods. At the same time, rapid population growth in the second half of the eighteenth century provided a pool of surplus labor for the new factories of the emerging British industry.

Britain also had a ready supply of capital for investment in the new industrial machines and the factories that were needed to house them. In addition to profits from trade and the cottage industry, Britain possessed an effective central bank and well-developed, flexible credit facilities. But capital is only part of the story. Britain had a fair number of individuals who were interested in making profits if the opportunity presented itself. No doubt the English revolutions of the seventeenth century had helped create an environment in Britain, unlike that of the absolutist states on the Continent, where political power rested in the hands of a progressive group of people who favored innovation in economic matters.

Britain also had ample supplies of important mineral resources, such as coal and iron ore, needed in the manufacturing process. It was also a small country, and the relatively short distances made transportation nonproblematic. Britain's government, too, played a significant role in the process of industrialization. Parliament contributed to the favorable business climate by providing a stable government and passing laws that protected private property.

Finally, in the course of its eighteenth-century wars and conquests, Great Britain had assembled a vast colonial empire at the expense of its leading rivals, the Dutch Republic and France. The many markets of that empire gave British industrialists a ready outlet for their manufactured goods. British exports quadrupled from 1660 to 1760. A crucial factor in Britain's successful industrialization was the ability to produce cheaply the articles in greatest demand. The traditional methods of the cottage industry could not keep up with the growing demand for cotton clothes throughout Britain and its vast colonial empire. This problem led British cloth manufacturers to seek and adopt the new methods of manufacturing that a series of inventions provided. In so doing, these individuals ignited the Industrial Revolution.

CHANGES IN TEXTILE PRODUCTION The invention of the flying shuttle made it possible to weave faster on a loom, enabling weavers to double their output. This created shortages of yarn until James Hargreaves's spinning jenny, perfected by 1768, allowed spinners to produce yarn in greater quantities. Edmund Cartwright's loom, powered by water and invented in 1787, allowed the weaving of cloth to catch up with the spinning of yarn. It was now more efficient to bring workers to the machines and organize their labor collectively in factories located next to rivers and streams, the sources of power for these early machines.

The cotton industry was then pushed to even greater heights of productivity by the invention of the steam engine. In the 1760s, a Scottish engineer, James Watt (1736–1819), built an engine powered by steam that could pump water from mines three times as quickly as previous engines, thereby allowing for more coal to be extracted from the mines. In 1782, Watt developed a rotary engine that could turn a shaft and thus drive machinery. Steam power could now be applied to spinning and weaving cotton, and before long, cotton mills using steam engines were multiplying across Britain. Fired by coal, these steam engines could be located anywhere.

The boost given to cotton textile production by these technological changes was readily apparent. In 1760, Britain had imported 2.5 million pounds of raw cotton, which was farmed out to cottage industries. In 1787, the British imported 22 million pounds of cotton; most of it was spun on machines, some powered by water in large mills. By 1840, some 366 million pounds of cotton—now Britain's most important product in value—were being imported. By this time, most cotton industry employees worked in factories, and British cotton goods were sold everywhere in the world.

OTHER TECHNOLOGICAL CHANGES The British iron industry was also radically transformed during the Industrial Revolution. Britain had always had large reserves of iron ore, but at the beginning of the eighteenth century, the basic process of producing iron had changed little since the Middle Ages and still depended heavily on charcoal. A better quality of iron came into being in the 1780s when Henry Cort developed a system called puddling, in which coke, derived from coal, was used to burn away impurities in pig iron (crude iron) and produce an iron of high quality. A boom then ensued in the British iron industry. In 1740, Britain produced 17,000 tons of iron; by the 1840s, more than 2 million tons; and by 1852, almost 3 million tons, more than the rest of the world combined.

The new high-quality wrought iron was in turn used to build new machines and ultimately new industries. In 1804, Richard Trevithick (TREV-uh-thik) pioneered the first steam-powered locomotive on an industrial rail line in southern Wales. It pulled 10 tons of ore and seventy people at 5 miles per hour. Better locomotives soon followed. Engines built by George Stephenson and his son proved superior, and it was Stephenson's *Rocket* that was used on the first public railway line, which opened in 1830, stretching 32 miles from Liverpool to Manchester. *Rocket* sped along at 16 miles per hour.

Within twenty years, locomotives had reached 50 miles per hour, an incredible speed to contemporary travelers. By 1840, Britain had almost 6,000 miles of railroads.

The railroad was important to the success and maturing of the Industrial Revolution. Railway construction created new job opportunities, especially for farm laborers and peasants who had long been accustomed to finding work outside their local villages. Perhaps most important, the proliferation of a cheaper and faster means of transportation had a ripple effect on the growth of the industrial economy. As the prices of goods fell, markets grew larger; increased sales meant more factories and more machinery, thereby reinforcing the self-sustaining aspect of the Industrial Revolution—a development that marked a fundamental break with the traditional European economy. Continuous, self-sustaining economic growth came to be seen as an essential characteristic of the new economy.

THE INDUSTRIAL FACTORY Another visible symbol of the Industrial Revolution was the factory (see the comparative illustration on p. 545). From its beginning, the factory created a new labor system. Factory owners wanted to use their new machines constantly. Workers were therefore obliged to work regular hours and in shifts to keep the machines producing at a steady rate. Early factory workers, however, came from rural areas, where they were used to a different pace of life. Peasant farmers worked hard, especially at harvest time, but they were also used to periods of inactivity.

Early factory owners therefore had to create a system of work discipline that would accustom employees to working regular hours and doing the same tasks over and over. Of course, such work was boring, and factory owners resorted to tough methods to accomplish their goals. They issued minute and detailed factory regulations (see the box on p. 546). For example, adult workers were fined for a wide variety of minor infractions, such as being a few minutes late for work, and dismissed for more serious misdoings, especially drunkenness, which set a bad example for younger workers and also courted disaster in the midst of dangerous machinery. Employers found that dismissals and fines worked well for adult employees; in a time when population growth had produced large masses of unskilled labor, dismissal could be

Railroad Line from Liverpool to Manchester. The railroad line from Liverpool to Manchester, which opened in 1830, relied on steam locomotives. As is evident in this illustration, carrying passengers was the railroad's main business. First-class passengers rode in covered cars; second- and third-class passengers, in open cars.

COMPARATIVE ILLUSTRATION

Textile Factories, West and East. The development of the factory changed the relationship between workers and employers as workers were encouraged to adjust to a new system of discipline that forced them to work regular hours under close supervision. At the top is an 1851 illustration that shows women working in a British cotton factory. The factory system came later to the rest of the world than it did to Britain. Shown at the bottom is one of the earliest industrial factories in Japan, the Tomioka silk factory, built in the 1870s. Note that although women are doing the work in both factories, the managers are men. Although these illustrations show mostly women working in the factories, both men and women were factory workers.

Q *What do you think were the major differences and similarities between British and Japanese factories (see also the box on p. 550)?*

disastrous. Children were less likely to understand the implications of dismissal, so they were sometimes disciplined more directly—often by beating. As the nineteenth century progressed, the second and third generations of workers came to view a regular workweek as a natural way of life.

By the mid-nineteenth century, Great Britain had become the world's first and richest industrial nation. Britain was the "workshop, banker, and trader of the world." It produced half of the world's coal and manufactured goods; its cotton industry alone in 1850 was equal in size to the industries of all other European countries combined.

The Spread of Industrialization

From Great Britain, industrialization spread to the Continental countries of Europe and the United States at different times and speeds during the nineteenth century. First to be industrialized on the Continent were Belgium, France, and the German states (see Map 19.1).

INDUSTRIALIZATION ON THE CONTINENT In 1815, Belgium, France, and the German states were still largely agrarian.

Although they had experienced some developments similar to those of Britain in the eighteenth century, these countries did not move in new industrial directions in the 1770s and 1780s because they lacked certain advantages that had made Britain's Industrial Revolution possible. Lack of good roads and problems with river transit made transportation difficult. Customs barriers along state boundaries increased the costs and prices of goods. Moreover, Continental businessmen were generally less enterprising than their British counterparts and tended to adhere to traditional business attitudes, including an unwillingness to take risks in investment. Consequently, industrialization on the Continent faced numerous hurdles, and as it proceeded in earnest after 1815, it did so along lines that were somewhat different from Britain's.

Lack of technical knowledge was initially a major obstacle to industrialization. But the Continental countries possessed an advantage here; they could simply borrow British techniques and practices. Gradually, the Continent achieved technological independence as local people learned all the skills their British teachers had to offer. Even more important, however, Continental countries, especially France and the German

Discipline in the New Factories

SCIENCE & TECHNOLOGY

Workers in the new factories of the Industrial Revolution had been accustomed to a lifestyle free of overseers. Unlike the cottages, where workers spun thread and wove cloth in their own rhythm and time, the factories demanded a new, rigorous discipline geared to the requirements of the machines. This selection is taken from a set of rules for a factory in Berlin in 1844. They were typical of company rules everywhere the factory system had been established.

Factory Rules, Foundry and Engineering Works, Royal Overseas Trading Company

In every large works, and in the coordination of any large number of workmen, good order and harmony must be looked upon as the fundamentals of success, and therefore the following rules shall be strictly observed.

1. The normal working day begins at all seasons at 6 A.M. precisely and ends, after the usual break of half an hour for breakfast, an hour for dinner, and half an hour for tea, at 7 P.M., and it shall be strictly observed. . . .

2. Workers arriving 2 minutes late shall lose half an hour's wages; whoever is more than 2 minutes late may not start work until after the next break, or at least shall lose his wages until then. Any disputes about the correct time shall be settled by the clock mounted above the gatekeeper's lodge. . . .

3. No workman, whether employed by time or piece, may leave before the end of the working day, without having first received permission from the overseer and having given his name to the gatekeeper. Omission of these two actions shall lead to a fine of ten silver groschen payable to the sick fund.

4. Repeated irregular arrival at work shall lead to dismissal. This shall also apply to those who are found idling by an official or overseer, and refuse to obey their order to resume work. . . .

6. No worker may leave his place of work otherwise than for reasons connected with his work.

7. All conversation with fellow-workers is prohibited; if any worker requires information about his work, he must turn to the overseer, or to the particular fellow-worker designated for the purpose.

8. Smoking in the workshops or in the yard is prohibited during working hours; anyone caught smoking shall be fined five silver groschen for the sick fund for every such offense. . . .

10. Natural functions must be performed at the appropriate places, and whoever is found soiling walls, fences, squares, etc., and similarly, whoever is found washing his face and hands in the workshop and not in the places assigned for the purpose, shall be fined five silver groschen for the sick fund. . . .

12. It goes without saying that all overseers and officials of the firm shall be obeyed without question, and shall be treated with due deference. Disobedience will be punished by dismissal.

13. Immediate dismissal shall also be the fate of anyone found drunk in any of the workshops. . . .

14. Every workman is obliged to report to his superiors any acts of dishonesty or embezzlement on the part of his fellow workmen. If he omits to do so, and it is shown after subsequent discovery of a misdemeanor that he knew about it at the time, he shall be liable to be taken to court as an accessory after the fact and the wage due to him shall be retained as punishment.

 What impact did factories have on the lives of workers? To what extent have such "rules" determined much of modern industrial life?

---

states, began to establish a wide range of technical schools to train engineers and mechanics.

That government played an important role in this regard brings us to a second difference between British and Continental industrialization. Governments in most of the Continental countries were accustomed to playing a significant role in economic affairs. Furthering the development of industrialization was a logical extension of that attitude. For example, the governments awarded grants to inventors and provided funds to build roads, canals, and railroads. By 1850, a network of iron rails had spread across Europe.

A third significant difference between British and Continental industrialization was the role of the **joint-stock investment bank** on the Continent. Such banks pooled the savings of thousands of small and large investors, creating a supply of capital that could then be plowed back into industry. These investments were essential to Continental industrialization. By starting with less expensive machines, the British had been able to industrialize largely through the private capital of successful individuals who reinvested their profits. On the Continent, advanced industrial machines necessitated large amounts of capital; joint-stock industrial banks provided it.

THE INDUSTRIAL REVOLUTION IN THE UNITED STATES The Industrial Revolution also transformed the new nation in North America, the United States. In 1800, six out of every seven American workers were farmers, and there were no

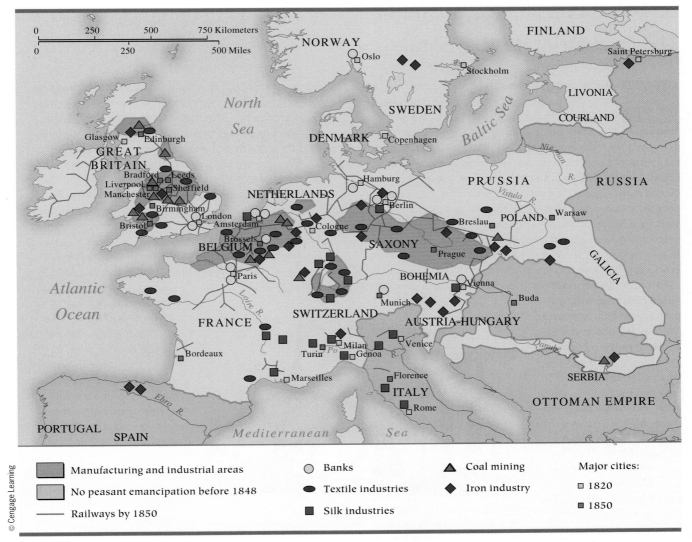

Manufacturing and industrial areas

No peasant emancipation before 1848

Railways by 1850

Banks

Textile industries

Silk industries

Coal mining

Iron industry

Major cities:
- 1820
- 1850

MAP 19.1 **The Industrialization of Europe by 1850.** Great Britain was Europe's first industrialized country; however, by the middle of the nineteenth century, several regions on the Continent, especially in Belgium, France, and the German states, had made significant advances in industrialization.

Q *What might explain why coal mining and iron industries were densely clustered in manufacturing and industrial areas?*

cities with more than 100,000 people. By 1860, however, the population had grown from 5 million to 30 million people, larger than Great Britain's; nine U.S. cities had populations over 100,000; and only 50 percent of American workers were farmers.

In sharp contrast to Britain, the United States was a large country. Thousands of miles of roads and canals were built linking east and west. The steamboat facilitated transportation on the Great Lakes, Atlantic coastal waters, and rivers. Most important in the development of an American transportation system was the railroad, which was needed to transport the abundant raw materials found throughout the country. Beginning with 100 miles in 1830, by 1865 the United States was crisscrossed by more than 35,000 miles of railroad track—more than three times the amount in Great Britain. This transportation revolution turned the United States into a single massive market for the manufactured

goods of the Northeast, the early center of American industrialization.

Labor for the growing number of factories in this area came primarily from rural New England. Many of the workers in the new textile and shoe factories of the region were women, who often accounted for more than 80 percent of the labor force. Factory owners sometimes sought entire families, including children, to work in their mills; one mill owner ran this advertisement in a newspaper in Utica, New York: "Wanted: A few sober and industrious families of at least five children each, over the age of eight years, are wanted at the Cotton Factory in Whitestown. Widows with large families would do well to attend this notice." A growing manufacturing sector, an abundance of raw materials, and an elaborate transportation system turned the United States into the world's second largest industrial nation by the end of the nineteenth century.

The Industrial Revolution

SCIENCE & TECHNOLOGY

Why some societies were able to embark on the road to industrialization during the nineteenth century and others were not has long been debated. Some historians have found an answer in the cultural characteristics of individual societies, such as the Protestant work ethic in parts of Europe or the tradition of social discipline and class hierarchy in Japan. Others have placed more emphasis on practical reasons. To historian Peter Stearns, for example, the availability of capital, natural resources, a network of trade relations, and navigable rivers all helped stimulate industrial growth in nineteenth-century Britain. By contrast, the lack of an urban market for agricultural products (which reduced landowners' incentives to introduce mechanized farming) is sometimes cited as a reason for China's failure to set out on its own path toward industrialization.

To some observers, the ability of western European countries to exploit the wealth and resources of their colonies in Asia, Africa, and Latin America was crucial to their industrial success. In this view, the Age of Exploration led to the creation of a new "world system" characterized by the emergence of global trade networks, propelled by the rising force of European capitalism in pursuit of precious metals, markets, and cheap raw materials.

These views are not mutually exclusive. In *The Great Divergence: China, Europe, and the Making of the Modern World Economy*, Kenneth Pomeranz has argued that access to coal resources and to the cheap raw materials of the Americas were both assets for Great Britain as it became the first to enter the industrial age.

The Steam Engine. Pictured here is an early steam engine developed by James Watt. The steam engine revolutionized the production of cotton goods and helped usher in the factory system.

© Oxford Science Archive, Oxford/HIP/Art Resource, NY

Clearly, there is no single answer to this controversy. In any event, the advent of the industrial age had a number of lasting consequences for the world at large. On the one hand, the material wealth of the nations that successfully passed through the process increased significantly. In many cases, the creation of advanced industrial societies strengthened democratic institutions and led to a higher standard of living for the majority of the population. It also helped reduce class barriers and bring about the emancipation of women from many of the legal and social restrictions that had characterized the previous era.

On the other hand, not all the consequences of the Industrial Revolution were beneficial. In the industrializing societies themselves, rapid economic change often led to widening disparities in the distribution of wealth and a sense of rootlessness and alienation among much of the population. Although some societies were able to manage these problems with a degree of success, others experienced a breakdown of social values and political instability. In the meantime, the transformation of Europe into a giant factory sucking up raw materials and spewing manufactured goods out to the entire world had a wrenching impact on traditional societies whose own economic, social, and cultural foundations were forever changed by their absorption into the new world order.

Q *What were the positive and negative consequences of the Industrial Revolution?*

Limiting the Spread of Industrialization in the Rest of the World

Before 1870, the industrialization that was transforming western and central Europe and the United States did not extend in any significant way to the rest of the world (see the comparative essay "The Industrial Revolution" above). Even in eastern Europe, industrialization lagged far behind. Russia, for example, was still largely rural and agricultural, ruled by an autocratic regime that preferred to keep the peasants in serfdom.

In other parts of the world, the newly industrialized European states pursued a deliberate policy of preventing the growth of mechanized industry in the areas where they had established control (see Chapter 21). India provides an excellent example. In the eighteenth century, India had become one of the world's greatest exporters of cotton cloth produced by hand labor. In the first half of the nineteenth century, much of India fell under the control of the British East India Company. With British control came inexpensive textiles produced in British factories. As the indigenous Indian textile industry declined, thousands of Indian spinners and handloom weavers lost their jobs, forcing many to turn to growing raw materials, such as cotton, wheat, and tea, for export to Britain, while buying British-made finished goods. In a similar fashion elsewhere, the rapidly industrializing nations of Europe worked to thwart the spread of the Industrial Revolution to their colonial dominions.

Social Impact of the Industrial Revolution

Eventually, the Industrial Revolution revolutionized the social life of Europe and the world. This change was already evident in the first half of the nineteenth century in the growth of cities and emergence of new social classes.

POPULATION GROWTH AND URBANIZATION The European population had begun to increase in the eighteenth century, but the pace accelerated dramatically in the nineteenth. In 1750, the total European population stood at an estimated 140 million; by 1850, it had almost doubled to 266 million. The key to the expansion of population was a decline in death rates evident throughout Europe. Wars and major epidemic diseases, such as plague and smallpox, became less frequent, which led to a drop in the number of deaths. Thanks to the increase in the food supply, more people were better fed and more resistant to disease.

Throughout Europe, cities and towns grew rapidly in the first half of the nineteenth century, a phenomenon related to industrialization. By 1850, especially in Great Britain and Belgium, cities were rapidly becoming home to many industries. With the steam engine, factory owners could locate their manufacturing plants in urban centers, where they had ready access to transportation facilities and large numbers of new arrivals from the country looking for work.

In 1800, Great Britain had one major city, London, with a population of one million and six cities with populations between 50,000 and 100,000. Fifty years later, London's population had swelled to 2,363,000, and there were nine cities over 100,000 and eighteen with populations between 50,000 and 100,000. By 1850, more than half of the British population lived in towns and cities. Urban populations also grew on the Continent, but at a less frenzied pace.

The dramatic growth of cities in the first half of the nineteenth century resulted in miserable living conditions for many of the inhabitants. Located in the center of most industrial towns were the row houses of the industrial workers. Rooms were not large and were frequently overcrowded, as a government report of 1838 in Britain revealed: "I entered several of the tenements. In one of them, on the ground floor, I found six persons occupying a very small room, two in bed, ill with fever. In the room above this were two more persons in one bed, ill with fever." Another report said, "There were 63 families where there were at least five persons to one bed; and there were some in which even six were packed in one bed, lying at the top and bottom—children and adults."[1]

Sanitary conditions in these towns were appalling; sewers and open drains were common on city streets: "In the center of this street is a gutter, into which the refuse of animal and vegetable matters of all kinds, the dirty water from the washing of clothes and of the houses, are all poured, and there they stagnate and putrefy."[2] Unable to deal with human wastes, cities in the early industrial era smelled horrible and were extraordinarily unhealthy. The use of coal blackened towns and cities with soot, as Charles Dickens described in one of his novels: "A long suburb of red brick houses—some with patches of garden ground, where coal-dust and factory smoke darkened the shrinking leaves, and coarse rank flowers; and where the struggling vegetation sickened and sank under the hot breath of kiln and furnace."[3] Towns and cities were death traps: deaths outnumbered births in most large cities in the first half of the nineteenth century; only a constant influx of people from the country kept them alive and growing.

THE INDUSTRIAL MIDDLE CLASS The rise of industrial capitalism produced a new kind of middle class. The bourgeoisie was not new; it had existed since the emergence of cities in the Middle Ages. Originally, the bourgeois or burgher was simply a town dweller, active as a merchant, official, artisan, lawyer, or man of letters. Because many of these people lived comfortable lives, the term took on a certain cachet. And so as other people began to accumulate wealth, the term *bourgeois* came to be applied to people involved in commerce, industry, and banking as well as professionals such as teachers, physicians, and government officials, regardless of where they lived.

The new industrial middle class was made up of the people who constructed the factories, purchased the machines, and figured out where the markets were (see the box on p. 550). Their qualities included resourcefulness, single-mindedness, resolution, initiative, vision, ambition, and often, of course, greed. As Jedediah Strutt, a cotton manufacturer said, "Getting of money . . . is the main business of the life of men."

Members of the industrial middle class not only sought to reduce the barriers between themselves and the landed elite, but also tried at the same time to separate themselves from the laboring classes below them. In the first half of the nineteenth century, the working class was actually a mixture of different groups, but in the course of the century, factory workers came to form an industrial **proletariat** that constituted a majority of the working class.

THE INDUSTRIAL WORKING CLASS Early industrial workers faced wretched working conditions. Work shifts ranged from twelve to sixteen hours a day, six days a week, with a half hour for lunch and dinner. There was no security of employment and no minimum wage. The worst conditions were in the cotton mills, where temperatures were especially debilitating. One report noted that "in the cotton-spinning work, these creatures are kept, fourteen hours in each day, locked up, summer and winter, in a heat of from eighty to eighty-four degrees." Mills were also dirty, dusty, and unhealthy.

Conditions in the coal mines were also harsh. Although steam-powered engines were used to lift coal from the mines to the top, inside the mines, men still bore the burden of digging the coal out while horses, mules, women, and children hauled coal carts on rails to the lift. Dangerous conditions,

Attitudes of the Industrial Middle Class in Britain and Japan

SCIENCE & TECHNOLOGY

In the nineteenth century, a new industrial middle class in Great Britain took the lead in creating the Industrial Revolution. Japan did not begin to industrialize until after 1870 (see Chapter 22). There, too, an industrial middle class emerged, although there were important differences in the attitudes of business leaders in Britain and Japan. Some of these differences can be seen in these documents. The first is an excerpt from the book *Self-Help* (first published in 1859) by Samuel Smiles, who espoused the belief that people succeed through "individual industry, energy, and uprightness." The other two selections are by Shibuzawa Eiichi (shih-boo-ZAH-wah EH-ee-chee), a Japanese industrialist who supervised textile factories. Although he began his business career in 1873, he did not write his autobiography, the source of his first excerpt, until 1927.

Samuel Smiles, *Self-Help*

"Heaven helps those who help themselves" is a well-worn maxim, embodying in a small compass the results of vast human experience. The spirit of self-help is the root of all genuine growth in the individual; and, exhibited in the lives of many, it constitutes the true source of national vigor and strength. Help from without is often enfeebling in its effects, but help from within invariably invigorates. Whatever is done for men or classes, to a certain extent takes away the stimulus and necessity of doing for themselves; and where men are subjected to overguidance and overgovernment, the inevitable tendency is to render them comparatively helpless. . . .

National progress is the sum of individual industry, energy, and uprightness, as national decay is of individual idleness, selfishness, and vice. What we are accustomed to decry as great social evils, will, for the most part, be found to be only the outgrowth of our own perverted life; and though we may endeavor to cut them down and extirpate them by means of law, they will only spring up again with fresh luxuriance in some other form, unless the individual conditions of human life and character are radically improved. If this view be correct, then it follows that the highest patriotism and philanthrophy consist, not so much in altering laws and modifying institutions as in helping and stimulating men to elevate and improve themselves by their own free and independent action as individuals. . . .

Many popular books have been written for the purpose of communicating to the public the grand secret of making money. But there is no secret whatever about it, as the proverbs of every nation abundantly testify. . . . "A penny saved is a penny gained."—"Diligence is the mother of good-luck."—"No pains, no gains."—"No sweat, no sweet."— "Sloth, the Key of poverty."—"Work, and thou shalt have."—"He who will not work, neither shall he eat."—"The world is his, who has patience and industry."

Shibuzawa Eiichi, *Autobiography*

I . . . felt that it was necessary to raise the social standing of those who engaged in commerce and industry. By way of setting an example, I began studying and practicing the teachings of the *Analects of Confucius*. It contains teachings first enunciated more than twenty-four hundred years ago. Yet it supplies the ultimate in practical ethics for all of us to follow in our daily living. It has many golden rules for businessmen. For example, there is a saying: "Wealth and respect are what men desire, but unless a right way is followed, they cannot be obtained; poverty and lowly position are what men despise, but unless a right way is found, one cannot leave that status once reaching it." It shows very clearly how a businessman must act in this world.

Shibuzawa Eiichi on Progress

One must beware of the tendency of some to argue that it is through individualism or egoism that the State and society can progress most rapidly. They claim that under individualism, each individual competes with the others, and progress results from this competition. But this is to see merely the advantages and ignore the disadvantages, and I cannot support such a theory. Society exists, and a State has been founded. Although people desire to rise to positions of wealth and honor, the social order and the tranquility of the State will be disrupted if this is done egoistically. Men should not do battle in competition with their fellow men. Therefore, I believe that in order to get along together in society and serve the State, we must by all means abandon this idea of independence and self-reliance and reject egoism completely.

 What are the major similarities and differences in the attitudes toward business of Samuel Smiles and Shibuzawa Eiichi? How do you explain the differences?

---

including cave-ins, explosions, and gas fumes, were a way of life. The cramped conditions in the mines—tunnels were often only 3 or 4 feet high—and their constant dampness led to deformed bodies and ruined lungs.

Both children and women worked in large numbers in early factories and mines. Children had been an important part of the family economy in preindustrial times, working in the fields or carding and spinning wool at home. In the

Women and Children in the Mines. Women and children were often employed in the factories and mines of the early nineteenth century. These illustrations are from the Report of the Children's Employment Commission in Great Britain in 1842. The top image shows a woman dragging a cart loaded with coal. The lower image shows a boy walking backward in a mine, pulling a cart filled with coal. Both images show the trying conditions under which both women and children worked in the early Industrial Revolution. In 1842, the British Mines Act forbade the use of children younger than thirteen and women of any age in the mines.

Industrial Revolution, however, child labor was exploited more than ever (see the box on p. 552). The owners of cotton factories found child labor very helpful. Children had an especially delicate touch as spinners of cotton. Their smaller size made it easier for them to crawl under machines to gather loose cotton. Moreover, children were more easily trained to do factory work. Above all, children represented a cheap source of labor. In 1821, about half of the British population was under twenty years of age. Hence, children made up an abundant supply of labor, and they were paid only about one-sixth to one-third of what a man was paid. Children as young as seven worked twelve to fifteen hours per day, six days a week, in the cotton mills.

By 1830, women and children provided two-thirds of the cotton industry's labor. Under the Factory Act of 1833, however, which prohibited employment of children under the age of nine and restricted the working hours of those under eighteen, the number of children employed declined. The new law did not end child labor, however, as many parents needed the income of working children to support the family. In 1838, children under eighteen still made up 29 percent of the total workforce. Moreover, as the number of children employed declined, their places were taken by women, who came to dominate the labor forces of the early factories. Women made up 50 percent of the labor force in textile (cotton and woolen) factories before 1870. They were mostly unskilled labor and were paid half or less of what men received.

Laws that limited the work hours of children and women also led to a new pattern of work based on a separation of work and home. Men were expected to be responsible for the primary work obligations, while women assumed daily control of the family and performed low-paying jobs such as laundry work that could be done in the home. Domestic industry made it possible for women to continue their contributions to family survival.

DID INDUSTRIALIZATION BRING AN IMPROVED STANDARD OF LIVING? During the first half of the nineteenth century, industrialization altered the lives of Europeans, especially the British, as they left their farms, moved to cities, and found work in factories. Historians have debated whether industrialization improved the standard of living during this time. Some historians have argued that industrialization increased employment and lowered the price of consumer goods, thereby improving the way people lived. They also maintain that household income rose because multiple members of the family could now hold wage-paying jobs. Other historians argue that wage labor made life worse for many families during the first half of the nineteenth century. They maintain that employment in the early factories was highly volatile as employers quickly dismissed workers whenever demand declined. Wages were not uniform, and inadequate housing in cities forced families to live in cramped and unsanitary conditions. Families continued to spend the majority of their incomes on food and clothing. Most historians agree that members of the middle class were the real gainers in the early Industrial Revolution and that industrial workers had to wait until the second half of the nineteenth century to begin to reap the benefits of industrialization.

Child Labor: Discipline in the Textile Mills

FAMILY & SOCIETY

Child labor was not new, but in the early Industrial Revolution, it was exploited more systematically. These selections are taken from the Report of Sadler's Committee, which was commissioned in 1832 to inquire into the condition of child factory workers.

How They Kept the Children Awake

It is a very frequent thing at Mr. Marshall's where the least children were employed (for there were plenty working at six years of age), for Mr. Horseman to start the mill earlier in the morning than he formerly did; and provided a child should be drowsy, the overlooker walks round the room with a stick in his hand, and he touches that child on the shoulder, and says, "Come here." In a corner of the room there is an iron cistern; it is filled with water; he takes this boy, and takes him up by the legs, and dips him over head in the cistern, and sends him to work for the remainder of the day. . . .

What means were taken to keep the children to their work?—Sometimes they would tap them over the head, or nip them over the nose, or give them a pinch of snuff, or throw water in their faces, or pull them off where they were, and job them about to keep them waking.

The Sadistic Overlooker

Samuel Downe, age 29, factory worker living near Leeds; at the age of about ten began work at Mr. Marshall's mill at Shrewsbury, where the customary hours when work was brisk were generally 5 A.M. to 8 P.M., sometimes from 5:30 A.M. to 8 or 9.

What means were taken to keep the children awake and vigilant, especially at the termination of such a day's labour as you have described?—There was generally a blow or a box, or a tap with a strap, or sometimes the hand.

Have you yourself been strapped?—Yes, most severely, till I could not bear to sit upon a chair without having pillows, and through that I left. I was strapped both on my own legs, and then I was put upon a man's back, and then strapped and buckled with two straps to an iron pillar, and flogged, and all by one overlooker; after that he took a piece of tow [rope], and twisted it in the shape of a cord, and put it in my mouth, and tied it behind my head.

He gagged you?—Yes; and then he ordered me to run round a part of the machinery where he was overlooker, and he stood at one end, and every time I came there he struck me with a stick, which I believe was an ash plant, and which he generally carried in his hand, and sometimes he hit me, and sometimes he did not; and one of the men in the room came and begged me off, and that he let me go, and not beat me any more, and consequently he did.

You have been beaten with extraordinary severity?—Yes, I was beaten so that I had not power to cry at all, or hardly speak at one time. What age were you at that time?—Between 10 and 11.

What kind of working conditions did children face in the mills during the early Industrial Revolution? Why were they beaten?

EFFORTS AT CHANGE In the first half of the nineteenth century, the pitiful conditions found in the slums, mines, and factories of the Industrial Revolution gave rise to efforts for change. One of them was a movement known as **socialism**. The term eventually became associated with a Marxist analysis of human society (see "Organizing the Working Classes" later in this chapter), but early socialism was largely the product of intellectuals who believed in the equality of all people and wanted to replace competition with cooperation in industry. To later socialists, especially the followers of Karl Marx, such ideas were merely impractical dreams, and they contemptuously labeled these theorists **utopian socialists**. The term has lasted to this day.

Robert Owen, a British cotton manufacturer, was one such utopian socialist. He believed that humans would show their true natural goodness if they lived in a cooperative environment. At New Lanark in Scotland, he transformed a squalid factory town into a flourishing, healthy community. But when he tried to create such a cooperative community at New Harmony, Indiana, in the United States in the 1820s, fighting within the community eventually destroyed his dream.

Another movement for change came through the formation of labor organizations to gain decent wages and working conditions. Known as **trade unions**, these new associations were formed by skilled workers in a number of new industries, including ironworkers and coal miners. Some trade unions were even willing to strike (refuse to work) to win improvements for the members of their trades. In the 1820s and 1830s, the union movement began to focus on the creation of national unions. The largest and most successful of these unions in Britain was the Amalgamated Society of Engineers, formed in 1851. Its provision of generous unemployment benefits in return for a small weekly payment was precisely the kind of practical gains that the trade unions sought.

The Growth of Industrial Prosperity

FOCUS QUESTIONS: What was the Second Industrial Revolution, and what effects did it have on economic and social life? What were the main ideas of Karl Marx, and what role did they play in politics and the union movement in the late nineteenth and early twentieth centuries?

After 1870, the Western world experienced a dynamic boom in material prosperity. The new industries, new sources of energy, and new goods of the Second Industrial Revolution led people to believe that their material progress reflected human progress.

New Products

The first major change in industrial development after 1870 was the substitution of steel for iron. New methods for shaping steel made it useful in the construction of lighter, smaller, and faster machines and engines as well as railways, ships, and armaments. In 1860, Great Britain, France, Germany, and Belgium produced 125,000 tons of steel; by 1913, the total was 32 million tons.

Electricity was a major new form of energy that could be easily converted into other forms—such as heat, light, and motion—and moved relatively effortlessly through space by means of transmitting wires. In the 1870s, the first commercially practical generators of electrical current were developed, and by 1910, hydroelectric power stations and coal-fired steam-generating plants enabled homes and factories in whole neighborhoods to be tied in to a single, common source of power.

Electricity spawned a number of inventions. The lightbulb, developed independently by the American Thomas Edison and the Briton Joseph Swan, permitted homes and cities to be illuminated by electric lights. By the 1880s, electricity-powered streetcars and subways had appeared in major European cities. Electricity also transformed the factory. Conveyor belts, cranes, machines, and machine tools could all be powered by electricity and located anywhere. Thanks to electricity, all countries could now enter the industrial age. A revolution in communications began when Alexander Graham Bell invented the telephone in 1876 and Guglielmo Marconi (gool-YEL-moh mahr-KOH-nee) sent the first radio waves across the Atlantic in 1901.

The development of the internal combustion engine, fired by oil and gasoline, provided a new source of power in transportation and gave rise to ocean liners as well as airplanes and automobiles. In 1900, world production stood at 9,000 cars, but an American, Henry Ford, revolutionized the automotive industry with the mass production of the Model T. By 1916, Ford's factories were producing 735,000 cars a year. In 1903, at Kitty Hawk, North Carolina, brothers Orville and Wilbur Wright made the first flight in a fixed-wing airplane. The first regular passenger air service was established in 1919.

Photo courtesy private collection

An Age of Progress. The Second Industrial Revolution led many Europeans to believe that most human problems would be solved through scientific achievements. This illustration is from a special issue of the *Illustrated London News* celebrating the Diamond Jubilee of Queen Victoria in 1897. On the left are scenes from 1837, when Victoria came to the British throne; on the right are scenes from 1897. The vivid contrast underscored the magazine's conclusion: "The most striking . . . evidence of progress during the reign is the ever increasing speed which the discoveries of physical science have forced into everyday life. Steam and electricity have conquered time and space to a greater extent during the last sixty years than all the preceding six hundred years witnessed."

New Patterns

Industrial production grew rapidly at this time because of the greatly increased sales of manufactured goods. An increase in real wages for workers after 1870, combined with lower prices for manufactured goods because of reduced transportation costs, made it easier for Europeans to buy consumer products. In the cities, the first department stores began to sell a whole new range of consumer goods made possible by the development of the steel and electrical industries (see the box on p. 554). The desire to own sewing machines, clocks, bicycles, electric lights, and typewriters was rapidly generating a new consumer ethic that has been a crucial part of the modern economy.

Not all nations benefited from the Second Industrial Revolution, however. Between 1870 and 1914, Germany replaced Great Britain as the industrial leader of Europe. Moreover, by 1900, Europe was divided into two economic zones. Great Britain, Belgium, France, the Netherlands, Germany, the western part of the Austro-Hungarian Empire, and northern Italy constituted an advanced industrialized core that had a

The Department Store and the Beginnings of Mass Consumerism

SCIENCE & TECHNOLOGY

Domestic markets were especially important for the sale of the goods being turned out by Europe's increasing number of industrial plants. New techniques of mass marketing arose to encourage the sale of the new consumer goods. The Parisians pioneered in the development of the department store, and this selection is taken from a contemporary's account of the growth of these stores in the French capital city.

E. Lavasseur, *On Parisian Department Stores*, 1907

It was in the reign of Louis-Philippe [1830–1848] that department stores for fashion goods and dresses, extending to material and other clothing, began to be distinguished. . . . These stores have increased in number and several of them have become extremely large. Combining in their different departments all articles of clothing, toilet articles, furniture and many other ranges of goods, it is their special object so to combine all commodities as to attract and satisfy customers who will find conveniently together an assortment of a mass of articles corresponding to all their various needs. They attract customers by permanent display, by free entry into the shops, by periodic exhibitions, by special sales, by fixed prices, and by their ability to deliver the goods purchased to customers' homes, in Paris and to the provinces. Turning themselves into direct intermediaries between the producer and the consumer, even producing sometimes some of their articles in their own workshops, buying at lowest prices because of their large orders and because they are in a position to profit from bargains, working with large sums, and selling to most of their customers for cash only, they can transmit these benefits in lowered selling prices. They can even decide to sell at a loss, as an advertisement or to get rid of out-of-date fashions. Taking 5–6 percent on 100 million [francs] brings them in more than 20 percent would bring to a firm doing a turnover of 50,000 francs.

The success of these department stores is only possible thanks to the volume of their business, and this volume needs considerable capital and a very large turnover. Now capital, having become abundant, is freely combined nowadays in large enterprises, although French capital has the reputation of being more wary of the risks of industry than of State or railway securities. On the other hand, the large urban agglomerations, the ease with which goods can be transported by the railways, the diffusion of some comforts to strata below the middle classes, have all favored these developments.

As example we may cite some figures relating to these stores. . . .

Le Louvre, dating to the time of the extension of the rue de Rivoli under the Second Empire [1855], did in 1893 a business of 120 million at a profit of 6.4 percent. *Le Bon Marché*, which was a small shop when Mr. Boucicaut entered it in 1852, already did a business of 20 million at the end of the Empire [1870]. During the republic its new buildings were erected; Mme. Boucicaut turned it by her will into a kind of cooperative society, with shares and an ingenious organization; turnover reached 150 million in 1893, leaving a profit of 5 percent. . . .

According to the tax records of 1891, these stores in Paris, numbering 12, employed 1,708 persons and were rated on their site values at 2,159,000 francs; the largest had then 542 employees. These same stores had, in 1901, 9,784 employees; one of them over 2,000 and another over 1,600; their site value has doubled (4,089,000 francs).

 Did the invention of department stores respond to or create the new "consumer ethic" in industrialized societies? What was this new turn-of-the-century ethic? According to Lavasseur, what were the positive effects of department stores on Parisian society?

---

high standard of living, decent systems of transportation, and relatively healthy and educated peoples (see Map 19.2). Another part of Europe, the backward and little industrialized area to the south and east, consisting of southern Italy, most of Austria-Hungary, Spain, Portugal, the Balkan kingdoms, and Russia, was still largely agricultural and relegated by the industrial countries to the function of providing food and raw materials.

Emergence of a World Economy

The economic developments of the late nineteenth century, combined with the transportation revolution that saw the growth of marine transport and railroads, fostered a true

world economy. International trade increased dramatically between 1850 and 1914. By 1900, Europeans were receiving beef and wool from Argentina and Australia, coffee from Brazil, nitrates from Chile, iron ore from Algeria, and sugar from Java. Until the Industrial Revolution, European countries had imported more from Asia than they had exported, but now foreign countries provided markets for the surplus manufactured goods of Europe. European capital was also invested abroad to develop railways, mines, electrical power plants, and banks. High rates of return, such as 11.3 percent on Latin American banking shares that were floated in London, provided plenty of incentive for investors. With its capital,

Shopping at Le Bon Marché. Early department stores benefited from the use of steel in building construction, which allowed for large open spaces and natural lighting for the goods on display. Le Bon Marché featured wrought-iron beams, an iron and glass roof, balconies, and iron bridges that enabled customers to view the goods and the scene below. By the 1890s, between 15,000 and 18,000 people entered the department store daily.

industries, and military might, Europe dominated the world economy by the beginning of the twentieth century.

The Spread of Industrialization

At the same time, after 1870, industrialization began to spread beyond western and central Europe and North America. Especially noticeable was its rapid development, fostered by governments, in Russia and Japan. A surge of industrialization began in Russia in the 1890s under the guiding hand of Sergei Witte (syir-GYAY VIT-uh), the minister for finance. Witte pushed the government toward a program of massive railroad construction. By 1900, some 35,000 miles of track had been laid. Witte's program also made possible the rapid growth of a modern steel and coal industry, making Russia by 1900 the fourth-largest producer of steel, behind the United States, Germany, and Great Britain. Russia was also turning out half of the world's production of oil.

In Japan, the imperial government took the lead in promoting industry (see Chapter 22). The government financed industries, built railroads, brought foreign experts to train Japanese employees in new industrial techniques, and instituted a universal educational system based on applied science. By the end of the nineteenth century, Japan had developed key industries in tea, silk, armaments, and shipbuilding.

Women and Work: New Job Opportunities

During the course of the nineteenth century, working-class organizations persisted in the belief that women should remain at home to bear and nurture children and not be allowed in the industrial workforce. Working-class men argued that keeping women out of the factories would ensure the moral and physical well-being of families. In reality, however, if their husbands were unemployed, women had to do low-wage work or labor part-time in sweatshops to support their families.

The Second Industrial Revolution opened the door to new jobs for women. The development of larger industrial plants and the expansion of government services created a variety of service or white-collar jobs. The increased demand for white-collar workers at relatively low wages coupled with a shortage of male workers led employers to hire women. Big businesses and retail shops needed clerks, typists, secretaries, file clerks, and salesclerks. The expansion of government services opened opportunities for women to be secretaries and telephone operators and to take jobs in health and social services. Compulsory education necessitated more teachers, while the development of modern hospital services opened the way for an increase in the number of nurses.

Many of the new white-collar jobs were far from exciting. The work was routine and, except for teaching and nursing, required few skills beyond basic literacy. Nevertheless, these jobs had distinct advantages for many women. For some middle-class women, the new jobs offered freedom from the domestic patterns expected of them. Moreover, because middle-class women did not receive an education comparable to that of men, they were limited in the careers they could pursue. Thus, they found it easier to fill the jobs at the lower end of middle-class occupations, such as teaching and civil service jobs, especially in the post office. Most of the new white-collar jobs, however, were filled by working-class women who saw the job as an opportunity to escape from the physical labor of the lower-class world.

Organizing the Working Classes

The desire to improve their working and living conditions led many industrial workers to form socialist political parties and socialist labor unions. These emerged after 1870, but the theory that made them possible had been developed more than two decades earlier in the work of Karl Marx. **Marxism** made its first appearance on the eve of the revolutions of 1848 with the publication of a short treatise titled *The Communist*

Railroad development
— Lines completed by 1848
— Area of main railroad completed by 1870
— Other major lines

▲ Steel
◆ Engineering
● Chemicals
■ Electrical industry

🛒 Low-grade coal
🛒 High-grade coal
⚒ Iron ore deposits
🛢 Petroleum deposits

◯ Oil production

Industrial concentration:
□ Cities
▨ Areas

© Cengage Learning

MAP 19.2 The Industrial Regions of Europe at the End of the Nineteenth Century. By the end of the nineteenth century, the Second Industrial Revolution—in steelmaking, electricity, petroleum, and chemicals—had spurred substantial economic growth and prosperity in western and central Europe; it also sparked economic and political competition between Great Britain and Germany.

Q *Look back at Map 19.1. What parts of Europe not industrialized in 1850 had become industrialized in the ensuing decades?*

Manifesto, written by two Germans, Karl Marx (1818–1883) and Friedrich Engels (FREE-drikh ENG-ulz) (1820–1895).

MARXIST THEORY Marx and Engels began their treatise with the statement that "the history of all hitherto existing society is the history of class struggles." Throughout history, then, oppressor and oppressed have "stood in constant opposition to one another."[4] One group of people—the oppressors—owned the means of production and thus had the power to control government and society. Indeed, government itself was but an instrument of the ruling class. The other group, which depended on the owners of the means of production, were the oppressed.

This **class struggle** continued in the industrialized societies of Marx's day. According to Marx and Engels, "Society as a whole is more and more splitting up into two great hostile camps, into two great classes directly facing each other: Bourgeoisie and Proletariat." Marx predicted that the struggle between the bourgeoisie and the proletariat would finally break into open revolution, "where the violent overthrow of the bourgeoisie lays the foundation for the sway of the proletariat." The fall of the bourgeoisie "and the victory of the proletariat are equally inevitable."[5] For a while, the proletariat would form a dictatorship to reorganize the means of production, and then the state—itself an instrument of the bourgeois interests—would wither away. Since classes had arisen from

Photo courtesy private collection

"Proletarians of the World, Unite." To improve their working and living conditions, many industrial workers, inspired by the ideas of Karl Marx, joined working-class or socialist parties. Pictured here is a socialist-sponsored poster that proclaims in German the closing words of *The Communist Manifesto*: "Proletarians of the World, Unite!"

the economic differences that would have been abolished, the end result would be a classless society (see the box on p. 558).

SOCIALIST PARTIES In time, Marx's ideas were picked up by working-class leaders who formed socialist parties. Most important was the German Social Democratic Party (SPD), which emerged in 1875 and espoused revolutionary Marxist rhetoric while organizing itself as a mass political party competing in elections for the Reichstag (RYKHSS-tahk), the lower house of parliament. Once in the Reichstag, SPD delegates sought to pass legislation to improve the condition of the working class. Despite government efforts to destroy it, the SPD continued to grow. In the 1912 elections, it received 4 million votes, making it the largest party in Germany.

Socialist parties also emerged in other European states, although not with the kind of success achieved by the German Social Democrats. In 1889, leaders of the various socialist parties formed the Second International, an association of national socialist groups dedicated to fighting against capitalism worldwide. (The First International had failed in 1872.) The Second International took some coordinated actions—May Day (May 1), for example, was made an international

labor holiday—but differences often wreaked havoc at the organization's congresses.

REVISIONISM AND TRADE UNIONS Marxist parties divided over the issue of **revisionism**. Pure Marxists believed in violent revolution that would bring the collapse of capitalism and socialist ownership of the means of production. But others, called revisionists, rejected **revolutionary socialism** and argued that workers must organize mass political parties and work together with other progressive elements to gain reforms. Having won the right to vote, workers were in a better position than ever to achieve their aims through democratic channels. Evolution by democratic means, not revolution, would achieve the desired goal of socialism.

Another force working for evolutionary rather than revolutionary socialism was the development of trade unions. In Great Britain, unions won the right to strike in the 1870s. Soon after, the masses of workers in factories were organized into trade unions in order to use the instrument of the strike. By 1900, there were 2 million workers in British trade unions; fourteen years later, there were almost 4 million. Trade unions in the rest of Europe had varying degrees of success, but by the outbreak of World War I, they had made considerable progress in improving the living and working conditions of the laboring classes.

Reaction and Revolution: The Growth of Nationalism

 FOCUS QUESTIONS: What were the major ideas associated with conservatism, liberalism, and nationalism, and what role did each ideology play in Europe between 1800 and 1870? What were the causes of the revolutions of 1848, and why did these revolutions fail?

Industrialization was a major force for change in the nineteenth century as it led the West into the machine-dependent modern world. Another major force of change was nationalism, which transformed the political map of Europe in the nineteenth century.

The Conservative Order

After the defeat of Napoleon, European rulers moved to restore much of the old order. This was the goal of the great powers—Great Britain, Austria, Prussia, and Russia—when they met at the Congress of Vienna in September 1814 to arrange a final peace settlement after the Napoleonic wars. The leader of the congress was the Austrian foreign minister, Prince Klemens von Metternich (KLAY-menss fun MET-ayr-nikh) (1773–1859), who claimed that he was guided at Vienna by the principle of **legitimacy**. To reestablish peace and stability in Europe, he considered it necessary to restore the legitimate monarchs who would preserve traditional institutions. This had already been done in France with the restoration of the Bourbon monarchy and in a number of other

The Classless Society

FAMILY & SOCIETY

In *The Communist Manifesto*, Karl Marx and Friedrich Engels projected that the struggle between the bourgeoisie and the proletariat would end in the creation of a classless society. In this selection, they discuss the steps by which that classless society would be reached.

Karl Marx and Friedrich Engels, *The Communist Manifesto*

We have seen . . . that the first step in the revolution by the working class is to raise the proletariat to the position of ruling class. . . . The proletariat will use its political supremacy to wrest, by degrees, all capital from the bourgeoisie; to centralize all instruments of production in the hands of the State, i.e., of the proletariat organized as the ruling class; and to increase the total of productive forces as rapidly as possible.

Of course, in the beginning, this cannot be effected except by means of despotic inroads on the rights of property, and on the conditions of bourgeois production; by means of measures, therefore, which appear economically insufficient and untenable, but which, in the course of the movement, outstrip themselves, necessitate further inroads upon the old social order, and are unavoidable as a means of entirely revolutionizing the mode of production.

These measures will of course be different in different countries.

Nevertheless, in the most advanced countries, the following will be pretty generally applicable:

1. Abolition of property in land and application of all rents of land to public purposes.
2. A heavy progressive or graduated income tax.
3. Abolition of all right of inheritance. . . .
5. Centralization of credit in the hands of the State, by means of a national bank with State capital and an exclusive monopoly.

6. Centralization of the means of communication and transport in the hands of the State.
7. Extension of factories and instruments of production owned by the State. . . .
8. Equal liability of all to labor. Establishment of industrial armies, especially for agriculture.
9. Combination of agriculture with manufacturing industries; gradual abolition of the distinction between town and country, by a more equable distribution of the population over the country.
10. Free education for all children in public schools. Abolition of children's factory labor in its present form. . . .

When, in the course of development, class distinctions have disappeared, and all production has been concentrated in the whole nation, the public power will lose its political character. Political power, properly so called, is merely the organized power of one class for oppressing another. If the proletariat during its contest with the bourgeoisie is compelled, by the force of circumstances, to organize itself as a class, if, by means of a revolution, it makes itself the ruling class, and, as such, sweeps away by force the old conditions of production, then it will, along with these conditions, have swept away the conditions for the existence of class antagonisms and of classes generally, and will thereby have abolished its own supremacy as a class.

In place of the old bourgeois society, with its classes and class antagonisms, we shall have an association, in which the free development of each is the condition for the free development of all.

How did Marx and Engels define the proletariat? The bourgeoisie? Why did Marxists come to believe that this distinction was paramount for understanding history and shaping the future?

---

states, but it did not stop the great powers from also grabbing land to add to their states (see Map 19.3).

The peace arrangements of 1815 were only the beginning of a conservative reaction determined to contain the liberal and nationalist forces unleashed by the French Revolution. Metternich and his kind were representatives of the ideology known as **conservatism**. Most conservatives favored obedience to political authority, believed that organized religion was crucial to social order, hated revolutionary upheavals, and were unwilling to accept either the liberal demands for civil liberties and representative governments or the nationalistic aspirations generated by the French revolutionary era. After 1815, the political philosophy of conservatism was supported by hereditary monarchs, government bureaucracies, landowning aristocracies, and revived churches, be they Protestant or Catholic. The conservative forces were dominant after 1815.

One method used by the great powers to maintain the new status quo they had constructed was the Concert of Europe, according to which Great Britain, Russia, Prussia, and Austria (and later France) agreed to meet periodically in conferences to take steps that would maintain the peace in Europe. Eventually, the great powers adopted a principle of **intervention**, asserting the right to send armies into countries where there were revolutions to restore legitimate monarchs to their thrones.

© Cengage Learning

MAP 19.3 Europe After the Congress of Vienna, 1815. The Congress of Vienna imposed order on Europe based on the principles of monarchical government and a balance of power. Monarchs were restored in France, Spain, and other states recently under Napoleon's control, and much territory changed hands, often at the expense of small, weak states.

Q How did Europe's major powers manipulate territory to decrease the probability that France could again threaten the Continent's stability?

Forces for Change

After 1815, conservative governments throughout Europe worked to maintain the old order. But powerful forces for change—liberalism and nationalism—were also at work. **Liberalism** owed much to the Enlightenment of the eighteenth century and the American and French Revolutions; it was based on the idea that people should be as free from restraint as possible.

Politically, liberals came to hold a common set of beliefs. Chief among them was the protection of civil liberties, or the basic rights of all people, which included equality before the law; freedom of assembly, speech, and the press; and freedom from arbitrary arrest. All of these freedoms should be guaranteed by a written document, such as the American Bill of Rights or the French Declaration of the Rights of Man and the Citizen. In addition to religious toleration for all, most liberals advocated separation of church and state. Liberals also demanded the right of peaceful opposition to the government in and out of parliament and the making of laws by a representative assembly (legislature) elected by qualified voters. Thus, many liberals believed in a constitutional monarchy or constitutional state with limits on the powers of government to prevent despotism and in written constitutions that would guarantee these rights. Liberals were not democrats, however. They thought that the right to vote and hold office should be

open only to men who owned property. Liberals also believed in economic values based upon *laissez-faire* principles that rejected state interference in the regulation of wages and work hours. As a political philosophy, liberalism was adopted by middle-class men, especially the industrial bourgeoisie, who favored voting rights for themselves so that they could share power with the landowning classes.

Nationalism was an even more powerful ideology for change in the nineteenth century. Nationalism arose out of an awareness of being part of a community that has common institutions, traditions, language, and customs. This community constitutes a "nation," and it would be the focus of the individual's primary political loyalty. Nationalism did not become a popular force for change until the French Revolution. From then on, nationalists came to believe that each nationality should have its own government. Thus, the Germans, who were not united, wanted national unity in a German nation-state with one central government. Subject peoples, such as the Hungarians, wanted the right to establish their own autonomy rather than be subject to a German minority in the multinational Austrian Empire.

Nationalism, then, was a threat to the existing political order. A united Germany, for example, would upset the balance of power established at Vienna in 1815. At the same time, an independent Hungarian state would mean the breakup of the Austrian Empire. Because many European states were multinational, conservatives tried hard to repress the radical threat of nationalism.

At the same time, in the first half of the nineteenth century, nationalism and liberalism became strong allies. Most liberals believed that liberty could be realized only by peoples who ruled themselves. Many nationalists believed that once each people obtained their own state, all nations could be linked together into a broader community of all humanity. In fact, the nationalism that later triumphed in the second half of the nineteenth century—a new, loud nationalism—divided people rather than unifying them as the new national states became embroiled in bitter competition.

Revolution and Reform, 1830–1832

The conservative order dominated much of Europe after 1815, but the forces of liberalism and nationalism, first generated by the French Revolution, continued to grow as that second great revolution, the Industrial Revolution, expanded and brought new groups of people who wanted change. In 1830 in France, these forces for change erupted as a revolution overthrew the Bourbon monarch and created a limited constitutional monarchy under Louis-Philippe (1830–1848), soon called the "bourgeois monarch" because political support for his rule came from the upper middle class. Great Britain, by contrast, avoided revolutionary upheaval by passing a Reform Bill in 1832 that increased the numbers of male voters, primarily benefiting the members of the upper middle class who favored liberal ideas.

Supporters of liberalism played a primary role in the revolution in France and British reform in 1832, but nationalism was the crucial force in three other revolutionary outbursts in 1830. Belgium, which had been annexed to the Dutch Republic in 1815 to create a larger state to act as a barrier against French aggression, rebelled against the Dutch and established an independent constitutional monarchy. Two other revolutions, however, failed. Russian forces crushed the Poles' attempt to liberate themselves from foreign domination, while Austrian troops intervened in Italy to uphold reactionary governments in a number of Italian states. But the forces of liberalism and nationalism continued to grow and gave rise to new revolutions in 1848.

The Revolutions of 1848

Revolution in France was the spark for revolts in other countries. A severe industrial and agricultural depression beginning in 1846 brought hardship in France to the lower middle class, workers, and peasants, while the government's persistent refusal to extend the suffrage angered the disenfranchised members of the middle class. When the government of King Louis-Philippe refused to make changes, opposition grew and finally overthrew the monarchy on February 24, 1848. A group of moderate and radical republicans established a provisional government and called for the election by universal male suffrage of a "constituent assembly" that would draw up a new constitution.

The new constitution, ratified on November 4, 1848, established the Second Republic, with a single legislature elected to three-year terms by universal male suffrage and a president, also elected by universal male suffrage to a four-year term. In the elections for the presidency held in December 1848, Charles Louis Napoleon Bonaparte (1808–1873), the nephew of the famous ruler, won a resounding victory. Within four years, President Louis Napoleon would become Emperor Napoleon III and establish an authoritarian regime.

REVOLUTION IN CENTRAL EUROPE News of the 1848 revolution in France led to upheaval in central Europe as well (see the box on p. 561). The Vienna settlement in 1815 had recognized the existence of thirty-eight sovereign states (called the Germanic Confederation) in what had once been the Holy Roman Empire. Austria and Prussia were the two great powers in terms of size and might; the other states varied considerably. In 1848, cries for change caused many German rulers to promise constitutions, a free press, jury trials, and other liberal reforms. In Prussia, King Frederick William IV (1840–1861) agreed to establish a new constitution and work for a united Germany.

The promise of unity reverberated throughout all the German states as governments allowed elections by universal male suffrage for deputies to an all-German parliament called the Frankfurt Assembly. Its purpose was to fulfill a liberal and nationalist dream—the preparation of a constitution for a new united Germany. But the Frankfurt Assembly failed to achieve its goal. The members had no real means of compelling the German rulers to accept the constitution they had drawn up. German unification was not achieved; the revolution had failed.

The Austrian Empire needed only the news of the revolution in Paris to erupt in flames in March 1848. The Austrian Empire was a multinational state, a collection of at least eleven ethnically distinct peoples, including Germans, Czechs, Magyars (Hungarians), Slovaks, Romanians, Serbs, and Italians, who had pledged their loyalty to the Habsburg emperor. The Germans, though only a quarter of the population, were economically dominant and played a leading role in governing Austria. The Hungarians, however, wanted their own legislature. In March, demonstrations in Buda, Prague, and Vienna led to the dismissal of Metternich, the Austrian foreign minister and the archsymbol of the conservative order, who fled abroad. In Vienna, revolutionary forces took control of the capital and demanded a liberal constitution. Hungary was given its own legislature and a separate national army. In Bohemia, the Czechs began to clamor for their own government as well.

Austrian officials had made concessions to appease the revolutionaries, but they were determined to reestablish firm control. As in the German states, they were increasingly encouraged by the divisions between radical and moderate revolutionaries and played on the middle-class fear of a working-class social revolution. In June 1848, Austrian military forces ruthlessly suppressed the Czech rebels in Prague. By the end of October, radical rebels had been crushed in Vienna, but it was only with the assistance of a Russian army of 140,000 men that the Hungarian revolution was finally put down in 1849. The revolutions in the Austrian Empire had failed.

Response to Revolution: Two Perspectives

POLITICS & GOVERNMENT

Based on their political beliefs, Europeans responded differently to the specter of revolution that haunted Europe in the first half of the nineteenth century. The first excerpt is taken from a speech given by Thomas Babington Macaulay (muh-KAHL-lee) (1800–1859), a historian and a member of Parliament. Macaulay spoke in Parliament on behalf of the Reform Act of 1832, which extended the right to vote to the industrial middle classes of Britain. The revolution of 1830 in France had influenced his belief that it was better to reform than to have a political revolution.

The second excerpt is taken from the *Reminiscences* of Carl Schurz (SHOORTS) (1829–1906). Like many liberals and nationalists in Germany, Schurz received the news of the February Revolution of 1848 in France with much excitement and great expectations for revolutionary change in the German states. After the failure of the German revolution, Schurz made his way to the United States and eventually became a U.S. senator.

Thomas Babington Macaulay, Speech of March 2, 1831

My hon[orable] friend the member of the University of Oxford tells us that, if we pass this law, England will soon be a Republic. The reformed House of Commons will, according to him, before it has sat ten years, depose the King, and expel the Lords from their House. Sir, if my hon[orable] friend could prove this, he would have succeeded in bringing an argument for democracy infinitely stronger than any that is to be found in the works of Paine. His proposition is, in fact, this—that our monarchical and aristocratical institutions have no hold on the public mind of England; that these institutions are regarded with aversion by a decided majority of the middle class. . . . Now, sir, if I were convinced that the great body of the middle class in England look with aversion on monarchy and aristocracy, I should be forced, much against my will, to come to this conclusion, that monarchical and aristocratical institutions are unsuited to this country. Monarchy and aristocracy, valuable and useful as I think them, are still valuable and useful as means, and not as ends. The end of government is the happiness of the people; and I do not conceive that, in a country like this, the happiness of the people can be promoted by a form of government in which the middle classes place no confidence, and which exists only because the middle classes have no organ by which to make their sentiments known. But, sir, I am fully convinced that the middle classes sincerely wish to uphold the royal prerogatives, and the constitutional rights of the Peers. . . .

But let us know our interest and our duty better. Turn where we may—within, around—the voice of great events is proclaiming to us, "Reform, that you may preserve." Now, therefore, while everything at home and abroad forebodes ruin to those who persist in a hopeless struggle against the spirit of the age; now, while the crash of the proudest throne of the Continent is still resounding in our ears; . . . now, while the heart of England is still sound; now, while the old feelings and the old associations retain a power and a charm which may too soon pass away; now, in this your accepted time; now, in this your day of salvation, take counsel, not of prejudice, not of party spirit . . . but of history, of reason, of the ages which are past, of the signs of this most portentous time. Pronounce in a manner worthy of the expectation with which this great debate has been anticipated, and of the long remembrance which it will leave behind. Renew the youth of the State. Save property divided against itself. Save the multitude, endangered by their own ungovernable passions. Save the aristocracy, endangered by its own unpopular power. Save the greatest, and fairest, and most highly civilized community that ever existed, from calamities which may in a few days sweep away all the rich heritage of so many ages of wisdom and glory. The danger is terrible. The time is short. If this Bill should be rejected, I pray to God that none of those who concur in rejecting it may ever remember their votes with unavailing regret, amidst the wreck of laws, the confusion of ranks, the spoliation of property, and the dissolution of social order.

Carl Schurz, *Reminiscences*

One morning, toward the end of February, 1848, I sat quietly in my attic-chamber, working hard at my tragedy of "Ulrich von Hutten" [a sixteenth-century German knight], when suddenly a friend rushed breathlessly into the room, exclaiming: "What, you sitting here! Do you not know what has happened?"

"No; what?"

"The French have driven away Louis Philippe and proclaimed the republic."

I threw down my pen—and that was the end of "Ulrich von Hutten." I never touched the manuscript again. We tore down the stairs, into the street, to the market-square, the accustomed meeting-place for all the student societies after their midday dinner. Although it was still forenoon, the market was already crowded with young men talking excitedly. There was no shouting, no noise, only agitated conversation. What did we want there? This probably no one knew. But since the French had driven away Louis Philippe and proclaimed the republic, something of course must happen here, too. . . . We were dominated by a vague feeling as if a great outbreak of elemental forces had begun, as if an earthquake

(continued)

(Opposing Viewpoints continued)

was impending of which we had felt the first shock, and we instinctively crowded together. . . .

The next morning there were the usual lectures to be attended. But how profitless! The voice of the professor sounded like a monotonous drone coming from far away. What he had to say did not seem to concern us. The pen that should have taken notes remained idle. At last we closed with a sigh the notebook and went away, impelled by a feeling that now we had something more important to do—to devote ourselves to the affairs of the fatherland. And this we did by seeking as quickly as possible again the company of our friends, in order to discuss what had happened and what was to come. In these conversations, excited as they were, certain ideas and catchwords worked themselves to the surface, which expressed more or less the feelings of the people. Now had arrived in Germany the day for the establishment of "German Unity," and the founding of a great, powerful national German Empire. In the first line the convocation of a national parliament. Then the demands for civil rights and liberties, free speech, free press, the right of free assembly, equality before the law, a freely elected representation of the people with legislative power, responsibility of ministers, self-government of the communes, the right of the people to carry arms, the formation of a civic guard with elective officers, and so on—in short, that which was called a "constitu-

tional form of government on a broad democratic basis." Republican ideas were at first only sparingly expressed. But the word *democracy* was soon on all tongues, and many, too, thought it a matter of course that if the princes should try to withhold from the people the rights and liberties demanded, force would take the place of mere petition. Of course the regeneration of the fatherland must, if possible, be accomplished by peaceable means. . . . Like many of my friends, I was dominated by the feeling that at last the great opportunity had arrived for giving to the German people the liberty which was their birthright and to the German fatherland its unity and greatness, and that it was now the first duty of every German to do and to sacrifice everything for this sacred object.

 What arguments did Macaulay use to support the Reform Bill of 1832? Was he correct? Why or why not? Why was Carl Schurz so excited when he heard the news about the revolution in France? Do you think being a university student helps explain his reaction? Why or why not? What differences do you see in the approaches of these two writers? What do these selections tell you about the development of politics in the German states and Britain in the nineteenth century?

REVOLTS IN THE ITALIAN STATES Revolutions in Italy also failed. The Congress of Vienna had established nine states in Italy, including the kingdom of Sardinia in the north, ruled by the house of Savoy; the kingdom of the Two Sicilies (Naples and Sicily); the Papal States; a handful of small duchies; and the important northern provinces of Lombardy and Venetia (vuh-NEE-shuh), which were now part of the Austrian Empire. Italy was largely under Austrian domination, but a new movement for Italian unity, known as Young Italy, led to initially successful revolts in 1848. Within a year, however, the Austrians had reestablished complete control over Lombardy and Venetia, and the old order also prevailed in the rest of Italy.

Throughout Europe in 1848, popular revolutions had led to liberal constitutions and liberal governments. Moderate, middle-class liberals and radical workers soon divided over their aims, however, and the failure of the revolutionaries to stay united soon led to the reestablishment of authoritarian regimes. In other parts of the Western world, revolutions took somewhat different directions.

Nationalism in the Balkans: The Ottoman Empire and the Eastern Question

The Ottoman Empire had long been in control of much of southeastern Europe, an area known as the Balkans. In the first half of the nineteenth century, a number of states in the Balkans sought to free themselves from the Ottomans. Serbia,

for example, won its autonomy in 1817. As the Ottoman Empire began to decline and authority over its outlying territories in southeastern Europe waned, European governments began to take an active interest in its disintegration. The "Eastern Question," as it came to be called, troubled European diplomats throughout the nineteenth century. Russia's proximity to the Ottoman Empire and the religious bonds between the Russians and the Greek Orthodox Christians in Turkish-dominated southeastern Europe naturally gave Russia special opportunities to enlarge its sphere of influence. The Austrian Empire feared Russian ambitions and had its own interest in the apparent demise of the Ottoman Empire. France and Britain were interested in commercial opportunities and naval bases in the eastern Mediterranean.

In 1821, the Greeks revolted against their Turkish masters. Although subject to Muslim control for four hundred years, the Greeks

The Balkans in 1830

had been allowed to maintain their language and their Greek Orthodox faith. The Greek revolt was soon transformed into a noble cause by an outpouring of European sentiment for the Greeks' struggle. In 1827, a combined British and French fleet went to Greece and defeated a large Turkish fleet. A year later, Russia declared war on the Ottoman Empire. In 1829, the Turks agreed to allow Russia, France, and Britain to decide the fate of Greece, and one year later, the three powers declared Greece an independent kingdom.

The Crimean War

THE CRIMEAN WAR The Crimean War was another episode in the story of the Eastern Question. In 1853, war had erupted again between the Russians and Turks over Russian demands for the right to protect Christian shrines in Palestine, a privilege that had already been extended to the French. When the Turks refused, the Russians invaded Turkish Moldavia (mohl-DAY-vee-uh) and Wallachia (wah-LAY-kee-uh). Failure to resolve the problem by negotiations led the Turks to declare war on Russia on October 4, 1853. In the following year, on March 28, Great Britain and France, fearful that the Russians would gain at the expense of the disintegrating Ottoman Empire, declared war on Russia.

The Crimean War was poorly planned and poorly fought. Britain and France decided on an attack on Russia's Crimean peninsula in the Black Sea. After a long siege and at a terrible cost in troops on both sides, the main Russian fortress of Sevastopol (suh-VAS-tuh-pohl) fell in September 1855, and the Russians soon sued for peace. Under the Treaty of Paris, signed in March 1856, Russia was forced to give up Bessarabia at the mouth of the Danube and accept the neutrality of the Black Sea. In addition, the Danubian principalities of Moldavia and Wallachia were placed under the protection of all the great powers.

The Crimean War proved costly to both sides. More than 250,000 soldiers died in the war, 60 percent of them from disease (primarily cholera). Even more would have died on the British side if it had not been for the efforts of Florence Nightingale (1820–1910). Her insistence on strict sanitary conditions saved many lives and helped make nursing a profession of trained, middle-class women.

The Crimean War destroyed the Concert of Europe. Austria and Russia, the two chief powers maintaining the status quo in the first half of the nineteenth century, were now enemies because of Austria's unwillingness to support Russia in the war. Russia, defeated and humiliated by the obvious failure of its armies, withdrew from European affairs for the next two decades. Great Britain, disillusioned by its role in the war, also pulled back from Continental affairs. Austria, paying the price for its neutrality, was now without friends among the great powers. This new international situation opened the door for the unification of Italy and Germany.

Florence Nightingale. Florence Nightingale is shown caring for wounded British soldiers in the military hospital at Scutari during the Crimean War. After a British journalist, W. H. Russell, issued a scathing denunciation of the quality of medical care afforded to wounded British soldiers, the British government allowed Nightingale to take a group of nurses to the Crimean warfront. Through her efforts in the Crimean War, Nightingale helped make nursing an admirable profession for middle-class women. At the right is a photograph of Nightingale.

National Unification and the National State, 1848–1871

> **Q FOCUS QUESTION:** What actions did Cavour and Bismarck take to bring about unification in Italy and Germany, respectively, and what role did war play in their efforts?

The revolutions of 1848 had failed, but within twenty-five years, many of the goals sought by liberals and nationalists during the first half of the nineteenth century were achieved. Italy and Germany became nations, and many European states were led by constitutional monarchs.

The Unification of Italy

The Italians were the first people to benefit from the breakdown of the Concert of Europe. In 1850, Austria was still the dominant power on the Italian peninsula. After the failure of the revolution of 1848–1849, more and more Italians looked to the northern Italian state of Piedmont, ruled by the royal house of Savoy, as their best hope to achieve the unification of Italy. It was, however, doubtful that the little state could provide the leadership needed to unify Italy until King Victor Emmanuel II (1849–1878) named Count Camillo di Cavour (kuh-MEEL-oh dee kuh-VOOR) (1810–1861) prime minister in 1852.

As prime minister, Cavour pursued a policy of economic expansion that increased government revenues and enabled Piedmont to equip a large army. Cavour, however, knew that Piedmont's army was not strong enough to beat the Austrians; consequently, he made an alliance with the French emperor Napoleon III and then provoked the Austrians into invading Piedmont in 1859. After French armies defeated the Austrians, a peace settlement gave the French Nice (NEES) and Savoy, which they had been promised for making the alliance, and Lombardy went to Piedmont. Cavour's success caused nationalists in some northern Italian states (Parma, Modena, and Tuscany) to overthrow their governments and join Piedmont.

Meanwhile, in southern Italy, Giuseppe Garibaldi (joo-ZEP-pay gar-uh-BAHL-dee) (1807–1882), a dedicated Italian patriot, raised an army of a thousand volunteers called the Red Shirts because of the color of their uniforms. Garibaldi's forces swept through Sicily and then crossed over to the mainland and began a victorious march up the Italian peninsula (see the box on p. 565). Naples, and with it the kingdom of the Two Sicilies, fell in early September 1860. Ever the patriot, Garibaldi chose to turn

The Unification of Italy

Map legend:
- Kingdom of Piedmont, before 1859
- To Kingdom of Piedmont, 1859
- To Kingdom of Piedmont, 1860
- To Kingdom of Italy, 1866, 1870

over his conquests to Cavour's Piedmontese forces. On March 17, 1861, the new kingdom of Italy was proclaimed under a centralized government subordinated to the control of Piedmont and King Victor Emmanuel II of the house of Savoy.

The task of unification was not yet complete, however. Venetia in the north was still held by Austria, and Rome was under papal control, supported by French troops. In the Austro-Prussian War of 1866, the new Italian state became an ally of Prussia. Although the Italian army was defeated by the Austrians, Prussia's victory left the Italians with Venetia. In 1870, the Franco-Prussian War resulted in the withdrawal of French troops from Rome. The Italian army then annexed the city on September 20, 1870, and Rome became the new capital of the united Italian state.

The Unification of Germany

After the failure of the Frankfurt Assembly to achieve German unification in 1848–1849, more and more Germans looked to Prussia for leadership in the cause of German unification. Prussia had become a strong, prosperous, and authoritarian state, with the Prussian king in firm control of both the government and the army. In the 1860s, King William I (1861–1888) attempted to enlarge and strengthen the Prussian army. When the Prussian legislature refused to levy new taxes for the proposed military changes, William appointed a new prime minister, Count Otto von Bismarck (OT-toh fun BIZ-mark) (1815–1898). Bismarck ignored the legislative opposition to the military reforms, arguing instead that "Germany does not look to Prussia's liberalism but to her power. . . . Not by speeches and majorities will the great questions of the day be decided—that was the mistake of 1848–1849—but by iron and blood."[6] Bismarck collected the taxes, reorganized the army anyway, and governed Prussia by simply ignoring parliament. In the meantime, opposition to his domestic policy determined Bismarck on an active foreign policy, which led to war and German unification. Bismarck has often been portrayed as the ultimate realist, the foremost nineteenth-century practitioner of *Realpolitik* (ray-AHL-poh-lee-teek)—the "politics of reality."

After defeating Denmark with Austrian help in 1864 and gaining control over the duchies of Schleswig (SHLESS-vik) and Holstein (HOHL-shtyn), Bismarck created friction with the Austrians and goaded them into a war on June 14, 1866. The Austrians were barely defeated at Königgrätz (kur-nig-GRETS) on July 3, but Prussia now organized the German states north of the Main River into the North German Confederation. The southern German states, largely Catholic, remained independent but

Garibaldi and Romantic Nationalism

POLITICS & GOVERNMENT

Giuseppe Garibaldi was one of the more colorful figures involved in the unification of Italy. Accompanied by only a thousand of his famous Red Shirts, the Italian soldier of fortune left Genoa on the night of May 5, 1860, for an invasion of the kingdom of the Two Sicilies. The ragged band entered Palermo, the chief city on the island of Sicily, on May 31. This selection is taken from an account by a correspondent for the *Times* of London, the Hungarian-born Nandor Eber.

Times, June 13, 1860

Palermo, May 31—Anyone in search of violent emotions cannot do better than set off at once for Palermo. However blasé he may be, or however milk-and-water his blood, I promise it will be stirred up. He will be carried away by the tide of popular feeling. . . .

In the afternoon Garibaldi made a tour of inspection round the town. I was there, but find it really impossible to give you a faint idea of the manner in which he was received everywhere. It was one of those triumphs which seem to be almost too much for a man. . . . The popular idol, Garibaldi, in his red flannel shirt, with a loose colored handkerchief round his neck, and his worn "wide-awake" [a soft-brimmed felt hat], was walking on foot among those cheering, laughing, crying, mad thousands; and all his few followers could do was to prevent him from being bodily carried off the ground. The people threw themselves forward to kiss his hands, or, at least, to touch the hem of his garment, as if it contained the panacea for all their past and perhaps coming suffering. Children were brought up, and mothers asked on their knees for his blessing; and all this while the object of this idolatry was calm and smiling as when in the deadliest fire, taking up the children and kissing them, trying to quiet the crowd, stopping at every moment to hear a long complaint of houses burned and property sacked by the retreating soldiers, giving good advice, comforting, and promising that all damages should be paid for. . . .

One might write volumes of horrors on the vandalism already committed, for every one of the hundred ruins has its story of brutality and inhumanity. . . . In these small houses a dense population is crowded together even in ordinary times. A shell falling on one, and crushing and burying the inmates, was sufficient to make people abandon the neighboring one and take refuge a little further on, shutting themselves up in the cellars. When the Royalists retired they set fire to those of the houses which had escaped the shells, and numbers were thus burned alive in their hiding places. . . .

If you can stand the exhalation, try and go inside the ruins, for it is only there that you will see what the thing means and you will not have to search long before you stumble over the remains of a human body, a leg sticking out here, an arm there, a black face staring at you a little further on. You are startled by a rustle. You look round and see half a dozen gorged rats scampering off in all directions, or you see a dog trying to make his escape over the ruins. . . . I only wonder that the sight of these scenes does not convert every man in the town into a tiger and every woman into a fury. But these people have been so long ground down and demoralized that their nature seems to have lost the power of reaction.

 This article from the London Times *is the first newspaper primary source document to appear in this textbook. How does this new source of information reflect the growth of an industrial middle class?*

---

signed military alliances with Prussia due to their fear of France, their western neighbor.

Prussia now dominated all of northern Germany, but problems with France soon arose. Bismark realized that France would never be content with a strong German state to its east because of the potential threat to French security. In 1870, Prussia and France became embroiled in a dispute over the candidacy of a relative of the Prussian king for the throne of Spain. Bismarck manipulated the misunderstandings between the French and Prussians to goad the French into declaring war on Prussia on July 15, 1870. The southern German states honored their military alliances with Prussia and joined the war effort against the French. The Prussian armies advanced into France, and at Sedan (suh-DAHN) on September 2, 1870, captured an entire French army and Napoleon III himself. Paris capitulated on January 28, 1871. France had to pay an indemnity of 5 billion francs (about $1 billion) and give up the provinces of Alsace (al-SASS) and Lorraine (luh-RAYN) to the new German state, a loss that left the French burning for revenge.

CHRONOLOGY	The Unification of Italy
Victor Emmanuel II	1849–1878
Count Cavour becomes prime minister of Piedmont	1852
Garibaldi's invasion of the Two Sicilies	1860
Kingdom of Italy is proclaimed	March 17, 1861
Italy's annexation of Venetia	1866
Italy's annexation of Rome	1870

The Unification of Germany

The Unification of Germany. Under Prussian leadership, a new German empire was proclaimed on January 18, 1871, in the Hall of Mirrors in the palace at Versailles. King William of Prussia became Emperor William I of the Second German Empire. Otto von Bismarck, the man who had been so instrumental in creating the new German state, is shown here, resplendently attired in his white uniform, standing at the foot of the throne.

CHRONOLOGY	The Unification of Germany
King William I of Prussia	1861–1888
Danish War	1864
Austro-Prussian War	1866
Franco-Prussian War	1870–1871
German Empire is proclaimed	January 18, 1871

Even before the war had ended, the southern German states had agreed to enter the North German Confederation. On January 18, 1871, in the Hall of Mirrors in Louis XIV's palace at Versailles, William I was proclaimed kaiser (KY-zur) (emperor) of the Second German Empire (the first was the medieval Holy Roman Empire). German unity had been achieved by the Prussian monarchy and the Prussian army. The Prussian leadership of German unification meant the triumph of authoritarian, militaristic values over liberal, constitutional sentiments in the development of the new German state. With its industrial resources and military might, the new state had become the strongest power on the Continent. A new European balance of power was at hand.

Nationalism and Reform: The European National State at Mid-Century

While European affairs were dominated by the unification of Italy and Germany, other states in the Western world were also undergoing change.

GREAT BRITAIN Unlike the nations on the Continent, Great Britain managed to avoid the revolutionary upheavals of the first half of the nineteenth century. In the early part of the century, Britain was governed by the aristocratic landowning classes that dominated both houses of Parliament. But in 1832, to avoid the turmoil on the Continent, Parliament passed a reform bill that increased the number of male voters, chiefly members of the industrial middle class (see the box on p. 561). By joining the industrial middle class to the landed interest in ruling Britain, Britain avoided revolution in 1848.

Another reason for Britain's stability was its continuing economic growth. After 1850, middle-class prosperity was at last coupled with some improvements for the working classes as real wages for laborers increased more than 25 percent between 1850 and 1870. The British sense of national pride was well represented in Queen Victoria (1837–1901), whose sense of duty and moral respectability reflected the attitudes of her age, which has ever since been known as the Victorian Age (see the Film & History feature on p. 567).

In the 1850s and 1860s, the British liberal parliamentary system also made both social and political reforms that enabled the country to remain stable. Although the Whigs (now called the Liberals), who had been responsible for the Reform Act of 1832, talked about passing additional reform legislation, it was actually the Tories (now called the Conservatives) who carried it through. Under the leadership of Benjamin Disraeli (diz-RAY-lee) (1804–1881), the Tory leader in Parliament, the Reform Act of 1867 added an important step in the democratization of Britain. The number of voters increased from 1 million to slightly over 2 million. At the

The Young Victoria (2009)

Directed by Jean-Marc Vallée, *The Young Victoria* is an imaginative and yet relatively realistic portrayal of the early struggles of the young woman who became Britain's longest-reigning monarch. The film begins in 1836 when the seventeen-year-old Victoria (Emily Blunt) is the heir to the throne. Her controlling mother, the duchess of Kent (Miranda Richardson), schemes to prevent her daughter from ascending the throne by trying to create a regency for herself and her close adviser and paramour, Sir John Conroy (Mark Strong). Conroy is accurately shown trying to force the young Victoria to sign a paper establishing a regency. The mother and Conroy fail, and Victoria succeeds to the throne after the death of her uncle, King William IV (Jim Broadbent), on June 20, 1837, about one month after she turned eighteen. The movie also shows the impact that Lord Melbourne (Paul Bettany), the prime minister, had on the young queen as her private secretary and adviser. Indeed, Victoria's attachment to Melbourne led to considerable discontent among her subjects. Central to the film, however, is the romantic portrayal of the wooing of Victoria by her young German cousin, Prince Albert of Saxe-Coburg-Gotha (Rupert Friend), the nephew of the king of Belgium. The film accurately conveys the close bond and the deep and abiding love that developed between Victoria and Albert.

The film is a visual treat, re-creating the life of the young Victoria in a number of castle and cathedral settings. As a romantic dramatization of some of the main events before and after the coronation of Victoria, the film also contains some noticeable flaws. Victoria is shown painting with her right hand, although she was actually left-handed. The facts are also embellished at times in order to dramatize the story. Although there was an assassination attempt on the queen, Prince Albert was not shot while trying to

GK Films/The Kobal Collection

The coronation of Victoria (Emily Blunt) as queen of England

protect her. Both shots fired by Edward Oxford, her would-be assassin, went wide of the mark. The character of Victoria's other uncle, King Leopold I of Belgium (Thomas Kretschmann), is also not quite accurate. He was not as selfish as he is portrayed in pushing Albert to marry Victoria. The banquet scene in which King William IV insults the duchess of Kent is quite accurate (it actually uses many of the exact words the king uttered), but its consequences were not. The duchess did not leave the room, and Victoria did not remain calm, but broke into tears. Finally, except for a passing reference to Victoria's concern for workers' housing conditions, this romantic movie makes no attempt to understand the political and social issues that troubled the British Empire of Victoria's time.

---

same time, the extension of the right to vote had an important by-product as it forced the Liberals and Conservatives to organize carefully in order to manipulate the electorate. Party discipline intensified, and the rivalry between the Liberals and Conservatives became a regular feature of parliamentary life.

FRANCE Events in France after the revolution of 1848 moved toward the restoration of monarchy. Four years after his election as president, Louis Napoleon returned to the people to ask for the restoration of the empire. Ninety-seven percent responded in the affirmative, and on December 2, 1852, Louis Napoleon assumed the title of Napoleon III (the first Napoleon had abdicated in favor of his son, Napoleon II, on April 6, 1814). The Second Empire had begun.

The first five years of Napoleon III's reign were a spectacular success. He took many steps to expand industrial growth.

Government subsidies helped foster the rapid construction of railroads as well as harbors, roads, and canals. The major French railway lines were completed during Napoleon's reign, and iron production tripled. In the midst of this economic expansion, Napoleon III also undertook a vast reconstruction of the city of Paris. The medieval Paris of narrow streets and old city walls was destroyed and replaced by a modern Paris of broad boulevards, spacious buildings, circular plazas, public squares, an underground sewage system, a new public water supply, and gas streetlights.

In the 1860s, as opposition to his rule began to mount, Napoleon III liberalized his regime. He gave the Legislative Corps more say in affairs of state, including debate over the budget. Liberalization policies worked initially; in a plebiscite in May 1870 on whether to accept a new constitution that might have inaugurated a parliamentary regime, the French people gave Napoleon another resounding victory. This triumph was short-lived, however. War with Prussia in 1870 brought Napoleon's ouster, and a republic was proclaimed.

THE AUSTRIAN EMPIRE Although nationalism was a major force in nineteenth-century Europe, one of the region's most powerful states, the Austrian Empire, managed to frustrate the desire of its numerous ethnic groups for self-determination. After the Habsburg rulers had crushed the revolutions of 1848–1849, they restored centralized, autocratic government to the empire. But Austria's defeat at the hands of the Prussians in 1866 forced the Austrians to deal with the fiercely nationalistic Hungarians.

The result was the negotiated *Ausgleich* (OWSS-glykh), or Compromise, of 1867, which created the Dual Monarchy of Austria-Hungary. Each part of the empire now had its own constitution, its own legislature, its own governmental bureaucracy, and its own capital (Vienna for Austria and Buda for Hungary). Holding the two states together was a single monarch—Francis Joseph (1848–1916) was emperor of Austria and king of Hungary—as well as a common army, foreign policy, and system of finances. The *Ausgleich* did not, however, satisfy the other nationalities that made up the Austro-Hungarian Empire.

RUSSIA At the beginning of the nineteenth century, Russia was overwhelmingly rural, agricultural, and autocratic. The Russian tsar was still regarded as a divine-right monarch with unlimited power. The Russian imperial autocracy, based on soldiers, secret police, and repression, had withstood the revolutionary fervor of the first half of the nineteenth century. But defeat in the Crimean War in 1856 led even staunch conservatives to realize that Russia was falling hopelessly behind the western European powers. Tsar Alexander II (1855–1881) decided to make serious reforms.

Serfdom was the most burdensome problem in tsarist Russia. On March 3, 1861, Alexander issued his emancipation edict (see the box on p. 569). Peasants were now free to own property and marry as they chose. The lands given to the peasants, however, were purchased by the state from the landlords, who kept the best parcels, leaving the Russian peasants without enough arable land to support themselves. Peasants were also expected to repay the state in long-term installments. To ensure that the payments were made, peasants were subjected to the authority of their *mir* (MEER), or village commune, which was collectively responsible for the land payments to the government. And since the village communes were responsible for the payments, they were reluctant to allow peasants to leave their land. Emancipation, then, led not to a free, landowning peasantry along the Western model but to an unhappy, land-starved peasantry that largely followed the old ways of agricultural production.

Alexander II attempted other reforms as well, but he soon found that he could please no one. Reformers wanted more and rapid change; conservatives thought that the tsar was attempting to undermine the basic institutions of Russian society. When one group of radicals assassinated Alexander II in 1881, his son and successor, Alexander III, turned against reform and returned to the traditional methods of repression.

The European State, 1871–1914

 FOCUS QUESTIONS: What general political trends were evident in the nations of western Europe in the late nineteenth and early twentieth centuries, and to what degree were those trends also apparent in the nations of central and eastern Europe? How did the growth of nationalism affect international affairs during the same period?

Throughout much of the Western world by 1870, the national state had become the focus of people's loyalties and the arena for political activity. Only in Russia, eastern Europe, Austria-Hungary, and Ireland did national groups still struggle for independence.

Within the major European states, considerable progress was made in achieving such liberal practices as constitutions and parliaments, but it was largely in western European states that **mass politics** became a reality. Reforms encouraged the expansion of political democracy through voting rights for men and the creation of mass political parties. At the same time, however, these latter developments were strongly resisted in parts of Europe where the old political forces remained strong.

Western Europe: The Growth of Political Democracy

By 1871, Great Britain had a functioning two-party parliamentary system. For fifty years, the Liberals and Conservatives alternated in power at regular intervals, although they also shared some common features. Both were dominated by a ruling class made up of a coalition of aristocratic landowners, who were also frequently involved in industrial and financial activities, and upper-middle-class businesspeople. The two parties competed with each other in supporting legislation that expanded the right to vote. By 1918, all males over twenty-one and women over thirty could vote. Political democracy was soon accompanied by social welfare measures for the working class.

The growth of trade unions, which advocated more radical change of the economic system, and the emergence in 1900 of the Labour Party, which dedicated itself to workers' interests, caused the Liberals, who held the government from 1906 to 1914, to realize that they would have to create a program of social welfare or lose the support of the workers. Therefore, they voted for a series of social reforms. The National Insurance Act of 1911 provided benefits for workers in case of sickness and unemployment, to be paid for by compulsory contributions from workers, employers, and the state. Additional legislation provided a small pension for Britons over age seventy and compensation for those injured in accidents at work. Although both the benefits of the program and the tax increases were modest, they were the first hesitant steps toward the future British welfare state.

In France, the confusion that ensued after the collapse of the Second Empire ended in 1875 when an improvised constitution established a republican form of government. This constitution established a bicameral legislature, with an upper house, the Senate, elected indirectly and a lower house, the Chamber of Deputies, chosen by universal male suffrage.

Emancipation: Serfs and Slaves

FAMILY & SOCIETY

Although overall their histories have been quite different, Russia and the United States shared a common feature in the 1860s. They were the only states in the Western world that still had large enslaved populations (the Russian serfs were virtually slaves). The leaders of both countries issued emancipation proclamations within two years of each other. The first excerpt is taken from the imperial decree of March 3, 1861, which freed the Russian serfs. The second excerpt is from Abraham Lincoln's Emancipation Proclamation, issued on January 1, 1863.

Tsar Alexander II's Imperial Decree, March 3, 1861

By the grace of God, we, Alexander II, Emperor and Autocrat of all the Russias, King of Poland, Grand Duke of Finland, etc., to all our faithful subjects, make known:

Called by Divine Providence and by the sacred right of inheritance to the throne of our ancestors, we took a vow in our innermost heart to respond to the mission which is intrusted to us as to surround with our affection and our Imperial solicitude all our faithful subjects of every rank and of every condition, from the warrior, who nobly bears arms for the defense of the country, to the humble artisan devoted to the works of industry; from the official in the career of the high offices of the State to the laborer whose plough furrows the soil. . . .

We thus came to the conviction that the work of a serious improvement of the condition of the peasants was a sacred inheritance bequeathed to us by our ancestors, a mission which, in the course of events, Divine Providence called upon us to fulfill. . . .

In virtue of the new dispositions above mentioned, the peasants attached to the soil will be invested within a term fixed by the law with all the rights of free cultivators. . . .

At the same time, they are granted the right of purchasing their close [a parcel of land], and, with the consent of the proprietors, they may acquire in full property the arable lands and other appurtenances which are allotted to them as a permanent holding. By the acquisition in full property of the quantity of land fixed, the peasants are free from their obligations toward the proprietors for land thus purchased, and they enter definitely into the condition of free peasant-landholders.

Abraham Lincoln's Emancipation Proclamation, January 1, 1863

Now therefore, I, Abraham Lincoln, President of the United States, by virtue of the power in me vested as Commander-in-Chief of the Army and Navy of the United States in time of actual armed rebellion against the authority and government of the United States, and as a fit and necessary war measure for suppressing such rebellion, do, on this 1st day of January, A.D. 1863, and in accordance with my purpose to do so, . . . order and designate as the States and parts of States wherein the people thereof, respectively, are this day in rebellion against the United States the following, to wit:

Arkansas, Texas, Louisiana, . . . Mississippi, Alabama, Florida, Georgia, South Carolina, North Carolina, and Virginia. . . .

And by virtue of the power for the purpose aforesaid, I do order and declare that all persons held as slaves within said designated States and parts of States are, and henceforward shall be free; and that the Executive Government of the United States, including the military and naval authorities thereof, will recognize and maintain the freedom of said persons.

 What changes did Tsar Alexander II's emancipation of the serfs initiate in Russia? What effect did Lincoln's Emancipation Proclamation have on the southern "armed rebellion"? What reasons did each leader give for his action?

The powers of the president, selected by the legislature to be the executive of the government for a term of seven years, were deliberately left vague. The premier (or prime minister) led the government, and he and his ministers were responsible not to the president but to the Chamber of Deputies.

The Constitution of 1875, intended only as a stopgap measure, solidified the Third Republic, which lasted sixty-five years. France's parliamentary system was weak, however, because the existence of a dozen political parties forced the premier to depend on a coalition of parties to stay in power. The Third Republic was notorious for its changes of government. Nevertheless, by 1914, the republic commanded the loyalty of most French people.

By 1870, Italy had emerged as a geographically united state with pretensions to great power status. Its internal weaknesses, however, gave that claim a particularly hollow ring. Sectional differences—a poverty-stricken south and an industrializing north—thwarted any sense of national unity. Chronic turmoil between labor and industry undermined the social fabric. The Italian government was unable to deal effectively with these problems because of extensive corruption among government officials and a lack of stability created by ever-changing government coalitions.

Central and Eastern Europe: Persistence of the Old Order

The constitution of the new imperial Germany begun by Bismarck in 1871 provided for a bicameral legislature. The lower house of the German parliament, the Reichstag, was elected on the basis of universal male suffrage, but it did not have ministerial responsibility. Ministers of government, among whom the most important was the chancellor, were responsible not to the parliament but to the emperor. The emperor also commanded the armed forces and controlled foreign policy and internal administration.

During the reign of Emperor William II (1888–1918), Germany continued as an "authoritarian, conservative, military-bureaucratic power state." By the end of William's reign, Germany had become the strongest military and industrial power on the Continent. More than 50 percent of German workers had jobs in industry, while only 30 percent of the workforce was still in agriculture. Urban centers had mushroomed in number and size. These rapid changes helped produce a society torn between modernization and traditionalism. With the expansion of industry and cities came demands for true democracy. Conservative forces, especially the landowning nobility and representatives of heavy industry, two of the powerful ruling groups in Germany, tried to block it by supporting William II's activist foreign policy. Expansion abroad, they believed, would divert people's attention from the yearning for democracy at home.

The tensions in German society created by the conflict between modernization and traditionalism were also manifested in radicalized right-wing politics. A number of nationalist pressure groups arose to support nationalistic goals. Antisocialist and antiliberal, such groups as the Pan-German League stressed strong German nationalism and advocated imperialism as a tool to overcome social divisions and unite all classes. They also denounced the Jews as the destroyers of the German national community, fueling the flames of **anti-Semitism**.

After the creation of the Dual Monarchy of Austria-Hungary in 1867, the Austrian part received a constitution that theoretically established a parliamentary system. Emperor Francis Joseph largely ignored parliament, however, ruling by decree when parliament was not in session.

Nicholas II. The last tsar of Russia hoped to preserve the traditional autocratic ways of his predecessors. In this photograph, Nicholas II and his wife, Alexandra, are shown around 1907 with their four daughters and son on holiday on the deck of a ship.

The problem of the various nationalities remained a difficult one. The German minority that governed Austria felt increasingly threatened by the Czechs, Poles, and other Slavic groups within the empire. The granting of universal male suffrage in 1907 served only to exacerbate the problem when nationalities that had played no role in the government now agitated in the parliament for autonomy. This led prime ministers after 1900 to ignore the parliament and rely increasingly on imperial emergency decrees to govern. On the eve of World War I, the Austro-Hungarian Empire was as far away as ever from solving its minorities problem.

By 1870, Russia was witnessing an increasing number of reform movements. Intellectuals known as **Westernizers** believed that Western ways were the solutions to Russia's problems and advocated the creation of parliamentary institutions and a policy of industrialization. Westernizers, however, were opposed by **Slavophiles**, who maintained that Russia's tsarist system, peasant villages, and Orthodox religious faith were superior to any Western ideals. Other Russians rejected both the Westernizers and Slavophiles and called for a more radical approach to reform. Among these were the **anarchists**, who believed that small groups of well-trained fanatical revolutionaries could perpetrate so much violence that the state and all its institutions would disintegrate. For the anarchist revolutionaries, assassination was the primary instrument of terror, and one group was successful in killing Tsar Alexander II in 1881.

This act had unexpected repercussions for the anarchists. Alexander III (1881–1894), the son and successor of the assassinated tsar, was now convinced that his father's attempts at reform had been a mistake, and he lost no time in persecuting both reformers and revolutionaries. When Alexander III died,

CHRONOLOGY The European State, 1871–1914	
Great Britain	
Formation of Labour Party	1900
National Insurance Act	1911
France	
Republican constitution (Third Republic)	1875
Germany	
Bismarck as chancellor	1871–1890
Emperor William II	1888–1918
Austria-Hungary	
Emperor Francis Joseph	1848–1916
Russia	
Tsar Alexander III	1881–1894
Tsar Nicholas II	1894–1917
Russo-Japanese War	1904–1905
Revolution	1905

his weak son and successor, Nicholas II (1894–1917), began his rule with his father's conviction that the absolute power of the tsars should be preserved: "I shall maintain the principle of autocracy just as firmly and unflinchingly as did my unforgettable father."[7] But conditions were changing, especially with the growth of industrialization.

Industrialization progressed rapidly in Russia after 1890, and with it came factories, an industrial working class, and the development of socialist parties, although repression in Russia soon forced the socialists to go underground and turn revolutionary. The social revolutionaries worked to overthrow the tsarist autocracy and establish peasant socialism. Growing opposition to the tsar finally exploded into revolution in 1905.

The defeat of the Russians by the Japanese in 1904–1905 encouraged antigovernment groups to rebel against the tsarist regime. Nicholas II granted civil liberties and agreed to create a legislative assembly, the Duma (DOO-muh), elected directly by a broad franchise. But real constitutional monarchy proved short-lived. Already by 1907, the tsar had curtailed the power of the Duma and relied again on the army and bureaucracy to rule Russia.

International Rivalries and the Winds of War

Between 1871 and 1914, Europe was mostly at peace. Wars did occur (including wars of conquest in the non-Western world), but none involved the great powers. A series of crises occurred, however, that might easily have led to war. Until 1890, Bismarck, the chancellor of Germany, exercised a restraining influence on Europeans. He realized that the emergence in 1871 of a unified Germany as the most powerful state on the Continent had upset the balance of power established at Vienna in 1815 (see Map 19.4). Fearful of a possible anti-German alliance involving France and Russia and possibly even Austria-Hungary, Bismarck made a defensive alliance with Austria in 1879. Both powers agreed to support each other in the event of an attack by Russia. In 1882, this German-Austrian alliance was enlarged by the addition of Italy, angry with the French over conflicting colonial ambitions in North Africa. The Triple Alliance of 1882 committed Germany, Austria-Hungary, and Italy to unite in their defense against France. Bismarck also signed a separate treaty with Russia.

When Emperor William II cashiered Bismarck in 1890 and took over direction of Germany's foreign policy, he embarked on an activist foreign policy dedicated to enhancing German power by finding, as he put it, Germany's rightful "place in the sun." One of his changes in Bismarck's foreign policy was to drop the treaty with Russia, which he viewed as being at odds with Germany's alliance with Austria. The ending of the alliance brought France and Russia together, and in 1894, the two powers concluded a military alliance. During the next ten years, German policies abroad caused the British to draw closer to France. By 1907, a loose confederation of Great Britain, France, and Russia—known as the Triple Entente (ahn-TAHNT)—stood opposed to the Triple Alliance of Germany, Austria-Hungary, and Italy. Europe was now divided into two opposing camps that became more and more inflexible and unwilling to compromise. A series of crises in the Balkans between 1908 and 1913 over the remnants of the Ottoman Empire set the stage for World War I.

The Ottoman Empire and Nationalism in the Balkans

Like the Austro-Hungarian Empire, the Ottoman Empire was severely troubled by the nationalist aspirations of its subject peoples, especially in the Balkans. Corruption and inefficiency had so weakened the Ottoman Empire that only the interference of the great European powers, who were fearful of each other's designs on the empire, kept it alive.

In the course of the nineteenth century, the Balkan provinces of the Ottoman Empire gradually gained their freedom, although the rivalry in the region between Austria and Russia complicated the process. By 1878, Greece, Serbia, Romania, and Montenegro (mahn-tuh-NEE-groh) had become independent. Bulgaria did not become totally independent but was allowed to operate autonomously under Russian protection. The Balkan territories of Bosnia and Herzegovina (HAYRT-suh-guh-VEE-nuh) were placed under the protection of Austria-Hungary. Austria could occupy but not annex them.

The Balkans in 1913

CRISES IN THE BALKANS, 1908–1913 In 1908, Austria took the drastic step of annexing the Slavic-speaking territories of Bosnia and Herzegovina. Serbia was outraged because the annexation dashed the Serbs' hopes of creating a large Serbian kingdom that would include most of the southern Slavs. But the Austrians had annexed Bosnia explicitly to prevent that eventuality. The creation of a large Serbia would be a threat to the unity of their empire with its large Slavic population. The Russians, as protectors of their fellow Slavs and also desiring to increase their own authority in the Balkans, supported the Serbs and opposed the Austrian action. Backed by the Russians, the Serbs prepared for war against Austria. At this point, William II intervened and demanded that the

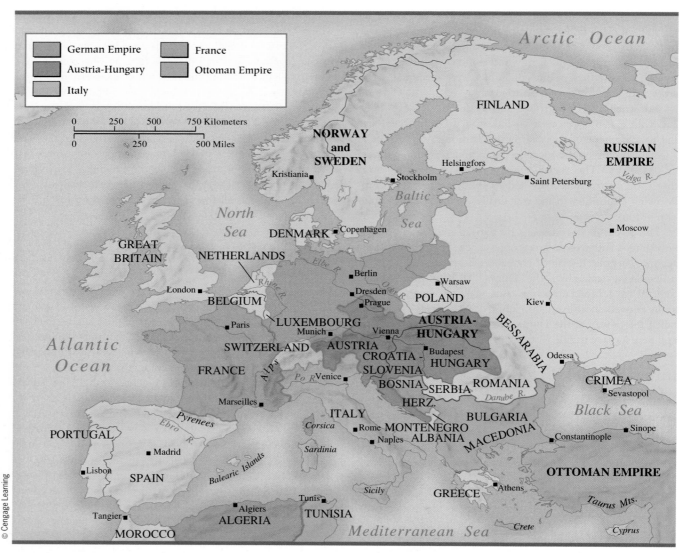

MAP 19.4 **Europe in 1871.** German unification in 1871 upset the balance of power established at Vienna in 1815 and eventually led to a realignment of European alliances. By 1907, Europe was divided into two opposing camps: the Triple Entente of Great Britain, Russia, and France and the Triple Alliance of Germany, Austria-Hungary, and Italy.

Q How was Germany affected by the formation of the Triple Entente?

Russians accept Austria's annexation of Bosnia and Herzegovina or face war with Germany. Weakened from their defeat in the Russo-Japanese War in 1904–1905, the Russians backed down but vowed revenge. Two wars between the Balkan states in 1912–1913 further embittered the inhabitants of the region and generated more tensions among the great powers.

Serbia's desire to create a large Serbian kingdom remained unfulfilled. In frustration, Serbian nationalists blamed the Austrians. Austria-Hungary was convinced that Serbia was a mortal threat to its empire and must at some point be crushed. As Serbia's chief supporters, the Russians were determined not to back down again in the event of a confrontation with Austria or Germany in the Balkans. The allies of Austria-Hungary and Russia were also determined to be more supportive of their respective allies in another crisis. By the beginning of 1914, two armed camps viewed each other with suspicion.

CHAPTER SUMMARY

In 1815, a conservative order had been reestablished throughout Europe, but the forces of liberalism and nationalism, unleashed by the French Revolution and now reinforced by the spread of industrialization, were pushing Europe into a new era of political and social change. Industrialization spread rapidly from Great Britain to the Continent and United States. As cities grew, the plight of Europe's new working class became the focus of new political philosophies. Utopian socialists championed better living conditions for the working poor, while the work of Karl Marx sought to liberate the oppressed proletariat. At the same time, middle-class industrialists adopted the political philosophy of liberalism, espousing freedom in politics and in economic activity. By the mid-nineteenth century, nationalism threatened the status quo in divided Germany and Italy and the multiethnic Austrian Empire.

The revolutionary waves of the 1820s and 1830s made it clear that the ideologies of liberalism and nationalism were still alive and active in the Western world. In 1848, revolutions erupted once more. A republic with universal manhood suffrage was established in France, but conflict emerged between socialist demands and the republican political agenda. The Frankfurt Assembly worked to create a unified Germany, but it also failed. In the Austrian Empire, the liberal demands of the Hungarians and other nationalities were eventually put down. In Italy, too, uprisings against Austrian rule failed when conservatives regained control.

By 1871, nationalist forces had prevailed in Germany and Italy. The combined activities of Count Cavour and Giuseppe Garibaldi finally led to the unification of Italy in 1870. Under the guidance of Otto von Bismarck, Prussia engaged in wars with Denmark, Austria, and France before it finally achieved the goal of German national unification in 1871. Reform characterized developments in other Western states. Austria created the Dual Monarchy of Austria-Hungary. Russia's defeat in the Crimean War led to reforms under Alexander II, which included the freeing of the Russian serfs.

Between 1871 and 1914, the national state began to expand its functions by adopting such social insurance measures as protection against accidents, illnesses, and old age in order to appease the working masses. Liberal and democratic reforms, especially in western Europe, brought new possibilities for greater participation in the political process. Nevertheless, significantly large minorities, especially in the multiethnic empires controlled by the Austrians, Ottomans, and Russians, had not achieved the goal of their own national states. Meanwhile, the collapse of the Ottoman Empire caused Russia and Austria to set their sights on territories in the Balkans. As Germany's power increased, the European nations formed new alliances that helped maintain a balance of power but also led to the creation of large armies. The alliances also generated tensions that were unleashed when Europeans were unable to resolve a series of crises in the Balkans and rushed into the catastrophic carnage of World War I.

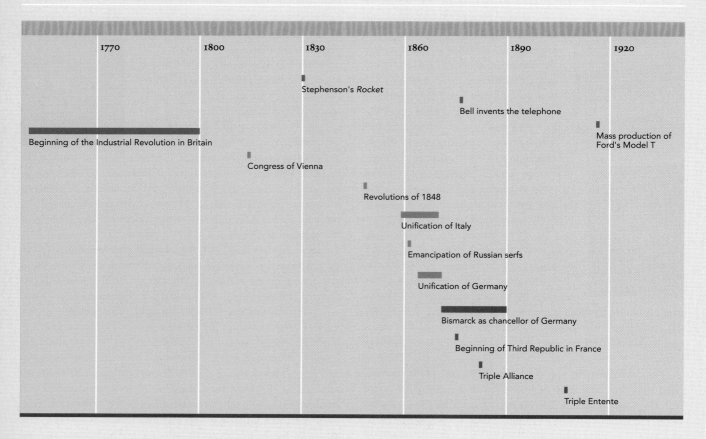

1770　1800　1830　1860　1890　1920

Stephenson's *Rocket*

Bell invents the telephone

Beginning of the Industrial Revolution in Britain

Mass production of
Ford's Model T

Congress of Vienna

Revolutions of 1848

Unification of Italy

Emancipation of Russian serfs

Unification of Germany

Bismarck as chancellor of Germany

Beginning of Third Republic in France

Triple Alliance

Triple Entente

CHAPTER REVIEW

Upon Reflection

Q What are the major similarities and differences between the First and Second Industrial Revolutions?

Q What were the chief ideas associated with the ideologies of liberalism and nationalism, and how were these ideas put into practice in the first half of the nineteenth century?

Q Between 1871 and 1914, two major domestic political goals involved the achievement of liberal practices and the growth of political democracy. To what extent were these realized in Great Britain, France, Germany, Austria-Hungary, and Russia?

Key Terms

joint-stock investment bank (p. 546)
proletariat (p. 549)
socialism (p. 552)
utopian socialists (p. 552)
trade unions (p. 552)
Marxism (p. 555)
class struggle (p. 556)
revisionism (p. 557)
revolutionary socialism (p. 557)
legitimacy (p. 557)

conservatism (p. 558)
intervention (p. 558)
liberalism (p. 559)
Realpolitik (p. 564)
Ausgleich (p. 568)
mass politics (p. 568)
anti-Semitism (p. 570)
Westernizers (p. 570)
Slavophiles (p. 570)
anarchists (p. 570)

Suggested Reading

THE INDUSTRIAL REVOLUTION AND ITS IMPACT A good introduction to the Industrial Revolution is **J. Horn,** *The Industrial Revolution* (Westport, Conn., 2007). On the role of the British, see **K. Morgan,** *The Birth of Industrial Britain: Social Change, 1750–1850* (New York, 2004). A work on female labor patterns is **J. Rendall,** *Women in an Industrializing Society: England, 1750–1880* (Oxford, 2002).

For a global approach to the modern economy, see **K. Pomeranz,** *The Great Deliverance: China, Europe, and the Making of the Modern World Economy* (Princeton, N.J., 2002).

THE GROWTH OF INDUSTRIAL PROSPERITY The Second Industrial Revolution is well covered in **A. S. Milward** and **S. B. Saul,** *The Development of the Economies of Continental Europe, 1850–1914*

(Cambridge, Mass., 1977). The impact of the new technology on European thought is imaginatively discussed in **S. Kern,** *The Culture of Time and Space, 1880–1918,* rev. ed. (Cambridge, Mass., 2003). On Marx, the standard work is **D. McLellan,** *Karl Marx: His Life and Thought,* 4th ed. (New York, 2006).

THE GROWTH OF NATIONALISM, 1814–1848 For a good survey of the nineteenth century, see **R. Gildea,** *Barricades and Borders: Europe, 1800–1914,* 3rd ed. (Oxford, 2003). Also valuable is **T. C. W. Blanning, ed.,** *Nineteenth Century: Europe, 1789–1914* (Oxford, 2000). For a survey of the period 1814–1848, see **M. Lyons,** *Postrevolutionary Europe, 1815–1856* (New York, 2006). The best introduction to the revolutions of 1848 is **J. Sperber,** *The European Revolutions, 1848–1851,* 2nd ed. (New York, 2005).

NATIONAL UNIFICATION AND THE NATIONAL STATE, 1848–1871 The unification of Italy can be examined in **B. Derek** and **E. F. Biagini,** *The Risorgimento and the Unification of Italy,* 2nd ed. (London, 2002). The unification of Germany can be pursued first in a biography of Bismarck, **E. Feuchtwanger,** *Bismarck* (London, 2002).

Louis Napoleon's role can be examined in **J. F. McMillan,** *Napoleon III* (New York, 1991). On the Austrian Empire, see **R. Okey,** *The Habsburg Monarchy* (New York, 2001). Imperial Russia is covered in **T. Chapman,** *Imperial Russia, 1801–1905* (London, 2001). On Victorian Britain, see **W. L. Arnstein,** *Queen Victoria* (New York, 2005).

THE EUROPEAN STATE, 1871–1914 The domestic politics of the period can be examined in the general works listed above. See also **J. Sperber,** *Europe 1850–1914* (New York, 2009).

Go to the CourseMate website at **www.cengagebrain.com** for additional study tools and review materials—including audio and video clips—for this chapter.

The Americas and Society and Culture in the West

A portrait of Toussaint L'Ouverture, leader of the Haitian independence movement

CHAPTER OUTLINE AND FOCUS QUESTIONS

Latin America in the Nineteenth and Early Twentieth Centuries

Q What role did liberalism and nationalism play in Latin America between 1800 and 1870? What were the major economic, social, and political trends in Latin America in the late nineteenth and early twentieth centuries?

The North American Neighbors: The United States and Canada

Q What role did nationalism and liberalism play in the United States and Canada between 1800 and 1870? What economic, social, and political trends were evident in the United States and Canada between 1870 and 1914?

The Emergence of Mass Society in the West

Q What is meant by the term *mass society*, and what were its main characteristics?

Cultural Life: Romanticism and Realism in the Western World

Q What were the main characteristics of Romanticism and Realism?

Toward the Modern Consciousness: Intellectual and Cultural Developments

Q What intellectual and cultural developments in the late nineteenth and early twentieth centuries "opened the way to a modern consciousness," and how did this consciousness differ from earlier worldviews?

CRITICAL THINKING

Q In what ways were the intellectual and cultural developments in the Western world between 1800 and 1914 related to the economic, social, and political developments?

NATIONALISM—one of the major forces for change in Europe in the nineteenth century—also affected Latin America as the colonial peoples there overthrew their Spanish and Portuguese masters and began the process of creating new national states. An unusual revolution in Haiti preceded the main independence movements. François-Dominique Toussaint L'Ouverture (frahn-SWAH-doh-muh-NEEK too-SANH loo-vayr-TOOR), the grandson of an African king, was born a slave in Saint-Domingue (san doh-MAYNG)—the western third of the island of Hispaniola, a French sugar colony—in 1746. Educated by his godfather, Toussaint was able to amass a small private fortune through his own talents and the generosity of his French master. When black slaves in Saint-Domingue, inspired by news of the French Revolution, revolted in 1791, Toussaint became their leader. For years, Toussaint and his ragtag army struck at the French. By 1801, after his army had come to control Saint-Domingue, Toussaint assumed the role of ruler and issued a constitution that freed all slaves.

But Napoleon Bonaparte refused to accept Toussaint's control of France's richest colony and sent a French army of 23,000 men under General Leclerc (luh-KLAHR), his brother-in-law, to crush the rebellion. Although yellow fever took its toll on the French army, the superior size and arms of the French forces enabled them to gain the upper hand. Toussaint was tricked into surrendering in 1802 with Leclerc's promise: "You will not find a more sincere friend than myself." What a friend! Toussaint was arrested, put in chains, and shipped to France, where he died a year later in a dungeon. The western part of Hispaniola, now called Haiti, however, became the first independent state in Latin America when Toussaint's lieutenants drove out the French forces in 1804. Haiti was only one of a number of places in the Americas where new nations were formed during the nineteenth century. Indeed, nation building was prominent in North America as the United States and Canada expanded.

As national states in both the Western Hemisphere and Europe were evolving in the nineteenth century, significant changes were occurring in society and culture. The rapid economic changes of the nineteenth century led to the emergence of mass society in the Western world, which meant improvements for the lower classes, who benefited from the extension of voting rights, a better standard of living, and universal education. The coming of mass society also created new roles for the governments of nation-states, which now fostered national loyalty, created mass armies by conscription, and took more responsibility for public health and housing measures in their cities. Cultural and intellectual changes also paralleled these social developments, and after 1870, Western philosophers, writers, and artists began exploring modern cultural expressions that questioned traditional ideas and increasingly provoked a crisis of confidence.

Latin America in the Nineteenth and Early Twentieth Centuries

Q FOCUS QUESTIONS: What role did liberalism and nationalism play in Latin America between 1800 and 1870? What were the major economic, social, and political trends in Latin America in the late nineteenth and early twentieth centuries?

The Spanish and Portuguese colonial empires in Latin America had been integrated into the traditional monarchical structure of Europe for centuries. When that structure was challenged, first by the ideas of the Enlightenment and then by the upheavals of the Napoleonic era, Latin America encountered the possibility of change. How it responded to that possibility, however, was determined in part by conditions unique to the region.

The Wars for Independence

By the end of the eighteenth century, the ideas of the Enlightenment and the new political ideals stemming from the successful revolution in North America were beginning to influence the creole elites (descendants of Europeans who became permanent inhabitants of Latin America). The principles of the equality of all people in the eyes of the law, free trade, and a free press proved very attractive. Sons of creoles, such as Simón Bolívar (see-MOHN boh-LEE-var) (1783–1830) and José de San Martín (hoh-SAY day san mar-TEEN) (1778–1850), who

became leaders of the independence movement, even went to European universities, where they imbibed the ideas of the Enlightenment. These Latin American elites, joined by a growing class of merchants, especially resented the domination of their trade by Spain and Portugal.

NATIONALISTIC REVOLTS IN LATIN AMERICA The creole elites soon began to use their new ideas to denounce the rule of the Iberian monarchs and the peninsulars (Spanish and Portuguese officials who resided in Latin America for political and economic gain). As Bolívar said in 1815, "It would be easier to have the two continents meet than to reconcile the spirits of Spain and America."[1] Bolívar reflected the growing nativism among the creole elites and their resentment of the Spanish peninsulars, who dominated Latin America and drained the people of their wealth. At the beginning of the nineteenth century, Napoleon's Continental wars provided the creoles with an opportunity for change. When Bonaparte toppled the monarchies of Spain and Portugal, the authority of the Spaniards and Portuguese in their colonial empires was weakened, and between 1807 and 1825, a series of revolts enabled most of Latin America to become independent.

As described in the chapter-opening vignette, the first revolt was actually a successful slave rebellion. Led by Toussaint L'Ouverture (1746–1803), the revolt resulted in the formation of Haiti as the first independent postcolonial state in Latin America in 1804.

In 1810, Mexico, too, experienced a revolt, fueled initially by the desire of the creole elites to overthrow the rule of the peninsulars. The first real hero of the Mexican independence movement, however, was Miguel Hidalgo y Costilla (mee-GEL ee-THAHL-goh ee kahs-TEE-yuh), a parish priest in a small village about 100 miles from Mexico City. Hidalgo, who had studied the French Revolution, roused the local Indians and mestizos, many of whom were suffering from a major famine in 1810, to free themselves from the Spanish: "My children, this day comes to us as a new dispensation. Are you ready to receive it? Will you be free? Will you make the effort to recover from the hated Spaniards the lands stolen from your forefathers three hundred years ago?"[2] On September 16, 1810, a crowd of Indians and mestizos, armed with clubs, machetes, and a few guns, quickly formed a mob army and attacked the Spaniards, shouting, "Long live independence and death to the Spaniards." But Hidalgo was not a good organizer, and his forces were soon crushed. A military court sentenced Hidalgo to death, but his memory lived on. In fact, September 16, the first day of the uprising, is celebrated as Mexico's Independence Day.

The participation of Indians and mestizos in the revolt against Spanish control frightened both creoles and peninsulars in Mexico. Fearful of the masses, they cooperated in defeating the popular revolutionary forces. The elites—both creoles and peninsulars—then decided to overthrow Spanish rule as a way of preserving their own power. They selected a creole military leader, Augustín de Iturbide (ah-goo-STEEN day ee-tur-BEE-day), as their leader and the first emperor of Mexico in 1821. Simón Bolívar said of Iturbide that he had become emperor "by the grace of God and bayonets." The new government fostered neither political nor economic changes, and it soon became apparent that Mexican independence benefited primarily the creole elites.

Independence movements elsewhere in Latin America were likewise the work of elites—primarily creoles—who overthrew Spanish rule and set up new governments that they could dominate. The masses of people—Indians, blacks, mestizos, and mulattoes—gained little from the revolts. José de San Martín of Argentina and Simón Bolívar of Venezuela, the leaders of the independence movement who were hailed as the liberators of South America, were both members of the creole elite.

THE EFFORTS OF BOLÍVAR AND SAN MARTÍN   Simón Bolívar has long been regarded as the George Washington of Latin America. Born into a wealthy Venezuelan family, he was introduced as a young man to the ideas of the Enlightenment. While in Rome in 1805 to witness the coronation of Napoleon as king of Italy, he committed himself to free his people from Spanish control. He vowed, "I swear before the God of my fathers, by my fathers themselves, by my honor and by my country, that my arm shall not rest nor my mind be at peace until I have broken the chains that bind me by the will and power of Spain."[3] When he returned to South America, Bolívar began to lead the bitter struggle for independence in

Venezuela as well as other parts of northern South America. Although he was acclaimed as the "liberator" of Venezuela in 1813 by the people, it was not until 1821 that he definitively defeated Spanish forces there. He went on to liberate Colombia, Ecuador, and Peru. Already in 1819, he had become president of Venezuela, at the time part of a federation that included Colombia and Ecuador. Bolívar was well aware of the difficulties in establishing stable republican governments in Latin America (see the box on p. 579).

While Bolívar was busy liberating northern South America from the Spanish, José de San Martín was concentrating his efforts on the southern part of the continent. Son of a Spanish army officer in Argentina, San Martín himself went to Spain and pursued a military career in the Spanish army. In 1811, after serving twenty-two years, he learned of the liberation movement in his native Argentina, abandoned his military career in Spain, and returned to his homeland in March 1812. Argentina had already been freed from Spanish control, but San Martín believed that the Spaniards must be removed from all of South America if any nation was to remain free. In January 1817, he led his forces over the high Andes Mountains, an amazing feat in itself. Two-thirds of their pack mules and horses died during the difficult journey. Many of the soldiers suffered from lack of oxygen and severe cold while crossing mountain passes that were more than 2 miles above

The Liberators of South America. José de San Martín and Simón Bolívar are hailed as the leaders of the South American independence movement. In the painting on the left, by Theodore Géricault (zhay-rih-KOH), a French Romantic painter, San Martín is shown leading his troops at the Battle of Chacabuco in Chile in 1817. The painting at the right shows Bolívar leading his troops across the Andes in 1823 to fight in Peru. This depiction of impeccably uniformed troops moving in perfect formation through the snow of the Andes, by the Chilean artist Franco Gomez, is, of course, highly unrealistic.

Simón Bolívar on Government in Latin America

POLITICS & GOVERNMENT

Simón Bolívar is acclaimed as the man who liberated Latin America from Spanish control. His interest in history and the ideas of the Enlightenment also led him to speculate on how Latin American nations would be governed after their freedom was obtained. This selection is taken from a letter that he wrote to the English governor of Jamaica.

Simón Bolívar, *The Jamaica Letter*

It is . . . difficult to foresee the future fate of the New World, to set down its political principles, or to prophesy what manner of government it will adopt. . . . We inhabit a world apart, separated by broad seas. We are young in the ways of almost all the arts and sciences, although in a certain manner, we are old in the ways of civilized society. . . . But we scarcely retain a vestige of what once was; we are, moreover, neither Indian nor European, but a species midway between the legitimate proprietors of this country and the Spanish usurpers. In short, though Americans by birth we derive our rights from Europe, and we have to assert these rights against the rights of the natives, and at the same time we must defend ourselves against the invaders. This places us in a most extraordinary and involved situation. . . .

The role of the inhabitants of the American hemisphere has for centuries been purely passive. Politically they were nonexistent. We are still in a position lower than slavery, and therefore it is more difficult for us to rise to the enjoyment of freedom. . . . States are slaves because of either the nature or the misuse of their constitutions; a people is therefore enslaved when the government, by its nature or its vices, infringes on and usurps the rights of the citizen or subject. Applying these principles, we find that America was denied not only its freedom but even an active and effective tyranny. Under absolutism there are no recognized limits to the exercise of governmental powers. . . .

So negative was our existence that I can find nothing comparable in any other civilized society, examine as I may the entire history of time and the politics of all nations. Is it not an outrage and a violation of human rights to expect a land so splendidly endowed, so vast, rich, and populous, to remain merely passive?

As I have just explained, we were cut off and, as it were, removed from the world in relation to the science of government and administration of the state. We were never viceroys or governors, save in the rarest of instances; seldom archbishops and bishops; diplomats never; as military men, only subordinates; as nobles, without royal privileges. In brief, we were neither magistrates nor financiers and seldom merchants—all in flagrant contradiction to our institutions. . . .

It is harder, Montesquieu has written, to release a nation from servitude than to enslave a free nation. This truth is proven by the annals of all times, which reveal that most free nations have been put under the yoke, but very few enslaved nations have recovered their liberty. Despite the convictions of history, South Americans have made efforts to obtain liberal, even perfect, institutions, doubtless out of that instinct to aspire to the greatest possible happiness, which, common to all men, is bound to follow in civil societies founded on the principles of justice, liberty, and equality. But are we capable of maintaining in proper balance the difficult charge of a republic? Is it conceivable that a newly emancipated people can soar to the heights of liberty, and, unlike Icarus, neither have its wings melt nor fall into an abyss? Such a marvel is inconceivable and without precedent. There is no reasonable probability to bolster our hopes.

More than anyone, I desire to see America fashioned into the greatest nation in the world, greatest not so much by virtue of her area and wealth as by her freedom and glory. Although I seek perfection for the government of my country, I cannot persuade myself that the New World can, at the moment, be organized as a great republic. Since it is impossible, I dare not desire it; yet much less do I desire to have all America a monarchy because this plan is not only impracticable but also impossible. Wrongs now existing could not be righted, and our emancipation would be fruitless. The American states need the care of paternal governments to heal the sores and wounds of despotism and war.

 What problems did Bolívar foresee for Spanish America's political future? Do you think he believed in democracy? Why or why not?

---

sea level. The arrival of San Martín's troops in Chile completely surprised the Spaniards, whose forces were routed at the Battle of Chacabuco (chahk-ah-BOO-koh) on February 12, 1817. One of San Martín's military leaders was Bernardo O'Higgins, a fierce proponent of Chilean independence, who was now made "supreme dictator" of Chile.

In 1821, San Martín moved on to Lima, Peru, the center of Spanish authority. Convinced that he was unable to complete the liberation of all of Peru, San Martín welcomed the arrival of Bolívar and his forces. As he wrote to Bolívar, "For me it would have been the height of happiness to end the war of

independence under the orders of a general to whom [South] America owes its freedom. Destiny orders it otherwise, and one must resign oneself to it."[4] Highly disappointed, San Martín left South America for Europe, where he remained until his death outside Paris in 1850. Meanwhile, Bolívar took on the task of crushing the last significant Spanish army at Ayacucho (ah-ya-KOO-choh) on December 9, 1824. By then, Peru, Uruguay, Paraguay, Colombia, Venezuela, Argentina, Bolivia, and Chile had all become free states (see Map 20.1). In 1823, the Central American states became independent and in 1838–1839 divided into five republics (Guatemala, El Salvador,

© Cengage Learning

MAP 20.1 Latin America in the First Half of the Nineteenth Century. Latin American colonies took advantage of Spain's weakness during the Napoleonic wars to fight for independence, beginning with Argentina in 1810 and spreading throughout the region over the next decade with the help of leaders like Simón Bolívar and José de San Martín.

Q *How many South American countries are sources of rivers that feed the Amazon, and roughly what percentage of the continent is contained within the Amazon's watershed?*

Honduras, Costa Rica, and Nicaragua). Earlier, in 1822, the prince regent of Brazil had declared Brazil's independence from Portugal.

Simón Bolívar, who had accomplished so much as the liberator of South America, grew increasingly pessimistic about his achievements. Shortly before his death from tuberculosis in 1830, at the age of forty-seven, he wrote to one of his Venezuelan generals, "You know I have been in command for twenty years; and . . . I have derived only a few sure conclusions: first, [South] America is ungovernable; . . . fourth, this country will fall without fail into the hands of an unbridled multitude, to pass later to petty, almost imperceptible, tyrants of all colors and races."[5]

INDEPENDENCE AND THE MONROE DOCTRINE In the early 1820s, only one major threat remained to the newly won independence of the Latin American states. Reveling in their success in crushing rebellions in Spain and Italy, the victorious Continental powers favored the use of troops to restore Spanish control in Latin America. This time, Britain's opposition to intervention prevailed. Eager to gain access to an entire continent for investment and trade, the British proposed joint action with the United States against European interference in Latin America. Distrustful of British motives, President James Monroe acted alone in 1823, guaranteeing the independence of the new Latin American nations and warning against any further European intervention in the

Americas under what is known as the Monroe Doctrine. Even more important to Latin American independence than American words was Britain's navy. All of the Continental powers were reluctant to challenge British naval power, which stood between Latin America and any European invasion force.

The Difficulties of Nation Building

As Simón Bolívar had foreseen, the new Latin American nations, most of which began as republics, faced a number of serious problems between 1830 and 1870. The wars for independence themselves had resulted in a staggering loss of population, property, and livestock. Despite the Monroe Doctrine, fear of European intervention persisted, and disputes arose between nations over their precise boundaries. Poor transportation and communication systems fostered regionalism and made national unity difficult.

POLITICAL DIFFICULTIES The new nations of Latin America established republican governments, but they had had no experience in ruling themselves. Due to the insecurities prevalent after independence, strong leaders known as **caudillos** (kah-DEEL-yohz *or* kow-THEEL-yohz) came to power. Although caudillos could be found at both the regional and national levels, national caudillos were generally one of two types. One group, who supported the elites, consisted of autocrats who controlled (and often abused) state revenues, centralized power, and kept the new national states together. Sometimes they were also modernizers who built roads and canals, ports, and schools. Others were destructive, such as Antonio Lopez de Santa Anna (ahn-TOHN-yoh LOH-pes day SAHN-tuh AH-nah), who ruled Mexico from 1829 to 1855. He misused state funds, curtailed reforms, created chaos, and helped lose some of Mexico's territory to the United States. Caudillos were usually supported by the Catholic Church, the rural aristocracy, and the army, which emerged from the wars of independence as a powerful political force that often made and deposed governments. Many caudillos, in fact, were former army leaders.

In contrast, other caudillos were supported by the masses, became extremely popular, and served as instruments for radical change. Juan Manuel de Rosas (WAHN mahn-WEL day ROH-sas), for example, who led Argentina from 1829 to 1852, became very popular by favoring Argentine interests against foreigners. Rafael Carrera (rah-fah-EL kuh-RERR-uh), who ruled Guatemala from 1839 to 1865, supported native Indian cultures and pursued a policy of land redistribution to aid the natives. But he was disliked by the elites, who wanted to Europeanize the economy and Guatemalan culture, and his efforts were undone by his successor, Justo Rufino Barrios (HOO-stoh roo-FEE-noh BAHR-yohs) (1873–1885). A caudillo who was supported by the elites, Barrios pushed the economy to coffee production and forced the Indians to give up their lands and become wage laborers to serve the interests of large plantation owners.

ECONOMIC PATTERNS Although political independence brought economic independence, old patterns of capital flows and trade were quickly reestablished. Instead of Spain and Portugal, Great Britain now dominated the Latin American economy. British merchants arrived in large numbers, and British investors poured in funds, especially into the mining industry. Since Latin America served as a source of raw materials and foodstuffs for the industrializing nations of Europe and the United States, exports—especially wheat, tobacco, wool, sugar, coffee, and hides—to the North Atlantic countries increased noticeably. At the same time, finished consumer goods, especially textiles, were imported in increasing quantities, causing a decline in industrial production in Latin America. The emphasis on exporting raw materials and importing finished products ensured the ongoing domination of the Latin American economy by foreigners.

SOCIAL CONDITIONS A fundamental underlying problem for all of the new Latin American nations was the persistent domination of society by the landed elites. Large estates remained an important aspect of Latin America's economic and social life (see the box on p. 582). After independence, the size of these estates expanded even more. By 1848, the Sánchez Navarro (SAHN-ches nuh-VAH-roh) family in Mexico owned seventeen haciendas (hah-see-EN-duhz), or plantations, covering 16 million acres. Governments facilitated this process by selling off church lands, public domains, and the lands of Indian communities. In Argentina, five hundred people bought 21 million acres of public land. Estates were often so large that they could not be farmed efficiently. As one Latin American newspaper put it, "The huge fortunes have the unfortunate tendency to grow even larger, and their owners possess vast tracts of land, which lie fallow and abandoned. Their greed for land does not equal their ability to use it intelligently and actively."[6]

Land remained the basis of wealth, social prestige, and political power throughout the nineteenth century. The Latin American elites tended to identify with European standards of progress, which worked to their benefit, while the masses gained little. Landed elites ran governments, controlled courts, and maintained the system of debt peonage that provided large landowners with a supply of cheap labor. These landowners made enormous profits by concentrating on specialized crops for export, such as coffee, while the masses, left without land to grow basic food crops, lived in dire poverty.

CHURCH AND STATE Conflicts between church and state were also common in the new nations. The Catholic Church had enormous landholdings in Latin America and through its amassed wealth exercised great power. After independence, clerics often took positions in the new governments and wielded considerable influence. Throughout Latin America, a division arose between liberals who wished to curtail the temporal powers of the church and conservatives who hoped to maintain all of the church's privileges and prerogatives. In Mexico, this division even led to civil war, the bloody War of Reform fought between 1858 and 1861, in which Catholic clergy and the military lined up against a liberal government.

A Radical Critique of the Land Problem in Mexico

POLITICS & GOVERNMENT

The domination of Mexico by elites who owned large estates remained a serious problem throughout the nineteenth century. Conservatives, of course, favored the great estates as the foundation stones of their own political power, while even liberals shied away from any extremist attack on property rights. Nevertheless, there were some strong voices of protest, as this excerpt from a speech delivered in 1857 by the social liberal Ponciano Arriaga (pahn-SYAHN-oh ah-RYAH-guh) demonstrates. Arriaga's appeal went unheeded; conservatives called him a "communist."

Ponciano Arriaga, Speech to the Constitutional Convention of 1856–1857

One of the most deeply rooted evils of our country—an evil that merits the close attention of legislators when they frame our fundamental law—is the monstrous division of landed property.

While a few individuals possess immense areas of uncultivated land that could support millions of people, the great majority of Mexicans languish in a terrible poverty and are denied property, homes, and work. . . .

There are Mexican landowners who occupy (if one can give that name to a purely imaginary act) an extent of land greater than the areas of some of our sovereign states, greater even than that of one of several European states.

In this vast area, much of which lies idle, deserted, abandoned, awaiting the arms and labor of men, live four or five million Mexicans who know no other industry than agriculture, yet are without land or the means to work it, and who cannot emigrate in the hope of bettering their fortunes. They must either vegetate in idleness, turn to banditry, or accept the yoke of a landed monopolist who subjects them to intolerable conditions of life. . . .

How can a hungry, naked, miserable people practice popular government? How can we proclaim the equal rights of men and leave the majority of the nation in conditions worse than those of helots or pariahs? How can we condemn slavery in words, while the lot of most of our fellow citizens is more grievous than that of the black slaves of Cuba or the United States? . . .

With some honorable exceptions, the rich landowners of Mexico, or the administrators who represent them, resemble the feudal lords of the Middle Ages. On his seignorial land, . . . the landowner makes and executes laws, administers justice and exercises civil power, imposes taxes and fines, has his own jails and irons, metes out punishments and tortures, monopolizes commerce, and forbids the conduct without his permission of any business but that of the estate. The judges or officials who exercise on the hacienda the powers attached to public authority are usually the master's servants or tenants, his retainers, incapable of enforcing any law but the will of the master.

An astounding variety of devices are employed to exploit the peons or tenants, to turn a profit from their sweat and labor. They are compelled to work without pay even on days traditionally set aside for rest. They must accept rotten seeds or sick animals whose cost is charged to their miserable wages. They must pay enormous parish fees that bear no relation to the scale of fees that the owner or majordomo [manager] has arranged beforehand with the parish priest. They must make all their purchases on the hacienda, using tokens or paper money that do not circulate elsewhere. At certain seasons of the year they are assigned articles of poor quality, whose price is set by the owner or majordomo, constituting a debt which they can never repay. They are forbidden to use pastures and woods, firewood and water, or even the wild fruit of the fields, save with the express permission of the master. In fine, they are subject to a completely unlimited and irresponsible power.

 What serious problems for Latin American politics were created by the concentration of land ownership in the hands of the elites? How did such large estates affect the structure of Latin American societies?

Tradition and Change in the Latin American Economy and Society

After 1870, Latin America began to experience rapid economic growth based to a large extent on the export of a few basic items, such as wheat and beef from Argentina, coffee from Brazil, nitrates from Chile, coffee and bananas from Central America, and sugar and silver from Peru. Exports from Argentina doubled between 1873 and 1893; Mexican exports quadrupled between 1877 and 1900. These foodstuffs and raw materials were generally exchanged for finished goods—textiles, machines, and luxury goods—from Europe and the United States. With economic growth came a boom in foreign investment. Between 1870 and 1913, British invest-ments—mostly in railroads, mining, and public utilities—grew from 85 million pounds to 757 million pounds, which constituted two-thirds of all foreign investment in Latin America. As Latin Americans struggled to create more balanced economies after 1900, they focused on increasing industrialization, especially in textiles, food processing, and construction materials.

Nevertheless, the growth of the Latin American economy continued to come largely from the export of raw materials, and economic modernization in the region simply added to its growing dependence on the capitalist nations of the West. Modernization was basically a surface feature of Latin American society, where, for the most part, old patterns still prevailed. Rural elites continued to dominate their estates and their rural workers. Although slavery was abolished by 1888, former slaves and their descendants remained at the bottom of their society. The Indians remained poverty-stricken, debt servitude was still a way of life, and the inhabitants continued to be economically dependent on foreigners. Despite its economic growth, Latin America was still an underdeveloped region of the world.

The prosperity that arose from Latin America's export-based economy had both social and political repercussions. One result was the modernization of the elites, who were determined to pursue their vision of progress. Large landowners sought to rationalize their production methods in order to increase their profits. Consequently, cattle ranchers in Argentina and coffee barons in Brazil became more aggressive entrepreneurs.

Another result of the new prosperity was some growth in the middle sectors of Latin American society—lawyers, merchants, shopkeepers, businessmen, schoolteachers, professors, bureaucrats, and military officers. These sectors, which made up only 5 to 10 percent of the population, depending on the country, were hardly large enough in numbers to constitute a true middle class. Nevertheless, after 1900, the middle sectors continued to expand. Regardless of the country, they shared some common characteristics. They lived in the cities, sought education and decent incomes, and increasingly looked to the United States as a model to emulate, especially in regard to industrialization and education.

The middle sectors in Latin America sought liberal reform, not revolution, and the elites found it relatively easy to co-opt them by giving them the right to vote. Although the middle sectors were not large and remained dependent on the agrarian sector of the economy, in some places they were able to enhance their political power. In Costa Rica, the middle sectors played an important role in maintaining a constitutional government from 1882 to 1917. An alliance of the middle sectors with the working classes won control of Chile's government in 1918. In Argentina, the extension of suffrage to the middle sectors in 1912 enabled a middle party to win power in 1916.

As Latin American exports increased, so did the working class, and that in turn led to the growth of labor unions, especially after 1914. Radical unions often advocated the use of the general strike as an instrument for change. By and large, however, the governing elites succeeded in stifling the political influence of the workers by restricting their right to vote. The need for industrial labor also led Latin American countries to encourage immigration from Europe. Between 1880 and 1914, 3 million Europeans, primarily Italians and Spaniards, settled in Argentina. More than 100,000 Europeans, mostly Italian, Portuguese, and Spanish, arrived in Brazil each year between 1891 and 1900.

As in Europe and the United States, industrialization led to urbanization, evident in both the emergence of new cities and the rapid growth of old ones. Buenos Aires (the "Paris" of South America) had 750,000 inhabitants by 1900 and 2 million by 1914—a fourth of Argentina's population. By that time, urban dwellers made up 53 percent of Argentina's population overall. Brazil and Chile also witnessed a dramatic increase in their urban populations.

Political Change in Latin America

Latin America also experienced a political transformation after 1870. Large landowners began to take a more direct interest in national politics, sometimes actually becoming involved in governing. In Argentina and Chile, for example, landholding elites controlled the government, and although they produced constitutions similar to those of the United States and the European nations, they were careful to restrict voting rights to ensure that they would maintain power.

In some countries, large landowners relied on a dictator to protect their interests. José de la Cruz Porfirio Díaz (hoh-SAY day lah KROOZ por-FEER-yoh DEE-ahs), who ruled Mexico from 1876 to 1910, established a conservative, centralized government with the support of the army, foreign capitalists, large landowners, and the Catholic Church. But there were forces for change in Mexico that led to a revolution in 1910.

During Díaz's dictatorial regime, the real wages of the working class declined. Moreover, 95 percent of the rural population owned no land, while about a thousand families owned almost all of Mexico. When a liberal landowner, Francisco Madero (frahn-SEES-koh muh-DERR-oh), forced Díaz from power, he opened the door to a wider revolution. Madero's ineffectiveness triggered a demand for agrarian reform led by Emiliano Zapata (eh-mee-LYAH-noh zup-PAH-tuh), who aroused the masses of landless peasants and began to seize the haciendas of the wealthy landholders (see the box on p. 585). The ensuing revolution caused untold destruction to the Mexican economy. Finally, a new constitution in 1917 established a strong presidency, initiated land reform policies, established limits on foreign investors, and set an agenda for social welfare for workers. The revolution also led to an outpouring of nationalistic pride. Intellectuals and artists in particular sought to capture what was unique about Mexico, with special emphasis on its Indian past. As the Mexican minister of education said, "Tired, disgusted of all this copied civilization, . . . we wish to cease being Europe's spiritual colonies."

By this time, a new power had begun to wield its influence over Latin America. At the beginning of the twentieth century, the United States, emerging as a world power, increasingly interfered in the affairs of its southern neighbors. As a result of the Spanish-American War (1898), Cuba became an American protectorate, and Puerto Rico was annexed outright. American investments in Latin America soon followed; so did American resolve to protect these investments. Between 1898 and 1934, U.S. military forces were sent to Cuba, Mexico, Guatemala,

CHRONOLOGY	Latin America
Revolution in Mexico	1810
Bolívar and San Martín free most of South America	1810–1824
Augustín de Iturbide becomes emperor of Mexico	1821
Brazil gains independence from Portugal	1822
Monroe Doctrine	1823
Rule of Porfirio Díaz in Mexico	1876–1910
Mexican Revolution begins	1910

Emiliano Zapata. The inability of Mexican president Francisco Madero to carry out far-reaching reforms led to a radical upheaval in the countryside. Emiliano Zapata led a band of Indians in a revolt against the large landowners of southern Mexico and issued his own demands for land reform. Joining forces with Pancho Villa in 1914, he fought against the regime of President Venustiano Carranza until he was killed in an ambush by army troops in 1919.

Honduras, Nicaragua, Panama, Colombia, Haiti, and the Dominican Republic to protect American interests. Some expeditions remained for many years; U.S. Marines were in Haiti from 1915 to 1934, and Nicaragua was occupied from 1909 to 1933. At the same time, the United States became the chief foreign investor in Latin America.

The North American Neighbors: The United States and Canada

Q **FOCUS QUESTIONS:** What role did nationalism and liberalism play in the United States and Canada between 1800 and 1870? What economic, social, and political trends were evident in the United States and Canada between 1870 and 1914?

Whereas Latin America had been colonized by Spain and Portugal, the colonies established in North America were part of the British Empire. Although they gained their freedom from

the British at different times, both the United States and Canada emerged as independent and prosperous nations whose political systems owed much to British political thought. In the nineteenth century, both the United States and Canada faced difficult obstacles in achieving national unity.

The Growth of the United States

The U.S. Constitution, ratified in 1789, committed the United States to two of the major influences of the first half of the nineteenth century, liberalism and nationalism. Initially, this constitutional commitment to national unity was challenged by divisions over the power of the federal government vis-à-vis the individual states. Bitter conflict erupted between the Federalists and the Republicans. Led by Alexander Hamilton (1757–1804), the Federalists favored a financial program that would establish a strong central government. The Republicans, guided by Thomas Jefferson (1743–1826) and James Madison (1751–1836), feared centralization and its consequences for popular liberties. These divisions were intensified by European rivalries because the Federalists were pro-British and the Republicans pro-French. The successful conclusion of the War of 1812 brought an end to the Federalists, who had opposed the war, while the surge of national feeling generated by the war served to heal the nation's divisions. (Over the next decades, the Republicans of this era gave rise to the Democratic Party, while a new Republican Party was formed in the 1850s as an antislavery party.)

Another strong force for national unity came from the Supreme Court while John Marshall (1755–1835) was chief justice from 1801 to 1835. Marshall made the Supreme Court into an important national institution by asserting the right of the Court to overrule an act of Congress if the Court found it to be in violation of the Constitution. Under Marshall, the Supreme Court contributed further to establishing the supremacy of the national government by curbing the actions of state courts and legislatures.

The election of Andrew Jackson (1767–1845) as president in 1828 opened a new era in American politics, the era of mass democracy. The electorate was expanded by dropping property qualifications; by the 1830s, suffrage had been extended to almost all adult white males. During the period from 1815 to 1850, the traditional liberal belief in the improvement of human beings was also given concrete expression through the establishment of detention schools for juvenile delinquents and new penal institutions; both were motivated by the belief that the right kind of environment would rehabilitate wayward individuals.

SLAVERY AND THE COMING OF WAR By the mid-nineteenth century, however, American national unity was increasingly threatened by the issue of slavery. Both North and South had grown dramatically in population during the first half of the nineteenth century, but in different ways. The cotton economy and social structure of the South were based on the exploitation of enslaved black Africans and their descendants. The importance of cotton is evident from production figures. In 1810, the South produced a raw cotton crop of 178,000 bales worth $10 million. By 1860, it was generating 4.5 million bales of cotton

Zapata and Land Reform

POLITICS & GOVERNMENT

Emiliano Zapata was a sharecropper on a sugar plantation in Morelos (moh-RAY-lohs), a mountainous state in southern Mexico. Using the slogan "Land and Liberty," Zapata formed a guerrilla band of Indians and led them in revolt against the haciendas of southern Mexico, burning the houses and sugar refineries. Convinced that the new president of Mexico, Francisco Madero, would not go far enough with land reform, Zapata issued his own plan, the Plan of Ayala (ah-yah-LUH), from which these excerpts are taken.

The Plan of Ayala

The Liberating Plan of the sons of the State of Morelos, members of the insurgent army that demands the . . . reforms that it judges convenient and necessary for the welfare of the Mexican Nation.

We, the undersigned, constituted as a Revolutionary Junta, in order to maintain and obtain the fulfillment of the promises made by the revolution of November 20, 1910, solemnly proclaim in the face of the civilized world . . . , so that it may judge us, the principles that we have formulated in order to destroy the tyranny that oppresses us. . . .

1. Considering that the President of the Republic, Don Francisco I. Madero, has made a bloody mockery of Effective Suffrage by . . . entering into an infamous alliance with the . . . enemies of the Revolution that he proclaimed, in order to forge the chains of a new dictatorship more hateful and terrible than that of Porfirio Díaz . . . we declare the said Francisco I. Madero unfit to carry out the promises of the Revolution of which he was the author. . . .

4. The Revolutionary Junta of the State of Morelos formally proclaims to the Mexican people: that it endorses the Plan of San Luis Potosí [Madero's revolutionary plan] with the additions stated below for the benefit of the oppressed peoples, and that it will defend its principles until victory or death. . . .

6. As an additional part of the plan we proclaim, be it known: that the lands, woods, and waters usurped . . . through tyranny and venal justice henceforth belong to the towns or citizens who have corresponding titles to those properties, of which they were despoiled by the bad faith of our oppressors. They shall retain possession of the said properties at all costs, arms in hand. The usurpers who think they have a right to the said lands may state their claims before special tribunals to be established upon the triumph of the Revolution.

7. Since the immense majority of Mexican towns and citizens own nothing but the ground on which they stand and endure a miserable existence, denied the opportunity to improve their social condition or to devote themselves to industry or agriculture because a few individuals monopolize the lands, woods, and waters—for these reasons the great estates shall be expropriated, with indemnification to the owners of one-third of such monopolies, in order that the towns and citizens of Mexico may obtain colonies, town sites, and arable lands. Thus, the welfare of the Mexican people shall be promoted in all respects.

8. The properties of those [landowners] who directly or indirectly oppose the present Plan shall be seized by the nation, and two thirds of their value shall be used for war indemnities and pensions for the widows and orphans of the soldiers who may perish in the struggle for this Plan.

Why did the hacienda system and its abuses prompt Zapata to issue the Plan of Ayala? Why did both his origins and this proposal endear him to the common people of Mexico?

---

with a value of $249 million. Fully 93 percent of southern cotton in 1850 was produced by a slave population that had grown dramatically since the beginning of the century. Although the importation of new slaves had been barred in 1808, there were 4 million slaves in the South by 1860—four times the number sixty years earlier. The cotton economy depended on plantation-based slavery, and the attempt to maintain it in the first half of the nineteenth century led the South to become increasingly defiant as the rise of an abolitionist movement in the North challenged the southern order and created an "emotional chain reaction" that ultimately led to civil war.

The push of the nation westward was a major factor in bringing the issue of slavery to the forefront of U.S. politics. Although slavery was permitted by the Constitution, all the states in the North had abolished it. Should new states be admitted to the Union as free or slave states? The issue first arose in the 1810s as new states were being created by the rush of settlers beyond the Mississippi. The free states of the North feared the prospect of a slave-state majority in the national government. Attempts at compromise did not solve this divisive issue but merely postponed it.

By the 1850s, the slavery question had caused the Whig Party to become defunct and the Democrats to split along North-South lines. Passage of the Kansas-Nebraska Act of 1854, which allowed slavery in the Kansas and Nebraska territories to be determined by popular sovereignty, unleashed a firestorm in the North and led to the creation of a new sectional party. The Republicans were united by antislavery principles and were especially driven by the fear that the "slave power" of the South would attempt to spread the slave system throughout the country.

As the country became increasingly polarized over the issue of slavery, compromise became less feasible. When Abraham Lincoln, the man who had said in a speech in Illinois in 1858 that "this government cannot endure permanently half slave and half free," was elected president in November 1860, the die was cast. Lincoln, the Republicans' second presidential candidate, carried only 2 of the 1,109 counties in the South; the Republican Party was not even on the ballot in ten southern states. On December 20, 1860, a South Carolina convention voted to repeal the state's ratification of the U.S. Constitution. In February 1861, six more southern states did the same, and a rival nation, the Confederate States of America, was formed (see Map 20.2). In April, fighting erupted between North and South—the first shots were fired at Fort Sumter in South Carolina, which fell to the Confederates on April 13.

THE CIVIL WAR The American Civil War (1861–1865) was an extraordinarily bloody struggle, a foretaste of the total war to come in the twentieth century. More than 600,000 soldiers died, either in battle or from deadly infectious diseases spawned by filthy camp conditions. The northern, or Union, forces enjoyed a formidable advantage in numbers of troops and material resources, but to southerners, those assets were not decisive. As they saw it, the Confederacy only had to defend the South from invasion, whereas the Union had to conquer the South. Furthermore, the South's aristocratic landowning society had a far stronger military tradition than the business-oriented North, so many of the most promising young military officers were southerners. Southerners also believed that the dependence of manufacturers in the North and the European countries on southern raw cotton would lead to antiwar sentiment in the North and support abroad for the South.

All these southern calculations meant little in the long run. Over a period of four years, the Union states of the North mobilized their superior assets and gradually wore down the

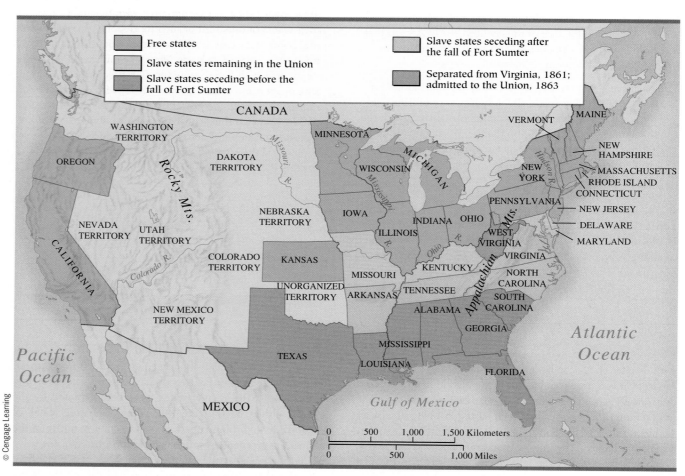

MAP 20.2 The United States: The West and the Civil War. By 1860, the North had developed an economy based on industry and commerce, whereas the South had remained a primarily agrarian economy based on black slave labor. The question of the continuance of slavery itself and the expansion of slavery into western territories led to the Civil War, in which the South sought to create an independent country.

Q *Why would its inhabitants want to create the separate state of West Virginia?*

Confederate forces of the South. As the war dragged on, it had the effect of radicalizing public opinion in the North. What began as a war to save the Union became a war against slavery. On January 1, 1863, Lincoln issued his Emancipation Proclamation, declaring most of the nation's slaves "forever free" (see the box on p. 569). An increasingly effective Union blockade of the ports of the South, combined with a shortage of fighting men, made the Confederate cause desperate by the end of 1864. The final push of Union troops under General Ulysses S. Grant forced General Robert E. Lee's Confederate Army to surrender on April 9, 1865. Although problems lay ahead, the Union victory reunited the country and confirmed that the United States would thereafter again be "one nation, indivisible."

The Rise of the United States

Four years of bloody civil war had restored American national unity. The old South had been destroyed; one-fifth of its adult white male population had been killed, and 4 million black slaves had been freed. For a while at least, a program of radical change in the South was attempted. Slavery was formally abolished by the Thirteenth Amendment to the Constitution in 1865, and the Fourteenth and Fifteenth Amendments extended citizenship to blacks and gave black men the right to vote. Radical Reconstruction in the early 1870s tried to create a new South based on the principle of the equality of black and white people, but the changes were soon mostly undone. Militia organizations, such as the Ku Klux Klan, used violence to discourage blacks from voting. A new system of sharecropping made blacks once again economically dependent on white landowners. New state laws made it nearly impossible for blacks to exercise their right to vote. By the end of the 1870s, supporters of white supremacy were back in power everywhere in the South.

PROSPERITY AND PROGRESSIVISM Between 1860 and 1914, the United States made the shift from an agrarian to a mighty industrial nation. American heavy industry stood unchallenged in 1900. In that year, the Carnegie Steel Company alone produced more steel than Great Britain's entire steel industry. Industrialization also led to urbanization. While established cities, such as New York, Philadelphia, and Boston, grew even larger, other moderate-sized cities, such as Pittsburgh, grew by leaps and bounds because of industrialization. Whereas 20 percent of Americans lived in cities in 1860, more than 40 percent did in 1900. Four-fifths of the population growth in cities came from migration. Eight to 10 million Americans moved from rural areas into the cities, and 14 million foreigners came from abroad.

The United States had become the world's richest nation and greatest industrial power. Yet serious questions remained about the quality of American life. In 1890, the richest 9 percent of Americans owned an incredible 71 percent of all the wealth. Workers' concerns over unsafe working conditions, strict work discipline, and periodic cycles of devastating unemployment led to the formation of unions. By the turn of the century, one national organization, the American Federation of Labor, had emerged as labor's dominant voice. Its lack of real power, however, was reflected in its membership figures. In 1900, it included only 8.4 percent of the American industrial labor force.

During the so-called Progressive Era after 1900, the reform of many features of American life became a primary issue. Efforts to improve living conditions in the cities included attempts to eliminate corrupt machine politics. At the state level, reforming governors sought to achieve clean government by introducing elements of direct democracy, such as direct primaries for selecting nominees for public office. State governments also enacted economic and social legislation, such as laws that governed hours, wages, and working conditions, especially for women and children.

Private Collection/© Peter Newark Military Pictures/The Bridgeman Art Library

The Dead at Antietam. National unity in the United States dissolved over the issue of slavery and led to a bloody civil war that cost 600,000 American lives. This photograph shows the southern dead after the Battle of Antietam on September 17, 1862. The invention of photography in the 1830s made it possible to document the horrors of war in the most graphic manner.

United States	
Election of Andrew Jackson	1828
Kansas-Nebraska Act	1854
Election of Abraham Lincoln and secession of South Carolina	1860
Civil War	1861–1865
Lincoln's Emancipation Proclamation	1863
Surrender of Robert E. Lee's Confederate Army	April 9, 1865
Spanish-American War	1898
Presidency of Woodrow Wilson	1913–1921
Canada	
Rebellions	1837–1838
Formation of the Dominion of Canada	1867
Transcontinental railroad	1885
Wilfred Laurier as prime minister	1896

The realization that state laws were ineffective in dealing with nationwide problems, however, led to a Progressive movement at the national level. The Meat Inspection Act and Pure Food and Drug Act provided for a limited degree of federal regulation of industrial practices. The presidency of Woodrow Wilson (1913–1921) witnessed the enactment of a graduated federal income tax and the establishment of the Federal Reserve System, which permitted the national government to play a role in important economic decisions formerly made by bankers. Like European nations, the United States was slowly adopting policies that broadened the functions of the state.

THE UNITED STATES AS A WORLD POWER   At the end of the nineteenth century, the United States began to expand abroad. The Samoan Islands in the Pacific became the first important American colony; the Hawaiian Islands were next. By 1887, American settlers had gained control of the sugar industry on the Hawaiian Islands. As more Americans settled in Hawaii, they sought political power. When Queen Liliuokalani (LIL-ee-uh-woh-kuh-LAH-nee) tried to strengthen the monarchy in order to keep the islands for the Hawaiian people, the U.S. government sent Marines to "protect" American lives. The queen was deposed, and Hawaii was annexed by the United States in 1898.

The defeat of Spain in the Spanish-American War in 1898 expanded the American empire to include Cuba, Puerto Rico, Guam, and the Philippines. Although the Filipinos appealed for independence, the Americans refused to grant it. As President William McKinley said, the United States had the duty "to educate the Filipinos and uplift and Christianize them," a remarkable statement in view of the fact that most of

them had been Roman Catholics for centuries. It took three years and 60,000 troops to pacify the Philippines and establish U.S. control. By the beginning of the twentieth century, the United States had become another Western imperialist power.

The Making of Canada

North of the United States, the process of nation building was also making progress. Under the Treaty of Paris in 1763, Canada—or New France, as it was called—passed into the hands of the British. By 1800, most Canadians favored more autonomy, although the colonists disagreed on the form this autonomy should take. The residents of Upper Canada (now Ontario) were predominantly English speaking, whereas Lower Canada (now Quebec) was dominated by French Canadians. A dramatic increase in immigration to Canada from Great Britain (almost one million immigrants between 1815 and 1850) also fueled the desire for self-government.

In 1837, a number of Canadian groups rose in rebellion against British authority. Rebels in Lower Canada demanded separation from Britain, creation of a republic, universal male suffrage, and freedom of the press. Although the rebellions were crushed by the following year, the British government now began to seek ways to satisfy some of the Canadian demands. The U.S. Civil War proved to be a turning point. Fearful of American designs on Canada during the war and eager to reduce the costs of maintaining the colonies, the British government finally capitulated to Canadian demands. In 1867, Parliament established the Dominion of Canada, with its own constitution. Canada now possessed a parliamentary system and ruled itself, although foreign affairs still remained under the control of the British government.

Canada faced problems of national unity between 1870 and 1914. At the beginning of 1870, the Dominion of Canada had only four provinces: Quebec, Ontario, Nova Scotia, and New Brunswick. With the addition of two more provinces in 1871—Manitoba and British Columbia—the Dominion of Canada now extended from the Atlantic Ocean to the Pacific. As the first prime minister, John Macdonald (1815–1891) moved to strengthen Canadian unity. He pushed for the construction of a transcontinental railroad, which was completed in 1885 and opened the western lands to industrial and commercial development. This also led to the incorporation of two more provinces—Alberta and Saskatchewan—into the Dominion of Canada in 1905.

Real unity was difficult to achieve, however, because of the distrust between the English-speaking majority and the French-speaking Canadians, living primarily in Quebec. Wilfred Laurier (LOR-ee-ay), who became the first French Canadian prime minister in 1896, was able to reconcile Canada's two major groups and resolve the issue of separate schools for French Canadians. During Laurier's administration, industrialization boomed, especially the production of textiles, furniture, and railway equipment.

Canada, 1914

Hundreds of thousands of immigrants, primarily from central and eastern Europe, also flowed into Canada. Many settled on lands in the west, thus helping to populate Canada's vast territories.

The Emergence of Mass Society in the West

 FOCUS QUESTION: What is meant by the term *mass society*, and what were its main characteristics?

While new states were developing in the Western Hemisphere in the nineteenth century, a new kind of society—a **mass society**—was emerging in Europe, especially in the second half of the nineteenth century, as a result of rapid economic and social changes. For the lower classes, mass society brought voting rights, an improved standard of living, and access to education. At the same time, however, mass society also made possible the development of organizations that manipulated the populations of the **nation-states**. To understand this mass society, we need to examine some aspects of its structure.

The New Urban Environment

One of the most important consequences of industrialization and the population explosion of the nineteenth century was urbanization. In the course of the nineteenth century, more and more people came to live in cities. In 1800, city dwellers constituted 40 percent of the population in Britain, 25 percent in France and Germany, and only 10 percent in eastern Europe. By 1914, urban residents had increased to 80 percent of the population in Britain, 45 percent in France, 60 percent in Germany, and 30 percent in eastern Europe. The size of cities also expanded dramatically, especially in industrialized countries. Between 1800 and 1900, London's population grew from 960,000 to 6.5 million and Berlin's from 172,000 to 2.7 million.

Urban populations grew faster than the general population primarily because of the vast migration from rural areas to cities. But cities also grew faster in the second half of the nineteenth century because health and living conditions were improving as reformers and city officials used new technology to improve urban life. In the 1840s, a number of urban reformers had pointed to filthy living conditions as the primary cause of epidemic diseases. Following the advice of reformers, city governments set up boards of health to boost the quality of housing and instituted regulations requiring all new buildings to have running water and internal drainage systems.

Essential to the public health of the modern European city was the ability to bring in clean water and to expel sewage. The problem of fresh water was solved by a system of dams and reservoirs that stored the water and aqueducts and tunnels that carried it from the countryside to the city and into individual dwellings. Gas heaters in the 1860s, and later electric heaters, made regular hot baths available to many people. The treatment of sewage was also improved by laying mammoth underground pipes that carried raw sewage far from the city for disposal. The city of Frankfurt, Germany, for example, began its program after a lengthy public campaign enlivened by the slogan "From the Toilet to the River in Half an Hour."

Middle-class reformers also focused on the housing needs of the working class. Overcrowded, disease-ridden slums were viewed as dangerous not only to physical health but also to the political and moral health of the entire nation. V. A. Huber, the foremost early German housing reformer, wrote in 1861, "Certainly it would not be too much to say that the home is the communal embodiment of family life. Thus, the purity of the dwelling is almost as important for the family as is the cleanliness of the body for the individual."[7] To Huber, good housing was a prerequisite for stable family life, and without stable family life, society would fall apart.

Early efforts to attack the housing problem emphasized the middle-class, liberal belief in the power of private, or free, enterprise. Reformers such as Huber believed that the construction of model dwellings renting at a reasonable price would force other private landlords to elevate their housing standards. A fine example of this approach was the work of Octavia Hill (see the box on p. 590). As cities continued to grow in number and size, by the 1880s governments concluded that private enterprise could not solve the housing crisis. In 1890, a British law empowered local town councils to construct cheap housing for the working classes. Similar activity was set in motion in Germany. More and more, governments were stepping into areas of activity that they would not have touched earlier.

The Social Structure of Mass Society

At the top of European society stood a wealthy elite, constituting only 5 percent of the population but controlling between 30 and 40 percent of the wealth. In the course of the nineteenth century, landed aristocrats had joined with the most successful industrialists, bankers, and merchants (the wealthy upper middle class) to form a new elite. Members of this elite, whether aristocratic or middle class in background, assumed leadership roles in government bureaucracies and military hierarchies. Marriage also united the two groups. Daughters of business tycoons gained titles, while aristocratic heirs gained new sources of cash. When the American Consuelo Vanderbilt married the duke of Marlborough, the new duchess brought $10 million to her husband.

The middle classes included a variety of groups. Below the upper middle class was a group that included lawyers, doctors, and members of the civil service, as well as business managers, engineers, architects, accountants, and chemists benefiting from industrial expansion. Beneath this solid and comfortable middle group was a lower middle class of small shopkeepers, traders, small manufacturers, and prosperous peasants.

Standing between the lower middle class and the lower classes were new groups of white-collar workers who were the product of the Second Industrial Revolution—the salespeople, bookkeepers, bank tellers, telephone operators, and secretaries. Though often paid little more than skilled laborers, these white-collar workers were committed to middle-class ideals.

The middle classes shared a certain lifestyle and values that dominated much of nineteenth-century society. This was especially evident in Victorian Britain, often considered a model of

The Housing Venture of Octavia Hill

FAMILY & SOCIETY

Octavia Hill was a practical-minded British housing reformer who believed that workers and their families were entitled to happy homes. At the same time, she was convinced that the poor needed guidance and encouragement, not charity. In this selection, she describes her housing venture.

Octavia Hill, *Homes of the London Poor*

About four years ago I was put in possession of three houses in one of the worst courts of Marylebone. Six other houses were bought subsequently. All were crowded with inmates.

The first thing to be done was to put them in decent tenantable order. The set last purchased was a row of cottages facing a bit of desolate ground, occupied with wretched, dilapidated cowsheds, manure heaps, old timber, and rubbish of every description. The houses were in a most deplorable condition—the plaster was dropping from the walls; on one staircase a pail was placed to catch the rain that fell through the roof. All the staircases were perfectly dark; the banisters were gone, having been burnt as firewood by tenants. The grates, with large holes in them, were falling forward into the rooms. The wash-house, full of lumber belonging to the landlord, was locked up; thus, the inhabitants had to wash clothes, as well as to cook, eat and sleep in their small rooms. The dustbin [trash receptacle], standing in the front part of the houses, was accessible to the whole neighbourhood, and boys often dragged from it quantities of unseemly objects and spread them over the court. The state of the drainage was in keeping with everything else. The pavement of the backyard was all broken up, and great puddles stood in it, so that the damp crept up the outer walls. . . .

As soon as I entered into possession, each family had an opportunity of doing better: those who would not pay, or who led clearly immoral lives, were ejected. The rooms they vacated were cleansed; the tenants who showed signs of improvement moved into them, and thus, in turn, an oppor-

tunity was obtained for having each room distempered [painted] and papered. The drains were put in order, a large slate cistern was fixed, the wash-house was cleared of its lumber, and thrown open on stated days to each tenant in turn. The roof, the plaster, the woodwork was repaired; the staircase walls were distempered; new grates were fixed; the layers of paper and rag (black with age) were torn from the windows, and glass was put in; out of 192 panes only eight were found unbroken. The yard and footpath were paved.

The rooms, as a rule, were re-let at the same prices at which they had been let before; but tenants with large families were counselled to take two rooms, and for these much less was charged than if let singly: this plan I continue to pursue. Incoming tenants are not allowed to take a decidedly insufficient quantity of room, and no subletting is permitted. . . .

The pecuniary result has been very satisfactory. Five per-cent has been paid on all the capital invested. A fund for the repayment of capital is accumulating. A liberal allowance has been made for repairs. . . .

My tenants are mostly of a class far below that of mechanics. They are, indeed, of the very poor. And yet, although the gifts they have received have been next to nothing, none of the families who have passed under my care during the whole four years have continued in what is called "distress," except such as have been unwilling to exert themselves. Those who will not exert the necessary self-control cannot avail themselves of the means of livelihood held out to them. But, for those who are willing, some small assistance in the form of work has, from time to time, been provided—not much, but sufficient to keep them from want or despair.

 Did Octavia Hill's housing venture generate financial returns on her initial investment? What benefits did her tenants receive in turn? What feelings and beliefs about the lower classes are evident in Hill's account?

---

middle-class society. The European middle classes believed in hard work, which they viewed as open to everyone and guaranteed to have positive results. They were also regular churchgoers who believed in the good conduct associated with traditional Christian morality. The middle class was concerned with propriety, the right way of doing things, which gave rise to an incessant stream of books aimed at the middle-class market with such titles as *The Habits of Good Society* or *Don't: A Manual of Mistakes and Improprieties More or Less Prevalent in Conduct and Speech.*

Below the middle classes on the social scale were the working classes, who constituted almost 80 percent of the European population. Many of them were landholding peasants, agricultural laborers, and sharecroppers, especially in eastern Europe. The urban working class consisted of many different

groups, including skilled artisans in such traditional trades as cabinetmaking, printing, and the making of jewelry, along with semiskilled laborers, who included carpenters, bricklayers, and many factory workers. At the bottom of the urban working class stood the largest group of workers, the unskilled laborers. They included day laborers, who worked irregularly for very low wages, and large numbers of domestic servants, most of whom were women.

The Experiences of Women

In the nineteenth century, women remained legally inferior, economically dependent, and largely defined by family and household roles. Many women still aspired to the ideal of

Octavia Hill and Working-Class Housing in London. Although urban workers experienced some improvements in the material conditions of their lives after 1870, working-class housing remained drab and depressing as shown in the top photograph, taken in 1912. Rows of similar-looking buildings line treeless streets in the East End of London; most of these houses had no gardens or green areas. The bottom photograph shows new cottage-style housing constructed in southern London by reformer Octavia Hill following the success of her housing project for the poor in Marylebone (see the box on p. 590). Overlooking Red Cross Garden, Hill's small cottages offered more fresh air and light and allowed the residents to have gardens. Hill argued that these houses provided better living conditions for urban workers.

femininity popularized by writers and poets. Alfred, Lord Tennyson's poem *The Princess* expressed it well:

> *Man for the field and woman for the hearth:*
> *Man for the sword and for the needle she:*
> *Man with the head and woman with the heart:*
> *Man to command and woman to obey;*
> *All else confusion.*

This traditional characterization of the sexes, based on socially defined gender roles, was elevated to the status of universal male and female attributes in the nineteenth century, due largely to the impact of the Industrial Revolution on the family. As the chief family wage earners, men worked outside the home for pay, while women were left with the care of the family, for which they were paid nothing.

MARRIAGE AND THE FAMILY   For most of the nineteenth century, marriage was viewed as the only honorable career available to most women. Although the middle class glorified the ideal of domesticity, for most women marriage was a matter of economic necessity. The lack of meaningful work and the lower wages paid to women for their work made it difficult for single women to earn a living. Most women chose to marry.

The most significant development in the modern family was the decline in the number of offspring born to the average woman. Although some historians attribute the decline to more widespread use of coitus interruptus, or male withdrawal before ejaculation, others have emphasized female control of family size through abortion and even infanticide or abandonment. That a change in attitude occurred was apparent in the development of a movement to increase awareness of birth control methods. Europe's first birth control clinic, founded by Dr. Aletta Jacob, opened in Amsterdam in 1882.

The family was the central institution of middle-class life. Men provided the family income while women focused on household and child care. The use of domestic servants in many middle-class homes, made possible by an abundant supply of cheap labor, reduced the amount of time middle-class women had to spend on household work. At the same time, by having fewer children, mothers could devote more time to child care and domestic leisure.

The middle-class family fostered an ideal of togetherness. The Victorians created the family Christmas with its Yule log, Christmas tree, songs, and exchange of gifts. In the United States, Fourth of July celebrations changed from drunken revels to family picnics by the 1850s.

Women in working-class families were more accustomed to hard work. Daughters were expected to work until they married; even after marriage, they often did piecework at home to help support the family. For the children of the working classes, childhood was over by the age of nine or ten when they became apprentices or were employed in odd jobs.

Between 1890 and 1914, however, family patterns among the working class began to change. High-paying jobs in heavy industry and improvements in the standard of living made it possible for working-class families to depend on the income of husbands and the wages of grown children. By the early twentieth century, some working-class mothers could afford to stay at home, following the pattern of middle-class women. At the same time, working-class families also aspired to buy new consumer products, such as sewing machines, clocks, bicycles, and cast-iron stoves.

THE MOVEMENT FOR WOMEN'S RIGHTS In the 1830s, a number of women in the United States and Europe, who worked together in several reform movements, argued for the right of women to divorce and own property. These early efforts were not particularly successful, however. Women did not gain the right to their own property until 1870 in Britain, 1900 in Germany, and 1907 in France.

Divorce and property rights were only a beginning for the women's movement, however. Some middle- and upper-middle-class women gained access to higher education, while others sought entry into occupations dominated by men. The first to fall was teaching. As medical training was largely closed to women, they sought alternatives through the development of nursing. Nursing pioneers included the British nurse Florence Nightingale, whose efforts during the Crimean War (1854–1856), along with those of Clara Barton in the American Civil War (1861–1865), transformed nursing into a profession of trained, middle-class "women in white."

By the 1840s and 1850s, the movement for women's rights had entered the political arena with the call for equal political rights. Many feminists believed that the right to vote was the key to all other reforms to improve the position of women. **Suffragists** had one basic aim: the right of women to full citizenship in the nation-state.

The British women's movement was the most vocal and active in Europe. Emmeline Pankhurst (PANK-hurst) (1858–1928) and her daughters, Christabel and Sylvia, founded the Women's Social and Political Union in 1903, which enrolled mostly middle- and upper-class women. The members of Pankhurst's organization realized the value of the media and used unusual publicity stunts to call attention to their demands. Derisively labeled "suffragettes" by male politicians, they pelted government officials with eggs, chained themselves to lampposts, smashed the windows of department stores on fashionable shopping streets, burned railroad cars, and went on hunger strikes in jail.

Before World War I, the demands for women's rights were being heard throughout Europe and the United States, although only in Norway and some American states did women actually receive the right to vote before 1914. It would take the dramatic upheaval of World War I before male-dominated governments capitulated on this basic issue.

Women reformers also took on issues besides suffrage. In many countries, women supported peace movements. Bertha von Suttner (BAYR-tuh fun ZOOT-nuh) (1843–1914) became head of the Austrian Peace Society and protested against the growing arms race of the 1890s. Her novel *Lay Down Your Arms* became a best-seller and brought her the Nobel Peace Prize in 1905. Lower-class women also took up the cause of peace. A group of women workers marched in Vienna in 1911 and demanded, "We want an end to armaments, to the means of murder, and we want these millions to be spent on the needs of the people."

Bertha von Suttner was but one example of the "new women" who were becoming more prominent at the turn of the century. These women rejected traditional feminine roles (see the box on p. 593) and sought new freedom outside the household and roles other than those of wife and mother.

© Harrogate Museums and Arts, UK/The Bridgeman Art Library

A Middle-Class Family. Nineteenth-century middle-class moralists considered the family the fundamental pillar of a healthy society, and togetherness constituted one of the important ideals of the middle-class family. This painting by William P. Frith, titled *Many Happy Returns of the Day*, shows grandparents, parents, and children taking part in a family birthday celebration for a little girl. The servant at the left holds the presents for the little girl.

Advice to Women: Two Views

FAMILY & SOCIETY

Industrialization had a strong impact on middle-class women as strict gender-based social roles became the norm. Men worked outside the home to support the family, while women provided for the needs of their children and husband at home. In the first selection, *Woman in Her Social and Domestic Character* (1842), Elizabeth Poole Sanford gives advice to middle-class women on their proper role and behavior.

Although a majority of women probably followed the nineteenth-century middle-class ideal of women as keepers of the household and nurturers of husband and children, an increasing number of women fought for women's rights. The second selection is taken from the third act of Henrik Ibsen's 1879 play *A Doll's House,* in which the character Nora Helmer declares her independence from her husband's control.

Elizabeth Poole Sanford, *Woman in Her Social and Domestic Character*

The changes wrought by Time are many. It influences the opinions of men as familiarity does their feelings; it has a tendency to do away with superstition, and to reduce every thing to its real worth.

It is thus that the sentiment for woman has undergone a change. The romantic passion which once almost deified her is on the decline; and it is by intrinsic qualities that she must now inspire respect. She is no longer the queen of song and the star of chivalry. But if there is less of enthusiasm entertained for her, the sentiment is more rational, and, perhaps, equally sincere; for it is in relation to happiness that she is chiefly appreciated.

And in this respect it is, we must confess, that she is most useful and most important. Domestic life is the chief source of her influence; and the greatest debt society can owe to her is domestic comfort; for happiness is almost an element of virtue; and nothing conduces more to improve the character of men than domestic peace. A woman may make a man's home delightful, and may thus increase his motives for virtuous exertion. She may refine and tranquilize his mind—may turn away his anger or allay his grief. Her smile may be the happy influence to gladden his heart, and to disperse the cloud that gathers on his brow. And in proportion to her endeavors to make those around her happy, she will be esteemed and loved. She will secure by her excellence that interest and that regard which she might formerly claim as the privilege of her sex, and will really merit the deference which was then conceded to her as a matter of course. . . .

Perhaps one of the first secrets of her influence is adaptation to the tastes, and sympathy in the feelings, of those around her. This holds true in lesser as well as in graver points. It is in the former, indeed, that the absence of interest in a companion is frequently most disappointing. Where want of congeniality impairs domestic comfort, the fault is generally chargeable on the female side. It is for woman, not for man, to make the sacrifice, especially in indifferent matters. She must, in a certain degree, be plastic herself if she would mold others. . . .

Nothing is so likely to conciliate the affections of the other sex as a feeling that woman looks to them for support and guidance. In proportion as men are themselves superior, they are accessible to this appeal. On the contrary, they never feel interested in one who seems disposed rather to offer than to ask assistance. There is, indeed, something unfeminine in independence. It is contrary to nature, and therefore it offends. We do not like to see a woman affecting tremors, but still less do we like to see her acting the amazon. A really sensible woman feels her dependence. She does what she can; but she is conscious of inferiority, and therefore grateful for support. She knows that she is the weaker vessel, and that as such she should receive honor. In this view, her weakness is an attraction, not a blemish.

In every thing, therefore, that women attempt, they should show their consciousness of dependence. If they are learners, let them evince a teachable spirit; if they give an opinion, let them do it in an unassuming manner. There is something so unpleasant in female self-sufficiency that it not unfrequently deters instead of persuading, and prevents the adoption of advice which the judgment even approves.

Henrik Ibsen, *A Doll's House*

NORA *(Pause)*: Does anything strike you as we sit here?

HELMER: What should strike me?

NORA: We've been married eight years; does it not strike you that this is the first time we two, you and I, man and wife, have talked together seriously?

HELMER: Seriously? What do you mean, *seriously*?

NORA: For eight whole years, and more—ever since the day we first met—we have never exchanged one serious word about serious things. . . .

HELMER: Why, my dearest Nora, what have you to do with serious things?

NORA: There we have it! You have never understood me. I've had great injustice done to me, Torvald; first by Father, then by you.

HELMER: What! Your father *and* me? We, who have loved you more than all the world!

NORA *(Shaking her head)*: You have never loved me. You just found it amusing to think you were in love with me.

HELMER: Nora! What a thing to say!

NORA: Yes, it's true, Torvald. When I was living at home with Father, he told me his opinions and mine were the

(continued)

same. If I had different opinions, I said nothing about them, because he would not have liked it. He used to call me his doll-child and played with me as I played with my dolls. Then I came to live in your house.

HELMER: What a way to speak of our marriage!

NORA (Undisturbed): I mean that I passed from Father's hands into yours. You arranged everything to your taste and I got the same tastes as you; or pretended to—I don't know which—both, perhaps; sometimes one, sometimes the other. When I look back on it now, I seem to have been living here like a beggar, on handouts. I lived by performing tricks for you, Torvald. But that was how you wanted it. You and Father have done me a great wrong. It is your fault that my life has come to naught.

HELMER: Why, Nora, how unreasonable and ungrateful! Haven't you been happy here?

NORA: No, never. I thought I was, but I never was.

HELMER: Not—not happy! . . .

NORA: I must stand quite alone if I am ever to know myself and my surroundings; so I cannot stay with you.

HELMER: Nora! Nora!

NORA: I am going at once. I daresay [my friend] Christina will take me in for tonight.

HELMER: You are mad! I shall not allow it! I forbid it!

NORA: It's no use your forbidding me anything now. I shall take with me only what belongs to me; from you I will accept nothing, either now or later.

HELMER: This is madness!

NORA: Tomorrow I shall go home—I mean to what was my home. It will be easier for me to find a job there.

HELMER: Oh, in your blind inexperience—

NORA: I must try to gain experience, Torvald.

HELMER: Forsake your home, your husband, your children! And you don't consider what the world will say.

NORA: I can't pay attention to that. I only know that I must do it.

HELMER: This is monstrous! Can you forsake your holiest duties?

NORA: What do you consider my holiest duties?

HELMER: Need I tell you that? Your duties to your husband and children.

NORA: I have other duties equally sacred.

HELMER: Impossible! What do you mean?

NORA: My duties toward myself.

HELMER: Before all else you are a wife and a mother.

NORA: That I no longer believe. Before all else I believe I am a human being just as much as you are—or at least that I should try to become one. I know that most people agree with you, Torvald, and that they say so in books. But I can no longer be satisfied with what most people say and what is in books. I must think things out for myself and try to get clear about them.

 According to Elizabeth Sanford, what is the proper role of women? What forces in nineteenth-century European society merged to shape Sanford's understanding of "proper" gender roles? In Ibsen's play, what challenges does Nora Helmer make to Sanford's view of the proper role and behavior of wives? Why is her husband so shocked? Why did Ibsen title this play A Doll's House?

Education in an Age of Mass Society

Universal education was a product of the mass society of the late nineteenth and early twentieth centuries. Education in the early nineteenth century was primarily for the elite or the wealthier middle class, but after 1870, most Western governments began to offer at least primary education to both boys and girls between the ages of six and twelve. States also assumed responsibility for better training of teachers by establishing teacher-training schools. By the beginning of the twentieth century, many European states, especially in northern and western Europe, provided state-financed primary schools, salaried and trained teachers, and free, compulsory elementary education.

Why did Western nations make this commitment to **mass education**? One reason was industrialization. The new firms of the Second Industrial Revolution demanded skilled labor. Both boys and girls with an elementary education had new possibilities of jobs beyond their villages or small towns, including white-collar jobs with railways and subways, in post offices, with banking and shipping firms, and in teaching and nursing. Mass education furnished the trained workers industrialists needed. For most students, elementary education led to apprenticeship and a job.

The chief motive for mass education, however, was political. With the expansion of suffrage came a need for a more educated electorate. In parts of Europe where the Catholic Church remained in control of education, implementing a mass education system reduced the influence of the church over the electorate. Even more important, however, mass compulsory education instilled patriotism and nationalized the masses, providing an opportunity for even greater national integration. As people lost their ties to local regions and even to religion, nationalism supplied a new faith. The use of a single national language created greater national unity than loyalty to a ruler did (see the comparative essay "The Rise of Nationalism" on p. 595).

Compulsory elementary education created a demand for teachers, and most of them were women. Many men viewed the teaching of children as an extension of women's "natural role" as nurturers of the young. Moreover, females were paid lower salaries, in itself a considerable incentive for governments to encourage the establishment of teacher-training institutes for women. The first female colleges were teacher-training schools. It was not until the beginning of the twentieth century that women were permitted to enter the male-dominated universities.

The Rise of Nationalism

POLITICS & GOVERNMENT

Like the Industrial Revolution, the concept of nationalism originated in eighteenth-century Europe, where it was the product of a variety of factors, including the spread of printing and the replacement of Latin with vernacular languages, the secularization of the age, and the experience of the French revolutionary and Napoleonic eras. The French were the first to show what a nation in arms could accomplish, but peoples conquered by Napoleon soon created their own national armies. At the beginning of the nineteenth century, peoples who had previously focused their identity on a locality or a region, on loyalty to a monarch or to a particular religious faith, now shifted their political allegiance to the idea of a nation, based on ethnic, linguistic, or cultural factors. The idea of the nation had explosive consequences: by the end of the first two decades of the twentieth century, the three largest multiethnic states in the world—Imperial Russia, Austria-Hungary, and the Ottoman Empire—had all given way to a number of individual nation-states.

The idea of establishing political boundaries on the basis of ethnicity, language, or culture had a broad appeal throughout Western civilization, but it had unintended consequences. Although the concept provided the basis for a new sense of community that was tied to liberal thought in the first half of the nineteenth century, it also gave birth to ethnic tensions and hatreds in the second half of the century that resulted in bitter disputes and contributed to the competition between nation-states that eventually erupted into world war. Governments, following the lead of the radical government in Paris during the French

Garibaldi. Giuseppe Garibaldi was a dedicated patriot and an outstanding example of the Italian nationalism that led to the unification of Italy by 1870.

© The Art Archive/Museo Civico, Modigliana/Alfredo Dagli Orti

Revolution, took full advantage of the rise of a strong national consciousness and transformed war into a matter of national honor that would require the commitment of the entire population. Universal schooling enabled states to arouse patriotic enthusiasm and create national unity. Most soldiers who joyfully went to war in 1914 were convinced that their nation's cause was just.

But if the concept of nationalism was initially the product of conditions in modern Europe, it soon spread to other parts of the world. Although a few societies, such as Vietnam, had already developed a strong sense of national identity, most of the peoples living in Asia and Africa lived in multiethnic and multireligious communities and were not yet ripe for the spirit of nationalism. As we shall see, the first attempts to resist European colonial rule were often based on religious or ethnic identity, rather than on the concept of denied nationhood. But the imperialist powers, which at first benefited from the lack of political cohesion among their colonial subjects, eventually reaped what they had sown. As the colonial peoples became familiar with Western concepts of democracy and self-determination, they too began to manifest a sense of common purpose that helped knit together the different elements in their societies to oppose colonial regimes and create the conditions for the emergence of future nations. For good or ill, the concept of nationalism had now achieved global proportions. We shall explore such issues, and their consequences, in greater detail in the chapters that follow.

 What is nationalism? How did it arise, and what impact did it have on the history of the nineteenth and twentieth centuries?

The most immediate result of mass education was an increase in literacy. In Germany, Great Britain, France, and the Scandinavian countries, adult illiteracy was virtually eliminated by 1900. Where there was less schooling, the story was quite different. Adult illiteracy rates were 79 percent in Serbia, 78 percent in Romania, and 79 percent in Russia.

Leisure in an Age of Mass Society

With the Industrial Revolution came new forms of leisure. Work and leisure became opposites as leisure came to be viewed as what people do for fun when they are not at work. The new leisure hours created by the industrial system—evening hours after work, weekends, and later a week or two in the summer—largely determined the contours of the new **mass leisure**.

New technology created novel experiences for leisure, such as the Ferris wheel at amusement parks, while the introduction of subways and streetcars in the 1880s meant that even the working classes were no longer dependent on neighborhood facilities but could make their way to athletic games, amusement parks, and dance halls. Railroads could take people to the beaches on weekends.

By the late nineteenth century, team sports had also developed into another important form of mass leisure. Unlike the old rural games, which were spontaneous and often chaotic activities, the new sports were strictly organized with sets of rules and officials to enforce them. These rules were the products of organized athletic groups, such as the English Football Association (1863) and the American Bowling Congress (1895). The development of urban transportation systems made possible the construction of stadiums where thousands could attend, making mass spectator sports into a big business.

Cultural Life: Romanticism and Realism in the Western World

Q FOCUS QUESTION: What were the main characteristics of Romanticism and Realism?

At the end of the eighteenth century, a new intellectual movement known as **Romanticism** emerged to challenge the ideas of the Enlightenment. To the Enlightenment, reason was the chief means for discovering truth. Although the Romantics by no means disparaged reason, they tried to balance its use by stressing the importance of feeling, emotion, and imagination as sources of knowing.

The Characteristics of Romanticism

Romantic writers emphasized emotion and sentiment and believed that these inner feelings were understandable only to the person experiencing them. In their novels, Romantic writers created figures who were often misunderstood and rejected by society but who continued to believe in their own worth through their inner feelings.

Many Romantics also possessed a passionate interest in the past. They revived medieval Gothic architecture and left European countrysides adorned with pseudo-medieval castles and cities bedecked with grandiose neo-Gothic cathedrals, city halls, and parliamentary buildings. Literature, too, reflected this historical consciousness. The novels of Walter Scott (1771–1832) became European best-sellers in the first half of the nineteenth century. *Ivanhoe*, in which Scott sought to evoke the clash between Saxon and Norman knights in medieval England, became one of his most popular works.

Many Romantics had a deep attraction to the exotic and unfamiliar. For some, this meant a fascination with historical figures from the non-Western parts of the world, evident in Samuel Taylor Coleridge's *Kubla Khan*, a poem about the ruler who established a new Chinese dynasty in the thirteenth century. For others, this preoccupation with the exotic took an exaggerated form in so-called **Gothic literature**, chillingly evident in Mary Shelley's *Frankenstein* and Edgar Allan Poe's short stories of horror (see the box on p. 597). Some Romantics even tried to bring the unusual into their own lives by experimenting with cocaine, opium, and hashish to achieve drug-induced altered states of consciousness.

To the Romantics, poetry ranked above all other literary forms because they believed it was the direct expression of the soul. Romantic poetry gave full expression to one of the most important characteristics of Romanticism: love of nature, especially evident in the poetry of William Wordsworth (1770–1850). His experience of nature was almost mystical as he claimed to receive "authentic tidings of invisible things":

> One impulse from a vernal wood
> May teach you more of man,
> Of Moral Evil and of good,
> Than all the sages can.[8]

Romantics believed that nature served as a mirror into which humans could look to learn about themselves.

Like the literary arts, the visual arts were also deeply affected by Romanticism. To Romantic artists, all artistic expression was a reflection of the artist's inner feelings; a painting should mirror the artist's vision of the world and be the instrument of his own imagination.

The early life experiences of Caspar David Friedrich (kass-PAR dah-VEET FREED-rikh) (1774–1840) left him with a lifelong preoccupation with God and nature. Friedrich painted landscapes with an interest that transcended the mere presentation of natural details. His portrayals of mountains shrouded in mist, gnarled trees bathed in moonlight, and the stark ruins of monasteries surrounded by withered trees all conveyed a feeling of mystery and mysticism. For Friedrich, nature was a manifestation of divine life, as is evident in *Man and Woman Gazing at the Moon*. To Friedrich, the artistic process depended on the use of an unrestricted imagination that could only be achieved through inner vision.

Eugène Delacroix (oo-ZHEN duh-lah-KRWAH) (1798–1863) was one of the most famous French exponents of the Romantic school of painting. Delacroix visited North Africa in 1832 and was strongly impressed by its vibrant colors and the brilliant dress of the people. His paintings came to exhibit two primary characteristics, a fascination with the exotic and a passion for color. Both are apparent in his *Women of Algiers*. Significant for its use of light and its patches of interrelated color, this portrayal of the world of harem concubines in exotic Algeria was considered somewhat scandalous in the early nineteenth century. In Delacroix, theatricality and movement combined with a daring use of color. Many of his works reflect his own belief that "a painting should be a feast to the eye."

Gothic Literature: Edgar Allan Poe

ART & IDEAS

American writers and poets made significant contributions to the movement of Romanticism. Although Edgar Allan Poe (1809–1849) was influenced by the German Romantic school of mystery and horror, many literary historians give him the credit for pioneering the modern short story. This selection from the conclusion of "The Fall of the House of Usher" gives a sense of the nature of so-called Gothic literature.

Edgar Allan Poe, "The Fall of the House of Usher"

[The narrator resumes a story he has been telling Usher.] No sooner had these syllables passed my lips, than—as if a shield of brass had indeed, at the moment, fallen heavily upon a floor of silver—I became aware of a distinct, hollow, metallic, and clangorous, yet apparently muffled, reverberation. Completely unnerved, I leaped to my feet; but the measured rocking movement of Usher was undisturbed. I rushed to the chair in which he sat. His eyes were bent fixedly before him, and throughout his whole countenance there reigned a stony rigidity. But, as I placed my hand upon his shoulder, there came a strong shudder over his whole person; a sickly smile quivered about his lips; and I saw that he spoke in a low, hurried, and gibbering murmur, as if unconscious of my presence. Bending closely over him, I at length drank in the hideous import of his words.

"Not hear it?—yes, I hear it, and have heard it. Long-long-long-many minutes, many hours, many days, have I heard it—yet I dared not—oh, pity me, miserable wretch that I am!—I dared not—I dared not speak! We have put her living in the tomb! Said I not that my senses were acute? I now tell you that I heard her first feeble movements in the hollow coffin. I heard them—many, many days ago—yet I dared not—I dared not speak! And now— to-night—. . . the rending of her coffin, and the grating of the iron hinges of her prison, and her struggles within the coppered archway of the vault! Oh whither shall I fly? Will she not be here anon? Is she not hurrying to upbraid me for my haste? Have I not heard her footstep on the stair? Do I not distinguish that heavy and horrible beating of her heart? MADMAN!"—here he sprang furiously to his feet, and shrieked out his syllables, as if in the effort he were giving up his soul—"MADMAN! I TELL YOU THAT SHE NOW STANDS WITHOUT THE DOOR!"

As if in the superhuman energy of his utterance there had been found the potency of a spell, the huge antique panels to which the speaker pointed threw slowly back, upon the instant, their ponderous and ebony jaws. It was the work of the rushing gust—but then without those doors there DID stand the lofty and enshrouded figure of the lady Madeline of Usher. There was blood upon her white robes, and the evidence of some bitter struggle upon every portion of her emaciated frame. For a moment she remained trembling and reeling to and fro upon the threshold, then, with a low moaning cry, fell heavily inward upon the person of her brother, and in her violent and now final death-agonies, bore him to the floor a corpse, and a victim to the terrors he had anticipated.

What were the aesthetic aims of Gothic literature? How did it come to be called "Gothic"? How did its values relate to those of the Romantic movement as a whole?

Caspar David Friedrich, *Man and Woman Gazing at the Moon.* The German artist Caspar David Friedrich sought to express in painting his own mystical view of nature. "The divine is everywhere," he once wrote, "even in a grain of sand." In this painting, a man and a woman are shown from the back, gazing at the moon. They are overwhelmed by the powerful presence of nature and the immensity of the universe.

Eugène Delacroix, *Women of Algiers.* Also characteristic of Romanticism was its love of the exotic and unfamiliar. This fascination is evident in Delacroix's portrayal of harem concubines in North Africa. The women's clothes and jewelry combine with their calm facial expressions to create an atmosphere of peaceful sensuality. At the same time, Delacroix's painting reflects his preoccupation with light and color.

Louvre, Paris//© Erich Lessing/Art Resource, NY

A New Age of Science

The Scientific Revolution had created a modern, rational approach to the study of the natural world, but even in the eighteenth century, these intellectual developments had remained the preserve of an educated elite and resulted in few practical applications. With the Industrial Revolution, however, came a renewed interest in basic scientific research. By the 1830s, new scientific discoveries had led to many practical benefits that caused science to have an ever-greater impact on European life.

In biology, the Frenchman Louis Pasteur (LWEE pass-TOOR) (1822–1895) came up with the germ theory of disease, which had enormous practical applications in the development of modern scientific medical practices. In chemistry, the Russian Dmitri Mendeleev (di-MEE-tree men-duh-LAY-ef) (1834–1907) in the 1860s classified all the material elements then known on the basis of their atomic weights and provided the systematic foundation for the periodic law. The Briton Michael Faraday (1791–1867) put together a primitive generator that laid the foundation for the use of electricity.

The popularity of scientific and technological achievement produced a widespread acceptance of the **scientific method** as the only path to objective truth and objective reality. This undermined the faith of many people in religious revelation. It is no accident that the nineteenth century was an age of increasing **secularization**, evident in the belief that truth was to be found in the concrete material existence of human beings. No one did more to create a picture of humans as material beings that were simply part of the natural world than Charles Darwin.

In 1859, Charles Darwin (1809–1882) published *On the Origin of Species by Means of Natural Selection*. The basic idea of this book was that all plants and animals had evolved over a long period of time from earlier and simpler forms of life, a principle known as **organic evolution**. In every species, he argued, "many more individuals of each species are born than can possibly survive." This results in a "struggle for existence." Darwin believed that some organisms were more adaptable to the environment than others, a process that Darwin called **natural selection**. Those that were naturally selected for survival ("survival of the fit") reproduced and thrived. The unfit did not and became extinct. The fit who survived passed on small variations that enhanced their survival until, from Darwin's point of view, a new and separate species emerged. In *The Descent of Man*, published in 1871, he argued for the animal origins of human beings: "Man is the co-descendant with other mammals of a common progenitor." Humans were not an exception to the rule governing other species.

Realism in Literature and Art

The name **Realism** was first applied in 1850 to a new style of painting and soon spread to literature. The literary Realists of the mid-nineteenth century rejected Romanticism. They wanted to deal with ordinary characters from actual life rather than Romantic heroes in exotic settings. They also sought to avoid emotional language by using close observation and precise description, an approach that led them to write novels rather than poems.

The leading novelist of the 1850s and 1860s, the Frenchman Gustave Flaubert (goo-STAHV floh-BAYR) (1821–1880),

Gustave Courbet, *The Stonebreakers*. Realism, largely developed by French painters, aimed at lifelike portrayals of the daily activities of ordinary people. Gustave Courbet was the most famous of the Realist artists. As is evident in *The Stonebreakers*, he sought to portray things as they really appear. He shows an old road builder and his young assistant in their tattered clothes, engrossed in their dreary work of breaking stones to construct a road.

perfected the Realist novel. His *Madame Bovary* (1857) was a straightforward description of barren and sordid provincial life in France. Emma Bovary is trapped in a marriage to a drab provincial doctor. Impelled by the images of romantic love she has read about in novels, she seeks the same thing for herself in adulterous love affairs but is ultimately driven to suicide.

The British novelist Charles Dickens (1812–1870) achieved extraordinary success with his novels focusing on the lower and middle classes in Britain's early industrial age. His descriptions of the urban poor and the brutalization of human life were vividly realistic.

Realism also made inroads in Latin America by the second half of the nineteenth century. There, Realist novelists focused on the injustices of Latin American society, evident in the work of Clorinda Matto de Turner (kloh-RIN-duh MAH-toh day TUR-nerr) (1852–1909). Her *Aves sin Nido* (*Birds Without a Nest*) was a brutal revelation of the pitiful living conditions of the Indians in Peru. She especially blamed the Catholic Church for much of their misery.

In art, too, Realism became dominant after 1850. Realist art demonstrated three major characteristics: a desire to depict the everyday life of ordinary people, whether peasants, workers, or prostitutes; an attempt at photographic accuracy; and an interest in the natural environment. The French became leaders in Realist painting.

Gustave Courbet (goo-STAHV koor-BAY) (1819–1877), the most famous artist of the Realist school, reveled in realistic portrayals of everyday life. His subjects were factory workers, peasants, and the wives of saloonkeepers. "I have never seen either angels or goddesses, so I am not interested in painting them," he exclaimed. One of his famous works, *The Stonebreakers*, painted in 1849, shows two road workers engaged in the deadening work of breaking stones to build a road. This representation of human misery was a scandal to those who objected to Courbet's "cult of ugliness."

Toward the Modern Consciousness: Intellectual and Cultural Developments

 FOCUS QUESTION: What intellectual and cultural developments in the late nineteenth and early twentieth centuries "opened the way to a modern consciousness," and how did this consciousness differ from earlier worldviews?

Before 1914, many people in the Western world continued to believe in the values and ideals of the Scientific Revolution and the Enlightenment. The idea that human beings could improve themselves and achieve a better society seemed to be proved by a rising standard of living, urban comforts, and mass education. Such products of modern technology as electric lights and automobiles reinforced the popular prestige of science. It was easy to think that the human mind could make sense of the universe. Between 1870 and 1914, radically new ideas challenged these optimistic views and opened the way to a modern consciousness.

A New Physics

Science was one of the chief pillars underlying the optimistic and rationalistic view of the world that many Westerners shared in the nineteenth century. Supposedly based on hard facts and cold reason, science offered a certainty of belief in the orderliness of nature. The new physics dramatically altered that perspective.

Throughout much of the nineteenth century, Westerners adhered to the mechanical conception of the universe postulated by the classical physics of Isaac Newton. In this perspective, the universe was viewed as a giant machine in which time, space, and matter were objective realities that existed

Marie Curie. Marie Curie was born in Warsaw, Poland, but studied at the University of Paris, where she received degrees in both physics and mathematics. She was the first woman to win two Nobel Prizes, one in 1903 in physics and another in chemistry in 1911. She is shown here in her Paris laboratory in 1921. She died of leukemia, a result of her laboratory work with radioactivity.

independently of the people observing them. Matter was thought to be composed of indivisible and solid material bodies called atoms.

These views were first seriously questioned at the end of the nineteenth century. The French scientist Marie Curie (kyoo-REE) (1867–1934) and her husband, Pierre Curie (1859–1906), discovered that an element called radium gave off rays of radiation that apparently came from within the atom itself. Atoms were not simply hard, material bodies but small worlds containing such subatomic particles as electrons and protons, which behaved in seemingly random and inexplicable fashion.

Building on this work, in 1900 a Berlin physicist, Max Planck (PLAHNK) (1858–1947), rejected the belief that a heated body radiates energy in a steady stream but maintained instead that it did so discontinuously, in irregular packets of energy that he called "quanta." The quantum theory raised fundamental questions about the subatomic realm of the atom. By 1900, the old view of atoms as the basic building blocks of the material world was being seriously questioned.

Albert Einstein (YN-styn) (1879–1955), a German-born patent officer working in Switzerland, pushed these new theories into new terrain. In 1905, Einstein published a paper titled "The Electro-Dynamics of Moving Bodies" that contained his special theory of relativity. According to **relativity theory**, space and time are not absolute but relative to the observer, and both are interwoven into what Einstein called a four-dimensional space-time continuum. Neither space nor time had an existence independent of human experience. As Einstein later explained simply to a journalist, "It was formerly believed that if all material things disappeared out of the universe, time and space would be left. According to the relativity theory, however, time and space disappear together with the things."[9] Moreover, matter and energy reflected the relativity of time and space. Einstein concluded that matter was nothing but another form of energy. His epochal formula $E = mc^2$—indicating that the energy of each particle of matter is equivalent to its mass times the square of the velocity of light—was the key theory explaining the vast energies contained within the atom. It led to the atomic age.

Sigmund Freud and Psychoanalysis

At the turn of the twentieth century, the Viennese physician Sigmund Freud (SIG-mund *or* ZIG-munt FROID) (1856–1939) advanced a series of theories that undermined optimism about the rational nature of the human mind. Freud's thought, like the new physics, added to the uncertainties of the age. His major ideas were published in 1900 in *The Interpretation of Dreams*.

According to Freud, human behavior was strongly determined by the unconscious, by past experiences and internal forces of which people were largely oblivious. For Freud, human behavior was no longer truly rational but rather instinctive or irrational. He argued that painful and unsettling experiences were blotted from conscious awareness but still continued to influence behavior since they had become part of the unconscious (see the box on p. 601). Repression of these thoughts began in childhood. Freud devised a method, known as **psychoanalysis**, by which a psychotherapist and patient could probe deeply into the memory in order to retrace the chain of repression all the way back to its childhood origins. By making the conscious mind aware of the unconscious and its repressed contents, the patient's psychic conflict was resolved.

The Impact of Darwin: Social Darwinism and Racism

In the second half of the nineteenth century, scientific theories were sometimes wrongly applied to achieve other ends. For example, the application of Charles Darwin's principle of organic evolution to the social order came to be known as **social Darwinism**, the belief that societies were organisms that evolved through time from a struggle with their environment. Progress came from the "struggle for survival," as the "fit"—the strong—advanced while the weak declined.

Freud and the Concept of Repression

ART & IDEAS

Sigmund Freud's psychoanalytical theories resulted from his attempt to understand the world of the unconscious. This excerpt is taken from a lecture given in 1909 in which Freud described how he arrived at his theory of the role of repression. Although Freud valued science and reason, his theories of the unconscious produced a new image of the human being as governed less by reason than by irrational forces.

Sigmund Freud, *Five Lectures on Psychoanalysis*

I did not abandon [the technique of encouraging patients to reveal forgotten experiences], however, before the observations I made during my use of it afforded me decisive evidence. I found confirmation of the fact that the forgotten memories were not lost. They were in the patient's possession and were ready to emerge in association to what was still known by him; but there was some force that prevented them from becoming conscious and compelled them to remain unconscious. The existence of this force could be assumed with certainty, since one became aware of an effort corresponding to it if, in opposition to it, one tried to introduce the unconscious memories into the patient's consciousness. The force which was maintaining the pathological condition became apparent in the form of resistance on the part of the patient.

It was on this idea of resistance, then, that I based my view of the course of psychical events in hysteria. In order to effect a recovery, it had proved necessary to remove these resistances. Starting out from the mechanism of cure, it now became possible to construct quite definite ideas of the origin of the illness. The same forces which, in the form of resistance, were now offering opposition to the forgotten material's being made conscious, must formerly have brought about the forgetting and must have pushed the pathogenic experiences in question out of consciousness. I gave the name of "repression" to this hypothetical process, and I considered that it was proved by the undeniable existence of resistance.

The further question could then be raised as to what these forces were and what the determinants were of the repression in which we now recognized the pathogenic mechanism of hysteria. A comparative study of the pathogenic situations which we had come to know through the cathartic procedure made it possible to answer this question. All these experiences had involved the emergence of a wishful impulse which was in sharp contrast to the subject's other wishes and which proved incompatible with the ethical and aesthetic standards of his personality. There had been a short conflict, and the end of this internal struggle was that the idea which had appeared before consciousness as the vehicle of this irreconcilable wish fell a victim to repression, was pushed out of consciousness with all its attached memories, and was forgotten. Thus, the incompatibility of the wish in question with the patient's ego was the motive for the repression; the subject's ethical and other standards were the repressing forces. An acceptance of the incompatible wishful impulse or a prolongation of the conflict would have produced a high degree of unpleasure; this unpleasure was avoided by means of repression, which was thus revealed as one of the devices serving to protect the mental personality.

 According to Freud, how did he discover the existence of repression? What function does repression perform?

Darwin's ideas were also applied to human society in an even more radical way by rabid nationalists and racists. In their pursuit of national greatness, extreme nationalists often insisted that nations, too, were engaged in a struggle for existence in which only the fittest survived. The German general Friedrich von Bernhardi (FREED-rikh fun bayrn-HAR-dee) argued in 1907, "War is a biological necessity of the first importance, . . . since without it an unhealthy development will follow, which excludes every advancement of the race, and therefore all real civilization. 'War is the father of all things.'"[10]

Perhaps nowhere was the combination of extreme nationalism and racism more evident or more dangerous than in Germany. One of the chief propagandists of German racism was Houston Stewart Chamberlain (1855–1927), a Briton who became a German citizen. According to Chamberlain, modern-day Germans were the only pure successors of the **Aryans**, who were portrayed as the true and original founders of Western culture. The Aryan race, under German leadership, must be prepared to fight for Western civilization and save it from the destructive assaults of such lower races as Jews, Negroes, and Orientals. Chamberlain singled out the Jews as the racial enemy who wanted to destroy the Aryan race.

ANTI-SEMITISM Anti-Semitism had a long history in European civilization, but in the nineteenth century, as a result of the ideals of the Enlightenment and the French Revolution,

Jews were increasingly granted legal equality in many European countries. Many Jews now left the ghetto and became assimilated into the cultures around them. Many became successful as bankers, lawyers, scientists, scholars, journalists, and stage performers.

These achievements represent only one side of the picture, however. In Germany and Austria during the 1880s and 1890s, conservatives founded right-wing anti-Jewish parties that used anti-Semitism to win the votes of traditional lower-middle-class groups who felt threatened by the new economic forces of the times. The worst treatment of Jews at the turn of the century, however, occurred in eastern Europe, where 72 percent of the world's Jewish population lived. Russian Jews were forced to live in certain regions of the country, and persecutions and pogroms were widespread. Hundreds of thousands of Jews decided to emigrate to escape the persecution.

Many Jews went to the United States, although some moved to Palestine, which soon became the focus of a Jewish nationalist movement called **Zionism**. For many Jews, Palestine, the land of ancient Israel, had long been the land of their dreams. A key figure in the growth of political Zionism was Theodor Herzl (TAY-oh-dor HAYRT-sul) (1860–1904), who predicted in his book *The Jewish State*, "The Jews who wish it will have their state" (see the box on p. 604).

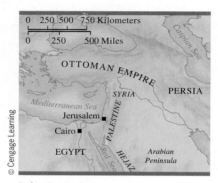

Palestine in 1900

Settlement in Palestine was difficult, however, because it was then part of the Ottoman Empire, which was opposed to Jewish immigration. Despite the problems, however, the first Zionist Congress, which met in Switzerland in 1897, proclaimed as its aim the creation of a "home in Palestine secured by public law" for the Jewish people. In 1900, about a thousand Jews migrated to Palestine, and the trickle rose to about three thousand a year between 1904 and 1914, keeping the Zionist dream alive.

The Culture of Modernity

The revolution in physics and psychology was paralleled by a revolution in literature and the arts. Before 1914, writers and artists were rebelling against the traditional literary and artistic styles that had dominated European cultural life since the Renaissance. The changes that they produced have since been called **Modernism**.

At the beginning of the twentieth century, a group of writers known as the Symbolists caused a literary revolution. Primarily interested in writing poetry and strongly influenced by the ideas of Freud, the Symbolists believed that an objective knowledge of the world was impossible. The external world was not real but only a collection of symbols that reflected the true reality of the individual human mind. Art, they believed, should function for its own sake instead of serving, criticizing, or seeking to understand society.

The period from 1870 to 1914 was one of the most fertile in the history of art. Since the Renaissance, the task of artists had been to represent reality as accurately as possible. By the late nineteenth century, artists were seeking new forms of expression. The preamble to modern painting can be found in **Impressionism**, a movement that originated in France in the 1870s when a group of artists rejected the studios and museums and went out into the countryside to paint nature directly. Camille Pissarro (kah-MEEl pee-SAH-roh) (1830–1903), one of Impressionism's founders, expressed what they sought:

> Precise drawing is dry and hampers the impression of the whole, it destroys all sensations. Do not define too closely the outlines of things; it is the brush stroke of the right value and color which should produce the drawing. . . . Work at the same time upon sky, water, branches, ground, keeping everything going on an equal basis and unceasingly rework until you have got it. . . . Don't proceed according to rules and principles, but paint what you observe and feel. Paint generously and unhesitatingly, for it is best not to lose the first impression.[11]

An important Impressionist painter was Berthe Morisot (BAYRT mor-ee-ZOH) (1841–1895), who believed that women had a special vision, which was, as she said, "more delicate than that of men." She made use of lighter colors and flowing brush strokes (see the comparative illustration on p. 603). Near the end of her life, she lamented the refusal of men to take her work seriously: "I don't think there has ever been a man who treated a woman as an equal, and that's all I would have asked, for I know I'm worth as much as they."[12]

In the 1880s, a new movement known as **Post-Impressionism** arose in France and soon spread to other European countries. A famous Post-Impressionist was the tortured and tragic figure Vincent van Gogh (van GOH *or* vahn GOK) (1853–1890). For van Gogh, art was a spiritual experience. He was especially interested in color and believed that it could act as its own form of language. Van Gogh maintained that artists should paint what they feel.

By the beginning of the twentieth century, the belief that the task of art was to represent "reality" had lost much of its meaning. By that time, the new psychology and the new physics had made it evident that many people were not sure what constituted reality anyway. Then, too, the growth of photography gave artists another reason to reject Realism. Invented in the 1830s, photography became popular and widespread after George Eastman created the first Kodak camera in 1888 for the mass market. What was the point of an artist's doing what the camera did better? Unlike the camera, which could only mirror reality, artists could create reality. Like the Symbolist writers of the time, artists sought meaning in individual consciousness.

By 1905, one of the most important figures in modern art was just beginning his career. Pablo Picasso (PAHB-loh pi-KAH-soh) (1881–1973) was from Spain but settled in Paris in 1904. Picasso was extremely flexible and painted

Musée Fabre, Montpellier//© Erich Lessing/Art Resource, NY

© Christie's Images/SuperStock

COMPARATIVE ILLUSTRATION

ART & IDEAS

Painting—West and East. Berthe Morisot, the first female painter to join the Impressionists, developed her own unique style. Her gentle colors and strong use of pastels are especially evident in *Young Girl by the Window*, seen at the left. The French Impressionist style also spread abroad. One of the most outstanding Japanese artists of the time was Kuroda Seiki (koor-OH-duh SAY-kee) (1866–1924), who returned from nine years in Paris to open a Western-style school of painting in Tokyo. Shown at the right is his *Under the Trees*, painted in 1898, an example of the fusion of contemporary French Impressionist painting with the Japanese tradition of courtesan prints.

 What differences and similarities do you notice in these two paintings?

in a remarkable variety of styles. He was instrumental in the development of a new style called **Cubism** that used geometrical designs as visual stimuli to re-create reality in the viewer's mind.

The modern artist's flight from "visual reality" reached a high point in 1910 with the beginning of abstract painting. A Russian who worked in Germany, Wassily Kandinsky (vus-YEEL-yee kan-DIN-skee) (1866–1944) was one of the

Digital Image © The Museum of Modern Art/Licensed by SCALA/Art Resource, NY

Vincent van Gogh, *The Starry Night*. The Dutch painter Vincent van Gogh was a major figure among the Post-Impressionists. His originality and power of expression made a strong impact on his artistic successors. In *The Starry Night*, van Gogh's subjective vision was given full play as the dynamic swirling forms of the heavens above overwhelm the village below. The heavens seem alive with a mysterious spiritual force.

The Voice of Zionism: Theodor Herzl and the Jewish State

POLITICS & GOVERNMENT

The Austrian Jewish journalist Theodor Herzl wrote *The Jewish State* in the summer of 1895 in Paris while he was covering the Dreyfus (DRY-fuss) case for his Vienna newspaper. (Alfred Dreyfus, a French army officer who was also Jewish, was accused and wrongly convicted of selling military secrets. Although he was later exonerated, the case revealed the depth of anti-Semitism in France.) In several weeks, during a period of feverish composition, he set out to analyze the fundamental causes of anti-Semitism and devise a solution to the "Jewish problem." In this selection, he discusses two of his major conclusions.

Theodor Herzl, *The Jewish State*

I do not intend to arouse sympathetic emotions on our behalf. That would be a foolish, futile, and undignified proceeding. I shall content myself with putting the following questions to the Jews: Is it true that, in countries where we live in perceptible numbers, the position of Jewish lawyers, doctors, technicians, teachers, and employees of all descriptions becomes daily more intolerable? True, that the Jewish middle classes are seriously threatened? True, that the passions of the mob are incited against our wealthy people? True, that our poor endure greater sufferings than any other proletariat?

I think that this external pressure makes itself felt everywhere. In our economically upper classes it causes discomfort, in our middle classes continual and grave anxieties, in our lower classes absolute despair.

Everything tends, in fact, to one and the same conclusion, which is clearly enunciated in that classic Berlin phrase: "Juden raus!" (Out with the Jews!)

I shall now put the Jewish Question in the curtest possible form: Are we to "get out" now? And if so, to what place?

Or, may we yet remain? And if so, how long?

Let us first settle the point of staying where we are. Can we hope for better days, can we possess our souls in patience, can we wait in pious resignation till the princes and peoples of this earth are more mercifully disposed toward us? I say that we cannot hope for a change in the current of feeling. And why not? . . . The nations in whose midst Jews live are all, either covertly or openly, Anti-Semitic. . . .

The whole plan is in its essence perfectly simple, as it must necessarily be if it is to come within the comprehension of all.

Let the sovereignty be granted us over a portion of the globe large enough to satisfy the rightful requirements of a nation; the rest we shall manage for ourselves.

The creation of a new State is neither ridiculous nor impossible. We have in our day witnessed the process in connection with nations which were not in the bulk of the middle class, but poorer, less educated, and consequently weaker than ourselves. The Governments of all countries scourged by Anti-Semitism will be keenly interested in assisting us to obtain the sovereignty we want. . . .

Palestine is our ever memorable historic home. The very name of Palestine would attract our people with a force of marvelous potency. Supposing his Majesty the Sultan [of the Ottoman Empire] were to give us Palestine, we could in return undertake to regulate the whole finances of Turkey. We should there form a portion of the rampart of Europe against Asia, an outpost of civilization as opposed to barbarism. We should as a neutral State remain in contact with all Europe, which would have to guarantee our existence. The sanctuaries of Christendom would be safeguarded by assigning to them an extraterritorial status such as is well known to the law of nations. We should form a guard of honor about these sanctuaries, answering for the fulfillment of this duty with our existence. This guard of honor would be the great symbol of the solution of the Jewish Question after eighteen centuries of Jewish suffering.

Why did Herzl believe that Palestine was necessary for Jews? How does he seek to gain the acceptance of the Ottoman sultan and the Christian nations of Europe?

---

founders of **abstract painting**. As is evident in his *Square with White Border*, Kandinsky sought to avoid representation altogether. He believed that art should speak directly to the soul. To do so, it must avoid any reference to visual reality and concentrate on line and color.

Modernism in the arts revolutionized architecture and architectural practices. A new principle known as **functionalism** motivated this revolution. Functionalism meant that buildings, like the products of machines, should be "functional" or useful, fulfilling the purpose for which they were constructed. Art and engineering were to be unified, and all unnecessary ornamentation was to be stripped away.

The United States was a leader in these pioneering architectural designs. Unprecedented urban growth and the absence of restrictive architectural traditions allowed for new building methods, especially in the relatively new city of Chicago. The Chicago School of the 1890s, led by Louis H. Sullivan (1856–1924), used reinforced concrete, steel frames,

Pablo Picasso, *Les Demoiselles d'Avignon.* Pablo Picasso, a major pioneer and activist of modern art, experimented with a remarkable variety of modern styles. *Les Demoiselles d'Avignon* (lay dem-wah-ZEL dah-vee-NYONH) (1907) was the first great example of Cubism, which one art historian has called "the first style of [the twentieth] century to break radically with the past." Geometrical shapes replace traditional forms, forcing the viewer to re-create reality in his or her own mind. The head at the upper right of the painting reflects Picasso's attraction to aspects of African art, as is evident from the mask shown at the left.

© Dr. Werner Muensterberger Collection, London/The Bridgeman Art Library

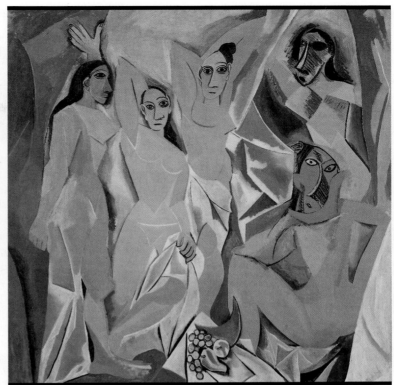

© 2011 Estate of Pablo Picasso/Artists Rights Society (ARS), New York//Digital Image
© The Museum of Modern Art/Licensed by Scala/Art Resource, NY

and electric elevators to build skyscrapers virtually free of external ornamentation. One of Sullivan's most successful pupils was Frank Lloyd Wright (1867–1959), who became known for innovative designs in domestic architecture. Wright's private houses, built chiefly for wealthy patrons, featured geometrical structures with long lines, overhanging roofs, and severe planes of brick and stone. The interiors were open spaces and included cathedral ceilings and built-in furniture and lighting. Wright pioneered the modern American house.

© 2011 Artists Rights Society (ARS), New York/ADAGP, Paris,/Russian State Museum, St. Petersburg,/Digital Image Scala/Art Resource, NY

Wassily Kandinsky, *Square with White Border.* One of the originators of abstract painting was the Russian Wassily Kandinsky, who sought to eliminate representation altogether by focusing on color and avoiding any resemblance to visual reality. In *Square with White Border*, Kandinsky used color "to send light into the darkness of men's hearts." He believed that color, like music, could fulfill a spiritual goal of appealing directly to the human being.

Since the sixteenth century, much of the Western Hemisphere had been under the control of Great Britain, Spain, and Portugal. But between 1776 and 1826, an age of revolution in the Atlantic world led to the creation of the United States and nine new nations in Latin America. Canada and other nations in Latin America followed in the course of the nineteenth century. This age of revolution was an expression of the force of nationalism, which had first emerged as a political ideology at the end of the eighteenth century. Influential, too, were the ideas of the Enlightenment that had made an impact on intellectuals and political leaders in both North and South America.

The new nations that emerged in the Western Hemisphere did not, however, develop without challenges to their national unity. Latin American nations often found it difficult to establish stable republics and resorted to strong leaders who used military force to govern. And although Latin American nations had achieved political independence, they found themselves economically dependent on Great Britain as well as their northern neighbor. The United States dissolved into four years of bloody civil war before reconciling, and Canada achieved only questionable unity owing to distrust between the English-speaking majority and the French-speaking minority.

By the second half of the nineteenth century, much of the Western world was experiencing a new mass society in which the lower classes in particular benefited from the right to vote, a higher standard of living, and new schools that provided them with some education. New forms of mass transportation, combined with new work patterns, enabled large numbers of people to enjoy weekend trips to amusement parks and seaside resorts, as well as to participate in new mass leisure activities.

The cultural revolutions before 1914 produced anxiety and a crisis of confidence in Western civilization. Albert Einstein showed that time and space were relative to the observer, that matter was simply another form of energy, and that the old Newtonian view of the universe was no longer valid. Sigmund Freud added to the uncertainties of the age with his argument that human behavior was governed not by reason but by the unconscious. Some intellectuals used the ideas of Charles Darwin to argue that in the struggle of race and nations, only the fittest survive. Collectively, these

new ideas helped create a modern consciousness that questioned most Europeans' optimistic faith in reason, the rational structure of nature, and the certainty of progress. As we shall see in Chapter 23, the devastating experiences of World War I would turn this culture of uncertainty into a way of life after 1918.

CHAPTER TIMELINE

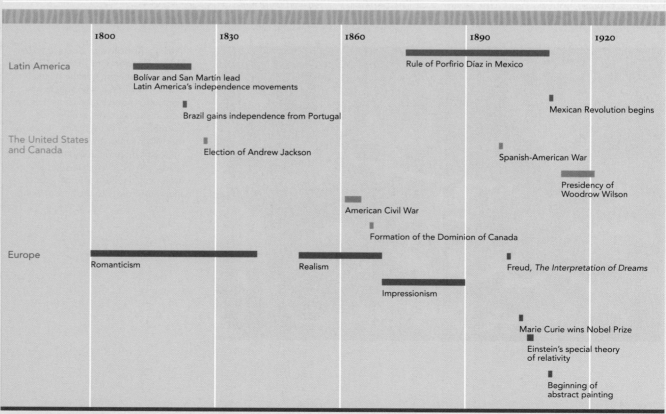

Upon Reflection

Q What were the similarities and dissimilarities in the development of Latin American nations, the United States, and Canada in the nineteenth century?

Q How were the promises and problems of the new mass society reflected in education, leisure, and the experiences of women?

Q How is Modernism evident in literature and the arts between 1870 and 1914? How do these literary and artistic products reflect the political and social developments of the age?

Key Terms

caudillos (p. 581)
mass society (p. 589)
nation-states (p. 589)
suffragists (p. 592)
mass education (p. 594)
mass leisure (p. 596)
Romanticism (p. 596)
Gothic literature (p. 596)
scientific method (p. 598)
secularization (p. 598)
organic evolution (p. 598)
natural selection (p. 598)
Realism (p. 598)
relativity theory (p. 600)
psychoanalysis (p. 600)
social Darwinism (p. 600)
Aryans (p. 601)
Zionism (p. 602)
Modernism (p. 602)
Impressionism (p. 602)
Post-Impressionism (p. 602)
Cubism (p. 603)
abstract painting (p. 604)
functionalism (p. 604)

Suggested Reading

LATIN AMERICA For general surveys of Latin American history, see **M. C. Eakin**, *The History of Latin America: Collision of Cultures* (New York, 2007), and **P. Bakewell**, *A History of Latin America* (Oxford, 1997). On the wars for independence, see **J. C. Chasteen**, *Americanos: Latin America's Struggle for Independence* (Oxford, 2008). On the economic history of Latin America, see **V. Bulmer-Thomas**, *The Economic History of Latin America Since Independence,* 2nd ed. (New York, 2003).

THE UNITED STATES AND CANADA On the United States in the first half of the nineteenth century, see **D. W. Howe**, *What God Hath Wrought: The Transformation of America, 1815–1848* (Oxford, 2007). The definitive one-volume history of the American Civil War is **J. M. McPherson**, *Battle Cry of Freedom: The Civil War Era* in the Oxford History of the United States series (New York, 2003). On the second half of the nineteenth century, see **L. Gould**, *America in the Progressive Era, 1890–1914* (New York, 2001). For a general history of Canada, see **S. W. See**, *History of Canada* (Westport, N.Y., 2001).

THE EMERGENCE OF MASS SOCIETY IN THE WEST For a good introduction to housing reform on the Continent, see **N. Bullock** and **J. Read**, *The Movement for Housing Reform in Germany and France, 1840–1914* (Cambridge, 1985). There are good overviews of women's experiences in the nineteenth century in **B. Smith**, *Changing Lives: Women in European History Since 1700,* rev. ed. (Lexington, Mass., 2005). On various aspects of education, see **M. J. Maynes**, *Schooling in Western Europe: A Social History* (Albany, N.Y., 1985). A concise and well-presented survey of leisure patterns is **G. Cross**, *A Social History of Leisure Since 1600* (State College, Pa., 1989).

ROMANTICISM AND REALISM On the ideas of the Romantics, see **M. Cranston**, *The Romantic Movement* (Oxford, 1994). For an introduction to the arts, see **W. Vaughan**, *Romanticism and Art* (New York, 1994). On Realism, **J. Malpas**, *Realism* (Cambridge, 1997), is a good introduction.

TOWARD THE MODERN CONSCIOUSNESS: INTELLECTUAL AND CULTURAL DEVELOPMENTS On Freud, see **P. D. Kramer**, *Sigmund Freud: Inventor of the Modern Mind* (New York, 2006). European racism is analyzed in **N. MacMaster**, *Racism in Europe, 1870–2000* (New York, 2001). On Modernism, see **P. Gay**, *Modernism: The Lure of Heresy* (New York, 2007). Very valuable on modern art are **G. Crepaldi**, *The Impressionists* (New York, 2002), and **T. Parsons**, *Post-Impressionism: The Rise of Modern Art* (London, 1992).

Go to the CourseMate website at **www.cengagebrain.com** for additional study tools and review materials—including audio and video clips—for this chapter.

The High Tide of Imperialism

Revere the conquering heroes: Establishing British rule in Africa

CHAPTER OUTLINE AND FOCUS QUESTIONS

The Spread of Colonial Rule

Q What were the causes of the new imperialism of the nineteenth century, and how did it differ from European expansion in earlier periods?

The Colonial System

Q What types of administrative systems did the various colonial powers establish in their colonies, and how did these systems reflect the general philosophy of colonialism?

India Under the British Raj

Q What were some of the major consequences of British rule in India, and how did they affect the Indian people?

Colonial Regimes in Southeast Asia

Q Which Western countries were most active in seeking colonial possessions in Southeast Asia, and what were their motives in doing so?

Empire Building in Africa

Q What factors were behind the "scramble for Africa," and what impact did it have on the continent?

The Emergence of Anticolonialism

Q How did the subject peoples respond to colonialism, and what role did nationalism play in their response?

CRITICAL THINKING

Q What were the consequences of the new imperialism of the nineteenth century for the colonies of the European powers? How should the imperialist countries be evaluated in terms of their motives and stated objectives?

IN 1877, THE YOUNG BRITISH empire builder Cecil Rhodes drew up his last will and testament. He bequeathed his fortune, achieved as a diamond magnate in South Africa, to two of his close friends and acquaintances. He also instructed them to use the inheritance to form a secret society with the aim of bringing about "the extension of British rule throughout the world, the perfecting of a system of emigration from the United Kingdom . . . especially the occupation by British settlers of the entire continent of Africa, the Holy Land, the valley of the Euphrates, the Islands of Cyprus and Candia [Crete], the whole of South America. . . . The ultimate recovery of the United States of America as an integral part of the British Empire . . . then finally the foundation of so great a power as to hereafter render wars impossible and promote the best interests of humanity."[1]

Preposterous as such ideas sound today, they serve as a graphic reminder of the hubris that characterized the worldview of Rhodes and many of his contemporaries during the age of imperialism, as well as the complex union of moral concern and vaulting ambition that motivated their actions on the world stage.

Through their efforts, Western colonialism spread throughout much of the non-Western world during the nineteenth and early twentieth centuries. Spurred by the

© Time Life Pictures/Getty Images

demands of the Industrial Revolution, a few powerful Western states—notably, Great Britain, France, Germany, Russia, and the United States—competed avariciously for consumer markets and raw materials for their expanding economies. By the end of the nineteenth century, virtually all of the traditional societies in Asia and Africa were under direct or indirect colonial rule. As the new century began, the Western imprint on Asian and African societies, for better or for worse, appeared to be a permanent feature of the political and cultural landscape.

The Spread of Colonial Rule

Q FOCUS QUESTION: What were the causes of the new imperialism of the nineteenth century, and how did it differ from European expansion in earlier periods?

In the nineteenth century, a new phase of Western expansion into Asia and Africa began. Whereas European aims in the East before 1800 could be summed up in Vasco da Gama's famous phrase "Christians and spices," now a new relationship took shape as European nations began to view Asian and African societies as sources of industrial raw materials and as markets for Western manufactured goods. No longer were Western gold and silver exchanged for cloves, pepper, tea, silk, and porcelain. Now the prodigious output of European factories was sent to Africa and Asia in return for oil, tin, rubber, and the other resources needed to fuel the Western industrial machine. This relationship between the West and Asian and African societies has been called the new **imperialism** (see the comparative essay "Imperialisms Old and New" on p. 610).

The Motives

The reason for this change, of course, was the Industrial Revolution, which began in England in the late eighteenth century and spread to the Continent a few decades later. Now industrializing countries in the West needed vital raw materials that were not available at home, as well as a reliable market for the goods produced in their factories. The latter factor became increasingly crucial as producers began to discover that their home markets could not always absorb domestic output and that they had to export their manufactures to make a profit. When consumer demand lagged, economic depression threatened.

The relationship between colonialism and national survival was expressed directly in a speech by the French politician Jules Ferry (ZHOOL feh-REE) in 1885. A policy of "containment or abstinence," he warned, would set France on "the broad road to decadence" and initiate its decline into a "third- or fourth-rate power." British imperialists agreed, convinced by social Darwinism (the application of Charles Darwin's theory of evolution to society) that in the struggle between nations, only the fit are victorious and survive. As the British professor of mathematics Karl Pearson argued in 1900, "The path of progress is strewn with the wrecks of

nations; traces are everywhere to be seen of the [slaughtered remains] of inferior races. . . . Yet these dead people are, in very truth, the stepping stones on which mankind has arisen to the higher intellectual and deeper emotional life of today."[2]

For some, colonialism had a moral purpose, whether to promote Christianity or to build a better world. The British colonial official Henry Curzon (CURR-zun) declared that the British Empire "was under Providence, the greatest instrument for good that the world has seen." To Cecil Rhodes, the most famous empire builder of his day, the extraction of material wealth from the colonies was only a secondary matter. "My ruling purpose," he remarked, "is the extension of the British Empire."[3] That British Empire, on which, as the saying went, "the sun never set," was the envy of its rivals and was viewed as the primary source of British global dominance during the second half of the nineteenth century.

The Tactics

With the change in European motives for colonization came a corresponding shift in tactics. Earlier, when their economic interests were more limited, European states had generally been satisfied to deal with existing independent countries rather than attempting to establish direct control over vast territories. There had been exceptions where state power at the local level was at the point of collapse (as in India), where European economic interests were especially intense (as in Latin America and the East Indies), or where there was no centralized authority (as in North America and the Philippines). But for the most part, the Western presence in Asia and Africa had been limited to controlling the regional trade network and establishing a few footholds where the foreigners could carry on trade and missionary activity.

After 1800, the demands of industrialization in Europe created a new set of dynamics. Maintaining access to industrial raw materials such as tin and rubber and setting up reliable markets for European manufactured products required more extensive control over colonial territories. As competition for colonies increased, the imperialist powers sought to solidify their hold over their territories to protect them from attack by their rivals. During the last two decades of the nineteenth century, the quest for colonies became a scramble as all the major European states, now joined by the United States and Japan, engaged in a global land grab. In many cases, economic interests were secondary to security concerns or the requirements of national prestige. In Africa, for example, the British engaged in a struggle with their rivals to protect their interests in the Suez Canal and the Red Sea. In Southeast Asia, the United States seized the Philippines from Spain at least partly to keep them out of the hands of the Japanese, and the French took over Indochina for fear that it would otherwise be occupied by Germany, Japan, or the United States.

By 1900, almost all the societies of Africa and Asia were either under full colonial rule or, as in the case of China and the Ottoman Empire, at a point of virtual collapse. Only a handful of states, such as Japan in East Asia, Thailand in Southeast Asia, Afghanistan and Persia in the Middle East, and mountainous Ethiopia in East Africa, managed to escape

COMPARATIVE ESSAY

Imperialisms Old and New

INTERACTION & EXCHANGE

The Random House Dictionary of the English Language defines *imperialism* as "the policy of extending the rule or authority of an empire or nation over foreign countries, or of acquiring and holding colonies and dependencies." The word derives from the Latin verb meaning "to command, or rule" and has been applied to certain types of political entities since the days of the Roman Empire.

At first, the term was used in situations described by the first part of the dictionary definition. An empire was larger than a kingdom and was composed of "an aggregate of nations and peoples," all ruled by an emperor who represented one dominant ethnic or religious group within the territory under his command. The lands under imperial rule were usually, but not always, contiguous. Good examples include the Roman Empire—whose sway extended well beyond the shores of the Italian peninsula—the Chinese Empire, the Mongolian Empire in Central Asia, the empires of Ghana and Mali in West Africa, and perhaps the Inkan Empire in South America.

More recently, the second part of the definition has come to the fore. As Western expansion into Asia and Africa gathered strength during the nineteenth century, it became fashionable to call that process "imperialism" as well. In this instance, the expansion was motivated by the efforts of capitalist states in the West to seize markets, cheap raw materials, and lucrative avenues for investment in the countries beyond Western civilization. Eventually, it resulted in the creation of colonies ruled by the imperialist power. In this interpretation, the primary motives behind imperial expansion were economic. The best-known promoter of this view was the British political economist John A. Hobson, who published a major analysis, *Imperialism: A Study*, in 1902. In this influential book, Hobson maintained that modern imperialism was a direct consequence of the modern industrial economy.

As historians began to analyze the phenomenon, however, many became convinced that the motivations of the imperial powers were not simply economic. As Hobson himself conceded, economic concerns were inevitably tinged with political overtones and questions of national grandeur and moral

purpose as well. To nineteenth-century Europeans, economic wealth, national status, and political power went hand in hand with the possession of a colonial empire. To global strategists, colonies brought tangible benefits in the world of balance-of-power politics as well as economic profits, and many nations pursued colonies as much to gain advantage over their rivals as to acquire territory for its own sake.

After World War II, when colonies throughout Asia and Africa were replaced by independent nations, a new term *neocolonialism* appeared to describe the situation in which imperialist nations cede a formal degree of political independence to their former colonies, but continue to exercise control by various political and economic means. Hence, in the view of many critics in the former colonial territories, Western imperialism has not disappeared but has simply found other ways to maintain its influence. We will discuss this issue further in Part V.

 What were the principal motives of the major trading nations for seizing colonies in Asia and Africa in the late nineteenth century?

© William J. Duiker

Gateway to India. Built in the Roman imperial style by the British to commemorate the visit to India of King George V and Queen Mary in 1911, the Gateway to India was erected at the water's edge in the harbor of Bombay (now Mumbai), India's greatest port city. For thousands of British citizens arriving in India, the Gateway to India was the first view of their new home and a symbol of the power and majesty of the British raj.

internal disintegration or subjection to colonial rule. For the most part, the exceptions were the result of good fortune rather than design. Thailand escaped subjugation primarily because officials in London and Paris found it more convenient to transform the country into a buffer state than to fight over it. Ethiopia and Afghanistan survived not only because

of their long tradition of fierce resistance to outside threats, but also because of their remote locations and mountainous terrain. Only Japan managed to avoid the common fate through a concerted strategy of political and economic reform. By the end of the nineteenth century, Japan itself had become engaged in the pursuit of colonies (see Chapter 22).

The Colonial System

FOCUS QUESTION: What types of administrative systems did the various colonial powers establish in their colonies, and how did these systems reflect the general philosophy of colonialism?

Once they had control of most of the world, what did the colonial powers do with it? As we have seen, their primary objective was to exploit the natural resources of the subject areas and to open up markets for manufactured goods and capital investment from the mother country. In some cases, that goal could be realized in cooperation with local political elites, whose loyalty could be earned, or purchased, by economic rewards or by confirming them in their positions of authority and status in a new colonial setting. Sometimes, however, this policy of **indirect rule** was not feasible because local leaders refused to cooperate with their colonial masters or even actively resisted the foreign conquest. In such cases, the local elites were removed from power and replaced with a new set of officials recruited from the mother country.

In general, the societies most likely to actively resist colonial conquest were those with a long tradition of national cohesion and independence, such as Burma and Vietnam in Asia and the African Muslim states in northern Nigeria and Morocco. In those areas, the colonial powers encountered higher levels of resistance and consequently tended to dispense with local collaborators and govern directly. In some parts of Africa, the Indian subcontinent, and the Malay peninsula, where the local authorities, for whatever reason, were willing to collaborate with the imperialist powers, indirect rule was more common.

The distinctions between **direct rule** and indirect rule were not merely academic and often had fateful consequences for the peoples involved. Where colonial powers encountered resistance and were forced to overthrow local political elites, they often adopted policies designed to eradicate the source of resistance and destroy the traditional culture. Such policies often had quite corrosive effects on the indigenous societies and provoked resentment and resistance that not only marked the colonial relationship but even affected relations after the restoration of national independence. The bitter struggles after World War II in Algeria, the Dutch East Indies, and Vietnam can be ascribed in part to that phenomenon.

The Philosophy of Colonialism

To justify their rule, the colonial powers appealed in part to the time-honored maxim of "might makes right." By the end of the nineteenth century, that attitude received pseudoscientific validation from the concept of social Darwinism, which maintained that only societies that moved aggressively to adapt to changing circumstances would survive and prosper in a world governed by the Darwinian law of "survival of the fittest."

Some people, however, were uncomfortable with such a brutal view of the law of nature and sought a moral justification that appeared to benefit the victim. Here again, social Darwinism pointed the way. By bringing the benefits of Western democracy, capitalism, and Christianity to the tradition-ridden societies of Africa and Asia, the colonial powers were enabling primitive peoples to adapt to the challenges of the modern world. Buttressed by such comforting theories, sensitive Western minds could ignore the brutal aspects of colonialism and persuade themselves that in the long run the results would be beneficial for both sides. Few were as adept at describing the "civilizing mission" of colonialism as the French administrator and twice governor-general of French Indochina Albert Sarraut (ahl-BAYR sah-ROH). While admitting that colonialism was originally an "act of force" undertaken for commercial profit, he insisted that by redistributing the wealth of the earth, the colonial process would result in a better life for all:

> Is it just, is it legitimate that such [an uneven distribution of resources] should be indefinitely prolonged? . . . No! . . . Humanity is distributed throughout the globe. No race, no people has

© Art Media, Victoria and Albert Museum, London/HIP/The Image Works

The Company Resident and His Puppet. The British of the East India Company gradually replaced the sovereigns of the once independent Indian states with puppet rulers who carried out the company's policies. Here we see the company's resident dominating a procession in Tanjore in 1825, while the Indian ruler, Sarabhoji, follows like an obedient shadow. As a boy, Sarabhoji had been educated by European tutors and had filled his life and home with English books and furnishings.

White Man's Burden, Black Man's Sorrow

ART & IDEAS

One of the justifications for modern imperialism was the notion that the allegedly "more advanced" white peoples had the moral responsibility to raise "ignorant" indigenous peoples to a higher level of civilization. Few captured this notion better than the British poet Rudyard Kipling (1865–1936) in his famous poem *The White Man's Burden*. His appeal, directed to the United States, became one of the most famous verses in the English-speaking world.

That sense of moral responsibility, however, was often misplaced or, even worse, laced with hypocrisy. All too often, the consequences of imperial rule were detrimental to everyone living under colonial authority. Few observers described the destructive effects of Western imperialism on the African people as well as Edmund Morel, a British journalist whose book *The Black Man's Burden* pointed out some of the more harmful aspects of colonialism in the Belgian Congo. The brutal treatment of Congolese workers involved in gathering rubber, ivory, and palm oil for export aroused an international outcry and in 1903 led to the formation of a commission under British consul Roger Casement to bring about reforms.

Rudyard Kipling, *The White Man's Burden*

Take up the White Man's burden—
Send forth the best ye breed—
Go bind your sons to exile
To serve your captives' need;
To wait in heavy harness,
On fluttered folk and wild—
Your new-caught sullen peoples,
Half-devil and half-child.

Take up the White Man's burden—
In patience to abide,
To veil the threat of terror
And check the show of pride;
By open speech and simple,
An hundred times made plain
To seek another's profit,
And work another's gain.

Take up the White Man's burden—
The savage wars of peace—
Fill full the mouth of Famine
And bid the sickness cease;
And when your goal is nearest
The end for others sought,
Watch Sloth and heathen Folly
Bring all your hopes to nought.

Edmund Morel, *The Black Man's Burden*

It is [the Africans] who carry the "Black man's burden." They have not withered away before the white man's occupation. Indeed . . . Africa has ultimately absorbed within itself every Caucasian and, for that matter, every Semitic invader, too. In hewing out for himself a fixed abode in Africa, the white man has massacred the African in heaps. The African has survived, and it is well for the white settlers that he has. . . .

What the partial occupation of his soil by the white man has failed to do; what the mapping out of European political "spheres of influence" has failed to do; what the Maxim and the rifle, the slave gang, labour in the bowels of the earth and the lash, have failed to do; what imported measles, smallpox and syphilis have failed to do; whatever the overseas slave trade failed to do; the power of modern capitalistic exploitation, assisted by modern engines of destruction, may yet succeed in accomplishing.

For from the evils of the latter, scientifically applied and enforced, there is no escape for the African. Its destructive effects are not spasmodic; they are permanent. In its permanence resides its fatal consequences. It kills not the body merely, but the soul. It breaks the spirit. It attacks the African at every turn, from every point of vantage. It wrecks his polity, uproots him from the land, invades his family life, destroys his natural pursuits and occupations, claims his whole time, enslaves him in his own home.

According to Kipling, why should Western nations take up the "white man's burden"? What was the "black man's burden," in the eyes of Edmund Morel?

---

the right or power to isolate itself egotistically from the movements and necessities of universal life.[4]

But what about the possibility that historically and culturally the societies of Asia and Africa were fundamentally different from those of the West and could not, or would not, be persuaded to transform themselves along Western lines? Was the human condition universal, or were human beings so shaped by their history and geographic environment that their civilizations would inevitably remain distinct? In that case, a policy of cultural transformation could not be expected to succeed and could even lead to disaster (see the box above).

ASSIMILATION AND ASSOCIATION   In fact, colonial theorists never decided this issue one way or the other. The French, who were most inclined to philosophize about the problem, adopted the terms **assimilation** (which implied an effort to transform colonial societies in the Western image) and **association** (implying collaboration with local elites while leaving local traditions alone) to describe the two alternatives

Indian in Blood, English in Taste and Intellect

INTERACTION & EXCHANGE

Thomas Babington Macaulay (1800–1859) was named a member of the Supreme Council of India in the early 1830s. In that capacity, he was responsible for drawing up a new educational policy for British subjects in the area. In his *Minute on Education*, he considered the claims of English and various local languages to become the vehicle for educational training and decided in favor of the former. It is better, he argued, to teach Indian elites about Western civilization so as "to form a class who may be interpreters between us and the millions whom we govern; a class of persons, Indian in blood and color, but English in taste, in opinions, in morals, and in intellect." Later Macaulay became a prominent historian. The debate in India over the relative benefits of English and the various Indian languages continues today.

Thomas Babington Macaulay, *Minute on Education*

We have a fund to be employed as government shall direct for the intellectual improvement of the people of this country. The simple question is, what is the most useful way of employing it?

All parties seem to be agreed on one point, that the dialects commonly spoken among the natives of this part of India contain neither literary or scientific information, and are, moreover, so poor and rude that, until they are enriched from some other quarter, it will not be easy to translate any valuable work into them. . . .

What, then, shall the language [of education] be? One half of the Committee maintain that it should be the English. The other half strongly recommend the Arabic and Sanskrit. The whole question seems to me to be, which language is the best worth knowing?

I have no knowledge of either Sanskrit or Arabic—but I have done what I could to form a correct estimate of their value. I have read translations of the most celebrated Arabic and Sanskrit works. I have conversed both here and at home with men distinguished by their proficiency in the Eastern tongues. I am quite ready to take the Oriental learning at the valuation of the Orientalists themselves. I have never found one among them who could deny that a single shelf of a good European library was worth the whole native literature of India and Arabia. . . .

It is, I believe, no exaggeration to say, that all the historical information which has been collected from all the books written in the Sanskrit language is less valuable than what may be found in the most paltry abridgments used at preparatory schools in England. In every branch of physical or moral philosophy the relative position of the two nations is nearly the same.

How did Macaulay justify the teaching of the English language in India? Do you find his arguments persuasive? How might a critic respond?

---

and then proceeded to vacillate between them. French policy in Indochina, for example, began as one of association but switched to assimilation under pressure from those who felt that colonial powers owed a debt to their subject peoples. But assimilation (which in any case was never accepted as feasible or desirable by many colonial officials) aroused resentment among the local population, many of whom opposed the destruction of their culture and traditions. In the end, the French abandoned the attempt to justify their presence and fell back on a policy of ruling by force of arms.

Other colonial powers had little interest in the issue. The British, whether out of a sense of pragmatism or of racial superiority, refused to entertain the possibility of assimilation and treated their subject peoples as culturally and racially distinct. In formulating a colonial policy for the Philippines, the United States adopted a policy of assimilation in theory but did not always put it into practice.

To many of the colonial peoples, such questions must have appeared academic, since in their eyes the primary objectives of all colonial officials were economic exploitation and the retention of power. Like the British soldier in Kipling's poem "On the Road to Mandalay," all too many Westerners living in the colonies believed that the Great Lord Buddha was nothing but a "bloomin' idol made of mud."

COLONIALISM IN ACTION In practice, colonialism in India, Southeast Asia, and Africa exhibited many similarities but also some differences. Some of these variations can be traced to political or social differences among the colonial powers themselves. The French, for example, often tried to impose a centralized administrative system on their colonies that mirrored the system in use in France, while the British sometimes attempted to transform local aristocrats into the equivalent of the landed gentry at home in Britain (see the box above). Other differences stemmed from conditions in the colonies themselves and the colonizers' aspirations for them. For instance, the Western powers believed that they could obtain only limited economic benefits from some areas and therefore treated those colonies somewhat differently than areas where they perceived that large profits could be made.

India Under the British Raj

FOCUS QUESTION: What were some of the major consequences of British rule in India, and how did they affect the Indian people?

By 1800, the once glorious empire of the Mughals (MOO-guls) had been reduced by British military power to a shadow of its former greatness. During the next few decades, the British sought to consolidate their control over the Indian subcontinent, expanding from their base areas along the coast into the interior. Some territories were taken over directly, first by the East India Company and later by the British crown; others were ruled indirectly through their local maharajas (mah-huh-RAH-juhs) and rajas (RAH-juhs).

Colonial Reforms

Not all of the effects of British rule were bad. British governance over the subcontinent brought order and stability to a society that had been rent by civil war. By the early nineteenth century, British control had been consolidated and led to a relatively honest and efficient government that in many respects operated to the benefit of the average Indian. One of the benefits of the period was the heightened attention given to education. Through the efforts of the British administrator Thomas Babington Macaulay (muh-KAHL-lee), a new school system was established to train the children of Indian elites, and the British civil service examination was introduced. The instruction of young girls also expanded, with the primary purpose of making them better wives and mothers for the educated male population. In 1875, a Madras (muh-DRAS *or* muh-DRAHS) medical college admitted an Indian woman for the first time.

British rule also brought an end to some of the more inhumane aspects of Indian tradition. The practice of *sati* (suh-TEE) was outlawed, and widows were legally permitted to remarry. The British also attempted to put an end to the endemic brigandage (known as *thuggee*, which gave rise to the English word *thug*) that had plagued travelers in India since time immemorial. Railroads, the telegraph, and the postal service were introduced to India shortly after they appeared in Great Britain itself. Work began on the main highway from Calcutta to Delhi (DEL-ee) in 1839 (see Map 21.1), and the first rail network was opened in 1853. A new penal code based on the British model was adopted, and health and sanitation conditions were improved.

The Cost of Colonialism

But the Indian people paid a high price for the peace and stability brought by the British **raj** (RAHJ) (from the Indian *raja,* or prince). Perhaps the most flagrant cost was economic. While British entrepreneurs and a small percentage of the Indian population attached to the imperial system reaped financial benefits from British rule, it brought hardship to millions of others in both the cities and the rural areas. The introduction of British textiles, for example, put thousands of Bengali women out of work and severely damaged the local textile industry.

In rural areas, the British introduced the *zamindar* (zuh-meen-DAHR) system (see Chapter 16) in the misguided expectation that it would both facilitate the collection of agricultural taxes and create a new landed gentry, who could, as in Britain, become the conservative foundation of imperial rule. But the local gentry took advantage of this new authority to increase taxes and force

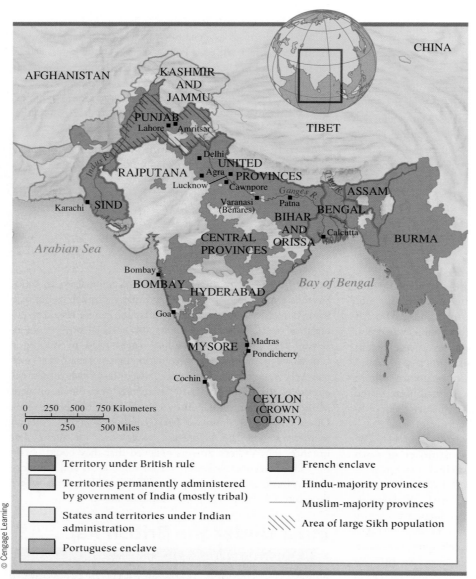

MAP 21.1 India Under British Rule, 1805–1931. This map shows the different forms of rule that the British applied in India during the period it was under their control.

Q Where were the major cities of the subcontinent located, and under whose rule did they fall?

COMPARATIVE ILLUSTRATION

INTERACTION & EXCHANGE

Cultural Influences—East and West. When Europeans moved into Asia in the nineteenth century, some Asians began to imitate European customs for prestige or social advancement. Seen at the left, for example, is a young Vietnamese during the 1920s dressed in Western sports clothes, learning to play tennis. Sometimes, however, the cultural influence went the other way. At the right, an English nabob, as European residents in India were often called, apes the manner of an Indian aristocrat, complete with harem and hookah, the Indian water pipe. The paintings on the wall, however, are in the European style.

 Compare and contrast the artistic styles in these two paintings. What message do they send to the viewer?

the less fortunate peasants to become tenants or lose their land entirely. When rural unrest threatened, the government passed legislation protecting farmers against eviction and unreasonable rent increases, but this measure had little effect outside the southern provinces, where it had originally been enacted. Similarly, British officials made few efforts during the nineteenth century to introduce democratic institutions or values to the Indian people. As one senior political figure remarked in Parliament in 1898, democratic institutions "can no more be carried to India by Englishmen . . . than they can carry ice in their luggage."[5]

British colonialism was also remiss in bringing the benefits of modern science and technology to India. Some limited forms of industrialization took place, notably in the manufacturing of textiles and jute (used in making rope). The first textile mill opened in 1856. Seventy years later, there were eighty mills in the city of Bombay alone. Nevertheless, the lack of local capital and the advantages given to British imports prevented the emergence of other vital new commercial and manufacturing operations.

Foreign rule also had a psychological effect on the Indian people. Although many British colonial officials sincerely tried to improve the lot of the people under their charge, British arrogance and contempt for local tradition cut deeply into the pride of many Indians, especially those of high caste, who were

accustomed to a position of superior status in India. Educated Indians trained in the Anglo-Indian school system for a career in the civil service, as well as Eurasians born to mixed marriages, often imitated the behavior and dress of their rulers, speaking English, eating Western food, and taking up European leisure activities, but many rightfully wondered where their true cultural loyalties lay (see the comparative illustration above). This cultural collision was poignantly described in the novel *A Passage to India* by the British writer E. M. Forster, which relates the story of a visiting Englishwoman who becomes interested in the Indian way of life, much to the dismay of the local European community.

Colonial Regimes in Southeast Asia

 FOCUS QUESTION: Which Western countries were most active in seeking colonial possessions in Southeast Asia, and what were their motives in doing so?

In 1800, only two societies in Southeast Asia were under effective colonial rule: the Spanish Philippines and the Dutch East Indies. During the nineteenth century, however, European interest in Southeast Asia increased rapidly, and by 1900, virtually the entire area had come under Western domination (see Map 21.2).

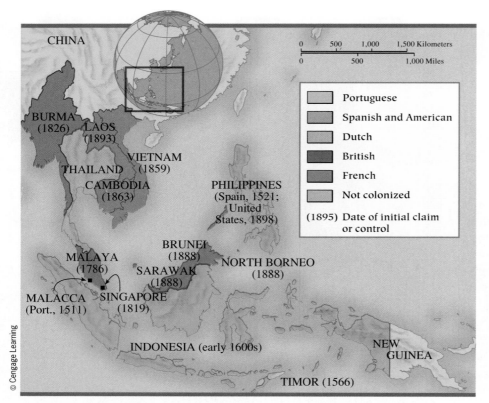

MAP 21.2 Colonial Southeast Asia. This map shows the spread of European colonial rule into Southeast Asia from the sixteenth century to the end of the nineteenth. Malacca, initially seized by the Portuguese in 1511, was taken by the Dutch in the seventeenth century and then by the British one hundred years later.

 What was the significance of Malacca?

"Opportunity in the Orient": The Colonial Takeover in Southeast Asia

The process began after the Napoleonic Wars, when the British, by agreement with the Dutch, abandoned their claims to territorial possessions in the East Indies in return for a free hand in the Malay peninsula. In 1819, the colonial administrator Stamford Raffles (1781–1826) founded a new British colony on the island of Singapore at the tip of the peninsula. When the invention of steam power enabled merchant ships to save time and distance by passing through the Strait of Malacca rather than sailing with the westerlies across the southern Indian Ocean, Singapore became a major stopping point for traffic en route to and from China and other commercial centers in the region.

During the next few decades, the pace of European penetration into Southeast Asia accelerated as the British attacked lower Burma in 1826 and eventually established control over the country, arousing fears in France that its British rival might soon establish a monopoly of trade in South China. The French still maintained a clandestine missionary organization in Vietnam despite harsh persecution by the local authorities, who viewed Christianity as a threat to Confucian doctrine. In 1857, the French government decided to compel the Vietnamese to accept French protection. A naval attack launched a year later was not a total success, but the French eventually forced the Nguyen (NGWEN) dynasty in Vietnam to cede territories in the Mekong River delta. A generation later, French rule was extended over the remainder of the country. By 1900, French seizure of neighboring Cambodia and Laos had led to the creation of the French-ruled Indochinese Union.

After the French conquest of Indochina, Thailand was the only remaining independent state on the Southeast Asian mainland. Under the astute leadership of two remarkable rulers, King Mongkut (MAHNG-koot) (1851–1868) and his son, King Chulalongkorn (CHOO-luh-lahng-korn) (1868–1910), the Thai attempted to introduce Western learning and maintain relations with the major European powers without undermining internal stability or inviting an imperialist attack. In 1896, the British and the French agreed to preserve Thailand as an independent buffer zone between their possessions in Southeast Asia.

The final piece in the colonial edifice in Southeast Asia was put in place in 1898, when U.S. naval forces under Commodore George Dewey defeated the Spanish fleet in Manila Bay. President William McKinley agonized over the fate of the Philippines but ultimately decided that the moral thing to do was to turn the islands into an American colony to prevent them from falling into the hands of the Japanese. In fact, the Americans (like the Spanish before them) found the islands convenient as a jumping-off point for the China trade (see Chapter 22). The mixture of moral idealism and the desire for profit was reflected in a speech given in the Senate in January 1900 by Senator Albert Beveridge of Indiana:

> Mr. President, the times call for candor. The Philippines are ours forever, "territory belonging to the United States," as the Constitution calls them. And just beyond the Philippines are China's illimitable markets. We will not retreat from either. . . . We will not renounce our part in the mission of our race, trustee, under God, of the civilization of the world. And we will move forward to our work, not howling out regrets like slaves whipped to their burdens, but with gratitude for a task worthy of our strength, and thanksgiving to Almighty God that He has marked us as His chosen people, henceforth to lead in the regeneration of the world.[6]

Not all Filipinos agreed with Senator Beveridge's portrayal of the situation. Under the leadership of Emilio Aguinaldo (ay-MEEL-yoh ah-gwee-NAHL-doh), guerrilla forces fought

Government Hill in Singapore. After occupying the island of Singapore early in the nineteenth century, the British turned what was once a pirate lair at the entrance to the Strait of Malacca into one of the most important commercial seaports in Asia. By the end of the century, Singapore was home to a rich mixture of peoples, both European and Asian. This painting by a British artist in the mid-nineteenth century graphically displays the multiracial character of the colony as strollers of various ethnic backgrounds share space on Government Hill, with the busy harbor in the background. Almost all colonial port cities became melting pots of people from various parts of the world. Many of the immigrants served as merchants, urban laborers, and craftsmen in the new imperial marketplace.

bitterly against U.S. troops to establish their independence from both Spain and the United States. But America's first war against guerrilla forces in Asia was a success, and the bulk of the resistance collapsed in 1901. President McKinley had his stepping-stone to the rich markets of China.

The Nature of Colonial Rule

In Southeast Asia, economic profit was the immediate and primary aim of colonial enterprise. For that purpose, imperial powers tried wherever possible to work with local elites to facilitate the exploitation of natural resources. Indirect rule reduced the cost of training European administrators and had a less corrosive impact on the local culture. In the Dutch East Indies, for example, officials of the Dutch East India Company (or VOC, the initials of its Dutch name) entrusted local administration to the indigenous landed aristocracy, who maintained law and order and collected taxes in return for a payment from the VOC (see the box on p. 618). The British followed a similar practice in Malaya. While establishing direct rule over the crucial commercial centers of Singapore and Malacca, the British allowed local Muslim rulers to maintain princely power in the interior of the peninsula.

ADMINISTRATION AND EDUCATION Indirect rule, however convenient and inexpensive, was not always feasible. In some instances, local resistance to the colonial conquest made such a policy impossible. In Burma, the staunch opposition of the

monarchy and other traditionalist forces caused the British to abolish the monarchy and administer the country directly through their colonial government in India. In Indochina, the French used both direct and indirect means. They imposed direct rule on the southern provinces in the Mekong delta. In the north, however, in the 1880s, they established a protectorate, with the emperor retaining titular authority from his palace in Hué (HWAY). During the same period, the French adopted a similar policy in Cambodia and Laos, where local rulers were left in charge with French advisers to counsel them.

Whatever method was used, colonial regimes in Southeast Asia, as elsewhere, were slow to create democratic institutions. The first legislative councils and assemblies were composed almost exclusively of European residents in the colony. The first representatives from the indigenous population were wealthy and conservative in their political views. When Southeast Asians complained, colonial officials gradually and reluctantly began to broaden the franchise. The French colonial official Albert Sarraut advised patience in awaiting the full benefits of colonial policy: "I will treat you like my younger brothers, but do not forget that I am the older brother. I will slowly give you the dignity of humanity."[7]

Colonial officials were also slow to adopt educational reforms. Although the introduction of Western education was one of the justifications of imperialism, colonial officials soon discovered that educating indigenous elites could backfire. Often there were few jobs for highly trained lawyers, engineers, and architects in colonial societies, leading to the

The Effects of Dutch Colonialism in Java

INTERACTION & EXCHANGE

Eduard Douwes Dekker (AY-dooart DOW-uss DEK-er) was a Dutch colonial official who served in the East Indies for nearly twenty years. In 1860, he published a critique of the Dutch colonial system that had an impact in the Netherlands similar to that of Harriet Beecher Stowe's *Uncle Tom's Cabin* in the United States. In the following excerpt from his book *Max Havelaar, or Coffee Auctions of the Dutch Trading Company*, Douwes Dekker described the system as it was applied on the island of Java, in the Indonesian archipelago.

Dutch administrative buildings in Batavia.

Eduard Douwes Dekker, *Max Havelaar*

The Javanese is by nature a husbandman; the ground whereon he is born, which gives much for little labor, allures him to it, and, above all things, he devotes his whole heart and soul to the cultivating of his rice fields, in which he is very clever. He grows up in the midst of his *sawahs* [rice fields] . . . ; when still very young, he accompanies his father to the field, where he helps him in his labor with plow and spade, in constructing dams and drains to irrigate his fields; he counts his years by harvests; he estimates time by the color of the blades in his field; he is at home amongst the companions who cut paddy with him; he chooses his wife amongst the girls of the *dessah* [village], who every evening tread the rice with joyous songs. The possession of a few buffaloes for plowing is the ideal of his dreams. The cultivation of rice is in Java what the vintage is in the Rhine provinces and in the south of France. But there came foreigners from the West, who made themselves masters of the country. They wished to profit by the fertility of the soil, and ordered the native to devote a part of his time and labor to the cultivation of other things which should produce higher profits in the markets of Europe. To persuade the lower orders to do so, they had only to follow a very simple policy. The Javanese obeys his chiefs; to win the chiefs, it

was only necessary to give them a part of the gain,—and success was complete.

To be convinced of the success of that policy we need only consider the immense quantity of Javanese products sold in Holland; and we shall also be convinced of its injustice, for, if anybody should ask if the husbandman himself gets a reward in proportion to that quantity, then I must give a negative answer. The Government compels him to cultivate certain products on his ground; it punishes him if he sells what he has produced to any purchaser but itself; and it fixes the price actually paid. The expenses of transport to Europe through a privileged trading company are high; the money paid to the chiefs for encouragement increases the prime cost; and because the entire trade must produce profit, that profit cannot be got in any other way than by paying the Javanese just enough to keep him from starving, which would lessen the producing power of the nation.

 According to Douwes Dekker, what was the impact of Dutch colonial policies on Javanese peasants? How might a colonial official respond to the criticism?

---

threat of an indigestible mass of unemployed intellectuals who would take out their frustrations on the colonial regime. Educational opportunities for the common people were even harder to come by. In French-controlled Vietnam in 1917, only 3,000 of the 23,000 villages in the country had a public school. The French had opened a university in Hanoi (ha-NOY), but it was immediately closed as a result of student demonstrations. As one French official noted in voicing his opposition to increasing the number of schools in Vietnam, educating the Vietnamese meant not "one coolie less, but one rebel more."

ECONOMIC DEVELOPMENT Colonial powers were equally reluctant to take up the "white man's burden" in the area of economic development. As we have seen, their primary goals were to secure a source of cheap raw materials and to maintain markets for manufactured goods. Such objectives would be undermined by the emergence of advanced industrial economies. So colonial policy concentrated on the export of raw materials—teakwood from Burma; rubber and tin from Malaya; spices, tea and coffee, and palm oil from the East Indies; and sugar and copra (coconut meat) from the Philippines.

The Royal Palace at Bangkok. Few societies in Asia have been as adept at absorbing Western influence without destroying their own institutions and customs as the Thai. In some cases, this talent has extended to the field of architecture. The illustration shown here depicts a late-nineteenth-century building on the grounds of the royal palace in Bangkok. Note how the architect has attempted to synthesize classical Western techniques with the rooftop design and Buddhist stupas characteristic of traditional religious buildings in Thailand.

In some Southeast Asian colonial societies, a measure of industrial development did take place to meet the needs of the European population and local elites. Major manufacturing cities such as Rangoon in lower Burma, Batavia (buh-TAY-vee-uh) on the island of Java, and Saigon (sy-GAHN) in French Indochina grew rapidly. Although the local middle class benefited from the increased economic activity, most large industrial and commercial establishments were owned and managed by Europeans or, in some cases, by Indian or Chinese merchants. In Saigon, for example, even the production of *nuoc mam* (NWAHK MAHM), the traditional Vietnamese fish sauce, was under Chinese ownership. In most cities, foreigners controlled banking, major manufacturing activities, and the import-export trade. The local residents were more apt to work in a family business, in factory or assembly plants, or as peddlers, day laborers, or rickshaw pullers—in other words, at less profitable and less capital-intensive businesses.

COLONIALISM AND THE COUNTRYSIDE Despite the growth of an urban economy, the vast majority of people in the colonial societies continued to farm the land. Many continued to live by subsistence agriculture, but the colonial policy of emphasizing cash crops for export also led to the creation of a form of plantation agriculture in which peasants were recruited to work as wage laborers on rubber and tea plantations owned by Europeans. To maintain a competitive edge, the plantation owners kept the wages of their workers at poverty level. Many plantation workers were "shanghaied" (the English term originated from the practice of recruiting

laborers, often from the docks and streets of Shanghai, by unscrupulous means such as the use of force, alcohol, or drugs) to work on plantations, where conditions were often so inhumane that thousands died. High taxes, enacted by colonial governments to pay for administrative costs or improvements in the local infrastructure, were an additional heavy burden for poor peasants.

The situation was made even more difficult by the steady growth of the population. Peasants in Asia had always had large families on the assumption that a high proportion of their children would die in infancy. But improved sanitation and medical treatment resulted in lower rates of infant mortality and a staggering increase in population. The population of the island of Java, for example, increased from about a million in the precolonial era to about 40 million at the end of the nineteenth century. Under these conditions, the rural areas could no longer support the growing populations, and many young people fled to the cities to seek jobs in factories or shops. The migratory pattern gave rise to squatter settlements in the suburbs of the major cities.

As in India, colonial rule did bring some benefits to Southeast Asia. It led to the beginnings of a modern economic infrastructure and to what is sometimes called a "modernizing elite" dedicated to the creation of an advanced industrialized society. The development of an export market helped create an entrepreneurial class in rural areas. This happened, for example, on the outer islands of the Dutch East Indies (such as Borneo and Sumatra), where small growers of rubber trees, palm trees for oil, coffee, tea, and spices began to share in the profits of the colonial enterprise.

A balanced assessment of the colonial legacy in Southeast Asia must take into account that the early stages of industrialization are difficult in any society. Even in western Europe, industrialization led to the creation of an impoverished and

CHRONOLOGY	Imperialism in Asia
Stamford Raffles arrives in Singapore	1819
British attack lower Burma	1826
British rail network opens in northern India	1853
Sepoy Rebellion	1857
French attack Vietnam	1858
British and French agree to neutralize Thailand	1896
Commodore Dewey defeats Spanish fleet in Manila Bay	1898
French create Indochinese Union	1900

The Production of Rubber. Natural rubber was one of the most important cash crops in the European colonies in Asia. Rubber trees, native to the Amazon River basin in Brazil, were eventually transplanted to Southeast Asia, where they became a major source of profit. Workers on the plantations received few benefits, however. Once the sap of the tree, called latex, was extracted, as shown on the left, it was hardened and pressed into sheets (right photo) and then sent to Europe for refining.

powerless proletariat, urban slums, and displaced peasants driven from the land. In much of Europe and Japan, however, the bulk of the population eventually enjoyed better material conditions as the profits from manufacturing and plantation agriculture were reinvested in the national economy and gave rise to increased consumer demand. In contrast, in Southeast Asia, most of the profits were repatriated to the colonial mother country, while displaced peasants fleeing to cities like Rangoon, Batavia, and Saigon found little opportunity for employment. Many were left with seasonal employment, with one foot on the farm and the other in the factory. The old world was being destroyed while the new one had yet to be born.

Empire Building in Africa

Q FOCUS QUESTION: What factors were behind the "scramble for Africa," and what impact did it have on the continent?

Up to the beginning of the nineteenth century, the relatively limited nature of European economic interests in Africa had provided little temptation for the penetration of the interior or the political takeover of the coastal areas. The slave trade, the main source of European profit during the eighteenth century, could be carried on by using African rulers and merchants as intermediaries. Disease, political instability, lack of transportation, and the generally unhealthy climate all deterred the Europeans from more extensive efforts in Africa. The situation began to change in the nineteenth century, as the growing need for industrial products, along with heightened competition from both European and African interests, created an incentive for imperialist countries to increase their economic presence in the continent.

The Growing European Presence in West Africa

As the new century dawned, the slave trade was in a state of decline. One reason was the growing sense of outrage among humanitarians in several European countries over the purchase, sale, and exploitation of human beings. Dutch merchants effectively ceased trafficking in slaves in 1795, and the Danes stopped in 1803. A few years later, in 1808 the slave trade was declared illegal in both Great Britain and the United States. The British began to apply pressure on other nations to follow suit, and most did so after the end of the Napoleonic Wars in 1815, leaving only Portugal and Spain as European practitioners of the trade south of the equator. In the meantime, the demand for slaves began to decline in the Western Hemisphere, and by the 1880s, slavery had been abolished in all major countries of the world. It continued to exist, although at a reduced rate, along the Swahili Coast of East Africa.

Economic as well as humanitarian interests contributed to the end of the slave trade. The cost of slaves had begun to rise after the middle of the eighteenth century, and the growth of the slave population reduced the need for additional labor on the plantations in the Americas. The British, with some reluctant assistance from France and the United States, added to the costs by actively using their navy to

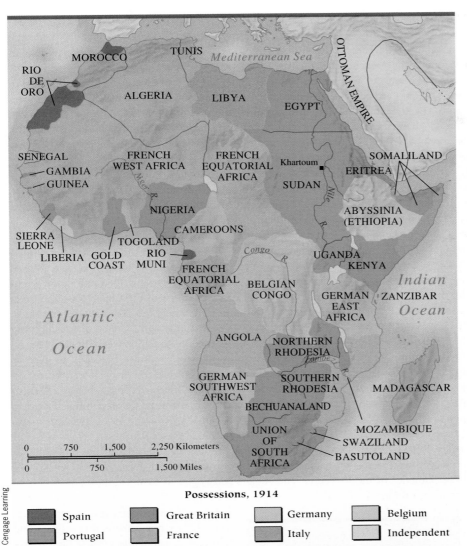

Possessions, 1914

Spain	Great Britain	Germany	Belgium
Portugal	France	Italy	Independent

© Cengage Learning

MAP 21.3 Africa in 1914. By the start of the twentieth century, virtually all of Africa was under some form of European rule. The territorial divisions established by colonial powers on the continent of Africa on the eve of World War I are shown here.

Q *Which European countries possessed the most colonies in Africa? Why did Ethiopia remain independent?*

capture slave ships and free the occupants. When slavery was abolished in the United States in 1863 and in Cuba and Brazil seventeen years later, the slave trade across the Atlantic was effectively brought to an end.

As the slave trade in the Atlantic declined during the first half of the nineteenth century, European interest in what was sometimes called "legitimate trade" in natural resources increased. Exports of peanuts, timber, hides, and palm oil from West Africa increased substantially during the first decades of the century, while imports of textile goods and other manufactured products rose.

Stimulated by growing commercial interests in the area, European governments began to push for a more permanent presence along the coast. During the first decades of the nineteenth century, the British established settlements along the Gold Coast and in Sierra Leone, where they set up agricultural plantations for freed slaves who had returned from the Western Hemisphere or had been liberated by British ships while en route to the Americas. A similar haven for ex-slaves was developed with the assistance of the United States in Liberia. The French occupied the area around the Senegal River near Cape Verde, where they attempted to develop peanut plantations (see Map 21.3).

The heightened European presence in West Africa led to the emergence of a new class of Africans educated in Western culture and often employed by Europeans. Many became Christians, and some studied in European or American universities. Eventually, a few became alarmed at the exploitation suffered by their fellow Africans and began to call for efforts to defend African interests, including the formation of nation-states on the Western model.

The growing numbers of Europeans also inevitably led to increasing tensions with African governments in the area. British efforts to increase trade with Ashanti (uh-SHAN-tee *or* uh-SHAHN-tee) led to conflict in the 1820s, but nevertheless British influence in the area intensified in later decades. Most African states, especially those with a fairly high degree of political integration, were able to maintain their independence from this creeping European encroachment, called "**informal empire**" by some historians, but the prospects for the future were ominous. When local groups attempted to organize to protect their interests, the British stepped in and annexed the coastal states as the British colony of Gold Coast in 1874. At about the same time, the British extended an informal protectorate over warring ethnic groups in the Niger delta.

Imperialist Shadow over the Nile

A similar process was under way in the Nile valley. There had long been interest in shortening the trade route to the East by digging a canal across the low, swampy isthmus separating the Mediterranean from the Red Sea. The Turks had considered constructing a canal from Cairo to Suez in the sixteenth century, as had the French king Louis XIV a century later, but the French did nothing about it until the end of the eighteenth century. At that time, Napoleon planned a military takeover of Egypt to cement French power in the eastern Mediterranean and open a faster route to India.

Napoleon's plan proved abortive. French troops landed in Egypt in 1798 and toppled the ramshackle Mamluk (MAM-look) regime in Cairo, but the British counterattacked, destroying the French fleet and eventually forcing the French to evacuate in disarray. The British restored the Mamluks to power, but in 1805, Muhammad Ali (1769–1849), an Ottoman army officer of Turkish or Albanian extraction, seized control.

During the next three decades, Muhammad Ali introduced a series of reforms to bring Egypt into the modern world. He modernized the army, set up a public educational system (supplementing the traditional religious education provided in Muslim schools), and sponsored the creation of a small industrial sector producing refined sugar, textiles, munitions, and even ships. Muhammad Ali also extended Egyptian authority southward into the Sudan and across the Sinai peninsula into Arabia, Syria, and northern Iraq and even briefly threatened to seize Istanbul itself. To prevent the possible collapse of the Ottoman Empire, the British and the French recognized Muhammad Ali as the hereditary **pasha** (PAH-shuh), later to be known as the khedive (kuh-DEEV), of Egypt under the loose authority of the Ottoman government.

The Suez Canal

The growing economic importance of the Nile valley, along with the development of steam navigation, made the heretofore visionary plans for a Suez canal more urgent. In 1854, the French entrepreneur Ferdinand de Lesseps (fer-DEE-nahn duh le-SEPS) signed a contract to begin construction of the canal, and it was completed in 1869. The project brought little immediate benefit to Egypt, however. The construction not only cost thousands of lives but also left the Egyptian government deep in debt, forcing it to depend increasingly on foreign financial support. When an army revolt against growing foreign influence broke out in 1881, the British stepped in to protect their investment (they had bought Egypt's canal company shares in 1875) and established an informal protectorate that would last until World War I.

Rising discontent in the Sudan added to Egypt's growing internal problems. In 1881, the Muslim cleric Muhammad Ahmad (AH-mahd) (1844–1885), known as the Mahdi (MAH-dee) (in Arabic, the "rightly guided one"), led a religious revolt that brought much of the upper Nile under his control. The famous British general Charles Gordon (1833–1885), who had earlier commanded Manchu armies fighting against the Taiping Rebellion in China (see Chapter 22), led a military force to Khartoum (kahr-TOOM) to restore Egyptian authority, but his besieged army was captured in 1885 by the Mahdi's troops, thirty-six hours before a British rescue mission reached Khartoum. Gordon himself died in the battle, which became one of the most dramatic news stories of the last quarter of the century.

The weakening of Turkish rule in the Nile valley had a parallel farther to the west, where local viceroys in Tripoli, Tunis, and Algiers had begun to establish their autonomy. In 1830, the French, on the pretext of protecting European shipping in the Mediterranean from pirates, seized the area surrounding Algiers and integrated it into the French Empire. By the mid-1850s, more than 150,000 Europeans had settled in the fertile region adjacent to the coast. In 1881, the French imposed a protectorate on neighboring Tunisia. Only Tripoli and Cyrenaica (seer-uh-NAY-uh-kuh), the Ottoman provinces that comprise modern Libya, remained under Turkish rule until the Italians seized them in 1911–1912.

Arab Merchants and European Missionaries in East Africa

As always, events in East Africa followed their own distinctive pattern of development. Although the Atlantic slave trade was declining, demand for slaves was increasing on the other side of the continent due to the growth of plantation agriculture in the region and on the islands off the coast. The French introduced sugar to the island of Réunion (ray-yoo-NYAHN)

The Opening of the Suez Canal. The Suez Canal, which connected the Mediterranean and Red Seas, was constructed under the direction of the French promoter Ferdinand de Lesseps. Still in use today, the canal is Egypt's greatest revenue producer. This sketch shows the ceremonial passage of the first ships through the canal in 1869. Note the combination of sail and steam power, reflecting the transition to coal-powered ships in the mid-nineteenth century.

FILM & HISTORY

Khartoum (1966)

The mission of General Charles "Chinese" Gordon to Khartoum in 1884 was one of the most dramatic news stories of the last quarter of the nineteenth century. Gordon was already renowned in his native Great Britain for his successful efforts to bring an end to the practice of slavery in North Africa. He had also attracted attention—and acquired the nickname "Chinese"—for helping the Manchu Empire suppress the Taiping Rebellion in China in the 1860s (see Chapter 22). But the Khartoum affair not only marked the culmination of his storied career but also symbolized in broader terms the epic struggle in Britain between advocates and opponents of imperial expansion. The battle for Khartoum thus became an object lesson in modern British history.

Proponents of British imperial expansion argued that the country must project its power in the Nile River valley to protect the Suez Canal as its main trade route to the East. Critics argued that imperial overreach would inevitably entangle the country in unwinnable wars in far-off places. The movie *Khartoum* (1966), filmed in Egypt and London, dramatically captures the ferocity of the battle for the Nile as well as its significance for the future of the British Empire. General Gordon, stoically played by the American actor Charlton Heston, is a devout Christian who has devoted his life to carrying out the moral imperative of imperialism in the continent of Africa. When peace in the Sudan (then a British protectorate in the upper Nile River valley) is threatened by the forces of radical Islam led by the Muslim mystic Muhammad Ahmad—known as the Mahdi—Gordon leads a mission to Khartoum under orders to prevent catastrophe there. But Prime Minister William Ewart Gladstone, admirably portrayed by the consummate British actor Ralph Richardson, fears that Gordon's messianic desire to save the Sudan will entrap his government

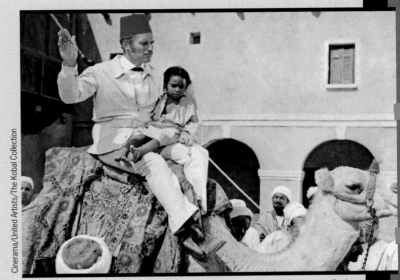

General Charles Gordon (Charlton Heston) astride his camel in Khartoum, Sudan.

Cinerama/United Artists/The Kobal Collection

in an unwinnable war; he thus orders Gordon to lead an evacuation of the city. The most fascinating character in the film is the Mahdi himself (played brilliantly by Sir Laurence Olivier), who firmly believes that he has a sacred mandate to carry the Prophet's words to the global Muslim community.

The conclusion of the film, set in the breathtaking beauty of the Nile River valley, takes place as the clash of wills reaches a climax in the battle for Khartoum. Although the film's portrayal of a face-to-face meeting between Gordon and the Mahdi is not based on fact, the narrative serves as an object lesson on the dangers of imperial overreach and as an eerie foretaste of the clash between Islam and Christendom in our own day.

---

early in the century, and plantations of cloves (introduced from the Moluccas in the eighteenth century) were established under Omani Arab ownership on the island of Zanzibar (ZAN-zi-bar). Zanzibar itself became the major shipping port along the entire east coast during the early nineteenth century, and the sultan of Oman (oh-MAHN), who had reasserted Arab suzerainty over the region in the aftermath of the collapse of Portuguese authority, established his capital at Zanzibar in 1840.

From Zanzibar, Arab merchants fanned out into the interior plateaus in search of slaves, ivory (known as "white gold"), and other local products. The competition for slaves spread as far as Lake Victoria and the lower Sudan as traders from the north launched their own raids to obtain conscripts for the Egyptian army. The khedive sent General Charles Gordon to Uganda to stop the practice, but in the absence of

alternative sources of income, local merchants could not easily be persuaded to give up a lucrative occupation.

The tenacity of the slave trade in East Africa—Zanzibar had now become the largest slave market in Africa—was undoubtedly a major reason for the rise of Western interest and Christian missionary activity in the region during the middle of the century. The most renowned missionary was the Scottish doctor David Livingstone (LIV-ing-stuhn) (1813–1873), who arrived in Africa in 1841. Because Livingstone spent much of his time exploring the interior of the continent, discovering Victoria Falls in the process, he was occasionally criticized for being more explorer than missionary. But Livingstone was convinced that it was his divinely appointed task to bring Christianity to the far reaches of the continent, and his passionate opposition to slavery did far more to win public support for the abolitionist cause than the efforts of any other figure of his generation. Public outcries provoked the British to redouble their attempts to bring the slave trade in East Africa to an end, and in 1873, the slave market at Zanzibar was finally closed as the result of pressure from London. Shortly before, Livingstone had died of illness in Central Africa, but some of his followers brought his body to the coast for burial. His legacy is still visible today in the form of an Anglican cathedral that was erected on the site of the slave market at Zanzibar.

Bantus, Boers, and British in the South

Nowhere in Africa did the European presence grow more rapidly than in the south. During the eighteenth century, the Boers (BOORS *or* BORS), Afrikaans-speaking farmers descended from the original Dutch settlers of the Cape Colony, began to migrate eastward. After the British seized control of the cape from the Dutch during the Napoleonic Wars, the Boers' eastward migration intensified, culminating in the Great Trek of the mid-1830s. In part, the Boers' departure was provoked by the different attitude of the British to the

indigenous population. Slavery was abolished in the British Empire in 1834, and the British government was generally more sympathetic to the rights of the local African population than were the Afrikaners (ah-fri-KAH-nurz), many of whom believed that white superiority was ordained by God and fled from British rule to control their own destiny. Eventually, the Boers formed their own independent republics—the Orange Free State and the South African Republic, usually called the Transvaal (trans-VAHL) (see Map 21.4).

Although the Boer occupation of the eastern territory was initially facilitated by internecine warfare among the local inhabitants of the region, the new settlers met some resistance. In the early nineteenth century, the Zulus (ZOO-looz), a Bantu people led by a talented ruler named Shaka (SHAH-kuh), engaged in a series of wars with the Europeans that ended only when Shaka was overthrown. The local Khoisan (KOI-sahn) people also sometimes reacted with violence when the Boers attempted to drive them off their grazing lands. One Dutch official complained that the Khoisan were driving settlers from their farms "for no other reason than because they saw that we were breaking up the best land and grass, where their cattle were accustomed to graze."[8] Ultimately, most of the black Africans in the Boer republics began to be resettled in reservation-like homelands created by the white government.

The Scramble for Africa

At the beginning of the 1880s, most of Africa was still independent. European rule was limited to the fringes of the continent, such as Algeria, the Gold Coast, and South Africa. Other areas like Egypt, lower Nigeria, Senegal (sen-ni-GAHL), and Mozambique (moh-zam-BEEK) were under various forms of loose protectorate. But the pace of European penetration was accelerating, and the constraints that had limited European rapaciousness were fast disappearing.

The scramble began in the mid-1880s when several European states, including Belgium, France, Germany, Great Britain, and Portugal, engaged in a feeding frenzy to seize a piece of the African cake before the plate had been picked clean. By 1900, virtually all of the continent had been placed under some form of European rule. The British had consolidated their authority over the Nile valley and seized additional territories in East Africa (see Map 21.3 on p. 621). The French retaliated by advancing eastward from Senegal into the central Sahara. They also occupied the island of Madagascar and other territories in West and Central Africa. In between, the Germans claimed the hinterland opposite Zanzibar, as well as coastal strips in West and Southwest Africa north of the cape, and King Leopold (LAY-oh-polt) II (1835–1909) of Belgium claimed the Congo for his own personal use. Eventually, Italy entered the contest and seized the territories that comprise modern Libya in 1911–1912; earlier it had claimed some of the Somali coast. In the mid-1890s, Italian forces had sought to extend

MAP 21.4 **The Struggle for Southern Africa.** European settlers from the Cape Colony expanded into adjacent areas of southern Africa in the nineteenth century. The arrows indicate the routes taken by Afrikaans-speaking Boers.

Q *Who were the Boers, and why did they migrate eastward?*

The Sunday Battle. When Boer "trekkers" seeking to escape British rule arrived in the Transvaal in the 1830s and 1840s, they were bitterly opposed by the Zulus, a Bantu-speaking people who resisted European encroachments on their territory for decades. In the battle shown in this 1847 lithograph, thousands of Zulu warriors engaged in a battle with their European rivals. Zulu resistance was not finally quelled until the end of the nineteenth century.

their control from the coast of the Red Sea into the mountainous highlands of Ethiopia, but were soundly defeated by the well-trained army of Emperor Menelik (MEN-il-ik), who had prudently purchased modern weapons from European sources. It was one of the more notable setbacks for European arms on the African continent.

What had happened to spark the sudden imperialist hysteria that brought an end to African independence? Although the level of trade between Europe and Africa had increased substantially during the latter part of the nineteenth century, it was probably not sufficient, by itself, to justify the risks and expense of conquest. More important than economic interests were the intensified rivalries among the European states that led them to engage in imperialist takeovers out of fear that if they did not, another state might do so, leaving them at a disadvantage. As one British diplomat remarked, a protectorate at the mouth of the Niger River would be an "unwelcome burden," but a French protectorate there would be "fatal." As occurred in Southeast Asia, as described earlier, statesmen felt compelled to obtain colonies as a hedge against future actions by rivals. In the most famous example, the British solidified their control over the entire Nile valley to protect the Suez Canal from seizure by the French.

Another consideration might be called the "missionary factor," as European missionary interests lobbied with their governments for colonial takeovers to facilitate their efforts to convert the African population to Christianity. The concept of social Darwinism and the "white man's burden" persuaded many that it was in the interests of the African people, as well as their conquerors, to be introduced more rapidly to the

benefits of Western civilization (see the box on p. 612). Even David Livingstone had become convinced that missionary work and economic development had to go hand in hand, pleading to his fellow Europeans to introduce the "three C's" (Christianity, commerce, and civilization) to the continent. How much easier such a task would be if African peoples were under benevolent European rule!

There were more prosaic reasons as well. Advances in Western technology and European superiority in firearms made it easier than ever for a small European force to defeat superior numbers. Furthermore, life expectancy for Europeans living in Africa had improved. With the discovery that quinine (extracted from the bark of the cinchona tree) could provide partial immunity from the ravages of malaria, the mortality rate for Europeans living in Africa dropped dramatically in the 1840s. By the end of the century, European residents in tropical Africa faced only slightly higher risks of death by disease than individuals living in Europe.

Under these circumstances, King Leopold of Belgium used missionary activities as an excuse to claim vast territories in the Congo River basin—Belgium, he said, as "a small country, with a small people," needed a colony to enhance its image.[9] The royal land grab set off a desperate race among European nations to stake claims throughout sub-Saharan Africa. Leopold ended up with the territories south of the Congo River, while France occupied areas to the north. Rapacious European adventurers established plantations in the new Belgian Congo to grow rubber, palm oil, and other valuable export products. Conditions for African workers on the

Dutch abolish slave trade in Africa	1795
Napoleon invades Egypt	1798
Slave trade declared illegal in Great Britain	1808
French seize Algeria	1830
Boers' Great Trek in southern Africa	1830s
Sultan of Oman establishes capital at Zanzibar	1840
David Livingstone arrives in Africa	1841
Slavery abolished in the United States	1863
Suez Canal completed	1869
Zanzibar slave market closed	1873
British establish Gold Coast colony	1874
British establish informal protectorate over Egypt	1881
Berlin Conference on Africa	1884
Charles Gordon killed at Khartoum	1885
Confrontation at Fashoda	1898
Boer War	1899–1902
Casement Commission report on Belgian Congo	1904
Union of South Africa established	1910

© Father Browne/Universal Images Group/Getty Images

Legacy of Shame. By the mid-nineteenth century, most European nations had prohibited the trade in African slaves, but slavery continued to exist in Africa well into the next century. The most flagrant example was in the Belgian Congo, where the mistreatment of conscript laborers led to a popular outcry and the formation of a commission to look into the situation and recommend reforms. Shown here are two manacled members of a chain gang in the Belgian Congo. The photograph was taken in 1904.

plantations were so abysmal that an international outcry eventually led to the formation of a commission under British consul Roger Casement to investigate. The commission's report, issued in 1904, helped to bring about reforms.

Meanwhile, on the eastern side of the continent, Germany (through the activities of an ambitious missionary and with the agreement of the British, who needed German support against the French) annexed the colony of Tanganyika (tan-gan-YEE-kuh). To avert the possibility of violent clashes among the great powers, the German chancellor, Otto von Bismarck, convened a conference in Berlin in 1884 to set ground rules for future annexations of African territory by European nations. The conference combined high-minded resolutions with a hardheaded recognition of practical interests. The delegates called for free commerce in the Congo—where Leopold's efforts to squeeze out foreign competition had provoked widespread opposition—and along the Niger River as well as for further efforts to end the slave trade. At the same time, the participants recognized the inevitability of the imperialist dynamic, agreeing only that future annexations of African territory should not be given international recognition until effective occupation had been demonstrated. No African delegates were present.

The Berlin Conference had been convened to avert war and reduce tensions among European nations competing for the spoils of Africa. It proved reasonably successful at achieving the first objective but less so at the second. During the next few years, African territories were annexed without provoking a major confrontation between the Western powers, but in the late 1890s, Britain and France reached the brink of conflict at Fashoda (fuh-SHOH-duh), a small town on the Nile River in the Sudan. The French had been advancing eastward across the Sahara with the transparent objective of controlling the regions around the upper Nile. In 1898, British

and Egyptian troops seized the Sudan from successors of the Mahdi and then marched southward to head off the French. After a tense face-off at Fashoda, the French government backed down, and British authority over the area was secured. Except for the Mediterranean littoral and their small possessions of Djibouti (juh-BOO-tee) and a portion of the Somali coast, the French were restricted to equatorial Africa.

Ironically, the only major clash between Europeans over Africa took place in southern Africa, where competition among the European imperialist powers was almost nonexistent. The discovery of gold and diamonds in the Boer republic of the Transvaal was the source of the problem. Clashes between the Afrikaner population and foreign (mainly British) miners and developers led to an attempt by Cecil Rhodes, prime minister of the Cape Colony and a prominent entrepreneur in the area, to subvert the government in Transvaal and bring the republic under British rule. In 1899, the so-called Boer War broke out between Britain and the Transvaal, which was backed by its fellow republic, the Orange Free State. Guerrilla resistance by the Boers was fierce, but the vastly superior forces of the British were able to prevail by

© Snark/Art Resource, NY

The Scramble for Africa. The rivalry among Western powers for territory in Africa at the end of the nineteenth century inspired much controversy in Europe between supporters and opponents of the imperialist enterprise. In this cartoon, published in the contemporary French journal *L'Assiette au Beurre* (*The Butter Plate*), the anonymous artist lampoons the struggle between the British and the French, resulting here in a torn map of Africa. Significantly, the cartoon does not take a position on the issue but implies that the results will not be beneficial for either side.

1902. To compensate the defeated Afrikaner population for the loss of independence, the British government agreed that only whites would vote in the now essentially self-governing colony. The Boers were placated, but the brutalities committed during the war (the British introduced an institution later to be known as the concentration camp) created bitterness on both sides that continued to fester through future decades.

Colonialism in Africa

As we have seen, European economic interests were initially somewhat more limited in Africa than elsewhere. Having seized the continent in what could almost be described as a fit of hysteria, the European powers had to decide what to do with it. With economic concerns relatively limited except for isolated areas like the gold mines in the Transvaal and copper deposits in the Belgian Congo, interest in Africa declined, and most European governments turned their attention to suppressing continued local resistance and then to governing their new territories with the least effort and expense possible. In many cases, this meant a form of indirect rule similar to what the British used in the princely states in India. The British, with their tradition of decentralized government at home, were especially prone to adopt this approach.

INDIRECT RULE In the minds of British administrators, the stated goal of indirect rule was to preserve African political traditions. The desire to limit cost and inconvenience was one reason for this approach, but it may also have been due to the conviction that Africans were inherently inferior to the white race and thus incapable of adopting European customs and institutions. In any event, indirect rule entailed relying to the greatest extent possible on existing political elites and institutions. Initially, in some areas the British simply asked a local ruler to formally accept British authority and to fly the Union Jack over official buildings.

Nigeria offers a typical example of British indirect rule. British officials maintained the central administration, but local authority was assigned to Nigerian chiefs, with British district officers serving as intermediaries with the central administration. Where an aristocracy did not exist, the British assigned administrative responsibility to clan heads from communities in the vicinity. The local authorities were expected to maintain law and order and to collect taxes from the indigenous population. As a general rule, local customs were left undisturbed, although the institution of slavery was abolished (see the box on p. 628). A dual legal system was instituted that applied African laws to Africans and European laws to foreigners.

One advantage of such an administrative system was that it did not severely disrupt local customs and institutions. Nevertheless, it had several undesirable consequences. In the first place, it was essentially a fraud, since all major decisions were made by the British administrators while the African authorities served primarily as a mechanism for enforcing those decisions. Among some peoples, indirect rule served to perpetuate the autocratic system in use prior to colonial takeover. It was official policy to inculcate respect for authority in areas under British rule, and colonial administrators had a natural tendency to view the local aristocracy as the African equivalent of the British ruling class. Such a policy provided few opportunities for ambitious and talented young Africans from outside the traditional elite and thus sowed the seeds for generational and class tensions after the restoration of independence in the twentieth century.

THE BRITISH IN EAST AFRICA The situation was somewhat different in East Africa, especially in Kenya, which had a relatively large European population attracted by the temperate climate in the central highlands. The local government had encouraged white settlers to migrate to the area as a means of promoting economic development and encouraging financial self-sufficiency. To attract Europeans, fertile farmlands in the central highlands were reserved for European settlement, while, as in South Africa, specified reserve lands were set aside for Africans. The presence of a substantial European minority (although in fact they represented only about 1 percent of the entire population) had an impact on Kenya's political development. The white settlers actively sought self-government and dominion status similar to that granted to such former British possessions as Canada and Australia. The British government, however,

The British in Hausaland: A Memoir

FAMILY & SOCIETY

Most Africans living outside the port cities had little idea of what to expect from the arrival of the white man and the new colonial authority. Thanks to these memoirs, recounted a half-century later by Baba, an African woman from northern Nigeria, we are offered an intimate glimpse into the arrival of the British at the end of the nineteenth century. As this excerpt makes clear, reaction to the arrival of European rule varied depending on conditions in the affected area. In northern Nigeria, local Hausa (HOW-suh) trading people still harbored considerable resentment toward the Fulani (FOO-lah-nee), a predominantly pastoral people who had seized the area centuries earlier.

It is also interesting to note that slavery among Africans was still a long-established tradition in the area. In a later passage, Baba remarks that her family lost income from the flight of its slaves, but the loss was offset by a reduction in taxes that African farmers had traditionally been compelled to pay to fill the pockets of local officials and chiefs.

Baba, a Hausa Woman of Nigeria

When I was a maiden the Europeans first arrived. Ever since we were quite small the *malams* [Muslim scholars] had been saying that the Europeans would come with a thing called a train, they would come with a thing called a motor-car. . . . They would stop wars, they would repair the world, they would stop oppression and lawlessness, we should live at peace with them. We used to go and sit quietly and listen to the prophecies. . . .

I remember when a European came to Karo on a horse, and some of his foot soldiers went into the town. Everyone came out to look at them. . . . Everyone at Karo ran away— "There's a European, there's a European!" . . .

At that time Yusufu was the [Fulani] king of Kano. He did not like the Europeans, he did not wish them, he would not sign their treaty. Then he saw that perforce he would have to agree, so he did. We Habe wanted them to come, it was the Fulani who did not like it. When the Europeans came the Habe saw that if you worked for them they paid you for it, they didn't say, like the Fulani, "Commoner, give me this! Commoner, bring me that!" Yes, the Habe wanted them. . . .

The Europeans said that there were to be no more slaves; if someone said "Slave!" you could complain to the *alkali* [judge] who would punish the master who said it, the judge said, "That is what the Europeans have decreed." . . . When slavery was stopped, nothing much happened at our *rinji* [the farm where their slaves lived] except that some slaves whom we had bought in the market ran away. Our own father went to his farm and worked, he and his son took up their large hoes. . . . They farmed guinea-corn and millet and groundnuts and everything; before this they had supervised the slaves' work—now they did their own. When the midday food was ready, the women of the compound would give us children the food, one of us drew water, and off we went to the farm to take the men their food at the foot of a tree.

Why did the Fulani and the Habe peoples respond in different ways to the arrival of the Europeans? How did the Europeans affect the institution of slavery in the area?

---

was not willing to run the risk of provoking racial tensions with the African majority and agreed only to establish separate government organs for the European and African populations.

BRITISH RULE IN SOUTH AFRICA The British used a different system in southern Africa, where there was a high percentage of European settlers. The situation was further complicated by the division between English-speaking and Afrikaner elements within the European population. In 1910, the British agreed to the creation of the independent Union of South Africa, which combined the old Cape Colony and Natal (nuh-TAHL) with the Boer republics. The new union adopted a representative government, but only for the European population, while the African reserves of Basutoland (buh-SOO-toh-land), now Lesotho (luh-SOH-toh); Bechuanaland (bech-WAH-nuh-land), now Botswana (baht-SWAH-nuh); and Swaziland (SWAH-zee-land) were subordinated directly to the crown. The union was now free to manage its own domestic affairs and possessed considerable autonomy in foreign relations. Formal British rule was also extended to the remaining lands south of the Zambezi River, which were eventually divided into the territories of Northern and Southern Rhodesia. Southern Rhodesia attracted many British immigrants, and in 1922, after a popular referendum, it became a crown colony.

DIRECT RULE, FRENCH STYLE Most other European nations governed their African possessions through a form of direct rule. The prototype was the French system, which reflected the centralized administrative system introduced in France itself by Napoleon. As in the British colonies, at the top of the pyramid was a French official, usually known as the governor-general, who was appointed from Paris and governed with the aid of a bureaucracy in the capital city. At the provincial level, French commissioners were assigned to deal with

Serving the White Ruler. Although European governments claimed to be carrying out a civilizing mission in Africa, all too often the local population was forced to labor in degrading conditions to serve the economic interests of the occupying power. Here, African workers carry British officers across a mangrove swamp in Central Africa. Two porters in the rear bring the liquor.

local administrators, but the latter were required to be conversant in French and could be transferred to a new position at the needs of the central government.

Moreover, the French ideal was to assimilate their African subjects into French culture rather than preserving their local traditions. Africans were eligible to run for office and to serve in the French National Assembly, and a few were appointed to high positions in the colonial administration. Such policies reflected the relative lack of color consciousness in French society, as well as the conviction among the French of the superiority of Gallic culture and their revolutionary belief in the universality of human nature.

HIGH COLONIALISM After World War I, European colonial policy in Africa entered a new and more formal phase that specialists in African studies call "**high colonialism**." The colonial administrative network was extended to a greater degree into outlying areas, where it was represented by a district official and defended by a small African army under European command. Greater attention was given to improving social services, including education, medicine and sanitation, and communications. The colonial system was now viewed more formally as a moral and social responsibility, a "sacred trust" to be maintained by the "civilized" countries until the Africans became capable of self-government. More emphasis was placed on economic development and on the exploitation of natural resources to provide the colonies with the means of achieving self-sufficiency. More Africans were now serving in colonial administrations, although relatively few were placed in positions of responsibility.

At the same time, race consciousness probably increased during this period. Segregated clubs, schools, and churches were established as more European officials brought their wives and began to raise families in the colonies. European feelings of superiority to their African subjects led to countless examples of cruelty similar to Western practices in Asia. While the institution of slavery was discouraged, African workers were often subjected to unbelievably harsh conditions as they were put to use in promoting the cause of imperialism.

WOMEN IN COLONIAL AFRICA The establishment of colonial rule had a mixed impact on the rights and status of women in Africa. Sexual relationships changed profoundly during the colonial era, sometimes in ways that could justly be described as beneficial. Colonial governments attempted to bring an end to forced marriage, bodily mutilation such as clitoridectomy (clit-er-ih-DEK-toh-mee), and polygamy. Missionaries introduced women to Western education and encouraged them to organize themselves to defend their interests.

But the colonial system had some unfavorable consequences as well. African women had traditionally benefited from the prestige of matrilineal systems and were empowered by their traditional role as the primary agricultural producers in their community. Under colonialism, the widespread conscription of males for forced labor on plantations and building projects left many woman behind to fend for their families on their own. Moreover, European settlers not only took the best land for themselves but also, in introducing new agricultural techniques, tended to deal exclusively with males, encouraging them to develop lucrative cash crops, while women were restricted to traditional farming methods. Whereas African men applied chemical fertilizer to the fields, women used manure. While men began to use bicycles, and eventually trucks, to transport goods, women still carried their goods on their heads, a practice that continues today. In British colonies, Victorian attitudes of female subordination led to restrictions on women's freedom, and positions in government that they had formerly held were now closed to them.

The Emergence of Anticolonialism

 FOCUS QUESTION: How did the subject peoples respond to colonialism, and what role did nationalism play in their response?

Thus far we have looked at the colonial experience primarily from the point of view of the European colonial powers. Equally important is the way the subject peoples reacted to the experience. In this chapter, we will deal with the initial response, which can be described in most cases by the general term "traditional resistance." Later, however, many in the colonized societies began to turn to the concept of nationalism as a means of preserving their ethnic, cultural, or religious identity. We will deal with that stage in more detail in Chapter 24.

Stirrings of Nationhood

As noted earlier, nationalism refers to a state of mind rising out of an awareness of being part of a community that possesses common institutions, traditions, language, and customs (see the comparative essay "The Rise of Nationalism" in Chapter 20). In the nineteenth century, few societies around the world met such criteria. Even today, most modern states contain a variety of ethnic, religious, and linguistic communities, each with its own sense of cultural and national identity. To cite one example, should Canada, which includes peoples of French, English, and Native American heritage, be considered a nation? Another question is how nationalism differs from other forms of tribal, religious, or linguistic affiliation. Should every group that resists assimilation into a larger political entity be called nationalist?

Such questions complicate the study of nationalism even in Europe and North America and make agreement on a definition elusive. They create even greater dilemmas in discussing Asia and Africa, where most societies are deeply divided by ethnic, linguistic, and religious differences and the very term *nationalism* is a foreign concept imported from the West. Prior to the colonial era, most traditional societies in Africa and Asia were formed on the basis of religious beliefs, ethnic loyalties, or devotion to hereditary monarchies. Although individuals in some countries may have identified themselves as members of a particular national group, others viewed themselves as subjects of a king, members of a lineage group, or adherents to a particular religion.

The advent of European colonialism brought the consciousness of modern nationhood to many of the societies of Asia and Africa. The creation of European colonies with defined borders and a powerful central government led to the weakening of local ethnic and religious loyalties and a significant reorientation in the individual's sense of political identity. The introduction of Western ideas of citizenship and representative government—even though they usually were not replicated in the colonial territories themselves—produced a heightened desire for participation in the affairs of government. At the same time, the appearance of a new elite class based not on hereditary privilege or religious sanction

but on alleged racial or cultural superiority aroused a shared sense of resentment among the subject peoples, who felt a common commitment to the creation of an independent society ruled by their own kind. By the first quarter of the twentieth century, political movements dedicated to the overthrow of colonial rule and the creation of modern nations had arisen throughout much of the non-Western world.

Modern nationalism, then, was a product of colonialism and, in a sense, a reaction to it. But a sense of nationhood does not emerge full-blown in a society. The rise of modern nationalism is a process that begins among a few members of the educated elite (most commonly among articulate professionals such as lawyers, teachers, journalists, and doctors) and then spreads only gradually to the mass of the population. Even after national independence has been realized, as we shall see, it is often questionable whether a mature sense of nationhood has been created, since local ethnic, linguistic, or religious ties often continue to predominate over loyalty to the larger community (see Chapter 29).

Traditional Resistance: A Precursor to Nationalism

The beginnings of modern nationalism can be found in the initial resistance by the indigenous peoples to the colonial conquest. Although, strictly speaking, such resistance was not "nationalist" because it was essentially motivated by the desire to defend traditional institutions, it did reflect a primitive concept of nationhood in that it aimed at protecting the homeland from the invader. After independence was achieved, governments of new nations often hailed early resistance movements as the precursors of twentieth-century nationalist movements. Thus, traditional resistance to colonial conquest may logically be viewed as the first stage in the development of modern nationalism.

Such resistance took various forms. For the most part, it was led by the existing ruling class, although in some instances traditionalists continued to oppose foreign conquest even after resistance had collapsed at the center. In India, Tipu Sultan (tih-POO SUL-tun) fought the British in the Deccan after the collapse of the Mughal dynasty. Similarly, after the decrepit monarchy in Vietnam had bowed to French pressure, a number of civilian and military officials set up an organization called Can Vuong (kahn VWAHNG) (literally, "save the king") and continued their own resistance campaign without imperial sanction.

Sometimes traditional resistance to Western penetration went beyond elite circles. Most commonly, it appeared in the form of peasant revolts. Rural rebellions were not uncommon in traditional Asian societies as a means of expressing peasant discontent with high taxes, official corruption, rising rural debt, and famine in the countryside. Under colonialism, rural conditions often deteriorated as population density increased and peasants were driven off the land to make way for plantation agriculture. Angry peasants then vented their frustration at the foreign invaders. For example, in Burma, the Buddhist monk Saya San (SAH-yuh SAHN) led a peasant uprising against the British many years after they had completed

The Ndebele Rebellion

SCIENCE & TECHNOLOGY

As British forces advanced northward from the Cape Colony toward the Zambezi River in the 1890s, they overran the Ndebele (uhn-duh-BEE-lee) people, who occupied rich lands in the region near the site of the ruins of Great Zimbabwe (zim-BAHB-way). Angered by British brutality, Ndebele warriors revolted in 1896 to throw off their oppressors. Despite the Ndebele's great superiority in numbers, British units possessed the feared Maxim gun, which mowed down African attackers by the hundreds. Faced with defeat, the Ndebele king, Lobengula (loh-beng-GOO-luh), fled into the hills and committed suicide. In the following account, a survivor describes the conflict.

Ndansi Kumalo, *A Personal Account*

We surrendered to the white people and were told to go back to our homes and live our usual lives and attend to our crops. But the white men sent native police who did abominable things; they were cruel and assaulted a lot of our people and helped themselves to our cattle and goats. . . . They interfered with our wives and molested them. . . . We thought it best to fight and die rather than bear it. . . .

We knew that we had very little chance because their weapons were so much superior to ours. But we meant to fight to the last, feeling that even if we could not beat them we might at least kill a few of them and so have some sort of revenge. . . .

I remember a fight . . . when we charged the white men. There were some hundreds of us; the white men also were many. We charged them at close quarters: we thought we had a good chance to kill them but the Maxims were too much for us. . . . Many of our people were killed in this fight. . . .

We were still fighting when we heard that [Cecil] Rhodes was coming and wanted to make peace with us. It was best to come to terms he said, and not go shedding blood like this on both sides. . . . So peace was made. Many of our people had been killed, and now we began to die of starvation; and then came the rinderpest [an infectious disease] and the cattle that were still left to us perished. We could not help thinking that all these dreadful things were brought by the white people.

 Compare this account with that of the Hausa woman from Nigeria in the document on p. 628. What factors might account for the differences?

---

their takeover. Similar forms of unrest occurred in various parts of India, where *zamindars* and rural villagers alike resisted government attempts to increase tax revenues. Yet another peasant uprising took place in Algeria in 1840.

OPPOSITION TO COLONIAL RULE IN AFRICA Because of the sheer size of Africa and its ethnic, religious, and linguistic diversity, resistance to the European seizure of territory in that continent was often sporadic and uncoordinated, but fierce nonetheless. The uprising led by the Mahdi in the Sudan was only the most dramatic example. In South Africa, as we have seen, the Zulus engaged in a bitter war of resistance to Boer colonists arriving from the Cape Colony. Later they fought against the British occupation of their territory and were not finally subdued until the end of the century. In West Africa, the Ashanti ruling class led a bitter struggle against the British with broad-based popular support. The lack of modern weapons was decisive, however, and African resistance forces eventually suffered defeat throughout the continent (see the box above). The one exception was Ethiopia where, at the Battle of Adowa (AH-doo-wah) in 1896, the modernized army created by Emperor Menelik was able to fend off an Italian invasion force and preserve the country's national independence well into the next century.

THE SEPOY REBELLION Perhaps the most famous uprising against European authority in the mid-nineteenth century was the revolt of the **sepoys** (SEE-poiz) in India. The sepoys (from the Turkish *sipahis*, cavalrymen or soldiers) were Indian troops hired by the East India Company to protect British interests in the region. Unrest within Indian units of the colonial army had been common since early in the century, when it had been sparked by economic issues, religious sensitivities, or nascent anticolonial sentiment. Such attitudes intensified in the mid-1850s when the British instituted a new policy of shipping Indian troops abroad—a practice that exposed Hindus to pollution by foreigners. In 1857, tension erupted when the British adopted the new Enfield rifle for use by sepoy infantrymen. The new weapon was a muzzle-loader that used paper cartridges covered with animal fat and lard; because the cartridge had to be bitten off, it broke strictures against high-class Hindus' eating animal products and Muslim prohibitions against eating pork. Protests among sepoy units in northern India turned into a full-scale mutiny, supported by uprisings in rural districts in various parts of the country. But the revolt lacked clear goals, and rivalries between Hindus and Muslims and discord among the leaders within each community prevented them from coordinating operations. Although the Indian troops often fought bravely

The Civilizing Mission in Egypt

INTERACTION & EXCHANGE

In many parts of the colonial world, European occupation served to sharpen class divisions in traditional societies. Such was the case in Egypt, where the British protectorate, established in the early 1880s, benefited many elites, who profited from the introduction of Western culture. Ordinary Egyptians, less inclined to adopt foreign ways, seldom profited from the European presence. In response, British administrators showed little patience for their subjects who failed to recognize the superiority of Western civilization. This view found expression in the words of the governor-general, Lord Cromer (KROH-mer), who remarked in exasperation, "The mind of the Oriental, . . . like his picturesque streets, is eminently wanting in symmetry. His reasoning is of the most slipshod description." Cromer was especially irritated at the local treatment of women, arguing that the seclusion of women and the wearing of the veil were the chief causes of Islamic backwardness.

Such views were echoed by some Egyptian elites, who were utterly seduced by Western culture and embraced the colonialists' condemnation of local traditions. The French-educated lawyer Qassim Amin (KAH-sum AH-meen) was one example. His book, *The Liberation of Women*, published in 1899 and excerpted here, precipitated a heated debate between those who considered Western nations the liberators of Islam and those who reviled them as oppressors.

Qassim Amin, *The Liberation of Women*

European civilization advances with the speed of steam and electricity, and has even overspilled to every part of the globe so that there is not an inch that he [European man] has not trodden underfoot. Any place he goes he takes control of its resources . . . and turns them into profit . . . and if he does harm to the original inhabitants, it is only that he pursues happiness in this world and seeks it wherever he may find it. . . . For the most part he uses his intellect, but when circumstances require it, he deploys force. He does not seek glory from his possessions and colonies, for he has enough of this through his intellectual achievements and scientific inventions. What drives the Englishman to dwell in India and the French in Algeria . . . is profit and the desire to acquire resources in countries where the inhabitants do not know their value or how to profit from them.

When they encounter savages they eliminate them or drive them from the land, as happened in America . . . and is happening now in Africa. . . . When they encounter a nation like ours, with a degree of civilization, with a past, and a religion . . . and customs and . . . institutions . . . they deal with its inhabitants kindly. But they do soon acquire its most valuable resources, because they have greater wealth and intellect and knowledge and force. . . . [The veil constituted] a huge barrier between woman and her elevation, and consequently a barrier between the nation and its advance.

 Why did Qassim Amin believe that Western culture would be beneficial to Egyptian society? How might a critic of colonialism have responded?

---

and outnumbered the British six to one, they were poorly organized, and the British forces (supplemented in many cases by sepoy troops) suppressed the rebellion.

Still, the revolt frightened the British and led to a number of major reforms. The proportion of Indian troops in the army was reduced, and precedence was given to ethnic groups likely to be loyal to the British, such as the Sikhs (SEEKS *or* see-ikhz) of Punjab (pun-JAHB) and the Gurkhas (GUR-kuhz), an upland people from Nepal (nuh-PAHL) in the Himalaya Mountains. To avoid religious conflicts, ethnic groups were spread throughout the service rather than assigned to special units. The British also decided to suppress the final remnants of the hapless Mughal dynasty, which had supported the mutiny, and turned responsibility for the administration of the subcontinent over to the crown.

Like the Sepoy Rebellion, traditional resistance movements usually met with little success. Peasants armed with pikes and spears were no match for Western armies possessing the most terrifying weapons then known to human society. In a few cases, such as the revolt of the Mahdi at Khartoum, the local peoples were able to defeat the invaders temporarily. But such successes were rare, and the late nineteenth century witnessed the seemingly inexorable march of the Western powers, armed with the Gatling gun (the first rapid-fire weapon and the precursor of the modern machine gun), to mastery of the globe.

THE PATH OF COLLABORATION Not all Asians and Africans reacted to a colonial takeover by choosing the path of violent resistance. Some found elements to admire in Western civilization and compared it favorably with their own traditional practices and institutions (see the box above). Even in sub-Saharan Africa, where the colonial record was often at its most brutal, some elites elected to support the imposition of colonial authority, as the following letter to Queen Victoria from African leaders in Cameroons indicates:

We *wish* to have your laws in our towns. We want to have every *fashion* altered; also we will do according to your Consul's *word*. Plenty wars here in our country. Plenty murder and plenty idol worshippers. Perhaps these *lines* of our writing will *look* to you as an *idle* tale.

We have *spoken* to the English consul plenty times about having an English *government* here. We never have answer from you, so we wish to write you *ourselves*.[10]

The decision to collaborate with the colonial administration was undoubtedly motivated in many cases by the desire for personal survival or self-aggrandizement. Such instances frequently aroused scorn and even hostility among the collaborators' contemporaries, and especially among those who chose to oppose the occupation by force of arms. On occasion, however, the decision was reached only after an excruciating and painful examination of equally unpleasant alternatives. Whatever the circumstances, the decision often divided friends and families, as occurred with two onetime childhood friends in central Vietnam, when one chose resistance and the other collaboration (see the box on p. 634).

Not all colonial subjects, of course, felt required to choose between resistance and collaboration. Most simply lived out their lives without engaging in the political arena. Even so, in some cases their actions had an impact on the future of their country. A prime example was Ram Mohan Roy (RAHM moh-HUHN ROI). A *brahmin* from Bengal (ben-GAHL), Roy founded the Brahmo Samaj (BRAH-moh suh-MAHJ) (Society of Brahma) in 1828. He probably had no intention of promoting Indian independence when he created the new organization as a means of helping his fellow religionists defend the Hindu faith against verbal attacks from their British acquaintances. Roy was by no means a hidebound traditionalist. He opposed such practices as *sati* and recognized the benefit of introducing the best aspects of European culture into Indian society. But in encouraging his countrymen to defend their traditional values and institutions against the onslaught of Western civilization, he helped to promote the first stirrings of nationalist sentiment in nineteenth-century India.

Imperialism: The Balance Sheet

Few periods of history are as controversial among scholars and casual observers as the era of imperialism. To defenders of the colonial enterprise like the poet Rudyard Kipling, imperialism was the "white man's burden," a disagreeable but necessary phase in the evolution of human society, lifting up the toiling races from tradition to modernity and bringing an end to poverty, famine, and disease (see the box on p. 612).

Critics take exception to such views, portraying imperialism as a tragedy of major proportions. The insatiable drive of the advanced economic powers for access to raw materials and markets created an exploitative environment that transformed the vast majority of colonial peoples into a permanent underclass while restricting the benefits of modern technology to a privileged few. Kipling's "white man's burden" was dismissed as a hypocritical gesture to hoodwink the naive and

salve the guilty feelings of those who recognized imperialism for what it was—a savage act of rape. In the blunt words of two Western critics of imperialism: "Why is Africa (or for that matter Latin America and much of Asia) so poor? . . . The answer is very brief: we have made it poor."[11]

Defenders of the colonial enterprise sometimes concede that there were gross inequities in the colonial system but point out that there was a positive side to the experience as well. The expansion of markets and the beginnings of a modern transportation and communications network, while bringing few immediate benefits to the colonial peoples, laid the groundwork for future economic growth. At the same time, the introduction of new ways of looking at human freedom, the relationship between the individual and society, and democratic principles set the stage for the adoption of such ideas after the restoration of independence following World War II. Finally, the colonial experience offered a new approach to the traditional relationship between men and women. Although colonial rule was by no means uniformly beneficial to the position of women in African and Asian societies, growing awareness of the struggle by women in the West to seek equality offered their counterparts in the colonial territories a weapon to fight against the long-standing barriers of custom and legal discrimination.

Between these two irreconcilable views, where does the truth lie? This chapter has contended that neither extreme position is justified. In fact, the consequences of colonialism have been more complex than either its defenders or its critics would have us believe. While the colonial peoples received little immediate benefit from the imposition of foreign rule, overall the imperialist era brought about a vast expansion of the international trade network and created at least the potential for societies throughout Africa and Asia to play an active and rewarding role in the new global economic arena. If, as the historian William McNeill believes, the introduction of new technology through cross-cultural encounters is the driving force of change in world history, then Western imperialism, whatever its faults, served a useful purpose in opening the door to such change, much as the rise of the Arab empire and the Mongol invasions hastened the process of global economic development in an earlier time.

Still, the critics have a point. Although colonialism did introduce the peoples of Asia and Africa to new technology and the expanding economic marketplace, it was unnecessarily brutal in its application and all too often failed to realize the exalted claims and objectives of its promoters. Existing economic networks—often potentially valuable as a foundation for later economic development—were ruthlessly swept aside in the interests of providing markets for Western manufactured goods. Potential sources of local industrialization were nipped in the bud to avoid competition for factories in Amsterdam, London, Pittsburgh, or Manchester. Training in Western democratic ideals and practices was ignored out of fear that the recipients might use them as weapons against the ruling authorities.

The fundamental weakness of colonialism, then, was that it was ultimately based on the self-interests of the citizens of the colonial powers. Where those interests collided with the needs of the colonial peoples, those of the former always triumphed. However sincerely the David Livingstones, Albert

OPPOSING ＜ VIEWPOINTS

To Resist or Not to Resist

How to respond to the imposition of colonial rule was sometimes an excruciating problem for political elites in many Asian countries, since resistance often seemed futile while simply adding to the suffering of the indigenous population. Hoang Cao Khai (HWANG cow KY) and Phan Dinh Phung (FAN din FUNG) were members of the Confucian scholar-gentry from the same village in Vietnam. Yet they reacted in dramatically different ways to the French conquest of their country. Their exchange of letters, reproduced here, illustrates the dilemmas they faced.

Hoang Cao Khai's Letter to Phan Dinh Phung

Soon, it will be seventeen years since we ventured upon different paths of life. How sweet was our friendship when we both lived in our village. . . . At the time when the capital was lost and after the royal carriage had departed, you courageously answered the appeals of the King by raising the banner of righteousness. It was certainly the only thing to do in those circumstances. No one will question that.

But now the situation has changed and even those without intelligence or education have concluded that nothing remains to be saved. How is it that you, a man of vast understanding, do not realize this? . . . You are determined to do whatever you deem righteous. . . . But though you have no thoughts for your own person or for your own fate, you should at least attend to the sufferings of the population of a whole region. . . .

Until now your actions have undoubtedly accorded with your loyalty. May I ask however what sin our people have committed to deserve so much hardship? I would understand your resistance, did you involve but your family for the benefit of a large number. As of now, hundreds of families are subject to grief; how do you have the heart to fight on? I venture to predict that, should you pursue your struggle, not only will the population of our village be destroyed but our entire country will be transformed into a sea of blood and a mountain of bones. It is my hope that men of your superior morality and honesty will pause a while to appraise the situation.

Reply of Phan Dinh Phung to Hoang Cao Khai

In your letter, you revealed to me the causes of calamities and of happiness. You showed me clearly where advantages and disadvantages lie. All of which sufficed to indicate that

your anxious concern was not only for my own security but also for the peace and order of our entire region. I understood plainly your sincere arguments.

I have concluded that if our country has survived these past thousand years when its territory was not large, its army not strong, its wealth not great, it was because the relationships between king and subjects, fathers and children, have always been regulated by the five moral obligations. In the past, the Han, the Sung, the Yuan, the Ming time and again dreamt of annexing our country and of dividing it up into prefectures and districts within the Chinese administrative system. But never were they able to realize their dream. Ah! if even China, which shares a common border with our territory, and is a thousand times more powerful than Vietnam, could not rely upon her strength to swallow us, it was surely because the destiny of our country had been willed by Heaven itself.

The French, separated from our country until the present day by I do not know how many thousand miles, have crossed the oceans to come to our country. Wherever they came, they acted like a storm, so much so that the Emperor had to flee. The whole country was cast into disorder. Our rivers and our mountains have been annexed by them at a stroke and turned into a foreign territory.

Moreover, if our region has suffered to such an extent, it was not only from the misfortunes of war. You must realize that wherever the French go, there flock around them groups of petty men who offer plans and tricks to gain the enemy's confidence. . . . They use every expedient to squeeze the people out of their possessions. That is how hundreds of misdeeds, thousands of offenses have been perpetrated. How can the French not be aware of all the suffering that the rural population has had to endure? Under these circumstances, is it surprising that families should be disrupted and the people scattered?

My friend, if you are troubled about our people, then I advise you to place yourself in my position and to think about the circumstances in which I live. You will understand naturally and see clearly that I do not need to add anything else.

 Explain briefly the reasons advanced by each writer to justify his actions. Which argument do you believe would earn more support from contemporaries? Why?

Sarrauts, and William McKinleys of the world were convinced of the rightness of their civilizing mission, the ultimate result was to deprive the colonial peoples of the right to make their own choices about their own destiny. Sophisticated, age-old societies that could have been left to respond to the technological revolution in their own way were thus

squeezed dry of precious national resources under the false guise of a "civilizing mission." As the sociologist Clifford Geertz remarked in his book *Agricultural Involution: The Processes of Ecological Change in Indonesia*, the tragedy is not that the colonial peoples suffered through the colonial era but that they suffered for nothing.

CHAPTER SUMMARY

By the first quarter of the twentieth century, virtually all of Africa and a good part of South and Southeast Asia were under some form of colonial rule. With the advent of the age of imperialism, a global economy was finally established, and the domination of Western civilization over those of Africa and Asia appeared to be complete.

The imperialist rush for colonies did not take place without opposition. In most areas of the world, local governments and peoples resisted the onslaught, sometimes to the bitter end. But with few exceptions, they were unable to overcome the fearsome new warships and firearms that the Industrial Revolution in Europe had brought into being. Although the material benefits and democratic values of the occupying powers aroused admiration from observers in much of the colonial world, in the end it was weapons, more than ideas, that ushered in the age of imperialism.

Africa and southern Asia were not the only areas of the world that were buffeted by the winds of Western expansionism in the late nineteenth century. The nations of eastern Asia, and those of Latin America and the Middle East as well, were also affected in significant ways. The consequences of Western political, economic, and military penetration varied substantially from one region to another, however, and therefore require separate treatment. The experience of East Asia will be dealt with in the next chapter. That of Latin America and the Middle East will be discussed in Chapter 24.

In these areas, new rivals—notably the United States, Russia, and Japan—entered the scene and played an active role in the process. By the end of the nineteenth century, the rush to secure colonies had circled the world.

CHAPTER TIMELINE

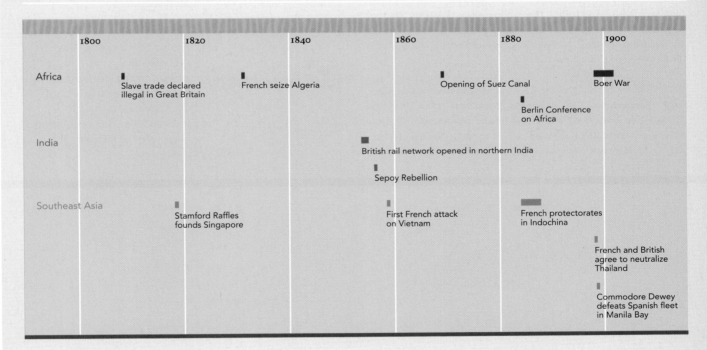

	1800	1820	1840	1860	1880	1900
Africa	Slave trade declared illegal in Great Britain	French seize Algeria		Opening of Suez Canal	Berlin Conference on Africa	Boer War
India			British rail network opened in northern India / Sepoy Rebellion			
Southeast Asia		Stamford Raffles founds Singapore		First French attack on Vietnam	French protectorates in Indochina	French and British agree to neutralize Thailand / Commodore Dewey defeats Spanish fleet in Manila Bay

CHAPTER REVIEW

Upon Reflection

Q What arguments have been advanced to justify the European takeover of colonies in Asia and Africa during the latter part of the nineteenth century? To what degree are such arguments justified?

Q The colonial powers adopted two basic philosophies in seeking to govern their conquered territories in Asia and Africa—assimilation and association. What were the principles behind these philosophies, and how did they work in practice? Which do you believe was more successful?

Q What was the purpose of the Berlin Conference of 1884, and how successful was it at achieving that purpose? What was the impact of the conference for the European powers and for Africa?

Key Terms

imperialism (p. 609)
indirect rule (p. 611)
direct rule (p. 611)
assimilation (p. 612)
association (p. 612)
raj (p. 614)
informal empire (p. 621)
pasha (p. 622)
high colonialism (p. 629)
sepoys (p. 631)

Suggested Reading

IMPERIALISM AND COLONIALISM There are a number of good works on the subject of imperialism and colonialism. For a study that focuses directly on the question of whether colonialism was beneficial to subject peoples, see **D. K. Fieldhouse**, *The West and the Third World: Trade, Colonialism, Dependence, and Development* (Oxford, 1999). Also see **D. B. Abernathy**, *Global Dominance: European Overseas Empires, 1415–1980* (New Haven, Conn., 2000). For a defense of the British imperial mission, see **N. Ferguson**, *Empire: The Rise and Demise of the British World Order* (New York, 2003).

IMPERIALIST AGE IN AFRICA On the imperialist age in Africa, see **B. Vandervoort**, *Wars of Imperial Conquest in Africa, 1830–1914* (Bloomington, Ind., 1998), and **T. Pakenham**, *The Scramble for Africa* (New York, 1991). The three-sided conflict in South Africa is ably analyzed in **M. Meredith**, *Diamonds, Gold, and War: The British, the Boers,* *and the Making of South Africa* (New York, 2007). The scandal in the Belgian Congo is chronicled in **A. Hothschild**, *King Leopold's Ghost: A Story of Greed, Terror, and Heroism in Central Africa* (New York, 1999). Also informative is **R. O. Collins, ed.,** *Historical Problems of Imperial Africa* (Princeton, N.J., 1994).

INDIA For an overview of the British takeover and administration of India, see **S. Wolpert**, *A New History of India,* 8th ed. (New York, 2008). **C. A. Bayly**, *Indian Society and the Making of the British Empire* (Cambridge, 1988), is a scholarly analysis of the impact of British conquest on the Indian economy. Also see **A. Wild's** elegant *East India Company: Trade and Conquest from 1600* (New York, 2000). In a provocative work, *Ornamentalism: How the British Saw Their Empire* (Oxford, 2000), **D. Cannadine** argues that it was class and not race that motivated British policy in the subcontinent. In *The Last Mughal: The Fall of a Dynasty: Delhi 1857* (New York, 2007), **W. Dalrymple** argues that religion was the key issue in provoking the Sepoy Rebellion. Also see **N. Dirks**, *The Scandal of Empire: India and the Creation of Imperial Britain* (Cambridge, Mass., 2007).

COLONIAL AGE IN SOUTHEAST ASIA General studies of the colonial period in Southeast Asia are rare because most authors focus on specific areas. For an overview by several authors, see **N. Tarling, ed.,** *The Cambridge History of Southeast Asia,* vol. 3 (Cambridge, 1992).

 CourseMate

Go to the CourseMate website at **www.cengagebrain.com** for additional study tools and review materials—including audio and video clips—for this chapter.

Shadows over the Pacific: East Asia Under Challenge

The Macartney mission to China, 1793

CHAPTER OUTLINE AND FOCUS QUESTIONS

The Decline of the Manchus

Q Why did the Qing dynasty decline and ultimately collapse, and what role did the Western powers play in this process?

Chinese Society in Transition

Q What political, economic, and social reforms were instituted by the Qing dynasty during its final decades, and why were they not more successful in reversing the decline of Manchu rule?

A Rich Country and a Strong State: The Rise of Modern Japan

Q To what degree was the Meiji Restoration a "revolution," and to what extent did it succeed in transforming Japan?

CRITICAL THINKING

Q How did China and Japan each respond to Western pressures in the nineteenth century, and what implications did their different responses have for each nation's history?

THE BRITISH EMISSARY Lord Macartney had arrived in Beijing in 1793 with a caravan loaded with six hundred cases of gifts for the emperor. Flags and banners provided by the Chinese proclaimed in Chinese characters that the visitor was an "ambassador bearing tribute from the country of England." But the tribute was in vain, for Macartney's request for an increase in trade between the two countries was flatly rejected, and he left Beijing in October with nothing to show for his efforts. Not until half a century later would the Qing dynasty—at the point of a gun—agree to the British demand for an expansion of commercial ties.

In fact, the Chinese emperor Qianlong had responded to the requests of his visitor with polite but poorly disguised condescension. To Macartney's proposal that a British ambassador be stationed in the capital of Beijing, the emperor replied that such a request was "not in harmony with the state system of our dynasty and will definitely not be permitted." As for the British envoy's suggestion that regular trade relations be established between the two countries, that proposal was also rejected. We receive all sorts of precious things, replied the Celestial Emperor, as gifts from myriad nations. "Consequently," he added, "there is nothing we lack, as your principal envoy and others have themselves observed. We have never set much store on strange or ingenious objects, nor do we need more of your country's manufactures."

Historians have often viewed the failure of Macartney's mission as a reflection of the disdain of Chinese rulers toward their counterparts in other countries and their serene confidence in the superiority of Chinese civilization in a world inhabited by barbarians. If that was the case, Qianlong's confidence was misplaced, for as the eighteenth century came to an end, his country faced a growing challenge not only from the escalating power and ambitions of the West but from its own growing internal weakness as well. When insistent British demands for the right to carry out trade and missionary activities in China were rejected, Britain resorted to force and in the Opium War, which broke out in 1839, gave Manchu troops a sound thrashing. A humiliated China was finally forced to open its doors.

The Decline of the Manchus

Q FOCUS QUESTION: Why did the Qing dynasty decline and ultimately collapse, and what role did the Western powers play in this process?

In 1800, the Qing (CHING) (Ch'ing) or Manchu dynasty was at the height of its power. China had experienced a long period of peace and prosperity under the rule of two great emperors, Kangxi (kang-SHEE) and Qianlong (CHAN-loong). Its borders were secure, and its culture and intellectual achievements were the envy of the world. Its rulers, hidden behind the walls of the Forbidden City in Beijing (bay-ZHING), had every reason to describe their patrimony as the "Central Kingdom." But a little over a century later, humiliated and harassed by the black ships and big guns of the Western powers, the Qing dynasty, the last in a series that had endured for more than two thousand years, collapsed in the dust (see Map 22.1).

Historians once assumed that the primary reason for the rapid decline and fall of the Manchu dynasty was the intense pressure applied to a proud but somewhat complacent traditional society by the modern West. Now, however, most historians believe that internal changes played a major role in the dynasty's collapse and point out that at least some of the problems suffered by the Manchus during the nineteenth century were self-inflicted.

Both explanations have some validity. Like so many of its predecessors, after an extended period of growth, the Qing dynasty began to suffer from the familiar dynastic ills of official corruption, peasant unrest, and incompetence at court. Such weaknesses were probably exacerbated by the rapid growth in population. The long era of peace and stability, the introduction of new crops from the Americas, and the cultivation of new,

MAP 22.1 The Qing Empire. Shown here is the Qing Empire at the height of its power in the late eighteenth century, as well as its shrunken sphere of influence at the moment of dissolution in 1911.

Q *How do China's tributary states on this map differ from those in Map 17.2 on p. 485? Which of them fell under the influence of foreign powers during the nineteenth century?*

A Letter of Advice to the Queen

INTERACTION & EXCHANGE

Lin Zexu was the Chinese imperial commissioner in Canton at the time of the Opium War. Prior to the conflict, he attempted to use reason and the threat of retaliation to persuade the British to cease importing opium illegally into southern China. The following selection is an excerpt from a letter that he wrote to Queen Victoria. In it, he appeals to her conscience while showing the condescension that the Chinese traditionally displayed to the rulers of other countries.

Lin Zexu, Letter to Queen Victoria

The kings of your honorable country by a tradition handed down from generation to generation have always been noted for their politeness and submissiveness. . . . Privately we are delighted with the way in which the honorable rulers of your country deeply understand the grand principles and are grateful for the Celestial grace. . . . The profit from trade has been enjoyed by them continuously for two hundred years. This is the source from which your country has become known for its wealth.

But after a long period of commercial intercourse, there appear among the crowd of barbarians both good persons and bad, unevenly. Consequently there are those who smuggle opium to seduce the Chinese people and so cause the spread of the poison to all provinces. . . .

The wealth of China is used to profit the barbarians. That is to say, the great profit made by barbarians is all taken from the rightful share of China. By what right do they then in return use the poisonous drug to injure the Chinese people? . . . Let us ask, where is your conscience? I have heard that the smoking of opium is very strictly forbidden by your country; that is because the harm caused by opium is clearly understood. Since it is not permitted to do harm to your own country, then even less should you let it be passed on to the harm of other countries—how much less to China! Of all that China exports to foreign countries, there is not a single thing which is not beneficial to people. . . . Is there a single article from China which has done any harm to foreign countries? Take tea and rhubarb, for example; the foreign countries cannot get along for a single day without them. . . . On the other hand, articles coming from the outside to China can only be used as toys. We can take them or get along without them. Nevertheless our Celestial Court lets tea, silk, and other goods be shipped without limit and circulated everywhere without begrudging it in the slightest. This is for no other reason but to share the benefit with the people of the whole world. . . .

May you, O King, check your wicked and sift your vicious people before they come to China, in order to guarantee the peace of your nation, to show further the sincerity of your politeness and submissiveness, and to let the two countries enjoy together the blessings of peace. . . . After receiving this dispatch will you immediately give us a prompt reply regarding the details and circumstances of your cutting off the opium traffic. Be sure not to put this off.

How did the imperial commissioner seek to persuade Queen Victoria to prohibit the sale of opium in China? How persuasive are his arguments?

---

fast-ripening strains of rice had enabled the Chinese population to double between 1550 and 1800. The population continued to grow after 1800, reaching the unprecedented level of 400 million by the end of the century and putting enormous pressure on the agricultural sector to increase the yield of lands under cultivation. Even without the irritating presence of the Western powers, the Manchus were probably destined to repeat the fate of their imperial predecessors. The ships, guns, and ideas of the foreigners simply highlighted the growing weakness of the Manchu dynasty and likely hastened its demise. In doing so, Western imperialism still exerted an indelible impact on the history of modern China—but as a contributing, not a causal, factor.

Opium and Rebellion

By 1800, Westerners had been in contact with China for more than two hundred years, but after an initial period of flourishing relations, Western traders had been limited to a small commercial outlet at Canton. This arrangement was not acceptable to the British, however. Not only did they chafe at being restricted to a tiny enclave, but the growing British appetite for Chinese tea created a severe balance-of-payments problem. After the failure of the Macartney mission in 1793, another mission, led by Lord Amherst, arrived in China in 1816. But it too achieved little except to worsen the already strained relations between the two countries. The British solution was opium. A product more addictive than tea, opium was grown in northeastern India and then shipped to China. Opium had been grown in southwestern China for several hundred years but had been used primarily for medicinal purposes. Now, as imports increased, popular demand for the product in southern China became insatiable despite an official prohibition on its use. Soon bullion was flowing out of the Chinese imperial treasury into the pockets of British merchants.

The Chinese became concerned and tried to negotiate. In 1839, Lin Zexu (LIN dzeh-SHOO) (Lin Tse-hsu; 1785–1850), a Chinese official appointed by the court to curtail the opium trade, appealed to Queen Victoria on both moral and practical grounds and threatened to prohibit the sale of rhubarb (widely used as a laxative in nineteenth-century Europe) to Great Britain if she did not respond (see the box above). But moral principles, then as now, paled before the lure of profits, and the British continued to promote the opium trade, arguing that if the Chinese did not want the opium, they did not have to buy it. Lin Zexu attacked on three fronts, imposing penalties on smokers, arresting dealers, and seizing supplies from importers as they attempted to smuggle the drug into China. The last tactic caused his downfall. When he blockaded the foreign factory (warehouse) area in Canton to force traders to hand over their remaining chests of opium, the British government, claiming that it could not permit British subjects "to be exposed to insult and injustice," launched a naval expedition to punish the Manchus and force the court to open China to foreign trade.[1]

THE OPIUM WAR The Opium War (1839–1842) demonstrated the superiority of British firepower and military tactics (including the use of a shallow-draft steamboat that effectively harassed Chinese coastal defenses). British warships destroyed Chinese coastal and river forts and seized the offshore island of Zhoushan (JOH-shahn), not far from the mouth of the Yangtze River. When a British fleet sailed virtually unopposed up the Yangtze to Nanjing (nan-JING) and cut off the supply of "tribute grain" from southern to northern China, the Qing finally agreed to British terms. In the Treaty of Nanjing in 1842, the Chinese agreed to open five coastal ports to British trade, limit tariffs on imported British goods, grant extraterritorial rights to British citizens in China, and pay a substantial indemnity to cover the costs of the war. China also agreed to cede the island of Hong Kong (dismissed by a senior British official as a "barren rock") to Great Britain. Nothing was said in the treaty about the opium trade, which continued unabated until it was brought under control through Chinese government efforts in the early twentieth century.

Although the Opium War has traditionally been considered the beginning of modern Chinese history, it is unlikely that many Chinese at the time would have seen it that way. This was not the first time that a ruling dynasty had been forced to make concessions to foreigners, and the opening of five coastal ports to the British hardly constituted a serious threat to the security of the empire. Although a few concerned Chinese argued that the court should learn more about European civilization, others contended that China had nothing to learn from the barbarians and that borrowing foreign ways would undercut the purity of Confucian civilization.

For the time being, the Manchus attempted to deal with the problem in the traditional way of playing the foreigners off against each other. Concessions granted to the British were offered to other Western nations, including the United States, and soon thriving foreign concession areas were operating in treaty ports along the southern Chinese coast from Canton to Shanghai (SHANG-hy).

THE TAIPING REBELLION In the meantime, the Qing court's failure to deal with pressing internal economic problems led to a major peasant revolt that shook the foundations of the

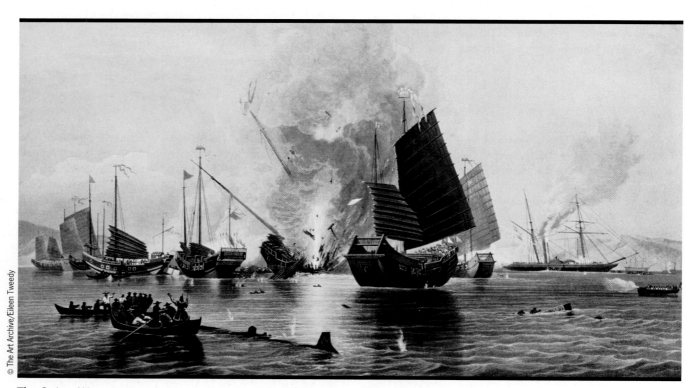

The Opium War. The Opium War, waged between China and Great Britain between 1839 and 1842, was China's first conflict with a European power. Lacking modern military technology, the Chinese suffered a humiliating defeat. In this painting, heavily armed British steamships destroy unwieldy Chinese junks along the Chinese coast. China's humiliation at sea was a legacy of its rulers' lack of interest in maritime matters since the middle of the fifteenth century, when Chinese junks were among the most advanced sailing ships in the world.

empire. On the surface, the Taiping (TY-ping) (T'ai-p'ing) Rebellion owed something to the Western incursion. The leader of the uprising, Hong Xiuquan (HOONG shee-oo-CHWAHN) (Hung Hsiu-ch'uan), a failed examination candidate, was a Christian convert who viewed himself as a younger brother of Jesus and hoped to establish what he referred to as a "Heavenly Kingdom of Supreme Peace" in China. But there were many local causes as well. The rapid increase in population forced millions of peasants to eke out a living as sharecroppers or landless laborers. Official corruption and incompetence led to the whipsaw of increased taxes and a decline in government services; even the Grand Canal was allowed to silt up, hindering the shipment of grain. In 1853, the rebels seized the old Ming capital of Nanjing, but that proved to be the rebellion's high-water mark. Plagued by factionalism, the rebellion gradually lost momentum until it was finally suppressed in 1864, but by then it had had devastating effects on Chinese society. More than 25 million people were killed, the vast majority of them civilians.

One reason for the dynasty's failure to deal effectively with the internal unrest was the continuing difficulties with the Western imperialists. In 1856, the British and the French, still smarting from trade restrictions and limitations on their missionary activities, launched a new series of attacks against China and seized Beijing in 1860. As punishment, British troops destroyed the imperial summer palace just outside the city. In the ensuing Treaty of Tianjin (TYAHN-jin) (Tientsin), the Qing agreed to humiliating new concessions: the legalization of the opium trade, the opening of additional ports to foreign trade, and the cession of the peninsula of Kowloon (KOW-loon) (opposite the island of Hong Kong) to the British (see Map 22.2). Additional territories in the north were ceded to Russia.

Efforts at Reform

By the late 1870s, the old dynasty was well on the road to internal disintegration. In fending off the Taiping Rebellion, the Manchus had been compelled to rely on armed forces under regional command. After quelling the revolt, many of these regional commanders refused to disband their units and, with the support of the local gentry, continued to collect local taxes for their

The Taiping Rebellion

own use. The dreaded pattern of imperial breakdown, so familiar in Chinese history, was beginning to appear once again.

In its weakened state, the court finally began to listen to the appeals of reform-minded officials, who called for a new policy of what they called **self-strengthening**, in which Western technology would be adopted while Confucian principles and institutions were maintained intact. This policy, popularly known by its slogan "East for Essence, West for Practical Use," remained the guiding standard for Chinese foreign and domestic policy for nearly a quarter of a century. Some even called for reforms in education and in China's hallowed political institutions (see the box on p. 642). Pointing to the power and prosperity of Great Britain, the journalist Wang Tao (wahng TOW ["ow" as in "how"]) (Wang T'ao; 1828–1897) remarked, "The real strength of England . . . lies in the fact that there is a sympathetic understanding between the governing and the governed, a close relationship between the ruler and the people. . . . My observation is that the daily domestic political life of England actually embodies the traditional ideals of our ancient Golden Age."[2] Such democratic ideas were too radical for most moderate reformers, however. One of the leading court officials of the day, Zhang Zhidong (JANG jee-DOONG) (Chang Chih-tung), countered:

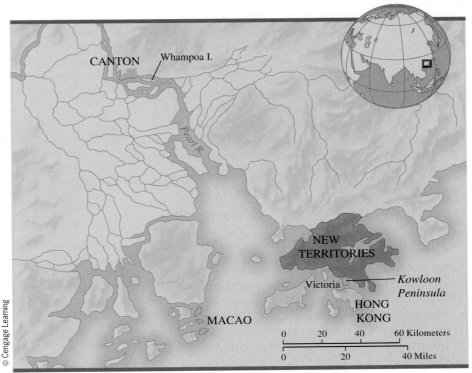

MAP 22.2 Canton and Hong Kong. This map shows the estuary of the Pearl River in southern China, an important area of early contact between China and Europe.

 What was the importance of Canton? What were the New Territories, and when were they annexed by the British?

An Appeal for Change in China

After the humiliating defeat at the hands of the British in the Opium War, a few Chinese intellectuals began to argue that China must change its ways if it were to survive. One of these reformist thinkers was the journalist and author Wang Tao. After a trip to Europe in the late 1860s, Wang returned to China convinced of the technological superiority of the West and the need for his country to adopt reforms that would enable it to compete effectively in a changing world. He had only limited success in persuading his contemporaries of the need for dramatic change. Many Chinese were undoubtedly reluctant to believe his claim that China was not the Middle Kingdom or "all under Heaven" but only one nation among many in a rapidly changing world.

Wang Tao on Reform

I know that within a hundred years China will adopt all Western methods and excel in them. For though both are vessels, a sailboat differs in speed from a steamship; though both are vehicles, a horse-drawn carriage cannot cover the same distance as a locomotive train. Among weapons, the power of the bow and arrow, sword and spear, cannot be compared with that of firearms; and of firearms, the old types do not have the same effect as the new. Although it be the same piece of work, there is a difference in the ease with which it can be done by machine and by human labor. When new methods do not exist, people will not think of changes; but when there are new instruments, to copy them is certainly possible. Even if the Westerners should give no guidance, the Chinese must surely exert themselves to the utmost of their ingenuity and resources on these things.

Alas! People all understand the past, but they are ignorant of the future. Only scholars whose thoughts run deep and far can grasp the trends. As the mind of Heaven changes above, so do human affairs below. Heaven opens the minds of the Westerners and bestows upon them intelligence and wisdom. Their techniques and skills develop without bound. They sail eastward and gather in China. This constitutes an unprecedented situation in history, and a tremendous change in the world. The foreign nations come from afar with their superior techniques, contemptuous of us in our deficiencies. They show off their prowess and indulge in insults and oppression; they also fight among themselves. Under these circumstances, how can we not think of making changes? . . .

If China does not make any change at this time, how can she be on a par with the great nations of Europe, and compare with them in power and strength? Nevertheless, the path of reform is beset with difficulties. What the Western countries have today are regarded as of no worth by those who arrogantly refuse to pay attention. Their argument is that we should use our own laws to govern the empire, for that is the Way of our sages. They do not know that the Way of the sages is valued only because it can make proper accommodations according to the times. If Confucius lived today, we may be certain that he would not cling to antiquity and oppose making changes. . . .

But how is this to be done? First, the method of recruiting civil servants should be changed. The examination essays, coming down to the present, have gone from bad to worse and should be discarded. And yet we are still using them to select civil servants.

Second, the method of training soldiers should be changed. Now our army units and naval forces have only names registered on books, but no actual persons enrolled. The authorities consider our troops unreliable and so they recruit militia who, however, can be assembled but cannot be disbanded. . . . The arms of the Manchu banners and the ships of the naval forces should all be changed. . . . If they continue to hold on to their old ways and make no plans for change, it may be called "using untrained people to fight," which is no different from driving them to their deaths.

 What arguments did Wang Tao use in his efforts to persuade readers to accept his point of view? Would Confucius have found Wang Tao's arguments persuasive? Why or why not?

The doctrine of people's rights will bring us not a single benefit but a hundred evils. Are we going to establish a parliament? . . . Even supposing the confused and clamorous people are assembled in one house, for every one of them who is clear-sighted, there will be a hundred others whose vision is beclouded; they will converse at random and talk as if in a dream—what use will it be?[3]

For the time being, Zhang Zhidong's arguments won the day. During the last quarter of the century, the Manchus attempted to modernize their military establishment and build up an industrial base without disturbing the essential elements of traditional Chinese civilization. Railroads, weapons arsenals, and shipyards were built, but the value system remained essentially unchanged.

The Climax of Imperialism

In the end, the results spoke for themselves. During the last two decades of the nineteenth century, the European penetration of China, both political and military, intensified. Rapacious imperialists began to bite off the outer edges of the Qing Empire. The Gobi Desert north of the Great Wall, Central Asia, and Tibet, all inhabited by non-Chinese peoples and

© Cengage Learning

MAP 22.3 Foreign Possessions and Spheres of Influence About 1900. At the end of the nineteenth century, China was being carved up like a melon by foreign imperialist powers. Colored areas indicate territories that had recently come under foreign influence.

Q *Which of the areas marked on the map were removed from Chinese control during the nineteenth century?*

disintegration gathered speed in 1897, when Germany, a new entry in the race for spoils in East Asia, used the pretext of the murder of two German missionaries by Chinese rioters to demand the cession of territories in the Shandong (SHAHN-doong) (Shantung) peninsula. The approval of the demand by the imperial court set off a scramble for territory by other interested powers (see Map 22.3). Russia now demanded the Liaodong (LYOW-doong) peninsula with its ice-free port at Port Arthur, and Great Britain weighed in with a request for a coaling station in northern China and, in order to obtain fresh water and agricultural produce for the growing population on Hong Kong island, obtained a hundred-year lease on the so-called New Territories, located on the mainland adjacent to the island.

The government responded to the challenge with yet another effort at reform. In the spring of 1898, an outspoken advocate of change, the progressive Confucian scholar Kang Youwei (KAHNG yow-WAY) (K'ang Yu-wei), won the support of the young emperor Guangxu (gwahng-SHOO) (Kuang Hsu) for a comprehensive reform program patterned after recent measures in Japan. Without change, Kang argued, China would perish. During the next several weeks, the emperor issued edicts calling for major political, administrative, and educational reforms. Not surprisingly, Kang's proposals were opposed by many conservatives, who saw little advantage and much risk in copying the West. More important, the new program was opposed by the emperor's aunt, the Empress Dowager Cixi (TSEE-shee) (Tz'u Hsi; 1835–1908)), the real power at court (see the comparative illustration on p. 644). Cixi had begun her political career as a concubine to an earlier emperor. After his death, she became a dominant force at court and in 1878 placed her infant nephew, the future Emperor Guangxu, on the throne. For two decades, she ruled in his name as regent. Cixi interpreted Guangxu's action as a British-supported effort to reduce her influence at court. With the aid of conservatives in the army, she arrested and executed several of the reformers and had the emperor incarcerated in the palace. Kang Youwei succeeded in fleeing abroad. With Cixi's palace coup, the so-called One Hundred Days of reform came to an end.

OPENING THE DOOR During the next two years, foreign pressure on the dynasty intensified. With encouragement from the British, who hoped to avert a total collapse of the

never fully assimilated into the Chinese Empire, were gradually lost. In the north and northwest, the main beneficiary was Russia, which took advantage of the dynasty's weakness to force the cession of territories north of the Amur (ah-MOOR) River in Siberia. In Tibet, competition between Russia and Great Britain prevented either power from seizing the territory outright but at the same time enabled Tibetan authorities to revive local autonomy never recognized by the Chinese. In the south, British and French advances in mainland Southeast Asia removed Burma and Vietnam from their traditional vassal relationship to the Manchu court. Even more ominous were the foreign spheres of influence in the Chinese heartland, where local commanders were willing to sell exclusive commercial, railroad-building, or mining privileges.

The crumbling of the Manchu dynasty accelerated at the end of the nineteenth century. In 1894, the Qing went to war with Japan over Japanese incursions into the Korean peninsula, which threatened China's long-held suzerainty over the area (see "Joining the Imperialist Club" later in this chapter). To the surprise of many observers, the Chinese were roundly defeated, confirming to some critics the devastating failure of the policy of self-strengthening by halfway measures. China's

COMPARATIVE ILLUSTRATION

POLITICS & GOVERNMENT

Female Rulers—East and West. Rulers of major states in the late nineteenth century included two prominent women: Empress Dowager Cixi of China and Queen Victoria of Great Britain. Cixi, shown at the left, was the most powerful figure in late-nineteenth-century China. Originally a concubine at the imperial court, she later placed her young nephew on the throne and dominated the political scene for a quarter of a century until her death in 1908. Conservative in her views, she staunchly resisted her advisers' suggestions for changes to help China face the challenge posed by the West. Queen Victoria, shown at the right, had the longest reign in British history (1837–1901). During this time, the British Empire reached the height of its power, but by the turn of the twentieth century, the monarchy was increasingly less relevant in Britain's liberal parliamentary system of government. Nevertheless, Victoria's dedication to duty and propriety reflected important values of her era, which is appropriately known as the Victorian Age.

Q *What other examples of influential female rulers can you recall from previous chapters in this book? What is distinctive about the two shown here?*

Manchu Empire, in 1899 U.S. Secretary of State John Hay presented the other imperialist powers with a proposal to ensure equal economic access to the China market for all states. Hay also suggested that all powers join together to guarantee the territorial and administrative integrity of the Chinese Empire. Though probably motivated more by the United States' preference for open markets than by a benevolent wish to protect China, the so-called **Open Door Notes** did have the practical effect of reducing the imperialist hysteria over access to the China market. That hysteria, a product of decades of mythologizing among Western commercial interests about the 400 million Chinese customers, had accelerated at the end of the century as fear of China's imminent collapse increased.

The "gentlemen's agreement" about the Open Door (it was not a treaty, merely a pious and nonbinding expression of intent) served to deflate fears in Britain, France, Germany, and Russia that other powers would take advantage of China's weakness to dominate the China market.

THE BOXER REBELLION In the long run, then, the Open Door policy was a positive step that brought a measure of sanity to imperialist meddling in East Asia. Unfortunately, it came too late to stop the domestic explosion known as the Boxer Rebellion. The Boxers, so-called because of the physical exercises they performed (which closely resembled the more martial forms of tai chi), were members of a secret

The International Expeditionary Force Advances to Beijing to Suppress the Boxers

society operating primarily in rural areas in northern China. Provoked by a damaging drought and high unemployment caused in part by foreign economic activity (the introduction of railroads and steamships, for example, undercut the livelihood of barge workers on the rivers and canals), the Boxers attacked foreign residents and besieged the foreign legation quarter in Beijing until the foreigners were rescued by an international expeditionary force in the late summer of 1900. As punishment, the foreign troops destroyed a number of temples in the capital suburbs, and the Chinese government was compelled to pay a heavy indemnity to the foreign governments involved in suppressing the uprising.

Justice or Mercy? Uncle Sam Decides. In the summer of 1900, Chinese rebels known as Boxers besieged Western embassies in the imperial capital of Beijing. Western nations, including the United States, dispatched troops to North China to rescue their compatriots. In the cartoon, which appeared in a contemporary American newsmagazine, China figuratively seeks pardon from a stern Uncle Sam.

Collapse of the Old Order

During the next few years, the old dynasty tried desperately to reform itself. The empress dowager, who had long resisted change, now embraced a number of reforms. The venerable civil service examination system was replaced by a new educational system based on the Western model. In 1905, a commission was formed to study constitutional changes; over the next few years, legislative assemblies were established at the provincial level, and elections for a national assembly were held in 1910.

Such moves helped shore up the dynasty temporarily, but history shows that the most dangerous period for an authoritarian system is when it begins to reform itself, because change breeds instability and performance rarely matches rising expectations. Such was the case in China. The emerging provincial elite, composed of merchants, professionals, and reform-minded gentry, soon became impatient with the slow pace of political change and were disillusioned to find that the new assemblies were intended to be primarily advisory rather than legislative. The government also alienated influential elements by financing railway development projects through foreign firms rather than local investors. The reforms also had little meaning for peasants, artisans, miners, and transportation workers, whose living conditions were being eroded by rising taxes and official venality. Rising rural unrest, as yet poorly organized and often centered on secret societies such as the Boxers, was an ominous sign of deep-seated resentment to which the dynasty would not or could not respond.

THE RISE OF SUN YAT-SEN To China's reformist elite, such signs of social discontent were a threat to be avoided. To its tiny revolutionary movement, they were a harbinger of promise. The first physical manifestations of future revolution appeared during the last decade of the nineteenth century with the formation of the Revive China Society by the young radical Sun Yat-sen (SOON yaht-SEN) (1866–1925). Born in a village south of Canton, Sun was educated in Hawaii and returned to China to practice medicine. Soon he turned his full attention to the ills of Chinese society.

CHRONOLOGY	China in the Era of Imperialism
Lord Macartney's mission to China	1793
Opium War	1839–1842
Taiping rebels seize Nanjing	1853
Taiping Rebellion suppressed	1864
Cixi becomes regent for nephew, Guangxu	1878
Sino-Japanese War	1894–1895
One Hundred Days reform	1898
Open Door policy	1899
Boxer Rebellion	1900
Commission to study constitution formed	1905
Deaths of Cixi and Guangxu	1908
Revolution in China	1911

Program for a New China

POLITICS & GOVERNMENT

In 1905, Sun Yat-sen united a number of anti-Manchu groups into a single patriotic organization called the Revolutionary Alliance (Tongmenghui). The new organization eventually formed the core of his Guomindang (gwoh-min-DAHNG), or Nationalist Party. This excerpt is from the organization's manifesto, published in 1905 in Tokyo. Note that Sun believed that the Chinese people were not ready for democracy and required a period of tutelage to prepare them for the final era of constitutional political government. This was a formula that would be adopted by many other political leaders in Asia and Africa after World War II.

Sun Yat-sen, *Manifesto for the Tongmenghui*

By order of the Military Government, . . . the Commander-in-Chief of the Chinese National Army proclaims the purposes and platform of the Military Government to the people of the nation:

Therefore we proclaim to the world in utmost sincerity the outline of the present revolution and the fundamental plan for the future administration of the nation.

1. *Drive out the Tartars:* The Manchus of today were originally the eastern barbarians beyond the Great Wall. They frequently caused border troubles during the Ming dynasty; then when China was in a disturbed state they came inside Shanhaikuan [the eastern terminus of the Great Wall], conquered China, and enslaved our Chinese people. . . . The extreme cruelties and tyrannies of the Manchu government have now reached their limit. With the righteous army poised against them, we will overthrow that government, and restore our sovereign rights.

2. *Restore China:* China is the China of the Chinese. The government of China should be in the hands of the Chinese. After driving out the Tartars we must restore our national state. . . .

3. *Establish the Republic:* Now our revolution is based on equality, in order to establish a republican government. All our people are equal and all enjoy political rights. . . .

4. *Equalize land ownership:* The good fortune of civilization is to be shared equally by all the people of the nation. We should improve our social and economic organization, and assess the value of all the land in the country. Its present price shall be received by the owner, but all increases in value resulting from reform and social improvements after the revolution shall belong to the state, to be shared by all the people, in order to create a socialist state, where each family within the empire can be well supported, each person satisfied, and no one fail to secure employment. . . .

The above four points will be carried out in three steps in due order. The first period is government by military law. When the righteous army has arisen, various places will join the cause. . . . Evils like the oppression of the government, the greed and graft of officials, . . . the cruelty of tortures and penalties, the tyranny of tax collections, the humiliation of the queue [the requirement that all Chinese males braid their hair]—shall all be exterminated together with the Manchu rule. Evils in social customs, such as the keeping of slaves, the cruelty of foot binding, the spread of the poison of opium, should also all be prohibited. . . .

The second period is that of government by a provisional constitution. When military law is lifted in each *hsien* [district], the Military Government shall return the right of self-government to the local people. . . .

The third period will be government under the constitution. Six years after the provisional constitution has been enforced a constitution shall be made. The military and administrative powers of the Military Government shall be annulled; the people shall elect the president, and elect the members of parliament to organize the parliament.

 How do Sun Yat-sen's proposals compare with those advanced by Wang Tao earlier in this chapter? Can Sun be described as a Chinese nationalist?

At first, Sun's efforts yielded few positive results, but in a convention in Tokyo in 1905, he managed to unite radical groups from across China in the so-called Revolutionary Alliance, or Tongmenghui (toong-meng-HWAY) (T'ung Meng Hui). The new organization's program was based on Sun's **"three people's principles"** of nationalism (meaning primarily the elimination of Manchu rule over China), democracy, and people's livelihood. It called for a three-stage process beginning with a military takeover and ending with a constitu-

tional democracy (see the box above). Although the new organization was small and relatively inexperienced, it benefited from rising popular discontent.

THE REVOLUTION OF 1911 In October 1911, Sun's followers launched an uprising in the industrial center of Wuhan (WOO-HAHN), in central China. With Sun traveling in the United States, the insurrection lacked leadership, but the decrepit government's inability to react quickly encouraged

The Last Emperor (1987)

On November 14, 1908, the Chinese emperor Guangxu died in Beijing. One day later, Empress Dowager Cixi—the real power behind the throne—passed away as well. A three-year-old boy, to be known in history as Henry Puyi, ascended the throne. Four years later, the Qing dynasty collapsed, and the deposed monarch lived out the remainder of his life in a China lashed by political turmoil and violence. He finally died in 1967 at the height of the Great Proletarian Cultural Revolution.

The Last Emperor (1987), directed by the Italian filmmaker Bernardo Bertolucci, is a brilliant portrayal of the experience of one hapless individual in a nation caught up in the throes of a seemingly endless revolution. The film evokes the fading majesty of the last days of imperial China but also the chaos of the warlord era and the terrors of the Maoist period, when the last shreds of the ex-emperor's personality were shattered under the pressure of Communist brainwashing techniques. Puyi (John Lone), who never appears to grasp what is happening to his country, lives and dies a nonentity.

The film, based on Puyi's autobiography, benefits from having been filmed partly on site in the Imperial City. In addition to the Chinese American actors John Lone and

Yanco/Tao/Recorded Picture Co/The Kobal Collection

Three-year-old Puyi (Richard Vuu), the last emperor of China, watches an emissary approach at the Imperial Palace.

Joan Chen, the cast includes the veteran film star Peter O'Toole, who plays Puyi's tutor when he was an adolescent.

---

political forces at the provincial level to take measures into their own hands. The dynasty was now in a state of virtual collapse: the empress dowager had died in 1908, one day after her nephew Guangxu; the throne was now occupied by China's "last emperor," the infant Puyi (POO-YEE) (P'u Yi). Sun's party had neither the military strength nor the political base necessary to seize the initiative, however, and was forced to turn to a representative of the old order, General Yuan Shikai (yoo-AHN shee-KY) (Yuan Shih-k'ai; 1859–1916). A prominent figure in military circles since the beginning of the century, Yuan had been placed in charge of the imperial forces sent to suppress the rebellion, but now he abandoned the Manchus and acted on his own behalf. In negotiations with representatives of Sun Yat-sen's party (Sun himself had arrived in China in January 1912), he agreed to serve as president of a new Chinese republic. The old dynasty and the age-old system that it had attempted to preserve were no more (see the Film & History feature above).

Although the dynasty was gone, Sun and his followers were unable to consolidate their gains. The program of the Revolutionary Alliance was based on Western liberal democratic principles aimed at the urban middle class. That class and program had provided the foundation for the capitalist democratic revolutions in western Europe and North America in the late eighteenth and nineteenth centuries, but the middle class in China was still too small to form the basis for

a new political order. The vast majority of the Chinese people still lived on the land. Sun had hoped to win their support with a land reform program, but few peasants had participated in the 1911 revolution. In failing to create new institutions and values to provide a framework for a changing society, the events of 1911 were less a revolution than a collapse of the old order. Under the weight of Western imperialism and its own internal weaknesses, the old dynasty had crumbled before new political and social forces were ready to fill the void.

What China had experienced was part of a historical process that was bringing down traditional empires across the globe, both in regions threatened by Western imperialism and in Europe itself, where tsarist Russia, the Austro-Hungarian Empire, and the Ottoman Empire all came to an end within a few years after the collapse of the Qing. The circumstances of their demise were not all the same. The Austro-Hungarian Empire, for example, was dismembered by the victorious allies after World War I, and the fate of tsarist Russia was directly linked to that conflict (see Chapter 23). Still, all four regimes bore some responsibility for their fate in that they had failed to meet the challenges posed by the times. All had responded to the forces of industrialization and popular participation in the political process with hesitation and reluctance, and their attempts at reform were too little and too late. All paid the supreme price for their folly.

© Hulton Archive/Getty Images

Sun Yat-sen, Father of Modern China. The son of a peasant in southern China, Sun Yat-sen rose to become a prominent revolutionary and the founder of the first Chinese republic. This photograph shows Sun as he assumed office as provisional president in January 1912. Shortly thereafter, he was forced to resign in favor of General Yuan Shikai, who moved the capital from Nanjing to Beijing.

Chinese Society in Transition

 FOCUS QUESTION: What political, economic, and social reforms were instituted by the Qing dynasty during its final decades, and why were they not more successful in reversing the decline of Manchu rule?

The growing Western presence in China during the late nineteenth and early twentieth centuries obviously had a major impact on Chinese society. Hence, until recently historians commonly asserted that the arrival of the Europeans shook China out of centuries of slumber and launched it on the road to revolutionary change. As we now know, however, Chinese society was already in a state of transition when the European economic penetration began to accelerate in the mid-nineteenth century. The growth of industry and trade was particularly noticeable in the cities, where a national market for such commodities as oil, copper, salt, tea, and porcelain had developed. The foundation of an infrastructure more conducive to the rise of a money economy appeared to be in place. In the

countryside, new crops introduced from abroad significantly increased food production and aided population growth. The Chinese economy had never been more productive or more complex.

The Economy: The Drag of Tradition

Whether these changes by themselves in the absence of outside intervention would eventually have led to an industrial revolution and the rise of a capitalist economy on the Western model is a hypothetical question that historians cannot answer. Certainly, a number of obstacles would have made it difficult for China to embark on the Western path if it had wished to do so.

Although industrial production was on the rise, it was still based almost entirely on traditional methods. There was no uniform system of weights and measures, and the banking system was still primitive by European standards. The use of paper money, invented by the Chinese centuries earlier, was still relatively limited. The transportation system, which had been neglected since the end of the Yuan dynasty, was increasingly chaotic. There were few paved roads, and the Grand Canal, long the most efficient means of carrying goods from north to south, was silting up. As a result, merchants had to rely more and more on the coastal route, where they faced increasing competition from foreign shipping.

Although foreign concession areas in the coastal cities provided a conduit for the importation of Western technology and modern manufacturing methods, the Chinese borrowed less than they might have. Foreign manufacturing enterprises could not legally operate in China until the last decade of the nineteenth century, and their methods had little influence beyond the concession areas. Chinese efforts to imitate Western methods, notably in shipbuilding and weapons manufacture, were dominated by the government and often suffered from mismanagement.

Equally serious problems persisted in the countryside. The rapid increase in population had led to smaller plots and burgeoning numbers of tenant farmers. Whether per capita consumption of food was on the decline is not clear from the available evidence, but apparently rice as a staple of the diet was increasingly being replaced by less nutritious foods, many of which depleted the soil, already under pressure from the dramatic increase in population. Some farmers benefited from switching to commercial agriculture to supply the markets of the growing coastal cities, but the shift entailed a sizable investment. Many farmers went so deeply into debt that they eventually lost their land. In the meantime, the traditional patron-client relationship was frayed as landlords moved to the cities to take advantage of the glittering urban lifestyle introduced by the West.

Some of these problems can undoubtedly be ascribed to the challenges presented by the growing Western presence. But the court's hesitant efforts to cope with these challenges suggest that the most important obstacle was at the top: Qing officials often seemed overwhelmed by the combination of external pressure and internal strife. At a time when a number of other traditional societies, such as Russia, the Ottoman Empire, and Japan, were making vigorous attempts to modernize their economies, the Manchu court, along with much of the elite class, still exhibited an alarming degree of complacency and was unable to bring the Chinese economy up to the standards being applied in the industrial world.

The Impact of Imperialism

In any event, with the advent of the imperialist era in the second half of the nineteenth century, the question of whether China left to itself would have experienced an industrial revolution became academic. Imperialism caused serious distortions in the local economy that resulted in massive changes in Chinese society during the twentieth century. Whether the Western intrusion was beneficial or harmful is debated to this day. The Western presence undoubtedly accelerated the development of the Chinese economy in some ways: the introduction of modern means of production, transport, and communications; the creation of an export market; and the steady integration of the Chinese market into the nineteenth-century global economy. To many Westerners at the time, it was self-evident that such changes would ultimately benefit the Chinese people (see the comparative essay "Imperialism and the Global Environment" on p. 650). In this view, Western civilization represented the most advanced stage of human development. By supplying (in the catchphrase of the day) "oil for the lamps of China," it was providing a backward society with an opportunity to move up a notch or two on the ladder of human evolution.

Not everyone agreed. The Russian Marxist Vladimir Lenin contended that Western imperialism actually hindered the process of structural change in preindustrial societies because the imperialist powers thwarted the rise of local industrial and commercial sectors in order to maintain colonies and semicolonies as a market for Western manufactured goods and a source of cheap labor and materials. Fellow Marxists in China such as Mao Zedong (see Chapter 24) later took up Lenin's charge and asserted that if the West had not intervened, China would have found its own road to capitalism and thence to socialism and communism.

Many historians today would say that the issue is too complex for such simplistic explanations. By shaking China out of its traditional mind-set, imperialism accelerated the process of change that had begun in the late Ming and early Qing periods and forced the Chinese to adopt new ways of thinking and acting. At the same time, China paid a heavy price in the destruction of its local industry while many of the profits flowed abroad. Although the Industrial Revolution was a painful process whenever and wherever it occurred, the Chinese found the experience doubly painful because it was foisted on China from the outside.

Daily Life in Qing China

At the beginning of the nineteenth century, daily life for most Chinese was not substantially different from what it had been in earlier centuries. Most were farmers, living in thousands of villages in rice fields and on hillsides throughout the country. Their lives were governed by the harvest cycle, village custom, and family ritual. Their roles in society were firmly fixed by the time-honored principles of Confucian social ethics. Male children, at least the more fortunate ones, were educated in the Confucian classics, while females remained in the home or in the fields. All children were expected to obey their parents, and wives to submit to their husbands.

A visitor to China a hundred years later would have seen a very different society, although still recognizably Chinese. Change was most striking in the coastal cities, where the educated and affluent had been visibly affected by the growing Western cultural presence. Confucian social institutions and behavioral norms were declining rapidly in influence, while those of Europe and North America were on the ascendant. Change was much less noticeable in the countryside, but even there, the customary bonds had been dangerously frayed by the rapidly changing times.

Some of the change can be traced to the educational system. During the nineteenth century, the importance of a Confucian education steadily declined as up to half of the degree holders had purchased their degrees. After 1906, when the government abolished the civil service examinations, a Confucian education ceased to be the key to a successful career, and Western-style education became more desirable. The old dynasty attempted to modernize by establishing an educational system on the Western model with universal education at the elementary level. Such plans had some effect in the cities, where public schools, missionary schools, and other private institutions educated a new generation of Chinese with little knowledge of or respect for the past.

CHANGING ROLES FOR WOMEN The status of women was also in transition. During the mid-Qing era, women were expected to remain in the home. Their status as useless sex

Women with Bound Feet. To ensure the best possible marriages for their daughters, upper-class families began to perform foot binding during the Song dynasty. Eventually, the practice spread to all social classes in China. Although small feet were supposed to denote a woman of leisure, most Chinese women with bound feet contributed to the labor force, working mainly in textiles and handicrafts to supplement the family income.

COMPARATIVE ESSAY

Imperialism and the Global Environment

EARTH & ENVIRONMENT

Beginning in the 1870s, European states engaged in an intense scramble for overseas territory. This "new imperialism" led Europeans to carve up Asia and Africa and create colonial empires. Within these empires, European states exercised complete political control over the indigenous societies and redrew political boundaries to meet their needs. In Africa, for example, in drawing the boundaries that separated one colony from another (boundaries that often became the boundaries of the modern countries of Africa), Europeans paid no attention to existing political, linguistic, or religious divisions; they often divided distinctive communities between colonies or included two hostile communities within the same colony.

In a similar fashion, Europeans paid little or no heed to the economic requirements of their colonial subjects but instead organized the economies of their empires to meet their own needs in the world market. In the process, Europeans often dramatically altered the global environment, a transformation that was visible in a variety of ways. Westerners built railways and ports, erected telegraph lines, drilled for oil, and dug mines for gold, tin, iron ore, and copper. Although the extraction of such resources often resulted in enormous profits, citizens of the colonial powers, not the indigenous population, were the prime beneficiaries. At the same time, these projects transformed and often scarred the natural landscape.

Landscapes were even more dramatically altered by Europe's demand for cash crops. Throughout vast regions of Africa and Asia, woodlands were cleared to make way for plantations where crops for export could be cultivated. In Ceylon (modern Sri Lanka) and India, the British cut down vast tropical forests to plant row upon row of tea bushes. The Dutch razed forests in the East Indies to plant cinchona trees imported from Peru. (Quinine, derived from the trees' bark, dramatically reduced the death rate for malaria and made it possible for Europeans to live more securely in the tropical regions of Africa and Asia.) In Indochina, the French replaced extensive forests with rubber, sugar, and coffee plantations. Local workers, who were usually paid pitiful wages by their European overseers, provided the labor for all of these vast plantations.

In many areas, precious farmland was turned over to the cultivation of cash crops. In the Dutch East Indies, farmers were forced to plow up some of their rice fields to make way

for the cultivation of sugar. In West Africa, overplanting of cash crops damaged fragile grasslands and turned parts of the Sahel (suh-HAYL or suh-HEEL) into a wasteland.

European states, however, greatly profited from this transformed environment. In *Agriculture in the Tropics: An Elementary Treatise*, written in 1909, the British botanist John Christopher Willis expressed his thoughts on this European policy:

> Whether planting in the tropics will always continue to be under European management is another question, but the northern powers will not permit that the rich and as yet comparatively undeveloped countries of the tropics should be entirely wasted by being devoted merely to the supply of the food and clothing wants of their own people, when they can also supply the wants of the colder zones in so many indispensable products.

In Willis's eyes, the imperialist transformation of the environments of Asia and Africa to serve European needs was entirely justified.

 How did the effects of imperialism on the environment in colonial countries compare with the impact of the Industrial Revolution in Europe and North America?

Picking Tea Leaves in Ceylon. In this 1900 photograph, women on a plantation in Ceylon (Sri Lanka) pick tea leaves for shipment abroad. The British cut down vast stands of tropical forests in Ceylon and India to grow tea to satisfy demand back home.

---

objects was painfully symbolized by the practice of foot binding, a custom that had probably originated among court entertainers in the Tang dynasty and later, during the Song dynasty, spread to the upper classes and then to the common people. By the mid-nineteenth century, more than half of all adult women probably had bound feet.

During the second half of the nineteenth century, signs of change began to appear. Women began to seek employment

in factories—notably in cotton mills and in the silk industry, established in Shanghai in the 1890s. Some women were active in dissident activities, such as the Taiping Rebellion and the Boxer movement, and a few fought beside men in the 1911 revolution. Qiu Jin (chee-oo JIN), a well-known female revolutionary, wrote a manifesto calling for women's liberation and then organized a revolt against the Manchu government, only to be captured and executed at the age of thirty-two in 1907.

By the end of the century, educational opportunities for women began to appear for the first time. Christian missionaries began to open girls' schools, mainly in the foreign concession areas. Although only a relatively small number of women were educated in these schools, they had a significant impact on Chinese society as progressive intellectuals began to argue that ignorant women produced ignorant children. In 1905, the court announced its intention to open public schools for girls, but few such schools ever materialized. Private schools for girls were established in some urban areas. The government also began to take steps to discourage the practice of foot binding, initially with only minimal success.

A Rich Country and a Strong State: The Rise of Modern Japan

 FOCUS QUESTION: To what degree was the Meiji Restoration a "revolution," and to what extent did it succeed in transforming Japan?

By the beginning of the nineteenth century, the Tokugawa (toh-KOO-gah-wah) shogunate had ruled the Japanese islands for two hundred years. It had revitalized the old governmental system, which had virtually disintegrated under its predecessors. It had driven out the foreign traders and missionaries and reduced Japanese contacts with the Western world. The Tokugawa maintained formal relations only with Korea, although informal trading links with Dutch and Chinese merchants continued at Nagasaki (nah-gah-SAH-kee). Isolation, however, did not mean stagnation. Although the vast majority of Japanese still depended on agriculture for their livelihood, a vigorous manufacturing and commercial sector had begun to emerge during the long period of peace and prosperity. As a result, Japanese society had begun to undergo deep-seated changes, and traditional class distinctions were becoming blurred. Eventually, these changes would end Tokugawa rule and destroy the traditional feudal system.

Some historians speculate that the Tokugawa system was beginning to come apart, just as the medieval order in Europe had started to disintegrate at the beginning of the Renaissance. Factionalism and corruption plagued the central bureaucracy, while rural unrest, provoked by a series of poor harvests brought about by bad weather, swept the countryside. Farmers fled to the towns, where anger was already rising as a result of declining agricultural incomes and shrinking stipends for the samurai. Many of the samurai lashed out at the perceived incompetence and corruption of the government. In response, the *bakufu* (buh-KOO-foo *or* bah-KOO-fuh) became increasingly rigid, persecuting its critics and attempting to force fleeing peasants to return to their lands.

The government also intensified its efforts to limit contacts with the outside world, driving away the foreign ships that were beginning to prowl along the Japanese coast in increasing numbers. For many years, Japan had financed its imports of silk and other needed products from other countries in Asia with the output of its silver and copper mines. But as these mines became exhausted during the eighteenth century, the *bakufu* cut back on foreign trade, while encouraging the domestic production of goods that had previously been imported. Thus, the Tokugawa sought to adopt a policy of *sakoku* (sah-KOH-koo), or closed country, even toward many of the Asian neighbors with which Japan had once had active relations.

Opening to the World

To the Western powers, Japan's refusal to open its doors to Western goods was an affront and a challenge. Driven by the growing rivalry among themselves and convinced that the expansion of trade on a global basis would benefit all nations, Western nations began to approach Japan in the hope of opening up the kingdom to foreign economic interests.

The first to succeed was the United States. American steamships crossing the northern Pacific needed a fueling station before going on to China and other ports in the area. In the summer of 1853, an American fleet of four warships under Commodore Matthew C. Perry arrived in Edo (now Tokyo) Bay with a letter from President Millard Fillmore asking for the opening of foreign relations between the two countries (see the box on p. 652). A few months later, Perry returned with a larger fleet for an answer. In his absence, Japanese officials had hotly debated the issue. Some argued that contacts with the West would be both politically and morally disadvantageous to Japan, while others pointed to U.S. military superiority and recommended concessions. For the shogunate in Edo (EH-doh), the black guns of Perry's ships proved decisive, and Japan agreed to the Treaty of Kanagawa (kah-nah-GAH-wah), which provided for the return of shipwrecked American sailors, the opening of two ports, and the establishment of a U.S. consulate on Japanese soil. In 1858, U.S. consul Townsend Harris negotiated a more elaborate commercial treaty calling for the opening of several ports to U.S. trade and residence, the exchange of ministers, and the granting of extraterritorial privileges for U.S. residents in Japan. Similar treaties were soon signed with several European nations.

The decision to open relations with the Western barbarians was highly unpopular in some quarters, particularly in regions distant from the shogunate headquarters in Edo. Resistance was especially strong in two of the key outside daimyo (DYM-yoh) territories in the south, Satsuma (sat-SOO-muh) and Choshu (CHOH-shoo), both of which had strong military traditions. In 1863, the "Sat-Cho" alliance forced the hapless shogun to promise to end relations with the West. The shogun eventually reneged on the agreement, but the rebellious groups soon learned of their own weakness. When Choshu troops fired on Western ships in the Strait of Shimonoseki (shee-moh-noh-SEK-ee), the Westerners fired back and destroyed the Choshu fortifications. The incident convinced the rebellious samurai of the need to strengthen their own military and intensified their unwillingness to give in to the West. Having strengthened their

A Letter to the Shogun

INTERACTION & EXCHANGE

When Commodore Matthew Perry arrived in Tokyo Bay on his first visit to Japan in July 1853, he carried a letter from the president of the United States, Millard Fillmore. The letter requested that trade relations between the two countries be established. The United States was already becoming a major participant in the race for the East Asian market. Little did the president know how momentous the occasion was or with what eagerness the Japanese would eventually respond to the challenge.

A Letter from the President of the United States

Millard Fillmore
President of the United States of America

To His Imperial Majesty,
The Emperor of Japan

Great and Good Friend!
I send you this public letter by Commodore Matthew C. Perry, an officer of the highest rank in the Navy of the United States, and commander of the squadron now visiting your Imperial Majesty's dominions.

I have directed Commodore Perry to assure your Imperial Majesty that I entertain the kindest feelings towards your Majesty's person and government; and that I have no other object in sending him to Japan, but to propose to your Imperial Majesty that the United States and Japan should live in friendship, and have commercial intercourse with each other. The constitution and laws of the United States forbid all interference with the religious or political concerns of other nations. I have particularly charged Commodore Perry to abstain from every act which could possibly disturb the tranquillity of your Imperial Majesty's dominions.

The United States of America reach from ocean to ocean, and our territory of Oregon and state of California lie directly opposite to the dominions of your Imperial Majesty. Our steamships can go from California to Japan in eighteen days. . . .

Japan is also a rich and fertile country, and produces many very valuable articles. . . . I am desirous that our two countries should trade with each other, for the benefit both of Japan and the United States.

We know that the ancient laws of your Imperial Majesty's government do not allow of foreign trade except with the Dutch. But as the state of the world changes, and new governments are formed, it seems to be wise from time to time to make new laws. . . . If your Imperial Majesty were so far to change the ancient laws as to allow a free trade between the two countries, it would be extremely beneficial to both. . . .

Many of our ships pass every year from California to China; and great numbers of our people pursue the whale fishery near the shores of Japan. It sometimes happens in stormy weather that one of our ships is wrecked on your Imperial Majesty's shores. In all such cases we ask and expect, that our unfortunate people should be treated with kindness, and that their property should be protected, till we can send a vessel and bring them away. . . .

May the Almighty have your Imperial Majesty in his great and holy keeping! . . .

Your Good Friend,
Millard Fillmore

 Why did President Fillmore want to establish relations with Japan? Why were Japanese leaders reluctant to agree to his request?

---

influence at the imperial court in Kyoto, they demanded the shogun's resignation and the restoration of the emperor's power. In January 1868, rebel armies attacked the shogun's palace in Kyoto and proclaimed the restored authority of the emperor. After a few weeks, resistance collapsed, and the venerable shogunate system was brought to an end.

The Meiji Restoration

Although the victory of the Sat-Cho faction had appeared on the surface to be a triumph of tradition over change, the new leaders soon realized that Japan must modernize to survive. Accordingly, they embarked on a policy of comprehensive reform that would lay the foundations of a modern industrial nation within a generation.

The symbol of the new era was the young emperor himself, who had taken the reign name Meiji (MAY-jee), meaning "enlightened rule," on ascending the throne after the death of his father in 1867. Although the post-Tokugawa period was termed a "restoration," the Meiji ruler, who shared the modernist outlook newly adopted by the Sat-Cho group, was controlled by the new leadership just as the shogunate had controlled his predecessors. In tacit recognition of the real source of political power, the new capital was located at Edo, now renamed Tokyo ("eastern capital"), and the imperial court was moved to the shogun's palace in the center of the city.

THE TRANSFORMATION OF JAPANESE POLITICS Once in power, the new leaders launched a comprehensive reform of Japanese political, social, economic, and cultural institutions and values. They moved first to abolish the remnants of the old order and strengthen executive power in their hands. To undercut the power of the daimyo, hereditary privileges were abolished in 1871, and the great lords lost title to their lands. As compensation, they were given government bonds and

© The Art Archive/British Museum, London

Black Ships in Tokyo Bay. The arrival of a U.S. fleet commanded by Commodore Matthew Perry in 1853 caused consternation among many Japanese observers, who were intimidated by the size and ominous presence of the American ships. This nineteenth-century woodblock print shows curious Japanese paddling out to greet the arrivals.

were named governors of the territories formerly under their control. The samurai, comprising about 8 percent of the total population, received a lump-sum payment to replace their traditional stipends, but they were forbidden to wear the sword, the symbol of their hereditary status.

The Meiji modernizers also set out to create a modern political system based roughly on the Western model. In the

(vertical text, left margin of image) Collection Ministry of Foreign Affairs, Tokyo//© Art Resource, NY

Emperor Meiji and the Charter Oath. In 1868, reformist elements overthrew the Tokugawa shogunate in an era of rapid modernization in Japanese society. Their intentions were announced in a charter oath of five articles promulgated in April 1868. In this contemporary print, the young Emperor Meiji listens to the reading of the Charter Oath in his palace in Kyoto.

Charter Oath of 1868, the new leaders promised to create a new deliberative assembly within the framework of continued imperial rule. They also called for the elimination of the "evil customs" of the past and the implementation of a vigorous program of reform based on international practices in order to "strengthen the foundations of imperial rule." Although senior positions in the new government were given to the daimyo, the key posts were dominated by modernizing samurai, eventually to be known as the *genro* (gen-ROH *or* GEN-roh), or elder statesmen, from the Sat-Cho clique.

During the next two decades, the Meiji government undertook a systematic study of Western political systems. A constitutional commission under Ito Hirobumi (ee-TOH HEE-roh-BOO-mee) (1841–1909) traveled to several Western countries, including Great Britain, Germany, Russia, and the United States, to study their political systems. As the process evolved, a number of factions appeared, each representing different political ideas. The most prominent were the Liberal Party and the Progressive Party. The Liberal Party favored political reform on the Western liberal democratic model, with supreme authority vested in the parliament as the representative of the people. The Progressive Party called for the distribution of power between the legislative and executive branches, with a slight nod to the latter. There

A Rich Country and a Strong State: The Rise of Modern Japan ❦ **653**

was also an imperial party, which advocated the retention of supreme authority exclusively in the hands of the emperor.

THE CONSTITUTION OF 1890 During the 1870s and 1880s, these factions competed for preeminence. Ito Hirobumi himself harbored doubts about the Western system of liberal democracy, fearing that it might not be appropriate for Japan. In the end, the Progressives emerged victorious. The Meiji Constitution, which was adopted in 1890, was based on the Bismarckian model with authority vested in the executive branch; the imperialist faction was pacified by the statement that the constitution was the gift of the emperor. Members of the cabinet were to be handpicked by the Meiji oligarchs. The upper house of parliament was to be appointed and have equal legislative powers with the lower house, called the Diet, whose members would be elected. The core ideology of the state, called the *kokutai* (koh-kuh-TY), or national polity, embodied (although in very imprecise form) the concept of the uniqueness of the Japanese system based on the supreme authority of the emperor. At the suggestion of a German adviser, the ancient practice of Shinto was transformed into a virtual national religion, and its traditional ritual ceremonies were performed at all important events in the imperial court.

The result was a system that was democratic in form but despotic in practice, modern in appearance but still traditional in that power remained in the hands of a ruling oligarchy. The system permitted the traditional ruling class to retain its influence and economic power while acquiescing in the emergence of new institutions and values.

MEIJI ECONOMICS With the end of the daimyo domains, the government needed to establish a new system of land ownership that would transform the mass of the rural population from indentured serfs into citizens. To do so, it enacted a land reform program that redefined the domain lands as the private property of the tillers while compensating the previous owner with government bonds. One reason for the new policy was that the government needed operating revenues. At the time, public funds came mainly from customs fees, which were limited by agreement with the foreign powers to 5 percent of the value of the product. To remedy the problem, the Meiji leaders added a new agriculture tax, which was set at an annual rate of 3 percent of the estimated value of the land. The new tax proved to be a lucrative and dependable source of income for the government, but it was onerous for the farmers, who had previously paid a fixed percentage of their harvest to the landowner. As a result, in bad years, many peasants were unable to pay their taxes and were forced to sell their lands to wealthy neighbors. Eventually, the government reduced the tax to 2.5 percent of the land value. Still, by the end of the century, about 40 percent of all farmers were tenants.

With its budget needs secured, the government turned to the promotion of industry with the basic objective of guaranteeing Japan's survival against the challenge of Western imperialism. Building on the small but growing industrial economy that existed under the Tokugawa, the Meiji reformers supplied a massive stimulus to Japan's industrial revolution. The government provided financial subsidies to needy industries, training, foreign advisers, improved transport and communications, and a universal educational system emphasizing applied science. In contrast to China, Japan was able to achieve results with minimal reliance on foreign capital. Although the first railroad—built in 1872—was financed by a loan from Great Britain, future projects were all backed by local funds. The foreign currency holdings came largely from tea and silk, which were exported in significant quantities during the latter half of the nineteenth century.

During the late Meiji era, Japan's industrial sector began to grow. Besides tea and silk, other key industries were weaponry, shipbuilding, and sake (SAH-kee) (fermented rice wine). From the start, the distinctive feature of the Meiji model was the intimate relationship between government and private business in terms of operations and regulations. Once an individual enterprise or industry was on its feet (or, sometimes, when it had ceased to make a profit), it was turned over entirely to private ownership, although the government often continued to play some role even after it was no

Collection Ministry of Foreign Affairs, Tokyo//© Art Resource, NY

The Emperor Inspects His Domain. A crucial challenge for the Japanese government during the Meiji era was to increase the country's food supply by improving the productivity of agricultural workers. In this painting, Emperor Meiji inspects a flooded field where farmers are planting rice seedlings. The practice of showing the imperial face in public was an innovation introduced by Emperor Meiji that earned him the affection of his subjects.

longer directly involved in management. Historians have explained the process:

> [The Meiji government] pioneered many industrial fields and sponsored the development of others, attempting to cajole businessmen into new and risky kinds of endeavor, helping assemble the necessary capital, forcing weak companies to merge into stronger units, and providing private entrepreneurs with aid and privileges of a sort that would be corrupt favoritism today. All this was in keeping with Tokugawa traditions that business operated under the tolerance and patronage of government. Some of the political leaders even played a dual role in politics and business.[4]

From the workers' perspective, the Meiji reforms had a less attractive side. As we have seen, the new land tax provided the funds to subsidize the growth of the industrial sector, but it imposed severe hardships on the rural population, forcing many people to abandon their farms and flee to the cities, where they provided an abundant source of cheap labor for Japanese industry. As in Europe during the early decades of the Industrial Revolution, workers toiled for long hours in the coal mines and textile mills, often under horrendous conditions. Reportedly, coal miners employed on a small island in Nagasaki harbor worked naked in temperatures up to 130 degrees Fahrenheit. If they tried to escape, they were shot.

BUILDING A MODERN SOCIAL STRUCTURE By the late Tokugawa era, the rigidly hierarchical social order was showing signs of disintegration. Rich merchants were buying their way into the ranks of the samurai, and Japanese of all classes were beginning to abandon their rice fields and move into the growing cities. Nevertheless, community and hierarchy still formed the basis of Japanese society. The lives of all Japanese were determined by their membership in various social groups—the family, the village, and their social class. Membership in a particular social class determined a person's occupation and social relationships with others. Women in particular were constrained by the "**three obediences**" imposed on their sex: child to father, wife to husband, and widow to son. Husbands could easily obtain a divorce, but wives could not (supposedly, a husband could divorce his spouse if she drank too much tea or talked too much). Marriages were arranged, and the average age at marriage for women was sixteen years. Females did not share inheritance rights with males, and few received any education outside the family.

The Meiji reformers dismantled much of the traditional social system in Japan. With the abolition of hereditary rights in 1871, the legal restrictions of the past were brought to an end with a single stroke. Special privileges for the aristocracy were abolished, as were the legal restrictions on the *eta* (AY-tuh), the traditional slave class (numbering about 400,000 in the 1870s). Another key focus of the reformers was the army. The Sat-Cho reformers had been struck by the weakness of the Japanese forces in clashes with Western powers and embarked on a major program to create a military force that could compete in the modern world. The old feudal army based on the traditional warrior class was abolished, and an imperial army based on universal conscription was formed in 1871. For many rural males, the army became a route of upward mobility.

Education also underwent major changes. The Meiji leaders recognized the need for universal education, including technical subjects, and after a few years of experimenting, they adopted the American model of a three-tiered system culminating in a series of universities and specialized institutes. In the meantime, they sent bright students to study abroad and brought foreign scholars to Japan to teach in the new schools, where much of the content was inspired by Western models. In another break with tradition, women for the first time were given an opportunity to get an education.

These changes were included in the Imperial Rescript on Education that was issued in 1890, but the rescript also placed strong emphasis on the traditional Confucian virtues of filial piety and loyalty to the state (see the box on p. 656). One reason for issuing the Imperial Rescript was the official concern that libertarian and individualistic ideas from the West might dilute the traditional Japanese emphasis on responsibility to the community.

Indeed, Western ideas and fashions had become the rage in elite circles, and the ministers of the first Meiji government were known as the "dancing cabinet" because of their addiction to Western-style ballroom dancing. Young people, increasingly exposed to Western culture and values, began to imitate the clothing styles, eating habits, and social practices of their European and American counterparts (see the box on p. 657). They even took up American sports when baseball was introduced.

TRADITIONAL VALUES AND WOMEN'S RIGHTS Nonetheless, the self-proclaimed transformation of Japan into a "modern society" by no means detached the country entirely from its traditional moorings. Although an educational order in 1872 increased the percentage of Japanese women exposed to public education, conservatives soon began to impose restrictions and bring about a return to more traditional social relationships. As we have seen, the Imperial Rescript on Education in 1890 stressed the Confucian virtues of filial piety, patriotism, and loyalty to the family and community. Traditional values were given a firm legal basis in the Constitution of 1890, which restricted the franchise to males and defined individual liberties as "subject to the limitations imposed by law," and by the Civil Code of 1898, which de-emphasized individual rights and essentially placed women within the context of their role in the family.

By the end of the nineteenth century, however, changes were under way as women began to play a crucial role in their nation's effort to modernize. Urged by their parents to augment the family income, as well as by the government to fulfill their patriotic duty, young girls were sent en masse to work in textile mills. From 1894 to 1912, women represented 60 percent of the Japanese labor force. Thanks to them, by 1914, Japan was the world's leading exporter of silk and dominated cotton manufacturing. If it had not been for the export revenues earned from textile exports, Japan might not have been able to develop its heavy industry and military prowess without an infusion of foreign capital.

Japanese women received few rewards, however, for their contribution to the nation. In 1900, new regulations prohibited women from joining political organizations or attending public meetings. Beginning in 1905, a group of independent-minded women petitioned the Japanese parliament to rescind this

The Rules of Good Citizenship in Meiji Japan

POLITICS & GOVERNMENT

After seizing power from the Tokugawa shogunate in 1868, the new Japanese leaders turned their attention to the creation of a new political system that would bring the country into the modern world. After exploring various systems in use in the West, a constitutional commission decided to adopt the system used in imperial Germany because of its paternalistic character. To promote civic virtue and obedience among the citizenry, the government then drafted an imperial rescript that was to be taught to every schoolchild in the country. The rescript instructed all children to obey their sovereign and place the interests of the community and the state above their own personal desires.

Imperial Rescript on Education, 1890

Know ye, Our subjects:

Our Imperial Ancestors have founded Our Empire on a basis broad and everlasting, and have deeply and firmly implanted virtue. Our subjects ever united in loyalty and filial piety have from generation to generation illustrated the beauty thereof. This is the glory of the fundamental character of Our Empire, and herein also lies the source of Our education. Ye, Our subjects, be filial to your parents, affectionate to your brothers and sisters, as husbands and wives be harmonious, as friends true; bear yourselves in modesty and moderation; extend your benevolence to all; pursue learning and cultivate arts, and thereby develop intellectual faculties and perfect moral powers; furthermore, advance public good and promote common interests; always respect the Constitution and observe the laws; should emergency arise, offer yourselves to the State; and thus guard and maintain the prosperity of Our Imperial Throne coeval with heaven and earth. So shall ye not only be Our good and faithful subjects, but render illustrious the best traditions of your forefathers.

Q *According to the Imperial Rescript, what was the primary purpose of education in Meiji Japan? How did these goals compare with those in China and the West?*

---

restriction. Although the regulation was not repealed until 1922, movements got under way to bring about an extension of women's rights in Japanese society (see the box on p. 658).

Joining the Imperialist Club

Traditionally, Japan had not been an expansionist country. As we have seen, except for sporadic forays against Korea, the Japanese had generally been satisfied to remain on their home islands and had even deliberately isolated themselves from their neighbors during the Tokugawa era. Now, however, the Japanese did not just imitate the domestic policies of their Western mentors; they also emulated the Western approach to foreign affairs. This is perhaps not surprising. The Japanese regarded themselves as particularly vulnerable in the world economic arena. Their territory was small, lacking in resources, and densely populated, and they had no natural outlet for expansion. To observant Japanese, the lessons of history were clear. Western nations had amassed wealth and power not only because of their democratic systems and high level of education but also because of their colonies.

The Japanese began their program of territorial expansion close to home (see Map 22.4). In 1874, the Japanese claimed compensation from China for fifty-four sailors from the Ryukyu (RYOO-kyoo) Islands who had been killed by the local population on the island of Taiwan (TY-WAHN) and sent a Japanese fleet to Taiwan to punish the perpetrators. When the Qing dynasty evaded responsibility for the incident while agreeing to pay an indemnity to Japan to cover the cost of the

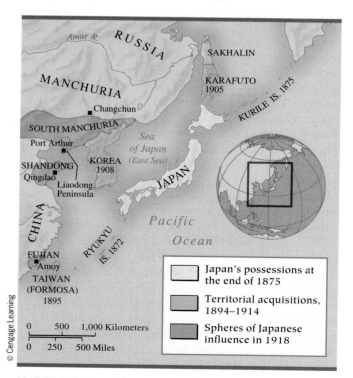

© Cengage Learning

MAP 22.4 Japanese Overseas Expansion During the Meiji Era. Beginning in the late nineteenth century, Japan ventured beyond its home islands and became an imperialist power. The extent of Japanese colonial expansion through World War I is shown here.

Q *Which parts of the Chinese Empire came under Japanese influence?*

The Wonders of Western Civilization: Two Views

INTERACTION & EXCHANGE

As information about Western institutions and values began to penetrate East Asian societies during the nineteenth century, it aroused considerable interest and discussion, at least in educated circles. Some found much to admire in Western science and democracy, as the first selection demonstrates. Published in 1891 by the Chinese intellectual Wang Xiji (wahng SHEE-jee) (Wang Hsi-ch'i), it is a description of European society written in a generally laudatory manner by a hypothetical Chinese visitor.

To other Asian observers, however, the lavish praise and imitation of Western ways was a source of irritation and even ridicule. In the second selection, published in 1871, the Japanese writer Kanagaki Rebun (REE-bun) mocks his compatriots who admire Western civilization and seek to bring it to his country. He begins by heaping scorn on those Japanese who now enjoy eating beef simply because it is a popular food in the West.

Wang Xiji, *A Chinese Description of Europe*

Europe (*Ou-lo-pa*) is one of the five great continents. . . . Though it is smaller than the other four continents, its soil is fertile, its products are plentiful, it has many talented people and many famous places. For this reason, Europe's power in the present world is pre-eminent, and it has become a leading force in the five continents. Yet in ancient times its people hunted for a living, ate meat, and wore skins. Their customs were barbaric, and their spirit was wild and free. But during our own Shang period (2000 B.C.E.) Greece and other countries gradually came under the influence of the Orient. For the first time they began to till fields and manufacture products, build cities, and dig lakes. They began to do all kinds of things. Before long, writing and civilization began to flourish. Thus, they became beautiful like the countries of the East. . . .

Europe's people are all tall and white. Only those who live in the northeast where it is very cold are short, and dwarfish. They have big noses and deep eyes. But their eyes are not of the same color, with brown, green, and black being most frequent. They have heavy beards that go up to their temples, or are wound around their jaws. . . .

Now for their machines. When they first invented them, they just relied on common sense. They tried this and rejected that, without ever finding out from anyone else how it ought to be done. However, they did some research and found people who investigated the fine points and propagated their usage. In this way they gradually developed all their machines such as steamships, steam trains, spinning machines, mining and canal-digging machines, and all machines for making weapons and gunpowder. Things improved day to day and helped enrich the nation and benefit the people. Day by day they became more prosperous and will keep on becoming so.

Kanagaki Rebun, *The Beefeater*

Excuse me, but the beef is certainly a most delicious thing, isn't it? Once you get accustomed to its taste, you can never go back to deer or wild boar again. I wonder why we in Japan haven't eaten such a clean thing before? For over 1,620—or is it 1,630—years people in the West have been eating huge quantities of beef. . . . We really should be grateful that even people like ourselves can now eat beef, thanks to the fact that Japan is steadily becoming a truly civilized country.

In the West they're free of superstitions. There it's the custom to do everything scientifically, and that's why they've invented amazing things like the steamship and the steam engine. Did you know that they engrave the plates for printing newspapers with telegraphic needles? And that they bring down wind from the sky with balloons? Aren't they wonderful inventions! Of course, there are good reasons behind these inventions. If you look at a map of the world you'll see some countries marked "tropical," which means that's where the sun shines closest. The people in those countries are all burnt black by the sun. The king of that part of the world tried all kinds of schemes before he hit on what is called a balloon. That's a big round bag they fill with air high up in the sky. They bring the bag down and open it, causing the cooling air inside the bag to spread out all over the country. That's a great invention. On the other hand, in Russia, which is a cold country where the snow falls even in summer and the ice is so thick that people can't move, they invented the steam engine. You've got to admire them for it. I understand that they modeled the steam engine after the flaming chariot of hell, but anyway, what they do is to load a crowd of people on a wagon and light a fire in a pipe underneath. They keep feeding the fire inside the pipe with a coal, so that the people riding on top can travel a great distance completely oblivious to the cold. Those people in the West can think up inventions like that, one after the other. . . . You say you must be going? Well, good-bye. Waitress! Another small bottle of sake. And some pickled onions to go with it!

Which of these two views of European society in the late nineteenth century appears to be more accurate? Why?

"In the Beginning, We Were the Sun"

FAMILY & SOCIETY

One aspect of Western thought that the Meiji reformers did not seek to imitate was the idea of gender equality. Although Japanese women sometimes tried to be "modern" like their male counterparts, Japanese society as a whole continued to treat women differently, as had been the case during the Tokugawa era. In 1911, a young woman named Hiratsuka Raicho (hee-RAHT-soo-kuh RAY-choh) founded a journal named *Seito* (SAY-toh) (*Blue Stockings*) to promote the liberation of women in Japan. The goal of the new movement was to encourage women to develop their own latent talents, rather than to demand legal changes in Japanese society. The following document is the proclamation that was issued at the creation of the Seito Society. Compare it with Mary Wollstonecraft's discussion of the rights of women in Chapter 18.

Hiratsuka Raicho, Proclamation at the Founding of the Seito Society

Freedom and Liberation! Oftentimes we have heard the term "liberation of women." But what is it then? Are we not seriously misunderstanding the term freedom or liberation? Even if we call the problem the liberation of women, are there not many other issues involved? Assuming that women are freed from external oppression, liberated from constraint, given the so-called higher education, employed in various occupations, given [the] franchise, and provided an opportunity to be independent from the protection of their parents and husbands, and to be freed from the little confinement of their homes, can all of these be called liberation of women? They may provide proper surroundings and opportunities to let us fulfill the true goal of liberation. Yet they remain merely the means, and do not represent our goal or ideals.

However, I am unlike many intellectuals in Japan who suggest that higher education is not necessary for women. Men and women are endowed by nature to have equal faculties. Therefore, it is odd to assume that one of the sexes requires education while the other does not. This may be tolerated in a given country and in a given age, but it is fundamentally a very unsound proposition.

I bemoan the facts that there is only one private college for women in Japan, and that there is no tolerance on man's part to permit entrance of women into many universities maintained for men. However, what benefit is there when the intellectual level of women becomes similar to that of men? Men seek knowledge in order to escape from their lack of wisdom and lack of enlightenment. They want to free themselves. . . . Yet multifarious thought can darken true wisdom, and lead men away from nature. . . .

Now, what is the true liberation which I am seeking? It is none other than to provide an opportunity for women to develop fully their hidden talents and hidden abilities. We must remove all the hindrances that stand in the way of women's development, whether they be external oppression or lack of knowledge. And above and beyond these factors, we must realize that we are the masters in possession of great talents, for we are the bodies which enshrine the great talents.

 What did Hiratsuka Raicho think was necessary to bring about the liberation of women in Meiji Japan? Were her proposals similar to those set forth by her counterparts in the West?

---

expedition, it weakened its claim to ownership of the island of Taiwan. Japan was then able to claim suzerainty over the Ryukyu Islands, long tributary to the Chinese Empire. Two years later, Japanese naval pressure forced Korea to open three ports to Japanese commerce.

Korea had long followed Japan's example and attempted to isolate itself from outside contact except for periodic tribute missions to China. Christian missionaries, mostly Chinese or French, were vigorously persecuted. But Korea's problems were basically internal. In the early 1860s, a peasant revolt, inspired in part by the Taiping Rebellion in China, caused considerable devastation before being crushed in 1864. In succeeding years, the Yi (YEE) dynasty sought to strengthen the country by returning to traditional values and fending off outside intrusion, but rural poverty and official corruption remained rampant. A U.S. fleet, following the example of Commodore Perry in Japan, sought to open the country in 1871 but was driven off with considerable loss of life.

Korea's most persistent suitor, however, was Japan, which was determined to bring an end to Korea's dependency status with China and modernize it along Japanese lines. In 1876, the two countries signed an agreement opening three treaty ports to Japanese commerce in return for Japanese recognition of Korean independence. During the 1880s, Sino-Japanese rivalry over Korea intensified. China supported conservatives at the Korean court, while Japan promoted a more radical faction that was determined to break loose from lingering Chinese influence. When a new rural rebellion broke out in Korea in 1894, China and Japan intervened on opposite sides. During the war, the Japanese navy destroyed the Chinese fleet and seized the Manchurian city of Port Arthur (see the box on p. 659). In the Treaty of Shimonoseki in 1895, China was forced to recognize the independence of Korea and cede Taiwan and the Liaodong peninsula with its strategic naval base at Port Arthur to Japan.

Shortly thereafter, under pressure from the European powers, the Japanese returned the Liaodong peninsula to

Two Views of the World

INTERACTION & EXCHANGE

During the nineteenth century, China's hierarchical way of looking at the outside world came under severe challenge, not only from European countries avid for new territories in Asia but also from the rising power of Japan, which accepted the Western view that a colonial empire was the key to national greatness. Japan's first objective was Korea, long a dependency of China, and in 1894, the competition between China and Japan in the peninsula led to war. The following declarations of war by the rulers of the two countries are revealing. Note the Chinese use of the derogatory term *Wojen* ("dwarf people") in referring to the Japanese.

Declaration of War Against China

Korea is an independent state. She was first introduced into the family of nations by the advice and guidance of Japan. It has, however, been China's habit to designate Korea as her dependency, and both openly and secretly to interfere with her domestic affairs. At the time of the recent insurrection in Korea, China despatched troops thither, alleging that her purpose was to afford a succor to her dependent state. We, in virtue of the treaty concluded with Korea in 1882, and looking to possible emergencies, caused a military force to be sent to that country.

Wishing to procure for Korea freedom from the calamity of perpetual disturbance, and thereby to maintain the peace of the East in general, Japan invited China's cooperation for the accomplishment of the object. But China, advancing various pretexts, declined Japan's proposal. . . . Such conduct on the part of China is not only a direct injury to the rights and interests of this Empire, but also a menace to the permanent peace and tranquility of the Orient. . . . In this situation, . . . we find it impossible to avoid a formal declaration of war against China.

Declaration of War Against Japan

Korea has been our tributary for the past two hundred odd years. She has given us tribute all this time, which is a matter known to the world. For the past dozen years or so Korea has been troubled by repeated insurrections and we, in sympathy with our small tributary, have as repeatedly sent succor to her aid. . . . This year another rebellion was begun in Korea, and the King repeatedly asked again for aid from us to put down the rebellion. We then ordered Li Hung-chang to send troops to Korea; and they having barely reached Yashan the rebels immediately scattered. But the *Wojen*, without any cause whatever, suddenly sent their troops to Korea, and entered Seoul, the capital of Korea, reinforcing them constantly until they have exceeded ten thousand men. In the meantime the Japanese forced the Korean king to change his system of government, showing a disposition every way of bullying the Koreans. . . .

As Japan has violated the treaties and not observed international laws, and is now running rampant with her false and treacherous actions commencing hostilities herself, and laying herself open to condemnation by the various powers at large, we therefore desire to make it known to the world that we have always followed the paths of philanthropy and perfect justice throughout the whole complications, while the *Wojen*, on the other hand, have broken all the laws of nations and treaties which it passes our patience to bear with. Hence we commanded Li Hung-chang to give strict orders to our various armies to hasten with all speed to root the *Wojen* out of their lairs.

Compare the worldviews of China and Japan at the end of the nineteenth century, as expressed in these declarations. Which point of view do you find more persuasive?

China, but in the early twentieth century, they went back on the offensive. Rivalry with Russia over influence in Korea led to increasingly strained relations between the two countries. In 1904, Japan launched a surprise attack on the Russian naval base at Port Arthur, which Russia had taken from China in 1898. The Japanese armed forces were weaker, but Russia faced difficult logistical problems along its new Trans-Siberian Railway and severe political instability at home. In 1905, after Japanese warships sank almost the entire Russian fleet off the coast of Korea, the Russians agreed to a humiliating peace, ceding the strategically located Liaodong peninsula back to Japan, as well as southern Sakhalin (SAK-uh-leen *or* suh-khuh-LYEEN) and the Kurile (KOOR-il *or* koo-REEL) Islands. Russia also agreed to abandon its political and economic influence in Korea and southern Manchuria, which now came increasingly under Japanese control. The Japanese victory stunned the world, including the colonial peoples of Southeast Asia, who now began to realize that the white race was not necessarily invincible.

During the next few years, the Japanese consolidated their position in northeastern Asia, annexing Korea in 1908 as an integral part of Japan. When the Koreans protested the seizure, Japanese reprisals resulted in thousands of deaths. The United States was the first nation to recognize the annexation, in return for Tokyo's declaration of respect for U.S. authority in the Philippines and Japanese acceptance of the principles of the Open Door. But mutual suspicion between the two countries was growing, sparked in part by U.S. efforts to restrict immigration from all Asian countries. President Theodore

Total Humiliation. Whereas China had persevered in hiding behind the grandeur of its past, Japan had embraced the West, modernizing politically, militarily, and culturally. China's humiliation at the hands of its newly imperialist neighbor is evident in this scene, where the differences in dress and body posture of the officials negotiating the treaty after the war reflect China's disastrous defeat by the Japanese in 1895.

Roosevelt, who mediated the Russo-Japanese War, had aroused the anger of many Japanese by turning down a Japanese demand for reparations from Russia. In turn, some Americans began to fear the rise of a "yellow peril" manifested by Japanese expansion in East Asia.

Japanese Culture in Transition

The wave of Western technology and ideas that entered Japan in the second half of the nineteenth century greatly altered the shape of traditional Japanese culture. Literature in particular was affected as European models eclipsed the repetitive and frivolous tales of the Tokugawa era. Dazzled by this "new" literature, Japanese authors began translating and imitating the imported models. Experimenting with Western verse, Japanese poets were at first influenced primarily by the British but eventually adopted such styles as Symbolism,

Dadaism (DAH-duh-iz-um), and Surrealism, although some traditional poetry was still composed.

As the Japanese invited technicians, engineers, architects, and artists from Europe and the United States to teach their "modern" skills to a generation of eager students, the Meiji era became a time of massive consumption of Western artistic techniques and styles. Japanese architects and artists created huge buildings of steel and reinforced concrete adorned with Greek columns and cupolas, oil paintings reflecting the European concern with depth perception and shading, and bronze sculptures of secular subjects. All expressed the individual creator's emotional and aesthetic preferences.

Cultural exchange also went the other way as Japanese arts and crafts, porcelains, textiles, fans, folding screens, and woodblock prints became the vogue in Europe and North America. Japanese art influenced Western painters such as Vincent van Gogh, Edgar Degas (duh-GAH), and James Whistler, who experimented with flatter compositional perspectives and unusual poses. Japanese gardens, with their exquisite attention to the positioning of rocks and falling water, became especially popular in the United States.

After the initial period of mass absorption of Western art, a national reaction occurred at the end of the nineteenth century as many artists returned to pre-Meiji techniques. In 1889, the Tokyo School of Fine Arts (today the Tokyo National University of Fine Arts and Music) was founded to promote traditional Japanese art. Over the next several decades, Japanese art underwent a dynamic resurgence, reflecting the nation's emergence as a prosperous and powerful state. While some artists attempted to synthesize Japanese and foreign techniques, others returned to past artistic traditions for inspiration.

In architecture, Japan's split personality revealed itself most effectively in the Diet building. As the home of the new

CHRONOLOGY	Japan and Korea in the Era of Imperialism
Commodore Perry arrives in Tokyo Bay	1853
Townsend Harris Treaty	1858
Fall of Tokugawa shogunate	1868
U.S. fleet fails to open Korea	1871
Feudal titles abolished in Japan	1871
Japanese imperial army formed	1871
Meiji Constitution adopted	1890
Imperial Rescript on Education	1890
Treaty of Shimonoseki awards Taiwan to Japan	1895
Russo-Japanese War	1904–1905
Korea annexed by Japan	1908

The Ginza in Downtown Tokyo.
This 1877 woodblock print shows the Ginza, a major commercial thoroughfare in downtown Tokyo, with modern brick buildings and a horse-drawn streetcar. The centerpiece and focus of public attention is a new electric streetlight. In combining traditional form with modern content, this painting symbolizes the unique ability of the Japanese to borrow ideas from abroad while preserving much of the essence of their traditional culture.

Japanese parliament, it was supposed to reflect both progress and the nation and culture of Japan. For half a century, conflicting views over the priority of these concepts delayed its construction. After a number of proposals were rejected, the government held a competition in 1919, but none of the designs won general approval. Finally, in 1936 the government decided on the final design, which followed neither traditional styles nor European architecture of the period.

The Meiji Restoration: A Revolution from Above

Japan's transformation from a feudal, agrarian society to an industrializing, technologically advanced society in little more than half a century has frequently been described by outside observers (if not by the Japanese themselves) in almost miraculous terms. Some historians have questioned this characterization, pointing out that the achievements of the Meiji leaders were spotty. In *Japan's Emergence as a Modern State*, the Canadian historian E. H. Norman lamented that the **Meiji Restoration** was an "incomplete revolution" because it had not ended the economic and social inequities of feudal society or enabled the common people to participate fully in the governing process. Although the *genro* were enlightened in many respects, they were also despotic and elitist, and the distribution of wealth remained as unequal as it had been under the old system.[5]

It has also been noted that Japan's transformation into a major industrial nation was by no means complete by the beginning of the new century. Until at least the outbreak of World War I in 1914, the majority of goods produced by the manufacturing sector came from traditional cottage industries, rather than from modern factories based on the principle of large-scale output. The integration of the Japanese economy into the global marketplace was also limited, and foreign investment played a much smaller role than in most comparable economies in the West.

These criticisms are persuasive, although most of them could also be applied to many other societies going through the early stages of industrialization. In any event, from an economic perspective, the Meiji Restoration was one of the great success stories of modern times. Not only did the Meiji leaders put Japan firmly on the path to economic and political development, but they also managed to remove the unequal treaty provisions that had been imposed at mid-century. Japanese achievements are especially impressive when compared with the difficulties experienced by China, which was not only unable to realize significant changes in its traditional society but had not even reached a consensus on the need for doing so. Japan's achievements more closely resemble those of Europe, but whereas the West needed a century and a half to achieve a significant level of industrial development, the Japanese realized it in forty years.

One of the distinctive features of Japan's transition from a traditional to a modern society during the Meiji era was that it took place for the most part without violence or the kind of social or political revolution that occurred in so many other countries. The Meiji Restoration, which began the process, has been called a "revolution from above," a comprehensive restructuring of Japanese society by its own ruling group.

Technically, of course, the Meiji Restoration was not a revolution, since it was not violent and did not result in the displacement of one ruling class by another. The existing elites undertook to carry out a series of major reforms that transformed society but left their own power intact. In the words of one historian, it was "a kind of amalgamation, in which the enterprising, adaptable, or lucky individuals of the old privileged classes [were] for most practical purposes tied up with those individuals of the old submerged classes, who, probably through the same gifts, were able to rise." In that respect, the Meiji Restoration resembles the American Revolution more than the French Revolution; it was a "conservative revolution" that resulted in gradual change rather than rapid and violent change.[6]

WHAT EXPLAINS JAPANESE UNIQUENESS? The differences between the Japanese response to the West and the response of China and many other nations in the region have sparked considerable debate among students of comparative history. In this and previous chapters we have already discussed some of the reasons why China—along with most other countries in Asia and Africa—had not yet begun to enter their own industrial revolutions by the end of the nineteenth century. The puzzle, then, becomes, why was Japan apparently uniquely positioned to make the transition to an advanced industrial economy?

A number of explanations have been offered. Some have argued that Japan's success was partly due to good fortune. Lacking abundant natural resources, it was exposed to less pressure from the West than many of its neighbors. That argument is problematic, however, and would probably not have been accepted by Japanese observers at the time. Nor does it explain why nations under considerably less pressure, such as Laos and Nepal, did not advance even more quickly. All in all, the luck hypothesis is not very persuasive.

Some explanations have already been suggested in this book. Japan's unique geographic position in Asia was certainly a factor. China, a continental nation with a heterogeneous ethnic composition, was distinguished from its neighbors by its Confucian culture. By contrast, Japan was an island nation, ethnically and linguistically homogeneous, and had never been conquered. Unlike the Chinese or many other peoples in the region, the Japanese had little to fear from cultural change in terms of its effect on their national identity. The fact that the emperor, the living symbol of the nation, had adopted change ensured that his subjects could follow in his footsteps without fear.

In addition, a number of other factors may have played a role. The nature of the Japanese value system, with its emphasis on practicality and military achievement, may have contributed. Finally, the Meiji also benefited from the fact that the pace of urbanization and commercial and industrial development had already begun to quicken under the Tokugawa. Having already lost their traditional feudal role and much of the revenue from their estates, the Japanese aristocracy—daimyo and samurai alike—could discard sword and kimono and don modern military uniforms or Western business suits and still feel comfortable in both worlds.

Whatever the case, as the historian W. G. Beasley has noted, the Meiji Restoration was possible because aristocratic and capitalist elements managed to work together to bring about drastic change. Japan, it was said, was ripe for change, and nothing could have been more suitable as an antidote for the collapsing old system than the Western emphasis on wealth and power. It was a classic example of challenge and response.

THE FUSION OF EAST AND WEST The final product was an amalgam of old and new, Japanese and foreign, forming a new civilization that was still uniquely Japanese. There were some undesirable consequences, however. Because Meiji politics was essentially despotic, Japanese leaders were able to fuse key traditional elements such as the warrior ethic and the concept of feudal loyalty with the dynamics of modern industrial capitalism to create a state totally dedicated to the possession of material wealth and national power. This combination of *kokutai* and capitalism, which one scholar has described as a form of "Asian fascism," was highly effective but explosive in its international manifestation. Like modern Germany, which also entered the industrial age directly from feudalism, Japan eventually engaged in a policy of repression at home and expansion abroad in order to achieve its national objectives. In Japan, as in Germany, it took defeat in war to disconnect the drive for national development from the feudal ethic and bring about the transformation to a pluralistic society dedicated to living in peace and cooperation with its neighbors.

CHAPTER SUMMARY

Few areas of the world resisted the Western incursion as stubbornly and effectively as East Asia. Although military, political, and economic pressure by the European powers was relatively intense during this era, two of the main states in the area were able to retain their independence, while the third—Korea—was temporarily absorbed by one of its larger neighbors. Why the Chinese and the Japanese were able to prevent a total political and military takeover by foreign powers is an interesting question. One key reason was that both had a long history as well-defined states with a strong sense of national community and territorial cohesion. Although China had frequently been conquered, it had retained its sense of unique culture and identity. Geography, too, was in its favor. As a continental nation, China was able to survive partly because of its sheer size. Japan possessed the advantage of an island location.

Even more striking, however, is the different way in which the two states attempted to deal with the challenge. While the Japanese chose to face the problem in a pragmatic manner, borrowing foreign ideas and institutions that appeared to be of value and at the same time not in conflict with traditional attitudes and customs, China agonized over the issue for half a century while conservative elements fought a desperate battle to retain a maximum of the traditional heritage intact.

This chapter has discussed some of the possible reasons for those differences. In retrospect, it is difficult to avoid the conclusion that the Japanese approach was the more effective one. Whereas the Meiji leaders were able to set in motion an orderly transition from a traditional to an advanced society, in China the old system collapsed in disorder, leaving chaotic conditions that were still not rectified a generation later. China would pay a heavy price for its failure to respond coherently to the challenge.

But the Japanese "revolution from above" was by no means an unalloyed success. Ambitious efforts by Japanese leaders to carve out a share in the spoils of empire led to escalating conflict with China as well as with rival Western powers and in the early 1940s to global war. We will deal with that issue in Chapter 25. Meanwhile, in Europe, a combination of old rivalries and the effects of the Industrial Revolution were leading to a bitter regional conflict that eventually engulfed the entire world.

CHAPTER TIMELINE

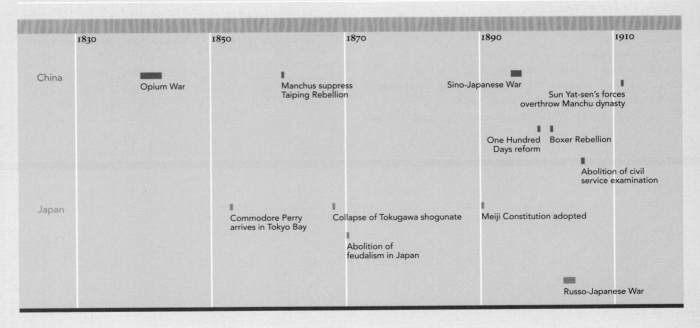

Upon Reflection

Q What were some of the key reasons why the Meiji reformers were so successful in launching Japan on the road to industrialization? Which of those reasons also applied to China under the Manchus?

Q What impact did colonial rule have on the environment in the European colonies in Asia and Africa during the nineteenth century? Did some of these same factors apply in China and Japan?

Q How did Western values and institutions influence Chinese and Japanese social mores and traditions during the imperialist era?

Key Terms

self-strengthening (p. 641)
Open Door Notes (p. 644)
three people's principles (p. 646)
sakoku (p. 651)
genro (p. 653)
kokutai (p. 654)
three obediences (p. 655)
eta (p. 655)
Meiji Restoration (p. 661)

Suggested Reading

CHINA For a general overview of modern Chinese history, see **I. C. Y. Hsu,** *The Rise of Modern China,* 6th ed. (Oxford, 2000). Also see **J. Spence's** stimulating work *The Search for Modern China* (New York, 1990).

On the Taiping Rebellion, **J. Spence,** *God's Chinese Son: The Taiping Heavenly Kingdom of Hong Xiuquan* (New York, 1996), has become a classic. Social issues are dealt with in **E. S. Rawski,** *The Last Emperors: A Social History of Qing Imperial Institutions* (Berkeley, Calif., 1998). On the Manchus' attitude toward modernization, see **D. Pong,** *Shen Pao-chen and China's Modernization in the Nineteenth Century* (New York, 1994). For a series of stimulating essays on various aspects of China's transition to modernity, see **Wen-hsin Yeh, ed.,** *Becoming Chinese: Passages to Modernity and Beyond* (Berkeley, Calif., 2000).

Sun Yat-sen's career is explored in **M. C. Bergère,** *Sun Yat-sen,* trans. **J. Lloyd** (Stanford, Calif., 2000). **S. Seagraves's** *Dragon Lady: The Life and Legend of the Last Empress of China* (New York, 1992), is a revisionist treatment of Empress Dowager Cixi. On the Boxer Rebellion, see **D. Preston,** *The Boxer Rebellion: The Dramatic Story of China's War on Foreigners That Shook the World in the Summer of 1900* (Berkeley, Calif., 2001).

JAPAN The Meiji period of modern Japan is covered in **M. B. Jansen, ed.,** *The Emergence of Meiji Japan* (Cambridge, 1995). Also see **D. Keene,** *Emperor of Japan: Meiji and His World, 1852–1912* (New York, 2000). See also **C. Gluck,** *Japan's Modern Myths: Ideology in the Late Meiji Period* (Princeton, N.J., 1985). To understand the role of the samurai in the Meiji Revolution, see **E. Ikegami,** *The Taming of the Samurai: Honorific Individualism and the Making of Modern Japan* (Cambridge, 1995).

On the international scene, **W. Lafeber,** *The Clash: U.S.-Japanese Relations Throughout History* (New York, 1997), is slow reading but a good source of information. The U.S. role in opening Japan to the West is analyzed in **G. Feifer,** *Breaking Open Japan: Commodore Perry, Lord Abe, and American Imperialism in 1853* (Washington, D.C., 2007). On the Russo-Japanese War, **R. Connaughton,** *Rising Sun and Tumbling Bear: Russia's War with Japan* (London, 2003), is one of several good offerings. The best introduction to Japanese art is **P. Mason,** *History of Japanese Art* (New York, 1993).

Go to the CourseMate website at **www.cengagebrain.com** for additional study tools and review materials— including audio and video clips—for this chapter.

The Beginning of the Twentieth-Century Crisis: War and Revolution

Canadian soldiers prepare for an attack at the Battle of the Somme

© Hulton Archive/Getty Images

CHAPTER OUTLINE AND FOCUS QUESTIONS

The Road to World War I

Q What were the long-range and immediate causes of World War I?

The Great War

Q Why did the course of World War I turn out to be so different from what the belligerents had expected? How did World War I affect the belligerents' governmental and political institutions, economic affairs, and social life?

War and Revolution

Q What were the causes of the Russian Revolution of 1917, and why did the Bolsheviks prevail in the civil war and gain control of Russia?

An Uncertain Peace

Q What was the aftermath of World War I, and what problems did Europe and the United States face in the 1920s?

In Pursuit of a New Reality: Cultural and Intellectual Trends

Q How did the cultural and intellectual trends of the post–World War I years reflect the crises of the time as well as the lingering effects of the war?

CRITICAL THINKING

Q What was the relationship between World War I and the Russian Revolution?

ON JULY 1, 1916, BRITISH and French infantry forces attacked German defensive lines along a 25-mile front near the Somme (SUHM) River in France. Each soldier carried almost 70 pounds of equipment, making it "impossible to move much quicker than a slow walk." German machine guns soon opened fire: "We were able to see our comrades move forward in an attempt to cross No-Man's-Land, only to be mown down like meadow grass," recalled one British soldier. "I felt sick at the sight of this carnage and remember weeping." In one day, more than 21,000 British soldiers died. After six months of fighting, the British had advanced 5 miles; one million British, French, and German soldiers had been killed or wounded.

Philip Gibbs, an English war correspondent, described what he saw in the German trenches that the British forces overran: "Victory! . . . Some of the German dead were young boys, too young to be killed for old men's crimes, and others might have been old or young. One could not tell because they had no faces, and were just masses of raw flesh in rags of uniforms. Legs and arms lay separate without any bodies thereabout."

World War I (1914–1918) was the defining event of the twentieth-century Western world. Overwhelmed by the scale of its battles, the extent of its casualties, and its impact on all facets of life, contemporaries referred to it simply as the "Great War." The Great War was all the more disturbing to Europeans because it came after what many believed to have been an age of progress. Material prosperity and a fervid belief in scientific and technological progress had convinced many people that the world stood on the verge of creating the utopia that humans had dreamed of for centuries. The historian Arnold Toynbee expressed what the era before the war had meant to his generation:

[We had expected] that life throughout the world would become more rational, more humane, and more democratic and that, slowly, but surely, political democracy would produce greater social justice. We had also expected that the progress of science and technology would make mankind richer, and that this increasing wealth would gradually spread from a minority to a majority. We had expected that all this would happen peacefully. In fact we thought that mankind's course was set for an earthly paradise.[1]

After 1918, it was no longer possible to maintain naive illusions about the progress of Western civilization. As World War I was followed by revolutionary upheavals, the mass murder machines of totalitarian regimes, and the destructiveness of World War II, it became all too apparent that instead of a utopia, Western civilization had become a nightmare. World War I and the revolutions it spawned can properly be seen as the first stage in the crisis of the twentieth century.

The Road to World War I

Q **FOCUS QUESTION:** What were the long-range and immediate causes of World War I?

On June 28, 1914, the heir to the Austrian throne, the Archduke Francis Ferdinand, was assassinated in the Bosnian city of Sarajevo (sar-uh-YAY-voh). Although this event precipitated the confrontation between Austria and Serbia that led to World War I, underlying forces had been propelling Europeans toward armed conflict for a long time.

Nationalism and Internal Dissent

The system of nation-states that had emerged in Europe in the second half of the nineteenth century (see Map 23.1) had led to severe competition. Rivalries over colonies and trade intensified during a frenzied imperialist expansion, while the division of Europe's great powers into two loose alliances (one consisting of Germany, Austria, and Italy; the other of France, Great Britain, and Russia) only added to the tensions. The series of crises that tested these alliances in the 1900s and early 1910s had left European states embittered, eager for revenge, and willing to revert to war as an acceptable way to preserve the power of their national states (see Chapter 19).

The growth of nationalism in the nineteenth century had yet another serious consequence. Not all ethnic groups had achieved the goal of nationhood. Slavic minorities in the Balkans and the multiethnic Habsburg Empire, for example, still dreamed of creating their own national states. So did the Irish in the British Empire and the Poles in the Russian Empire.

National aspirations, however, were not the only source of internal strife at the beginning of the twentieth century. Socialist labor movements had grown more powerful and were increasingly inclined to use strikes, even violent ones, to achieve their goals. Some conservative leaders, alarmed at the increase in labor strife and class division, even feared that European nations were on the verge of revolution. Did these statesmen opt for war in 1914 because they believed that

"prosecuting an active foreign policy," as some Austrian leaders expressed it, would smother "internal troubles"? Some historians have argued that the desire to suppress internal disorder may have encouraged some leaders to take the plunge into war in 1914.

Militarism

The growth of large mass armies after 1900 not only heightened the existing tensions in Europe but also made it inevitable that if war did come, it would be extremely destructive. **Conscription**—obligatory military service—had been established as a regular practice in most Western countries before 1914 (the United States and Britain were major exceptions). European military machines had doubled in size between 1890 and 1914. With its 1.3 million men, the Russian army had grown to be the largest, but the French and Germans were not far behind, with 900,000 each. The British, Italian, and Austrian armies numbered between 250,000 and 500,000 soldiers.

Militarism, however, involved more than just large armies. As armies grew, so did the influence of military leaders, who drew up vast and complex plans for quickly mobilizing millions of men and enormous quantities of supplies in the event of war. Fearful that changing these plans would cause chaos in the armed forces, military leaders insisted that the plans could not be altered. In the crises during the summer of 1914, the generals' lack of flexibility forced European political leaders to make decisions for military instead of political reasons.

The Outbreak of War: Summer 1914

Militarism, nationalism, and the desire to stifle internal dissent may all have played a role in the coming of World War I, but the decisions made by European leaders in the summer of 1914 directly precipitated the conflict. It was another crisis in the Balkans that forced this predicament on Europe's statesmen.

As we have seen, states in southeastern Europe had struggled to free themselves from Ottoman rule in the course of the nineteenth and early twentieth centuries. But the rivalry between Austria-Hungary and Russia for domination of these new states created serious tensions in the region. By 1914, Serbia, supported by Russia, was determined to create a large, independent Slavic state in the Balkans, while Austria, which had its own Slavic minorities to contend with, was equally set on preventing that possibility. Many Europeans perceived the inherent dangers in this combination of Serbian ambition bolstered by Russian hatred of Austria and the Austrian conviction that Serbia's success would mean the end of its empire. The British ambassador to Vienna wrote in 1913:

Serbia will some day set Europe by the ears, and bring about a universal war on the Continent. . . . I cannot tell you how exasperated people are getting here at the continual worry which that little country causes to Austria under encouragement from Russia. . . . It will be lucky if Europe succeeds in avoiding war as a result of the present crisis. The next time a Serbian crisis

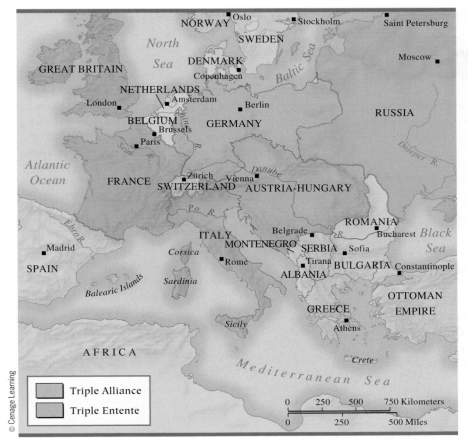

© Cenage Learning

MAP 23.1 **Europe in 1914.** By 1914, two alliances dominated Europe: the Triple Entente of Britain, France, and Russia and the Triple Alliance of Germany, Austria-Hungary, and Italy. Russia sought to bolster fellow Slavs in Serbia, whereas Austria-Hungary was intent on increasing its power in the Balkans and thwarting Serbia's ambitions. Thus, the Balkans became the flash point for World War I.

 Which nonaligned nations were positioned between the two alliances?

Much historical debate has focused on this "blank check" extended to the Austrians. Did the Germans realize that an Austrian-Serbian war could lead to a wider war? If so, did they actually want one? Historians are still divided on the answers to these questions.

Strengthened by German support, Austrian leaders issued an ultimatum to Serbia on July 23 in which they made such extreme demands that Serbia had little choice but to reject some of them in order to preserve its sovereignty. Austria then declared war on Serbia on July 28. Although Austria had hoped to keep the war limited to Serbia and Austria in order to ensure its success in the Balkans, these hopes soon vanished.

DECLARATIONS OF WAR Still smarting from its humiliation in the Bosnian crisis of 1908, Russia was determined to support Serbia's cause. On July 28, Tsar Nicholas II ordered partial mobilization of the Russian army against Austria. The Russian General Staff informed the tsar that their mobilization plans were based on a war against both Germany and Austria simultaneously. They could not execute partial mobilization without creating chaos in the army. Consequently, the Russian government ordered full mobilization of the Russian army on July 29, knowing that the Germans would consider this an act of war against them (see the box on p. 668). Germany quickly responded with an ultimatum that the Russians must halt their mobilization within twelve hours. When the Russians ignored it, Germany declared war on Russia on August 1.

France now became involved in the war. Under the guidance of General Alfred von Schlieffen (AHL-fret fun SHLEE-fun), chief of staff from 1891 to 1905, the German General Staff had devised a military plan based on the assumption of a two-front war with France and Russia because the two powers had formed a military alliance in 1894. The Schlieffen Plan called for a minimal troop deployment against Russia while most of the German army would make a rapid invasion of France before Russia could become effective in the east or before the British could cross the English Channel to help France. This meant invading France by advancing through neutral Belgium, with its level coastal plain on which the army could move faster than on the rougher terrain to the southeast. After the planned quick defeat of the French, the German army expected to redeploy to the east against Russia. Under the Schlieffen Plan, Germany could not mobilize its troops solely against Russia and therefore declared war on France on August 3 after it had issued an ultimatum

arises . . . , I feel sure that Austria-Hungary will refuse to admit of any Russian interference in the dispute and that she will proceed to settle her differences with her little neighbor by herself.[2]

It was against this backdrop of mutual distrust and hatred that the events of the summer of 1914 were played out.

THE ASSASSINATION OF FRANCIS FERDINAND: A "BLANK CHECK"? The assassination of the Austrian Archduke Francis Ferdinand and his wife, Sophia, on June 28, 1914, was carried out by a Bosnian activist who worked for the Black Hand, a Serbian terrorist organization dedicated to the creation of a pan-Slavic kingdom. Although the Austrian government did not know whether the Serbian government had been directly involved in the archduke's assassination, it saw an opportunity to "render Serbia innocuous once and for all by a display of force," as the Austrian foreign minister put it. Fearful of Russian intervention on Serbia's behalf, Austrian leaders sought the backing of their German allies. Emperor William II and his chancellor responded with the infamous "blank check," their assurance that Austria-Hungary could rely on Germany's "full support," even if "matters went to the length of a war between Austria-Hungary and Russia."

"You Have to Bear the Responsibility for War or Peace"

POLITICS & GOVERNMENT

After Austria declared war on Serbia on July 28, 1914, Russian support of Serbia and German support of Austria threatened to escalate the conflict in the Balkans into a wider war. As we can see in these last-minute telegrams between the Russians and Germans, neither side was able to accept the other's line of reasoning.

Communications Between Berlin and Saint Petersburg on the Eve of World War I

Emperor William II to Tsar Nicholas II, July 28, 10:45 P.M.

I have heard with the greatest anxiety of the impression which is caused by the action of Austria-Hungary against Servia [Serbia]. The inscrupulous agitation which has been going on for years in Servia has led to the revolting crime of which Archduke Franz Ferdinand has become a victim. The spirit which made the Servians murder their own King and his consort still dominates that country. Doubtless You will agree with me that both of us, You as well as I, and all other sovereigns, have a common interest to insist that all those who are responsible for this horrible murder shall suffer their deserved punishment. . . .

Your most sincere and devoted friend and cousin

(*Signed*) WILHELM

Tsar Nicholas II to Emperor William II, July 29, 1:00 P.M.

I am glad that you are back in Germany. In this serious moment I ask You earnestly to help me. An ignominious war has been declared against a weak country and in Russia the indignation which I fully share is tremendous. I fear that very soon I shall be unable to resist the pressure exercised upon me and that I shall be forced to take measures which will lead to war. To prevent a calamity as a European war would be, I urge You in the name of our old friendship to do all in Your power to restrain Your ally from going too far.

(*Signed*) NICOLAS

Emperor William II to Tsar Nicholas II, July 29, 6:30 P.M.

I have received Your telegram and I share Your desire for the conservation of peace. However: I cannot—as I told You in my first telegram—consider the action of Austria-Hungary as an "ignominious war." Austria-Hungary knows from experience that the promises of Servia as long as they are merely on paper are entirely unreliable. . . . I believe

that a direct understanding is possible and desirable between Your Government and Vienna, an understanding which—as I have already telegraphed You—my Government endeavors to aid with all possible effort. Naturally military measures by Russia, which might be construed as a menace by Austria-Hungary, would accelerate a calamity which both of us desire to avoid and would undermine my position as mediator which—upon Your appeal to my friendship and aid—I willingly accepted.

(*Signed*) WILHELM

Emperor William II to Tsar Nicholas II, July 30, 1:00 A.M.

My Ambassador has instructions to direct the attention of Your Government to the dangers and serious consequences of a mobilization. I have told You the same in my last telegram. Austria-Hungary has mobilized only against Servia, and only a part of her army. If Russia, as seems to be the case, according to Your advice and that of Your Government, mobilizes against Austria-Hungary, the part of the mediator with which You have entrusted me in such friendly manner and which I have accepted upon Your express desire, is threatened if not made impossible. The entire weight of decision now rests upon Your shoulders; You have to bear the responsibility for war or peace.

(*Signed*) WILHELM

German Chancellor to German Ambassador at Saint Petersburg, July 31, URGENT

In spite of negotiations still pending and although we have up to this hour made no preparations for mobilization, Russia has mobilized her entire army and navy, hence also against us. On account of these Russian measures, we have been forced, for the safety of the country, to proclaim the threatening state of war, which does not yet imply mobilization. Mobilization, however, is bound to follow if Russia does not stop every measure of war against us and against Austria-Hungary within 12 hours, and notifies us definitely to this effect. Please to communicate this at once to M. Sazonoff and wire hour of communication.

How do the telegrams exchanged between William II and Nicholas II reveal why the Europeans foolishly went to war in 1914? What do they tell us about the nature of the relationship between these two monarchs?

to Belgium on August 2, demanding the right of German troops to pass through Belgian territory. On August 4, Great Britain declared war on Germany, officially over this violation of Belgian neutrality but in fact over the British desire to maintain world power. As one British diplomat argued, if Germany and Austria were to win the war, "what would be the position of a friendless England?" By August 4, all the great powers of Europe were at war.

The Excitement of War

The incredible outpouring of patriotic enthusiasm that greeted the declaration of war at the beginning of August 1914 demonstrated the power that nationalistic feeling had attained in the early twentieth century. Many Europeans seemingly believed that the war had given them a higher purpose, a renewed dedication to the greatness of their nations. These selections are taken from three sources: the autobiography of Stefan Zweig (SHTE-fahn TSVYK), an Austrian writer; the memoirs of Robert Graves, a British writer; and a letter by a German soldier, Walter Limmer, to his parents.

Stefan Zweig, *The World of Yesterday*

The next morning I was in Austria. In every station placards had been put up announcing general mobilization. The trains were filled with fresh recruits, banners were flying, music sounded, and in Vienna I found the entire city in a tumult. . . . There were parades in the street, flags, ribbons, and music burst forth everywhere, young recruits were marching triumphantly, their faces lighting up at the cheering. . . .

And to be truthful, I must acknowledge that there was a majestic, rapturous, and even seductive something in this first outbreak of the people from which one could escape only with difficulty. And in spite of all my hatred and aversion for war, I should not like to have missed the memory of those days. As never before, thousands and hundreds of thousands felt what they should have felt in peace time, that they belonged together. A city of two million, a country of nearly fifty million, in that hour felt that they were participating in world history, in a moment which would never recur, and that each one was called upon to cast his infinitesimal self into the glowing mass, there to be purified of all selfishness. All differences of class, rank, and language were flooded over at that moment by the rushing feeling of fraternity. . . .

What did the great mass know of war in 1914, after nearly half a century of peace? They did not know war, they had hardly given it a thought. It had become legendary, and distance had made it seem romantic and heroic. They still saw it in the perspective of their school readers and of paintings in museums; brilliant cavalry attacks in glittering uniforms, the fatal shot always straight through the heart, the entire campaign a resounding march of victory—"We'll be home at Christmas," the recruits shouted laughingly to their mothers in August of 1914. . . . A rapid excursion into the romantic, a wild, manly adventure—that is how the war of 1914 was painted in the imagination of the simple man, and the younger people were honestly afraid that they might miss this most wonderful and exciting experience of their lives; that is why they hurried and thronged to the colors, and that is why they shouted and sang in the trains that carried them to the slaughter; wildly and feverishly the red wave of blood coursed through the veins of the entire nation.

Robert Graves, *Goodbye to All That*

I had just finished with Charterhouse and gone up to Harlech, when England declared war on Germany. A day or two later I decided to enlist. In the first place, though the papers predicted only a very short war—over by Christmas at the outside—I hoped that it might last long enough to delay my going to Oxford in October, which I dreaded. Nor did I work out the possibilities of getting actively engaged in the fighting, expecting garrison service at home, while the regular forces were away. In the second place, I was outraged to read of the Germans' cynical violation of Belgian neutrality. Though I discounted perhaps twenty percent of the atrocity details as wartime exaggeration, that was not, of course, sufficient.

Walter Limmer, Letter to His Parents

In any case I mean to go into this business. . . . That is the simple duty of every one of us. And this feeling is universal among the soldiers, especially since the night when England's declaration of war was announced in the barracks. We none of us got to sleep till three o'clock in the morning, we were so full of excitement, fury, and enthusiasm. It is a joy to go to the Front with such comrades. We are bound to be victorious! Nothing else is possible in the face of such determination to win.

 What do these excerpts reveal about the motivations of people to join and support World War I? Do the passages reveal anything about the power of nationalism in Europe in the early twentieth century?

The Great War

Q FOCUS QUESTIONS: Why did the course of World War I turn out to be so different from what the belligerents had expected? How did World War I affect the belligerents' governmental and political institutions, economic affairs, and social life?

Before 1914, many political leaders had become convinced that war involved so many political and economic risks that it was not worth fighting. Others had believed that "rational" diplomats could control any situation and prevent the outbreak of war. At the beginning of August 1914, both of these prewar illusions were shattered, but the new illusions that replaced them soon proved to be equally foolish.

1914–1915: Illusions and Stalemate

Many Europeans went to war with remarkable enthusiasm (see the box above). Government propaganda had been

The Excitement of War. World War I was greeted with incredible enthusiasm. Each of the major belligerents was convinced of the rightness of its cause, demonstrating the power of nationalism. Even socialists supported their governments rather than maintaining the solidarity of the working classes regardless of nationality. Everywhere in Europe, jubilant civilians sent their troops off to battle with joyous fervor, as is evident in this photograph of French troops marching off to war. The belief that the soldiers would be home by Christmas proved to be a pathetic illusion.

successful in stirring up national antagonisms before the war. Now, in August 1914, the urgent pleas of governments for defense against aggressors found many receptive ears in every belligerent nation. Middle-class crowds, often composed of young students, were especially enthusiastic, though workers in the cities and peasants in the countryside were considerably less eager for war. Once the war began, however, most people seemed genuinely convinced that their nation's cause was just.

A new set of illusions also fed the enthusiasm for war. In August 1914, almost everyone believed that the war would be over in a few weeks. People were reminded that the major battles in European wars since 1815 had ended in a matter of weeks, thus conveniently overlooking the American Civil War (1861–1865), which was a better prototype for World War I. Both the soldiers who exuberantly boarded the trains for the war front in August 1914 and the jubilant citizens who bombarded them with flowers as they departed believed that the warriors would be home by Christmas.

German hopes for a quick end to the war rested on a military gamble. The Schlieffen Plan had called for the German army to proceed through Belgium into northern France with a vast encircling movement that would sweep around Paris and surround most of the French army. But the plan suffered a major defect from the beginning: it called for a strong right flank for the encircling of Paris, but German military leaders, concerned about a Russian invasion in the east, had moved forces from the right flank to strengthen the German army in the east.

As a result, the German advance was halted only 20 miles from Paris at the First Battle of the Marne (September 6–10). The war quickly turned into a stalemate as neither the Germans nor the French could dislodge the other from the trenches they had begun to dig for shelter. Two lines of trenches soon extended from the English Channel to the frontiers of Switzerland (see Map 23.2). The Western Front had become bogged down in **trench warfare**, which kept both sides immobilized in virtually the same positions for four years.

In contrast to the Western Front, the war in the east was marked by much more mobility, although the cost in lives was equally enormous. At the beginning of the war, the Russian army moved into eastern Germany but was decisively defeated at the Battles of Tannenberg on August 30 and the Masurian Lakes on September 15. The Russians were no longer a threat to German territory.

The Austrians, Germany's allies, fared less well initially. They had been defeated by the Russians in Galicia (guh-LISH-ee-uh) and thrown out of Serbia as well. To make matters worse, the Italians betrayed the Germans and Austrians and entered the war on the Allied side by attacking Austria in May 1915. By this time, the Germans had come to the aid of the Austrians. A German-Austrian army defeated and routed the Russian army in Galicia and pushed the Russians back 300 miles into their own territory. Russian casualties stood at 2.5 million killed, captured, or wounded; the Russians had almost been knocked out of the war. Buoyed by their success, the Germans and Austrians, joined by the Bulgarians in September 1915, attacked and eliminated Serbia from the war.

1916–1917: The Great Slaughter

The successes in the east enabled the Germans to move back to the offensive in the west. The early trenches dug in 1914, stretching from the English Channel to the frontiers of Switzerland, had by now become elaborate systems of defense. Both lines of trenches were protected by barbed-wire entanglements 3 to 5 feet high and 90 feet wide, concrete machine-gun nests, and mortar batteries, supported farther back by heavy artillery. Troops lived in holes in the ground, separated from each other by a "no-man's land."

The unexpected development of trench warfare on the Western Front baffled military leaders, who had been trained to fight wars of movement and maneuver. Periodically, the high command on either side would order an offensive that would begin with an artillery barrage to flatten the enemy's barbed wire and leave the enemy in a state of shock. After "softening up" the enemy in this fashion, a mass of soldiers would climb out of their trenches with fixed bayonets and hope to work their way toward the enemy trenches. The attacks rarely worked, as the machine gun put hordes of men advancing unprotected across open fields at a severe disadvantage. In 1916 and 1917, millions of young men were sacrificed in the search for the elusive

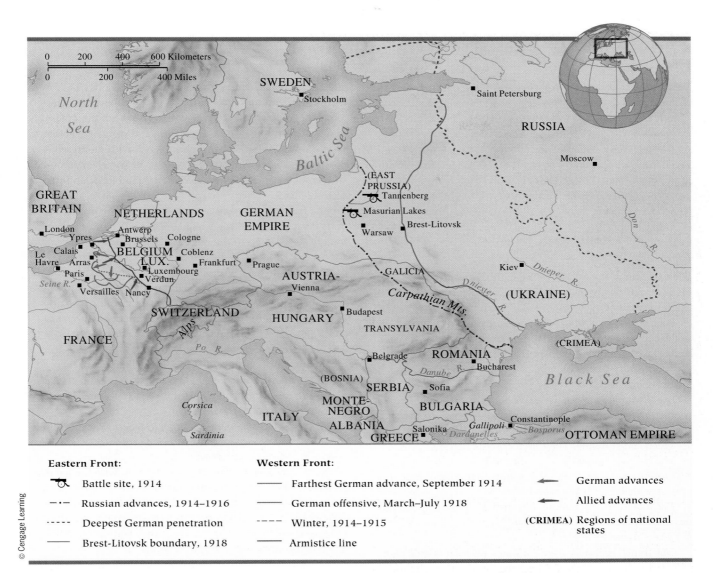

Eastern Front:

⚔ Battle site, 1914

—·— Russian advances, 1914–1916

‑ ‑ ‑ Deepest German penetration

——— Brest-Litovsk boundary, 1918

Western Front:

——— Farthest German advance, September 1914

——— German offensive, March–July 1918

‑ ‑ ‑ Winter, 1914–1915

——— Armistice line

← German advances

← Allied advances

(CRIMEA) Regions of national states

MAP 23.2 World War I, 1914–1918. This map shows how greatly the Western and Eastern Fronts of World War I differed. After initial German gains in the west, the war became bogged down in trench warfare, with little change in the battle lines between 1914 and 1918. The Eastern Front was marked by considerable mobility, with battle lines shifting by hundreds of miles.

 How do you explain the difference in the two fronts?

breakthrough. In ten months at Verdun (ver-DUHN) in 1916, 700,000 men lost their lives over a few miles of terrain.

Warfare in the trenches of the Western Front produced unimaginable horrors (see the box on p. 672 and the Film & History feature on p. 673). Battlefields were hellish landscapes of barbed wire, shell holes, mud, and injured and dying men. The introduction of poison gas in 1915 produced new forms of injuries, as one British writer described them:

> I wish those people who write so glibly about this being a holy war could see a case of mustard gas . . . could see the poor things burnt and blistered all over with great mustard-coloured suppurating blisters with blind eyes all sticky . . . and stuck together, and always fighting for breath, with voices a mere whisper, saying that their throats are closing and they know they will choke.[3]

Soldiers in the trenches also lived with the persistent presence of death. Since combat went on for months, soldiers had to carry on in the midst of countless bodies of dead men or the remains of men dismembered by artillery barrages. Many soldiers remembered the stench of decomposing bodies and the swarms of rats that grew fat in the trenches.

The Widening of the War

As another response to the stalemate on the Western Front, both sides looked for new allies who might provide a winning advantage. The Ottoman Empire had already come into the war on Germany's side in August 1914. Russia, Great Britain, and France declared war on the Ottoman Empire in November. Although the Allies attempted to open a Balkan front by landing forces at Gallipoli (gah-LIP-poh-lee), southwest of

The Reality of War: Trench Warfare

POLITICS & GOVERNMENT

The romantic illusion about the excitement and adventure of war that filled the minds of so many young men who marched off to battle quickly disintegrated after a short time in the trenches on the Western Front. This description of trench warfare is taken from the most famous novel that emerged from World War I, Erich Maria Remarque's *All Quiet on the Western Front*, published in 1929. Remarque had fought in the trenches in France.

Erich Maria Remarque, *All Quiet on the Western Front*

We wake up in the middle of the night. The earth booms. Heavy fire is falling on us. We crouch into corners. We distinguish shells of every calibre.

Each man lays hold of his things and looks again every minute to reassure himself that they are still there. The dugout heaves, the night roars and flashes. We look at each other in the momentary flashes of light, and with pale faces and pressed lips shake our heads.

Every man is aware of the heavy shells tearing down the parapet, rooting up the embankment and demolishing the upper layers of concrete. . . . Already by morning a few of the recruits are green and vomiting. They are too inexperienced. . . .

The bombardment does not diminish. It is falling in the rear too. As far as one can see it spouts fountains of mud and iron. A wide belt is being raked.

The attack does not come, but the bombardment continues. Slowly we become mute. Hardly a man speaks. We cannot make ourselves understood.

Our trench is almost gone. At many places it is only eighteen inches high; it is broken by holes, and craters, and mountains of earth. A shell lands square in front of our post. At once it is dark. We are buried and must dig ourselves out. . . .

Towards morning, while it is still dark, there is some excitement. Through the entrance rushes in a swarm of fleeing rats that try to storm the walls. Torches light up the confusion. Everyone yells and curses and slaughters. The madness and despair of many hours unloads itself in this outburst. Faces are distorted, arms strike out, the beasts scream; we just stop in time to avoid attacking one another. . . .

Suddenly it howls and flashes terrifically, the dugout cracks in all its joints under a direct hit, fortunately only a light one that the concrete blocks are able to withstand. It rings metallically; the walls reel; rifles, helmets, earth, mud, and dust fly everywhere. Sulfur fumes pour in. . . . The recruit starts to rave again and two others follow suit. One jumps up and rushes out, we have trouble with the other two. I start after the one who escapes and wonder whether to shoot him in the leg—then it shrieks again; I fling myself down and when I stand up the wall of the trench is plastered with smoking splinters, lumps of flesh, and bits of uniform. I scramble back.

The first recruit seems actually to have gone insane. He butts his head against the wall like a goat. We must try tonight to take him to the rear. Meanwhile we bind him, but so that in case of attack he can be released.

Suddenly the nearer explosions cease. The shelling continues but it has lifted and falls behind us; our trench is free. We seize the hand grenades, pitch them out in front of the dugout, and jump after them. The bombardment has stopped and a heavy barrage now falls behind us. The attack has come.

No one would believe that in this howling waste there could still be men; but steel helmets now appear on all sides out of the trench, and fifty yards from us a machine gun is already in position and barking.

The wire entanglements are torn to pieces. Yet they offer some obstacle. We see the storm troops coming. Our artillery opens fire. Machine guns rattle, rifles crack. The charge works its way across. Haie and Kropp begin with the hand grenades. They throw as fast as they can; others pass them, the handles with the strings already pulled. Haie throws seventy-five yards, Kropp sixty; it has been measured; the distance is important. The enemy as they run cannot do much before they are within forty yards.

We recognize the distorted faces, the smooth helmets: they are French. They have already suffered heavily when they reach the remnants of the barbed-wire entanglements. A whole line has gone down before our machine guns; then we have a lot of stoppages and they come nearer.

I see one of them, his face upturned, fall into a wire cradle. His body collapses, his hands remain suspended as though he were praying. Then his body drops clean away and only his hands with the stumps of his arms, shot off, now hang in the wire.

What is causing the "madness and despair" Remarque describes in the trenches? Why does the recruit in this scene apparently go insane?

Constantinople, in April 1915, the entry of Bulgaria into the war on the side of the Central Powers (as Germany, Austria-Hungary, and the Ottoman Empire were called) and a disastrous campaign at Gallipoli caused them to withdraw. The Italians, as we have seen, also entered the war on the Allied side after France and Britain promised to further their

FILM & HISTORY

Paths of Glory (1957)

Paths of Glory, directed by Stanley Kubrick, is a powerful antiwar film made in 1957 and based on the novel with the same name by Humphrey Cobb. Set in France in 1916, the film deals with the time during World War I when the Western Front had become bogged down in brutal trench warfare. The novel was based loosely on a true story of five French soldiers who were executed for mutiny. In the film, General George Broulard (Adolphe Menjou) of the French General Staff suggests to his subordinate, General Mireau (George Macready), that he launch what would amount to a suicidal attack on the well-defended Ant Hill. Mireau refuses until Broulard mentions the possibility of a promotion, at which point Mireau abruptly changes his mind and accepts the challenge. He walks through the trenches preparing his men with a stock question: "Hello there, soldier, are you ready to kill more Germans?" Mireau persuades Colonel Dax (Kirk Douglas) to mount the attack, despite Dax's protest that it will be a disaster. Dax proves to be right. None of the French soldiers reach the German lines, and one-third of the troops are not even able to leave their trenches because of enemy fire.

To avoid blame for the failure, General Mireau accuses his men of cowardice, and three of them (one from each company, chosen in purely arbitrary fashion) are brought before a hastily arranged court-martial. Dax defends his men but to no avail. The decision has already been made, and the three men are shot in front of the assembled troops. As General Broulard cynically comments, "One way to maintain discipline is to shoot a man now and then." After the execution, when General Broulard offers Dax a promotion, Dax responds, "Would you like me to suggest what you can do with that promotion?" Replies Broulard, "You're an idealist; I pity you." But Dax has the last word: "I pity you for not seeing the wrongs you have done." The film ends with the troops being ordered back to the front.

The film realistically portrays the horrors of trench warfare in World War I—the senseless and suicidal attacks through no-man's land against well-entrenched machine-gun batteries. The film is also scathing in its portrayal of military leaders. The generals are shown drinking cognac in the palaces they requisitioned for their headquarters while the troops live in the mud and filth of the trenches. Both generals are portrayed as arrogant, ego-driven individuals who think nothing of the slaughter of their men in battle. The men condemned to die for cowardice are scapegoats sacrificed to cover up the mistakes of their superior officers, who are determined to pursue "paths of glory" to advance themselves. The film's portrayal of the military executions was not accurate, however. The French army did not choose individuals at random for punishment, although it did execute some soldiers on charges of cowardice, as did the armies of the other belligerents.

This realistic indictment of war and the military elites offended some countries. French authorities saw it as an insult to the honor of the army and did not allow it to be shown in France until 1975. The military regime of Francisco Franco in Spain also banned the film for its antimilitary content. Kubrick himself went on to make two other antiwar films, capturing the Vietnam War in *Full Metal Jacket* and the Cold War in *Dr. Strangelove*.

United Artists/The Kobal Collection

Colonel Dax (Kirk Douglas) begins to lead his men out of the trenches to attack Ant Hill.

---

acquisition of Austrian territory. In the long run, however, Italian military incompetence forced the Allies to come to the assistance of Italy.

A GLOBAL CONFLICT Because the major European powers controlled colonial empires in other parts of the world, the war in Europe soon became a world war (see the comparative illustration on p. 675). In the Middle East, the British officer T. E. Lawrence (1888–1935), who came to be known as Lawrence of Arabia, incited Arab princes to revolt against their Ottoman overlords in 1916. In 1918, British forces from Egypt and Mesopotamia destroyed the rest of the Ottoman Empire in the Middle East. For their Middle East campaigns, the British mobilized forces from India, Australia, and New Zealand.

The Allies also took advantage of Germany's preoccupation in Europe and lack of naval strength to seize German colonies in Africa. But there too the war did not end quickly. The first British shots of World War I were actually fired in Africa when British African troops moved into the German colony of Togoland near the end of August 1914. But in East Africa, the German commander Colonel Paul von Lettow-Vorbeck (POWL fun LEH-toh-FOR-bek) managed to keep

The Horrors of War. The slaughter of millions of men in the trenches of World War I created unimaginable horrors for the participants. For the sake of survival, many soldiers learned to harden themselves against the stench of decomposing bodies and the sight of bodies horribly dismembered by artillery barrages.

his African troops fighting one campaign after another for four years; he did not surrender until two weeks after the armistice ended the war in Europe.

In the battles in Africa, Allied governments drew mainly on African soldiers, but some states, especially France, also recruited African troops to fight in Europe. The French drafted more than 170,000 West African soldiers, many of whom fought in the trenches on the Western Front. African troops were also used as occupation forces in the German Rhineland at the end of the war. About 80,000 Africans were killed or injured in Europe, where they were often at a distinct disadvantage due to the unfamiliar terrain and climate.

Hundreds of thousands of Africans were also used for labor, especially for carrying supplies and building roads and bridges. In East Africa, both sides drafted African laborers as carriers for their armies. More than 100,000 of these laborers died from disease and starvation caused by neglect.

The immediate impact of World War I in Africa was the extension of colonial rule since Germany's African colonies were simply transferred to the winning powers, especially the British and the French. But the war also had unintended consequences for the Europeans. African soldiers who had gone to war for the Allies, especially those who left Africa and fought in Europe, became politically aware and began to advocate

German Possessions in Africa, 1914

political and social equality. As one African who had fought for the French said, "We were not fighting for the French, we were fighting for ourselves [to become] French citizens."[4] Moreover, educated African elites, who had aided their colonial overlords in enlisting local peoples to fight, did so in the belief that they would be rewarded with citizenship and new political possibilities after the war. When their hopes were frustrated, they soon became involved in anticolonial movements (see Chapter 24).

In East Asia and the Pacific, Japan joined the Allies on August 23, 1914, primarily to seize control of German territories in Asia. As one Japanese statesman declared, the war in Europe was "divine aid . . . for the development of the destiny of Japan."[5] The Japanese took possession of German territories in China, as well as the German-occupied islands in the Pacific. New Zealand and Australia quickly joined the Japanese in conquering the German-held parts of New Guinea.

ENTRY OF THE UNITED STATES Most important to the Allied cause was the entry of the United States into the war. The impetus for American involvement grew out of the naval conflict between Germany and Great Britain. Britain used its superior naval power to maximum effect by imposing a naval blockade on Germany. Germany retaliated with a counterblockade enforced by submarine warfare. Strong American protests over the German sinking of passenger liners, especially the British ship *Lusitania* on May 7, 1915, when more than a hundred Americans lost their lives, forced the German government to suspend unrestricted submarine warfare in September 1915 to avoid further antagonizing the Americans.

In January 1917, however, eager to break the deadlock in the war, the Germans decided on another military gamble by returning to unrestricted submarine warfare. German naval officers convinced Emperor William II that the use of unrestricted submarine warfare could starve the British into submission within five months, before the Americans could act. The return to unrestricted submarine warfare brought the United States into the war on April 6, 1917. Although American troops did not arrive in Europe in large numbers until 1918, the entry of the United States into the war in 1917 gave the Allied Powers a psychological boost when they needed it.

The year 1917 had not been a good year for them. Allied offensives on the Western Front were disastrously defeated. The Italian armies were smashed in October, and in November a revolution in Russia (see "The Russian Revolution" later in this chapter) led to Russia's withdrawal from the war and left Germany free to concentrate entirely on the Western Front. The cause of the Central Powers looked favorable,

COMPARATIVE ILLUSTRATION

POLITICS & GOVERNMENT

Soldiers from around the World.
Although World War I began in Europe, it
soon became a global conflict fought in different areas of the world and with soldiers
from all parts of the globe. France, especially, recruited
troops from its African colonies to fight in Europe. The
photo at the top shows French African troops fighting in
the trenches on the Western Front. About 80,000 Africans
were killed or injured in Europe. The photo at the bottom
shows a group of German soldiers in their machine-gun
nest on the Western Front.

Q *What do these photographs reveal about the
nature of World War I and the role of African
troops in the conflict?*

although war weariness in the Ottoman Empire, Bulgaria,
Austria-Hungary, and Germany was beginning to take its toll.
The home front was rapidly becoming a cause for as much
concern as the war front.

A New Kind of Warfare

By the end of 1915, airplanes appeared on the battlefront. The
planes were first used to spot the enemy's position, but soon
they began to attack ground targets, especially enemy communications. Fights for control of the air occurred and increased
over time. At first, pilots fired at each other with handheld pistols, but later machine guns were mounted on the noses of
planes, which made the skies considerably more dangerous.

The Germans also used their giant airships—the zeppelins
(ZEP-puh-lins)—to bomb London and eastern England. This
caused little damage but frightened many people. Germany's
enemies, however, soon found that zeppelins, which were
filled with hydrogen gas, quickly became raging infernos
when hit by antiaircraft guns.

TANKS Tanks were also introduced to the battlefields of
Europe in 1916. The first tank—a British model—used cater-
pillar tracks, which enabled it to move across rough terrain.
Armed with mounted guns, tanks could attack enemy
machine-gun positions as well as enemy infantry. But the
first tanks were not very effective, and it was not until
1918, with the introduction of the British Mark V model,
that tanks had more powerful engines and greater maneuverability. They could now be used in large numbers, and
coordinated with infantry and artillery, they became effective instruments in pushing back the retreating German
army.

The tank came too late to have a great effect on the outcome of World War I, but the lesson was not lost on those
who realized the tank's potential for creating a whole new
kind of warfare. In World War II (see Chapter 25), lightning
attacks that depended on tank columns and massive air power
enabled armies to cut quickly across battle lines and encircle
entire enemy armies. It was a far cry from the trench warfare
of World War I.

The Home Front: The Impact of Total War

The prolongation of World War I made it a **total war** that affected the lives of all citizens, however remote they might be from the battlefields. The need to organize masses of men and matériel for years of combat (Germany alone had 5.5 million men in active units in 1916) led to increased centralization of government powers, economic regimentation, and manipulation of public opinion to keep the war effort going.

POLITICAL CENTRALIZATION AND ECONOMIC REGIMENTATION

Because the war was expected to be short, little thought had been given to economic considerations or long-term wartime needs. Governments had to respond quickly, however, when the war machines failed to achieve their knockout blows and made ever-greater demands for men and matériel. To meet these needs, governments expanded their powers. Countries drafted tens of millions of young men for that elusive breakthrough to victory.

Throughout Europe, wartime governments expanded their powers over their economies. Free market capitalistic systems were temporarily shelved as governments experimented with price, wage, and rent controls; rationed food supplies and materials; and nationalized transportation systems and industries. In effect, to mobilize all national resources for the war effort, European nations moved toward planned economies directed by government agencies. Under total war mobilization, the distinction between soldiers at war and civilians at home was narrowed. In the view of political leaders, all citizens constituted a national army dedicated to victory. As the American president Woodrow Wilson expressed it, the men and women "who remain to till the soil and man the factories are no less a part of the army than the men beneath the battle flags."

PUBLIC ORDER AND PUBLIC OPINION

As the Great War dragged on and casualties mounted, the patriotic enthusiasm that had marked the early stages of the conflict waned. By 1916, there were numerous signs that civilian morale was beginning to crack under the pressure of total war. War governments, however, fought back against the growing opposition to the war. Authoritarian regimes, such as those of Germany, Russia, and Austria-Hungary, had always relied on force to subdue their populations, but under the pressures of the war, even parliamentary regimes resorted to an expansion of police powers to stifle internal dissent. At the very beginning of the war, the British Parliament passed the Defense of the Realm Act (DORA), which allowed the public authorities to arrest dissenters as traitors. Newspapers were censored, and sometimes their publication was even suspended. In 1917, government authorities in France began to suppress basic civil liberties.

Wartime governments made active use of propaganda to arouse enthusiasm for the war. At first, public officials needed to do little to achieve this goal. The British and French, for example, exaggerated German atrocities in Belgium and found that their citizens were only too willing to believe

British Recruiting Poster. As the conflict persisted month after month, governments resorted to active propaganda campaigns to generate enthusiasm for the war. In this British recruiting poster, the government tried to pressure men into volunteering for military service. By 1916, the British were forced to adopt compulsory military service.

these accounts. But as the war dragged on and morale sagged, governments were forced to devise new techniques for stimulating enthusiasm. In one British recruiting poster, for example, a small daughter asked her father, "Daddy, what did YOU do in the Great War?" while her younger brother played with toy soldiers and cannons.

Total war made a significant impact on European society, most visibly by bringing an end to unemployment. The withdrawal of millions of men from the labor market to fight, combined with the heightened demand for wartime products, led to jobs for everyone able to work.

WOMEN IN THE WAR EFFORT

World War I also created new roles for women. With so many men off fighting at the front, women were called on to assume jobs and responsibilities that had not been open to them before. Overall, 1,345,000 women in Britain obtained new jobs or replaced men during the war. Women were also now employed in jobs that had been considered "beyond the capacity of women." These included such occupations as chimney sweeps, truck drivers, farm laborers, and factory workers in heavy industry (see the box on p. 677). In Germany, 38

Women in the Factories

During World War I, women were called on to assume new job responsibilities, including factory work. In this selection, Naomi Loughnan, a young, upper-middle-class woman, describes the experiences in a munitions plant that considerably broadened her perspective on life.

Naomi Loughnan, "Munition Work"

We little thought when we first put on our overalls and caps and enlisted in the Munition Army how much more inspiring our life was to be than we had dared to hope. Though we munition workers sacrifice our ease, we gain a life worth living. Our long days are filled with interest, and with the zest of doing work for our country in the grand cause of Freedom. As we handle the weapons of war we are learning great lessons of life. In the busy, noisy workshops we come face to face with every kind of class, and each one of these classes has something to learn from the others. . . .

Engineering mankind is possessed of the unshakable opinion that no woman can have the mechanical sense. If one of us asks humbly why such and such an alteration is not made to prevent this or that drawback to a machine, she is told, with a superior smile, that a man has worked her machine before her for years, and that therefore if there were any improvement possible it would have been made. As long as we do exactly what we are told and do not attempt to use our brains, we give entire satisfaction, and are treated as nice, good children. Any swerving from the easy path prepared for us by our males arouses the most scathing contempt in their manly bosoms. . . . Women have, however, proved that their entry into the munition world has increased the output. Employers who forget things personal in their patriotic desire for large results are enthusiastic over the success of women in the shops. But their workmen have to be handled with the utmost tenderness and caution lest they should actually imagine it was being suggested that women could do their work equally well, given equal conditions of training—at least where muscle is not the driving force. . . .

The coming of the mixed classes of women into the factory is slowly but surely having an educative effect upon the men. "Language" is almost unconsciously becoming subdued. There are fiery exceptions, who make our hair stand up on end under our close-fitting caps, but a sharp rebuke or a look of horror will often straighten out the most savage. . . . It is grievous to hear the girls also swearing and using disgusting language. Shoulder to shoulder with the children of the slums, the upper classes are having their eyes opened at last to the awful conditions among which their sisters have dwelt. Foul language, immorality, and many other evils are but the natural outcome of overcrowding and bitter poverty. . . . Sometimes disgust will overcome us, but we are learning with painful clarity that the fault is not theirs whose actions disgust us, but must be placed to the discredit of those other classes who have allowed the continued existence of conditions which generate the things from which we shrink appalled.

 What did Naomi Loughnan learn about men and lower-class women while working in the munitions factory? What did she learn about herself?

---

percent of the workers in the Krupp (KROOP) armaments works in 1918 were women. Nevertheless, despite the noticeable increase in women's wages that resulted from government regulations, women's industrial wages were still not equal to men's wages by the end of the war.

Even worse, women's place in the workforce was far from secure. Both men and women seemed to assume that many of the new jobs for women were only temporary, an expectation quite evident in the British poem "War Girls," written in 1916:

> There's the girl who clips your ticket for the train,
> And the girl who speeds the lift from floor to floor,
> There's the girl who does a milk-round in the rain,
> And the girl who calls for orders at your door.
> Strong, sensible, and fit,
> They're out to show their grit,
> And tackle jobs with energy and knack.
> No longer caged and penned up,
> They're going to keep their end up
> Till the khaki soldier boys come marching back.[6]

At the end of the war, governments moved quickly to remove women from the jobs they had encouraged them to take earlier. By 1919, there were 650,000 unemployed women in Britain, and wages for women who were still employed were lowered. The work benefits for women from World War I seemed to be short-lived as demobilized men returned to the job market.

Nevertheless, in some countries, the role played by women in the wartime economies did have a positive impact on the women's movement for social and political emancipation. The most obvious gain was the right to vote, given to women in Germany and Austria immediately after the war (in Britain a few months earlier). Contemporary media, however, tended to focus on the more noticeable yet in some ways more superficial social emancipation of upper- and middle-class women. In ever-larger numbers, these young women took jobs, had their own apartments, and showed their new independence by smoking in public and wearing shorter dresses, cosmetics, and new hairstyles.

War and Revolution

 FOCUS QUESTION: What were the causes of the Russian Revolution of 1917, and why did the Bolsheviks prevail in the civil war and gain control of Russia?

By 1917, total war was creating serious domestic turmoil in all of the European belligerent states. Only one, however, experienced the kind of complete collapse that others were predicting might happen throughout Europe. Out of Russia's collapse came the Russian Revolution.

The Russian Revolution

After the Revolution of 1905 had failed to bring any substantial changes to Russia, Tsar Nicholas II relied on the army and bureaucracy to uphold his regime. But World War I magnified Russia's problems and severely challenged the tsarist government. The tsar, possessed of a strong sense of moral duty to his country, was the only European monarch to take personal charge of the armed forces, despite a lack of training for such an awesome responsibility. Russian industry was unable to produce the weapons needed for the army. Ill-led and ill-armed, Russian armies suffered incredible losses. Between 1914 and 1916, 2 million soldiers were killed while another 4 to 6 million were wounded or captured.

The tsarist government was unprepared for the tasks that it faced in 1914. The surge of patriotic enthusiasm that greeted the outbreak of war was soon dissipated by a government that distrusted its own people. Although the middle classes and liberal aristocrats still hoped for a constitutional monarchy, they were sullen over the tsar's revocation of the political concessions made during the Revolution of 1905. Peasant discontent flourished as conditions worsened. The concentration of Russian industry in a few large cities made workers' frustrations all the more evident and dangerous. In the meantime, Nicholas was increasingly insulated from events by his wife, Alexandra.

Tsarina Alexandra, a well-educated German-born princess, had fallen under the influence of Rasputin (rass-PYOO-tin), a Siberian peasant whom the tsarina regarded as a holy man because he alone seemed able to stop the bleeding of her hemophiliac son, Alexis. Rasputin's influence made him a power behind the throne, and he did not hesitate to interfere in government affairs. As the leadership at the top experienced a series of military and economic disasters, the middle class, aristocrats, peasants, soldiers, and workers grew more and more disenchanted with the tsarist regime. Even conservative aristocrats who supported the monarchy felt the need to do something to reverse the deteriorating situation. For a start, they assassinated Rasputin in December 1916. By then it was too late to save the monarchy, and its fall came quickly at the beginning of March 1917.

THE MARCH REVOLUTION In early 1917, a series of strikes broke out in the capital city of Petrograd (formerly Saint Petersburg). Here the actions of working-class women helped change the course of Russian history. Weeks earlier, the government had introduced bread rationing in the capital city after the price of bread had skyrocketed. Many of the women who stood in the lines waiting for bread were also factory workers who had put in twelve-hour days. The Russian government soon became aware of the volatile situation in the capital. One police report stated:

> Mothers of families, exhausted by endless standing in line at stores, distraught over their half-starving and sick children, are today perhaps closer to revolution than [the liberal opposition leaders] and of course they are a great deal more dangerous because they are the combustible material for which only a single spark is needed to burst into flame.[7]

On March 8, a day celebrated since 1910 as International Women's Day, about ten thousand Petrograd women marched in parts of the city chanting "Peace and Bread" and "Down with Autocracy." Soon the women were joined by other workers, and together they called for a general strike that succeeded in shutting down all the factories in the city two days later. The tsarina wrote to Nicholas at the battlefront that "this is a hooligan movement. If the weather were very cold they would all probably stay at home." Believing his wife, Nicholas responded to his military leaders, "I command you tomorrow to stop the disorders in the capital, which are unacceptable in the difficult time of war with Germany and Austria."[8] The troops were ordered to disperse the crowds, shooting them if necessary. Initially, the troops cooperated, but soon significant numbers of the soldiers joined the demonstrators. The Duma (DOO-muh) or legislative body, which the tsar had tried to dissolve, met anyway and on March 12 declared that it was assuming governmental responsibility. It established a provisional government on March 15; the tsar abdicated the same day.

The Provisional Government, which came to be led in July by Alexander Kerensky (kuh-REN-skee) (1881–1970), decided to carry on the war to preserve Russia's honor—a major blunder because it satisfied neither the workers nor the peasants, who above all wanted an end to the war. The Provisional Government also faced another authority, the **soviets**, or councils of workers' and soldiers' deputies. The Petrograd soviet had been formed in March 1917; at the same time, soviets sprang up spontaneously in army units, factory towns, and rural areas. The soviets represented the more radical interests of the lower classes and were largely composed of socialists of various kinds. Among them was the Marxist Social Democratic Party, which had formed in 1898 but divided in 1903 into two factions known as the Mensheviks (MENS-shuh-viks) and the Bolsheviks (BOHL-shuh-viks). The Mensheviks wanted the Social Democrats to be a mass electoral socialist party based on a Western model.

LENIN AND THE BOLSHEVIK REVOLUTION The Bolsheviks were a small faction of Russian Social Democrats who had come under the leadership of Vladimir Ulianov (VLAD-ih-

The Women's March in Petrograd. After the imposition of bread rationing in Petrograd, ten thousand women engaged in mass demonstrations and demanded "Peace and Bread" for the families of soldiers. This photograph shows the women marching through the streets of Petrograd on March 8, 1917.

meer ool-YA-nuf), known to the world as Lenin (LEH-nin) (1870–1924). Trained as a lawyer, he had earlier turned into a dedicated enemy of tsarist Russia when his older brother was executed for planning to assassinate the tsar. Arrested for his revolutionary activity, Lenin was shipped to Siberia. After his release, he chose to go into exile in Switzerland and eventually assumed the leadership of the Bolshevik wing of the Russian Social Democratic Party. Under Lenin's direction, the Bolsheviks became a party dedicated to violent revolution. He believed that only a revolution could destroy the capitalist system and that a "vanguard" of activists must form a small party of well-disciplined professional revolutionaries to accomplish the task. Between 1900 and 1917, Lenin spent most of his time in Switzerland. When the Provisional Government was formed in March 1917, he believed that an opportunity for the Bolsheviks to seize power had come. Just weeks later, with the connivance of the German High Command, who hoped to create disorder in Russia, Lenin was shipped to Russia in a sealed train by way of Finland.

Lenin's arrival in Russia on April 3 opened a new stage of the Russian Revolution. Lenin maintained that the soviets of soldiers, workers, and peasants were ready-made instruments of power. The Bolsheviks must work toward gaining control of these groups and then use them to overthrow the Provisional Government (see the box on p. 680). At the same time, Bolshevik propaganda must seek mass support through promises geared to the needs of the people: an end to the war, redistribution of all land to the peasants, the transfer of factories and industries from capitalists to committees of workers, and the relegation of government power from the Provisional Government to the soviets. Three simple slogans summed up the Bolshevik program: "Peace, Land, Bread,"

"Worker Control of Production," and "All Power to the Soviets."

By the end of October, the Bolsheviks had achieved a slight majority in the Petrograd and Moscow soviets. The number of party members had also grown, from 50,000 to 240,000. With Leon Trotsky (TRAHT-skee) (1877–1940), a fervid revolutionary, as chairman of the Petrograd soviet, Lenin and the Bolsheviks were in a position to seize power in the name of the soviets. During the night of November 6, pro-soviet and pro-Bolshevik forces took control of Petrograd; the Provisional Government quickly collapsed, with little bloodshed. The following night, the all-Russian Congress of Soviets, representing local soviets from all over the country, affirmed the transfer of power. At the second session, the night of November 8, Lenin announced the new Soviet government, the Council of People's Commissars, with himself as its head.

But the Bolsheviks, soon renamed the Communists, still had a long way to go. For one thing, Lenin had promised peace, and that, he realized, was not an easy task because of the humiliating losses of Russian territory that it would entail. There was no real choice, however. On March 3, 1918, Lenin signed the Treaty of Brest-Litovsk (BREST-li-TUFFSK) with Germany and gave up eastern Poland, Ukraine, and the Baltic provinces. To his critics, Lenin argued that it made no difference because the spread of socialist revolution throughout Europe would make the treaty largely irrelevant. In any case, he had promised peace to the Russian people, but real peace did not come, for the country soon sank into civil war.

CIVIL WAR There was great opposition to the new Communist regime, not only from groups loyal to the tsar but also from bourgeois and aristocratic liberals and anti-Leninist

Soldier and Peasant Voices

In 1917, Russia experienced a cataclysmic upheaval as two revolutions overthrew first the tsarist regime and then the Provisional Government that replaced it. Peasants, workers, and soldiers poured out their thoughts and feelings on these events, some of them supporting the Bolsheviks and others denouncing the Bolsheviks for betraying their socialist revolution. These selections are taken from two letters, the first from a soldier and the second from a peasant. Both are addressed to Bolshevik leaders.

Letter from a Soldier in Leningrad to Lenin, January 6, 1918

Bastard! What the hell are you doing? How long are you going to keep on degrading the Russian people? After all, it's because of you they killed the former minister . . . and so many other innocent victims. Because of you, they might kill even other former ministers belonging to the [Socialist Revolutionary] party because you call them counterrevolutionaries and even monarchists. . . . And you, you Bolshevik gang leader hired either by Nicholas II or by Wilhelm II, are waging this pogrom propaganda against men who may have done time with you in exile.

Scoundrel! A curse on you from the politically conscious Russian proletariat, the conscious ones and not the kind who are following you—that is, the Red Guards, the tally clerks, who, when they are called to military service, all hide at the factories and now are killing . . . practically their own father, the way the soldiers did in 1905 when they killed their own, or the way the police and gendarmes did in [1917]. That's who they're more like. They're not pursuing the ideas of socialism because they don't understand them (if they did they wouldn't act this way) but because they get paid a good salary both at the factory and in the Red Guards. But not all the workers are like that—there are very politically aware ones and the soldiers—again not all of them—are like that but only former policemen, constables, gendarmes and the very very ignorant ones who under the old regime tramped with hay on one foot and straw on the other because they couldn't tell their right foot from their left and they are pursuing not the ideas of socialism that you advocate but to be able to lie on their cots in the barracks and do absolutely nothing not even to be asked to sweep the floor, which is already piled with several inches of filth. And so the entire proletariat of Russia is following you, but count fewer than are against you, but they are only physically or rather technically stronger than the majority, and that is what you're abusing when

you disbanded the Constituent Assembly the way Nicholas II disbanded the Duma. You point out that counterrevolutionaries gathered there. You lie, scoundrel, there wasn't a single counterrevolutionary and if there was then it was you, the Bolsheviks, which you proved by your actions when you encroached on the gains of the revolution: you are shutting down newspapers, even socialist ones, arresting socialists, committing violence and deceiving the people; you promised loads but did none of it.

Letter from a Peasant to the Bolshevik Leaders, January 10, 1918

TO YOU!

Rulers, plunderers, rapists, destroyers, usurpers, oppressors of Mother Russia, citizens Lenin, Trotsky, Uritsky, Zinoviev, Antonov, Lunacharsky, Krylenko, and Co. [leaders of the Bolshevik party]:

Allow me to ask you how long you are going to go on degrading Russia's millions, its tormented and exhausted people. Instead of peace, you signed an armistice with the enemy, and this gave our opponent a painful advantage, and you declared war on Russia. You moved the troops you had tricked to the Russian-Russian front and started a fratricidal war. Your mercenary Red Guards are looting, murdering, and raping everywhere they go. A fire has consumed all our dear Mother Russia. Rail transport is idle, as are the plants and factories; the entire population has woken up to find itself in the most pathetic situation, without bread or kerosene or any of the other essentials, unclothed or unshod in unheated houses. In short: hungry and cold. . . . You have strangled the entire press, and freedom with it, you have wiped out the best freedom fighters, you have destroyed all Russia. Think it over, you butchers, you hirelings of the Kaiser [William II]. Isn't your turn about up, too? For all you are doing, we, politically aware Great Russians, are sending you butchers, you hirelings of the Kaiser, our curse. May you be damned, you accursed one, you bloodthirsty butchers, you hirelings of the Kaiser—don't think you're in the clear, because the Russian people will sober up and that will be the end of you. I'm writing in red ink to show that you are bloodthirsty. . . . I'm writing these curses, a great Russian native of Orel Province, peasant of Mtsensk Uezd.

What arguments do both of the writers of these letters use against Lenin and the Bolsheviks? Why do they feel so betrayed by the Bolsheviks?

---

socialists. In addition, thousands of Allied troops were eventually sent to different parts of Russia in the hope of bringing Russia back into the war.

Between 1918 and 1921, the Red (Bolshevik) Army was forced to fight on many fronts. The first serious threat to the Bolsheviks came from Siberia, where White (anti-Bolshevik)

Lenin and Trotsky. Vladimir Lenin and Leon Trotsky were important figures in the Bolsheviks' successful seizure of power in Russia. On the left, Lenin is seen addressing a rally in Moscow in 1917. On the right, Trotsky, who became commissar of war in the new regime, is shown haranguing his troops.

forces attacked westward and advanced almost to the Volga River before being stopped. Attacks also came from the Ukrainians in the southeast and from the Baltic regions. In mid-1919, White forces swept through Ukraine and advanced almost to Moscow. By 1920, the major White forces had been defeated and Ukraine retaken. The next year, the Communist regime regained control over the independent nationalist governments in the Caucasus: Georgia, Russian Armenia, and Azerbaijan (az-ur-by-JAHN).

The royal family was yet another victim of the civil war. After the tsar had abdicated, he, his wife, and their five children had been taken into captivity. They were moved in August 1917 to Tobolsk in Siberia and in April 1918 to Ekaterinburg (i-kat-tuh-RIN-burk), a mining town in the Urals. On the night of July 16, members of the local soviet murdered the tsar and his family and burned their bodies in a nearby mine shaft.

How had Lenin and the Bolsheviks triumphed over what seemed at one time to be overwhelming forces? For one thing, the Red Army became a well-disciplined and formidable fighting force, largely due to the organizational genius of Leon Trotsky. As commissar of war, Trotsky reinstated the draft and insisted on rigid discipline; soldiers who deserted or refused to obey orders were summarily executed.

The disunity of the anti-Communist forces seriously weakened their efforts. Political differences created distrust among the Whites and prevented them from cooperating effectively with each other. Some Whites insisted on restoring the tsarist regime, while others understood that only a more liberal democratic program had any chance of success. It was difficult enough to achieve military cooperation; political differences made it virtually impossible.

The Whites' inability to agree on a common goal was in sharp contrast to the Communists' single-minded sense of purpose. Inspired by their vision of a new socialist order, the Communists had the advantage of possessing the determination that comes from revolutionary fervor and revolutionary convictions.

The Communists also succeeded in translating their revolutionary faith into practical instruments of power. A policy of **war communism**, for example, was used to ensure regular supplies for the Red Army. War communism included the nationalization of banks and most industries, the forcible requisition of grain from peasants, and the centralization of state power under Bolshevik control. Another Bolshevik instrument was "revolutionary terror." A new Red secret police, known as the Cheka (CHEK-uh), instituted the Red Terror, aimed at nothing less than the destruction of all opponents of the new regime.

Finally, the intervention of foreign armies enabled the Communists to appeal to the powerful force of Russian patriotism. Although the Allied Powers had intervened initially in Russia to encourage the Russians to remain in the war, the end of the war on November 11, 1918, had made that purpose inconsequential. Nevertheless, Allied troops remained, and even more were sent, as Allied countries did not hide their

	1916
Murder of Rasputin	December
	1917
March of women in Petrograd	March 8
General strike in Petrograd	March 10
Establishment of Provisional Government	March 12
Tsar Nicholas II abdicates	March 15
Formation of Petrograd soviet	March
Lenin arrives in Russia	April 3
Bolsheviks gain majority in Petrograd soviet	October
Bolsheviks overthrow Provisional Government	November 6–7
	1918
Treaty of Brest-Litovsk	March 3
Murder of royal family	July 16
Civil war	1918–1921

anti-Bolshevik feelings. At one point, more than 100,000 foreign troops, mostly Japanese, British, American, and French, were stationed on Russian soil. This intervention by the Allies enabled the Communist government to appeal to patriotic Russians to fight the attempts of foreigners to control their country.

By 1921, the Communists were in control of Russia. In the course of the civil war, the Bolshevik regime had also transformed Russia into a bureaucratically centralized state dominated by a single party. It was also a state that was largely hostile to the Allied Powers that had sought to assist the Bolsheviks' enemies in the civil war. To most historians, the Russian Revolution is unthinkable without the total war of World War I, for only the collapse of Russia made it possible for a radical minority like the Bolsheviks to seize the reins of power. In turn, the Russian Revolution had an impact on the course of World War I.

The Last Year of the War

For Germany, the withdrawal of the Russians from the war in March 1918 offered renewed hope for a favorable end to the war. The victory over Russia persuaded Erich von Ludendorff (LOO-dun-dorf) (1865–1937), who guided German military operations, and most German leaders to make one final military gamble—a grand offensive in the west to break the military stalemate. The German attack was launched in March and lasted into July, but an Allied counterattack, supported by the arrival of 140,000 fresh American troops, defeated the Germans at the Second Battle of the Marne on July 18. Ludendorff's gamble had failed. With the arrival of 2 million more American troops on the Continent, Allied forces began to advance steadily toward Germany.

On September 29, 1918, General Ludendorff informed German leaders that the war was lost and demanded that the government sue for peace at once. When German officials discovered, however, that the Allies were unwilling to make peace with the autocratic imperial government, reforms were instituted to create a liberal government. But these constitutional reforms came too late for the exhausted and angry German people. On November 3, naval units in Kiel (KEEL) mutinied, and within days, councils of workers and soldiers were forming throughout northern Germany and taking over the supervision of civilian and military administrations. William II capitulated to public pressure and abdicated on November 9, and the Socialists under Friedrich Ebert (FREED-rikh AY-bert) (1871–1925) announced the establishment of a republic. Two days later, on November 11, 1918, the new German government agreed to an armistice. The war was over.

THE CASUALTIES OF THE WAR World War I devastated European civilization. Between 8 and 9 million soldiers died on the battlefields; another 22 million were wounded. Many of those who survived later died from war injuries or lived on with missing arms or legs or other forms of mutilation. The birthrate in many European countries declined noticeably as a result of the death or maiming of so many young men.

Nor did the killing affect only soldiers. Untold numbers of civilians died from war injuries or starvation. In 1915, using the excuse of a rebellion by the Armenian minority and their supposed collaboration with the Russians, the Turkish government began systematically to kill Armenian men and expel women and children. Within seven months, 600,000 Armenians had been killed, and 500,000 had been deported. Of the latter, 400,000 died while marching through the deserts and swamps of Syria and Mesopotamia. By September 1915, an estimated one million Armenians were dead, the victims of genocide.

The Peace Settlement

In January 1919, the delegations of twenty-seven victorious Allied nations gathered in Paris to conclude a final settlement of the Great War. Over a period of years, the reasons for fighting World War I had been transformed from selfish national interests to idealistic principles.

PEACE AIMS No one expressed these principles better than U.S. President Woodrow Wilson. Wilson's proposals for a truly just and lasting peace included "open covenants of peace, openly arrived at" instead of secret diplomacy; the reduction of national armaments to a "point consistent with domestic safety"; and the self-determination of people so that "all well-defined national aspirations shall be accorded the utmost satisfaction." Wilson characterized World War I as a people's war waged against "absolutism and militarism," which could be eradicated only by creating democratic governments and a "general association of nations" that would guarantee the "political independence and territorial integrity to great and small states alike" (see the box on p. 684). As the spokesman for a new world order based on democracy and international cooperation, Wilson was enthusiastically cheered by many Europeans when he arrived in Europe for the peace conference, held at the palace of Versailles. Wilson's rhetoric on self-determination also inspired peoples in the colonial world, in Africa, Asia, and the Middle East, and was influential in developing anticolonial nationalist movements in these areas (see Chapter 24).

Wilson soon found, however, that more practical motives guided other states at the peace table. The secret treaties and agreements that had been made before the war could not be totally ignored, even if they did conflict with the principle of self-determination enunciated by Wilson. National interests also complicated the deliberations of the Paris Peace Conference. David Lloyd George (1863–1945), prime minister of Great Britain, had won a decisive electoral victory in December 1918 on a platform of making the Germans pay for this dreadful war.

France's approach to peace was determined primarily by considerations of national security. To Georges Clemenceau (ZHORZH kluh-mahn-SOH) (1841–1929), the feisty premier of France who had led his country to victory, the French people had borne the brunt of German aggression. They deserved revenge and security against future German encroachment.

The most important decisions at the Paris Peace Conference were made by Wilson, Clemenceau, and Lloyd George. Italy was considered one of the so-called Big Four powers but played a much less important role than the other three countries. Germany, of course, was not invited to attend, and Russia could not because of its civil war.

In view of the many conflicting demands at Versailles, it was inevitable that the Big Three would quarrel. Wilson was determined to create a "league of nations" to prevent future wars. Clemenceau and Lloyd George were equally determined to punish Germany. In the end, only compromise made it possible to achieve a peace settlement. Wilson's wish that the creation of an international peacekeeping organization be the first order of business was granted, and on January 25, 1919, the conference adopted the principle of the League of Nations. In return, Wilson agreed to make compromises on territorial arrangements to guarantee the establishment of the League, believing that a functioning League could later rectify bad arrangements. Clemenceau also compromised to obtain some guarantees for French security. He renounced France's desire for a separate Rhineland and instead accepted a defensive alliance with Great Britain and the United States. Both states pledged to help France if it were attacked by Germany.

THE TREATY OF VERSAILLES The final peace settlement consisted of five separate treaties with the defeated nations—Germany, Austria, Hungary, Bulgaria, and Turkey. The Treaty of Versailles with Germany, signed on June 28, 1919, was by far the most important one. The Germans considered it a harsh peace and were particularly unhappy with Article 231, the so-called **War**

CHRONOLOGY	World War I
	1914
Battle of Tannenberg	August 26–30
First Battle of the Marne	September 6–10
Battle of Masurian Lakes	September 15
	1915
Battle of Gallipoli begins	April 25
Italy declares war on Austria-Hungary	May 23
	1916
Battle of Verdun	February 21–December 18
	1917
United States enters the war	April 6
	1918
Last German offensive	March 21–July 18
Second Battle of the Marne	July 18
Allied counteroffensive	July 18–November 10
Armistice between Allies and Germany	November 11

Guilt Clause, which declared Germany (and Austria) responsible for starting the war and ordered Germany to pay **reparations** for all the damage to which the Allied governments and their people were subjected as a result of the war "imposed upon them by the aggression of Germany and her allies."

The military and territorial provisions of the treaty also rankled Germans. Germany had to reduce its army to

The Big Four at Paris. Shown here are the Big Four negotiators at the Paris Peace Conference: David Lloyd George of Britain, Vittorio Orlando of Italy, Georges Clemenceau of France, and Woodrow Wilson of the United States. Although Italy was one of the Big Four powers, Britain, France, and the United States (the Big Three) made the major decisions at the peace conference.

Three Voices of Peacemaking

POLITICS & GOVERNMENT

When the Allied Powers met in Paris in January 1919, it soon became apparent that the victors had different opinions on the kind of peace they expected. The first selection is a series of excerpts from the speeches of Woodrow Wilson in which the American president presented his idealistic goals for a peace based on justice and reconciliation.

The French leader, Georges Clemenceau, had a vision of peacemaking quite different from Wilson's. The French sought revenge and security. In the selection from his book *Grandeur and Misery of Victory*, Clemenceau revealed his fundamental dislike and distrust of Germany.

A third voice of peacemaking was heard in Paris in 1919, although not at the peace conference. W. E. B. Du Bois (doo BOYZ), an African American writer and activist, had organized the Pan-African Congress to meet in Paris during the Paris Peace Conference. The goal of the Pan-African Congress was to present a series of resolutions that promoted the cause of Africans and people of African descent. As can be seen in the selection presented here, the resolutions did not call for immediate independence for African nations.

Woodrow Wilson, Speeches

May 26, 1917

We are fighting for the liberty, the self-government, and the undictated development of all peoples, and every feature of the settlement that concludes this war must be conceived and executed for that purpose. Wrongs must first be righted and then adequate safeguards must be created to prevent their being committed again. . . .

No people must be forced under sovereignty under which it does not wish to live. No territory must change hands except for the purpose of securing those who inhabit it a fair chance of life and liberty. No indemnities must be insisted on except those that constitute payment for manifest wrongs done. No readjustments of power must be made except such as will tend to secure the future peace of the world and the future welfare and happiness of its peoples.

And then the free peoples of the world must draw together in some common covenant, some genuine and practical cooperation that will in effect combine their force to secure peace and justice in the dealings of nations with one another.

April 6, 1918

We are ready, whenever the final reckoning is made, to be just to the German people, deal fairly with the German power, as with all others. There can be no difference between peoples in the final judgment, if it is indeed to be a righteous judgment. To propose anything but justice, even-handed and dispassionate justice, to Germany at any time, whatever the outcome of

the war, would be to renounce and dishonor our own cause. For we ask nothing that we are not willing to accord.

January 3, 1919

Our task at Paris is to organize the friendship of the world, to see to it that all the moral forces that make for right and justice and liberty are united and are given a vital organization to which the peoples of the world will readily and gladly respond. In other words, our task is no less colossal than this, to set up a new international psychology, to have a new atmosphere.

Georges Clemenceau, *Grandeur and Misery of Victory*

War and peace, with their strong contrasts, alternate against a common background. For the catastrophe of 1914 the Germans are responsible. Only a professional liar would deny this. . . .

What after all is this war, prepared, undertaken, and waged by the German people, who flung aside every scruple of conscience to let it loose, hoping for a peace of enslavement under the yoke of a militarism, destructive of all human dignity? It is simply the continuance, the recrudescence, of those never-ending acts of violence by which the first savage tribes carried out their depredations with all the resources of barbarism. . . .

I have sometimes penetrated into the sacred cave of the Germanic cult, which is, as every one knows, the *Bierhaus* [beer hall]. A great aisle of massive humanity where there accumulate, amid the fumes of tobacco and beer, the popular rumblings of a nationalism upheld by the sonorous brasses blaring to the heavens the supreme voice of Germany, *Deutschland über alles! Germany above everything!* Men, women, and children, all petrified in reverence before the divine stoneware pot, brows furrowed with irrepressible power, eyes lost in a dream of infinity, mouths twisted by the intensity of willpower, drink in long draughts the celestial hope of vague expectations. These only remain to be realized presently when the chief marked out by Destiny shall have given the word. There you have the ultimate framework of an old but childish race.

Pan-African Congress

Resolved

That the Allied and Associated Powers establish a code of law for the international protection of the natives of Africa. . . .

The Negroes of the world demand that hereafter the natives of Africa and the peoples of African descent be governed according to the following principles:

1. The Land: the land and its natural resources shall be held in trust for the natives and at all times they shall have effective ownership of as much land as they can profitably develop. . . .

(continued)

(Opposing Viewpoints continued)

3. Labor: slavery and corporal punishment shall be abolished and forced labor except in punishment for crime. . . .

5. The State: the natives of Africa must have the right to participate in the government as fast as their development permits, in conformity with the principle that the government exists for the natives, and not the natives for the government.

 How did the peacemaking aims of Wilson and Clemenceau differ? How did their different views affect the deliberations of the Paris Peace Conference and the nature of the final peace settlement? How and why did the views of the Pan-African Congress differ from those of Wilson and Clemenceau?

100,000 men, cut back its navy, and eliminate its air force. German territorial losses included the return of Alsace and Lorraine to France and sections of Prussia to the new Polish state (see Map 23.3). German land west and as far as 30 miles east of the Rhine was established as a demilitarized zone and stripped of all armaments or fortifications to serve as a barrier to any future German military moves westward against France. Outraged by the "dictated peace," the new German government complained but accepted the treaty.

THE OTHER PEACE TREATIES The separate peace treaties made with the other Central Powers extensively redrew the map of eastern Europe. Many of these changes merely ratified what the war had already accomplished. Both the German and Russian empires lost considerable territory in eastern Europe, and the Austro-Hungarian Empire disappeared altogether. New nation-states emerged from the lands of these three empires: Finland, Latvia, Estonia, Lithuania, Poland, Czechoslovakia, Austria, and Hungary. Territorial

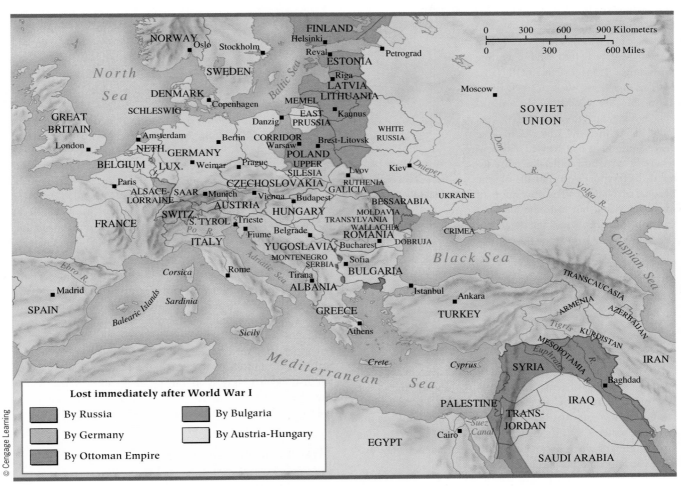

MAP 23.3 Territorial Changes in Europe and the Middle East After World War I. The victorious Allies met in Paris to determine the shape and nature of postwar Europe. At the urging of U.S. President Woodrow Wilson, many nationalist aspirations of former imperial subjects were realized with the creation of several new countries from the prewar territory of Austria-Hungary, Germany, Russia, and the Ottoman Empire.

 What new countries emerged in Europe and the Middle East?

rearrangements were also made in the Balkans. Romania acquired land from Russia, Hungary, and Bulgaria. Serbia formed the nucleus of a new southern Slavic kingdom, later called Yugoslavia, which united Serbs, Croats, and Slovenes under a single monarch.

Although the Paris Peace Conference was supposedly guided by the principle of self-determination, the mixtures of peoples in eastern Europe made it impossible to draw boundaries along neat ethnic lines. As a result of compromises, virtually every eastern European state was left with a minorities problem that could lead to future conflicts. Germans in Poland; Hungarians, Poles, and Germans in Czechoslovakia; Hungarians in Romania; and the combination of Serbs, Croats, Slovenes, Macedonians, and Albanians in Yugoslavia all became sources of later conflict.

Yet another centuries-old entity, the Ottoman Empire, was dismembered by the peace settlement after the war. To gain Arab support against the Ottoman Turks during the war, the Western Allies had promised to recognize the independence of Arab states in the Middle Eastern lands of the Ottoman Empire. But the imperialist habits of Western nations died hard. After the war, France was given control of Lebanon and Syria, while Britain received Iraq and Palestine (including Trans-Jordan). Officially, both acquisitions were called **mandates**. Because Woodrow Wilson had opposed the outright annexation of colonial territories by the Allies, the peace settlement had created a system whereby a nation officially administered a territory on behalf of the League of Nations. The invention of mandates could not hide the fact that the principle of national self-determination at the Paris Peace Conference was largely for Europeans.

The Middle East in 1919

An Uncertain Peace

FOCUS QUESTION: What was the aftermath of World War I, and what problems did Europe and the United States face in the 1920s?

Four years of devastating war had left many Europeans with a profound sense of despair and disillusionment. The Great War indicated to many people that something was dreadfully wrong with Western values. In *The Decline of the West*, the German writer Oswald Spengler (1880–1936) reflected this disillusionment when he emphasized the decadence of Western civilization and posited its collapse.

The Impact of World War I

The enormous suffering and the deaths of almost 10 million people shook traditional society to its foundations and undermined the whole idea of progress. New propaganda techniques had manipulated entire populations into maintain-

ing involvement in senseless slaughter. How did Europeans deal with such losses? In France, for example, probably two-thirds of the population was in mourning over the deaths of these young people.

An immediate response was the erection of war memorials accompanied by ceremonies to honor the dead. Battlefields also became significant commemorative sites with memorial parks, large monuments, and massive cemeteries, including ossuaries, vaults where the bones of thousands of unidentified soldiers were interred. Virtually all belligerent countries adopted national ceremonies for the burial of a symbolic "unknown soldier," a telling reminder of the brutality of World War I. Moreover, businesses, schools, universities, and other corporate bodies all set up their own war memorials.

It is impossible to calculate the social impact of the mourning for the lost soldiers. One French mother explained, "No matter how proud as Frenchwomen we poor mothers may be of our sons, we nevertheless carry wounds in our hearts that nothing can heal. It is strongly contrary to nature for our children to depart before us."[9] Another Frenchman wrote, "Why should the old people remain alive, when the children who might have initiated the most beautiful era in French history march off to the sacrifice?"[10]

World War I created a "lost generation" of war veterans who had become inured to violence; indeed, in the course of the war, brutality became a way of life and a social reality. As one Frenchman recounted, "Not only did war make us dead, impotent or blind. In the midst of beautiful actions, of sacrifice and self-abnegation, it also awoke in us . . . ancient instincts of cruelty and barbarity. At times, I, who have never punched anyone, who loathes disorder and brutality, took pleasure in killing."[11] After the war, some veterans became pacifists, but for many veterans, the viciousness of the war became a starting point for the use of violence in the new political movements of the 1920s and 1930s (see "Retreat from Democracy: Dictatorial Regimes" in Chapter 25). These men were fiercely nationalistic and eager to restore the national interests they felt had been betrayed in the peace treaties. They would later band together in support of Mussolini and Hitler in their tyrannical bids for power.

The Search for Security

The peace settlement at the end of World War I had tried to fulfill the nineteenth-century dream of nationalism by creating secure boundaries and new states. From its inception, however, this peace settlement had left nations unhappy and eager to revise it.

U.S. President Woodrow Wilson had recognized that the peace treaties contained unwise provisions that could serve as new causes for conflicts and had placed many of his hopes for the future in the League of Nations. The League, however, was not particularly effective in maintaining the peace. The failure of the United States to join the League in a backlash of isolationist sentiment undermined its effectiveness from the beginning. Moreover, the League could use only economic sanctions to halt aggression.

THE FRENCH POLICY OF COERCION (1919–1924) The weakness of the League of Nations and the failure of both the United States and Great Britain to honor their defensive military alliances with France left France embittered and alone. France's search for security between 1919 and 1924 was founded primarily on a strict enforcement of the Treaty of Versailles. This tough policy toward Germany began with the issue of the reparations payments that the Germans were supposed to make to compensate for war damage. In April 1921, the Allied Reparations Commission settled on a sum of 132 billion marks ($33 billion), payable in annual installments of 2.5 billion (gold) marks. The new German Republic made its first payment in 1921, but by the following year, facing financial problems, the Germans announced that they were unable to pay more. Outraged, the French government sent troops to occupy the Ruhr valley, Germany's chief industrial and mining center. If the Germans would not pay reparations, the French would collect reparations in kind by operating and using the Ruhr's mines and factories.

Both Germany and France suffered from the French occupation of the Ruhr. The German government adopted a policy of passive resistance to French occupation that was largely financed by printing more paper money. This only intensified the inflationary pressures that had begun in Germany toward the end of the war. The German mark became worthless, and economic disaster fueled political upheavals. All the nations, including France, were happy to cooperate with the American suggestion for a new conference of experts to reassess the reparations problem.

THE HOPEFUL YEARS (1924–1929) In August 1924, an international commission produced a new plan for reparations. The Dawes Plan, named after the American banker who chaired the commission, reduced reparations and stabilized Germany's payments on the basis of its ability to pay. The Dawes Plan also granted an initial $200 million loan for German recovery, which opened the door to heavy American investments in Europe that helped create an era of European prosperity between 1924 and 1929.

With prosperity came a new age of European diplomacy. A spirit of cooperation was fostered by the foreign ministers of Germany and France, Gustav Stresemann (GOOS-tahf SHTRAY-zuh-mahn) and Aristide Briand (ah-ruh-STEED bree-AHNH), who concluded the Treaty of Locarno (loh-KAHR-noh) in 1925. This guaranteed Germany's new western borders with France and Belgium. Although Germany's new eastern borders with Poland were conspicuously absent from the agreement, the Locarno pact was viewed by many as the beginning of a new era of European peace. On the day after the pact was concluded, the *New York Times* proclaimed,

"France and Germany Ban War Forever," and the *London Times* declared, "Peace at Last."[12]

The spirit of Locarno was based on little real substance, however. Germany lacked the military power to alter its western borders even if it wanted to. And the issue of disarmament soon proved that even the spirit of Locarno could not bring nations to cut back on their weapons. The League of Nations had suggested the "reduction of national armaments to the lowest point consistent with national safety." Germany, of course, had been disarmed with the expectation that other states would do likewise. Numerous disarmament conferences, however, failed to achieve anything substantial as states were unwilling to trust their security to anyone but their own military forces.

The Great Depression

After World War I, most European states hoped to return to the liberal ideal of a market economy based on private enterprise and largely free of state intervention. But the war had vastly strengthened business cartels and labor unions, making some government regulation of these powerful organizations necessary. At the same time, reparations and war debts had severely damaged the postwar international economy, making the prosperity that did occur between 1924 and 1929 exceedingly fragile and the dream of returning to the liberal ideal of a self-regulating market economy merely an illusion. What destroyed the concept altogether was the Great Depression.

CAUSES Two factors played a major role in the coming of the Great Depression: a downturn in domestic economies and an international financial crisis created by the collapse of the American stock market in 1929. Already in the mid-1920s, prices for agricultural goods were beginning to decline rapidly due to overproduction of basic commodities such as wheat. In 1925, states in central and eastern Europe began to impose tariffs to close their markets to other countries' goods. An increase in the use of oil and hydroelectricity led to a slump in the coal industry even before 1929.

In addition to these domestic economic troubles, much of the European prosperity between 1924 and 1929 had been built on American bank loans to Germany. In 1928, American investors had begun to pull money out of Germany in order to invest in the booming New York stock market. The crash of the U.S. stock market in October 1929 led panicky American investors to withdraw even more of their funds from Germany and other European markets. The withdrawal of funds seriously weakened the banks of Germany and other central European states. The Credit-Anstalt, Vienna's most prestigious bank, collapsed on May 31, 1931. By that time, trade was slowing down, industrialists were cutting back production, and unemployment was increasing as the ripple effects of international bank failures had a devastating impact on domestic economies.

REPERCUSSIONS Economic depression was by no means a new phenomenon in European history. But the depth of the economic downturn after 1929 fully justifies the Great

The Great Depression: Bread Lines in Paris. The Great Depression devastated the European economy and had serious political repercussions. Because of its more balanced economy, France did not feel the effects of the depression as quickly as other European countries. By 1931, however, even France was experiencing lines of unemployed people at free-food centers.

The Democratic States

The Great Depression had political as well as economic consequences for all of the democratic states. In some, especially the United States, it became the impetus for new social reform measures.

GREAT BRITAIN After World War I, Great Britain went through a period of serious economic difficulties. During the war, Britain had lost many of the markets for its industrial products, especially to the United States and Japan. The postwar decline of such staple industries as coal, steel, and textiles led to a rise in unemployment, which reached the 2 million mark in 1921. But Britain soon rebounded and from 1925 to 1929 experienced an era of renewed prosperity, even though unemployment remained at the startling level of 10 percent.

By 1929, Britain faced the growing effects of the Great Depression. The Labour Party, which had become the largest party in Britain, failed to solve the nation's economic problem and fell from power in 1931. A national government (a coalition of Liberals and Conservatives) claimed credit for bringing Britain out of the worst stages of the depression, primarily by using the traditional policies of balanced budgets and protective tariffs. British politicians had largely ignored the new ideas of a Cambridge economist, John Maynard Keynes (KAYNZ) (1883–1946), who published his *General Theory of Employment, Interest and Money* in 1936. He condemned the traditional view that in a free economy, depressions should be left to work themselves out. Instead, Keynes argued that unemployment stemmed not from overproduction but from a decline in demand and that demand could be increased by putting people back to work constructing highways and public buildings. Such public works should be used to stimulate the economy even if the government had to go into debt to pay for them, a concept known as **deficit spending**.

FRANCE After the defeat of Germany, France had become the strongest power on the European continent. Its greatest need was to rebuild the devastated areas of northern and eastern France, but no French government seemed capable of solving the nation's financial problems between 1921 and 1926. Like other European countries, though, France did experience a period of relative prosperity between 1926 and 1929.

Because it had a more balanced economy than other nations, France did not begin to feel the full effects of the Great Depression until 1932. Economic instability soon had political repercussions. During a nineteen-month period in 1932 and 1933, six different cabinets were formed as France faced political chaos. Finally, in June 1936, a coalition of leftist parties—Communists, Socialists, and Radicals—formed a Popular Front government.

Depression label. During 1932, the worst year of the downturn, one British worker in four was unemployed, and 6 million workers, or 40 percent of the German labor force, were out of work. Between 1929 and 1932, industrial production plummeted almost 50 percent in the United States and nearly as much in Germany. Unemployed and homeless people filled the streets of cities throughout the advanced industrial world (see the box on p. 689).

The economic crisis also had unexpected social repercussions. Women were often able to secure low-paying jobs as servants, housecleaners, or laundresses, while many men remained unemployed, either begging on the streets or staying at home to do household tasks. Many unemployed men, resenting this reversal of traditional gender roles, were open to the shrill cries of demagogues with simple solutions to the economic crisis. In addition, high unemployment rates among young males often led them to join gangs that gathered in parks or other public places, creating fear among local residents.

Governments seemed powerless to deal with the crisis. The classical liberal remedy for depression, a deflationary policy of balanced budgets, which involved cutting costs by lowering wages and raising tariffs to exclude other countries' goods from home markets, only served to worsen the economy and cause even greater mass discontent. This in turn led to serious political repercussions. Increased government activity in the economy was one reaction. Another effect was a renewed interest in Marxist doctrines. Hadn't Marx predicted that capitalism would destroy itself through overproduction? Communism took on new popularity, especially with workers and intellectuals. Finally, the Great Depression increased the attractiveness of simplistic dictatorial solutions, especially from a new movement known as fascism. Everywhere, democracy seemed on the defensive in the 1930s (see Chapter 25).

The Great Depression: Unemployed and Homeless in Germany

FAMILY & SOCIETY

In 1932, Germany had 6 million unemployed workers, many of them wandering aimlessly about the country, begging for food and seeking shelter in city lodging houses for the homeless. The Great Depression was an important factor in the rise to power of Adolf Hitler and the Nazis. This selection presents a description of the unemployed homeless in 1932.

Heinrich Hauser, "With Germany's Unemployed"

An almost unbroken chain of homeless men extends the whole length of the great Hamburg-Berlin highway. . . . All the highways in Germany over which I have traveled this year presented the same aspect. . . .

Most of the hikers paid no attention to me. They walked separately or in small groups, with their eyes on the ground. And they had the queer, stumbling gait of barefooted people, for their shoes were slung over their shoulders. Some of them were guild members—carpenters . . . milkmen . . . and bricklayers . . . —but they were in a minority. Far more numerous were those whom one could assign to no special profession or craft—unskilled young people, for the most part, who had been unable to find a place for themselves in any city or town in Germany, and who had never had a job and never expected to have one. There was something else that had never been seen before—whole families that had piled all their goods into baby carriages and wheelbarrows that they were pushing along as they plodded forward in dumb despair. It was a whole nation on the march.

I saw them—and this was the strongest impression that the year 1932 left with me—I saw them, gathered into groups of fifty or a hundred men, attacking fields of potatoes. I saw them digging up the potatoes and throwing them into sacks while the farmer who owned the field watched them in despair and the local policeman looked on gloomily from the distance. I saw them staggering toward the lights of the city as night fell, with their sacks on their backs. What did it remind me of? Of the War, of the worst periods of starvation in 1917 and 1918, but even then people paid for the potatoes. . . .

I saw that the individual can know what is happening only by personal experience. I know what it is to be a tramp.

I know what cold and hunger are. . . . But there are two things that I have only recently experienced—begging and spending the night in a municipal lodging house.

I entered the huge Berlin municipal lodging house in a northern quarter of the city. . . .

Distribution of spoons, distribution of enameled-ware bowls with the words "Property of the City of Berlin" written on their sides. Then the meal itself. A big kettle is carried in. Men with yellow smocks have brought it in, and men with yellow smocks ladle out the food. These men, too, are homeless and they have been expressly picked by the establishment and given free food and lodging and a little pocket money in exchange for their work about the house.

Where have I seen this kind of food distribution before? In a prison that I once helped to guard in the winter of 1919 during the German civil war. There was the same hunger then, the same trembling, anxious expectation of rations. Now the men are standing in a long row, dressed in their plain nightshirts that reach to the ground, and the noise of their shuffling feet is like the noise of big wild animals walking up and down the stone floor of their cages before feeding time. The men lean far over the kettle so that the warm steam from the food envelops them, and they hold out their bowls as if begging and whisper to the attendant, "Give me a real helping. Give me a little more." A piece of bread is handed out with every bowl.

My next recollection is sitting at a table in another room on a crowded bench that is like a seat in a fourth-class railway carriage. Hundreds of hungry mouths make an enormous noise eating their food. The men sit bent over their food like animals who feel that someone is going to take it away from them. They hold their bowl with their left arm partway around it, so that nobody can take it away, and they also protect it with their other elbow and with their head and mouth, while they move the spoon as fast as they can between their mouth and the bowl.

Why did Hauser compare the scene he describes from 1932 with conditions in the years 1917 and 1918? Why did he compare the hungry men to animals?

Although the Popular Front initiated a program for workers that included the right of collective bargaining, a forty-hour workweek, two-week paid vacations, and minimum wages, its policies failed to solve the problems of the depression. By 1938, the French were experiencing a serious decline of confidence in their political system.

GERMANY After the imperial Germany of William II had come to an end in 1918 with Germany's defeat in World War I, a German democratic state known as the Weimar (VY-mar) Republic was established. From the very start, the Weimar Republic was plagued by problems. It had no truly outstanding political leaders, and in 1925, Paul von Hindenburg

(POWL fun HIN-den-boork), a World War I army commander, was elected president at the age of seventy-seven. Hindenburg was a traditional military man, monarchist in sentiment, who at heart was not in favor of the republic he had been elected to serve.

The Weimar Republic also faced serious economic difficulties. Germany experienced runaway inflation in 1922 and 1923; widows, orphans, the retired elderly, army officers, teachers, civil servants, and others who lived on fixed incomes all watched their monthly stipends become worthless and their lifetime savings evaporate. Their economic losses increasingly pushed the middle class to the rightist parties that were hostile to the republic. To make matters worse, after a period of prosperity from 1924 to 1929, Germany faced the Great Depression. Unemployment increased to 3 million in March 1930 and 4.4 million by December of the same year. The depression paved the way for the rise of extremist parties.

UNITED STATES After Germany, no Western nation was more affected by the Great Depression than the United States. By 1932, U.S. industrial production had fallen to half what it had been in 1929. By 1933, there were 15 million unemployed. Under these circumstances, the Democratic presidential candidate, Franklin Delano Roosevelt (1882–1945), was able to win a landslide electoral victory in 1932. He and his advisers pursued a policy of active government intervention in the economy with a stepped-up program of public works that came to be known as the **New Deal**. The Works Progress Administration (WPA), a government organization established in 1935, employed 2 to 3 million people building bridges, roads, post offices, and airports. The Roosevelt administration was also responsible for new social legislation that launched the American welfare state. In 1935, the Social Security Act created a system of old-age pensions and unemployment insurance.

The New Deal provided some social reform measures that perhaps averted the possibility of social revolution in the United States. It did not, however, solve the unemployment problems of the Great Depression. In May 1937, during what was considered a period of full recovery, American unemployment still stood at 7 million. Only World War II and the subsequent growth of the armaments industry brought American workers back to full employment.

Socialism in Soviet Russia

With their victory in the civil war, Bolshevik leaders could now turn to the challenging task of building the first socialist society in a world dominated by their capitalist enemies. But the civil war had taken an enormous toll of life. During the civil war, Lenin had pursued a policy of war communism, but once the war was over, peasants began to sabotage the program by hoarding food. Added to this problem was drought, which caused a great famine between 1920 and 1922 that claimed as many as 5 million lives. Industrial collapse paralleled the agricultural disaster. By 1921, industrial output was only 20 percent of its 1913 levels. Russia was exhausted.

A peasant banner proclaimed, "Down with Lenin and horseflesh, Bring back the Tsar and pork." As Leon Trotsky said, "The country, and the government with it, were at the very edge of the abyss."[13]

NEW POLICIES In March 1921, Lenin pulled Russia back from the abyss by adopting his **New Economic Policy** (NEP), a modified version of the old capitalist system. Forced requisitioning of food from the peasants was halted, and peasants were now allowed to sell their produce openly. Retail stores and small industries that employed fewer than twenty people could now operate under private ownership, although heavy industry, banking, utilities, and mines remained in the hands of the government.

In 1922, Lenin and the Communists formally created a new state called the Union of Soviet Socialist Republics, known as the USSR by its initials or the Soviet Union by its shortened form. Already by that year, a revived market and a good harvest had brought the famine to an end; Soviet agricultural production climbed to 75 percent of its prewar level. Overall, the NEP had saved the nation from complete economic disaster even though Lenin and other leading Communists intended it to be only a temporary, tactical retreat from the goals of communism.

The new government also introduced a number of social changes. Alexandra Kollontai (kul-lun-TY) (1872–1952), who had become a supporter of revolutionary socialism while in exile in Switzerland, took the lead in pushing a Bolshevik program for women's rights and social welfare reforms. As minister of social welfare, she tried to provide health care for women and children by establishing Palaces for the Protection of Maternity and Children. Between 1918 and 1920, the new regime issued a series of reforms that made marriage a civil act, legalized divorce, decreed the equality of men and women, and permitted abortions. Kollontai was also instrumental in establishing an agency within the Communist Party known as Zhenotdel (zhen-ut-DEL) that sent men and women to all parts of the Russian Empire to explain the new social order. In the provinces in the east, Zhenotdel members were often brutally murdered by angry men who objected to any kind of liberation for their wives and daughters. Much to Kollontai's disappointment, many of these early Communist social reforms were later undone as the Communists came to face more pressing matters, including survival of the new regime.

THE STRUGGLE FOR POWER Lenin's death in 1924 inaugurated a struggle for power among the seven members of the Politburo (POL-it-byoor-oh), the institution that had become the leading organ of the party. The Politburo was severely divided over the future direction of the nation. The Left, led by Leon Trotsky, wanted to end the NEP and launch the nation on the path of rapid industrialization, primarily at the expense of the peasantry. This same group wanted to continue the revolution, believing that the survival of the Russian Revolution ultimately depended on the spread of communism abroad. Another group in the Politburo, called the Right, rejected the cause of world revolution and wanted to concentrate instead on constructing a socialist state. The members of this group also favored a continuation of Lenin's NEP because they believed that rapid industrialization would harm the living standards of the peasantry.

These ideological divisions were underscored by an intense personal rivalry between Leon Trotsky and Joseph Stalin (1879–1953). In 1924, Trotsky held the post of commissar of war and was the leading spokesman for the Left in the Politburo. Stalin was content to hold the dull bureaucratic job of party general secretary, while other Politburo members held party positions that enabled them to display their brilliant oratorical abilities. Stalin was skilled at avoiding allegiance to either the Left or the Right faction in the Politburo. He was also a good organizer (his fellow Bolsheviks called him "Comrade Card-Index"), and the other members of the Politburo soon found that the position of party secretary was really the most important in the party hierarchy. Stalin used his post to gain complete control of the Communist Party. Trotsky was expelled from the party in 1927. By 1929, Stalin had succeeded in eliminating the Old Bolsheviks of the revolutionary era from the Politburo and establishing a dictatorship so powerful that the Russian tsars of old would have been envious.

In Pursuit of a New Reality: Cultural and Intellectual Trends

Q FOCUS QUESTION: How did the cultural and intellectual trends of the post–World War I years reflect the crises of the time as well as the lingering effects of the war?

Four years of devastating war left many Europeans with a profound sense of despair and a conviction that something was dreadfully wrong with Western values. The Great Depression only added to the desolation left behind by World War I.

Political and economic uncertainties were paralleled by social innovations. The Great War had served to break down many traditional middle-class attitudes, especially toward sexuality. In the 1920s, women's physical appearance changed dramatically. Short skirts, short hair, the use of cosmetics that were once thought to be the preserve of prostitutes, and the new practice of suntanning gave women a new image. This change in physical appearance, which stressed more exposure of a woman's body, was also accompanied by frank discussions of sexual matters. In 1926, the Dutch physician Theodor van de Velde (TAY-oh-dor vahn duh VEL-duh) published *Ideal Marriage: Its Physiology and Technique*. Translated into a number of languages, it became an international best-seller. Van de Velde described female and male anatomy, discussed birth control techniques, and glorified sexual pleasure in marriage.

Nightmares and New Visions

Uncertainty also pervaded the cultural and intellectual achievements of the postwar years. Artistic trends were largely a working out of the implications of prewar developments. Abstract painting, for example, became ever more popular as many pioneering artists of the early twentieth century matured

(see the comparative essay "A Revolution in the Arts" on p. 692). In addition, prewar fascination with the absurd and the unconscious contents of the mind seemed even more appropriate after the nightmare landscapes of World War I battlefronts. This gave rise to both the Dada movement and Surrealism.

THE DADA MOVEMENT Dadaism (DAH-duh-iz-um) attempted to enshrine the purposelessness of life. Tristan Tzara (TRISS-tun TSAHR-rah) (1896–1945), a Romanian-French poet and one of the founders of Dadaism, expressed the Dadaist contempt for the Western tradition in a lecture in 1922: "The acts of life have no beginning or end. Everything happens in a completely idiotic way. . . . Like everything in life, Dada is useless." Revolted by the insanity of life, the Dadaists tried to give it expression by creating anti-art. The 1918 Berlin Dada Manifesto maintained that "Dada is the international expression of our times, the great rebellion of artistic movements." Many Dadaists took pieces of junk (wire, string, rags, scraps of newspaper, nails, washers) and assembled them into collages, believing that they were transforming the refuse of their culture into art.

In the hands of Hannah Höch (HURKH) (1889–1978), Dada became an instrument to comment on women's roles

Hannah Höch, *Cut with the Kitchen Knife Dada Through the Last Weimar Beer Belly Cultural Epoch of Germany.* Hannah Höch, a prominent figure in the postwar Dada movement, used photomontage to create images that reflected on women's issues. In *Cut with the Kitchen Knife* (1919), she combined pictures of German political leaders with sports stars, Dada artists, and scenes from urban life. One major theme emerged: the confrontation between the anti-Dada world of German political leaders and the Dada world of revolutionary ideals. Höch associated women with Dada and the new world.

A Revolution in the Arts

ART & IDEAS

The period between 1880 and 1930 witnessed a revolution in the arts throughout Western civilization. Fueled in part by developments in physics and psychology, artists and writers rebelled against the traditional belief that the task of art was to represent "reality" and experimented with innovative new techniques in order to approach reality from a totally fresh perspective. Their daring break with the past reflected both the exhilaration of an age propelled by technological discoveries and a fascination with the unconscious contents of the human mind.

From Impressionism and Expressionism to Cubism, abstract art, Dadaism, and Surrealism, painters seemed intoxicated with the belief that their canvases would help reveal the radically changing world. Especially after the cataclysm of World War I, which shattered the image of a rational society, artists sought an absolute freedom of expression, confident that art could redefine humanity in the midst of chaos. Other arts soon followed their lead: James Joyce turned prose on its head by focusing on his characters' innermost thoughts; Arnold Schönberg (AR-nawlt SHURN-bayrk) created atonal music by using a scale composed of twelve notes independent of any tonal key; and Le Corbusier (luh kor-boo-ZYAY) launched a revolution in architecture by using concrete slabs to make "machines for living."

This revolutionary spirit had already been exemplified by Pablo Picasso's canvas *Les Demoiselles d'Avignon*, painted in 1907 (see the illustration on p. 605). Picasso used geometrical designs to create a new reality and appropriated non-Western cultural resources in the desire to revitalize Western art. Reflecting the prevailing European view that African masks were primitive oddities, Picasso ignored the cultural and religious significance of such carvings. Although some African observers charged that Picasso had exploited African culture just as European governments had exploited their colonies, Picasso had succeeded in helping revitalize Western art.

Another illustration of the revolutionary approach to art was the decision by the French artist Marcel Duchamp (mar-SEL duh-SHAHN) to enter a porcelain urinal in a 1917 art exhibit held in New York City. By signing it and giving it the title *Fountain*, Duchamp proclaimed that he had transformed the urinal into a work of art. His "ready-mades" (as such art would henceforth be labeled) declared that art was whatever the artist proclaimed as art. The Dadaist Kurt Schwitters (KOORT SCHVIT-urz) brought together postage stamps, old

Kurt Schwitters, *Der Harz.* Kurt Schwitters became identified with the Dada movement when he began to create his collages. He wrote in 1928, "Fundamentally, I cannot understand why one is not able to use in a picture, exactly in the same way as commercially made color . . . all the old junk which piles up in closets or the rubbish heaps."

handbills, streetcar tickets, newspaper scraps, and pieces of cardboard to form his works of art.

Such intentionally irreverent acts were a slap in the face of the established art world and demystified the nearly sacred reverence that had traditionally been attached to works of art. Essentially, Duchamp, Schwitters, and others claimed that anything under the sun could be selected as a work of art because the mental choice itself equaled the act of artistic creation. Therefore, art need not be a manual construct; it need only be a mental conceptualization. This liberating concept opened the floodgates of the art world, causing the new century to swim in this free-flowing, exploratory torrent.

 How was the revolution in the arts between 1880 and 1930 related to the political, economic, and social developments of the same period?

in the new mass culture. Höch was the only female member of the Berlin Dada Club, which featured photomontage. Her work was part of the first Dada show in Berlin in 1920. In *Dada Dance*, she seemed to criticize the "new woman" by making fun of the way women were inclined to follow fashion trends. In other works, however, she projected positive images of the modern woman and expressed a keen interest in new freedoms for women.

SURREALISM AND MODERN ARCHITECTURE Perhaps more important as an artistic movement was **Surrealism**, which sought a reality beyond the material, sensible world and found it in the world of the unconscious through the portrayal of fantasies, dreams, or nightmares. Employing logic to convey the illogical, the Surrealists created disturbing and evocative images. The Spaniard Salvador Dalí (sahl-vah-DOR dah-LEE) (1904–1989) became the high priest of Surrealism and in his mature phase became a master of representational Surrealism. In *The Persistence of Memory*, Dalí portrayed recognizable objects divorced from their normal context. By placing these objects in unrecognizable relationships, Dalí created a disturbing world in which the irrational had become tangible.

The move toward functionalism in modern architecture also became more widespread in the 1920s and 1930s. Especially important in the spread of functionalism was the Bauhaus (BOW-howss) school of art, architecture, and design, founded in 1919 at Weimar, Germany, by the Berlin architect Walter Gropius (VAHL-tuh GROH-pee-uss). The Bauhaus teaching staff included architects, artists, and designers, who worked together to blend the study of fine arts (painting and sculpture) with the applied arts (printing, weaving, and furniture making). Gropius urged his followers to foster a new union of arts and crafts in order to create the buildings and objects of the future.

Probing the Unconscious

The interest in the unconscious, evident in Surrealism, was also apparent in the new literary techniques that emerged in the 1920s. One of its most apparent manifestations was the "stream of consciousness" technique, in which the writer presented an interior monologue, or a report of the innermost thoughts of each character. One example of this genre was written by the Irish exile James Joyce (1882–1941). His *Ulysses*, published in 1922, told the story of one day in the life of ordinary people in Dublin by following the flow of their inner dialogue. Disconnected ramblings and veiled allusions pervade Joyce's work.

The German writer Hermann Hesse (hayr-MAHN HESS-uh) (1877–1962) dealt with the unconscious in a considerably different fashion. His novels reflected the influence of both the psychological theories of Carl Jung (YOONG) and Eastern religions and focused, among other things, on the spiritual loneliness of modern human beings in a mechanized urban society. *Demian* was a psychoanalytic study of incest, and *Steppenwolf* mirrored the psychological confusion of modern existence. Hesse's novels made a large impact on German youth in the 1920s (see the box on p. 694). He won the Nobel Prize in Literature in 1946.

For much of the Western world, the best way to find (or escape) reality was in the field of mass entertainment. The 1930s represented the heyday of the Hollywood studio system, which in the single year of 1937 turned out nearly six hundred feature films. Supplementing the movies were cheap paperback books and radio, which brought sports, soap operas, and popular music to the masses.

Mass forms of communication and entertainment were not new. But the increased size of audiences and the ability of radio and cinema, unlike the printed word, to provide an immediate mass experience did add new dimensions to mass culture. Favorite film actors and actresses became stars whose lives then became subject to public adoration and scrutiny. Sensuous actresses such as Marlene Dietrich, whose appearance in the early sound film *The Blue Angel* catapulted her to fame, projected new images of women's sexuality.

Salvador Dalí, *The Persistence of Memory.* Surrealism was an important artistic movement in the 1920s. Influenced by the theories of Freudian psychology, Surrealists sought to reveal the world of the unconscious, or the "greater reality" that they believed existed beyond the world of physical appearances. As is evident in this painting, Salvador Dalí sought to portray the world of dreams by painting recognizable objects in unrecognizable relationships.

Hesse and the Unconscious

ART & IDEAS

The novels of Hermann Hesse made a strong impact on young people, first in Germany in the 1920s and then in the United States in the 1960s after they had been translated into English. Many of these young people shared Hesse's fascination with the unconscious and his dislike of modern industrial civilization. This excerpt from *Demian* spoke directly to many of them.

Hermann Hesse, *Demian*

The following spring I was to leave the preparatory school and enter a university. I was still undecided, however, as to where and what I was to study. I had grown a thin mustache, I was a full-grown man, and yet I was completely helpless and without a goal in life. Only one thing was certain: the voice within me, the dream image. I felt the duty to follow this voice blindly wherever it might lead me. But it was difficult and each day I rebelled against it anew. Perhaps I was mad, as I thought at moments; perhaps I was not like other men? But I was able to do the same things the others did; with a little effort and industry I could read Plato, was able to solve problems in trigonometry or follow a chemical analysis. There was only one thing I could not do: wrest the dark secret goal from myself and keep it before me as others did who knew exactly what they wanted to be—professors, lawyers, doctors, artists, however long this would take them and whatever difficulties and advantages this decision would bear in its wake. This I could not do. Perhaps I would become something similar, but how was I to know? Perhaps I would have to continue my search for years on end and would not become anything, and would not reach a goal. Perhaps I would reach this goal but it would turn out to be an evil, dangerous, horrible one?

I wanted only to try to live in accord with the promptings which came from my true self. Why was that so very difficult?

 How does Hesse's interest in the unconscious appear in this excerpt? Why was a dislike of mechanized society particularly intense after World War I?

CHAPTER SUMMARY

The assassination of Archduke Francis Ferdinand of Austria-Hungary in the summer of 1914 in the Bosnian capital of Sarajevo led within six weeks to a major war among the major powers of Europe. The Germans drove the Russians back in the east, but in the west a stalemate developed, with trenches defended by barbed wire and machine guns extending from the Swiss border to the English Channel. After German submarine attacks, the United States entered the war in 1917, but even from the beginning of the war, battles also took place in the African colonies of Europe's great powers as well as in the East, making this a truly global war.

Unprepared for war, Russia soon faltered and collapsed, leading to a revolution against the tsar. But the new provisional government in Russia also soon failed, enabling the revolutionary Bolsheviks of V. I. Lenin, to seize power. Lenin established a dictatorship and made a costly peace with Germany. After American troops entered the war, the German government collapsed, leading to an armistice on November 11, 1918.

World War I was the defining event of the twentieth century. The incredible destruction and the deaths of almost 10 million people undermined the whole idea of progress. World War I was also a total war that required a mobilization of resources and populations and increased the centralization of government power. Civil liberties, such as freedom of the press, speech, and assembly, were circumscribed in the name of national security. Governments' need to plan the distribution of goods restricted economic freedom. World War I made the practice of strong central authority a way of life.

Finally, World War I ended the age of European hegemony over world affairs. In 1917, the Russian Revolution had laid the foundation for the creation of a new Eurasian power, the Soviet Union, and the United States had entered the war. The waning of the European age was not immediately evident to all, however, for it was clouded by American isolationism and the withdrawal of the Soviets from world affairs while they nurtured the growth of their own socialist system. These developments, though temporary, created a political vacuum in Europe that all too soon would be filled by the revival of German power.

Although World War I destroyed the liberal optimism of the prewar era, many people in the 1920s still hoped that the progress of Western civilization could somehow be restored. These hopes proved largely unfounded. France, feeling vulnerable to another invasion, sought to weaken Germany. European recovery, largely the result of American loans and investments, ended with the Great Depression at the end of the 1920s. Democratic states, such as Great Britain, France, and the United States, spent much of the 1930s trying to recover from the Great Depression. In the Soviet Union, Lenin's New Economic Policy helped to stabilize the economy, but on his death a struggle for power ensued that ended with the establishment of a dictatorship under Joseph Stalin.

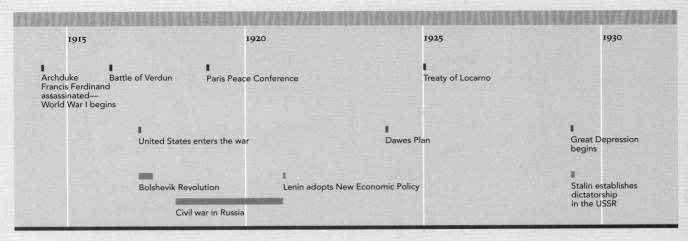

	1915		1920		1925		1930

Archduke Francis Ferdinand assassinated— World War I begins

Battle of Verdun

Paris Peace Conference

Treaty of Locarno

United States enters the war

Dawes Plan

Great Depression begins

Bolshevik Revolution

Lenin adopts New Economic Policy

Stalin establishes dictatorship in the USSR

Civil war in Russia

CHAPTER REVIEW

Upon Reflection

Q What nation, if any, was the most responsible for causing World War I? Why?

Q How did Lenin and the Bolsheviks manage to seize and hold power despite their small numbers?

Q What were the causes of the Great Depression, and how did European states respond to it?

Key Terms

conscription (p. 666)
militarism (p. 666)
trench warfare (p. 670)
total war (p. 676)
soviets (p. 678)
war communism (p. 681)
War Guilt Clause (p. 683)
reparations (p. 683)
mandates (p. 686)
deficit spending (p. 688)
New Deal (p. 690)
New Economic Policy (p. 690)
Dadaism (p. 691)
Surrealism (p. 693)

Suggested Reading

GENERAL WORKS ON TWENTIETH-CENTURY EUROPE A number of general works on European history in the twentieth century provide a context for understanding both World War I and the Russian Revolution. Especially valuable is **N. Ferguson**, *The War of the World: Twentieth-Century Conflict and the Descent of the West* (New York, 2006). See also **R. Paxton**, *Europe in the Twentieth Century,* 4th ed. (New York, 2004).

CAUSES OF WORLD WAR I The historical literature on the causes of World War I is vast. Good starting points are the works by **J. Joll** and **G. Martel**, *The Origins of the First World War,* 3rd ed. (London, 2006), and **A. Mombauer**, *The Origins of the First World War:*

Controversies and Consensus (London, 2002). On the events leading to war, see **D. Fromkin**, *Europe's Last Summer: Who Started the Great War in 1914?* (New York, 2004).

WORLD WAR I The best brief account of World War I is **H. Strachan**, *The First World War* (New York, 2004). On the global nature of World War I, see **M. S. Neiberg**, *Fighting the Great War: A Global History* (Cambridge, Mass., 2005). For a more recent interpretation, see **D. Stevenson**, *Cataclysm: The First World War as Political Tragedy* (New York, 2004). On the role of women in World War I, see **S. Grayzel**, *Women and the First World War* (London, 2002).

On the Paris Peace Conference, see **M. MacMillan**, *Paris, 1919: Six Months That Changed the World* (New York, 2002). On the impact of Woodrow Wilson's ideas on the colonial world, see **E. Manela**, *The Wilsonian Moment: Self-Determination and the International Origins of Anticolonial Nationalism* (Oxford, 2007).

THE RUSSIAN REVOLUTION A good introduction to the Russian Revolution can be found in **R. A. Wade**, *The Russian Revolution, 1917,* 2nd ed. (Cambridge, 2005), and **S. Fitzpatrick**, *The Russian Revolution, 1917–1932,* 2nd ed. (New York, 2001). On Lenin, see **R. Service**, *Lenin: A Biography* (Cambridge, Mass., 2000).

THE 1920S For a general introduction to the post–World War I period, see **M. Kitchen**, *Europe Between the Wars,* 2nd ed. (London, 2006). On European security issues after the Peace of Paris, see **S. Marks**, *The Illusion of Peace: Europe's International Relations, 1918–1933,* 2nd ed. (New York, 2003). On the Great Depression, see **C. P. Kindleberger**, *The World in Depression, 1929–39,* rev. ed. (Berkeley, Calif., 1986).

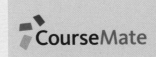

Go to the CourseMate website at **www.cengagebrain.com** for additional study tools and review materials— including audio and video clips—for this chapter.

Nationalism, Revolution, and Dictatorship: Asia, the Middle East, and Latin America from 1919 to 1939

Mohandas "Mahatma" Gandhi, the "Soul of India"

CHAPTER OUTLINE AND FOCUS QUESTIONS

The Rise of Nationalism

Q What were the various stages in the rise of nationalist movements in Asia and the Middle East, and what challenges did they face?

Revolution in China

Q What problems did China encounter between the two world wars, and what solutions did the Nationalists and the Communists propose to solve them?

Japan Between the Wars

Q How did Japan address the problems of nation building in the first decades of the twentieth century, and why did democratic institutions not take hold more effectively?

Nationalism and Dictatorship in Latin America

Q What problems did the nations of Latin America face in the interwar years? To what degree were the problems a consequence of foreign influence?

CRITICAL THINKING

Q How did the societies discussed in this chapter deal with the political, economic, and social challenges that they faced after World War I, and how did these challenges differ from one region to another?

IN 1930, MOHANDAS GANDHI, the sixty-one-year-old leader of the nonviolent movement for Indian independence from British rule, began a march to the sea with seventy-eight followers. Their destination was Dandi, a little coastal town some 240 miles away. The group covered about 12 miles a day. As they went, Gandhi preached his doctrine of nonviolent resistance to British rule in every village he passed through: "Civil disobedience is the inherent right of a citizen. He dare not give it up without ceasing to be a man." By the time he reached Dandi, twenty-four days later, his small group had become an army of thousands. When they arrived at Dandi, Gandhi picked up a pinch of salt from the sand. All along the coast, thousands did likewise, openly breaking British laws that prohibited Indians from making their own salt. The British had long profited from their monopoly on the making and sale of salt. By this simple act of disobedience, Gandhi and the Indian people had taken a bold step on their long march toward independence.

The salt march was but one of many nonviolent activities that Gandhi undertook between World War I and World War II to win India's independence from British rule. World War I had not only deeply affected the lives of Europeans but had also undermined the prestige of Western civilization in the minds of many observers in the rest of the world. As the Europeans devastated their own civilization on the battlefields of Europe, the subject peoples of their vast colonial empires were quick to recognize the opportunity to shake free of foreign domination. In those areas, movements for national independence began to take shape. Some were inspired by the nationalist and liberal movements of the West, while others began to look toward the new Marxist model provided by the victory of the Communists in Soviet Russia, who soon worked to spread their revolutionary vision to African and Asian societies. In the Middle East, World War I ended the rule of the Ottoman Empire and led to the creation of new states, many of which were placed under Western domination.

The societies of Latin America were no longer under direct colonial rule and thus, for the most part, did not face the same types of challenges as their less fortunate counterparts in Asia and Africa. Nevertheless, in some cases the economies of the Latin American countries were virtually controlled by foreign interests. A similar situation prevailed in China and Japan, which had managed with some difficulty to retain at least a degree of political independence, despite severe pressure from the West during the era of high imperialism. But the political flux and economic disruption that characterized much of the world during the two decades following World War I had affected Latin America, China, and Japan as well, leading many in these regions to heed the siren call of fascist dictatorship or social revolution. For all the peoples of Asia, the Middle East, and Latin America, the end of the Great War had not created a world safe for democracy, as Woodrow Wilson had hoped, but an age of great peril and uncertainty.

The Rise of Nationalism

Q FOCUS QUESTION: What were the various stages in the rise of nationalist movements in Asia and the Middle East, and what challenges did they face?

World War I sundered the political and social foundations of the West and severely undermined its self-confidence. In Europe, doubts about the future viability of Western civilization were widespread, especially among the intellectual elite. These doubts were quick to reach the perceptive observers in Asia and Africa and contributed to a rising tide of unrest against Western political domination throughout the colonial and semicolonial world. That unrest took a variety of forms but was most notably displayed in increasing worker activism, rural protest, and a sense of national fervor among anticolonialist intellectuals. In areas of Asia, the Middle East, and Latin America where independent states had successfully resisted the Western onslaught, the discontent fostered by the war and later by the Great Depression led to a loss of confidence in democratic institutions and the rise of political dictatorships.

Modern Nationalism

The first stage of resistance to the West in Asia and Africa (see Chapter 21) had resulted in humiliation and failure and must have confirmed many Westerners' conviction that colonial peoples lacked both the strength and the know-how to create modern states and govern their own destinies. But the process was just beginning. The next phase—the rise of modern nationalism—began to take shape at the beginning of the twentieth century and was the product of the convergence of

several factors. The most vocal source of anticolonialist sentiment was a new urban middle class of westernized intellectuals. In many cases, these merchants, petty functionaries, clerks, students, and professionals had been educated in Western-style schools. A few had spent time in the West. Many spoke Western languages, wore Western clothes, and worked in occupations connected with the colonial regime. Some even wrote in the languages of their colonial masters.

The results were paradoxical. On the one hand, this "new class" admired Western culture and sometimes harbored a deep sense of contempt for traditional ways. On the other hand, many strongly resented the foreigners and their arrogant contempt for colonial peoples. Though eager to introduce Western ideas and institutions into their own societies, these intellectuals were dismayed at the gap between ideal and reality, theory and practice, in colonial policy. Although Western political thought exalted democracy, equality, and individual freedom, democratic institutions were primitive or nonexistent in the colonies.

Equality in economic opportunity and social life was also noticeably lacking. Normally, the middle classes did not suffer in the same manner as impoverished peasants or menial workers in coal mines or on sugar or rubber plantations, but they, too, had complaints. They were usually relegated to low-level jobs in the government or business and were paid less than Europeans in similar positions. The superiority of the Europeans was expressed in a variety of ways, including "whites only" clubs and the use of the familiar form of the language (normally used by adults to children) when addressing the local peoples.

Under these conditions, many of the new urban educated class were ambivalent toward their colonial masters and the civilization that they represented. Out of this mixture of hopes and resentments emerged the first stirrings of modern nationalism in Asia and Africa. During the first quarter of the century, in colonial and semicolonial societies from the Suez Canal to the shores of the Pacific Ocean, educated indigenous peoples began to organize political parties and movements seeking reforms or the end of foreign rule and the restoration of independence.

RELIGION AND NATIONALISM At first, many of the leaders of these movements did not focus clearly on the idea of nationhood but tried to defend indigenous economic interests or religious beliefs. In Burma, for example, the first expression of modern nationalism came from students at the University of Rangoon, who protested against official persecution of the Buddhist religion and British failure to observe local customs in Buddhist temples, such as not removing their footwear. As part of the protest against British arrogance and lack of respect for local religious traditions, the students adopted the name Thakin (TAHK-in)—a polite term in the Burmese language that means "lord" or "master," thereby emphasizing their demand for the right to rule themselves. Only in the 1930s did the Thakins begin to focus specifically on national independence.

In the Dutch East Indies, Sarekat (SAR-eh-kaht) Islam (Islamic Association) began as a self-help society among

The Dilemma of the Intellectual

INTERACTION & EXCHANGE

Sutan Sjahrir was a prominent leader of the Indonesian nationalist movement who briefly served as prime minister of the Republic of Indonesia in the 1950s. Like many Western-educated Asian intellectuals, he was tortured by the realization that by education and outlook he was closer to his colonial masters—in his case, the Dutch—than to his own people. He wrote the following passage in a letter to his wife in 1935 and later included it in his book *Out of Exile.*

Sutan Sjahrir, *Out of Exile*

Am I perhaps estranged from my people? . . . Why are the things that contain beauty for them and arouse their gentler emotions only senseless and displeasing for me? In reality, the spiritual gap between my people and me is certainly no greater than that between an intellectual in Holland . . . and the undeveloped people of Holland. . . . The difference is rather . . . that the intellectual in Holland does not feel this gap because there is a portion—even a fairly large portion—of his own people on approximately the same intellectual level as himself. . . .

This is what we lack here. Not only is the number of intellectuals in this country smaller in proportion to the total population—in fact, very much smaller—but in addition, the few who are here do not constitute any single entity in spiritual outlook, or in any spiritual life or single culture whatsoever. . . . It is for them so much more difficult than for the intellectuals in Holland. In Holland they build—both consciously and unconsciously—on what is already there. . . .

Even if they oppose it, they do so as a method of application or as a starting point.

In our country this is not the case. Here there has been no spiritual or cultural life, and no intellectual progress for centuries. There are the much-praised Eastern art forms but what are these except bare rudiments from a feudal culture that cannot possibly provide a dynamic fulcrum for people of the twentieth century? . . . Our spiritual needs are needs of the twentieth century; our problems and our views are of the twentieth century. Our inclination is no longer toward the mystical, but toward reality, clarity, and objectivity. . . .

We intellectuals here are much closer to Europe or America than we are to the Borobudur or Mahabharata or to the primitive Islamic culture of Java and Sumatra. . . .

So, it seems, the problem stands in principle. It is seldom put forth by us in this light, and instead most of us search unconsciously for a synthesis that will leave us internally tranquil. We want to have both Western science and Eastern philosophy, the Eastern "spirit," in the culture. But what is this Eastern spirit? It is, they say, the sense of the higher, of spirituality, of the eternal and religious, as opposed to the materialism of the West. I have heard this countless times, but it has never convinced me.

Why did Sutan Sjahrir feel estranged from his own culture? What was his answer to the challenges faced by his country in coming to terms with the modern world?

Muslim merchants to fight domination of the local economy by Chinese interests. Eventually, activist elements began to realize that the source of the problem was not the Chinese merchants but the colonial presence, and in the 1920s, Sarekat Islam was transformed into a new organization, the Nationalist Party of Indonesia (PNI), that focused on national independence. Like the Thakins in Burma, this party would eventually lead the country to independence after World War II.

INDEPENDENCE OR MODERNIZATION? THE NATIONALIST QUANDARY Building a new nation, however, requires more than a shared sense of grievances against the foreign invader. A host of other issues also had to be resolved. Soon patriots throughout the colonial world were engaged in a lively and sometimes acrimonious debate over such questions as whether independence or modernization should be their primary objective. The answer depended in part on how the colonial regime was perceived. If it was viewed as a source of needed reforms in a traditional society, a gradualist approach

made sense. But if it was seen primarily as an impediment to change, the first priority, in the minds of many, was to bring it to an end. The vast majority of patriotic individuals were convinced that to survive, their societies must adopt much of the Western way of life; yet many were equally determined that the local culture would not, and should not, become a carbon copy of the West. What was the national identity, after all, if it did not incorporate national traditions?

Another reason for using traditional values was to provide ideological symbols that the common people could understand and would rally around. Though aware that they needed to enlist the mass of the population in the common struggle, most urban intellectuals had difficulty communicating with the teeming population in the countryside who did not understand such complicated and unfamiliar concepts as democracy and nationhood. As the Indonesian intellectual Sutan Sjahrir (SOO-tan syah-REER) (1909–1966) lamented, many westernized intellectuals had more in common with their colonial rulers than with the rural population in the villages (see the box above). As one French colonial official remarked in some surprise to a French-educated Vietnamese reformist, "Why, Monsieur, you are more French than I am!"

Gandhi and the Indian National Congress

Nowhere in the colonial world were these issues debated more vigorously than in India. Before the Sepoy Rebellion (see Chapter 21), Indian consciousness had focused primarily on the question of religious identity. After all, the subcontinent had not been ruled by a dynasty of purely indigenous origins since the Guptas in the middle of the first millennium C.E. But in the latter half of the nineteenth century, a stronger sense of national consciousness began to emerge, provoked by the conservative policies and racial arrogance of the British colonial authorities.

The first Indian nationalists were upper class and educated. Many of them were from urban areas such as Bombay (now Mumbai), Madras (now Chennai), and Calcutta (now Kolkata). Some were trained in law and were members of the civil service. At first, many tended to prefer reform to revolution and believed that India needed modernization before it could handle independence. An exponent of this view was Gopal Gokhale (goh-PAHL GOH-kuh-lay) (1866–1915), a moderate nationalist who hoped that he could convince the British to bring about needed reforms in Indian society. Gokhale and other like-minded reformists did have some effect. In the 1880s, the government introduced a measure of self-government for the first time. All too often, however, such efforts were sabotaged by local British officials.

British India Between the Wars

The slow pace of reform convinced many Indian nationalists that relying on British benevolence was futile. In 1885, a small group of Indians, with some British participation, met in Bombay to form the Indian National Congress (INC). They hoped to speak for all India, but most were high-caste English-trained Hindus. Like their reformist predecessors, members of the INC did not demand immediate independence and accepted the need for reforms to end traditional abuses like child marriage and *sati*. At the same time, they called for an Indian share in the governing process and more spending on economic development and less on military campaigns along the frontier. The British responded with a few concessions, but change was glacially slow. As impatient members of the INC became disillusioned, the radicals split off and formed the New Party, which called for the use of terrorism and violence to achieve national independence.

The INC also had difficulty reconciling religious differences within its ranks. The stated goal of the INC was to seek self-determination for all Indians regardless of class or religious affiliation, but many of its leaders were Hindu and inevitably reflected Hindu concerns. In the first decade of the twentieth century, the separate Muslim League was created to represent the interests of the millions of Muslims in Indian society.

NONVIOLENT RESISTANCE In 1915, a young Hindu lawyer returned from South Africa to become active in the INC. He transformed the movement and galvanized India's struggle for independence and identity. Mohandas Gandhi (moh-HAHN-dus GAHN-dee) (1869–1948) was born in Gujarat (goo-juh-RAHT), in western India, the son of a government minister. In the late nineteenth century, he studied in London and became a lawyer. In 1893, he went to South Africa to work in a law firm serving Indian émigrés working as laborers there. He soon became aware of the racial prejudice and exploitation experienced by Indians living in the territory and tried to organize them to protect their interests.

On his return to India, Gandhi immediately became active in the independence movement. Using his experience in South Africa, he set up a movement based on nonviolent resistance—the Hindi term was *satyagraha* (SUHT-yuh-grah-hah), meaning "hold fast to the truth"—to try to force the British to improve the lot of the poor and grant independence to India. His goal was twofold: to convert the British to his views while simultaneously strengthening the unity and sense of self-respect of his compatriots. Gandhi was particularly concerned about the plight of the millions of untouchables, whom he called *harijans* (HAR-ih-jans), or "children of God." When the British attempted to suppress dissent, he called on his followers to refuse to obey British regulations. He began to manufacture his own clothes, now dressing in a simple *dhoti* (DOH-tee) made of coarse homespun cotton, and adopted the spinning wheel as a symbol of Indian resistance to imports of British textiles.

Gandhi, now increasingly known as Mahatma (mah-HAHT-muh), or India's "Great Soul," organized mass protests to achieve his aims, but in 1919 they got out of hand and led to violence and British reprisals. British troops killed hundreds of unarmed protesters in the enclosed square in the city of Amritsar (am-RIT-sur) in northwestern India. When the protests spread, Gandhi was horrified at the violence. Nevertheless, he was arrested for his role in the protests and spent several years in prison.

Gandhi combined his anticolonial activities with an appeal to the spiritual instincts of all Indians. Though he had been born and raised a Hindu, his universalist approach to the idea of God transcended individual religion, albeit shaped by the historical themes of Hindu belief. At a speech given in London in September 1931, he expressed his view of the nature of God as "an indefinable mysterious power that pervades everything . . . , an unseen power which makes itself felt and yet defies all proof."[1]

While Gandhi was in prison, the political situation continued to evolve. In 1921, the British passed the Government of

Gandhi (1982)

To many of his contemporaries, Mohandas Gandhi—usually referred to as the Mahatma, or "Great Soul"—was the conscience of India. Son of a senior Indian official from the state of Gujarat and trained as a lawyer at University College in London, Gandhi first dealt with racial discrimination when he sought to provide legal assistance to Indian laborers living under the apartheid regime in South Africa. On his return to India in 1915, he rapidly emerged as a fierce critic of British colonial rule over his country. His message of *satyagraha* ("hold fast to the truth"), embodying the idea of a steadfast but nonviolent resistance to the injustice and inhumanity inherent in the colonial enterprise, inspired millions of his compatriots in their long struggle for national independence. It also earned the admiration and praise of sympathetic observers around the world. His death by assassination at the hands of a Hindu fanatic in 1948 shocked the world.

Time, however, has somewhat dimmed his message. Gandhi's vision of a future India was symbolized by the spinning wheel—he rejected the industrial age and material pursuits in favor of the simple pleasures of the traditional Indian village. Since achieving independence, however, India has followed the path of national wealth and power laid out by Gandhi's friend and colleague Jawaharlal Nehru. Gandhi's appeal for religious tolerance and mutual respect at home rapidly gave way to a bloody conflict between Hindus and Muslims that has not yet been eradicated in our own day. On the global stage, his vision of world peace and brotherly love has similarly been ignored, first during the Cold War and more recently during the "clash of civilizations" between Western countries and the forces of militant Islam.

It was at least partly in an effort to revive and perpetuate the message of the Mahatma that in 1982 the British filmmaker Richard Attenborough directed the film *Gandhi*. Epic in its length and scope, the film seeks to present a faithful rendition of the life of its subject, from his introduction to apartheid in South Africa at the turn of the century to his tragic death after World War II. Actor Ben Kingsley, son of an Indian father and an English mother, plays the title role with intensity and conviction. The film was widely praised and earned eight Academy Awards. Kingsley received an Oscar in the Best Actor category.

© Columbia Pictures/Courtesy The Everett Collection, Inc.

Jawaharlal Nehru (Roshan Seth), Mahatma Gandhi (Ben Kingsley), and Muhammad Ali Jinnah (Alyque Padamsee) confer before the partition of India into Hindu and Muslim states.

India Act, transforming the heretofore advisory Legislative Council into a bicameral parliament, two-thirds of whose members would be elected. Similar bodies were created at the provincial level. In a stroke, 5 million Indians were enfranchised. But such reforms were no longer enough for many members of the INC, who wanted to push aggressively for full independence. The British exacerbated the situation by increasing the salt tax and prohibiting the Indian people from manufacturing or harvesting their own salt. Gandhi, now released from prison, returned to his earlier policy of **civil disobedience** by openly joining several dozen supporters in a 240-mile walk to the sea, where he picked up a lump of salt and urged Indians to ignore the law (see the Film & History feature above). Gandhi and many other members of the INC were arrested.

Indian women were also active in the movement. The first organizations to promote women's rights had been established in the early years of the century, and they quickly became involved in a variety of efforts to bring about social reforms. Women accounted for about 20,000, or nearly 10 percent, of people arrested and jailed for taking part in demonstrations during the interwar period. Women marched, picketed foreign shops, and promoted the spinning and wearing of homemade cloth. By the 1930s, women's associations were actively promoting a number of reforms, including women's education, the introduction of birth control devices, the abolition of child marriage, and universal suffrage. In 1929, the Sarda Act raised the minimum age of marriage to fourteen.

NEW LEADERS AND NEW PROBLEMS In the 1930s, a new figure entered the movement in the person of Jawaharlal Nehru (juh-WAH-hur-lahl NAY-roo) (1889–1964), son of an earlier INC leader. Educated in the law in Great Britain and a *brahmin* by birth, Nehru personified the new Anglo-Indian politician: secular, rational, upper class, and intellectual. In fact, he appeared to be everything that Gandhi was not. With Nehru's emergence, the independence movement embarked on two paths, religious and secular, Indian and Western, traditional and modern. The dual character of the INC leadership may well have strengthened the movement by bringing together the two primary impulses behind the desire for independence: elite nationalism and the primal force of Indian traditionalism. But it portended trouble for the nation's new leadership in defining India's future path in the contemporary world. In the meantime, Muslim discontent with Hindu dominance over the INC was increasing. In 1940, the Muslim League called for the creation of a separate Muslim state of Pakistan ("land of the pure") in the northwest (see the box on p. 703). As communal strife between Hindus and Muslims increased, many Indians came to realize with sorrow (and some British colonialists with satisfaction) that British rule was all that stood between peace and civil war.

The Nationalist Revolt in the Middle East

In the Middle East, as in Europe, World War I hastened the collapse of old empires. The Ottoman Empire, which had dominated the eastern Mediterranean since the seizure of Constantinople in 1453, had been growing weaker since the end of the eighteenth century, troubled by rising governmental corruption, a decline in the effectiveness of the sultans, and the loss of considerable territory in the Balkans and southwestern Russia. In North Africa, Ottoman authority, tenuous at best, had disintegrated in the nineteenth century, enabling the French to seize Algeria and Tunisia and the British to establish a protectorate over the Nile River valley.

DECLINE OF THE OTTOMAN EMPIRE Reformist elements in Istanbul, to be sure, had tried from time to time to resist the trend, but military defeats continued: Greece declared its independence, and Ottoman power declined steadily in the Middle East. A rising sense of nationality among Serbs, Armenians, and other minority peoples threatened the internal stability and cohesion of the empire. In the 1870s, a new generation of Ottoman reformers seized power in Istanbul and pushed through a constitution aimed at forming a legislative assembly that would represent all the peoples in the state. But the sultan they placed on the throne suspended the new charter and attempted to rule by traditional authoritarian means.

By the end of the nineteenth century, the defunct 1876 constitution had become a symbol of change for reformist elements, now grouped together under the common name **Young Turks** (undoubtedly borrowed from the Young Italy nationalist movement earlier in the century). They found support in the Ottoman army and administration and among Turks living in exile. In 1908, the Young Turks forced the sultan to restore the constitution, and he was removed from power the following year.

But the Young Turks had appeared at a moment of extreme fragility for the empire. Internal rebellions, combined with Austrian annexations of Ottoman territories in the Balkans, undermined support for the new government and provoked the army to step in. With most minorities from the old empire now removed from Istanbul's authority, many ethnic Turks began to embrace a new concept of a Turkish state based on Turkish nationality.

The final blow to the old empire came in World War I, when the Ottoman government allied with Germany in the hope of driving the British from Egypt and restoring Ottoman rule over the Nile valley. In response, the British declared an official protectorate over Egypt and, aided by the efforts of the dashing, if eccentric, British adventurer T. E. Lawrence (popularly known as Lawrence of Arabia), sought to undermine Ottoman rule in the Arabian peninsula by encouraging Arab nationalists there. In 1916, the local governor of Mecca, encouraged by the British, declared Arabia independent from Ottoman rule, while British troops, advancing from Egypt, seized Palestine. In October 1918, having suffered more than 300,000 casualties during the war, the Ottoman Empire negotiated an armistice with the Allied Powers.

MUSTAFA KEMAL AND THE MODERNIZATION OF TURKEY During the next few years, the tottering empire began to fall apart as the British and the French made plans to divide up Ottoman territories in the Middle East and the Greeks won Allied approval to seize the western parts of the Anatolian peninsula for their dream of re-creating the substance of the old Byzantine Empire. The impending collapse energized key elements in Turkey under the leadership of a war hero, Colonel Mustafa Kemal (moos-tah-FAH kuh-MAHL) (1881–1938), who had commanded Turkish forces in their successful defense of the Dardanelles against a British invasion during World War I. Now he resigned from the army and convoked a national congress that called for an elected government and the preservation of the remaining territories of the old empire in a new republic of Turkey. Establishing his capital at Ankara (AN-kuh-ruh), Kemal's forces drove the Greeks from the Anatolian peninsula and persuaded the British to agree to a new treaty. In 1923, the last of the Ottoman sultans fled the country, which was now declared a Turkish republic. The Ottoman Empire had come to an end.

During the next few years, President Mustafa Kemal, now popularly known as Atatürk (ah-tah-TIRK), or "Father Turk," attempted to transform Turkey into a modern secular republic. The trappings of a democratic system were put in place, centered on an elected Grand National Assembly, but the president was relatively intolerant of opposition and harshly suppressed critics of his rule. Turkish nationalism was emphasized, and the Turkish language, now written in the Roman alphabet, was shorn of many of its Arabic elements. Popular education was emphasized, old aristocratic titles like *pasha* and *bey* were abolished, and all Turkish citizens were given family names in the European style.

Atatürk also took steps to modernize the economy, overseeing the establishment of a light industrial sector producing textiles, glass, paper, and cement and instituting a five-year plan on the Soviet model to provide for state direction over the economy. Atatürk was no admirer of Soviet communism, however, and the Turkish economy can be better described as a form of state capitalism. He also encouraged the modernization of the agricultural sector by establishing training institutions and model farms, but such reforms had relatively little effect on the nation's generally conservative peasantry.

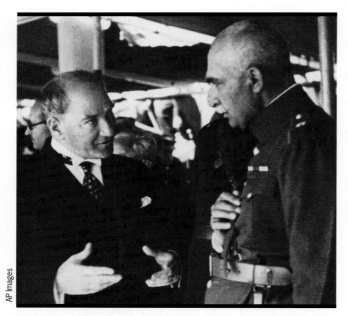

Mustafa Kemal Atatürk. The war hero Mustafa Kemal took the initiative in creating the republic of Turkey. As president of the new republic, Atatürk ("Father Turk"), as he came to be called, worked hard to transform Turkey into a modern secular state by restructuring the economy, adopting Western dress, and breaking the powerful hold of Islamic traditions. He is now reviled by Muslim fundamentalists for his opposition to an Islamic state. In this photograph, Atatürk, at the left in civilian clothes, hosts the shah of Persia during the latter's visit to Turkey in July 1934.

Perhaps the most significant aspect of Atatürk's reform program was his attempt to break the power of the Islamic clerics and transform Turkey into a secular state. The caliphate was formally abolished in 1924 (see the box on p. 703), and *Shari'a* (Islamic law) was replaced by a revised version of the Swiss law code. The fez (the brimless cap worn by Turkish Muslims) was abolished, and women were discouraged from wearing the traditional Islamic veil. Women received the right to vote in 1934 and were legally guaranteed equal rights with men in all aspects of marriage and inheritance. Education and the professions were now open to citizens of both sexes, and some women even began to participate in politics. All citizens were given the right to convert to another religion at will. Finally, Atatürk attempted to break the waning power of the various religious orders of Islam by abolishing all monasteries and brotherhoods.

The legacy of Mustafa Kemal Atatürk was enormous. Although not all of his reforms were widely accepted in practice, especially by devout Muslims, most of the changes he introduced were retained after his death in 1938. In virtually every respect, the Turkish republic was the product of his determined efforts to create a modern Turkish nation.

MODERNIZATION IN IRAN In the meantime, a similar process was under way in Persia. Under the Qajar (kuh-JAHR) dynasty (1794–1925), the country had not been very successful in resisting Russian advances in the Caucasus or resolving its domestic problems. To secure themselves from foreign influence, the Qajars moved the capital from Tabriz to Tehran (teh-RAHN), in a mountainous area just south of the Caspian Sea.

During the mid-nineteenth century, one modernizing shah attempted to introduce political and economic reforms but faced resistance from tribal and religious—predominantly Shi'ite—forces. To buttress its rule, the dynasty turned increasingly to Russia and Great Britain to protect itself from its own people.

Eventually, the growing foreign presence led to the rise of an indigenous Persian nationalist movement. Its efforts were largely directed against Russian advances in the northwest and the growing European influence in the small modern industrial sector, the profits from which left the country or disappeared into the hands of the dynasty's ruling elite. Supported actively by Shi'ite religious leaders, opposition to the regime rose steadily among both peasants and merchants in the cities, and in 1906, popular pressures forced the reigning shah to grant a constitution on the Western model. It was an eerie foretaste of the revolution of 1979 (see Chapter 29).

As in the Ottoman Empire and Manchu China, however, the modernizers had moved too soon, before their power base was secure. With the support of the Russians and the British, the shah was able to retain control, while the two foreign powers began to divide the country into separate spheres of influence. One reason for the growing foreign presence in Persia was the discovery of oil reserves in the southern part of the country in 1908. Within a few years, oil exports increased rapidly, with the bulk of the profits going into the pockets of British investors.

Iran Under the Pahlavi Dynasty

In 1921, an officer in the Persian army by the name of Reza Khan (ree-ZAH KAHN) (1878–1944) led a mutiny that seized power in Tehran. The new ruler had originally intended to establish a republic, but resistance from traditional forces impeded his efforts, and in 1925 the new Pahlavi (PAH-luh-vee) dynasty, with Reza Khan as shah, replaced the now defunct Qajar dynasty. During the next few years, Reza Khan attempted to follow the example of Atatürk in Turkey, introducing a number of reforms to strengthen the central government, modernize the civilian and military bureaucracy, and establish a modern economic infrastructure. In 1935, he officially changed the name of the nation to Iran.

Unlike Atatürk, Reza Khan did not attempt to destroy the power of Islamic beliefs, but he did encourage the establishment of a Western-style educational system and forbade women to wear the veil in public. Women continued to be exploited, however. Like the textile industry in Meiji Japan (see Chapter 22), the Iranian carpet industry was based on the intensive labor of women; the carpets they produced were a valuable export—second only to oil—in the interwar period. To strengthen the sense of Iranian nationalism and reduce the power of Islam, Reza Khan attempted to popularize the symbols and beliefs of pre-Islamic times. Like his Qajar

Islam in the Modern World: Two Views

POLITICS & GOVERNMENT

As part of his plan to transform Turkey into a modern society, Mustafa Kemal Atatürk sought to free his country from what he considered to be outdated practices imposed by traditional beliefs. The first selection is from a speech in which he proposed bringing an end to the caliphate, which had been in the hands of Ottoman sultans since the formation of the empire. But not all Muslims wished to move in the direction of a more secular society. Mohammed Iqbal (ik-BAHL), a well-known Muslim poet in colonial India, was a prominent advocate of the creation of a separate state for Muslims in South Asia. The second selection is from an address he presented to the All-India Muslim League in December 1930, explaining the rationale for his proposal.

Atatürk, Speech to the Assembly (October 1924)

The sovereign entitled Caliph was to maintain justice among the three hundred million Muslims on the terrestrial globe, to safeguard the rights of these peoples, to prevent any event that could encroach upon order and security, and confront every attack which the Muslims would be called upon to encounter from the side of other nations. It was to be part of his attributes to preserve by all means the welfare and spiritual development of Islam. . . .

If the Caliph and Caliphate, as they maintained, were to be invested with a dignity embracing the whole of Islam, ought they not to have realized in all justice that a crushing burden would be imposed on Turkey, on her existence; her entire resources and all her forces would be placed at the disposal of the Caliph? . . .

For centuries our nation was guided under the influence of these erroneous ideas. But what has been the result of it? Everywhere they have lost millions of men. "Do you know," I asked, "how many sons of Anatolia have perished in the scorching deserts of the Yemen? Do you know the losses we have suffered in holding Syria and Egypt and in maintaining our position in Africa? And do you see what has come out of it? Do you know?

"Those who favor the idea of placing the means at the disposal of the Caliph to brave the whole world and the power to administer the affairs of the whole of Islam must not appeal to the population of Anatolia alone but to the great Muslim agglomerations which are eight or ten times as rich in men.

"New Turkey, the people of New Turkey, have no reason to think of anything else but their own existence and their own welfare. She has nothing more to give away to others."

Mohammed Iqbal, Speech to the All-India Muslim League (1930)

It cannot be denied that Islam, regarded as an ethical ideal plus a certain kind of polity—by which expression I mean a social structure regulated by a legal system and animated by a specific ethical ideal—has been the chief formative factor in the life history of the Muslims of India. It has furnished those basic emotions and loyalties which gradually unify scattered individuals and groups and finally transform them into a well-defined people. Indeed it is no exaggeration to say that India is perhaps the only country in the world where Islam, as a people-building force, has worked at its best. In India, as elsewhere, the structure of Islam as a society is almost entirely due to the working of Islam as a culture inspired by a specific ethical ideal. What I mean to say is that Muslim society, with its remarkable homogeneity and inner unity, has grown to be what it is under the pressure of the laws and institutions associated with the culture of Islam.

Communalism in its higher aspect, then, is indispensable to the formation of a harmonious whole in a country like India. The units of Indian society are not territorial as in European countries. India is a continent of human groups belonging to different religions. Their behavior is not at all determined by a common race consciousness. Even the Hindus do not form a homogeneous group. The principle of European democracy cannot be applied to India without recognizing the fact of communal groups. The Muslim demand for the creation of a Muslim India within India is, therefore, perfectly justified. . . .

I therefore demand the formation of a consolidated Muslim State in the best interests of India and Islam. For India it means security and peace resulting from an internal balance of power; for Islam an opportunity to rid itself of the stamp that Arabian imperialism was forced to give it, to mobilize its law, its education, its culture, and to bring them into closer contact with its own original spirit and with the spirit of modern times.

 Why did Mustafa Kemal believe that the caliphate no longer met the needs of the Turkish people? Why did Mohammed Iqbal believe that a separate state for Muslims in India would be required? How did he attempt to persuade non-Muslims that this would be to their benefit as well?

predecessors, however, he was hindered by strong foreign influence. When the Soviet Union and Great Britain decided to send troops into the country during World War II, he resigned in protest and died three years later.

NATION BUILDING IN IRAQ One other consequence of the collapse of the Ottoman Empire was the emergence of a new political entity along the Tigris and Euphrates Rivers, once the heartland of ancient empires. Lacking defensible borders and sharply divided along ethnic and religious lines—a Shi'ite majority in rural areas was balanced by a vocal Sunni minority in the cities and a largely Kurdish population in the northern mountains—the area had been under Ottoman rule since the seventeenth century. With the advent of World War I, the lowland area from Baghdad southward to the Persian Gulf was occupied by British forces, who hoped to protect oil-producing regions in neighboring Persia from a German takeover.

Although the British claimed to have arrived as liberators, in 1920 the country now known as Iraq was placed under British control as a mandate of the League of Nations. Civil unrest and growing anti-Western sentiment rapidly dispelled any immediate plans for the emergence of an independent government, and in 1921, after the suppression of resistance forces, the country was placed under the titular authority of King Faisal (FY-suhl) of Syria, a descendant of the Prophet Muhammad. Faisal relied for support primarily on the politically more sophisticated urban Sunni population, although they represented less than a quarter of the population. The discovery of oil near Kirkuk (kir-KOOK) in 1927 increased the value of the area to the British, who granted formal independence to the country in 1932, although British advisers retained a strong influence over the fragile government.

THE RISE OF ARAB NATIONALISM As we have seen, the Arab uprising during World War I helped bring about the demise of the Ottoman Empire. There had been resistance against Ottoman rule in the Arabian peninsula since the eighteenth century, when the devoutly Muslim Wahhabi (wuh-HAH-bee) sect revolted in an attempt to drive out outside influences and cleanse Islam of corrupt practices that had developed in past centuries. The revolt was eventually suppressed, but Wahhabi influence persisted.

World War I offered an opportunity for the Arabs to throw off the shackles of Ottoman rule—but what would replace them? The Arabs were not a nation but an idea, a loose collection of peoples who often did not see eye to eye on matters that affected their community. Disagreement over what constitutes an Arab has plagued generations of political leaders who have sought unsuccessfully to knit together the disparate peoples of the region into a single Arab nation.

When the Arab leaders in Mecca declared their independence from Ottoman rule in 1916, they had hoped for British support, but—despite the efforts of T. E. Lawrence—they were to be sorely disappointed. At the close of the war, the British and French agreed to create a number of mandates in the area under the general supervision of the League of Nations (see Chapter 23). Iraq was assigned to the British; Syria and Lebanon (the two areas were separated so that Christian peoples in Lebanon could be placed under Christian administration) were given to the French.

In the early 1920s, a leader of the Wahhabi movement, Ibn Saud (IB-un sah-OOD) (1880–1953), united Arab tribes in the northern part of the Arabian peninsula and drove out the remnants of Ottoman rule. Ibn Saud was a descendant of the family that had led the Wahhabi revolt in the eighteenth century. Devout and gifted, he won broad support among Arab tribal peoples and established the kingdom of Saudi Arabia throughout much of the peninsula in 1932.

At first, his new kingdom, consisting essentially of the vast desert wastes of central Arabia, was desperately poor. Its financial resources were limited to the income from Muslim pilgrims visiting the holy sites in Mecca and Medina. But during the 1930s, American companies began to explore for oil, and in 1938, Standard Oil made a successful strike at Dhahran (dah-RAHN), on the Persian Gulf. Soon an Arabian-American oil conglomerate, popularly called Aramco, was established, and the isolated kingdom was suddenly inundated by Western oilmen and untold wealth.

THE ISSUE OF PALESTINE The land of Palestine—once the home of the Jews but now inhabited primarily by Muslim Arabs—became a separate mandate and immediately became a thorny problem for the British. In 1897, the Austrian-born journalist Theodor Herzl (1860–1904) (see Chapter 20) had convened an international conference in Basel, Switzerland, which led to the creation of a World Zionist Organization (WZO). The aim of the organization was to create a homeland in Palestine for the Jewish people, who had long been dispersed widely throughout Europe, North Africa, and the Middle East.

Over the next decade, Jewish immigration into Palestine, then under Ottoman rule, increased with WZO support. By the outbreak of World War I, about 85,000 Jews lived in Palestine, representing about 15 percent of the total population. In 1917, responding to appeals from the British chemist Chaim Weizmann (KY-im VYTS-mahn), British Foreign Secretary Lord Arthur Balfour (BAL-foor) issued a declaration saying Palestine was to be a national home for the Jews. The Balfour Declaration, which was later confirmed by the League of Nations, was ambiguous on the legal status of the territory and promised that the decision would not undermine the rights of the non-Jewish peoples currently living in the area. But Arab nationalists were incensed. How could a national home for the Jewish people be established in a territory where the majority of the population was Muslim?

After World War I, more Jewish settlers began to arrive in Palestine in response to the promises made in the Balfour Declaration. As tensions between the new arrivals and existing Muslim residents began to escalate, the British tried to restrict Jewish immigration into the territory while Arab voices rejected the concept of a separate state. In a bid to relieve Arab sensitivities, Great Britain created the separate

European Jewish Refugees. After the 1917 Balfour Declaration promised a Jewish homeland in Palestine, increasing numbers of European Jews emigrated there. Their goal was to build a new life in a Jewish land. Like the refugees aboard this ship, they celebrated as they reached their new homeland. The sign reads "Keep the gates open, we are not the last"—a reference to British efforts to slow the pace of Jewish immigration in response to protests by Muslim residents of Palestine.

emirate of Trans-Jordan out of the eastern portion of Palestine. After World War II, it would become the independent kingdom of Jordan. The stage was set for the conflicts that would take place in the region after World War II.

THE BRITISH IN EGYPT Great Britain had maintained a loose protectorate over Egypt since the middle of the nineteenth century, although the area remained nominally under Ottoman rule. London formalized its protectorate in 1914 to protect the Suez Canal and the Nile River valley from possible seizure by the Central Powers. After the war, however, nationalist elements became restive and formed the Wafd (WAHFT) Party, a secular organization dedicated to the creation of an independent Egypt based on the principles of representative government. The Wafd received the support of many middle-class Egyptians who, like Kemal Atatürk in Turkey, hoped to meld Islamic practices with the secular tradition of the modern West. This modernist form of Islam did not have broad appeal outside the cosmopolitan centers, however, and in 1928 the Muslim cleric Hasan al-Bana (hah-SAHN al-BAN-ah) organized the Muslim Brotherhood, which demanded strict adherence to the traditional teachings of the Prophet, as set forth in the Qur'an. The Brotherhood rejected Western ways and sought to create a new Egypt

The Middle East After World War I

based firmly on the precepts of the *Shari'a*. By the 1930s, the organization had as many as a million members.

Nationalism and Revolution

Before the Russian Revolution, to most intellectuals in Asia and Africa, "westernization" referred to the capitalist democratic civilization of western Europe and the United States, not the doctrine of social revolution developed by Karl Marx. Until 1917, Marxism was regarded as a utopian idea rather than a concrete system of government. Moreover, to many intellectuals, Marxism appeared to have little relevance to conditions in Asia and Africa. Marxist doctrine, after all, declared that a communist society would arise only from the ashes of an advanced capitalism that had already passed through the Industrial Revolution. From the perspective of Marxist historical analysis, most societies in Asia and Africa were still at the feudal stage of development; they lacked the economic conditions and political awareness to achieve a socialist revolution that would bring the working class to power. Finally, the Marxist view of nationalism and religion had little appeal to many patriotic intellectuals in the non-Western world. Marx believed that nationhood and religion were essentially false ideas that diverted the attention of the oppressed masses from the critical issues of class struggle and, in his phrase, the exploitation of one person by another. Instead, Marx stressed an "internationalist" outlook based on class consciousness and the eventual creation of a classless society with no artificial divisions based on culture, nation, or religion.

For these reasons, many patriotic non-Western intellectuals initially deemed Marxism both irrelevant and unappealing. That situation began to change after the Russian Revolution in 1917. The rise to power of Lenin's Bolsheviks demonstrated that a revolutionary party espousing Marxist principles could overturn a corrupt, outdated system and launch a new experiment dedicated to ending human inequality and achieving a paradise on earth. In 1920, Lenin proposed a new revolutionary strategy designed to relate Marxist doctrine and practice to non-Western societies. His reasons were not entirely altruistic. Soviet Russia, surrounded by capitalist powers, desperately needed allies in its struggle to survive in a hostile world.

LENIN AND THE EAST To Lenin, the anticolonial movements emerging in North Africa, Asia, and the Middle East after World War I were natural allies of the beleaguered new regime in Moscow. In the spring of 1913, he had written, "Was it so long ago that China was considered typical of the lands that had been standing still for centuries? Today China is a land of seething political activity, the scene of a virile social movement and of a democratic upsurge."[2] Similar conditions, he added, were spreading the democratic revolution to other parts of Asia—to Turkey, Persia, and Iraq. Ferment was on the rise even in British India. Lenin was convinced that only the ability of the imperialist powers to find markets, raw materials, and sources of capital investment in the non-Western world kept capitalism alive. If the tentacles of capitalist influence in Asia and Africa could be severed, imperialism would weaken and collapse.

Establishing such an alliance was not easy, however. Most nationalist leaders in colonial countries belonged to the urban middle class, and many abhorred the idea of a comprehensive revolution to create a totally egalitarian society. In addition, many still adhered to traditional religious beliefs and were opposed to the atheistic principles of classical Marxism.

Since it was unrealistic to expect bourgeois nationalist support for social revolution, Lenin sought a compromise that would enable Communist Parties to be organized among the working classes in the preindustrial societies of Asia and Africa. These parties would then forge informal alliances with existing middle-class parties to struggle against the common enemies of feudal reaction (the remnants of the traditional ruling class) and Western imperialism. Such an alliance, of course, could not be permanent because many bourgeois nationalists in Asia and Africa would reject an egalitarian, classless society. Once the imperialists had been overthrown, therefore, the Communist Parties would turn against their erstwhile nationalist partners to seize power on their own and carry out the socialist revolution. Lenin thus proposed a two-stage revolution: an initial "national democratic" stage followed by a "proletarian socialist" stage.

Lenin's strategy became a major element in Soviet foreign policy in the 1920s. Soviet agents fanned out across the world to carry Marxism beyond the boundaries of industrial Europe. The primary instrument of this effort was the Third International, usually known as the **Communist International, or Comintern** for short. Formed in 1919 at Lenin's prodding, the Comintern was a worldwide organization of Communist Parties dedicated to the advancement of world revolution. At its headquarters in Moscow, agents from around the world were trained in the precepts of world communism and then sent back to their countries to form Marxist parties and promote the cause of social revolution. By the end of the 1920s, almost every colonial or semicolonial society in Asia had a party based on Marxist principles. The Soviets had less success in the Middle East, where Marxist ideology appealed mainly to minorities such as Jews and Armenians in the cities, or in black Africa, where Soviet strategists in any case felt that conditions were not sufficiently advanced for the creation of Communist organizations.

THE APPEAL OF COMMUNISM According to Marxist doctrine, the rank and file of Communist Parties should be urban factory workers alienated from capitalist society by inhumane working conditions. In practice, many of the leaders even in European Communist Parties tended to be urban intellectuals or members of the lower middle class (in Marxist parlance, the "petty bourgeoisie"). That phenomenon was even more true in the non-Western world, where most early Marxists were rootless intellectuals. Some were probably drawn into the movement for patriotic reasons and saw Marxist doctrine as a new and more effective means of modernizing their societies and removing the colonial exploiters (see the box on p. 707).

Others were attracted by the message of egalitarian communism and the utopian dream of a classless society. For those who had lost their faith in traditional religion, communism often served as a new secular ideology, dealing not with the hereafter but with the here and now or, indeed, with a remote future when the state would wither away and the "classless society" would replace the lost truth of traditional faiths.

Of course, the new doctrine's appeal was not the same in all non-Western societies. In Confucian societies such as China and Vietnam, where traditional belief systems had been badly discredited by their failure to counter the Western challenge, communism had an immediate impact and rapidly became a major factor in the anticolonial movement. In Buddhist and Muslim societies, where traditional religion remained strong and actually became a cohesive factor in the resistance movement, communism had less success. To maximize their appeal and minimize potential conflict with traditional ideas, Communist Parties frequently attempted to adapt Marxist doctrine to indigenous values and institutions. In the Middle East, for example, the Ba'ath (BAHTH) Party in Syria adopted a hybrid socialism combining Marxism with Arab nationalism. In Egypt, however, the Wafd Party, formed by modernist intellectuals in 1918, focused its efforts on the creation of an independent government based on Western democratic principles but gave little thought to measures designed to alleviate problems of poverty in urban and rural areas.

In some instances, the Communists were briefly able to establish a cooperative relationship with the bourgeois parties. The most famous example was the alliance between the Chinese Communist Party and Sun Yat-sen's Nationalist Party (discussed in the next section). In the Dutch East Indies, the Indonesian Communist Party (known as the PKI) allied with the middle-class nationalist group Sarekat Islam but later broke loose in an effort to organize its own mass movement among the poor peasants. In French Indochina, Vietnamese Communists organized by the Moscow-trained revolutionary Ho Chi Minh (HOH CHEE MIN) sought at first to cooperate with bourgeois nationalist parties against the colonial regime. These efforts were abandoned in 1928, however, when the Comintern, reacting to Chiang Kai-shek's betrayal of the alliance with the Chinese Communist Party, declared that Communist Parties should restrict their recruiting efforts to the most revolutionary elements in society—notably, the urban intellectuals and the working class. Harassed by colonial authorities and saddled with strategic directions from Moscow that often had little relevance to local conditions, Communist Parties in most colonial societies had little success in

The Path of Liberation

POLITICS & GOVERNMENT

In 1919, the Vietnamese revolutionary Ho Chi Minh (1890–1969) was living in exile in France, where he first became acquainted with the new revolutionary experiment in Bolshevik Russia. Later he became a leader of the Vietnamese Communist movement. In the following passage, written in 1960, he reminisces about his reasons for becoming a Communist. The Second International mentioned in the text was an organization created in 1889 by moderate socialists who pursued their goal by parliamentary means. Lenin created the Third International, or Comintern, in 1919 to promote violent revolution.

Ho Chi Minh, "The Path Which Led Me to Leninism"

After World War I, I made my living in Paris, now as a retoucher at a photographer's, now as a painter of "Chinese antiquities" (made in France!). I would distribute leaflets denouncing the crimes committed by the French colonialists in Vietnam.

At that time, I supported the October Revolution [in Russia] only instinctively, not yet grasping all its historic importance. I loved and admired Lenin because he was a great patriot who liberated his compatriots; until then, I had read none of his books.

The reason for my joining the French Socialist Party was that these "ladies and gentlemen"—as I called my comrades at that moment—had shown their sympathy toward me, toward the struggle of the oppressed peoples. But I understood neither what was a party, a trade union, nor what was Socialism nor Communism.

Heated discussions were then taking place in the branches of the Socialist Party, about the question whether the Socialist Party should remain in the Second International, should a Second-and-a-Half International be founded, or should the Socialist Party join Lenin's Third International? I attended the meetings regularly, twice or three times a week, and attentively listened to the discussion. First, I could not understand thoroughly. Why were the discussions so heated? Either with the Second, Second-and-a-Half, or Third International, the revolution could be waged. What was the use of arguing then? As for the First International, what had become of it?

What I wanted most to know—and this precisely was not debated in the meetings—was: which International sides with the peoples of colonial countries?

I raised this question—the most important in my opinion—in a meeting. Some comrades answered: It is the Third, not the Second International. And a comrade gave me Lenin's "Thesis on the national and colonial questions," published by *l'Humanité*, to read.

There were political terms difficult to understand in this thesis. But by dint of reading it again and again, finally I could grasp the main part of it. What emotion, enthusiasm, clearsightedness, and confidence it instilled in me! I was overjoyed to tears. Though sitting alone in my room, I shouted aloud as if addressing large crowds: "Dear martyrs, compatriots! This is what we need, this is the path to our liberation!"

After that, I had entire confidence in Lenin, in the Third International.

 Why did Ho Chi Minh believe that the Third International was the key to the liberation of the colonial peoples? What were the essential elements of Lenin's strategy for bringing that about?

---

the 1930s and failed to build a secure base of support among the mass of the population.

Revolution in China

 FOCUS QUESTION: What problems did China encounter between the two world wars, and what solutions did the Nationalists and the Communists propose to solve them?

Overall, revolutionary Marxism had its greatest impact in China, where a group of young radicals, including several faculty and staff members from Peking (Beijing) University, founded the Chinese Communist Party (CCP) in 1921. The rise of the CCP was a consequence of the failed revolution of 1911. When political forces are too weak or too divided to consolidate their power during a period of instability, the military usually steps in to fill the vacuum. In China, Sun Yat-sen (SOON yaht-SEN) and his colleagues had accepted General Yuan Shikai (yoo-AHN shee-KY) as president of the new Chinese republic in 1911 because they lacked the military force to compete with his control over the army (see Chapter 22). Moreover, many feared, perhaps rightly, that if the revolt lapsed into chaos, the Western powers would intervene and the last shreds of Chinese sovereignty would be lost. But some had misgivings about Yuan's intentions. As one remarked in a letter to a friend, "We don't know whether he will be a George Washington or a Napoleon."

Nguyen the Patriot at Tours. At a meeting held on Christmas Day in 1920, the French progressive movement split into two separate organizations, the French Socialist Party (FSP) and the French Communist Party (FCP). One participant at the congress—held in the French industrial city of Tours—was a young Vietnamese radical who took the pseudonym Nguyen Ai Quoc (Nguyen the Patriot). In this photograph, Nguyen announces his decision to join the new FCP on the grounds that it alone could help bring about the liberation of the oppressed peoples of Asia and Africa from colonial rule. A quarter of a century later, Nguyen would resurface as the Comintern agent and Vietnamese revolutionary leader Ho Chi Minh.

As it turned out, he was neither. Showing little comprehension of the new ideas sweeping into China from the West, Yuan ruled in a traditional manner, reviving Confucian rituals and institutions and eventually trying to found a new imperial dynasty. Yuan's dictatorial inclinations rapidly led to clashes with Sun's party, now renamed the Guomindang (gwoh-min-DAHNG) (Kuomintang), or Nationalist Party. When Yuan dissolved the new parliament, the Nationalists launched a rebellion; it failed, and Sun fled to Japan.

Yuan was strong enough to brush off the challenge from the revolutionary forces but not to turn back the clock of history. He died in 1916 (apparently of natural causes, although legend holds that his heart was broken by popular resistance to his imperial pretensions) and was succeeded by one of his military subordinates. For the next several years, China slipped into semianarchy as the power of the central government disintegrated and military warlords seized power in the provinces.

Mr. Science and Mr. Democracy: The New Culture Movement

Although the failure of the 1911 revolution was a clear sign that China was not yet ready for radical change, discontent with existing conditions continued to rise in various sectors of Chinese society. The most vocal protests came from radical intellectuals, who opposed Yuan Shikai's conservative rule but were now convinced that political change could not take place until the Chinese people were more familiar with

trends in the outside world. Braving the displeasure of Yuan and his successors, progressive intellectuals at Peking University launched the **New Culture Movement**, aimed at abolishing the remnants of the old system and introducing Western values and institutions into China. Using the classrooms of China's most prestigious university as well as the pages of newly established progressive magazines and newspapers, the intellectuals introduced a bewildering mix of new ideas, from the philosophy of Friedrich Nietzsche (FREED-rikh NEE-chuh) and Bertrand Russell to the educational views of the American John Dewey and the feminist plays of Henrik Ibsen. As such ideas flooded into China, they stirred up a new generation of educated Chinese youth, who chanted "Down with Confucius and sons" and talked of a new era dominated by "Mr. Sai" (Mr. Science) and "Mr. De" (Mr. Democracy). No one was a greater defender of free thought and speech than the chancellor of Peking University, Cai Yuanpei (TSY yoo-wahn-PAY) (Ts'ai Yüan-p'ei):

> So far as theoretical ideas are concerned, I follow the principles of "freedom of thought" and an attitude of broad tolerance in accordance with the practice of universities the world over. . . . Regardless of what school of thought a person may adhere to, so long as that person's ideas are justified and conform to reason and have not been passed by through the process of natural selection, although there may be controversy, such ideas have a right to be presented.[3]

The problem was that appeals for American-style democracy and women's liberation had little relevance to Chinese peasants, most of whom were still illiterate and concerned above all with survival. Consequently, the New Culture Movement did not win widespread support outside the urban areas. It certainly earned the distrust of conservative military officers, one of whom threatened to lob artillery shells into Peking University to destroy the poisonous new ideas and eliminate their advocates.

Discontent among intellectuals, however, was soon joined by the rising chorus of public protest against Japan's efforts to expand its influence on the mainland. During the first decade of the twentieth century, Japan had taken advantage of the Qing's decline to extend its domination over Manchuria and Korea (see Chapter 22). In 1915, the Japanese government insisted that Yuan Shikai accept a series of twenty-one demands that would have given Japan a virtual protectorate over the Chinese government and economy. Yuan was able to fend off the most far-reaching Japanese demands by arousing popular outrage in China, but at the Paris Peace Conference four years later, Japan received Germany's sphere of influence in Shandong (SHAHN-doong) Province as a reward for its support of the Allied cause in World War I. On hearing that the Chinese government had accepted the decision, on May 4, 1919, patriotic students, supported by other sectors of the urban population, demonstrated in Beijing and other major cities of the country (see the comparative illustration on p. 808). Although this May Fourth Movement did not lead to the restoration of Shandong to Chinese rule, it did alert a substantial part of the politically literate population to the threat to national survival and the incompetence of the warlord government.

The Nationalist-Communist Alliance

By 1920, central authority had almost ceased to exist in China. Two competing political forces now began to emerge from the chaos. One was Sun Yat-sen's Nationalist Party. Driven from the political arena seven years earlier by Yuan Shikai, the party now reestablished itself on the mainland by making an alliance with the warlord ruler of Guangdong (gwahng-DOONG) (Kwangtung) Province in southern China. From Canton, Sun sought international assistance to carry out his national revolution. The other was the CCP. Following Lenin's strategy, Comintern agents advised the new party to link up with the more experienced Nationalists. Sun Yat-sen needed the expertise and the diplomatic support that Soviet Russia could provide because his anti-imperialist rhetoric had alienated many Western powers; one English-language newspaper in Shanghai remarked, "All his life, all his influence, are devoted to ideas which keep China in turmoil, and it is utterly undesirable that he should be allowed to prosecute those aims here."[4] In 1923, the two parties formed an alliance to oppose the warlords and drive the imperialist powers out of China.

For three years, with the assistance of a Comintern mission in Canton, the two parties submerged their mutual suspicions and mobilized and trained a revolutionary army to march north and seize control of China. The so-called Northern Expedition began in the summer of 1926 (see Map 24.1). By the following spring, revolutionary forces were in control of all Chinese territory south of the Yangtze River, including the major river ports of Wuhan (WOO-HAHN) and Shanghai (SHANG-hy). But tensions between the two parties now surfaced. Sun Yat-sen had died of cancer in 1925 and was succeeded as head of the Nationalist Party by his military subordinate, Chiang Kai-shek (CHANG ky-SHEK) (see the comparative illustration on p. 710). Chiang feigned support for the alliance with the Communists but actually planned to destroy them. In April 1927, he struck against the Communists and their supporters in Shanghai, killing thousands. After the massacre, most of the Communist

MAP 24.1 **The Northern Expedition and the Long March.** This map shows the routes taken by the combined Nationalist-Communist forces during the Northern Expedition of 1926–1928. The blue arrow indicates the route taken by Communist units during the Long March led by Mao Zedong.

 Where did Mao establish his new headquarters after the Long March?

leaders went into hiding in the city, where they attempted to revive the movement in its traditional base among the urban working class. Some party members, however, led by the young Communist organizer Mao Zedong (mow zee-DOONG ["ow" as in "how"]) (Mao Tse-tung), fled to the hilly areas south of the Yangtze River.

Unlike most CCP leaders, Mao was convinced that the Chinese revolution must be based not on workers in the big cities but on the impoverished peasants in the countryside. The son of a prosperous farmer, Mao had helped organize a peasant movement in southern China during the early 1920s and then served as an agitator in rural villages in his home province of Hunan (HOO-NAHN) during the Northern Expedition in the fall of 1926. At that time, he wrote a report to the party leadership suggesting that the CCP support peasant demands for a land revolution (see the box on p. 711). But his superiors refused, fearing that such radical policies would destroy the alliance with the Nationalists.

The Nanjing Republic

In 1928, Chiang Kai-shek founded a new Chinese republic at Nanjing, and over the next three years, he managed to reunify China by a combination of military operations and inducements (known as "silver bullets") to various northern warlords to join his movement. He also attempted to put an end to the Communists, rooting them out of their urban base in Shanghai and their rural redoubt in the rugged hills of

AP Images/Max Desfor

Private Collection//© Archives Charmet/The Bridgeman Art Library

COMPARATIVE ILLUSTRATION

POLITICS & GOVERNMENT

Masters and Disciples. When the founders of nationalist movements passed leadership over to their successors, the result was often a change in the strategy and tactics of the organizations. When Jawaharlal Nehru (left photo, on the left) replaced Mahatma Gandhi (wearing a simple Indian *dhoti* rather than the Western dress favored by his colleagues) as leader of the Indian National Congress, the movement adopted a more secular posture. In China, Chiang Kai-shek (right photo, standing) took Sun Yat-sen's Nationalist Party in a more conservative direction after Sun's death in 1925.

Q *How do these four leaders compare in terms of their roles in furthering political change in their respective countries?*

Jiangxi (JAHNG-shee) (Kiangsi) Province. He succeeded in the first task in 1931, when most party leaders were forced to flee Shanghai for Mao's base in southern China. Three years later, using their superior military strength, Chiang's troops surrounded the Communist base in Jiangxi, inducing Mao's young People's Liberation Army (PLA) to abandon its guerrilla lair and embark on the famous Long March, an arduous journey of thousands of miles on foot through mountains, marshes, and deserts to the small provincial town of Yan'an (yuh-NAHN) (Yenan) 200 miles north of the city of Xian (SHEE-ahn) in the dusty hills of northern China (see Map 24.1). Of the 90,000 who embarked on the journey in October 1934, only 10,000 arrived in Yan'an a year later. Contemporary observers must have thought that the Communist threat to the Nanjing regime had been averted forever.

Meanwhile, Chiang was trying to build a new nation. When the Nanjing Republic was established in 1928, Chiang publicly declared his commitment to Sun Yat-sen's "three people's principles." In a program announced in 1918, Sun had written about the all-important second stage of "political tutelage":

China . . . needs a republican government just as a boy needs school. As a schoolboy must have good teachers and helpful friends, so the Chinese people, being for the first time under republican rule, must have a farsighted revolutionary government for their training. This calls for the period of political tutelage, which is a necessary transitional stage from monarchy to republicanism. Without this, disorder will be unavoidable.[5]

In keeping with Sun's program, Chiang announced a period of political indoctrination to prepare the Chinese people for a final stage of constitutional government. In the meantime, the Nationalists would use their dictatorial power to carry out a land reform program and modernize the urban industrial sector.

But it would take more than paper plans to create a new China. Years of neglect and civil war had severely frayed the political, economic, and social fabric of the nation. There were faint signs of an impending industrial revolution in the major urban centers, but most of the people in the countryside, drained by warlord exactions and civil strife, were still grindingly poor and overwhelmingly illiterate. A westernized middle class had begun to emerge in the cities and formed much of the natural constituency of the Nanjing government. But this new westernized elite, preoccupied with bourgeois values of individual advancement and material accumulation, had few links with the peasants in the countryside or the rickshaw drivers "running in this world of suffering," in the poignant words of a Chinese poet. In an expressive phrase,

A Call for Revolt

POLITICS & GOVERNMENT

In the fall of 1926, Nationalist and Communist forces moved north from Canton on their Northern Expedition in an effort to defeat the warlords. The young Communist Mao Zedong accompanied revolutionary troops into his home province of Hunan, where he submitted a report to the CCP Central Committee calling for a massive peasant revolt against the ruling order. The report shows his confidence that peasants could play an active role in the Chinese revolution despite the skepticism of many of his colleagues.

Mao Zedong, "The Peasant Movement in Hunan"

During my recent visit to Hunan I made a firsthand investigation of conditions. . . . In a very short time, . . . several hundred million peasants will rise like a mighty storm, . . . a force so swift and violent that no power, however great, will be able to hold it back. They will smash all the trammels that bind them and rush forward along the road to liberation. They will sweep all the imperialists, warlords, corrupt officials, local tyrants, and evil gentry into their graves. Every revolutionary party and every revolutionary comrade will be put to the test, to be accepted or rejected as they decide. There are three alternatives. To march at their head and lead them? To trail behind them, gesticulating and criticizing? Or to stand in their way and oppose them? Every Chinese is free to choose, but events will force you to make the choice quickly.

The main targets of attack by the peasants are the local tyrants, the evil gentry and the lawless landlords, but in passing they also hit out against patriarchal ideas and institutions, against the corrupt officials in the cities and against bad practices and customs in the rural areas. . . . As a result, the privileges which the feudal landlords enjoyed for thousands of years are being shattered to pieces. . . . With the collapse of the power of the landlords, the peasant associations have now become the sole organs of authority, and the popular slogan "All power to the peasant associations" has become a reality.

The peasants' revolt disturbed the gentry's sweet dreams. When the news from the countryside reached the cities, it caused immediate uproar among the gentry. . . . From the middle social strata upwards to the Kuomintang [Nationalist] right-wingers, there was not a single person who did not sum up the whole business in the phrase, "It's terrible!" . . . Even quite progressive people said, "Though terrible, it is inevitable in a revolution." In short, nobody could altogether deny the word "terrible." But . . . the fact is that the great peasant masses have risen to fulfill their historic mission. . . . What the peasants are doing is absolutely right; what they are doing is fine! "It's fine!" is the theory of the peasants and of all other revolutionaries. Every revolutionary comrade should know that the national revolution requires a great change in the countryside. The Revolution of 1911 did not bring about this change, hence its failure. This change is now taking place, and it is an important factor for the completion of the revolution. Every revolutionary comrade must support it, or he will be taking the stand of counterrevolution.

 Why did Mao Zedong believe that rural peasants could help bring about a social revolution in China? How does his vision compare with the reality of the Bolshevik Revolution in Russia?

© Rene Burri/Magnum Photos

Mao Zedong on the Long March. In 1934, the Communist leader Mao Zedong led his bedraggled forces on the famous Long March from southern China to a new location at Yan'an, in the hills just south of the Gobi Desert. The epic journey has ever since been celebrated as a symbol of the party's willingness to sacrifice for the revolutionary cause. In this photograph, Mao sits astride a white horse as he accompanies his followers on the march. Reportedly, he was the only participant allowed to ride a horse en route to Yan'an.

some critics dismissed Chiang and his chief followers as "banana Chinese"—yellow on the outside, white on the inside.

THE BEST OF EAST AND WEST   Chiang was aware of the difficulty of introducing exotic foreign ideas into a society still culturally conservative. While building a modern industrial sector, he attempted to synthesize modern Western ideas with traditional Confucian values of hard work, obedience, and moral integrity. In the officially promoted New Life Movement, sponsored by his Wellesley-educated wife, Mei-ling Soong (may-LING SOONG), Chiang sought to propagate traditional Confucian social ethics such as integrity, propriety, and righteousness while rejecting what he considered the excessive individualism and material greed of Western capitalism.

Unfortunately for Chiang, Confucian ideas—at least in their institutional form—had been widely discredited by the failure of the traditional system to solve China's growing problems. With only a tenuous hold over the Chinese provinces (the Nanjing government had total control over only a handful of provinces in the Yangtze valley), a growing Japanese threat in the north, and a world suffering from the Great Depression, Chiang made little progress with his program. Lacking the political sensitivity of Sun Yat-sen and fearing Communist influence, Chiang repressed all opposition and censored free expression, thereby alienating many intellectuals and political moderates. Since the urban middle class and landed gentry were his natural political constituency, he shunned programs that would lead to a redistribution of wealth. A land reform program was enacted in 1930 but had little effect.

Chiang Kai-shek's government had little more success in promoting industrial development. During the decade of precarious peace following the Northern Expedition, industrial growth averaged only about 1 percent annually. Much of the national wealth was in the hands of the senior officials and close subordinates of the ruling elite. Military expenses consumed half the budget, and distressingly little was devoted to social and economic development.

The new government, then, had little success in dealing with China's deep-seated economic and social problems. The deadly combination of internal disintegration and foreign pressure now began to coincide with the virtual collapse of the global economic order during the Great Depression and the rise of militant political forces in Japan determined to extend Japanese influence and power in an unstable Asia. These forces and the turmoil they unleashed will be examined in the next chapter.

"Down with Confucius and Sons": Economic, Social, and Cultural Change in Republican China

The transformation of the old order that had commenced at the end of the Qing era extended into the period of the early Chinese republic. The industrial sector continued to grow, albeit slowly. Although about 75 percent of all industrial goods were still manually produced in the early 1930s, mechanization was gradually beginning to replace manual labor in a number of traditional industries, notably in the manufacture of textile goods. Traditional Chinese exports, such as silk and tea, were hit hard by the Great Depression, however, and manufacturing suffered a decline during the 1930s. It is difficult to gauge conditions in the countryside during the early republican era, but there is no doubt that farmers were often victimized by high taxes imposed by local warlords and the endemic political and social conflict.

SOCIAL CHANGES   Social changes followed shifts in the economy and the political culture. By 1915, the assault on the old system and values by educated youth was intense. The main focus of the attack was the Confucian concept of the family—in particular, filial piety and the subordination of women (see the comparative essay "Out of the Doll's House" on p. 713). Young people called for the right to choose their own mates and their own careers. Inspired by the American women's advocate Margaret Sanger who visited China in 1922, women began to demand rights and opportunities equal to those enjoyed by men. More broadly, progressives called for an end to the concept of duty to the community and praised the Western individualist ethos. The popular short story writer Lu Xun (loo SHUN) (Lu Hsun) criticized the Confucian concept of family as a "man-eating" system that degraded humanity. In a famous short story "Diary of a Madman," the protagonist remarks:

> I remember when I was four or five years old, sitting in the cool of the hall, my brother told me that if a man's parents were ill, he should cut off a piece of his flesh and boil it for them if he wanted to be considered a good son. I have only just realized that I have been living all these years in a place where for four thousand years they have been eating human flesh.[6]

Such criticisms did have some beneficial results. During the early republic, the tyranny of the old family system began to decline, at least in urban areas, under the impact of economic changes and the urgings of the New Culture intellectuals. Women began to escape their cloistered existence and seek education and employment alongside their male contemporaries. Free choice in marriage and a more relaxed attitude toward sex became commonplace among affluent families in the cities, where the teenage children of westernized elites aped the clothing, social habits, and musical tastes of their contemporaries in Europe and the United States.

But, as a rule, the new emphasis on individualism and women's rights did not penetrate to the textile factories, where more than a million women worked in slave labor conditions, or to the villages, where traditional attitudes and customs held sway. Arranged marriages continued to be the rule

COMPARATIVE ESSAY

Out of the Doll's House

FAMILY & SOCIETY

In Henrik Ibsen's 1879 play *A Doll's House*, Nora Helmer informs her husband, Torvald, that she will no longer accept his control over her life and announces her intention to leave home to start her life anew (see the box on p. 593). When the outraged Torvald cites her sacred duties as wife and mother, Nora replies that she has other duties just as sacred, those to herself. "I can no longer be satisfied with what most people say," she declares. "I must think things out for myself and try to get clear about them."

To Ibsen's contemporaries, such remarks were revolutionary. In nineteenth-century Europe, the traditional characterization of the sexes, based on gender-defined social roles, had been elevated to the status of a universal law. As the family wage earners, men were expected to go off to work, while women were responsible for caring for home and family. Women were advised to accept their lot and play their role as effectively and as gracefully as possible. In other parts of the world, women generally had even fewer rights than their male counterparts. Often, as in traditional China, they were viewed as sex objects.

The ideal, however, did not always match the reality. With the advent of the Industrial Revolution, many women in Europe, especially those in the lower classes, were driven by the need for supplemental income to seek employment outside the home, often in the form of menial labor. Some women, inspired by the ideals of human dignity and freedom expressed during the Enlightenment and the French Revolution, began to protest against a tradition of female inferiority that had long kept them in a "doll's house" of male domination and to claim equal rights before the law.

The Art Archive/Private Collection/Marc Charmet

The Chinese "Doll's House." A woman in traditional China binding her feet.

The movement to liberate women from the iron cage of legal and social inferiority first began to gain ground in English-speaking countries such as Great Britain and the United States, but it gradually spread to the continent of Europe and then to colonial areas in Africa and Asia. By the first decades of the twentieth century, women's liberation movements were under way in parts of North Africa, the Middle East, and East Asia, voicing a growing demand for access to education, equal treatment before the law, and the right to vote. Nowhere was this more true than in China, where a small minority of educated women began to agitate for equal rights with men.

Progress, however, was often agonizingly slow, especially in societies where age-old traditional values had not yet been undermined by the corrosive force of the Industrial Revolution. In many colonial societies, the effort to improve the condition of women was subordinated to the goal of gaining national independence. In some instances, women's liberation movements were led by educated elites who failed to include the concerns of working-class women in their agendas. Colonialism, too, was a double-edged sword, as the sexist bias of European officials combined with indigenous traditions of male superiority to marginalize women even further. As men moved to the cities to exploit opportunities provided by the new colonial administration, women were left to cope with their traditional responsibilities in the villages, often without the safety net of male support that had sustained them during the precolonial era.

Based on the information presented in this textbook, to what extent, if at all, did the imperial policies applied in colonial territories serve to benefit women's rights?

rather than the exception, and concubinage remained common. According to a survey taken in the 1930s, well over two-thirds of the marriages even among urban couples had been arranged by their parents (see the box on p. 714), and in one rural area, only 3 out of 170 villagers interviewed had even heard of the idea of "modern marriage." Even the tradition of binding the feet of female children continued despite efforts by the Nationalist government to eradicate the practice.

A NEW CULTURE? Nowhere was the struggle between traditional and modern more visible than in the field of culture. Beginning with the New Culture era, radical reformists criticized traditional culture as the symbol and instrument of feudal oppression that must be entirely eradicated before a new China could stand with dignity in the modern world. During the 1920s and 1930s, Western literature and art became highly popular, especially among the urban middle class. Traditional culture continued to prevail among more conservative elements, and

An Arranged Marriage

FAMILY & SOCIETY

Under Western influence, Chinese social customs changed dramatically for many urban elites in the interwar years. A vocal women's movement, inspired in part by translations of Henrik Ibsen's play *A Doll's House*, campaigned aggressively for universal suffrage and an end to sexual discrimination. Some progressives called for free choice in marriage and divorce and even for free love. By the 1930s, the government had taken some steps to free women from patriarchal marriage constraints and realize sexual equality. But life was generally unaffected in the villages, where traditional patterns held sway. This often created severe tensions between older and younger generations, as this passage from a novel by the popular twentieth-century writer Ba Jin (BAH JIN) shows.

Ba Jin, *Family*

Brought up with loving care, after studying with a private tutor for a number of years, Chueh-hsin entered middle school. One of the school's best students, he graduated four years later at the top of his class. He was very interested in physics and chemistry and hoped to study abroad, in Germany. His mind was full of beautiful dreams. At that time he was the envy of his classmates.

In his fourth year at middle school, he lost his mother. His father later married again, this time to a younger woman who had been his mother's cousin. Chueh-hsin was aware of his loss, for he knew full well that nothing could replace the love of a mother. But her death left no irreparable wound in his heart; he was able to console himself with rosy dreams of his future. Moreover, he had someone who understood him and could comfort him—his pretty cousin Mei, "mei" for "plum blossom."

But then, one day, his dreams were shattered, cruelly and bitterly shattered. The evening he returned home carrying his diploma, the plaudits of his teachers and friends still ringing in his ears, his father called him into his room and said:

"Now that you've graduated, I want to arrange your marriage. Your grandfather is looking forward to having a great-grandson, and I, too, would like to be able to hold a grandson in my arms. You're old enough to be married; I won't feel easy until I fulfill my obligation to find you a wife. Although I didn't accumulate much money in my years away from home as an official, still I've put by enough for us to get along on. My health isn't what it used to be; I'm thinking of spending my time at home and having you help me run the household affairs. All the more reason you'll be needing a wife. I've already arranged a match with the Li family. The thirteenth of next month is a good day. We'll announce the engagement then. You can be married within the year. . . ."

Chueh-hsin did not utter a word of protest, nor did such a thought ever occur to him. He merely nodded to indicate his compliance with his father's wishes. But after he returned to his own room, and shut the door, he threw himself down on his bed, covered his head with the quilt and wept. He wept for his broken dreams.

He was deeply in love with Mei, but now his father had chosen another, a girl he had never seen, and said that he must marry within the year. What's more, his hopes of continuing his studies had burst like a bubble. It was a terrible shock to Chueh-hsin. His future was finished, his beautiful dreams shattered.

He cried his disappointment and bitterness. But the door was closed and Chueh-hsin's head was beneath the bedding. No one knew. He did not fight back, he never thought of resisting. He only bemoaned his fate. But he accepted it. He complied with his father's will without a trace of resentment. But in his heart he wept for himself, wept for the girl he adored—Mei, his "plum blossom."

 Why does Chueh-hsin comply with the wishes of his father in the matter of his marriage? Why were arranged marriages so prevalent in traditional China?

---

some intellectuals argued for a new art that would synthesize the best of Chinese and foreign culture. But the most creative artists were interested in imitating foreign trends, while traditionalists were more concerned with preservation.

Literature in particular was influenced by foreign ideas as Western genres like the novel and the short story attracted a growing audience. Although most Chinese novels written after World War I dealt with Chinese subjects, they reflected the Western tendency toward social realism and often dealt with the new westernized middle class, as in *Midnight* by Mao Dun (mow DOON ["ow" as in "how"]), which describes the changing mores of Shanghai's urban elites. Another favorite theme was the disintegration of the traditional Confucian

family—Ba Jin's famous novel *Family* is an example. Most of China's modern authors displayed a clear contempt for the past.

Japan Between the Wars

 FOCUS QUESTION: How did Japan address the problems of nation building in the first decades of the twentieth century, and why did democratic institutions not take hold more effectively?

During the first two decades of the twentieth century, Japan made remarkable progress toward the creation of an advanced society on the Western model. The political system based on the Meiji Constitution of 1890 began to evolve along Western pluralistic lines, and a multiparty system took shape, while the economic and social reforms launched during the Meiji era led to increasing prosperity and the development of a modern industrial and commercial sector. Optimists had reason to hope that Japan was on the road to becoming a full-fledged democracy.

Experiment in Democracy

As the twentieth century progressed, the Japanese political system appeared to evolve significantly toward the pluralistic democratic model. Political parties expanded their popular following and became increasingly competitive, and universal male suffrage was instituted in the 1920s. Individual pressure groups began to appear in Japanese society, along with an independent press and a bill of rights. The influence of the old ruling oligarchy, the *genro*, had not yet been significantly challenged, however, nor had that of its ideological foundation, the *kokutai* (koh-kuh-TY) (see Chapter 22).

These fragile democratic institutions were able to survive through the 1920s, often called the era of **Taisho** (TY-SHOH) **democracy**, from the reign title of the ruling emperor. During that period, the military budget was reduced, and a suffrage bill enacted in 1925 granted the vote to all Japanese males, thus continuing the process of democratization begun earlier in the century. Women remained disenfranchised, but women's associations became increasingly visible during the

1920s, and many women were active in the labor movement and in campaigns for various social reforms.

But the era was also marked by growing social turmoil, and two opposing forces within the system were gearing up to challenge the prevailing wisdom. On the left, a Marxist labor movement, which reflected the tensions in the working class and the increasing radicalism among the rural poor, began to take shape in the early 1920s in response to growing economic difficulties. Attempts to suppress labor disturbances led to further radicalization. On the right, ultranationalist groups called for a rejection of Western models of development and a more militant approach to realizing national objectives. In 1919, the radical nationalist Kita Ikki (KEE-tuh IK-kee) called for a military takeover and the establishment of a new system bearing strong resemblance to what would later be called National Socialism in Germany.

This cultural conflict between old and new, indigenous and foreign, was reflected in literature. Japanese self-confidence had been restored after the victories over China and Russia and launched an age of cultural creativity in the early twentieth century. Fascination with Western literature gave birth to a striking new genre called the "I novel." Defying traditional Japanese reticence, some authors reveled in self-exposure with confessions of their innermost thoughts. Others found release in the "proletarian literature" movement of the early 1920s. Inspired by Soviet literary examples, these authors wanted literature to serve socialist goals and improve the lives of the working class. Finally, some Japanese writers

Geishas, Old and New. The geisha (GAY-shuh) ("accomplished person") was a symbol of old Japan. Dressed in traditional costumes, her body movements highly stylized, she served not only as an entertainer and an ornament but also as a beautiful purveyor of elite Japanese culture. That image was dramatically transformed in a new Japan that had been inundated by the influence of the modern West. In the photo on the left, geishas in early-twentieth-century Tokyo mimic Western fashions and dance positions. In the photo on the right, three young Japanese women in traditional costumes stroll in contemporary Kyoto.

The Clash of East and West

ART & IDEAS

The deep-seated conflict between Eastern and Western culture manifested itself in early-twentieth-century Japan through the writings of Nagai Kafu (NAH-gy KAH-foo) (1879–1959). Although Kafu had become a fervent admirer of French culture after living for a time in Europe, he decried the vulgarity and pretentiousness of the westernized Tokyo of his day. In his fiction, he sought to extol the virtues of an idealized "Edo" of the past, wandering through the narrow streets of the city in search of old houses that had not been transformed by the passion for modernization. In the following passage, Kafu expressed his frustration at the superficial absorption of Western ideas during the Meiji era, an effort that only served to mask Japan's feudal heritage. Although more conflicted in his views than many of his contemporaries, Kafu reflected the cultural confusion stemming from Japan's attempt to imitate Western ways.

Nagai Kafu, "Commentary on *Reisho (Sneers)*"

My primary purpose in writing *Sneers* was to attempt a serious critique of the confused, tasteless externals of Tokyo life in 1909; to lament the difficulty of living peacefully in the atmosphere of this period; and, finally, to try to study and seek out places where genuine Japanese features might still be found.

I did not say this in so many words, but it was my intention to convey here and there in the work my conviction that the present-day importation of Western culture has been no more than superficial, and that the Japanese by no means rejoice in the profound content of Western thought. Rather, there lurks in Japan a xenophobia that is far stronger than the doctrine of the Yellow Peril that has been advanced in the West. Even now, when we have a constitutional government, there is something oriental and despotic in the atmosphere enveloping Japan to which it would be hard to give a name but which has not changed in the least since feudal times. I cannot help but feeling that, no matter how the external forms have changed, the natural features, the climate, and all the invisible things seem to harbor malice toward freedom of human wishes and the liberation of ideas. Perhaps I am mistaken, but I believe that nowhere else in the world do people resign themselves so quickly, without really thinking through problems.

What aspects of Japanese tradition were retained in the new Japan that emerged during the Meiji era? Do you believe that a society can totally remake itself in the image of another culture?

---

blended Western psychology with Japanese sensibility in exquisite novels reeking with nostalgia for the old Japan (see the box above). One well-known example is *Some Prefer Nettles* (1929) by Junichiro Tanizaki (jun-ih-CHEE-roh tan-ih-ZAH-kee), which delicately juxtaposed the positive aspects of both traditional and modern Japan. By the 1930s, however, military censorship increasingly inhibited free literary expression.

A *Zaibatsu* Economy

Japan also continued to make impressive progress in economic development. Spurred by rising domestic demand as well as continued government investment in the economy, the production of raw materials tripled between 1900 and 1930, and industrial production increased more than twelvefold. Much of the increase went into exports, and Western manufacturers began to complain about increasing competition from the Japanese.

As often happens, rapid industrialization was accompanied by some hardship and rising social tensions. In the Meiji model, various manufacturing processes were concentrated in a single enterprise, the **zaibatsu** (zy-BAHT-soo *or* DZY-

bahtss), or financial clique. Some of these firms were existing merchant companies, such as Mitsui (MIT-swee) and Sumitomo (soo-mee-TOH-moh), that had the capital and the foresight to move into new areas of opportunity. Others were formed by enterprising samurai, who used their status and experience in management to good account in a new environment. Whatever their origins, these firms gradually developed, often with official encouragement, into large conglomerates that controlled a major segment of the Japanese economy. By 1937, the four largest *zaibatsu*—Mitsui, Mitsubishi (mit-soo-BEE-shee), Sumitomo, and Yasuda (yah-SOO-duh)—controlled 21 percent of the banking industry, 26 percent of mining, 35 percent of shipbuilding, 38 percent of commercial shipping, and more than 60 percent of paper manufacturing and insurance.

This concentration of power and wealth in a few major industrial combines created problems in Japanese society. In the first place, it resulted in the emergence of a dual economy: on the one hand, a modern industry characterized by up-to-date methods and massive government subsidies, and on the other, a traditional manufacturing sector characterized by conservative methods and small-scale production techniques.

The Great Tokyo Earthquake. On September 1, 1923, a massive earthquake struck the central Japanese island of Honshu, causing more than 130,000 deaths and virtually demolishing the capital city of Tokyo. Although the quake was a national tragedy, it also came to symbolize the ingenuity of the Japanese people, whose efforts led to a rapid reconstruction of the city in a new and more modern style. That unity of national purpose would be demonstrated again a quarter of a century later in Japan's swift recovery from the devastation of World War II. An earthquake off the northern coast of Japan triggered a massive tsunami that caused an equivalent level of damage in 2011.

Concentration of wealth also led to growing economic inequalities. As we have seen, economic growth had been achieved at the expense of the peasants, many of whom fled to the cities to escape rural poverty. That labor surplus benefited the industrial sector, but the urban proletariat was still poorly paid and ill housed. Rampant inflation in the price of rice led to food riots shortly after World War I. A rapid increase in population (the total population of the Japanese islands increased from an estimated 43 million in 1900 to 73 million in 1940) led to food shortages and the threat of rising unemployment. In the meantime, those left on the farm continued to suffer. As late as 1940, an estimated half of all Japanese farmers were tenants.

Shidehara Diplomacy

A final problem for Japanese leaders in the post-Meiji era was the familiar colonial dilemma of finding sources of raw materials and foreign markets for the nation's manufactured goods. Until World War I, Japan had dealt with the problem by seizing territories such as Taiwan, Korea, and southern Manchuria and transforming them into colonies or protectorates of the growing Japanese empire. That policy had succeeded brilliantly, but it had also begun to arouse the concern and in some cases the hostility of the Western nations. China was also becoming apprehensive; as we have seen, Japanese demands for Shandong Province at the Paris Peace Conference in 1919 aroused massive protests in major Chinese cities.

The United States was especially concerned about Japanese aggressiveness. Although the United States had been less active than some European states in pursuing colonies in the Pacific, it had a strong interest in keeping the area open for U.S. commercial activities. In 1922, in Washington, D.C., the United States convened a major conference of nations with interests in the Pacific to discuss problems of regional security. The Washington Conference led to agreements on several issues, but the major accomplishment was a nine-power treaty recognizing the territorial integrity of China and the Open Door. The other participants induced Japan to agree to these provisions by accepting its special position in Manchuria.

During the remainder of the 1920s, Japanese governments attempted to play by the rules laid down at the Washington Conference. Known as Shidehara (shee-deh-HAH-rah) diplomacy, after the Japanese foreign minister (and later prime minister) who attempted to carry it out, this policy sought to use diplomatic and economic means to realize Japanese interests in Asia. But this approach came under severe pressure as Japanese industrialists began to move into new areas, such as heavy industry, chemicals, mining, and the manufacturing of appliances and automobiles. Because such industries desperately needed resources not found in abundance locally, the Japanese government came under increasing pressure to find new sources abroad.

THE RISE OF MILITANT NATIONALISM In the early 1930s, with the onset of the Great Depression and growing tensions in the international arena, nationalist forces rose to dominance in the Japanese government. The changes that occurred in the 1930s, which we shall discuss in Chapter 25, were not in the constitution or the institutional structure, which remained essentially intact, but in the composition and attitudes of the ruling group. Party leaders during the 1920s had attempted to realize Tokyo's aspirations within the existing global political and economic framework. The dominant elements in the government in the 1930s, a mixture of military officers and ultranationalist politicians, were convinced that the diplomacy of the 1920s had failed and advocated a more aggressive approach to protecting national interests in a brutal and competitive world.

TAISHO DEMOCRACY: AN ABERRATION?

The dramatic shift in Japanese political culture that occurred in the early 1930s has caused some historians to question the breadth and depth of the trend toward democratic practices in the immediate post–World War I era. Was Taisho democracy merely a fragile attempt at comparative liberalization in a framework dominated by the Meiji vision of empire and *kokutai*? Or was the militant nationalism of the 1930s an aberration brought on by the Great Depression, which caused the inexorable emergence of democracy in Japan to stall?

Clearly, there is some truth in both contentions. A process of democratization was taking place in Japan during the first decades of the twentieth century, but without shaking the essential core of the Meiji concept of the state. When the "liberal" approach of the 1920s failed to solve the problems of the day, the shallow roots of the democracy movement in Japan became exposed, and the shift toward a more aggressive approach was inevitable.

Still, the course of Japanese history after World War II (see Chapter 30) suggests that the emergence of multiparty democracy in the 1920s was not simply an aberration but a natural consequence of evolutionary trends in Japanese society. The seeds of democracy nurtured during the Taisho era were nipped in the bud by the cataclysmic effects of the Great Depression of the 1930s, but in the more conducive climate after World War II, a democratic system—suitably adjusted to Japanese soil—reached full flower.

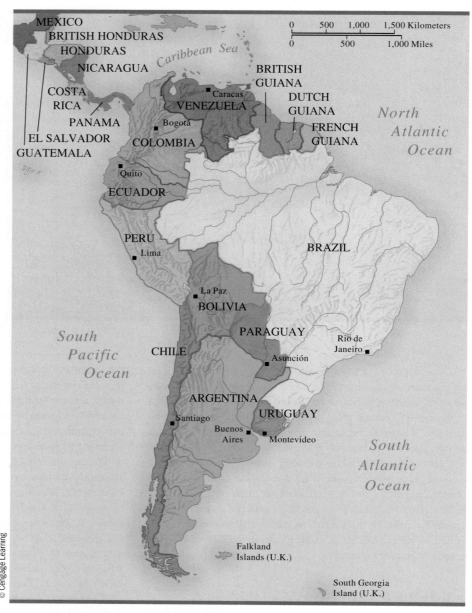

MAP 24.2 **Latin America in the First Half of the Twentieth Century.** Shown here are the boundaries dividing the countries of Latin America after the independence movements of the nineteenth century.

 Which areas remained under European rule?

Nationalism and Dictatorship in Latin America

Q FOCUS QUESTIONS: What problems did the nations of Latin America face in the interwar years? To what degree were the problems a consequence of foreign influence?

Although the nations of Latin America played almost no role in World War I, that conflict nevertheless exerted an impact on them, especially on their economies, as the region continued to be strongly affected by decisions reached in the advanced industrial nations. By the end of the 1920s, Latin America was also strongly influenced by another event of global proportions—the Great Depression.

A Changing Economy

At the beginning of the twentieth century, virtually all of Latin America, except for the three Guianas, British Honduras, and some of the Caribbean islands, had achieved independence. The economy of the region (see Map 24.2) was still based largely on the export of foodstuffs and raw

A Pledge of Cooperation

INTERACTION & EXCHANGE

During the first three decades of the twentieth century, the United States intervened periodically in the affairs of various countries in Latin America to protect the lives of U.S. citizens and its growing economic interests. By the late 1920s, that policy had aroused considerable resentment among governments throughout the region. U.S. President Franklin D. Roosevelt attempted to allay their concerns by announcing the Good Neighbor policy toward other nations in the hemisphere. This selection is from a speech given in August 1936, in which he discussed this policy.

Franklin D. Roosevelt's Good Neighbor Policy

Long before I returned to Washington as President of the United States, I made up my mind that . . . the United States could best serve the cause of peaceful humanity by setting an example. That was why on the 4th of March, 1933, I made the following declaration:

> In the field of world policy I would dedicate this nation to the policy of the good neighbor—the neighbor who resolutely respects himself and because he does so, respects the rights of others—the neighbor who respects his obligations and respects the sanctity of his agreements in and with a world of neighbors.

In the whole of the Western Hemisphere our good neighbor policy had produced results that are especially heartening. . . . The American republics to the south of us have been ready always to cooperate with the United States on a basis of equality and mutual respect, but before we inaugurated the good neighbor policy there was among them resentment and fear, because certain administrations in Washington had slighted their national pride and their sovereign rights.

In pursuance of the good neighbor policy, and because in my younger days I had learned many lessons in the hard school of experience, I stated that the United States was opposed definitely to armed intervention.

We have negotiated a Pan-American convention embodying the principles of nonintervention. We have abandoned the Platt amendment which gave us the right to intervene in the internal affairs of the Republic of Cuba. We have withdrawn American marines from Haiti. We have signed a new treaty which places our relations with Panama on a mutually satisfactory basis. We have undertaken a series of trade agreements with other American countries to our mutual commercial profit. . . .

Throughout the Americas the spirit of the good neighbor is a practical and living fact. The twenty-one American republics are not only living together in friendship and in peace; they are united in the determination so to remain.

How did President Roosevelt define the concept of a "good neighbor" in this speech? What previous U.S. policies toward Latin America does he suggest will be discarded?

---

materials. Some countries relied on exports of only one or two products. Argentina, for example, exported primarily beef and wheat; Chile, nitrates and copper; Brazil and the Caribbean nations, sugar; and the Central American states, bananas. A few reaped large profits from these exports, but for the majority of the population, the returns were meager.

THE ROLE OF THE YANKEE DOLLAR World War I led to a decline in European investment in Latin America and a rise in the U.S. role in the local economies. By the late 1920s, the United States had replaced Great Britain as the foremost source of investment in Latin America. Unlike the British, however, U.S. investors put their funds directly into production enterprises, causing large segments of the area's export industries to fall into American hands. A number of Central American states, for example, were popularly labeled "banana republics" because of the power and influence of the U.S.-owned United Fruit Company. American firms also dominated the copper mining industry in Chile and Peru and the oil industry in Mexico, Peru, and Bolivia.

Increasing economic power reinforced the traditionally high level of U.S. political influence in Latin America. This influence was especially evident in Central America and the Caribbean, regions that many Americans considered their backyard and hence vital to U.S. national security. The growing U.S. presence in the region provoked hostility and a growing national consciousness among Latin Americans, who viewed the United States as an aggressive imperialist power. Some charged that Washington worked to keep ruthless dictators, such as Juan Vicente Gómez (WAHN vee-SEN-tay GOH-mez) of Venezuela and Fulgencio Batista (full-JEN-see-oh bah-TEES-tuh) of Cuba, in power in order to preserve U.S. economic influence; sometimes the United States even intervened militarily. In a bid to improve relations with Latin American countries, in 1933 President Franklin D. Roosevelt promulgated the **Good Neighbor policy**, which rejected the use of U.S. military force in the region (see the box above). To underscore his sincerity, Roosevelt ordered the withdrawal of U.S. marines from the island nation of Haiti in 1936. For the first time in thirty years, there were no U.S. occupation troops in Latin America.

Because so many Latin American nations depended for their livelihood on the export of raw materials and food products, the Great Depression of the 1930s was a disaster for the

Hipólito Irigoyen becomes president of Argentina	1916
Argentine military overthrows Irigoyen	1930
Rule of Getúlio Vargas in Brazil	1930–1945
Presidency of Lázaro Cárdenas in Mexico	1934–1940
Beginning of U.S. Good Neighbor policy	1933

region. In 1930, the value of Latin American exports fell to only half of the amount that had been exported in each of the previous five years. Spurred by the decline in foreign revenues, Latin American governments began to encourage the development of new industries. In some cases—the steel industry in Chile and Brazil, the oil industry in Argentina and Mexico—government investment made up for the absence of local sources of capital.

The Effects of Dependency

During the late nineteenth century, most governments in Latin America had been increasingly dominated by landed or military elites, who controlled the mass of the population—mostly impoverished peasants—by the blatant use of military force. This trend toward authoritarianism increased during the 1930s as domestic instability caused by the effects of the Great Depression led to the creation of military dictatorships throughout the region. This trend was especially evident in Argentina, Brazil, and Mexico—three countries that together possessed more than half of the land and wealth of Latin America.

ARGENTINA Political domination by an elite minority often had disastrous effects. The government of Argentina, controlled by landowners who had benefited from the export of beef and wheat, was slow to recognize the growing importance of establishing a local industrial base. In 1916, Hipólito Irigoyen (ee-POH-lee-toh ee-ree-GOH-yen) (1852–1933), head of the Radical Party, was elected president on a program to improve conditions for the middle and lower classes. Little was achieved, however, as the party became increasingly corrupt and drew closer to the large landowners. In 1930, the army overthrew Irigoyen's government and reestablished the power of the landed class. But efforts to return to the previous export economy and suppress the growing influence of labor unions failed, and in 1946 General Juan Perón (WAHN puh-ROHN)—claiming the support of the *descamisados* (days-kah-mee-SAH-dohs) ("shirtless ones")—seized sole power (see Chapter 28).

BRAZIL Brazil followed a similar path. In 1889, the army replaced the Brazilian monarchy, installed by Portugal years before, with a republic. But it was controlled by landed elites, many of whom had grown wealthy through their ownership of vast rubber and coffee plantations. Exports of Brazilian rubber dominated the world market until just before World War I. When it proved easier to produce rubber in Southeast

Asia, however, Brazilian exports suddenly collapsed, leaving the economy of the Amazon River basin in ruins.

To make matters worse, the coffee industry also suffered problems. In 1900, three-quarters of the world's coffee was grown in Brazil. As in Argentina, the ruling oligarchy ignored the importance of establishing an urban industrial base. When the Great Depression ravaged profits from coffee exports, a wealthy rancher, Getúlio Vargas (zhi-TOO-lyoo VAHR-guhs) (1883–1954), seized power and ruled the country as president from 1930 to 1945. At first, Vargas sought to appease workers by instituting an eight-hour workday and a minimum wage, but influenced by the apparent success of fascist regimes in Europe, he ruled by increasingly autocratic means and relied on a police force that used torture to silence his opponents. His industrial policy was relatively enlightened, however, and by the end of World War II, Brazil had become Latin America's major industrial power. In 1945, the army, fearing that Vargas might prolong his power illegally after calling for new elections, forced him to resign.

The Tango, National Dance of Argentina. In the early twentieth century, the gaucho (GOW-choh), or cowboy, came to epitomize the self-image of the Argentinean people. Immigrants from southern Europe who had come to Latin America in search of work and a better life, they eventually settled in the vast grassy plains called the pampas (PAM-puhz *or* PAHM-pahs), becoming key participants in the emerging cattle industry that transformed the country into a major exporter of beef and hides. For entertainment, many visited the bawdyhouses and brothels of Buenos Aires, where the tango—a soulful and nostalgic dance based on Iberian rhythms—symbolized the hopes and frustrations of the immigrant experience. Once exported abroad, the tango became an overnight sensation in Europe and North America, where its sensuous movements aroused stern criticism in religious circles.

The Opera House at Manaus. The discovery of rubber in the mid-nineteenth century was one of the most significant events in the history of Brazil. Derived from the sap of a tree native to the Amazon River basin, rubber became the source of great wealth for Brazilian plantation owners until the rubber boom declined after 1900. The most visible symbol of "king rubber" is the Opera House at Manaus (mah-NOWSS), the largest city on the Amazon. Built in 1896 in an opulent style including the profligate use of Italian marble, it fell into disrepair when the rubber trade moved from Brazil to Southeast Asia in the first quarter of the twentieth century. Thus, the Opera House is a vivid example of the vicissitudes that developing countries may experience as a result of economies based on exports of primary products. The building has recently been renovated and stands as a beacon of promise for one of Latin America's fastest growing regions.

MEXICO After the dictator Porfirio Díaz (por-FEER-yoh DEE-ahs) was ousted from power in 1910 (see Chapter 20), Mexico entered a state of turbulence that lasted for years. The ineffective leaders who followed Díaz were unable either to solve the country's economic problems or to bring an end to the civil strife. Declining real wages were squeezing the working class, while in the countryside almost all of the land was controlled by about a thousand families. In southern Mexico, the landless peasants responded eagerly to Emiliano Zapata (ee-mee-LYAH-noh zup-PAH-tuh) (1879–1919) when he called for land redistribution and began to seize the estates of wealthy landholders.

For the next several years, Zapata and rebel leader Pancho Villa (pahn-CHOH VEE-uh) (1878–1923), who operated in the northern state of Chihuahua (chih-WAH-wah), became an important political force in the country by publicly advocating efforts to redress the economic grievances of the poor. But neither had a broad grasp of the challenges facing the country, and power eventually gravitated to a more moderate group of reformists around the Constitutionalist Party. The latter were intent on breaking the power of the great landed families and U.S. corporations, but without engaging in radical land reform or the nationalization of property. After a bloody conflict that cost the lives of thousands, the moderates consolidated power, and in 1917, they promulgated a new constitution that established a strong presidency, initiated land reform policies, established limits on foreign investment, and set an agenda for social welfare programs.

In 1920, the Constitutionalist Party leader Alvaro Obregón (AHL-vah-roh oh-bree-GAHN) assumed the presidency and began to carry out his reform program. But real change did not take place until the presidency of General Lázaro Cárdenas (LAH-zah-roh KAHR-day-nahss) (1895–1970) in 1934. Cárdenas won wide popularity with the peasants by ordering the redistribution of 44 million acres of land controlled by landed elites. He also seized control of the oil industry, which had hitherto been dominated by major U.S. oil companies. Alluding to the Good Neighbor policy, President Roosevelt refused to intervene, and eventually Mexico agreed to compensate U.S. oil companies for their lost property. It then set up PEMEX, a governmental organization, to run the oil industry. By now, the revolution was democratic in name only, as the official political party, known as the Institutional Revolutionary Party (PRI), controlled the levers of power throughout society. Every six years, for more than half a century, PRI presidential candidates automatically succeeded each other in office.

Latin American Culture

The first half of the twentieth century witnessed a dramatic increase in literary activity in Latin America, a result in part of its ambivalent relationship with Europe and the United States. Many authors, while experimenting with imported modernist styles, felt compelled to proclaim their region's unique identity through the adoption of Latin American themes and social issues. In *The Underdogs* (1915), for example, Mariano Azuela (mahr-YAHN-oh ah-SWAY-luh) (1873–1952) presented a sympathetic but not uncritical portrait of the Mexican Revolution as his country entered an era of unsettling change.

In their determination to commend Latin America's distinctive characteristics, some writers extolled the promise of the region's vast virgin lands and the diversity of its peoples. In *Don Segundo Sombra*, published in 1926, Ricardo Guiraldes (ree-KAHR-doh gwee-RAHL-dess) (1886–1927) celebrated the life of the ideal gaucho (cowboy), defining Argentina's hope and strength through the enlightened management of its fertile earth. Likewise, in *Dona Barbara*, Rómulo Gallegos (ROH-moo-loh gah-YAY-gohs) (1884–1969) wrote in a similar vein about his native Venezuela. Other authors pursued the theme of solitude and detachment,

Struggle for the Banner. Like Diego Rivera, David Alfaro Siqueiros (dah-VEED al-FAHR-oh see-KAY-rohss) (1896–1974) decorated public buildings with large murals that celebrated the Mexican Revolution and the workers' and peasants' struggle for freedom. Beginning in the 1930s, Siqueiros expressed sympathy for the exploited and downtrodden peoples of Mexico in dramatic frescoes such as this one. He painted similar murals in Uruguay, Argentina, and Brazil and was once expelled from the United States, where his political art and views were considered too radical.

a product of the region's physical separation from the rest of the world.

Latin American artists followed their literary counterparts in joining the Modernist movement in Europe, yet they too were eager to promote the emergence of a new regional and national essence. In Mexico, where the government provided financial support for painting murals on public buildings, the artist Diego Rivera (DYAY-goh rih-VAIR-uh) (1886–1957) began to produce monumental murals that served two purposes: to illustrate the national past by portraying Aztec legends and folk customs and to popularize a political message in favor of realizing the social goals of the Mexican Revolution. His wife, Frida Kahlo (FREE-duh KAH-loh) (1907–1954), incorporated Surrealist whimsy in her own paintings, many of which were portraits of herself and her family.

CHAPTER SUMMARY

The turmoil brought about by World War I not only resulted in the destruction of several of the major Western empires and a redrawing of the map of Europe but also opened the door to political and social upheavals elsewhere in the world. In the Middle East, the decline and fall of the Ottoman Empire led to the creation of the secular republic of Turkey. The state of Saudi Arabia emerged in the Arabian peninsula, and Palestine became a source of tension between newly arrived Jewish settlers and longtime Muslim residents.

Other parts of Asia and Africa also witnessed the rise of movements for national independence. In many cases, these movements were spearheaded by local leaders who had been educated in Europe or the United States. In India, Mahatma Gandhi and his campaign of civil disobedience played a crucial role in his country's bid to be free of British rule. Communist movements also began to emerge in Asian societies as radical elements sought new methods of bringing about the overthrow of Western imperialism. Japan continued to follow its own path to modernization, which, although successful from an economic perspective, took a menacing turn during the 1930s.

 Between 1919 and 1939, China experienced a dramatic struggle to establish a modern nation. Two dynamic political organizations—the Nationalists and the Communists—competed for legitimacy as the rightful heirs of the old order. At first, they formed an alliance in an effort to defeat their common adversaries, but cooperation ultimately turned to conflict. The Nationalists under Chiang Kai-shek emerged supreme, but Chiang found it difficult to control the remnants of the warlord regime in China, while the Great Depression undermined his efforts to build an industrial nation.

During the interwar years, the nations of Latin America faced severe economic problems because of their dependence on exports. Increasing U.S. investments in Latin America contributed to growing hostility toward the powerful neighbor to the north. The Great Depression forced the region to begin developing new industries, but it also led to the rise of authoritarian governments, some of them modeled after the fascist regimes of Italy and Germany.

By demolishing the remnants of their old civilization on the battlefields of World War I, Europeans had inadvertently encouraged the subject peoples of their vast colonial empires to begin their own movements for national independence. The process was by no means completed in the two decades following the Treaty of Versailles, but the bonds of imperial rule had been severely strained. Once Europeans began to weaken themselves in the even more destructive conflict of World War II, the hopes of African and Asian peoples for national independence and freedom could at last be realized. It is to that devastating world conflict that we must now turn.

CHAPTER TIMELINE

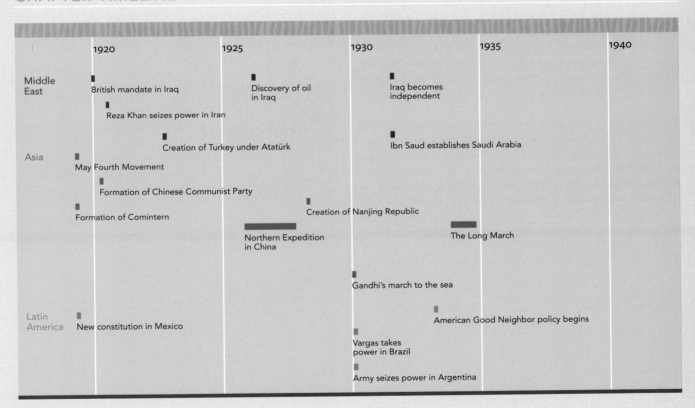

	1920	1925	1930	1935	1940
Middle East	British mandate in Iraq	Discovery of oil in Iraq	Iraq becomes independent		
	Reza Khan seizes power in Iran				
		Creation of Turkey under Atatürk	Ibn Saud establishes Saudi Arabia		
Asia	May Fourth Movement				
	Formation of Chinese Communist Party				
	Formation of Comintern		Creation of Nanjing Republic		
		Northern Expedition in China		The Long March	
			Gandhi's march to the sea		
Latin America	New constitution in Mexico			American Good Neighbor policy begins	
			Vargas takes power in Brazil		
			Army seizes power in Argentina		

CHAPTER REVIEW

Upon Reflection

Q In what ways did Japan's political system and social structure in the interwar years combine modern and traditional elements? How successful was the attempt to create a modern political system while retaining indigenous traditions of civil obedience and loyalty to the emperor?

Q During the early twentieth century did conditions for women change for the better or for the worse in the countries discussed in this chapter? Why?

Q Communist Parties were established in many Asian societies in the years immediately following the Bolshevik Revolution. How successful were these parties in winning popular support and achieving their goals?

Key Terms

satyagraha (p. 699)

harijans (p. 699)

civil disobedience (p. 700)

Young Turks (p. 701)

Communist International (Comintern) (p. 706)

New Culture Movement (p. 708)

Taisho democracy (p. 715)

zaibatsu (p. 716)

Good Neighbor policy (p. 719)

descamisados (p. 720)

Suggested Reading

NATIONALISM   The most up-to-date survey of modern nationalism is **E. Gellner**, *Nations and Nationalism,* 2nd ed. (Ithaca, N.Y., 2009), but it has little to say about the non-Western world. For a provocative study of the roots of nationalism in Asia, see **B. Anderson**, *Imagined Communities: Reflections on the Origins and Spread of Nationalism* (London, 1983).

INDIA   There have been a number of studies of Mahatma Gandhi and his ideas. See, for example, **S. Wolpert**, *Gandhi's Passion: The Life and Legacy of Mahatma Gandhi* (Oxford, 1999), and **D. Dalton**, *Mahatma Gandhi: Nonviolent Power in Action* (New York, 1995). For a study of Nehru, see **J. M. Brown**, *Nehru* (New York, 2000).

MIDDLE EAST   For a general survey of events in the Middle East in the interwar era, see **E. Bogle**, *The Modern Middle East: From Imperialism to Freedom* (Upper Saddle River, N.J., 1996). For more specialized studies, see **I. Gershoni et al.**, *Egypt, Islam, and the Arabs: The Search for Egyptian Nationhood* (Oxford, 1993), and **W. Laqueur**, *A History of Zionism: From the French Revolution to the Establishment of the State of Israel* (New York,

1996). The role of Atatürk is examined in **A. Mango**, *Atatürk: The Biography of the Founder of Modern Turkey* (New York, 2000). The Palestinian issue is dealt with in **B. Morris**, *Righteous Victims: The Palestinian Conflict, 1880–2000* (New York, 2001). On the founding of Iraq, see **S. Mackey**, *The Reckoning: Iraq and the Legacy of Saddam Hussein* (New York, 2002). For a penetrating account of the fall of the Ottoman Empire and its consequences for the postwar era, see **D. Fromkin**, *A Peace to End All Peace: The Fall of the Ottoman Empire and the Creation of the Modern Middle East* (New York, 2001).

CHINA AND JAPAN   On the early Chinese republic, a good study is **J. Fitzgerald**, *Awakening China: Politics, Culture, and Class in the Nationalist Revolution* (Stanford, Calif., 1996). The rise of the Chinese Communist Party is charted in **A. Dirlik**, *The Origins of Chinese Communism* (Oxford, 1989). Also see **J. Taylor**, *The Generalissimo: Chiang Kai-shek and the Struggle for Modern China* (Cambridge, Mass., 2009). On Japan, see **J. McLain**, *Japan: A Modern History* (New York, 2001).

LATIN AMERICA   For an overview of Latin American history during the interwar period, see **J. Chasteen**, *Born in Blood and Fire: A Concise History of Latin America,* 2nd ed. (New York, 2005). For documents, see **J. Wood** and **J. Chasteen, eds.**, *Problems in Latin American History: Sources and Interpretations,* 3rd ed. (New York, 2009).

Go to the CourseMate website at **www.cengagebrain.com** for additional study tools and review materials—including audio and video clips—for this chapter.

The Crisis Deepens: World War II

Adolf Hitler salutes military leaders and soldiers during a Nazi party rally.

© Hugo Jaeger/Time Life Pictures/Getty Images

CHAPTER OUTLINE
AND FOCUS QUESTIONS

Retreat from Democracy: Dictatorial Regimes

Q What are the characteristics of totalitarian states, and to what degree were these characteristics present in Fascist Italy, Nazi Germany, and Stalinist Russia? To what extent was Japan a totalitarian state?

The Path to War

Q What were the underlying causes of World War II, and what specific steps taken by Nazi Germany and Japan led to war?

World War II

Q What were the main events of World War II in Europe and Asia?

The New Order

Q What was the nature of the new orders that Germany and Japan attempted to establish in the territories they occupied?

The Home Front

Q What were conditions like on the home front for the major belligerents in World War II?

Aftermath of the War

Q What were the costs of World War II? How did World War II affect the European nations' colonial empires? How did the Allies' visions of the postwar world differ, and how did these differences contribute to the emergence of the Cold War?

CRITICAL THINKING

Q What was the relationship between World War I and World War II, and how did the ways in which the wars were fought differ?

ON FEBRUARY 3, 1933, only four days after he had been appointed chancellor of Germany, Adolf Hitler met secretly with Germany's leading generals. He revealed to them his desire to remove the "cancer of democracy," create a new authoritarian leadership, and forge a new domestic unity. All Germans would need to realize that "only a struggle can save us and that everything else must be subordinated to this idea." Youth especially must be trained and their wills strengthened "to fight with all means." Since Germany's living space was too small for its people, Hitler said, Germany must rearm and prepare for "the conquest of new living space in the east and its ruthless Germanization." Even before he had consolidated his power, Adolf Hitler had a clear vision of his goals, and their implementation meant another war.

World War II in Europe was clearly Hitler's war. Although other countries may have helped make the war possible by not resisting Hitler's Germany earlier, it was Nazi Germany's actions that made World War II inevitable.

But World War II was more than just Hitler's war. It was in fact two separate and parallel conflicts, one provoked by the ambitions of Germany in Europe and the other by the ambitions of Japan in Asia. Around the same time that Hitler was consolidating his power in the early 1930s, the United States and major European nations raised the tariffs they imposed on Japanese imports in a desperate effort to protect local businesses and jobs. In response, militant groups in

Tokyo began to argue that Japan must obtain by violent action what it could not secure by peaceful means. By 1941, when the United States became embroiled in both wars, the two had merged into a single global conflict.

Although World War I has been described as a total war, World War II was even more so and was fought on a scale unheard of in history. Almost everyone in the warring countries was involved in one way or another: as soldiers; as workers in wartime industries; as ordinary citizens subject to invading armies, military occupation, or bombing raids; as refugees; or as victims of mass extermination. The world had never witnessed such widespread human-induced death and destruction.

Retreat from Democracy: Dictatorial Regimes

Q FOCUS QUESTIONS: What are the characteristics of totalitarian states, and to what degree were these characteristics present in Fascist Italy, Nazi Germany, and Stalinist Russia? To what extent was Japan a totalitarian state?

The rise of dictatorial regimes in the 1930s had a great deal to do with the coming of World War II. The apparent triumph of liberal democracy in 1919 had proved extremely short-lived. By 1939, only two major states in Europe (Great Britain and France) and several minor ones (the Low Countries, the Scandinavian states, Switzerland, and Czechoslovakia) remained democratic. Italy and Germany had succumbed to the political movement called fascism, and Soviet Russia under Joseph Stalin moved toward repressive totalitarianism. A host of other European states and Latin American countries adopted authoritarian structures of different kinds, while a militarist regime in Japan moved that country down the path of war. What had happened to Woodrow Wilson's claim that World War I had been fought to make the world safe for democracy? Actually, World War I turned out to have had the opposite effect.

Stepping Back from Democracy

The postwar expansion of the electorate made mass politics a reality and seemed to enhance the spread of democracy in Europe. But the war itself had created conditions that led the new mass electorate to distrust democracy and move toward a more radicalized politics.

Many postwar societies were badly divided, especially along class lines. During the war, to maintain war production, governments had been forced to make concessions to trade unions and socialist parties, which strengthened the working class after the war. At the same time, the position of many middle-class people had declined as consumer industries had been curtailed during the war and war bonds, which had been purchased by the middle classes as their patriotic contribution to the war effort, sank in value and even became worthless in some countries.

Gender divisions also weakened social cohesion. After the war, as soldiers returned home, women were forced out of jobs they had taken during the war, jobs that many newly independent women wanted to retain. The loss of so many men during the war had also left many younger women with no marital prospects and widows with no choice but to find jobs in the labor force. At the same time, fears about a declining population because of the war led many male political leaders to encourage women to return to their traditional roles of wives and mothers. Many European countries outlawed abortion and curtailed the sale of birth control devices while providing increased welfare benefits to entice women to remain at home and bear children.

The Great Depression served to deepen social conflict. Larger and larger numbers of people felt victimized, first by the war and now by socioeconomic conditions that seemed beyond their control. Postwar politics became more and more polarized as people reverted to the wartime practice of dividing into friends and enemies, downplaying compromise and emphasizing conflict. Moderate centrist parties that supported democracy soon found themselves with fewer and fewer allies as people became increasingly radicalized politically, supporting the extremes of left-wing communism or right-wing fascism.

The dictatorial regimes between the wars assumed both old and new forms. Dictatorship was not new, but the modern **totalitarian state** was. The totalitarian regimes, best exemplified by Stalinist Russia and Nazi Germany, greatly extended the functions and power of the central state. The modern totalitarian state went beyond the ideal of passive obedience expected in a traditional dictatorship or authoritarian monarchy. The new "total states" expected the active loyalty and commitment of citizens to the regime's goal, whether it be war, a socialist society, or a thousand-year Reich (RYKH) (empire). They used modern mass propaganda techniques and high-speed communications to conquer the minds and hearts of their subjects. The total state sought to control not only the economic, political, and social aspects of life but the intellectual and cultural aspects as well.

The modern totalitarian state was to be led by a single leader and a single party. It ruthlessly rejected the liberal ideal of limited government power and constitutional guarantees of individual freedoms. Indeed, individual freedom was to be subordinated to the collective will of the masses, organized and determined for them by the leader. Modern technology also gave total states unprecedented police controls to force their wishes on their subjects.

The Birth of Fascism

In the early 1920s, Benito Mussolini (buh-NEE-toh moos-suh-LEE-nee) bestowed on Italy the first successful fascist movement in Europe. Mussolini (1883–1945) began his political career as a socialist, but in 1919, he established a new political group, the *Fascio di Combattimento* (FASH-ee-oh dee com-bat-ee-MEN-toh) (League of Combat), which won support from middle-class industrialists fearful of working-class agitation and large landowners who objected to strikes by farmworkers. Mussolini also perceived that Italians were angry over Italy's failure to receive more territory after World War I. In 1920 and 1921, bands of armed Fascists called *squadristi* (skwah-DREES-tee) were formed and turned loose to attack socialist offices and newspapers. The movement gained momentum as Mussolini's nationalist rhetoric and the middle-class fear of socialism, Communist revolution, and disorder made the Fascists seem more and more attractive. On October 29, 1922, after Mussolini and the Fascists threatened to march on Rome if they were not given power, King Victor Emmanuel (1900–1946) capitulated and made Mussolini prime minister of Italy.

By 1926, Mussolini had established the institutional framework for a Fascist dictatorship. Press laws gave the government the right to suspend any publications that fostered disrespect for the Catholic Church, the monarchy, or the state. The prime minister was made "head of government" with the power to legislate by decree. A law empowered the police to arrest and confine anybody for both nonpolitical and political crimes without pressing charges. The government was given the power to dissolve political and cultural associations. In 1926, all anti-Fascist parties were outlawed, and a secret police force was established. By the end of the year, Mussolini ruled Italy as *Il Duce* (eel DOO-chay), the leader.

Mussolini conceived of the Fascist state as totalitarian: "Fascism is totalitarian, and the Fascist State, the synthesis and unity of all values, interprets, develops and gives strength to the whole life of the people."[1] Mussolini did try to create a police state, but it was not very effective. Police activities in Italy were never as repressive, efficient, or savage as those of Nazi Germany. Likewise, the Italian Fascists' attempt to exercise control over all forms of mass media, including newspapers, radio, and cinema, so that they could use propaganda as an instrument to integrate the masses into the state, was rarely effective. Most commonly, Fascist propaganda was disseminated through simple slogans, such as "Mussolini is always right," plastered on walls all over Italy.

Mussolini and the Fascists also attempted to mold Italians into a single-minded community by developing Fascist organizations. Because the secondary schools maintained considerable freedom from Fascist control, the regime relied more and more on the activities of youth organizations, known as the Young Fascists, to indoctrinate the young people of the nation in Fascist ideals, especially the need for discipline and preparation for war.

The Fascists portrayed the family as the pillar of the state and women as the basic foundation of the family. "Woman into the home" became the Fascist slogan. Women were to be homemakers and baby producers, "their natural and fundamental mission in life," according to Mussolini, for population growth was viewed as an indicator of national strength. Employment outside the home was an impediment distracting women from conception: "It forms an independence and consequent physical and moral habits contrary to child bearing."[2]

Despite the instruments of repression, the use of propaganda, and the creation of numerous Fascist organizations, Mussolini never achieved the degree of totalitarian control attained in Hitler's Germany or Stalin's Soviet Union. Mussolini and the Fascist Party did not completely destroy the old power structure. Some institutions, including the Catholic Church, the armed forces, and the monarchy, were never absorbed into the Fascist state and managed to maintain their independence. In all areas of Italian life under Mussolini and the Fascists, there was a noticeable dichotomy between Fascist ideals and practice. The Italian Fascists promised much but actually delivered considerably less, and they were soon overshadowed by a much more powerful fascist movement to the north.

AP Images

Mussolini, the Iron Duce. One of Mussolini's favorite images of himself was that of the Iron Duce—the strong leader who is always right. Consequently, he was often seen in military-style uniforms and military poses. This photograph shows Mussolini in one of his numerous uniforms with his Blackshirt bodyguards giving the Fascist salute.

Hitler and Nazi Germany

In 1923, a small south German rightist party known as the Nazis, led by an obscure Austrian rabble-rouser named Adolf Hitler (1889–1945), created a stir when it tried to seize power in southern Germany in conscious imitation of Mussolini's march on Rome in 1922. Although the attempt failed, Hitler and the Nazis achieved sudden national prominence. Within ten years, they had taken over complete power.

HITLER AND THE EARLY NAZI PARTY At the end of World War I, after four years of service on the Western Front, Adolf Hitler went to Munich and decided to enter politics. In 1919, he joined the obscure German Workers' Party, one of a number of right-wing extreme nationalist parties in Munich. By the summer of 1921, he had assumed control of the party, which he renamed the National Socialist German Workers' Party (NSDAP), or Nazi for short (from the pronunciation of the first two syllables of the name in German). Hitler worked assiduously to develop the party into a mass political movement with flags, badges, uniforms, its own newspaper, and its own police force or party militia known as the SA, the *Sturmabteilung* (SHTOORM-ap-ty-loonk) (Storm Troops). The SA was used to defend the party in meeting halls and break up the meetings of other parties. Hitler's own oratorical skills were largely responsible for attracting an increasing number of followers. By 1923, the party's membership had grown from its early hundreds to 55,000, of whom 15,000 served in the SA.

Overconfident, Hitler staged an armed uprising against the government in Munich in November 1923. The so-called Beer Hall Putsch was quickly crushed, and Hitler was sentenced to prison. During his brief stay in jail, he wrote *Mein Kampf* (myn KAHMPF) (*My Struggle*), an autobiographical account of his movement and its underlying ideology. Extreme German nationalism, virulent anti-Semitism, and anticommunism are linked together by a social Darwinian theory of struggle that stresses the right of superior nations to *Lebensraum* (LAY-benz-rown) (living space) through expansion and the right of superior individuals to secure authoritarian leadership over the masses.

During his imprisonment, Hitler also came to the realization that the Nazis would have to come to power by constitutional means, not by overthrowing the Weimar (VY-mar) Republic. This implied the formation of a mass political party that would actively compete for votes with the other political parties. After his release from prison, Hitler reorganized the Nazi Party on a regional basis and expanded it to all parts of Germany. By 1929, the Nazis had a national party organization.

THE RISE TO POWER Three years later, the Nazi Party had 800,000 members and had become the largest party in the Reichstag (RYKHSS-tahk). Germany's economic difficulties were a crucial factor in the Nazis' rise to power. Unemployment rose dramatically, from just over 4 million in 1931 to 6 million by the winter of 1932. The economic and psychological impact of the Great Depression made extremist parties promising dramatic quick fixes more attractive. The Nazis maintained that they stood above classes and parties. Hitler

vowed to create a new Germany free of class differences and party infighting. His appeal to national pride, national honor, and traditional militarism struck chords of emotion in his listeners. After attending one of Hitler's rallies, a schoolteacher in Hamburg said, "When the speech was over, there was roaring enthusiasm and applause. . . . Then he went—how many look up to him with touching faith as their savior, their deliverer from unbearable distress."[3]

Increasingly, the right-wing elites of Germany—the industrial magnates, landed aristocrats, military establishment, and higher bureaucrats—came to see Hitler as the man who had the mass support to establish a right-wing, authoritarian regime that would save Germany and their privileged positions from a Communist takeover. Under pressure, since the Nazi Party had the largest share of seats in the Reichstag, President Paul von Hindenburg agreed to allow Hitler to become chancellor (on January 30, 1933) and create a new government.

Within two months, Hitler had laid the foundations for the Nazis' complete control over Germany. The crowning step in Hitler's "legal seizure" of power came on March 23, when the Reichstag passed the Enabling Act by a two-thirds vote. This legislation, which empowered the government to dispense with constitutional forms for four years while it issued laws that dealt with the country's problems, provided the legal basis for Hitler's subsequent acts. In effect, Hitler became a dictator appointed by the parliamentary body itself.

With their new source of power, the Nazis acted quickly to coordinate all institutions under Nazi control. The civil service was purged of Jews and democratic elements, concentration camps were established for opponents of the new regime, the autonomy of the federal states was eliminated, trade unions were dissolved, and all political parties except the Nazis were abolished. By the end of the summer of 1933, less than seven months after being appointed chancellor, Hitler and the Nazis had established the foundations for a totalitarian state. When Hindenburg died on August 2, 1934, the office of Reich president was abolished, and Hitler became sole ruler of Germany. Public officials and soldiers were all required to take a personal oath of loyalty to Hitler as the "Führer (FYOOR-ur) (leader) of the German Reich and people."

THE NAZI STATE, 1933–1939 Having smashed the parliamentary state, Hitler now felt that the real task was at hand: to develop the "total state." Hitler's goal was the development of an "Aryan" racial state that would dominate Europe and possibly the world for generations to come. That required a movement in which the German people would be actively involved, not passively cowed by force. Hitler stated:

> We must develop organizations in which an individual's entire life can take place. Then every activity and every need of every individual will be regulated by the collectivity represented by the party. There is no longer any arbitrary will; there are no longer any free realms in which the individual belongs to himself. . . . The time of personal happiness is over.[4]

The Nazis pursued the creation of this totalitarian state in a variety of ways. Mass demonstrations and spectacles were

Propaganda and Mass Meetings in Nazi Germany

POLITICS & GOVERNMENT

Propaganda and mass rallies were two of the chief instruments that Hitler used to prepare the German people for the tasks he set before them. In the first selection, taken from *Mein Kampf*, Hitler explains the psychological importance of mass meetings in creating support for a political movement. In the second excerpt, taken from his speech to a crowd at Nuremberg, he describes the kind of mystical bond he hoped to create through his mass rallies.

Adolf Hitler, *Mein Kampf*

The mass meeting is also necessary for the reason that in it the individual, who at first, while becoming a supporter of a young movement, feels lonely and easily succumbs to the fear of being alone, for the first time gets the picture of a larger community, which in most people has a strengthening, encouraging effect. . . . When from his little workshop or big factory, in which he feels very small, he steps for the first time into a mass meeting and has thousands and thousands of people of the same opinions around him, when, as a seeker, he is swept away by three or four thousand others into the mighty effect of suggestive intoxication and enthusiasm, when the visible success and agreement of thousands confirm to him the rightness of the new doctrine and for the first time arouse doubt in the truth of his previous conviction—then he himself has succumbed to the magic influence of what we designate as "mass suggestion." The will, the longing, and

also the power of thousands are accumulated in every individual. The man who enters such a meeting doubting and wavering leaves it inwardly reinforced: he has become a link in the community.

Adolf Hitler, Speech at the Nuremberg Party Rally, 1936

Do we not feel once again in this hour the miracle that brought us together? Once you heard the voice of a man, and it struck deep into your hearts; it awakened you, and you followed this voice. Year after year you went after it, though him who had spoken you never even saw. You heard only a voice, and you followed it. When we meet each other here, the wonder of our coming together fills us all. Not every one of you sees me, and I do not see every one of you. But I feel you, and you feel me. It is the belief in our people that has made us small men great, that has made us poor men rich, that has made brave and courageous men out of us wavering, spiritless, timid folk; this belief made us see our road when we were astray; it joined us together into one whole! . . . You come, that . . . you may, once in a while, gain the feeling that now we are together; we are with him and he with us, and we are now Germany!

In Hitler's view, what would mass meetings accomplish for his movement? How do mass rallies further the development of nationalism?

---

employed to integrate the German nation into a collective fellowship and to mobilize it as an instrument for Hitler's policies (see the box above). These mass demonstrations, especially the Nuremberg party rallies that were held every September, combined the symbolism of a religious service with the merriment of a popular amusement. They had great appeal and usually evoked mass enthusiasm and excitement.

The apparatus of Hitler's total state had some confusing features. One usually thinks of Nazi Germany as having an all-powerful government that maintained absolute control and order. In truth, Nazi Germany was the scene of almost constant personal and institutional conflict, which resulted in administrative chaos. Incessant struggle characterized the relationships within the party, within the state, and between party and state. Hitler, of course, remained the ultimate decision maker and absolute ruler.

In the economic sphere, Hitler and the Nazis also established control. Although the regime pursued the use of public works projects and "pump-priming" grants to private construction firms to foster employment and end the depression, there is little doubt that rearmament contributed far more to

solving the unemployment problem. Unemployment, which had stood at 6 million in 1932, dropped to 2.6 million in 1934 and less than 500,000 in 1937. The regime claimed full credit for solving Germany's economic woes, and this was an important factor in convincing many Germans to accept the new regime, despite its excesses.

For Germans who needed coercion, the Nazi total state had its instruments of terror. Especially important were the *Schutzstaffel* (SHOOTS-shtah-fuhn) (guard squadrons), known simply as the SS. Originally created as Hitler's personal bodyguard, the SS, under the direction of Heinrich Himmler (1900–1945), came to control all of the regular and secret police forces. Himmler and the SS functioned on the basis of two principles: terror and ideology. Terror included the instruments of repression and murder: the secret police, criminal police, concentration camps, and later the execution squads and death camps for the extermination of the Jews. For Himmler, the SS was a crusading order whose primary goal was to further the Aryan master race.

Other institutions, such as the Catholic and Protestant churches, primary and secondary schools, and universities,

The Nazi Mass Spectacle. Hitler and the Nazis made clever use of mass spectacles to rally the German people behind the Nazi regime. These mass demonstrations evoked intense enthusiasm, as is evident in this photograph of Hitler arriving at the Bückeberg (BOOK-uh-bayrk) near Hamelin for the Harvest Festival in 1937. Almost one million people were present for the celebration.

were also brought under the control of the Nazi totalitarian state. Nazi professional organizations and leagues were formed for civil servants, teachers, women, farmers, doctors, and lawyers. Since the early indoctrination of youth would create the foundation for a strong totalitarian state for the future, youth organizations—the *Hitler Jugend* (HIT-luh YOO-gunt) (Hitler Youth) and its female counterpart, the *Bund Deutscher Mädel* (BOONT DOIT-chur MAY-dul) (League of German Maidens)—were given special attention. The oath required of Hitler Youth members demonstrates the degree of dedication expected of youth in the Nazi state: "In the presence of this blood banner, which represents our Führer, I swear to devote all my energies and my strength to the savior of our country, Adolf Hitler. I am willing and ready to give up my life for him, so help me God."

The creation of the Nazi total state also had an impact on women. Women played a crucial role in the Aryan racial state as bearers of the children who would bring about the triumph of the Aryan race. To the Nazis, the differences between men and women were natural: men were warriors and political leaders, while women were destined to be wives and mothers.

Nazi ideas determined employment opportunities for women. The Nazis hoped to drive women out of certain areas of the labor market, including heavy industry or other jobs that might hinder them from bearing healthy children. Certain professions, including university teaching, medicine, and law, were also considered inappropriate for women, especially married women. Instead, the Nazis encouraged women to pursue professional occupations that had direct practical application, such as social work and nursing. The Nazi regime pursued its campaign against working women

with such poster slogans as "Get hold of pots and pans and broom and you'll sooner find a groom!"

The Nazi total state was intended to be an Aryan racial state. From its beginning, the Nazi Party reflected Hitler's strong anti-Semitic beliefs. In September 1935, the Nazis announced new racial laws at the annual party rally in Nuremberg. These "Nuremberg laws" excluded German Jews from German citizenship and forbade marriages and extramarital relations between Jews and German citizens. The Nuremberg laws essentially separated Jews from the Germans politically, socially, and legally and were the natural extension of Hitler's stress on the creation of a "pure" Aryan race.

A more violent phase of anti-Jewish activity took place in 1938 and 1939, initiated on November 9–10, 1938, by the infamous *Kristallnacht* (kri-STAHL-nahkht), or night of shattered glass. The assassination of a secretary in the German embassy in Paris became the pretext for a Nazi-led rampage against the Jews in which synagogues were burned, 7,000 Jewish businesses were destroyed, and at least one hundred Jews were killed. Moreover, 20,000 Jewish males were rounded up and sent to concentration camps. Jews were barred from all public buildings and prohibited from owning, managing, or working in any retail store. Finally, under the direction of the SS, Jews were encouraged to "emigrate from Germany."

The Stalinist Era in the Soviet Union

Joseph Stalin made a significant shift in Soviet economic policy in 1928 when he launched his first five-year plan. Its real goal was nothing less than the transformation of the agrarian Soviet Union into an industrial country virtually overnight. Instead of consumer goods, the first five-year plan emphasized maximum production of capital goods and armaments and succeeded in quadrupling the production of heavy machinery and doubling oil production. Between 1928 and 1937, during the first two five-year plans, steel production increased from 4 million to 18 million tons per year.

Rapid industrialization was accompanied by an equally rapid collectivization of agriculture. Stalin believed that the capital needed for industrial growth could be obtained through agricultural surpluses that would be created by eliminating private farms and pushing people onto collective farms (see the box on p. 731). By eliminating private property, a Communist ideal would also be achieved.

By 1934, Russia's 26 million family farms had been collectivized into 250,000 units. This was done at tremendous cost, since Stalin did not hesitate to starve the peasants, especially

The Formation of Collective Farms

FAMILY & SOCIETY

Accompanying the rapid industrialization of the Soviet Union was the collectivization of agriculture, a feat that involved nothing less than transforming Russia's 26 million family farms into 250,000 collective farms called *kolkhozes* (kuhl-KAHZ-zuhz). This selection provides a firsthand account of how the process worked.

Max Belov, *The History of a Collective Farm*

General collectivization in our village was brought about in the following manner: Two representatives of the [Communist] Party arrived in the village. All the inhabitants were summoned by the ringing of the church bell to a meeting at which the policy of general collectivization was announced. . . . The upshot was that although the meeting lasted two days, from the viewpoint of the Party representatives nothing was accomplished.

After this setback the Party representatives divided the village into two sections and worked each one separately. Two more officials were sent to reinforce the first two. A meeting of our section of the village was held in a stable which had previously belonged to a kulak [wealthy farmer]. The meeting dragged on until dark. Suddenly someone threw a brick at the lamp, and in the dark the peasants began to beat the Party representatives, who jumped out the window and escaped from the village barely alive. The following day seven people were arrested. The militia was called in and stayed in the village until the peasants, realizing their helplessness, calmed down. . . .

By the end of 1930 there were two kolkhozes in our village. Though at first these collectives embraced at most only 70 percent of the peasant households, in the months that followed they gradually absorbed more and more of them.

In these kolkhozes the great bulk of the land was held and worked communally, but each peasant household owned a house of some sort, a small plot of ground and perhaps some livestock. All the members of the kolkhoz were required to work on the kolkhoz a certain number of days each month;

the rest of the time they were allowed to work on their own holdings. They derived their income partly from what they grew on their garden strips and partly from their work in the kolkhoz.

When the harvest was over, and after the farm had met its obligations to the state and to various special funds (for insurance, seed, etc.) and had sold on the market whatever undesignated produce was left, the remaining produce and the farm's monetary income were divided among the kolkhoz members according to the number of "labor days" each one had contributed to the farm's work. . . . It was in 1930 that the kolkhoz members first received their portions out of the "communal kettle." After they had received their earnings, at the rate of 1 kilogram of grain and 55 kopecks per labor day, one of them remarked, "You will live, but you will be very, very thin."

In the spring of 1931 a tractor worked the fields of the kolkhoz for the first time. The tractor was "capable of plowing every kind of hard soil and virgin sod," as Party representatives told us at the meeting in celebration of its arrival. The peasants did not then know that these "steel horses" would carry away a good part of the harvest in return for their work. . . .

By late 1932 more than 80 percent of the peasant households . . . had been collectivized. . . . That year the peasants harvested a good crop and had hopes that the calculations would work out to their advantage and would help strengthen them economically. These hopes were in vain. The kolkhoz workers received only 200 grams of flour per labor day for the first half of the year; the remaining grain, including the seed fund, was taken by the government. The peasants were told that industrialization of the country, then in full swing, demanded grain and sacrifices from them.

 What was the purpose of collectivizing Soviet agriculture? According to Belov, why did the peasants of his village assault the Communist Party representatives? What was the result of their protest?

---

in Ukraine, to force them to comply with the policy of collectivization. Stalin himself supposedly told Winston Churchill during World War II that 10 million peasants died in the artificially created famines of 1932 and 1933. The only concession Stalin made to the peasants was to allow each household to have one tiny, privately owned garden plot.

Stalin's program of rapid industrialization entailed additional costs as well. To achieve his goals, Stalin strengthened the party bureaucracy under his control. Anyone who resisted was sent into forced labor camps in Siberia. Stalin's desire for

sole control of decision making also led to purges of the Old Bolsheviks. Between 1936 and 1938, the most prominent Old Bolsheviks were put on trial and condemned to death. During this same time, Stalin undertook a purge of army officers, diplomats, union officials, party members, intellectuals, and numerous ordinary citizens. One old woman was sent to Siberia for saying, "If people prayed, they would work better." Estimates are that 8 million Russians were arrested; millions died in Siberian forced labor camps. This gave Stalin the distinction of being one of the greatest mass murderers in

Fascist Italy	
Creation of Fascist Party	1919
Mussolini is made prime minister	October 29, 1922
Establishment of Fascist dictatorship	1926
Nazi Germany	
Hitler as Munich politician	1919–1923
Beer Hall Putsch	1923
Hitler is made chancellor	January 30, 1933
Enabling Act	March 23, 1933
Hindenburg dies; Hitler as sole ruler	August 2, 1934
Nuremberg laws	1935
Kristallnacht	November 9–10, 1938
Soviet Union	
First five-year plan begins	1928
Stalin's purges	1936–1938

human history. The Stalinist bloodbath made what some Western intellectuals had hailed as the "new civilization" much less attractive by the late 1930s.

Disturbed by a rapidly declining birthrate, Stalin also reversed much of the permissive social legislation of the early 1920s. Advocating complete equality of rights for women, the Communists had made divorce and abortion easy to obtain while also encouraging women to work outside the home and to set their own moral standards. After Stalin came to power, the family was praised as a miniature collective in which parents were responsible for inculcating values of duty, discipline, and hard work. Abortion was outlawed, and divorced fathers who failed to support their children were fined heavily.

The Stalinist era did witness some positive aspects in the everyday lives of Soviet citizens. To create leaders for the new Communist society, Stalin began a program to enable workers, peasants, and young Communists to receive higher education, especially in engineering. There was also tremendous growth in part-time schools where large numbers of adults took courses to become literate so that they could advance to technical school or college. Increasing numbers of people saw education as the key to better jobs and upward mobility in Soviet society. One woman of peasant background recounted, "In Moscow I had a burning desire to study. Where or what wasn't important; I wanted to study." For what purpose? "We had a saying at work: 'Without that piece of paper [the diploma], you are an insect; with it, a human being.' My lack of higher education prevented me from getting decent wages."[5]

The Rise of Militarism in Japan

The rise of militarism in Japan resulted not from a seizure of power by a new political party but from the growing influence of militant forces at the top of the political hierarchy. During the 1920s, a multiparty system based on democratic practices appearing to be emerging. Two relatively moderate political parties, the Minseito (men-SAY-toh) and the Seiyukai (say-YOO-ky), dominated the legislature and took turns providing executive leadership in the cabinet. Nevertheless, the political system was probably weaker than it seemed at the time. Both of the major parties were heavily dependent on campaign contributions from powerful corporations, and conservative forces connected to the military or the old landed aristocracy were still highly influential behind the scenes. As in the Weimar Republic in Germany during the same period, the actual power base of modern political forces was weak, and politicians unwittingly undermined the fragile system by engaging in bitter attacks on each other.

In the early 1930s, the growing confrontation with China in Manchuria, combined with the onset of the Great Depression, brought an end to the fragile stability of the immediate postwar years. The depression had a disastrous effect on Japan. The value of Japanese exports dropped by 50 percent from 1929 to 1931, and wages dropped nearly as much. Hardest hit were farmers as the price of rice and other staple food crops plummeted.

During the early 1930s, civilian cabinets managed to cope with the economic challenges presented by the depression. By abandoning the gold standard, Prime Minister Inukai Tsuyoshi (ih-NOO-ky tsoo-YOH-shee) was able to lower the price of Japanese goods on the world market, and exports climbed back to earlier levels. But the political parties were no longer able to stem the growing influence of militant nationalist elements.

In May 1932, Tsuyoshi was assassinated by right-wing extremists. He was succeeded by a moderate, Admiral Saito Makoto (sy-TOH muh-KAH-toh), but extremist patriotic societies composed of ultranationalists began to terrorize opponents, assassinating businessmen and public figures identified with the Shidehara (shee-deh-HAH-rah) policy of conciliation toward the outside world (see Chapter 24). Some, such as the publicist Kita Ikki (KEE-tuh IK-kee), were convinced that the parliamentary system had been corrupted by materialism and Western values and should be replaced by a system that would return to traditional Japanese values and imperial authority. His message, "Asia for the Asians," had not won widespread support during the relatively prosperous 1920s but increased in popularity after the Great Depression, which convinced many Japanese that capitalism was unsuitable for Japan. These same people advocated the use of military force to create a self-sufficient Japan that would acquire the resources and raw materials it needed by controlling East Asia.

During the mid-1930s, the government steadily came under the influence of the military and extreme nationalists. Minorities and left-wing elements were persecuted, and moderates were intimidated into silence. Terrorists on trial for participating in assassination attempts portrayed themselves as selfless patriots and received light sentences. Japan continued to hold national elections, and moderate candidates continued to receive substantial popular support, but the cabinets were dominated by the military or advocates of Japanese expansionism. In February 1936, junior army officers led a coup, briefly occupying the Diet building and other key government installations in Tokyo and assassinating several members of the cabinet. The ringleaders were quickly tried and convicted of treason, but under conditions that further strengthened the influence of the military.

The Path to War

 FOCUS QUESTION: What were the underlying causes of World War II, and what specific steps taken by Nazi Germany and Japan led to war?

Only twenty years after the "war to end war," the world plunged back into the nightmare. The efforts at collective security in the 1920s—the League of Nations, the attempts at disarmament, the pacts and treaties—all proved meaningless in view of the growth of Nazi Germany and the rise of Japan.

The Path to War in Europe

World War II in Europe had its beginnings in the ideas of Adolf Hitler, who believed that only so-called Aryans were capable of building a great civilization. But to Hitler, the Germans, the leading group of Aryans, were threatened from the east by a large mass of "inferior" peoples, the Slavs, who had learned to use German weapons and technology. Germany needed more land to support a larger population and be a great power. Already in the 1920s, in the second volume of *Mein Kampf*, Hitler had indicated where a National Socialist regime would find this land: "And so we National Socialists . . . take up where we broke off six hundred years ago. We stop the endless German movement to the south and west, and turn our gaze toward the land in the east. . . . If we speak of soil in Europe today, we can primarily have in mind only Russia and her vassal border states."[6] Once Russia had been conquered, its land could be resettled by German peasants while the Slavic population could be used as slave labor to build the Aryan racial state that would dominate Europe for a thousand years. Hitler's conclusion was apparent: Germany must prepare for its inevitable war with the Soviet Union.

A DIPLOMATIC REVOLUTION: SCRAPPING THE TREATY OF VERSAILLES When Hitler became chancellor on January 30, 1933, Germany's situation in Europe seemed weak. The Versailles treaty had created a demilitarized zone on Germany's western border that would allow the French to move into the heavily industrialized parts of Germany in the event of war. To Germany's east, the smaller states, such as Poland and Czechoslovakia, had defensive treaties with France. The Versailles treaty had also limited Germany's army to 100,000 troops, with no air force and only a small navy.

Posing as a man of peace in his public speeches, Hitler emphasized that Germany wished only to revise the unfair provisions of Versailles by peaceful means and achieve Germany's rightful place among the European states. On March 9, 1935, he announced the creation of a new air force and one week later the introduction of a military draft that would expand Germany's army from 100,000 to 550,000 troops. Hitler's unilateral repudiation of the Versailles treaty brought a swift reaction, as France, Great Britain, and Italy condemned Germany's action and warned against future aggressive steps. But nothing concrete was done.

On March 7, 1936, buoyed by his conviction that the Western democracies had no intention of using force to maintain the Treaty of Versailles, Hitler sent German troops into the demilitarized Rhineland. According to the Versailles treaty, the French had the right to use force against any violation of the demilitarized Rhineland. But France would not act without British support, and the British viewed the occupation of German territory by German troops as reasonable action by a dissatisfied power. The *London Times* noted that the Germans were only "going into their own back garden."

Meanwhile, Hitler gained new allies. In October 1935, Benito Mussolini had committed Fascist Italy to imperial expansion by invading Ethiopia. Angered by French and British opposition to his invasion, Mussolini welcomed Hitler's support and began to draw closer to the German dictator he had once called a buffoon. The joint intervention of Germany and Italy on behalf of General Francisco Franco in the Spanish Civil War in 1936 also drew the two nations closer. In October 1936, Mussolini and Hitler concluded an agreement that recognized their common political and economic interests, and one month later, Mussolini referred publicly to the new Rome-Berlin Axis. Also in November, Germany and Japan (the rising military power in the Far East) concluded the Anti-Comintern Pact and agreed to maintain a common front against communism.

By the end of 1936, Hitler and Nazi Germany had achieved a "diplomatic revolution" in Europe. The Treaty of Versailles had been virtually scrapped, and Germany was once more a "world power," as Hitler proclaimed. Hitler was convinced that neither the French nor the British would provide much opposition to his plans and decided in 1938 to move on Austria. By threatening Austria with invasion, Hitler coerced the Austrian chancellor into putting Austrian Nazis in charge of the government. The new government promptly invited German troops to enter Austria and assist in maintaining law and order. One day later, on March 13, 1938, after his triumphal return to his native land, Hitler formally annexed Austria to Germany. Great Britain's ready acknowledgment of Hitler's action only increased the German dictator's contempt for Western weakness.

THE TAKEOVER OF CZECHOSLOVAKIA The annexation of Austria improved Germany's strategic position in central Europe and put Hitler in position to achieve his next objective—the destruction of Czechoslovakia. This goal might have seemed unrealistic, as democratic Czechoslovakia was fully prepared to defend itself and was well supported by pacts with France and the Soviet Union. Hitler believed, however, that France and Britain would not use force to defend Czechoslovakia.

He was right again. On September 15, 1938, Hitler demanded the cession of the Sudetenland (soo-DAY-tun-land) (an area in northwestern Czechoslovakia inhabited largely by ethnic Germans) to Germany and expressed his willingness to risk "world war" if he was refused. Instead of

Hitler Arrives in Vienna. By threatening to invade Austria, Hitler forced the Austrian government to capitulate to his wishes. Austria was annexed to Germany. Shown here is the triumphal arrival of Hitler in Vienna on March 13, 1938. Seated beside him is Arthur Seyss-Inquart, Hitler's new handpicked governor of Austria.

objecting, the British, French, Germans, and Italians—at a hastily arranged conference at Munich—reached an agreement that essentially met all of Hitler's demands. German troops were allowed to occupy the Sudetenland as the Czechs, abandoned by their Western allies and the Soviet Union, stood by helplessly. The Munich Conference was the high point of Western **appeasement** of Hitler. When Neville Chamberlain, the British prime minister, returned to England from Munich, he boasted that the Munich agreement meant "peace for our time." Hitler had promised Chamberlain that he had made his last demand. Like scores of politicians before him, Chamberlain had believed Hitler's promises (see the box on p. 735).

POLAND Munich confirmed Hitler's perception that the Western democracies were weak and would not fight. Hitler was increasingly convinced of his own infallibility, and he had been pleased but by no means satisfied at Munich. In March 1939, Germany occupied all the Czech lands (Bohemia and Moravia) while the Slovaks, with his encouragement, declared their independence of the Czechs and became a puppet state (Slovakia) of Nazi Germany. On the evening of March 15, 1939, Hitler triumphantly declared in Prague that he would be known as the greatest German of them all.

At last, the Western states realized that they had to react vigorously to the Nazi threat. Hitler's unremitting aggression made clear that his promises were worthless. When he began to demand the return to Germany of Danzig, which had been made a free city by the Treaty of Versailles to serve as a seaport for Poland, Britain recognized the danger and offered to protect Poland in the event of war. At the same time, both France and Britain realized that, among the European powers, only the Soviet Union was powerful enough to counter Nazi aggression and so began political and military negotiations with Stalin. Their distrust of Soviet communism, however, made an alliance unlikely.

Meanwhile, Hitler pressed on in the belief that Britain and France would not fight over Poland. To preclude an alliance between the western European states and the Soviet Union, which would create the danger of a two-front war, Hitler, ever the opportunist, negotiated his own nonaggression pact with Stalin and shocked the world with its announcement, on August 23, 1939. The treaty with the Soviet Union gave Hitler the freedom to attack Poland. He told his generals, "Now Poland is in the position in which I wanted her. . . . I am only afraid that at the last moment some swine or other will yet submit to me a plan for mediation."[7] He need not have worried. On September 1, German forces invaded Poland; two days later, Britain and France declared war on Germany. Europe was again at war.

The Path to War in Asia

In September 1931, on the pretext that the Chinese had attacked a Japanese railway near Mukden (MOOK-dun) (the "Mukden incident" had actually been carried out by Japanese saboteurs), Japanese military units seized Manchuria. Japanese officials in Tokyo were divided over the wisdom of the takeover, but the moderates were unable to control the army. Eventually, worldwide protests against the Japanese action led the League of Nations to send an investigative commission to Manchuria. When the commission issued a report condemning the seizure, Japan withdrew from the League. Over the next several years, the Japanese consolidated their hold on Manchuria, renaming it Manchukuo (man-CHOO-kwoh) and placing it under the titular authority of the former Chinese emperor and now Japanese puppet Puyi (POO-YEE). Japan now began to expand into northern China.

Not all politicians in Tokyo agreed with this aggressive policy, but right-wing terrorists assassinated some of the key critics and intimidated others into silence. By the mid-1930s, militants connected with the government and the armed forces were effectively in control of Japanese politics. The United States refused to recognize the Japanese takeover of Manchuria but was unwilling to threaten the use of force. Instead, the Americans attempted to appease Japan in the hope of encouraging Japanese moderates. As a senior U.S. diplomat with long experience in Asia warned in a memorandum to the president:

Utter defeat of Japan would be no blessing to the Far East or to the world. It would merely create a new set of stresses, and substitute for Japan the USSR as the successor to Imperial Russia—as a contestant (and at least an equally unscrupulous and dangerous one) for the mastery of the East. Nobody except perhaps Russia would gain from our victory in such a war.[8]

The Munich Conference

At the Munich Conference, the leaders of France and Great Britain capitulated to Hitler's demands on Czechoslovakia. Although the British prime minister, Neville Chamberlain, defended his actions at Munich as necessary for peace, another British statesman, Winston Churchill, characterized the settlement at Munich as "a disaster of the first magnitude."

Winston Churchill, Speech to the House of Commons, October 5, 1938

I will begin by saying what everybody would like to ignore or forget but which must nevertheless be stated, namely, that we have sustained a total and unmitigated defeat, and that France has suffered even more than we have. . . . The utmost my right honorable Friend the Prime Minister . . . has been able to gain for Czechoslovakia and in the matters which were in dispute has been that the German dictator, instead of snatching his victuals from the table, has been content to have them served to him course by course. . . . And I will say this, that I believe the Czechs, left to themselves and told they were going to get no help from the Western Powers, would have been able to make better terms than they have got. . . .

We are in the presence of a disaster of the first magnitude which has befallen Great Britain and France. Do not let us blind ourselves to that. . . .

And do not suppose that this is the end. This is only the beginning of the reckoning. This is only the first sip, the first foretaste of a bitter cup which will be proffered to us year by year unless by a supreme recovery of moral health and mar-

tial vigor, we arise again and take our stand for freedom as in the olden time.

Neville Chamberlain, Speech to the House of Commons, October 6, 1938

That is my answer to those who say that we should have told Germany weeks ago that, if her army crossed the border of Czechoslovakia, we should be at war with her. We had no treaty obligations and no legal obligations to Czechoslovakia. When we were convinced, as we became convinced, that nothing any longer would keep the Sudetenland within the Czechoslovakian State, we urged the Czech Government as strongly as we could to agree to the cession of territory, and to agree promptly. . . . It was a hard decision for anyone who loved his country to take, but to accuse us of having by that advice betrayed the Czechoslovakian State is simply preposterous. What we did was to save her from annihilation and give her a chance of new life as a new State, which involves the loss of territory and fortifications, but may perhaps enable her to enjoy in the future and develop a national existence under a neutrality and security comparable to that which we see in Switzerland today. Therefore, I think the Government deserve the approval of this House for their conduct of affairs in this recent crisis which has saved Czechoslovakia from destruction and Europe from Armageddon.

 What were the opposing views of Churchill and Chamberlain on the Munich Conference? Why did they disagree so much? With whom do you agree? Why?

JAPANESE AGGRESSION IN CHINA For the moment, the prime victim of Japanese aggression was China. Chiang Kai-shek attempted to avoid a confrontation with Japan so that he could deal with the Communists, whom he considered the greater threat. When clashes between Chinese and Japanese troops broke out, he sought to appease the Japanese by granting them the authority to administer areas in northern China. But as Japan moved steadily southward, popular protests in Chinese cities against Japanese aggression intensified. In December 1936, Chiang was briefly kidnapped by military forces commanded by General Zhang Xueliang (JAHNG scheh-LEE-AHNG), who compelled him to end his military efforts against the Communists in Yan'an and form a new united front against the Japanese. After Chinese and Japanese forces clashed at Marco Polo Bridge, south of Beijing, in July 1937, China refused to apologize, and hostilities spread.

Japan had not planned to declare war on China, but neither side would compromise, and the 1937 incident eventually turned into a major conflict. The Japanese advanced up the Yangtze

River valley and seized the Chinese capital of Nanjing in December, but Chiang Kai-shek refused to capitulate and moved his government upriver to Hankou (HAHN-kow). When the Japanese seized that city, he moved on to Chongqing (chung-CHING), in remote Sichuan (suh-CHWAHN) province. Japanese strategists had hoped to force Chiang to join a Japanese-dominated New Order in East Asia, comprising Japan, Manchuria, and China. This was part of a larger plan to seize Soviet Siberia with its rich resources and create a new "Monroe Doctrine for Asia" under which Japan would guide its Asian neighbors on the path to development and prosperity (see the box on p. 736). After all, who better to instruct Asian societies on modernization than the one Asian country that had already achieved it?

ADVANCE TO THE SOUTH During the late 1930s, Japan began to cooperate with Nazi Germany on the assumption that the two countries would ultimately launch a joint attack on the Soviet Union and divide up its resources between them. But when Germany surprised the world by signing a

Japan's Justification for Expansion

POLITICS & GOVERNMENT

Advocates of Japanese expansion justified their proposals by claiming both economic necessity and moral imperatives. Note the familiar combination of motives in this passage written by an extremist military leader in the late 1930s.

Hashimoto Kingoro on the Need for Emigration and Expansion

We have already said that there are only three ways left to Japan to escape from the pressure of surplus population. We are like a great crowd of people packed into a small and narrow room, and there are only three doors through which we might escape, namely emigration, advance into world markets, and expansion of territory. The first door, emigration, has been barred to us by the anti-Japanese immigration policies of other countries. The second door, advance into world markets, is being pushed shut by tariff barriers and the abrogation of commercial treaties. What should Japan do when two of the three doors have been closed against her?

It is quite natural that Japan should rush upon the last remaining door.

It may sound dangerous when we speak of territorial expansion, but the territorial expansion of which we speak does not in any sense of the word involve the occupation of the possessions of other countries, the planting of the Japanese flag thereon, and the declaration of their annexation to Japan. It is just that since the Powers have suppressed the circulation of Japanese materials and merchandise abroad, we are looking for some place overseas where Japanese capital, Japanese skills and Japanese labor can have free play, free from the oppression of the white race.

We would be satisfied with just this much. What moral right do the world powers who have themselves closed to us the two doors of emigration and advance into world markets have to criticize Japan's attempt to rush out of the third and last door?

If they do not approve of this, they should open the doors which they have closed against us and permit the free movement overseas of Japanese emigrants and merchandise. . . .

At the time of the Manchurian incident, the entire world joined in criticism of Japan. They said that Japan was an untrustworthy nation. They said that she had recklessly brought cannon and machine guns into Manchuria, which was the territory of another country, flown airplanes over it, and finally occupied it. But the military action taken by Japan was not in the least a selfish one. Moreover, we do not recall ever having taken so much as an inch of territory belonging to another nation. The result of this incident was the establishment of the splendid new nation of Manchuria. The Powers are still discussing whether or not to recognize this new nation, but regardless of whether or not other nations recognize her, the Manchurian empire has already been established, and now, seven years after its creation, the empire is further consolidating its foundations with the aid of its friend, Japan.

And if it is still protested that our actions in Manchuria were excessively violent, we may wish to ask the white race just which country it was that sent warships and troops to India, South Africa, and Australia and slaughtered innocent natives, bound their hands and feet with iron chains, lashed their backs with iron whips, proclaimed these territories as their own, and still continues to hold them to this very day.

What arguments does Hashimoto Kingoro make in favor of territorial expansion? What is his reaction to the condemnation of his proposal by western European nations?

---

nonaggression pact with the Soviets in August 1939, Japanese strategists were compelled to reevaluate their long-term objectives. Japan was not strong enough to defeat the Soviet Union alone, as a small but bitter border war along the Siberian frontier near Manchuria had amply demonstrated. So the Japanese began to shift their sights southward to the vast resources of Southeast Asia—the oil of the Dutch East Indies, the rubber and tin of Malaya, and the rice of Burma and Indochina.

A move southward, of course, would risk war with the European colonial powers and the United States. Japan's attack on China in the summer of 1937 had already aroused strong criticism abroad, particularly from the United States, where President Franklin Roosevelt threatened to "quarantine" the aggressors after Japanese military units bombed an American naval ship operating in China. Public fear of

involvement forced the president to draw back, but when Japan suddenly demanded the right to occupy airfields and exploit economic resources in French Indochina in the summer of 1940, the United States warned the Japanese that it would cut off the sale of oil and scrap iron unless Japan withdrew from the area and returned to its borders of 1931.

The Japanese viewed the American threat of retaliation as an obstacle to their long-term objectives. Japan badly needed oil and scrap iron from the United States. Should they be cut off, Japan would have to find them elsewhere. The Japanese were thus caught in a vise. To obtain guaranteed access to natural resources that were necessary to fuel the Japanese military machine, Japan must risk being cut off from its current source of raw materials that would be needed in case of a conflict. After much debate, the Japanese decided to launch

© Keystone/Getty Images

A Japanese Victory in China. After consolidating its authority over Manchuria, Japan began to expand into northern China. Direct hostilities between Japanese and Chinese forces began in 1937. This photograph shows victorious Japanese forces in January 1938 riding under the arched Chungshan Gate in Nanjing after they had conquered the Chinese capital city. By 1939, Japan had conquered most of eastern China.

a surprise attack on American and European colonies in Southeast Asia in the hope of a quick victory that would evict the United States from the region.

World War II

> **Q** FOCUS QUESTION: What were the main events of World War II in Europe and Asia?

Unleashing an early form of **Blitzkrieg** (BLITZ-kreeg), or "lightning war," Hitler stunned Europe with the speed and efficiency of the German attack. Moving into Poland with about 1.5 million troops from two fronts, German forces used armored columns or panzer divisions (a *panzer division* was a strike force of about three hundred tanks and accompanying forces and supplies) supported by airplanes to break quickly through Polish lines and encircle the outnumbered and poorly equipped Polish armies. The coordinated air and ground assaults included the use of Stuka dive bombers; as they descended from the skies, their sirens emitted a blood-curdling shriek, adding a frighteningly destructive element to the German attack. Regular infantry units, still on foot with their supplies drawn by horses, then marched in to hold the newly conquered territory. Soon afterward, Soviet military forces attacked eastern Poland. Within four weeks, Poland had surrendered. On September 28, 1939, Germany and the Soviet Union officially divided Poland between them.

Europe at War

Although Hitler's hopes to avoid a war with the western European states were dashed when France and Britain

declared war on September 3, he was confident that he could control the situation. After a winter of waiting (called the "phony war"), Hitler resumed his aggression on April 9, 1940, with another Blitzkrieg, against Denmark and Norway (see Map 25.1). One month later, on May 10, the Germans launched an attack on the Netherlands, Belgium, and France. The main assault through Luxembourg and the Ardennes forest was completely unexpected by the French and British forces. German panzer divisions broke through the weak French defensive positions there and raced across northern France, splitting the Allied armies and trapping French troops and the entire British army on the beaches of Dunkirk. Only by heroic efforts did the British succeed in a gigantic evacuation of 330,000 Allied (mostly British) troops. The French capitulated on June 22. German armies occupied about three-fifths of France, while the French hero of World War I, Marshal Henri Pétain (AHN-ree pay-TANH) (1856–1951), established an authoritarian regime—known as Vichy (VISH-ee) France—over the remainder. Germany was now in control of western and central Europe, but Britain still had not been defeated.

THE PROBLEM OF BRITAIN As Hitler realized, an amphibious invasion of Britain would be possible only if Germany

CHRONOLOGY The Path to War, 1931–1939	
Japan seizes Manchuria	September 1931
Hitler becomes chancellor of Germany	January 30, 1933
Hitler announces a German air force	March 9, 1935
Hitler announces military conscription	March 16, 1935
Mussolini invades Ethiopia	October 1935
Hitler occupies the demilitarized Rhineland	March 7, 1936
Mussolini and Hitler intervene in the Spanish Civil War	1936
Rome-Berlin Axis formed	October 1936
Anti-Comintern Pact (Japan and Germany)	November 1936
Japan invades China	July 1937
Germany annexes Austria	March 13, 1938
Munich Conference: Sudetenland goes to Germany	September 29, 1938
Germany occupies the rest of Czechoslovakia	March 1939
German-Soviet Nonaggression Pact	August 23, 1939
Germany invades Poland	September 1, 1939
Britain and France declare war on Germany	September 3, 1939

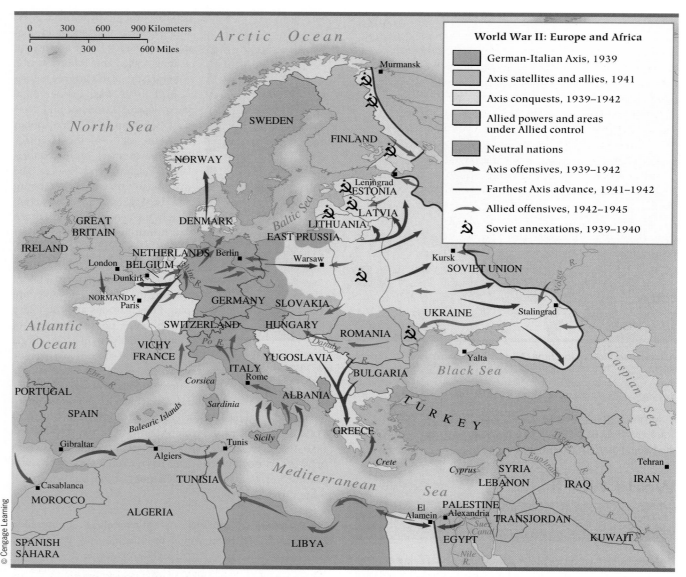

MAP 25.1 **World War II in Europe and North Africa.** With its fast and effective military, Germany quickly overwhelmed much of western Europe. Hitler had overestimated his country's capabilities, however, and underestimated those of his foes. By late 1942, his invasion of the Soviet Union was failing, and the United States had become a major factor in the war. The Allies successfully invaded Italy in 1943 and France in 1944.

 Which countries were neutral, and how did geography help make their neutrality an option?

gained control of the air. At the beginning of August 1940, the German air force, or Luftwaffe (LOOFT-vahf-uh), launched a major offensive against British air and naval bases, harbors, communication centers, and war industries. The British fought back doggedly, supported by an effective radar system that gave them early warning of German attacks. Nevertheless, the British air force suffered critical losses by the end of August and was probably saved by a change in Hitler's strategy. In September, in retaliation for a British attack on Berlin, Hitler ordered a shift from military targets to massive bombing of British cities to break British morale. The British rebuilt their air strength quickly and were soon inflicting major losses on Luftwaffe bombers. By the end of September, Germany had lost the Battle of Britain, and the invasion of Britain had to be postponed.

At this point, Hitler pursued the possibility of a Mediterranean strategy, which would involve capturing Egypt and the Suez Canal and closing the Mediterranean to British ships, thereby shutting off Britain's supply of oil. Hitler's commitment to the Mediterranean was never wholehearted, however. His initial plan was to let the Italians defeat the British in North Africa, but this strategy failed when the British routed the Italian army. Although Hitler then sent German troops to the North African theater of war, his primary concern lay elsewhere; he had already reached the decision to fulfill his lifetime obsession with the acquisition of territory in the east.

INVASION OF THE SOVIET UNION Although he had no desire for a two-front war, Hitler became convinced that

Britain was remaining in the war only because it expected Soviet support. If the Soviet Union were smashed, Britain's last hope would be eliminated. Moreover, Hitler had convinced himself that the Soviet Union, with what he contemptuously regarded as its Jewish-Bolshevik leadership and a pitiful army, could be defeated quickly and decisively. Although the invasion of the Soviet Union was scheduled for spring 1941, the attack was delayed because of problems in the Balkans. Hitler had already obtained the political cooperation of Hungary, Bulgaria, and Romania, but Mussolini's disastrous invasion of Greece in October 1940 exposed Hitler's southern flank to British air bases in that country. To secure his Balkan flank, German troops seized both Yugoslavia and Greece in April 1941. Feeling reassured, Hitler turned to the east and invaded the Soviet Union, believing that the Soviets could still be decisively defeated before winter set in.

On June 22, 1941, Nazi Germany launched its attack on the Soviet Union, by far the largest invasion the Germans had yet attempted. The German force consisted of 180 divisions, including 20 panzer divisions, 8,000 tanks, and 3,200 airplanes. German troops were stretched out along an 1,800-mile front. The Soviets had 160 infantry divisions but were able to mobilize another 300 divisions out of reserves within half a year. Hitler had badly miscalculated the potential power of the Soviets. The German troops advanced rapidly, capturing 2 million Soviet soldiers. By November, one German army group had swept through Ukraine, while a second was besieging Leningrad; a third approached within 25 miles of Moscow, the Russian capital.

An early winter and unexpected Soviet resistance, however, brought the German advance to a halt. Armor and transport vehicles stalled in temperatures of 30 degrees below zero. Hitler's commanders wished to withdraw and regroup for the following spring, but Hitler refused. Fearing the disintegration of his lines, he insisted that there would be no retreat. A Soviet counterattack in December 1941 by an army supposedly exhausted by Nazi victories came as an ominous ending to the year. Although the Germans managed to hold on and reestablish their lines, a war diary kept by a soldier in Panzer Group Three described the desperate situation: "Discipline is breaking down. More and more soldiers are heading west on foot without weapons. . . . The road is under constant air attack. Those killed by bombs are no longer being buried. All the hangers-on (cargo troops, Luftwaffe, supply trains) are pouring to the rear in full flight."[9] By December 1941, another of Hitler's decisions—the declaration of war on the United States—probably made his defeat inevitable and turned another European conflict into a global one.

Japan at War

On December 7, 1941, Japanese carrier-based aircraft attacked the U.S. naval base at Pearl Harbor in the Hawaiian Islands. The same day, other units launched assaults on the Philippines and began advancing toward the British colony of Malaya (see Map 25.2). Shortly thereafter, Japanese forces invaded the Dutch East Indies and occupied a number of islands in the Pacific Ocean. In some cases, as on the Bataan (buh-TAN or buh-TAHN) peninsula and the island of Corregidor (kuh-REG-ih-dor) in the Philippines, resistance was fierce, but by the spring of 1942, almost all of Southeast Asia and much of the western Pacific had fallen into Japanese hands. Japan then announced its intention to liberate the colonies of Southeast Asia from Western rule. For the moment, however, it needed the resources of the region for its war machine and placed its conquests on a wartime basis.

Japanese leaders had hoped that their lightning strike at American bases would destroy the U.S. Pacific fleet and persuade the Roosevelt administration to accept Japanese domination of the Pacific. The American people, in the eyes of Japanese leaders, had been made soft by material indulgence. But the Japanese had miscalculated. The attack on Pearl Harbor galvanized American public opinion and won broad support for Roosevelt's war policy. The United States now joined with European nations and Nationalist China in a combined effort to defeat Japan and bring an end to its hegemony in the Pacific. Believing that American involvement in the Pacific would render the United States ineffective in the European theater of war, Hitler declared war on the United States four days after Pearl Harbor.

The Turning Point of the War, 1942–1943

The entry of the United States into the war created a coalition (the Grand Alliance) that ultimately defeated the Axis Powers (Germany, Italy, and Japan). Nevertheless, the three major Allies—Britain, the United States, and the Soviet Union—had to overcome mutual suspicions before they could operate as an effective alliance. Two factors aided that process. First, Hitler's declaration of war on the United States made it easier for the Americans to accept the British and Russian contention that the defeat of Germany should be the first priority of the United States. For that reason, the United States, under its lend-lease program (which had begun before U.S. entry into the war), sent large amounts of military aid, including $50 billion worth of trucks, planes, and other arms, to the British and the Soviets. Also important to the alliance was the tacit agreement of the three chief Allies to stress military operations while ignoring political differences and larger strategic issues concerning any postwar settlement. At the beginning of 1943, the Allies agreed to fight until the Axis Powers surrendered unconditionally. Although this principle of **unconditional surrender** prevented a repeat of the mistake of World War I, which ended in 1918 with an armistice rather than a total victory, it likely discouraged dissident Germans and Japanese from attempting to overthrow their governments in order to arrange a negotiated peace. At the same time, it did have the effect of cementing the Grand Alliance by making it nearly impossible for Hitler to divide his foes.

Defeat, however, was far from Hitler's mind at the beginning of 1942. As Japanese forces advanced into Southeast Asia and the Pacific after crippling the American naval fleet at Pearl Harbor, Hitler and his European allies continued the war in Europe against Britain and the Soviet Union. Until the fall of 1942, it appeared that the Germans might still prevail on the battlefield. Reinforcements in North Africa enabled

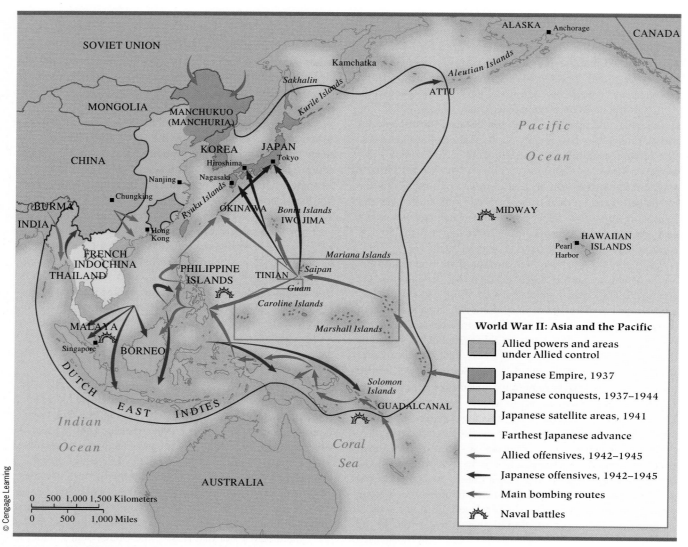

MAP 25.2 World War II in Asia and the Pacific. In 1937, Japan invaded northern China, beginning its effort to create a "Great East-Asia Co-Prosperity Sphere." Further expansion led the United States to end iron and oil sales to Japan. Deciding that war with the United States was inevitable, Japan engineered a surprise attack on Pearl Harbor.

 Why was control of the islands in the western Pacific of great importance both to the Japanese and to the Allies?

the Afrika Korps under General Erwin Rommel (RAHM-ul) to break through the British defenses in Egypt and advance toward Alexandria. In the spring of 1942, a renewed German offensive in the Soviet Union led to the capture of the entire Crimea, causing Hitler to boast in August 1942:

> As the next step, we are going to advance south of the Caucasus and then help the rebels in Iran and Iraq against the English. Another thrust will be directed along the Caspian Sea toward Afghanistan and India. Then the English will run out of oil. In two years we'll be on the borders of India. Twenty to thirty elite German divisions will do. Then the British Empire will collapse.[10]

But this would be Hitler's last optimistic outburst. By the fall of 1942, the war had turned against the Germans.

NORTH AFRICA AND THE EASTERN FRONT In North Africa, British forces had stopped Rommel's troops at El Alamein

(ell ah-lah-MAYN), Egypt, in the summer of 1942 and then forced them back across the desert. In November 1942, British and American forces invaded French North Africa and forced the German and Italian troops to surrender in May 1943. On the Eastern Front, the turning point of the war occurred at Stalingrad. After the capture of the Crimea, Hitler's generals wanted him to concentrate on the Caucasus and its oil fields, but Hitler decided that Stalingrad, a major industrial center on the Volga, should be taken first. Between November 1942 and February 1943, German troops were stopped, then encircled, and finally forced to surrender on February 2, 1943 (see the box on p. 741). The entire German Sixth Army of 300,000 men was lost. By February 1943, German forces in Russia were back to their positions of June 1942. By the spring of 1943, long before western Allied troops returned to the European continent, even Hitler knew that the Germans would not defeat the Soviet Union.

A German Soldier at Stalingrad

POLITICS & GOVERNMENT

The Soviet victory at Stalingrad was a major turning point in World War II. This excerpt comes from the diary of a German soldier who fought and died in the Battle of Stalingrad. His dreams of victory and a return home with medals were soon dashed by the realities of Soviet resistance.

Diary of a German Soldier

Today, after we'd had a bath, the company commander told us that if our future operations are as successful, we'll soon reach the Volga, take Stalingrad, and then the war will inevitably soon be over. Perhaps we'll be home by Christmas.

July 29. The company commander says the Russian troops are completely broken, and cannot hold out any longer. To reach the Volga and take Stalingrad is not so difficult for us. The Führer knows where the Russians' weak point is. Victory is not far away. . . .

August 10. The Führer's orders were read out to us. He expects victory of us. We are all convinced that they can't stop us.

August 12. This morning outstanding soldiers were presented with decorations. . . . Will I really go back to Elsa without a decoration? I believe that for Stalingrad the Führer will decorate even me. . . .

September 4. We are being sent northward along the front toward Stalingrad. We marched all night and by dawn had reached Voroponovo Station. We can already see the smoking town. It's a happy thought that the end of the war is getting nearer. That's what everyone is saying. . . .

September 8. Two days of nonstop fighting. The Russians are defending themselves with insane stubbornness. Our regiment has lost many men. . . .

September 16. Our battalion, plus tanks, is attacking the [grain storage] elevator, from which smoke is pouring—the grain in it is burning; the Russians seem to have set light to it themselves. Barbarism. The battalion is suffering heavy losses. . . .

October 10. The Russians are so close to us that our planes cannot bomb them. We are preparing for a decisive attack. The Führer has ordered the whole of Stalingrad to be taken as rapidly as possible. . . .

October 22. Our regiment has failed to break into the factory. We have lost many men; every time you move you have to jump over bodies. . . .

November 10. A letter from Elsa today. Everyone expects us home for Christmas. In Germany everyone believes we already hold Stalingrad. How wrong they are. If they could only see what Stalingrad has done to our army. . . .

November 21. The Russians have gone over to the offensive along the whole front. Fierce fighting is going on. So, there it is—the Volga, victory, and soon home to our families! We shall obviously be seeing them next in the other world.

November 29. We are encircled. It was announced this morning that the Führer has said: "The army can trust me to do everything necessary to ensure supplies and rapidly break the encirclement."

December 3. We are on hunger rations and waiting for the rescue that the Führer promised. . . .

December 14. Everybody is racked with hunger. Frozen potatoes are the best meal, but to get them out of the ice-covered ground under fire from Russian bullets is not so easy. . . .

December 26. The horses have already been eaten. I would eat a cat; they say its meat is also tasty. The soldiers look like corpses or lunatics, looking for something to put in their mouths. They no longer take cover from Russian shells; they haven't the strength to walk, run away, and hide. A curse on this war!

 What did this soldier believe about the Führer? Why? What was the source of his information? Why is the battle for Stalingrad considered a major turning point in World War II?

ASIA The tide of battle in the Far East also turned dramatically in 1942. In the Battle of the Coral Sea on May 7 and 8, 1942, American naval forces stopped the Japanese advance and temporarily relieved Australia of the threat of invasion. On June 4, at the Battle of Midway Island, American carrier planes destroyed all four of the attacking Japanese aircraft carriers and established American naval superiority in the Pacific. The victory came at high cost; about two-fifths of the American planes were shot down in the encounter. By the fall of 1942, Allied forces were beginning to gather for offensive operations in three areas: from bases in north Burma and India into the rest of Burma; in the Solomon Islands and on New Guinea, with forces under the direction of American general Douglas MacArthur moving toward the Philippines; and across the Pacific where combined U.S. Army, Marine, and Navy forces would mount attacks against Japanese-held islands. After a series of bitter engagements in the waters of the Solomon Islands from August to November 1942, Japanese fortunes began to fade.

The Last Years of the War

By the beginning of 1943, the tide of battle had turned against Germany, Italy, and Japan. After the Axis forces had surrendered in Tunisia on May 13, 1943, the Allies crossed the Mediterranean and carried the war to Italy. After taking Sicily, Allied troops began the invasion of mainland Italy in September. In the meantime, after the ouster and arrest of Benito Mussolini, a new Italian government offered to surrender to Allied forces. But Mussolini was liberated by the Germans in

The Battle of Stalingrad. The Battle of Stalingrad was a major turning point on the Eastern Front. Shown in the first photograph is a German infantry platoon in the ruins of a tractor factory they had captured in the northern part of Stalingrad. This victory took place on October 15, 1942, at a time when Hitler still believed he was winning the battle for Stalingrad. That belief was soon dashed as a Soviet counteroffensive in November led to a total defeat for the Germans. The second photograph shows thousands of captured soldiers being marched across frozen Soviet soil to prison camps. The soldiers in white fur hats are Romanian. Fewer than 6,000 captured soldiers survived to go home; the remainder—almost 85,000 prisoners—died in captivity.

a daring raid and then set up as the head of a puppet German state in northern Italy while German troops moved in and occupied much of the rest of the country. The new defensive lines established by the Germans in the hills south of Rome were so effective that the Allied advance up the Italian peninsula was a painstaking affair accompanied by heavy casualties. Rome did not fall to the Allies until June 4, 1944. By that time, the Italian war had assumed a secondary role anyway as the Allies prepared to open their long-awaited "second front" in western Europe.

ALLIED ADVANCES IN EUROPE Since the autumn of 1943, the Allies had been planning a cross-channel invasion of France from Britain. Under the direction of the American general Dwight D. Eisenhower (1890–1969), the Allies landed five assault divisions on the beaches of Normandy on June 6, 1944, in history's greatest naval invasion. An initially indecisive German response enabled the Allied forces to establish a beachhead. Within three months, they had landed 2 million men and a half-million vehicles that pushed inland and broke through German defensive lines.

After the breakout, Allied troops moved south and east and liberated Paris by the end of August. By March 1945, they had crossed the Rhine River and advanced farther into Germany. At the end of April 1945, Allied armies in northern Germany moved toward the Elbe River, where they finally linked up with the Soviets. The Soviets had come a long way since the Battle of Stalingrad in 1943. In the summer of 1943, Hitler had gambled on taking the offensive by making use of newly developed heavy tanks, but the German forces were soundly defeated by the Soviets at the Battle of Kursk (KOORSK) (July 5–12), the greatest tank battle of World War II. Soviet forces then began a relentless advance westward. The Soviets had reoccupied Ukraine by the end of 1943 and lifted the siege of Leningrad and moved into the Baltic states by the beginning of 1944. Advancing along a northern front, Soviet troops occupied Warsaw in January 1945 and entered Berlin in April. Meanwhile, Soviet troops along a southern front swept through Hungary, Romania, and Bulgaria.

In January 1945, Hitler had moved into a bunker 55 feet under Berlin to direct the final stages of the war. In his final political testament, Hitler, consistent to the end in his rabid anti-Semitism, blamed the Jews for the war: "Above all I charge the leaders of the nation and those under them to scrupulous observance of the laws of race and to merciless

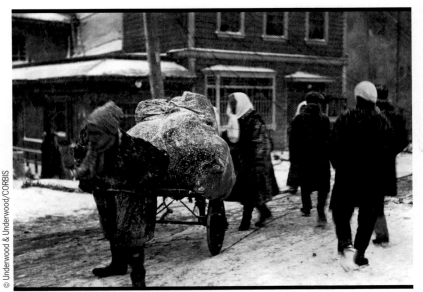

Refugees Flee Japanese Cities. American bombing attacks on Japanese cities began in earnest in November 1944. Built of flimsy materials, Japan's crowded cities were soon devastated by these air raids. This photograph shows refugees carrying a few belongings as they flee the city of Hakodate.

opposition to the universal poisoner of all peoples, international Jewry."[11] Hitler committed suicide on April 30, two days after Mussolini had been shot by partisan Italian forces. On May 7, German commanders surrendered. The war in Europe was over.

DEFEAT OF JAPAN The war in Asia continued. Beginning in 1943, American forces had gone on the offensive and advanced their way, slowly at times, across the Pacific. The Americans took an increasing toll of enemy resources, especially at sea and in the air. As Allied military power drew inexorably closer to the main Japanese islands in the first months of 1945, President Harry Truman, who had succeeded to the presidency on the death of Franklin Roosevelt in April, had an excruciatingly difficult decision to make. Should he use atomic weapons (at the time, only two bombs had been developed, and their effectiveness had not been demonstrated) to bring the war to an end without the necessity of an Allied invasion of the Japanese homeland? As the world knows, Truman answered that question in the affirmative. The first bomb was dropped on the city of Hiroshima (hee-roh-SHEE-muh) on August 6. Truman then called on Japan to surrender or expect a "rain of ruin from the air." When the Japanese did not respond, a second bomb was dropped on Nagasaki (nah-gah-SAH-kee). Japan surrendered unconditionally on August 14. World War II was finally over.

The New Order

 FOCUS QUESTION: What was the nature of the new orders that Germany and Japan attempted to establish in the territories they occupied?

The initial victories of the Germans and the Japanese gave them the opportunity to create new orders in Europe and

Asia. Although both countries presented positive images of these new orders for publicity purposes, in practice both followed policies of ruthless domination of their subject peoples.

The New Order in Europe

After the German victories, Nazi propagandists conjured up glowing images of a **Nazi New Order** in Europe based on "equal chances" for all nations and an integrated economic community. This was not Hitler's conception of a European New Order. He regarded the Europe he had conquered simply as subject to German domination. Only the Germans, he once said, "can really organize Europe."

THE NAZI EMPIRE The Nazi empire stretched across continental Europe from the English Channel in the west to the outskirts of Moscow in the east. In no way was this empire organized systematically or governed efficiently. Some areas, such as western Poland, were directly annexed by Nazi Germany and made into German provinces. The rest of occupied Europe was administered by German military or civilian officials in combination with varying degrees of indirect control from collaborationist regimes.

Racial considerations played an important role in determining how conquered peoples were treated. German civil administrations were established in Norway, Denmark, and the Netherlands because the Nazis considered their peoples

CHRONOLOGY The Course of World War II	
Germany and the Soviet Union divide Poland	September 28, 1939
Blitzkrieg against Denmark and Norway	April 1940
Blitzkrieg against Belgium, Netherlands, and France	May 1940
France surrenders	June 22, 1940
Battle of Britain	Summer-Fall 1940
Nazi seizure of Yugoslavia and Greece	April 1941
Germany invades the Soviet Union	June 22, 1941
Japanese attack Pearl Harbor	December 7, 1941
Battle of the Coral Sea	May 7–8, 1942
Battle of Midway Island	June 4, 1942
Allied invasion of North Africa	November 1942
Germans surrender at Stalingrad	February 2, 1943
Axis forces surrender in North Africa	May 1943
Battle of Kursk	July 5–12, 1943
Invasion of mainland Italy	September 1943
Allied invasion of France	June 6, 1944
Hitler commits suicide	April 30, 1945
Germany surrenders	May 7, 1945
Atomic bomb dropped on Hiroshima	August 6, 1945
Japan surrenders	August 14, 1945

Hitler's Plans for a New Order in the East

POLITICS & GOVERNMENT

Hitler's nightly monologues to his postdinner guests, which were recorded by the Führer's private secretary, Martin Bormann, reveal much about the New Order he wished to create. On the evening of October 17, 1941, Hitler expressed his views on what the Germans would do with their newly conquered territories in the east.

Hitler's Secret Conversations, October 17, 1941

In comparison with the beauties accumulated in Central Germany, the new territories in the East seem to us like a desert. . . . This Russian desert, we shall populate it. . . . We'll take away its character of an Asiatic steppe; we'll Europeanize it. With this object, we have undertaken the construction of roads that will lead to the southernmost point of the Crimea and to the Caucasus. These roads will be studded along their whole length with German towns, and around these towns our colonists will settle.

As for the two or three million men whom we need to accomplish this task, we'll find them quicker than we think. They'll come from Germany, Scandinavia, the Western countries, and America. I shall no longer be here to see all that, but in twenty years the Ukraine will already be a home for twenty million inhabitants besides the natives. In three hundred years, the country will be one of the loveliest gardens in the world.

As for the natives, we'll have to screen them carefully. The Jew, that destroyer, we shall drive out. . . . We shan't settle in the Russian towns, and we'll let them fall to pieces without intervening. And, above all, no remorse on this subject! We're not going to play at children's nurses; we're absolutely without obligations as far as these people are concerned. To struggle against the hovels, chase away the fleas, provide German teachers, bring out newspapers—very little of that for us! We'll confine ourselves, perhaps, to setting up a radio transmitter, under our control. For the rest, let them know just enough to understand our highway signs, so that they won't get themselves run over by our vehicles. . . . There's only one duty: to Germanize this country by the immigration of Germans, and to look upon the natives as Redskins. If these people had defeated us, Heaven have mercy! But we don't hate them. That sentiment is unknown to us. We are guided only by reason. . . .

All those who have the feeling for Europe can join in our work.

In this business I shall go straight ahead, cold-bloodedly. What they may think about me, at this juncture, is to me a matter of complete indifference. I don't see why a German who eats a piece of bread should torment himself with the idea that the soil that produces this bread has been won by the sword.

 What were Hitler's plans for the conquered eastern territories and the peoples who inhabited these lands? Concerning eastern Europeans, do you believe Hitler's statements that "we don't hate them" and "we are guided only by reason"? What motivations do you see behind this monologue?

Aryan, racially kin to the Germans and hence worthy of more lenient treatment. "Inferior" Latin peoples, such as the occupied French, were given military administrations. By 1943, however, as Nazi losses continued to multiply, all the occupied territories of northern and western Europe were ruthlessly exploited for material goods and manpower for Germany's labor needs.

PLANS FOR AN ARYAN RACIAL EMPIRE Because the conquered lands in the east contained the living space for German expansion and were populated in Nazi eyes by racially inferior Slavic peoples, Nazi administration there was considerably more ruthless. Hitler's racial ideology and his plans for an Aryan empire were so important to him that he and the Nazis began to implement their race-based program soon after the conquest of Poland. Heinrich Himmler, a strong believer in Nazi racial ideology and the leader of the SS, was put in charge of German resettlement plans in the east. Himmler's task was to evacuate the inferior Slavic peoples and replace them with Germans, a policy first applied to the new German provinces carved out of western Poland. One million Poles were uprooted and dumped in southern Poland. Hundreds of thousands of ethnic Germans (descendants of Germans who had migrated decades earlier from Germany to different parts of southern and eastern Europe) were encouraged to colonize designated areas in Poland. By 1942, 2 million ethnic Germans had been settled in Poland.

The invasion of the Soviet Union inflated Nazi visions of German colonization in the east. Hitler spoke to his intimate circle of a colossal project of social engineering after the war, in which Poles, Ukrainians, and Russians would become slave labor while German peasants settled on the abandoned lands and Germanized them (see the box above). Nazis involved in this planning were well aware of the human costs. Himmler told a gathering of SS officers that although the destruction of 30 million Slavs was a prerequisite for German plans in the east, "whether nations live in prosperity or starve to death interests me only insofar as we need them as slaves for our culture. Otherwise it is of no interest."[12]

USE OF FOREIGN WORKERS Labor shortages in Germany led to a policy of ruthless mobilization of foreign labor for

Germany. After the invasion of the Soviet Union, the 4 million Russian prisoners of war captured by the Germans along with more than 2 million workers conscripted in France became a major source of heavy labor, but it was wasted by allowing more than 3 million of them to die from neglect. In 1942, a special office was created to recruit labor for German farms and industries. By the summer of 1944, 7 million foreigners were laboring in Germany, constituting 20 percent of the nation's workforce. At the same time, another 7 million workers were supplying forced labor in their own countries on farms, in industries, and even in military camps. Forced labor, however, often proved counterproductive because it created economic chaos in occupied countries and disrupted industrial production that could have helped Germany. The brutality of Germany's recruitment policies often led more and more people to resist the Nazi occupation forces.

The Holocaust

No aspect of the Nazi New Order was more terrifying than the deliberate attempt to exterminate the Jewish people of Europe. Racial struggle was a key element in Hitler's ideology and meant to him a clearly defined conflict of opposites: the Aryans, creators of human cultural development, against the Jews, parasites who were trying to destroy the Aryans. By the beginning of 1939, Nazi policy focused on promoting the "emigration" of German Jews from Germany. Once the war began in September 1939, the so-called Jewish problem took on new dimensions. For a while, there was discussion of the Madagascar Plan, which aspired to the mass shipment of Jews to the island of Madagascar off the east coast of Africa. When war contingencies made this plan impractical, an even more drastic policy was conceived (see the Film & History feature on p. 746).

THE SS AND THE *EINSATZGRUPPEN* Himmler and the SS organization shared Hitler's racial ideology. The SS was given responsibility for what the Nazis called their **Final Solution** to the Jewish problem—the annihilation of the Jewish people. Reinhard Heydrich (RYN-hart HY-drikh) (1904–1942), head of the SS's Security Service, was given administrative responsibility for the Final Solution. After the defeat of Poland, Heydrich ordered the *Einsatzgruppen* (YN-zahtz-groop-un), special strike forces that he had created, to round up all Polish Jews and concentrate them in ghettos established in a number of Polish cities.

In June 1941, the *Einsatzgruppen* were given new responsibilities as mobile killing units. These SS death squads followed the regular army's advance into the Soviet Union. Their job was to round up Jews in the villages and execute and bury them in mass graves, often giant pits dug by the victims themselves before they were shot. Such constant killing produced morale problems among the SS executioners. During a visit to Minsk in the Soviet Union, Himmler tried to build morale by pointing out that "he would not like it if Germans did such a thing gladly. But their conscience was in no way impaired, for they were soldiers who had to carry out every order unconditionally. He alone had responsibility before

God and Hitler for everything that was happening, . . . and he was acting from a deep understanding of the necessity for this operation."[13]

THE DEATH CAMPS Although it has been estimated that as many as a million Jews were killed by the *Einsatzgruppen*, this approach to solving the Jewish problem was soon perceived as inadequate. So the Nazis opted for the systematic annihilation of the European Jewish population in death camps. The plan was simple: Jews from countries occupied by Germany (or sympathetic to Germany) would be rounded up, packed like cattle into freight trains, and shipped to Poland, where six extermination centers were built for this purpose. The largest and most famous was Auschwitz-Birkenau (OW-shvitz-BEER-kuh-now). Medical technicians chose Zyklon B (the commercial name for hydrogen cyanide) as the most effective gas for quickly killing large numbers of people in gas chambers designed to look like shower rooms to facilitate the cooperation of the victims.

Library of Congress (2391, folder 401)

The Holocaust: Mission of the *Einsatzgruppen*. The activation of mobile killing units known as the *Einsatzgruppen* marked the first stage in implementing Hitler's Final Solution, the mass murders of the Holocaust. This picture shows the execution of a Jew by a member of one of these SS killing squads. Onlookers include members of the German army, the German Labor Service, and even Hitler Youth. When it became apparent that this method of killing individuals one by one was inefficient, it was replaced by the death camps, where large groups could be put to death at once.

Europa, Europa (1990)

Directed by Agnieszka Holland, *Europa, Europa* (known as *Hitlerjunge Salomon* [Hitler Youth Salomon] in Germany) is the harrowing story of one Jewish boy's escape from the horrors of Nazi persecution. It is based on the memoirs of Salomon Perel, a German Jew of Polish background who survived by pretending to be a pure Aryan. The film begins in 1938 during *Kristallnacht* when the family of Solly (Salomon's nickname) is attacked in their hometown of Peine, Germany. Solly's sister is killed, and the family moves back to Poland. When the Nazis invade Poland, Solly (Marco Hofschneider) and his brother are sent east, but the brothers become separated, and Solly is placed in a Soviet orphanage in Grodno in the eastern part of Poland occupied by the Soviets.

For two years, Solly becomes a dedicated Communist youth, but when the Germans invade in 1941, he falls into their hands and quickly assumes a new identity in order to survive. He becomes Josef "Jupp" Peters, supposedly the son of German parents from Latvia. Fluent in both Russian and German, Solly/Jupp becomes a translator for the German forces. After an unintended act of bravado, he is rewarded by being sent to a Hitler Youth school where he lives in fear of being exposed as a Jew because of his circumcised penis. He manages to survive the downfall of Nazi Germany and at the end of the war makes his way to Palestine with his brother, who has also survived. Throughout much of the movie, Solly/Jupp lives in constant fear that his true identity as a Jew will be recognized, but his luck, charm, and resourcefulness enable him to survive a series of extraordinary events.

Although there is no way of knowing if each detail of this movie is historically accurate (and a few are clearly inaccurate, such as a bombing run by a plane that was not developed until after the war), overall the story has the ring of truth. The fanaticism of both the Soviet and the Nazi officials who indoctrinate young people seems real. The scene in the Hitler Youth school on how to identify a Jew is realistic, even when it is made ironic by the instructor's choice of Solly/Jupp to demonstrate the characteristics of a true Aryan. The movie also realistically portrays the fearful world in which Jews had to live under the Nazis before the war and the horrible conditions of the Jewish ghettos in Polish cities during the war. The film shows how people had to fight for their survival in a world of

Salomon Perel/Josef Peters (Marco Hofschneider) as a Hitler Youth member

Les Films Du Losange/CCC Filmkunst/The Kobal Collection

ideological madness, when Jews were killed simply for being Jews. The attitudes of the German soldiers also seem real. Many are shown following orders and killing Jews based on the beliefs in which they have been indoctrinated. But the movie also portrays some German soldiers whose humanity did not allow them to kill Jews. One homosexual soldier discovers that Solly/Jupp is a Jew when he tries—unsuccessfully—to have sex with him. The soldier then becomes the boy's protector until he himself is killed in battle.

Many movies have been made about the horrible experiences of Jews during World War II, but this one is quite different from most of them. It might never have been made except for the fact that Salomon Perel, who was told by his brother not to tell his story because no one would believe it, was inspired to write his memoirs after a 1985 reunion with his former Hitler Youth group leader. This passionate and intelligent film is ultimately a result of that encounter.

The death camps were up and running by the spring of 1942. Although initial priority was given to the elimination of the ghettos in Poland, by that summer, Jews were also being shipped from France, Belgium, and the Netherlands. Even as the Allies were making significant advances in 1944, Jews were being shipped from Greece and Hungary. These shipments depended on the cooperation of Germany's Transport Ministry, and despite desperate military needs, the Final Solution was given priority in using railroad cars for the transportation of Jews to death camps.

A harrowing experience awaited the Jews when they arrived at one of the six camps. Rudolf Höss (HESS), commandant at Auschwitz-Birkenau, described it:

We had two SS doctors on duty at Auschwitz to examine the incoming transports of prisoners. The prisoners would be marched by one of the doctors, who would make spot decisions as they walked by. Those who were fit for work were sent into the camp. Others were sent immediately to the extermination plants. Children of tender years were invariably exterminated

The Holocaust: The Camp Commandant and the Camp Victims

POLITICS & GOVERNMENT

The systematic annihilation of millions of men, women, and children in extermination camps makes the Holocaust one of the most horrifying events in history. The first document is taken from an account by Rudolf Höss, commandant of the extermination camp at Auschwitz-Birkenau. In the second document, a French doctor explains what happened to the victims at one of the crematoria described by Höss.

Commandant Höss Describes the Equipment

The two large crematoria, Nos. I and II, were built during the winter of 1942–43. . . . They each . . . could cremate c. 2,000 corpses within twenty-four hours. . . . Crematoria I and II both had underground undressing and gassing rooms which could be completely ventilated. The corpses were brought up to the ovens on the floor above by lift. The gas chambers could hold c. 3,000 people.

The firm of Topf had calculated that the two smaller crematoria, III and IV, would each be able to cremate 1,500 corpses within twenty-four hours. However, owing to the wartime shortage of materials, the builders were obliged to economize and so the undressing rooms and gassing rooms were built above ground and the ovens were of a less solid construction. But it soon became apparent that the flimsy construction of these two four-retort ovens was not up to the demands made on it. No. III ceased operating altogether after a short time and later was no longer used. No. IV had to be repeatedly shut down since after a short period in operation of 4–6 weeks, the ovens and chimneys had burnt out. The victims of the gassing were mainly burnt in pits behind crematorium IV.

The largest number of people gassed and cremated within twenty-four hours was somewhat over 9,000.

A French Doctor Describes the Victims

It is mid-day, when a long line of women, children, and old people enter the yard. The senior official in charge . . . climbs on a bench to tell them that they are going to have a bath and that afterward they will get a drink of hot coffee. They all undress in the yard. . . . The doors are opened and an indescribable jostling begins. The first people to enter the gas chamber begin to draw back. They sense the death which awaits them. The SS men put an end to this pushing and shoving with blows from their rifle butts beating the heads of the horrified women who are desperately hugging their children. The massive oak double doors are shut. For two endless minutes one can hear banging on the walls and screams which are no longer human. And then—not a sound. Five minutes later the doors are opened. The corpses, squashed together and distorted, fall out like a waterfall. . . . The bodies which are still warm pass through the hands of the hairdresser who cuts their hair and the dentist who pulls out their gold teeth. One more transport has just been processed through No. IV crematorium.

What equipment does Höss describe? What process does the French doctor describe? It there any sympathy for the victims in either account? Why or why not? How could such a horrifying process have been allowed to occur?

---

since by reason of their youth they were unable to work. . . . At Auschwitz we endeavored to fool the victims into thinking that they were to go through a delousing process. Of course, frequently they realized our true intentions and we sometimes had riots and difficulties due to that fact.[14]

About 30 percent of the arrivals at Auschwitz were sent to a labor camp; the remainder went to the gas chambers (see the box above). After they had been gassed, the bodies were burned in specially built crematoria. The victims' goods and even their bodies were used for economic gain. Women's hair was cut off, collected, and used to stuff mattresses or make cloth. Some inmates were also subjected to cruel and painful "medical" experiments. Altogether, the Germans killed between 5 and 6 million Jews, more than 3 million of them in the death camps. About 90 percent of the Jewish populations of Poland, the Baltic countries, and

Germany were exterminated. Overall, the Holocaust was responsible for the death of nearly two of every three Jews in Europe.

THE OTHER HOLOCAUST The Nazis were also responsible for another Holocaust, the death by shooting, starvation, or overwork of at least another 9 to 10 million people. Because the Nazis also considered the Gypsies of Europe (like the Jews) a race containing alien blood, they were systematically rounded up for extermination. About 40 percent of Europe's one million Gypsies were killed in the death camps. The leading elements of the "subhuman" Slavic peoples—the clergy, intelligentsia, civil leaders, judges, and lawyers—were arrested and deliberately killed. Probably an additional 4 million Poles, Ukrainians, and Byelorussians lost their lives as slave laborers for Nazi Germany, and 3 to 4 million Soviet

Japan's Plan for Asia

POLITICS & GOVERNMENT

The Japanese objective in World War II was to create a vast Great East-Asia Co-Prosperity Sphere to provide Japan with needed raw materials and a market for its exports. The following passage is from a secret document produced by a high-level government committee in January 1942.

Draft Plan for the Establishment of the Great East-Asia Co-Prosperity Sphere

The Plan. The Japanese empire is a manifestation of morality and its special characteristic is the propagation of the Imperial Way. It is necessary to foster the increased power of the empire, to cause East Asia to return to its original form of independence and co-prosperity by shaking off the yoke of Europe and America, and to let its countries and peoples develop their respective abilities in peaceful cooperation and secure livelihood.

The Form of East Asiatic Independence and Co-Prosperity. The states, their citizens, and resources, comprised in those areas pertaining to the Pacific, Central Asia, and the Indian Oceans formed into one general union are to be established as an autonomous zone of peaceful living and common prosperity on behalf of the peoples of the nations of East Asia. The area including Japan, Manchuria, North China, lower Yangtze River, and the Russian Maritime Province, forms the nucleus of the East Asiatic Union. The Japanese empire possesses a duty as the leader of the East Asiatic Union.

The above purpose presupposes the inevitable emancipation or independence of Eastern Siberia, China, Indo-China, the South Seas, Australia, and India. . . .

Outline of East Asiatic Administration. It is intended that the unification of Japan, Manchukuo, and China in neighborly friendship be realized by the settlement of the Sino-Japanese problems through the crushing of hostile influences in the Chinese interior, and through the construction of a new China. . . . Aggressive American and British influences in East Asia shall be driven out of the area of Indo-China and the South Seas, and this area should be brought into our defense

sphere. The war with Britain and America shall be prosecuted for that purpose. . . .

Chapter 3: Political Construction

Basic Plan. The realization of the great ideal of constructing Greater East Asia Co-Prosperity requires not only the complete prosecution of the current Greater East Asia War but also presupposes another great war in the future. . . .

The following are the basic principles for the political construction of East Asia. . . .

The desires of the peoples in the sphere for their independence shall be respected, and endeavors shall be made for their fulfillment, but proper and suitable forms of government shall be decided for them in consideration of military and economic requirements and of the historical, political, and cultural elements peculiar to each area.

It must also be noted that the independence of various peoples of East Asia should be based on the idea of constructing East Asia as "independent countries existing within the New Order of East Asia" and that this conception differs from an independence based on the idea of liberalism and national self-determination. . . .

Western individualism and materialism shall be rejected, and a moral worldview, the basic principle of whose morality shall be the Imperial Way, shall be established. The ultimate object to be achieved is not exploitation but co-prosperity and mutual help, not competitive conflict but mutual assistance and mild peace, not a formal view of equality but a view of order based on righteous classification, not an idea of rights but an idea of service, and not several worldviews but one unified worldview.

 What were Japan's proposals for a Japanese-led Asia? What distinction did the government committee that drafted this document draw between "Western individualism and materialism" and the "Imperial Way"? Based on this document, were individualism and materialism a part of the Imperial Way?

---

prisoners of war were killed in captivity. The Nazis also singled out homosexuals for persecution, and thousands lost their lives in concentration camps.

The New Order in Asia

Once the takeover was completed, Japanese war policy in the occupied areas in Asia became essentially defensive, as Japan hoped to use its new possessions to meet its burgeoning needs for raw materials, such as tin, oil, and rubber, and also as an outlet for Japanese manufactured goods. To provide an

organizational structure for the arrangement, Japanese leaders set up the Great East-Asia Co-Prosperity Sphere, a self-sufficient economic community designed to provide mutual benefits to the occupied areas and the home country (see the box above). The Ministry for Great East Asia, staffed by civilians, was established in Tokyo in October 1942 to handle arrangements between Japan and the conquered territories.

JAPANESE POLICIES The Japanese conquest of Southeast Asia had been accomplished under the slogan "Asia for the Asiatics," and many Japanese probably sincerely believed that their government was bringing about the liberation of the Southeast Asian peoples from European colonial rule. Japanese officials in the occupied territories quickly made contact with anticolonialist elements and promised that independent governments would be established under Japanese tutelage. Such governments were eventually established in Burma, the Dutch East Indies, Vietnam, and the Philippines.

In fact, however, real power rested with the Japanese military authorities in each territory, and the local Japanese military command was directly subordinated to the army general staff in Tokyo. The economic resources of the colonies were exploited for the benefit of the Japanese war machine, while local peoples were recruited to serve in local military units or conscripted to work on public works projects. In some cases, the people living in the occupied areas were subjected to severe hardships. In Indochina, for example, forced requisitions of rice by the local Japanese authorities for shipment abroad created a food shortage that caused the starvation of more than a million Vietnamese in 1944 and 1945.

The Japanese planned to implant a new moral and social order as well as a new political and economic order in the occupied areas. Occupation policy stressed traditional values such as obedience, community spirit, filial piety, and discipline that reflected the prevailing political and cultural bias in Japan, while supposedly Western values such as materialism, liberalism, and individualism were strongly discouraged. To promote this New Order, occupation authorities gave particular support to local religious organizations but discouraged the formation of formal political parties.

RESENTMENT AND RESISTANCE At first, many Southeast Asian nationalists took Japanese promises at face value and agreed to cooperate with their new masters. In Burma, an independent government was established in 1943 and subsequently declared war on the Allies. But as the exploitative nature of Japanese occupation policies became increasingly clear, sentiment turned against the New Order. Japanese officials sometimes unwittingly provoked resentment by their arrogance and contempt for local customs. In the Dutch East Indies, for example, Indonesians were required to bow in the direction of Tokyo and recognize the divinity of the Japanese emperor—practices that were repugnant to Muslims. In Burma, Buddhist pagodas were sometimes used as military latrines.

Like German soldiers in occupied Europe, Japanese military forces often had little respect for the lives of their subject peoples. In their conquest of Nanjing, China, in 1937, Japanese soldiers had devoted several days to killing, raping, and looting. Almost 800,000 Koreans were sent overseas, most of them as forced laborers, to Japan. Tens of thousands of women from Korea and the Philippines were forced to serve as "comfort women" (prostitutes) for Japanese troops. In construction projects to help their war effort, the Japanese also made extensive use of labor forces composed of both prisoners of war and local peoples. In building the Burma-Thailand railway in 1943, for example, the Japanese used 61,000 Australian, British, and Dutch prisoners of war and almost 300,000 workers from Burma, Malaya, Thailand, and the Dutch East Indies. By the time the railway was completed,

12,000 Allied prisoners of war and 90,000 local workers had died from the inadequate diet and appalling working conditions in an unhealthy climate.

Such Japanese behavior created a dilemma for many nationalists, who had no desire to see the return of the colonial powers. Some turned against the Japanese, while others lapsed into inactivity. Indonesian patriots tried to have it both ways, feigning support for Japan while attempting to sabotage the Japanese administration. In French Indochina, Ho Chi Minh's Indochinese Communist Party established contacts with American military units in southern China and agreed to provide information on Japanese troop movements and rescue downed American flight crews in the area. In Malaya, where Japanese treatment of ethnic Chinese residents was especially harsh, many joined a guerrilla movement against the occupying forces. By the end of the war, little support remained in the region for the erstwhile "liberators."

The Home Front

 FOCUS QUESTION: What were conditions like on the home front for the major belligerents in World War II?

World War II was even more of a total war than World War I. Fighting was much more widespread and covered most of the planet. Economic mobilization was more extensive; so was the mobilization of women. The number of civilians killed was far higher: almost 20 million were killed from bombing raids, mass extermination policies, and attacks by invading armies.

Mobilizing the People

The home fronts of the major belligerents varied considerably, based on local circumstances.

THE SOVIET UNION World War II had an enormous impact on the Soviet Union. Known to the Soviets as the Great Patriotic War, the German-Soviet war witnessed the greatest land battles in history as well as incredible ruthlessness. To Nazi Germany, it was a war of oppression and annihilation that called for merciless measures. Two out of every five persons killed in World War II were Soviet citizens.

The initial defeats of the Soviet Union led to drastic emergency mobilization measures that affected the civilian population. Leningrad, for example, experienced nine hundred days of siege, during which its inhabitants became so desperate for food that they ate dogs, cats, and mice. As the German army made its rapid advance into Soviet territory, the factories in the western part of the Soviet Union were dismantled and shipped to the interior—to the Urals, western Siberia, and the Volga region. Machines were placed on the bare ground, and walls went up around them as workers began their work.

This widespread military, industrial, and economic mobilization created yet another industrial revolution for the Soviet Union (see the comparative essay "Paths to Modernization" on p. 750). Stalin labeled the war effort a "battle of machines," and the Soviets won, producing 78,000 tanks and

Paths to Modernization

POLITICS & GOVERNMENT

To the casual observer, the most important feature of the first half of the twentieth century was the rise of a virulent form of competitive nationalism that began in Europe and ultimately descended into the cauldron of two destructive world wars. Behind the scenes, however, another competition was taking place over the most effective path to modernization.

The traditional approach, in which modernization was fostered by an independent urban merchant class, had been adopted by Great Britain, France, and the United States and led to the emergence of democratic societies on the capitalist model. In the second approach, adopted in the late nineteenth century by imperial Germany and Meiji Japan, modernization was carried out by traditional elites in the absence of a strong independent bourgeois class. Both Germany and Japan relied on strong government intervention to promote the growth of national wealth and power, and in both nations, modernization led ultimately to the formation of fascist and militarist regimes during the depression years of the early 1930s.

The third approach, selected by Vladimir Lenin after the Bolshevik Revolution in 1917, was designed to carry out an industrial revolution without going through an intermediate capitalist stage. Under the guidance of the Communist Party in the almost total absence of an urban middle class, an advanced industrial society would be created by destroying the concept of private property. Although Lenin's plans ultimately called for the "withering away of the state," the party adopted totalitarian methods to eliminate enemies of the revolution and carry out the changes needed to create a future classless utopia.

How did these various approaches contribute to the crises that afflicted the world during the first half of the twentieth century? The democratic-capitalist approach proved to be a considerable success in an economic sense, leading to advanced economies that could produce manufactured goods at a rate never seen before. Societies just beginning to undergo their own industrial revolutions tried to imitate the success of the capitalist nations by carrying out their own "revolutions from above," as in Germany and Japan. But the Great Depression and competition over resources and markets soon led to an intense rivalry between the established

The Soviet Path to Modernization. One aspect of the Soviet effort to create an advanced industrial society was the collectivization of agriculture, which included the rapid mechanization of food production. In this photograph, peasants are watching a new tractor at work.

capitalist states and their ambitious late arrivals, a rivalry that ultimately erupted into global conflict.

In the first decade of the twentieth century, imperial Russia appeared ready to launch its own bid to join the ranks of the industrialized nations. But that effort was derailed by its entry into World War I, and before that conflict had come to an end, the Bolsheviks were in power. Isolated from the capitalist marketplace by mutual consent, the Soviet Union was able to avoid being dragged into the Great Depression but, despite Stalin's efforts, was unsuccessful in staying out of the "battle of imperialists" that followed at the end of the 1930s. As World War II came to an end, the stage was set for a battle of the victors—the United States and the Soviet Union—over political and ideological supremacy.

 What were the three major paths to modernization in the first half of the twentieth century, and why did they lead to conflict?

98,000 artillery pieces. Fully 55 percent of Soviet national income went for war matériel, compared to 15 percent in 1940. As a result of the emphasis on military goods, Soviet citizens experienced extreme shortages of both food and housing.

Soviet women played a major role in the war effort. Women and girls worked in industries, mines, and railroads. Overall, the number of women working in industry increased almost 60 percent. Soviet women were also expected to dig antitank ditches and work as air-raid wardens. In addition, the

Soviet Union was the only country in World War II to use women as combatants. Soviet women functioned as snipers and also as air crews in bomber squadrons. The female pilots who helped defeat the Germans at Stalingrad were known as the "Night Witches."

THE UNITED STATES The home front in the United States was quite different from that of its chief wartime allies, largely because the United States faced no threat of war on its own

Women in the Factories. Although only the Soviet Union used women in combat positions, the number of women working in industry increased dramatically in most belligerent countries. British women are shown here in a British munitions factory during World War II, probably in 1943.

territory. Although the economy and labor force were slow to mobilize, eventually the United States became the arsenal of the Allied Powers, producing the military equipment they needed.

The immediate impact of mobilization was a dramatic expansion of the U.S. economy, which ultimately brought an end to the Great Depression. Old factories were converted from peacetime goods to war goods, and many new factories were built. American industry not only supplied the American armed forces but also provided U.S. allies with the huge quantities of tanks, trucks, jeeps, and airplanes needed to win the war. During the war years, gross national product (GNP) rose by 15 percent a year. During the high point of war production in the United States in November 1943, the nation was constructing six ships a day and $6 billion worth of other military equipment a month. Airplane production increased from 6,000 in 1939 to over 96,000 in 1944.

The mobilization of the American economy created social problems, however. Boomtowns sprang up near the new factories where thousands came to work but then faced a shortage of houses, health facilities, and schools. The dramatic expansion of small towns into large cities often brought a breakdown in traditional social mores, especially evident in an increase in teenage prostitution. Economic mobilization also led to extensive movements of people, which in turn created new social tensions. Sixteen million men and women were enrolled in the military, and another 16 million, mostly wives and sweethearts of the servicemen or workers looking for jobs, also relocated. More than a million blacks migrated from the rural South to the industrial cities of the North and West, looking for jobs in industry. The presence of blacks in areas where they had not lived before led to racial tensions and sometimes even racial riots. In Detroit in June 1943, white mobs roamed the streets attacking blacks. Many of the one million blacks who enrolled in the military, only to be segregated in their own battle units, were angered by the way they were treated. Some became militant and prepared to fight for their civil rights.

Japanese Americans were treated even more shabbily. On the West Coast, 110,000 Japanese Americans, 65 percent of whom had been born in the United States, were removed to camps encircled by barbed wire and made to take loyalty oaths. Although public officials claimed this policy was necessary for security reasons, no similar treatment of German Americans or Italian Americans ever took place. The racism inherent in this treatment of Japanese Americans was evident when the governor of California, Culbert Olson, said, "You know, when I look out at a group of Americans of German or Italian descent, I can tell whether they're loyal or not. I can tell how they think and even perhaps what they are thinking. But it is impossible for me to do this with inscrutable orientals, and particularly the Japanese."[15]

GERMANY In August 1914, Germans had enthusiastically cheered their soldiers marching off to war. In September 1939, the streets were quiet. Many Germans were apathetic or, even worse for the Nazi regime, had a foreboding of disaster. Hitler was very aware of the importance of the home front. He believed that the collapse of the home front in World War I had caused Germany's defeat, and in his determination to avoid a repetition of that experience, he adopted economic policies that may indeed have cost Germany the war.

To maintain the morale of the home front during the first two years of the war, Hitler refused to cut the production of consumer goods or increase the production of armaments. Blitzkrieg allowed the Germans to win quick victories, after which they believed they could plunder the food and raw materials of the conquered countries to avoid diverting resources from the civilian economy. After German defeats on the Russian front and the American entry into the war, the economic situation changed. Early in 1942, Hitler finally ordered a massive increase in armaments production and in the size of the army. Hitler's architect, Albert Speer (AHL-bert SHPAYR), was made minister for armaments and munitions that year. By eliminating waste and rationalizing procedures, Speer was able to triple the production of armaments between 1942 and 1943 despite the intense Allied air raids. Speer's urgent plea for a total mobilization of resources for the war effort went unheeded, however. Hitler, fearful of civilian morale problems that would undermine the home front, refused any dramatic cuts in the production of consumer goods. A total mobilization of the economy was not implemented until 1944, when schools, theaters, and cafés were closed and Speer was finally permitted to use all remaining resources for the production of a few basic military items. By that time, it was in vain. Total war mobilization in July 1944 was too little and too late to save Germany from defeat.

The war caused a reversal in Nazi attitudes toward women. Nazi resistance to female employment declined as the war progressed and more and more men were called up for military service. Nazi magazines now proclaimed, "We see the woman as the eternal mother of our people, but also as the working and fighting comrade of the man."[16] But the number of women working in industry, agriculture, commerce, and domestic service increased only slightly. The total number of employed women in September 1944 was 14.9 million, compared to 14.6 million in May 1939. Many women, especially those of the middle class, resisted regular employment, particularly in factories. Even the introduction of labor conscription for women in January 1943 failed to achieve much as women found ingenious ways to avoid the regulations.

JAPAN In Japan, society was placed on a wartime footing even before the attack on Pearl Harbor. A conscription law was passed in 1938, and economic resources were put under strict government control. Two years later, all political parties were merged into the Imperial Rule Assistance Association. Labor unions were dissolved, and education and culture were purged of all "corrupt" Western ideas in favor of traditional values emphasizing the divinity of the emperor and the higher spirituality of Japanese civilization. During the war, individual rights were severely curtailed as the entire population was harnessed to the needs of the war effort. Traditional habits of obedience and hierarchy were emphasized to encourage citizens to sacrifice their resources, and sometimes their lives, for the national cause. Especially important was the code of Bushido (BOO-shee-doh), or the way of the warrior, the old code of morality of the samurai, who had played a prominent military role in medieval and early modern Japan. The code of Bushido was revived during the nationalistic fervor of the 1930s. Based on an ideal of loyalty and service, the code emphasized the obligation to honor and defend emperor, country, and family and to sacrifice one's life if one failed in this sacred mission. The system culminated in the final years of the war, when young Japanese were encouraged to volunteer en masse to serve as pilots in suicide missions—known as *kamikaze* (kah-mi-KAH-zee), or "divine wind"—against U.S. warships.

Women's rights, too, were to be sacrificed to the greater national cause. Already by 1937, Japanese women were being exhorted to fulfill their patriotic duty by bearing more children and by espousing the slogans of the Greater Japanese Women's Association. Nevertheless, Japan was extremely reluctant to mobilize women on behalf of the war effort. General Hideki Tojo (hee-DEK-ee TOH-joh), prime minister from 1941 to 1944, opposed female employment, arguing that "the weakening of the family system would be the weakening of the nation. . . . We are able to do our duties only because we have wives and mothers at home."[17] Female employment increased during the war, but only in areas, such as the textile industry and farming, where women had traditionally worked. Instead of using women to meet labor shortages, the Japanese government brought in Korean and Chinese laborers.

The Bombing of Cities

Bombing was used in World War II against nonhuman military targets, against enemy troops, and against civilian populations. The bombing of civilians made World War II as devastating for noncombatants as it was for frontline soldiers. A small number of bombing raids in the last year of World War I had given rise to the argument, crystallized in 1930 by the Italian general Giulio Douhet (JOOL-yoh doo-AY), that the public outcry in reaction to the bombing of civilian populations would be an effective way to coerce governments into making peace. Consequently, European air forces began to develop long-range bombers in the 1930s.

LUFTWAFFE ATTACKS The first sustained use of civilian bombing contradicted Douhet's theory. Beginning in early September 1940, the German Luftwaffe subjected London and many other British cities and towns to nightly air raids, making the Blitz (as the British called the German air raids) a national experience. Londoners took the first heavy blows and set the standard for the rest of the British population by refusing to panic. But London morale was helped by the fact that German raids were widely dispersed over a very large city. Smaller communities were more directly affected by the devastation. On November 14, 1940, for example, the Luftwaffe destroyed hundreds of shops and 100 acres of the city center of Coventry. The destruction of smaller cities did produce morale problems as rumors of social collapse spread quickly in these communities (see the comparative illustration on p. 753). Nevertheless, morale was soon restored. In any case, war production in these areas seems to have been little affected by the raids.

THE BOMBING OF GERMANY The British failed to learn from their own experience, however, and soon retaliated by bombing Germany. Prime Minister Winston Churchill (1874–1965) and his advisers believed that destroying German communities would break civilian morale and bring victory. Major bombing raids began in 1942 under the direction of Arthur Harris, the wartime leader of the British air force's Bomber Command, which was rearmed with four-engine heavy bombers capable of taking the war into the center of occupied Europe. On May 31, 1942, Cologne became the first German city to be subjected to an attack by a thousand bombers.

The entry of the Americans into the war produced a new bombing strategy. American planes flew daytime missions aimed at the precision bombing of transportation facilities and wartime industries, while the British Bomber Command continued nighttime saturation bombing of all German cities with populations over 100,000. Bombing raids added an element of terror to circumstances already made difficult by growing shortages of food, clothing, and fuel. Germans especially feared the incendiary bombs, which set off firestorms that swept destructive paths through the cities. Four raids on Hamburg in August 1943 produced temperatures of 1,800 degrees Fahrenheit, obliterated half the city's buildings, and

COMPARATIVE ILLUSTRATION

The Bombing of Civilians—East and West. World War II was the most destructive war in world history, not only for frontline soldiers but for civilians at home as well. The most devastating bombing of civilians came near the end of the war when the United States dropped atomic bombs on the Japanese cities of Hiroshima and Nagasaki. At the left is a panoramic view of Hiroshima after the bombing that shows the incredible devastation produced by the atomic bomb. The photograph at the right shows a street in Clydebank, near Glasgow in Scotland, the day after the city was bombed by the Germans in March 1941. Only 7 of the city's 12,000 houses were left undamaged; 35,000 of the 47,000 inhabitants became homeless overnight.

Q *What was the rationale for bombing civilian populations? Did such bombing achieve its goal?*

killed thousands of civilians. The ferocious bombing of Dresden for three days in 1945 (February 13–15) created a firestorm that may have killed as many as 35,000 inhabitants and refugees. Even some Allied leaders began to criticize what they saw as the unnecessary terror bombing of German cities.

Germany suffered enormously from the Allied bombing raids. Millions of buildings were destroyed, and possibly half a million civilians died from the raids. Nevertheless, it is highly unlikely that Allied bombing sapped the morale of the German people. Instead, Germans, whether pro-Nazi or anti-Nazi, fought on stubbornly, often driven simply by a desire to live. Nor did the bombing destroy Germany's industrial capacity. The Allied Strategic Bombing survey revealed that the production of war matériel actually increased between 1942 and 1944. Even in 1944 and 1945, Allied raids cut German armaments production by only 7 percent. Nevertheless, the widespread destruction of transportation systems and fuel supplies made it extremely difficult for the new materials to reach the German military.

THE BOMBING OF JAPAN: THE ATOMIC BOMB In Japan, the bombing of civilians reached a new level with the use of the first atomic bomb. Japan was especially vulnerable to air raids because its air force had been virtually destroyed in the course of the war and its crowded cities were built of flimsy materials. Attacks on Japanese cities by the new American B-29 Superfortresses, the biggest bombers of the war, began

in June 1944. By the summer of 1945, many of Japan's industries had been destroyed, along with one-fourth of its dwellings. After the Japanese government ordered the mobilization of all people between the ages of thirteen and sixty into the People's Volunteer Corps, President Truman and his advisers feared that Japanese fanaticism might mean a million American casualties. This concern led them to drop the atomic bomb on Hiroshima (August 6) and Nagasaki (August 9). The destruction was incredible. Of 76,000 buildings near the center of the explosion in Hiroshima, 70,000 were flattened, and 140,000 of the city's 400,000 inhabitants died by the end of 1945. Over the next five years, another 50,000 had perished from the effects of radiation. The dropping of the first atomic bomb marked the start of the nuclear age.

After the war, Truman's decision to approve the use of nuclear weapons to compel Japan to surrender was harshly criticized, not only for causing thousands of civilian casualties but also for introducing a frightening new weapon that could threaten the survival of the human race. Some have even charged that Truman's real purpose in ordering the nuclear strikes was to intimidate the Soviet Union. Defenders of the decision argue that the human costs of invading the Japanese home islands would have been infinitely higher had the bombs not been dropped, and that the Soviet Union would have had ample time to consolidate its control over Manchuria.

Aftermath of the War

FOCUS QUESTIONS: What were the costs of World War II? How did World War II affect the European nations' colonial empires? How did the Allies' visions of postwar Europe differ, and how did these differences contribute to the emergence of the Cold War?

World War II was the most destructive war in history. Much had been at stake. Nazi Germany followed a worldview based on racial extermination and the enslavement of millions in order to create an Aryan racial empire. The Japanese, fueled by extreme nationalist ideals, also pursued dreams of empire in Asia that led to mass murder and untold devastation. Fighting the Axis Powers in World War II required the mobilization of millions of ordinary men and women in the Allied countries who rose to the occasion and struggled to preserve a different way of life. As Winston Churchill once put it, "War is horrible, but slavery is worse."

The Costs of World War II

The costs of World War II were enormous. At least 21 million soldiers died. Civilian deaths were even greater and are now estimated at around 40 million, of whom more than 28 million were Russian and Chinese. The Soviet Union experienced the greatest losses: 10 million soldiers and 19 million civilians. In 1945, millions of people around the world faced starvation; in Europe, 100 million people depended on food relief of some kind.

Millions of people had also been uprooted by the war and became "displaced persons." Europe alone may have had 30 million displaced persons, many of whom found it hard to return home. After the war, millions of Germans were expelled from the Sudetenland in Czechoslovakia, and millions more were ejected from former eastern German territories turned over to Poland, all of which seemed reasonable to people who had suffered so much at the hands of the Germans. In Asia, millions of Japanese were returned from the former Japanese empire to Japan, while thousands of Korean forced laborers returned to Korea.

Devastation was everywhere. Most areas of Europe had been damaged or demolished, China was in shambles after eight years of conflict, the Philippines had suffered heavy damage, and large parts of the major cities in Japan had been destroyed in air raids. Millions of tons of shipping now lay beneath the seas; factories, farms, transportation systems, bridges, and dams lay in ruins. The total monetary cost of the war has been estimated at $4 trillion. The economies of most belligerents, with the exception of the United States, were left drained and on the brink of disaster.

World War II and the European Colonies: Decolonization

As we saw in Chapter 24, movements for independence had begun in earnest in Africa and Asia in the years between World War I and World War II. After World War II, these movements grew even louder. The ongoing subjugation of peoples by colonial powers seemed at odds with the goals the Allies had pursued in overthrowing the repressive regimes of Germany, Italy, and Japan. Then, too, indigenous peoples everywhere took up the call for national self-determination and expressed their determination to fight for independence.

The ending of the European powers' colonial empires did not come easy, however. In 1941, Churchill had said, "I have not become His Majesty's Chief Minister in order to preside over the liquidation of the British Empire." Britain and France in particular seemed reluctant to let go of their colonies, but for a variety of reasons both eventually gave in to the obvious—the days of empire were over.

During the war, the Japanese had already humiliated the Western states by overrunning their colonial empires. In addition, colonial soldiers who had fought on behalf of the Allies (India, for example, had contributed large numbers of troops to the British Indian Army) were well aware that Allied war aims included the principle of self-determination for the peoples of the world. Equally important to the process of **decolonization** after the war, the power of the European states had been destroyed by the exhaustive struggles of World War II. The greatest colonial empire builder, Great Britain, no longer had the energy or the wealth to maintain its colonial empire. Given the combination of circumstances, a rush of decolonization swept the world after World War II.

The Allied War Conferences

The total victory of the Allies in World War II was not followed by a real peace but by the emergence of a new conflict known as the **Cold War**, which dominated world politics until the end of the 1980s. The Cold War grew out of military, political, and ideological differences, especially between the Soviet Union and the United States, that became apparent at the Allied war conferences held in the last years of the war. Although Allied leaders were mostly preoccupied with ending the war, they were also strongly motivated by differing, and often conflicting, visions of the postwar world.

THE CONFERENCE AT TEHRAN Stalin, Roosevelt, and Churchill, the leaders of the Big Three of the Grand Alliance, met at Tehran, the capital of Iran, in November 1943 to decide the future course of the war. Their major tactical decision concerned the final assault on Germany. Stalin and Roosevelt argued successfully for an American-British invasion of the Continent through France, which they scheduled for the spring of 1944. The acceptance of this plan had important consequences. It meant that Soviet and British-American forces would meet in defeated Germany along a north-south dividing line and that eastern Europe would most likely be liberated by Soviet forces. The Allies also agreed to a partition of postwar Germany until denazification could take place.

THE YALTA CONFERENCE By the time of the conference at Yalta in southern Russia in February 1945, the defeat of Germany was a foregone conclusion. The Western powers, which had earlier believed that the Soviets were in a weak position, now faced the reality of 11 million Red Army soldiers taking possession of eastern and central Europe. Like

The Victorious Allied Leaders at Yalta. Even before World War II ended, the leaders of the Big Three of the Grand Alliance, Churchill, Roosevelt, and Stalin (shown from left to right), met in wartime conferences to plan the final assault on Germany and negotiate the outlines of the postwar settlement. At the Yalta meeting (February 5–11, 1945), the three leaders concentrated on postwar issues. The American president, who died two months later, was already a worn-out man at Yalta.

Churchill, Stalin was still operating under the notion of spheres of influence. He was deeply suspicious of the Western powers and desired a buffer to protect the Soviet Union from possible future Western aggression. At the same time, however, Stalin was eager to obtain economically important resources and strategic military positions. Roosevelt by this time was moving away from the notion of spheres of influence toward the more Wilsonian ideal of self-determination. He called for "the end of the system of unilateral action, exclusive alliances, and spheres of influence." The Grand Alliance approved a declaration on liberated Europe. This was a pledge to assist Europeans in the creation of "democratic institutions of their own choice." Liberated countries were to hold free elections to determine their political systems.

At Yalta, Roosevelt sought Soviet military help against Japan. The atomic bomb was not yet assured, and American military planners feared the possibility of heavy losses in amphibious assaults on the Japanese home islands. Roosevelt therefore agreed to Stalin's price for military assistance against Japan: possession of Sakhalin and the Kurile Islands, as well as two warm-water ports and railroad rights in Manchuria.

The creation of the United Nations was a major American concern at Yalta. Roosevelt hoped to ensure the participation of the Big Three powers in a postwar international organization before difficult issues divided them into hostile camps. After a number of compromises, both Churchill and Stalin accepted Roosevelt's plans for a United Nations organization and set the first meeting for San Francisco in April 1945.

The issues of Germany and eastern Europe were treated less decisively. The Big Three reaffirmed that Germany must surrender unconditionally and created four occupation zones (see Map 25.3). German reparations were set at $20 billion. A compromise was also worked out in regard to Poland. Stalin agreed to free elections in the future to determine a new government. But the issue of free elections in eastern Europe caused a serious rift between the Soviets and the Americans. The principle was that eastern European governments would be freely elected, but they were also supposed to be pro-Soviet. As Churchill expressed it, "The Poles will have their future in their own hands, with the single limitation that they must honestly follow in harmony with their allies, a policy friendly to Russia."[18] This attempt to reconcile two irreconcilable goals was doomed to failure, as soon became evident at the next conference of the Big Three powers.

THE POTSDAM CONFERENCE Even before the conference at Potsdam took place in July 1945, Western relations with the Soviets were deteriorating rapidly. The Grand Alliance had been a collaboration of necessity in which ideological incompatibility had been subordinated to the pragmatic concerns of the war. The Allies' only common aim was the defeat of Nazism. Once this aim had been accomplished, the many differences that antagonized East-West relations came to the surface. The Potsdam conference of July 1945 consequently began under a cloud of mistrust. Roosevelt had died on April 12 and had been succeeded as president by Harry Truman. During the conference, Truman received word that the atomic bomb had been successfully tested. Some historians have argued that this knowledge resulted in Truman's stiffened resolve against the Soviets. Whatever the reasons, there was a new coolness in the relations between the Soviets and Americans. At Potsdam, Truman demanded free elections throughout eastern Europe. Stalin responded, "A freely elected government in any of these east European countries would be anti-Soviet, and that we cannot allow."[19] After a bitterly fought and devastating war, Stalin sought absolute military security. To him, it could be gained only by the presence of Communist states in eastern Europe. Free elections might result in governments hostile to the Soviets. By the middle of 1945, only an invasion by Western forces could undo developments in eastern Europe, and after the world's most destructive conflict had ended, few people favored such a policy.

EMERGENCE OF THE COLD WAR As the war slowly receded into the past, the reality of conflicting ideologies had reappeared. Many in the West interpreted Soviet policy as part of a worldwide Communist conspiracy. The Soviets viewed Western, especially American, policy as nothing less than

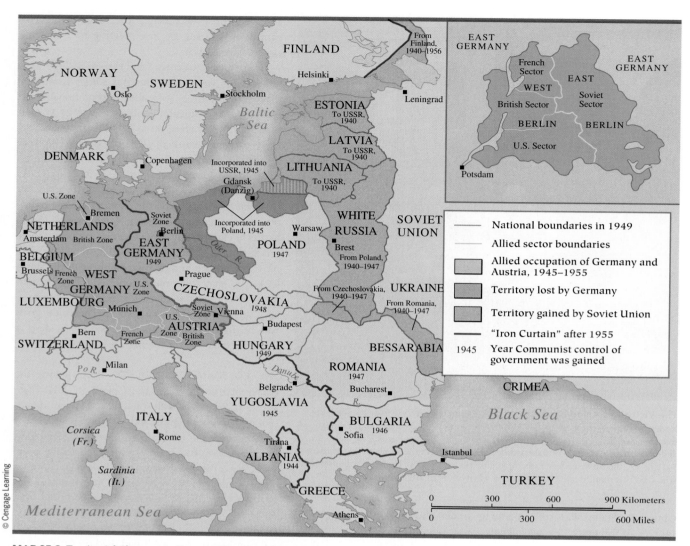

MAP 25.3 Territorial Changes in Europe After World War II. In the last months of World War II, the Red Army occupied much of eastern Europe. Stalin sought pro-Soviet satellite states in the region as a buffer against future invasions from western Europe, whereas Britain and the United States wanted democratically elected governments. Soviet military control of the territory settled the question.

 Which country gained the greatest territory at the expense of Germany?

global capitalist expansionism or, in Leninist terms, economic imperialism. Vyacheslav Molotov (vyich-chiss-SLAHF MAHL-uh-tawf), the Russian foreign minister, referred to the Americans as "insatiable imperialists" and "war-mongering groups of adventurers."[20] In March 1946, in a speech to an American audience, the former British prime minister

Winston Churchill declared that "an iron curtain" had "descended across the continent," dividing Europe into two hostile camps. Stalin branded Churchill's speech a "call to war with the Soviet Union." Only months after the world's most devastating conflict had ended, the world seemed once again to be bitterly divided.

CHAPTER SUMMARY

Between 1933 and 1939, Europeans watched as Adolf Hitler rebuilt Germany into a great military power. For Hitler, military power was an absolute prerequisite for the creation of a German racial empire that would dominate Europe and the world for generations to come. During that same period, the

nation of Japan fell under the influence of military leaders who conspired with right-wing forces to push a program of expansion at the expense of China and the Soviet Union as well as territories in Southeast Asia. The ambitions of Germany in Europe and those of Japan in Asia led to a global conflict that became the most devastating war in human history.

The Axis nations, Germany, Italy, and Japan, proved victorious during the first two years of the war, which began after the German invasion of Poland on September 1, 1939. By 1942, the war had begun to turn in favor of the Allies, an alliance of Great Britain, the Soviet Union, and the United States. The Japanese advance was ended at the Battles of the Coral Sea and Midway in 1942. In February 1943, the Soviets won the Battle of Stalingrad and began a push westward. By mid-1943, Germany and Italy had been driven out of North Africa; in June 1944, Rome fell to the Allies, and an Allied invasion force landed in Normandy in France. After the Soviets linked up with British and American forces in April 1945, Hitler committed suicide, and the war in Europe came to an end. After atomic bombs were dropped on Hiroshima and Nagasaki in August 1945, the war in Asia also ended.

During its domination of Europe, the Nazi empire brought death and destruction to many, especially Jews, minorities, and others that the Nazis considered racially inferior peoples. The Japanese New Order in Asia, while claiming to promote a policy of "Asia for the Asians" also brought economic exploitation, severe hardship, and often death for the peoples under Japanese control. All sides bombed civilian populations, making World War II as devastating for civilians as for the frontline soldiers.

If Hitler had been successful, the Nazi New Order, built on authoritarianism, racial extermination, and the brutal oppression of peoples, would have meant a triumph of barbarism and the end of freedom and equality, which, however imperfectly realized, had become important ideals in Western civilization.

The Nazis lost, but only after tremendous sacrifices and costs. Much of European civilization lay in ruins, and the old Europe had disappeared forever. Europeans, who had been accustomed to dominating the world at the beginning of the twentieth century, now watched helplessly at mid-century as the two new superpowers created by the two world wars took control of their destinies. Even before the last battles had been fought, the United States and the Soviet Union had arrived at different versions of the postwar European world. No sooner had the war ended than their differences gave rise to a new and potentially even more devastating conflict known as the Cold War.

CHAPTER TIMELINE

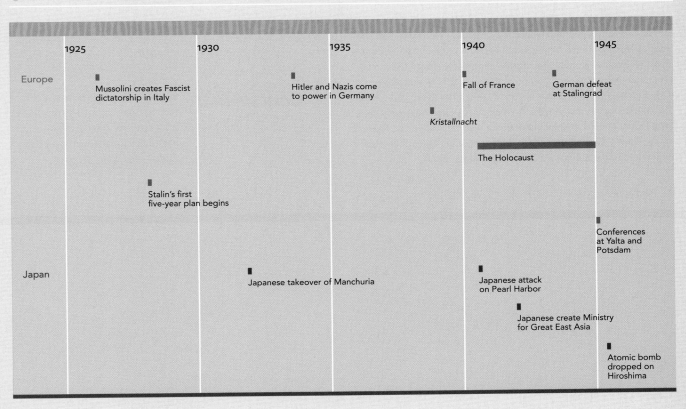

Europe

| 1925 | 1930 | 1935 | 1940 | 1945 |

- Mussolini creates Fascist dictatorship in Italy
- Hitler and Nazis come to power in Germany
- Fall of France
- German defeat at Stalingrad
- *Kristallnacht*
- The Holocaust
- Stalin's first five-year plan begins
- Conferences at Yalta and Potsdam

Japan

- Japanese takeover of Manchuria
- Japanese attack on Pearl Harbor
- Japanese create Ministry for Great East Asia
- Atomic bomb dropped on Hiroshima

CHAPTER REVIEW

Upon Reflection

Q How do you account for the early successes of the Germans from 1939 to 1941?

Q How did the Nazis attempt to establish a New Order in Europe after their military victories, and what were the results of their efforts?

Q How did the attempt to arrive at a peace settlement after World War II lead to the beginnings of a new conflict known as the Cold War?

Key Terms

totalitarian state (p. 726)
squadristi (p. 727)
appeasement (p. 734)
Blitzkrieg (p. 737)
unconditional surrender (p. 739)
Nazi New Order (p. 743)
Final Solution (p. 745)
Einsatzgruppen (p. 745)
decolonization (p. 754)
Cold War (p. 754)

Suggested Reading

THE DICTATORIAL REGIMES   The best biography of Mussolini is **R. J. B. Bosworth**, *Mussolini* (London, 2002). A brief but sound survey of Nazi Germany is **J. J. Spielvogel** and **D. Redles**, *Hitler and Nazi Germany: A History,* 6th ed. (Upper Saddle River, N.J., 2010). The best biography of Hitler is **I. Kershaw**, *Hitler, 1889–1936: Hubris* (New York, 1999), and *Hitler: Nemesis* (New York, 2000). On the Nazis in power, see **R. J. Evans**, *The Third Reich in Power, 1933–1939* (New York, 2005). The collectivization of agriculture in the Soviet Union is examined in **S. Fitzpatrick**, *Stalin's Peasants: Resistance and Survival in the Russian Village After Collectivization* (New York, 1995). On Stalin himself, see **R. Service**, *Stalin: A Biography* (Cambridge, Mass., 2006).

THE PATH TO WAR   On the causes of World War II, see **A. J. Crozier**, *Causes of the Second World War* (Oxford, 1997). On the origins of the war in the Pacific, see **A. Iriye**, *The Origins of the Second World War in Asia and the Pacific* (London, 1987).

WORLD WAR II   The best general work on World War II is **G. Weinberg**, *A World at Arms: A Global History of World War II,* 2nd ed. (Cambridge, 2005). A good military history of World War II can be found in **W. Murray** and **A. R. Millett**, *A War to Be Won: Fighting the Second World War* (Cambridge, Mass., 2000).

THE HOLOCAUST   Excellent studies of the Holocaust include **S. Friedänder**, *The Years of Extermination: Nazi Germany and the Jews, 1939–1945* (New York, 2007), and **L. Yahil**, *The Holocaust* (New York, 1990). For a brief study, see **D. Dwork** and **R. J. van Pelt**, *Holocaust: A History* (New York, 2002).

THE HOME FRONT   On the home front in Germany, see **M. Kitchen**, *Nazi Germany at War* (New York, 1995). The Soviet Union during the war is examined in **M. Harrison**, *Soviet Planning in Peace and War, 1938–1945* (Cambridge, 1985). On the American home front, see the collection of essays in **K. P. O'Brien** and **L. H. Parsons**, *The Home-Front War: World War II and American Society* (Westport, Conn., 1995). The Japanese home front is examined in **T. R. H. Havens**, *The Valley of Darkness: The Japanese People and World War Two* (New York, 1978). On the Allied bombing campaign against Germany, see **R. Hansen**, *Fire and Fury: The Allied Bombing of Germany, 1942–1945* (London, 2008).

Go to the CourseMate website at **www.cengagebrain.com** for additional study tools and review materials—including audio and video clips—for this chapter.

PART V

Toward a Global Civilization?
The World Since 1945

AS WORLD WAR II came to an end, the survivors of that bloody struggle could afford to face the future with a cautious optimism. There was reason to hope that the bitter rivalry that had marked relations among the Western powers would finally be put to an end and that the wartime alliance of the United States, Great Britain, and the Soviet Union could be maintained into the postwar era.

More than sixty-five years later, these hopes have been only partly realized. In the decades following the war, the Western capitalist nations managed to recover from the economic depression that had led into World War II and advanced to a level of economic prosperity never seen before. The bloody conflicts that had erupted among European nations during the first half of the twentieth century ended, and Germany and Japan were fully reintegrated into the world community.

At the same time, the prospects for a stable, peaceful world and an end to balance-of-power politics were hampered by the emergence of the grueling and sometimes tense ideological struggle between the socialist and capitalist camps, a competition headed by the only remaining great powers, the Soviet Union and the United States.

In the shadow of this rivalry, the Western European states made a remarkable economic recovery and reached untold levels of prosperity. In Eastern Europe, Soviet domination, both political and economic, seemed so complete that many people doubted it could ever be undone. But communism had never put down deep roots in Eastern Europe, and in the late 1980s, when Soviet leader Mikhail Gorbachev indicated that his government would no longer intervene militarily to keep the Eastern European states in line, they were quick to embrace their freedom and adopt new economic structures based on Western models.

The peoples of Africa and Asia had their own reasons for optimism as World War II came to a close. In the Atlantic Charter, Franklin Roosevelt and Winston Churchill had set forth a joint declaration of their peace aims calling for the self-determination of all peoples and self-government and sovereign rights for all nations that had been deprived of them.

As it turned out, some colonial powers were reluctant to divest themselves of their colonies. Still, World War II had severely undermined the stability of the colonial order, and by the end of the 1940s, most colonies in Asia had received their independence. Africa followed a decade or two later.

Broadly speaking, the leaders of these newly liberated countries set forth three goals at the outset of independence. They wanted to throw off the shackles of Western economic domination and ensure material prosperity for all of their citizens. They wanted to introduce new political institutions that would enhance the right of self-determination of their peoples. And they wanted to develop a sense of common nationhood within the population and establish secure territorial boundaries. Most opted to follow a capitalist or a moderately socialist path toward economic development. In a few cases—most notably in China and Vietnam—revolutionary leaders opted for the communist mode of development.

Regardless of the path chosen, to many the results were often disappointing. Much of Africa and Asia remained economically dependent on the advanced industrial nations Some societies faced severe problems of urban and rural poverty. Others were rent by bitter internal conflicts.

What had happened to tarnish the bright dream of economic affluence? During the late 1950s and early 1960s, the dominant school of thought among scholars and government officials in the United States was what is known as modernization theory. This school took the view that the problems faced by the newly independent countries were a consequence of the difficult transition from a traditional to a modern society. Modernization theorists were convinced that agrarian countries were destined to follow the path of the West toward the creation of modern industrial societies but would need both time and substantial amounts of economic and technological assistance from the West to complete the journey.

Eventually, modernization theory came under attack from a new generation of scholars. In their view, the responsibility for continued economic underdevelopment in the postcolonial world lay not with the countries themselves but with their continued domination by the former colonial powers. In this view, known as dependency theory, the countries of Asia, Africa, and Latin America were the victims of the international marketplace, in which high prices were charged for the manufactured goods of the West while low prices were paid to the preindustrial countries for their raw material exports. Efforts by such countries to build up their industrial sectors and move into the stage of self-sustaining growth were hampered by foreign control of many of their resources via European- and American-owned corporations. To end this "neocolonial" relationship, the dependency theory advocates argued, developing societies should reduce their economic ties with the West and institute a policy of economic self-reliance, thereby taking control of their own destinies.

Leaders of African and Asian countries also encountered problems creating new political cultures responsive to the needs of their citizens. At first, most accepted the concept of democracy as the defining theme of that culture. Within a decade, however, democratic systems throughout the developing world were replaced by military dictatorships or one-party governments that redefined the concept of democracy to fit their own preferences. It was clear that the difficulties in building democratic political institutions in developing societies had been underestimated.

The problem of establishing a common national identity has in some ways been the most daunting of all the challenges facing the new nations of Asia and Africa. Many of these new states were a composite of various ethnic, religious, and linguistic groups that found it difficult to agree on common symbols of nationalism or national values. The process of establishing an official language and delineating territorial boundaries left over from the colonial era created difficulties in many countries. Internal conflicts spawned by deep-rooted historical and ethnic hatreds have proliferated throughout the world, causing vast numbers of people to move across state boundaries in migrations as large as any since the great migrations of the thirteenth and fourteenth centuries.

The introduction of Western cultural values and customs has also had a destabilizing effect in many areas. Though welcomed by some groups, such ideas are firmly resisted by others. Where Western influence has the effect of undermining traditional customs and religious beliefs, it often provokes violent hostility and sparks tension and even conflict within individual societies. Much of the anger recently directed at the United States in Muslim countries has undoubtedly been generated by such feelings.

Nonetheless, social and political attitudes are changing rapidly in many Asian and African countries as new economic circumstances have led to a more secular worldview, a decline in traditional hierarchical relations, and a more open attitude toward sexual practices. In part, these changes are a consequence of the influence of Western music, movies, and television. But they are also a product of the growth of an affluent middle class in many societies of Asia and Africa.

Today, we live not only in a world economy but in a world society, where a revolution in the Middle East can cause a rise in the price of oil in the United States and a change in social behavior in Malaysia and Indonesia, where the collapse of an empire in Asia can send shock waves as far as Hanoi and Havana, and where a terrorist attack in New York City or London can disrupt financial markets around the world. ◈

East and West in the Grip of the Cold War

Churchill, Roosevelt, and Stalin at Yalta

CHAPTER OUTLINE AND FOCUS QUESTIONS

The Collapse of the Grand Alliance

Q Why were the United States and the Soviet Union suspicious of each other after World War II, and what events between 1945 and 1949 heightened the tensions between the two nations?

Cold War in Asia

Q How and why did Mao Zedong and the Communists come to power in China, and what were the Cold War implications of their triumph?

From Confrontation to Coexistence

Q What events led to the era of coexistence in the 1960s, and to what degree did each side contribute to the reduction in international tensions?

An Era of Equivalence

Q Why did the Cold War briefly flare up again in the 1980s, and why did it come to a definitive end at the end of the decade?

CRITICAL THINKING

Q How have historians answered the question of whether the United States or the Soviet Union bears the primary responsibility for the Cold War, and what evidence can be presented on each side of the issue?

"OUR MEETING HERE in the Crimea has reaffirmed our common determination to maintain and strengthen in the peace to come that unity of purpose and of action which has made victory possible and certain for the United Nations in this war. We believe that this is a sacred obligation which our Governments owe to our peoples and to all the peoples of the world."[1]

With these ringing words, drafted at the Yalta Conference in February 1945, U.S. President Franklin D. Roosevelt, Soviet leader Joseph Stalin, and British Prime Minister Winston Churchill affirmed their common hope that the Grand Alliance that had been victorious in World War II could be sustained into the postwar era. Only through continuing and growing cooperation and understanding among the three Allies, the statement asserted, could a secure and lasting peace be realized that, in the words of the Atlantic Charter, would "afford assurance that all the men in all the lands may live out their lives in freedom from fear and want."

Roosevelt hoped that the decisions reached at Yalta would provide the basis for a stable peace in the postwar era. Allied occupation forces—American, British, and French in the west and Soviet in the east—were to bring about the end of Axis administration and organize the free election of democratic governments throughout Europe. To foster mutual trust and end the suspicions that had marked relations between the capitalist world and the Soviet Union prior to the war, Roosevelt tried to assure Stalin that Moscow's legitimate territorial aspirations and genuine security needs would be adequately met in a durable peace settlement.

It was not to be. Within months after the German surrender, the mutual trust among the Allies—if it had ever truly existed—rapidly disintegrated, and the dream of a stable peace was replaced by the specter of a potential nuclear holocaust. The United Nations, envisioned by its founders as a mechanism for adjudicating international disputes, became mired in partisan bickering. As the Cold War between Moscow and Washington intensified, Europe was divided into two armed camps, while the two superpowers, glaring at each other across a deep ideological divide, held the survival of the entire world in their hands.

The Collapse of the Grand Alliance

Q FOCUS QUESTION: Why were the United States and the Soviet Union suspicious of each other after World War II, and what events between 1945 and 1949 heightened the tensions between the two nations?

The problems started in Europe. At the end of the war, Soviet military forces occupied all of Eastern Europe and the Balkans (except Greece, Albania, and Yugoslavia), while U.S. and other Allied forces secured the western part of the Continent. Roosevelt had assumed that free elections, administered promptly by "democratic and peace-loving forces," would lead to democratic governments responsive to the local population. But it soon became clear that the Soviet Union interpreted the Yalta agreement differently. When Soviet occupation authorities began forming a new Polish government, Stalin refused to accept the Polish government-in-exile—headquartered in London during the war and composed primarily of landed aristocrats who harbored a deep distrust of the Soviet Union—and instead set up a government composed of Communists who had spent the war in Moscow. Roosevelt complained to Stalin but eventually agreed to a compromise whereby two members of the London government were included in the new Communist regime. A week later, Roosevelt was dead of a cerebral hemorrhage, leaving the challenge to a new U.S. president, Harry Truman (1884–1972), who lacked experience in foreign affairs.

Soviet Domination of Eastern Europe

Similar developments took place in all of the states occupied by Soviet troops. Coalitions of all political parties (except fascist or right-wing parties) were formed to run the government, but within a year or two, the Communist Party in each coalition had assumed the lion's share of power. It was then a short step to the establishment of one-party Communist governments. Between 1945 and 1947, Communist governments became firmly entrenched in East Germany, Bulgaria, Romania, Poland, and Hungary. In Czechoslovakia, with its strong tradition of democratic institutions, the Communists did not achieve their goals until 1948. After the Czech elections of 1946, the Communist Party shared control of the government with the non-Communist parties. When it appeared that the latter might win new elections early in 1948, the Communists seized control of the government on February 25. All other parties were dissolved, and the Communist leader Klement Gottwald (KLEM-ent GUT-vald) (1896–1953) became the new president of Czechoslovakia.

Yugoslavia was a notable exception to the pattern of Soviet dominance in Eastern Europe. The Communist Party there had led the resistance to the Nazis during the war and easily assumed power when the war ended. Josip Broz (yaw-SEEP BRAWZ), known as Tito (TEE-toh) (1892–1980), the leader of the Communist resistance movement, appeared to be a loyal Stalinist. After the war, however, he moved to establish an independent Communist state. Stalin hoped to take control of Yugoslavia, but Tito refused to capitulate to Stalin's demands and gained the support of the people (and some sympathy in the West) by portraying the struggle as one of Yugoslav national freedom. In 1958, the Yugoslav party congress asserted that Yugoslav Communists did not see themselves as deviating from communism, only from Stalinism. They considered their more decentralized system, in which workers managed themselves and local communes exercised some political power, closer to the Marxist-Leninist ideal.

To Stalin (who had once boasted, "I will shake my little finger, and there will be no more Tito"), the creation of pliant pro-Soviet regimes throughout Eastern Europe to serve as a buffer zone against the capitalist West may simply have represented his interpretation of the Yalta peace agreement and a reward for sacrifices suffered during the war. If the Soviet leader had any intention of promoting future Communist revolutions in Western Europe—and there is some indication that he did—such developments would have to await the appearance of a new capitalist crisis a decade or more into the future. As Stalin undoubtedly recalled, Lenin had always maintained that revolutions come in waves, and he was willing to wait for the next one to come along.

Eastern Europe in 1948

Descent of the Iron Curtain

To the United States, however, the Soviet takeover of Eastern Europe represented an ominous development that threatened Roosevelt's vision of a durable peace. Public suspicion of Soviet intentions grew rapidly, especially among the millions of Americans who had relatives living in Eastern Europe. Winston Churchill was quick to put such fears into words. In a highly publicized speech at Westminster College in Fulton, Missouri, in March 1946, Churchill said that an "iron curtain" had "descended across the Continent," dividing Germany and Europe itself into two hostile camps. Stalin responded that Churchill's speech was a "call to war with the Soviet Union." But he need not have worried. Although public opinion in the United States put increasing pressure on Harry Truman, Roosevelt's successor, to devise an effective strategy to counter Soviet advances abroad, the American people were in no mood for another war.

A Call to Arms. Within five years after the end of World War II, the Grand Alliance that had brought victory over the Axis Powers was in tatters. In March 1946, the former British prime minister Winston Churchill, in an address given at Westminster College in Fulton, Missouri, declared that Soviet occupation of Eastern Europe had divided the Continent into two hostile camps, separated by an "iron curtain." The speech is often credited with launching the first salvo in the Cold War.

The first threat of a U.S.-Soviet confrontation took place in the Middle East. During World War II, British and Soviet troops had been stationed in Iran to prevent Axis occupation of the rich oil fields in that country. Both nations had promised to withdraw their forces after the war, but at the end of 1945, there were ominous signs that Moscow might attempt to use its troops as a bargaining chip to annex Iran's northern territories—known as Azerbaijan (az-ur-by-JAHN)—into the Soviet Union. When the government of Iran, with strong U.S. support, threatened to take the issue to the United Nations, the Soviets backed down and removed their forces from that country in the spring of 1946.

The Truman Doctrine

A civil war in Greece created another potential arena for confrontation between the superpowers and an opportunity for the Truman administration to take a stand. Communist guerrilla forces supported by Tito's Yugoslavia had taken up arms against the pro-Western government in Athens. Great Britain had initially assumed primary responsibility for promoting postwar reconstruction in the eastern Mediterranean, but in 1947, continuing economic problems caused the British to withdraw from the active role they had been playing in both Greece and Turkey. President Truman, alarmed by British weakness and the possibility of Soviet expansion into the eastern Mediterranean, responded with the **Truman Doctrine**, which said in essence that the United States would provide financial aid to countries that claimed they were threatened by Communist expansion (see the box on p. 765). If the Soviets were not stopped in Greece, the Truman argument ran, then the United States would have to face the spread of communism throughout the free world. As Dean Acheson, the U.S. secretary of state, explained, "Like apples in a barrel infected by disease, the corruption of Greece would infect Iran and all the East . . . likewise Africa . . . Italy . . . France. . . . Not since Rome and Carthage has there been such a polarization of power on this earth."[2]

The somewhat apocalyptic tone of Acheson's statement was intentional. Not only were the American people in no mood for foreign adventures, but the administration's Republican opponents in Congress were in an isolationist frame of mind. Only the prospect of a dire threat from abroad, the president's advisers argued, could persuade the nation to take action. The tactic worked, and Congress voted to provide the aid Truman had requested.

The U.S. suspicion that Moscow was actively supporting the insurgent movement in Greece turned out to be unfounded, however. Stalin was apparently unhappy with Tito's role in the conflict, not only because he suspected that the latter was attempting to create his own sphere of influence in the Balkans but also because it risked provoking a direct confrontation between the United States and the Soviet Union. But the Truman Doctrine had its intended effect in the United States, as public concern about the future intentions of the Soviets rose to new heights.

The Marshall Plan

The proclamation of the Truman Doctrine was followed in June 1947 by the European Recovery Program, better known as the **Marshall Plan**, which provided $13 billion in U.S. assistance for the economic recovery of war-torn Europe. Underlying the program was the belief that Communist aggression fed off economic turmoil. General George C. Marshall had noted in a speech at Harvard University, "Our policy is not directed against any country or doctrine but against hunger, poverty, desperation, and chaos."[3]

From the Soviet perspective, the Marshall Plan was capitalist imperialism, a thinly veiled attempt to buy the support of the smaller European countries "in return for the relinquishing . . . of their economic and later also their political independence."[4] A Soviet spokesperson described the United States as the "main force in the imperialist camp," whose ultimate goal was "the strengthening of imperialism, preparation for a new imperialist war, a struggle against socialism and democracy, and the support of reactionary and antidemocratic, profascist regimes and movements." Although the Marshall Plan was open to the Soviet Union and its Eastern European satellite states, Soviet leaders viewed the offer as a devious capitalist ploy and refused to participate. Under heavy pressure from Moscow, Eastern European governments did so as well. The Soviets were in no position to compete financially with the United States, however, and could do little to counter the Marshall Plan except tighten their control in Eastern Europe.

The Truman Doctrine

POLITICS & GOVERNMENT

In 1947, the battle lines in the Cold War had been clearly drawn. This excerpt is taken from a speech by President Harry Truman to the U.S. Congress in which he justified his request for aid to Greece and Turkey. Truman expressed the urgent need to contain the expansion of communism. Compare this statement with that of Soviet leader Leonid Brezhnev cited on p. 779.

Truman's Speech to Congress, March 12, 1947

The gravity of the situation which confronts the world today necessitates my appearance before a joint session of the Congress. The foreign policy and the national security of this country are involved.

One aspect of the present situation, which I wish to present to you at this time for your consideration and decision, concerns Greece and Turkey.

The United States has received from the Greek Government an urgent appeal for financial and economic assistance. Preliminary reports from the American Economic Mission now in Greece and reports from the American Ambassador in Greece corroborate the statement of the Greek Government that assistance is imperative if Greece is to survive as a free nation.

I do not believe that the American people and the Congress wish to turn a deaf ear to the appeal of the Greek Government.

Greece is not a rich country. Lack of sufficient natural resources has always forced the Greek people to work hard to make both ends meet. Since 1940, this industrious and peace loving country has suffered invasion, four years of cruel enemy occupation, and bitter internal strife . . . .

The peoples of a number of countries of the world have recently had totalitarian regimes forced upon them against their will. The Government of the United States has made frequent protests against coercion and intimidation, in violation of the Yalta agreement, in Poland, Rumania, and Bulgaria. I must also state that in a number of other countries there have been similar developments.

At the present moment in world history nearly every nation must choose between alternative ways of life. The choice is too often not a free one.

One way of life is based upon the will of the majority, and is distinguished by free institutions, representative government, free elections, guarantees of individual liberty, freedom of speech and religion, and freedom from political oppression.

The second way of life is based upon the will of a minority forcibly imposed upon the majority. It relies upon terror and oppression, a controlled press and radio; fixed elections, and the suppression of personal freedoms.

I believe that it must be the policy of the United States to support free peoples who are resisting attempted subjugation by armed minorities or by outside pressures.

I believe that we must assist free peoples to work out their own destinies in their own way.

I believe that our help should be primarily through economic and financial aid which is essential to economic stability and orderly political processes.

The world is not static, and the status quo is not sacred. But we cannot allow changes in the status quo in violation of the Charter of the United Nations by such methods as coercion, or by such subterfuges as political infiltration. In helping free and independent nations to maintain their freedom, the United States will be giving effect to the principles of the Charter of the United Nations.

It is necessary only to glance at a map to realize that the survival and integrity of the Greek nation are of grave importance in a much wider situation. If Greece should fall under the control of an armed minority, the effect upon its neighbor, Turkey, would be immediate and serious. Confusion and disorder might well spread throughout the entire Middle East.

Moreover, the disappearance of Greece as an independent state would have a profound effect upon those countries in Europe whose peoples are struggling against great difficulties to maintain their freedoms and their independence while they repair the damages of war.

It would be an unspeakable tragedy if these countries, which have struggled so long against overwhelming odds, should lose that victory for which they sacrificed so much. Collapse of free institutions and loss of independence would be disastrous not only for them but for the world. Discouragement and possibly failure would quickly be the lot of neighboring peoples striving to maintain their freedom and independence.

Should we fail to aid Greece and Turkey in this fateful hour, the effect will be far reaching to the West as well as to the East.

We must take immediate and resolute action . . . .

The assistance that I am recommending for Greece and Turkey amounts to little more than 1 tenth of 1 per cent of this investment. It is only common sense that we should safeguard this investment and make sure that it was not in vain.

The seeds of totalitarian regimes are nurtured by misery and want. They spread and grow in the evil soil of poverty and strife. They reach their full growth when the hope of a people for a better life has died. We must keep that hope alive.

The free peoples of the world look to us for support in maintaining their freedoms.

If we falter in our leadership, we may endanger the peace of the world—and we shall surely endanger the welfare of our own nation.

Great responsibilities have been placed upon us by the swift movement of events.

I am confident that the Congress will face these responsibilities squarely.

How did President Truman defend his request for aid to Greece and Turkey? What role did this decision play in intensifying the Cold War?

Europe Divided

By 1947, the split in Europe between East and West had become a fact of life. At the end of World War II, the United States had favored a quick end to its commitments in Europe. But American fears of Soviet aims caused the United States to play an increasingly important role in Europe. In an article in *Foreign Affairs* in July 1947, George Kennan, a well-known U.S. diplomat with much knowledge of the Soviet Union, advocated a policy of **containment** against further aggressive Soviet moves. Kennan favored the "adroit and vigilant application of counter-force at a series of constantly shifting geographical and political points, corresponding to the shifts and maneuvers of Soviet policy." When the Soviets blockaded Berlin in 1948, containment of the Soviet Union became formal U.S. policy.

THE BERLIN BLOCKADE The fate of Germany had become a source of heated contention between East and West. Aside from **denazification** (dee-naht-sih-fuh-KAY-shun)—the removal of all pro-Nazi elements from positions of influence in German society—and the partitioning of Germany (and Berlin) into four occupied zones, the Allied Powers had agreed on little with regard to the conquered nation. The Soviet Union, hardest hit by the war, took reparations from Germany by pillaging German industry. The technology-starved Soviets dismantled and removed to Russia 380 factories from the western zones of Berlin before transferring their control to the Western powers. By the summer of 1946, two hundred chemical, paper, and textile factories in the East German zone had likewise been shipped to the Soviet Union. At the same time, the German Communist Party was reestablished under the control of Walter Ulbricht (VAHL-tuh OOL-brikkt) (1893–1973), and it was soon in charge of the political reconstruction of the Soviet zone in eastern Germany.

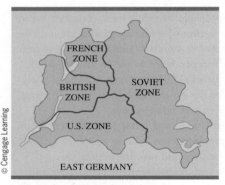

Berlin at the Start of the Cold War

© Cengage Learning

Although the foreign ministers of the four occupying powers kept meeting in an attempt to arrive at a final peace treaty with Germany, they moved further and further apart. At the same time, the British, French, and Americans gradually began to merge their zones economically and by February 1948 were making plans for unification of these sectors and the formation of a national government. In an effort to secure all of Berlin and to halt the creation of a West German government, the Soviet Union imposed a blockade of West Berlin that prevented all traffic from entering the city's western zones through Soviet-controlled territory in East Germany.

The Western powers faced a dilemma. Direct military confrontation seemed dangerous, especially at a time when the U.S. military presence in Europe had been severely reduced, and no one wished to risk World War III. Therefore, an attempt to break through the blockade with tanks and trucks was ruled out. The solution was to deliver supplies for the city's inhabitants by plane. At its peak, the Berlin Airlift flew 13,000 tons of supplies daily into Berlin. The Soviets, also not wanting war, did not interfere and finally lifted the blockade in May 1949. But the blockade had severely increased tensions between the United States and the Soviet Union and brought about the separation of Germany into two states. The Federal Republic of Germany was formally created from the three western zones in September 1949, and a month later, the separate German Democratic Republic (GDR) was established in East Germany. Berlin remained a divided city and the source of much contention between East and West.

NATO AND THE WARSAW PACT The search for security in the Cold War also led to the formation of military alliances. The North Atlantic Treaty Organization (NATO) was formed in April 1949 when Belgium, Britain, Denmark, France, Iceland, Italy, Luxembourg, the Netherlands, Norway, and Portugal signed a treaty with the United States and Canada. All the powers agreed to provide mutual assistance if any one of them was attacked. A few years later, West Germany and Turkey joined NATO. In the meantime, the United States engaged in an arms buildup aimed at preventing the further expansion of communism anywhere in the world.

The Eastern European states soon followed suit. In 1949, they formed the Council for Mutual Economic Assistance (COMECON) for economic cooperation. Then, in 1955, Albania, Bulgaria, Czechoslovakia, East Germany, Hungary, Poland, Romania, and the Soviet Union organized a formal military alliance, the Warsaw Pact. Once again, Europe was tragically divided into hostile alliance systems (see Map 26.1 on p. 768).

WHO STARTED THE COLD WAR? There has been considerable historical debate over who bears responsibility for starting the Cold War. In the 1950s, most scholars in the West assumed that the bulk of the blame must fall on the shoulders of Stalin, whose determination to impose Soviet rule on Eastern Europe snuffed out hopes for freedom and self-determination there and aroused justifiable fears of Communist expansion in the West. During the next decade, however, revisionist historians—influenced in part by their hostility to aggressive U.S. policies in Southeast Asia—began to argue that the fault lay primarily in Washington, where Truman and his anti-Communist advisers abandoned the precepts of Yalta and sought to encircle the Soviet Union with a tier of pliant U.S. client states. More recently, many historians have adopted a more nuanced view, noting that both the United States and the Soviet Union took some unwise steps that contributed to rising tensions at the end of World War II.

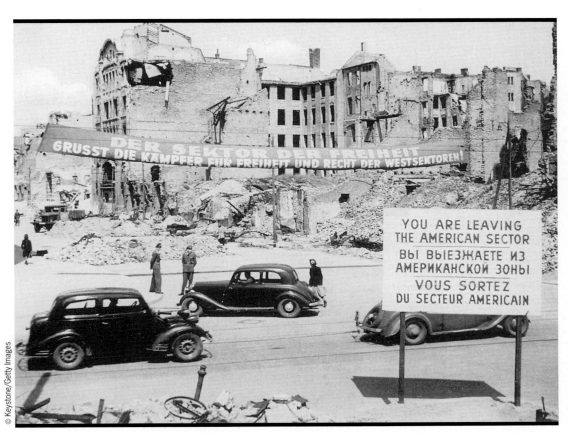

A City Divided. In 1948, U.S. planes airlifted supplies into Berlin to break the blockade that Soviet troops had imposed to isolate the city. Shown here is "Checkpoint Charlie," located at the boundary between the U.S. and Soviet zones of Berlin, just as Soviet roadblocks are about to be removed. The banner at the entrance to the Soviet sector reads, ironically, "The sector of freedom greets the fighters for freedom and rights of the Western sectors."

In fact, both nations were working within a framework conditioned by the past. The rivalry between the two superpowers ultimately stemmed from their different historical perspectives and their irreconcilable political ambitions. Intense competition for political and military supremacy had long been a regular feature of Western civilization. The United States and the Soviet Union were the heirs of that European tradition of power politics, and it should come as no surprise that two such different systems would seek to extend their way of life to the rest of the world. Because of its need to secure its western border, the Soviet Union was not prepared to give up the advantages it had gained in Eastern Europe from Germany's defeat. But neither were Western leaders prepared to accept without protest the establishment of a system of Soviet satellites that not only threatened the security of Western Europe but also deeply offended Western sensibilities because of its blatant disregard of the Western concept of human rights.

This does not necessarily mean that both sides bear equal responsibility for starting the Cold War. Some revisionist historians have claimed that the U.S. doctrine of containment was a provocative action that aroused Stalin's suspicions and drove him into a position of hostility toward the West. This charge lacks credibility. Although it is understandable that the Soviets were concerned that the United States might use its monopoly of nuclear weapons to attempt to intimidate them, information now available from the Soviet archives and other sources makes it increasingly clear that Stalin's suspicions of the West were rooted in his Marxist-Leninist worldview and long predated Washington's enunciation of the doctrine of containment. As his foreign minister, Vyacheslav Molotov, once remarked, Soviet policy was inherently aggressive and would be triggered whenever the opportunity offered. Although Stalin apparently had no master plan to advance Soviet power into Western Europe, he was probably prepared to make every effort to do so once the next revolutionary wave arrived. Western leaders were fully justified in reacting to this possibility by strengthening their own lines of defense. On the other hand, a case can be made that in deciding to respond to the Soviet challenge in a primarily military manner, Western leaders overreacted to the situation and virtually guaranteed that the Cold War would be transformed into an arms race that could conceivably result in a new and uniquely destructive war. George Kennan, the original architect of the doctrine of containment, had initially proposed a primarily political approach and eventually disavowed the means by which the containment strategy was carried out.

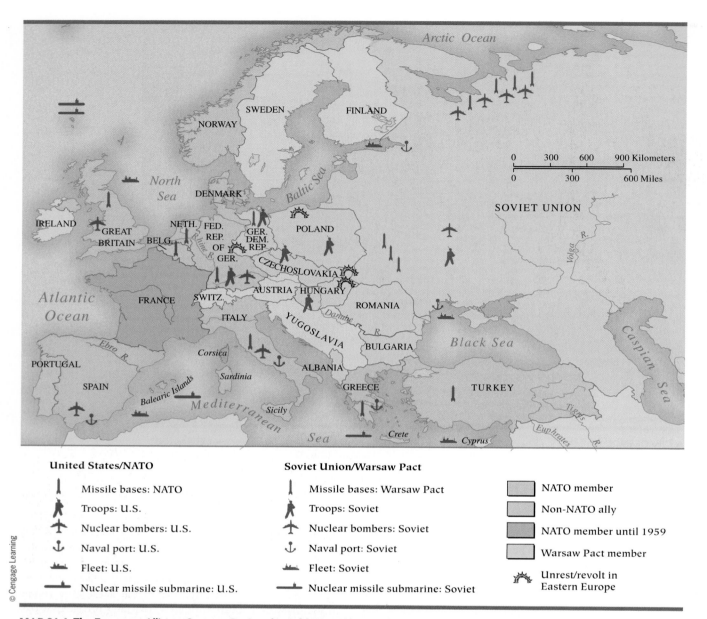

United States/NATO

⚔	Missile bases: NATO
🧍	Troops: U.S.
✈	Nuclear bombers: U.S.
⚓	Naval port: U.S.
⛴	Fleet: U.S.
⎯	Nuclear missile submarine: U.S.

Soviet Union/Warsaw Pact

⚔	Missile bases: Warsaw Pact
🧍	Troops: Soviet
✈	Nuclear bombers: Soviet
⚓	Naval port: Soviet
⛴	Fleet: Soviet
⎯	Nuclear missile submarine: Soviet

▢	NATO member
▢	Non-NATO ally
▢	NATO member until 1959
▢	Warsaw Pact member
☢	Unrest/revolt in Eastern Europe

MAP 26.1 The European Alliance Systems During the Cold War. This map shows Europe as it was divided during the Cold War into two contending power blocs, the NATO alliance and the Warsaw Pact. Major military and naval bases are indicated by symbols on the map.

Q *Where on the map was the Iron Curtain?*

Cold War in Asia

Q FOCUS QUESTION: How and why did Mao Zedong and the Communists come to power in China, and what were the Cold War implications of their triumph?

The Cold War was somewhat slower to make itself felt in Asia. At Yalta, Stalin formally agreed to enter the Pacific war against Japan three months after the close of the conflict with Germany. As a reward for Soviet participation in the struggle against Japan, Roosevelt promised that Moscow would be granted "preeminent interests" in Manchuria (reminiscent of the interests possessed by imperial Russia prior to its defeat at the hands of Japan in 1904–1905) and allowed to establish a Soviet naval base at Port Arthur. In return, Stalin promised to sign a treaty of alliance with the Republic of China, thus implicitly committing the Soviet Union not to assist the Chinese Communists in a possible future civil war. Although many observers would later question Stalin's sincerity in making such a commitment to the vocally anti-Communist Chiang Kai-shek, in Moscow the decision probably had a logic of its own. Stalin had no particular liking for the independent-minded Mao Zedong (he once derisively labeled the Chinese leader a "radish Communist"—red on the outside and white on the inside) and indeed did not anticipate a Communist victory in any civil war in China. Only an agreement with Chiang could provide the Soviet Union with a strategically vital economic and political presence in northern China.

The Truman administration was equally reluctant to get embroiled in a confrontation with Moscow over the unfolding events in East Asia. Suspicion of Chiang Kai-shek ran high in Washington, and as we shall see, many key U.S. policymakers hoped to avoid a deeper involvement in China by brokering a compromise agreement between Chiang and his Communist rival, Mao.

Despite such misgivings, the Allied agreements soon broke down, and East Asia was sucked into the vortex of the Cold War by the end of the 1940s. The root of the problem lay in the underlying weakness of Chiang's regime, which threatened to create a political vacuum in East Asia that both Moscow and Washington would be tempted to fill.

The Chinese Civil War

As World War II came to an end in the Pacific, relations between the government of Chiang Kai-shek in China and its powerful U.S. ally had become frayed. Although Roosevelt had hoped that republican China would be the keystone of his plan for peace and stability in Asia after the war, U.S. officials became disillusioned with the corruption of Chiang's government and his unwillingness to risk his forces against the Japanese (he hoped to save them for use against the Communists after the war in the Pacific ended). Hence, China was no longer the object of Washington's close attention as the war came to a close. Nevertheless, U.S. military and economic aid to China had been substantial, and at war's end, the new Truman administration still hoped that it could rely on Chiang to support U.S. postwar goals in the region.

While Chiang wrestled with Japanese aggression and problems of national development, the Communists were building up their strength in northern China. To enlarge their political base, they carried out a "mass line" policy (a term in Communist jargon that meant responding to the immediate needs and demands of the mass of the Chinese population), reducing land rents and confiscating the lands of wealthy landlords. By the end of World War II, 20 to 30 million Chinese were living under the administration of the Communists, and their People's Liberation Army (PLA) included nearly one million troops.

As the war came to an end, world attention began to focus on the prospects for renewed civil strife in China. Members of a U.S. liaison team stationed in Yan'an (yuh-NAHN) were impressed by the performance of the Communists, and some recommended that the United States should support them or at least remain neutral in a possible conflict between Communists and Nationalists for control of China. The Truman administration, though skeptical of Chiang's ability to forge a strong and prosperous country, was increasingly concerned about the spread of communism in Europe and tried to find a peaceful solution through the formation of a coalition government of all parties in China.

THE COMMUNIST TRIUMPH The effort failed. By 1946, full-scale war between the Nationalist government, now reinstalled in Nanjing, and the Communists resumed. Initially, most of the fighting took place in Manchuria, where newly arrived Communist units began to surround Nationalist forces occupying the major cities. Now Chiang Kai-shek's errors came home to roost. In the countryside, millions of peasants, attracted to the Communists by promises of land and social justice, flocked to serve in Mao Zedong's PLA. In the cities, middle-class Chinese, normally hostile to communism, were alienated by Chiang's brutal suppression of all dissent and his government's inability to slow the ruinous rate of inflation or solve the economic problems it caused. By the end of 1947, almost all of Manchuria was under Communist control.

The Truman administration reacted to the spread of Communist power in China with acute discomfort. Washington had no desire to see a Communist government on the mainland, but it had little confidence in Chiang Kai-shek's ability

Chiang Kai-shek and Mao Zedong Exchange a Toast. After World War II, the United States sent General George C. Marshall to China in an effort to prevent civil war between Chiang Kai-shek's government and Mao Zedong's Communists. Marshall's initial success was symbolized by this toast between Chiang (at the right) and Mao. But suspicion ran too deep, and soon conflict ensued, resulting in a Communist victory in 1949. Chiang's government retreated to the island of Taiwan.

© Jack Wilkes/Time Life Pictures/Getty Images

to realize Roosevelt's dream of a strong, united, and prosperous China. In December 1945, President Truman sent General George C. Marshall to China in a last-ditch effort to bring about a peaceful settlement, but anti-Communist elements in the Republic of China resisted U.S. pressure to create a coalition government with the Chinese Communist Party (CCP). During the next two years, the United States gave limited military support to Chiang's regime but refused to commit U.S. power to guarantee its survival. The administration's hands-off policy deeply angered many members of Congress, who charged that the White House was "soft on communism" and called for increased military assistance to the Nationalist government.

With morale dropping in the cities, Chiang's troops began to defect to the Communists. Sometimes whole divisions, officers as well as ordinary soldiers, changed sides. By 1948, the PLA was advancing south out of Manchuria and had encircled Beijing. Communist troops took the old imperial capital, crossed the Yangtze the following spring, and occupied the commercial hub of Shanghai (see Map 26.2). During the next few months, Chiang's government and 2 million of his followers fled to Taiwan, which the Japanese had returned to Chinese control after World War II.

With the Communist victory in China, Asia became a major theater of the Cold War and an integral element in American politics. In a white paper issued by the State Department in the fall of 1949, the Truman administration placed most of the blame for the debacle on Chiang Kai-shek's regime (see the box on p. 771). Republicans in Congress, however,

disagreed, arguing that Roosevelt had betrayed Chiang Kai-shek at Yalta by granting privileges in Manchuria to the Soviet Union. In their view, Soviet troops had hindered the dispatch of Nationalist forces to the area and provided the PLA with weapons to use against their rivals.

In later years, sources in Moscow and Beijing made clear that in actuality the Soviet Union gave little assistance to the CCP in its postwar struggle against the Nanjing regime. In fact, Stalin—likely concerned at the prospect of a military confrontation with the United States—advised Mao against undertaking the effort. Although Communist forces undoubtedly received some assistance from Soviet occupation troops in Manchuria, their victory ultimately stemmed from conditions inside China. Nevertheless, the White House responded to its critics. During the spring of 1950, under pressure from Congress and public opinion to define U.S. interests in Asia, the Truman administration adopted a new national security policy that implied that the United States would take whatever steps were necessary to stem the further expansion of communism in the region. Containment had come to East Asia.

The New China

In their new capital of Beijing, China's Communist leaders probably hoped that their accession to power in 1949 would bring about an era of temporary peace in the region and permit their new government to concentrate on domestic goals. But the desire for peace was tempered by their determination to erase a century of humiliation at the hands of imperialist powers and to restore the traditional outer frontiers of the empire. In addition to recovering territories that had been part of the Manchu Empire, such as Manchuria, Taiwan, and Tibet, the Chinese leaders also hoped to restore Chinese influence in former tributary areas such as Korea and Vietnam.

It soon became clear that these two goals were not always compatible. Negotiations between Mao Zedong and Joseph Stalin, held in Moscow in January 1950, led to Soviet recognition of Chinese sovereignty over Manchuria and Xinjiang (SHIN-jyahng)—the desolate lands north of Tibet that were known as Chinese Turkestan because many of the peoples in the area were of Turkic origin—although the Soviets retained a measure of economic influence in both areas. Chinese troops occupied Tibet in 1950 and brought it under Chinese administration for the first time in more than a century. But in Korea and Taiwan, China's efforts to re-create the imperial buffer zone provoked new conflicts with foreign powers.

The problem of Taiwan was a consequence of the Cold War. As the civil war in China came to an end, the Truman administration appeared determined to avoid entanglement in China's internal affairs and indicated that it would not seek to prevent a Communist takeover of the island, now occupied by Chiang Kai-shek's Republic of China. But as tensions between the United States and the

MAP 26.2 The Chinese Civil War. After the close of the Pacific war in 1945, the Nationalist Chinese government and the Chinese Communists fought a bitter civil war that ended with a Communist victory in 1949. The path of the Communist advance is shown on the map.

Q *Where did Chiang Kai-shek's government retreat to after its defeat?*

Who Lost China?

POLITICS & GOVERNMENT

In 1949, with China about to fall under the control of the Communists, President Truman instructed the State Department to prepare a detailed "white paper" report explaining why the U.S. policy of seeking to avoid a Communist victory in China had failed. The authors of the report concluded that responsibility lay at the door of Nationalist Chinese leader Chiang Kai-shek and that there was nothing the United States could have done to alter the result. Most China observers today would accept that assessment, but it did little at the time to deflect criticism of the administration for selling out the interests of our ally in China.

U.S. State Department White Paper on China, 1949

When peace came the United States was confronted with three possible alternatives in China: (1) it could have pulled out lock, stock, and barrel; (2) it could have intervened militarily on a major scale to assist the Nationalists to destroy the Communists; (3) it could, while assisting the Nationalists to assert their authority over as much of China as possible, endeavor to avoid a civil war by working for a compromise between the two sides.

The first alternative would, and I believe American public opinion at the time so felt, have represented an abandonment of our international responsibilities and of our traditional policy of friendship for China before we had made a determined effort to be of assistance. The second alternative policy, while it may look attractive theoretically, in retrospect was wholly impracticable. The Nationalists had been unable to destroy the Communists during the ten years before the war. Now after the war the Nationalists were . . . weakened, demoralized, and unpopular. They had quickly dissipated their popular support and prestige in the areas liberated from the Japanese

by the conduct of their civil and military officials. The Communists on the other hand were much stronger than they had ever been and were in control of most of North China. Because of the ineffectiveness of the Nationalist forces, which was later to be tragically demonstrated, the Communists probably could have been dislodged only by American arms. It is obvious that the American people would not have sanctioned such a colossal commitment of our armies in 1945 or later. We therefore came to the third alternative policy whereunder we faced the facts of the situation and attempted to assist in working out a modus vivendi which would avert civil war but nevertheless preserve and even increase the influence of the National Government. . . .

The distrust of the leaders of both the Nationalist and Communist Parties for each other proved too deep-seated to permit final agreement, notwithstanding temporary truces and apparently promising negotiations. The Nationalists, furthermore, embarked in 1946 on an overambitious military campaign in the face of warnings by General Marshall that it not only would fail but would plunge China into economic chaos and eventually destroy the National Government. . . .

The unfortunate but inescapable fact is that the ominous result of the civil war in China was beyond the control of the government of the United States. Nothing that this country did or could have done within the reasonable limits of its capabilities could have changed that result; nothing that was left undone by this country has contributed to it. It was the product of internal Chinese forces, forces which this country tried to influence but could not. A decision was arrived at within China, if only a decision by default.

 How did the authors of the white paper explain the Communist victory in China? According to their argument, what actions might have prevented it?

---

new Chinese government escalated during the winter of 1949–1950, influential figures in the United States began to argue that Taiwan was crucial to U.S. defense strategy in the Pacific.

The Korean War

The sudden outbreak of war in Korea intensified the Cold War in East Asia. After the Sino-Japanese War in 1894–1895, Korea, long a Chinese tributary, had fallen increasingly under the rival influences of Japan and Russia. After the Japanese defeated the Russians in 1905, Korea became an integral part of the Japanese Empire and remained so until 1945. The removal of Korea from Japanese control had been one of the stated objectives of the Allies in World War II, and on the eve of Japanese surrender in August 1945, the Soviet Union

and the United States agreed to divide the country into two separate occupation zones at the 38th parallel. They originally planned to hold national elections after the restoration of peace to reunify Korea under an independent government. But as U.S.-Soviet relations deteriorated, two separate governments emerged in Korea, a Communist one in the north and an anti-Communist one in the south.

Tensions between the two governments ran high along the dividing line, and on June 25, 1950, with the apparent approval of Stalin, North Korean troops invaded the south. The Truman administration immediately ordered U.S. naval and air forces to support South Korea, and the United Nations Security Council (with the Soviet delegate absent to protest the refusal of the UN to assign China's seat to the new government in Beijing) passed a resolution calling on member

A Pledge of Eternal Friendship. After the Communist victory in the Chinese civil war, in 1950 Chairman Mao Zedong traveled to Moscow, where he negotiated a treaty of friendship and cooperation with the Soviet Union. The poster shown here trumpets the results of the meeting: "Long live and strengthen the unbreakable friendship and cooperation of the Soviet and Chinese peoples!" The two leaders, however, did not get along. Mao reportedly complained to colleagues that obtaining assistance from Stalin was "like taking meat from a tiger's mouth."

MAP 26.3 The Korean Peninsula. In June 1950, North Korean forces crossed the 38th parallel in a sudden invasion of the south. Shown here is the cease-fire line that brought an end to the war in 1953.

 What is the significance of the Yalu River?

nations to jointly resist the invasion, in line with the security provisions in the United Nations Charter. By September, UN forces under the command of U.S. General Douglas MacArthur marched northward across the 38th parallel with the aim of unifying Korea under a single, non-Communist government.

President Truman worried that by approaching the Chinese border at the Yalu (YAH-loo) River, the UN troops—the majority of whom were from the United States—could trigger Chinese intervention, but MacArthur assured him that China would not respond. In November, however, Chinese "volunteer" forces intervened in force on the side of North Korea and drove the UN troops southward in disarray. A static defense line was eventually established near the original dividing line at the 38th parallel (see Map 26.3), although the war continued.

To many Americans, the Chinese intervention in Korea was clear evidence that China intended to promote communism throughout Asia, and recent evidence suggests that Mao, now convinced that a revolutionary wave was on the rise in Asia, had given his blessing to the North Korean invasion of the south. China's decision to enter the war, however, was probably motivated in large part by the fear that hostile U.S. forces might be stationed on the Chinese frontier and perhaps even launch an attack across the border. MacArthur intensified such fears by calling publicly for air attacks on Manchurian cities in preparation for an attack on Communist China.

In any case, the outbreak of the Korean War was particularly unfortunate for China. Immediately after the invasion,

President Truman dispatched the U.S. Seventh Fleet to the Taiwan Strait to prevent a possible Chinese invasion of Taiwan. Even more unfortunate, the invasion hardened Western attitudes against the new Chinese government and led to China's isolation from the major capitalist powers for two decades. The United States continued to regard the Nationalist government in Taiwan as the only legal representative of the Chinese people and to support its retention of China's seat on the UN Security Council. As a result, mainland China was cut off from all forms of economic and technological assistance and was forced to rely almost entirely on the Soviet Union.

Conflict in Indochina

During the mid-1950s, Communist leaders in Beijing began to back away from their confrontational stance toward the West and sought to build contacts with the nonsocialist world. A cease-fire agreement brought the Korean War to an end in July 1953, and China signaled its desire to live in peaceful coexistence with other independent countries in the region. But Bejing's message of peace was clouded by its role in a bitter conflict that began to intensify on China's southern flank, in French Indochina. The struggle had begun after Japan's surrender at the end of World War II, when the Indochinese Communist Party led by Ho Chi Minh (HOH CHEE MIN) (1890–1969), at the head of a multiparty nationalist alliance called the Vietminh (vee-et-MIN) Front, seized power in northern and central Vietnam. After abortive negotiations between Ho's government and the returning French, war

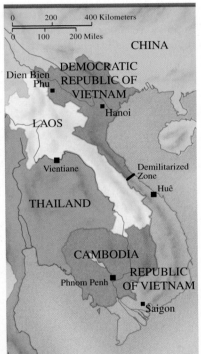

Ho Chi Minh Plans an Attack on the French. Unlike many of the peoples of Southeast Asia, the Vietnamese had to fight for their independence after World War II. That fight was led by the talented Communist leader Ho Chi Minh. In this 1950 photograph taken at his secret base in the mountains of North Vietnam, Ho plans an attack on French positions. He changed the location of his headquarters on several occasions to evade capture by French forces.

© AFP/Getty Images

broke out in December 1946. French forces occupied the cities and the densely populated lowlands, while the Vietminh took refuge in the mountains.

For three years, the Vietminh waged a "people's war" of national liberation from colonial rule, gradually increasing in size and effectiveness. At the time, however, the conflict in Indochina attracted relatively little attention from world leaders, who viewed the events there as only one aspect of the transition to independence of colonialized territories in postwar Asia. The Truman administration was uneasy about Ho's long-standing credentials as a Soviet agent but was equally reluctant to anger anticolonialist elements in the region by intervening on behalf of the French. Moscow had even less interest in the issue. Stalin—still hoping to see the Communist Party come to power in Paris—ignored Ho's request for recognition of his movement as the legitimate representative of the national interests of the Vietnamese people.

But what had begun as an anticolonial struggle by the Vietminh Front against the French became entangled in the Cold War after the CCP came to power in China. In early 1950, Beijing began to provide military assistance to the Vietminh to burnish its revolutionary credentials and protect its own borders from hostile forces. The Truman administration, increasingly concerned that a revolutionary "Red tide" was sweeping through the region, decided to provide financial and technical assistance to the French while pressuring them to prepare for an eventual transition to independent non-Communist governments in Vietnam, Laos, and Cambodia.

Despite growing U.S. involvement in the war, Vietminh forces continued to gain strength, and in the spring of 1954, with Chinese assistance, they besieged a French military outpost at Dien Bien Phu, (DEE-en bee-en FOO) not far from the border of Laos. The French sent reinforcements, and the decisive battle of the conflict was under way.

With casualties mounting and the French public tired of fighting the "dirty war" in Indochina, the French had agreed to hold peace talks with the Vietminh in May of 1954. On the day before the peace conference convened in Geneva, Switzerland,

Vietminh forces overran the French bastion at Dien Bien Phu. The humiliating defeat weakened French resolve to maintain a presence in Indochina. In July, the two sides agreed to a settlement. Vietnam was temporarily divided into a northern Communist half, known as the Democratic Republic of Vietnam (DRV), and a non-Communist southern half based in Saigon (sy-GAHN) (now Ho Chi Minh City) that eventually came to be known as the Republic of Vietnam. A demilitarized zone separated the two at the 17th parallel.

Indochina After 1954

© Cengage Learning

Elections were to be held in two years to create a unified government. Cambodia and Laos were both declared independent under neutral governments. French forces were withdrawn from all three countries.

China had played an active role in bringing about the settlement and clearly hoped that it would reduce tensions in the area, but subsequent efforts to improve relations between China and the United States foundered on the issue of Taiwan. In the fall of 1954, the United States signed a mutual security treaty with the Republic of China guaranteeing U.S. military support in case of an invasion of Taiwan. When Beijing demanded U.S. withdrawal from Taiwan as the price for improved relations, diplomatic talks between the two countries collapsed.

From Confrontation to Coexistence

Q FOCUS QUESTION: What events led to the era of coexistence in the 1960s, and to what degree did each side contribute to the reduction in international tensions?

The decade of the 1950s had opened with the world teetering on the edge of a nuclear holocaust. The Soviet Union had detonated its first nuclear device in 1949, and the two blocs—capitalist and socialist—viewed each other across an ideological divide that grew increasingly bitter with each passing year. Yet as the decade drew to a close, a measure of sanity crept into the Cold War, and the leaders of the major world powers began to seek ways to coexist in a peaceful and stable world (see Map 26.4).

The first clear sign of change occurred after Stalin's death in early 1953. His successor, Georgy Malenkov (gyee-OR-gyee muh-LEN-kawf) (1902–1988), openly hoped to improve relations with the Western powers in order to reduce defense expenditures and shift government spending to growing consumer needs. Nikita Khrushchev (nuh-KEE-tuh KHROOSH-chawf) (1894–1971), who replaced Malenkov in 1955, continued his predecessor's efforts to reduce tensions with the West and improve the living standards of the Soviet people.

In an adroit public relations touch, Khrushchev called for a policy of **peaceful coexistence** with the West. In 1955, he surprisingly agreed to negotiate an end to the postwar occupation of Austria by the victorious Allies and allow the creation of a neutral country with strong cultural and economic ties with the West. He also called for a reduction in defense expenditures and reduced the size of the Soviet armed forces.

Ferment in Eastern Europe

At first, Western leaders were suspicious of Khrushchev's motives, especially in light of events that were taking place in Eastern Europe. The key to security along the western frontier of the Soviet Union was the string of Eastern European satellite states that had been assembled in the aftermath of World War II (see Map 26.1). Once Communist domination had been assured, a series of "little Stalins" put into power by Moscow instituted Soviet-type five-year plans that emphasized

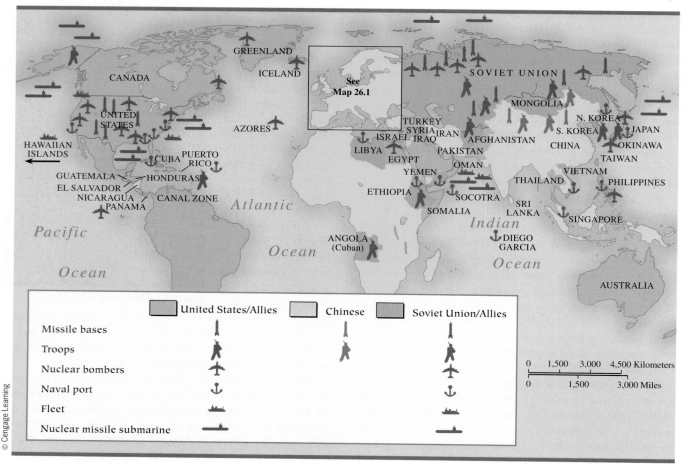

MAP 26.4 The Global Cold War. This map shows the location of the major military bases and missile sites maintained by the three contending power blocs at the height of the Cold War.

Q *Which continents were the most heavily armed? Why?*

heavy industry rather than consumer goods, the collectivization of agriculture, and the nationalization of industry. They also appropriated the political tactics that Stalin had perfected in the Soviet Union, eliminating all non-Communist parties and establishing the classic institutions of repression—the secret police and military forces. Dissidents were tracked down and thrown into prison, and "national Communists" who resisted total subservience to the Soviet Union were charged with treason in mass show trials and executed.

Despite these repressive efforts, popular discontent became increasingly evident in several Eastern European countries. Hungary, Poland, and Romania harbored bitter memories of past Russian domination and suspected that Stalin, under the guise of proletarian internationalism, was seeking to revive the empire of the tsars. For the vast majority of the residents of Eastern Europe, the imposition of the so-called people's democracies (a term invented by Moscow to refer to a society in the early stage of socialist transition) resulted in economic hardship and severe threats to the most basic political liberties. The first indications of unrest appeared in East Berlin, where popular riots broke out against Communist rule in 1953. The riots eventually subsided, but the virus had spread to neighboring countries.

In Poland, public demonstrations against an increase in food prices in 1956 escalated into widespread protests against the regime's economic policies, restrictions on the freedom of Catholics to practice their religion, and the continued presence of Soviet troops (as called for by the Warsaw Pact) on Polish soil. In a desperate effort to defuse the unrest, the party leader stepped down and was replaced by Wladyslaw Gomulka (vlah-DIS-lahf goh-MOOL-kuh) (1905–1982), a popular party figure who had previously been demoted for his "nationalist" tendencies. When Gomulka took steps to ease the crisis, Khrushchev flew to Warsaw to warn him against adopting policies that could undermine the political dominance of the party and weaken security links with the Soviet Union. After a tense confrontation, Poland agreed to remain in the Warsaw Pact and to maintain the sanctity of party rule; in return, Gomulka was authorized to adopt domestic reforms, such as easing restrictions on religious practice and ending the policy of forced collectivization in rural areas.

THE HUNGARIAN REVOLUTION The developments in Poland sent shock waves throughout the region. The impact was strongest in neighboring Hungary, where the methods of the local "little Stalin," Mátyás Rákosi (MAH-tyash RAH-koh-see) (1892–1971), were so brutal that he had been summoned to Moscow for a lecture ("He distrusts everybody," remarked one Soviet official). In late October 1956, student-led popular riots broke out in the capital of Budapest and soon spread to other towns and villages throughout the country. Rákosi was forced to resign and was replaced by Imre Nagy (IM-ray NAHJ) (1896–1958), a "national Communist" who attempted to satisfy popular demands without arousing the anger of Moscow. Unlike Gomulka, however, Nagy was unable to contain the zeal of leading members of the protest movement, who sought major political reforms and the

How the Mighty Have Fallen. In the fall of 1956, Hungarian freedom fighters rose up against Communist domination of their country in the short-lived Hungarian Revolution. Their actions threatened Soviet hegemony in Eastern Europe, however, and in late October, Soviet leader Nikita Khrushchev dispatched troops to quell the uprising. In the meantime, the Hungarian people had voiced their discontent by toppling a gigantic statue of Joseph Stalin in the capital of Budapest. Statues of the Soviet dictator had been erected in all the Soviet satellites after World War II. ("W.C." identifies a public toilet in European countries.)

withdrawal of Hungary from the Warsaw Pact. On November 1, Nagy promised free elections, which, given the mood of the country, would probably have brought an end to Communist rule. After a brief moment of uncertainty, Khrushchev decided on firm action. Soviet troops, recently withdrawn at Nagy's request, returned to Budapest and installed a new government under the more pliant party leader János Kádár (YAH-nush KAH-dahr) (1912–1989). While Kádár rescinded many of Nagy's measures, Nagy sought refuge in the Yugoslav embassy. A few weeks later, he left the embassy under the promise of safety but was quickly arrested, convicted of treason, and executed (see the box on p. 776).

DIFFERENT ROADS TO SOCIALISM The dramatic events in Poland and Hungary graphically demonstrated the vulnerability of the Soviet satellite system in Eastern Europe, and many observers throughout the world anticipated that the United States would intervene on behalf of the freedom fighters in Hungary. After all, President Dwight D. Eisenhower (1890–1969) and his administration had promised that they would "roll back" communism, and radio broadcasts by the U.S.-sponsored Radio Liberty and Radio Free Europe had encouraged the peoples of Eastern Europe to rise up against Soviet domination. In reality, the United States was well aware that U.S. intervention could lead to nuclear war and limited its response to protesting Soviet brutality in crushing the uprising.

The year of discontent was not without consequences, however. Soviet leaders now recognized that they could maintain control over the satellites in Eastern Europe only by granting them the leeway to adopt domestic policies appropriate to local conditions. Khrushchev had already embarked on this path in 1955 when he assured Tito that there were "different roads to socialism." Some Eastern European

Soviet Repression in Eastern Europe: Hungary, 1956

INTERACTION & EXCHANGE Developments in Poland in 1956 inspired the Communist leaders of Hungary to begin to extricate their country from Soviet control. But there were limits to Khrushchev's tolerance, and he sent Soviet troops to crush Hungary's movement for independence. The first selection is a statement by the Soviet government justifying its use of troops, while the second is the brief and tragic final statement from Imre Nagy, the Hungarian leader.

Statement of the Soviet Government, October 30, 1956

The Soviet Government regards it as indispensable to make a statement in connection with the events in Hungary.

The course of the events has shown that the working people of Hungary, who have achieved great progress on the basis of their people's democratic order, correctly raise the question of the necessity of eliminating serious shortcomings in the field of economic building, the further raising of the material well-being of the population, and the struggle against bureaucratic excesses in the state apparatus.

However, this just and progressive movement of the working people was soon joined by forces of black reaction and counterrevolution, which are trying to take advantage of the discontent of part of the working people to undermine the foundations of the people's democratic order in Hungary and to restore the old landlord and capitalist order.

The Soviet Government and all the Soviet people deeply regret that the development of events in Hungary has led to bloodshed. On the request of the Hungarian People's Government the Soviet Government consented to the entry into Budapest of the Soviet Army units to assist the Hungarian People's Army and the Hungarian authorities to establish order in the town.

The Last Message of Imre Nagy, November 4, 1956

This fight is the fight for freedom by the Hungarian people against the Russian intervention, and it is possible that I shall only be able to stay at my post for one or two hours. The whole world will see how the Russian armed forces, contrary to all treaties and conventions, are crushing the resistance of the Hungarian people. They will also see how they are kidnapping the Prime Minister of a country which is a Member of the United Nations, taking him from the capital, and therefore it cannot be doubted at all that this is the most brutal form of intervention. I should like in these last moments to ask the leaders of the revolution, if they can, to leave the country. I ask that all that I have said in my broadcast, and what we have agreed on with the revolutionary leaders during meetings in Parliament, should be put in a memorandum, and the leaders should turn to all the peoples of the world for help and explain that today it is Hungary and tomorrow, or the day after tomorrow, it will be the turn of other countries because the imperialism of Moscow does not know borders, and is only trying to play for time.

 How did the United States and its allies respond to the events in Hungary? Why did the United States decide not to intervene in support of the dissident forces?

Communist leaders now took Khrushchev at his word and adopted reform programs to make socialism more palatable to their subject populations. Even Kádár, derisively labeled the "butcher of Budapest," managed to preserve many of Nagy's reforms to allow a measure of capitalist incentive and freedom of expression in Hungary.

CRISIS OVER BERLIN But in the late 1950s, a new crisis erupted over the status of Berlin. The Soviet Union had launched its first intercontinental ballistic missile (ICBM) in August 1957, arousing U.S. fears of a missile gap between the United States and the Soviet Union. Khrushchev attempted to take advantage of the U.S. frenzy over missiles to solve the problem of West Berlin, which had remained a "Western island" of prosperity inside the relatively poverty-stricken state of East Germany (the GDR). Many East Germans sought to escape to West Germany by fleeing through West Berlin, a serious blot on the GDR's credibility and a potential source of instability in East-West relations. In November 1958, Khrushchev announced that unless the West removed its forces from West Berlin within six months, he would turn over control of the access routes to the East Germans. Unwilling to accept an ultimatum that would have abandoned West Berlin to the Communists, President Eisenhower and the West stood firm, and Khrushchev eventually backed down.

Despite such periodic crises in East-West relations, there were tantalizing signs that an era of true peaceful coexistence between the two power blocs could be achieved. In the late 1950s, the United States and the Soviet Union initiated a cultural exchange program. While Leningrad's Kirov Ballet appeared at theaters in the United States, clarinetist Benny Goodman and the film *West Side Story* played in Moscow. In 1958, Khrushchev visited the United States and had a brief but friendly encounter with President Eisenhower at the presidential retreat in northern Maryland.

The Kitchen Debate. During the late 1950s, the United States and the Soviet Union sought to defuse Cold War tensions by encouraging cultural exchanges between the two countries. On one occasion, U.S. Vice President Richard M. Nixon visited Moscow in conjunction with the arrival of an exhibit to introduce U.S. culture and society to the Soviet people. Here, Nixon lectures Soviet Communist Party chief Nikita Khrushchev on the technology of the U.S. kitchen. Beside Nixon at the far right is future Soviet president Leonid Brezhnev.

Rivalry in the Third World

Yet Khrushchev could rarely avoid the temptation to gain an advantage over the United States in the competition for influence throughout the world, a posture that exacerbated the unstable relationship between the two global superpowers. Unlike Stalin, who had exhibited a profound distrust of all political figures who did not slavishly follow his lead, Khrushchev viewed the dismantling of colonial regimes in Asia, Africa, and Latin America as a potential advantage for the Soviet Union. When neutralist leaders like Nehru in India, Tito in Yugoslavia, and Sukarno (soo-KAHR-noh) in Indonesia founded the **Non-aligned Movement** in 1955 to provide an alternative to the two major power blocs, Khrushchev took every opportunity to promote Soviet interests in the Third World (as the nonaligned countries of Asia, Africa, and Latin America were now popularly called). Khrushchev openly sought alliances with strategically important neutralist countries such as India, Indonesia, and Egypt, while the United States' ability to influence events at the United Nations began to wane.

In January 1961, just as John F. Kennedy (1917–1963) assumed the U.S. presidency, Khrushchev unnerved the new president at an informal summit meeting in Vienna by declaring that the Soviet Union would provide active support to national liberation movements throughout the world. Increasingly, Washington was becoming concerned about Soviet meddling in such sensitive trouble spots as Southeast Asia, where insurgent activities in Indochina continued to simmer; Central Africa, where the pro-Soviet tendencies of radical leader Patrice Lumumba (puh-TREES loo-MOOM-buh) (1925–1961) aroused U.S. suspicions; and the Caribbean, where a little-known Cuban revolutionary named Fidel Castro threatened to transform his country into an advance base for Soviet expansion in the Americas.

The Cuban Missile Crisis and the Move Toward Détente

In 1959, the left-wing revolutionary Fidel Castro (fee-DELL KASS-troh) (b. 1926/1927) overthrew the Cuban dictator Fulgencio Batista (full-JEN-see-oh bah-TEES-tuh) and established a Soviet-supported totalitarian regime. As tensions increased between the new government in Havana and the United States, the Eisenhower administration broke relations with Cuba and drafted plans to overthrow Castro, who reacted by drawing closer to Moscow.

Soon after taking office in early 1961, Kennedy approved a plan drawn up under his predecessor to support an invasion of Cuba by anti-Castro exiles. But the attempted landing at the Bay of Pigs in southern Cuba was an utter failure. At Castro's invitation, the Soviet Union then began to station nuclear missiles in Cuba, within striking distance of the American mainland. (That the United States had placed nuclear weapons in Turkey within easy range of the Soviet Union was a fact that Khrushchev was quick to point out.) When U.S. intelligence discovered that a Soviet fleet carrying more missiles was heading to Cuba, Kennedy decided to dispatch U.S. warships into the Atlantic to prevent the fleet from reaching its destination.

This approach to the problem was risky but had the benefit of delaying confrontation and giving the two sides time to find a peaceful solution. After a tense standoff during which the two countries came frighteningly close to a direct nuclear confrontation (the Soviet missiles already in Cuba were launch-ready), Khrushchev finally sent a conciliatory letter to Kennedy agreeing to turn back the fleet if Kennedy pledged not to invade Cuba. In a secret concession not revealed until many years later, the president also promised to dismantle U.S. missiles in Turkey. To the world (and to an angry Castro), however, it appeared that Kennedy had bested Khrushchev. "We were eyeball to eyeball," noted U.S. Secretary of State Dean Rusk, "and they blinked" (see the Film & History feature on p. 778).

The ghastly realization that the world might have faced annihilation in a matter of days had a profound effect on both sides. A communication hotline between Moscow and Washington was installed in 1963 to expedite rapid communication between the two superpowers in time of crisis. In the same year, the two powers agreed to ban nuclear tests in the atmosphere, a step that served to lessen the tensions between the two nations.

The Missiles of October (1973)

Never has the world been closer to nuclear holocaust than in October 1962, when U.S. and Soviet leaders found themselves in a direct confrontation over Nikita Khrushchev's decision to install Soviet missiles in Cuba, just 90 miles from the coast of the United States. When President John F. Kennedy announced that U.S. warships would intercept Soviet freighters destined for Cuban ports, the two countries teetered on the verge of war. Only after protracted and delicate negotiations was the threat defused. The confrontation sobered leaders on both sides of the Iron Curtain and led to the signing of the first test ban treaty, as well as the opening of a hotline between Moscow and Washington.

The Missiles of October, a made-for-TV film produced in 1973, is a tense political drama that is all the more riveting because it is based on fact. Although it is less well known than the more recent *Thirteen Days*, released in 2000, it is in many ways more persuasive, and the acting is demonstrably superior. The film stars William Devane as John F. Kennedy and Martin

Courtesy The Everett Collection, Inc.

John Kennedy (William Devane, seated) and Robert Kennedy (Martin Sheen) confer with advisers.

Sheen as his younger brother, Robert. Based in part on Robert Kennedy's *Thirteen Days* (New York, 1969), a personal account of the crisis that was published shortly after his assassination in 1968, the film traces the tense discussions that took place in the White House as the president's key advisers debated how to respond to the Soviet challenge. President Kennedy remains cool as he reins in his more bellicose advisers to bring about a compromise solution that successfully avoids the seemingly virtual certainty of a nuclear confrontation with Moscow.

Because the film is based on the recollections of Robert F. Kennedy, it presents a favorable portrait of his brother's handling of the crisis, as might be expected, and the somewhat triumphalist attitude at the end of the film is perhaps a bit exaggerated. But Khrushchev's colleagues in the Kremlin and his Cuban ally, Fidel Castro, viewed the U.S.-Soviet agreement as a humiliation for Moscow that nevertheless set the two global superpowers on the road to a more durable and peaceful relationship. It was one Cold War story that had a happy ending.

The Sino-Soviet Dispute

Nikita Khrushchev had launched his appeal for peaceful coexistence as a means of improving relations with the capitalist powers; ironically, one result of the campaign was to undermine Moscow's ties with its close ally China. During Stalin's lifetime, Beijing had accepted the Soviet Union as the acknowledged leader of the socialist world. After Stalin's death, however, relations began to deteriorate. Part of the reason may have been Mao Zedong's contention that he, as the most experienced Marxist leader, should now be acknowledged as the most authoritative voice in the socialist community. But another determining factor was that just as Soviet policies were moving toward moderation, China's were becoming more radical.

Several other issues were involved, including territorial disputes along the Sino-Soviet border and China's unhappiness with limited Soviet economic assistance. But the key sources of disagreement involved ideology and the Cold War. Chinese leaders were convinced that the successes of

the Soviet space program confirmed that the socialists were now technologically superior to the capitalists (the East Wind, trumpeted the Chinese official press, had now triumphed over the West Wind), and they urged Khrushchev to go on the offensive to promote world revolution. Specifically, China wanted Soviet assistance in retaking Taiwan from Chiang Kai-shek. But Khrushchev was trying to improve relations with the West and rejected Chinese demands for support against Taiwan.

By the end of the 1950s, the Soviet Union had begun to remove its advisers from China, and in 1961, the dispute broke into the open. Increasingly isolated, China voiced its hostility to what Mao described as the "urban industrialized countries" (which included the Soviet Union) and portrayed itself as the leader of the "rural underdeveloped countries" of Asia, Africa, and Latin America in a global struggle against imperialist oppression. In effect, China had applied Mao Zedong's concept of people's war in an international framework (see the box on p. 779).

OPPOSING VIEWPOINTS

Peaceful Coexistence or People's War?

INTERACTION & EXCHANGE

The Soviet leader Vladimir Lenin had contended that war between the socialist and imperialist camps was inevitable because the imperialists would never give up without a fight. That assumption had probably guided the thoughts of Joseph Stalin, who told colleagues shortly after World War II that a new war would break out in fifteen to twenty years. But Stalin's successor, Nikita Khrushchev, feared that a new world conflict could result in a nuclear holocaust and contended that the two sides must learn to coexist, although peaceful competition would continue. In this speech given in Beijing in 1959, Khrushchev attempted to persuade the Chinese to accept his views. But Chinese leaders argued that the "imperialist nature" of the United States would never change and countered that the crucial area of competition was in the Third World, where "people's wars" would bring down the structure of imperialism. That argument was presented in 1966 by Marshall Lin Biao (LIN BYOW) of China, at that time one of Mao Zedong's closest allies.

Nikita Khrushchev, Speech to the Chinese, 1959

Comrades! Socialism brings to the people peace—that greatest blessing. The greater the strength of the camp of socialism grows, the greater will be its possibilities for successfully defending the cause of peace on this earth. The forces of socialism are already so great that real possibilities are being created for excluding war as a means of solving international disputes. . . .

When I spoke with President Eisenhower—and I have just returned from the United States of America—I got the impression that the President of the U.S.A.—and not a few people support him—understands the need to relax international tension. . . .

There is only one way of preserving peace—that is the road of peaceful coexistence of states with different social systems. The question stands thus: either peaceful coexistence or war with its catastrophic consequences. Now, with the present relation of forces between socialism and capitalism being in favor of socialism, he who would continue the "cold war" is moving towards his own destruction. . . .

It is not at all because capitalism is still strong that the socialist countries speak out against war, and for peaceful coexistence. No, we have no need of war at all. If the people do not want it, even such a noble and progressive system as socialism cannot be imposed by force of arms. The socialist countries therefore, while carrying through a consistently peace-loving policy, concentrate their efforts on peaceful construction; they fire the hearts of men by the force of their example in building socialism, and thus lead them to follow in their footsteps. The question of when this or that country will take the path to socialism is decided by its own people. This, for us, is the holy of holies.

Lin Biao, "Long Live the Victory of People's War"

Many countries and peoples in Asia, Africa, and Latin America are now being subjected to aggression and enslavement on a serious scale by the imperialists headed by the United States and their lackeys. . . . As in China, the peasant question is extremely important in these regions. The peasants constitute the main force of the national-democratic revolution against the imperialists and their lackeys. In committing aggression against these countries, the imperialists usually begin by seizing the big cities and the main lines of communication. But they are unable to bring the vast countryside completely under their control. . . . The countryside, and the countryside alone, can provide the revolutionary basis from which the revolutionaries can go forward to final victory. Precisely for this reason, Mao Tse-tung's theory of establishing revolutionary base areas in the rural districts and encircling the cities from the countryside is attracting more and more attention among the people in these regions.

Taking the entire globe, if North America and Western Europe can be called "the cities of the world," then Asia, Africa, and Latin America constitute "the rural areas of the world." Since World War II, the proletarian revolutionary movement has for various reasons been temporarily held back in the North American and West European capitalist countries, while the people's revolutionary movement in Asia, Africa, and Latin America has been growing vigorously. In a sense, the contemporary world revolution also presents a picture of the encirclement of cities by the rural areas. In the final analysis, the whole cause of world revolution hinges on the revolutionary struggles of the Asian, African, and Latin American peoples, who make up the overwhelming majority of the world's population. The socialist countries should regard it as their internationalist duty to support the people's revolutionary struggles in Asia, Africa, and Latin America. . . .

Ours is the epoch in which world capitalism and imperialism are heading for their doom and communism is marching to victory. Comrade Mao Tse-tung's theory of people's war is not only a product of the Chinese revolution, but has also the characteristic of our epoch. The new experience gained in the people's revolutionary struggles in various countries since World War II has provided continuous evidence that Mao Tse-tung's thought is a common asset of the revolutionary people of the whole world.

Why did Nikita Khrushchev feel that the conflict between the socialist and capitalist camps that Lenin had predicted was no longer necessary? How did Lin Biao respond?

Combating the Americans

POLITICS & GOVERNMENT

In December 1960, the National Front for the Liberation of South Vietnam, or NLF, was born. Composed of political and social leaders opposed to the anti-Communist government of Ngo Dinh Diem in South Vietnam, it operated under the direction of the Vietnam Workers' Party in North Vietnam and served as the formal representative of revolutionary forces in the south throughout the remainder of the Vietnam War. When, in the spring of 1965, President Lyndon Johnson began to dispatch U.S. combat troops to Vietnam to prevent a Communist victory there, the NLF issued the following declaration.

Statement of the National Front for the Liberation of South Vietnam

American imperialist aggression against South Vietnam and interference in its internal affairs have now continued for more than ten years. More American troops and supplies, including missile units, Marines, B-57 strategic bombers, and mercenaries from South Korea, Taiwan, the Philippines, Australia, Malaysia, etc., have been brought to South Vietnam. . . .

The Saigon puppet regime, paid servant of the United States, is guilty of the most heinous crimes. These despicable traitors, these boot-lickers of American imperialism, have brought the enemy into our country. They have brought to South Vietnam armed forces of the United States and its satellites to kill our compatriots, occupy and ravage our sacred soil and enslave our people.

The Vietnamese, the peoples of all Indo-China and Southeast Asia, supporters of peace and justice in every part of the world, have raised their voice in angry protest against this criminal unprovoked aggression of the United States imperialists.

In the present extremely grave situation, the South Vietnam National Liberation Front considers it necessary to proclaim anew its firm and unswerving determination to resist the U.S. imperialists and fight for the salvation of our country. . . . [It] will continue to rely chiefly on its own forces and potentialities, but it is prepared to accept any assistance, moral and material, including arms and other military equipment, from all the socialist countries, from nationalist countries, from international organizations, and from the peace-loving peoples of the world.

 How did the NLF justify its claim to represent the legitimate aspirations of the people of South Vietnam? Was its claim justified?

The Second Indochina War

China's radicalism was intensified in the early 1960s by the renewal of war in Indochina. The Eisenhower administration had opposed the peace settlement at Geneva in 1954, which divided Vietnam temporarily into two separate regroupment zones, specifically because the provision for future national elections opened up the possibility that the entire country would come under Communist rule. But Eisenhower had been unwilling to introduce U.S. military forces to continue the conflict without the full support of the British and the French, who preferred to seek a negotiated settlement. In the end, Washington promised not to break the provisions of the agreement but refused to commit itself to the results.

During the next several months, the United States began to provide aid to the new government in South Vietnam. Under the leadership of the anti-Communist politician Ngo Dinh Diem (NGHOH din DEE-em) (1901–1963), the government began to root out dissidents. With the tacit approval of the United States, Diem refused to hold the national elections called for by the Geneva Accords. It was widely anticipated, even in Washington, that the Communists would win such elections. In 1959, Ho Chi Minh, despairing of the peaceful unification of the country under Communist rule, returned to a policy of revolutionary war in the south.

Late the following year, a political organization that was designed to win the support of a wide spectrum of the population was founded in an isolated part of South Vietnam. Called the National Front for the Liberation of South Vietnam (NLF), it purported to be an independent organization representing the interests of the population in the south, but was actually under the secret but firm leadership of high-ranking Communists in the DRV (North Vietnam) (see the box above).

By 1963, South Vietnam was on the verge of collapse. Diem's autocratic methods and inattention to severe economic inequality had alienated much of the population, and revolutionary forces, popularly known as the Viet Cong (Vietnamese Communists) and supported by the Communist government in the north, expanded their influence throughout much of the country. In the fall of 1963, with the approval of the Kennedy administration, senior military officers overthrew the Diem regime. But factionalism kept the new military leadership from reinvigorating the struggle against the insurgent forces, and the situation in South Vietnam grew worse. By early 1965, the Viet Cong, their ranks now swelled by military units infiltrating from North Vietnam, were on the verge of seizing control of the entire country. In March, President Lyndon Johnson (1908–1973) decided to send U.S.

AP Images

© Three Lions/Getty Images

COMPARATIVE
ILLUSTRATION

**POLITICS &
GOVERNMENT**

War in the Rice Paddies.
The first stage of the Vietnam
War consisted primarily of
guerrilla conflict, as Viet Cong insurgents
relied on guerrilla tactics to bring down the
U.S.-supported government in Saigon. In
1965, however, President Lyndon Johnson
ordered U.S. combat troops into South Vietnam (top photo) in a desperate bid to prevent
a Communist victory in that beleaguered
country. The Communist government in
North Vietnam responded in kind, sending
its own regular forces down the Ho Chi
Minh Trail to confront U.S. troops on the
battlefield. In the photo on the bottom,
North Vietnamese troops storm the U.S.
Marine base at Khe Sanh (KAY SARN), near
the demilitarized zone, in 1968, the most violent year of the war. Although U.S. military
commanders believed that helicopters would
be a key factor in defeating the insurgent
forces in Vietnam, this was one instance
when technological superiority did not
produce a victory on the battlefield.

Q *How do you think helicopters were
used to assist U.S. operations in
South Vietnam? Why didn't their
use result in a U.S. victory?*

combat troops to South Vietnam to prevent the total defeat of the anti-Communist government in Saigon. Over the next three years, U.S. troop levels steadily increased as the White House counted on U.S. firepower to persuade Ho Chi Minh to abandon his quest to unify Vietnam under Communist leadership.

THE ROLE OF CHINA Chinese leaders observed the gradual escalation of the conflict in South Vietnam with mixed feelings. They were undoubtedly pleased to have a firm Communist ally—one that had in many ways followed the path of Mao Zedong—just beyond their southern frontier. Yet they were concerned that bloodshed in South Vietnam might enmesh China in a new conflict with the United States. Nor did they welcome the specter of a powerful and ambitious united Vietnam, which might wish to extend its influence throughout mainland Southeast Asia, an area that Beijing considered its own backyard.

Chinese leaders therefore tiptoed delicately through the minefield of the Indochina conflict. As the war escalated in 1964 and 1965, Beijing publicly announced that the Chinese people fully supported their comrades seeking national liberation but privately assured Washington that China would not directly enter the conflict unless U.S. forces threatened its southern border. Beijing also refused to cooperate fully with Moscow in shipping Soviet goods to North Vietnam through Chinese territory.

Despite its dismay at the lack of full support from China, the Communist government in North Vietnam responded to U.S. escalation by infiltrating more of its own regular troops into the south, and by 1968, the war had reached a stalemate (see the comparative illustration above). The Communists were not strong enough to overthrow the government in Saigon, whose weakness was shielded by the presence of half a million U.S. troops, but President Johnson was reluctant to engage in all-out war on North Vietnam for fear of provoking a global nuclear conflict. In the fall, after the Communist-led

Tet offensive undermined claims of progress in Washington and aroused intense antiwar protests in the United States, peace negotiations began in Paris.

THE QUEST FOR PEACE Richard Nixon (1913–1994) came into the White House in 1969 on a pledge to bring an honorable end to the Vietnam War. With U.S. public opinion sharply divided on the issue, he began to withdraw U.S. troops while continuing to hold peace talks in Paris. But the centerpiece of his strategy was to improve relations with China and thus undercut Chinese support for the North Vietnamese war effort. During the 1960s, relations between Moscow and Beijing had reached a point of extreme tension, and thousands of troops were stationed on both sides of their long common frontier. To intimidate their Communist rivals, Soviet sources hinted that they might launch a preemptive strike to destroy Chinese nuclear facilities in Xinjiang. Sensing an opportunity to split the two onetime allies, Nixon sent his emissary, Henry Kissinger, on a secret trip to China. Responding to assurances that the United States was determined to withdraw from Indochina and hoped to improve relations with the mainland regime, Chinese leaders invited President Nixon to visit China in early 1972. Nixon accepted, and the two sides agreed to set aside their differences over Taiwan to pursue a better mutual relationship.

THE FALL OF SAIGON Incensed at the apparent betrayal by their close allies, North Vietnamese leaders decided to seek a temporary settlement of the war in the south. In January 1973, a peace treaty was signed in Paris calling for the removal of all U.S. forces from South Vietnam. In return, the Communists agreed to halt military operations and to engage in negotiations to resolve their differences with the Saigon regime. But negotiations over the political settlement soon broke down, and in early 1975, the Communists resumed the offensive. At the end of April, under a massive assault by North Vietnamese military forces, the South Vietnamese government surrendered. A year later, the country was unified under Communist rule.

The Communist victory in Vietnam was a severe humiliation for the United States. But its strategic impact was limited because of the new relationship with China. During the next decade, Sino-American relations continued to improve. In 1979, the two countries established diplomatic ties as the United States renounced its mutual security treaty with the Republic of China in return for a pledge from China to seek reunification with Taiwan by peaceful means (see the box on p. 783). By the end of the 1970s, China and the United States had forged a "strategic relationship" in which they would cooperate against the common threat of Soviet hegemony in Asia.

Why had the United States failed to achieve its objective of preventing a Communist victory in Vietnam? One leading member of the Johnson administration later commented that Washington had underestimated the determination of its adversary in Hanoi and overestimated the patience of the American people. Deeper reflection suggests, however, that another factor was equally important: the United States had overestimated the ability of its client state in South Vietnam to defend itself against a disciplined adversary. In subsequent years, the Vietnam War became a crucial lesson to the Americans on the perils of nation building.

AP Images

A Bridge Across the Cold War Divide. In January 1972, U.S. President Richard Nixon startled the world by visiting mainland China and beginning the long process of restoring normal relations between the two countries. Despite Nixon's reputation as a dedicated anti-Communist, the visit was a success as the two sides agreed to put aside their most bitter differences in an effort to reduce tensions in Asia. Here Nixon and Chinese leader Mao Zedong exchange a historic handshake in Beijing.

A New Beginning in Sino-American Relations

INTERACTION & EXCHANGE

On January 1, 1979, the United States and the People's Republic of China agreed to establish diplomatic relations. It was the first time that the two countries had exchanged diplomatic representatives since 1949, when the Communist Party seized control of the mainland from Chiang Kai-shek's Nationalist government. To achieve their new relationship, both Beijing and Washington had to place several contentious issues on the back burner—notably, the continued existence of the Republic of China on the island of Taiwan. Note how the two statements carefully describe that issue to reflect their distinct points of view.

Statement of the United States of America

As of January 1, 1979, the United States of America recognizes the People's Republic of China as the sole legal government of China. On the same date, the People's Republic of China accords similar recognition to the United States of America. The United States thereby establishes diplomatic relations with the People's Republic of China.

On that same date, January 1, 1979, the United States of America will notify Taiwan that it is terminating diplomatic relations and that the Mutual Defense Treaty between the United States and the Republic of China is being terminated in accordance with the provisions of the Treaty. The United States also states that it will be withdrawing its remaining military personnel from Taiwan within four months.

In the future, the American people and the people of Taiwan will maintain commercial, cultural and other relations without official government representation and without diplomatic relations.

The Administration will seek adjustments to our laws and regulations to permit the maintenance of commercial, cultural and other non-governmental relationships in the new circumstances that will exist after normalization.

The United States is confident that the people of Taiwan face a peaceful and prosperous future. The United States continues to have an interest in the peaceful resolution of the Taiwan issue and expects that the Taiwan issue will be settled peacefully by the Chinese themselves.

The United States believes that the establishment of diplomatic relations with the People's Republic will contribute to the welfare of the American people, to the stability of Asia where the United States has major security and economic interests and to the peace of the entire world.

Statement of the People's Republic of China

As of January 1, 1979, the People's Republic of China and the United States of America recognize each other and establish diplomatic relations, thereby ending the prolonged abnormal relationship between them. This is a historic event in Sino-U.S. relations.

As is known to all, the Government of the People's Republic of China is the sole legal government of China and Taiwan is a part of China. The question of Taiwan was the crucial issue obstructing the normalization of relations between China and the United States. It has now been resolved between the two countries in the spirit of the Shanghai Communiqué and through their joint efforts, thus enabling the normalization of relations so ardently desired by the people of the two countries. As for the way of bringing Taiwan back to the embrace of the motherland and reunifying the country, it is entirely China's internal affair.

At the invitation of the U.S. Government, Teng Hsiaoping [Deng Xiaoping], vice-premier of the State Council of the People's Republic of China, will pay an official visit to the United States in January 1979, with a view to further promoting the friendship between the two peoples and good relations between the two countries.

What are the key differences between these two statements with regard to the Taiwan situation? Given these differences, why did China and the United States decide to resume diplomatic relations?

An Era of Equivalence

FOCUS QUESTION: Why did the Cold War briefly flare up again in the 1980s, and why did it come to a definitive end at the end of the decade?

When the Johnson administration sent U.S. combat troops to South Vietnam in 1965, Washington's main concern was with Beijing, not Moscow. By the mid-1960s, U.S. officials viewed the Soviet Union as an essentially conservative power, more concerned with protecting its vast empire than with expanding its borders. In fact, U.S. policymakers periodically requested Soviet assistance in seeking a peaceful settlement of the Vietnam War. As long as Khrushchev was in power, they found a receptive ear in Moscow. Khrushchev was firmly dedicated to promoting peaceful coexistence (at least on his terms) and sternly advised the North Vietnamese against a resumption of revolutionary war in South Vietnam.

After October 1964, when Khrushchev was replaced by a new leadership headed by party chief Leonid Brezhnev (lee-oh-NYEET BREZH-neff) (1906–1982) and Prime Minister Alexei Kosygin (uh-LEK-say kuh-SEE-gun) (1904–1980), Soviet attitudes about Vietnam became more ambivalent. On the one hand, the new Soviet leaders had no desire to see the Vietnam conflict poison relations between the great powers. On the other hand, Moscow was eager to demonstrate its

The Brezhnev Doctrine

POLITICS & GOVERNMENT

In the summer of 1968, when the new Communist Party leaders in Czechoslovakia were seriously considering proposals for reforming the totalitarian system there, the Warsaw Pact nations met under the leadership of Soviet party chief Leonid Brezhnev to assess the threat to the socialist camp. Soon afterward, military forces of several Soviet bloc nations entered Czechoslovakia and imposed a new government subservient to Moscow. The move was justified by the spirit of "proletarian internationalism" and was widely viewed as a warning to China and other socialist states not to stray too far from Marxist-Leninist orthodoxy, as interpreted by the Soviet Union. But Moscow's actions also raised tensions in the Cold War.

A Letter to the Central Committee of the Communist Party of Czechoslovakia

Dear comrades!

On behalf of the Central Committees of the Communist and Workers' Parties of Bulgaria, Hungary, the German Democratic Republic, Poland, and the Soviet Union, we address ourselves to you with this letter, prompted by a feeling of sincere friendship based on the principles of Marxism-Leninism and proletarian internationalism and by the concern of our common affairs for strengthening the positions of socialism and the security of the socialist community of nations.

The development of events in your country evokes in us deep anxiety. It is our firm conviction that the offensive of the reactionary forces, backed by imperialists, against your Party and the foundations of the social system in the Czechoslovak Socialist Republic, threatens to push your country off the road of socialism and that consequently it jeopardizes the interests of the entire socialist system. . . .

We neither had nor have any intention of interfering in such affairs as are strictly the internal business of your Party and your state, nor of violating the principles of respect, independence, and equality in the relations among the Communist Parties and socialist countries. . . .

At the same time we cannot agree to have hostile forces push your country from the road of socialism and create a threat of severing Czechoslovakia from the socialist community. . . . This is the common cause of our countries, which have joined in the Warsaw Treaty to ensure independence, peace, and security in Europe, and to set up an insurmountable barrier against the intrigues of the imperialist forces, against aggression and revenge. . . . We shall never agree to have imperialism, using peaceful or non-peaceful methods, making a gap from the inside or from the outside in the socialist system, and changing in imperialism's favor the correlation of forces in Europe. . . .

That is why we believe that a decisive rebuff of the anticommunist forces, and decisive efforts for the preservation of the socialist system in Czechoslovakia are not only your task but ours as well. . . .

We express the conviction that the Communist Party of Czechoslovakia, conscious of its responsibility, will take the necessary steps to block the path of reaction. In this struggle you can count on the solidarity and all-round assistance of the fraternal socialist countries.

Warsaw, July 15, 1968.

How did Leonid Brezhnev justify the Soviet decision to invade Czechoslovakia? To what degree do you find his arguments persuasive?

---

support for the North Vietnamese to deflect Chinese charges that the Soviet Union had betrayed the interests of the oppressed peoples of the world. As a result, Soviet officials publicly voiced sympathy for the U.S. predicament in Vietnam but put no pressure on their allies to bring an end to the war. Indeed, the Soviet Union became Hanoi's main supplier of advanced military equipment in the final years of the war.

The Brezhnev Doctrine

In the meantime, new Cold War tensions were brewing in Eastern Europe, where discontent with Stalinist policies began to emerge in Czechoslovakia. The Czechs had not shared in the thaw of the mid-1950s and remained under the rule of the hardliner Antonín Novotný (AHN-toh-nyeen NOH-vaht-nee) (1904–1975), who had been placed in power by Stalin himself. By the late 1960s, however, Novotný's policies had led to widespread popular alienation, and in 1968, with the support of

intellectuals and reformist party members, Alexander Dubček (DOOB-check) (1921–1992) was elected first secretary of the Communist Party. He immediately attempted to implement what was popularly called "socialism with a human face," relaxing restrictions on freedom of speech and the press and the right to travel abroad. Economic reforms were announced, and party control over all aspects of society was reduced. A period of euphoria erupted that came to be known as the "Prague Spring."

It proved to be short-lived. Encouraged by Dubček's actions, some Czechs called for more far-reaching reforms, including neutrality and withdrawal from the Soviet bloc. To forestall the spread of this "spring fever," the Soviet Red Army, supported by troops from other Warsaw Pact states, invaded Czechoslovakia in August 1968 and crushed the reform movement. Gustav Husák (goo-STAHV HOO-sahk) (1913–1991), a committed Stalinist, replaced Dubček and restored the old order, while Moscow attempted to justify its action by issuing the so-called **Brezhnev Doctrine** (see the box on p. 784).

In East Germany as well, Stalinist policies continued to hold sway. The ruling Communist government, led by Walter Ulbricht, had consolidated its position in the early 1950s and had become a faithful Soviet satellite. Industry was nationalized and agriculture collectivized. After a workers' revolt was crushed by Soviet tanks in 1953, a steady flight of East Germans to West Germany ensued, primarily through the city of Berlin. This exodus of mostly skilled laborers ("Soon only party chief Ulbricht will be left," remarked one Soviet observer sardonically) created economic problems and in 1961 led the East German government to erect a wall separating East Berlin from West Berlin, as well as even more fearsome barriers along the entire border with West Germany.

After building the Berlin Wall, East Germany succeeded in developing the strongest economy among the Soviet Union's Eastern European satellites. In 1971, Ulbricht was succeeded by Erich Honecker (AY-reekh HON-nek-uh) (1912–1994), a party hard-liner. Propaganda increased, and the use of the Stasi (SHTAH-see), the secret police, became a hallmark of Honecker's virtual dictatorship. Honecker ruled unchallenged for the next eighteen years.

An Era of Détente

Still, under Brezhnev and Kosygin, the Soviet Union continued to pursue peaceful coexistence with the West and adopted a generally cautious posture in foreign affairs. By the early 1970s, a new phase in Soviet-American relations had emerged, often referred to as **détente** (day-TAHNT), a French term meaning a reduction of tensions between the two sides. One symbol of the new relationship was the Antiballistic Missile (ABM) Treaty, often called SALT I because it emerged from the first round of Strategic Arms Limitation Talks (SALT). In the treaty, which was signed in 1972, the two nations agreed to limit the size of their ABM systems.

The U.S. objective in pursuing the treaty was to make it unlikely that either superpower could win a nuclear exchange by launching a preemptive strike against the other. U.S. officials believed that a policy of "equivalence," in which there was a roughly equal power balance between the two sides, was the best way to avoid a nuclear confrontation. Détente was pursued in other ways as well. When President Nixon took office in 1969, he sought to increase trade and cultural contacts with the Soviet Union. His purpose was to set up a series of "linkages" in U.S.-Soviet relations that would persuade Moscow of the economic and social benefits of maintaining good relations with the West.

The Helsinki Accords were a symbol of that new relationship. Signed in 1975 by the United States, Canada, and all European nations on both sides of the Iron Curtain, these accords recognized all borders in Europe that had been established since the end of World War II, thereby formally acknowledging for the first time the Soviet sphere of influence in Eastern Europe. The Helsinki Accords also committed the signatories to recognize and protect the human rights of their citizens, a clear effort by the Western states to improve the performance of the Soviet Union and its allies in that area.

Renewed Tensions in the Third World

Protection of human rights became one of the major foreign policy goals of the next U.S. president, Jimmy Carter (b. 1924). Ironically, just at the point when U.S. involvement in Vietnam came to an end and relations with China began to improve, U.S.-Soviet relations began to sour, for several reasons. Some Americans had become increasingly concerned about aggressive new tendencies in Soviet foreign policy. The first indication came in Africa. Soviet influence was on the rise in Somalia, across the Red Sea from South Yemen, and later in neighboring Ethiopia. In Angola, once a colony of Portugal, an insurgent movement supported by Cuban troops came to power. In 1979, Soviet troops were sent across the border into Afghanistan to protect a newly installed Marxist regime facing internal resistance from fundamentalist Muslims. Some observers suspected that the ultimate objective of the Soviet advance into hitherto neutral Afghanistan was to extend Soviet power into the oil fields of the Persian Gulf. To deter such a possibility, the White House promulgated the Carter Doctrine, which stated that the United States would use its military power, if necessary, to safeguard Western access to the oil reserves in the Middle East. In fact, sources in Moscow later disclosed that the Soviet advance had little to do with the oil of the Persian Gulf but was an effort to increase Soviet influence in a region increasingly beset by Islamic fervor. Soviet officials feared that Islamic activism could spread to the Muslim populations in the Soviet republics in Central Asia and were confident that the United States was too distracted by the so-called **Vietnam syndrome** (the public fear of U.S. involvement in another Vietnam-type conflict) to respond. Such attitudes were undoubtedly a factor in encouraging Moscow to become more aggressive in pursuing influence in Africa.

CHRONOLOGY	The Cold War to 1980	
Truman Doctrine		1947
Formation of NATO		1949
Soviet Union explodes first nuclear device		1949
Communists come to power in China		1949
Nationalist government retreats to Taiwan		1949
Korean War		1950–1953
Geneva Conference ends Indochina War		1954
Warsaw Pact created		1955
Khrushchev calls for peaceful coexistence		1955–1956
Sino-Soviet dispute breaks into the open		1961
Cuban Missile Crisis		1962
SALT I treaty signed		1972
Nixon's visit to China		1972
Fall of South Vietnam		1975
Soviet invasion of Afghanistan		1979

Another reason for the growing suspicion of the Soviet Union in the United States was that some U.S. defense analysts began to charge that the Soviet Union had abandoned the policy of equivalence and was seeking strategic superiority in nuclear weapons. Accordingly, they argued for a substantial increase in U.S. defense spending. Such charges, combined with evidence of Soviet efforts in Africa and the Middle East and reports of the persecution of Jews and dissidents in the Soviet Union, helped undermine public support for détente in the United States. These changing attitudes were reflected in the failure of the Carter administration to obtain congressional approval of a new arms limitation agreement (SALT II), signed with the Soviet Union in 1979.

Countering the Evil Empire

The early years of the administration of President Ronald Reagan (1911–2004) witnessed a return to the harsh rhetoric, if not all of the harsh practices, of the Cold War. President Reagan's anti-Communist credentials were well known. In a speech given shortly after his election in 1980, he referred to the Soviet Union as an "evil empire" and frequently voiced his suspicion of its motives in foreign affairs. In an effort to eliminate perceived Soviet advantages in strategic weaponry, the White House began a military buildup that stimulated a renewed arms race. In 1982, the Reagan administration introduced the nuclear-tipped cruise missile, whose ability to fly at low altitudes made it difficult to detect by enemy radar. Reagan also became an ardent exponent of the Strategic Defense Initiative (SDI), nicknamed **Star Wars**. Its purposes were to create a space shield that could destroy incoming missiles and to force Moscow into an arms race that it could not hope to win.

The Reagan administration also adopted a more activist, if not confrontational, stance in the Third World. That attitude was most directly demonstrated in Central America, where the revolutionary Sandinista (san-duh-NEES-tuh) regime had been established in Nicaragua after the overthrow of the Somoza dictatorship in 1979. Charging that the Sandinista regime was supporting a guerrilla insurgency movement in nearby El Salvador, the Reagan administration began to provide material aid to the government in El Salvador while simultaneously supporting an anti-Communist guerrilla movement (the **Contras**) in Nicaragua. Though the administration insisted that it was countering the spread of communism in the Western Hemisphere, its Central American policy aroused considerable

© Cengage Learning

Northern Central America

controversy in Congress, where some members charged that growing U.S. involvement could lead to a repeat of the nation's bitter experience in Vietnam.

The Reagan administration also took the offensive in other areas. By providing military support to the anti-Soviet insurgents in Afghanistan, the White House helped maintain a Vietnam-like war in Afghanistan that would embed the Soviet Union in its own quagmire. Like the Vietnam War, the conflict in Afghanistan resulted in heavy casualties and demonstrated that the influence of a superpower was limited in the face of strong nationalist, guerrilla-type opposition.

Toward a New World Order

In 1985, Mikhail Gorbachev (meek-HAYL GOR-buh-chawf) (b. 1931) was elected secretary of the Communist Party of the Soviet Union. During Brezhnev's last years and the brief tenures of his two successors (see Chapter 27), the Soviet Union had entered an era of serious economic decline, and the dynamic new party chief was well aware that drastic changes would be needed to rekindle the dreams that had inspired the Bolshevik Revolution. During the next few years, he launched a program of restructuring, or *perestroika* (per-uh-STROI-kuh), to revitalize the Soviet system. As part of that program, he set out to improve relations with the United States and the rest of the capitalist world. When he met with President Reagan in Reykjavik (RAY-kyuh-vik), the capital of Iceland, the two leaders agreed to set aside their ideological differences.

Gorbachev's desperate effort to rescue the Soviet Union from collapse was too little and too late. In 1989, popular demonstrations against Communist rule broke out across Eastern Europe. The contagion soon spread eastward, and in 1991 the Soviet Union, so long an apparently permanent fixture on the global scene, suddenly disintegrated. In its place arose fifteen new nations. That same year, the string of Soviet satellites in Eastern Europe broke loose from Moscow's grip and declared their independence from Communist rule. The Cold War was over (see Chapter 27).

The end of the Cold War lulled many observers into the seductive vision of a new world order that would be characterized by peaceful cooperation and increasing prosperity. Sadly, such hopes have not been realized (see the comparative essay "Global Village or Clash of Civilizations?" on p. 787). A bitter civil war in the Balkans in the mid-1990s graphically demonstrated that old fault lines of national and ethnic hostility still divided the post–Cold War world. Elsewhere, bloody ethnic and religious disputes broke out in Africa and the Middle East. Then, on September 11, 2001, the world entered a dangerous new era when terrorists attacked the nerve centers of U.S. power in New York City and Washington, D.C., inaugurating a new round of tension between the West and the forces of militant Islam. These events will be discussed in greater detail in the chapters that follow.

In the meantime, other issues beyond the headlines clamor for attention. Environmental problems and the threat of global

COMPARATIVE ESSAY

Global Village or Clash of Civilizations?

INTERACTION & EXCHANGE

As the Cold War came to an end in 1991, policymakers, scholars, and political pundits began to forecast the emergence of a "new world order." One hypothesis, put forth by the political philosopher Francis Fukuyama, was that the decline of communism signaled that the industrial capitalist democracies of the West had triumphed in the world of ideas and were now poised to remake the rest of the world in their own image.

Not everyone agreed with this optimistic view of the world situation. In *The Clash of Civilizations and the Remaking of the World Order*, the historian Samuel P. Huntington suggested that the post–Cold War era, far from marking the triumph of Western ideals, would be characterized by increased global fragmentation and a "clash of civilizations" based on ethnic, cultural, or religious differences. According to Huntington, the twenty-first century would be dominated by disputatious cultural blocs in East Asia, Western Europe and the United States, Eurasia, and the Middle East. The dream of a universal order—a global village—dominated by Western values, he concluded, is a fantasy.

Recent events have lent some support to Huntington's hypothesis. The collapse of the Soviet Union led to the emergence of an atmosphere of conflict and tension all along the perimeter of the old Soviet empire. More recently, the terrorist attack on the United States in September 2001 set the advanced nations of the West and much of the Muslim world on a collision course. As for the new economic order—now enshrined as official policy in Western capitals—public anger at the impact of globalization has reached disturbing levels in many countries, leading to a growing demand for self-protection and group identity in an impersonal and rapidly changing world.

Are we then headed toward multiple power blocs divided by religion and culture as Huntington predicted? His thesis is indeed a useful corrective to the complacent tendency of many observers to view Western civilization as the zenith of human achievement. By dividing the world into competing cultural blocs, however, Huntington has underestimated the

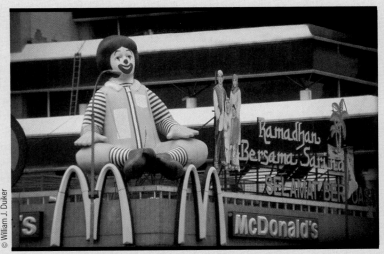

Ronald McDonald in Indonesia. This giant statue welcomes young Indonesians to a McDonald's restaurant in the capital city, Jakarta. McDonald's restaurant chain symbolizes the globalization of today's world civilization.

centrifugal forces at work in the various regions of the world. As the industrial and technological revolutions spread across the face of the earth, their impact is measurably stronger in some societies than in others, thereby intensifying historical rivalries in a given region while establishing links between individual societies and counterparts in other parts of the world. In recent years, for example, Japan has had more in common with the United States than with its traditional neighbors, China and Korea.

The most likely scenario for the next few decades, then, is more complex than either the global village hypothesis or its rival, the clash of civilizations. The twenty-first century will be characterized by simultaneous trends toward globalization and fragmentation as the thrust of technology and information transforms societies and gives rise to counterreactions among societies seeking to preserve a group identity and sense of meaning and purpose in a confusing world.

  How has the recent global economic recession affected the issues discussed in this essay?

warming, the growing gap between rich and poor nations, and tensions caused by migrations of peoples all present a growing threat to political stability and the pursuit of happiness. The recent financial crisis, which has severely undermined the overall health of the global economy, is an additional impediment. As the twenty-first century progresses, the task of guaranteeing the survival of the human race appears to be just as challenging, and even more complex, than it was during the Cold War.

CHAPTER SUMMARY

At the end of World War II, a new conflict arose as the two superpowers, the United States and the Soviet Union, began to compete for political domination. This ideological division soon spread throughout the world as the United States fought in Korea and Vietnam to prevent the spread of communism, promoted by the new Maoist government in China, while the Soviet Union used its influence to prop up pro-Soviet regimes in Asia, Africa, and Latin America.

What had begun, then, as a confrontation across the great divide of the Iron Curtain in Europe eventually took on global significance, much as the major European powers had jostled for position and advantage in Africa and eastern Asia prior to World War I. As a result, both Moscow and Washington became entangled in areas that in themselves had little importance in terms of real national security interests.

As the twentieth century wore on, however, there were tantalizing signs of a thaw in the Cold War. In 1979, China and the United States established mutual diplomatic relations, a consequence of Beijing's decision to focus on domestic reform and stop supporting wars of national liberation in Asia. Six years later, the ascent of Mikhail Gorbachev to leadership, which culminated in the dissolution of the Soviet Union in 1991, brought an end to almost half a century of bitter rivalry between the world's two superpowers.

The Cold War thus ended without the horrific vision of a mushroom cloud. Unlike the earlier rivalries that had resulted in two world wars, this time the antagonists had gradually come to realize that the struggle for supremacy could be carried out in the political and economic arena rather then on the battlefield. And in the final analysis, it was not military superiority but political, economic, and cultural factors that brought about the triumph of Western civilization over the Marxist vision of a classless utopia. The world's policymakers could now shift their focus to other problems of mutual concern.

CHAPTER TIMELINE

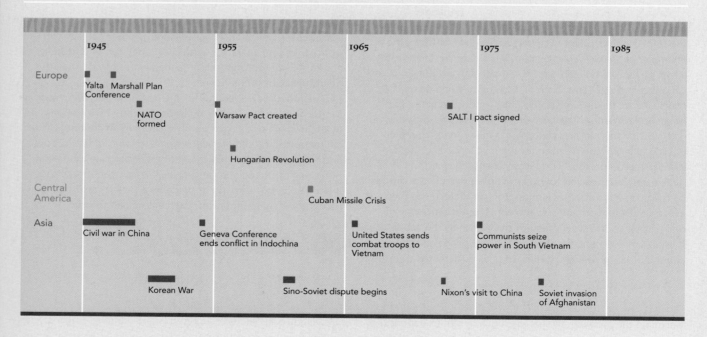

	1945	1955	1965	1975	1985
Europe	Yalta Conference / Marshall Plan; NATO formed	Warsaw Pact created; Hungarian Revolution		SALT I pact signed	
Central America			Cuban Missile Crisis		
Asia	Civil war in China; Korean War	Geneva Conference ends conflict in Indochina; Sino-Soviet dispute begins	United States sends combat troops to Vietnam	Communists seize power in South Vietnam; Nixon's visit to China; Soviet invasion of Afghanistan	

CHAPTER REVIEW

Upon Reflection

Q This chapter has described the outbreak of the Cold War as virtually inevitable, given the ambitions of the two superpowers and their ideological differences. Do you agree? How might the Cold War have been avoided?

Q What disagreements brought about an end to the Sino-Soviet alliance in 1961? Which factors appear to have been most important?

Q How did the wars in Korea and Vietnam relate to the Cold War and affect its course?

Key Terms

Truman Doctrine (p. 764)
Marshall Plan (p. 764)
containment (p. 766)
denazification (p. 766)
peaceful coexistence (p. 774)
Nonaligned Movement (p. 777)
Brezhnev Doctrine (p. 785)
détente (p. 785)
Vietnam syndrome (p. 785)
Star Wars (p. 786)
Contras (p. 786)

Suggested Reading

COLD WAR   Literature on the Cold War is abundant. Revisionist studies have emphasized U.S. responsibility for the Cold War, especially its global aspects. See, for example, **W. La Feber**, *America, Russia, and the Cold War, 1945–1966*, 8th ed. (New York, 2002). For a highly competent retrospective analysis of the Cold War era, see **J. L. Gaddis**, *We Now Know: Rethinking Cold War History* (Oxford, 1997). Also see his more general work *The Cold War: A New History* (New York, 2005). For the perspective of a veteran journalist, see **M. Frankel**, *High Noon in the Cold War: Kennedy, Khrushchev, and the Cuban Missile Crisis* (New York, 2004).

A number of studies of the early stages of the Cold War are based on documents unavailable until the late 1980s or early 1990s. See, for example, **O. A. Westad**, *Cold War and Revolution: Soviet-American Rivalry and the Origins of the Chinese Civil War* (New York, 1993), and **Chen Jian**, *China's Road to the Korean War: The Making of the Sino-American Confrontation* (New York, 1994). **S. Goncharov, J. W. Lewis,** and **Xue Litai**, *Uncertain Partners: Stalin, Mao, and the Korean War* (Stanford, Calif., 1993), provides a fascinating view of the war from several perspectives. For a perspective that places much of the blame for the Korean War on the United States, see **B. Cumings**, *The Korean War: A History* (New York, 2010).

CHINA   There are several informative surveys of Chinese foreign policy since the Communist rise to power. A particularly insightful account is **Chen Jian**, *Mao's China and the Cold War* (Chapel Hill, N.C., 2001). On Chinese policy in Korea, see **Shu Guang Zhang**, *Mao's Military Romanticism: China and the Korean War* (Lawrence, Kans., 2001), and **Xiaobing Li et al.**, *Mao's Generals Remember Korea* (Lawrence, Kans., 2001). On Sino-Vietnamese relations, see **Ang Cheng Guan**, *Vietnamese Communists' Relations with China and the Second Indochina Conflict* (Jefferson, N.C., 1997).

THE COLD WAR ENDS   Two recent works that deal with the end of the Cold War are the gripping account by **M. E. Sarotte**, *1989: The Struggle to Create Post–Cold War Europe* (Princeton, N.J., 2009), and **V. Sebestyen**, *Revolution 1989: The Fall of the Soviet Empire* (New York, 2008).

Go to the CourseMate website at **www.cengagebrain.com** for additional study tools and review materials—including audio and video clips—for this chapter.

Brave New World: Communism on Trial

Shopping in Moscow

CHAPTER OUTLINE
AND FOCUS QUESTIONS

The Postwar Soviet Union

Q How did Nikita Khrushchev change the system that the Soviet dictator Joseph Stalin had put in place before his death in 1953? To what degree did his successors adopt Khrushchev's policies?

The Disintegration of the Soviet Empire

Q What were the key components of *perestroika*, which Mikhail Gorbachev espoused during the 1980s? Why did it fail?

The East Is Red: China Under Communism

Q What were Mao Zedong's chief goals for China, and what policies did he institute to try to achieve them?

"Serve the People": Chinese Society Under Communism

Q What significant political, economic, and social changes have taken place in China since the death of Mao Zedong? How successful have they been at improving the quality of life in China?

CRITICAL THINKING

Q Why has communism survived in China when it failed to survive in Eastern Europe and Russia? Are Chinese leaders justified in claiming that without party leadership, the country would fall into chaos?

ACCORDING TO KARL MARX, capitalism is a system that involves the exploitation of man by man; under socialism, it is the other way around. That wry joke was typical of popular humor in post–World War II Moscow, where the dreams of a future utopia had faded in the grim reality of life in the Soviet Union.

For the average Soviet citizen after World War II, few images better displayed the shortcomings of the Soviet system than a long line of people queuing up outside an official state store selling consumer goods. Because the command economy was so inefficient, items of daily use were chronically in such short supply that when a particular item became available, people often lined up immediately to buy several for themselves and their friends.

Despite the evident weaknesses of the centralized Soviet economy, the Communist monopoly on power seemed secure, as did Moscow's hold over its client states in Eastern Europe. In fact, for three decades after the end of World War II, the Soviet empire appeared to be a permanent feature of the international landscape. But by the early 1980s, it had become clear that there were cracks in the Kremlin wall. The Soviet economy was stagnant, the minority nationalities were restive, and Eastern European leaders were increasingly emboldened to test the waters of the global capitalist marketplace. In the United States, the newly elected president, Ronald Reagan, boldly predicted the imminent collapse of the "evil empire."

At the time many observers questioned that prediction, but it soon seemed uncannily clairvoyant. Within a span of less than three years (1989–1991), the Soviet Union ceased to exist as a nation as Russia and other former Soviet republics declared their separate independence, Communist regimes in

Eastern Europe were toppled, and the long-standing division of postwar Europe came to an end.

The fate of communism in China has been quite different. Despite some turbulence, the Communist Party has managed to retain power in China, even as that nation takes giant strides toward becoming an economic superpower. Yet as China's leaders struggle to bring the nation into the modern age, many of the essential principles of Marxist-Leninist dogma have been tacitly abandoned, and cynicism among the nation's youth is widespread. Whether communism will continue to provide a realistic framework for the challenges that lie ahead remains an open question. The "brave new world" forecast by Karl Marx remains but a figment of his imagination.

The Postwar Soviet Union

 FOCUS QUESTIONS: How did Nikita Khrushchev change the system that the Soviet dictator Joseph Stalin had put in place before his death in 1953? To what degree did his successors adopt Khrushchev's policies?

At the end of World War II, the Soviet Union was one of the world's two superpowers, and its leader, Joseph Stalin, was in a position of strength. He and his Soviet colleagues were now in control of a vast empire (see Map 27.1) that included Eastern Europe, much of the Balkans, and new territory gained from Japan in East Asia.

From Stalin to Khrushchev

World War II devastated the Soviet Union. Twenty million citizens lost their lives, and cities such as Kiev (KEE-yev), Kharkov (KHAR-kawf), and Leningrad suffered enormous physical destruction. As the lands that had been occupied by the German forces were liberated, the Soviet government turned its attention to restoring their economic structures. Nevertheless, in 1945, agricultural production was only 60 percent and steel output only 50 percent of prewar levels. The Soviet people faced incredibly difficult conditions: they worked longer hours than before the war, ate less, and were ill-housed and poorly clothed.

STALINISM IN ACTION In the immediate postwar years, the Soviet Union removed goods and materials from occupied Germany and extorted valuable raw materials from its satellite states in Eastern Europe. More important, however, to create a new industrial base, Stalin returned to the method he had used in the 1930s—the extraction of development capital from Soviet labor. Working hard for little pay and for precious few consumer goods, Soviet laborers were expected to produce goods for export with little in return for themselves. The incoming capital from abroad could then be used to purchase machinery and Western technology. The loss of millions of men in the war meant that much of this tremendous

workload fell on Soviet women, who performed almost 40 percent of the heavy manual labor.

The pace of economic recovery in the years immediately after the war was impressive. By 1947, industrial production had attained 1939 levels; three years later, it had surpassed those levels by 40 percent. New power plants, canals, and giant factories were built, and industrial enterprises and oil fields were established in Siberia and Soviet Central Asia. Stalin's new five-year plan, announced in 1946, reached its goals in less than five years.

Although Stalin's economic strategy was successful in promoting growth in heavy industry, primarily for the benefit of the military, consumer goods remained scarce, and long-suffering Soviet citizens were still being asked to sacrifice for a better tomorrow. The development of thermonuclear weapons, MIG fighter planes, and the first space satellite (*Sputnik*) in the 1950s may have elevated the nation's reputation as a world power abroad, but domestically, the people of the Soviet Union were shortchanged. Heavy industry grew at a rate three times that of personal consumption. Moreover, housing was in short supply, and living conditions were especially difficult in the overcrowded cities.

When World War II ended in 1945, Stalin had been in power for more than fifteen years. During that time, he had quashed all opposition to his rule and emerged as the undisputed master of the Soviet Union. Political terror enforced by several hundred thousand secret police ensured that he would remain in power. By the late 1940s, an estimated 9 million Soviet citizens were in Siberian concentration camps.

Increasingly distrustful of potential competitors, Stalin exercised sole authority and pitted his subordinates against one another. His morbid suspicions extended to even his closest colleagues. In 1948, Andrei Zhdanov (ahn-DRAY ZHDAH-nawf), his presumed successor and head of the Leningrad party organization, died under mysterious circumstances, almost certainly at Stalin's order. Within weeks, the Leningrad party organization was purged of several top leaders, many of whom were accused of having traitorous connections with Western intelligence agencies.

In succeeding years, Stalin directed his suspicions at other members of the inner circle, including Foreign Minister Vyacheslav Molotov. Known as "Old Stone Butt" in the West for his stubborn defense of Soviet security interests, Molotov had been a loyal lieutenant since the early years of Stalin's rise to power. Now Stalin distrusted Molotov and had his Jewish wife sent to a Siberian concentration camp. This intimidated virtually all of Stalin's colleagues. As Stalin remarked mockingly on one occasion, "When I die, the imperialists will strangle all of you like a litter of kittens."[1]

Stalin died—presumably of natural causes—in 1953 and, after some bitter infighting within the party leadership, was succeeded by Georgy Malenkov, a veteran administrator and ambitious member of the Politburo (POL-it-byoor-oh), the party's governing body. Malenkov came to power with a clear agenda. In foreign affairs, he hoped to promote an easing of Cold War tensions and improve relations with the Western powers. For Moscow's Eastern European allies, he advocated a so-called **new course** in their mutual relations

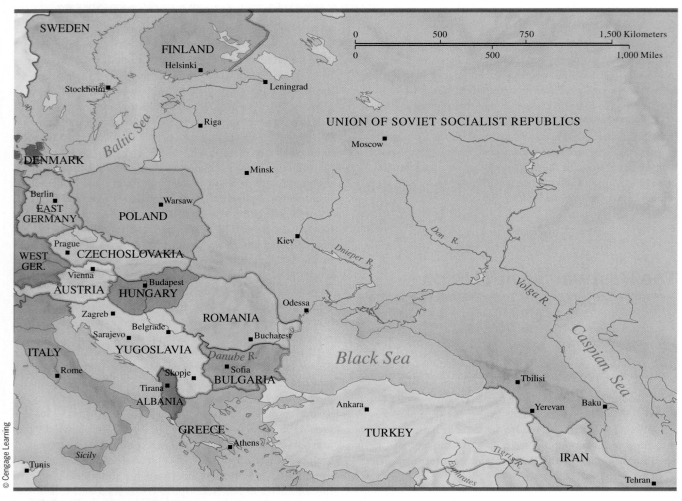

MAP 27.1 Eastern Europe and the Soviet Union. After World War II, the boundaries of Eastern Europe were redrawn as a result of Allied agreements reached at the Tehran and Yalta Conferences. This map shows the new boundaries that were established throughout the region, placing Soviet power at the center of Europe.

 How had the boundaries changed from the prewar era?

and a decline in Stalinist methods of rule. Inside the Soviet Union, he hoped to reduce defense expenditures and improve the standard of living. Such goals were laudable and probably had the support of the majority of the people, but they did not necessarily appeal to key groups, including the army, the Communist Party, the managerial elite, and the security services (now known as the Committee on Government Security, or KGB). Malenkov was soon removed from his position, and power shifted to his rival, the new party general secretary, Nikita Khrushchev.

THE RISE AND FALL OF KHRUSHCHEV During the struggle for power with Malenkov, Khrushchev had outmaneuvered his rival by calling for heightened defense expenditures and a continuing emphasis on heavy industry. Once in power, however, Khrushchev showed the political dexterity displayed by many American politicians and reversed his priorities. He now resumed the efforts of his predecessor to reduce tensions with the West and boost the standard of living of the Russian people. He moved vigorously to improve the performance of

the Soviet economy and revitalize Soviet society. By nature, Khrushchev was a man of enormous energy and creativity. In an attempt to release the stranglehold of the central bureaucracy over the national economy, he abolished dozens of government ministries and split up the party and government apparatus. Khrushchev also attempted to rejuvenate the stagnant agricultural sector, long the Achilles's heel of the Soviet economy. He attempted to spur production by increasing profit incentives and opened thousands of acres in Soviet Kazakhstan (ka-zak-STAN *or* kuh-zahk-STAHN) to cultivation.

Like any innovator, however, Khrushchev had to overcome the inherently conservative instincts of the Soviet bureaucracy, as well as of the mass of the Soviet population. His plan to remove the "dead hand" of the state, however laudable in intent, alienated much of the Soviet official class, and his effort to split the Communist Party angered those who saw it as the central force in the Soviet system. Khrushchev's agricultural schemes inspired similar opposition. Although the Kazakhstan wheat lands would eventually demonstrate their importance, progress was slow, and his effort to

Behind the Kremlin Walls. A historic walled city in the heart of Moscow, the Kremlin long served as the home of the tsars during the imperial era. After the Bolshevik Revolution, it was occupied by Stalin and his successors. Its physical appearance reflects its varied history, as forbidding structures like the Communist Party headquarters (below) were balanced by the fairy-tale domes and cupolas of Russian Orthodox churches (right)—relics of a faith that came under harsh attacks during the many decades of Soviet rule.

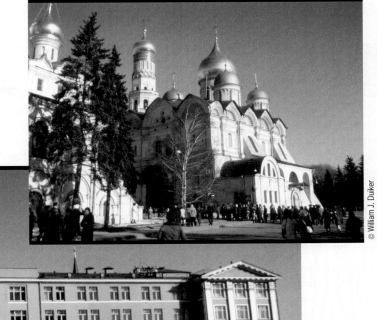

© William J. Duiker

persuade Russians to eat more corn (an idea he had apparently picked up during a visit to the United States) earned him the mocking nickname "Cornman." The combination of disappointing agricultural production and high military spending hurt the Soviet economy. The industrial growth rate, which had soared in the early 1950s, now declined dramatically, from 13 percent annually in 1953 to 7.5 percent in 1964.

Khrushchev was probably best known for his policy of **de-Stalinization**. Khrushchev had risen in the party hierarchy as a Stalin protégé, but he had been deeply disturbed by his mentor's excesses and, once in a position of authority, moved to excise the Stalinist legacy from Soviet society. The campaign began at the Twentieth National Congress of the Communist Party in February 1956, when Khrushchev gave a long speech in private criticizing some of Stalin's major shortcomings. The speech apparently had not been intended for public distribution, but it was quickly leaked to the Western press and created a sensation throughout the world (see the box on p. 794). During the next few years, Khrushchev encouraged more freedom for writers, artists, and composers, arguing that "readers should be given the chance to make their own judgments" about the acceptability of controversial literature and that "police measures shouldn't be used."[2] Under Khrushchev's instructions, thousands of prisoners were released from concentration camps.

Khrushchev's personality, however, did not endear him to higher Soviet officials, who frowned at his tendency to crack jokes and play the clown. Nor were the higher members of the party bureaucracy pleased when Khrushchev tried to curb their privileges. Foreign policy failures further damaged Khrushchev's reputation among his colleagues. His plan to install missiles in Cuba was the final straw (see Chapter 26). While he was on vacation in 1964, a special meeting of the Soviet Politburo voted him out of office (citing "deteriorating health") and forced him into retirement. Although a team of leaders succeeded him, real power came into the hands of Leonid Brezhnev (1906–1982), the "trusted" supporter of Khrushchev who had engineered his downfall.

The Brezhnev Years (1964–1982)

The ouster of Nikita Khrushchev in October 1964 vividly demonstrated the challenges that would be encountered by any leader sufficiently bold to try to reform the Soviet system. In democratic countries, pressure on the government comes from various sources in society at large—the business community and labor unions, innumerable interest groups, and the general public. In the Soviet Union, pressure on government and party leaders originated from sources essentially operating inside the system—the government bureaucracy, the party apparatus, the KGB, and the armed forces.

Khrushchev Denounces Stalin

POLITICS & GOVERNMENT

Three years after Stalin's death, the new Soviet premier, Nikita Khrushchev, addressed the Twentieth Congress of the Communist Party and denounced the former Soviet dictator for his crimes. This denunciation was the beginning of a policy of de-Stalinization. When it was secretly leaked to Western news organizations, it provoked excited debate in countries around the world and great consternation among conservative elements in the Soviet Union. One member of the Congress reportedly died of a heart attack shortly after the speech.

Khrushchev Addresses the Twentieth Party Congress, February 1956

A lot has been said about the cult of the individual and about its harmful consequences. . . . The cult of the person of Stalin . . . became at a certain specific stage the source of a whole series of exceedingly serious and grave perversions of Party principles, of Party democracy, of revolutionary legality.

Stalin absolutely did not tolerate collegiality in leadership and in work and . . . practiced brutal violence, not only toward everything which opposed him, but also toward that which seemed, to his capricious and despotic character, contrary to his concepts.

Stalin abandoned the method of ideological struggle for that of administrative violence, mass repressions and terror. . . . Arbitrary behavior by one person encouraged and permitted arbitrariness in others. Mass arrests and deportations of many thousands of people, execution without trial and without normal investigation created conditions of insecurity, fear, and even desperation.

Stalin showed in a whole series of cases his intolerance, his brutality, and his abuse of power. . . . He often chose the path of repression and annihilation, not only against actual enemies, but also against individuals who had not committed any crimes against the Party and the Soviet government. . . .

Many Party, Soviet, and economic activists who were branded in 1937 and 1938 as "enemies" were actually never enemies, spies, wreckers, and so on, but were always honest communists; they were only so stigmatized, and often, no longer able to bear barbaric tortures, they charged themselves (at the order of the investigative judges-falsifiers) with all kinds of grave and unlikely crimes.

This was the result of the abuse of power by Stalin, who began to use mass terror against the Party cadres. . . . Stalin put the Party and the NKVD [the Soviet police agency] up to the use of mass terror when the exploiting classes had been liquidated in our country and when there were no serious reasons for the use of extraordinary mass terror. The terror was directed . . . against the honest workers of the Party and the Soviet state. . . .

Stalin was a very distrustful man, sickly, suspicious. . . . Everywhere and in everything he saw "enemies," "two-facers," and "spies." Possessing unlimited power, he indulged in great willfulness and choked a person morally and physically. A situation was created where one could not express one's own will. When Stalin said that one or another would be arrested, it was necessary to accept on faith that he was an "enemy of the people." What proofs were offered? The confession of the arrested. . . . How is it possible that a person confesses to crimes that he had not committed? Only in one way—because of application of physical methods of pressuring him, tortures, bringing him to a state of unconsciousness, deprivation of his judgment, taking away of his human dignity.

 What were the key charges that Khrushchev made against Stalin? Can it be said that Khrushchev corrected these problems?

Leonid Brezhnev, the new party chief, was undoubtedly aware of these realities of Soviet politics, and his long tenure in power was marked, above all, by the desire to avoid changes that might provoke instability, either at home or abroad. Brezhnev was himself a product of the Soviet system. He had entered the ranks of the party leadership under Stalin, and although he was not a particularly avid believer in party ideology—indeed, there were innumerable stories about his addiction to "bourgeois pleasures," including expensive country houses and fast cars (many of them gifts from foreign leaders)—he was no partisan of reform.

Still, Brezhnev sought domestic stability. He and his prime minister, Alexei Kosygin, undertook what might be described as a program of "de-Khrushchevization," returning the responsibility for long-term planning to the central ministries and reuniting the Communist Party apparatus. Despite some cautious attempts to stimulate the stagnant agricultural sector, there was no effort to revise the basic system of collective farms. In the industrial sector, the regime launched a series of reforms designed to give factory managers (themselves employees of the state) more responsibility for setting prices, wages, and production quotas. These "Kosygin reforms" had little effect, however, because they were stubbornly resisted by the bureaucracy and were adopted by relatively few enterprises in the vast state-owned industrial sector.

A CONTROLLED SOCIETY Brezhnev also initiated a significant retreat from Khrushchev's policy of de-Stalinization. Criticism of the "Great Leader" had angered conservatives both within the party hierarchy and among the public at large, many of whom still revered Stalin as a hero and a defender of Russia against Nazi Germany. Many influential figures in the Kremlin feared that de-Stalinization could lead to internal instability and a decline in public trust in the legitimacy of party leadership—the hallowed "dictatorship of the proletariat." Early in Brezhnev's reign, Stalin's reputation began to revive. Although his alleged shortcomings were not totally ignored, he was now described in the official press as "an outstanding party leader" who had been primarily responsible for the successes achieved by the Soviet Union.

The regime also adopted a more restrictive policy toward dissidents in Soviet society. Critics of the Soviet system, such as the physicist Andrei Sakharov (ahn-DRAY SAH-kuh-rawf), were harassed and arrested or, like the famous writer Alexander Solzhenitsyn (sohl-zhuh-NEET-sin), forced to leave the country. There was also a return to the anti-Semitic policies and attitudes that had marked the Stalin era. Such indications of renewed repression aroused concern in the West and were instrumental in the inclusion of a statement on human rights in the 1975 Helsinki Accords (see Chapter 26).

Free expression was also restricted. The media were controlled by the state and presented only what the state wanted people to hear. The two major newspapers, *Pravda* ("Truth") and *Izvestia* ("News"), were the agents of the party and the government, respectively. Cynics joked that there was no news in *Pravda* (PRAHV-duh) and no truth in *Izvestia* (iz-VESS-tee-uh). According to Western journalists, airplane accidents in the Soviet Union were rarely publicized, out of concern that they would raise questions about the quality of the Soviet airline industry. Shortly after the disaster at the Chernobyl (chur-NOH-buhl) nuclear plant in 1986, a Soviet official testily assured me that foreign news reports about the seriousness of the incident were just Western propaganda.

The government also made strenuous efforts to prevent the Soviet people from being exposed to harmful foreign ideas, especially modern art, literature, and rock music. When the Summer Olympic Games were held in Moscow in 1980, Soviet newspapers advised citizens to keep their children indoors to keep them from being polluted with "bourgeois" ideas passed on by foreign visitors. But the effort proved fruitless, as Soviet adolescents nonetheless became enamored of forbidden Western rock music and clothing styles.

For citizens of Western democracies, such a political atmosphere would seem highly oppressive, but for the Russian people, an emphasis on law and order was an accepted aspect of everyday life inherited from the tsarist period. It was firmly enshrined in the Soviet constitution, in which individual freedom was subordinated to the interests of the state (see the box on p. 796). Conformity was the rule in virtually every corner of Soviet society, from the educational system (characterized at all levels by rote memorization and political indoctrination) to child rearing (it was forbidden, for example, to be left-handed) and even to yearly vacations (most workers took their vacations at resorts run by their employer, where the daily schedule of activities was highly regimented). Young Americans studying in the Soviet Union reported that their Soviet friends were often shocked to hear U.S. citizens criticizing their own president.

A STAGNANT ECONOMY Soviet leaders also failed to achieve their objective of revitalizing the national economy. Whereas growth rates during the early Khrushchev era had been impressive (prompting Khrushchev during a 1956 reception at the Kremlin to chortle to an American guest, "We will bury you"), under Brezhnev industrial growth declined to an annual rate of less than 4 percent in the early 1970s and less than 3 percent in the period from 1975 to 1980. Successes in the agricultural sector were equally meager. Grain production rose from less than 90 million tons in the early 1950s to nearly 200 million tons in the 1970s but then stagnated at that level.

One of the primary problems with the Soviet economy was the absence of incentives. Salary structures offered little reward for hard labor and extraordinary achievement. Pay differentials operated in a much narrower range than in most Western societies, and there was little danger of being dismissed. According to the Soviet constitution, every Soviet citizen was guaranteed an opportunity to work.

There were, of course, some exceptions to this general rule. Athletic achievement was highly prized, and a gymnast of Olympic stature would receive great rewards in the form of prestige and lifestyle. Senior officials did not receive high salaries but were provided with countless perquisites, such as access to foreign goods, official automobiles with chauffeurs, and entry into prestigious institutions of higher learning for their children. For the elite, it was *blat* (influence) that most often differentiated them from the rest of the population. The average citizen, however, had little material incentive to produce beyond the minimum acceptable level. It is hardly surprising that per capita productivity was only about half that realized in most capitalist countries. At the same time, the rudeness of Soviet clerks and waiters became legendary.

The problem of incentives existed at the managerial level as well, where centralized planning discouraged initiative and innovation. Factory managers, for example, were assigned monthly and annual quotas by the **Gosplan** (gaws-PLAHN)—the "state plan" drawn up by the central planning commission. Because state-owned factories faced little or no competition, managers did not care whether their products were competitive in terms of price and quality, as long as the quota was attained. One of the key complaints of Soviet citizens was the low quality of domestic consumer goods. Knowledgeable consumers quickly discovered that products manufactured at the end of the month were often of lower quality (because factory workers had to rush to meet their quotas) and attempted to avoid purchasing them.

Often consumer goods were simply unavailable. Whenever Soviet citizens saw a queue forming in front of a store, they automatically got in line, often without even knowing what people were lining up for, because they never knew when that item might be available again. When they reached the head of the line, most would purchase several of the same item in order to swap with their friends and neighbors. This "queue psychology," of course, was a time-consuming process and inevitably served to reduce the per capita rate of productivity.

Soviet citizens often tried to overcome the shortcomings of the system by resorting to the black market (buying "on the left," in Soviet parlance). Private economic activities, of course, were illegal, but many workers took to moonlighting to augment their meager salaries. An employee in a state-run

The Rights and Duties of Soviet Citizens

POLITICS & GOVERNMENT

In the Soviet Union, and in other countries modeled on the Soviet system, the national constitution was viewed not as a timeless document, but as a reflection of conditions at the time it was framed. As Soviet society advanced from a state of "raw communism" to a fully socialist society, new constitutions were drafted to reflect the changes taking place in society as a whole. The first two constitutions of the Soviet Union, promulgated in 1924 and 1936, declared that the state was a "dictatorship of the proletariat" guided by the Communist Party, the vanguard organization of the working class in the Soviet Union. But the so-called Brezhnev constitution of 1977 described the Soviet Union as a "state of all the people," composed of workers, farmers, and "socialist intellectuals," although it confirmed the role of Communist Party as the "leading force" in society. The provisions from the 1977 constitution presented here illustrate some of the freedoms and obligations of Soviet citizens. Especially noteworthy are Articles 39 and 62, which suggest that the interests and prestige of the state took precedence over individual liberties.

The Soviet Constitution of 1977

Chapter 1: The Political System

Article 6. The leading and guiding force of the Soviet society and the nucleus of its political system, of all state organizations and public organizations, is the Communist Party of the Soviet Union. The CPSU exists for the people and serves the people.

The Communist Party, armed with Marxism-Leninism, determines the general perspectives of the development of society and the course of the home and foreign policy of the USSR, directs the great constructive work of the Soviet people, and imparts a planned, systematic, and theoretically substantiated character to their struggle for the victory of communism.

Chapter 6: Equality of Citizens' Rights

Article 35. Women and men have equal rights in the USSR. Exercise of these rights is ensured by according women equal access with men to education and vocational and professional training, equal opportunities in employment, remuneration and promotion, and in social and political, and cultural activity, and by the special labor and health protection measures for women; by providing conditions enabling mothers to work; by legal protection, and material and moral support for mothers and children, including paid leaves and other benefits for expectant mothers and mothers, and gradual reduction of working time for mothers with small children.

Chapter 7: The Basic Rights, Freedoms, and Duties of Citizens of the USSR

Article 39. Citizens of the USSR enjoy in full the social, economic, political, and personal rights and freedoms proclaimed and guaranteed by the Constitution of the USSR and by Soviet laws. The socialist system ensures enlargement of the rights and freedoms of citizens and continuous improvement of their living standards as social, economic, and cultural development programs are fulfilled. Enjoyment by citizens of their rights and freedoms must not be to the detriment of the interests of society or the state, or infringe the rights of other citizens.

Article 62. Citizens of the USSR are obliged to safeguard the interests of the Soviet state, and to enhance its power and prestige. Defense of the Socialist Motherland is the sacred duty of every citizen of the USSR. Betrayal of the Motherland is the gravest of crimes against the people.

 Which of these provisions would seem out of place if they were to appear in the Constitution of the United States?

---

appliance store, for example, would promise to repair a customer's television set on his own time in return for a payment "under the table." Otherwise, servicing of the set might require several weeks. Knowledgeable observers estimated that as much as one-third of the entire Soviet economy operated outside the legal system.

Another major obstacle to economic growth was inadequate technology. Except in the area of national defense, the overall level of Soviet technology was not comparable to that of the West or the advanced industrial societies of East Asia. Part of the problem stemmed from issues already described. With no competition, factory managers had little incentive to improve the quality of their products. But another reason was the high priority assigned to national defense. The military

sector regularly received the most resources from the government and attracted the cream of the country's scientific talent.

AN AGING LEADERSHIP Such problems would be intimidating for any government, but they were particularly so for the elderly generation of party leaders surrounding Leonid Brezhnev, many of whom were cautious to a fault. Though some undoubtedly recognized the need for reform and innovation, they were paralyzed by the fear of instability and change. The problem worsened during the late 1970s when Brezhnev's health began to deteriorate.

Brezhnev died in November 1982 and was succeeded by Yuri Andropov (YOOR-ee ahn-DRAHP-awf) (1914–1984), a party veteran and head of the Soviet secret services. During his brief tenure as party chief, Andropov was a vocal advocate of reform, but most of his initiatives were limited to the familiar nostrums of punishment for wrongdoers and moral exhortations to Soviet citizens to work harder. At the same time, material incentives were still officially discouraged and generally ineffective. Andropov had been ailing when he was selected to succeed Brezhnev as party chief, and when he died after only a few months in office, little had been done to change the system. He was succeeded by a mediocre party stalwart, the elderly Konstantin Chernenko (kuhn-stuhn-TEEN chirn-YEN-koh) (1911–1985). With the Soviet system in crisis, Moscow seemed stuck in a time warp. As one concerned observer told an American journalist, "I had a sense of foreboding, like before a storm. That there was something brewing in people and there would be a time when they would say, 'That's it. We can't go on living like this. We can't. We need to redo everything.'"[3]

Cultural Expression in the Soviet Bloc

In his occasional musings about the future Communist utopia, Karl Marx had predicted that a new, classless society would replace the exploitative and hierarchical systems of feudalism and capitalism. Workers would engage in productive activities and share equally in the fruits of their labor. In their free time, they would produce a new, advanced culture, proletarian in character and egalitarian in content.

The reality in the post–World War II Soviet Union and Eastern Europe was somewhat different. Under Stalin, the Soviet cultural scene was a wasteland. Beginning in 1946, a series of government decrees made all forms of literary and scientific expression dependent on the state. All Soviet culture was expected to follow the party line. Historians, philosophers, and social scientists all grew accustomed to quoting Marx, Lenin, and, above all, Stalin as their chief authorities. Novels and plays, too, were supposed to portray Communist

Stalinist Heroic: An Example of Socialist Realism. Under Stalin and his successors, art was assigned the task of indoctrinating the Soviet population on the public virtues, such as hard work, loyalty to the state, and patriotism. Grandiose statuary erected to commemorate the heroic efforts of the Red Army during World War II appeared in every Soviet city. Here is an example in Minsk, today the capital of Belarus.

heroes and their efforts to create a better society. No criticism of existing social conditions was permitted. Even distinguished composers such as Dmitry Shostakovich (dih-MEE-tree shahs-tuh-KOH-vich) were compelled to heed Stalin's criticisms, including his view that contemporary Western music was nothing but a "mishmash." Some areas of intellectual activity were virtually abolished; the science of genetics disappeared, and few movies were made during Stalin's final years.

Stalin's death brought a modest respite from cultural repression. Writers and artists banned during the Stalin years were again allowed to publish. Still, Soviet authorities, including Khrushchev, were reluctant to allow cultural freedom to move far beyond official Soviet ideology.

These restrictions, however, did not prevent the emergence of some significant Soviet literature, although authors paid a heavy price if they alienated the Soviet authorities. Boris Pasternak (buh-REESS PASS-tur-nak) (1890–1960), who began his literary career as a poet, won the Nobel Prize in 1958 mainly for his celebrated novel *Doctor Zhivago*, written between 1945 and 1956 and published in Italy in 1957. But the Soviet government condemned Pasternak's anti-Soviet tendencies, banned the novel, and would not allow him to accept the prize. The author had alienated the authorities by describing a society scarred by the excesses of Bolshevik revolutionary zeal.

Alexander Solzhenitsyn (1918–2008) caused an even greater furor than Pasternak. Solzhenitsyn had spent eight years in forced labor camps for criticizing Stalin, and his novel *One Day in the Life of Ivan Denisovich*, one of the works for which he won the Nobel Prize in 1970, was an account of life in those camps. Khrushchev allowed the book's publication as part of his de-Stalinization campaign. In 1973, Solzhenitsyn's *Gulag Archipelago*, a detailed indictment of the whole system of Soviet oppression, was published in the West. Soviet authorities denounced Solzhenitsyn's efforts to inform the world of Soviet crimes against humanity and expelled him from the Soviet Union in the same year.

Although restrictive policies continued into the late 1980s, some Soviet authors learned how to minimize battles with the censors by writing under the guise of humor or fantasy. Two of the most accomplished and popular Soviet novelists of the period, Yury Trifonov (YOOR-ee trih-FAH-nawf) (1925–1981) and Fazil Iskander (fah-ZUHL is-KAN-der) (b. 1929), focused on the daily struggle of Soviet citizens to live with dignity. Trifonov depicted the everyday life of ordinary Russians with grim realism, while Iskander used humor to poke fun at the incompetence of the Soviet regime.

In the Eastern European satellites, cultural freedom varied considerably from country to country. In Poland, intellectuals had access to Western publications as well as greater freedom to travel to the West. Hungarian and Yugoslav Communists, too, tolerated a certain level of intellectual activity that was not liked but at least not prohibited. Elsewhere, intellectuals were forced to conform to the regime's demands. After the Soviet invasion of Czechoslovakia in 1968 (see Chapter 26), Czech Communists pursued a policy of strict cultural control.

The socialist camp also experienced the many facets of modern popular culture. By the early 1970s, there were 28 million television sets in the Soviet Union, although state authorities controlled the content of the programs that the Soviet people watched. Tourism, too, made inroads into the Communist world as state-run industries provided vacation time and governments established resorts for workers on the Black Sea and Adriatic coasts. In Poland, the number of vacationers who used holiday retreats increased from 700,000 in 1960 to 2.8 million in 1972.

Spectator sports became a large industry and were also highly politicized as a result of Cold War divisions. "Each new victory," one party leader stated, "is a victory for the Soviet form of society and the socialist sport system; it provides irrefutable proof of the superiority of socialist culture over the decaying culture of the capitalist states."[4] Accordingly, the state provided money for the construction of gymnasiums and training camps and portrayed athletes as superheroes.

Social Changes in the Soviet Union and Eastern Europe

The imposition of Marxist systems in Eastern Europe had far-reaching social consequences. Most Eastern European countries made the change from peasant societies to modern, industrialized economies. In Bulgaria, for example, 80 percent of the labor force was engaged in agriculture in 1950, but only 20 percent was still working there in 1980. Although the Soviet Union and its Eastern European satellites never achieved the high standards of living of the West, they did experience some improvement. In 1960, the average real income of Polish peasants was four times higher than before World War II. Consumer goods also became more widely available. In East Germany, only 17 percent of families had television sets in 1960, but 75 percent had acquired them by 1972.

According to Marxist doctrine, state control of industry and the elimination of private property were supposed to lead to a classless society. Although that ideal was never achieved, it did have important social consequences. For one thing, traditional ruling classes were stripped of their special status after 1945. The Potocki family in Poland, for example, which had owned 9 million acres of land before the war, lost all of its possessions, and family members were reduced to the ranks of common laborers.

EDUCATION The desire to create a classless society led to noticeable changes in education. In some countries, laws mandated quota systems based on class. In East Germany, for example, 50 percent of the students in secondary schools had to be children of workers and peasants. The sons of manual workers constituted 53 percent of university students in Yugoslavia in 1964 and 40 percent in East Germany, compared with only 15 percent in Italy and 5.3 percent in West Germany. Social mobility also increased. In Poland in 1961, half of all white-collar workers came from blue-collar families. A significant number of judges, professors, and industrial managers stemmed from working-class backgrounds.

Education became crucial in preparing for new jobs in the Communist system and led to higher enrollments in both secondary schools and universities. In Czechoslovakia, for example, the number of students in secondary schools tripled between 1945 and 1970, and the number of university students quadrupled between the 1930s and the 1960s. The type of education that students received also changed. In Hungary before World War II, 40 percent of students studied law, 9 percent engineering and technology, and 5 percent agriculture. In 1970, 35 percent were in engineering and technology, 9 percent in agriculture, and only 4 percent in law.

By the 1970s, the new managers of society, regardless of class background, realized the importance of higher education and used their power to gain special privileges for their children. By 1971, 60 percent of the children of white-collar workers attended university, and even though blue-collar families constituted 60 percent of the population, only 36 percent of their children attended institutions of higher learning. Even East Germany dropped its requirement that 50 percent of secondary students had to be the offspring of workers and peasants.

THE NEW ELITE This shift in educational preferences demonstrates yet another aspect of the social structure in the Communist world: the emergence of a new privileged class, made up of members of the Communist Party, state officials, high-ranking officers in the military and the secret police, and a few special professional groups. The new elite not only possessed political power but also received special privileges, including the right to purchase high-quality goods in special stores, paid vacations at special resorts, access to good housing and superior medical services, and advantages in education and jobs for their children. In 1980, in one Soviet province, 70 percent of Communist Party members came from the families of managers, technicians, and government and party bureaucrats.

Ideals of equality did not include women. Men dominated the leadership positions of the Communist Parties. Women did have greater opportunities in the workforce and even in the professions, however. In the Soviet Union, women comprised 51 percent of the labor force in 1980; by the mid-1980s, they constituted 50 percent of the engineers, 80 percent of the doctors, and 75 percent of the teachers and teachers' aides. But many of these were low-paying jobs; most female doctors, for example, worked in primary care and were paid less than skilled machinists. The chief administrators in hospitals and schools were still men.

Moreover, although women made up nearly half of the workforce, they were still expected to fulfill their traditional roles in the home (see the box on p. 799). Most women worked what came to be known as the "double shift." After spending eight hours in their jobs, they came home to do the housework and take care of the children. They might spend another two hours a day in long lines at a number of stores waiting to buy food and clothes. Because of the scarcity of housing, they had to use kitchens that were shared by a number of families.

Nearly three-quarters of a century after the Bolshevik Revolution, then, the Marxist dream of an advanced, egalitarian society was as far off as ever. Although in some respects conditions in the socialist camp were better than

"It's So Difficult to Be a Woman Here"

FAMILY & SOCIETY

One of the major problems for Soviet women was the need to balance work and family roles, a problem noticeably ignored by authorities. This selection is taken from a series of interviews of thirteen women in Moscow conducted by Swedish investigators in the late 1970s. As is evident in this interview with Anna, a young wife and mother, these Soviet women took pride in their achievements but were also frustrated with their lives. It is hardly surprising that the conflicting pressures on women caught between the demands of the family and the state's push for industrialization would result in a drop in birthrates and a change in family structure.

Moscow Women: Interview with Anna

[Anna is twenty-one and married, has a three-month-old daughter, and lives with her husband and daughter in a one-room apartment with a balcony and a large bathroom. Anna works as a hairdresser; her husband is an unemployed writer.]

Are there other kinds of jobs dominated by women?
Of course! Preschool teachers are exclusively women. Also beauticians. But I guess that's about all. Here women work in every profession, from tractor drivers to engineers. But I think there ought to be more jobs specifically for women so that there are *some* differences. In this century women have to be equal to men. Now women wear pants, have short hair, and hold important jobs, just like men. There are almost no differences left. Except in the home.

Do women and men have the same goal in life?
Of course. Women want to get out of the house and have careers, just the same as men do. It gives women a lot of advantages, higher wages, and so on. In that sense we have the same goal, but socially I don't think so. The family is, after all, more important for a woman. A man can live without a family; all he needs is for a woman to come from time to time to clean for him and do his laundry. He sleeps with her

if he feels like it. Of course, a woman can adopt this lifestyle, but I still think that most women want their own home, family, children. From time immemorial, women's instincts have been rooted in taking care of their families, tending to their husbands, sewing, washing—all the household chores. Men are supposed to provide for the family; women should keep the home fires burning. This is so deeply ingrained in women that there's no way of changing it.

Whose career do you think is the most important?
The man's, naturally. The family is often broken up because women don't follow their men when they move where they can get a job. That was the case of my in-laws. They don't live together any longer because my father-in-law worked for a long time as far away as Smolensk. He lived alone, without his family, and then, of course, it was only natural that things turned out the way they did. It's hard for a man to live without his family when he's used to being taken care of all the time. Of course there are men who can endure, who continue to be faithful, etc., but for most men it isn't easy. For that reason I think a woman ought to go where her husband does. . . .

That's the way it is. Women have certain obligations, men others. One has to understand that at an early age. Girls have to learn to take care of a household and help at home. Boys too, but not as much as girls. Boys ought to be with their fathers and learn how to do masculine chores. . . .

It's so difficult to be a woman here. With emancipation, we lead such abnormal, twisted lives, because women have to work the same as men do. As a result, women have very little time for themselves to work on their femininity.

 What does this interview reveal about the role of women in the Soviet Union in the 1970s? In what ways did that role differ from that of women in the West during the same period?

---

before World War II, many problems and inequities were as intransigent as ever.

The Disintegration of the Soviet Empire

 FOCUS QUESTIONS: What were the key components of *perestroika*, which Mikhail Gorbachev espoused during the 1980s? Why did it fail?

On the death of Konstantin Chernenko in 1985, party leaders selected a talented and youthful Soviet official, Mikhail Gorbachev, to succeed him. The new Soviet leader had

shown early signs of promise. Born into a peasant family in 1931, Gorbachev combined farmwork with school and received the Order of the Red Banner for his agricultural efforts. This award and his good school record enabled him to study law at the University of Moscow. After receiving his law degree in 1955, he returned to his native southern Russia, where he eventually became first secretary of the Communist Party in the city of Stavropol (STAH-vruh-puhl *or* stav-ROH-puhl)—he had joined the party in 1952—and then first secretary of the regional party committee. In 1978, Gorbachev was made a member of the party's Central Committee in Moscow. Two years later, he became a full member of the ruling Politburo and secretary of the Central Committee.

COMPARATIVE ILLUSTRATION

POLITICS & GOVERNMENT

Sideline Industries: Creeping Capitalism in a Socialist Paradise. In the late 1980s, Communist leaders in both the Soviet Union and China began to encourage their citizens to engage in private commercial activities as a means of reviving moribund economies. In the photo on the left, a Soviet farmworker displays fruits and vegetables on a street corner in Odessa, a seaport on the Black Sea. On the right, a Chinese woman sells her dumplings to passersby in Shandong province. As her smile suggests, the Chinese took up the challenge of entrepreneurship with much greater success and enthusiasm than their Soviet counterparts did.

Q *Why did Chinese citizens adopt capitalist reforms in the countryside more enthusiastically than their Soviet counterparts?*

During the early 1980s, Gorbachev began to realize the immensity of Soviet problems and the crucial need to transform the system. During a visit to Canada in 1983, he discovered to his astonishment that Canadian farmers worked hard on their own initiative. "We'll never have this for fifty years," he reportedly remarked.[5] On his return to Moscow, he set up a number of committees to evaluate the situation and recommend measures to improve the system.

The Gorbachev Era

With his election as party general secretary in 1985, Gorbachev seemed intent on taking earlier reforms to their logical conclusions. The cornerstone of his program was ***perestroika*** (per-uh-STROI-kuh), or "restructuring." At first it meant only a reordering of economic policy, as Gorbachev called for the beginning of a market economy with limited free enterprise and some private property (see the comparative illustration above). Initial economic reforms were difficult to implement, however. Radicals criticized Gorbachev for his caution and demanded decisive measures; conservatives feared that rapid changes would be too painful. In his attempt to achieve compromise, Gorbachev often pursued partial liberalization, which satisfied neither faction and also failed to work, producing only more discontent.

Gorbachev soon perceived that in the Soviet system, the economy was intimately tied to the social and political spheres. Any efforts to reform the economy without political or social reform would be doomed to failure. One of the most important instruments of *perestroika* was ***glasnost*** (GLAHZ-nohst), or "openness." Soviet citizens and officials were encouraged to openly discuss the strengths and weaknesses of the Soviet Union. The effects of this policy could be seen in *Pravda*, the official newspaper of the Communist Party, which began to report news of disasters such as the nuclear accident at Chernobyl in 1986 and collisions of ships in the Black Sea. This more liberal approach was soon extended to include reports of official corruption, sloppy factory work, and protests against government policy. The arts also benefited from the new policy as previously banned works were now published and motion pictures were allowed to depict negative aspects of Soviet life. Music based on Western styles, such as jazz and rock, could now be performed openly. Religious activities, long banned by the government, were once again tolerated.

Political reforms were equally revolutionary. In June 1987, the principle of two-candidate elections was introduced; previously, voters had been presented with only one choice. Most dissidents, including Andrei Sakharov, who had spent years in internal exile, were released. At the Communist Party conference in 1988, Gorbachev called for the creation of a new Soviet parliament, the Congress of People's Deputies, whose members were to be chosen in competitive

Mikhail Gorbachev. After graduating from the University of Moscow with a law degree in 1955, Mikhail Gorbachev rose rapidly through the ranks of the Communist Party and was elected general secretary of the party in 1985. To colleagues who questioned Gorbachev's qualifications because of his relative youth, one of his supporters remarked, "He has a nice smile, but he has iron teeth." A pragmatist at heart, Gorbachev realized that drastic reforms were needed to prevent a total collapse of the Soviet system. During the late 1980s he liberalized economic policy and sought to achieve a new openness in Soviet politics. Unintentionally, he opened the door to the disintegration of the Soviet Union.

motivated slights. As violence erupted, the Soviet army, in disarray since the Soviet intervention in Afghanistan in 1979, had difficulty controlling the situation. In some cases, independence movements and ethnic causes became linked, as in Azerbaijan (az-ur-by-JAHN), where the National Front became the spokesgroup for the Muslim Azerbaijanis in the conflict with Christian Armenians.

The period from 1988 to 1990 witnessed the emergence of nationalist movements throughout the constituent republics of the Soviet Union. Often motivated by ethnic concerns, many of them called for independence from Russian-based rule centered in Moscow. Such movements sprang up first in Georgia in late 1988 and then in Latvia (LAT-vee-uh), Estonia (ES-toh-nee-uh), Moldavia (mohl-DAY-vee-uh), Uzbekistan (ooz-BEK-ih-stan), Azerbaijan, and Lithuania (lih- thuh-WAY-nee-ee-uh).

In December 1989, the Communist Party of Lithuania declared itself independent of the Communist Party of the Soviet Union. Gorbachev made it clear that he supported self-determination but not secession, which he believed would be detrimental to the Soviet Union. Nevertheless, on March 11, 1990, the Lithuanian Supreme Council unilaterally declared that the Lithuanian Soviet Socialist Republic was now the independent Lithuanian Republic. Four days later, the Soviet Congress of People's Deputies, though recognizing a general right to secede from the Union of Soviet Socialist Republics, proclaimed the Lithuanian declaration null and void, insisting that proper procedures must be followed before secession would be allowed. The Lithuanians paid this no mind.

elections. It convened in 1989, the first such meeting in the nation since 1918. Because of its size, the Congress chose a Supreme Soviet of 450 members to deal with day-to-day activities. The revolutionary nature of Gorbachev's political reforms was evident in Sakharov's rise from dissident to elected member of the Congress of People's Deputies. As a leader of the dissident deputies, Sakharov called for an end to the Communist monopoly of power, and on December 11, 1989, the day he died, he urged the creation of a new, non-Communist party. Early in 1990, Gorbachev legalized the formation of other political parties and struck out Article 6 of the Soviet constitution, which guaranteed the leading role of the Communist Party. Hitherto, the position of first secretary of the party was the most important post in the Soviet Union, but as the Communist Party became less closely associated with the state, the powers of this office diminished. Gorbachev attempted to consolidate his power by creating a new state presidency and in March 1990 became the Soviet Union's first president.

THE BEGINNING OF THE END One of Gorbachev's most serious problems stemmed from the nature of the Soviet Union. The Union of Soviet Socialist Republics was a truly multiethnic country, containing 92 nationalities and 112 recognized languages. Previously, the iron hand of the Communist Party, centered in Moscow, had kept a lid on the centuries-old ethnic tensions that had periodically erupted throughout the history of the region. As Gorbachev released this iron grip, tensions resurfaced, a by-product of *glasnost* that Gorbachev had not anticipated. Ethnic groups took advantage of the new openness to protest what they perceived to be ethnically

EVAPORATION OF AN EMPIRE In 1990 and 1991, Gorbachev struggled to deal with Lithuania and the other problems unleashed by his reforms. On the one hand, he tried to appease the conservative forces who complained about the growing disorder within the Soviet Union. On the other hand, he tried to accommodate the liberal forces, especially those in the Soviet republics, who increasingly favored a new kind of decentralized Soviet federation. Gorbachev especially labored to cooperate more closely with Boris Yeltsin (YELT-sun) (1931–2007), who was elected president of the Russian Republic in June 1991.

By that time, conservatives within the army, government, KGB, and military industries had grown increasingly worried about the possible dissolution of the Soviet Union and its impact on their own fortunes. On August 19, 1991, a group of these discontented rightists arrested Gorbachev and attempted to seize power. Gorbachev's unwillingness to work with the conspirators and the brave resistance in Moscow of

© Cengage Learning

MAP 27.2 Eastern Europe and the Former Soviet Union in 2011. After the disintegration of the Soviet Union at the end of 1991, the fifteen constituent Soviet republics became independent nations. This map shows the states that emerged from the former Soviet Union and also from the former Yugoslavia, which disintegrated more slowly in the 1990s and 2000s.

Q *What new nations have appeared in Europe and Central Asia since the end of the Cold War?*

Yeltsin and thousands of Russians who had grown accustomed to their new liberties caused the coup to fall apart rapidly. The actions of these right-wing plotters served to accelerate the very process they had hoped to stop—the disintegration of the Soviet Union.

Despite desperate pleas from Gorbachev, the Soviet republics soon opted for complete independence. On December 1, 1991, Ukraine voted for independence. A week later, the leaders of Russia, Ukraine, and Belarus (bell-uh-ROOSS) announced that the Soviet Union had "ceased to exist" and would be replaced by a "commonwealth of independent states." Gorbachev resigned on December 25, 1991, and turned over his responsibilities as commander in chief to Yeltsin, the president of Russia. By the end of 1991, one of the largest empires in world history had come to an end, and fifteen new nations had embarked on an uncertain future (see Map 27.2).

Eastern Europe: From Satellites to Sovereign Nations

The disintegration of the Soviet Union had an immediate impact on its neighbors to the west. First to respond, as in 1956, was Poland, where popular protests at high food prices had erupted in the early 1980s, leading to the rise of an independent labor movement called Solidarity. Led by Lech Walesa (LEK vah-WENT-sah) (b. 1943), Solidarity rapidly became an influential force for change and a threat to the government's monopoly of power. The union was outlawed in 1981, but martial law did not solve Poland's serious economic problems. In 1988, the Communist government

bowed to the inevitable and permitted free national elections to take place, resulting in the election of Walesa as president of Poland in December 1990. In contrast to 1956, when Khrushchev had intervened to prevent the collapse of the Soviet satellite system in Eastern Europe, in the late 1980s, Moscow—inspired by Gorbachev's policy of encouraging "new thinking" to improve relations with the Western powers—took no action to reverse the verdict in Warsaw.

In Hungary, as in Poland, the process of transition had begun many years earlier. After crushing the Hungarian revolution of 1956, the Communist government of János Kádár had tried to assuage popular opinion by enacting a series of far-reaching economic reforms (labeled "communism with a capitalist face-lift"). But as the 1980s progressed, the economy sagged, and in 1989, the regime permitted the formation of opposition political parties, leading eventually to the formation of a non-Communist coalition government in elections held in March 1990.

The transition in Czechoslovakia was more abrupt. After Soviet troops crushed the Prague Spring in 1968, hard-line Communists under Gustav Husák followed a policy of massive repression to maintain their power. In 1977, dissident intellectuals formed an organization called Charter 77 as a vehicle for protest against violations of human rights. Regardless of the repressive atmosphere, dissident activities continued to grow during the 1980s, and when massive demonstrations broke out in several major cities in 1989, President Husák's government, lacking popular support, collapsed. At the end of December, he was replaced by Václav Havel (VAHT-slahf HAH-vul) (b. 1936), a dissident playwright who had been a leading figure in Charter 77.

But the most dramatic events took place in East Germany, where a persistent economic slump and the ongoing oppression by the regime of Erich Honecker led to a flight of refugees and mass demonstrations against the regime in the summer and fall of 1989. Capitulating to popular pressure, the Communist government opened its entire border with the West. The Berlin Wall, the most tangible symbol of the Cold War, became the site of a massive celebration; most of it was dismantled by joyful Germans from both sides of the border. In March 1990, free elections led to the formation of a non-Communist government that rapidly carried out a program of political and economic reunification with West Germany.

The dissolution of the Soviet Union and its satellite system in Eastern Europe brought a dramatic end to the Cold War. By the beginning of the 1990s, a generation of global rivalry between two ideological systems had come to a close, and world leaders turned their attention to the construction of what U.S. President George H. W. Bush called the New World Order. But what sort of new order would it be?

Why Did the Soviet Union Collapse?

What caused the sudden disintegration of the Soviet system? It is popular in some quarters in the United States to argue that the ambitious defense policies adopted by the Reagan administration forced Moscow into an arms race that it could not afford and that ultimately led to the collapse of the Soviet economy. This contention has some superficial plausibility as Soviet leaders did indeed react to Reagan's "Star Wars" program by increasing their own defense expenditures, which put a strain on the Soviet budget.

Most knowledgeable observers, however, believe that the fall of the Soviet Union was primarily a consequence of conditions inherent in the system, several of which have been pointed out in this chapter. For years, if not decades, leaders in the Kremlin had disguised or ignored the massive inefficiencies in the Soviet economy. In the 1980s, time began to run out. The perceptive Mikhail Gorbachev tried to stem the decline by instituting radical reforms, but by then it was too late.

An additional factor should also be considered. One of the most vulnerable aspects of the Soviet Union was its multiethnic character, with only a little more than half of the total population composed of ethnic Russians. Many of the minority nationalities were becoming increasingly restive and were demanding more autonomy or even independence for their regions. By the end of the 1980s, such demands brought about the final collapse of the system. The Soviet empire died at least partly from imperial overreach.

The East Is Red: China Under Communism

 FOCUS QUESTION: What were Mao Zedong's chief goals for China, and what policies did he institute to try to achieve them?

"A revolution is not a dinner party, or writing an essay, or painting a picture, or doing embroidery; it cannot be so

CHRONOLOGY	The Soviet Bloc and Its Demise	
Death of Joseph Stalin		1953
Rise of Nikita Khrushchev		1955
Khrushchev's de-Stalinization speech		1956
Removal of Khrushchev		1964
Brezhnev era		1964–1982
Rule of Andropov and Chernenko		1982–1985
Gorbachev comes to power in Soviet Union		1985
Collapse of Communist governments in Eastern Europe		1989
Disintegration of Soviet Union		1991

refined, so leisurely and gentle, so temperate and kind, courteous, restrained, and magnanimous. A revolution is an insurrection, an act of violence by which one class overthrows another."[6] With these words—written in 1926, at a time when the Communists, in cooperation with Chiang Kai-shek's Nationalist Party, were embarked on their Northern Expedition to defeat the warlords and reunify China—the young revolutionary Mao Zedong warned his colleagues that the road to victory in the struggle to build a Communist society would be arduous and would inevitably involve acts of violence against the class enemy.

In the fall of 1949, China was at peace for the first time in twelve years. The newly victorious Communist Party, under the leadership of its chairman, Mao Zedong, turned its attention to consolidating its power base and healing the wounds of war. Its long-term goal was to construct a socialist society, but its leaders realized that popular support for the revolution was based on the party's platform of honest government, land reform, social justice, and peace rather than on the utopian goal of a classless society. Accordingly, the new regime temporarily set aside Mao Zedong's stirring exhortation of 1926 and followed Soviet precedent by adopting a moderate program of political and economic recovery known as New Democracy.

New Democracy

With **New Democracy**—patterned roughly after Lenin's New Economic Policy in Soviet Russia in the 1920s (see Chapter 23)—the new Chinese leadership tacitly recognized that time and extensive indoctrination would be needed to convince the Chinese people of the superiority of socialism. In the meantime, the party would rely on capitalist profit incentives to spur productivity. Manufacturing and commercial firms were permitted to remain under private ownership, although with stringent government regulations. To win the support of the poorer peasants, who made up the majority of the population, a land redistribution program was adopted, but the collectivization of agriculture was postponed.

In a number of key respects, New Democracy was a success. About two-thirds of the peasant households in the country received land and thus had reason to be grateful to the new regime. Spurred by official tolerance for capitalist activities and the end of internal conflict, the national economy

Land Reform in Action

FAMILY & SOCIETY

One of the great achievements of the new Communist regime in China was the land reform program, which resulted in the distribution of farmland to almost two-thirds of the rural population. The program consequently won the gratitude of millions of Chinese. But it also had a dark side as local land reform tribunals routinely convicted "wicked landlords" of crimes against the people and then put them to death. The following passage, written by a foreign observer, describes the process in one village.

Revolution in a Chinese Village

T'ien-ming [a Party cadre] called all the active young cadres and the militiamen of Long Bow [village] together and announced to them the policy of the county government, which was to confront all enemy collaborators and their backers at public meetings, expose their crimes, and turn them over to the county authorities for punishment. He proposed that they start with Kuo Te-yu, the puppet village head. Having moved the group to anger with a description of Te-yu's crimes, T'ien-ming reviewed the painful life led by the poor peasants during the occupation and recalled how hard they had all worked and how as soon as they harvested all the grain the puppet officials, backed by army bayonets, took what they wanted, turned over huge quantities to the Japanese devils, forced the peasants to haul it away, and flogged those who refused.

As the silent crowd contracted toward the spot where the accused man stood, T'ien-ming stepped forward. . . . "This is our chance. Remember how we were oppressed. The traitors seized our property. They beat us and kicked us. . . .

"Let us speak out the bitter memories. Let us see that the blood debt is repaid. . . ."

He paused for a moment. The peasants were listening to every word but gave no sign as to how they felt. . . .

"Come now, who has evidence against this man?"

Again there was silence.

Kuei-ts'ai, the new vice-chairman of the village, found it intolerable. He jumped up [and] struck Kuo Te-yu on the jaw with the back of his hand. "Tell the meeting how much you stole," he demanded.

The blow jarred the ragged crowd. It was as if an electric spark had tensed every muscle. Not in living memory had any peasant ever struck an official. . . .

The people in the square waited fascinated as if watching a play. They did not realize that in order for the plot to unfold they themselves had to mount the stage and speak out what was on their minds.

That evening T'ien-ming and Kuei-ts'ai called together the small groups of poor peasants from various parts of the village and sought to learn what it was that was really holding them back. They soon found the root of the trouble was fear of the old established political forces, and their military backers. The old reluctance to move against the power of the gentry, the fear of ultimate defeat and terrible reprisal that had been seared into the consciousness of so many generations, lay like a cloud over the peasants' minds and hearts.

Emboldened by T'ien-ming's words, other peasants began to speak out. They recalled what Te-yu had done to them personally. Several vowed to speak up and accuse him the next morning. After the meeting broke up, the passage of time worked its own leaven. In many a hovel and tumbledown house talk continued well past midnight. Some people were so excited they did not sleep at all. . . .

On the following day the meeting was livelier by far. It began with a sharp argument as to who would make the first accusation, and T'ien-ming found it difficult to keep order. Before Te-yu had a chance to reply to any questions, a crowd of young men, among whom were several militiamen, surged forward ready to beat him.

 What was the Communist Party's purpose in carrying out land reform in China? How did the tactics employed here support that strategy?

---

began to rebound, although agricultural production still lagged behind both official targets and the growing population, which was increasing at an annual rate of more than 2 percent. But not all benefited. In the course of carrying out land redistribution, thousands if not millions of landlords and well-to-do farmers lost their lands, their personal property, their freedom, and sometimes their lives. Many of those who died were tried and convicted of "crimes against the people" in tribunals set up under official sponsorship in towns and villages around the country. As Mao himself later conceded, many were innocent of any crime, but in the eyes of the party, their deaths were necessary to destroy the power of the landed gentry in the countryside (see the box above).

The Transition to Socialism

Originally, party leaders intended to follow the Leninist formula of delaying the building of a fully socialist society until China had a sufficient industrial base to permit the mechanization of agriculture. In 1953, they launched the nation's first five-year plan (patterned after similar Soviet plans), which called for substantial increases in industrial output. Lenin had believed that mechanization would induce Russian peasants to join collective farms, because the farms, with their greater size and efficiency, could purchase expensive farm machinery that individual farmers could not afford. But the difficulty of providing tractors and reapers for millions of rural villages eventually convinced Mao that it would take years, if not decades, for China's infant industrial base to meet the needs of a modernizing agricultural sector. He therefore decided to begin collectivization immediately, in the hope that collective farms would increase food production and release land, labor, and capital for the industrial sector. Accordingly, beginning in 1955, virtually all private farmland was collectivized (although peasant families were allowed to retain small private plots for their own use), and most businesses and industries were nationalized.

Collectivization was achieved without arousing the massive peasant unrest that had taken place in the Soviet Union during the 1930s, perhaps because the Chinese government followed a policy of persuasion rather than compulsion (Mao Zedong remarked that Stalin had "drained the pond to catch the fish") and because the Communist land redistribution program had already earned the support of millions of rural Chinese. But the hoped-for production increases did not materialize, and in 1958, at Mao's insistent urging, party leaders approved a more radical program known as the **Great Leap Forward**. Existing rural collectives, normally the size of a traditional village, were combined into vast "people's communes," each containing more than 30,000 people. These communes were to be responsible for all administrative and economic tasks at the local level. The party's official slogan promised "Hard work for a few years, happiness for a thousand."[7]

Some party members were concerned that this ambitious program would threaten the government's rural base of support, but Mao argued that Chinese peasants were naturally revolutionary in spirit. The Chinese rural masses, he said, are

> first of all, poor, and secondly, blank. That may seem like a bad thing, but it is really a good thing. Poor people want change, want to do things, want revolution. A clean sheet of paper has no blotches, and so the newest and most beautiful words can be written on it, the newest and most beautiful pictures can be painted on it.[8]

Those words, of course, were *socialism* and *communism*.

The communes were a disaster. Administrative bottlenecks, bad weather, and peasant resistance to the new system (which, among other things, attempted to eliminate work incentives and destroy the traditional family as the basic unit of Chinese society) combined to drive food production downward, and over the next few years, as many as 15 million people may have died of starvation. Many peasants were reportedly reduced to eating the bark off trees and in some cases allowing infants to starve. In 1960, the experiment was essentially abandoned. Although the commune structure was retained, ownership and management were returned to the collective level. Mao was severely criticized by some of his more pragmatic colleagues (one remarked bitingly that "one cannot reach Heaven in a single step"), causing him to complain that he had been relegated to the sidelines "like a Buddha on a shelf."

The Great Proletarian Cultural Revolution

But Mao was not yet ready to abandon either his power or his dream of a totally egalitarian society. In 1966, he returned to the attack, mobilizing discontented youth and disgruntled party members into revolutionary units, soon to be known as Red Guards, who were urged to take to the streets to cleanse Chinese society—from local schools and factories to government ministries in Beijing—of impure elements who (in Mao's mind, at least) were guilty of "taking the capitalist road." Supported by his wife, Jiang Qing (jahng CHING), and other radical party figures, Mao launched China on a new forced march toward communism.

The so-called **Great Proletarian Cultural Revolution** (literally, a "great revolution to create a proletarian culture") lasted for ten years, from 1966 to 1976. Some Western observers interpreted it as a simple power struggle between Mao Zedong and some of his key rivals such as Liu Shaoqi (lyoo show-CHEE ["ow" as in "how"]) (Liu Shao-ch'i), Mao's designated successor, and Deng Xiaoping (DUHNG show-PING ["ow" as in "how"] (Teng Hsiao-p'ing), the party's general secretary. Both were removed from their positions, and Liu later died, allegedly of torture, in a Chinese prison. But real policy disagreements were involved. Mao and his supporters feared that capitalist values and the remnants of "feudalist" Confucian ideas would undermine ideological fervor and betray the revolutionary cause. He was convinced that only an atmosphere of **uninterrupted revolution** could enable the Chinese to overcome the lethargy of the past and achieve the final stage of utopian communism. "I care not," he once wrote, "that the winds blow and the waves beat. It is better than standing idly in a courtyard."

His opponents argued for a more pragmatic strategy that gave priority to nation building over the ultimate Communist goal of spiritual transformation. But with Mao's supporters now in power, the party carried out vast economic and educational reforms that virtually eliminated any remaining profit incentives, established a new school system that emphasized "Mao Zedong thought," and stressed practical education at the elementary level at the expense of specialized training in science and the humanities in the universities. School learning was discouraged as a legacy of capitalism, and Mao's famous Little Red Book (officially, *Quotations of Chairman Mao Zedong*, a slim volume of Maoist aphorisms to encourage good behavior and revolutionary zeal) was hailed as the most important source of knowledge in all areas.

The radicals' efforts to destroy all vestiges of traditional society were reminiscent of the Reign of Terror in revolutionary France, when the Jacobins sought to destroy organized religion and even created a new revolutionary calendar. Red Guards rampaged through the country attempting to eradicate the "four olds" (old thought, old culture, old customs, and old habits). They destroyed temples and religious sculptures; they tore down street signs and replaced them with new ones carrying revolutionary names. At one point, the city of Shanghai even ordered that the significance of colors in stoplights be changed so that red (the revolutionary color) would indicate that traffic could move. That experiment was soon abandoned.

But a mood of revolutionary ferment and enthusiasm is difficult to sustain. Key groups, including bureaucrats, urban professionals, and many military officers, did not share Mao's

Punishing China's Enemies During the Cultural Revolution. The Cultural Revolution, which began in 1966, was a massive effort by Mao Zedong and his radical supporters to eliminate rival elements within the Chinese Communist Party and the government. Accused of being "capitalist roaders," such individuals were subjected to public criticism and removed from their positions. Some were imprisoned or executed. Here Red Guards parade a victim wearing a dunce cap through the streets of Beijing.

belief in the benefits of uninterrupted revolution and constant turmoil. Many were alienated by the arbitrary actions of the Red Guards, who indiscriminately accused and brutalized their victims in a society where legal safeguards had almost entirely vanished (see the box on p. 807). Inevitably, the sense of anarchy and uncertainty caused popular support for the movement to erode, and when the end came with Mao's death in 1976, the vast majority of the population may well have welcomed its demise.

Personal accounts by young Chinese who took part in the Cultural Revolution show that their initial enthusiasm often turned to disillusionment. In *Son of the Revolution*, Liang Heng (lee-ahng HUHNG) tells how at first he helped friends organize Red Guard groups: "I thought it was a great idea. We would be following Chairman Mao just like the grown-ups, and Father would be proud of me. I suppose I too resented the teachers who had controlled and criticized me for so long, and I looked forward to a little revenge."[9] Later he had reason to repent. His sister ran off to join the local Red Guard group. Prior to her departure, she denounced her mother and the rest of her family as "rightists" and enemies of the revolution. Their home was regularly raided by Red Guards, and their father was severely beaten and tortured for having three neckties and "Western shirts." Books, paintings, and writings were piled in the center of the floor and burned before his eyes. On leaving, a few of the Red Guards helped themselves to his monthly salary and his transistor radio.

From Mao to Deng

Mao Zedong died in September 1976 at the age of eighty-three. After a short but bitter succession struggle, the pragmatists led by Deng Xiaoping (1904–1997) seized power from the radicals and formally brought the Cultural Revolution to an end. Mao's widow, Jiang Qing, and three other radicals (derisively called the "Gang of Four" by their opponents) were placed on trial and sentenced to death or to long prison terms. The egalitarian policies of the previous decade were reversed, and a new program emphasizing economic modernization was introduced.

Under the leadership of Deng Xiaoping, who placed his supporters in key positions throughout the party and the government, attention focused on what were called the **Four Modernizations**: industry, agriculture, technology, and national defense. Deng had been a leader of the faction that opposed Mao's program of rapid socialist transformation, and during the Cultural Revolution, he had been forced to perform menial labor to "sincerely correct his errors." But Deng continued to espouse the pragmatic approach, which he often likened to the Chinese aphorism "cross the river by feeling the stones." Reportedly, he also once remarked, "Black cat, white cat, what does it matter so long as it catches the mice?" Under the program of Four Modernizations, many of the restrictions against private activities and profit incentives were eliminated, and people were encouraged to work hard to benefit themselves and Chinese society. The familiar slogan "Serve the people"

Make Revolution!

POLITICS & GOVERNMENT

In 1966, Mao Zedong unleashed the power of revolution on China. Rebellious youth in the form of Red Guards rampaged through all levels of society, exposing anti-Maoist elements, suspected "capitalist roaders," and those identified with the previous ruling class. In this poignant excerpt, Nien Cheng (nee-uhn CHUHNG), the widow of an official of Chiang Kai-shek's regime, describes a visit by Red Guards to her home during the height of the Cultural Revolution.

Nien Cheng, *Life and Death in Shanghai*

Suddenly the doorbell began to ring incessantly. At the same time, there was furious pounding of many fists on my front gate, accompanied by the confused sound of hysterical voices shouting slogans. The cacophony told me that the time of waiting was over and that I must face the threat of the Red Guards and the destruction of my home. . . .

Outside, the sound of voices became louder. "Open the gate! Open the gate! Are you all dead? Whey don't you open the gate?" Someone was swearing and kicking the wooden gate. The horn of the truck was blasting too. . . .

I stood up to put the book on the shelf. A copy of the Constitution of the People's Republic caught my eye. Taking it in my hand and picking up the bunch of keys I had ready on my desk, I went downstairs.

At the same moment, the Red Guards pushed open the front door and entered the house. There were thirty or forty senior high school students, aged between fifteen and twenty, led by two men and one woman much older.

The leading Red Guard, a gangling youth with angry eyes, stepped forward and said to me, "We are the Red Guards. We have come to take revolutionary action against you!"

Though I knew it was futile, I held up the copy of the Constitution and said calmly, "It's against the Constitution of

the People's Republic of China to enter a private house without a search warrant."

The young man snatched the document out of my hand and threw it on the floor. With his eyes blazing, he said, "The Constitution is abolished. It was a document written by the Revisionists within the Communist Party. We recognize only the teachings of our Great Leader Chairman Mao." . . .

Another young man used a stick to smash the mirror hanging over the blackwood chest facing the front door.

Mounting the stairs, I was astonished to see several Red Guards taking pieces of my porcelain collection out of their padded boxes. One young man had arranged a set of four Kangxi wine cups in a row on the floor and was stepping on them. I was just in time to hear the crunch of delicate porcelain under the sole of his shoe. The sound pierced my heart. Impulsively I leapt forward and caught his leg just as he raised his foot to crush the next cup. He toppled. We fell in a heap together. . . . The other Red Guards dropped what they were doing and gathered around us, shouting at me angrily for interfering in their revolutionary activities.

The young man whose revolutionary work of destruction I had interrupted said angrily, "You shut up! These things belong to the old culture. They are the useless toys of the feudal emperors and the modern capitalist class and have no significance to us, the proletarian class. They cannot be compared to cameras and binoculars, which are useful for our struggle in time of war. Our Great Leader Chairman Mao taught us, 'If we do not destroy, we cannot establish.' The old culture must be destroyed to make way for the new socialist culture."

 How do the tactics of the Red Guards compare with those employed by the land reform cadres in the box on p. 804? To what degree did they succeed in remaking the character of the Chinese people?

---

was replaced by a new one repugnant to the tenets of Mao Zedong thought: "Create wealth for the people."

Crucial to the program's success was the government's ability to attract foreign technology and capital. For more than two decades, China had been isolated from technological advances taking place elsewhere in the world. Now, to make up for lost time, the government abandoned its policy of self-reliance and sought to improve relations with the rest of the world. It encouraged foreign investment and sent thousands of students and specialists abroad to study capitalist techniques.

By adopting this pragmatic approach in the years after 1976, China made great strides in ending its chronic problems of poverty and underdevelopment. Per capita income roughly doubled during the 1980s; housing, education, and sanitation

improved, and both agricultural and industrial output skyrocketed.

But critics, both Chinese and foreign, complained that Deng's program had failed to achieve a "fifth modernization": democracy. Official sources denied such charges and spoke proudly of restoring "socialist legality" by doing away with the arbitrary punishments applied during the Cultural Revolution. Deng himself encouraged the Chinese people to speak out against earlier excesses. In the late 1970s, ordinary citizens pasted "big character posters" criticizing the abuses of the past on the so-called Democracy Wall near Tiananmen (tee-AHN-ahn-muhn) Square in downtown Beijing.

Yet it soon became clear that the new leaders would not tolerate any direct criticism of the Communist Party or of Marxist-

Leninist ideology. Dissidents were suppressed, and some were sentenced to long prison terms. Among them was the well-known astrophysicist Fang Lizhi (FAHNG lee-JURR) (Fang Li-chih), who spoke out publicly against official corruption and the continuing influence of Marxist-Leninist concepts in post-Mao China, telling an audience in Hong Kong that "China will not be able to modernize if it does not break the shackles of Maoist and Stalinist-style socialism." Fang immediately felt the weight of official displeasure. He was refused permission to travel abroad, and articles that he submitted to official periodicals were rejected.

The problem began to intensify in the late 1980s as more Chinese began to study abroad and more information about Western society reached educated individuals inside the country. Rising expectations aroused by the economic improvements of the early 1980s led to increasing pressure from students and other urban residents for better living conditions, relaxed restrictions on study abroad, and increased freedom to select employment after graduation.

Incident at Tiananmen Square

As long as economic conditions for the majority of Chinese were improving, other classes did not share the students' discontent, and the government was able to isolate them from other elements in society. But in the late 1980s, an overheated economy led to rising inflation and growing discontent among salaried workers, especially in the cities. At the same time, corruption, nepotism, and favored treatment for senior officials and party members were provoking increasing criticism. In May 1989, student protesters carried placards demanding "Science and Democracy" (reminiscent of the slogan of the May Fourth Movement, whose seventieth anniversary was celebrated in the spring of 1989), an end to official corruption, and the resignation of China's aging party leadership (see the comparative illustration below). These demands received widespread support from the urban population (although notably less in rural areas) and led to massive demonstrations in Tiananmen Square (see the box on p. 809).

COMPARATIVE ILLUSTRATION

POLITICS & GOVERNMENT

Student Demonstrations in Beijing. On May 4, 1919, students gathered at the Gate of Heavenly Peace in Beijing to protest the Japanese takeover of the Shandong peninsula after World War I (top photo). The protests triggered the famous May Fourth Movement, which highlighted the demand by progressive forces in China for political and social reforms. Seventy years later, students and their supporters gathered in the same spot to demand democracy and an end to official corruption in China (bottom photo). The Heroes' Monument and Mao's mausoleum are in the background.

Q *Compare and contrast the motives, participants, and consequences of the demonstrations that took place in 1919 and 1989.*

© Topham/The Image Works

© William J. Duiker

OPPOSING ⋝ VIEWPOINTS

Students Appeal for Democracy

POLITICS & GOVERNMENT

In the spring of 1989, thousands of students gathered in Tiananmen Square in downtown Beijing to provide moral support to their many compatriots who had gone on a hunger strike in an effort to compel the Chinese government to reduce the level of official corruption and enact democratic reforms, opening the political process to the Chinese people. The first selection is from an editorial published on April 26 by the official newspaper *People's Daily*. Fearing that the student demonstrations would get out of hand, as had happened during the Cultural Revolution, the editorial condemned the protests for being contrary to the Communist Party. The second selection is from a statement by Zhao Ziyang, the party general secretary, who argued that many of the students' demands were justified. On May 17, student leaders distributed flyers explaining the goals of the movement to participants and passersby, including the author of this chapter. The third selection is from one of these flyers.

People's Daily Editorial, April 26, 1989

This is a well-planned plot . . . to confuse the people and throw the country into turmoil. . . . Its real aim is to reject the Chinese Communist Party and the socialist system at the most fundamental level. . . . This is a most serous political struggle that concerns the whole Party and nation.

Statement by Party General Secretary Zhao Ziyang Before Party Colleagues, May 4, 1989

Let me tell you how I see all this. I think the student movement has two important characteristics. First, the students' slogans call for things like supporting the Constitution, promoting democracy, and fighting corruption. These demands all echo positions of the Party and the government. Second, a great many people from all parts of society are out there joining the demonstrations and backing the students. . . . This has grown into a nationwide protest. I think the best way to bring the thing to a quick end is to focus on the mainstream views of the majority.

"Why Do We Have to Undergo a Hunger Strike?"

By 2:00 P.M. today, the hunger strike carried out by the petition group in Tiananmen Square has been under way for 96 hours. By this morning, more than 600 participants have fainted. When these democracy fighters were lifted into the ambulances, no one who was present was not moved to tears.

Our petition group now undergoing the hunger strike demands that at a minimum the government agree to the following two points:

1. To engage on a sincere and equal basis in a dialogue with the "higher education dialogue group." In addition, to broadcast the actual dialogue in its entirety. We absolutely refuse to agree to a partial broadcast, to empty gestures, or to fabrications that dupe the people.
2. To evaluate in a fair and realistic way the patriotic democratic movement. Discard the label of "troublemaking" and redress the reputation of the patriotic democratic movement.

It is our view that the request for a dialogue between the people's government and the people is not an unreasonable one. Our party always follows the principle of seeking truths from actual facts. It is therefore only natural that the evaluation of this patriotic democratic movement should be done in accordance with the principle of seeking truths from actual facts.

Our classmates who are going through the hunger strike are the good sons and daughters of the people! One by one, they have fallen. In the meantime, our "public servants" are completely unmoved. Please, let us ask where your conscience is.

What were the key demands of the protesters in Tiananmen Square? Why were they rejected by the Chinese government?

The demonstrations divided the Chinese leaders. Reformist elements around party general secretary Zhao Ziyang (JOW dzee-YAHNG) were sympathetic to the protesters, but veteran leaders such as Deng Xiaoping saw the student demands for more democracy as a disguised call for an end to Chinese Communist Party (CCP) rule. After some hesitation, the government sent tanks and troops into Tiananmen Square to crush the demonstrators. Dissidents were arrested, and the regime once again began to stress ideological purity and socialist values. Although the crackdown came under widespread criticism abroad, Chinese leaders insisted that economic reforms could only take place in conditions of party leadership and political stability.

Deng Xiaoping and other aging party leaders turned to the army to protect their base of power and suppress what they described as "counterrevolutionary elements." Deng was undoubtedly counting on the fact that many Chinese, particularly in rural areas, feared a recurrence of the disorder of the Cultural Revolution and craved economic prosperity more than political reform. In the months following the confrontation, the government issued new regulations requiring courses on Marxist-Leninist ideology in the schools, sought out dissidents within the intellectual community, and made it clear that while economic reforms would continue, the CCP's monopoly of power would not be allowed to decay. Harsh punishments were imposed on those accused of undermining the Communist system and supporting its enemies abroad.

Back to Confucius?

In the 1990s, the government began to nurture urban support by reducing the rate of inflation and guaranteeing the availability of consumer goods in great demand among the rising middle class. Under Deng Xiaoping's successor, Jiang Zemin (JAHNG zuh-MIN) (b. 1926), who occupied the positions of both party chief and president of China, the government promoted rapid economic growth while cracking down harshly on political dissent. That policy paid dividends in bringing about a perceptible decline in alienation among the residents of the cities. Industrial production continued to increase rapidly, leading to predictions that China would become one of the economic superpowers of the twenty-first century. But discontent in rural areas began to grow, as lagging farm income, high taxes, and official corruption sparked resentment in the countryside.

Partly out of fear that such developments could undermine the socialist system and the rule of the CCP, conservative leaders attempted to curb Western influence and restore faith in Marxism-Leninism. In what may have been a tacit recognition that Marxist exhortations were no longer an effective means of enforcing social discipline, the party sought to make use of Confucianism. Ceremonies celebrating the birth of Confucius now received official sanction, and the virtues promoted by the Master, such as righteousness, propriety, and filial piety, were widely cited as an antidote to the tide of anti-social behavior. As a further indication of its willingness to employ traditional themes to further its national interest, the Chinese government has begun to sponsor the establishment of Confucian centers in countries around the world to promote its view that Confucian humanism is destined to replace traditional religious faiths in coming decades.

In effect, Chinese leaders have tacitly conceded that Marxism is increasingly irrelevant to today's China, which responds much more forcefully to the siren call of nationalism. In a striking departure from the precepts of Marxist internationalism, official sources in Beijing cite Confucian tradition to support their assertion that China is unique and will not follow the path of "peaceful evolution" (to use their term) toward a future democratic capitalist society.

That attitude is also reflected in foreign policy, as China is playing an increasingly active role in the region. To some of its neighbors, including Japan, India, and Russia, China's new posture is disquieting and raises suspicions that China is once again preparing to flex its muscle as it did in the imperial era. The first example of this new attitude took place as early as 1979, when Chinese forces briefly invaded Vietnam as punishment for the Vietnamese occupation of neighboring Cambodia. In the 1990s, China aroused concern in the region by claiming sole ownership over the Spratly (sprat-LEE) Islands in the South China Sea and over the Diaoyu (DYOW-you) Islands (also claimed by Japan, which calls them the Senkakus) near Taiwan (see Map 27.3).

To Chinese leaders, however, such actions represent legitimate efforts to resume China's rightful

MAP 27.3 **The People's Republic of China.** This map shows China's current boundaries. Major regions are indicated in capital letters.

Q *In which regions are there movements against Chinese rule?*

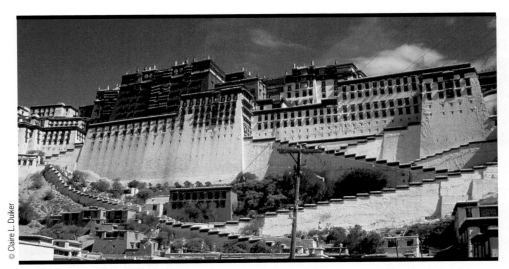

The Potala Palace in Tibet. Tibet was a distant and reluctant appendage of the Chinese Empire during the Qing dynasty. Since the rise to power of the Communist Party in 1949, the regime in Beijing has consistently sought to integrate the region into the People's Republic of China. Resistance to Chinese rule, however, has been widespread. In recent years, the Dalai Lama, the leading religious figure in Tibetan Buddhism, has attempted without success to persuade Chinese leaders to allow a measure of autonomy for the Tibetan people. In 2008, massive riots by frustrated Tibetans took place in the capital city of Lhasa (LAH-suh) just prior to the opening of the Olympic Games in Beijing. The Potala Palace, symbol of Tibetan identity, was constructed in the seventeenth century in Lhasa and serves today as the foremost symbol of the national and cultural aspirations of the Tibetan people.

role in the affairs of the region. After a century of humiliation at the hands of the Western powers and neighboring Japan, the nation, in Mao's famous words of 1949, "has stood up" and no one will be permitted to humiliate it again. For the moment, at least, a fervent patriotism seems to be on the rise in China, actively promoted by the party as a means of holding the country together. The decision by the International Olympic Committee to award the 2008 Summer Games to Beijing led to widespread celebration throughout the country. The event served to symbolize China's emergence as a major national power on the world stage.

Pumping up the spirit of patriotism, however, is not the solution to all problems. Unrest is growing among China's national minorities: in Xinjiang (SHIN-jyahng), where restless Muslim peoples are observing with curiosity the emergence of independent Islamic states in Central Asia, and in Tibet, where the official policy of quelling separatist sentiment has led to the violent suppression of Tibetan culture and an influx of thousands of ethnic Chinese immigrants. In the meantime, the Falun Gong (FAH-loon GONG) religious movement, which the government has attempted to eliminate as a potentially serious threat to its authority, is an additional indication that with the disintegration of the old Maoist utopia, the Chinese people will need more than a pallid version of Marxism-Leninism or a revived Confucianism to fill the gap.

Whether the current leadership will be able to prevent further erosion of the party's power and prestige is unclear. In the short term, efforts to slow the process of change may succeed because many Chinese are understandably fearful of punishment and concerned for their careers. And high economic growth rates can sometimes obscure a multitude of problems as many individuals will opt to chase the fruits of materialism rather than

the less tangible benefits of personal freedom. But in the long run, the party leadership must resolve the contradiction between political authoritarianism and economic prosperity.

New leaders installed in 2002 and 2003 appeared aware of the magnitude of the problem. Hu Jintao (HOO jin-TOW ["ow" as in "how"]) (b. 1943), who replaced Jiang Zemin as CCP general secretary and head of state, called for further reforms to open up Chinese society and bridge the yawning gap between rich and poor. In recent years, the government has shown a growing tolerance for the public exchange of ideas, which has surfaced with the proliferation of bookstores, avant-garde theater, experimental art exhibits, and the Internet. In 2005, an estimated 27 percent of all Chinese citizens possessed a cellphone, and the number has increased dramatically since then. Today, despite the government's efforts to restrict access to certain websites, more people are "surfing the Net" in China than in any other country except the United States. The Internet is wildly popular with those under thirty, who use it for online games, downloading videos and music, and instant messaging. The challenge, however, continues to be daunting. At the CCP's Seventeenth National Congress, held in October 2007, President Hu emphasized the importance of adopting a "scientific view of development," a vague concept calling for social harmony, improved material prosperity, and a reduction in the growing income gap between rich and poor in Chinese society. But he insisted that the Communist Party must remain the sole political force in charge of carrying out the revolution. Ever fearful of chaos, party leaders are convinced that only a firm hand at the tiller can keep the ship of state from crashing onto the rocks.

CHRONOLOGY	China Under Communist Rule
New Democracy	1949–1955
Era of collectivization	1955–1958
Great Leap Forward	1958–1960
Great Proletarian Cultural Revolution	1966–1976
Death of Mao Zedong	1976
Era of Deng Xiaoping	1978–1997
Tiananmen Square incident	1989
Presidency of Jiang Zemin	1993–2002
Hu Jintao becomes president	2002

"Serve the People": Chinese Society Under Communism

 FOCUS QUESTIONS: What significant political, economic, and social changes have taken place in China since the death of Mao Zedong? How successful have they been at improving the quality of life in China?

When the Communist Party came to power in 1949, Chinese leaders made it clear that their policies would differ from the Soviet model in one key respect. Whereas the Bolsheviks had distrusted nonrevolutionary elements in Russia and relied almost exclusively on the use of force to achieve their objectives, the CCP sought to win support from the mass of the population by carrying out reforms that could win popular support. This "mass line" policy, as it was called, worked fairly well until the late 1950s, when Mao and his radical allies adopted policies such as the Great Leap Forward that began to alienate much of the population. Ideological purity was valued over expertise in building an advanced and prosperous society.

Economics in Command

When he came to power in the late 1970s, Deng Xiaoping recognized the need to restore credibility to a system on the verge of breakdown and hoped that rapid economic growth would satisfy the Chinese people and prevent them from demanding political freedoms. The post-Mao leaders clearly placed economic performance over ideological purity. To stimulate the stagnant industrial sector, which had been under state control since the end of the New Democracy era, they reduced bureaucratic controls over state industries and allowed local managers to have more say over prices, salaries, and quality control. Productivity was encouraged by permitting bonuses for extra effort, a policy that had been discouraged during the Cultural Revolution. The regime also tolerated the emergence of a small private sector. The unemployed were encouraged to set up restaurants, bicycle or radio repair shops, and handicraft shops on their own initiative (see the comparative illustration on p. 800).

Finally, the regime opened up the country to foreign investment and technology. Special economic zones were established in urban centers near the coast (ironically, many were located in the old nineteenth-century treaty ports), where lucrative concessions were offered to encourage foreign firms to build factories. The tourist industry was encouraged, and students were sent abroad to study.

The new leaders especially stressed educational reform. The system adopted during the Cultural Revolution, emphasizing practical education and ideology at the expense of higher education and modern science, was rapidly abandoned (Mao's Little Red Book was even withdrawn from circulation and could no longer be found on bookshelves), and a new system based generally on the Western model was instituted. Admission to higher education was based on success in merit examinations, and courses on science and mathematics received high priority.

AGRICULTURAL REFORM No economic reform program could succeed unless it included the countryside. Three decades of socialism had done little to increase food production or to lay the basis for a modern agricultural sector. China, with a population now numbering one billion, could still barely feed itself. Peasants had little incentive to work and few opportunities to increase production through mechanization, the use of fertilizer, or better irrigation.

Under Deng Xiaoping, agricultural policy made a rapid about-face. Under the new **rural responsibility system**, adopted shortly after Deng had consolidated his authority, collectives leased land to peasant families, who paid the collective a quota as rent. Anything produced on the land beyond that payment could be sold on the private market or consumed. To soak up excess labor in the villages, the government encouraged the formation of so-called sideline industries, a modern equivalent of the traditional cottage industries in premodern China. Peasants raised fish or shrimp, made consumer goods, and even assembled living room furniture and appliances for sale to their newly affluent compatriots.

The reform program had a striking effect on rural production. Grain production increased rapidly, and farm income doubled during the 1980s. Yet it also created problems. In the first place, income at the village level became more unequal as some enterprising farmers (known locally as "ten-thousand-dollar households") earned profits several times those realized by their less fortunate or less industrious neighbors. When some farmers discovered that they could earn more by growing cash crops or other specialized commodities, they devoted less land to rice and other grain crops, thereby threatening to reduce the supply of China's most crucial staple. Finally, the agricultural policy threatened to undermine the government's population control program, which party leaders viewed as crucial to the success of the Four Modernizations.

Since a misguided period in the mid-1950s when Mao Zedong had argued that more labor would result in higher productivity, China has been attempting to limit its population growth. By 1970, the government had launched a stringent family planning program—including education, incentives, and penalties for noncompliance—to persuade the Chinese people to limit themselves to one child per family. The program did have some success, and population growth was reduced drastically in the early 1980s. The rural responsibility system, however, undermined the program because it encouraged farm families to pay the penalties for having additional children in the belief that their labor would increase family income and provide the parents with a form of social security for their old age.

EVALUATING THE FOUR MODERNIZATIONS Still, the overall effects of the modernization program were impressive. The standard of living improved for the majority of the population. Whereas a decade earlier, the average Chinese had struggled to earn enough to buy a bicycle, radio, watch, or washing machine, by the late 1980s, many were beginning to purchase videocassette recorders, refrigerators, and color television sets. Yet the rapid growth of the economy created its own problems: inflationary pressures, greed, envy, increased corruption, and—most dangerous of all for the regime—rising expectations. Young people in particular resented restrictions on employment (most young people in China are still required to accept the jobs that are offered to them by the government or school officials) and opportunities to study abroad. Disillusionment ran high, especially in the cities, where lavish living by officials and rising prices for goods aroused widespread alienation and cynicism and laid the groundwork for the massive protest demonstrations in 1989.

During the 1990s, growth rates in the industrial sector continued to be high as domestic capital became increasingly available to compete with the growing presence of foreign enterprises. The government finally recognized the need to close down inefficient state enterprises, and by the end of the decade, the private sector, with official encouragement, accounted for more than 10 percent of the nation's gross domestic product. A stock market opened, and with the country's entrance into the World Trade Organization (WTO) in 2001, China's prowess in the international marketplace improved dramatically. Today, China has the second-largest economy in the world and is the largest exporter of goods. Even the global economic crisis that struck the world in the fall of 2008 has not derailed the Chinese juggernaut, which quickly recovered from the sudden drop in demand for Chinese goods in countries still suffering from the economic downturn.

As a result of these developments, China now possesses a large and increasingly affluent middle class and a burgeoning domestic market for consumer goods. More than 80 percent

of all urban Chinese now own a color television set, a refrigerator, and a washing machine. One-third own their homes, and nearly as many have an air conditioner. For the more affluent, a private automobile is increasingly a possibility, and in 2010, more vehicles were sold in China than in the United States.

But as Chinese leaders have discovered, rapid economic change never comes without cost. The closing of state-run factories led to the dismissal of millions of workers each year, and the private sector, although growing at more than 20 percent annually, initially struggled to absorb them. Poor working conditions and low salaries in Chinese factories resulted in periodic outbreaks of labor unrest. Demographic conditions, however, are changing. The reduction in birthrates since the 1980s is creating a labor shortage, which is putting upward pressure on workers' salaries. As a result, China is facing inflation in the marketplace and increased competition from exports produced by factories located in lower-wage countries in South and Southeast Asia.

Discontent has also been increasing in the countryside, where farmers earn only about half as much as their urban counterparts (the government tried to increase the official purchase price for grain but rescinded the order when it became too expensive). China's entry into the World Trade Organization was greeted with great optimism but has been of little benefit to farmers facing the challenges of cheap foreign imports. Taxes and local corruption add to their complaints, and land seizures by the government or by local officials are a major source of anger in rural communities. In desperation, millions of rural Chinese have left for the big cities, where many of them are unable to find steady employment and are forced to live in squalid conditions in crowded tenements or in the sprawling suburbs. Millions of others remain on their farms and attempt to augment their income by producing for the market or, despite the risk of stringent penalties, by increasing the size of their families. A new land reform law passed in 2008 authorizes farmers to lease or transfer land use rights, although in principle all land in rural areas belongs to the local government.

Another factor hindering China's rush to economic advancement is the impact on the environment. With the rising population, fertile land is in increasingly short supply (China's population has doubled since 1950, but only two-thirds as much irrigable land is available). Soil erosion is a major problem, especially in the north, where the desert is encroaching on farmlands. Water is also a problem. An ambitious plan to transport water by canals from the Yangtze River to the more arid northern provinces has run into a number of roadblocks. Another massive project to construct dams on the Yangtze River has sparked protests from environmentalists, as well as from local peoples forced to migrate from the area. Air pollution is ten times the level in the United States, contributing to growing health concerns. To add to the challenge, more than 700,000 new cars and trucks appear on the country's roads each year. To reduce congestion on roadways, China is constructing an extensive rail network for high-speed bullet trains that will connect all the major regions in the country.

Silk Workers of the World, Unite! In recent years, many critics have charged that Chinese factories are able to market their goods at cheap prices abroad because their workers are paid low wages and often must labor in abysmal working conditions. The silk industry, which produces one of China's key high-end exports, is a case in point. At this factory in Wuxi, women workers spend ten-hour days with their hands immersed in boiling water as they unwind filaments from cocoons onto a spool of silk yarn. Their blistered red hands testify to the difficulty of their painful task.

AP Images/Xinhua Photo, Xia Lin

The Three Gorges Dam. The damming of the Yangtze River over the past two decades is one of the most massive and ambitious construction projects in human history. Designed to increase the amount of farmland in the Yangtze River valley and enable precious water resources to be redistributed to drought-prone regions of the country, the project has also caused considerable environmental damage throughout the Yangtze River valley and displaced several million Chinese from their ancestral homes. Shown here is the famous Three Gorges Dam at Yichang (EE-CHAHNG), a modern wonder of the world.

Social Problems

At the root of Marxist-Leninist ideology is the idea of building a new citizen free from the prejudices, ignorance, and superstition of the "feudal" era and the capitalist desire for self-gratification. This new citizen would be characterized not only by a sense of racial and sexual equality but also by the selfless desire to contribute his or her utmost for the good of all.

WOMEN AND THE FAMILY From the very start, the Chinese Communist government intended to bring an end to the Confucian legacy in modern China. Women were given the vote and encouraged to become active in the political process. At the local level, an increasing number of women became active in the CCP and in collective organizations. In 1950, a new marriage law guaranteed women equal rights with men. Most important, perhaps, it permitted women for the first time to initiate divorce proceedings against their husbands. Within a year, nearly one million divorces had been granted.

At first, the new government moved carefully on family issues to avoid unnecessarily alienating its supporters in the countryside. When collective farms were established in the mid-1950s, payment for hours worked in the form of ration coupons was made not to the individual but to the family head, thus maintaining the traditionally dominant position of the patriarch. When people's communes were established in the late 1950s, however, payments went to the individual.

During the political radicalism of the Great Leap Forward, children were encouraged to report to the authorities any comments by their parents that criticized the system. Such practices continued during the Cultural Revolution, when children were expected to tell on their parents, students on their teachers, and employees on their superiors. By encouraging the oppressed elements in society—the young, the

female, and the poor—to voice their bitterness, Mao was hoping to break the tradition of dependency. Such denunciations had been issued against landlords and other "local tyrants" in the land reform tribunals of the late 1940s and early 1950s. Later, during the Cultural Revolution, they were applied to other authority figures in Chinese society.

LIFESTYLE CHANGES The post-Mao era brought a decisive shift away from revolutionary utopianism and back toward the pragmatic approach to nation building. For most people, that meant improved living conditions and a qualified return to family traditions. For the first time, millions of Chinese saw the prospect of a house or an urban apartment with a washing machine, television set, and indoor plumbing. Young people whose parents had given them patriotic names such as Build the Country, Protect Mao Zedong, and Assist Korea began to choose more elegant and cosmopolitan names for their own children. Some names, such as Surplus Grain or Bring a Younger Brother, expressed hope for the future.

The new attitudes were also reflected in physical appearance. For a generation after the civil war, clothing had been restricted to the traditional baggy "Mao suit" in olive drab or dark blue, but by the 1980s, young people craved such fashionable Western items as designer jeans, trendy sneakers, and sweat suits (or reasonable facsimiles). Cosmetic surgery to create a more buxom figure or a more Western facial look became increasingly common among affluent young women in the cities. Many had the epicanthic fold over their eyelids removed or their noses enlarged—a curious decision in view of the tradition of referring derogatorily to foreigners as "big noses" (see the comparative essay "Family and Society in an Era of Change" on p. 815).

Religious practices and beliefs have also changed. As the government has become more tolerant of organized religion,

Family and Society in an Era of Change

FAMILY &
SOCIETY

One of the paradoxes of the modern world is that at a time of political stability and economic prosperity for many people in the advanced capitalist societies, public cynicism about the system is increasingly widespread. Alienation and drug use are at dangerously high levels, and the rate of criminal activities in most areas remains much higher than in the years immediately after World War II.

Although various reasons have been advanced to explain this paradox, many observers contend that the decline of the traditional family system is responsible for many contemporary social problems. There has been a steady rise in the percentage of illegitimate births and single-parent families in countries throughout the Western world. In the United States, approximately half of all marriages end in divorce. Even in two-parent families, more and more parents work full time, leaving the children to fend for themselves on their return from school. In many countries in Europe, the birthrate has dropped to alarming levels, leading to a severe labor shortage that is attracting a rising number of immigrants from other parts of the world.

Observers point to several factors to explain these conditions: the growing emphasis in advanced capitalist states on an individualistic lifestyle devoted to instant gratification, a phenomenon promoted vigorously by the advertising media; the rise of the feminist movement, which has freed women from the servitude imposed on their predecessors, but at the expense of removing them from full-time responsibility for the care of the next generation;

© William J. Duiker

China's "Little Emperors." Chinese leaders have launched a massive family planning program to curtail population growth. Urban families are restricted to a single child. In conformity with tradition, sons are especially prized, and some Chinese complain that many parents overindulge their children, turning them into spoiled "little emperors."

and the increasing mobility of contemporary life, which disrupts traditional family ties and creates a sense of rootlessness and impersonality in the individual's relationship to the surrounding environment.

These trends are not unique to Western civilization. The traditional nuclear family is also under attack in many societies around the world. Even in East Asia, where the Confucian tradition of family solidarity has been endlessly touted as a major factor in the region's economic success, the incidence of divorce and illegitimate births is on the rise, as is the percentage of women in the workforce. Older citizens frequently complain that the Asian youth of today are too materialistic, faddish, and steeped in the individualistic values of the West. Such criticisms are now voiced in mainland China as well as in the capitalist societies around its perimeter (see Chapter 30).

In societies less exposed to the individualist lifestyle portrayed so prominently in Western culture, traditional attitudes about the family continue to hold sway. In the Middle East, governmental and religious figures seek to prevent the Western media from undermining accepted mores. Success is sometimes elusive, however, as the situation in Iran demonstrates. Despite the zealous guardians of Islamic morality, many young Iranians are clamoring for the individual freedoms that have been denied to them since the Islamic Revolution took place more than three decades ago (see Chapter 29).

Q *To what degree and in what ways are young people in China becoming more like their counterparts in the West?*

some Chinese have begun to return to the traditional Buddhist faith or to folk religions, and Buddhist and Taoist temples are once again crowded with worshipers. Despite official efforts to suppress its more evangelical forms, Christianity has become increasingly popular as well; like the "rice Christians" (persons who supposedly converted for economic reasons) of the past, many now view it as a symbol of success and cosmopolitanism.

As with all social changes, China's reintegration into the outside world has had a price. Arranged marriages, nepotism, and mistreatment of females (for example, under the one-child rule, parents reportedly killed female infants to regain

the possibility of having a son) have returned, although such behavior likely survived under the cloak of revolutionary purity for a generation (see the box on p. 816). Materialistic attitudes are prevalent among young people, along with a corresponding cynicism about politics and the CCP. Expensive weddings are now increasingly common, and bribery and favoritism are all too frequent. Crime of all types, including an apparently growing incidence of prostitution and sex crimes against women, appears to be on the rise. To discourage sexual abuse, the government now seeks to provide free legal services for women living in rural areas.

Love and Marriage in China

FAMILY & SOCIETY

"What men can do, women can also do." So said Chairman Mao as he "liberated" and masculinized Chinese women to work alongside men. Women's individuality and sexuality were sacrificed for the collective good of his new socialist society. Marriage, which had traditionally been arranged by families for financial gain, was now dictated by duty to the state. The Western concept of romantic love did not enter into a Chinese marriage, as this interview of a schoolteacher by the reporter Zhang Xinxin (JANG SHEEN-SHEEN) in the mid-1980s illustrates. According to recent surveys, the same is true today.

Zhang Xinxin, *Chinese Lives*

My husband and I never did any courting—honestly! We registered our marriage a week after we'd met. He was just out of the forces and a worker in a building outfit. They'd been given a foreign-aid assignment in Zambia, and he was selected. He wanted to get his private life fixed up before he went, and someone introduced us. Seeing how he looked really honest, I accepted him.

No, you can't say I didn't know anything about him. The person who introduced us told me he was a Party member who'd been an organization commissar. Any comrade who's good enough to be an organization cadre is politically reliable. Nothing special about our standing of living—it's what we've earned. He's still a worker, but we live all right, don't we?

He went off with the army as soon as we'd registered our marriage and been given the wedding certificates. He was away three years. We didn't have the wedding itself before he went because we hadn't got a room yet.

Those three years were a test for us. The main problem was that my family was against it. They thought I was still only a kid and I'd picked the wrong man. What did they have against him? His family was too poor. Of course I won in the end—we'd registered and got our wedding certificates. We were legally married whether we had the family ceremony or not.

We had our wedding after he came back in the winter of 1973. His leaders and mine all came to congratulate us and give us presents. The usual presents those days were busts of Chairman Mao. I was twenty-six and he was twenty-nine. We've never had a row.

I never really wanted to take the college entrance exams. Then in 1978 the school leadership got us all to put our names forward. They said they weren't going to hold us back: the more of us who passed, the better it would be for the school. So I put my name forward, crammed for six weeks, and passed. I already had two kids then. . . .

I reckoned the chance for study was too good to miss. And my husband was looking after the kids all by himself. I usually only came back once a fortnight. So I couldn't let him down.

My instructors urged me to take the exams for graduate school, but I didn't. I was already thirty-four, so what was the point of more study? There was another reason too. I didn't want an even wider gap between us: he hadn't even finished junior middle school when he joined the army.

It's bad if the gap's too wide. For example, there's a definite difference in our tastes in music and art, I have to admit that. But what really matters? Now we've set up this family we have to preserve it. Besides, look at all the sacrifices he had to make to see me through college. Men comrades all like a game of cards and that, but he was stuck with looking after the kids. He still doesn't get any time for himself—it's all work for him.

We've got a duty to each other. Our differences? The less said about them the better. We've always treated each other with the greatest respect.

Of course some people have made suggestions, but my advice to him is to respect himself and respect me. I'm not going to be like those men who ditch their wives when they go up in the world.

I'm the head of our school now. With this change in my status I've got to show even more responsibility for the family. Besides, I know how much he's done to get me where I am today. I've also got some duties in the municipal Women's Federation and Political Consultative Conference. No, I'm not being modest. I haven't done anything worth talking about, only my duty.

We've got to do a lot more educating people. There have been two cases of divorce in our school this year.

Do you think the marriage described here is successful? Why or why not? What do you think this woman feels about her marriage?

There is also a price to pay for the trend toward privatization. Under the Maoist system, the elderly and the sick were provided with retirement benefits and health care by the state or by the collective organizations. Under current conditions, with the latter no longer playing such a social role and more workers operating in the private sector, the safety net has been removed. The government recently attempted to fill the gap by enacting a social security law, but because of lack of funds, eligibility is limited primarily to individuals in urban areas. Those living in the countryside—who still represent 60 percent of the population—are essentially unprotected, prompting legislation in 2010 to provide modest pensions and medical insurance to the poorest members of Chinese society. Yet much more needs to be done. As the population ages, the lack of a retirement system represents a potential time bomb.

China's Changing Culture

During the first half of the twentieth century, Chinese culture was strongly influenced by currents from the West (see Chapter 24). The rise to power of the Communists in 1949 added a new dimension to the debate over the future of culture in China. The new leaders rejected the Western attitude of "art for art's sake" and, like their Soviet counterparts, viewed culture as an important instrument of indoctrination. The standard would no longer be aesthetic quality or the personal preference of the artist but "art for life's sake," whereby culture would serve the interests of socialism.

CULTURE IN A REVOLUTIONARY ERA At first, the new emphasis on socialist realism did not entirely extinguish the influence of traditional culture. Mao and his colleagues tolerated—and even encouraged—efforts by artists to synthesize traditional ideas with socialist concepts and Western techniques. During the Cultural Revolution, however, all forms of traditional culture came to be viewed as reactionary. Socialist realism became the only acceptable standard in literature, art, and music. All forms of traditional expression were forbidden, and the deification of Mao and his central role in building a Communist paradise became virtually the only acceptable form of artistic expression.

Characteristic of the changing cultural climate in China was the experience of author Ding Ling (DING LING). Born in 1904 and educated in a school for women set up by leftist intellectuals during the hectic years after the May Fourth Movement, she began writing in her early twenties. After her husband, a struggling young poet and member of the CCP, was executed by Chiang Kai-shek's government in 1931, she became involved in party activities and sublimated her talent to the revolutionary cause.

In the late 1930s, Ding Ling settled in Yan'an, where she became a leader in the women's and literary associations of the CCP. Though she remained dedicated to revolution, years of service to the party did not stifle her individuality, and in 1942, she wrote critically of the incompetence, arrogance, and hypocrisy of many party officials, as well as the treatment of women in areas under Communist authority. Such comments raised eyebrows, but she was able to survive criticism and in 1948 wrote her most famous novel, *The Sun Shines over the Sangan River*, which described the CCP's land reform program in favorable terms. It was awarded the Stalin Prize three years later.

During the early 1950s, Ding Ling was one of the most prominent literary lights of the new China, but in the more ideological climate at the end of the decade, she was attacked for her individualism and her previous criticism of the party. Although temporarily rehabilitated, during the Cultural Revolution she was sentenced to hard labor on a commune in the far north and was not released until the late 1970s after the death of Mao Zedong. Although crippled and in poor health, she began writing a biography of her mother that examined the role of women in twentieth-century China. She died in 1981. Ding Ling's fate mirrored the fate of thousands of progressive Chinese intellectuals who, despite their efforts, were not able to satisfy the constantly changing demands of a repressive regime.

ART AND MUSIC After Mao's death, Chinese culture was finally released from the shackles of socialist realism. In painting, where for a decade the only acceptable standard for excellence was praise for the party and its policies, the new permissiveness led to a revival of interest in both traditional and Western forms. Although some painters continued to blend Eastern and Western styles, others imitated trends from abroad, experimenting with a wide range of previously prohibited art styles, including Cubism and abstract painting.

In the late 1980s, two avant-garde art exhibits shocked the Chinese public and provoked the wrath of the party. An exhibition of nude paintings, the first ever held in China, attracted many viewers but reportedly offended the modesty of many Chinese.

The Red Sun in Our Hearts. During the Great Proletarian Cultural Revolution, Chinese art was restricted to topics that promoted revolution and the thoughts of Chairman Mao Zedong. All the knowledge that the true revolutionary required was to be found in Mao's Little Red Book, a collection of his sayings on proper revolutionary behavior. In this painting, Chairman Mao's portrait hovers above a crowd of his admirers, who wave copies of the book as a symbol of their total devotion to him and his vision of a future China.

The second was an exhibit presenting the works of various schools of modern and postmodern art. The event resulted in considerable commentary and some expressions of public hostility. After a Communist critic lambasted the works as promiscuous and ideologically reactionary, the government declared that henceforth it would regulate all art exhibits. Since the 1990s, some Chinese artists, such as the world-famous Ai Weiwei (I WAY-WAY) (b. 1957), have aggressively challenged the government's authority. In response, the government razed Ai's art studio in Shanghai in 2011. He was subsequently taken into police custody on charges related to tax evasion. Nonetheless, Chinese contemporary art has expanded exponentially, attracting international attention and commanding exorbitant prices on the world market.

Like the fine arts, Western classical music was vigorously suppressed during the Cultural Revolution. Significant changes have occurred in the post-Mao era, however, as the government has encouraged public interest in classical music by opening conservatories, holding competitions, and building elaborate concert halls. China today is producing legions of professional musicians, who are filling orchestras and schools of music in Western countries.

LITERATURE The limits of freedom of expression were most apparent in literature. During the early 1980s, party leaders encouraged Chinese writers to express their views on the mistakes of the past, and a new "literature of the wounded" began to describe the brutal and arbitrary character of the Cultural Revolution.

One of the most prominent writers was Bai Hua (by HWA) (b. 1930), whose film script *Bitter Love* described the life of a young Chinese painter who joined the revolutionary movement during the 1940s but whose work was condemned as counterrevolutionary during the Cultural Revolution. In describing the excesses of the Cultural Revolution, Bai Hua was only responding to Deng Xiaoping's appeal for intellectuals to speak out, but he was soon criticized for failing to point out the essentially beneficial role of the CCP in recent Chinese history. The film was withdrawn from circulation in 1981, and Bai Hua was compelled to recant his errors and to state that the great ideas of Mao Zedong on art and literature were "still of universal guiding significance today."[10]

As the attack on Bai Hua illustrates, many party leaders remained suspicious of the impact that "decadent" bourgeois culture could have on the socialist foundations of Chinese society. The official press periodically warned that China should adopt only the "positive" aspects of Western culture (notably, its technology and its work ethic) and not the "negative" elements such as drug use, pornography, and hedonism.

One of the chief targets of China's recent "spiritual civilization" campaign is author Wang Shuo (wahng SHWOH) (b. 1958), whose writings have been banned for exhibiting a sense of "moral decay." In his novels *Playing for Thrills* (1989) and *Please Don't Call Me Human* (2000), Wang highlighted the seamier side of contemporary urban society, peopled with hustlers, ex-convicts, and other assorted hooligans. Spiritually depleted, hedonistic, and amoral in their approach to life, his characters represent the polar opposite of the socialist ideal.

Conservatives were especially incensed by the tendency of many writers to dwell on the shortcomings of the socialist system and to come uncomfortably close to direct criticism of the role of the CCP. One such writer is Mo Yan (muh YAHN) (b. 1956), whose novels *The Garlic Ballads* (1988) and *Life and Death Are Wearing Me Out* (2008) expose the rampant corruption of contemporary Chinese society, the roots of which he attributes to one-party rule. Yu Hua (yoo HWA) (b. 1960), another outstanding novelist, uses narratives marked by exaggerated and grotesque humor to criticize the cruelty of the Communist regime in *To Live* (2003). In *Brothers* (2009), he lambastes the vulgarity and moral depravity of China's newly rich.

Today, Chinese culture has been dramatically transformed by the nation's adoption of a market economy and the invasive spread of the Internet. A new mass literature, much of it written by and intended for China's new urban youth, explores the aspirations and frustrations of a generation obsessed with material consumption and the right of individual expression. Lost in the din are the voices of China's rural poor.

Confucius and Marx: The Tenacity of Tradition

Why has communism survived in China, albeit in a substantially altered form, when it failed in Eastern Europe and the Soviet Union? One of the primary factors is probably cultural. Although the doctrine of Marxism-Leninism originated in Europe, many of its main precepts, such as the primacy of the community over the individual and the denial of the concept of private property, run counter to trends in Western civilization. This inherent conflict is especially evident in the societies of central Europe, which were strongly influenced by Enlightenment philosophy and the Industrial Revolution. These forces were weaker farther to the east, although they had begun to penetrate tsarist Russia by the end of the nineteenth century.

In contrast, Marxism-Leninism found a more receptive climate in China and other countries in the region influenced by Confucian tradition. In its political culture, the Communist system exhibits many of the same characteristics as traditional Confucianism—a single truth, an elite governing class, and an emphasis on obedience to the community and its governing representatives. Although a significant and influential minority of the Chinese population—primarily urban and educated—finds the idea of personal freedom against the power of the state appealing, such concepts have little meaning in rural villages, where the interests of the community have always been emphasized over the desires of the individual. It is no accident that Chinese leaders now seek to reintroduce the precepts of State Confucianism to bolster a fading belief in the existence of a future Communist paradise.

Party leaders today are banking on the hope that China can be governed as it has always been—by an elite class of highly trained professionals dedicated to pursing a predefined objective. In fact, however, real changes are taking place in China today. Although the youthful protesters in Tiananmen Square were comparable in some respects to the reformist elements of the early republic, the China of today is fundamentally different from that of the early twentieth century. Literacy rates and the standard of living are far higher, the pressures of outside powers are less threatening, and China has entered its own industrial and technological revolution. Many Chinese depend more on independent talk radio and the Internet for news and views than on the official media.

Whereas Sun Yat-sen, Chiang Kai-shek, and even Mao Zedong broke their lances on the rocks of centuries of tradition, poverty, and ignorance, the present leaders rule a country much more aware of the world and China's place in it. Although the shift in popular expectations may be gradual, China today is embarked on a journey to a future for which the past no longer provides a roadmap.

CHAPTER SUMMARY

For four decades after the end of World War II, the two major Communist powers appeared to have become permanent features on the international landscape. Suddenly, though, in the late 1980s, the Soviet Union entered a period of internal crisis that shook the foundations of Soviet society. In 1991 the system collapsed, to be replaced by a series of independent states based primarily on ethnic and cultural differences that had existed long before the Bolshevik Revolution. China went through an even longer era of instability, beginning with the Cultural Revolution in 1966, but it managed to survive under a hybrid system that combines features of a Leninist command economy with capitalist practices adapted from the modern West.

Why were the outcomes so different? Although the cultural differences we have described were undoubtedly an important factor, the role of human action should not be ignored. Whereas Mikhail Gorbachev introduced the idea of *glasnost* to permit the emergence of a more pluralistic political system in the Soviet Union, Chinese leaders crushed the protest movement in the spring of 1989 and reasserted the authority of the Communist Party. Deng Xiaoping's gamble paid off, and today the party stands at the height of its power.

CHAPTER TIMELINE

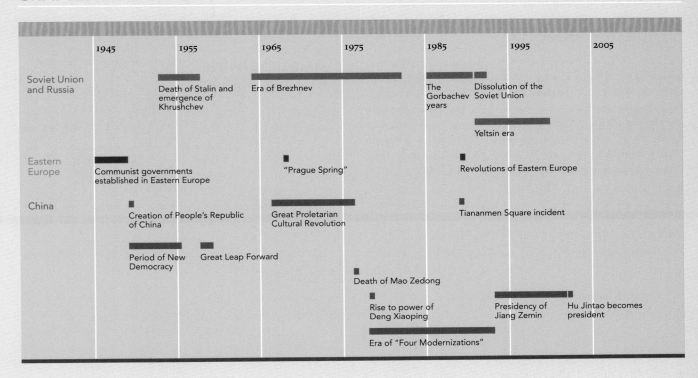

Upon Reflection

Q How have six decades of Communist rule affected the concept of the family in China? How does the current state of the family in China compare with the family in other parts of the world?

Q What strategies were used by the leaders of the Soviet Union and the People's Republic of China as they sought to build Communist societies in their countries? In what ways were the strategies different, and in what ways were they similar? To what degree were they successful?

Q How has the current generation of leadership in China made use of traditional values to solidify Communist control over the country? To what degree has this approach contradicted the theories of Karl Marx?

Key Terms

new course (p. 791)
de-Stalinization (p. 793)
Glosplan (p. 795)
perestroika (p. 800)
glasnost (p. 800)
New Democracy (p. 803)
Great Leap Forward (p. 805)
Great Proletarian Cultural Revolution (p. 805)
uninterrupted revolution (p. 805)
Four Modernizations (p. 806)
rural responsibility system (p. 812)

Suggested Reading

RUSSIA AND THE SOVIET UNION   For a general view of modern Russia, see **M. Malia**, *Russia Under Western Eyes* (Cambridge, Mass., 1999), and **M. T. Poe**, *The Russian Moment in World History* (Princeton, N.J., 2003). On the Khrushchev years, see **W. Taubman**, *Khrushchev: The Man and His Era* (New York, 2004). For an inquiry into the reasons for the Soviet collapse, see **R. Conquest**, *Reflections on a Ravaged Century* (New York, 1999), and **R. Strayer**, *Why Did the Soviet Union Collapse? Understanding Historical Change* (New York, 1998).

CHINA UNDER MAO ZEDONG   A number of useful surveys deal with China after World War II. The most comprehensive treatment of the Communist period is **M. Meisner**, *Mao's China and After: A History of the People's Republic* (New York, 1999). Also see **R. Macfarquhar, ed.,** *The Politics of China: The Eras of Mao and Deng* (Cambridge, 1997). A recent critical biography of China's "Great Helmsman" is **J. Chang** and **J. Halliday**, *Mao: The Unknown Story* (New York, 2005).

POST-MAO CHINA   The 1989 demonstrations and their aftermath are described in an eyewitness account by **L. Feigon**, *China Rising: The Meaning of Tiananmen* (Chicago, 1990). Documentary materials relating to the events of 1989 are chronicled in **A. J. Nathan** and **P. Link, eds.,** *The Tiananmen Papers* (New York, 2001). Subsequent events are analyzed in **J. Fewsmith**, *China Since Tiananmen: The Politics of Transition* (Cambridge, 2001). On China's challenge from the process of democratization, see **J. Gittings**, *The Changing Face of China: From Mao to Market* (Oxford, 2005). Also see **T. Saich**, *Governance and Politics in China* (New York, 2002). China's evolving role in the world is traced in **S. Shirk**, *China: Fragile Superpower* (Oxford, 2007).

CHINESE LITERATURE AND ART   For a comprehensive introduction to twentieth-century Chinese literature, consult **E. Widmer** and **D. Der-Wei Wang, eds.,** *From May Fourth to June Fourth: Fiction and Film in Twentieth-Century China* (Cambridge, Mass., 1993), and **J. Lau** and **H. Goldblett**, *The Columbia Anthology of Modern Chinese Literature* (New York, 1995). For the most comprehensive analysis of twentieth-century Chinese art, see **M. Sullivan**, *Arts and Artists of Twentieth-Century China* (Berkeley, Calif., 1996).

Europe and the Western Hemisphere Since 1945

Children play amid the ruins of Warsaw, Poland, at the end of World War II.

© Bettmann (Reginald Kenny)/CORBIS

CHAPTER OUTLINE AND FOCUS QUESTIONS

Recovery and Renewal in Europe

Q What problems have the nations of Western Europe faced since 1945, and what steps have they taken to try to solve these problems? What problems have Eastern European nations faced since 1989?

Emergence of the Superpower: The United States

Q What political, social, and economic changes has the United States experienced since 1945?

The Development of Canada

Q What political, social, and economic developments has Canada experienced since 1945?

Latin America Since 1945

Q What problems have the nations of Latin America faced since 1945, and what role has Marxist ideology played in their efforts to solve these problems?

Society and Culture in the Western World

Q What major social, cultural, and intellectual developments have occurred in Western Europe and North America since 1945?

CRITICAL THINKING

Q What were the similarities and differences between the major political, economic, and social developments in the first half of the twentieth century and those in the second half of the century?

THE END OF WORLD WAR II in Europe had been met with great joy. One visitor in Moscow reported, "I looked out of the window [at 2:00 A.M.]; almost everywhere there were lights in the windows—people were staying awake. Everyone embraced everyone else; someone sobbed aloud." But after the victory parades and celebrations, Europeans awoke to a devastating realization: their civilization was in ruins. Almost 40 million people (both soldiers and civilians) had been killed over the last six years. Massive air raids and artillery bombardments had reduced many of the great cities of Europe to heaps of rubble. The Polish capital of Warsaw had been almost completely obliterated. An American general described Berlin: "Wherever we looked, we saw desolation. It was like a city of the dead. Suffering and shock were visible in every face. Dead bodies still remained in canals and lakes and were being dug out from under bomb debris." Millions of Europeans faced starvation as grain harvests were only half what they had been in 1939. Millions were also homeless.

Yet by 1970, Europe had not only recovered from the devastating effects of World War II but had experienced an economic resurgence that seemed nothing less than miraculous. Economic growth and virtually full employment continued so long that the first postwar recession, in 1973, came as a shock. It was short-lived, however, and economic growth resumed. Important to this economic expansion was the creation of the welfare state—a prominent social development in postwar Europe. After the collapse of Communist governments in the revolutions of 1989, a number of Eastern European states sought to create market economies and join the military and economic unions first formed by Western European states.

The most significant development after 1945 was the emergence of the United States as the world's richest and most powerful nation. American prosperity reached new heights in the two decades after World War II, but a series of economic and social problems—including racial tensions and staggering budget deficits—left an imposing array of obstacles.

Latin America, to the south of the United States, had its own unique heritage. Although some Latin Americans in the nineteenth century had looked to the United States as a model for their own development, in the twentieth century many strongly criticized the United States for its military and economic domination of their countries. And even though they had escaped the turmoil of World War II, many Latin American countries struggled with economic and political instability in the postwar years.

Toward the end of the century, as the West adjusted from Cold War to post–Cold War realities, other changes were also shaping the Western outlook. The demographic face of European countries changed as massive numbers of immigrants introduced greater ethnic diversity. New artistic and intellectual currents, the continued advance of science and technology, the coming to grips with environmental problems, the surge of the women's liberation movement—all reflected a vibrant, ever-changing world. At the same time, a devastating series of terrorist attacks made the Western world vividly aware of its vulnerability to international terrorism.

Recovery and Renewal in Europe

Q **FOCUS QUESTIONS:** What problems have the nations of Western Europe faced since 1945, and what steps have they taken to try to solve these problems? What problems have Eastern European nations faced since 1989?

All the nations of Europe faced similar problems at the end of World War II. First and foremost, they needed to rebuild their shattered economies. Remarkably, within a few years after the defeat of Germany and Italy, an incredible economic revival brought renewed growth to Western Europe.

Western Europe: The Triumph of Democracy

With the economic aid of the Marshall Plan, the countries of Western Europe recovered relatively rapidly from the devastation of World War II. Between the early 1950s and the late 1970s, industrial production surpassed all previous records, and Western Europe experienced virtually full employment.

FRANCE: FROM DE GAULLE TO NEW UNCERTAINTIES The history of France for nearly a quarter-century after the war was dominated by one man—Charles de Gaulle (SHAHRL duh GOHL) (1890–1970). The founding of the Fourth Republic, with a parliamentary system based on parties that de Gaulle considered weak, led him to withdraw for a while

from politics. In 1958, however, frightened by the bitter divisions within France caused by the Algerian crisis (see Chapter 29), the panic-stricken leaders of the Fourth Republic offered to let de Gaulle take over the government and revise the constitution.

De Gaulle's constitution for the Fifth Republic greatly enhanced the power of the president, who now had the right to choose the prime minister, dissolve parliament, and supervise both national defense and foreign policy. Once elected to that office, de Gaulle sought to return France to the status of a great power. With that goal in mind, he invested heavily in the nuclear arms race. France exploded its first nuclear bomb in 1960. Nevertheless, de Gaulle did not really achieve his ambitious goals; in truth, France was too small for such global ambitions.

During de Gaulle's presidency, the French gross domestic product experienced an annual increase of 5.5 percent, greater than that of the United States. France became a major industrial producer and exporter, particularly in such areas as automobiles and armaments. But the expansion of traditional industries, such as coal, steel, and railroads, which had all been nationalized, led to large government deficits. The cost of living rose faster in France than in the rest of Europe. Increased dissatisfaction led to a series of student protests in May 1968, followed by a general strike by the labor unions. Although he restored order, de Gaulle became discouraged, resigned from office in April 1969, and died the next year.

The worsening of France's economic situation in the 1970s brought a political shift to the left. By 1981, the Socialists had

Charles de Gaulle. As president, Charles de Gaulle sought to revive the greatness of the French nation. He is shown here dressed in his military uniform during a formal state ceremony on a visit to Quebec, Canada, in July 1967.

become the dominant party in the National Assembly, and the Socialist leader, François Mitterrand (frahnh-SWAH MEE-tayr-rahnh) (1916–1995), was elected president. Mitterrand passed a number of measures to aid workers: a higher minimum wage, expanded social benefits, a mandatory fifth week of paid vacation for salaried workers, and a thirty-nine-hour workweek. The victory of the Socialists led them to enact some of their more radical reforms: the government nationalized the steel industry, major banks, the space and electronics industries, and important insurance firms.

The Socialist policies largely failed to work, however, and within three years, a decline in support for the Socialists caused the Mitterrand government to reprivatize portions of the economy. But France's economic decline continued. In 1993, French unemployment stood at 10.6 percent, and in the elections in March of that year, the Socialists won only 28 percent of the vote; a coalition of conservative parties ended up with 80 percent of the seats. The move to the right was strengthened when the conservative mayor of Paris, Jacques Chirac (ZHAHK shee-RAK) (b. 1932), was elected president in May 1995 and reelected in 2002. As high unemployment rates fueled resentment against foreign-born residents, many French voters called for restrictions on all new immigration. Chirac himself pursued a plan of sending illegal immigrants back to their home countries.

In the fall of 2005, however, antiforeign sentiment provoked a backlash of its own as young Muslims in the crowded suburbs of Paris rioted against dismal living conditions and the lack of employment opportunities for foreign residents in France. After the riots subsided, government officials promised to adopt measures to respond to the complaints, but tensions between the Muslim community and the remainder of the French population have become a chronic source of social unrest throughout the country—an unrest that Nicolas Sarkozy (nee-kohl-AH sar-koh-ZEE) (b. 1955), elected president in 2007, promised to address but without much success. In 2009, unemployment among those under age twenty-five was almost 22 percent, but in the suburbs that are home to many Muslims, youth joblessness exceeded 50 percent.

FROM WEST GERMANY TO ONE GERMANY As noted in Chapter 26, the three Western zones of Germany were unified as the Federal Republic of Germany in 1949. Konrad Adenauer (AD-uh-now-ur) (1876–1967), the leader of the Christian Democratic Union (CDU), served as chancellor from 1949 to 1963 and became the Federal Republic's "founding hero." Adenauer sought respect for postwar Germany by cooperating with the United States and the other Western European nations.

Adenauer's chancellorship is largely associated with the resurrection of the West German economy, even today regarded as a modern miracle. Although West Germany had only 52 percent of the territory of prewar Germany, by 1955 the West German gross domestic product exceeded that of prewar Germany. Real wages doubled between 1950 and 1965. Unemployment fell from 8 percent in 1950 to 0.4 percent in 1965.

After the Adenauer era, German voters moved politically from the center-right of the Christian Democrats to center-

left politics; in 1969, the Social Democrats became the leading party. The first Social Democratic chancellor was Willy Brandt (VIL-ee BRAHNT) (1913–1992), who was especially successful with his "opening toward the east"—known as *Ostpolitik* (OHST-poh-lee-teek)—for which he received the Nobel Peace Prize in 1972. On March 19, 1971, Brandt worked out the details of a treaty with East Germany (the former Russian zone) that led to greater cultural, personal, and economic contacts between West and East Germany.

In 1982, the Christian Democratic Union of Helmut Kohl (HEL-moot KOHL) (b. 1930) formed a new center-right government. Kohl was a clever politician who benefited greatly from an economic boom in the mid-1980s and the 1989 revolution in East Germany, which led in 1990 to the long-awaited reunification of the two Germanies, making the new restored Germany, with its 79 million people, the leading power in Europe.

But the excitement over reunification soon dissipated as new problems arose. All too soon, the realization set in that the revitalization of eastern Germany would take far more money than was originally thought, and Kohl's government was soon forced to face the politically undesirable task of raising taxes substantially. Moreover, the virtual collapse of the economy in eastern Germany led to extremely high levels of unemployment and severe discontent. East Germans were also haunted by another memory from their recent past. The opening of the files of the secret police—the *Stasi* (SHTAH-see)—revealed that millions of East Germans had spied on their neighbors and colleagues, and even their spouses and parents, during the Communist era (see the Film & History feature on p. 824). A few senior *Stasi* officials were put on trial for their past actions, but many Germans preferred simply to close the door on that unhappy period in their lives and face the challenges of the future.

As the century neared its close, then, Germans struggled to cope with the challenge of building a united nation. To reduce the debt incurred for economic reconstruction in the east, the government threatened to cut back on many of the social benefits West Germans had long been accustomed to receiving. This in turn sharpened resentments that were already beginning to emerge between western and eastern Germany.

In 1998, voters took out their frustrations at the ballot box. Helmut Kohl's conservative coalition was defeated, and a new prime minister, Social Democrat Gerhard Schröder (GAYR-hahrt SHRUR-dur) (b. 1944), came into office. But Schröder had little success at solving Germany's economic woes, and as a result of elections in 2005, Angela Merkel (AHNG-uh-luh MERK-uhl) (b. 1954), leader of the Christian Democrats, became the first female chancellor in German history. Merkel pursued health care reform and new energy policies at home while taking a leading role in the affairs of the European Union. After new elections in 2009, she began a second term as Germany's chancellor.

THE DECLINE OF GREAT BRITAIN The end of World War II left Britain with massive economic problems. In elections held immediately after the war, the Labour Party overwhelmingly

The Lives of Others (2006)

Directed by Florian Henckel von Donnersmarck, *The Lives of Others*, which won the Academy Award for Best Foreign Film, is a German film (*Das Leben der Anderen*) that brilliantly re-creates the depressing debilitation of East German society under its Communist regime, and especially the *Stasi*, the secret police. Georg Dreyman (Sebastian Koch) is a successful playwright in the German Democratic Republic (East Germany). Although he is a dedicated socialist who has not offended the authorities, they try to determine whether he is completely loyal by wiretapping his apartment, where he lives with his girlfriend, Christa-Maria Sieland (Martina Gedeck), an actress in some of Dreyman's plays. Captain Gerd Wiesler (Ulrich Mühe) of the *Stasi* takes charge of the spying operation. He is the epitome of the perfect functionary—a cold, calculating, dedicated professional who is convinced he is building a better society and is only too eager to fight the "enemies of socialism." But as he listens to the everyday details of Dreyman's life, Wiesler begins to develop a conscience and becomes sympathetic to the writer. After a close friend of Dreyman's commits suicide, Dreyman turns against the Communist regime and writes an article on the alarming number of suicides in East German society for *Der Spiegel*, a West German magazine. Though the article is published anonymously, Lieutenant Colonel Grubitz (Ulrich Tukur), Wiesler's boss, suspects that Dreyman is the author. His girlfriend is brought in for questioning and provides some damning information about Dreyman's involvement. Horrified by what she has done, she commits suicide, but Wiesler, who is now determined to save Dreyman, fudges his reports and protects him from being arrested. Wiesler's boss suspects what Wiesler has done and demotes him. The film ends after the fall of the Berlin Wall when the new German government opens the *Stasi* files. When Dreyman reads his file, he realizes how Wiesler saved him and writes a book dedicated to him.

The film brilliantly re-creates the stifling atmosphere of East Germany under Communist rule. The *Stasi* had about 90,000 employees but also recruited a network of hundreds of thousands of informers who submitted secret reports on their friends, family, bosses, and coworkers. Some volunteered the information, but as the film makes clear, others were bribed or blackmailed into collaborating with the authorities. As the movie demonstrates, the *Stasi* were experts at wiretapping dwellings and compiling detailed written reports about what they heard, including conversations, arguments, jokes, and even sexual activities. Ironically, Ulrich Mühe, who plays Captain Wiesler in the film, was an East German who himself had been spied on by the *Stasi*.

The Lives of Others has been praised by East Germans for accurately depicting the drab environment of their country and the role of the *Stasi* in fostering a society riddled by secrecy, fear, and the abuse of power. The dangers of governments that monitor their citizens are apparent and quite relevant in an age of legislation infringing on personal privacy in an attempt to fight terrorism. The police state is revealed for what it is, a soulless, hollow world with no redeeming features or values.

Georg Dreyman (Sebastian Koch) examines his *Stasi* files.

Creado Film/BR/Arte/The Kobal Collection

---

defeated Churchill's Conservatives. Labour had promised far-reaching reforms, particularly in the area of social welfare, and in a country with a tremendous shortage of consumer goods and housing, its platform was quite appealing. The new Labour government under Clement Attlee (1883–1967) proceeded to turn Britain into a modern **welfare state**.

The process began with the nationalization of the Bank of England, the coal and steel industries, public transportation, and public utilities, such as electricity and gas. In 1946, the new government established a comprehensive social security program and nationalized medical insurance, thereby enabling the state to subsidize the unemployed, the sick, and the aged. The health act established a system of **socialized medicine** that forced doctors and dentists to work with state hospitals, although private practices could be maintained. The British welfare state became the model for most European nations after the war.

Continuing economic problems, however, brought the Conservatives back into power from 1951 to 1964. Although the British economy had recovered from the war, its slow rate of improvement reflected a long-term economic decline. The war had cost Britain much of its prewar revenues from abroad but left a burden of debt from innumerable international commitments. And as the influence of the United States and the Soviet Union continued to rise, Britain's ability to play the role of a world power declined substantially. Between 1964 and 1979, Conservatives and Labour alternated in power, but neither party was able to heal Britain's ailing economy.

In 1979, the Conservatives returned to power under Margaret Thatcher (b. 1925), who became the first woman prime minister in British history. Thatcher pledged to lower taxes, reduce government bureaucracy, limit social welfare, restrict union power, and end inflation. The "Iron Lady," as she was called, did break the power of the labor unions. Although she did not eliminate the basic components of the social welfare system, she used austerity measures to control inflation. "Thatcherism," as her economic policy was termed, improved the British economic situation, but at a price. The south of England, for example, prospered, but the old industrial areas of the Midlands and north declined and were beset by high unemployment, poverty, and sporadic violence.

Thatcher dominated British politics in the 1980s. But in 1990, Labour's fortunes revived when Thatcher's government attempted to replace local property taxes with a flat-rate tax payable by every adult to a local authority. Many British citizens argued that this was nothing more than a poll tax that would allow the rich to get away with paying the same rate as the poor. In 1990, after antitax riots broke out, Thatcher's popularity plummeted, and a revolt within her own party

forced her to resign as prime minister. She was replaced by John Major (b. 1943), but his government failed to capture the imagination of most Britons. In new elections on May 1, 1997, the Labour Party won a landslide victory. The new prime minister, Tony Blair (b. 1953), was a moderate whose youthful energy immediately instilled a new vigor on the political scene. Adopting centrist policies reminiscent of those followed by President Bill Clinton in the United States, his party dominated British politics into the new century. Blair was one of the prominent leaders who joined an international coalition against terrorism after the September 11 terrorist attacks on the United States in 2001. Four years later, his support of the U.S. war in Iraq when a majority of Britons opposed it caused his popularity to plummet, although the failure of the Conservative Party to field a popular candidate kept him in power until the summer of 2007, when he stepped down and allowed the Labour leader Gordon Brown (b. 1951) to become prime minister.

In 2010, in the wake of climbing unemployment and a global financial crisis, the thirteen-year rule of Britain's Labour Party ended when Conservative Party candidate David Cameron (b. 1966) became prime minister on the basis of a coalition with the Liberal Democrats. Cameron has promised to decrease the government debt by reducing government waste and welfare benefits, cutting social services, and introducing legislation to overhaul Britain's health care system.

Eastern Europe After Communism

The fall of Communist governments in Eastern Europe during the revolutions of 1989 (see Chapter 27) brought a wave of euphoria to Europe. The new structures meant an end to a postwar European order that had been imposed on unwilling peoples by the victorious forces of the Soviet Union. In 1989 and 1990, new governments throughout Eastern Europe worked diligently to scrap the remnants of the old system

Margaret Thatcher. Great Britain's first female prime minister, Margaret Thatcher was a strong leader who dominated British politics in the 1980s and served in the post longer than any man in modern times. This picture of Thatcher was taken during a meeting with French president François Mitterrand in 1986.

© Peter Turnley/CORBIS

and introduce the democratic procedures and market systems they believed would revitalize their scarred lands. But this process proved to be neither simple nor easy.

Most Eastern European countries had little or virtually no experience with democratic systems. Then, too, ethnic divisions, which had troubled these areas before World War II and had been forcibly submerged under Communist rule, reemerged with a vengeance. Finally, the rapid conversion to market economies also proved painful. The adoption of "shock therapy" austerity measures caused much suffering. Unemployment, for example, climbed above 13 percent in Poland in 1992.

Nevertheless, by the beginning of the twenty-first century, many of these states, especially Poland and the Czech Republic, were making a successful transition to both free markets and democracy. In Poland, Aleksander Kwaśniewski (kwahsh-NYEF-skee) (b. 1954), a former Communist, was elected president in November 1995 and pushed Poland toward an increasingly prosperous free market economy. His successor, Lech Kaczyński (LEK kuh-ZIN-skee) (1949–2010), emphasized the need to combine modernization with tradition. In Czechoslovakia, the shift to non-Communist rule was complicated by old problems, especially ethnic issues. Czechs and Slovaks disagreed over the makeup of the new state but were able to agree to a peaceful division of the country. On January 1, 1993, Czechoslovakia split into the Czech Republic and Slovakia. Václav Havel (VAHT-slahf HAH-vul) (b. 1936) was elected the first president of the new Czech Republic (see the box on p. 827). In Romania, the current president, Traian Băsescu (trih-YAHN buh-SES-koo) (b. 1951), leads a country that is just beginning to experience economic growth and the rise of a middle class.

The revival of the post–Cold War Eastern European states is evident in their desire to join both NATO and the European Union (EU), the two major Cold War institutions of Western European unity (see "The Unification of Europe" later in this chapter). In 1997, Poland, the Czech Republic, and Hungary became full members of NATO. In 2004, ten nations—including Hungary, Poland, the Czech Republic, Slovenia, Estonia, Latvia, and Lithuania—joined the EU, and Romania and Bulgaria were added in 2007.

Not everyone is convinced that European integration is a good thing. Eastern Europeans fear that their countries will be dominated by investments from their prosperous neighbors, while their counterparts in Western Europe are concerned about a possible influx of low-wage workers from the new member countries. The global financial crisis of 2008–2009 also added to the economic problems of Eastern European countries.

THE DISINTEGRATION OF YUGOSLAVIA From its creation in 1918, Yugoslavia had been an artificial entity. Strong leaders—especially the dictatorial Marshal Tito after World War II—had managed to hold together the six disparate republics and two autonomous provinces that made up the country. After Tito's death in 1980, however, no successor emerged, and eventually Yugoslavia was caught up in the reform movements sweeping through Eastern Europe.

After negotiations among the six republics failed, Slovenia and Croatia declared their independence in June 1991. This action was opposed by Slobodan Milošević (sluh-BOH-dahn mih-LOH-suh-vich) (1941–2006), the leader of the republic of Serbia. He asserted that these republics could be independent only if new border arrangements were made to accommodate the Serb minorities in those republics who did not want to live outside the boundaries of Serbia. Serbian forces attacked both new states; although unsuccessful against Slovenia, they captured one-third of Croatia's territory.

The international recognition of independent Slovenia and Croatia in 1992 and of Macedonia and Bosnia and Herzegovina soon thereafter did not deter the Serbs, who now turned their guns on Bosnia. By mid-1993, Serbian forces had acquired 70 percent of Bosnian territory. The Serbian policy of **ethnic cleansing**—killing or forcibly removing Bosnian Muslims from their lands—revived memories of Nazi atrocities in World War II. This account by one Muslim survivor from the town of Srebrenica (sreb-bruh-NEET-suh) is eerily reminiscent of the activities of the Nazi *Einsatzgruppen* (see Chapter 25):

> When the truck stopped, they told us to get off in groups of five. We immediately heard shooting next to the trucks. . . . About ten Serbs with automatic rifles told us to lie down on the ground face first. As we were getting down, they started to shoot, and I fell into a pile of corpses. I felt hot liquid running down my face. I realized that I was only grazed. As they continued to shoot more groups, I kept on squeezing myself in between dead bodies.[1]

Almost eight thousand men and boys were killed in the Serbian massacre at Srebrenica. Nevertheless, despite worldwide outrage, European governments failed to take a forceful stand against the Serbs' actions, leaving the Muslim population of Bosnia in desperate straits. At long last, as the fighting spread, European nations and the United States began to intervene to stop the bloodshed, and in the fall of 1995, a fragile cease-fire agreement was reached. An international peacekeeping force was stationed in the area to maintain tranquillity.

Peace in Bosnia, however, did not bring peace to Yugoslavia. A new war erupted in 1999 over Kosovo (KAWSS-suh-voh), which had been made an autonomous province within the Serbian republic in 1974. Kosovo's inhabitants were mainly ethnic Albanians. But the province was also home to a Serbian minority. In 1989, Yugoslav president Milošević stripped Kosovo of its autonomous status. Four years later, some groups of ethnic Albanians founded the Kosovo Liberation Army (KLA) and began a campaign against Serbian rule in Kosovo. When Serb forces began to massacre ethnic Albanians in an effort to crush the KLA, the United States and its NATO allies mounted a bombing campaign that forced Milošević to stop. In elections held in the fall of 2000, Milošević himself was ousted from power and was later put on trial by an international tribunal for crimes against humanity for his ethnic cleansing policies. He died in prison in 2006 before his trial could be completed.

Troops from the European Union remain in Bosnia to keep the peace. NATO military forces were also brought into

Václav Havel: The Call for a New Politics

POLITICS & GOVERNMENT

In attempting to deal with the world's problems, some European leaders have pointed to the need for a new perspective, especially a moral one, if people are to live in a sane world. These two excerpts are taken from speeches by Václav Havel, who was elected president of Czechoslovakia at the end of 1989. The first is from his inaugural address as president on January 1, 1990; the second is from a speech given to the U.S. Congress.

Václav Havel, Address to the People of Czechoslovakia, January 1, 1990

But all this is still not the main problem [the environmental devastation of the country by its Communist leaders]. The worst thing is that we live in a contaminated moral environment. We fell morally ill because we became used to saying something different from what we thought. We learned not to believe in anything, to ignore each other, to care only about ourselves. Concepts such as love, friendship, compassion, humility, or forgiveness lost their depth and dimensions, and for many of us they represented only psychological peculiarities, or they resembled gone-astray greetings from ancients, a little ridiculous in the era of computers and spaceships. Only a few of us were able to cry out loud that the powers that be should not be all-powerful, and that special farms, which produce ecologically pure and top-quality food just for them should send their produce to schools, children's homes and hospitals if our agriculture was unable to offer them to all. The previous regime—armed with its arrogant and intolerant ideology—reduced man to a force of production and nature to a tool of production. In this it attacked both their very substance and their mutual relationship. It reduced gifted and autonomous people, skillfully working in their own country, to nuts and bolts of some monstrously huge, noisy, and stinking machine, whose real meaning is not clear to anyone.

Václav Havel, Speech to Congress, February 21, 1990

For this reason, the salvation of this human world lies nowhere else than in the human heart, in the human power to reflect, in human meekness and in human responsibility.

Without a global revolution in the sphere of human consciousness, nothing will change for the better in the sphere of our being as humans, and the catastrophe toward which this world is headed—be it ecological, social, demographic or a general breakdown of civilization—will be unavoidable. . . .

We are still a long way from that "family of man." In fact, we seem to be receding from the ideal rather than growing closer to it. Interests of all kinds—personal, selfish, state, nation, group, and if you like, company interests—still considerably outweigh genuinely common and global interests. We are still under the sway of the destructive and vain belief that man is the pinnacle of creation and not just a part of it and that therefore everything is permitted . . . .

In other words, we still don't know how to put morality ahead of politics, science and economics. We are still incapable of understanding that the only genuine backbone of all our actions, if they are to be moral, is responsibility.

Responsibility to something higher than my family, my country, my company, my success—responsibility to the order of being where all our actions are indelibly recorded and where and only where they will be properly judged.

The interpreter or mediator between us and this higher authority is what is traditionally referred to as human conscience.

How different is Havel's view of politics from the views of mainstream politicians? What broader forces working in modern European society do you believe shaped Havel's thinking? How can Havel's view of our common humanity and responsibility to conscience help revitalize Western civilization?

Kosovo while United Nations officials worked to set up democratic institutions there. In 2004, Yugoslavia ceased to exist when the new national government under Vojislav Kostunica (VOH-yee-slav kuh-STOO-nit-suh) (b. 1944) officially renamed the truncated country Serbia and Montenegro. Two years later, Montenegrins voted in favor of independence. Thus, by 2006, all six republics cobbled together to form Yugoslavia in 1918 were once again independent nations. Kosovo unilaterally proclaimed its independence from Serbia in 2008 and was recognized by most other world nations as the seventh sovereign state to emerge from the former Yugoslavia.

The New Russia

Soon after the disintegration of the Soviet Union in 1991, a new era began in Russia with the presidency of Boris Yeltsin (YELT-sun) (1931–2007). A new constitution created a two-chamber parliament and established a strong presidency. During the mid-1990s, Yeltsin sought to implement reforms that would place Russia on a firm course toward a pluralistic political system and a market economy. But the new post-Communist Russia remained as fragile as ever. Burgeoning economic inequality and rampant corruption aroused widespread criticism and shook the confidence of the Russian

The War in Bosnia. By mid-1993, irregular Serb forces had overrun much of Bosnia and Herzegovina amid scenes of untold suffering. This photograph shows a woman running past the bodies of victims of a mortar attack on Sarajevo on August 21, 1992. Three mortar rounds landed, killing at least three people.

people in the superiority of the capitalist system over the one that existed under Communist rule. A nagging war in the Caucasus—where the people of Chechnya (CHECH-nee-uh) sought national independence from Russia—drained the government budget and exposed the decrepit state of the once vaunted Red Army. In presidential elections held in 1996, Yeltsin was reelected although his precarious health raised serious questions about his ability to govern.

THE PUTIN ERA At the end of 1999, Yeltsin suddenly resigned and was replaced by Vladimir Putin (VLAD-ih-meer POO-tin) (b. 1952), a former member of the KGB. Putin vowed to strengthen the role of the central government in managing the affairs of state. During the succeeding months, the parliament approved his proposal to centralize power in the hands of the federal government in Moscow.

The new president also vowed to return the breakaway state of Chechnya to Russian authority and to adopt a more assertive role in international affairs. Fighting in Chechnya continued throughout 2000, nearly reducing the republic's capital city of Grozny (GRAWZ-nee) to ruins. In July 2001, Putin launched reforms, which included the unrestricted sale and purchase of land and tax cuts aimed at boosting economic growth and budget revenues. Although Russia soon experienced a budget surplus and a growing economy, serious problems remained.

Putin attempted to deal with the chronic problems in Russian society by centralizing his control over the system and by silencing critics—notably in the Russian media. Although he was criticized in the West for these moves, many Russians expressed sympathy with Putin's attempts to restore a sense of pride and discipline in Russian society.

In 2008, Dmitry Medvedev (di-MEE-tree mehd-VYEH-dehf) (b. 1965) became president of Russia when Putin could not run for reelection under Russia's constitution. Instead, Putin became prime minister, and the two men have since shared power.

The Unification of Europe

As we saw in Chapter 26, the divisions created by the Cold War led the nations of Western Europe to seek military security by forming the North Atlantic Treaty Organization (NATO) in 1949. The destructiveness of two world wars, however, caused many thoughtful Europeans to consider the need for some additional form of unity.

In 1957, France, West Germany, the Benelux countries (Belgium, the Netherlands, and Luxembourg), and Italy signed the Treaty of Rome, which created the European Economic Community (EEC). The EEC eliminated customs barriers for the six member nations and created a large free-trade area protected from the rest of the world by a common external tariff. All the member nations benefited economically. In 1973, Great Britain, Ireland, and Denmark gained membership in what now was called the European Community (EC). Greece joined in 1981, followed by Spain and Portugal in 1986. In 1995, Austria, Finland, and Sweden also became members of the EC.

THE EUROPEAN UNION The European Community was an economic union, not a political one. By 2000, the EC contained 370 million people and constituted the world's largest single trading entity, transacting one-fourth of the world's commerce. In the 1980s and 1990s, the EC moved toward even greater economic integration. The Treaty on European Union, which went into effect on January 1, 1994, turned the European Community into the European Union (EU), a true economic and monetary union of all EC members. One of its first goals was achieved in 1999 with the introduction of a common currency, the euro. On January 1, 2002, the euro officially replaced twelve national currencies. By 2011, the euro had been adopted in seventeen countries and was serving approximately 327 million people; it had become the second-largest reserve currency after the U.S. dollar.

A major crisis for the euro emerged in 2010, when Greece's burgeoning public debt threatened to cause the bankruptcy of that country as well as financial difficulties for many European banks. To avert a financial disaster, other EU members, led by Germany, labored to put together a financial rescue plan. Subsequently, Portugal and Ireland also asked for assistance.

In addition to creating a single internal market for its members and a common currency, the European Union also established a common agricultural policy, under which subsidies are provided to farmers to enable them to sell their goods competitively on the world market. The end of national passports has given millions of Europeans greater flexibility in travel. The EU has been less successful in setting common foreign policy goals, primarily because individual nations still see foreign policy as a national priority and are reluctant to give up this power to a single overriding institution. Nevertheless, the EU did create a military force of 60,000, which is used chiefly for humanitarian and peacekeeping purposes, as in Bosnia where EU troops have replaced NATO forces. Indeed, the focus of the EU is on peaceful conflict resolution, not making war.

In 2009, the European Union ratified the Lisbon Treaty, which created a full-time presidential post and a new voting system that reflects each country's population size. It also provided more power for the European Parliament in an effort to promote the EU's foreign policy goals.

But as successful as the European Union has been, problems exist. Europeans are often divided on the EU. Some oppose it because the official representatives of the EU are not democratically accountable to the people. Moreover, many Europeans do not see themselves as "Europeans" but remain committed to a national identity. The issue of bailouts has also created tensions between the bankrupt and solvent nations.

TOWARD A UNITED EUROPE At the beginning of the twenty-first century, the EU established a new goal: to incorporate into the union the states of eastern and southeastern Europe. Many of these states were considerably poorer than the current members, which raised the possibility that adding these nations might weaken the EU itself. To lessen the danger, EU members established a set of qualifications requiring candidates for membership to demonstrate a commitment both to market capitalism and to democracy, including not only the rule of law but also respect for minorities and human rights. Hence joining the EU might well add to the stability of these nations and make the dream of a united Europe a reality. In May 2004, the European Union took the

plunge and added ten new members: Cyprus, the Czech Republic, Estonia, Hungary, Latvia, Lithuania, Malta, Poland, Slovakia, and Slovenia, thus enlarging the population of the EU to 455 million people. In January 2007, the EU expanded again as Bulgaria and Romania joined (see Map 28.1).

Emergence of the Superpower: The United States

 FOCUS QUESTION: What political, social, and economic changes has the United States experienced since 1945?

At the end of World War II, the United States emerged as one of the world's two superpowers. As its Cold War confrontation with the Soviet Union intensified, the United States directed much of its energy toward combating the spread of communism throughout the world. With the collapse of the Soviet Union at the beginning of the 1990s, the United States became the world's foremost military power.

American Politics and Society Through the Vietnam Era

Franklin Roosevelt's New Deal of the 1930s initiated a basic transformation of American society that included a dramatic increase in the role and power of the federal government, the rise of organized labor as a significant force in the economy and politics, a commitment to the welfare state, a grudging acceptance of ethnic minorities, and a willingness to experiment with deficit spending as a means of spurring the economy. The New Deal in American politics was bolstered by the election of Democratic presidents—Harry Truman in 1948, John F. Kennedy in 1960, and Lyndon B. Johnson in 1964. Even the election of a Republican president, Dwight D. Eisenhower, in 1952 and 1956 did not significantly alter the fundamental direction of the New Deal. As Eisenhower observed in 1954, "Should any political party attempt to abolish Social Security and eliminate labor laws and farm programs, you would not hear of that party again in our political history."

The economic boom after World War II fueled confidence in the American way of life. A shortage of consumer goods during the war left Americans with both surplus income and the desire to purchase these goods after the war. Then, too, the development of organized labor enabled more and more workers to get the wage increases that spurred the growth of the domestic market. Between 1945 and 1973, real wages grew an average of 3 percent a year, the most prolonged advance in U.S. history.

Starting in the 1960s, problems that had been glossed over earlier came to the fore. The decade began on a youthful and optimistic note when John F. Kennedy (1917–1963), age forty-three, became the youngest elected president in the history of the United States and the first one born in the twentieth century. His own administration, cut short by an assassin's bullet on November 22, 1963, focused primarily on foreign affairs. Kennedy's successor, Lyndon B. Johnson (1908–1973), who

MAP 28.1 European Union, 2007. Beginning in 1957 as the European Economic Community, also known as the Common Market, the union of European states seeking to integrate their economies has gradually grown from six members to twenty-seven. By 2002, the European Union had achieved two major goals—the creation of a single internal market and a common currency—although it has been less successful at working toward common political and foreign policy goals.

Q *What additional nations do you think will eventually join the European Union?*

won a new term as president in a landslide in 1964, used his stunning mandate to pursue the growth of the welfare state begun in the New Deal. Johnson's programs included health care for the elderly and the War on Poverty, to be fought with food stamps and the Job Corps.

Johnson's other domestic passion was achieving equal rights for black Americans. In August 1963, the eloquent Martin Luther King Jr. (1929–1968), a Baptist minister and leader of a growing movement for racial equality, led the March on Washington for Jobs and Freedom to dramatize black Americans' desire for treatment no different from that accorded to whites. This march and King's impassioned plea for racial equality had an electrifying effect on the American people. President Johnson pursued the cause of civil rights. As a result of his initiative, Congress enacted the Civil Rights Act of 1964, which created the machinery to end segregation and discrimination in the workplace and in public accommodations. The Voting Rights Act the following year eliminated obstacles to black participation in elections in southern states. But laws alone could not guarantee the "Great Society" that Johnson envisioned, and soon the administration faced bitter social unrest.

In the North and the West, blacks had had voting rights for many years, but local patterns of segregation resulted in considerably higher unemployment rates for blacks (and Hispanics) than for whites and left blacks segregated in huge urban ghettos. In these ghettos, the calls for militant action by radical black nationalist leaders, such as Malcolm X (1925–1965) of the Black Muslims, attracted more attention than the nonviolent appeals of Martin Luther King. In the summer of 1965, race riots broke out in the Watts district of Los Angeles, leading to thirty-four deaths and the destruction of more than one thousand buildings. When King was assassinated in 1968, more than one hundred cities erupted in rioting, including Washington, D.C., the nation's capital. The combination of riots and extremist comments by radical black leaders led to a "white backlash" and a severe racial division in America.

Antiwar protests also divided the American people after President Johnson committed American troops to a costly war in Vietnam (see Chapter 26). Teach-ins, sit-ins, and occupations of university buildings alternated with more radical demonstrations that increasingly led to violence. The killing of four student protesters at Kent State University in 1970 by the Ohio National

The Civil Rights Movement. In the early 1960s, Martin Luther King Jr. and his Southern Christian Leadership Conference organized a variety of activities to pursue the goal of racial equality. He is shown here with his wife, Coretta Scott King (right), and Rosa Parks and Ralph Abernathy (far left) leading a march in 1965 against racial discrimination. He was assassinated three years later.

Guard shocked both activists and ordinary Americans, and thereafter the vehemence of the antiwar movement began to subside. But the combination of antiwar demonstrations and riots in the cities caused many people to call for "law and order," an appeal used by Richard Nixon (1913–1994), the Republican presidential candidate in 1968. Nixon's election in 1968 started a shift to the right in American politics.

The Shift Rightward After 1973

Nixon eventually ended U.S. involvement in Vietnam by gradually withdrawing American troops. Politically, he pursued a "southern strategy," carefully calculating that "law and order" issues would appeal to southern whites. The Republican strategy, however, also gained support among white Democrats in northern cities, where court-mandated busing of students to distant neighborhoods to achieve racial integration of the public schools had provoked a white backlash.

As president, Nixon was paranoid about conspiracies and resorted to subversive methods of gaining political intelligence on his political opponents. Nixon's zeal led to the Watergate scandal—a botched attempt to plant listening devices in the Democratic National Headquarters and the ensuing cover-up. Although Nixon repeatedly denied involvement in the affair, secret tapes he made of his own conversations in the White House revealed otherwise. On August 9, 1974, Nixon resigned in disgrace, an act that saved him from almost certain impeachment and conviction.

After Watergate, American domestic politics focused on economic issues. Gerald Ford (1913–2006) became president when Nixon resigned, only to lose in the 1976 election to the former governor of Georgia, Jimmy Carter (b. 1924), who campaigned as an outsider against the Washington establishment. By 1980, the Carter administration faced two devastating problems. High inflation and a decline in average weekly earnings were causing a perceptible drop in American living standards. At the same time, a crisis abroad had erupted when fifty-three Americans were taken hostage by the Iranian government of Ayatollah Khomeini and held for nearly fifteen months (see Chapter 29). Carter's inability to gain the release of the American hostages led to perceptions at home that he was a weak president. His overwhelming loss to Ronald Reagan (1911–2004) in the election of 1980 brought forward the chief exponent of right-wing Republican policies.

The Reagan Revolution, as it has been called, sent U.S. policy in a number of new directions. Reversing decades of changes, Reagan cut back on the welfare state by decreasing spending on food stamps, school lunch programs, and job programs. At the same time, his administration fostered the largest peacetime military buildup in American history. Total federal spending rose from $631 billion in 1981 to over $1 trillion by 1986. But instead of raising taxes to pay for the new expenditures, Reagan convinced Congress that massive tax cuts would supposedly stimulate rapid economic growth and produce new revenues. Reagan's policies seemed to work in the short run as the United States experienced an economic upturn that lasted until the end of the 1980s. But the administration's spending policies also produced record government deficits, which loomed as an obstacle to long-term growth. In 1980, the total government debt was around $930 billion; by 1988, the total debt had almost tripled, reaching $2.6 trillion.

The inability of Reagan's successor, George H. W. Bush (b. 1924), to deal with the deficit problem, coupled with an economic downturn, led to the election of a Democrat, Bill Clinton (b. 1946), in November 1992. The new president was a southerner who claimed to be a new Democrat, one who favored a number of the Republican policies of the 1980s—a clear indication that this Democratic victory had by no means ended the rightward drift in American politics. In fact, Clinton's reelection in 1996 was due in part to his adoption of conservative policies.

President Clinton's political fortunes were aided considerably by a lengthy economic revival. A steady reduction in the annual government budget deficit strengthened confidence in the performance of the national economy. Much of

Presidential Candidate Barack Obama. In this photograph, Barack Obama is seen speaking to an overflow crowd of his supporters at a campaign rally in Montana on May 19, 2008. By this time, Obama was ahead of his chief opponent, Senator Hillary Clinton, and after primary victories two weeks later in South Dakota and Montana, he finally clinched the nomination. Campaigning on the slogan, "Change We Can Believe In," Obama electrified his campaign audiences.

Clinton's second term, however, was overshadowed by charges of misconduct stemming from the president's affair with a White House intern. After a bitter partisan struggle, the U.S. Senate acquitted the president on two articles of impeachment brought by the House of Representatives. But Clinton's problems helped the Republican candidate, George W. Bush (b. 1946), win the presidential election in 2000. Although Bush lost the popular vote to Al Gore, he narrowly won the electoral vote after a highly controversial victory in the state of Florida decided ultimately by the U.S. Supreme Court.

The first four years of Bush's administration were largely occupied with the war on terrorism and the U.S.-led war on Iraq. The Department of Homeland Security was established after the 2001 terrorist assaults to help protect the United States from future terrorist acts. At the same time, Bush pushed tax cuts through Congress that mainly favored the wealthy and helped produce record deficits reminiscent of the Reagan years. Environmentalists were especially disturbed by the Bush administration's efforts to weaken environmental laws and impose regulations that would benefit American corporations. In November 2004, after a highly negative political campaign, Bush was narrowly elected to a second term. Thereafter, Bush's popularity plummeted drastically as discontent grew over the Iraq War and financial corruption in the Republican Party, as well as the administration's poor handling of relief efforts after Hurricane Katrina devastated the city of New Orleans and other areas of Louisiana and Mississippi in 2005.

The many failures of the Bush administration led to the lowest approval ratings for a modern president and opened the door for a dramatic change in American politics. The new and often inspiring voice of Barack Obama (b. 1961), who campaigned on a platform of change "we can believe in" and ending the war in Iraq, led to an overwhelming Democratic victory in the elections of 2008. The Democrats were also aided by the dramatic collapse of the American financial system in the fall of 2008. Obama moved quickly in 2009 to deal with the worst economic recession since the Great Depression. At the same time, Obama emphasized the need to deal with the health care crisis, climate change, the decline in the educational system, and failed economic policies.

The Development of Canada

 FOCUS QUESTION: What political, social, and economic developments has Canada experienced since 1945?

Canada's development in the postwar years has paralleled that of the United States. For twenty-five years after World War II, Canada experienced extraordinary economic prosperity as it set out on a path of industrial development. Canada had always had a strong export economy based on its abundant natural resources. Now it also developed electronic, aircraft, nuclear, and chemical engineering industries on a large scale. Much of the Canadian growth, however, was financed by capital from the United States, which resulted in American ownership of Canadian businesses. Though many Canadians welcomed the economic growth, others feared American economic domination of Canada and its resources.

A notable feature of Canada's postwar history has been its close relationship with the United States. In addition to fears of economic domination, Canadians have also worried about playing a subordinate role politically and militarily to the neighboring superpower. Canada agreed to join NATO in 1949 and even sent military contingents to fight in Korea the following year. But to avoid subordination to the United States or any other great power, Canada has consistently and actively supported the United Nations. Nevertheless, concerns about the United States have not kept Canada from maintaining a special relationship with its southern neighbor.

For three decades after 1945, the Liberal Party largely dominated Canadian politics and created Canada's welfare state by enacting a national social security system (the Canada Pension Plan) and a national health insurance program. The most prominent Liberal government was that of Pierre Trudeau (PYAYR troo-DOH) (1919–2000), who came to power in 1968. A French Canadian, Trudeau did not harbor separatist sentiments and was dedicated to Canada's federal union. In 1968, his government passed the Official Languages Act, which created a bilingual federal civil service and encouraged the growth of French culture and language in Canada. Although Trudeau's government vigorously pushed an industrialization program, high inflation and Trudeau's efforts to impose the will of the federal government on the powerful provincial governments alienated voters and weakened his government.

Economic recession in the early 1980s brought Brian Mulroney (b. 1939), leader of the Progressive Conservative Party, to power in 1984. Mulroney's government sought greater privatization of Canada's state-run corporations and negotiated a free-trade agreement with the United States. Bitterly resented by many Canadians, the agreement cost Mulroney's government much of its popularity. In 1993, the ruling Conservatives were overwhelmingly defeated, and the Liberal leader, Jean Chrétien (ZHAHNH kray-TEN) (b. 1934), became prime minister. Chrétien's conservative fiscal policies, combined with strong economic growth, enabled his government to have a budgetary surplus by the late 1990s and led to another Liberal victory in the elections of 1997. Charges of widespread financial corruption in the government, however, led to a Conservative victory early in 2006, and Stephen Harper (b. 1959) became the new prime minister. Harper's government collapsed in March 2011, but elections held in May resulted in Harper remaining as prime minister. The government has also faced an ongoing crisis over the French-speaking province of Quebec. In the late 1960s, the Parti Québécois (par-TEE kay-bek-KWAH), headed by René Lévesque (ruh-NAY lay-VEK) (1922–1987), campaigned on a platform of Quebec's secession from the Canadian

confederation. In 1970, the party won 24 percent of the popular vote in Quebec's provincial elections. To pursue their dream of separation, some underground separatist groups even used terrorist bombings and kidnapped two prominent government officials. In 1976,

Quebec

the Parti Québécois won Quebec's provincial elections and in 1980 called for a referendum that would enable the provincial government to negotiate Quebec's independence from the rest of Canada. Voters in Quebec narrowly rejected the plan in 1995, however, and debate over the province's future continues to divide Canada.

Latin America Since 1945

 FOCUS QUESTION: What problems have the nations of Latin America faced since 1945, and what role has Marxist ideology played in their efforts to solve these problems?

In many Latin American countries, the Great Depression of the 1930s had created political instability that led to military coups and militaristic regimes (see Chapter 24). But the depression also resulted in the transformation of Latin America from a traditional to a modern economic structure. Since the nineteenth century, Latin Americans had exported raw materials, especially minerals and foodstuffs, while buying the manufactured goods of the industrialized countries in Europe and the United States. As a result of the depression, however, exports were cut in half, and the revenues available to buy

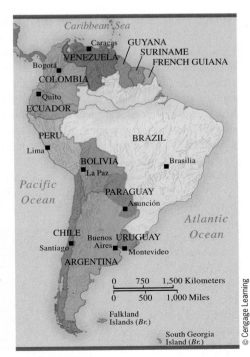

South America

manufactured goods declined. This encouraged many Latin American countries to develop industries to produce goods that were formerly imported. Due to a shortage of capital in the private sector, governments often invested in the new industries, thus leading, for example, to government-run steel industries in Chile and Brazil.

Despite these developments, in the 1960s Latin American countries still found themselves dependent on the United States, Europe, and now Japan, especially for the advanced technology needed for modern industries. Because of the great poverty in much of Latin America, domestic markets were limited in size, and many Latin American countries failed to find markets abroad for their products. These failures led to instability and a new reliance on military regimes, especially to curb the power of the new industrial middle class and working classes, which had increased in size and power as a result of industrialization. In the 1960s, repressive military regimes in Chile, Brazil, and Argentina abolished political parties and repeatedly returned to export-import economies financed by foreigners. They also invited multinational companies to come in. The companies that accepted the invitations did so primarily to take advantage of Latin America's raw materials and abundant supply of cheap labor, and thus only contributed to the ongoing dependency of Latin America on the industrially developed nations.

In the 1970s, Latin American regimes grew even more dependent, borrowing from abroad, especially from banks in Europe and the United States, to maintain their failing economies. Between 1970 and 1982, debt to foreigners increased from $27 billion to $315 billion. By 1982, a number of governments announced that they could no longer pay interest on their debts to foreign banks, and their economies began to crumble.

The debt crisis was paralleled by a movement toward democracy during the 1980s. In part, some military leaders were simply unwilling to deal with the monstrous debt problems. At the same time, many people realized that military power without popular consent was incapable of providing a strong state. Then, too, there was a swelling of popular support for basic rights and free and fair elections. By the 1980s and early 1990s, democratic regimes were in place everywhere except Cuba, some of the Central American states, Chile, and Paraguay. At the end of the twentieth century and beginning of the twenty-first, a noticeable political trend in Latin America was the election of left-wing governments, evident in the election of Hugo Chávez (OO-goh CHAH-vez) (b. 1954) in Venezuela in 1998, Luiz Inácio Lula da Silva in Brazil in 2002, Michelle Bachelet in Chile in 2006, and Daniel Ortega in Nicaragua in 2007.

The United States has also played an important role in Latin America since 1945. For years, the United States had intervened militarily in Latin American affairs, particularly in Central America and the Caribbean, a region it considered its "backyard" and thus of strategic

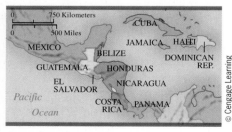

Central America

importance. As Chapter 24 described, in the 1920s the United States became the leading investor in Latin America, replacing Great Britain. By investing directly in Latin American firms, Americans succeeded in gaining control of a large portion of Latin America's export industries. Thus, copper mining in Chile and Peru and the oil industry in Bolivia, Mexico, and Peru came under American control, and the American-owned United Fruit Company gained a virtual monopoly over the banana trade in a number of Central American nations, turning them into "banana republics." The control of these industries by American investors reinforced a growing nationalist sentiment in Latin America against the United States as a neo-imperialist power.

But the United States also tried to pursue a new relationship with Latin America. In 1948, the nations of the Western Hemisphere formed the Organization of American States (OAS), which was intended to eliminate unilateral interference by one state in the internal or external affairs of any other state. But as the Cold War between the United States and the Soviet Union intensified, American policymakers grew anxious about the possibility of Communist regimes arising in Central America and the Caribbean and returned to a policy of unilateral action when they believed that Soviet agents were attempting to establish Communist governments. Especially after the success of Castro in Cuba (see the next section), the desire of the United States to prevent "another Cuba" largely determined American policy toward Latin America until the collapse of the Soviet Union in the early 1990s. The United States provided massive military aid to anti-Communist regimes, regardless of their nature.

The Threat of Marxist Revolutions

Until the 1960s, Marxism played little role in the politics of Latin America. The success of Fidel Castro in Cuba and his espousal of Marxism, however, opened the door for other Marxist movements that aimed to gain the support of peasants and industrial workers and bring radical change to Latin America.

THE CUBAN REVOLUTION A dictatorship, headed by Fulgencio Batista (full-JEN-ee-oh bah-TEES-tuh) (1901–1973) and closely tied economically to U.S. investors, had ruled Cuba since 1934. In the 1950s, Batista's government came under attack by a strong opposition movement, led by Fidel Castro (fee-DELL KASS-troh) (b. 1926) and assisted by Ernesto "Ché" Guevara (er-NAY-stoh CHAY guh-VAHR-uh) (1928–1967), an Argentinian who believed in the need for revolutionary upheaval (see the box on p. 835). When their initial assaults brought little success, Castro's forces turned to guerrilla warfare. Batista's regime responded with such brutality that he alienated his own supporters. The dictator fled in December 1958, and Castro's revolutionaries seized Havana on January 1, 1959.

Relations between Cuba and the United States quickly deteriorated when the Soviet Union early in 1960 agreed to buy Cuban sugar and provide $100 million in credits. On March 17, 1960, President Eisenhower directed the Central Intelligence Agency (CIA) to "organize the training of Cuban exiles, mainly in Guatemala, against a possible future day

Castro's Revolutionary Ideals

POLITICS & GOVERNMENT

On July 26, 1953, Fidel Castro and a small group of supporters launched an ill-fated attack on the Moncada Barracks in Santiago de Cuba. Castro was arrested and put on trial. This selection is taken from the speech he made in his defense, in which he discussed the goals of the revolutionaries.

Fidel Castro, "History Will Absolve Me"

I stated that the second consideration on which we based our chances for success was one of social order because we were assured of the people's support. When we speak of the people we do not mean the comfortable ones, the conservative elements of the nation, who welcome any regime of oppression, any dictatorship, and despotism, prostrating themselves before the master of the moment until they grind their foreheads into the ground. When we speak of struggle, the people means the vast unredeemed masses, to whom all make promises and whom all deceive; we mean the people who yearn for a better, more dignified, and more just nation; who are moved by ancestral aspirations of justice, for they have suffered injustice and mockery, generation after generation; who long for great and wise changes in all aspects of their life; people, who, to attain these changes, are ready to give even the very last breath of their lives—when they believe in something or in someone, especially when they believe in themselves.

In the brief of this cause there must be recorded the five revolutionary laws that would have been proclaimed immediately after the capture of the Moncada barracks and would have been broadcast to the nation by radio. . . .

The First Revolutionary Law would have returned power to the people and proclaimed the Constitution of 1940 the supreme Law of the land, until such time as the people should decide to modify or change it. . . .

The Second Revolutionary Law would have granted property, not mortgageable and not transferable, to all planters, subplanters, lessees, partners, and squatters who hold parcels of five or less *caballerias* of land [total of 166 acres], and the state would indemnify the former owners on the basis of the rental which they would have received for these parcels over a period of ten years.

The Third Revolutionary Law would have granted workers and employees the right to share 30 percent of the profits of all the large industrial, mercantile, and mining enterprises, including the sugar mills. . . .

The Fourth Revolutionary Law would have granted all planters the right to share 55 percent of the sugar production and a minimum quota of forty thousand *arrobas* [total of 500 tons] for all small planters who have been established for three or more years.

The Fifth Revolutionary Law would have ordered the confiscation of all holdings and ill-gotten gains of those who had committed frauds during previous regimes, as well as the holdings and ill-gotten gains of all their legatees and heirs. . . .

Furthermore, it was to be declared that the Cuban policy in the Americas would be one of close solidarity with the democratic people of this continent, and that those politically persecuted by bloody tyrants oppressing our sister nations would find generous asylum, brotherhood, and bread in [Cuba]. Not the persecution, hunger, and treason that they find today. Cuba should be the bulwark of liberty and not a shameful link in the chain of despotism.

 What did Fidel Castro intend to accomplish by his revolution in Cuba? On whose behalf did he fight this revolution?

---

when they might return to their homeland."[2] As arms from Eastern Europe began to arrive in Cuba, the United States cut its purchases of Cuban sugar, and the Cuban government retaliated by nationalizing U.S. companies and banks. In October 1960, the United States declared a trade embargo of Cuba, which drove Castro closer to the Soviet Union. In December 1960, Castro declared himself a Marxist.

On January 3, 1961, the United States broke diplomatic relations with Cuba. The new U.S. president, John F. Kennedy, supported a coup attempt against Castro's government, but the landing of 1,400 CIA-assisted Cuban exiles in Cuba at the Bay of Pigs on April 17, 1961, turned into a military disaster. The Soviets then attempted to install nuclear missiles in the country, an act that led to a showdown with the United States (see Chapter 26). As its part of the bargain to defuse the missile crisis, the United States agreed not to invade Cuba.

But the missile crisis affected Cuba in another way as well. Castro realized that the Soviet Union had been unreliable. If revolutionary Cuba was to be secure, the Cubans would have to instigate social revolution in the rest of Latin America. Castro judged Bolivia, Haiti, Venezuela, Colombia, Paraguay, and a number of Central American states to be especially open to radical revolution. He believed that once guerrilla wars were launched, peasants would flock to the movement and overthrow the old regimes. Guevara began a guerrilla war in Bolivia but was caught and killed by the Bolivian army in the fall of 1967. The Cuban strategy had failed.

Nevertheless, Castro's socialist revolution proceeded within Cuba, with mixed results. The Cuban Revolution did secure some social gains for the Cuban people, especially in health care and education. The regime provided free medical services for all citizens, and the population's health improved noticeably. Illiteracy was wiped out by developing new schools and establishing teacher-training institutes that tripled the number of teachers within ten years. The theoretical equality of women in Marxist thought was put into practice in Cuba by new laws, such as the

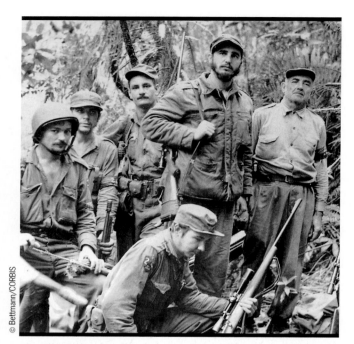

Fidel Castro. On January 1, 1959, a band of revolutionaries led by Fidel Castro overthrew the authoritarian government of Fulgencio Batista. Castro (second from the right) is shown here in 1957, surrounded by some of his followers at a secret base near the Cuban coast.

family code, which stated that husband and wife were equally responsible for the economic support of the family and household, as well as for child care. Such laws led to improvements but fell short of creating full equality for women.

Eschewing rapid industrialization, Castro encouraged agricultural diversification, but the Cuban economy continued to rely heavily on the production and sale of sugar. Economic problems forced the Castro regime to depend on Soviet subsidies and the purchase of Cuban sugar by Soviet bloc countries. After the collapse of these Communist regimes in 1989, Cuba lost their support. Although economic conditions continued to decline, Fidel Castro remained in power until illness forced him to resign the presidency in 2008, when his brother, Raúl Castro (rah-OOL KASS-troh) (b. 1931), succeeded him.

CHILE'S MARXIST ADVENTURE Another challenge to U.S. influence in Latin America came in 1970 when the Marxist Salvador Allende (sahl-vah-DOR al-YEN-day) (1908–1973) was elected president of Chile and attempted to create a socialist society by constitutional means. Chile suffered from a number of economic problems. Wealth was concentrated in the hands of large landowners and a few large corporations. Inflation, foreign debts, and a decline in the mining industry (copper exports accounted for 80 percent of Chile's export income) caused untold difficulties. Right-wing control of the government had failed to achieve any solutions, especially since foreign investments were allowed to expand. There was already growing resentment of U.S. corporations, especially Anaconda and Kennecott, which controlled the copper industry.

In the 1970 elections, a split in the moderate forces enabled Allende to become president of Chile as head of a coalition of Socialists, Communists, and Catholic radicals.

Allende increased the wages of industrial workers and began to move toward socialism by nationalizing the largest domestic and foreign-owned corporations. Nationalization of the copper industry—essentially without compensation for the owners—caused the Nixon administration to cut off all aid to Chile, creating serious problems for the Chilean economy. At the same time, the government offered only halfhearted resistance to radical workers who were beginning to take control of the landed estates.

In response, the upper and middle classes organized strikes against the government (with support from the American CIA). Allende attempted to stop the disorder by bringing three military officers into his cabinet. They succeeded in ending the strikes, but when Allende's coalition increased its vote in the congressional elections of March 1973, the Chilean army, under the direction of General Augusto Pinochet (aw-GOO-stoh pin-noh-chet *or* pee-noh-CHAY) (1915–2006), decided on a coup d'état. In September 1973, Allende and thousands of his supporters were killed. Contrary to the expectations of many right-wing politicians, the military remained in power and set up a dictatorship. The regime moved quickly to outlaw all political parties and restore many nationalized industries to their original owners. By the mid-1980s, the regime's horrible abuses of human rights led to growing unrest against the government.

In 1989, free elections produced a new president, Patricio Aylwin (pa-TREES-yoh YL-win) (b. 1918), who advocated free market economics. Despite some economic improvement, unemployment remained high. Early in 2004, Chile entered into a free-trade agreement with the United States in the hopes of boosting economic growth. In 2006, Michelle Bachelet (mih-SHELL BAHSH-uh-let) (b. 1951), a moderate Socialist running on a platform of increasing social welfare measures for the nation's poor, became the first woman to be elected president of Chile. In January 2010, following divisions in the Socialist Party, Chileans elected center-right National Renewal Party candidate Sebastián Piñera (say-bahs-TYAHN peen-YAIR-uh) (b.1949). A Harvard-educated billionaire, Piñera promised to uphold the social economic policies of the Socialists, while being tougher on crime.

NICARAGUA: FROM THE SOMOZAS TO THE SANDINISTAS During the early twentieth century, the United States intervened in Nicaraguan domestic affairs on several occasions, and U.S. marines even remained there for long periods of time. After the leader of the U.S.-supported National Guard, Anastasio Somoza (ah-nahs-TAH-see-oh suh-MOH-suh (1896–1956), seized control of the government in 1937, his family remained in power for forty-three years. U.S. support for the Somoza military regime enabled the family to overcome its opponents while enriching themselves at the expense of the state.

Opposition to the regime finally arose from Marxist guerrilla forces known as the Sandinista National Liberation Front. By mid-1979, military victories by the Sandinistas (san-duh-NEES-tuhz) left them in virtual control of the country. Inheriting a poverty-stricken nation, the Sandinistas organized a provisional government aligned with the Soviet Union. The Reagan and Bush administrations, believing that Central America faced the danger of another Communist state, financed Contra rebels in a guerrilla war against the Sandinista government. The Contra war and an American economic embargo damaged the Nicaraguan economy and undermined support for the Sandinistas. In 1990, they agreed to free elections and lost to a coalition headed by Violeta Barrios de Chamorro (vee-oh-LET-uh bah-REE-ohss day chah-MOH-roh) (b. 1929). Nevertheless, the Sandinistas remained the strongest single party in Nicaragua and finally won new elections in 2006. Daniel Ortega (dah-NYEL awr-TAY-guh) (b. 1945) became president in January 2007.

Nationalism and the Military: The Examples of Argentina and Brazil

The military became the power brokers of twentieth-century Latin America. Especially in the 1960s and 1970s, Latin American armies portrayed themselves as the guardians of national honor and orderly progress.

ARGENTINA Juan Perón (WAHN puh-ROHN) (1895–1974) first rose to prominence as a member of the military regime that had seized power in Argentina in 1943. As labor secretary in the military government, he used his position to curry favor with the workers. But as Perón grew more popular, other army officers began to fear his power and arrested him. An uprising by workers forced the officers to back down, and in 1946, Perón was elected president.

To please his chief supporters—labor and the urban middle class—Perón pursued a policy of increased industrialization. At the same time, he sought to free Argentina from foreign investors. The government bought the railways; took over the banking, insurance, shipping, and communications industries; and assumed regulation of imports and exports. But Perón's regime was also authoritarian. His wife, Eva Perón (1919–1952), organized women's groups to support the government, while Perón assembled fascist gangs, modeled after Hitler's Brown Shirts, that used violence to intimidate his opponents. But growing corruption in the Perón government and the alienation of more and more people by the regime's excesses encouraged the military to overthrow him in September 1955. Perón went into exile in Spain.

Overwhelmed by problems, however, military leaders eventually decided to allow Perón to return. Reelected president in September 1973, Perón died a year later. In 1976, the military installed a new regime. Tolerating no opposition, the military leaders encouraged the "disappearance" of their opponents. Perhaps 30,000 people, including 6,000 leftists, were killed as a result.

But economic problems remained. To divert people's attention, the military regime invaded the Falkland Islands off the coast of Argentina in April 1982. Great Britain, which had controlled the islands since the nineteenth century, sent ships and troops to defend the islands. When the Argentine forces surrendered to the British in July, angry Argentinians denounced the military regime. The loss discredited the military and opened the door to civilian rule. In 1983, Raúl Alfonsín (rah-OOL al-fahn-SEEN) (b. 1927) of the Radical Party was elected president and tried to restore democratic practices. In elections in 1989, the Perónist Carlos Saúl Menem (KAHR-lohs sah-OOL MEN-em) (b. 1930) won. This peaceful transfer of power gave hope that Argentina was moving on a democratic path. Despite problems of foreign debt and inflation, Argentina has witnessed economic growth since 2003, first under the government of President Nestor Kirchner (NAY-stor KEERCH-nehr) (1950–2010) and then under his wife, Christina Fernández de Kirchner (kris-TEE-nuh fehr-NAHN-des day KEERCH-nehr) (b. 1953), who in 2007 became the first woman to be elected president of Argentina.

BRAZIL After the military put an end to the authoritarian regime of Getúlio Vargas (zhi-TOO-lyoo VAHR-guhs) (1882–1954) in 1945, Brazil established a republic. Over the next two decades, various democratically elected presidents (including Vargas himself) struggled to solve Brazil's economic problems, especially its soaring inflation, but with little success. Finally, in the spring of 1964, the military decided to intervene and took over the government.

Unlike previous interventions by military leaders in politics, this time the armed forces remained in direct control of the country for twenty years. The military set course on a new economic direction, cutting back somewhat on state control of the economy and emphasizing market forces. Beginning in 1968, the new policies seemed to work, and Brazil experienced an "economic miracle" as it moved into self-sustaining economic growth, generally the hallmark of a modern economy. Economic growth

Juan and Eva Perón. Elected president of Argentina in 1946, Juan Perón soon established an authoritarian regime that nationalized some of Argentina's basic industries and organized fascist gangs to overwhelm its opponents. He is shown here with his wife, Eva, during the inauguration ceremonies initiating his second term as president, in 1952.

© Bettmann/CORBIS

Student Revolt in Mexico

POLITICS & GOVERNMENT

Growing conflict between government authorities and university students in Mexico came to a violent and bloody climax on October 2, 1968, when army troops killed and wounded large numbers of students in Mexico City. This excerpt is taken from an account of the events by the student National Strike Council.

National Strike Council, Events of October 2–3

After an hour and a half of a peaceful meeting attended by ten thousand people and witnessed by scores of domestic and foreign reporters, a helicopter gave the army the signal to attack by dropping flares into the crowd. Simultaneously, the plaza was surrounded and attacked by members of the army and all police forces, using weapons of every caliber, up to 9 mm.

The local papers have given the following information about the attack, confirmed by firsthand witnesses:

1. Numerous secret policemen had infiltrated the meeting in order to attack it from within, with orders to kill. They were known to each other by the use of a white handkerchief tied around their right hands. . . .
3. High caliber weaponry and expansion bullets were used. Seven hours after the massacre began, tanks cleaned up the residential buildings of Nonoalco-Tlaltelolco with short cannon blasts and machine-gun fire.
4. On the morning of October 3, the apartments of supposedly guilty individuals were still being searched, without a search warrant.
5. Doctors in the emergency wards of the city hospitals were under extreme pressure, being forced to forgo attention to the victims until they had been interrogated and placed under guard. Various interns who attended the demonstration for the purpose of giving medical aid had since disappeared.

6. The results of this brutal military operation include hundreds of dead (including women and children), thousands of wounded, an unwarranted search of all the apartments in the area, and thousands of violent arrests. Those arrested were taken to various illegal locations, such as Military Camp No. 1. It should be added that members of the National Strike Council who were captured were stripped and herded into a small archaeological excavation at Tlaltelolco, converted for the moment into a dungeon. Some of them were put up against a wall and shot.
7. Onesimo Mason, the general who directed the operation, praised the preparedness of his men, in contrast to the obvious lack of preparedness on the part of the students.

All this has occurred only ten days before the start of the Olympics. The repression is expected to become even greater after the Games, in view of the fact that national public opinion and the protest from the provinces are unified against a regime whose only interest lies in demonstrating its power to control.

Already individual liberties have been suspended, and restricted zones have been created where all vehicles are searched at gunpoint and personal identification is demanded. The Secretary of Defense declared that the friendly disposition of the regime will solve the conflict.

WE ARE NOT AGAINST THE OLYMPIC GAMES. WELCOME TO MEXICO.

Why did the Mexican army attack this peaceful student protest? Do you think that the timing of the Olympic Games in Mexico City was a factor? How does this event compare with what happened at Kent State University in 1970 and with the 1989 student protests in Tiananmen Square?

---

also included the economic exploitation of the Amazon basin, which the regime opened to farming; some experts believe that the resulting destruction of the extensive Amazon rain forests, which is still going on, poses a threat to the ecological balance not only of Brazil but of the earth itself. Rapid economic growth had additional drawbacks. Ordinary Brazilians hardly benefited at all as the gulf between rich and poor, always wide, grew even wider. In 1960, the wealthiest 10 percent of Brazil's population received 40 percent of the nation's income; in 1980, they received 51 percent. Then, too, rapid development led to an inflation rate of 100 percent a year, while an enormous foreign debt added to the problems. By the early 1980s, the economic miracle was turning into a nightmare. Overwhelmed, the generals retreated and opened the door for a return to democracy in 1985.

The new democratic government faced herculean obstacles—massive foreign debt, runaway inflation, and a lack

of social consensus. Nevertheless, by the 1990s, some stability was maintained as Brazil became committed to democratic elections. The enduring gulf between rich and poor helped lead to the election in 2002 of Luiz Inácio Lula da Silva (LWEES ee-NAH-syoh LOO-luh duh-SEEL-vuh) (b. 1945), who pursued a policy of increased trade and social reforms while continuing to increase exports. Despite economic growth, problems of crime and poor education still persisted in Brazil. In October 2010, Lula's chief of staff, Dilma Rousseff (DIL-muh ROO-seff) (b. 1947), became the first woman to be elected president of Brazil.

The Mexican Way

During the 1950s and 1960s, Mexico's ruling party (the Institutional Revolutionary Party, or PRI) focused on a balanced industrial program. Fifteen years of steady economic growth combined with low inflation and real gains in wages for more and more people made those years seem a golden age in Mexico's economic development. But at the end of the 1960s, the true nature of Mexico's domination by one party became apparent with the student protest movement. On October 2, 1968, a demonstration of university students in Tlaltelolco (tuh-lahl-teh-LOH-koh) Square in Mexico City was met by police forces, who opened fire and killed hundreds of students (see the box on p. 838). Leaders of the PRI became concerned about the need to change the system.

The next two presidents, Luis Echeverría (loo-EES eh-cheh-vahr-REE-uh) (b. 1922), who was elected in 1970, and José López Portillo (hoh-SAY LOH-pehz pohr-TEE-yoh) (b. 1920), who was elected in 1976, introduced political reforms. Rules for the registration of political parties were eased, making their growth more likely, and greater freedom of debate in the press and universities was allowed. But economic problems continued to trouble Mexico. In the late 1970s, vast new reserves of oil were discovered. As the sale of oil abroad increased dramatically, the government became even more dependent on oil revenues. When world oil prices dropped in the mid-1980s, Mexico was no longer able to make payments on its foreign debt, which had reached $80 billion in 1982. The government was forced to adopt new economic policies, including the increased sale of publicly owned companies to private parties.

The debt crisis and rising unemployment increased dissatisfaction with the government, which was especially evident in the 1988 election, when the PRI's choice for president, Carlos Salinas (KAHR-lohs sah-LEE-nahs) (b. 1948), who was expected to win in a landslide, won by only a 50.3 percent majority. Increasing dissatisfaction with the government's economic policies finally led to the unthinkable: in 2000, Vicente Fox (vee-SEN-tay FOKS) (b. 1942) defeated the PRI candidate for the presidency. Despite high hopes, Fox's presidency failed to deal with police corruption and bureaucratic inefficiency in the government. His successor, Felipe Calderón (feh-LEE-pay kahl-duh-ROHN) (b. 1962), has made immigration reform a major priority, with little success. He has also waged war on Mexico's powerful drug cartels.

Society and Culture in the Western World

 FOCUS QUESTION: What major social, cultural, and intellectual developments have occurred in Western Europe and North America since 1945?

Socially, culturally, and intellectually, the post–World War II Western world has been marked by much diversity, and although many trends represent a continuation of prewar modern developments, they have affected society in unpredictable ways.

The Emergence of a New Society

During the first decades after World War II, such products of new technologies as computers, television, jet planes, contra-

CHRONOLOGY Latin America Since 1945	
Juan Perón becomes president of Argentina	1946
Creation of the Organization of American States	1948
Castro's forces seize Cuba	1959
Bay of Pigs invasion	1961
Cuban Missile Crisis	1962
Death of Ché Guevara in Bolivia	1967
Presidency of Luis Echeverría in Mexico	1970–1976
Overthrow of Salvador Allende in Chile	1973
Perón returns to power	1973
Presidency of José López Portillo in Mexico	1976–1982
Sandinistas establish provisional government in Nicaragua	1979
Falklands War	1982
Election of Carlos Salinas in Mexico	1988
Election of Vicente Fox in Mexico	2000
Election of Luiz Inácio Lula da Silva in Brazil	2002
Election of Michelle Bachelet as the first woman president of Chile	2006
Election of Christina Fernández de Kirchner as the first woman president of Argentina	2007
Raúl Castro becomes president of Cuba	2008
Election of Dilma Rousseff as the first woman president of Brazil	2010

ceptive devices, and new surgical techniques all dramatically altered the pace and nature of human life. The rapid changes in society were fueled by scientific advances and vigorous economic growth. Called a *technocratic society* by some and the **consumer society** by others, postwar Western society has been characterized by an evolving social structure and new movements for change.

European society was dramatically altered after 1945. Especially noticeable were the changes in the middle class. As large companies and government agencies began employing large numbers of white-collar supervisory and administrative personnel, people in managerial and technological occupations greatly augmented the ranks of such traditional middle-class groups as businesspeople and professionals in law, medicine, and academia. In both Eastern and Western Europe, the new managers and experts were very much alike. Everywhere their positions depended on specialized knowledge acquired through higher education, and everywhere they focused on the effective administration of their corporations.

A SOCIETY OF CONSUMERS Changes also occurred among the traditional lower classes. Especially noticeable was the dramatic shift of people from rural to urban areas. The number of people in agriculture declined drastically; by the 1950s, the number of farmers throughout most of Europe had dropped by 50 percent. Nor did the size of the industrial working class expand. In West Germany, industrial workers made up 48 percent of the labor force throughout the 1950s and 1960s. Thereafter, the number of industrial workers began to dwindle as the number of white-collar service employees increased. At the same time, a substantial increase in their real wages enabled the working classes to aspire to the consumption patterns of the middle class. Buying on the installment plan, introduced in the 1930s, became widespread in the 1950s and gave workers a chance to imitate the middle class by buying such products as televisions, washing machines, refrigerators, vacuum cleaners, and stereos. But the most visible symbol of mass consumerism was the automobile. Before World War II, cars were reserved mostly for the European upper classes. In 1948, there were 5 million cars in all of Europe, but by 1957, the number had tripled. By the 1960s, there were almost 45 million cars.

Rising incomes, combined with shorter working hours, created an even greater market for mass leisure activities. Between 1900 and 1980, the workweek was reduced from sixty hours to a little more than forty hours, and the number of paid holidays increased. All aspects of popular culture—music, sports, media—became commercialized and offered opportunities for leisure activities.

Another very visible symbol of mass leisure was the growth of tourism. Before World War II, most persons who traveled for pleasure were from the upper and middle classes. After the war, the combination of more vacation time, increased prosperity, and the flexibility provided by package tours with their lower rates and budget-priced accommodations enabled millions to expand their travel possibilities.

A Revolt in Sexual Mores

The **permissive society** was yet another label critics applied to postwar Europe. World War I had seen the first significant crack in the rigid code of manners and morals of the nineteenth century. Subsequently, the 1920s had witnessed experimentation with drugs, the appearance of hard-core pornography, and a new sexual freedom (police in Berlin, for example, issued cards that permitted female and male homosexual prostitutes to ply their trade). But these indications of a new attitude appeared mostly in major cities and touched only small numbers of people. After World War II, changes in manners and morals were far more extensive and far more noticeable.

Sweden took the lead in the propagation of the so-called sexual revolution of the 1960s, but the rest of Europe and the United States soon followed. Sex education in the schools and the decriminalization of homosexuality were

but two aspects of Sweden's liberal legislation. The introduction of the birth control pill, which became widely available by the mid-1960s, gave people more freedom in sexual behavior. Meanwhile, sexually explicit movies, plays, and books broke new ground in the treatment of once hidden subjects. Cities like Amsterdam, which allowed open prostitution and the public sale of hard-core pornography, attracted thousands of curious tourists.

The new standards were evident in the breakdown of the traditional family. Divorce rates increased dramatically, especially in the 1960s, while the incidence of premarital and extramarital sexual experiences also rose substantially. A survey in the Netherlands in 1968 revealed that 78 percent of men and 86 percent of women had participated in extramarital sex.

Youth Protest and Student Revolt

The 1960s also saw the emergence of a drug culture. Marijuana, though illegal, was widely used by college and university students. For young people more interested in higher levels of consciousness, Timothy Leary, who had done research at Harvard on the psychedelic effects of LSD (lysergic acid diethylamide), became the high priest of hallucinogenic experiences.

New attitudes toward sex and the use of drugs were only two manifestations of a growing youth movement in the 1960s that questioned authority and fostered rebellion against the older generation. Spurred by opposition to the Vietnam War and a growing political consciousness, the youth rebellion became a full-fledged protest movement by the second half of the 1960s (see the box on p. 841).

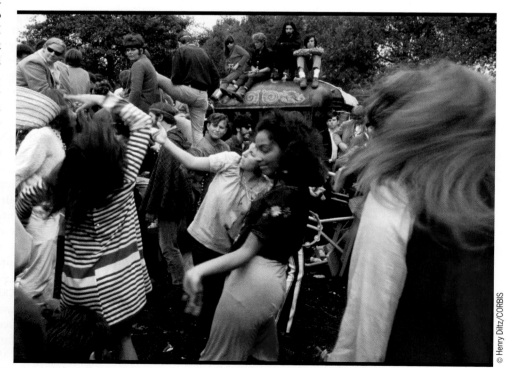

The "Love-In." In the 1960s, a number of outdoor public festivals for young people combined music, drugs, and sex. Flamboyant dress, face painting, free-form dancing, and drugs were vital ingredients in creating an atmosphere dedicated to "love and peace." Shown here are "hippies" dancing around a decorated bus at a "love-in" during 1967's Summer of Love.

© Henry Diltz/CORBIS

"The Times They Are A-Changin'": The Music of Youthful Protest

ART & IDEAS

In the 1960s, the lyrics of rock music reflected the rebellious mood of many young people. Bob Dylan (b. 1941), a vastly influential performer and recording artist, expressed the feelings of the younger generation. His song "The Times They Are A-Changin'," released in 1964, has been called an "anthem for the protest movement."

Bob Dylan, "The Times They Are A-Changin'"

Come gather 'round people
Wherever you roam
And admit that the waters
Around you have grown
And accept it that soon
You'll be drenched to the bone
If your time to you
Is worth savin'
Then you better start swimmin'
Or you'll sink like a stone
For the times they are a-changin'

Come writers and critics
Who prophesize with your pen
And keep your eyes wide
The chance won't come again
And don't speak too soon
For the wheel's still in spin
And there's no tellin' who
That it's namin'
For the loser now
Will be later to win
For the times they are a-changin'

Come senators, congressmen
Please heed the call
Don't stand in the doorway

Don't block up the hall
For he that gets hurt
Will be he who has stalled
There's a battle outside
And it is ragin'
It'll soon shake your windows
And rattle your walls
For the times they are a-changin'

Come mothers and fathers
Throughout the land
And don't criticize
What you can't understand
Your sons and your daughters
Are beyond your command
Your old road
Is rapidly agin'
Please get out of the new one
If you can't lend your hand
For the times they are a-changin'

The line it is drawn
The curse it is cast
The slow one now
Will later be fast
As the present now
Will later be past
The order is
Rapidly fadin'
And the first one now
Will later be last
For the times they are a-changin'

What prompted the student campus revolts of the 1960s? According to Bob Dylan, who and what are causing the problem?

Before World War II, higher education had remained largely the preserve of Europe's wealthier classes. After the war, European states began to foster greater equality of opportunity in higher education by eliminating fees, and universities experienced an influx of students from the middle and lower classes. Enrollments grew dramatically; in France, 4.5 percent of young people went to a university in 1950. By 1965, the figure had increased to 14.5 percent.

But there were problems. Overcrowded classrooms, professors who paid little attention to students, administrators who acted in an authoritarian fashion, and an education that to many seemed irrelevant to the modern age led to an outburst of student revolts in the late 1960s. One of the major issues that mobilized youthful European protesters was the United States' war in Vietnam, which they viewed as an act of aggression and imperialism. In 1968, demonstrations broke out in universities in Italy, France, and Britain. In part, these were an extension of the protests against the Vietnam War in American universities in the mid-1960s. In London, 30,000 demonstrators took to the streets protesting America's involvement in Vietnam. But student protests in Europe also backfired in that they provoked a reaction from people who favored order over the lawlessness of privileged young people. As Pier Paolo Pasolini (PYER PAH-loh pah-SOH-lee-nee)

(1922–1975), an Italian poet and intellectual, wrote, "Now all the journalists of the world are licking your arses . . . but not me, my dears. You have the faces of spoiled brats, and I hate you, like I hate your fathers. . . . When yesterday at Valle Giulia [in Rome] you beat up the police, I sympathized with the police because they are the sons of the poor."[3]

There were other reasons for the student radicalism besides protesting the Vietnam War. Some students were genuinely motivated by a desire to reform the university. They also attacked other aspects of Western society, such as its materialism, and expressed concern about becoming cogs in the large and impersonal bureaucratic jungles of the modern world. For many students, the calls for democratic decision making in the universities were a reflection of their deeper concerns about the direction of Western society.

Women in the Postwar Western World

Despite their enormous contributions to the war effort, women at the end of World War II were removed from the workforce to free up jobs for the soldiers returning home. After the horrors of war, people seemed willing for a while to return to traditional family practices. Female participation in the workforce declined, and birthrates began to rise, creating a "baby boom." The boost in the birthrate lasted until the early 1960s, when family size began to decline primarily because of the widespread practice of birth control. Invented in the nineteenth century, the condom was already in wide use, but the development in the 1960s of oral contraceptives, known as birth control pills, provided a reliable means of birth control that quickly spread to all Western countries.

The trend toward smaller families contributed to changes in women's employment in both Europe and the United States, mainly because women now needed to devote far fewer years to rearing children. That led to a large increase in the number of married women in the workforce. At the beginning of the twentieth century, even working-class wives tended to stay at home if they could afford to do so. In the postwar period, this was no longer the case. In the United States, for example, married women made up about 15 percent of the female labor force in 1900; by 1970, their number had increased to 62 percent.

But the increased presence of women in the workforce did not change some old patterns. Working-class women in particular still earned salaries lower than those of men performing equivalent work. In the 1960s, women earned only 60 percent of men's wages in Britain, 50 percent in France, and 63 percent in West Germany. In addition, women still tended to enter traditionally female jobs. As one Swedish woman guidance counselor remarked in 1975, "Every girl now thinks in terms of a job. This is progress. They want children, but they don't pin their hopes on marriage. They don't intend to be housewives for some future husband. But there has been no change in their vocational choices."[4] Many European women also still faced the double burden of earning income on the one hand and raising a family and maintaining the household on the other. Such inequalities led increasing numbers of women to rebel.

THE FEMINIST MOVEMENT: THE QUEST FOR LIBERATION The participation of women in World Wars I and II helped them achieve one of the major aims of the nineteenth-century feminist movement—the right to vote. Already after World War I, many governments acknowledged the contributions of women to the war effort by granting them the franchise. Sweden, Great Britain, Germany, Poland, Hungary, Austria, and Czechoslovakia did so in 1918, followed by the United States in 1920. Women in France and Italy did not obtain the vote until 1945. After World War II, European women tended to fall back into the traditional roles expected of them, and little was heard of feminist concerns. But by the late 1960s, women began to assert their rights again and speak as feminists. Along with the student upheavals of the late 1960s came renewed interest in feminism, or the **women's liberation movement**, as it was now called. Increasingly, women protested that the acquisition of political and legal equality had not brought true equality with men:

> We are economically oppressed: in jobs we do full work for half pay; in the home we do unpaid work full-time. We are commercially exploited by advertisement, television, and the press;

The Women's Liberation Movement. In the late 1960s, as women began once again to assert their rights, a revived women's liberation movement emerged. Feminists in the movement maintained that women themselves must alter the conditions of their lives. During this women's liberation rally, some women climbed the statue of Admiral Farragut in Washington, D.C., to exhibit their signs.

The Voice of the Women's Liberation Movement

Simone de Beauvoir was an important figure in the emergence of the postwar women's liberation movement. This selection is taken from her book *The Second Sex,* in which she argued that women have been forced into a position subordinate to men.

Simone de Beauvoir, *The Second Sex*

Now, woman has always been man's dependent, if not his slave; the two sexes have never shared the world in equality. And even today woman is heavily handicapped, though her situation is beginning to change. Almost nowhere is her legal status the same as man's, and frequently it is much to her disadvantage. Even when her rights are legally recognized in the abstract, long-standing custom prevents their full expression in the mores. In the economic sphere men and women can almost be said to make up two castes; other things being equal, the former hold the better jobs, get higher wages, and have more opportunity for success than their new competitors. In industry and politics men have a great many more positions and they monopolize the most important posts. In addition to all this, they enjoy a traditional prestige that the education of children tends in every way to support, for the present enshrines the past—and in the past all history has been made by men. At the present time, when women are beginning to take part in the affairs of the world, it is still a world that belongs to men—they have no doubt of it at all and women have scarcely any. To decline to be the *Other,* to refuse to be a party to a deal—this would be for women to renounce all the advantages conferred upon them by their alliance with the superior caste. Man-the-sovereign will provide woman-the-liege with material protection and will undertake the moral justification of her existence; thus, she can evade at once both economic risk and the metaphysical risk of a liberty in which ends and aims must be contrived without assistance. Indeed, along with the ethical urge of each individual to affirm his subjective existence, there is also the temptation to forgo liberty and become a thing. This is an inauspicious road, for he who takes it—passive, lost, ruined— becomes henceforth the creature of another's will, frustrated in his transcendence and deprived of every value. But it is an easy road; on it one avoids the strain involved in undertaking an authentic existence. When man makes of woman the *Other,* he may, then, expect her to manifest deep-seated tendencies toward complicity. Thus, woman may fail to lay claim to the status of subject because she lacks definite resources, because she feels the necessary bond that ties her to man regardless of reciprocity, and because she is often very well pleased with her role as the *Other.*

Now, what peculiarly signalizes the situation of woman is that she—a free and autonomous being like all human creatures—nevertheless finds herself living in a world where men compel her to assume the status of the *Other.*

 What did Simone de Beauvoir mean by the "second sex"? By "the Other"? What is the difference between being a "thing" and having an "authentic existence"? According to de Beauvoir, how do women fall prey to the former?

---

legally we often have only the status of children. We are brought up to feel inadequate, educated to narrower horizons than men. This is our specific oppression as women. It is as women that we are, therefore, organizing.[5]

These were the words of a British Women's Liberation Workshop in 1969.

Of great importance to the emergence of the postwar women's liberation movement was the work of a Frenchwoman, Simone de Beauvoir (see-MUHN duh boh-VWAR) (1908–1986). Born into a Catholic middle-class family and educated at the Sorbonne in Paris, de Beauvoir supported herself as a teacher and later as a novelist and writer. De Beauvoir believed that she lived a "liberated" life for a twentieth-century European woman, but for all her freedom, she still came to perceive that as a woman she faced limits that men did not. In 1949, she published her highly influential work *The Second Sex,* in which she argued that as a result of male-dominated societies, women had been defined by their differences from men and consequently received second-class status (see the box above).

Another important influence in the growth of the women's movement in the 1960s was Betty Friedan (free-DAN) (1921–2006). A journalist and the mother of three children, Friedan grew increasingly uneasy with her attempt to fulfill the traditional role of the "ideal housewife and mother." In 1963, she published *The Feminine Mystique,* in which she analyzed the problems of middle-class American women in the 1950s and argued that women were being denied equality with men. *The Feminine Mystique* became a best-seller and made Friedan a celebrity.

TRANSFORMATION IN WOMEN'S LIVES To ensure the natural replacement of a country's population, women need to produce an average of 2.1 children each. Many European countries fall short of this mark; their populations stopped growing in the 1960s, and the trend has continued since then.

By the 1990s, among the nations of the European Union, the average number of children per woman of childbearing age was 1.4. At 1.31 in 2009, Spain's rate is among the lowest in the world.

At the same time, the presence of women in the workforce has continued to rise. In Britain, for example, the number of women in the labor force went from 32 percent to 44 percent between 1970 and 1990. Moreover, women have entered new employment areas. Greater access to universities and professional schools has enabled women to take jobs in law, medicine, government, business, and education. In the Soviet Union, for example, about 70 percent of doctors and teachers were women. Nevertheless, economic inequality still often prevails; women are paid lower wages than men for comparable work and receive fewer promotions to management positions.

Feminists in the women's liberation movement came to believe that women themselves must transform the fundamental conditions of their lives. Women sought and gained a measure of control over their own bodies by seeking to legalize both contraception and abortion. In the 1960s and 1970s, hundreds of thousands of European women worked to repeal laws that prohibited contraception and abortion and began to meet with success. Even in Catholic countries, where the church remained strongly opposed to both procedures, legislation allowing contraception and abortion was passed in the 1970s and 1980s.

As more women became activists, they also became involved in new issues. In the 1980s and 1990s, women faculty in universities concentrated on developing more enlightened cultural attitudes through the new academic field of women's studies. Such courses, which stressed the role and contributions of women in history, mushroomed in colleges and universities on both sides of the Atlantic.

Other women began to try to affect the political environment by allying with the antinuclear movement. In 1981, a group of women in Britain protested American nuclear missiles by chaining themselves to the fence of an American military base. Thousands more joined in creating a peace camp around the military compound. Enthusiasm ran high; one participant said, "I'll never forget that feeling; it'll live with me forever. . . . As we walked round, and we clasped hands . . . it was for women; it was for peace; it was for the world."[6]

Some women joined the ecological movement. As one German writer who was concerned with environmental issues said, it is women "who must give birth to children, willingly or unwillingly, in this polluted world of ours." Especially prominent was the number of women members in the Green Party in Germany (see "The Environment and the Green Movements" later in this chapter).

Women in the West have also reached out to work with women from the rest of the world in international conferences to change the conditions of their lives. Between 1975 and 1995, the United Nations held conferences in Mexico City, Copenhagen, Nairobi, and Beijing. These meetings made the differences between women from Western and non-Western countries very clear. Whereas women from Western countries spoke of political, economic, cultural, and sexual rights, women from developing countries in Latin America, Africa, and Asia focused on bringing an end to the violence, hunger, and disease that haunt their lives. Despite these differences, these meetings demonstrated that women in both developed and developing nations were organizing to increase awareness of women's issues among all people, male and female.

The Growth of Terrorism

Acts of terror by individuals and groups opposed to governments have become a frightening aspect of modern Western society. During the late 1970s and early 1980s, small bands of terrorists used assassination, indiscriminate killing of civilians, the taking of hostages, and the hijacking of airplanes to draw attention to their demands or to destabilize governments in the hope of achieving their political goals. Terrorist acts garnered considerable media attention. When Palestinian terrorists kidnapped and killed eleven Israeli athletes at the Munich Olympic Games in 1972, hundreds of millions of people watched the drama unfold on television. Indeed, some observers believe that media exposure has been an important catalyst for some terrorist groups.

Motivations for terrorist acts vary considerably. Left- and right-wing terrorist groups flourished in the late 1970s and early 1980s, but terrorist acts have also stemmed from militant nationalists who wish to create separatist states. Most prominent was the Irish Republican Army (IRA), which resorted to vicious attacks against the ruling government and innocent civilians in Northern Ireland.

Although left- and right-wing terrorist activities declined in Europe in the 1980s, international terrorism continued. Angered by the loss of their territory to Israel, some militant Palestinians responded with a policy of terrorist attacks against Israel's supporters. Palestinian terrorists operated throughout European countries, attacking both Europeans and American tourists; Palestinian terrorists massacred vacationers at airports in Rome and Vienna in 1985. State-sponsored terrorism was often an integral part of international terrorism. Militant governments, especially in Iran, Libya, and Syria, assisted terrorist organizations that launched attacks on Europeans and Americans. On December 21, 1988, Pan American flight 103 from Frankfurt to New York exploded over Lockerbie, Scotland, killing all 259 passengers and crew members. A massive investigation revealed that the bomb responsible for the explosion had been planted by two Libyan terrorists.

TERRORIST ATTACK ON THE UNITED STATES One of the most destructive acts of terrorism occurred on September 11, 2001, in the United States. Terrorists hijacked four commercial jet airplanes after takeoff from Boston, Newark, and Washington, D.C. The hijackers flew two of the airplanes directly into the twin towers of the World Trade Center in New York City, causing these buildings, as well as a number of surrounding buildings, to collapse. A third hijacked plane slammed into the Pentagon near Washington, D.C. The fourth plane, apparently headed for Washington, crashed instead in an isolated area of Pennsylvania. In total, nearly

Terrorist Attack on the World Trade Center in New York City. On September 11, 2001, hijackers flew two commercial jetliners into the twin towers of the World Trade Center. Shown at the left are the two towers in the New York skyline before the attack. The middle picture shows the second of the two jetliners about to hit one of the towers while smoke billows from the site of the first attack. In the scene below, firefighters are making their way through what was left of the 110-story towers after their collapse.

three thousand people were killed, including everyone aboard the four airliners.

These coordinated acts of terror were carried out by hijackers connected to an international terrorist organization known as al-Qaeda, run by Osama bin Laden (1957–2011). A native of Saudi Arabia of Yemeni extraction, bin Laden used an inherited fortune to set up terrorist training camps in Afghanistan, under the protection of the nation's militant fundamentalist Islamic rulers known as the Taliban.

U.S. President George W. Bush vowed to wage a lengthy and thorough war on terrorism and worked to create a coalition of nations to assist in ridding the world of al-Qaeda and other terrorist groups. Within weeks of the attack on America, U.S. and NATO air forces began bombing Taliban-controlled command centers, airfields, and al-Qaeda hiding places in Afghanistan. On the ground, Afghan forces, assisted by U.S. special forces, pushed the Taliban out and gained control of the country by the end of November 2001. A democratic multiethnic government was installed but has faced problems from revived Taliban activity (see Chapter 29).

THE WEST AND ISLAM One of the major sources of terrorist activity against the West, especially the United States, has come from parts of the Muslim world. The ongoing Israeli-Palestinian conflict, in which the United States has steadfastly supported Israel, has certainly fed anti-Western and especially anti-American feelings among many Muslims. In 1979, the revolution in Iran that led to the overthrow of the Western-oriented shah and the establishment of a new Islam-based government also stoked anti-Western sentiment (see Chapter 29).

The involvement of the United States in the liberation of Kuwait in the Persian Gulf War in 1991 also had unexpected consequences in the relationship of Islam and the West. After Iraq invaded Kuwait, the United States stationed forces in Saudi Arabia, the location of many sacred Islamic sites. The presence of American forces was considered an affront to Islam by certain anti-Western Islamic groups, especially that of Osama bin Laden and his followers. These anti-Western attitudes came to be shared by a number of radical Islamic groups, as is evident in the 2004 bombing in Madrid and the 2005 bombing on subway trains in London.

The U.S. invasion of Iraq in 2003 (see Chapter 29) further inflamed Islamic groups against the United States and the West. Although there was no evidence of a relationship between al-Qaeda terrorists and the regime of Iraqi dictator Saddam Hussein, this claim was one of the excuses used by the United States to launch a preemptive war against Iraq. Although many Iraqis welcomed the overthrow of Saddam Hussein, the subsequent deaths of innocent civilians, the torturing of Muslim prisoners by American soldiers, and the prolonged American occupation of Iraq in the heart of the Middle East served to deepen anti-American resentment throughout the Muslim world.

Guest Workers and Immigrants

As the economies of the Western European countries revived in the 1950s and 1960s, a severe labor shortage forced them to rely on foreign workers. Thousands of Turks and eastern and southern Europeans relocated to Germany, North Africans to France, and people from the Caribbean, India, and Pakistan to Great Britain. Overall, there were probably 15 million **guest workers** in Europe in the 1980s.

Although these workers had been recruited for economic reasons, their presence caused social and political problems for their host countries. The concentration of guest workers in certain cities and even certain sections of those cities often created tensions with the local native populations. Foreign workers constituted almost one-fifth of the population in the German cities of Frankfurt, Munich, and Stuttgart. Having become settled in their new countries, many were unwilling to leave, even after the end of the postwar boom in the early 1970s led to mass unemployment.

In the 1980s, there was an influx of other refugees, especially to West Germany, which had liberal immigration laws that permitted people seeking asylum from political persecution to enter the country. During the 1970s and 1980s, West Germany absorbed more than a million refugees from Eastern Europe and East Germany. In 1986 alone, 200,000 political refugees from Pakistan, Bangladesh, and Sri Lanka entered the country. Other parts of Europe saw a similar influx of foreigners. Between 1992 and 2002, London and the southeast region of England witnessed an increase of 700,000 new foreigners, primarily from Yugoslavia, Southeast Asia, the Middle East, and Africa. A survey in 1998 showed that English was not the first language of one-third of inner-city children in London.

This great influx of foreigners, many of them nonwhite, has strained not only the social services of European countries but also the patience of native residents who oppose making their countries ethnically diverse. Antiforeign sentiment, increased by growing unemployment, has been encouraged by new right-wing political parties that cater to people's complaints. Thus, the National Front in France, organized by Jean-Marie Le Pen (ZHAHNH-muh-REE leh PEN) (b. 1928), and the Republican Party in Germany, led by Franz Schönhuber (FRAHNTS SHURN-hoo-bur) (1923–2005), a former SS officer, advocate restricting all new immigration and limiting the assimilation of settled immigrants. Much more frightening, however, have been organized campaigns of violence, especially against African and Asian immigrants, by radical right-wing groups.

Even nations that have been especially tolerant in opening their borders to immigrants and seekers of asylum are changing their policies. In the Netherlands, 19 percent of the people have a foreign background, representing almost 180 nationalities. In 2004, however, the Dutch government passed tough new immigration laws, including a requirement that newcomers pass a Dutch language and culture test before being admitted to the Netherlands.

Sometimes these policies have been aimed at religious practices. Another effect of the influx of foreigners into Europe has been a dramatic increase in the number of Muslims. Although Christians still constitute a majority (though many no longer practice their faith), the number of Muslims has mushroomed in France, Britain, Belgium, the Netherlands, and Germany. It has been estimated that at least 15 million Muslims were living in European Union nations at the beginning of the twenty-first century.

In some nations, concern that Muslim immigration will result in the erosion of national values has led to attempts to restrict the display of Islamic symbols. In 2004, France enacted a law prohibiting female students from wearing a headscarf (*hijab*) to school. Article 1 stated: "In public elementary, middle and high schools, the wearing of signs or clothing which conspicuously manifest students' religious affiliations is prohibited." The law further clarified "conspicuous" to mean "a large cross, a veil, or a skullcap."[7] Small religious symbols, such as small crosses or medallions, were not included. Critics of this law argue that it will exacerbate ethnic and religious tensions in France, while supporters stress that it upholds the tradition of secularism and equality for women in France (see the box on p. 847).

The Environment and the Green Movements

Beginning in the 1970s, environmentalism has become a major item on the European political agenda. By that time, serious ecological problems had become all too apparent. Air pollution, produced by nitrogen oxide and sulfur dioxide emissions from road vehicles, power plants, and industrial factories, was causing respiratory illnesses and having corrosive effects on buildings and monuments. Many rivers, lakes, and seas had become so polluted that they posed serious health risks. Dying forests and disappearing wildlife alarmed more and more people. The opening of Eastern Europe after the revolutions of 1989 brought to the world's attention the incredible environmental destruction of that region caused by unfettered industrial pollution.

Environmental concerns have forced the major political parties in Europe to advocate new regulations for the protection of the environment. The Soviet nuclear power disaster at Chernobyl in Ukraine in 1986 made Europeans even more aware of potential environmental hazards, and 1987 was touted as the "year of the environment." Many European states established government ministries to oversee environmental issues.

Growing ecological awareness also gave rise to Green movements and Green Parties that emerged throughout Europe in the 1970s. Most visible was the Green Party in Germany, which was officially organized in 1979 and had elected forty-two delegates to the West German parliament by 1987. Green Parties have also competed successfully in Sweden, Austria, and Switzerland.

Islam and the West: Secularism in France

FAMILY & SOCIETY

The banning of headscarves in schools was preceded by a debate on the secular state in France. Secularism in France extends beyond the separation of church and state: while recognizing the right to religious expression, French law dictates that religious expression must remain in the private sphere. Before the law was enacted, President Jacques Chirac set up the Stasi Commission (named after its chair, Bernard Stasi) to interview school, religious, and political leaders on the issue. The commission decided in favor of prohibiting all conspicuous religious symbols in schools.

The first selection is taken from a speech by President Chirac, who favored the ban. The second is taken from interviews with French Muslim women, many of them from the Maghreb (the Arabic term for Northwest Africa). Many of these women questioned how the law protects their individual rights and freedom of religious expression.

French President Jacques Chirac on Secularism in French Society

The debate on the principle of secularism goes to the very heart of our values. It concerns our national cohesion, our ability to live together, our ability to unite on what is essential. . . . Many young people of immigrant origin, whose first language is French, and who are in most cases of French nationality, succeed and feel at ease in a society which is theirs. This kind of success must also be made possible by breaking the wall of silence and indifference which surrounds the reality of discrimination today. I know about the feeling of being misunderstood, of helplessness, sometimes even of revolt, among young French people of immigrant origin whose job applications are rejected because of the way their names sound, and who are too often confronted with discrimination in the fields of access to housing or even simply of access to leisure facilities. . . . All of France's children, whatever their history, whatever their origin, whatever their beliefs, are the daughters and sons of the republic. They have to be recognized as such, in law but above all in reality. By ensuring respect for this requirement, by reforming our integration policy, by our ability to bring equal opportunities to life, we shall bring national cohesion to life again. We shall also do so by bringing to life the principle of secularism, which is a pillar of our constitution. It expresses our wish to live together in respect, dialogue and tolerance. Secularism guarantees freedom of conscience. It protects the freedom to believe or not to believe. . . . We also need to reaffirm secularism in schools, because schools must be preserved absolutely. . . .

There is of course no question of turning schools into a place of uniformity, of anonymity, where religious life or belonging would be banned. It is a question of enabling teachers and head teachers, who are today in the front-line and confronted with real difficulties, to carry out their mission serenely with the affirmation of a clear rule. Until recently, as a result of a reasonable custom which was respected spontaneously, nobody ever doubted that pupils, who are naturally free to live their faith, should nevertheless not arrive in schools, secondary schools or A-level colleges, in religious clothes. It is not a question of inventing new rules or of shifting the boundaries of secularism. It is a question of expressing, with respect but clearly and firmly, a rule which has been part of our customs and practices for a very long time. I have consulted, I have studied the report of the Stasi Commission, I have examined the arguments put forward by the National Assembly committee [on secularism], by political parties, by religious authorities, by major representatives of major currents of thought. In all conscience, it is my view that the wearing of clothes or of symbols which conspicuously demonstrate religious affiliations must be banned in state schools.

North African Women in France Respond to the Headscarf Ban

Labiba (Thirty-Five-Year-Old Algerian)

I don't feel that they should interfere in the private life of people in the respect that we're in a secular country; France shouldn't take a position toward one religion to the detriment of another. . . . I think that in a secular school, we should all be secular, otherwise we need to have religious school and then everyone is free to wear what he wants.

Nour (Thirty-Four-Year-Old Algerian)

Honestly, you know the secular school, it doesn't miss celebrating Easter, and when they celebrate Easter, it doesn't bother me. My daughter comes home with painted Easter eggs and everything; it's pretty; it's cute. There are classes that are over 80 percent Maghrebin in the suburbs, and they celebrate Easter, they celebrate Christmas, you see? And that's not a problem for the secular school. And I don't find that fair.

I find that when it's Ramadan, they should talk about Ramadan. Honestly, me, it wouldn't be a problem. On the contrary, someone who comes into class . . . with a veil, that would pose a question actually, that we could discuss in class, to know why this person wears the veil. So why punish them, amputate them from that part of their culture without discussing it? Why is it so upsetting to have someone in class who

(Continued)

wears a veil, when we could make it a subject of discussion on all religions? Getting stuck on the veil hides the question. They make such a big deal out of it, the poor girls, they take them out of school; people turn them into extraterrestrials. In the end we turn them into people who will have problems in their identities, in their culture and everything . . . . For a country that is home to so many cultures, there's no excuse.

Isma (Thirty-Six-Year-Old Algerian)

The girls who veil in France, especially the high school and junior high students, it's first of all a question of identity, because these girls are born in France to foreign parents. . . .

At a given time an adolescent want to affirm himself, to show that he's someone, that he's an individual, so he thinks, I'd say, he thinks that it's by his clothes that he shows that he comes from somewhere, that he's from someone. So then, I think you should let them do it, and afterwards, by themselves, people come back to who they really are.

 What were the perspectives of the French president and the French Muslim women who were interviewed? How do they differ? Do you think there might be a way to reconcile the opposing positions? Why or why not?

Although the Green movements and parties have played an important role in making people aware of ecological problems, they have not supplanted the traditional political parties, as some political analysts in the mid-1980s forecast. For one thing, the coalitions that made up the Greens found it difficult to agree on all issues and tended to splinter into different cliques. Moreover, traditional political parties have co-opted the environmental issues of the Greens. By the 1990s, more and more European governments were beginning to sponsor projects to safeguard the environment and clean up the worst sources of pollution.

GREEN URBAN PLANNING By the beginning of the twenty-first century, many European cities began to recognize the need for urban sustainability. Many cities have enacted laws that limit the amount of new construction, increase the quantity and quality of green spaces within the city, and foster the construction of new public transportation systems. The use of such alternatives as rail, metro, bus, and bicycle has created more options for public transportation (see the comparative illustration on p. 849). In Stockholm, Sweden, 70 percent of all trips are made by public transit. Moreover, the emphasis on public transportation has served to limit the growth of urban sprawl. Many cities, such as Vienna, where 50 percent of the city's land is in green space, are also enacting new laws to protect urban parks and forests.

Western Culture Since 1945

Intellectually and culturally, the Western world since World War II has been notable for its diversity and innovation. Especially since 1970, new directions have led some observers to speak of a "Postmodern" cultural world.

POSTWAR LITERATURE One of the most original trends in postwar literature was known as the Theater of the Absurd. Its most famous proponent was the Irishman Samuel Beckett (1906–1990), who lived in France. In Beckett's play *Waiting for Godot* (1952), the action on the stage is not drawn from real life. Two men talk as they wait for someone with whom they may or may not have an appointment. No background

information on the two men is provided. During the course of the play, nothing seems to happen. The audience is never told if the action in front of them is real or imagined. Unlike traditional theater, suspense is maintained not by having the audience wonder what is going to happen next but by having them wonder what is happening now.

The Theater of the Absurd reflected its time. The immediate postwar period was a time of disillusionment with fixed ideological beliefs in politics or religion. The same disillusionment that inspired the **existentialism** of Albert Camus (ahl-BAYR ka-MOO) (1913–1960) and Jean-Paul Sartre (ZHAHNH-POHL SAR-truh) (1905–1980), with its sense of the world's meaninglessness, underscored the bleak worldview of absurdist drama and literature. The starting point of the existentialism of Sartre and Camus was the absence of God in the universe. Although the death of God was tragic, it meant that humans had no preordained destiny and were utterly alone in the universe, with no future and no hope. As Camus expressed it:

> A world that can be explained even with bad reasons is a familiar world. But, on the other hand, in a universe suddenly divested of illusions and lights, man feels an alien, a stranger. His exile is without remedy since he is deprived of the memory of a lost home or the hope of a promised land. This divorce between man and his life, the actor and his setting, is properly the feeling of absurdity.[8]

According to Camus, then, the world was absurd and without meaning; humans, too, are without meaning and purpose. Reduced to despair and depression, humans have but one source of hope—themselves.

POSTMODERNISM The term *Postmodern* covers a variety of intellectual and artistic styles and ways of thinking prominent since the 1970s. In the broadest sense, **Postmodernism** rejects the modern Western belief in an objective truth and instead focuses on the relative nature of reality and knowledge.

While existentialism wrestled with notions of meaning and existence, a group of French philosophers in the 1960s

© Jake Wyman/Getty Images

© Nightman1965/Dreamstime.com

attempted to understand how meaning and knowledge operate through the study of language and signs. **Poststructuralism**, or **deconstruction**, formulated by Jacques Derrida (ZHAHK DEH-ree-duh) (1930–2004), holds that culture is created and can therefore be analyzed in a variety of ways, according to the manner in which people create their own meaning. Hence there is no fixed truth or universal meaning.

Michel Foucault (mih-SHELL foo-KOH) (1926–1984) drew on Derrida to explore relationships of power. Believing that "power is exercised rather than possessed," Foucault argued that the diffusion of power and oppression marks all relationships. For example, any act of teaching entails components of assertion and submission, as the student adopts the ideas of the person in power. Therefore, all norms are culturally produced and entail some degree of power struggle.

Postmodernism was also evident in literature. In the Western world, the best examples were found in Latin America, in a literary style called *magic realism*, and in Central and Eastern Europe. Magic realism combined realistic events with dreamlike or fantastic backgrounds. One of the finest examples of magic realism can be found in the novel *One Hundred Years of Solitude*, written by Gabriel García Márquez (gahb-ree-EL gar-SEE-uh MAHR-kes) (b. 1928), a Colombian who won the Nobel Prize for Literature in 1982. The novel is the story of the fictional town of Macondo as seen by several generations of the Buendias, its founding family. The author slips back and forth between fact and fantasy. Villagers are not surprised when a local priest rises into the air and floats. But when wandering gypsies introduce these villagers to magnets, telescopes, and magnifying glasses, the villagers are dumbfounded by what they see as magic. According to the author, fantasy and fact depend on one's point of view.

The other center of Postmodernism was in Central and Eastern Europe, especially in the work of Milan Kundera (MEE-lahn koon-DAYR-uh) (b. 1929) of Czechoslovakia. Like the magic realists of Latin America, Kundera blended fantasy with realism. Unlike the magic realists, though, Kundera used fantasy to examine moral issues and remained optimistic about the human condition. Indeed, in his first novel, *The Unbearable Lightness of Being*, published in 1984, Kundera does not despair because of the political repression in his native land that he so aptly describes, but allows his characters to use love as a way to a better life. The human spirit can be diminished but not destroyed.

Trends in Art

Following the war, the United States dominated the art world, much as it did the world of popular culture. New York City replaced Paris as the artistic center of the West. The Guggenheim Museum, the Museum of Modern Art, and the Whitney Museum of Modern Art, together with New York's numerous art galleries, promoted modern art and helped determine artistic tastes throughout much of the world. One of the styles that became synonymous with the emergence of the New York art scene was **Abstract Expressionism**.

Dubbed "action painting" by one critic, Abstract Expressionism was energetic and spontaneous, qualities evident in

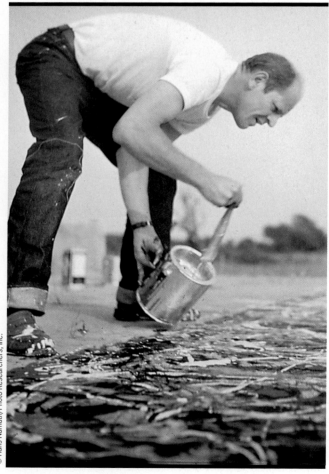

© Hans Namuth/Photo Researchers, Inc.

Jackson Pollock at Work. After World War II, Abstract Expressionism moved to the center of the artistic mainstream. One of its best-known practitioners was the American Jackson Pollock, who achieved his ideal of total abstraction in his drip paintings. He is shown here painting in his Long Island studio. Pollock found it easier to cover his large canvases with spontaneous patterns of color when he put them on the floor.

the enormous canvases of Jackson Pollock (1912–1956). In such works as *Lavender Mist* (1950), paint seems to explode, enveloping the viewer with emotion and movement. Pollock's swirling forms and seemingly chaotic patterns broke all conventions of form and structure. His drip paintings, with their total abstraction, were extremely influential with other artists, and he eventually became a celebrity. Inspired by Native American sand painters, Pollock painted with the canvas on the floor. He explained, "On the floor I am more at ease. I feel nearer, more a part of the painting, since this way I can walk around it, work from four sides and be literally *in* the painting. When I am in the painting, I am not aware of what I am doing. There is pure harmony."

The early 1960s saw the emergence of Pop Art, which took images of popular culture and transformed them into works of fine art. Andy Warhol (1930–1987), who began as an advertising illustrator, was the most famous of the pop artists. Warhol adapted images from commercial art, such as cans of Campbell's soup, and photographs of such celebrities as Marilyn Monroe. Other artists drew their inspiration from comic strips. Derived from mass culture, these works were mass-produced and deliberately "of the moment," expressing the fleeting whims of popular culture.

Postmodernism's eclectic commingling of past tradition with Modernist innovation became increasingly evident in architecture. One example is provided by Charles Moore (1929–1993). His *Piazza d'Italia* (1976–1980) in New Orleans is an outdoor plaza that combines classical Roman columns with stainless steel and neon lights. This blending of modern-day materials with historical references distinguished the Postmodern architecture of the late 1970s and 1980s from the Modernist glass box.

ART IN THE AGE OF COMMERCE: THE 1980S AND 1990S Throughout the 1980s and 1990s, the art and music industries increasingly adopted the techniques of marketing and advertising. With large sums of money invested in painters and musicians, pressure mounted to achieve critical and commercial success. Negotiating the distinction between art and popular culture was essential as many people equated merit with sales or economic value rather than aesthetic considerations.

In the art world, Neo-Expressionism reached its zenith in the mid-1980s. The economic boom and free spending of the Reagan years contributed to a thriving art scene in the United States. Neo-Expressionist artists like Anselm Kiefer (AN-selm KEEF-uhr) (b. 1945) became increasingly popular as the art market soared. Born in Germany the year the war ended, Kiefer combines aspects of Abstract Expressionism, collage, and German Expressionism to create works that are stark and haunting.

The World of Science and Technology

Many of the scientific and technological achievements since World War II have revolutionized people's lives. During World War II, university scientists were recruited to work for their governments and develop new weapons and practical instruments of war. British physicists played a crucial role

in the development of an improved radar system that helped defeat the German air force in the Battle of Britain in 1940. German scientists created self-propelled rockets as well as jet airplanes to keep Hitler's hopes alive for a miraculous turnaround in the war. The computer, too, was a wartime creation. The British mathematician Alan Turing designed a primitive computer to assist British intelligence in breaking the secret codes of German ciphering machines. The most famous product of wartime scientific research was the atomic bomb, created by a team of American and European scientists under the guidance of the physicist J. Robert Oppenheimer. Many wartime devices were created for destructive purposes, but computers and breakthrough technologies such as nuclear energy were soon adapted for peacetime uses.

The sponsorship of research by governments and the military during World War II created a new scientific model. Science had become very complex, and only large organizations with teams of scientists, huge laboratories, and complicated equipment could undertake large-scale scientific projects. The requisite facilities were so expensive that they could be provided only by governments or large corporations.

There was no more stunning example of how the new scientific establishment operated than the space race of the 1960s. The announcement by the Soviets in 1957 that they had sent the first space satellite, *Sputnik*, into orbit around the earth spurred the United States to launch an ambitious project to land a manned spacecraft on the moon within a decade. Massive amounts of government money financed the scientific research and technological advances that attained this goal in 1969.

In 2004, two vehicles sent by the National Aeronautics and Space Administration (NASA) arrived on the planet Mars. These Mars rovers, called *Spirit* and *Opportunity*, landed three weeks apart on different parts of the planet. Both contained instruments that determine the chemical content of rocks. Based on the minerals found in Mars rocks, NASA scientists were able to conclude that the now barren planet once had generous supplies of water. NASA plans additional missions to Mars to help prepare for the eventual landing of humans on the planet.

The postwar alliance of science and technology led to an accelerated rate of change that has become a fact of life in Western society (see the comparative essay "From the Industrial Age to the Technological Age" on p. 852). One product of this alliance—the computer—may yet prove to be the most revolutionary of all the technological inventions of the twentieth century. Early computers, which required thousands of vacuum tubes to function, were large and hot and took up considerable space. The development of the transistor and then the silicon chip produced a revolutionary new approach to computer design. With the invention in 1971 of the microprocessor, a machine that combines the equivalent of thousands of transistors on a single, tiny silicon chip, the road was open for the development of the personal computer. By the 1990s, the personal computer had become a regular fixture in businesses, schools, and homes. The Internet—the world's largest computer network, launched in the 1980s by the U.S. government—provides millions of people around the world with quick access to immense quantities of information, as well as rapid communication and commercial transactions. By 2000, an estimated 500 million people were using the Internet.

Despite the marvels produced by science and technology, some people came to question the underlying assumption of this alliance—that scientific knowledge gave human beings the ability to manipulate the environment for their benefit. They maintained that some technological advances had far-reaching side effects damaging to the environment. The chemical fertilizers, for example, that were touted for producing larger crops wreaked havoc with the ecological balance of streams, rivers, and woodlands.

Varieties of Religious Life

Existentialism was one response to the despair generated by the apparent collapse of civilized values in the twentieth century. A revival of religion was another. Ever since the Enlightenment of the eighteenth century, Christianity had been on the defensive. But in the twentieth century, a number of religious leaders attempted to bring new life to the faith.

In the Catholic Church, attempts at religious renewal came from two charismatic popes—John XXIII and John Paul II. Pope John XXIII (1881–1963) reigned for only a short time (1958–1963) but sparked a dramatic revival of Catholicism when he summoned the twenty-first ecumenical council of the church. Known as Vatican Council II, it liberalized a number of Catholic practices. The Mass was henceforth to be celebrated in the vernacular languages rather than Latin. New avenues of communication with other Christian faiths were also opened for the first time since the Reformation.

John Paul II (1920–2005), who had been the archbishop of Krakow in Poland before his elevation to the papacy in 1978, was the first non-Italian to be elected pope since the sixteenth century. Although he alienated a number of people by reasserting traditional Catholic teaching on such issues as birth control, women in the priesthood, and clerical celibacy, John Paul's numerous travels around the world helped strengthen the Catholic Church throughout the non-Western world. A strong believer in social justice, the charismatic John Paul II was a powerful figure reminding Europeans of their spiritual heritage and the need to temper the pursuit of materialism with spiritual concerns.

FUNDAMENTALISM Despite the revival of religion after World War II, church attendance in Europe and the United States declined dramatically in the 1960s and 1970s as a result of growing secular attitudes. Yet even though the numbers of regular churchgoers in established Protestant and Catholic churches continued to decline, the number of fundamentalist churches and churchgoers has been growing, especially in the United States.

Fundamentalism was originally a movement within Protestantism that arose early in the twentieth century. Its goal was to maintain a strict traditional interpretation of the Bible and the Christian faith, especially in opposition to the theory of Darwinian evolution and secularism. In the 1980s and

From the Industrial Age to the Technological Age

SCIENCE & TECHNOLOGY

As many observers have noted, a key aspect of the world economy is that it is in the process of transition to what has been called a "postindustrial age," characterized by a system that is not only increasingly global in scope but also increasingly technology-intensive. Since World War II, a stunning array of technological changes—especially in transportation, communications, space exploration, medicine, and agriculture—have transformed the world in which we live. Technological changes have also raised new questions and concerns and led to unexpected results. Some scientists have worried that genetic engineering might accidentally result in new strains of deadly bacteria that cannot be controlled outside the laboratory. Some doctors have recently raised the alarm that the overuse of antibiotics has created supergerms that are resistant to antibiotic treatment. The Technological Revolution has also led to the development of more advanced methods of destruction. Most frightening have been nuclear weapons.

The transition to a technology-intensive postindustrial world, which the futurologist Alvin Toffler has dubbed the Third Wave (the first two being the Agricultural and Industrial Revolutions), has produced difficulties for people in many walks of life—for blue-collar workers, whose high wages price them out of the market as firms begin to move their factories abroad; for the poor and uneducated, who lack the technical skills to handle complex tasks in the contemporary economy; and even for some

© Adastra/Getty Images

The Technological Age. A communication satellite is seen orbiting above the earth.

members of the middle class, who have been fired or forced into retirement as their employers seek to reduce payrolls or outsource jobs to compete in the global marketplace.

It is now increasingly clear that the Technological Revolution, like the Industrial Revolution that preceded it, will entail enormous consequences and may ultimately give birth to a new era of social and political instability. The success of advanced capitalist states in the post–World War II era has been built on a broad consensus on the importance of two propositions: (1) the need for high levels of government investment in education, communications, and transportation as a means of meeting the challenges of continued economic growth and technological innovation and (2) the desirability of cooperative efforts in the international arena as a means of maintaining open markets for the free exchange of goods.

In the twenty-first century, these assumptions are increasingly under attack as citizens refuse to support education and oppose the formation of trading alliances to promote the free movement of goods and labor across national borders. The breakdown of the public consensus that brought modern capitalism to a pinnacle of achievement raises serious questions about the likelihood that the coming challenges of the Third Wave can be successfully met without a growing measure of political and social tension.

 What is implied by the term Third Wave, *and what challenges does the Third Wave present to humanity?*

1990s, fundamentalists became involved in a struggle against such nontheistic belief systems as secular humanism and communism, as well as legalized abortion and homosexuality. Especially in the United States, fundamentalists organized politically to elect candidates who supported their views. This so-called Christian right played an influential role in electing Ronald Reagan and both George Bushes to the presidency.

THE GROWTH OF ISLAM Fundamentalism, however, was not unique to Protestantism. In Islam, the term *fundamentalism* is used to refer to a return to traditional Islamic values, especially in opposition to a perceived weakening of moral strictures due to the corrupting influence of Western ideas and practices. After the Iranian Revolution of 1979, the term was also applied to militant Islamic movements, such as the

Taliban in Afghanistan, that favored militant action against Western influence.

Despite wariness about Islamic radicalism in the aftermath of the September 11, 2001 terrorist attacks on the United States, Islam is growing in both Europe and the United States, thanks primarily to the migration of people from Muslim countries. As Muslim communities became established in France, Germany, Britain, Italy, and Spain during the 1980s and 1990s, they built mosques for religious worship and religious education.

The Explosion of Popular Culture

Especially since World War II, popular culture has played an important role in helping Western people define themselves. It also reflects the economic system that supports it, for this system manufactures, distributes, and sells the images that people consume as popular culture. Modern popular culture is therefore an integral part of the mass consumer society in which it has emerged.

The United States has been the most influential force in shaping popular culture in the West and, to a lesser degree, the rest of the world. Through movies, music, advertising, and television, the United States has spread its particular form of consumerism and the American dream around the globe. Already in 1923, the New York *Morning Post* noted that "the film is to America what the flag was once to Britain. By its means Uncle Sam may hope some day . . . to Americanize the world."[9]

Motion pictures were the primary vehicle for the diffusion of American popular culture in the years immediately following the war and continued to dominate both European and American markets in the next decades. Although developed in the 1930s, television did not become readily available until the late 1940s. By 1954, there were 32 million sets in the United States as television became the centerpiece of middle-class life. In the 1960s, as television spread around the world, American networks exported their products to Europe and developing countries at extraordinarily low prices.

The United States has also dominated popular music since the end of World War II. Jazz, blues, rhythm and blues, rap, rock-and-roll, and hip-hop have been by far the most popular music forms in the Western world—and much of the non-Western

world—during this time. All of them originated in the United States, and all are rooted in African American musical innovations. As these forms spread to the rest of the world, they inspired local artists, who then transformed the music in their own way.

The introduction of the video music channel MTV in the early 1980s radically changed the music scene by making image as important as sound in selling records. Artists like Michael Jackson and Madonna became superstars by treating the music video as an art form. Rather than merely a recorded performance, many videos were short films involving elaborate staging and special effects set to music. Technological advances became prevalent in the music of the 1980s with the advent of the synthesizer, an electronic piano that produced computerized sounds.

Sports have become a major product of both popular culture and the leisure industry. The development of satellite television and various electronic breakthroughs helped make sports a global phenomenon. The Olympic Games can now be broadcast around the world instantly from anyplace on earth. In 2010, approximately 715 million people, or one out of every ten people in the world, watched the World Cup championship match between Spain and the Netherlands. Sports has also become a cheap form of entertainment for consumers as spectators do not have to leave their homes to watch athletic competitions. As sports television revenue has escalated, many sports have come to receive the bulk of their yearly revenue from television contracts.

CHAPTER SUMMARY

Western Europe reinvented itself in the 1950s and 1960s as a remarkable economic recovery fostered a new optimism. Western European states embraced political democracy, and with the development of the European Community, many of them began to move toward economic unity. A new European society also emerged after World War II. White-collar workers increased in number, and installment plan buying helped create a consumer society. The welfare state provided both pensions and health care. Birth control led to smaller families, and more women joined the workforce.

Although many people were optimistic about a "new world order" after the collapse of communism, uncertainties still prevailed. Germany was successfully reunited, and the European Union became even stronger with the adoption of a common currency in the euro. Yugoslavia, however, disintegrated into warring states that eventually all became independent, and ethnic groups that had once been forced to live under distinct national banners began rebelling to form autonomous states. Although some were successful, others were brutally repressed.

In the Western Hemisphere, the United States and Canada built prosperous economies and relatively stable communities in the 1950s, but there, too, new problems, including ethnic,

racial, and linguistic differences, along with economic difficulties, dampened the optimism of earlier decades. Although some Latin American nations shared in the economic growth of the 1950s and 1960s, it was not accompanied by political stability. Not until the 1980s did democratic governments begin with consistency to replace oppressive military regimes.

While the "new world order" was fitfully developing, other challenges emerged. The arrival of many foreigners, especially in Western Europe, not only strained the social services of European countries but also led to antiforeign sentiment and right-wing political parties that encouraged it. Environmental abuses led to growing threats not only to Europeans but also all humans. Terrorism, especially that caused by some parts of the Muslim world, emerged as a threat to many

Western states. Since the end of World War II, terrorism seems to have replaced communism as the number one enemy of the West. At the beginning of the twenty-first century, a major realization has been the recognition that the problems afflicting the Western world have become global problems.

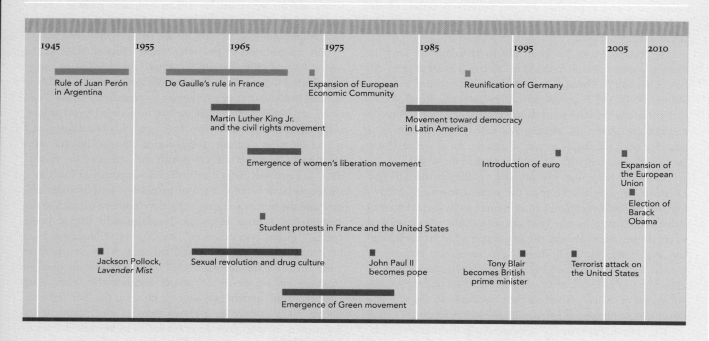

1945	1955	1965	1975	1985	1995	2005	2010

Rule of Juan Perón in Argentina

De Gaulle's rule in France

Expansion of European Economic Community

Reunification of Germany

Martin Luther King Jr. and the civil rights movement

Movement toward democracy in Latin America

Emergence of women's liberation movement

Introduction of euro

Expansion of the European Union

Election of Barack Obama

Student protests in France and the United States

Jackson Pollock, *Lavender Mist*

Sexual revolution and drug culture

John Paul II becomes pope

Tony Blair becomes British prime minister

Terrorist attack on the United States

Emergence of Green movement

CHAPTER REVIEW

Upon Reflection

Q What were the major successes and failures of the Western European democracies between 1945 and 2010?

Q What directions did Eastern European nations take after they became free from Soviet control? Why did they react as they did?

Q What role did popular culture play in the Western world after 1945?

Key Terms

welfare state (p. 824)
socialized medicine (p. 824)
ethnic cleansing (p. 826)
consumer society (p. 839)
permissive society (p. 840)
women's liberation movement (p. 842)
guest workers (p. 846)
existentialism (p. 848)
Postmodernism (p. 848)
poststructuralism (deconstruction) (p. 849)
Abstract Expressionism (p. 850)
fundamentalism (p. 851)

Suggested Reading

EUROPE SINCE 1945 For a well-written survey on Europe since 1945, see **T. Judt**, *Postwar: A History of Europe Since 1945* (New York, 2005). See also **W. I. Hitchcock**, *The Struggle for Europe: The Turbulent History of a Divided Continent, 1945–2002* (New York, 2002). On the

building of common institutions in Western Europe, see **S. Henig**, *The Uniting of Europe: From Discord to Concord* (London, 1997). On Eastern Europe, see **P. Kenney**, *The Burden of Freedom: Eastern Europe Since 1989* (London, 2006).

THE UNITED STATES AND CANADA For a general survey of U.S. history since 1945, see **W. H. Chafe**, *Unfinished Journey: America Since World War II* (Oxford, 2006). More detailed accounts can be found in two volumes by **J. T. Patterson** in the Oxford History of the United States series: *Grand Expectations: The United States, 1945–1974* (Oxford, 1997) and *Restless Giant: The United States from Watergate to Bush v. Gore* (Oxford, 2005). Information on Canada can be found in **C. Brown, ed.**, *The Illustrated History of Canada,* 4th ed. (Toronto, 2003).

LATIN AMERICA For general surveys of Latin American history, see **M. C. Eakin**, *The History of Latin America: Collision of Cultures* (New York, 2007), and **E. Bradford Burns** and **J. A. Charlip**, *Latin America: An Interpretive History,* 8th ed. (Upper Saddle River, N.J., 2007). The twentieth century is the focus of **T. E. Skidmore** and **P. H. Smith**, *Modern Latin America,* 6th ed. (Oxford, 2004).

SOCIETY IN THE WESTERN WORLD On the turbulent 1960s, see **A. Marwick**, *The Sixties: Social and Cultural Transformation in Britain, France, Italy, and the United States* (Oxford, 1999). On the sexual revolution of the 1960s, see **D. Allyn**, *Make Love, Not War: The Sexual Revolution—An Unfettered History* (New York, 2000).

The changing role of women is examined in **R. Rosen**, *The World Split Open: How the Modern Women's Movement Changed America* (New York, 2001). On terrorism, see **C. E. Simonsen** and **J. R. Spendlove**, *Terrorism Today: The Past, the Players, the Future,* 3rd ed. (Upper Saddle River, N.J., 2006). The problems of guest workers and immigrants are examined in **W. Laqueur,** *The Last Days of Europe: Epitaph for an Old Continent* (New York, 2007).

WESTERN CULTURE SINCE 1945 For a general view of postwar thought and culture, see **J. A. Winders,** *European Culture Since 1848: From Modern to Postmodern and Beyond,* rev. ed. (New York, 2001). On Postmodernism, see **C. Butler,** *Postmodernism: A Very Short Introduction* (Oxford, 2002). On the arts, see **A. Marwick,** *Arts in the West Since 1945* (Oxford, 2002).

Go to the CourseMate website at **www.cengagebrain.com** for additional study tools and review materials—including audio and video clips—for this chapter.

Challenges of Nation Building in Africa and the Middle East

© William J. Duiker

The African community, soul of a continent

CHAPTER OUTLINE AND FOCUS QUESTIONS

Uhuru: The Struggle for Independence in Africa

Q What role did nationalist movements play in the transition to independence in Africa, and how did such movements differ from their counterparts elsewhere?

The Era of Independence

Q How have dreams clashed with realities in the independent nations of Africa, and how have African governments sought to meet these challenges?

Continuity and Change in Modern African Societies

Q How did the rise of independent states affect the lives and the role of women in African societies? How does that role compare with the role played by women in other parts of the contemporary world?

Crescent of Conflict

Q What problems have the nations of the Middle East faced since the end of World War II, and to what degree have they managed to resolve them?

Society and Culture in the Contemporary Middle East

Q How have religious issues affected economic, social, and cultural conditions in the Middle East in recent decades?

CRITICAL THINKING

Q What factors can be advanced to explain the chronic instability and internal conflict that have characterized conditions in Africa and the Middle East since World War II?

BY THE END OF World War II, many societies in Asia and Africa had endured more than half a century of colonial rule. Although Europeans complacently assumed that colonialism was a necessary step in the process of introducing civilization to "backward" peoples around the globe, many of their colonial subjects disagreed. Some even argued that the Western drive for political hegemony and economic profit, far from being a panacea for the world's ills, was a plague that threatened ultimately to destroy human civilization.

Few were more outspoken in their contempt for Western culture than the Ghanaian official Michael Francis Dei-Anang (DAY-ahn-NAHNG). In *Whither Bound Africa*, written in 1946, he scathingly unmasked the pretensions of Western superiority:

> *Forward! To what?*
> *To the reeking round*
> *Of medieval crimes,*
> *Where the greedy hawks*
> *of Aryan stock*
> *Prey with bombs and guns*
> *On men of lesser breed?*
> *Forward to CIVILIZATION.*[1]

To observers like Dei-Anang, the new Africa that emerged from imperialist rule had a duty to seek its own ways of resolving the problems of humanity.

One of the aspects of Western civilization that some thoughtful Asians and Africans rejected was the concept of the nation-state as the natural unit of communal identity in the modern world. In their view, nationalism was at the root of many of the evils of the twentieth century and should be abandoned as a model for development in the postwar period. In Africa, some intellectuals pointed to the traditional village community as a unique symbol of the humanistic and spiritual qualities of the people; they felt that the village might serve as a common bond that would knit all the peoples of the continent into a cohesive African community. The nation-state was similarly repudiated by some observers in the Middle East, where many Muslims viewed Western materialist culture as a threat to the fundamental principles of Islam. To fend off the new threat from their old adversary, some leaders dreamed of resurrecting the concept of a global caliphate (see Chapter 7) to unify all Muslim peoples and allow them to pursue their common destiny throughout the Islamic world.

Time has not been kind to such dreams of transnational solidarity and cooperation in the postwar world. Although the peoples of Africa and the Middle East were gradually liberated from the formal trappings of European authority, most political elites in both regions adopted the model of the nation-state with enthusiasm. The results have been mixed, and sometimes costly. Political inexperience and continued European economic domination have frustrated efforts to achieve political stability. At the same time, arbitrary boundaries imposed by the colonial powers, in combination with ethnic and religious divisions, have led to bitter conflicts that undermine attempts to realize the dream of solidarity and cooperation. Today, these two regions, although blessed with enormous potential, are among the most volatile and conflict-ridden areas in the world.

Uhuru: The Struggle for Independence in Africa

 FOCUS QUESTION: What role did nationalist movements play in the transition to independence in Africa, and how did such movements differ from their counterparts elsewhere?

After World War II, Europeans reluctantly recognized that the end result of colonial rule in Africa would be African self-government, if not full independence. Accordingly, the African population would have to be trained to handle the responsibilities of representative government. In many cases, however, relatively little had been done to prepare the local people for self-rule. During the late nineteenth century, African administrators had held influential positions in several British colonies, and one even served as governor of the Gold Coast. But with the formal institution of colonial rule, senior positions were reserved for the British, while local authority remained in the hands of African rulers.

After World War II, most British colonies introduced reforms that increased the representation of the local population. Members of legislative and executive councils were increasingly chosen through elections, and Africans came to constitute a majority of these bodies. Elected councils at the local level were introduced in the 1950s to reduce the power of the chiefs and clan heads, who had controlled local government under indirect rule. An exception was South Africa, where European domination continued. In the Union of South Africa, the franchise was restricted to whites except in the former territory of the Cape Colony, where persons of mixed ancestry had enjoyed the right to vote since the mid-nineteenth century. Black Africans did win some limited electoral rights in Northern and Southern Rhodesia (now Zambia and Zimbabwe, respectively), although whites generally dominated the political scene.

A similar process of political liberalization was taking place in the French colonies. At first, the French tried to integrate the African peoples into French culture. By the 1920s, however, racist beliefs in Western cultural superiority and the tenacity of traditional beliefs and practices among Africans had somewhat discredited this ideal. The French therefore substituted a more limited program of assimilating African elites into Western culture and using them as administrators at the local level as a link to the remainder of the population.

The Colonial Legacy

As in Asia, colonial rule had a mixed impact on the societies and peoples of Africa. The Western presence brought a number of short-term and long-term benefits to Africa, such as improved transportation and communication facilities, and in a few areas laid the foundation for a modern industrial and commercial sector. Improved sanitation and medical care increased life expectancy. The introduction of selective elements of Western political systems laid the groundwork for the gradual creation of democratic societies.

Yet the benefits of westernization were distributed very unequally, and the vast majority of Africans found their lives little improved, if at all. Only South Africa and French-held Algeria, for example, developed modern industrial sectors, extensive railroad networks, and modern communications systems. In both countries, European settlers were numerous, most investment capital for industrial ventures was European, and whites comprised almost the entire professional and managerial class. Members of the local population were generally restricted to unskilled or semiskilled jobs at wages less than one-fifth those enjoyed by Europeans.

Many colonies concentrated on export crops—peanuts in Senegal and Gambia, cotton in Egypt and Uganda, coffee in Kenya, palm oil and cocoa products in the Gold Coast. In some cases, the crops were grown on plantations, which were usually owned by Europeans. But plantation agriculture was not always suitable in Africa, and much farming was done by free or tenant farmers. In some areas, where land ownership was traditionally vested in the community, the land was owned and leased by the corporate village. The vast majority of the profits from the exports, however, accrued to Europeans or to merchants from other foreign countries, such as India and the Arab emirates.

While a fortunate few benefited from the increase in exports, the vast majority of Africans continued to be subsistence farmers growing food for their own consumption. The gap was particularly wide in places like Kenya, where the best lands were reserved for European settlers to make the colony self-sufficient. As in other parts of the world, the early stages of the Industrial Revolution were especially painful for the rural population, and ordinary subsistence farmers reaped few benefits from colonial rule. To make matters worse, in some areas—notably in West Africa—the cultivation of cash crops eroded the fragile soil base and turned farmland into desert.

The Rise of Nationalism

Political organizations for African rights did not arise until after World War I, and then only in a few areas, such as British-ruled Kenya and the Gold Coast. At first, organizations such as the National Congress of British West Africa (formed in 1919 in the Gold Coast) and Jomo Kenyatta's Kikuyu Central Association focused on improving living conditions in the colonies rather than on national independence. After World War II, however, following the example of independence movements elsewhere, these groups became organized political parties with independence as their objective. In the Gold Coast, Kwame Nkrumah (KWAH-may en-KROO-muh) (1909–1972) led the Convention People's Party, the first formal political party in black Africa. In the late 1940s, Jomo Kenyatta (JOH-moh ken-YAHT-uh) (1894–1978) founded the Kenya African National Union (KANU), which focused on economic issues but had an implied political agenda as well.

For the most part, these political activities were nonviolent and were led by Western-educated African intellectuals. Their constituents were primarily urban professionals, merchants, and members of labor unions. But the demand for independence was not restricted to the cities. In Kenya, for example, the widely publicized Mau Mau (MOW MOW ["ow" as in "how"]) movement among the Kikuyu (ki-KOO-yoo) people used guerrilla tactics as an element of its program to achieve *uhuru* (oo-HOO-roo) (Swahili for "freedom") from the British. One of the primary reasons for the revolt was to protest against the unlawful seizure of African lands by European plantation owners. Although only about a hundred Europeans were killed compared with an estimated two thousand Africans who died at the hands of either Mau Mau units or the British, the specter of a nationwide revolt alarmed the European population and convinced the British government in 1959 to promise eventual independence.

In South Africa and Algeria where the political system was also dominated by European settlers, the transition to independence was more complicated. In South Africa, political activity by local Africans began with the formation of the African National Congress (ANC) in 1912. Initially, the ANC was dominated by Western-oriented intellectuals and had limited mass support. Its goal was to achieve economic and political reforms, including full equality for educated Africans, within the framework of the existing system. But the ANC's efforts met with little success, while conservative white parties managed to stiffen the segregation laws and impose a policy of full legal segregation, called **apartheid** (uh-PAHRT-hyt), in 1948. In response, the ANC became increasingly radicalized, and by the 1950s, the prospects for violence rather than conciliation were growing.

In Algeria, resistance to French rule by Berbers and Arabs in rural areas had never ceased. After World War II, urban agitation intensified, leading to a widespread rebellion against colonial rule in the mid-1950s. At first, the French government tried to maintain its authority in Algeria, which was considered an integral part of metropolitan France. But when Charles de Gaulle became president of France in 1958, he reversed French policy, and Algeria became an independent republic four years later, with Ahmad Ben Bella (AH-muhd ben BELL-luh) (1918–2004) as its president. The armed struggle in Algeria hastened the transition to statehood in its neighbors as well. Tunisia won its independence in 1956 after some urban agitation and rural unrest but retained close ties with Paris. The French attempted to suppress the nationalist movement in French Morocco by sending Sultan Muhammad V into exile, but the effort failed, and in 1956, he returned as the ruler of the independent state of Morocco.

Most black African nations achieved their independence in the late 1950s and 1960s, beginning with the Gold Coast, renamed Ghana, in 1957 (see Map 29.1). It was soon followed by Nigeria; the Belgian Congo, renamed Zaire (zah-EER) and then the Democratic Republic of the Congo; Kenya; Tanganyika (tang-an-YEE-kuh), later joined with Zanzibar (ZAN-zi-bar) and renamed Tanzania (tan-zuh-NEE-uh); and several other countries. Most of the French colonies agreed to accept independence within the framework of de Gaulle's French Community. By the late 1960s, only parts of southern Africa and the Portuguese possessions of Mozambique and Angola remained under European rule.

Independence thus came later to Africa than to most of Asia. Several factors help explain the delay. For one thing, colonialism was established in Africa somewhat later than in most areas of Asia, and the inevitable reaction from the local population was consequently later in coming. Furthermore, with the exception of a few areas in West Africa and along the Mediterranean, coherent states with a strong sense of cultural, ethnic, and linguistic unity did not exist in most of Africa. Most traditional states, such as Ashanti (uh-SHAN-tee *or* uh-SHAHN-tee) in West Africa, Songhai (song-HY) in the southern Sahara, and Kongo in the Congo River basin, were collections of heterogeneous peoples with little sense of national or cultural unity. Even after colonies were established, the European powers often practiced a policy of "divide and rule," and the British encouraged political decentralization by retaining the authority of the traditional local chieftains. It is hardly surprising that when opposition to colonial rule emerged, unity was difficult to achieve.

MAP 29.1 **Modern Africa.** This map shows the fifty-four independent states in Africa today.

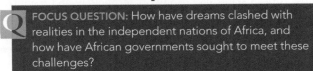

Why was unity so difficult to achieve in African regions?

The Era of Independence

FOCUS QUESTION: How have dreams clashed with realities in the independent nations of Africa, and how have African governments sought to meet these challenges?

The newly independent African states faced intimidating challenges. They had been profoundly affected by colonial rule, but the experience had been highly unsatisfactory in most respects. Although Western political institutions, values, and technology had been introduced, at least in the cities, the exposure to European civilization had been superficial at best for most Africans and tragic for many. At the outset of independence, most African societies were still primarily agrarian and traditional, and their modern sectors depended mainly on imports from the West.

The Destiny of Africa: Unity or Diversity?

Like their counterparts in South and Southeast Asia, most of Africa's new leaders came from the urban middle class. They had studied in Europe or the United States and spoke and read European languages. Although most were profoundly critical of colonial policies, they appeared for the most part to accept the Western model of governance and Western democratic values.

Their views on economics were somewhat more diverse. Some, like Jomo Kenyatta of Kenya and General Mobutu Sese Seko (moh-BOO-too SES-ay SEK-oh) (1930–1997) of Zaire, were advocates of Western-style capitalism. Others, like Julius Nyerere (ny-REHR-ee) (1922–1999) of Tanzania, Kwame Nkrumah of Ghana, and Sékou Touré (say-KOO too-RAY) (1922–1984) of Guinea, preferred an "African form of socialism," which bore scant resemblance to the Marxist-Leninist socialism practiced in the Soviet Union. According to its advocates, it was descended from traditional communal practices in precolonial Africa.

At first, most of the new African leaders accepted the national boundaries established during the colonial era. But as we have noted, these boundaries were artificial creations of the colonial powers. Virtually all of the new states included widely diverse ethnic, linguistic, and territorial groups. Zaire, for example, was composed of more than two hundred territorial groups speaking seventy-five different languages. Such conditions posed a severe challenge to the task of forming cohesive nation-states.

A number of leaders—including Nkrumah of Ghana, Touré of Guinea, and Nyerere of Tanganyika—were enticed by **Pan-Africanism**, the concept of a continental unity that transcended national boundaries. Nkrumah in particular hoped that a pan-African union could be established that would unite all of the new countries of the continent in a broader community. His dream was not widely shared by other African political figures, however, who eventually settled on a more innocuous concept of regional cooperation on key issues. The concrete manifestation of this idea was the Organization of African Unity (OAU), founded in Addis Ababa (AH-diss AH-bah-buh) in 1963 (see the box on p. 860).

Toward African Unity

In May 1963, the leaders of thirty-two African states met in Addis Ababa, the capital of Ethiopia, to discuss the creation of an organization that would represent the interests of all the newly independent countries of Africa. The result was the Organization of African Unity. An excerpt from its charter is presented here. Although the organization did not realize all of the aspirations of its founders, it provided a useful forum for the discussion and resolution of its members' common problems. In 2001, it was replaced by the African Union, which was designed to bring about increased cooperation among the states on the continent; unlike the OAU, the African Union has recognized the need on occasion to intervene in the internal affairs of member nations.

Charter of the Organization of African Unity

We, the Heads of African States and Governments assembled in the City of Addis Ababa, Ethiopia;

CONVINCED that it is the inalienable right of all people to control their own destiny;

CONSCIOUS of the fact that freedom, equality, justice, and dignity are essential objectives for the achievement of the legitimate aspirations of the African peoples;

CONSCIOUS of our responsibility to harness the natural and human resources of our continent for the total advancement of our peoples in spheres of human endeavor;

INSPIRED by a common determination to promote understanding among our peoples and cooperation among our States in response to the aspirations of our peoples for brotherhood and solidarity, in a larger unity transcending ethnic and national differences;

CONVINCED that, in order to translate this determination into a dynamic force in the cause of human progress, conditions for peace and security must be established and maintained;

DETERMINED to safeguard and consolidate the hard-won independence as well as the sovereignty and territorial integrity of our States, and to fight against neocolonialism in all its forms;

DEDICATED to the general progress of Africa; . . .

DESIROUS that all African States should henceforth unite so that the welfare and well-being of their peoples can be assured;

RESOLVED to reinforce the links between our states by establishing and strengthening common institutions;

HAVE agreed to the present Charter.

 What are the key objectives expressed in this charter? To what degree have they been achieved?

Dream and Reality: Political and Economic Conditions in Independent Africa

The program of the OAU called for an Africa based on freedom, equality, justice, and dignity and on the unity, solidarity, prosperity, and territorial integrity of African states. It did not take long for reality to set in. Vast disparities in education and wealth and the lingering effects of colonial domination made it hard to establish material prosperity in much of Africa. Expectations that independence would lead to stable political structures based on "one person, one vote" were soon disappointed as the initial phase of pluralistic governments gave way to a series of military regimes and one-party states. Between 1957 and 1982, more than seventy leaders of African countries were overthrown by violence.

THE PROBLEM OF NEOCOLONIALISM Part of the problem was the residual impact of colonialism. Most new countries in Africa were dependent on the export of a single crop or natural resource. When prices fluctuated or dropped, these countries were at the mercy of the international market. In several cases, the resources were still controlled by foreigners, leading to the charge that colonialism had been succeeded by **neocolonialism**, in which Western domination was maintained primarily by economic rather than political or military means.

World trade patterns often exacerbated these problems. Most African states had to import technology and manufactured goods from the West, and the prices of those goods rose more rapidly than those of the export products. Many of the exports were raw materials, and their prices were often subject to rapid fluctuations.

The new states contributed to their own problems. Treasury funds were squandered on military equipment or expensive consumer goods rather than applied to building up the infrastructure to support and sustain an industrial economy. Corruption, a painful reality throughout the modern world, became almost a way of life in Africa as bribery became necessary to obtain even the most basic services (see the box on p. 861).

AFRICA IN THE COLD WAR Many of the problems encountered by the new nations of Africa have also been ascribed to the fact that independence has not ended Western interference in Africa's political affairs. Many African leaders were

Stealing the Nation's Riches

ART & IDEAS

After 1965, African novelists transferred their anger from the foreign oppressor to their own national leaders, deploring their greed, corruption, and inhumanity. One of the most pessimistic expressions of this betrayal of newly independent Africa is found in *The Beautiful Ones Are Not Yet Born*, a novel published by the Ghanaian author Ayi Kwei Armah (AY-yee KWAY AR-mah) in 1968. The author decried the government of Kwame Nkrumah and was unimpressed with the rumors of a military coup, which, he predicted, would simply replace the regime with a new despot and his entourage of "fat men." Ghana today has made significant progress in reducing the level of corruption.

Ayi Kwei Armah, *The Beautiful Ones Are Not Yet Born*

The net had been made in the special Ghanaian way that allowed the really big corrupt people to pass through it. A net to catch only the small, dispensable fellows, trying in their anguished blindness to leap and to attain the gleam and the comfort the only way these things could be done. And the big ones floated free, like all the slogans. End bribery and corruption. Build Socialism. Equality. Shit. A man would just have to make up his mind that there was never going to be anything but despair, and there would be no way of escaping it. . . .

In the life of the nation itself, maybe nothing really new would happen. New men would take into their hands the power to steal the nation's riches and to use it for their own satisfaction. That, of course, was to be expected. New people would use the country's power to get rid of men and women who talked a language that did not flatter them. There would be nothing different in that. That would only be a continuation of the Ghanaian way of life. But here was the real change. The individual man of power now shivering, his head filled with the fear of the vengeance of those he had wronged. For him everything was going to change. And for those like him who had grown greasy and fat singing the praises of their chief, for those who had been getting themselves ready for the enjoyment of hoped-for favors, there would be long days of pain ahead. The flatterers with their new white Mercedes cars would have to find ways of burying old words. For those who had come directly against the old power, there would be much happiness. But for the nation itself there would only be a change of embezzlers and a change of the hunters and the hunted. A pitiful shrinking of the world from those days Teacher still looked back to, when the single mind was filled with the hopes of a whole people. A pitiful shrinking, to days when all the powerful could think of was to use the power of a whole people to fill their own paunches. Endless days, same days, stretching into the future with no end anywhere in sight.

According to Ayi Kwei Armah, who was to blame for conditions in his country? Did the charter of the OAU (see the box on p. 860) make provisions for dealing with situations such as this?

---

angered when Western powers led by the United States conspired to overthrow the left-leaning politician Patrice Lumumba (puh-TREES loo-MOOM-buh) (1925–1961) in the Congo in the early 1960s. Lumumba, who had been educated in the Soviet Union, aroused fears in Washington that he might promote Soviet influence in Central Africa (see Chapter 26). Eventually, he was assassinated under mysterious circumstances.

The episode was a major factor influencing African leaders to form the OAU as a means of reducing Western influence on the continent, but the strategy achieved few results. Although many African leaders agreed to adopt a neutral stance in the Cold War, competition between Moscow and Washington throughout the region was fierce, often undermining the efforts of fragile governments to build stable new nations. To make matters worse, African states had difficulty achieving a united position on many issues, and their disagreements left the region vulnerable to external influence and conflict. Border disputes festered in many areas of the continent, and in some cases—as with Morocco and a rebel movement in the Western Sahara and between Kenya and Uganda—flared into outright war.

Even within many new African nations, the concept of nationhood was undermined by the lingering force of regionalism or ethnic rivalries. Nigeria, with the largest population on the continent, was rent by civil strife during the late 1960s when dissident Ibo (EE-boh) groups in the southeast attempted unsuccessfully to form the independent state of Biafra (bee-AH-fruh). Another force undermining nationalism in Africa was that of pan-Islamism. Its prime exponent in Africa was the Egyptian president Gamal Abdul Nasser (guh-MAHL AB-dool NAH-sur) (see "Nasser and Pan-Arabism" later in this chapter). After Nasser's death in 1970, the torch of Islamic unity in Africa was carried by the Libyan president Muammar Qaddafi (moo-AHM-ahr guh-DAH-fee) (b. 1942), whose ambitions to create a greater Muslim nation in the Sahara under his authority led to conflict with neighboring Chad. The Islamic resurgence also surfaced in Nigeria and other nations of West Africa, where divisions between Muslims and Christians began to emerge and have recently erupted into violence.

THE POPULATION BOMB Finally, rapid population growth crippled efforts to create modern economies. By the 1980s, annual population growth averaged nearly 3 percent throughout Africa, the highest rate of any continent. Drought conditions and the inexorable spread of the Sahara (usually known as *desertification*), caused partly by overcultivation of the land, led to widespread hunger and starvation, first in West African countries such as Niger and Mali and then in Ethiopia, Somalia, and the Sudan.

Predictions are that the population of Africa will increase by at least 200 million over the next ten years, but that estimate does not take into account the prevalence of AIDS, which has reached epidemic proportions in Africa. According to a United Nations study, at least 5 percent of the entire population of sub-Saharan Africa is infected with the virus, including a high percentage of the urban middle class. More than 65 percent of the AIDS cases reported around the world are on the continent of Africa. Some observers estimate that without measures to curtail the effects of the disease, it will have a significant impact on several African countries by reducing population growth.

Today poverty is widespread in Africa, particularly among the three-quarters of the population still living off the land. Urban areas have grown tremendously, but as in much of Asia, most are surrounded by massive squatter settlements of rural peoples who have fled to the cities in search of a better life. The expansion of the cities has overwhelmed fragile transportation and sanitation systems and led to rising pollution and perpetual traffic jams, while millions are forced to live without running water and electricity. Meanwhile, the fortunate few (all too often government officials on the take) live the high life and emulate the consumerism of the West (in a particularly expressive phrase, the rich in many East African countries are known as *wabenzi*, or "Mercedes-Benz people").

In "Pedestrian, to Passing Benz-Man," the Kenyan poet Albert Ojuka (oh-JOO-kuh) voiced the popular discontent with economic inequality in the 1970s:

> You man, lifted gently
> out of the poverty and suffering
> we so recently shared; I say—
> why splash the muddy puddle on to
> my bare legs, as if, still unsatisfied
> with your seated opulence
> you must sully the unwashed
> with your diesel-smoke and mud-water
> and force him to buy, beyond his means
> a bar of soap from your shop?
> a few years back we shared a master
> today you have none, while I have
> exchanged a parasite for something worse.
> But maybe a few years is too long a time.[2]

It is a lament still voiced today.

The Search for Solutions

While the problems of nation building described here have to one degree or another afflicted all of the emerging states of Africa, each has sought to deal with the challenge in its own way, sometimes with strikingly different consequences. Some African countries have made dramatic improvements in the past two decades, but others have encountered increasing difficulties. Despite all its shared problems, Africa today remains one of the most diverse regions of the globe.

TANZANIA: AN AFRICAN ROUTE TO SOCIALISM

Concern over the dangers of economic inequality inspired a number of African leaders to restrict foreign investment and nationalize the major industries and utilities while promoting democratic ideals and values. Julius Nyerere of Tanzania was the most consistent, promoting the ideals of socialism and self-reliance through his Arusha (uh-ROO-shuh) Declaration of 1967, which set forth the principles for building a socialist society in Africa. Nyerere did not seek to establish a Leninist-style dictatorship of the proletariat in Tanzania, but neither was he a proponent of a multiparty democracy, which in his view would be divisive under the conditions prevailing in Africa:

> Where there is one party—provided it is identified with the nation as a whole—the foundations of democracy can be firmer, and the people can have more opportunity to exercise a real choice, than when you have two or more parties.

Manioc, Food for the Millions. Manioc (also called cassava or yuca), a tuber like the potato, was brought to Africa from South America soon after the voyages of Columbus. Although low in nutrient value, it can be cultivated in poor soil with little moisture and is the staple food for nearly one-third of the population of sub-Saharan Africa. Manioc is also widely grown in other parts of Asia and South America and is familiar to Westerners as the source of tapioca. In the photograph shown here, village women in Senegal rhythmically pound manioc to remove traces of naturally occurring cyanide that would otherwise poison those who rely on the tuber as a basic commodity. As the threat of chronic drought becomes an ever more common reality in parts of Africa, dry crops like manioc will acquire increasing importance in the diet of the African people.

To import the Western parliamentary system into Africa, he argued, could lead to violence because the opposition parties would be viewed as traitors by the majority of the population.[3]

Taking advantage of his powerful political influence, Nyerere placed limits on income and established village collectives to avoid the corrosive effects of economic inequality and government corruption. Sympathetic foreign countries provided considerable economic aid to assist the experiment, and many observers noted that levels of corruption, political instability, and ethnic strife were lower in Tanzania than in many other African countries. Nyerere's vision was not shared by all of his compatriots, however. Political elements on the island of Zanzibar, citing the stagnation brought by two decades of socialism, agitated for autonomy or even total separation from the mainland. Tanzania also has poor soil, inadequate rainfall, and limited resources, all of which have contributed to its slow growth and continuing rural and urban poverty.

In 1985, Nyerere voluntarily retired from the presidency. In his farewell speech, he confessed that he had failed to achieve many of his ambitious goals to create a socialist society in Africa. In particular, he admitted that his plan to collectivize the traditional private farm (*shamba*) had run into strong resistance from conservative peasants. "You can socialize what is not traditional," he remarked. "The *shamba* can't be socialized." But Nyerere insisted that many of his policies had succeeded in improving social and economic conditions, and he argued that the only real solution was to consolidate the multitude of small countries in the region into a larger East African Federation. Today, a quarter of a century later, Nyerere's party, the Party of the Revolution, continues to rule the country. The current president, Jakaya Kikwete (jah-KAH-yah kee-KWEH-tee) (b. 1950), was reelected in 2010 by a comfortable margin, although there were charges of electoral fraud.

KENYA: THE PERILS OF CAPITALISM The countries that opted for capitalism faced their own dilemmas. Neighboring Kenya, blessed with better soil in the highlands, a local tradition of aggressive commerce, and a residue of European settlers, welcomed foreign investment and profit incentives. The results have been mixed. Kenya has a strong current of indigenous African capitalism and a substantial middle class, mostly based in the capital, Nairobi (ny-ROH-bee). But landlessness, unemployment, and income inequities are high, even by African standards (almost one-fifth of the country's 41 million people are squatters, and unemployment is currently estimated at 40 percent). The rate of population growth—about 2.5 percent annually—is one of the higher rates in the world. Almost 80 percent of the population remains rural, and 50 percent of the people live below the poverty line. The result has been widespread unrest in a country formerly admired for its successful development.

Kenya's problems have been exacerbated by chronic disputes between disparate ethnic groups and simmering tensions between farmers and pastoralists, leading some to question whether the country is capable of achieving political stability (see the box on p. 864). For many years, the country

maintained a fragile stability under the dictatorial rule of President Daniel arap Moi (ah-RHAP moh-YEE) (b. 1924), one of the most authoritarian of African leaders. Plagued by charges of corruption, Moi finally agreed to retire in 2002, but under his successor, Mwai Kibaki (MWY kih-BAH-kee) (b. 1931), the twin problems of political instability and widespread poverty continue to afflict the country. When presidential elections held in January 2008 led to a victory for Kibaki's party, opposition elements—angered by the government's perceived favoritism toward Kibaki's Kikuyu constituency—launched numerous protests, and violent riots occurred throughout the country. A fragile truce was eventually put in place, but popular anger at current conditions smolders just beneath the surface.

ANGOLA AND ETHIOPIA: EXPERIMENTS IN MARXISM Beginning in the mid-1970s, a few African nations decided to adopt Soviet-style Marxism-Leninism. In Angola and Ethiopia, Marxist parties followed the Soviet model and attempted to create fully socialist societies with the assistance of Soviet experts and Cuban troops and advisers. Economically, the results were disappointing, and both countries faced severe internal opposition. In Ethiopia, the revolt by Muslim guerrilla fighters in the province of Eritrea (er-ih-TREE-uh) led to the fall of the Marxist leader Mengistu Haile Mariam (men-GIS-too HY-lee MAHR-ee-uhm) (b. 1937) and his regime in 1990 and the eventual independence of Eritrea. A similar revolt erupted against the government in Angola, with the rebel group UNITA controlling much of the rural population and for a time threatening the capital city of Luanda (loo-AHN-duh). With the death of the rebel leader Julius Savimbi (suh-VIM-bee) in 2002, the civil war finally appeared to be at an end.

SOUTH AFRICA: AN END TO APARTHEID Perhaps Africa's greatest success story is in South Africa, where the white government, which long maintained a policy of racial segregation (apartheid) and restricted black sovereignty to a series of small "Bantustans" in relatively infertile areas of the country, finally accepted the inevitability of African involvement in the political process and the national economy. A key factor in the decision was growing international pressure in the form of a campaign to persuade foreign investors to withdraw funds from the country. In 1990, the government of President F. W. (Frederik Willem) de Klerk (b. 1936) released African National Congress leader Nelson Mandela (man-DELL-uh) (b. 1918) from prison, where he had been held since 1964. In 1993, the two leaders agreed to hold democratic national elections the following spring. In the meantime, ANC representatives agreed to take part in a transitional coalition government with de Klerk's National Party. Those elections resulted in a substantial majority for the ANC, and Mandela became president.

In May 1996, a new constitution was approved, calling for a multiracial state. The National Party immediately went into opposition, claiming that the new charter did not adequately provide for joint decision making by members of the coalition. The third group in the coalition government, the

Meeting the Challenges of Independence

POLITICS & GOVERNMENT

Tom Mboya (uhm-BOY-yuh) (1930–1969) was an inspiring political figure in Kenya during the era of early independence. As minister of labor during the transition to statehood, he urged his fellow Kenyans to believe in the prospect of independence, while calming the anxieties of European residents by assuring them that their lives and property would not be threatened or confiscated. This selection is from a speech he delivered in July 1962, in which he recognized the challenges of independence while expressing confidence that the experiment would inevitably succeed. In 1969, Mboya was assassinated by a political opponent.

Tom Mboya, "Kenya as a Nation," July 23, 1962

It is suggested by some people that there is no such thing as a Kenya nation. All kinds of arguments and recriminations are thrown up to try to prove that any nationalist ambitions for Kenya must encounter more difficulties than could ever be overcome. Noisy minorities in all walks of life, both here and in their contact with overseas interests, keep plugging away at their "no confidence" theme. Some people say that Kenya is heading for economic disaster and political chaos and tribal war. . . .

When I talk now about a "Kenya nation," I am not speaking as a political romantic, but as a realist. Any sincere politician or leader must have some vision in front of him. There must be something much more than notoriety to attract him toward unceasing work, the bitterness of struggle, the temptations, and the pressures. There must be a factor of dedication, an undeniable impulse to build and to serve. In this he must satisfy himself. There are very few other rewards.

It is not only the vision of the leaders that dictates our struggle. There are the deep-rooted aspirations of our people. These people may appear simple and uneducated; they may not be articulate, but they are human beings and not stones. They have an inborn pride and a genuine desire for self-improvement and self-fulfilment. These are facts which may have dodged many people in the past but with which we all must reckon in the future. To ignore this force would be to lead to frustrations and explosions—indeed we have already had such an experience in Kenya.

It is not, however, the fear of this force that should dictate our decisions. There is the positive side of this force, namely, its ability to face the challenge of nation building. We have to release this force of our people for new and constructive purposes. We have to harness the enthusiasm for self-improvement to form the spearhead in our efforts for nation-building.

True, we have tribal differences and sensitivities. So often people point at the Congo and warn that Kenya is doomed to become another Congo. I do not share this view. We have passed the stage when this could have happened. We have passed through more trials than most African countries, and I believe we have come to appreciate freedom to a point where we would be prepared to defend it with our lives. We do not intend to exchange British colonialism for either local dictatorship or Soviet and American colonialism.

 Why is the author of this document confident that the people of Kenya can surmount the challenges of nationhood?

Zulu-based Inkatha Freedom Party, agreed to remain within the government, but rivalry between the ANC and Zulu elites intensified. Zulu chief Mangosuthu Buthelezi (MANG-goh-soo-too boo-tuh-LAY-zee) (b. 1928), drawing on the growing force of Zulu nationalism, began to invoke the memory of the great nineteenth-century Zulu ruler Shaka in a possible bid at future independence.

In 1999, a major step toward political stability was taken when Nelson Mandela stepped down from the presidency and was replaced by his longtime disciple Thabo Mbeki (TAH-boh uhm-BAY-kee) (b. 1942). The new president faced a number of intimidating problems, including rising unemployment, widespread lawlessness, chronic corruption, and an ominous flight of capital and professional personnel from the country. Mbeki's conservative economic policies earned the support of some white voters and the country's new black elite but were criticized by labor unions, which contended that the benefits of the new black leadership were not seeping down to the poor. The government's promises to

carry out an extensive land reform program—aimed at providing farmland to the nation's 40 million black farmers—were not fulfilled, leading some squatters to seize unused private lands near Johannesburg.

In 2008, Mbeki was forced out of office by disgruntled ANC party members. A year later, his onetime vice president and rival Jacob Zuma (ZOO-muh) (b. 1942) was elected president. Although the country faces serious challenges, South Africa remains the wealthiest and most industrialized state in Africa and the best hope that a multiracial society can succeed on the continent. The country's black elite now number nearly one-quarter of its wealthiest households, compared with only 9 percent in 1991.

NIGERIA: A NATION DIVIDED If the situation in South Africa provides grounds for modest optimism, the situation in Nigeria provides reason for serious concern. Africa's largest country in terms of population and one of its wealthiest because of substantial oil reserves, Nigeria was for many years in the

New Housing for the Poor. Under apartheid, much of the black population in South Africa was confined to so-called townships, squalid slums located along the fringes of the country's major cities. The top photo shows a crowded township on the edge of Cape Town, one of the most modern cities on the continent of Africa. Today, the government is actively building new communities that provide better housing, running water, and electricity for their residents. The photo on the bottom shows a new township rising on the outskirts of the city of New London. The township has many modern facilities and even a new shopping mall with consumer goods for local residents.

grip of military strongmen. During his rule, General Sani Abacha (SAH-nee ah-BAH-chuh) (1943–1998) ruthlessly suppressed all opposition and in late 1995 ordered the execution of author Ken Saro-Wiwa (SAH-roh-WEE-wah) (1941–1995) despite widespread protests from human rights groups abroad. Saro-Wiwa had criticized environmental damage caused by foreign oil interests in southern Nigeria, but the regime's major concern was his support for separatist activities in the area that had launched the Biafran insurrection in the late 1960s. When Abacha died in 1998 under mysterious circumstances, national elections led to the creation of a civilian government under Olusegun Obasanjo (ohl-OO-seh-goon oh-buh-SAHN-joh) (b. 1937).

Civilian leadership has not been a panacea for Nigeria's problems, however. Although Obasanjo promised reforms to bring an end to the corruption and favoritism that had long plagued Nigerian politics, the results were disappointing (the

state power company—known as NEPA—was so inefficient that Nigerians joked that the initials stood for "never expect power again"). When presidential elections held in 2007 led to the election of Umaru Yar'Adua (oo-MAHR-oo YAHR-ah-doo-uh (b. 1951–2010), an obscure member of Obasanjo's ruling political party, opposition forces and neutral observers complained that the vote had been seriously flawed. After Yar'Adua died from an illness in 2010, he was succeeded by his vice president, Goodluck Jonathan (b. 1951), who was elected president in his own right in 2011.

One of the most critical problems facing the Nigerian government in recent years has been rooted in religious disputes. In early 2000, riots between Christians and Muslims broke out in several northern cities as a result of the decision by Muslim provincial officials to apply *Shari'a* throughout their jurisdictions. The violence abated as local officials managed to craft compromise policies that limit the application of some of the harsher aspects of Muslim law, but the dispute continues to threaten the fragile unity of Africa's most populous country. The election of Goodluck Jonathan, a Christian, in 2011 led to new protests among Muslims in the northern part of the country. Under an unwritten agreement, the presidency has alternated between Muslims and Christians, and some Muslims argued that a Muslim should hold the office because Yar'Adua, a Muslim, had died before he could serve a second term.

TENSIONS IN THE DESERT The religious tensions that erupted in Nigeria have spilled over into neighboring states on the border of the Sahara. Pressure to apply *Sha-ri'a* is spreading to Nigeria's northern neighbor, Niger, where the government has opposed Islamic law on the grounds that it would unsettle the country. Christian churches have been attacked, and bars and brothels have been sacked and burned to the ground.

A similar rift between farmers and herders has been at the root of the lengthy civil war that has been raging in Sudan. Conflict between Muslim pastoralists—supported by the central government in Khartoum—and predominantly Christian black farmers in the southern part of the country was finally brought to an end in 2004, and the government agreed to permit a plebiscite in the south under the sponsorship of the United Nations to determine whether the local population there wished to secede from the country. In elections held in early 2011, voters overwhelmingly supported independence as the new nation of the Republic of South Sudan.

In the meantime, the violence in the south had spread to western Darfur province, where clashes between farmers and armed pastoral people led to reports of widespread starvation among the local villagers. The United Nations, joined by other African countries, has sought to bring an end to the bloodshed. The violence continues, however, and now threatens to overflow into neighboring Chad.

The dispute between Muslims and Christians throughout the southern Sahara is a contemporary variant of the traditional tensions that have existed between farmers and pastoralists throughout recorded history. Muslim cattle herders, migrating southward to escape the increasing desiccation of the grasslands south of the Sahara, compete for precious land with primarily Christian farmers. As a result of the religious revival now under way throughout the continent, the confrontation often leads to outbreaks of violence with strong religious and ethnic overtones (see the comparative essay "Religion and Society" on p. 867).

CENTRAL AFRICA: CAULDRON OF CONFLICT The most tragic situation is in the Central African states of Rwanda and Burundi, where a chronic conflict between the minority Tutsis and the Hutu majority has led to a bitter civil war, with thousands of refugees fleeing to the neighboring Congo. The Tutsis, supported by the colonial Belgian government, had long dominated the sedentary Hutu population. The Hutus' attempt to bring an end to Tutsi domination initiated the most recent conflicts, which have been marked by massacres on both sides. In the meantime, the presence of large numbers of foreign troops and refugees intensified centrifugal forces inside Zaire, where General Mobutu Sese Seko had long ruled with an iron hand. In 1997, military forces led by Mobutu's longtime opponent Laurent-Désiré Kabila (loh-RAHN-DAY-zee-

Morning in Timbuktu. The boundary between pastoral and agricultural peoples—the steppe and the sown—has been one of the crucial fault lines in human history. Nowhere is this more true today than in West Africa, where Muslim herders compete with Christian farmers for precious land and water resources. The dispute is at the root of the ethnic and religious conflicts that are now erupting throughout the region. In this photo, a pastoral family greets the new day just outside the historic city of Timbuktu, in the state of Mali. Once an important commercial hub on the trans-Saharan trade routes, Timbuktu is today a sleepy river port on the edge of the vast Sahara.

© Ruth Petzold

COMPARATIVE ESSAY

Religion and Society

RELIGION & PHILOSOPHY

The nineteenth and twentieth centuries witnessed a steady trend toward the secularization of society as people increasingly turned from religion to science for explanations of natural phenomena and for answers to the challenges of everyday life.

In recent years, however, the trend has reversed as religious faith in all its guises appears to be reviving in much of the world. Although the percentage of people attending religious services on a regular basis or professing firm religious convictions has been dropping steadily in many countries, the intensity of religious belief appears to be growing among the faithful. This phenomenon has been widely publicized in the United States, where the evangelical movement has become a significant force in politics and an influential factor in defining many social issues. But it has also occurred in Latin America, where a drop in membership in the Roman Catholic Church has been offset by significant increases in the popularity of evangelical Protestant sects. In the Muslim world, the influence of traditional Islam has been steadily on the rise, not only in the Middle East but also in non-Arab countries such as Malaysia and Indonesia (see Chapter 30). In Africa, as we observe in this chapter, the appeal of both Christianity and Islam appears to be on the rise. Even in Russia and China, where half a century of Communist government sought to eradicate religion as the "opiate of the people," the popularity of religion is growing.

One major reason for the increasing popularity of religion in contemporary life is the desire to counter the widespread sense of malaise brought on by the absence of any sense of meaning and purpose in life—a purpose that religious faith provides. For many

evangelical Christians in the United States, for example, the adoption of a Christian lifestyle is seen as a necessary prerequisite for resolving problems of crime, drugs, and social alienation. It is likely that a similar phenomenon is present with other religions and in other parts of the world. Religious faith also provides a sense of community at a time when village and family ties are declining in many countries.

Historical evidence suggests, however, that although religious fervor may enhance the sense of community and commitment among believers, it can have a highly divisive impact on society as a whole, as the examples of Northern Ireland, Yugoslavia, Africa, and the Middle East vividly attest. Even if less dramatically, as in the United States and Latin America, religion divides as well as unites, and it will be a continuing task for religious leaders of all faiths to promote tolerance for peoples of other persuasions.

Another challenge for contemporary religion is to find ways to coexist with expanding scientific knowledge. Influential figures in the evangelical movement in the United States, for example, not only support a conservative social agenda but are also suspicious of the role of technology and science in the contemporary world. Similar views are often expressed by significant factions in other world religions. Although fear of the impact of science on contemporary life is widespread, efforts to turn the clock back to a mythical golden age are not likely to succeed in the face of powerful forces for change set in motion by advances in scientific knowledge.

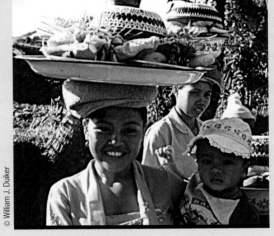

© William J. Duiker

Carrying Food to the Temple. Bali is the only island in Indonesia where the local population adheres to the Hindu faith. Here worshipers carry food to the local temple to be blessed before being consumed.

 What are some of the reasons for the growing intensity of religious faith in many parts of the world today?

---

ray kah-BEE-luh) (1939–2001) managed to topple the general's corrupt government. Once in power, Kabila renamed the country the Democratic Republic of the Congo and promised a return to democratic practices. The new government systematically suppressed political dissent, however, and in January 2001, Kabila was assassinated. He was succeeded by his son Joseph Kabila (b. 1971). Peace talks to end the conflict began that fall, but the fighting has continued.

Africa: A Continent in Flux

The brief survey of events in some of the more important African countries provided here illustrates the enormous

difficulty that historians of Africa face in drawing any general conclusions about the pace and scope of change that has taken place in the continent in recent decades. Progress in some areas has been countered by growing problems elsewhere, and signs of hope in one region contrast with feelings of despair in another.

The shifting fortunes experienced throughout the continent are most prominently illustrated in the political arena. Over the past two decades, the collapse of one-party regimes has led to the emergence of fragile democracies in several countries. In other instances, however, democratic governments erupted in civil war or were replaced by authoritarian leaders. One prominent example of the latter is the Ivory Coast, long considered one of West Africa's most stable and prosperous countries. After the death of President Félix Houphouet-Boigny (fay-LEEKS oo-FWAY-bwah-NYEE) in 1993, long-simmering resentment between Christians in the south and newly arrived Muslim immigrants in the north erupted into open conflict. National elections held in 2010 led to sporadic violence and a standoff between opposition forces and the sitting president, who was forced to resign the following year. By contrast, in Liberia, a bitter civil war recently gave way to the emergence of a stable democratic government under Ellen Johnson-Sirleaf (b. 1938), one of the continent's first female presidents.

The economic picture in Africa has also been mixed. It is clear that African societies have not yet begun to surmount the challenges they have faced since independence. Most African states are still poor and their populations illiterate. Moreover, African concerns continue to carry little weight in the international community. A recent agreement by the World Trade Organization (WTO) on the need to reduce agricultural subsidies in the advanced nations has been widely ignored. In 2000, the General Assembly of the United Nations passed the Millennium Declaration, which called for a dramatic reduction in the incidence of poverty, hunger, and illiteracy worldwide by the year 2015. So far, however, efforts to realize these ambitious goals have been limited. At a conference on the subject in September 2005, the participants squabbled over how to fund the effort. Some delegations, including that of the United States, argued that external assistance cannot succeed unless the nations of Africa adopt measures to bring about good government and sound economic policies.

Despite the African continent's chronic economic problems, however, there are signs of hope. The overall rate of economic growth for the region as a whole is twice what it was during the 1980s and 1990s. African countries were also less affected by the recent economic downturn than was much of the rest of the world. Although poverty, AIDs, and a lack of education and infrastructure are still major impediments in much of the region, rising commodity prices—most notably, an increase in oil revenues—are enabling many countries to make additional investments and reduce their national debt. One promising sign is that the African people as a whole are not about to despair. In a recent survey of public opinion throughout the continent, the majority of respondents were optimistic about the future and confident that they would be economically better off in five years.

Certainly, part of the solution to the continent's multiple problems must come from within. Although there are gratifying signs of progress toward political stability in some countries, others are still governed by brutal dictatorships or racked by civil strife. Corruption and political inexperience are serious problems as well. But many of Africa's difficulties are a consequence of interference by foreign governments and international corporations. Efforts by Western governments to protect their local farmers by providing subsidies or levying high tariffs have hurt African growers in countries where agricultural products are a major export crop. Foreign corporations interfere in local politics and impede the normal political process, often to the detriment of local populations.

THE AFRICAN UNION: A GLIMMER OF HOPE A significant part of the problem is that Africans must find better ways to cooperate with one another and to protect and promote their own interests. A first step in that direction was taken in 1991, when the OAU agreed to establish the African Economic Community (AEC). In 2001, the OAU was replaced by the **African Union**, which is intended to provide greater political and economic integration throughout the continent on the pattern of the European Union (see Chapter 28). The new organization has already sought to mediate several of the conflicts in the region.

As Africa evolves, it is useful to remember that economic and political change is often an agonizingly slow and painful process. Introduced to industrialization and concepts of Western democracy only a century ago, African societies are still groping for ways to graft Western political institutions and economic practices onto a structure still significantly influenced by traditional values and attitudes.

Continuity and Change in Modern African Societies

 FOCUS QUESTIONS: How did the rise of independent states affect the lives and the role of women in African societies? How does that role compare with the role played by women in other parts of the contemporary world?

In general, the impact of the West has been greater on urban and educated Africans and more limited on their rural and illiterate compatriots. One reason is that the colonial presence was first and most firmly established in the cities. Many cities, including Dakar, Lagos, Johannesburg, Cape Town, Brazzaville, and Nairobi, are direct products of the colonial experience. Most African cities today look like their counterparts elsewhere in the world. They have high-rise buildings, blocks of residential apartments, wide boulevards, neon lights, movie theaters, and traffic jams.

Education

The educational system has been the primary means of introducing Western values and culture. In the precolonial era, formal schools did not really exist in Africa except for parochial schools in Christian Ethiopia and academies to train young males in Islamic doctrine and law in Muslim societies in North and West Africa. For the average African, education took place at the home or in the village courtyard and stressed socialization and vocational training. Traditional education in Africa was not necessarily inferior to that in Europe. Social values and customs were transmitted to the young by storytellers, often village elders, who could gain considerable prestige through their performance.

Europeans introduced modern Western education into Africa in the nineteenth century. At first, the schools

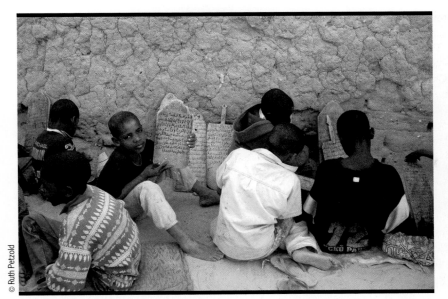

Learning the ABCs in Niger. Educating the young is one of the most crucial problems for many African societies today. Few governments are able to allocate the funds necessary to meet the challenge, so religious organizations—Muslim or Christian—often take up the slack. In this photo, students at a madrasa—a Muslim school designed to teach the Qur'an—are learning how to read Arabic, the language of Islam's holy scripture. Madrasas are one of the most prominent forms of schooling in Muslim societies in West Africa today.

on p. 870): they farm or hunt by traditional methods, practice time-honored family rituals, and believe in the traditional deities. Even here, however, change is taking place. Slavery has been eliminated, for the most part, although there have been persistent reports of raids by slave traders on defenseless villages in the southern Sudan. Economic need, though, has brought about massive migrations as some leave to work on plantations, others move to the cities, and still others flee abroad or to refugee camps to escape starvation. Migration itself is a wrenching experience, disrupting familiar family and village ties and enforcing new social relationships.

Nowhere, in fact, is the dichotomy between old and new, local and foreign, rural and urban so clear and painful as in Africa. Urban dwellers regard the village as the repository of all that is backward in the African past, while rural peoples view the growing urban areas as a source of corruption, prostitution, hedonism, and the destruction of communal customs and values. The tension between traditional ways and Western culture is particularly strong among African intellectuals, many of whom are torn between their admiration for things Western and their desire to retain an African identity.

concentrated on vocational training, with some instruction in European languages and Western civilization. Eventually, pressure from Africans led to the introduction of professional training, and the first institutes of higher learning were established in the early twentieth century.

With independence, African countries established their own state-run schools. The emphasis was on the primary level, but high schools and universities were established in major cities. The basic objectives have been to introduce vocational training and improve literacy rates. Unfortunately, both funding and trained teachers are scarce in most countries, and few rural areas have schools. As a result, illiteracy remains high, estimated at about 70 percent of the population across the continent. There has been a perceptible shift toward education in the vernacular languages. In West Africa, only about one in four adults is conversant in a Western language.

Urban and Rural Life

The cities are where the African elites live and work. Affluent Africans, like their contemporaries in other developing countries, have been strongly attracted to the glittering material aspects of Western culture. They live in Western-style homes or apartments and eat Western foods stored in Western refrigerators, and those who can afford it drive Western cars. It has been said, not wholly in praise, that there are more Mercedes-Benz automobiles in Nigeria than in Germany, where they are manufactured.

Outside the major cities, where about three-quarters of the continent's inhabitants live, Western influence has had less impact. Millions of people throughout Africa (as in Asia) live much as their ancestors did, in thatch huts without modern plumbing and electricity (see the comparative illustration

African Women

As noted in Chapter 21, one of the consequences of colonialism in Africa was a change in the relationship between men and women. Some of these changes could be described as beneficial, but others were not. Women were often introduced to Western education and given legal rights denied to them in the precolonial era. But they also became a labor source and were sometime recruited or compelled to work on construction projects.

Independence also had a significant impact on gender roles in African society. Almost without exception, the new governments established the principle of sexual equality and permitted women to vote and run for political office. Yet as elsewhere, women continue to operate at a disability in a world dominated by males. Politics remains a male preserve, and although a few professions, such as teaching, child care, and clerical work, are dominated by women, most African women are employed in menial positions such as agricultural labor, factory work, and retail trade or as domestics. Education is open to all at the elementary level, but women comprise less than 20 percent of students at the upper levels in most African societies today.

URBAN WOMEN Not surprisingly, women have made the greatest strides in the cities. Most urban women, like men, now marry on the basis of personal choice, although a significant minority are still willing to accept their parents' choice.

Continuity and Change in Modern African Societies ❧ **869**

COMPARATIVE ILLUSTRATION

EARTH & ENVIRONMENT

Traditional Patterns in the Countryside. In various parts of the world, many people continue to follow patterns of living that are centuries old. In Africa, the houses of rural peoples are often constructed from a wooden frame woven from poles and branches, known as wattle, that is daubed with mud and then covered with a thatched roof. At the left is a scene from a Kenyan village not far from the Indian Ocean, where a young man is applying mud to the wall of his future house. The photo at the right shows a village in India, where house styles and village customs have changed little since they were first described by Portuguese travelers in the sixteenth century. Note the thatched roofs and the mud-and-straw walls plastered with dung used in constructing these houses, reminiscent of those found in Africa.

Q *What might be the advantages and disadvantages of mud-and-thatch houses for rural peoples in contemporary Africa and Asia?*

After marriage, African women appear to occupy a more equal position than their counterparts in most Asian countries. Each marriage partner tends to maintain a separate income, and women often have the right to possess property separate from their husbands. Though many wives still defer to their husbands in the traditional manner, others are like the woman in Abioseh Nicol's story "A Truly Married Woman," who, after years of living as a common-law wife with her husband, is finally able to provide the price and finalize the marriage. After the wedding, she declares, "For twelve years I have got up every morning at five to make tea for you and breakfast. Now I am a truly married woman, [and] you must treat me with a little more respect. You are now my husband and not a lover. Get up and make yourself a cup of tea."[4]

In the cities, a feminist movement is growing, but it is firmly based on conditions in the local environment. Many African women writers, for example, opt for a brand of African feminism much like that of Ama Ata Aidoo (AH-mah AH-tah ah-EE-doo) (b. 1942), a Ghanaian novelist, whose ultimate objective is to free African society as a whole, not just its female inhabitants. After receiving her education at a girls' school in the preindependence Gold Coast and attending Stanford University in the United States, she embarked on a writing career. Every African woman and every man, she insists, "should be a feminist, especially if they believe that Africans should take charge of our land, its wealth, our lives,

and the burden of our development. Because it is not possible to advocate independence for our continent without also believing that African women must have the best that the environment can offer."[5]

WOMEN IN RURAL AREAS Feminism has had less impact on women in rural areas, where traditional attitudes continue to exert a strong influence. In some societies, female genital mutilation, the traditional rite of passage for a young girl's transit to womanhood, is still widely practiced. Polygamy is also not uncommon, and arranged marriages are still the rule rather than the exception. In some Muslim societies, efforts to apply *Shari'a* law have led to greater restrictions on the freedom of women. In northern Nigeria, a women was recently sentenced to death for committing adultery. The sentence was later reversed on appeal.

The dichotomy between rural and urban values can lead to acute tensions. Many African villagers regard the cities as the fount of evil, decadence, and corruption. Women in particular have suffered from the tension between the pull of the city and the village. As men are drawn to the cities in search of employment and excitement, their wives and girlfriends are left behind, both literally and figuratively, in the village. Fortunately, there are some signs of change. In 2006, Ellen Johnson-Sirleaf was elected president of Liberia—the first woman to be elected chief executive of a country on the African continent.

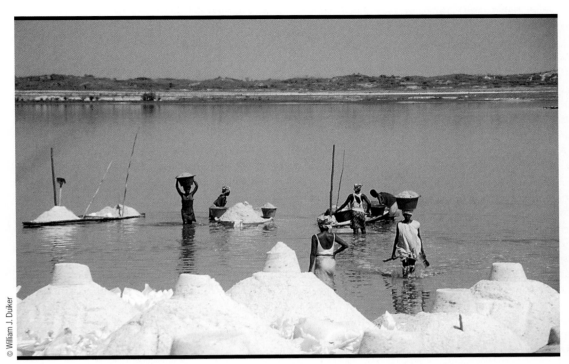

Salt of the Earth. During the precolonial era, many West African societies were forced to import salt from Mediterranean countries in exchange for tropical products and gold. Today, the people of Senegal satisfy their domestic needs by mining salt deposits contained in lakes like this one in the interior of the country. These lakes are the remnants of vast seas that covered the region of the Sahara in prehistoric times. Note that women are doing much of the heavy labor while men occupy the managerial positions.

African Culture

Inevitably, the tension between traditional and modern, local and foreign, and individual and communal that has permeated contemporary African society has spilled over into culture. In general, in the visual arts and music, utility and ritual have given way to pleasure and decoration. In the process, Africans have been affected to a certain extent by foreign influences but have retained their distinctive characteristics. Wood carving, metalwork, painting, and sculpture, for example, have preserved their traditional forms but are now increasingly adapted to serve the tourist industry and the export market.

LITERATURE No area of African culture has been so strongly affected by political and social events as literature. Except for Muslim areas in North and East Africa, precolonial Africans did not have a written literature, although their tradition of oral storytelling served as a rich repository of history, custom, and folk culture. The first written literature in the vernacular or in European languages emerged during the nineteenth century in the form of novels, poetry, and drama.

Angry at the negative portrayal of Africa in Western literature (see the box on p. 872), African authors initially wrote primarily for a European audience as a means of establishing black dignity and purpose. In response to condescending Western attitudes about African history, many glorified the emotional and communal aspects of the traditional African experience. The Nigerian Chinua Achebe (CHIN-wah ah-CHAY-bay) (b. 1930) is considered the first major African novelist to write in the English language. In his writings, he attempted to interpret African history from an African perspective and to forge a new sense of African identity. In his trailblazing novel *Things Fall Apart* (1958), he recounted the story of a Nigerian who refused to submit to the new British order and eventually committed suicide. Criticizing his contemporaries who accepted foreign rule, the protagonist lamented that the white man "has put a knife on the things that held us together and we have fallen apart."

In recent decades, the African novel has taken a dramatic turn, shifting its focus from the brutality of the foreign oppressor to the shortcomings of the new African leaders. Having gained independence, African politicians are portrayed as mimicking and even outdoing the injustices committed by their colonial predecessors. A prominent example of this genre is the work of the Kenyan Ngugi Wa Thiong'o (GOO-gee wah tee-AHNG-goh) (b. 1938). His first novel, *A Grain of Wheat*, takes place on the eve of independence. Although it mocks local British society for its racism, snobbishness, and superficiality, its chief interest lies in its unsentimental and even unflattering portrayal of ordinary Kenyans in their daily struggle for survival.

Like most of his predecessors, Ngugi initially wrote in English, but he eventually decided to write in his native Kikuyu as a means of broadening his readership. For that reason, perhaps, in the late 1970s, he was placed under house arrest for writing subversive literature. There, he secretly wrote *Devil on the Cross*, which urged his compatriots to overthrow the ruling government. Published in 1980, the book

Africa: Dark Continent or Radiant Land?

INTERACTION & EXCHANGE

Colonialism camouflaged its economic objectives under the cloak of a "civilizing mission," which in Africa was aimed at illuminating the so-called Dark Continent with Europe's brilliant civilization. In 1899, the Polish-born English author Joseph Conrad (1857–1924) fictionalized his harrowing journey up the Congo River in the novella *Heart of Darkness*. Conrad's protagonist, Marlow, travels upriver to locate a Belgian trader who has mysteriously disappeared. The novella describes Marlow's gradual recognition of the egregious excesses of colonial rule, as well as his realization that such evil lurks in everyone's heart. The story concludes with a cry: "The horror! The horror!" Voicing views that expressed his Victorian perspective, Conrad described an Africa that was incomprehensible, sensual, and primitive.

Over the years, Conrad's work has provoked much debate. Author Chinua Achebe, for one, lambasted *Heart of Darkness* as a radical diatribe. Since independence, many African writers have been prompted to counter Conrad's portrayal by reaffirming the dignity and purpose of the African people. One of the first to do so was the Guinean author Camara Laye (1928–1980), who in 1954 composed a brilliant novel, *The Radiance of the King*, which can be viewed as the mirror image of Conrad's *Heart of Darkness*. In Laye's work, Clarence, another European protagonist, undertakes a journey into the impenetrable heart of Africa. This time, however, he is enlightened by the process, obtaining self-knowledge and ultimately salvation.

Joseph Conrad, *Heart of Darkness*

We penetrated deeper and deeper into the heart of darkness. It was very quiet there. At night sometimes the roll of drums behind the curtain of trees would run up the river and remain sustained faintly, as if hovering in the air high over our heads, till the first break of day. Whether it meant war, peace, or prayer we could not tell. . . . But suddenly, as we struggled round a bend, there would be a glimpse of rush walls, of peaked grass-roofs, a burst of yells, a whirl of black limbs, a mass of hands clapping, of feet stamping, of bodies swaying, of eyes rolling, under the droop of heavy and motionless foliage. The steamer toiled along slowly on the edge of a black and incomprehensible frenzy. The prehistoric man was cursing us, praying to us, welcoming us—who could tell? We were cut off from the comprehension of our surroundings; we glided past like phantoms, wondering and secretly appalled, as sane men would be before an enthusiastic outbreak in a madhouse.

Camara Laye, *The Radiance of the King*

At that very moment the king turned his head, turned it imperceptibly, and his glance fell upon Clarence. . . .

"Yes, no one is as base as I, as naked as I," he thought. "And you, lord, you are willing to rest your eyes upon me!" Or was it because of his very nakedness? . . . "Because of your very nakedness!" the look seemed to say. "That terrifying void that is within you and which opens to receive me; your hunger which calls to my hunger; your very baseness which did not exist until I gave it leave; and the great shame you feel. . . ."

When he had come before the king, when he stood in the great radiance of the king, still ravaged by the tongue of fire, but alive still, and living only through the touch of that fire, Clarence fell upon his knees, for it seemed to him that he was finally at the end of his seeking, and at the end of all seekings.

Compare the depiction of the continent of Africa in these two passages. Is Laye making a response to Conrad? If so, what is it?

---

sold widely and was eventually read aloud by storytellers throughout Kenyan society. Fearing an attempt on his life, Ngugi has since lived in exile.

Many of Ngugi's contemporaries have followed his lead and focused their frustration on the failure of the continent's new leadership to carry out the goals of independence. One of the most outstanding is the Nigerian Wole Soyinka (woh-LAY soh-YEENK-kuh) (b. 1934). His novel *The Interpreters* (1965) lambasted the corruption and hypocrisy of Nigerian politics. Succeeding novels and plays have continued that tradition, resulting in a Nobel Prize in Literature in 1986. In 1994, however, Soyinka barely managed to escape arrest, and he entered a self-imposed exile abroad until the Abacha regime in Nigeria came to an end. In a protest against the brutality of the regime, he published from exile a harsh exposé of the crisis. His book, *The Open Sore of a Continent*, placed the primary responsibility for failure not on Nigeria's long list of dictators but on the very concept of the modern nation-state, which was introduced to Africa arbitrarily by Europeans. A nation, he contends, can only emerge spontaneously from below, as the expression of the moral and political will of the local inhabitants; it cannot be imposed artificially from above.

A number of Africa's most prominent writers today are women. Traditionally, African women were valued for their talents as storytellers, but writing was strongly discouraged by both traditional and colonial authorities on the grounds that women should occupy themselves with their domestic obligations. In recent years, however, a number of women have emerged as prominent writers of African fiction. Two examples are Buchi Emecheta (BOO-chee ay-muh-CHAY-tuh) (b. 1940) of Nigeria and Ama Ata Aidoo of Ghana. Beginning with *Second Class Citizen* (1975), which chronicled the breakdown of her own marriage, Emecheta has published numerous works exploring the role of women in contemporary African society and decrying the practice of polygamy. Ata Aidoo has focused on the identity of today's African women and the changing relations between men and women in society. In her novel *Changes: A Love Story* (1991), she chronicles the lives of three women, none presented as a victim but all caught up in the struggle for survival and happiness. Of late, two young authors have garnered great acclaim for their novels about Nigeria's political and social upheavals—Chimamanda Ngozi Adichie (chim-muh-MAHN-duh en-GOH-zee ah-DEECH-ee) (b. 1977) in *Half a Yellow Sun* (2006) and Sefi Atta (b. 1964) in *Everything Good Will Come* (2005).

MUSIC Contemporary African music also reflects a hybridization or fusion with Western culture. Having traveled to the Americas via the slave trade centuries earlier, African drum beats evolved into North American jazz and Latin American dance rhythms, only to return to reenergize African music. In fact, today music is one of Africans' most effective weapons for social and political protest. Easily accessible to all, African music, whether Afro-beat in Nigeria, *rai* in Algeria, or *reggae* in Benin, represents the "weapon of the future," contemporary musicians say; "it helped free Nelson Mandela" and "will put Africa back on the map." Censored by all the African dictatorial regimes, these courageous musicians persist in their struggle against corruption, what one singer calls the second slavery, "the cancer that is eating away at the system." Their voices echo the chorus "Together we can build a nation / Because Africa has brains, youth, knowledge."[6]

What Is the Future of Africa?

Nowhere in the developing world is the dilemma of continuity and change more agonizing than in Africa. Mesmerized by the spectacle of Western affluence yet repulsed by the bloody trail from slavery to World War II and the atomic bombs over Hiroshima and Nagasaki, African intellectuals have been torn between the dual images of Western materialism and African uniqueness. For the average African, of course, such intellectual dilemmas pale before the daily challenge of survival. But the fundamental gap between traditional and modern is perhaps wider in Africa than anywhere else in the world and may well be harder to bridge.

What is the future of Africa? It seems almost foolhardy to seek an answer to such a question, given the degree of ethnic, linguistic, and cultural diversity that exists throughout the vast continent. Not surprisingly, visions of the future are equally diverse. Some Africans still yearn for the dreams embodied in the program of the OAU. Novelist Ngugi Wa Thiong'o calls for "an internationalization of all the democratic and social struggles for human equality, justice, peace, and progress."[7] Others have discarded the democratic ideal and turned their attention to systems based on the subordination of the individ-

ual to the community as the guiding principle of national development. Like all peoples, Africans must ultimately find their own solutions within the context of their own traditions, not by seeking to imitate the example of others.

Crescent of Conflict

 FOCUS QUESTION: What problems have the nations of the Middle East faced since the end of World War II, and to what degree have they managed to resolve them?

"We Muslims are of one family even though we live under different governments and in various regions."[8] So said Ayatollah Ruholla Khomeini (ah-yah-TUL-uh roo-HUL-uh khoh-MAY-nee), the Islamic religious figure and leader of the 1979 revolution that overthrew the shah in Iran. The ayatollah's remark was dismissed by some as just a pious wish by a religious mystic. In fact, however, it illustrates one crucial aspect of the political dynamics of the region.

If the concept of cultural uniqueness has been presented as a potential alternative to the system of nation-states in Africa, a similar role has been played in the Middle East by the religion of Islam. In both regions, a yearning for a sense of community beyond national borders tugs at the emotions and intellect of their inhabitants and counteracts the dynamic pull of nationalism that has led to political turmoil and conflict in much of the rest of the world.

A dramatic example of the powerful force of pan-Islamic sentiment took place on September 11, 2001, when Muslim terrorists hijacked four U.S. airliners and turned them into missiles aimed at the center of world capitalism (see Chapter 28). Although the organizers of the attack—known as al-Qaeda—were located in Afghanistan, the terrorists themselves came from other Muslim states, primarily Saudi Arabia. In the months that followed, support for al-Qaeda and its elusive leader, Osama bin Laden, intensified throughout the Muslim world. To many observers, it was clear that bin Laden and his cohorts had tapped into a wellspring of hostility and resentment directed at the Western world.

What were the sources of Muslim anger? In a speech released on videotape shortly after the attack, bin Laden declared that the attacks were a response to the "humiliation and disgrace" inflicted on the Islamic world for more than eighty years, a period dating back to the end of World War I. For the Middle East, the period between the two world wars was an era of transition. With the fall of the Ottoman and Persian Empires, new modernizing regimes emerged in Turkey and Iran, and a more traditionalist but fiercely independent government was established in Saudi Arabia. Elsewhere, European influence continued to be strong; the British and French had mandates in Syria, Lebanon, Jordan, and Palestine, and British influence persisted in Iraq, in southern Arabia, and throughout the Nile valley. **Pan-Arabism**—the concept of the unity of all Arab peoples—was on the rise, but it lacked focus and coherence.

During World War II, the Middle East became the cockpit of European rivalries, as it had been during World War I.

The region was more significant to the warring powers than previously because of the growing importance of oil and the Suez Canal's position as a vital sea route. For a brief period, the German Afrika Korps threatened to seize Egypt and the Suez Canal, but British troops defeated the German forces at El Alamein, west of Alexandria, in 1942. Thereafter, the entire region from the Mediterranean Sea eastward was under secure Allied occupation until the end of the war.

The Question of Palestine

As in other areas of Asia, the end of World War II led to the emergence of a number of independent states in the Middle East. Jordan, Lebanon, and Syria, all European mandates before the war, became independent. Egypt, Iran, and Iraq, though still under a degree of Western influence, became increasingly autonomous. Sympathy for the idea of Arab unity led to the formation of the Arab League in 1945, but different points of view among its members prevented it from achieving anything of substance.

The one issue on which all Muslim states in the area could agree was the question of Palestine. As tensions between Jews and Arabs in that mandate intensified during the 1930s, the British attempted to limit Jewish immigration into the area and firmly rejected proposals for independence, despite the promise made in the 1917 Balfour Declaration (see Chapter 24).

After World War II ended, the situation drifted rapidly toward crisis, as thousands of Jewish refugees, many of them from displaced persons camps in Europe, sought to migrate to Palestine despite British efforts to prevent their arrival. As violence between Muslims and Jews intensified in the fall of 1947, the issue was taken up in the United Nations General Assembly. After an intense debate, the assembly voted to approve the partition of Palestine into two separate states, one for the Jews and one for the Arabs. The city of Jerusalem was to be placed under international control. A UN commission was established to iron out the details and determine the future boundaries.

During the next several months, growing hostility between Jewish and Arab forces—the latter increasingly supported by neighboring Muslim states—caused the British to announce that they would withdraw their own peacekeeping forces by May 15, 1948. Shortly after the stroke of midnight, as the British mandate formally came to a close, the Zionist leader David Ben-Gurion (ben-GOOR-ee-uhn) (1886–1973) announced the independence of the state of Israel. Later that same day, the new state was formally recognized by the United States, while military forces from several neighboring Muslim states—all of which had vigorously opposed the formation of a Jewish state in the region—entered Israeli territory but were beaten back. Thousands of Arab residents of the new state fled. Internal dissonance among the Arabs, combined with the strength of Jewish resistance groups, contributed to the failure of the invasion, but the bitterness between the two sides did not subside. The Muslim states refused to recognize the new state of Israel, which became a member of the United Nations, legitimizing it in the eyes of the rest of the world. The stage for future conflict was set.

The exodus of thousands of Palestinian refugees into neighboring Muslim states had repercussions that are still felt today. Jordan, which had become an independent kingdom under its Hashemite (HASH-uh-myt) ruler, was flooded by the arrival of one million urban Palestinians. They overwhelmed the half million Jordanians, most of whom were Bedouins. To the north, the state of Lebanon had been created to provide the local Christian community with a country of their own, but the arrival of the Palestinian refugees upset the delicate balance between Christians and Muslims. Moreover, the creation of Lebanon had angered the Syrians, who had lost that land as well as other territories to Turkey as a result of European decisions before and after World War II.

Nasser and Pan-Arabism

The dispute over Palestine put Egypt in an uncomfortable position. Technically, Egypt was not an Arab state. King Farouk (fuh-ROOK) (1920–1965), who had acceded to power in 1936, had frequently declared support for the Arab cause, but the Egyptian people were not Bedouins and shared little of the culture of the peoples across the Red Sea. Nevertheless, Farouk committed Egyptian armies to the disastrous war against Israel.

In 1952, Farouk, whose corrupt habits had severely eroded his early popularity, was overthrown by a military coup engineered by young military officers, and the monarchy was replaced by a republic. The real force behind the scenes was Colonel Gamal Abdul Nasser (1918–1970), the son of a minor government functionary who, like many of his fellow officers, had been angered by the army's inadequate preparation for the war against Israel four years earlier.

In 1954, Nasser seized power in his own right and immediately instituted a land reform program. He also adopted a policy of neutrality in foreign affairs and expressed sympathy for the Arab cause. The British presence had rankled many Egyptians for years, for even after granting Egypt independence, Britain had retained control over the Suez Canal. In 1956, Nasser suddenly nationalized the Suez Canal Company, which had been under British and French administration. Seeing a threat to their route to the Indian Ocean, the British and the French launched a joint attack on Egypt to protect their investment. They were joined by Israel, whose leaders had grown exasperated at sporadic Arab commando raids launched from the Egyptian Sinai (SY-ny) peninsula against Israeli territory and now decided to strike back. But the Eisenhower administration in the United States, concerned that the attack smacked of a revival of colonialism, supported Nasser and brought about the withdrawal of foreign forces from Egypt and of Israeli troops from the Sinai.

THE UNITED ARAB REPUBLIC Nasser now turned to pan-Arabism. Egypt had won the admiration of other states in the area for its successful eviction of the British and the French from the Suez Canal and for its sponsorship of efforts to replace Israel by an independent Palestinian state. The Ba'ath (BAHTH) Party, which advocated the unity of all Arab states in a new socialist society, assumed power in Syria in 1957 and opened talks with Egypt on a political union between the two countries, which took place in March 1958 following a plebiscite. Nasser was named president of the new United Arab Republic (UAR).

Egypt and Syria hoped that the union would eventually expand to include all Arab states, but other Arab leaders, including the kings of Jordan, Iraq, and Saudi Arabia, were suspicious. The latter two in particular feared pan-Arabism on the reasonable assumption that they would be asked to share their vast oil revenues with the poorer states of the Middle East. Indeed, in Nasser's view, through Arab unity, this wealth could be used to improve the standard of living in the area. To achieve a more equitable division of the wealth of the region, natural resources and major industries would be nationalized; central planning would guarantee that resources were exploited efficiently, but private enterprise would continue at the local level.

In the end, however, Nasser's determination to extend state control over the economy brought an end to the UAR. When the government announced the nationalization of a large number of industries and utilities in 1961, a military coup overthrew the Ba'ath leaders in Damascus, and the new authorities declared that Syria would end its relationship with Egypt.

The breakup of the UAR did not necessarily end Nasser's dream of pan-Arabism. In 1962, Algeria finally received its independence from France and, under its new president, Ahmad Ben Bella, established close relations with Egypt, as did a new republic in Yemen. During the mid-1960s, Egypt took the lead in promoting Arab unity against Israel. At a meeting of Arab leaders held in Jerusalem in 1964, the Palestine Liberation Organization (PLO) was set up under Egyptian sponsorship to represent the interests of the Palestinians. According to the charter of the PLO, only the Palestinian people (and hence not Jewish immigrants) had the right to form a state in the old British mandate. A guerrilla movement called al-Fatah (al-FAH-tuh), led by the dissident PLO figure Yasir Arafat (yah-SEER ah-ruh-FAHT) (1929–2004), began to carry out terrorist attacks on Israeli territory, prompting the Israeli government to raid PLO bases in Jordan in 1966.

The Arab-Israeli Dispute

Growing Arab hostility was a constant threat to the security of Israel. In the years after independence, Israeli leaders dedicated themselves to creating a Jewish homeland. Aided by reparations paid by the postwar German government and private funds provided by Jews living abroad, notably in the United States, the government attempted to build a modern democratic state that would be a magnet for Jews throughout the world and a symbol of Jewish achievement.

Ensuring the survival of the tiny state surrounded by antagonistic Arab neighbors was a considerable challenge, made more difficult by divisions within the Israeli population. Some were immigrants from Europe, while others came from other states in the Middle East. Some were secular and even socialist in their views, while others were politically and religiously conservative. The state was also home to Christians as well as Muslim Palestinians who had not fled to other

countries. To balance these diverse interests, Israel established a parliament, called the Knesset (kuh-NESS-it), on the European model, with proportional representation based on the number of votes each party received in the general election. The parties were so numerous that none ever received a majority of votes, and all governments had to be formed from a coalition of several parties. As a result, moderate secular leaders such as longtime prime minister David Ben-Gurion had to cater to more marginal parties composed of conservative religious groups.

During the late 1950s and 1960s, the dispute between Israel and other states in the Middle East intensified (see the box on p. 876). Essentially alone except for the sympathy of the United States and a handful of Western European countries, Israel adopted a policy of determined resistance to and immediate retaliation against PLO and Arab provocations. By the spring of 1967, relations between Israel and its Arab neighbors had deteriorated as Nasser attempted to improve his standing in the Arab world by imposing a blockade against Israeli commerce through the Gulf of Aqaba (AH-kah-buh), a move that he had attempted before in 1956.

THE SIX-DAY WAR Concerned that it might be isolated, and lacking firm support from Western powers (which had originally guaranteed Israel the freedom to use the Gulf of Aqaba), in June 1967 Israel suddenly launched air strikes against Egypt and several of its Arab neighbors. Israeli armies then broke the blockade at the head of the Gulf of Aqaba and occupied the Sinai peninsula. Other Israeli forces attacked Jordanian territory on the West Bank of the Jordan River (Jordan's King Hussein had recently signed an alliance with Egypt and placed his army under Egyptian command), occupied the city of Jerusalem, and seized Syrian military positions in the Golan Heights, along the Israeli-Syrian border (see Map 29.2 on p. 877).

Despite limited Soviet support for Egypt and Syria, in a war lasting only six days, Israel had mocked Nasser's pretensions of Arab unity and tripled the size of its territory, thus enhancing its precarious security. But the new Israel aroused even more bitter hostility among the Arabs and added one million Palestinians inside its borders, most of them on the West Bank of the Jordan River.

During the next few years, the focus of the Arab-Israeli dispute shifted as Arab states demanded the return of the territories lost in the 1967 war. Meanwhile, many Israelis argued that the new lands improved the security of the beleaguered state and should be retained. Concerned that the dispute might lead to a confrontation between the superpowers, with the Soviet Union backing the Arabs, the Nixon administration tried to achieve a peace settlement. The peace effort received a mild stimulus when Nasser died of a heart attack in September 1970 and was succeeded by his vice president, ex-general Anwar al-Sadat (ahn-WAHR al-sah-DAHT) (1918–1981). Sadat soon showed himself to be more pragmatic than his predecessor, dropping the now irrelevant name United Arab Republic in favor of the Arab Republic of Egypt and replacing Nasser's socialist policies with a new strategy based on free enterprise and encouragement of Western investment. He also agreed to sign a peace treaty with Israel on condition that

A Plea for Peace in the Middle East

POLITICS & GOVERNMENT

In an effort to end an Egyptian blockade of the Gulf of Aqaba against Israeli shipping, Israel joined Great Britain and France in attacking Egypt during the Suez Canal crisis in October 1956. Israel quickly captured the Sinai peninsula, but the United Nations condemned the attack and pressured Great Britain, France, and Israel to withdraw their troops. For four months, Israel refused, demanding that the Arab states respect its right to use the Gulf of Aqaba. In March 1957, however, the Israeli government agreed to withdraw from the Sinai and the Gaza Strip. This selection is from the speech in which Golda Meir, Israel's foreign minister, announced the withdrawal.

Golda Meir Announces an Israeli Withdrawal from the Sinai

Interference, by armed force, with ships of Israeli flag exercising free and innocent passage in the Gulf of Aqaba and through the Straits of Tiran, will be viewed by Israel as an attack entitling it to exercise its inherent right of self-defense under article 51 of the United Nations Charter and to take all such measures as are necessary to ensure the free and innocent passage of its ships in the Gulf and in the Straits. We make this announcement in accordance with the accepted principles of international law under which all states have an inherent right to use their forces to protect their ships and their rights against interference by armed force. My government naturally hopes that this contingency will not occur. In a public address on 20 February 1957, President Eisenhower states: "We should not assume that, if Israel withdraws, Egypt will prevent Israel shipping from using the Suez Canal or the Gulf of Aqaba." This declaration has weighed heavily with my government in determining its action today. Israel is now prepared to withdraw its forces from the regions of the Gulf of Aqaba and the Straits of Tiran in the confidence that there will be continued freedom of navigation for international and Israeli shipping in the Gulf of Aqaba and through the Straits of Tiran. . . .

May I now add these few words to the states in the Middle East area and, more specifically, to the neighbors of Israel. We all come from an area which is a very ancient one. The hills and the valleys have been witnesses to many wars and many conflicts. But that is not the only thing which characterizes that part of the world from which we come. It is also a part of the world which is of an ancient culture. It is that part of the world which has given to humanity three great religions. It is also that part of the world which has given a code of ethics to all humanity. In our countries, in the entire region, all our peoples are anxious for and in need of a higher standard of living, of great programs of development and progress. Can we, from now on—all of us—turn a new leaf and, instead of fighting with each other, can we all, united, fight poverty and disease and illiteracy? Is it possible for us to put all our efforts and all our energy into one single purpose, the betterment and progress and development of all our lands and all our peoples? I can here pledge the government and the people of Israel to do their part in this united effort. There is no limit to what we are prepared to contribute so that all of us, together, can live to see a day of happiness for our peoples and can see again from that region a great contribution to peace and happiness for all humanity.

 How did neighboring states react to Golda Meir's offer of cooperation? Why did they react the way they did?

Israel withdraw to its pre-1967 frontiers. Concerned that other Arab countries would refuse to make peace and take advantage of its presumed weakness, Israel refused.

Rebuffed in his offer of peace, smarting from criticism of his moderate stand from other Arab leaders, and increasingly concerned over Israeli plans to build permanent Jewish settlements in the West Bank, Sadat attempted once again to renew Arab unity through a new confrontation with Israel. On Yom Kippur (the Jewish Day of Atonement), an Israeli national holiday, Egyptian forces suddenly launched an air and artillery attack on Israeli positions in the Sinai just east of the Suez Canal. Syrian armies attacked Israeli positions in the Golan Heights. After early Arab successes, the Israelis managed to recoup some of their losses on both fronts. As a superpower confrontation between the United States and the Soviet Union loomed, a cease-fire was finally reached. The focus of tension, however, now switched to Lebanon, where many Palestinians had found refuge and the PLO had set up its headquarters. Rising tension along the border was compounded by increasingly hostile disputes between Christians and Muslims over control of the capital, Beirut (bay-ROOT).

THE CAMP DAVID ACCORDS After his election as U.S. president in 1976, Jimmy Carter began to press for a compromise peace based on Israel's return of territories occupied during the 1967 war and Arab recognition of the state of Israel. In September 1978, Sadat and Israeli prime minister Menachem Begin (muh-NAH-kuhm BAY-gin) (1913–1992) met with Carter at Camp David, the presidential retreat in Maryland. In the first treaty signed with a Muslim state, Israel agreed to withdraw from the Sinai but not from other occupied territories unless it was recognized by other Arab countries.

© Cengage Learning

0 50 100 150 Kilometers

0 50 100 Miles

MAP 29.2 Israel and Its Neighbors. This map shows the evolution of the state of Israel since its founding in 1948. Areas occupied by Israel after the Six-Day War in 1967 are indicated in green.

Q *What is the significance of the West Bank?*

The promise of the Camp David accords was not fulfilled. One reason was the assassination of Sadat by Islamic militants in October 1981. But there were deeper causes, including the continued unwillingness of Muslim governments to recognize Israel and the Israeli government's encouragement of Jewish settlements in the occupied West Bank.

THE PLO AND THE *INTIFADA* During the early 1980s, the militancy of the Palestinians increased, leading to rising unrest, popularly labeled the *intifada* (in-tuh-FAH-duh) (uprising), among PLO supporters living inside Israel. To control the situation, in 1982 a new Israeli government under Prime Minister Yitzhak Shamir (yits-HAHK shuh-MEER) (b. 1915) invaded southern Lebanon to destroy PLO commando bases near the Israeli border. The invasion aroused controversy abroad and further destabilized the perilous balance between Muslims and Christians in Lebanon. In the early 1990s, U.S.-sponsored peace talks opened between Israel and a number of its neighbors, leading to a breakthrough in 1993, when Israel and the PLO reached an agreement in Oslo, Norway, calling for Palestinian autonomy in selected areas of Israel in return for PLO recognition of the legitimacy of the state of Israel.

Progress in implementing the agreement, however, was slow. Terrorist attacks by Palestinian militants resulted in heavy casualties and shook the confidence of many Jewish citizens that their security needs could be protected under the agreement. At the same time, Jewish residents of the West Bank resisted the extension of Palestinian authority in the area. In November 1995, Prime Minister Yitzhak Rabin (rah-BEEN) (1922–1995) was assassinated by an Israeli opponent of the accords. National elections held a few months later led to the formation of a new government under Benjamin Netanyahu (net-ahn-YAH-hoo) (b. 1949), which adopted a tougher stance in negotiations with the Palestinian Authority under Yasir Arafat.

When Netanyahu was replaced as prime minister by Ehud Barak (EH-hud bah-RAHK) (b. 1942), the new Labour government promised to revitalize the peace process. Negotiations continued with the PLO and also got under way in 1999 with Syria over a peace settlement in Lebanon and the possible return of the Golan Heights. But peace talks broke down over the future of the city of Jerusalem, leading to massive riots by Palestinians, a tough Israeli response, and the election in 2000 of a new and more hard-line Israeli prime minister, the former defense minister Ariel Sharon (ah-REE-ul shuh-ROHN) (b. 1928). Sharon's ascent to leadership was accompanied by a rash of suicide attacks by Palestinians against Israeli targets, an intensive Israeli military crackdown on suspected terrorist sites inside Palestinian territory, and a dramatic increase in bloodshed on both sides.

The death of Arafat in 2004 and his replacement by the Palestinian moderate Mahmoud Abbas (mah-MOOD ah-BAHS) (b. 1935), followed by the unilateral evacuation of Israeli settlers from the Gaza Strip a year later, raised modest hopes for progress in peace talks (key issues that remain unresolved include the future status of Jerusalem and the presence of Jewish settlements in the occupied territories). But the incapacitation of Prime Minister Sharon by a stroke and the victory of Hamas (HAH-mahs), a militant organization that calls for the destruction of the state of Israel, in Palestinian elections held in late 2005 undermined the search for peace. In 2006, rocket attacks launched by guerrillas from **Hezbollah** (hes-bah-LAH *or* HEZ-bull-lah), a militant Shi'ite organization and political party based in Lebanon, provoked an Israeli invasion of southern Lebanon to wipe out the source

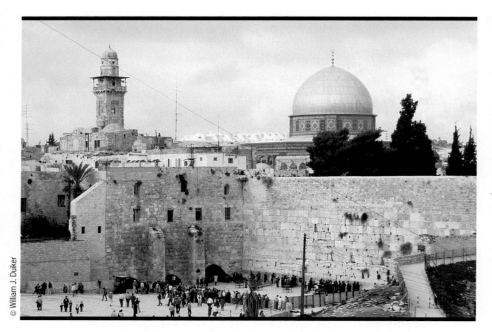

The Temple Mount at Jerusalem. The Temple Mount is one of the most sacred spots in the city of Jerusalem. Originally, it was the site of the Temple built during the reign of Solomon, king of the Israelites, about 1000 B.C.E. The Western Wall of the Temple is shown in the foreground. Beyond the wall is the Dome of the Rock complex, built on the place from which Muslims believe that Muhammad ascended to heaven. Sacred to both Judaism and Islam, the Temple Mount is now a major bone of contention between Muslims and Jews and a prime obstacle to a final settlement of the Arab-Israeli dispute.

of the assault, thereby raising the specter of a wider conflict. As attitudes on both sides hardened, national elections in 2009 led to the return to office of former prime minister Benjamin Netanyahu.

Revolution in Iran

The Arab-Israeli dispute also provoked an international oil crisis. In 1960, a number of oil-producing states formed the Organization of Petroleum Exporting Countries (OPEC) to gain control over oil prices, but the organization was not recognized by the foreign oil companies. During the 1973 Yom Kippur War, some OPEC nations announced significant increases in the price of oil to foreign countries. The price hikes were accompanied by an apparent oil shortage and created serious economic problems in the United States and Europe as well as in the Third World. They also proved to be a boon to oil-exporting countries, such as Libya, now under the leadership of the militantly anti-Western Colonel Muammar Qaddafi.

One of the key oil-exporting countries was Iran. Under the leadership of Shah Mohammad Reza Pahlavi (ree-ZAH PAH-luh-vee) (1919–1980), who had taken over from his father in 1941, Iran had become one of the richest countries in the Middle East. Relations with the West had occasionally been fragile, especially after Prime Minister Muhammad Mossadegh (MOH-sah-dek) (1882–1967) attempted to nationalize the oil industry in 1951. Mossadegh was overthrown in 1953 with covert U.S. assistance, and during the next twenty years, Iran became a prime U.S. ally. With encouragement from the United States, which hoped that Iran could become a force for stability in the Persian Gulf, the shah attempted to carry out a series of social and economic reforms to transform the country into the most advanced in the region.

Statistical evidence suggested that his efforts were succeeding. Per capita income increased dramatically, literacy rates improved, a modern communications infrastructure took shape, and an affluent middle class emerged in the capital of Tehran (teh-RAHN). Under the surface, however, trouble was brewing. Despite an ambitious land reform program, many peasants were still landless, unemployment among intellectuals was dangerously high, and the urban middle class was squeezed by high inflation. Housing costs had skyrocketed, in part because of a massive influx of foreigners attracted by oil money.

THE FALL OF THE SHAH Some of the unrest took the form of religious discontent as millions of devout Muslims looked with distaste at a new Iranian civilization based on greed, sexual license, and a decline in religious values. Religious conservatives opposed rampant government corruption, the ostentation of the shah's court, and the extension of voting rights to women. Some opposition elements resorted to terrorism against wealthy Iranians or foreign residents in an attempt to initiate social and political disorder. In response, the shah's U.S.-trained security police, the SAVAK, imprisoned and sometimes tortured thousands of dissidents.

Leading the opposition was Ayatollah Ruholla Khomeini (1900–1989), an austere Shi'ite cleric who had been exiled to Iraq and then to France because of his outspoken opposition to the shah's regime. From Paris, Khomeini continued his attacks in print, on television, and in radio broadcasts. By the late 1970s, large numbers of Iranians—especially Shi'ite Muslims, whose approach to religion is sometimes more mystical and messianic than that of their Sunni counterparts—began to respond to Khomeini's diatribes against the "satanic regime," and demonstrations by his supporters were repressed with ferocity by the police. But workers' strikes grew in intensity. In 1979, the government collapsed and was replaced by a hastily formed Islamic republic headed by the returning Ayatollah Khomeini. The new government, dominated by Shi'ite clergy, immediately began to introduce traditional

FILM & HISTORY

Persepolis (2007)

The Iranian author Marjane Satrapi (b. 1969) has re-created *Persepolis*, her autobiographical graphic novel, as an enthralling animated film of the same name. Using simple black-and-white animation, the movie recounts key stages in the turbulent history of modern Iran as seen through the eyes of a spirited young girl, also named Marjane. The dialogue is in French with English subtitles (a version dubbed in English is also available), and the voices of the characters are rendered beautifully by Danielle Darrieux, Catherine Deneuve, Chiara Mastroianni, and other European film stars.

In the film, Marjane is the daughter of middle-class left-wing intellectuals who abhor the dictatorship of the shah and actively participate in his overthrow in 1979. After the revolution, however, the severity of the ayatollah's Islamic rule arouses their secularist and democratic impulses. Encouraged by her loving grandmother, who reinforces her modernist and feminist instincts, Marjane resents having to wear a head scarf and the educational restrictions imposed by the puritanical new Islamic regime, but to little avail. Emotionally exhausted and fearful of political retribution from the authorities, her family finally sends her to study in Vienna.

Study abroad, however, is not a solution to Marjane's problems. She is distressed by the nihilism and emotional shallowness of her new Austrian school friends, who seem oblivious to the contrast between their privileged lives and her own experience of living under the shadow of a tyrannical regime. Disillusioned by the loneliness of exile and several failed love affairs, she descends into a deep depression and then decides to return to Tehran. When she discovers that her family is still suffering from political persecution, however, she decides to leave the country permanently and settles in Paris.

Observing the events, first through the eyes of a child and then through the perceptions of an innocent schoolgirl, the viewer of the film is forced to fill in the blanks, as Marjane initially cannot comprehend the meaning of the adult conversations swirling around her. As Marjane passes through adolescence into adulthood, the realization of the folly of human intransigence and superstition becomes painfully clear, both to her and to the audience. Although animated films have long been a staple in the cinema, thanks in part to Walt Disney, both the novel and the film *Persepolis* demonstrate how graphic design can depict a momentous event in history with clarity and compassion.

Islamic law (see the Film & History feature above). A new reign of terror ensued as supporters of the shah were rounded up and executed.

Though much of the outside world focused on the U.S. embassy in Tehran, where militants held a number of foreign hostages, the Iranian Revolution involved much more. In the eyes of the ayatollah and his followers, the United States was "the great Satan," the powerful protector of Israel and enemy of Muslims everywhere. Furthermore, it was responsible for the corruption of Iranian society under the shah. With economic conditions in Iran rapidly deteriorating, the Islamic revolutionary government finally agreed to free the hostages in return for the release of Iranian assets in the United States.

During the next few years, the intensity of the Iranian Revolution moderated slightly as the government displayed a modest tolerance for a loosening of clerical control over freedom of expression and social activities. In 1997, a moderate Muslim cleric, Mohammad Khatami (KHAH-tah-mee) (b. 1943), was elected president of Iran. Khatami, whose surprising victory reflected a growing desire among many Iranians for a more pluralistic society open to the outside world, signaled the tantalizing possibility that Iran might wish to improve relations with the United States. During the next few years, press censorship was relaxed, leading to the emergence of several reformist newspapers and magazines, and restrictions on women's activities were loosened. But the new president faced severe pressures from conservative elements to maintain the purity of Islamic laws, and in April 2000, the judiciary ordered several reformist publications to close because they had printed materials that "disparaged Islam." Although student protests erupted into the streets in 2003, hard-liners continued to reject proposals to expand civil rights and limit the power of the clerics.

In 2005, the presidential elections brought a new leader, Mahmoud Ahmadinejad (mah-MOOD ah-mah-dee-nee-ZHAHD) (b. 1956), to power in Tehran. He immediately inflamed the situation by calling publicly for the destruction of the state of Israel, while his government aroused unease throughout the world by indicating its determination to

CHRONOLOGY	The Modern Middle East
King Farouk overthrown in Egypt	1952
Egypt nationalizes the Suez Canal	1956
Formation of the United Arab Republic	1958
First oil crisis	1973
Iranian Revolution	1979
Iran-Iraq War begins	1980
Iraqi invasion of Kuwait	1990
Persian Gulf War	1991
Al-Qaeda terrorist attack on the United States	2001
U.S.-led forces invade Iraq	2003
Ahmadinejad elected president of Iran	2005
Popular riots in Middle East	2011
Overthrow of Egyptian president Hosni Mubarak	2011

develop a nuclear energy program, ostensibly for peaceful purposes. Despite worsening conditions inside Iran that eroded the government's popularity, Ahmadinejad was reelected in June 2009, although charges of voting irregularities aroused a widespread wave of protest.

Crisis in the Persian Gulf

Although much of the Iranians' anger was directed against the United States during the early phases of the revolution, Iran had enemies closer to home. To the north, the immensely powerful Soviet Union, driven by atheistic communism, was viewed as the latest incarnation of the Russian threat of previous centuries. To the west was a militant and hostile Iraq, under the leadership of the ambitious and brutal Saddam Hussein (sah-DAHM hoo-SAYN) (1937–2006). Iraq had just passed through a turbulent period. The monarchy had been overthrown by a military coup in 1958, but conflicts within the military ruling junta led to chronic instability, and in 1979 Colonel Saddam Hussein, a prominent member of the local Ba'athist Party, seized power on his own.

THE VISION OF SADDAM HUSSEIN Saddam Hussein was a fervent believer in the Ba'athist vision of a single Arab state in the Middle East and soon began to persecute non-Arab groups in Iraq, including Persians and Kurds. He then turned his sights to territorial expansion to the east.

Iraq and Iran had long had an uneasy relationship, fueled by religious differences (Iranian Islam is predominantly Shi'ite, while the ruling caste in Iraq was Sunni) and a perennial dispute over borderlands adjacent to the Persian Gulf, the vital waterway for the export of oil from both countries. Like several of its neighbors, Iraq had long dreamed of unifying the Arabs but had been hindered by internal factions and suspicion among its neighbors.

During the mid-1970s, Iran gave some support to a Kurdish rebellion in the mountains of Iraq. In 1975, the government of the shah agreed to stop aiding the rebels in return for territorial concessions at the head of the Gulf. Five years later, however, the Kurdish revolt had been suppressed.

Saddam Hussein now saw his opportunity; accusing Iran of violating the territorial agreement, in 1980 he launched an attack on his neighbor. The war was a bloody one and lasted nearly ten years. Poison gas was used against civilians, and children were employed to clear minefields. Finally, with both sides virtually exhausted, a cease-fire was arranged in the fall of 1988.

The bitter conflict with Iran had not slaked Saddam Hussein's appetite for territorial expansion. In early August 1990, Iraqi military forces suddenly moved across the border and occupied the small neighboring country of Kuwait at the head of the Gulf. The immediate pretext was the claim that Kuwait was pumping oil from fields inside Iraqi territory. Baghdad was also angry over the Kuwaiti government's demand for repayment of loans it had made to Iraq during the war with Iran. But the underlying reason was Iraq's contention that Kuwait was legally a part of Iraq. Kuwait had been part of the Ottoman Empire until the beginning of the twentieth century, when the local prince had agreed to place his patrimony under British protection. When Iraq became independent in 1932, it claimed the area on the grounds that the state of Kuwait had been created by British imperialism, but opposition from major Western powers and other countries in the region, which feared the consequences of a "greater Iraq," prevented an Iraqi takeover.

THE PERSIAN GULF WAR The Iraqi invasion of Kuwait in 1990 sparked an international outcry, and the United States assembled a multinational coalition that, under the name Operation Desert Storm, liberated the country and destroyed a substantial part of Iraq's armed forces in 1991. But the allied forces did not occupy Baghdad at the end of the war out of fear that doing so would cause a breakup of the country, an eventuality that would operate to the benefit of Iran. The allies hoped instead that Saddam's regime would be ousted by an internal revolt. In the meantime, harsh economic sanctions were imposed on the Iraqi government as the condition for peace. The anticipated overthrow of Saddam Hussein did not materialize, however, and his tireless efforts to evade the conditions of the cease-fire continued to bedevil U.S. President Bill Clinton and his successor, George W. Bush.

© Cengage Learning

- ☐ Predominantly Sunni areas
- ☐ Predominantly Shi'ite areas
- ☐ Predominantly Kurdish areas

Iraq

Conflicts in Afghanistan and Iraq

The terrorist attacks launched against U.S. targets in September 2001 added a new dimension to the Middle Eastern equation. After the failure of the Soviet Union to quell the rebellion in Afghanistan during the 1980s, a fundamentalist Muslim group known as the Taliban, supported covertly by the United States, seized power in Kabul and ruled the country with a fanaticism reminiscent of the Cultural Revolution in China. Backed by conservative religious forces in Pakistan, the Taliban provided a base of operations for

Afghanistan and Pakistan

Osama bin Laden's al-Qaeda terrorist network. After the attacks of September 11, a coalition of forces led by the United States overthrew the Taliban and attempted to build a new and moderate government. But the country's history of bitter internecine warfare among tribal groups remained a severe challenge to those efforts, and Taliban forces have managed to regroup and continue to operate in the mountainous region adjacent to the Pakistani border. The terrorist threat from al-Qaeda, however, was dealt a major blow in May 2011, when Osama bin Laden was killed by U.S. special operations forces during a raid on his hideout in northern Pakistan.

After moving against the Taliban at the end of 2001 the administration of George W. Bush, charging that Iraqi dictator Saddam Hussein had not only provided support to bin Laden's terrorist organization but also stockpiled weapons of mass destruction for use against his enemies, threatened to invade Iraq and remove him from power. It was the president's hope that the overthrow of the Iraqi dictator would promote the spread of democracy throughout the region. The plan, widely debated in the media and opposed by many of the United States' traditional allies, disquieted Arab leaders and fanned anti-American sentiment throughout the Muslim world. Nevertheless, in March 2003, U.S.-led forces attacked Iraq and overthrew Saddam Hussein's regime. In the months that followed, occupation forces sought to restore stability to the country while setting out plans on which to build a democratic society. But although Saddam Hussein was captured by U.S. troops and later executed, armed resistance by militant Muslim elements continued.

When Barack Obama came into office in 2009, he promised to bring about the withdrawal of U.S. combat forces from Iraq, while training an Iraqi military force capable of defeating the remaining insurgents. In the meantime, a fragile government has been formed in Baghdad, the embryo of a possible pro-Western state that could serve as an emblem of democracy in the Middle East. Squabbling among Sunni, Shi'ite, and Kurdish elements within the country, however, is a vivid reminder that a similar effort by the British eighty years earlier ended with minimal success.

Revolution in the Middle East

In the early months of 2011, popular protests against current conditions broke out in several countries in the Middle East. Beginning in Tunisia, the riots spread rapidly to Egypt— where they brought about the abrupt resignation of longtime president Hosni Mubarak (HAHS-nee moo-BAH-rahk) (b.1929)—and then to other countries in the region, such as Syria, Libya, and Yemen, where political leaders sought to quell the unrest, often by violent means. The uprisings aroused hopes around the world that the seeds of democracy had been planted in a region long dominated by autocratic governments, but also provoked widespread concern that unstable conditions could lead to further violence and a rise in international terrorism. In the months following the outbreak of unrest, the prognosis for the future of the region was still unclear.

Society and Culture in the Contemporary Middle East

 FOCUS QUESTION: How have religious issues affected economic, social, and cultural conditions in the Middle East in recent decades?

In the Middle East today, all aspects of society and culture— from political and economic issues to literature, art, and the role of the family—are intertwined with questions of religious faith.

Varieties of Government: The Politics of Islam

To many seasoned observers, the strategy applied by President George W. Bush in Iraq appeared unrealistic, since democratic values are not deeply rooted in the culture of the Middle East. In many countries, feudal rulers remain securely in power. The kings of Saudi Arabia, for example, continue to govern by traditional precepts and, citing the distinctive character of Muslim society, have been reluctant to establish representative political institutions. These rulers insist that strict observance of traditional customs be maintained. Religious police are responsible for enforcing the Muslim dress code, maintaining the prohibition against alcohol, and making sure that offices close during the time of prayer.

To be sure, there have been some variations in government throughout the region. In some societies, traditional authority has been replaced by charismatic one-party rule or military dictatorships. Nasser's Egypt was a single-party state where the leader won political power by the force of his presence or personality. The regimes of Ayatollah Khomeini in Iran, Muammar Qaddafi in Libya, and Saddam Hussein in Iraq could also trace much of their power to the personal appeal of the leader.

In other states, charismatic rule has given way to modernizing bureaucratic regimes. Examples include the governments of Syria, Yemen, Turkey, and Egypt since Nasser, where Anwar al-Sadat and his successor, Hosni Mubarak, focused on performance. Most of these regimes have remained highly autocratic in character, however, except in Turkey, where free elections and the sharing of power have become more prevalent in recent years. Only in the Jewish state of Israel are democratic institutions firmly established.

A few Arab nations, such as Bahrain, Kuwait, and Jordan, have engaged in limited forms of democratic experimentation. Most of the region's recent leaders, however, have maintained that Western-style democracy is not appropriate for their societies. Bashar al-Assad (bah-SHAHR al-ah-SAHD) (b. 1965), the president of Syria, once remarked that he would tolerate only "positive criticism" of his policies. "We have to have our own democracy to match our history and culture," he said, "arising from the needs of our people and our reality."[9] President Mubarak of Egypt often insisted to foreign critics that only authoritarian rule could prevent the spread of Islamic radicalism throughout his country. The

Islam and Democracy

RELIGION & PHILOSOPHY

One of George W. Bush's objectives in launching the invasion of Iraq was to promote the emergence of democratic states in the Middle East. According to U.S. officials, one reason for the formation of terrorist movements in Muslim societies is the prevalence of dictatorial governments that do not serve the interests of their citizens. According to the author of this editorial, an Indian Muslim, the problem lies as much with the actions of Western countries as it does with political attitudes in the Muslim world.

M. J. Akbar, "Linking Islam to Dictatorship"

Let us examine a central canard, that Islam and democracy are incompatible. This is an absurdity. There is nothing Islamic or un-Islamic about democracy. Democracy is the outcome of a political process, not a religious process.

It is glibly suggested that "every" Muslim country is a dictatorship, but the four largest Muslim populations of the world—in Indonesia, India, Bangladesh, and Turkey—vote to change governments. Pakistan could easily have been on this list.

Voting does not make these Muslims less or more religious. There are dictators among Muslims just as there are dictators among Christians, Buddhists, and Hindus. . . . Christian Latin America has seen ugly forms of dictatorship, as has Christian Africa.

What is unique to the Muslim world is not the absence of democracy but the fact that in 1918, after the defeat of the Ottoman Empire, every single Muslim in the world lived under foreign subjugation. . . .

The West, in the shape of Britain, France, or America, was never interested in democracy when a helpful dictator or king would serve. When people got a chance to express their wish, it was only logical that they would ask for popular rule. It was the street that brought Mossadegh to power in Iran and drove the shah of Iran to tearful exile in Rome. Who brought the shah of Iran and autocracy back to Iran? The CIA.

If Iranian democracy had been permitted a chance in 1953, there would have been no uprising led by Ayatollah Khomeini in 1979. In other countries, where the struggle for independence was long and brutal, as in Algeria and Indonesia, the militias who had fought the war institutionalized army authority. In other instances, civilian heroes confused their own well-being with national health. They became regressive dictators. Once again, there was nothing Islamic about it.

Muslim countries will become democracies, too, because it is the finest form of modern governance. But it will be a process interrupted by bloody experience as the street wrenches power from usurpers. . . .

Democracy has become the latest rationale for the occupation of Iraq. . . . Granted, democracy is always preferable to tyranny no matter how it comes. But Iraqis are not dupes. They will take democracy and place it at the service of nationalism. . . .

There is uncertainty and apprehension across the Muslim nations: uncertainty about where they stand, and apprehension about both American power and the repugnant use of terrorism that in turn invites the exercise of American power. There is also anger that a legitimate cause like that of Palestine can get buried in the debris of confusion. Muslims do not see Palestinians as terrorists.

 How does the author of this editorial answer the charge that democracy and Islam are incompatible? To what degree, in his view, is the West responsible for the problems of the Middle East?

recent electoral victory of the militant group Hamas in Palestine may be a case in point.

For many years, most world leaders have accepted the logic of these contentions, provoking some critics to charge that Western governments coddle Middle Eastern dictatorships as a means of maintaining stability in the region and preserving their access to the vast oil reserves located on the Arabian peninsula (see the box on p. 882). For their part, authoritarian leaders in the region sought to deflect, often with great success, popular discontent with local conditions onto the West.

The recent outbreak of popular unrest that has erupted from North Africa to the Arabian peninsula raises questions about the potential for democratic changes to emerge in the countries throughout the region. Are democratic institutions and the principles of human freedom truly antithetical to the culture of the Middle East and the principles of Islam? As we await the consequences of the current wave of popular unrest, the fate of the region hangs in the balance.

The Economics of the Middle East: Oil and Sand

Few areas exhibit a greater disparity of individual and national wealth than the Middle East. While millions live in abject poverty, a fortunate few rank among the wealthiest people in the world. The primary reason for this disparity is oil. Unfortunately for most of the peoples of the region, oil

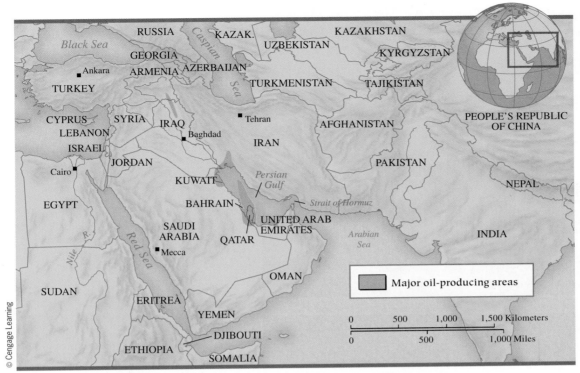

MAP 29.3 The Modern Middle East. Shown here are the boundaries of the independent states in the contemporary Middle East.

 Which are the major oil-producing countries?

reserves are distributed unevenly and all too often are located in areas where the population density is low (see Map 29.3). Egypt and Turkey, with more than 75 million inhabitants apiece, have almost no oil reserves. The combined population of Kuwait, the United Arab Emirates, and Saudi Arabia is about 35 million people. This disparity in wealth inspired Nasser's quest for Arab unity but has also posed a major obstacle to that unity.

ECONOMICS AND ISLAM Not surprisingly, considering their different resources and political systems, the states of the Middle East have adopted diverse approaches to the problem of developing strong and stable economies. Some, like Nasser in Egypt and the leaders of the Ba'ath Party in Syria, attempted to create a form of Arab socialism, favoring a high level of government involvement in the economy to relieve the inequities of the free enterprise system. Others turned to the Western capitalist model to maximize growth while using taxes or massive development projects to build a modern infrastructure, redistribute wealth, and maintain political stability and economic opportunity for all (see the comparative illustration on p. 884).

Whatever their approach, all the states have attempted to develop their economies in accordance with Islamic beliefs. Although the Qur'an has little to say about economics and cannot be said to be either capitalist or socialist, it is clear in its opposition to charging interest and in its concern for the material welfare of the Muslim community, the *umma*. How these goals are to be achieved, though, is a matter of interpretation.

Socialist theories of economic development such as Nasser's were often suggested as a way to promote economic growth while meeting the requirements of Islamic doctrine. State intervention in the economic sector would bring about rapid development, while land redistribution and the nationalization or regulation of industry would minimize the harsh inequities of the marketplace. In general, however, the socialist approach has had little success, and most governments, including those of Egypt and Syria, eventually shifted to a more free enterprise approach while encouraging foreign investment to compensate for a lack of capital or technology.

AGRICULTURAL POLICIES Although the amount of arable land is relatively small, most countries in the Middle East rely on farming to supply food for their growing populations. Much of the fertile land was owned by wealthy absentee landlords, but land reform programs in several countries have attempted to alleviate this problem.

The most comprehensive and probably the most successful land reform program was instituted in Egypt, where Nasser and his successors managed to reassign nearly a quarter of all cultivable lands by limiting the amount a single individual could hold. Similar programs in Iran, Iraq, Libya, and Syria generally had less effect. After the 1979 revolution in Iran, many farmers forcibly seized lands from the landlords, raising questions of ownership that the revolutionary government has tried to resolve with only minimal success.

COMPARATIVE ILLUSTRATION

POLITICS & GOVERNMENT

Wealth and Poverty in the Middle East. Although many of the countries in the Middle East are relatively poor by world standards, a favored few have amassed great wealth as a result of their fortunate geographic location. Such is the case with the United Arab Emirates, a small country situated strategically on the eastern edge of the Arabian peninsula and located directly over some of the most abundant oil reserves in the world. The modern city of Dubai (top photo), resplendent in its opulence, serves today as a playground for the rich and a vivid symbol of the wealth that has flowed into the region because of the world's thirst for energy. At the opposite extreme is Yemen, on the southern edge of the Arabian peninsula. Lacking valuable resources, the people of Yemen, live by traditional pursuits, as shown in the photo at the bottom.

 Which are the wealthiest states in the region? Which are the poorest?

Agricultural productivity throughout the region has been plagued by a lack of water. With populations growing at more than 2 percent annually on average in the Middle East (more than 3 percent in some countries), several governments have tried to increase the amount of water available for irrigation. Many attempts have been sabotaged by government ineptitude, political disagreements, and territorial conflicts, however. For example, disputes between Israel and its neighbors over water rights and between Iraq and its neighbors over the exploitation of the Tigris and Euphrates Rivers have caused serious tensions in recent years. Today, the dearth of water in the region is reaching crisis proportions.

MIGRATORY WORKERS Another way that governments have attempted to deal with rapid population growth is to encourage emigration. Oil-producing states with small populations, such as Saudi Arabia and the United Arab Emirates, have imported labor from other countries in the region, mostly to work in the oil fields. Since the mid-1980s, the majority of the population in those states has been composed of foreign nationals, who often send the bulk of their salaries back to their families in their home countries. When oil revenues declined in the 1980s and 1990s, however, several governments took measures to reduce their migrant population. Today migrant workers are a volatile force in the politics of the region.

The Islamic Revival

In recent years, developments in the Middle East have often been described in terms of a resurgence of traditional values and customs in response to Western influence. Indeed, some conservative religious forces in the area have consciously attempted to replace foreign culture and values with allegedly "pure" Islamic forms of belief and behavior.

MODERNIST ISLAM Initially, many Muslim intellectuals responded to Western influence by trying to create a "modernized" set of Islamic beliefs and practices that would not clash with the demands of the twentieth century. This process took place to some degree in most Islamic societies, but it was especially prevalent in Turkey, Egypt, and Iran. Mustafa Kemal Atatürk embraced the strategy when he attempted to secularize the Islamic religion in the new Turkish republic. The Turkish model was followed by Shah Reza Khan and his son Mohammad Reza Pahlavi in Iran and then by Nasser in postwar Egypt, all of whom attempted to honor Islamic values while asserting the primacy of other issues such as political and economic development. Religion, in effect, had become the handmaiden of political power, national identity, and economic prosperity.

These secularizing trends were particularly noticeable among the political, intellectual, and economic elites in urban areas. They had less influence in the countryside, among the poor, and among devout elements within the clergy. Many of the clerics believed that Western influence in the cities had given birth to political and economic corruption, sexual promiscuity, hedonism, individualism, and the prevalence of alcohol, pornography, and drugs. Although such practices had long existed in the Middle East, they were now far more visible and socially acceptable.

RETURN TO TRADITION Reaction among conservatives against the modernist movement was quick to emerge in several countries and reached its zenith in the late 1970s with the return of the Ayatollah Khomeini to Iran. It is not surprising that Iran took the lead in light of its long tradition of ideological purity within the Shi'ite sect as well as the uncompromisingly secular character of the shah's reforms in the postwar era. In Iran today, traditional Islamic beliefs are all-pervasive and extend into education, clothing styles, social practices, and the legal system. In recent years, for example, Iranian women have been heavily fined or even flogged for violating the Islamic dress code.

The cultural and social effects of the Iranian Revolution soon began to spread. In Algeria, the political influence of fundamentalist Islamic groups enabled them to win a stunning victory

in the national elections in 1992. When the military stepped in to cancel the second round of elections and crack down on the militants, the latter responded with a campaign of terrorism against moderates that claimed thousands of lives.

A similar trend emerged in Egypt, where militant groups such as the Muslim Brotherhood, formed in 1928 as a means of promoting personal piety, engaged in terrorism, including the assassination of President Anwar al-Sadat and attacks on foreign tourists, who are considered carriers of corrupt Western influence.

Even in Turkey, generally considered the most secular of Islamic societies, a Muslim political group took power in a coalition government formed in 1996. The new government adopted a pro-Arab stance in foreign affairs and threatened to reduce the country's economic and political ties to Europe. Worried moderates voiced their concern that the secular legacy of Kemal Atatürk was being eroded, and eventually the government resigned under heavy pressure from the military. But a new Islamist organization, known as the Justice and Development Party (the AK Party), won elections held in 2007 and has signaled its intention to guarantee the rights of devout Muslims to display their faith publicly. In elections held in June 2011, the AK Party won a clear victory with about 50 percent of the vote.

Throughout the Middle East, even governments and individuals who do not support efforts to return to pure Islamic principles have adjusted their behavior and beliefs in subtle

© Patrick Robert/Sygma/CORBIS

Answering the Call of the *Muezzin*. With the renewed fervor of Muslims in the world today, scenes such as this one in Kuwait exemplify the adherents' humble submission to God. Required to pray five times a day—at dawn, noon, midafternoon, sunset, and early evening—a Muslim, after ritual ablutions, prostrates himself facing Mecca to proclaim, "There is no god but Allah, and Muhammad is his prophet." Responding to the call of the *muezzin*, which today is often a recorded message from the minaret of a mosque, the faithful can perform their prayers in a few minutes, wherever they are, at home or in any public place. There are an estimated 1.3 billion Muslims in the world today, 175 million of whom are in Indonesia, 105 million in India, and 15 million in Europe.

ways. In Egypt, for example, the government now encourages television programs devoted to religion in preference to comedies and adventure shows imported from the West, and alcohol is discouraged or at least consumed more discreetly.

Women in the Middle East

Nowhere have the fault lines between tradition and modernity in Muslim societies in the Middle East been so sharp as in the ongoing debate over the role of women. At the beginning of the twentieth century, women's place in Middle Eastern society had changed little since the death of the prophet Muhammad. Women were secluded in their homes and had few legal, political, or social rights.

During the first decades of the twentieth century, advocates of modernist views began to contend that Islamic doctrine was not inherently opposed to women's rights. To modernists, Islamic traditions such as female seclusion, wearing the veil, and polygamy were actually pre-Islamic folk traditions that had been tolerated in the early Islamic era and continued to be practiced in later centuries. Such views had a considerable impact on a number of Middle Eastern societies, including Turkey and Iran. As we have seen, greater rights for women were a crucial element in the social revolution promoted by Kemal Atatürk in Turkey. In Iran, Shah Reza Khan and his son granted female suffrage and encouraged the education of women. In Egypt, a vocal feminist movement arose in educated women's circles in Cairo as early as the 1920s. With the exception of Orthodox religious communities, women in Israel have achieved substantial equality with men and are active in politics, the professions, and even the armed forces. Golda Meir (may-EER) (1898–1978), prime minister of Israel from 1969 to 1974, became an international symbol of the ability of women to be world leaders.

In recent years, a more traditional view of women's role has tended to prevail in many Middle Eastern countries. Attacks by religious conservatives on the growing role of women contributed to the emotions underlying the Iranian Revolution of 1979. Iranian women were instructed to wear the veil and to dress modestly in public. Films produced in postrevolutionary Iran rarely featured women, and when they did, physical contact between men and women was prohibited. The events in Iran had repercussions in secular Muslim societies such as Egypt, Turkey, and far-off Malaysia, where women began to dress more modestly in public and criticism of open sexuality in the media became increasingly frequent.

The most conservative nation by far remains Saudi Arabia, where following Wahhabi tradition, women are not only segregated and expected to wear the veil in public but also restricted in education and forbidden to drive automobiles (see the box on p. 887). Still, women's rights have been extended in a few countries. In 1999, women obtained the right to vote in Kuwait, and they have been granted an equal right with their husbands to seek a divorce in Egypt. Even in Iran, women have many freedoms that they lacked before the twentieth century; for example, they can receive military training, vote, practice birth control, and publish fiction. Most important, today nearly 60 percent of university entrants in Iran are women.

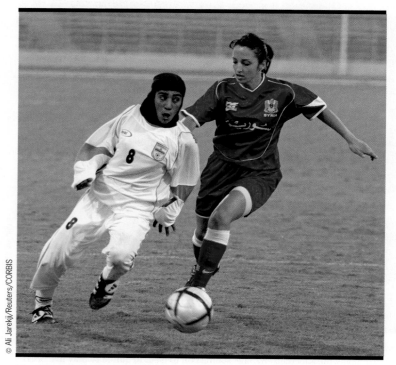

Playing Soccer. Despite having to cover their bodies in public, young Iranian women play soccer and other sports, attend schools and universities, and partake in other activities of the modern world. Here we see a young woman from Iran in a black-hooded garment and another from Syria playing a game of soccer. Today, about 2 million Iranian women take part in sports, whereas they rarely did so before the Islamic Revolution.

Literature and Art

As in other areas of Asia and Africa, the encounter with the West in the nineteenth and twentieth centuries stimulated a cultural renaissance in the Middle East. Muslim authors translated Western works into Arabic and Persian and began to experiment with new literary forms.

NATIONAL LITERATURES Iran has produced one of the most prominent national literatures in the contemporary Middle East. Since World War II, Iranian literature has been hampered somewhat by political considerations, since it has been expected to serve first the Pahlavi monarchy and then the Islamic republic. Nevertheless, Iranian writers are among the most prolific in the region and often write in prose, which has finally been accepted as the equal of poetry. Perhaps the most outstanding Iranian author of the twentieth century was the short-story writer Sadeq Hedayat (sah-DEK HAY-dy-yaht) (1903–1951). Hedayat was obsessed with the frailty and absurdity of life and wrote with compassion about the problems of ordinary human beings. Frustrated and disillusioned at the government's suppression of individual liberties, he committed suicide in 1951. Like Japan's Mishima Yukio, Hedayat later became a cult figure among his country's youth.

Keeping the Camel out of the Tent

FAMILY & SOCIETY

"Almighty God created sexual desire in ten parts; then he gave nine parts to women and one to men." So pronounced Ali, Muhammad's son-in-law, as he explained why women are held morally responsible as the instigators of sexual intercourse. Consequently, over the centuries, Islamic women have been secluded, veiled, and in many cases genitally mutilated in order to safeguard male virtue. Women are forbidden to look directly at, speak to, or touch a man prior to marriage. Even today, they are often sequestered at home or limited to strictly segregated areas away from all male contact. Women normally pray at home or in an enclosed antechamber of the mosque so that their physical presence will not disturb men's spiritual concentration.

Especially limiting today are the laws governing women's behavior in Saudi Arabia. Schooling for girls has never been compulsory because fathers believe that "educating women is like allowing the nose of the camel into the tent; eventually the beast will edge in and take up all the room inside." The country did not establish its first girls' school until 1956. The following description of Saudi women is from *Nine Parts Desire: The Hidden World of Islamic Women* by the journalist Geraldine Brooks.

Geraldine Brooks, *Nine Parts Desire*

Women were first admitted to university in Saudi Arabia in 1962, and all women's colleges remain strictly segregated. Lecture rooms come equipped with closed-circuit TVs and telephones, so women students can listen to a male professor and question him by phone, without having to contaminate themselves by being seen by him. When the first dozen women graduated from university in 1973, they were devastated to find that their names hadn't been printed on the commencement program. The old tradition, that it dishonors women to mention them, was depriving them of recognition they believed they'd earned. The women and their families protested, so a separate program was printed and a segregated graduation ceremony was held for the students' female relatives. . . .

But while the opening of women's universities widened access to higher learning for women, it also made the educational experience much shallower. Before 1962, many progressive Saudi families had sent their daughters abroad for education. They had returned to the kingdom not only with a degree but with experience of the outside world. . . . Now a whole generation of Saudi women have completed their education entirely within the country. . . .

Lack of opportunity for education abroad means that Saudi women are trapped in the confines of an education system that still lags men's. Subjects such as geology and petroleum engineering—tickets to influential jobs in Saudi Arabia's oil economy—remain closed to women. . . . Few women's colleges have their own libraries, and libraries shared with men's schools are either entirely off limits to women or open to them only one day per week. . . .

But women and men sit for the same degree examinations. Professors quietly acknowledge the women's scores routinely outstrip the men's. "It's no surprise," said one woman professor. "Look at their lives. The boys have their cars, they can spend the evenings cruising the streets with their friends, sitting in cafés, buying black-market alcohol and drinking all night. What do the girls have? Four walls and their books. For them, education is everything."

 According to Geraldine Brooks, do women in Saudi Arabia have an opportunity to receive an education? To what degree do they take advantage of it?

Despite the male-oriented nature of Iranian society, many of the new writers have been women. Since the revolution, the veil and the *chador* (CHUH-der *or* CHAH-der), an all-enveloping cloak, have become the central metaphor in Iranian women's writing. Those who favor body covering praise it as the last bastion of defense against Western cultural imperialism. Behind the veil, the Islamic woman can breathe freely, unpolluted by foreign exploitation and moral corruption. Other Iranian women, however, consider the veil and *chador* a "mobile prison" or an oppressive anachronism from the Dark Ages. As one writer, Sousan Azadi, expressed it, "As I pulled the *chador* over me, I felt a heaviness descending over me. I was hidden and in hiding. There was nothing visible left of Sousan Azadi. I felt like an animal of the light suddenly trapped in a cave. I was just another faceless Moslem woman carrying a whole inner world hidden inside the *chador*."[10] Whether or not they accept the veil, women writers are a vital part of contemporary Iranian literature, addressing all aspects of social issues.

Like Iran, Egypt in the twentieth century experienced a flowering of literature accelerated by the establishment of the Egyptian republic in the early 1950s. The most illustrious contemporary Egyptian writer was Naguib Mahfouz (nah-GEEB mah-FOOZ) (1911–2006), who won the Nobel Prize for Literature in 1988. His *Cairo Trilogy* (1952) chronicles three generations of a merchant family in Cairo during the tumultuous years between the world wars. Mahfouz was particularly adept at blending panoramic historical events with the intimate lives of ordinary human beings. In recent years, several best-selling novels have been translated from Arabic into English.

In *The Yacoubian Building*, Alaa al-Aswany (ah-LAH al-as-WAH-nee) (b. 1957) deplores the problems of political corruption and religious fundamentalism that plagued Egypt under Mubarak's regime. Meanwhile, in *Girls of Riyadh*, the Saudi writer Rajaa Alsanea (rah-JAH al-sah-NAY-ah) (b. 1981) pleads for more freedom in relations between the sexes and extols the benefits of marriage for love rather than solely for convenience.

Although Israeli literature arises from a totally different tradition from that of its neighbors, it shares with them certain contemporary characteristics and a concern for ordinary human beings. Early writers identified with the aspirations of the new nation, trying to find a sense of order in the new reality, voicing terrors from the past and hopes for the future.

Some contemporary Israeli authors, however, have taken controversial positions on sensitive national issues. Three internationally renowned authors, Amos Oz (b. 1939), A.B. Yehoshua (YEH-hoh-shoo-uh) (b. 1936), and David Grossman (b. 1954), have long been vocal supporters of peace with the Palestinians. Their works address the difficulties of the Israeli situation as well as the bitterness of Palestinians living under Israeli occupation. In his extraordinary novel, *To the End of the Land* (2010), Grossman weaves together the daily joys and sorrows of an ordinary Israeli family with the constant undercurrent of conflict and loss. Having lost his own son in battle in 2006, Grosssman has been labeled by some the moral conscience of his country. With the Arabs feeling victimized by colonialism and the Jews by Nazi Germany, each side believes that it alone is the rightful proprietor of ancient Palestine. For these three authors, the only solution is compromise, which, however unsatisfactory to both sides, is preferable to mutual self-destruction.

As in other areas of the developing world, the reading of books has drastically declined in the Middle East, eclipsed by television and other forms of popular entertainment and discouraged by poverty and by government censorship reflecting political control or religious conservatism. The old maxim that "Cairo writes, Beirut publishes, and Baghdad reads" is no longer true. In Egypt, where even *The Arabian Nights* was banned, the Mubarak government censored most new fiction, while in Iraq, severe inflation has made the purchase price of books prohibitive. Another problem stems from the fact that the one common language of the Middle East—classical Arabic—is not conducive to expressing contemporary life; it is as stilted as Shakespearean English. Yet if authors choose to write in their own Arabic dialect, they greatly restrict their potential audience.

ART AND MUSIC Like literature, the art of the modern Middle East has been profoundly influenced by its exposure to Western culture. At first, artists tended to imitate Western models, but later they began to experiment with national styles, returning to earlier forms for inspiration. Some emulated the writers in returning to the village to depict peasants and shepherds, but others followed international trends and attempted to express the alienation and disillusionment that characterize so much of modern life.

The popular music of the contemporary Middle East has also been strongly influenced by that of the modern West, but to different degrees in different countries. In Israel, many contemporary young rock stars voice lyrics as irreverent toward the traditions of their elders as those of Europe and the United States. One idol of many Israeli young people, the rock star Aviv Geffen (b. 1973), declares himself "a person of no values," and his music carries a shock value that attacks the country's political and social shibboleths. The rock music popular among Palestinians, on the other hand, makes greater use of Arab musical motifs and is closely tied to a political message. One recording, "The Song of the Engineer," lauds Yahya Ayash (1966–1996), a Palestinian accused of manufacturing many of the explosive devices used in terrorist attacks on Israeli citizens. The lyrics have their own shock value: "Spread the flame of revolution. Your explosive will wipe the enemy out, like a volcano, a torch, a banner." When one Palestinian rock leader from Gaza was asked why his group employed a musical style that originated in the West, he explained, "For us, this is a tool like any other. Young people in Gaza like our music, they listen to us, they buy our cassettes, and so they spread our message."

CHAPTER SUMMARY

The Middle East is one of the most unstable regions in the world today. In part, this turbulence is due to the continued interference of outsiders attracted by the massive oil reserves under the parched wastes of the Arabian peninsula and in the vicinity of the Persian Gulf. Oil is indeed both a blessing and a curse to the peoples of the region. The similarities with Africa are striking, as governments in both regions struggle to achieve regional cooperation among themselves while fending off the influence of powerful foreign states or multinational corporations.

Some would argue, however, that anger at Western meddling in the Middle East began generations or even centuries earlier. According to the historian Bernard Lewis, the roots of Muslim resentment emerged centuries ago, when Arab hegemony in the region was replaced by European domination. That sense of humiliation culminated in the early twentieth century, when much of the Middle East was occupied by Western colonial regimes. Today, the world is reaping the harvest of that long-cultivated bitterness, as recruits flock to terrorist movements like al-Qaeda in response to Osama bin Laden's call to eliminate all Western influence in the Arab world.

Another factor contributing to the volatility of the Middle East is the tug-of-war between the sense of ethnic identity in the form of nationalism and the intense longing to be part of a broader Islamic community, a dream that dates back to the time of the prophet Muhammad. Sometimes, the motive for seeking Arab unity may simply be self-aggrandizement—two such examples are Nasser and Saddam Hussein. But there are undoubtedly others who see restoration of the caliphate as a means of reversing the stain of moral decline that they see taking place throughout the region. Muslims, of course, are not alone in believing that a purer form of religious faith is the best antidote for such social evils as hedonism, sexual license, and political corruption. But it is hard to deny that the issue has been pursued with more anger and passion in the Middle East than in almost any other part of the world. The current wave of popular protest has been focused primarily on internal political and economic concerns in each country. But whatever the outcome, the role of Islam in society will be one of the foremost issues that will face new leaders in the region. The consequences of this struggle cannot yet be foreseen.

CHAPTER TIMELINE

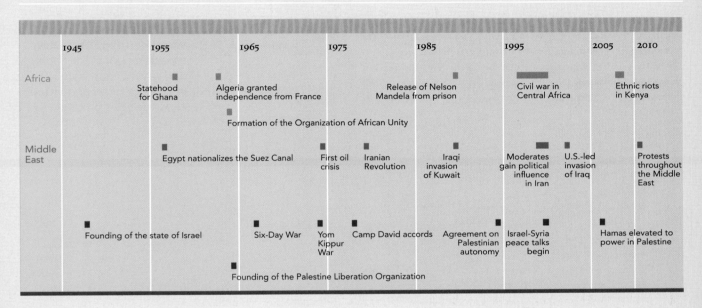

CHAPTER REVIEW

Upon Reflection

Q What are some of the key reasons advanced to explain why democratic institutions have been slow to take root in the Middle East?

Q Why do tensions between farmers and pastoral peoples appear to be on the rise in Africa today? In what parts of the continent is the problem most serious?

Q What are the main sources of discord in the Middle East today? How do they contribute to the popularity of radical terrorist organizations in the region?

Key Terms

uhuru (p. 858)
apartheid (p. 858)
pan-Africanism (p. 859)
neocolonialism (p. 860)
African Union (p. 868)

pan-Arabism (p. 873)
intifada (p. 877)
Hezbollah (p. 877)

Suggested Reading

AFRICA: GENERAL For general surveys of contemporary African history, see **P. Nugent,** *Africa Since Independence* (New York, 2004); **M. Meredith,** *The Fate of Africa* (New York, 2005); and **H. French,** *A Continent for the Taking: The Tragedy and Hope of Africa* (New York, 2004).

AFRICAN LITERATURE AND ART For a survey of African literature, see **A. Kalu, ed.,** *The Rienner Anthology of African Literatures* (London, 2007); **M. J. Hay,** *African Novels in the Classroom* (Boulder, Colo., 2000); and **M. J. Daymond et al., eds.,** *Women Writing Africa: The Southern Region* (New York, 2003). On art, see **S. L. Kasfir,** *Contemporary African Art* (London, 1999).

WOMEN IN AFRICA For interesting analyses of women's issues in the Africa of this time frame, see **M. Kevane,** *Women and Development in Africa: How Gender Works* (Boulder, Colo., 2004).

RECENT EVENTS IN AFRICA For contrasting views on the reasons for Africa's current difficulties, see **J. Marah**, *The African People in the Global Village: An Introduction to Pan-African Studies* (Lanham, Md., 1998), and **G. Ayittey**, *Africa in Chaos* (New York, 1998).

THE MIDDLE EAST A good general survey of the modern Middle East is **A. Goldschmidt Jr.**, *A Concise History of the Middle East* (Boulder, Colo., 2005).

ISRAEL AND PALESTINE On Israel and the Palestinian question, see **D. Ross**, *The Missing Peace: The Inside Story of the Fight for Middle East Peace* (New York, 2004). On Jerusalem, see **B. Wasserstein**, *Divided Jerusalem: The Struggle for the Holy City* (New Haven, Conn., 2000).

IRAN AND IRAQ On the Iranian Revolution, see **S. Bakash**, *The Reign of the Ayatollahs* (New York, 1984). Iran's role in Middle Eastern politics and diplomacy is analyzed in **T. Parsi**, *Treacherous Alliance: The Secret Dealings of Israel, Iran, and the United States* (New Haven, Conn., 2007). The Iran-Iraq War is discussed in **S. C. Pelletiere**, *The Iran-Iraq War: Chaos in a Vacuum* (New York, 1992). The issue of oil is examined in **D. Yergin et al.**, *The Prize: The Epic Quest for Oil, Money, and Power* (New York, 1993).

For historical perspective on the invasion of Iraq, see **J. Kendell**, *Iraq's Unruly Century* (New York, 2003). **R. Khalidi**, *Resurrecting Empire: Western Footprints and America's Perilous Path in the Middle East* (Boston, 2003), is a critical look at U.S. policy in the region.

For expert analysis of the situation in the region, see **B. Lewis**, *What Went Wrong? Western Impact and Middle Eastern Response* (Oxford, 2001), and **P. L. Bergen**, *Holy War, Inc.: Inside the Secret World of Osama bin Laden* (New York, 2001). Also see **M. Afkhami** and **E. Friedl**, *In the Eye of the Storm: Women in Post-Revolutionary Iran* (Syracuse, N.Y., 1994).

MIDDLE EASTERN LITERATURE For a scholarly but accessible overview of Arabic literature, see **M. M. Badawi**, *A Short History of Modern Arab Literature* (Oxford, 1993).

Go to the CourseMate website at **www.cengagebrain.com** for additional study tools and review materials—including audio and video clips—for this chapter.

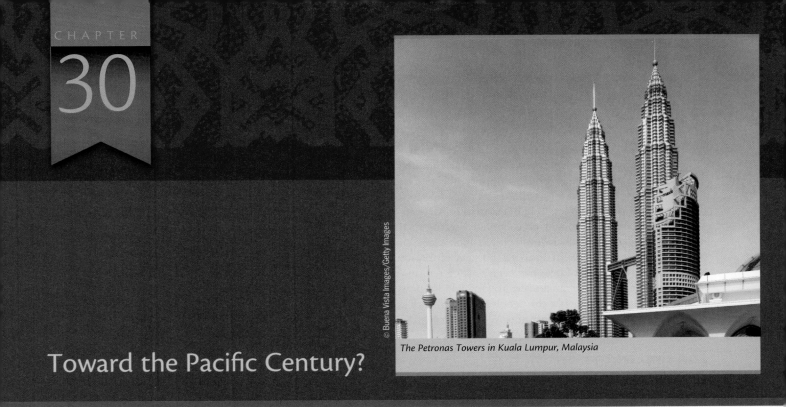

The Petronas Towers in Kuala Lumpur, Malaysia

Toward the Pacific Century?

CHAPTER OUTLINE
AND FOCUS QUESTIONS

South Asia

Q How did Gandhi's and Nehru's goals for India differ, and what role has each leader's views played in shaping modern India?

Southeast Asia

Q What kinds of problems have the nations of Southeast Asia faced since 1945, and how have they attempted to solve them?

Japan: Asian Giant

Q How did the Allied occupation after World War II change Japan's political and economic institutions, and what remained unchanged?

The Little Tigers

Q What factors have contributed to the economic success achieved by the Little Tigers? To what degree have they applied the Japanese model in forging their developmental strategies?

CRITICAL THINKING

Q What differences and similarities do you see in the performances of the nations of South, Southeast, and East Asia since World War II? What do you think accounts for the differences?

FIRST-TIME VISITORS to the Malaysian capital of Kuala Lumpur (KWAH-luh loom-POOR) are astonished to see a pair of twin towers thrusting up above the surrounding buildings into the clouds. The Petronas Towers rise 1,483 feet from ground level; they were the world's tallest buildings at the time of their completion in 1998. (They have since been surpassed by other structures such as Burj Khalifa, in Dubai, and Taipei 101, in Taiwan.)

Beyond their status as an architectural achievement, the Petronas Towers announced the emergence of Southeast Asia as a major player on the international scene. It is no accident that the foundations were laid on the site of the Selangor Cricket Club, symbol of British colonial hegemony in Southeast Asia. "These towers," commented one local official, "will do wonders for Asia's self-esteem and confidence, which I think is very important, and which I think at this moment are at the point of takeoff."[1]

The sky-piercing towers in Kuala Lumpur and Taipei (TY-PAY) are not alone in signaling Asia's new prominence on the world stage in the century now unfolding. Several other cities in the region, including Hong Kong, Singapore, Tokyo, and Shanghai, have become major capitals of finance and monuments of economic prowess, rivaling the traditional centers of New York, London, Berlin, and Paris.

That the nations of the Pacific Rim would become a driving force in global development was all but unimaginable after World War II, when the Communist triumph in China ushered in an era of intense competition between the capitalist and socialist camps. Bitter conflicts in Korea and Vietnam were visible manifestations of a region in turmoil. Yet today, many of the nations of eastern Asia have become models of successful nation building, characterized by economic prosperity and political stability. They have heralded the opening of what has been called the "Pacific Century."

South Asia

 Q FOCUS QUESTION: How did Gandhi's and Nehru's goals for India differ, and what role has each leader's views played in shaping modern India?

In 1947, nearly two centuries of British colonial rule came to an end when two new independent nations, India and Pakistan, came into being. Under British authority, the subcontinent of South Asia had been linked ever more closely to the global capitalist economy. Yet, as in other areas of Asia and in Africa, the experience brought only limited benefits to the local peoples; little industrial development took place, and the bulk of the profits went into the pockets of Western entrepreneurs. Nationalist forces had been seeking reforms in colonial policy and the eventual overthrow of colonial power for at least half a century, but the peoples of South Asia did not attain their independence until after World War II.

The End of the British Raj

During the 1930s, the nationalist movement in India was severely shaken by factional disagreements between Hindus and Muslims. The outbreak of World War II subdued these sectarian clashes, but they erupted again after the war ended in 1945. Battles between Hindus and Muslims broke out in several cities, and Muhammad Ali Jinnah (muh-HAM-ad ah-LEE JIN-uh) (1876–1948), leader of the Muslim League, demanded the creation of a separate state for each ethnic group. Meanwhile, the Labour Party, which had long been critical of British colonial policies on both moral and economic grounds, had come to power in Britain, and the new prime minister, Clement Attlee, announced that governing authority would be transferred to "responsible Indian hands" by June 1948.

But the imminence of independence had no effect on communal strife. As riots escalated, the British reluctantly accepted the inevitability of partition and declared that on August 15, 1947, two independent nations—Hindu India and Muslim Pakistan—would be established. Pakistan would consist of the main area of Muslim habitation in the Indus River valley in the west and a separate territory in eastern Bengal, 2,000 miles to the east. Although Mahatma Gandhi warned that partition would provoke "an orgy of blood,"[2] he was by now regarded as a figure of the past, and his views were ignored.

The British instructed the rulers in the princely states to choose which nation they would join by August 15, but problems arose in predominantly Hindu Hyderabad (HY-der-uh-bahd), where the governor was a Muslim, and in the mountainous province of Jammu (JUHM-oo) and Kashmir (KAZH-meer), usually referred to simply as Kashmir, where a Hindu prince ruled over a Muslim population. After independence was declared, the flight of millions of Hindus and Muslims across the borders led to violence and the deaths of more than a million people. One of the casualties was Gandhi, who was assassinated on January 30, 1948, on his way to morning prayer. The assassin, a Hindu militant, was apparently motivated by Gandhi's opposition to a strictly Hindu India.

Independent India

Upon independence, the Indian National Congress, now renamed the Congress Party, assumed governing responsibility under Jawaharlal Nehru (juh-WAH-hur-lahl NAY-roo), the new prime minister. The prospect must have been intimidating. The vast majority of India's 400 million people were poor and illiterate. The new nation encompassed a large number of ethnic groups and fourteen major languages. Although Congress leaders spoke bravely of building a new nation, Indian society still bore the scars of past wars and divisions.

The government's first problem was to resolve disputes left over from the transition period. The rulers of Hyderabad and Kashmir had both followed their own preferences rather than the wishes of their subject populations. Nehru was determined to include both states within India. In 1948, Indian troops invaded Hyderabad and annexed the area. India was also able to seize most of Kashmir, but at the cost of creating an intractable problem that has poisoned relations with Pakistan to the present day.

AN EXPERIMENT IN DEMOCRATIC SOCIALISM Under Nehru's leadership, India adopted a political system on the British model, with a figurehead president and a parliamentary form of government. A number of political parties operated legally, but the Congress Party, with its enormous prestige and charismatic leadership, was dominant at both the central and local levels.

Nehru had been influenced by British socialism and patterned his economic policy roughly after the program of the British Labour Party. The state took over ownership of the major industries and resources, transportation, and utilities, while private enterprise was permitted at the local and retail levels. Farmland remained in private hands, but rural cooperatives were officially encouraged. The government also sought to avoid excessive dependence on foreign investment and technological assistance. All businesses were required by law to have majority Indian ownership.

In other respects, Nehru was a devotee of Western materialism. He was convinced that to succeed, India must industrialize. In advocating industrialization, Nehru departed sharply from Gandhi, who believed that materialism was morally corrupting and that only simplicity and nonviolence (as represented by the traditional Indian village and the symbolic spinning wheel) could save India, and the world itself, from self-destruction (see the box on p. 893).

The primary themes of Nehru's foreign policy were anticolonialism and antiracism. Under his guidance, India took a neutral stance in the Cold War and sought to provide leadership to all newly independent nations in Asia, Africa, and Latin America. India's neutrality put it at odds with the United States, which during the 1950s was trying to mobilize all nations against what it viewed as the menace of international communism.

Relations with Pakistan continued to be troubled. India refused to consider Pakistan's claim to Kashmir, even though the majority of the population there were Muslims. Tension between the two countries persisted, erupting into war in 1965. In 1971, when riots against the Pakistani government

OPPOSING ⪦ VIEWPOINTS

Two Visions for India

POLITICS & GOVERNMENT

Although Jawaharlal Nehru and Mohandas "Mahatma" Gandhi agreed on their desire for an independent India, their visions of the future of their homeland were dramatically different. Nehru favored industrialization to build material prosperity, whereas Gandhi praised the simple virtues of manual labor. The first selection is from a speech by Nehru; the second is from a letter written by Gandhi to Nehru.

Nehru's Socialist Creed

I am convinced that the only key to the solution of the world's problems and of India's problems lies in socialism, and when I use this word I do so not in a vague humanitarian way but in the scientific economic sense. . . . I see no way of ending the poverty, the vast unemployment, the degradation and the subjection of the Indian people except through socialism. That involves vast and revolutionary changes in our political and social structure, the ending of vested interests in land and industry, as well as the feudal and autocratic Indian states system. That means the ending of private property, except in a restricted sense, and the replacement of the present profit system by a higher ideal of cooperative service. . . . In short, it means a new civilization, radically different from the present capitalist order. Some glimpse we can have of this new civilization in the territories of the USSR. Much has happened there which has pained me greatly and with which I disagree, but I look upon that great and fascinating unfolding of a new order and a new civilization as the most promising feature of our dismal age.

Mohandas Gandhi, A Letter to Jawaharlal Nehru

I believe that if India, and through India the world, is to achieve real freedom, then sooner or later we shall have to go and live in the villages—in huts, not in palaces. Millions of people can never live in cities and palaces in comfort and peace. Nor can they do so by killing one another, that is, by resorting to violence and untruth. . . . We can have the vision of . . . truth and nonviolence only in the simplicity of the villages. That simplicity resides in the spinning wheel and what is implied by the spinning wheel. . . .

You will not be able to understand me if you think that I am talking about the villages of today. My ideal village still exists only in my imagination. . . . In this village of my dreams the villager will not be dull—he will be all awareness. He will not live like an animal in filth and darkness. Men and women will live in freedom, prepared to face the whole world. There will be no plague, no cholera, and no smallpox. Nobody will be allowed to be idle or to wallow in luxury. Everyone will have to do body labor. Granting all this, I can still envisage a number of things that will have to be organized on a large scale. Perhaps there will even be railways and also post and telegraph offices. I do not know what things there will be or will not be. Nor am I bothered about it. If I can make sure of the essential thing, other things will follow in due course. But if I give up the essential thing, I give up everything.

What are the key differences between these two views on the future of India? Why do you think Nehru's proposals triumphed over Gandhi's?

---

broke out in East Pakistan, India intervened on the side of East Pakistan, which declared its independence as the new nation of Bangladesh (see Map 30.1 on p. 894).

THE POST-NEHRU ERA Nehru's death in 1964 aroused concern that Indian democracy was dependent on the Nehru mystique. When his successor, a Congress Party veteran, died in 1966, Congress leaders selected Nehru's daughter, Indira Gandhi (in-DEER-uh GAHN-dee) (1917–1984)—no relation to Mahatma Gandhi—as the new prime minister. Gandhi was inexperienced in politics, but she quickly showed the steely determination of her father.

Like Nehru, Gandhi embraced democratic socialism and a policy of neutrality in foreign affairs, but she was more activist in promoting her objectives than her father. To combat rural poverty, she nationalized banks, provided loans to peasants on easy terms, built low-cost housing, distributed land to the landless, and introduced electoral reforms to enfranchise the poor.

Gandhi was especially worried by India's growing population and in an effort to curb the growth rate adopted a policy of enforced sterilization. This policy proved unpopular, however, and along with growing official corruption and Gandhi's authoritarian tactics, it led to her defeat in the general election of 1975, the first time the Congress Party had failed to win a majority at the national level.

A minority government of procapitalist parties was formed, but within two years, Gandhi was back in power. She now faced a new challenge, however, in the rise of religious strife. The most dangerous situation was in the Punjab (pun-JAHB), located in the border region between India and Pakistan, where militant Sikhs (SEEKS *or* SEE-ikhz) were demanding autonomy or even independence from India. Gandhi did not shrink from a confrontation and attacked Sikh rebels hiding in their Golden Temple in the city of Amritsar (uhm-RIT-ser). The incident aroused widespread anger among the Sikh community, and in 1984, Sikh members of Gandhi's personal bodyguard assassinated her.

South Asia 🐚 **893**

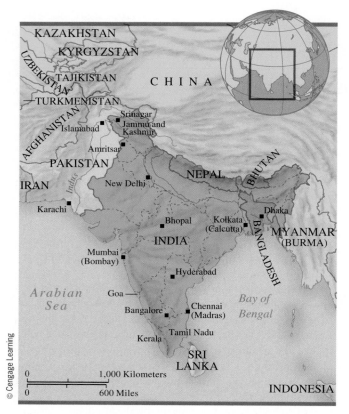

MAP 30.1 Modern South Asia. This map shows the boundaries of all the states in contemporary South Asia.

 Which of the countries on this map have a Muslim majority?

By now, Congress politicians were convinced that the party could not remain in power without a member of the Nehru family at the helm. Gandhi's son Rajiv Gandhi (rah-JEEV GAHN-dee) (1944–1991), a commercial airline pilot with little interest in politics, was persuaded to replace his mother as prime minister. Rajiv lacked the strong ideological

and political convictions of his mother and grandfather and allowed a greater role for private enterprise. But his government was criticized for cronyism, inefficiency, and corruption, as well as insensitivity to the poor.

Rajiv Gandhi also sought to play a role in regional affairs, mediating a dispute between the government in Sri Lanka and Tamil rebels (known as the Elam Tigers) who were ethnically related to the majority population in southern India. The decision cost him his life: while campaigning for reelection in 1991, he was assassinated by a member of the Tiger organization. India faced the future without a member of the Nehru family as prime minister.

During the early 1990s, Congress remained the leading party, but the powerful hold it had once had on the Indian electorate was gone. New parties, such as the militantly Hindu Bharatiya Janata (BAR-ruh-tee-uh JAH-nuh-tuh) Party (BJP), actively vied with Congress for control of the central and state governments. Growing political instability at the center was accompanied by rising tensions between Hindus and Muslims.

When a coalition government formed under Congress leadership collapsed, the BJP, under Prime Minister A. B. Vajpayee (VAHJ-py-ee) (b. 1924), ascended to power and played on Hindu sensibilities to build its political base. The new government based its success on an aggressive program of privatization in the industrial and commercial sectors and made a major effort to promote the nation's small but growing technological base. But BJP leaders had underestimated the discontent of India's less affluent citizens (an estimated 350 million Indians earn less than one U.S. dollar a day), and in the spring of 2004, a stunning defeat in national elections forced the Vajpayee government to resign. The Congress Party returned to power at the head of a coalition government based on a commitment to maintain economic growth while carrying out reforms in rural areas, including public works projects and hot lunch programs for all primary school children. But sectarian strife between Hindus and Muslims, as well as pervasive official corruption, continued to bedevil the government. In the fall of 2008, a terrorist attack in the city of Mumbai (MUM-by) left nearly 200 dead and raised serious questions about the effectiveness of Indian security procedures. Indian officials charged that the inspiration for the attack came from Pakistan. The Congress Party remained in power after national elections held in the spring of 2009.

The Land of the Pure: Pakistan Since Independence

When Pakistan achieved independence in August 1947, it was, unlike its neighbor India, in all respects a new nation, based on religious conviction rather than historical or ethnic tradition. The unique state consisted of two separate territories 2,000 miles apart. West Pakistan, including the Indus River basin and the West Punjab, was perennially short of water and was populated by dry crop farmers and peoples of the steppe. East Pakistan was made up of the marshy deltas of the Ganges and Brahmaputra Rivers. Densely populated with rice farmers, it was the home of the artistic and intellectual Bengalis (ben-GAH-leez).

CHRONOLOGY	South Asia Since 1945
India and Pakistan become independent	1947
Assassination of Mahatma Gandhi	1948
Death of Jawaharlal Nehru	1964
Indo-Pakistani War	1965
Indira Gandhi elected prime minister	1966
Bangladesh declares its independence	1971
Assassination of Indira Gandhi	1984
Assassination of Rajiv Gandhi	1991
Military coup overthrows civilian government in Pakistan	1999
U.S.-led forces oust Taliban in Afghanistan	2001
Congress Party returns to power in India	2004
Assassination of Benazir Bhutto in Pakistan	2007
Terrorist attack in Mumbai	2008
Massive floods in the Indus River valley	2010
Osama bin Laden killed in Pakistan	2011

The peoples of West Pakistan were especially diverse and included, among others, Pushtuns, Baluchis (buh-LOO-cheez), and Punjabis (pun-JAHB-eez). The Pushtuns are organized on a tribal basis and have kinship ties with the majority population across the border in neighboring Afghanistan. Many are nomadic and cross the border on a regular basis with their flocks. The Baluchis straddle the border with Iran, while the region of Punjab was divided between Pakistan and India at the moment of independence.

Even though the new state was an essentially Muslim society, its first years were marked by intense internal conflicts over religious, linguistic, and regional issues. Muhammad Ali Jinnah's vision of a democratic state that would assure freedom of religion and equal treatment for all was opposed by those who advocated a state based on Islamic principles.

Even more dangerous was the division between east and west. Many in East Pakistan felt that the government, based in the west, ignored their needs. In 1952, riots erupted in East Pakistan over the government's decision to adopt Urdu, a language derived from Hindi and used by Muslims in northern India, as the national language of the entire country. Most East Pakistanis spoke Bengali, an unrelated language. Tensions persisted, and in March 1971, East Pakistan declared its independence as the new nation of Bangladesh. Pakistani troops attempted to restore central government authority in the capital of Dhaka (DAK-uh *or* DAH-kuh), but rebel forces supported by India went on the offensive, and the government bowed to the inevitable and recognized independent Bangladesh.

The breakup of the union between East and West Pakistan undermined the fragile authority of the military regime that had ruled Pakistan since 1958 and led to its replacement by a civilian government under Zulfikar Ali Bhutto (ZOOL-fee-kahr ah-LEE BOO-toh) (1928–1979). But now religious tensions came to the fore, despite a new constitution that made a number of key concessions to conservative Muslims. In 1977, a new military government under General Zia Ul Ha'q (ZEE-ah ool HAHK) (1924–1988) came to power with a commitment to make Pakistan a true Islamic state. *Shari'a* became the basis for social behavior as well as for the legal system. Laws governing the consumption of alcohol and the role of women were tightened in accordance with strict Muslim beliefs. But after Zia was killed in a plane crash, Pakistanis elected Benazir Bhutto (ben-uh-ZEER BOO-toh) (1953–2007), the daughter of Zulfikar Ali Bhutto and a supporter of secularism who had been educated in the United States. She too was removed from power by a military regime, in 1990, on charges of incompetence and corruption. Reelected in 1993, she attempted to crack down on opposition forces but was removed once again in 1997 amid renewed charges of official corruption. Her successor soon came under fire for the same reason and in 1999 was ousted by a military coup led by General Pervaiz Musharraf (pur-VEZ moo-SHAHR-uf) (b. 1943), who promised to restore political stability and honest government.

In September 2001, Pakistan became the focus of international attention when a coalition of forces arrived in Afghanistan to overthrow the Taliban regime and destroy the al-Qaeda terrorist network. Despite considerable support for the Taliban among the local population, President Musharraf pledged his help in bringing terrorists to justice. He also promised to return his country to the secular principles espoused by Muhammad Ali Jinnah. His situation was complicated by renewed tensions with India over Kashmir and a series of violent clashes between Muslims and Hindus in India. In 2003, relations began to improve as both sides promised to seek a peaceful solution to the Kashmir dispute.

By then, however, problems had begun to escalate on the domestic front. As Musharraf sought to fend off challenges from radical Muslim groups—some of them allied with Taliban forces in neighboring Afghanistan—secular opposition figures criticized the authoritarian nature of his regime. When Benazir Bhutto returned from exile to present herself as a candidate in presidential elections to be held early in 2008, she was assassinated, leading to widespread suspicions of official involvement. In September 2008, amid growing political turmoil, Benazir Bhutto's widower, Asif Ali Zardari (AH-seef ah-LEE zahr-DAR-ree) (b. 1955), was elected president of Pakistan.

The new civilian government, which is composed of an uneasy coalition of several political parties, faces a number of challenges in coping with the multitude of problems affecting the country today. Half of the entire population of 150 million live in poverty, and illiteracy is widespread. Massive flooding of the Indus River in 2010 killed nearly 2,000 people and left millions homeless.

In a nation where much of the rural population still professes loyalty to traditional tribal leaders, the sense of nationalism remains fragile, while military elites, who have long played a central role in Pakistani politics, continue to press their own agenda. The internal divisions within the country's ruling class became painfully apparent when the al-Qaeda leader Osama bin Laden was killed in a U.S. raid on his compound in the spring of 2011. The terrorist leader had been living secretly in a villa in the military town of Abbottabad, within two hours' drive of the national capital of Islamabad. Many observers suspected that elements within the Pakistan military were aware of his presence there (see the box on p. 901).

Poverty and Pluralism in South Asia

The leaders of the new states that emerged in South Asia after World War II faced a number of problems. The peoples of the region were still overwhelmingly poor and illiterate, and the sectarian, ethnic, and cultural divisions that had plagued Indian society for centuries had not dissipated.

THE POLITICS OF COMMUNALISM Perhaps the most sincere effort to create democratic institutions was in India, where the new constitution called for social justice, liberty, equality of status and opportunity, and brotherhood. All citizens were guaranteed protection from discrimination on the grounds of religious belief, race, caste, sex, or place of birth.

In theory, then, India became a full-fledged democracy on the British parliamentary model. In actuality, a number of distinctive characteristics made the system less than fully democratic in the Western sense but may also have enabled it to survive. As we have seen, India became in essence a one-party state. By leading the independence movement, the Congress Party had amassed overwhelming public support, which enabled it to retain its preeminent position in Indian politics for three decades. The party also avoided being identified as a party exclusively for the Hindu majority by including prominent non-Hindus among its leaders and favoring measures to protect minority groups such as Sikhs and Muslims from discrimination.

After Nehru's death in 1964, however, challenges emerged that had been disguised by his adept maneuvering. Part of the problem was the familiar one of a party too long in power. Party officials became complacent and all too easily fell prey to the temptations of corruption and pork-barrel politics.

Another problem was **communalism**. Beneath the surface unity of the new republic lay age-old ethnic, linguistic, and religious divisions. Because of India's vast size and complex history, no national language had ever emerged. Hindi was the most prevalent, but it was the native language of less than one-third of the population. During the colonial period, English had served as the official language of government, and many non-Hindi speakers suggested making it the official language. But English was spoken only by the educated elite, and it represented an affront to national pride. Eventually, India recognized fourteen official tongues, making the parliament sometimes sound like the Tower of Babel.

Divisiveness increased after Nehru's death, and under his successors, official corruption grew. Only the lack of appeal of its rivals and the Nehru family charisma carried on by his daughter Indira Gandhi kept the party in power. But she was unable to prevent the progressive disintegration of the party's power base at the state level, where regional or ideological parties won the allegiance of voters by exploiting ethnic or social revolutionary themes.

During the 1980s, religious tensions began to intensify, not only among Sikhs in the northwest but also between Hindus and Muslims. As we have seen, Gandhi's uncompromising approach to Sikh separatism led to her assassination in 1984. Under her son, Rajiv Gandhi, Hindu militants at Ayodhya (ah-YOHD-yuh), in northern India, demanded the destruction of a mosque built on the traditional site of King Rama's birthplace, where a Hindu temple had previously existed. In 1992, Hindu demonstrators destroyed the mosque and erected a temporary temple at the site, provoking clashes between Hindus and Muslims throughout the country. In protest, rioters in neighboring Pakistan destroyed a number of Hindu shrines in that country. In 2010, an Indian court ordered that the land that had contained the mosque be divided between the Hindu and Muslim plaintiffs.

In the early years of the new century, communal divisions intensified as militant Hindu groups demanded a state that would cater to the Hindu majority, now numbering more than 700 million people. Some textbooks were rewritten to reflect a more Hindu-oriented version of history, including the contention that the Indus valley civilization was founded by Aryan peoples, the Hindus' ancestors (see Chapter 2). In the eastern state of Orissa, pitched battles broke out between Hindus and Christians over efforts by the latter to win converts to their faith. Manmohan Singh (MUHN-moh-hahn SING) (b. 1932),

India's prime minister since 2004, has lamented what he calls an assault on India's "composite culture."[3]

THE ECONOMY Nehru's answer to the social and economic inequality that had long afflicted the subcontinent was socialism. He instituted a series of five-year plans, which led to the creation of a relatively large and reasonably efficient state-run manufacturing sector, centered on steel, vehicles, and textiles. Industrial production almost tripled between 1950 and 1965, and per capita income rose by 50 percent between 1950 and 1980, although it was still less than $300 (in U.S. dollars).

By the 1970s, however, industrial growth had slowed. The lack of modern infrastructure was a problem, as was the rising price of oil, most of which had to be imported. The relative weakness of the state-owned sector, which grew at an annual rate of only about 2 percent in the 1950s and 1960s, versus 5 percent for the private sector, also became a serious obstacle.

India's major economic weakness, however, was in agriculture. At independence, mechanization was almost unknown, fertilizer was rarely used, and most farms were small and uneconomical because of the Hindu tradition of dividing the land equally among all male children. As a result, the vast majority of the Indian people lived in conditions of abject poverty. Landless laborers outnumbered landowners by almost two to one. The government attempted to relieve the problem by redistributing land to the poor, limiting the size of landholdings, and encouraging farmers to form voluntary cooperatives. But all three programs ran into widespread opposition and apathy.

Another problem was overpopulation. Even before independence, the country had had difficulty supporting its people. In the 1950s and 1960s, the population grew by more than 2 percent annually, twice the nineteenth-century rate. Beginning in the 1960s, the Indian government sought to curb population growth. Indira Gandhi instituted a program combining monetary rewards and compulsory sterilization. Males who had fathered too many children were sometimes forced to undergo a vasectomy. Popular resistance undermined the program, however, and the goals were scaled back in the 1970s. As a result, India has made little progress in holding down its burgeoning population, now estimated at more than one billion. One factor in the continued growth has been a decline in the death rate, especially the rate of infant mortality. Nevertheless, as a result of media popularization and better government programs, the trend today, even in poor rural villages, is toward smaller families. The average number of children a woman bears has been reduced from six in 1950 to three today. As has occurred elsewhere, the decline in family size began among the educated and is gradually spreading throughout Indian society. Still, India is on target to become the most populous nation in the world, surpassing China, by the year 2025.

The so-called **green revolution** that began in the 1960s helped reduce the severity of the population problem. The introduction of more productive, disease-resistant strains of rice and wheat doubled grain production between 1960 and 1980. But the green revolution also increased rural inequality. Only the wealthier farmers were able to purchase the necessary fertilizer, while poor peasants were often driven off the

Say No to McDonald's and KFC!

INTERACTION & EXCHANGE

One of the consequences of Rajiv Gandhi's decision to deregulate the Indian economy has been an increase in the presence of foreign corporations, including U.S. fast-food restaurant chains. Their arrival set off a storm of protest in India: from environmentalists concerned that raising grain for chickens is an inefficient use of land, from religious activists angry at the killing of animals for food, and from nationalists anxious to protect the domestic market from foreign competition. Fast-food restaurants now represent a growing niche in Indian society, but most cater to local tastes, avoiding beef products and offering many vegetarian dishes, such as the Veg Pizza McPuff. This piece, which appeared in the *Hindustan Times,* was written by Maneka Gandhi, a daughter-in-law of Indira Gandhi and a onetime minister of the environment who has emerged as a prominent rival of Congress Party president Sonia Gandhi.

Why India Doesn't Need Fast Food

India's decision to allow Pepsi Foods Ltd. to open 60 restaurants in India—30 each of Pizza Hut and Kentucky Fried Chicken—marks the first entry of multinational, meat-based junk-food chains into India. If this is allowed to happen, at least a dozen other similar chains will very quickly arrive, including the infamous McDonald's.

The implications of allowing junk-food chains into India are quite stark. As the name denotes, the foods served at Kentucky Fried Chicken (KFC) are chicken-based and fried. This is the worst combination possible for the body and can create a host of health problems, including obesity, high cholesterol, heart ailments, and many kinds of cancer. Pizza Hut products are a combination of white flour, cheese, and meat—again, a combination likely to cause disease. . . .

Then there is the issue of the environmental impact of junk-food chains. Modern meat production involves misuse of crops, water, energy, and grazing areas. In addition, animal agriculture produces surprisingly large amounts of air and water pollution.

KFC and Pizza Hut insist that their chickens be fed corn and soybeans. Consider the diversion of grain for this purpose. As the outlets of KFC and Pizza Hut increase in number, the poultry industry will buy up more and more corn to feed the chickens, which means that the corn will quickly disappear from the villages, and its increased price will place it out of reach for the common man. Turning corn into junk chicken is like turning gold into mud. . . .

It is already shameful that, in a country plagued by famine and flood, we divert 37 percent of our arable land to growing animal fodder. Were all of that grain to be consumed directly by humans, it would nourish five times as many people as it does after being converted into meat, milk, and eggs. . . .

Of course, it is not just the KFC and Pizza Hut chains of Pepsi Foods Ltd. that will cause all of this damage. Once we open India up by allowing these chains, dozens more will be eagerly waiting to come in. Each city in America has an average of 5,000 junk-food restaurants. Is that what we want for India?

Why does the author of this article oppose the introduction of fast-food restaurants in India? Do you think her complaints apply in the United States as well?

---

land. Millions fled to the cities, where they lived in vast slums, working at menial jobs or begging for a living.

After the death of Indira Gandhi in 1984, her son Rajiv proved more receptive to foreign investment and a greater role for the private sector in the economy. India began to export more manufactured goods, including computer software. The pace of change has accelerated under Rajiv Gandhi's successors, who have continued to transfer state-run industries to private hands. These policies have stimulated the growth of a prosperous new middle class, now estimated at more than 100 million. Consumerism has soared, and sales of television sets, DVD players, cellphones, and automobiles have increased dramatically. Equally important, Western imports are being replaced by new products manufactured in India with Indian brand names.

One consequence of India's entrance into the industrial age is the emergence of a small but vibrant technological sector that provides many important services to the world's advanced nations. The city of Bengaluru (BEHNG-uh-luh-roo) (Bangalore) in southern India has become an important technological center, benefiting from low wages and the presence of skilled labor with proficiency in the English language.

Nevertheless, Nehru's dream of a socialist society remains strong. State-owned enterprises still produce about half of all domestic goods, and high tariffs continue to stifle imports. Nationalist parties have played on the widespread fear of foreign economic influence to force the cancellation of some contracts and the relocation of some foreign firms. A combination of religious and environmental groups attempted unsuccessfully to prevent Kentucky Fried Chicken from establishing outlets in major Indian cities (see the box above). The fast-food invasion has led to a phenomenon occurring all over Asia: the growing incidence of obesity among children.

As in the industrialized countries of the West, economic growth has been accompanied by environmental damage. Water and air pollution has led to illness and death for many people, and an environmental movement has emerged. Some critics, reflecting the traditional anti-imperialist attitude of

COMPARATIVE ESSAY

One World, One Environment

EARTH & ENVIRONMENT

A crucial factor affecting the evolution of society and the global economy in the early twenty-first century is the growing concern over the impact of industrialization on the environment. Humans have always caused some harm to their natural surroundings, but never has the ecological damage been as significant and extensive as during the past century. Chemicals and other pollutants introduced into the atmosphere or into rivers, lakes, and oceans have increasingly threatened the health and well-being of all living species.

For many years, environmental concern was focused on the developed countries of the West, where industrial effluents, automobile exhausts, and the use of artificial fertilizers and insecticides led to urban smog, extensive damage to crops and wildlife, and a major reduction of the ozone layer in the upper atmosphere. In recent years, the problem has spread elsewhere. China's headlong rush to industrialization has resulted in major ecological damage in that country. Industrial smog has created almost unlivable conditions in many cities in Asia, while hillsides denuded of their forests have led to severe erosion and loss of farmlands. Destruction of the rain forest is a growing problem in many parts of the world, notably in Brazil and Indonesia. With the forest cover across the earth rapidly disappearing, there is less plant life to perform the crucial process of reducing carbon dioxide levels in the atmosphere.

One positive note is that environmental concerns have begun to take on a global character. While the causes of global warming have not

© Judyth Platt/Ecoscene/CORBIS

Destruction of the Environment. This stunted tree has been killed by acid rain; a combination of sulfuric and nitric acids mixed with moisture in the air. Entire forests of trees killed by acid rain are becoming common sights in Canada, the United States, and northern Europe.

yet been definitively proved, though the release of carbon dioxide and other gases into the atmosphere as a result of industrialization apparently plays a part, it has become a source of sufficient concern to be the subject of an international conference in Kyoto, Japan, in December 1997. If, as many scientists predict, worldwide temperatures continue to increase, the rise in sea levels could pose a significant threat to low-lying islands and coastal areas throughout the world, while climatic change could lead to severe droughts or excessive rainfall in cultivated areas.

It is one thing to recognize a problem, however, and another to solve it. So far, cooperative efforts among nations to alleviate environmental problems have all too often been hindered by economic forces or by political, ethnic, and religious disputes. The 1997 conference on global warming, for example, was marked by bitter disagreement over the degree to which developing countries should share the burden of cleaning up the environment. The fact is, few nations have been willing to take unilateral action that might pose an obstacle to economic development plans or lead to a rise in unemployment. In 2001, President George W. Bush refused to sign the Kyoto Agreement on the grounds that it discriminated against advanced Western countries. Subsequent conferences on the subject including the 2009 conference in Copenhagen, Denmark, have yielded few concrete results.

What kinds of environmental problems have recently taken place in the region of South Asia? Have they all been the result of human action?

Indian intellectuals, blame Western capitalist corporations for the problem, as in the highly publicized case of leakage from a foreign-owned chemical plant at Bhopal (boh-PAHL). Much of the problem, however, comes from state-owned factories erected with Soviet aid. And not all the environmental damage can be ascribed to industrialization. The Ganges River is so polluted by human overuse that it is risky for Hindu believers to bathe in it (see the comparative essay "One World, One Environment" above).

Moreover, many Indians have not benefited from the new prosperity. Nearly one-third of the population lives below the national poverty line. Millions continue to live in urban slums, such as the famous "City of Joy" in Kolkata (Calcutta),

and most farm families remain desperately poor. Despite the socialist rhetoric of India's leaders, the inequality of wealth in India is as pronounced as it is in capitalist nations in the West. Indeed, India has been described as two nations: an educated urban India of 100 million people surrounded by more than nine times that many impoverished peasants in the countryside (see the comparative illustration on p. 899).

The enormous gap between India's rich and poor is reflected in the educational system. For the children of affluent families, parental pressure to obtain a college degree is often intense, and many students devote long hours to studying for examinations to gain entrance to the country's many institutes of higher learning. Yet only about 12 percent

Two Indias. Contemporary India is a study in contrasts. In the photo on the top, middle-class students learn to use a computer, a symbol of their country's recent drive to join the global technological marketplace. Yet India today remains primarily a nation of villages. On the bottom, women in colorful saris fill their pails of water at the village well. As in many developing countries, the scarcity of water is one of India's most crucial problems.

Q *In what other regions of the world is lack of water a serious problem?*

© Indranil Mukherjee/AFP/Getty Images

© William J. Duiker

of India's nearly 200 million students are in college, one of the lowest ratios in the world.

Such problems are even more serious in neighboring Pakistan and Bangladesh. The overwhelming majority of Pakistan's citizens are poor, and at least half are illiterate. The recent flooding along the Indus River has had a devastating effect on people living in the region and was described by a United Nations official as the worst humanitarian crisis in the sixty-five years of the UN's existence. Prospects for the future are not bright, for Pakistan lacks a modern technological sector to serve as a magnet for the emergence of a modern middle class.

CASTE, CLASS, AND GENDER Drawing generalizations about the life of the average Indian is difficult because of ethnic, religious, and caste differences, which are compounded by the vast gulf between town and country.

Although the constitution of 1950 guaranteed equal treatment and opportunity for all, regardless of class and caste, and prohibited discrimination based on untouchability, prejudice is hard to eliminate. Untouchability persists, particularly in the villages, where *harijans* (HAR-ih-jans), now called *dalits* (DAH-lits), still perform menial tasks and are often denied fundamental human rights.

In general, urban Indians appear less conscious of caste distinctions. Material wealth rather than caste identity is increasingly defining status. Still, color consciousness based on the age-old distinctions between upper-class and lower-class Indians remains strong. Class-conscious Hindus still express a

A Marriage of Convenience

ART & IDEAS

One of independent India's foremost challenges has been to realize Mahatma's Gandhi's dream of integrating the country's multiple ethnic and religious groups into a cohesive society. Among the most serious issues is the uneasy relationship between the Muslim community and the Hindu majority. In *A Suitable Boy*, author Vikram Seth (b. 1952) describes the dilemma faced by a Hindu family when a daughter wishes to marry her Muslim boyfriend. Rupa Mehra is the mother of two daughters, Savita and Lata. Savita has married Pran, a fellow Hindu, but Lata has fallen in love with Kabir, a Muslim student at her university.

In the passage presented here, the author portrays the anguish experienced by family members as they seek to resolve the problem. At the end of 1,500 pages, Lata finally agrees to follow family tradition and marry the young Hindu her mother has chosen. Although it will initially be a "marriage of convenience," she hopes that respect for her husband will eventually turn to love, as happened with her sister Savita.

A Suitable Boy

Mrs. Rupa Mehra was not more prejudiced against Muslims than most upper-caste Hindu women of her age and background. As Lata had inopportunely pointed out, she even had friends who were Muslims, though almost all of them were not orthodox at all. The Nawab Sahib was perhaps, quite orthodox, but then he was, for Mrs. Rupa Mehra, more a social acquaintance than a friend.

The more Mrs. Rupa Mehra thought, the more agitated she became. Even marrying a non-*kshatriya* Hindu was bad enough. But this was unspeakable. It was one thing to mix socially with Muslims, entirely another to dream of polluting one's blood and sacrificing one's daughter.

Whom could she turn to in her hour of darkness? When Pran came home for lunch and heard the story, he suggested mildly that they meet the boy. Mrs. Rupa Mehra threw another fit. It was utterly out of the question. Pran then decided to stay out of things and to let them die down. He had not been hurt when he realized that Savita had kept her sister's confidence from him, and Savita loved him still more for that. She tried to calm her mother down, console Lata, and keep them in separate rooms—at least during the day.

Lata looked around the bedroom and wondered what she was doing in this house with her mother when her heart was entirely elsewhere, anywhere but here—a boat, a cricket field, a concert, a banyan grove, a cottage in the hills, Blandings Castle, anywhere, anywhere, so long as she was with Kabir. No matter what happened, she would meet him as planned, tomorrow. She told herself again and again that the path of true love never did run smooth.

 What is the source of Mrs. Rupa Mehra's objection to her daughter's planned marriage? How does her daughter respond?

Young Hindu Bride in Gold Bangles. Awaiting the marriage ceremony, a young bride sits with her female relatives at the Meenakshi Hindu temple, one of the largest in southern India. Although child marriage is illegal, Indian girls are still married at a young age. With the marital union arranged by the parents, this young bride may never have met her future husband. Bedecked in gold jewelry and rich silks—part of her dowry—she nervously awaits the priest's blessing before she moves to her husband's home. There she will begin a life of servitude to her in-laws' family.

© William J. Duiker

A Critique of Western Feminism

FAMILY & SOCIETY

Organized efforts to protect the rights of women have been under way in India since the 1970s, when the Progressive Organization for Women (POW) instituted a campaign against sexual harassment and other forms of discrimination against women in Indian society. Like many of their counterparts in other parts of Asia and Africa, however, many activists for women's rights in India contend that Western feminism is irrelevant to their own realities. Although Indian feminists feel a bond with their sisters all over the world, they insist on resolving Indian problems with Indian solutions. The author of this editorial is Madhu Kishwar, founder and editor of a women's journal in New Delhi.

Finding Indian Solutions to Women's Problems

Western feminism, exported to India and many other Third World countries in recent decades, has brought with it serious problems.

As products of a more homogenized culture, most Western feminists assume women's aspirations the world over must be quite similar. Yet a person's idea of a good life and her aspirations are closely related to what is valued in her particular society. This applies to feminism itself. An offshoot of individualism and liberalism, it posits that each individual is responsible primarily to herself....

In societies like India, most of us find it difficult to tune in to this extreme individualism. For instance, most Indian women are unwilling to assert rights in a way that estranges them not just from their family but also from their larger community... .

This isn't slavery to social opinion. Rather, many of us believe life is a poor thing if our own dear ones don't honor and celebrate our rights, if our freedom cuts us off from others. In our culture, both men and women are taught to value the interests of our families more than our self-interest....

Cultural issues aside, my most fundamental reservation regarding feminism is that it has strengthened the tendency among India's Western-educated elites to adopt the statist authoritarian route to social reform. The characteristic feminist response to most social issues affecting women—in the workplace, in the media, in the home—is to demand more and more stringent laws....

But dearly held and deeply cherished cultural norms cannot be changed simply by applying the instruments of state repression through legal punishment. Social reform is too complex and important a matter to be left to the police and courts. The best of laws will tend to fail if social opinion is contrary to them. Therefore, the statist route of using laws as a substitute for creating a new social consensus about women's rights tends to be counterproductive.

 How, according to the author of this article, do the needs of Indian women differ from those of women in Western countries? What are the author's criticisms of Western feminism? What differences between Indian and American society explain her attitude?

---

distinct preference for light-skinned marital partners. Marriage between Hindus and Muslims continues to be fraught with problems (see the box on p. 900).

In recent years, low-caste Indians (who represent more than 80 percent of the voting public) have begun to demand affirmative action to expand their opportunities and give them a more equal share in the national wealth. But opponents of such measures are often not reluctant to fight back against programs that guarantee opportunities for lower-caste Indians in education and government positions. Violent conflicts between caste groups have been on the rise in recent years, and in some areas, political parties are organized almost entirely on the basis of caste identity. The situation is different in parts of southern India, where for years members of lower castes have focused on education and economic achievement rather than on increasing their political influence in Indian society. As a result, many members of traditionally lower castes have become prominent in business, technological pursuits, and education.

After independence, India's leaders faced an equally serious challenge in seeking to equalize treatment of the sexes. The constitution expressly forbade discrimination based on gender and called for equal pay for equal work. Laws prohibited child marriage, *sati*, and the payment of a dowry by the bride's family. Women were encouraged to attend school and enter the labor market.

Such laws, along with the dynamics of economic and social change, have had a major impact on the lives of many Indian women. Middle-class women in urban areas are much more likely to seek employment outside the home, and many hold managerial and professional positions. Some Indian women, however, choose to play a dual role—a modern one in their work and in the marketplace and a more submissive, traditional one at home (see the box above).

Nothing more strikingly indicates the changing role of women in South Asia than the fact that in recent decades, three of the major countries in the area—India, Pakistan, and Sri Lanka—have had women prime ministers. It is worthy of mention, however, that all three—Indira Gandhi, Benazir Bhutto, and Srimivao Bandaranaike (see-ree-MAH-voh bahn-dur-uh-NY-uh-kuh)—came from prominent political families and owed their initial success to a husband or father who had served as prime minister before them.

Like other aspects of life, the role of women has changed much less in rural areas. In the early 1960s, many villagers still practiced the institution of *purdah*. Female children are still much less likely to receive an education. The overall literacy rate in India today is about 60 percent, but it is less than 50 percent among women. Laws relating to dowry, child marriage, and inheritance are routinely ignored in the countryside. There have been a few highly publicized cases of *sati*, although undoubtedly more women die of mistreatment at the hands of their husband or of other members of his family. In a few instances, widows have been forcibly thrown on the funeral pyre by their in-laws.

Perhaps the most tragic aspect of continued sexual discrimination in India is the high mortality rate among girls. One-quarter of the female children born in India die before the age of fifteen as a result of neglect or infanticide. Others are aborted before birth after gender-detection examinations. The results are striking. In India, according to one recent estimate, there are only 933 females to every 1,000 males.

South Asian Art and Literature Since Independence

Recent decades have witnessed a prodigious outpouring of literature in India. Most works have been written in one of the Indian languages and have not been translated into a foreign tongue. Fortunately, however, many authors choose to write in English. Known as Indo-Anglian literature, such works are written primarily for the Indian elite or for foreign audiences. For that reason, some critics charge that Indo-Anglian literature lacks authenticity.

Because of the vast quantity of works published (India is currently the third-largest publisher of English-language books in the world), only a few of the most prominent fiction writers can be mentioned here.

One of the most famous Indian-born authors is Salman Rushdie (b. 1947). In *Midnight's Children*, published in 1980, the author linked his protagonist, born on the night of independence, to the history of modern India, its achievements, and its frustrations. Like his contemporaries Günter Grass and Gabriel García Márquez, Rushdie used the technique of magical realism to jolt his audience into a recognition of the inhumanity of modern society and the need to develop a sense of moral concern for the fate of the Indian people and for the world as a whole.

Rushdie's later novels have tackled such problems as religious intolerance, political tyranny, social injustice, and greed and corruption. His attack on Islamic fundamentalism in *The Satanic Verses* (1988) won plaudits from literary critics but aroused widespread criticism among Muslims, including a death sentence by Iran's Ayatollah Khomeini. *The Moor's Last Sigh* (1995) examined what Rushdie perceives as the excesses of Hindu nationalism, and *Shalimar the Clown* (2005) addressed the quagmire in Kashmir. A number of younger writers are following Rushdie's lead and are providing their own critiques of India's evolving social problems. In *The White Tiger* (2008), Indian author Aravind Adiga (AR-vind ah-DEE-gah) (b. 1974) addresses the greed and corruption among India's newly rich as he traces the darkly mordant rise of a rickshaw driver to wealthy entrepreneur.

Anita Desai (dess-SY) (b. 1937) was one of the first prominent female writers to emerge from contemporary India. Her writing focuses on the struggle of Indian women to achieve a degree of independence. In her first novel, *Cry, the Peacock*, the heroine finally seeks liberation by murdering her husband, preferring freedom at any cost to remaining a captive of traditional society. Her daughter, Kiran Desai (b. 1971), also an author, has explored the contemporary issues of globalism and immigration in *The Inheritance of Loss* (2006).

Another female author, Taslima Nasrin (tah-SLEE-muh naz-REEN) (b. 1962) of Bangladesh, became famous when she was sentenced to death for her novel *Shame* (1993), in which she criticized official persecution of the Hindu minority. An outspoken feminist, she is critical of Islam for obstructing human progress and women's equality. In 2004, she moved to India, where the government was fearful that her presence would instigate Muslim unrest. She now lives in exile in Europe.

Like Chinese and Japanese artists, Indian artists have agonized over how best to paint with a modern yet indigenous mode of expression. During the colonial period, Indian art went in several directions at once. One school of painters favored traditional themes; another experimented with a colorful primitivism founded on folk art. Many Indian artists painted representational social art extolling the suffering and silent dignity of India's impoverished millions. After 1960, however, most Indian artists adopted abstract art as their medium. Surrealism in particular, with its emphasis on spontaneity and the unconscious, appeared closer to the Hindu tradition of favoring intuition over reason. Today a new generation of Indian artists and writers is addressing the excitement and anxiety of the era of globalization.

What Is the Future of India?

Indian society looks increasingly Western in form, if not in content. As in a number of other Asian and African societies, the distinction between traditional and modern, or indigenous and westernized, sometimes seems to be a simple dichotomy between rural and urban. The major cities appear modern and westernized, but the villages have changed little since precolonial days.

Yet traditional practices appear to be more resilient in India than in many other societies, and the result is often a synthesis rather than a clash between conflicting institutions and values. Unlike China under Mao Zedong, India did not reject its past but merely adjusted it to meet the needs of the present. Clothing styles in the streets where the *sari* and *dhoti* continue to be popular, religious practices in the temples, and social relationships in the home all testify to the importance of tradition in India.

One disadvantage of the eclectic approach, which seeks to blend the old and the new rather than choosing one over the other, is that sometimes contrasting traditions cannot be reconciled. In his book *India: A Wounded Civilization*, V. S. Naipaul (NY-pahl) (b. 1932), a Trinidadian of Indian descent who received the Nobel Prize for Literature in 2001, charged that Mahatma Gandhi's glorification of poverty and the simple Indian village was an obstacle to efforts to overcome the poverty, ignorance, and degradation of India's past and build a prosperous modern society. Gandhi's vision of a spiritual India, Naipaul complained, was a balm for defeatism and an excuse for failure.

Yet the appeal of Gandhi's philosophy remains a major part of the country's heritage. In July 2006, at a time when growing despair at economic conditions in the countryside resulted in a rash of suicides by poor farmers, Prime Minister Manmohan Singh called on the Indian people to reject the American model of "wasteful" consumer spending and return to the frugal teachings and spiritual vision of Mahatma Gandhi, which were, in his words, a "necessity" for a country as poor in material goods as India.[4]

Certainly, India faces a difficult dilemma. As historian Martha Nussbaum points out in *The Clash Within: Democracy, Religious Violence, and India's Future*, much of India's rural population continues to hold traditional beliefs, such as the concept of *karma* and inherent caste distinctions, that are incompatible with the capitalist work ethic and the democratic belief in equality before the law. Yet these beliefs provide a measure of identity and solace often lacking in other societies where such traditional spiritual underpinnings have eroded.

India, like Pakistan, also faces a number of other serious challenges. The Congress Party's vision of a diverse society composed of many distinct ethnic and religious communities is increasingly at odds with the virulent spirit of nationalism and religious identity sweeping the region today. It also must cope with severe environmental difficulties, including land erosion, overcrowding, and a scarcity of water and other vital resources, which will place severe limitations on the country's ability to transform itself into an economic powerhouse. As a democratic and pluralistic society, India is unable to launch major programs without popular consent and thus cannot move as quickly or often as effectively as an authoritarian system like China's. At the same time, India's institutions provide a mechanism to prevent the emergence of a despotic government elite interested only in its own survival. Nevertheless, whether India will be able to meet its challenges remains an open question.

Southeast Asia

 FOCUS QUESTION: What kinds of problems have the nations of Southeast Asia faced since 1945, and how have they attempted to solve them?

As we saw in Chapter 25, Japanese wartime occupation had a great impact on attitudes among the peoples of Southeast Asia. It demonstrated the vulnerability of colonial rule in the region and showed that an Asian power could defeat Europeans. The Allied governments themselves also contributed—sometimes unwittingly—to rising aspirations for independence by promising self-determination for all peoples at the end of the war. Although Winston Churchill later said that the Atlantic Charter did not apply to the colonial peoples, it would be difficult to put the genie back in the bottle again.

The End of the Colonial Era

Some did not try. In July 1946, the United States granted total independence to the Philippines. The Americans maintained a military presence on the islands, however, and U.S. citizens retained economic and commercial interests in the new country.

The British, too, under the Labour Party, were willing to bring an end to a century of imperialism in the region. In 1948, the Union of Burma received its independence. Malaya's turn came in 1957, after a Communist guerrilla movement had been suppressed.

The French and the Dutch, however, both regarded their colonies in the region as economic necessities as well as symbols of national grandeur and refused to turn them over to nationalist movements at the end of the war. The Dutch attempted to suppress a rebellion in the East Indies led by Sukarno (soo-KAHR-noh) (1901–1970), leader of the Indonesian Nationalist Party. But the United States, which feared a Communist victory there, pressured the Dutch to grant independence to Sukarno and his non-Communist forces, and in 1950 the Dutch finally agreed to recognize the new Republic of Indonesia.

The situation was somewhat different in Vietnam, where the Communists seized power throughout most of the country in the August Revolution of 1945. After the French refused to recognize the new government and sought to reimpose their rule, hostilities broke out between the French and the Vietminh Front in December 1946. At the time it was only an anticolonial war, but it would soon become much more (see Chapter 26).

In the Shadow of the Cold War

Many of the leaders of the newly independent states in Southeast Asia (see Map 30.2) admired Western political institutions and hoped to adapt them to their own countries. New constitutions were patterned on Western democratic models, and multiparty political systems quickly sprang into operation.

THE SEARCH FOR A NEW POLITICAL CULTURE By the 1960s, most of these budding experiments in pluralist democracy had been abandoned or were under serious threat. Some had been replaced by military or one-party autocratic regimes. In Burma, a moderate government based on the British parliamentary system and dedicated to Buddhism and nonviolent Marxism had given way to a military regime. In Thailand, too, the military ruled. In the Philippines, President Ferdinand Marcos (MAHR-kohs) (1917–1989) discarded democratic restraints and established his own centralized control. In South Vietnam, under pressure from Communist-led insurgents, Ngo Dinh Diem and his successors paid lip service to the Western democratic model but ruled by authoritarian means.

One problem faced by most of these states was that independence had not brought material prosperity or ended economic inequality and the domination of the local economies by foreign interests. As in Africa, most economies in the region were still characterized by tiny industrial sectors; they lacked technology, educational resources, capital investment, and leaders trained in developmental skills.

The presence of widespread ethnic, linguistic, religious, and economic differences also made the transition to

© Cengage Learning

MAP 30.2 Modern Southeast Asia. Shown here are the countries that comprise contemporary Southeast Asia. The names of major islands are indicated in italic type.

Q *Which of the countries in Southeast Asia have democratic governments?*

Western-style democracy difficult. In Malaya, for example, the majority Malays—most of whom were farmers and virtually all of whom were (and still are) Muslims—feared economic and political domination by the local Chinese minority, who were much more experienced in industry and commerce. In 1961, the Federation of Malaya, whose ruling party was dominated by Malays, integrated former British possessions on the island of Borneo into the new Union of Malaysia in a move to increase the non-Chinese proportion of the country's population. Yet periodic conflicts persisted as the Malaysian government attempted to guarantee Malay control over politics and a larger role in the economy.

Finally, the new nations of Southeast Asia were seeking to realize their ambitious objectives in a time of intense political turmoil throughout Asia. While their political leaders were under severe pressure to take sides in the ideological Cold War, revolutionary parties—many of them influenced by the Maoist strategy of "people's war"—operated outside the

system as they sought to bring about drastic change on the model of the new China.

SUKARNO AND "GUIDED DEMOCRACY" The most prominent example of a failed experiment in democracy was in Indonesia. In 1950, the new leaders drew up a constitution creating a parliamentary system under a titular presidency. Sukarno was elected the first president. A spellbinding orator, Sukarno played a major role in creating a sense of national identity among the disparate peoples of the Indonesian archipelago (see the box on p. 905).

In 1959, Sukarno, exasperated at the incessant maneuvering among Muslims, Communists, and the army, dissolved the constitution and attempted to rule on his own through what he called **guided democracy**. As he described it, guided democracy was closer to Indonesian traditions and superior to the Western variety. The weakness of the latter was that it allowed the majority to dominate the minority, whereas

The Golden Throat of President Sukarno

POLITICS & GOVERNMENT

President Sukarno of Indonesia was a spellbinding speaker and a charismatic leader of his nation's struggle for independence. These two selections are from speeches in which Sukarno promoted two of his favorite projects: Indonesian nationalism and "guided democracy." The force that would guide Indonesia, of course, was to be Sukarno himself.

Sukarno on Indonesian Greatness

What was Indonesia in 1945? What was our nation then? It was only two things, only two things. A flag and a song. That is all. (Pause, finger held up as afterthought.) But no, I have omitted the main ingredient. I have missed the most important thing of all. I have left out the burning fire of freedom and independence in the breast and heart of every Indonesian. That is the most important thing—this is the vital chord—the spirit of our people, the spirit and determination to be free. This was our nation in 1945—the spirit of our people!

And what are we today? We are a great nation. We are bigger than Poland. We are bigger than Turkey. We have more people than Australia, than Canada, we are bigger in area and have more people than Japan. In population now we are the fifth-largest country in the world. In area, we are even bigger than the United States of America. The American Ambassador, who is here with us, admits this. Of course, he points out that we have a lot of water in between our thousands of islands. But I say to him—America has a lot of mountains and deserts, too!

Sukarno on Guided Democracy

Indonesia's democracy is not liberal democracy. Indonesian democracy is not the democracy of the world of Montaigne or Voltaire. Indonesia's democracy is not à la America, Indonesia's democracy is not the Soviet—NO! Indonesia's democracy is the democracy which is implanted in the breasts of the Indonesian people, and it is that which I have tried to dig up again, and have put forward as an offering to you. . . . If you, especially the undergraduates, are still clinging to and being borne along the democracy made in England, or democracy made in France, or democracy made in America, or democracy made in Russia, you will become a nation of copyists!

 What are Sukarno's criticisms of Western democracy? Can you think of other instances in Asia or Africa where new leaders sought to adopt Western institutions to local realities?

---

guided democracy would reconcile different opinions and points of view in a government operated by consensus. Highly suspicious of the West, Sukarno nationalized foreign-owned enterprises and sought economic aid from China and the Soviet Union while relying for domestic support on the Indonesian Communist Party.

The army and many devout Muslims resented Sukarno's increasing reliance on the Communists, and the Muslims were further upset by his refusal to consider a state based on Islamic principles. In 1965, military officers launched a coup d'état that provoked a mass popular uprising, which resulted in the slaughter of several hundred thousand suspected Communists, many of whom were overseas Chinese, long distrusted by the Muslim majority (see the Film & History feature on p. 906). In 1967, a military government under General Suharto (soo-HAHR-toh) (1921–2008) was installed.

The new government made no pretensions of reverting to democratic rule, but it did restore good relations with the West and sought foreign investment to repair the country's ravaged economy. It also sought to placate the Muslims while refusing demands for an Islamic state. In a few areas, including western Sumatra, militant Muslims took up arms against the state.

The one country in Southeast Asia that openly rejected the Western model was North Vietnam. Ho Chi Minh and his colleagues opted for the Stalinist pattern of national development, based on Communist Party rule and socialist forms of ownership. In 1958, stimulated by the success of collectivization in neighboring China, the government launched a three-year plan to lay the foundation for a socialist society. Collective farms were established, and all industry and commerce above the family level were nationalized.

On the Road to Political Reform

With the end of the Vietnam War and the gradual rapprochement between China and the United States in the late 1970s, the ferment and uncertainty that had marked the first three decades of independence in Southeast Asia gradually gave way to an era of greater political stability. In the Philippines, the dictatorial regime of Ferdinand Marcos was overthrown by a popular uprising in 1986 and replaced by a democratically-elected government under President Corazon Aquino (KOR-uh-zahn ah-KEE-noh) (1933–2009), the widow of a popular politician assassinated a few years earlier. Aquino was unable to resolve many of the country's chronic economic and social difficulties, however, and political stability remained elusive. One of her successors, Joseph Estrada (b. 1937), a former actor, was forced to resign on charges of corruption, and Muslims on the southern island of Mindanao (min-duh-NAH-oh) have for many years carried on a terrorist campaign in their effort to obtain autonomy or independence.

The Year of Living Dangerously (1983)

President Sukarno of Indonesia was one of the most prominent figures in Southeast Asia in the first two decades after World War II. A key figure in the nationalist movement while the country was under Dutch colonial rule, he became the first elected president of the new republic when it was granted formal independence in 1950. The charismatic Sukarno initially won broad popular support for his efforts to end colonial dependency and improve living conditions for the impoverished local population. But the government's economic achievements failed to match his fiery oratory, and when political unrest began to spread through Indonesian society in the early 1960s, Sukarno dismantled the parliamentary system that had been installed at independence and began to crack down on dissidents.

These conditions are the setting for the Australian film *The Year of Living Dangerously* (1983). Based on the novel of the same name by Christian Koch, the movie takes place in the summer of 1965, when popular unrest against the dictatorial government had reached a crescendo and the country appeared about to descend into civil war. The newly arrived Australian reporter Guy Hamilton (Mel Gibson) is befriended by a diminutive Chinese-Indonesian journalist named Billy Kwan, effectively played by Linda Hunt who received an Academy Award for her performance. Kwan, who has become increasingly disenchanted with Sukarno's failure to live up his promises, introduces Hamilton to the seamy underside of Indonesian society, as well as to radical elements connected to the Communist Party who are planning a coup to seize power in Jakarta.

The movie reaches a climax as Hamilton—a quintessentially ambitious reporter out to get a scoop on the big story—inadvertently becomes involved in the Communist plot and arouses the suspicion of government authorities. As Indonesia appears ready to descend into chaos, Hamilton finally

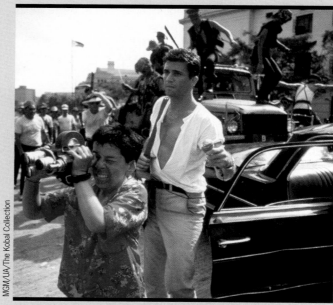

Photographer Billy Kwan (Linda Hunt) and reporter Guy Hamilton (Mel Gibson) film a political protest.

recognizes the extent of the danger and manages to board the last plane from Jakarta. Others are not so fortunate, as Sukarno's security police crack down forcefully on critics of his regime.

The Year of Living Dangerously (the title comes from a remark made by Sukarno during his presidential address in August 1964) is an important if underrated film that dramatically portrays a crucial incident in a volatile region caught in the throes of the global Cold War. The beautiful scenery (the film was shot in the Philippines because the story was banned in Indonesia) and a haunting film score help create a mood of tension spreading through a tropical paradise.

In other nations, the trends have been equally mixed. Malaysia is a practicing democracy, although a coalition of groups known as the United Malays National Organization (UMNO) has controlled the government since independence. In recent years, tensions between Malays and Chinese, as well as between secular and orthodox Muslims, have weakened UMNO's control over the apparatus of government.

In neighboring Thailand, a fragile democracy has functioned under the watchful eye of the military. Since 2008, however, political tensions have spilled into the streets and threatened to throw Thai society into a state of paralysis.

INDONESIA AFTER SUHARTO For years, a major exception to the trend toward political pluralism in the region was Indonesia, where Suharto ruled without restraints. But in 1996 and 1997, protests by students demanding increased freedoms and by Muslims demanding a larger role for Islam in society prompted Suharto's government to arrest many dissidents. In 1997, popular anger against the government (several members of Suharto's family had reportedly used their positions to amass considerable wealth) led to violent street riots and demands for his resignation. Forced to step down in the spring of 1998, Suharto was replaced by his deputy B. J. Habibie (hab-BEEB-ee) (b. 1936), who called for the establishment of a national assembly to select a new government based on popular aspirations. The assembly selected a moderate Muslim leader as president, but he was charged with corruption and incompetence and was replaced in 2001 by his vice president, Sukarno's daughter Megawati Sukarnoputri (meg-uh-WAH-tee soo-kahr-noh-POO-tree) (b. 1947).

The new government faced internal challenges from dissident elements seeking autonomy or separation from the republic, as well as from religious forces seeking to transform the country into an Islamic state. Under pressure from the

© William J. Duiker

© William J. Duiker

A Funeral in Torajaland. The Toraja (toh-RAH-jah) peoples on the island of Sulawesi (soo-lah-WAY-see) practice a faith that predates the arrival of Islam. Their elaborate funeral rites are only one of the unique aspects of their culture. After death, the deceased is placed in a house (left photo), where family members keep vigil—sometimes for years—until funds are available to stage a funeral. At that time, gifts of ox meat and pork are distributed to the entire village. The coffin is then placed in a niche high on a cliff face to protect it from grave robbers. Effigies of the deceased, called Tautaus, are placed in front of the burial niche (right photo), where they watch solicitously over the welfare of the community.

international community, Indonesia agreed to grant independence to the onetime Portuguese colony of East Timor, where the majority of the people are Roman Catholics. But violence provoked by pro-Indonesian militia units forced many refugees to flee the country. Religious tensions also erupted between Muslims and Christians elsewhere in the archipelago, and Muslim rebels in western Sumatra continue to agitate for a new state based on strict adherence to fundamentalist Islam. In the meantime, a terrorist attack directed at tourists on the island of Bali aroused fears that the Muslim nation had become a haven for terrorist elements throughout the region.

In direct elections held in 2004, General Susilo Yudhyono (soo-SEE-loh yood-heh-YOH-noh) (b. 1949) defeated Megawati Sukarnoputri and ascended to the presidency. The new chief executive promised a new era of political stability, honest government, and economic reform while ceding more authority to the country's thirty-three provinces. Pressure from traditional Muslims to abandon the nation's secular tradition and move toward the creation of an Islamic state continues, but the level of religious and ethnic tension has declined somewhat. In elections held in 2009, Yudhyono won a second term in office, while popular support for Islamic parties dropped from 38 percent to 26 percent. That the country was able to hold democratic elections in the midst of such tensions holds some promise for the future.

THE EXCEPTIONS: VIETNAM AND MYANMAR As always, Vietnam is a special case. After achieving victory over South

Vietnam with the fall of Saigon in the spring of 1975 (see Chapter 26), the Communist government in Hanoi pursued the rapid reunification of the two zones under Communist Party rule and laid plans to carry out a socialist transformation throughout the country, now renamed the Socialist Republic of Vietnam. The result was an economic disaster, and in 1986, party leaders followed the example of Mikhail Gorbachev in the Soviet Union and introduced their own version of *perestroika* in Vietnam (see Chapter 27). The trend in recent years has been toward a mixed capitalist-socialist economy along Chinese lines and a greater popular role in the governing process. Elections for the unicameral parliament are more open than in the past. The government remains suspicious of Western-style democracy, however, and represses any opposition to the Communist Party's guiding role over the state.

Only in Burma (in 1989 renamed Myanmar), where the military has been in complete control since the early 1960s, have the forces of greater popular participation been virtually silenced. Even there, however, the power of the ruling regime of General Ne Win (NAY WIN) (1911–2002) and his successors, known first as SLORC and after 1997 as the State Peace and Development Council (SPDC), was vocally challenged by Aung San Suu Kyi (AWNG SAHN SOO CHEE) (b. 1945), the admired daughter of one of the heroes of the country's struggle for national liberation after World War II. In 2011, the SPDC was officially abolished and replaced by a new constitution and an elected president, Thein Sein (TAY-en SAY-en) (b. 1945), a retired military officer. Nevertheless, the military remains in control, and opposition parties such as that led by Aung San Suu Kyi did not participate in the elections.

FINANCIAL CRISIS AND RECOVERY The trend toward more representative systems of government in the region has been due in part to increasing prosperity and the growth of an affluent and educated middle class. Although Myanmar and the three Indochinese states (Cambodia, Laos, and Vietnam) are still overwhelmingly agrarian, Indonesia, Malaysia, and Thailand have been undergoing relatively rapid economic development.

In the late summer of 1997, however, these economic gains were threatened and popular faith in the ultimate benefits of globalization was shaken as a financial crisis swept through the region. The crisis was triggered by a number of problems, including growing budget deficits caused by excessive government expenditures on ambitious development projects, irresponsible lending and investment practices by financial institutions, and an overvaluation of local currencies relative to the U.S. dollar. An underlying cause of these problems was the prevalence of backroom deals between politicians and business leaders that temporarily enriched both groups at the cost of eventual economic dislocation.

As local currencies plummeted in value, the International Monetary Fund agreed to provide assistance, but only on the condition that the governments concerned permit greater transparency in their economic systems and allow market forces to operate more freely, even at the price of bankruptcies and the loss of jobs. By the early 2000s, there were signs that the economies in the region had weathered the crisis and were beginning to recover. The massive tsunami that struck the region in December 2004 was a setback, as well as a human tragedy of enormous proportions, but as the decade wore on, progress resumed, and today the nations of Southeast Asia, with a few exceptions, are among the fastest growing in the world.

Indonesia is one of the region's foremost success stories. Blessed with abundant natural resources, including oil reserves, precious metals, and a variety of tropical products, it has surmounted the recent global economic slowdown and currently enjoys an annual growth rate of more than 6 percent. Indonesia continues to face a number of problems, including urban poverty and environmental pollution, but its prospects are brighter than could have been anticipated even a decade ago.

Regional Conflict and Cooperation: The Rise of ASEAN

Another problem for the Southeast Asian states has been the serious tensions that have risen among them. Some of these tensions were a consequence of historical rivalries and territorial disputes that had been submerged during the long era of colonial rule. In the 1960s, Indonesian president Sukarno briefly launched a policy of confrontation with the Federation of Malaya, contending that the Malay peninsula had once been part of empires based on the Indonesian islands. The claim was dropped after Sukarno's fall from power in 1965.

Another chronic border dispute has long festered between Cambodia and its two neighbors, Thailand and Vietnam, both of which once exercised suzerainty over Cambodian territories. The frontiers of independent Cambodia were originally drawn up by French colonial authorities for their own convenience.

After the reunification of Vietnam under Communist rule in 1975, the border dispute between Cambodia and Vietnam erupted again. In April 1975, a brutal revolutionary regime under the leadership of the Khmer Rouge (KMAIR ROOZH) dictator Pol Pot (POHL PAHT) came to power in Cambodia and proceeded to carry out the massacre of more than one million Cambodians. Then, claiming that vast territories in the Mekong delta had been seized from Cambodia by the Vietnamese in previous centuries, the Khmer Rouge regime launched attacks across the common border. In response, Vietnamese forces invaded Cambodia in December 1978 and installed a pro-Hanoi regime in Phnom Penh (puh-NAHM PEN). Fearful of Vietnam's increasing power in the region, China launched a brief attack on Vietnam to demonstrate its displeasure.

The outbreak of war among the erstwhile Communist allies aroused the concern of other countries in the neighborhood. In 1967, several non-Communist countries had established the Association of Southeast Asian Nations, or **ASEAN**. Composed of Indonesia, Malaysia, Thailand, Singapore, and the Philippines, ASEAN at first concentrated on cooperative social and economic endeavors, but after the end of the Vietnam War, it cooperated with other states in an effort to force the Vietnamese to withdraw from Cambodia. In 1991, the Vietnamese agreed to pull back, and a new government was formed in Phnom Penh.

The growth of ASEAN from a weak collection of diverse states into a stronger organization whose members cooperate

CHRONOLOGY Southeast Asia Since 1945	
August Revolution in Vietnam	1945
Philippines becomes independent	1946
Beginning of Franco-Vietminh War	1946
Burma becomes independent	1948
Republic of Indonesia becomes independent	1950
Malaya becomes independent	1957
Beginning of Sukarno's "guided democracy" in Indonesia	1959
Military seizes power in Indonesia	1965
Foundation of ASEAN	1967
Fall of Saigon to North Vietnamese forces	1975
Vietnamese invade Cambodia	1978
Corazon Aquino elected president in the Philippines	1986
Vietnamese withdraw from Cambodia	1991
Vietnam becomes a member of ASEAN	1996
Suharto steps down as president of Indonesia	1998
Tsunami causes widespread death and destruction throughout the region	2004
Reelection of President Yudhyono in Indonesia	2009

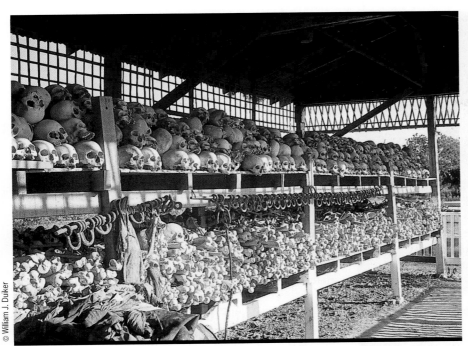

Holocaust in Cambodia. When the Khmer Rouge seized power in Cambodia in April 1975, they immediately emptied the capital of Phnom Penh and systematically began to eliminate opposition elements throughout the country. Thousands were tortured in the infamous Tuol Sleng prison and then marched out to the countryside, where they were massacred. Their bodies were thrown into massive pits. The succeeding government disinterred the remains, which are now displayed at an outdoor museum on the site.

militarily and politically has helped provide the nations of Southeast Asia with a more cohesive voice to represent their interests on the world stage. They will need it, for disagreements with Western countries over global economic issues and the rising power of China will present major challenges in coming years. That Vietnam was admitted into ASEAN in 1996 should provide both Hanoi and its neighbors with greater leverage in dealing with China, their powerful neighbor to the north.

Daily Life: Town and Country in Contemporary Southeast Asia

The urban-rural dichotomy observed in India is also found in Southeast Asia, where the cities resemble those in the West while the countryside often appears little changed from precolonial days. In cities such as Bangkok, Manila, and Jakarta, broad boulevards lined with skyscrapers alternate with muddy lanes passing through neighborhoods packed with wooden shacks topped by thatch or rusty tin roofs. Nevertheless, in recent decades, millions of Southeast Asians have fled to these urban slums. Although most available jobs are menial, the pay is better than in the villages.

TRADITIONAL CUSTOMS, MODERN VALUES The urban migrants change not only their physical surroundings but their attitudes and values as well. Sometimes the move leads to a decline in traditional religious faith. Belief in natural and ancestral spirits, for example, has declined among the urban populations of Southeast Asia. In Thailand, Buddhism has come under pressure from the rising influence of materialism, although temple schools still educate thousands of rural youths whose families cannot afford the cost of public education.

Nevertheless, Buddhist, Muslim, and Confucian beliefs remain strong, even in cosmopolitan cities such as Bangkok,

Jakarta, and Singapore. This preference for the traditional also shows up in lifestyle. Traditional dress—or an eclectic blend of Asian and Western dress—is still common. Asian music, art, theater, and dance remain popular, although Western music has become fashionable among the young, and Indonesian filmmakers complain that Western films are beginning to dominate the local market.

The increasing inroads made by Western culture have caused anxiety in some countries. In Malaysia, for example, fundamentalist Muslims criticize the prevalence of pornography, hedonism, drugs, and alcohol in Western culture and have tried to limit their presence in their own country. Many Indonesians have expressed concern in recent years that English has become the language of choice among the young, undercutting the role of Bahasa Indonesia, the composite language that has deliberately been employed to bring a degree of unity to the country's 250 different ethnic groups.

CHANGING ROLES FOR WOMEN One of the most significant changes that has taken place in Southeast Asia in recent decades is in the role of women in society. In general, women in the region have historically faced fewer restrictions on their activities and enjoyed a higher status than women elsewhere in Asia. Nevertheless, they were not the equal of men in every respect. With independence, Southeast Asian women gained new rights. Virtually all of the constitutions adopted by the newly independent states granted women full legal and political rights, including the right to work. Today, women have increased opportunities for education and have entered careers previously reserved for men. Women have become more active in politics, and as we have seen, some have served as heads of state.

Yet women are not truly equal to men in any country in Southeast Asia. Sometimes the distinction is simply a matter

The Teachings of the Buddha. Many young people in Thailand receive their education in a Buddhist temple, where they learn to read and write as well as study the teachings of the Buddha. After graduation, most of them return to the secular world to go on with their daily lives. In later life, some return to the temple to recharge their spirituality. In this illustration, novice monks pray at a Buddhist temple in Bangkok, Thailand. Although not observable in the photograph, one of the young monks is secretly reading a comic book.

of custom. In Vietnam, women are legally equal to men, yet until recently no women had served in the Communist Party's ruling Politburo. In Thailand, Malaysia, and Indonesia, women rarely hold senior positions in government service or in the boardrooms of major corporations. Similar restrictions apply in Myanmar, although Aung San Suu Kyi is the leading figure in the democratic opposition movement.

Sometimes, too, women's rights have been undermined by a social or religious backlash. The revival of Islamic fundamentalism has had an especially strong impact in Malaysia, where Malay women are expected to cover their bodies and wear the traditional Muslim headdress. Even in non-Muslim countries, women are expected to behave demurely and exercise discretion in all contacts with the opposite sex.

Cultural Trends

In most countries in Southeast Asia, writers, artists, and composers are attempting to synthesize international styles and themes with local tradition and experience. The novel has become increasingly popular as writers seek to find the best medium to encapsulate the dramatic changes that have taken place in the region in recent decades.

The best-known writer in postwar Indonesia—at least to readers abroad—was Pramoedya Toer (PRAHM-oh-DEE-

yah TOOR) (1925–2006). Born in eastern Java, he joined the Indonesian nationalist movement in his early twenties. Arrested in 1965 on the charge of being a Communist, he spent the next several years in prison. While incarcerated, he began writing his four-volume *Buru Quartet*, which recounts in fictional form the story of the struggle of the Indonesian people for freedom from colonial rule and the autocratic regimes of the independence period.

Among the most talented contemporary Vietnamese novelists is Duong Thu Huong (ZHWAHNG too HWAHNG) (b. 1947). A member of the Vietnamese Communist Party who served on the front lines during the Sino-Vietnamese war in 1979, she later became outspoken in criticizing the party's failure to carry out democratic reforms and was briefly imprisoned in 1991. Undaunted by official pressure, she has written several novels that express the horrors experienced by guerrilla fighters during the Vietnam War and the cruel injustices perpetrated by the regime in the cause of building socialism.

A Region in Flux

Today, the Western image of a Southeast Asia mired in the Vietnam conflict and the tensions of the Cold War is a distant memory. In ASEAN, the states in the region have created the framework for a regional organization that can serve their common political, economic, technological, and security interests. A few members of ASEAN are already on the road to advanced development.

To be sure, there are continuing signs of trouble. The financial crisis of the 1990s aroused serious political unrest in Indonesia. There are disquieting signs that terrorist groups inspired by al-Qaeda have established a presence in the region. Myanmar remains isolated and appears mired in a state of chronic underdevelopment and brutal military rule. Even after a devastating cyclone struck the country in the spring of 2008, the government refused to allow access to foreign aid workers. The three states of Indochina remain potentially unstable and have not yet been fully integrated into the region as a whole. All things considered, however, the situation is more promising today than would have seemed possible a generation ago. Unlike the case in Africa and the Middle East, the nations of Southeast Asia have put aside the bitter legacy of the colonial era to embrace the wave of globalization that has been sweeping the world in the post–World War II era.

Japan: Asian Giant

 FOCUS QUESTION: How did the Allied occupation after World War II change Japan's political and economic institutions, and what remained unchanged?

In August 1945, Japan was in ruins, its cities destroyed, its vast Asian empire in ashes, its land occupied by a foreign army. Half a century later, Japan had emerged as the second-greatest industrial power in the world, democratic in form and content and a source of stability throughout the region. Japan's achievement spawned a number of Asian imitators.

The Emperor Is Not Divine

POLITICS & GOVERNMENT

At the close of World War II, the United States agreed that Japan could retain its emperor, but only on the condition that he renounce his divinity. When the governments of Great Britain and the Soviet Union advocated that Hirohito be tried as a war criminal, General Douglas MacArthur, the supreme commander of Allied occupation forces in Japan, argued that the emperor had a greater grasp of democratic principles than most other Japanese and that his presence was vital to the success of Allied occupation policy. That argument prevailed. On New Year's Day 1946, the emperor issued a rescript denying his divinity. To many Japanese of the era, however, he remained a divine figure.

Hirohito, Rescript on Divinity

In greeting the New Year, we recall to mind that the Emperor Meiji proclaimed as the basis of our national policy the five clauses of the Charter at the beginning of the Meiji era. . . .

The proclamation is evident in its significance and high in its ideals. We wish to make this oath anew and restore the country to stand on its own feet again. We have to reaffirm the principles embodied in the Charter and proceed unflinchingly toward elimination of misguided practices of the past; and keeping in close touch with the desires of the people, we will construct a new Japan through thoroughly being pacific, the officials and the people alike obtaining rich culture and advancing the standard of living of the people.

The devastation of the war inflicted upon our cities, the miseries of the destitute, the stagnation of trade, shortage of food, and the great and growing number of unemployed are indeed heart-rending, but if the nation is firmly united in its resolve to face the present ordeal and to see civilization consistently in peace, a bright future will undoubtedly be ours, not only for our country but for the whole of humanity.

Love of the family and love of country are especially strong in this country. With more of this devotion should we now work toward love of mankind.

We feel deeply concerned to note that consequent upon the protracted war ending in our defeat our people are liable to grow restless and to fall into the slough of despond. Radical tendencies in excess are gradually spreading and the sense of morality tends to lose its hold on the people with the result that there are signs of confusion of thoughts.

We stand by the people and we wish always to share with them in their moment of joys and sorrows. The ties between us and our people have always stood upon mutual trust and affection. They do not depend upon mere legends and myths. They are not predicated on the false conception that the Emperor is divine and that the Japanese people are superior to other races and fated to rule the world.

Our Government should make every effort to alleviate their trials and tribulations. At the same time, we trust that the people will rise to the occasion and will strive courageously for the solution of their outstanding difficulties and for the development of industry and culture. Acting upon a consciousness of solidarity and of mutual aid and broad tolerance in their civil life, they will prove themselves worthy of their best tradition. By their supreme endeavors in that direction they will be able to render their substantial contribution to the welfare and advancement of mankind.

The resolution for the year should be made at the beginning of the year. We expect our people to join us in all exertions looking to accomplishment of this great undertaking with an indomitable spirit.

 What promises did the Japanese emperor make to his subjects in this statement? Did he apologize for mistakes made in the past?

Known as the "Little Tigers," the four industrializing societies of Taiwan, Hong Kong, Singapore, and South Korea achieved considerable success by following the path originally charted by Japan. Along with Japan, they became economic powerhouses and ranked among the world's top twenty trading nations. Other nations in Asia and elsewhere took note and began to adopt the Japanese formula. It is no wonder that observers relentlessly heralded the coming of the Pacific Century.

The Transformation of Modern Japan

For five years after the end of the war in the Pacific, Japan was governed by an Allied administration under the command of U.S. General Douglas MacArthur (1880–1964). The occupation regime was dominated by the United States, although the country was technically administered by a new Japanese government. As commander of the occupation administration, MacArthur was responsible for demilitarizing Japanese society, destroying the Japanese war machine, trying Japanese civilian and military officials charged with war crimes, and laying the foundations of postwar Japanese society.

During the war, senior U.S. officials had discussed whether to insist on the abdication of the emperor as the symbol of Japanese imperial expansion. During the summer of 1945, the United States rejected a Japanese request to guarantee that the position of the emperor would be retained in any future peace settlement and reiterated its demand for unconditional surrender. After the war, however, the United States agreed to the retention of the emperor after he agreed publicly to renounce his divinity (see the box above). Although many historians have suggested that Emperor Hirohito (heer-oh-HEE-toh) (1901–1989) opposed the war policy of his senior advisers, some historians have contended that he fully supported it.

THE MACARTHUR REFORMS Under MacArthur's firm tutelage, Japanese society was remodeled along Western lines. The centerpiece of occupation policy was the promulgation of a new constitution to replace the Meiji Constitution of 1890. The new charter, which was drafted by U.S. planners and imposed on the Japanese despite their objections to some of its provisions, was designed to transform Japan into a peaceful and pluralistic society that would no longer be capable of waging offensive war. The constitution specifically renounced war as a national policy, and Japan unilaterally agreed to maintain armed forces only sufficient for self-defense. Perhaps most important, the constitution established a parliamentary form of government based on a bicameral legislature, an independent judiciary, and a universal franchise; it also reduced the power of the emperor and guaranteed human rights.

But more than a written constitution was needed to demilitarize Japan and place it on a new course. Like the Meiji leaders in the late nineteenth century, occupation administrators wished to transform Japanese social institutions and hoped their policies would be accepted by the Japanese people as readily as those of the Meiji period had been. The Meiji reforms, however, had been crafted to reflect Japanese traditions and had set Japan on a path quite different from that of the modern West. Some Japanese observers believed that a fundamental reversal of trends begun with the Meiji Restoration would be needed before Japan would be ready to adopt the Western capitalist, democratic model.

One of the sturdy pillars of Japanese militarism had been the giant business cartels, known as *zaibatsu* (see Chapter 24). Allied policy was designed to break up the *zaibatsu* into smaller units in the belief that corporate concentration not only hindered competition but was inherently undemocratic and conducive to political authoritarianism. Occupation planners also intended to promote the formation of independent labor unions, lessen the power of the state over the economy, and provide a mouthpiece for downtrodden Japanese workers. Economic inequality in rural areas was to be reduced by a comprehensive land reform program that would turn the land over to the people who farmed it. Finally, the educational system was to be remodeled along American lines so that it would turn out independent individuals rather than automatons subject to manipulation by the state.

JAPAN IN THE COLD WAR The Allied program was an ambitious and even audacious plan to remake Japanese society and has been justly praised for its clear-sighted vision and altruistic motives. Parts of the program, such as the constitution, the land reforms, and the educational system, succeeded brilliantly. But as other concerns began to intervene, changes or compromises were made that were not always successful. In particular, with the rise of Cold War sentiment in the United States in the late 1940s, the goal of decentralizing the Japanese economy gave way to the desire to make Japan a key partner in the effort to defend East Asia against international communism. Convinced of the need to promote economic recovery in Japan, U.S. policymakers began to show more tolerance for the *zaibatsu*. Concerned at growing radicalism within the new labor movement, U.S. occupation authorities placed less emphasis on the independence of the labor unions.

Cold War concerns also affected U.S. foreign relations with Japan. On September 8, 1951, the United States and other former belligerent nations signed a peace treaty restoring Japanese independence. In turn, Japan renounced any claim to such former colonies or territories as Taiwan, Korea, and southern Sakhalin and the Kurile Islands (see Map 30.3). On the same day, Japan and the United States signed a defensive alliance and agreed that the latter could maintain military bases on the Japanese islands. Japan was now formally independent but in a new dependency relationship with the United States. Thus, by the early 1950s, Japan had regained partial control over its destiny.

POLITICS AND GOVERNMENT The Allied occupation administrators started with the conviction that Japanese expansionism was directly linked to the institutional and ideological foundations of the Meiji Constitution. Accordingly, they set

© Keystone/Getty Images

General MacArthur and Emperor Hirohito. After the end of World War II, U.S. General Douglas MacArthur was appointed supreme commander of the Allied Powers. In that capacity, he directed U.S. policy during the occupation of Japan from 1945 to 1950. Here MacArthur stands side by side with Emperor Hirohito of Japan. Note the cultural and attitudinal differences of the two leaders expressed by their contrasting body language.

© Cengage Learning

MAP 30.3 Modern Japan. Shown here are the four main islands that comprise the contemporary state of Japan.

Q *Which is the largest?*

government, however, quickly split into feuding factions, and in 1995, the Liberal Democrats returned to power. Successive prime ministers proved unable to carry out promised reforms, and in 2001, Junichiro Koizumi (joo-hee-CHAY-roh koh-ee-ZOO-mee) (b. 1942), a former minister of health and welfare, was elected prime minister. His personal charisma raised expectations that he might be able to bring about significant changes, but bureaucratic resistance to reform and chronic factionalism within the Liberal Democratic Party thwarted his efforts. In 2009, three years after he left office, the Liberal Democrats were once again voted out of power.

JAPAN, INCORPORATED One of the problems plaguing the current system has been the centralizing tendencies that it inherited from the Meiji period. The government is organized on a unitary rather than a federal basis; the local administrative units, called prefectures, have few of the powers of states in the United States. Moreover, the central government plays an active and sometimes intrusive role in various aspects of the economy, mediating management-labor disputes, establishing price and wage policies, and subsidizing vital industries and enterprises producing goods for export. This government intervention in the economy has traditionally been widely accepted and is often cited as a key reason for the efficiency of Japanese industry and the emergence of the country as an industrial giant.

In recent years, though, the tradition of active government involvement in the economy has increasingly come under fire. Japanese business, which previously sought government protection from imports, now argues that deregulation is needed to enable Japanese firms to innovate in order to keep up with the competition. Such reforms, however, have been resisted by powerful government ministries in Tokyo, which are accustomed to playing an active role in national affairs.

A third problem is that the Liberal Democratic Party has long been divided into factions that seek to protect their own interests and often resist changes that might benefit society as a whole. This tradition of factionalism has tended to insulate political figures from popular scrutiny and encouraged susceptibility to secret dealing and official corruption. A number of senior politicians, including two recent prime ministers, have been forced to resign because of serious questions about improper financial dealings with business associates. Concern over political corruption was undoubtedly a major factor in the defeats suffered by the Liberal Democrats in 1993 and 2009, and the issue continues to plague the political scene.

ATONING FOR THE PAST Lingering social problems also need to be addressed. Minorities such as the *eta*, now known as the **Burakumin** (BOOR-uh-koo-min), and Korean residents in Japan continue to be subjected to legal and social discrimination. For years, official sources were reluctant to divulge growing evidence that thousands of Korean women were conscripted to serve as prostitutes (euphemistically called "comfort women") for Japanese soldiers during World War II, and many Koreans living in Japan contend that such prejudicial attitudes continue to exist. Representatives of the "comfort

out to change Japanese politics into something closer to the pluralistic model used in most Western nations. Yet a number of characteristics of the postwar Japanese political system reflected the tenacity of the traditional political culture. Although Japan had a multiparty system with two major parties, the Liberal Democrats and the Socialists, in practice there was a "government party" and a permanent opposition—the Liberal Democrats, who had presided over an era of growing material prosperity, were not voted out of office for thirty years. Many of the leading Liberal Democrats controlled factions on a patron-client basis, and decisions on key issues, such as who should assume the prime ministership, were reached by a modern equivalent of the Meiji oligarchs.

That tradition changed suddenly in 1993 when the ruling Liberal Democrats, shaken by persistent reports of corruption and cronyism between politicians and business interests, failed to win a majority of seats in parliamentary elections. Morihiro Hosokawa (moh-ree-HEE-roh hoh-soh-KAH-wah) (b. 1938), the leader of one of several newly formed parties, was elected prime minister. The new coalition women" have demanded both financial compensation and a formal letter of apology from the Japanese government for the treatment they received during the Pacific War. Negotiations over the issue have been under way for several years.

Japan's behavior during World War II has been an especially sensitive issue. During the early 1990s, critics at home and abroad charged that textbooks printed under the guidance of the Ministry of Education did not adequately discuss the atrocities committed by the Japanese armed forces during World War II. Other Asian governments were particularly incensed at Tokyo's failure to accept responsibility for such behavior and demanded a formal apology. The government expressed remorse, but only in the context of the aggressive actions of all colonial powers during the imperialist era. In the view of many Japanese, the actions of their government during the Pacific War were a form of self-defense. When new textbooks were published that openly discussed instances of Japanese wartime misconduct, including sex slavery, the use of slave labor, and the Nanjing Massacre (see Chapter 25), many Japanese were outraged and initiated a campaign to delete or tone down references to atrocities committed by imperial troops during the Pacific War. Prime Minister Koizumi exacerbated the controversy by attending ceremonies at shrines dedicated to the spirits of Japan's war dead.

The issue is not simply an academic one, for fear of a revival of Japanese militarism is still strong in the region, where Japan's relations with other states have recently been strained by disputes with South Korea and China over ownership of small islands in the China Sea. The proper role of the military has been the subject of vigorous debate in Japan, where some observers have argued that their country should adopt a more assertive stance toward the United States and play a larger role in Asian affairs. These concerns have increased in recent years, as the potential nuclear threat from nearby North Korea (see "South Korea: A Peninsula Divided" later in this chapter) and a more aggressive posture by powerful China have reminded many Japanese that they live in a dangerous neighborhood.

The Economy

Nowhere are the changes in postwar Japan so visible as in the economic sector, where Japan developed into a major industrial and technological power in the space of a century, surpassing such advanced Western societies as Germany, France, and Great Britain.

Although this "Japanese miracle" has often been described as beginning after the war as a result of the Allied reforms, in fact Japanese economic growth began much earlier, with the Meiji reforms, which helped transform Japan from an autocratic society based on semifeudal institutions into an advanced capitalist democracy.

REFORMS DURING THE OCCUPATION As noted earlier, the officials of the Allied occupation identified the Meiji economic system with centralized power and the rise of Japanese militarism. Accordingly, they set out to break up the *zaibatsu* and decentralize Japanese industry and commerce. But with the rise of Cold War tensions, the policy was scaled back. Looser

ties between companies were still allowed, and a new type of informal relationship, sometimes called the *keiretsu* (key-RET-soo), or "interlocking arrangement," began to take shape. Through such arrangements among suppliers, wholesalers, retailers, and financial institutions, the *zaibatsu* system was reconstituted under a new name.

The occupation administration had more success with its program to reform the agricultural system. Half of the population still lived on farms, and half of all farmers were still tenants. Under the land reform program, all lands owned by absentee landlords and all cultivated landholdings over an established maximum were sold on easy credit terms to the tenants. The program created a strong class of yeoman farmers, and tenants declined to about 10 percent of the rural population.

THE "JAPANESE MIRACLE" During the next fifty years, Japan re-created the stunning results of the Meiji era. In 1950, the Japanese gross domestic product was about one-third that of Great Britain or France. Thirty years later, it was larger than both put together and well over half that of the United States. Japan became the greatest exporting nation in the world, and its per capita income equaled that of the most advanced Western states.

Explanations for Japan's success tended to fall into two major categories. Some analysts pointed to cultural factors: the Japanese are naturally group oriented and find it easy to cooperate with one another. Traditionally hardworking and frugal, they are more inclined to save than to consume, a trait that boosts the savings rate and labor productivity. Like all Confucian societies, the Japanese value education, and consequently the labor force is highly skilled. The literacy rate is almost 100 percent, and a significantly higher proportion of the population graduates from high school than in most advanced nations of the West.

Other observers gave more practical reasons for Japan's success. Paradoxically, Japan benefited from the total destruction of its industrial base during World War II, in that it did not have to contend with the antiquated plants that held back many industries in the United States. Secure under U.S. protection, Japan spends less than 1 percent of its gross domestic product on national defense (by comparison, the United States spends about 5 percent on defense). In addition, the Japanese government has actively promoted business interests. Some critics have charged that Japan went beyond promotion to unfair trade practices by subsidizing exports through the Ministry of International Trade and Industry (**MITI**), dumping goods at prices below cost to break into foreign markets, maintaining an artificially low standard of living at home to encourage exports, and unduly restricting imports from other countries.

There is some truth on both sides of the argument. Many of the practical steps Japan took were possible precisely because of the cultural factors described here. The tradition of loyalty to the firm, for example, derives from the communal tradition in Japanese society. The concept of sacrificing one's personal interests to those of the state, though not necessarily rooted in the traditional period, was certainly fostered by the *genro* oligarchy during the Meiji era.

A MIRACLE TARNISHED In recent years, the Japanese economy has run into serious difficulties, raising the question as to whether the vaunted Japanese model is as appealing as many observers earlier declared. A rise in the value of the yen hurt exports and burst the bubble of investment by Japanese banks that had taken place under the umbrella of government protection. Lacking a domestic market equivalent in size to the United States, in the 1990s the Japanese economy slipped into a recession that has not yet entirely abated. Today, about 16 percent of the Japanese population lives in poverty, a figure only slightly lower than in the United States.

These economic difficulties have placed heavy pressure on some of the vaunted features of the Japanese economy. The tradition of lifetime employment created a bloated white-collar workforce and has made downsizing difficult. Today, job security is on the decline as increasing numbers of workers are being laid off. A disproportionate burden has fallen on women, who lack seniority and continue to suffer from various forms of discrimination in the workplace. In the meantime, many older Japanese have seen their savings diminish, while retirement programs are increasingly strained by the demands of a rapidly aging population.

A final change is that slowly but inexorably, the Japanese market is beginning to open up to international competition. Foreign automakers are winning a growing share of the domestic market, and the government—concerned at the prospect of food shortages—has committed itself to facilitating the importation of rice from abroad. Greater exposure to foreign competition may improve the performance of Japanese manufacturers. In recent years, Japanese consumers have become increasingly critical of the quality of some domestic products, causing one cabinet minister to complain about "sloppiness and complacency" among Japanese firms (even the Japanese automaker Toyota, whose vehicles consistently rank high in quality tests, has been faced with quality problems in its best-selling fleet of motor vehicles). The massive earthquake and tsunami that struck the coast of Japan in 2011 added to the nation's difficulties when they exposed the failure of the government to maintain proper safeguards for its nuclear plants in the vicinity. The costs of rebuilding after the disaster will pose a major challenge to Japanese leaders, who already face a crisis of confidence from their constituents.

A Society in Transition

During the occupation, Allied planners set out to change social characteristics that they believed had contributed to Japanese aggressiveness before and during World War II. The new educational system removed all references to filial piety, patriotism, and loyalty to the emperor while emphasizing the individualistic values of Western civilization. The new constitution and a revised civil code eliminated remaining legal restrictions on women's rights to obtain a divorce, hold a job, or change their domicile. Women were guaranteed the right to vote and were encouraged to enter politics.

THE PRESSURE TO CONFORM Such efforts to remake Japanese behavior through legislation have had mixed success.

During the past sixty-five years, Japan has unquestionably become a more individualistic and egalitarian society. At the same time, many of the distinctive characteristics of traditional Japanese society have persisted to the present day, although in somewhat altered form. The emphasis on loyalty to the group and community relationships, for example, is reflected in the strength of corporate loyalties in contemporary Japan, although, as we have seen, the attitude has eroded in recent years.

Emphasis on the work ethic also remains strong. The tradition of hard work is taught at a young age. Japanese students attend school 240 days a year, compared with 180 days in the United States, and homework assignments tend to be more extensive. The results are impressive: Japanese schoolchildren consistently earn higher scores on achievement tests than children in other advanced countries. At the same time, this devotion to success has often been accompanied by bullying by teachers and an emphasis on conformity (see the box on p. 916).

Some young Japanese find suicide the only escape from the pressures emanating from society, school, and family. Parental pride often becomes a factor, with "education mothers" pressuring their children to work hard and succeed for the honor of the family. Ironically, once the student is accepted into college, the amount of work assigned tends to decrease because graduates of the best universities are virtually guaranteed lucrative employment offers. Nevertheless, the early training instills an attitude of deference to group interests that persists throughout life.

By all accounts, however, independent thinking is on the increase in Japan. In some cases, it leads to antisocial behavior, such as crime or membership in a teenage gang. Crime rates, while well below those in the United States, have risen dramatically, leading Prime Minister Koizumi to lament in 2003 that Japan is no longer "the world's safest country."[5] Antisocial feeling, however, is usually expressed in more indirect ways, such as the recent fashion among young people of dyeing their hair brown (known in Japanese as "tea hair"). Because the practice is banned in many schools and generally frowned on by the older generation (one police chief dumped a pitcher of beer on a student with brown hair whom he noticed in a bar), many young Japanese dye their hair as a gesture of independence. When seeking employment or getting married, however, they return their hair to its natural color.

WOMEN IN JAPANESE SOCIETY One of the most tenacious legacies of the past in Japanese society is sexual inequality. Although women are now legally protected against discrimination in employment, very few have reached senior levels in business, education, or politics. Women now comprise nearly 50 percent of the workforce, but most are in retail or service occupations. Less than 10 percent of managerial workers in Japan are women, compared with nearly half in the United States. There is a feminist movement in Japan, but it has none of the vigor and mass support of its counterpart in the United States.

There is no stigma attached to being a homemaker in Japan, where a woman has considerable responsibility. She is

Growing Up in Japan

FAMILY & SOCIETY

Japanese schoolchildren are exposed to a much more regimented environment than U.S. children experience. Most Japanese schoolchildren, for example, wear black-and-white uniforms to school. These regulations are examples of rules adopted by middle school systems in various parts of Japan. The Ministry of Education in Tokyo concluded that these regulations were excessive, but they are probably typical.

School Regulations, Japanese Style

1. Boys' hair should not touch the eyebrows, the ears, or the top of the collar.
2. No one should have a permanent wave or dye his or her hair. Girls should not wear ribbons or accessories in their hair. Hair dryers should not be used.
3. School uniform skirts should be _____ centimeters above the ground, no more and no less (differs by school and region).
4. Keep your uniform clean and pressed at all times. Girls' middy blouses should have two buttons on the back collar. Boys' pant cuffs should be of the prescribed width. No more than 12 eyelets should be on shoes. The number of buttons on a shirt and tucks in a shirt are also prescribed.
5. Wear your school badge at all times. It should be positioned exactly.
6. Going to school in the morning, wear your book bag strap on the right shoulder; in the afternoon on the way home, wear it on the left shoulder. Your book case thickness, filled and unfilled, is also prescribed.
7. Girls should wear only regulation white underpants of 100% cotton.
8. When you raise your hand to be called on, your arm should extend forward and up at the angle prescribed in your handbook.
9. Your own route to and from school is marked in your student rule handbook; carefully observe which side of each street you are to use on the way to and from school.
10. After school you are to go directly home, unless your parent has written a note permitting you to go to another location. Permission will not be granted by the school unless this other location is a suitable one. You must not go to coffee shops. You must be home by _____ o'clock.
11. It is not permitted to drive or ride a motorcycle, or to have a license to drive one.
12. Before and after school, no matter where you are, you represent our school, so you should behave in ways we can all be proud of.

 What is the apparent purpose of these regulations? Why does Japan appear to place more restrictions on adolescent behavior than the United States does?

---

expected to be a "good wife and wise mother" and has the primary responsibility for managing the family finances and raising the children. Japanese husbands (known derisively in Japan as the "wet leaf tribe") perform little work around the house, spending an average of nine minutes a day on housework, compared with twenty-six minutes for American husbands. At the same time, Japanese divorce rates are well below those of the United States.

THE DEMOGRAPHIC CRISIS Many of Japan's current dilemmas stem from its growing demographic problems. Today, Japan has the highest proportion of people older than sixty-five of any industrialized country—almost 23 percent of the country's total population. By the year 2024, an estimated one-third of the Japanese population will be over the age of sixty-five, and the median age will be fifty, ten years older than the median in the United States. This demographic profile is due both to declining fertility and a low level of immigration. Immigrants make up only 1 percent of the total population of Japan. Together, the aging population and the absence of immigrants are creating the prospect of a dramatic labor shortage in coming years. Nevertheless, prejudice against foreigners persists in Japan, and the government remains reluctant to ease restrictions against immigrants from other countries in the region.

Japan's aging population has many implications for the future. Traditionally, it was the responsibility of the eldest child in a Japanese family to care for aging parents, but that system is beginning to break down because of limited housing space and the growing tendency of working-age women to seek jobs in the marketplace. The proportion of Japanese older than sixty-five years of age who live with their children has dropped from 80 percent in 1970 to about 50 percent today. At the same time, public and private pension plans are under increasing financial pressure, partly because of the low birthrate and the graying population.

RELIGION When Japan was opened to the West in the nineteenth century, many Japanese became convinced of the superiority of foreign ideas and institutions and were especially interested in Western religion and culture. Although Christian converts were few, numbering less than 1 percent of the population, the influence of Christianity was out of proportion to the size of the community. Many intellectuals during

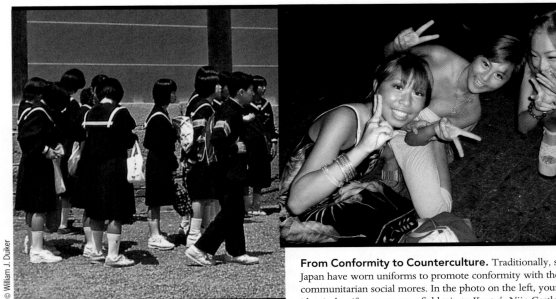

From Conformity to Counterculture. Traditionally, schoolchildren in Japan have worn uniforms to promote conformity with the country's communitarian social mores. In the photo on the left, young students dressed in identical uniforms are on a field trip to Kyoto's Nijo Castle, built in 1603 by Tokugawa Ieyasu. Recently, however, a youth counterculture has emerged in Japan. On the right, fashion-conscious teenagers with "tea hair"—heirs of Japan's long era of affluence—revel in their expensive hip-hop outfits, platform shoes, and layered dresses. Such fashion choices symbolize the growing revolt against conformity in contemporary Japan.

the Meiji era were impressed by the emotional commitment shown by missionaries in Japan and viewed Christianity as a contemporary version of Confucianism.

Today, Japan includes almost 1.5 million Christians, along with 93 million Buddhists. Many Japanese also follow Shinto, no longer identified with reverence for the emperor and the state. As in the West, increasing urbanization has led to a decline in the practice of organized religion, although evangelical sects have proliferated in recent years. The largest and best-known sect is Soka Gakkai (SOH-kuh GAK-ky), a lay Buddhist organization that has attracted millions of followers and formed its own political party, the Komeito (koh-MAY-toh). Zen Buddhism retains its popularity, and some businesspeople seek to use Zen techniques to learn how to focus on willpower as a means of outwitting a competitor. The head of one Zen monastery, however, has publicly apologized for the sect's role in promoting fanatical patriotism in the military before World War II.

Japanese Culture

Western literature, art, and music have had a major impact on Japanese society. After World War II, many of the writers who had been active before the war resurfaced, but now their writing reflected demoralization. Many were attracted to existentialism, and some turned to hedonism and nihilism. For these disillusioned authors, defeat was compounded by fear of the Americanization of postwar Japan. One of the best examples of this attitude was the novelist Yukio Mishima (yoo-KEE-oh mi-SHEE-muh) (1925–1970), who led a crusade to stem the tide of what he described as America's "universal and uniform 'Coca-Colonization'" of the world in

general and Japan in particular.[6] Mishima's ritual suicide in 1970 was the subject of widespread speculation and transformed him into a cult figure.

One of Japan's most serious-minded contemporary authors is Kenzaburo Oe (ken-zuh-BOO-roh OH-ay) (b. 1935). His work, rewarded with a Nobel Prize for Literature in 1994, presents Japan's ongoing quest for modern identity and purpose. His characters reflect the spiritual anguish precipitated by the collapse of the imperial Japanese tradition and the subsequent adoption of Western culture—a trend that Oe contends has culminated in unabashed materialism, cultural decline, and a moral void. Yet unlike Mishima, Oe does not wish to reinstill the imperial traditions of the past but rather seeks to regain spiritual meaning by retrieving the sense of communality and innocence found in rural Japan.

Haruki Murakami (HAR-oo-kee moo-rah-KAH-mee) (b. 1949), one of Japan's most popular authors today, was one of the first to discard the introspective and somber style of the earlier postwar period. Characters in his novels typically take the form of a detached antihero, reflecting the emptiness of corporate life in contemporary Japan. In *The Wind-Up Bird Chronicle* (1997), Murakami highlights the capacity for irrational violence in Japanese society and the failure of the nation to accept its guilt for the behavior of Japanese troops during World War II.

Since the 1970s, increasing affluence and a high literacy rate have contributed to a massive quantity of publications, ranging from popular potboilers to first-rate fiction. Much of this new literature deals with the common concerns of all affluent industrialized nations, including the effects of urbanization, advanced technology, and mass consumption. A wildly popular genre is the "art-manga," or graphic novel. Some members of the youth counterculture have used manga to rebel against Japan's rigid educational and conformist pressures.

Other aspects of Japanese culture have also been influenced by Western ideas, although without the intense preoccupation with synthesis that is evident in literature. Western music is very popular in Japan, and scores of Japanese classical musicians have succeeded in the West. Even rap music has gained a foothold among Japanese youth, although without the association with sex, drugs, and violence that it has in the United States. Although some of the lyrics betray an attitude of modest revolt against the uptight world of Japanese society, most lack any such connotations.

No longer are Japanese authors and painters seeking to revive the old Japan of the tea ceremony and falling plum blossoms. Raised in the crowded cities of postwar Japan, soaking up movies and television, rock music and jeans, Coca-Cola and McDonald's, many contemporary Japanese speak the universal language of today's world.

The Japanese Difference

Whether the unique character of modern Japan will endure is unclear. Confidence in the Japanese "economic miracle" has been shaken by the long recession, and there are indications of a growing tendency toward hedonism and individualism among Japanese youth. Older Japanese frequently complain that the younger generation lacks their sense of loyalty and willingness to sacrifice. There are also signs that the concept of loyalty to one's employer may be beginning to erode among Japanese youth. Some observers have predicted that with increasing affluence Japan will become more like the industrialized societies in the West. Although Japan is unlikely to evolve into a photocopy of the United States, the vaunted image of millions of dedicated "salarymen" heading off to work with their briefcases and their pin-striped suits may no longer be an accurate portrayal of reality in contemporary Japan.

The Little Tigers

Q FOCUS QUESTIONS: What factors have contributed to the economic success achieved by the Little Tigers? To what degree have they applied the Japanese model in forging their developmental strategies?

Postwar Japan's success in meeting the challenge from the capitalist West soon caught the eye of other Asian nations. By the 1980s, several smaller states in the region, known collectively as the Little Tigers, had embraced the Japanese example.

South Korea: A Peninsula Divided

While the world was focused on the economic miracle occurring on the Japanese islands, another miracle of sorts was taking place across the Sea of Japan on the Asian mainland. In 1953, the Korean peninsula was exhausted from three years of bitter fraternal war, a conflict that took the lives of an estimated 4 million Koreans on both sides of the 38th parallel and turned as much as one-quarter of the population into refugees. Although a cease-fire was signed in July 1953, it was a fragile peace that left two heavily armed and mutually hostile countries facing each other suspiciously.

North of the truce line was the People's Republic of Korea (PRK), a police state under the dictatorial rule of the Communist leader Kim Il Sung (KIM ILL SOONG) (1912–1994). To the south was the Republic of Korea, under the equally autocratic President Syngman Rhee (SING-muhn REE) (1875–1965), a fierce anti-Communist who had led the resistance to the northern invasion. But many Koreans resented Rhee's reliance on the wealthy landlord class. After several years of harsh rule, marked by government corruption, fraudulent elections, and police brutality, demonstrations broke out in the capital city of Seoul in the spring of 1960 and forced him into retirement.

The Korean Peninsula Since 1953

The Rhee era was followed by a brief period of multiparty democratic government, but in 1961, a coup d'état placed General Chung Hee Park (1917–1979) in power. The new regime promulgated a new constitution, and in 1963, Park was elected president of a civilian government. He set out to foster recovery of the economy from decades of foreign occupation and civil war. Because the private sector had been relatively weak under Japanese rule, the government played an active role in the process by instituting a series of five-year plans that targeted specific industries for development, promoted exports, and funded infrastructure development. Under a land reform program, large landowners were required to sell all their farmland above 7.4 acres to their tenants at low prices.

The program was a solid success. Benefiting from the Confucian principles of thrift, respect for education, and hard work, as well as from Japanese capital and technology, South Korea gradually emerged as a major industrial power in East Asia. The economic growth rate rose from less than 5 percent annually in the 1950s to an average of 9 percent under Chung Hee Park. The largest corporations—including Samsung, Daewoo, and Hyundai—were transformed into massive conglomerates called *chaebol* (jay-BOHL *or* je-BUHL), the Korean equivalent of the *zaibatsu* of prewar Japan. Taking advantage of relatively low wages and a stunningly high rate of saving, Korean businesses began to compete actively with the Japanese for export markets in Asia and throughout the world. Per capita income also increased dramatically, from less than $90 (in U.S. dollars) annually in 1960 to $1,560 (twice that of Communist North Korea) twenty years later.

But like many other countries in the region, South Korea was slow to develop democratic principles. Although his government functioned with the trappings of democracy, Park continued to rule by autocratic means and suppressed all forms of dissidence. In 1979, Park was assassinated. But after a brief interregnum of democratic rule, in 1980 a new military government under General Chun Doo Hwan (JUN DOH HWAHN) (b. 1931) seized power. The new regime was as authoritarian as its predecessors, and widespread student protests erupted against its autocratic rule in 1987.

National elections were finally held in 1989, and South Korea reverted to civilian rule. Successive presidents sought to rein in corruption while cracking down on the *chaebols* and initiating contacts with the Communist regime in the PRK on possible steps toward eventual reunification of the peninsula. After the Asian financial crisis in 1997, economic conditions temporarily worsened, but they have since recovered, and the country is increasingly competitive in world markets today. Symbolic of South Korea's growing self-confidence is the nation's new president, elected in 2007. An ex-mayor of Seoul, Lee Myung-bak (LEE MYUHNG BAHK) (b. 1941) is noted for his rigorous efforts to beautify the city and improve the quality of life of his compatriots, including the installation of a new five-day workweek.

In the meantime, relations with North Korea, now under the dictatorial rule of Kim Il Sung's son Kim Jong Il (b. 1941) and on the verge of becoming a nuclear power, remain tense. Multinational negotiations to persuade the regime to suspend its nuclear program have been under way for several years, so far without success.

Taiwan: The Other China

South Korea was not the only rising industrial power trying to imitate the success of the Japanese in East Asia. To the south on the island of Taiwan, the Republic of China began to do the same.

Modern Taiwan

After retreating to Taiwan following their defeat by the Communists, Chiang Kai-shek and his followers established a new capital at Taipei. The government, which continued to refer to itself as the Republic of China (ROC), contended that it remained the legitimate representative of the Chinese people and that it would eventually return in triumph to the mainland.

The Nationalists had much more success on Taiwan than they had achieved on the mainland. In the relatively safe and stable environment provided by a security treaty with the United States, signed in 1954, the ROC was able to concentrate on economic growth without worrying about a Communist invasion.

The government moved rapidly to create a solid agricultural base. A land reform program led to a reduction of rents, and landholdings over 3 acres were purchased by the government and resold to the tenants at reasonable prices. At the same time, local manufacturing and commerce were strongly encouraged. By the 1970s, Taiwan had become one of the most dynamic industrial economies in East Asia. The government played a major role in the process, targeting strategic industries for support and investing in infrastructure. At the same time, as in Japan, the government stressed the importance of private enterprise and encouraged foreign investment and a high rate of internal savings.

In contrast to the Communist regime in the People's Republic of China (PRC), the ROC actively maintained Chinese tradition, promoting respect for Confucius and the ethical principles of the past, such as hard work, frugality, and filial piety. Although there was some corruption in both the government and the private sector, income differentials between the wealthy and the poor were generally less than elsewhere in the region, and the overall standard of living increased substantially. Health and sanitation improved, literacy rates were quite high, and an active family planning program reduced the rate of population growth. Nevertheless, the total population on the island increased from about 7 million in 1945 to about 20 million in the mid-1980s.

Increasing prosperity, however, did not lead to the democratization of the political process. The Nationalists continued to rule by emergency decree and refused to permit the formation of opposition political parties on the ground that the danger of invasion from the mainland had not subsided. Some friction developed between the mainlanders, who numbered about 2 million and were dominant in the government, and the indigenous Taiwanese (mostly ethnic Chinese whose ancestors had emigrated to the island during the Qing dynasty). By the 1980s, however, these fissures in Taiwanese society had begun to diminish; by then, an ever-higher proportion of the population had been born on the island and identified themselves as Taiwanese.

After the death of Chiang Kai-shek in 1975, the ROC slowly began to move toward a more representative form of government, including elections and legal opposition parties. A national election in 1992 resulted in a bare majority for the Nationalists over strong opposition from the Democratic Progressive Party (DPP). But political liberalization had its dangers; some members of the DPP began to agitate for an independent Republic of Taiwan, a possibility that aroused concern within the Nationalist government in Taipei and frenzied hostility on the mainland. The election of DPP leader Chen Shuibian (CHUHN SHWAY-BEE-ahn) (b.1950) as ROC president in March 2000 angered Beijing, which threatened to invade Taiwan if the island continued to delay unification with the mainland. In 2007, the government returned to Nationalist control, a result that, at least for the time being, has eased relations with mainland China.

Whether Taiwan will remain an independent state or be united with the mainland is impossible to predict. Although

The Taiwan Democracy Memorial in Taipei. While the Chinese government on the mainland attempted to destroy all vestiges of traditional culture, the Republic of China on Taiwan sought to preserve the cultural heritage as a line between past and present. This policy was graphically displayed in the mausoleum for Chiang Kai-shek that was erected in downtown Taipei. The mausoleum, with its massive entrance gate, was designed not only to glorify the nation's deceased president but also to recall the grandeur of old China. In 2007, the mausoleum was renamed the Taiwan Democracy Memorial Hall in a bid by the government to downplay the island's historical ties to the mainland.

diplomatic ties have been severed, the United States continues to provide defensive military assistance to the Taiwanese armed forces and has made it clear that it supports self-determination for the people of Taiwan and that it expects the final resolution of the Chinese civil war to be by peaceful means. In the meantime, economic and cultural contacts between Taiwan and the mainland are steadily increasing. Nevertheless, the Taiwanese have shown no inclination to accept the PRC's offer of "one country, two systems," under which the ROC would accept the PRC as the legitimate government of China in return for autonomous control over the affairs of Taiwan.

Singapore and Hong Kong: The Littlest Tigers

The smallest but by no means least successful of the Little Tigers are Singapore and Hong Kong. Both are essentially city-states, with large populations densely packed into small territories. Singapore, once a British colony and briefly a part of the state of Malaysia, is now an independent nation. Hong Kong was a British colony for a century until it was returned to PRC control in 1997. In recent years, both have emerged as industrial powerhouses, with standards of living well above those of their neighbors.

The success of Singapore must be ascribed in good measure to the will and energy of its political leaders. When it became independent in August 1965, Singapore's longtime position as an entrepôt for trade between the Indian Ocean and the South China Sea was on the

MALAYSIA

SINGAPORE

Singapore R.

Singapore

0   10 Kilometers

0   6 Miles

Singapore Strait

© Cengage Learning

The Republic of Singapore

wane. With only 618 square miles of territory, much of it marshland and tropical jungle, Singapore had little to offer but the frugality and industriousness of its predominantly overseas Chinese population.

Within a decade, Singapore's role and reputation had dramatically changed. Under the leadership of Prime Minister Lee Kuan-yew (LEE kwahn-YOO) (b. 1923), once the firebrand leader of the radical People's Action Party, the government cultivated an attractive business climate while engaging in massive public works projects to feed, house, and educate its 2 million citizens. The major components of success have been shipbuilding, oil refineries, tourism, electronics, and finance—the city-state has become the banking hub of the entire region.

Like South Korea and Taiwan, Singapore relied on a combination of government planning, entrepreneurial spirit, export promotion, high productivity, and an exceptionally high rate of saving to achieve industrial growth rates of nearly 10 percent annually during the last quarter of the twentieth century. In recent years, however, the rate of growth has dropped dramatically, due primarily to increasing competition from China.

As in the other Little Tigers, an authoritarian political system has guaranteed a stable environment for economic growth. Until his retirement in 1990, Lee Kuan-yew and his People's Action Party dominated Singapore politics, and opposition elements were intimidated into silence or arrested. The prime minister openly declared that the Western model of pluralist democracy was not appropriate for Singapore and lauded the Meiji model of centralized development (see the box on p. 921). Confucian values of thrift, hard work, and obedience to authority have been promoted as the ideology of the state. The government has had a passion for cleanliness and at one time even undertook a campaign to persuade its citizens to flush the public urinals.

But economic success has begun to undermine the authoritarian foundations of the system as a more sophisticated citizenry voices aspirations for more political freedoms and an end to government paternalism. Lee Kuan-yew's successor, Goh Chok Tong (GO chawk-TONG) (b. 1941), promised a "kinder, gentler" Singapore, and political restrictions on individual behavior were gradually relaxed. The process continued under Goh's successor, Lee Hsien-loong (LEE HAZ-ee-en-LAHNG) (b. 1952), the son of Lee

To Those Living in Glass Houses

INTERACTION & EXCHANGE

Kishore Mahbubani (b. 1948) was permanent secretary in the Ministry of Foreign Affairs in Singapore from 1993 to 1998. Previously, he served as his country's ambassador to the United Nations. In this 1994 article, adapted from a piece in the *Washington Quarterly*, the author advises his audience to stop lecturing Asian societies on the issue of human rights and focus attention instead on problems in the United States. In his view, today the countries of the West have much to learn from their counterparts in East Asia. This viewpoint is shared by many other observers, political leaders, and foreign affairs specialists in the region.

Kishore Mahbubani, "Go East, Young Man"

In a major reversal of a pattern lasting centuries, many Western societies, including the U.S., are doing some major things fundamentally wrong, while a growing number of East Asian societies are doing the same things right. The results are most evident in the economic sphere. In purchasing power parity terms, East Asia's gross domestic product is already larger than that of either the U.S. or European community. Such economic prosperity, contrary to American belief, results not just from free-market arrangements but also from the right social and political choices. . . .

In most Asian eyes, the evidence of real social decay in the U.S. is clear and palpable. Since 1960, the U.S. population has grown by 41%. In the same period, there has been a 560% increase in violent crimes, a 419% increase in illegitimate births, a 400% increase in divorce rates, a 300% increase in children living in single-parent homes, a more than 200% increase in teenage suicide rates, and a drop of almost 80

points in [SAT] scores. A clear American paradox is that a society that places such a high premium on freedom has effectively reduced the physical freedom of most Americans, especially those who live in large cities. They live in heavily fortified homes, think twice before taking an evening stroll around their neighborhoods, and feel increasingly threatened by random violence when they are outside.

To any Asian, it is obvious that the breakdown of the family and social order in the U.S. owes itself to a mindless ideology that maintains that the freedom of a small number of individuals who are known to pose a threat to society (criminals, terrorists, street gang members, drug dealers) should not be constrained (for example, through detention without trial), even if to do so would enhance the freedom of the majority. . . . This belief is purely and simply a gross violation of common sense.

My hope is that Americans will come to visit East Asia in greater numbers. When they do, they will come to realize that their society has swung much too much in one direction: liberating the individual while imprisoning society. The relatively strong and stable family and social institutions of East Asia will appear more appealing. And as Americans experience the freedom of walking on city streets in Asia, they may begin to understand that freedom can also result from greater social order and discipline. Perhaps the best advice to give to a young American is: "Go East, Young Man."

 What are Mahbubani's criticisms of Western civilization? How does he justify the "Asian" approach to politics?

Kuan-yew. After the new prime minister assumed office in 2004, the government announced plans to relax restrictions on freedom of speech and assembly in the small island-state. Elections held in 2011 resulted in growing support for members of opposition parties.

The future of Hong Kong is not so clear-cut. As in Singapore, sensible government policies and the hard work of its people have enabled Hong Kong to thrive. At first, the prosperity of the colony depended on a plentiful supply of cheap labor. Inundated with refugees from the mainland during the

Hong Kong

1950s and 1960s, the population of Hong Kong burgeoned to more than 6 million. More recently, Hong Kong has benefited from increased tourism, manufacturing, and the growing economic prosperity of neighboring Guangdong province, the most prosperous region of the PRC. Unlike the other societies discussed in this chapter, Hong Kong has relied on an unbridled free market system rather than active state intervention in the economy. At the same time, by allocating substantial funds for transportation, sanitation, education, and public housing, the government has created favorable conditions for economic development.

When Britain's ninety-nine-year lease on the New Territories, the food basket of the colony, expired on July 1, 1997, Hong Kong returned to mainland authority. Although the Chinese promised the British that for fifty years the people of Hong Kong would live under a capitalist system and be essentially self-governing, recent statements by Chinese leaders have raised questions about the degree of autonomy Hong Kong will continue to receive under Chinese rule. In 2003, the local government's decision to expand security

The Hong Kong Skyline. Hong Kong reverted to Chinese sovereignty in 1997 after a century of British rule. To commemorate the occasion, the imposing Conference Center, shown here in the foreground, was built on reclaimed shore land in the Hong Kong harbor.

CHRONOLOGY	Japan and the Little Tigers Since World War II
End of World War II in the Pacific	1945
Chiang Kai-shek retreats to Taiwan	1949
End of U.S. occupation of Japan	1950
Korean War	1950–1953
United States–Republic of China security treaty	1954
Syngman Rhee overthrown in South Korea	1960
Rise to power of Chung Hee Park in South Korea	1961
Independence of Singapore	1965
Death of Chiang Kai-shek	1975
Chung Hee Park assassinated	1979
Student riots in South Korea	1987
Lee Kuan-yew era ends in Singapore	1990
First free general elections on Taiwan	1992
Return of Hong Kong to Chinese control	1997
Financial crisis hits the region	1997
Chen Shuibian elected president of Taiwan	2000
Junichiro Koizumi elected prime minister in Japan	2001
Koizumi era ends in Japan	2006
Nationalist Party returns to power in Taiwan	2007
Lee Myung-bak elected president of South Korea	2007
Earthquake and tsunami in Japan	2011

restrictions aroused widespread protests, and pro-democracy candidates have done well in recent local elections.

On the Margins of Asia: Postwar Australia and New Zealand

Geographically, Australia and New Zealand are not part of Asia, and throughout their short history, both countries have identified culturally and politically with the West rather than with their Pacific Rim neighbors. Their political institutions and values are derived from Europe, and their economies resemble those of the advanced countries of the world rather than the preindustrial societies of much of Southeast Asia. Both are currently members of the British Commonwealth and of the U.S.-led ANZUS alliance (Australia, New Zealand, and the United States).

Yet trends in recent years have been drawing both states, especially Australia, closer to Asia. In the first place, immigration from East and Southeast Asia has increased rapidly. More than one-half of current immigrants into Australia come from East Asia, and about 7 percent of the population of about 18 million people is now of Asian descent. In New Zealand, residents of Asian descent represent only about 3 percent of the population of 3.5 million, but about 12 percent of the population are Maoris, Polynesian peoples who settled on the islands about a thousand years ago. Second, trade relations with Asia are increasing rapidly. About 60 percent of Australia's export

© William J. Duiker

You *Can* Take It with You. In traditional China, wealthy Chinese buried clay models of personal possessions to accompany the departed to the next world, but ordinary people burned paper effigies, which were transported to the afterlife by means of the rising smoke. This custom survives in many Chinese communities today, as this photograph taken in modern-day Singapore demonstrates. Some merchants make their living by manufacturing paper replicas of elaborate houses as seen here, often featuring such embellishments as television sets, elegant furniture, and even Mercedes automobiles.

markets today are in East Asia, and the region is the source of about half of its imports. Asian trade with New Zealand is also on the increase.

At the same time, the links that bind both countries to Great Britain and the United States have been loosening. Although security ties with the United States remain important, the Australian government is seeking to establish closer ties with the ASEAN alliance. Farther removed from Asia both physically and psychologically, New Zealand assigns less importance to its security treaty with the United States and has been vocally critical of U.S. nuclear policies in the region.

Whether Australia and New Zealand will ever become an integral part of the Asia-Pacific region is uncertain. Cultural differences stemming from the European origins of the majority of the population in both countries hinder mutual understanding on both sides of the divide, and many ASEAN leaders express reluctance to accept the two countries as full members of the alliance. But economic and geographic realities act as a powerful force, and should the Pacific region continue on its current course toward economic prosperity and political stability, the role of Australia and New Zealand will assume greater significance.

Explaining the East Asian Miracle

What explains the striking ability of Japan and the four Little Tigers to transform themselves into export-oriented societies

capable of competing with the advanced nations of Europe and the Western Hemisphere? Some analysts point to the traditional character traits of Confucian societies, such as thrift, a work ethic, respect for education, and obedience to authority. In a recent poll of Asian executives, more than 80 percent expressed the belief that Asian values differ from those of the West, and most add that these values have contributed significantly to the region's recent success. Others place more emphasis on deliberate steps taken by government and economic leaders to meet the political, economic, and social challenges their societies face.

There seems no reason to doubt that cultural factors connected to East Asian social traditions have contributed to the economic success of these societies. Certainly, habits such as frugality, industriousness, and subordination of individual desires have all played a role in their governments' ability to concentrate on the collective interest. As this and preceding chapters have shown, however, without active encouragement by political elites, such traditions cannot be effectively harnessed for the good of society as a whole. The creative talents of the Chinese people, for example, were not efficiently utilized under Mao Zedong during the frenetic years of the Cultural Revolution. Only when Deng Xiaoping and other pragmatists took charge and began to place a high priority on economic development were the stunning advances of recent decades achieved. By the same token, political elites elsewhere in East Asia were aware of traditional values and willing to use them for national purposes.

One other factor should be taken into account. Japan and the Little Tigers were operating within a regional framework highly conducive to rapid economic development. The Little Tigers received substantial inputs of capital and technology from the advanced nations of the West—Taiwan and South Korea from the United States, Hong Kong and Singapore from Britain. Japan relied to a greater degree on its own efforts but received a significant advantage by being placed under the U.S. security umbrella and guaranteed access to markets and sources of raw materials in a region dominated by U.S. naval power. In effect, the rapid rise of East Asia in the postwar era was no miracle, but a fortuitous combination of favorable cultural factors and deliberate human action.

CHAPTER SUMMARY

In the years following the end of World War II, the peoples of Asia emerged from a century of imperial rule to face the challenge of building stable and prosperous independent states. Initially, progress was slow, as new political leaders were forced to deal with the legacy of colonialism and internal disagreements over their visions for the future. By the end of the century, however, most nations in the area were beginning to lay the foundations for the creation of advanced industrial societies. Today, major Asian states like China, Japan, and India have become major competitors of the advanced Western nations in the international marketplace.

To some observers, these economic achievements have come at a high price, in the form of political authoritarianism and a lack of attention to human rights. Rapid economic development has also exacted an environmental price. Industrial pollution in China and India and the destruction of the forest cover in Southeast Asia increasingly threaten the fragile ecosystem and create friction among nations in the region. Unless they learn to cooperate effectively to deal with the challenge in future years, it will ultimately undermine the dramatic economic and social progress that has taken place.

Still, a look at the historical record suggests that, for the most part, the nations of southern and eastern Asia have made dramatic progress in coping with the multiple challenges of independence. Political pluralism is often a by-product of economic growth, while a rising standard of living should enable the peoples of the region to meet the social and environmental challenges that lie ahead.

CHAPTER TIMELINE

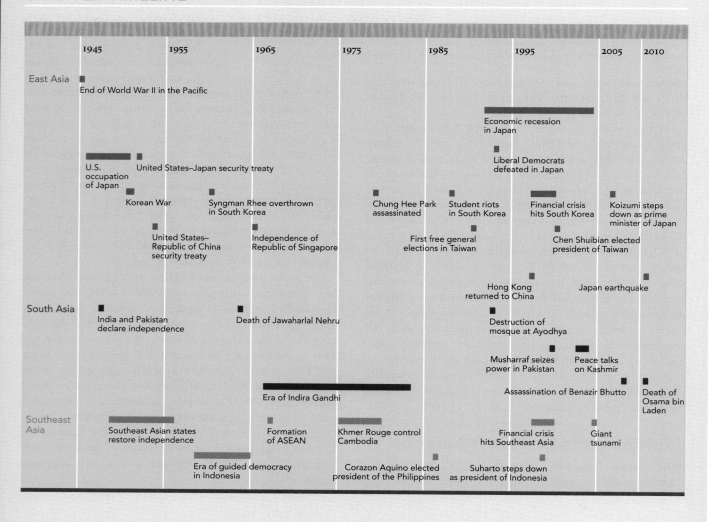

Upon Reflection

Q What kinds of environmental problems are currently being faced by the nations of southern and eastern Asia? How have the region's political leaders sought to deal with the problems?

Q How has independence affected the role of women in southern and eastern Asia? What factors are involved?

Q How have the nations in the region dealt with the challenge of integrating their ethnic and religious minorities into their political systems?

Key Terms

communalism (p. 896)
green revolution (p. 896)
dalits (p. 899)
guided democracy (p. 904)
ASEAN (p. 908)
Burakumin (p. 913)
keiretsu (p. 914)
MITI (p. 914)
chaebol (p. 918)

Suggested Reading

THE INDIAN SUBCONTINENT SINCE 1945 For a survey of postwar Indian history, see **S. Tharoor,** *India: From Midnight to the Millennium* (New York, 1997). On India's founding father, see **J. Brown,** *Nehru: A Political Life* (New Haven, Conn., 2003). The life and career of Indira Gandhi have been well chronicled. See **K. Frank,** *Indira: The Life of Indira Nehru Gandhi* (New York, 2000). On Pakistan, see **O. B. Jones,** *Pakistan: Eye of the Storm* (New Haven, Conn., 2002). Also of interest is **C. Baxter,** *Bangladesh: From a Nation to a State* (Boulder, Colo., 1997).

SOUTHEAST ASIA SINCE 1945 There are a number of standard surveys of the history of modern Southeast Asia. One is **N. Tarling,** *Southeast Asia: A Modern History* (Oxford, 2002). For a more scholarly approach, see **N. Tarling, ed.,** *The Cambridge History of Southeast Asia,* vol. 4 (Cambridge, 1999).

T. Friend, *Indonesian Destinies* (Cambridge, Mass., 2003), is a fine introduction to Indonesian society and culture. The rise of terrorism in the region is discussed in **Z. Abuza,** *Militant Islam in Southeast Asia: Crucible of Terror* (Boulder, Colo., 2003). For an overview of women's issues in contemporary South and Southeast Asia, consult **B. Ramusack** and **S. Sievers,** *Women in Asia* (Bloomington, Ind., 1999).

JAPAN SINCE 1945 For a balanced treatment of all issues relating to postwar Japan, see **J. McLain,** *Japan: A Modern History* (New York, 2001). **I. Buruma,** *Inventing Japan* (New York, 2002), offers a more journalistic approach that raises questions about the future of democracy in Japan.

THE LITTLE TIGERS On the four Little Tigers and their economic development, see **D. Oberdorfer,** *The Two Koreas: A Contemporary History* (Indianapolis, 1997); **Lee Kuan Yew,** *From Third World to First: The Singapore Story, 1965–2000* (New York, 2000); and **K. Rafferty,** *City on the Rocks: Hong Kong's Uncertain Future* (London, 1991). Also see **M. Rubinstein,** *Taiwan: A New History* (New York, 2001).

Go to the CourseMate website at **www.cengagebrain.com** for additional study tools and review materials— including audio and video clips—for this chapter.

ON A VISIT TO NUREMBERG, Germany, with his family in 2000, Jackson Spielvogel, one of the authors of this textbook, was startled to find that the main railroad station, where he had once arrived as a Fulbright student, was now ostentatiously adorned with McDonald's Golden Arches. McDonald's was the brainstorm of two brothers who opened a cheap burger restaurant in California in 1940. When they expanded their operations to Arizona, they began to use two yellow arches to make their building visible from blocks away. After Ray Kroc, an enterprising businessman, bought the burgeoning business from the brothers, McDonald's arches rapidly spread to all of the United States. And they didn't stop there. The so-called fast-food industry, which now relied on computers to maximize the automated processing of its food, found an international market. McDonald's spread to Japan in 1971 and to Russia and China in 1990; by 1995, more than half of all McDonald's restaurants were located outside the United States. By 2000, McDonald's was serving 50 million people a day.

McDonald's is but one of numerous U.S. companies that use the latest technology and actively seek global markets. Indeed, sociologists have coined the term *McDonaldization* to refer to "the process whereby the principles of the fast-food restaurant are coming to dominate more and more sectors of American society as well as the rest of the world."[1] Multinational corporations like McDonald's have brought about a worldwide homogenization of societies and made us aware of the political, economic, and social interdependence of the world's nations and the global nature of our contemporary problems. An important part of this global awareness is the technological dimension. The growth of new technology has made possible levels of world communication that simply did not exist before. At the same time that Osama bin Laden and al-Qaeda were denouncing the forces of modernization, they were promoting their message by using advanced telecommunication systems that have only recently been developed. The Technological Revolution has tied peoples and nations closely together and contributed to **globalization**, the term that is frequently used today to describe the process by which peoples and nations have become more interdependent.

Of course, as we have seen in world history, globalization is a process that is centuries old. Ever since *Homo sapiens sapiens* moved out of Africa and gradually populated the world, globalization has been occurring. During the Middle Ages, the Mongol conquests inaugurated what one scholar has called the "idea of the unified conceptualization of the globe," creating a "basic information circuit" that spread commodities, ideas, and inventions from one end of the Eurasian supercontinent to the other. Between 1500 and 1815, a maritime trade network extended throughout the entire populated world. And after 1815, the spread of Western imperialism to most parts of the

McDonald's in India. McDonald's has become an important symbol of U.S. cultural influence throughout the world. Seen here is a McDonald's located in a traditional building in New Delhi, India. The children outside are trying to make some money by selling balloons to other children who can afford to buy fast food.

© Mark Edwards/Peter Arnold/Photolibrary

world led to the domination of subject peoples but also tied the peoples of the world together in new ways. Aided by the technological advances of the twentieth and twenty-first centuries, globalization is now proceeding at an accelerated pace.

The Global Economy

Especially since the 1970s, the world has developed a **global economy** in which the production, distribution, and sale of goods are accomplished on a worldwide scale. Several international institutions have contributed to the rise of the global economy. Soon after the end of World War II, the United States and other nations established the World Bank and the International Monetary Fund (IMF) as a means of expanding global markets and avoiding dramatic economic crises such as the Great Depression of the 1930s. The World Bank is actually a group of five international organizations, largely controlled by developed countries, which provides grants, loans, and advice for economic development to developing countries. The goal of the IMF is to oversee the global financial system by supervising exchange rates and offering financial and technical assistance to developing nations. Today, 187 countries are members of the IMF. Critics have argued, however, that both the World Bank and the IMF sometimes push inappropriate Western economic practices on non-Western nations that only aggravate the poverty and debt of developing nations.

Another reflection of the new global economic order is the **multinational corporation** or **transnational corporation** (a company that has divisions in more than two countries). Prominent examples of multinational corporations include Siemens, General Electric, ExxonMobil, Mitsubishi, and Sony. These companies are among the two hundred largest multinational corporations, which are responsible for more than half of the world's industrial production. In 2000, some 71 percent of these corporations were headquartered in just three countries—the United States, Japan, and Germany. Changes in telecommunications and distribution have made it easier for corporations to be multinational. In addition, the electronics products so much in demand today, such as iPads, digital cameras, and computers, are much lighter and easier to transport than the steel, coal, and other heavy goods of earlier centuries. These supercorporations have come to dominate much of the world's investment capital, technology, and markets. A recent comparison of corporate sales and national gross domestic product found that only forty-nine of the world's hundred largest economic entities are nations; the remaining fifty-one are corporations. For this reason, some observers believe that economic globalization is more appropriately labeled "corporate globalization."

Another important component of economic globalization is free trade. In 1947, talks led to the creation of the General Agreement on Tariffs and Trade (GATT), a global trade organization that was replaced in 1995 by the World Trade Organization (WTO). Made up of more than 150 member nations, the WTO arranges trade agreements and settles trade disputes. The goal of the WTO is to open up world markets and maximize global production, but many critics charge that the WTO has ignored environmental and health concerns, harmed small and developing countries, and created an ever-growing gap between rich and poor nations.

The End of Excess

Despite an increase in production, capital, and trade as a result of globalization, the steps taken to promote the flow of goods worldwide also created an interconnected world of finance leading to one of the largest economic collapses since the Great Depression. The global economy experienced worldwide financial troubles beginning in 2007, following the collapse of the U.S. housing market. Spurred by low interest rates in the early 2000s, easily available mortgages drove up housing values in the United States. In response, investment banks began selling financial investments called collateralized debt obligations (CDOs), which were based on bundles of mortgages. Banks in New York sold CDOs to banks in Europe and elsewhere, spreading the wealth and the risk of investment. Many of the mortgages used as investments had been subprime—issued to borrowers with low credit ratings and a high likelihood of default. As the low introductory rates on the mortgages expired beginning in 2006, default rates increased, and all asset securities began to lose their value. By September 2008, a number of large financial institutions, including insurance and mortgage companies, investment firms, and banks, were approaching or had fallen into bankruptcy. The rapid collapse of CDO values and falling housing prices caused a precipitous decline in the U.S. stock market as stocks lost almost $8 trillion in value from mid-September to November 2008.

Ultimately, the crash of the U.S. housing market led to a worldwide recession. As the American economy slowed, trade decreased worldwide because American consumers, who had been consuming because of higher home values, could no longer afford to do so. Production in Asia decreased, and prices of commodities fell, including the price of oil, which had an impact on Middle Eastern countries and Russia as well.

The United States responded to the financial crisis with an emergency program to recapitalize financial institutions and a stimulus package to support growth and reduce unemployment. Although Europe initially faced less severe problems than the United States, several countries including Greece and Ireland have been forced to take loans from the IMF and the European Union. In eastern Europe, countries that only recently adopted free market economies experienced a drastic devaluation of their currencies as investors fled to the stronger dollar and euro. Many Asian nations faced a series of layoffs in the immediate wake of the crisis, although by 2010, production had begun to return to pre-crash levels. Latin America also escaped the brunt of the crisis as Brazil took the lead with oil, food, and mineral exports. Although government measures prevented a systemic failure of the world financial system, high unemployment and weak consumption will probably plague Western nations for several years to come, as people pay off their debts from the previous era of excess.

Global Culture and the Digital Age

Since the invention of the microprocessor in 1971, the capabilities of computers have expanded by leaps and bounds, resulting in what is often called the information age or digital age. By increasing access to information, the digital age enables billions of people to communicate directly in a relatively short time, while allowing multinational corporations to make transactions from any location that has Internet access. Beginning in the 1980s, computer and software companies such as Apple and Microsoft competed to create more powerful computers. By the 1990s, the booming technology industry had made Microsoft founder Bill Gates the richest man in the world. Much of this success was due to several innovations involving computers that made them indispensable devices for communication, information, and entertainment.

Global Communication

The advent of electronic mail, or e-mail, in the mid-1990s transformed the way that people communicate. As the capacity of computers to transmit data increased, e-mail messages could carry document and image attachments, making them a workable and speedier alternative to "snail mail," as conventional postal mail came to be called. Perhaps even more transformative was the Internet, a network of smaller, interlinking Web pages with sites devoted to news, commerce, entertainment, and academic scholarship. As Web capabilities have increased, new forms of communication have emerged including Twitter, a communications platform that allows people to send instant updates from their cellphones to their friends; Facebook, a social networking site; and YouTube, an Internet site now used for international news broadcasts and for President Obama's weekly radio addresses.

Advances in telecommunications led first to cellular or mobile phones and later to smartphones, which combine many capabilities including portable media players, cameras, GPS navigation features, Wi-Fi, and mobile broadband access. Though cellular phones existed in the 1970s and 1980s, it was not until the size of the digital components of these devices was reduced in the 1990s that cellphones became truly portable. Cellphones have since become enormously important, and not only for communication. Indeed, many nations have become financially dependent on their sales for economic growth. For example, the Nokia Corporation of Finland is largely responsible for that country's fiscal stability. Annual sales of Nokia phones, amounting to approximately $25 billion, nearly equal the entire Finnish budget. Worldwide the number of people with access to a mobile phone increased from 12.4 million in 1990 to almost 4.6 billion in 2009. The ubiquity of smartphones has transformed communication into a global endeavor as users can capture video, share text messages, and place images, video, and information on the World Wide Web.

A number of the innovations that have enhanced consumers' ability to share music, read newspapers, watch movies, and search the web were introduced by Apple, Inc., and subsequently imitated by other companies. In 2001, Apple introduced the iPod, a portable digital music player that allows users to download music from the Internet. This device revolutionized the music industry, as downloading music electronically from the Internet soon surpassed the purchasing of records (CDs, tapes, and other physical forms). CD sales declined nearly 25 percent from 2000 to 2006. Another Apple innovation, the iPhone, enables users to connect immediately to the Internet from their phone, allowing information to be instantly updated for various telecommunication sites, such as Twitter and Facebook. Apple's most recent introduction, the iPad, a handheld tablet computer, is challenging computer sales worldwide, as almost 7.5 million iPads were sold in the first six months.

These developments in communications are also affecting current events. Smartphones and the like recently played a role in the Arab Spring. Through social networking sites such as Facebook and Twitter, protesters in Arab countries were able to inform others and organize protests.

Reality in the Digital Age

Advances in communication and information during the digital age have led many people to believe that world cultures are increasingly interdependent and homogenized. Many contemporary artists have questioned the effects of the computer age on identity and material reality. According to some, the era of virtual reality has displaced cultural uniqueness and bodily presence.

THE BODY AND IDENTITY IN CONTEMPORARY ART By focusing on bodily experience and cultural norms, contemporary artists have attempted to restore what has been lost in the digital age. Kiki Smith (b. 1954), an American artist born in Germany, creates sculptures of the human body that often focus on anatomical processes. These works, commonly made of wax or plaster, question the politics surrounding the body, including AIDS and domestic abuse, while reconnecting to bodily experiences.

Contemporary artists also continue to explore the interaction between the Western and non-Western world, particularly with the **multiculturalism** generated by global migrations (see "The Social Challenges of Globalization" later in this Epilogue). For example, the art of Yinka Shonibare (YEEN-kuh SHOH-nih-bar-eh) (b. 1962), who was born in London, raised in Nigeria, and now resides in England, investigates the notion of hybrid identity as he creates clothing and tableaux that fuse European designs with African traditions.

MULTICULTURALISM IN LITERATURE The interaction of East and West has also preoccupied numerous authors since the late 1990s. Jhumpa Lahiri (JOOM-puh luh-HEER-ee) (b. 1967) has received international attention for writings that explore contemporary Indian life. Lahiri won the Pulitzer Prize for her collection of stories, *Interpreter of Maladies* (1999), and her acclaimed first novel, *The Namesake* (2003), chronicled the lives of Indian immigrants in the United States. Both works examine generation gaps, particularly the alienation and unique synthesis that can accompany cross-cultural exchange. The success of Lahiri's work indicates how, in the digital age, Western peoples remain interested in other cultures and traditions. This emergence of a global culture has become part of the new globalism of the twenty-first century.

Globalization and the Environmental Crisis

As many people take a global perspective in the twenty-first century, they are realizing that human beings everywhere on the planet are interdependent in terms of the air they breathe, the water they drink, the food they consume, and the climate that affects their lives. At the same time, however, human activities are creating environmental challenges that threaten the very foundation of human existence on earth (see the box on p. 931).

One problem is population growth. As of July 2011, the world population was estimated at more than 6.9 billion people, only twenty-three years after passing the 5 billion mark. At its current rate of growth, the world population could reach 12.8 billion by 2050, according to the United Nations' long-range population projections. The result has been an increased demand for food and other resources that has put great pressure on the earth's ecosystems. At the same time, the failure to grow enough food for more and more people, a problem exacerbated by drought conditions beginning to appear on several continents, has created a severe problem, as an estimated 1 billion people

Courtesy of NASA

The Earth. For many people in the West, as in the rest of the world, the view of the earth from outer space fostered a sense of global unity. The American astronaut Russell Schweickart wrote, "From where you see it, the thing is a whole, and it is so beautiful." In a similar reaction, Yuri Gagarin, the first Soviet cosmonaut, remarked, "What strikes me is not only the beauty of the continents . . . but their closeness to one another . . . their essential unity."

worldwide today suffer from hunger. Every year, more than 8 million people die of hunger, many of them young children.

Another problem is the pattern of consumption as the wealthy nations of the Northern Hemisphere consume vast quantities of the planet's natural resources. The United States, for example, which has 6 percent of the planet's people, consumes 30 to 40 percent of its resources. The spread of these consumption patterns to other parts of the world raises serious questions about the ability of the planet to sustain itself and its population. Within a few years, for example, more automobiles will be sold in China annually than in the United States.

Yet another threat to the environment is **global climate change**, which has the potential to create a worldwide crisis. Virtually all of the world's scientists agree that the **greenhouse effect**, the warming of the earth because of the buildup of carbon dioxide in the atmosphere, is contributing to devastating droughts and storms, the melting of the polar ice caps, and rising sea levels that could inundate coastal regions in the second half of the twenty-first century. Also alarming is the potential loss of biodiversity. Seven out of ten biologists believe the planet is now experiencing an alarming extinction of both plant and animal species.

The Social Challenges of Globalization

Since 1945, tens of millions of people have migrated from one part of the world to another. These migrations have occurred for many reasons. Persecution for political reasons caused many people from Pakistan, Bangladesh, Sri Lanka, and eastern Europe to seek refuge in western European countries, while brutal civil wars in Asia, Africa, the Middle East, and Europe

led millions of refugees to seek safety in neighboring countries. Most people who have migrated, however, have done so to find jobs. Latin Americans seeking a better life have migrated to the United States, while guest workers from Turkey, southern and eastern Europe, North Africa, India, and Pakistan have migrated to more prosperous western European countries. In 2005, nearly 200 million people, about 3 percent of the world's population, lived outside the country where they were born.

The migration of millions of people has also provoked a social backlash in many countries. Foreign workers have often become scapegoats when countries face economic problems. Political parties in France and Norway, for example, have called for the removal of blacks, Muslims, and Arabs in order to protect the ethnic or cultural purity of their nations, while in Asian countries, there is animosity against other Asian ethnic groups. The problem of foreigners has also led to a more general attack on globalization itself as being responsible for a host of social ills that are undermining national sovereignty.

Another challenge of globalization is the wide gap between rich and poor nations. The rich nations, or **developed nations**, are located mainly in the Northern Hemisphere. They include the United States, Canada, Germany, and Japan, which have well-organized industrial and agricultural systems, advanced technologies, and effective educational systems. The poor nations, or **developing nations**, include many nations in Africa, Asia, and Latin America, which often have primarily agricultural economies with little technology. A serious problem in many developing nations is explosive population growth, which has led to severe food shortages caused often by poor soil but also by economic factors. Growing crops for export to developed countries, for example, may lead to enormous profits for large landowners but leaves many small farmers with little land on which to grow food.

Civil wars have also created food shortages. Not only does war disrupt normal farming operations, but warring groups try to limit access to food to weaken or kill their enemies. In Sudan, 1.3 million people starved when combatants of a civil war in the 1980s prevented food from reaching them. As unrest continued during the early 2000s in Sudan's Darfur region, families were forced to leave their farms. As a result, an estimated 70,000 people starved by mid-2004.

Global Movements and New Hopes

As people have become aware that the problems humans face are not just national or regional but global in scope, they have responded to this challenge in different ways. One approach has been to develop grassroots social movements, including environmental, women's and men's liberation, human potential, appropriate technology, and nonviolence movements. "Think globally, act locally" is frequently the slogan of these grassroots groups. Related to the emergence of these social movements is the growth of **nongovernmental organizations (NGOs)**. According to one analyst, NGOs are an important instrument in the cultivation of global perspectives: "Since NGOs by definition are identified with interests that transcend national boundaries,

A Warning to Humanity

EARTH & ENVIRONMENT

As human threats to the environment grew, world scientists began to organize and respond to the crisis. One group, founded in 1969, was the Union of Concerned Scientists, a nonprofit organization of professional scientists and private citizens, now with more than 200,000 members. In November 1992, the Union of Concerned Scientists published an appeal from 1,700 of the world's leading scientists. The first selection is taken from this "Warning to Humanity."

Earlier, in 1988, in response to the threat of global warming, the United Nations established the Intergovernmental Panel on Climate Change (IPCC) to study the most up-to-date scientific information on global warming and climate change. In 2007, more than 2,500 scientists from more than 130 countries contributed to the group's most recent report, "Climate Change, 2007: The Fourth Assessment Report," released in November 2007. The second selection is taken from the Web page that summarizes the basic findings of the 2007 report.

World Scientists' Warning to Humanity, 1992

Human beings and the natural world are on a collision course. Human activities inflict harsh and often irreversible damage on the environment and on critical resources. If not checked, many of our current practices put at serious risk the future that we wish for human society and the plant and animal kingdoms, and may so alter the living world that it will be unable to sustain life in the manner that we know. Fundamental changes are urgent if we are to avoid the collision our present course will bring about. The environment is suffering critical stress:

The Atmosphere

Stratospheric ozone depletion threatens us with enhanced ultraviolet radiation at the earth's surface, which can be damaging or lethal to many life forms. Air pollution near ground level, and acid precipitation, are already causing widespread injury to humans, forests, and crops.

Water Resources

Heedless exploitation of depletable ground water supplies endangers food production and other essential human systems. Heavy demands on the world's surface waters have resulted in serious shortages in some 80 countries, containing 40% of the world's population. Pollution of rivers, lakes, and ground water further limits the supply.

Oceans

Destructive pressure on the oceans is severe, particularly in the coastal regions which produce most of the world's food fish. The total marine catch is now at or above the estimated maximum sustainable yield. Some fisheries have already shown signs of collapse.

Soil

Loss of soil productivity, which is causing extensive land abandonment, is a widespread by-product of current practices in agriculture and animal husbandry. Since 1945, 11% of the earth's vegetated surface has been degraded—an area larger than India and China combined—and per capita food production in many parts of the world is decreasing.

Forests

Tropical rain forests, as well as tropical and temperate dry forests, are being destroyed rapidly. At present rates, some critical forest types will be gone in a few years, and most of the tropical rain forest will be gone before the end of the next century. With them will go large numbers of plant and animal species.

Living Species

The irreversible loss of species, which by 2100 may reach one-third of all species now living, is especially serious. We are losing the potential they hold for providing medicinal and other benefits, and the contribution that genetic diversity of life forms gives to the robustness of the world's biological systems and to the astonishing beauty of the earth itself.

Much of this damage is irreversible on a scale of centuries, or permanent. Other processes appear to pose additional threats. Increasing levels of gases in the atmosphere from human activities, including carbon dioxide released from fossil fuel burning and from deforestation, may alter climate on a global scale.

Warning

We the undersigned, senior members of the world's scientific community, hereby warn all humanity of what lies ahead. A great change in our stewardship of the earth and the life on it is required, if vast human misery is to be avoided and our global home on this planet is not to be irretrievably mutilated.

Findings of the IPCC Fourth Assessment Report, 2007

Human Responsibility for Climate Change

The report finds that it is "very likely" that emissions of heat-trapping gases from human activities have caused "most of the observed increase in globally averaged temperatures since the mid-20th century." Evidence that human activities are the major cause of recent climate change is even stronger than in prior assessments.

(continued)

(continued)

Warming Is Unequivocal

The report concludes that it is "unequivocal" that Earth's climate is warming, "as is now evident from observations of increases in global average air and ocean temperatures, widespread melting of snow and ice, and rising global mean sea level." The report also confirms that the current atmospheric concentration of carbon dioxide and methane, two important heat-trapping gases, "exceeds by far the natural range over the last 650,000 years." Since the dawn of the industrial era, concentrations of both gases have increased at a rate that is "very likely to have been unprecedented in more than 10,000 years."

Additional IPCC Findings on Recent Climate Change

Rising Temperatures

- Eleven of the last 12 years rank among the 12 hottest years on record (since 1850, when sufficient worldwide temperature measurements began).
- Over the last 50 years, "cold days, cold nights, and frost have become less frequent, while hot days, hot nights, and heat waves have become more frequent."

Increasingly Severe Weather (storms, precipitation, drought)

- The intensity of tropical cyclones (hurricanes) in the North Atlantic has increased over the past 30 years, which correlates with increases in tropical sea surface temperatures.
- Storms with heavy precipitation have increased in frequency over most land areas. Between 1900 and 2005, long-term trends show significantly increased precipitation in eastern parts of North and South America, northern Europe, and northern and central Asia.
- Between 1900 and 2005, the Sahel (the boundary zone between the Sahara and more fertile regions of Africa to the south), the Mediterranean, southern Africa, and parts of southern Asia have become drier, adding stress to water resources in these regions.
- Droughts have become longer and more intense, and have affected larger areas since the 1970s, especially in the tropics and subtropics.

 What problems and challenges do these two reports present? What do these two reports have in common? How do they differ?

---

we expect all NGOs to define problems in global terms, to take account of human interests and needs as they are found in all parts of the planet."[2] NGOs are often represented at the United Nations and include professional, business, and cooperative organizations; foundations; religious, peace, and disarmament groups; youth and women's organizations; environmental and human rights groups; and research institutes. The number of international NGOs increased from 176 in 1910 to 37,000 in 2000.

And yet hopes for global approaches to global problems have also been hindered by political, ethnic, and religious differences. Pollution of the Rhine River by factories along its banks provokes angry disputes among European nations, and the United States and Canada have argued about the effects of acid rain on Canadian forests. Droughts in Russia and China threaten the world's food supply, while floods in Pakistan challenge the stability of Asia. The collapse of the Soviet Union and its satellite system seemed to provide an enormous boost to the potential for international cooperation on global issues, but it has had almost the opposite effect. The bloody conflict in the former Yugoslavia indicates the dangers inherent in the rise of nationalist sentiment among various ethnic and religious groups in eastern Europe. The widening gap between wealthy nations and poor, developing nations threatens global economic stability. Many conflicts begin with regional issues and then develop into international concerns. International terrorist groups seek to wreak havoc around the world.

Thus, even as the world becomes more global in culture and interdependent in its mutual relations, centrifugal forces are still at work attempting to redefine the political, cultural, and ethnic ways in which the world is divided. Such efforts are often disruptive and can sometimes work against measures to enhance our human destiny. But they also represent an integral part of human character and human history and cannot be suppressed in the relentless drive to create a world society.

There are already signs that as the common dangers posed by environmental damage, overpopulation, and scarcity of resources become ever more apparent, societies around the world will find ample reason to turn their attention from cultural differences to the demands of global interdependence. The greatest challenge of the twenty-first century may be to reconcile the drive for individual and group identity with the common needs of the human community.

Further Reading

Useful books on different facets of the new global civilization include **M. B. Steger,** *Globalization: A Very Short Introduction* (New York, 2003); **J. H. Mittelman,** *The Globalization Syndrome* (Princeton, N.J., 2000); **M. Waters,** *Globalization,* 2nd ed. (London, 2001); and **P. O'Meara et al., eds.,** *Globalization and the Challenges of the New Century* (Bloomington, Ind., 2000). For a comprehensive examination of the digital age, see **M. Castells,** *The Information Age,* 3 vols. (Oxford, 1996–1998). On the role of the media in the digital age, see **J. R. Dominick,** *Dynamics of Mass Communication: Media in the Digital Age* (New York, 2006).

abbess   the head of a convent or monastery for women.

abbot   the head of a monastery.

absolutism   a form of government in which the sovereign power or ultimate authority rested in the hands of a monarch who claimed to rule by divine right and was therefore responsible only to God.

Abstract Expressionism   a post–World War II artistic movement that broke with all conventions of form and structure in favor of total abstraction.

abstract painting   an artistic movement that developed early in the twentieth century in which artists focused on color to avoid any references to visual reality.

African National Congress   *see* ANC.

African Union   the organization that replaced the Organization of African Unity in 2001; designed to bring about increased political and economic integration of African states.

Agricultural (Neolithic) Revolution   *see* Neolithic Revolution.

Amerindians   the earliest inhabitants of North and South America. Original theories suggested migration from Siberia across the Bering Land Bridge; more recent evidence suggests migration also occurred by sea from regions of the South Pacific to South America.

Analects   the body of writing containing conversations between Confucius and his disciples that preserves his worldly wisdom and pragmatic philosophies.

anarchists   people who hold that all governments and existing social institutions are unnecessary and advocate a society based on voluntary cooperation.

ANC   the African National Congress. Founded in 1912, it was the beginning of political activity by South African blacks. Banned by the politically dominant whites in 1960, it was not officially "unbanned" until 1990. It is now the majority party in South Africa.

anti-Semitism   hostility toward or discrimination against Jews.

apartheid   the system of racial segregation practiced in the Republic of South Africa until the 1990s, which involved political, legal, and economic discrimination against nonwhites.

appeasement   the policy, followed by the European nations in the 1930s, of accepting Hitler's annexation of Austria and Czechoslovakia in the belief that meeting his demands would ensure peace and stability.

Aramaic   a Semitic language dominant in the Middle East in the first century B.C.E.; still in use in small regions of the Middle East and southern Asia.

aristocracy   a class of hereditary nobility in medieval Europe; a warrior class who shared a distinctive lifestyle based on the institution of knighthood, although there were social divisions within the group based on extremes of wealth.

Arthasastra   an early Indian political treatise that sets forth many fundamental aspects of the relationship of rulers and their subjects. It has been compared to Machiavelli's well-known book *The Prince* and provided principles on which many aspects of social organization developed in the region.

Aryans   Indo-European-speaking nomads who entered India from the Central Asian steppes between 1500 and 1000 B.C.E. and greatly affected Indian society, notably by establishing the caste system. The term *Aryan* was later adopted by German Nazis to describe their racial ideal.

asceticism   a lifestyle involving the denial of worldly pleasures. Predominantly associated with the Hindu, Buddhist, and Christian religions, adherents perceive their practices as a path to greater spirituality.

ASEAN   the Association for the Southeast Asian Nations, formed in 1967 to promote the prosperity and political stability of its member nations. Currently, Brunei, Cambodia, Indonesia, Laos, Malaysia, Myanmar, the Philippines, Singapore, Thailand, and Vietnam are members. Other countries in the region participate as "observer" members.

assimilation   the concept, originating in France, that the colonial peoples should be assimilated into the parent French culture.

association   the concept, developed by French colonial officials, that the colonial peoples should be permitted to retain their precolonial cultural traditions.

Atman   in Brahmanism, the individual soul.

Ausgleich   the "Compromise" of 1867 that created the dual monarchy of Austria-Hungary. Austria and Hungary each had its own capital, constitution, and legislative assembly but were united under one monarch.

authoritarian state   a state that has a dictatorial government and some other trappings of a totalitarian state but does not demand that the masses be actively involved in the regime's goals as totalitarian states do.

bakufu   the centralized government set up in Japan in the twelfth century. *See also* shogunate system.

banners   originally established in 1639 by the Qing dynasty, the eight banners were administrative divisions into which all Manchu families were placed. Banners quickly evolved into the basis of Manchu military organization, with each required to raise and support a prescribed number of troops.

Bao-jia system   the Chinese practice, reportedly originated by the Qin dynasty in the third century B.C.E., of organizing families into groups of five or ten to exercise mutual control and surveillance and reduce loyalty to the family.

bard   in Africa, a professional storyteller.

Baroque   a style that dominated Western painting, sculpture, architecture, and music from about 1580 to 1730, generally characterized by elaborate ornamentation and dramatic effects. Important practitioners included Bernini, Rubens, Handel, and Bach.

Bedouins   nomadic tribes originally from northern Arabia who became important traders after the domestication of the camel during the first millennium B.C.E. Early converts to Islam, their values and practices deeply affected Muhammad.

Berbers   an ethnic group indigenous to western North Africa.

bey   a provincial governor in the Ottoman Empire.

bhakti   in Hinduism, devotion as a means of religious observance open to all persons regardless of class.

Black Death   the outbreak of plague (mostly bubonic) in the mid-fourteenth century that killed from 25 to 50 percent of Europe's population.

Blitzkrieg   "lightning war." A war conducted with great speed and force, as in Germany's advance at the beginning of World War II.

bodhi   wisdom; sometimes described as complete awareness of the true nature of the universe.

bodhisattva   in some schools of Buddhism, an individual who has achieved enlightenment but, because of his great compassion, has chosen to renounce Nirvana and to remain on earth in spirit form to help all human beings achieve release from reincarnation.

Boers   the Afrikaans-speaking descendants of Dutch settlers in southern Africa who left the Cape Colony in the nineteenth century to settle in the Orange Free State and Transvaal; defeated by the British in the Boer War (1899–1902) and ultimately incorporated in the Union of South Africa.

Bolsheviks   a small faction of the Russian Social Democratic Party who were led by Lenin and dedicated to violent revolution; seized power in Russia in 1917 and were subsequently renamed the Communists.

bonsai   the cultivation of stunted trees and shrubs to create exquisite nature scenes in miniature; originated in China in the first millennium B.C.E. and imported to Japan between 700 and 900 C.E.

Brahman   the Hindu word roughly equivalent to God; the divine basis of all being; regarded as the source and sum of the cosmos.

Brahmanism   the early religious beliefs of the Aryan peoples in India, which eventually gave rise to Hinduism.

brahmin   a member of the Hindu priestly caste or class; literally "one who has realized or attempts to realize *Brahman*." Traditionally, duties of a *brahmin* included studying Hindu religious scriptures and transmitting them to others orally. The priests of Hindu temples are *brahmins*.

Brezhnev Doctrine   the doctrine, enunciated by Leonid Brezhnev, that the Soviet Union had a right to intervene if socialism was threatened in another socialist state; used to justify the use of Soviet troops in Czechoslovakia in 1968.

Buddhism   a religion and philosophy based on the teachings of Siddhartha Gautama around 500 B.C.E. Principally practiced in China, India, and other parts of Asia, Buddhism has 360 million followers and is considered a major world religion.

Burakumin   a Japanese minority similar to *dalits* (untouchables) in Indian culture. Past and current discrimination has resulted in lower educational attainment and socioeconomic status for members of this group. Movements with objectives ranging from "liberation" to integration have tried over the years to change this situation.

Bushido   the code of conduct observed by samurai warriors; comparable to the European concept of chilvalry.

caliph   the secular leader of the Islamic community.

calpulli   in Aztec society, a kinship group, often of a thousand or more, that served as an intermediary with the central government, providing taxes and conscript labor to the state.

capital   material wealth used or available for use in the production of more wealth.

caravels   mobile sailing ships with both lateen and square sails that began to be constructed in Europe in the sixteenth century.

cartel   a combination of independent commercial enterprises that work together to control prices and limit competition.

Cartesian dualism   Descartes's principle of the separation of mind and matter (and mind and body) that enabled scientists to view matter as something separate from themselves that could be investigated by reason.

caste system   a system of rigid social hierarchy in which all members of that society are assigned by birth to specific "ranks" and inherit specific roles and privileges.

Catholic Reformation   a movement for the reform of the Catholic Church in the sixteenth century.

caudillos   strong leaders in nineteenth-century Latin America who were usually supported by the landed elites and ruled chiefly by military force, though some were popular; they included both modernizers and destructive dictators.

censorate   one of the three primary Chinese ministries, originally established in the Qin dynasty, whose inspectors surveyed the efficiency of officials throughout the system.

centuriate assembly   the chief popular assembly of the Roman Republic. It passed laws and elected the chief magistrates.

chaebol   a South Korean business structure similar to the Japanese *keiretsu*.

Chan Buddhism   a Chinese sect (Zen in Japanese) influenced by Daoist ideas, which called for mind training and a strict regimen as a means of seeking enlightenment.

chinampas   in Mesoamerica, artificial islands crisscrossed by canals that provided water for crops and easy transportation to local markets.

chivalry   the ideal of civilized behavior that emerged among the European nobility in the eleventh and twelfth centuries under the influence of the church; a code of ethics knights were expected to uphold.

chonmin   in Korea, the lowest class in society consisting of slaves and workers in certain undesirable occupations such as butchers; literally, "base people."

Christian humanism   an intellectual movement in northern Europe in the late fifteenth and early sixteenth centuries that combined interest in the classics of the Italian Renaissance with an interest in the sources of early Christianity, including the New Testament and the writings of the church fathers.

chu nom   an adaptation of Chinese written characters to provide a writing system for spoken Vietnamese; in use by the ninth century C.E.

civil disobedience   the tactic of using illegal but nonviolent means of protest; designed by the Indian nationalist leader Mohandas Gandhi to resist British colonial rule. The tactic would later be adopted by nationalist and liberation forces in many other countries.

civilization   a complex culture in which large numbers of humans share a variety of common elements, including cities; religious, political, military, and social structures; writing; and significant artistic and intellectual activity.

civil rights   the basic rights of citizens, including equality before the law, freedom of speech and press, and freedom from arbitrary arrest.

civil service examination   an elaborate Chinese system of selecting bureaucrats on merit, first introduced in 165 C.E., developed by the Tang dynasty in the seventh century C.E., and refined under the Song dynasty; later adopted in Vietnam and with less success in Japan and Korea. It contributed to efficient government, upward mobility, and cultural uniformity.

class struggle   the basis of the Marxist analysis of history, which says that the owners of the means of production have always oppressed the workers and predicts an inevitable revolution. *See also* Marxism.

Cold War   the ideological conflict between the Soviet Union and the United States between the end of World War II and the early 1990s.

collective farms   large farms created in the Soviet Union by Stalin by combining many small holdings into large farms worked by the peasants under government supervision.

collective security   the use of an international army raised by an association of nations to deter aggression and keep the peace.

Columbian Exchange   the exchange of animals, plants, and culture, but also communicable diseases and human populations including slaves, between the Western and Eastern Hemispheres that occurred after Columbus's voyages to the Americas.

commercial capitalism   beginning in the Middle Ages, an economic system in which people invested in trade and goods in order to make profits.

common law   law common to the entire kingdom of England; imposed by the king's courts beginning in the twelfth century to replace the customary law used in county and feudal courts that varied from place to place.

communalism   in South Asia, the tendency of people to band together in mutually antagonistic social subgroups; elsewhere used to describe unifying trends in the larger community.

commune   in medieval Europe, an association of townspeople bound together by a sworn oath for the purpose of obtaining basic liberties from the lord of the territory in which the town was located; also, the self-governing town after receiving its liberties.

Communist International (Comintern)   a worldwide organization of Communist Parties, founded by Lenin in 1919, dedicated to the advancement of world revolution; also known as the Third International.

conciliarism   a movement in fourteenth- and fifteenth-century Europe that held that final authority in spiritual matters resided with a general church council, not the pope. It emerged in response to the Avignon papacy and the Great Schism and was used to justify the summoning of the Council of Constance (1414–1418).

Confucianism   a system of thought based on the teachings of Confucius (551–479 B.C.E.) that developed into the ruling ideology of the Chinese state. *See also* Neo-Confucianism.

conquistadors "conquerors." Leaders in the Spanish conquests in the Americas, especially Mexico and Peru, in the sixteenth century.

conscription a military draft.

conservatism an ideology based on tradition and social stability that favored the maintenance of established institutions, organized religion, and obedience to authority and resisted change, especially abrupt change.

consuls the chief executive officers of the Roman Republic. Two were chosen annually to administer the government and lead the army in battle.

consumer society a term applied to Western society after World War II as the working classes adopted the consumption patterns of the middle class and installment plans, credit cards, and easy credit made consumer goods such as appliances and automobiles widely available.

containment a policy adopted by the United States during the Cold War. It called for the use of any means, short of all-out war, to limit Soviet expansion.

Continental system Napoleon's effort to bar British goods from the Continent in the hope of weakening Britain's economy and destroying its capacity to wage war.

Contras in Nicaragua in the 1980s, an anti-Sandinista guerrilla movement supported by the U.S. Reagan administration.

Coptic a form of Christianity, originally Egyptian, that has thrived in Ethiopia since the fourth century C.E.

cosmopolitanism the quality of being sophisticated and having wide international experience.

cottage industry a system of textile manufacturing in which spinners and weavers worked at home in their cottages using raw materials supplied to them by capitalist entrepreneurs.

council of the plebs in the Roman Republic, a council only for the plebeians. After 287 B.C.E., however, its resolutions were binding on all Romans.

creoles in Latin America, American-born descendants of Europeans.

Crusade in the Middle Ages, a military campaign in defense of Christendom.

Cubism an artistic style developed at the beginning of the twentieth century, especially by Pablo Picasso, that used geometric designs to re-create reality in the viewer's mind.

cultural relativism the belief that no culture is superior to another because culture is a matter of custom, not reason, and derives its meaning from the group that created it.

cuneiform "wedge-shaped." A system of writing developed by the Sumerians that consisted of wedge-shaped impressions made by a reed stylus on clay tablets.

Dadaism an artistic movement in the 1920s and 1930s by artists who were revolted by the senseless slaughter of World War I and used their "anti-art" to express contempt for the Western tradition.

daimyo prominent Japanese families who provided allegiance to the local shogun in exchange for protection; similar to vassals in Europe.

dalits commonly referred to as untouchables; the lowest level of Indian society, technically outside the caste system and considered less than human; renamed *harijans* ("children of God") by Gandhi, they remain the object of discrimination despite affirmative action programs.

Dao a Chinese philosophical concept, literally "the Way," central to both Confucianism and Daoism, that describes the behavior proper to each member of society; somewhat similar to the Indian concept of *dharma*.

Daoism a Chinese philosophy traditionally ascribed to the perhaps legendary Lao Tzu, which holds that acceptance and spontaneity are the keys to harmonious interaction with the universal order; an alternative to Confucianism.

decolonization the process of becoming free of colonial status and achieving statehood; occurred in most of the world's colonies between 1947 and 1962.

deconstruction *see* poststructuralism.

deficit spending the concept, developed by John Maynard Keynes in the 1930s, that in times of economic depression, governments should stimulate demand by hiring people to do public works, such as building highways, even if this increases the public debt.

deism belief in God as the creator of the universe who, after setting it in motion, ceased to have any direct involvement in it and allowed it to run according to its own natural laws.

demesne the part of a manor retained under the direct control of the lord and worked by the serfs as part of their labor services.

denazification after World War II, the Allied policy of rooting out all traces of Nazism in German society by bringing prominent Nazis to trial for war crimes and purging any known Nazis from political office.

depression a very severe, protracted economic downturn with high levels of unemployment.

descamisados the working-class supporters of Juan Perón during his rise to power in Argentina in 1946; literally, the "shirtless ones."

de-Stalinization the policy of denouncing and undoing the most repressive aspects of Stalin's regime; begun by Nikita Khrushchev in 1956.

détente the relaxation of tension between the Soviet Union and the United States that occurred in the 1970s.

developed nations a term used to refer to rich nations, primarily in the Northern Hemisphere, that have well-organized industrial and agricultural systems, advanced technologies, and effective educational systems.

developing nations a term used to refer to poor nations, mainly in the Southern Hemisphere, that have primarily agricultural economies with little technology and serious population problems.

devshirme in the Ottoman Empire, a system (literally, "collection") of training talented children to be administrators or members of the sultan's harem; originally meritocratic, by the seventeenth century it had degenerated into a hereditary caste.

dharma in Hinduism and Buddhism, the law that governs the universe and specifically human behavior.

dictator in the Roman Republic, an official granted unlimited power to run the state for a short period of time, usually six months, during an emergency.

diffusion hypothesis the hypothesis that the Yellow River valley was the ancient heartland of Chinese civilization and that technological and cultural achievements radiated from there to other parts of East Asia. Recent discoveries of other early agricultural communities in China have led to some modification of the hypothesis to allow for other centers of civilization.

diocese the area under the jurisdiction of a Christian bishop; based originally on Roman administrative districts.

direct representation a system of choosing delegates to a representative assembly in which citizens vote directly for the delegates who will represent them.

direct rule a concept devised by European colonial governments to rule their colonial subjects without the participation of local authorities. It was most often applied in colonial societies in Africa.

divination the practice of seeking to foretell future events by interpreting divine signs, which could appear in various forms, such as in the entrails of animals, in patterns in smoke, or in dreams.

divine-right monarchy a monarchy based on the belief that monarchs receive their power directly from God and are responsible to no one except God.

domino theory the belief that if the Communists succeeded in Vietnam, other countries in Southeast and East Asia would also fall (like dominoes) to communism; a justification for the U.S. intervention in Vietnam.

dualism the belief that the universe is dominated by two opposing forces, one good and the other evil.

dyarchy during the Qing dynasty in China, a system in which all important national and provincial admininstrative positions were shared equally by Chinese and Manchus, which helped consolidate both the Manchus' rule and their assimilation.

dynastic state a state in which the maintenance and expansion of the interests of the ruling family are the primary consideration.

economic imperialism the process in which banks and corporations from developed nations invest in underdeveloped regions and establish a major presence there in the hope of making high profits; not necessarily the same as colonial expansion in that businesses invest where they can make a profit, which may not be in their own nation's colonies.

Einsatzgruppen in Nazi Germany, special strike forces in the SS that played an important role in rounding up and killing Jews.

El Niño periodic changes in water temperature at the surface of the Pacific Ocean, which can lead to major environmental changes and may have led to the collapse of the Moche civilization in what is now Peru.

emir "commander" in Arabic, a title used by Muslim rulers in southern Spain and elsewhere.

empiricism the practice of relying on observation and experiment.

encomienda a grant from the Spanish monarch to colonial conquistadors. *See also encomienda* system.

encomienda **system** the system by which Spain first governed its American colonies. Holders of an *encomienda* were supposed to protect the Indians as well as use them as laborers and collect tribute but in practice exploited them.

encyclical a letter from the pope to all the bishops of the Roman Catholic Church.

enlightened absolutism an absolute monarchy in which the ruler follows the principles of the Enlightenment by introducing reforms for the improvement of society, allowing freedom of speech and the press, permitting religious toleration, expanding education, and ruling in accordance with the laws.

Enlightenment an eighteenth-century intellectual movement, led by the philosophes, that stressed the application of reason and the scientific method to all aspects of life.

entrepreneur one who organizes, operates, and assumes the risk in a business venture in the expectation of making a profit.

Epicureanism a philosophy founded by Epicurus in the fourth century B.C.E. that taught that happiness (freedom from emotional turmoil) could be achieved through the pursuit of pleasure (intellectual rather than sensual pleasure).

eta in feudal Japan, a class of hereditary slaves who were responsible for what were considered degrading occupations, such as curing leather and burying the dead.

ethnic cleansing the policy of killing or forcibly removing people of another ethnic group; used by the Serbs against Bosnian Muslims in the 1990s.

Eucharist a Christian sacrament in which consecrated bread and wine are consumed in celebration of Jesus's Last Supper; also called the Lord's Supper or communion.

eunuch a man whose testicles have been removed. Eunuchs often played an important role at court in the Chinese imperial system, the Ottoman Empire, and the Mughal dynasty, among others.

existentialism a philosophical movement that arose after World War II that emphasized the meaninglessness of life, born of the desperation caused by two world wars.

fascism an ideology that exalts the nation above the individual and calls for a centralized government with a dictatorial leader, economic and social regimentation, and forcible suppression of opposition; in particular, the ideology of Mussolini's Fascist regime in Italy.

feminism the belief in the social, political, and economic equality of the sexes; also, organized activity to advance women's rights.

fief a landed estate granted to a vassal in exchange for military services.

filial piety in traditional China, in particular, a hierarchical system in which every family member has his or her place, subordinate to a patriarch who has certain reciprocal responsibilities.

Final Solution the Nazis' name for their attempted physical extermination of the Jewish people during World War II.

Five Pillars of Islam the core requirements of the Muslim faith: belief in Allah and his prophet, Muhammad; prescribed prayers; observation of Ramadan; pilgrimage to Mecca; and giving alms to the poor.

five relationships in traditional China, the hierarchical interpersonal associations considered crucial to social order, within the family, between friends, and with the king.

folk culture the traditional arts and crafts, literature, music, and other customs of the people; something that people make, as opposed to modern popular culture, which is something people buy.

foot binding an extremely painful process, common in China throughout the second millennium C.E., that compressed girls' feet to half their natural size, representing submissiveness and self-discipline, which were considered necessary attributes of an ideal wife.

Four Modernizations the radical reforms of Chinese industry, agriculture, technology, and national defense instituted by Deng Xiaoping after his accession to power in the late 1970s.

free trade the unrestricted international exchange of goods with low or no tariffs.

fudai **daimyo** during the Tokugawa shogunate in Japan, less powerful lords who were directly subordinate to the shogunate; literally, "inside daimyo."

functionalism the idea that the function of an object should determine its design and materials.

fundamentalism a movement that emphasizes rigid adherence to basic religious principles; often used to describe evangelical Christianity as well as the practices of Islamic conservatives.

genin landless laborers in feudal Japan, who were effectively slaves.

genro the ruling clique of aristocrats in Meiji Japan.

geocentric theory the idea that the earth is at the center of the universe and that the sun and other celestial objects revolve around the earth.

glasnost "openness"; Mikhail Gorbachev's policy of encouraging Soviet citizens to openly discuss the strengths and weaknesses of the Soviet Union.

global civilization human society considered as a single worldwide entity in which local differences are less important than overall similarities.

global climate change the changes in climate, including an increase in the temperature of the earth's atmosphere, caused by the greenhouse effect.

global economy an interdependent economy in which the production, distribution, and sale of goods are accomplished on a worldwide scale.

globalization a term referring to the trend by which peoples and nations have become more interdependent; often used to refer to the development of a global economy and culture.

good emperors the five emperors who ruled from 96 to 180 (Nerva, Trajan, Hadrian, Antoninus Pius, and Marcus Aurelius), a period of peace and prosperity for the Roman Empire.

Good Neighbor policy a policy adopted by the administration of President Franklin D. Roosevelt to practice restraint in U.S. relations with Latin American nations.

Gosplan in the Soviet Union, the "state plan" for the economy drawn up by the central planning commission.

Gothic a term used to describe the art and especially architecture of Europe in the twelfth, thirteenth, and fourteenth centuries.

Gothic literature a form of literature used by Romantics to emphasize the bizarre and unusual, especially evident in horror stories.

Grand Council the top of the government hierarchy in the Song dynasty in China.

grand vizier the chief minister in the Ottoman Empire, under the sultan.

Great Leap Forward a short-lived, radical experiment in China, started in 1958, that created vast rural communes in an attempt to replace the family as the fundamental social unit.

Great Proletarian Cultural Revolution an attempt to destroy all vestiges of tradition in China in order to create a totally egalitarian society. Launched by Mao Zedong in 1966, it devolved into virtual anarchy and lasted only until Mao's death in 1976.

greenhouse effect the warming of the earth caused by the buildup of carbon dioxide in the atmosphere as a result of human activity.

green revolution the introduction of technological agriculture, especially in India in the 1960s, which increased food production substantially but also exacerbated rural inequality because only the wealthier farmers could afford fertilizer.

guest workers foreign workers employed temporarily in European countries.

guided democracy the name given by President Sukarno of Indonesia in the late 1950s to his style of government, which theoretically operated by consensus.

guild an association of people with common interests and concerns, especially people working in the same craft. In medieval Europe, guilds came to control much of the production process and to restrict entry into various trades.

guru teacher, especially in the Hindu, Buddhist, and Sikh religious traditions, where the term is an important honorific.

Hadith a collection of the sayings of the Prophet Muhammad, used to supplement the revelations contained in the Qur'an.

harijans a name used by Mohandas Gandhi to refer to the untouchables in India; literally, "children of God." *See also dalits.*

harem the private living quarters of a ruler such as the sultan in the Ottoman Empire or the caliph of Baghdad; generally large and mostly inhabited by the extended family.

Hegira the flight of Muhammad from Mecca to Medina in 622, which marks the first date on the official calendar of Islam.

heliocentric theory the idea that the sun (not the earth) is at the center of the universe.

Hellenistic literally, "to imitate the Greeks"; the era after the death of Alexander the Great when Greek culture spread into the Near East and blended with the culture of that region.

helots serfs in ancient Sparta who were permanently bound to the land that they worked for their Spartan masters.

heresy the holding of religious doctrines different from the official teachings of the church.

Hezbollah a militant Shi'ite organization and political party based in modern Lebanon.

hieroglyphics a highly pictorial system of writing most often associated with ancient Egypt. Also used (with different "pictographs") by other ancient peoples such as the Maya.

high colonialism the more formal phase of European colonial policy in Africa after World War I when the colonial administrative network was extended to outlying areas and more emphasis was placed on improving social services and fostering economic development, especially the exploitation of natural resources, to enable the colonies to achieve self-sufficiency.

high culture the literary and artistic culture of the educated and wealthy ruling classes.

Hinayana the scornful name for Theravada Buddhism ("lesser vehicle") used by devotees of Mahayana Buddhism.

Hinduism the main religion in India. It emphasizes reincarnation, based on the results of the previous life, and the desirability of escaping this cycle. Its various forms feature both asceticism and the pleasures of ordinary life and encompass a multitude of gods as different manifestations of one ultimate reality.

Holocaust the mass slaughter of European Jews by the Nazis during World War II.

hominids the earliest humanlike creatures. They flourished in East and South Africa as long as 3 to 4 million years ago.

Hopewell culture a Native American society that flourished from about 200 B.C.E. to 400 C.E., noted for large burial mounds and extensive manufacturing. Largely based in Ohio, its traders ranged as far as the Gulf of Mexico.

hoplites heavily armed infantry soldiers used in ancient Greece in a phalanx formation.

hundred schools schools of philosophy in China around the third century B.C.E. that engaged in a wide-ranging debate over the nature of human beings, society, and the universe. The schools included Legalism and Daoism, as well as Confucianism.

hydraulic society a society organized around a large irrigation system.

iconoclasm an eighth-century Byzantine movement against the use of icons (pictures of sacred figures), which was condemned as idolatry.

iconoclast a member of an eighth-century Byzantine movement against the use of icons (pictures of sacred figures), which it condemned as idolatry.

ideology a political philosophy such as conservatism or liberalism.

imam an Islamic religious leader. Some traditions say there is only one per generation; others use the term more broadly.

imperialism the policy of extending one nation's power either by conquest or by establishing direct or indirect economic or cultural authority over another. Generally driven by economic self-interest, it can also be motivated by a sincere (if often misguided) sense of moral obligation.

Impressionism an artistic movement that originated in France in the 1870s. Impressionists sought to capture their impressions of the changing effects of light on objects in nature.

indirect representation a system of choosing delegates to a representative assembly in which citizens do not choose the delegates directly but instead vote for electors who choose the delegates.

indirect rule a colonial policy of foreign rule in cooperation with local political elites. Though implemented in much of India and Malaya and in parts of Africa, it was not feasible where resistance was greater.

individualism emphasis on and interest in the unique traits of each person.

indulgence the remission of part or all of the temporal punishment in purgatory due to sin; granted for charitable contributions and other good deeds. Indulgences became a regular practice of the Christian church in the High Middle Ages, and their abuse was instrumental in sparking Luther's reform movement in the sixteenth century.

infanticide the practice of killing infants.

inflation a sustained rise in the price level.

informal empire the growing presence of Europeans in Africa during the first decades of the nineteenth century. During this period, most African states were nonetheless still able to maintain their independence.

intendants royal officials in seventeenth-century France who were sent into the provinces to execute the orders of the central government.

interdict in the Catholic Church, a censure by which a region or country is deprived of receiving the sacraments.

intervention the idea, after the Congress of Vienna, that the great powers of Europe had the right to send armies into countries experiencing revolution to restore legitimate monarchs to their thrones.

intifada the "uprising" of Palestinians living under Israeli control, especially in the 1980s and 1990s.

Islam the religion derived from the revelations of Muhammad, the Prophet of Allah; literally, "submission" (to the will of Allah); also, the culture and civilization based on the faith.

isolationism a foreign policy in which a nation refrains from making alliances or engaging actively in international affairs.

Jainism an Indian religion, founded in the fifth century B.C.E., that stresses extreme simplicity.

Janissaries an elite core of eight thousand troops personally loyal to the sultan of the Ottoman Empire.

jati a kinship group, the basic social organization of traditional Indian society, to some extent specialized by occupation.

jihad in Islam, "striving in the way of the Lord." The term is ambiguous and has been subject to various interpretations, from the practice of conducting raids against local neighbors to the conduct of "holy war" against unbelievers.

joint-stock company a company or association that raises capital by selling shares to individuals who receive dividends on their investment while a board of directors runs the company.

joint-stock investment bank a bank created by selling shares of stock to investors. Such banks potentially have access to much more capital than private banks owned by one or a few individuals.

Jomon the earliest known Neolithic inhabitants of Japan, named for the cord pattern of their pottery.

justification by faith the primary doctrine of the Protestant Reformation; taught that humans are saved not through good works but by the grace of God, bestowed freely through the sacrifice of Jesus.

Kabuki a form of Japanese theater that developed in the seventeenth century C.E. Originally disreputable, it became a highly stylized art form.

kami spirits worshiped in early Japan that resided in trees, rivers, and streams. *See also* Shinto.

karma a fundamental concept in Hindu (and later Buddhist, Jain, and Sikh) philosophy, that rebirth in a future life is determined by actions in this or other lives. The word refers to the entire process, to the individual's actions, and also to the cumulative result of those actions (for instance, a store of good or bad *karma*).

keiretsu a type of powerful industrial or financial conglomerate that emerged in post–World War II Japan following the abolition of the *zaibatsu*.

khanates Mongol kingdoms, in particular the subdivisions of Genghis Khan's empire ruled by his heirs.

kokutai the core ideology of the Japanese state, particularly during the Meiji Restoration, stressing the uniqueness of the Japanese system and the supreme authority of the emperor.

kolkhoz a collective farm in the Soviet Union, in which the great bulk of the land was held and worked communally. Between 1928 and 1934, some 26 million family farms were reconfigured into 250,000 kolkhozes.

kowtow the ritual of prostration and touching the forehead to the ground, demanded of all foreign ambassadors to the Chinese court as a symbol of submission.

kshatriya originally, the warrior class of Aryan society in India; ranked below (sometimes equal to) *brahmins*; in modern times often government workers or soldiers.

laissez-faire French for "leave it alone." An economic doctrine that holds that an economy is best served when the government does not interfere but allows the economy to self-regulate according to the forces of supply and demand.

latifundia large landed estates in the Roman Empire (singular: *latifundium*).

lay investiture the practice in which a layperson chose a bishop and invested him with the symbols of both his temporal office and his spiritual office; led to the Investiture Controversy, which was ended by compromise in the Concordat of Worms in 1122.

Lebensraum "living space"; the doctrine, adopted by Hitler, that a nation's power depends on the amount of land it occupies. Thus, a nation must expand to be strong.

Legalism a Chinese philosophy that argued that human beings were by nature evil and would follow the correct path only if coerced by harsh laws and stiff punishments. Adopted as official ideology by the Qin dynasty, it was later rejected but remained influential.

legitimacy the idea that after the Napoleonic wars, peace could best be reestablished in Europe by restoring legitimate monarchs who would preserve traditional institutions; guided Metternich at the Congress of Vienna.

Leninism Lenin's revision of Marxism that held that Russia need not experience a bourgeois revolution before it could move toward socialism.

liberal arts the seven areas of study that formed the basis of education in medieval and early modern Europe; consisted of grammar, rhetoric, and dialectic or logic (the *trivium*) and arithmetic, geometry, astronomy, and music (the *quadrivium*).

liberalism an ideology based on the belief that people should be as free from restraint as possible. Economic liberalism is the idea that the government should not interfere in the workings of the economy. Political liberalism is the idea that there should be restraints on the exercise of power so that people can enjoy basic civil rights in a constitutional state with a representative assembly.

limited liability the principle that shareholders in a joint-stock corporation can be held responsible for the corporation's debts only up to the amount they have invested.

limited (constitutional) monarchy a system of government in which the monarch is limited by a representative assembly and by the duty to rule in accordance with the laws of the land.

lineage group the descendants of a common ancestor; relatives, often as opposed to immediate family.

Longshan a Neolithic society from near the Yellow River in China, sometimes identified by its black pottery.

maharaja originally, a king in the Aryan society of early India (a great raja); later used more generally to denote an important ruler.

Mahayana a school of Buddhism that promotes the idea of universal salvation through the intercession of bodhisattvas; predominant in north Asia.

majlis a council of elders among the Bedouins of the Roman era.

Malayo-Polynesian a family of languages whose speakers originated on Taiwan or in southeastern China and spread from there to the Malay peninsula, the Indonesian archipelago, and many islands of the South Pacific.

mandate of Heaven the justification for the rule of the Zhou dynasty in China. The king was charged to maintain order as a representative of Heaven, which was viewed as an impersonal law of nature.

mandates a system established after World War I whereby a nation officially administered a territory (mandate) on behalf of the League of Nations. Thus, France administered Lebanon and Syria as mandates, and Britain administered Iraq and Palestine.

Manichaeanism an offshoot of the ancient Zoroastrian religion that was later influenced by Christianity; became popular in central Asia in the eighth century C.E.

manor an agricultural estate operated by a lord and worked by peasants who performed labor services and paid various rents and fees to the lord in exchange for protection and sustenance.

mansa in the West African state of Mali, a chieftain who served as both religious and administrative leader and was responsible for forwarding tax revenues from the village to higher levels of government.

Marshall Plan the European Recovery Program, under which the United States provided financial aid to European countries to help them rebuild after World War II.

Marxism the political, economic, and social theories of Karl Marx, which included the idea that history is the story of class struggle and that ultimately the proletariat will overthrow the bourgeoisie and establish a dictatorship en route to a classless society.

mass education a state-run educational system, usually free of charge and compulsory, that aims to ensure that all children in society have at least a basic education.

mass leisure forms of leisure that appeal to large numbers of people in a society, including the working classes; emerged at the end of the nineteenth century to provide workers with amusements after work and on weekends; used during the twentieth century by totalitarian states to control their populations.

mass politics a political order characterized by mass political parties and universal male and (eventually) female suffrage.

mass society a society in which the concerns of the majority—the lower classes—play a prominent role; characterized by extension of voting rights, an improved standard of living for the lower classes, and mass education.

materialism the belief that everything mental, spiritual, or ideal is an outgrowth of physical forces and that truth is found in concrete material existence, not through feeling or intuition.

matrilinear passing through the female line—for example, from a father to his sister's son rather than his own—as practiced in some African societies; not necessarily or even usually combined with matriarchy, in which women rule.

megaliths large stones, widely used in Europe from around 4000 to 1500 B.C.E. to create monuments, including sophisticated astronomical observatories.

Meiji Restoration   the period during the late nineteenth and early twentieth centuries when fundamental economic and cultural changes occurred in Japan, tranforming it from a feudal and agrarian society to an industrial and technological one.

mercantilism   an economic theory that held that a nation's prosperity depended on its supply of gold and silver and that the total volume of trade is unchangeable; therefore advocated that the government play an active role in the economy by encouraging exports and discouraging imports, especially through the use of tariffs.

Mesoamerica   the region stretching roughly from modern central Mexico to Honduras, in which the Olmec, Maya, Aztec, and other civilizations developed.

Mesolithic Age   the period from 10,000 to 7000 B.C.E., characterized by a gradual transition from a food-gathering and hunting economy to a food-producing economy.

mestizos   the offspring of intermarriage between Europeans, originally Spaniards, and native American Indians.

Middle Passage   the journey of slaves from Africa to the Americas as the middle leg of the triangular trade.

Middle Path   a central concept of Buddhism, which advocates avoiding extremes of both materialism and asceticism; also known as the Eightfold Way.

mihrab   the niche in a mosque's wall that indicates the direction of Mecca, usually containing an ornately decorated panel representing Allah.

militarism   a policy of aggressive military preparedness; in particular, the large armies based on mass conscription and complex, inflexible plans for mobilization that most European nations had before World War I.

millet   an administrative unit in the Ottoman Empire used to organize religious groups.

ministerial responsibility   a tenet of nineteenth-century liberalism that held that ministers of the monarch should be responsible to the legislative assembly rather than to the monarch.

MITI   the Ministry of International Trade and Industry in Japan; responsible for formulating and directing much of Japanese industrial policy after World War II.

Modernism   the artistic and literary styles that emerged in the decades before 1914 as artists rebelled against traditional efforts to portray reality as accurately as possible (leading to Impressionism and Cubism) and writers explored new forms.

monasticism   a movement that began in early Christianity whose purpose was to create communities of men and women who practiced a communal life dedicated to God as a moral example to the world around them.

monk   a man who chooses to live a communal life divorced from the world in order to dedicate himself totally to the will of God.

monotheism   having only one god; the doctrine or belief that there is only one god.

muezzin   the man who calls Muslims to prayer at the appointed times; nowadays often a tape-recorded message played over loudspeakers.

mulattoes   the offspring of Africans and Europeans, particularly in Latin America.

multiculturalism   a term referring to the connection of several cultural or ethnic groups within a society.

multinational corporation   a company with divisions in more than two countries.

mutual deterrence   the belief that nuclear war could best be prevented if both the United States and the Soviet Union had sufficient nuclear weapons so that even if one nation launched a preemptive first strike, the other could respond and devastate the attacker.

mystery religions   religions that involve initiation into secret rites that promise intense emotional involvement with spiritual forces and a greater chance of individual immortality.

nationalism   a sense of national consciousness based on awareness of being part of a community—a "nation"—that has common institutions, traditions, language, and customs and that becomes the focus of the individual's primary political loyalty.

nationalization   the process of converting a business or industry from private ownership to government control and ownership.

nation in arms   the people's army raised by universal mobilization to repel the foreign enemies of the French Revolution.

nation-state   a form of political organization in which a relatively homogeneous people inhabits a sovereign state, as opposed to a state containing people of several nationalities.

NATO   the North Atlantic Treaty Organization; a military alliance formed in 1949 in which the signatories (Belgium, Canada, Denmark, France, Great Britain, Iceland, Italy, Luxembourg, the Netherlands, Norway, Portugal, and the United States) agreed to provide mutual assistance if any one of them was attacked; later expanded to include other nations, including former members of the Warsaw Pact—Poland, the Czech Republic, and Hungary.

natural law   a body of laws or specific principles held to be derived from nature and binding on all human society even in the absence of positive laws.

natural rights   certain inalienable rights to which all people are entitled. They include the right to life, liberty, and ownership of property; freedom of speech and religion; and equal treatment under the law.

natural selection   Darwin's idea that organisms that are most adaptable to their environment survive and pass on the variations that enabled them to survive while less adaptable organisms become extinct; known by the shorthand expression "survival of the fittest."

Nazi New Order   the Nazis' plan for their conquered territories; included the extermination of Jews and others considered inferior, ruthless exploitation of resources, German colonization in the east, and the use of Poles, Russians, and Ukrainians as slave labor.

neocolonialism   the use of economic rather than political or military means to maintain Western domination of developing nations.

Neo-Confucianism   the dominant ideology of China during the second millennium C.E.; combined the metaphysical speculations of Buddhism and Daoism with the pragmatic Confucian approach to society, maintaining that the world is real, not illusory, and that fulfillment comes from participation, not withdrawal. It encouraged an intellectual environment that valued continuity over change and tradition over innovation.

Neolithic Revolution   the development of agriculture, including the planting of food crops and the domestication of farm animals, around 10,000 B.C.E.

new course   a short-lived, liberalizing change in Soviet policy toward eastern European allies instituted after Stalin's death in 1953.

New Culture Movement   a protest launched by students at Beijing University after the failure of the 1911 revolution; aimed at abolishing the remnants of the old system and introducing Western values and institutions into China.

New Deal   the reform program implemented by President Franklin Roosevelt in the 1930s, which included large public works projects and the introduction of Social Security.

New Democracy   the initial program of the Chinese Communist government, from 1949 to 1955, focusing on honest government, land reform, social justice, and peace rather than on the utopian goal of a classless society.

New Economic Policy   a modified version of the old capitalist system introduced in the Soviet Union by Lenin in 1921 to revive the economy after the ravages of the civil war and war communism.

new imperialism   the revival of imperialism after 1880 in which European nations established colonies throughout much of Asia and Africa.

new monarchies   the governments of France, England, and Spain at the end of the fifteenth century, where the rulers were successful in reestablishing or extending centralized royal authority, suppressing the nobility, controlling the church, and insisting on the loyalty of all peoples living in their territories.

Nirvana   in Buddhist thought, enlightenment, the ultimate transcendence from the illusion of the material world; release from the "wheel of life."

Nok culture   in northern Nigeria, one of the most active early iron-working societies in Africa, artifacts from which date back as far as 500 B.C.E.

Nonaligned Movement   an organization of neutralist nations established in the 1950s to provide a counterpoise between the socialist bloc, headed by the Soviet Union, and the capitalist nations led by the United States. Chief sponsors of the movement were Jawaharlal Nehru of India, Gamal Abdul Nasser of Egypt, and Sukarno of Indonesia.

noncentralized societies   societies characterized by autonomous villages organized by clans and ruled by a local chieftain or clan head; typical of the southern half of the African continent before the eleventh century C.E.

nongovernmental organizations (NGOs)   organizations that have no government ties and work to address world problems.

northern Renaissance humanism   *see* Christian humanism.

nuclear family   a family group consisting only of father, mother, and children.

nun   a woman who withdraws from the world and joins a religious community; the female equivalent of a monk.

old regime/old order   the political and social system of France in the eighteenth century before the Revolution.

oligarchy   rule by a few.

Open Door Notes   a series of letters sent in 1899 by U.S. Secretary of State John Hay to Great Britain, France, Germany, Italy, Japan, and Russia, calling for equal economic access to the China market for all states and for the maintenance of the territorial and administrative integrity of the Chinese Empire.

opium trade   the sale of the addictive product of the poppy, specifically by British traders to China in the 1830s. Chinese attempts to prevent it led to the Opium War of 1839–1842, which resulted in British access to Chinese ports.

orders/estates   the traditional tripartite division of European society based on heredity and quality rather than wealth or economic standing, first established in the Middle Ages and continuing into the eighteenth century; traditionally consisted of those who pray (the clergy), those who fight (the nobility), and those who work (all the rest).

organic evolution   Darwin's principle that all plants and animals have evolved over a long period of time from earlier and simpler forms of life.

Organization of African Unity   an organization founded in Addis Ababa in 1963 to represent the interests of all the newly independent countries of Africa and provide a forum for the discussion of common problems; replaced by the African Union in 2001.

Oriental despotism   a theory identified with the Sinologist Karl Wittfogel that traditional societies organized on the basis of large-scale irrigation networks—many of them in eastern Asia—often possessed tendencies to create autocratic political systems.

Paleolithic Age   the period of human history when humans used simple stone tools (c. 2,500,000–10,000 B.C.E.).

pan-Africanism   the concept of African continental unity and solidarity in which the common interests of African countries transcend regional boundaries.

pan-Arabism   a movement promoted by Egyptian president Gamal Abdul Nasser and other Middle Eastern leaders to unify all Arab peoples in a single supra-national organization. After Nasser's death in 1971, the movement languished.

pantheism   a doctrine that equates God with the universe and all that is in it.

pariahs   members of the lowest level of traditional Indian society, technically outside the class system itself; also known as untouchables.

pasha   an administrative official of the Ottoman Empire, responsible for collecting taxes and maintaining order in the provinces. Some eventually became hereditary rulers.

paterfamilias   the dominant male in a Roman family whose powers over his wife and children were theoretically unlimited, though they were sometimes circumvented in practice.

patriarchal family   a family in which the man (husband and father) dominates his wife and children.

patriarchy   a society in which the father is supreme in the clan or family; more generally, a society dominated by men.

patricians   great landowners who became the ruling class in the Roman Republic; in early modern Europe, a term used to identify the ruling elites of cities.

patrilinear   passing through the male line, from father to son; often combined with patriarchy.

patronage   the practice of awarding titles and making appointments to government and other positions to gain political support.

Pax Romana   "Roman peace"; the stability and prosperity that Roman rule brought to the Mediterranean world and much of western Europe during the first and second centuries C.E.

peaceful coexistence   the policy adopted by the Soviet Union under Nikita Khrushchev in 1955 and continued by his successors that called for economic and ideological rivalry with the West rather than nuclear war.

peon   in Latin America, a peasant permanently dependent on the landowners.

people's democracies   a term invented by the Soviet Union to define a society in the early stage of socialist transition; applied to Eastern European countries in the 1950s.

perestroika   "restructuring"; the term applied to Mikhail Gorbachev's economic, political, and social reforms in the Soviet Union.

permissive society   a characterization of Western society after World War II to reflect its sexual freedom and the emergence of the drug culture.

Petrine supremacy   the doctrine that the bishop of Rome, the pope, as the successor of Saint Peter (traditionally considered the first bishop of Rome), should hold a preeminent position in the church.

phalanx   a rectangular formation of tightly massed infantry soldiers.

pharaoh   the most common title used for Egyptian kings. Pharaohs possessed absolute power and were seen as divine.

philosophes   intellectuals of the eighteenth-century Enlightenment who believed in applying a spirit of rational criticism to all things, including religion and politics, and who focused on improving and enjoying this world rather than on the afterlife.

plebeians   the class of Roman citizens who included nonpatrician landowners, craftspeople, merchants, and small farmers in the Roman Republic. Their struggle for equal rights with the patricians dominated much of the Republic's history.

pogroms   organized massacres of Jews.

polis   an ancient Greek city-state encompassing both an urban area and its surrounding countryside; a small but autonomous political unit where all major political and social activities were carried out in a central location (plural: *poleis*).

political democracy   a form of government characterized by universal suffrage and mass political parties.

polygyny   the practice of having more than one wife at a time.

polytheism   having many gods; belief in or the worship of more than one god.

popular culture   as opposed to high culture, the unofficial written and unwritten culture of the masses, much of which was passed down orally; centered on public and group activities such as festivals. In the twentieth century, the entertainment, recreation, and pleasures that people purchase as part of mass consumer society.

popular sovereignty   the doctrine that government is created by and subject to the will of the people, who are the source of all political power.

portolani   charts of landmasses and coastlines made by navigators and mathematicians in the thirteenth and fourteenth centuries.

Post-Impressionism   an artistic movement that began in France in the 1880s. Post-Impressionists sought to use color and line to express inner feelings and produce a personal statement of reality.

Postmodernism   a term used to cover a variety of artistic and intellectual styles and ways of thinking prominent since the 1970s.

poststructuralism (deconstruction)   a theory formulated by Jacques Derrida in the 1960s, holding that there is no fixed, universal truth because culture is created and can therefore be analyzed in various ways.

praetorian guard the military unit that served as the personal body-guard of the Roman emperors.

praetors the two senior Roman judges, who had executive author-ity when the consuls were away from the city and could also lead armies.

Prakrit an ancient Indian language, a simplified form of Sanskrit.

predestination the belief, associated with Calvinism, that God, as a consequence of his foreknowledge of all events, has predetermined who will be saved (the elect) and who will be damned.

price revolution the dramatic rise in prices (inflation) that occurred throughout Europe in the sixteenth and early seventeenth centuries.

primogeniture an inheritance practice in which the eldest son re-ceives all or the largest share of the parents' estate.

principate the form of government established by Augustus for the Roman Empire; continued the constitutional forms of the Republic and consisted of the *princeps* ("first citizen") and the senate, although the *princeps* was clearly the dominant partner.

proletariat the industrial working class; in Marxism, the class that will ultimately overthrow the bourgeoisie.

Protestant Reformation the western European religious reform movement in the sixteenth century that divided Christianity into Catholic and Protestant groups.

psychoanalysis a method developed by Sigmund Freud to resolve a patient's psychic conflict.

pueblo a three-story adobe communal house with a timbered roof. Pueblos were constructed by the Ancient Pueblo people in what is now the southwestern United States starting around the ninth cen-tury C.E.

Pueblo Bonito a large settlement built by the Ancient Pueblo people in what is now New Mexico in the ninth century C.E. It contained sev-eral hundred compounds housing several thousand residents.

puja in India, a populist tradition focused on personal worship that began to replace the Brahmanical emphasis on court sacrifice and asceticism during the early centuries of the first millennium C.E.; an aspect of the transition from Brahmanism to Hinduism.

purdah the Indian term for the practice among Muslims and some Hindus of isolating women and preventing them from associating with men outside the home.

Pure Land a Buddhist sect, originally Chinese but later popular in Japan, that taught that devotion alone could lead to enlightenment and release.

Puritans English Protestants inspired by Calvinist theology who wished to remove all traces of Catholicism from the Church of England.

quipu an Inka record-keeping system that used knotted strings rather than writing.

raj the British colonial regime in India.

raja originally, a chieftain in the Aryan society of early India, a repre-sentative of the gods; later used more generally to denote a ruler.

Ramadan the holy month of Islam, during which believers fast from dawn to sunset. Because the Islamic calendar is lunar, Ramadan mi-grates through the seasons.

rationalism a system of thought based on the belief that human rea-son and experience are the chief sources of knowledge.

Realism in medieval Europe, the school of thought that, following Plato, held that the individual objects we perceive are not real but merely manifestations of universal ideas existing in the mind of God. In the nineteenth century, a school of painting that emphasized the everyday life of ordinary people, depicted with photographic realism.

Realpolitik "politics of reality"; politics based on practical concerns rather than theory or ethics.

reason of state the principle that a nation should act on the basis of its long-term interests and not merely to further the dynastic interests of its ruling family.

reincarnation the idea that the individual soul is reborn in a different form after death. In Hindu and Buddhist thought, release from this cycle is the objective of all living souls.

relativity theory Einstein's theory that holds, among other things, that space and time are not absolute but are relative to the observer and interwoven into a four-dimensional space-time continuum and that matter is a form of energy, expressed by the equation $E = mc^2$.

relics the bones of Christian saints or objects intimately associated with saints that were considered worthy of veneration.

Renaissance the "rebirth" of Classical culture that occurred in Italy between c. 1350 and c. 1550; also, the earlier revivals of Classical cul-ture that occurred under Charlemagne and in the twelfth century.

Renaissance humanism an intellectual movement in Renaissance Italy based on the study of the Greek and Roman classics.

rentier a person who lives on income from property and is not person-ally involved in its operation.

reparations payments made by a defeated nation after a war to com-pensate another nation for damage sustained as a result of the war; required from Germany after World War I.

revisionism a socialist doctrine that rejected Marx's emphasis on class struggle and revolution and argued instead that workers should work through political parties to bring about gradual change.

revolution a fundamental change in the political and social organiza-tion of a state.

revolutionary socialism the socialist doctrine espoused by Georges Sorel, who held that violent action was the only way to achieve the goals of socialism.

rhetoric the art of persuasive speaking; in the Middle Ages, one of the seven liberal arts.

Rococo a style, especially of decoration and architecture, that devel-oped from the Baroque and spread throughout Europe by the 1730s. Though still elaborate, it emphasized curves, lightness, and charm in the pursuit of pleasure, happiness, and love.

Romanesque a term used to describe the art and especially architec-ture of Europe in the eleventh and twelfth centuries.

Romanticism a nineteenth-century intellectual and artistic movement that rejected the emphasis on reason of the Enlightenment. Instead, Romantics stressed the importance of intuition, feeling, emotion, and imagination as sources of knowing.

ronin Japanese warriors made unemployed by developments in the early modern era, since samurai were forbidden by tradition to en-gage in commerce.

rural responsibility system post-Maoist land reform in China, under which collectives leased land to peasant families, who could consume or sell their surplus production and keep the profits.

sacraments rites considered imperative for a Christian's salvation. By the thirteenth century, they consisted of the Eucharist or Lord's Supper, baptism, marriage, penance, extreme unction, holy orders, and confirmation of children; Protestant reformers of the sixteenth century generally recognized only two—baptism and communion (the Lord's Supper).

sakoku during the Tokugawa shogunate in Japan, the policy of closing the country to foreign trade with Europe and encouraging domestic production of goods that had previously been imported.

samurai literally, "retainers"; similar to European knights. Usually in service to a particular shogun, these Japanese warriors lived by a strict code of ethics and duty.

Sanskrit an early Indo-European language, in which the Vedas were composed, beginning in the second millennium B.C.E. It survived as the language of literature and the bureaucracy in India for centuries after its decline as a spoken tongue.

sans-culottes the common people who did not wear the fine clothes of the upper classes (*sans-culottes* means "without breeches") and played an important role in the radical phase of the French Revolution.

sati the Hindu ritual requiring a wife to throw herself on her de-ceased husband's funeral pyre.

satori enlightenment, in the Japanese (especially Zen) Buddhist tradition.

satrap a governor with both civil and military duties in the ancient Persian Empire, which was divided into satrapies, or provinces, each administered by a satrap.

satrapy one of the provinces of the ancient Persian Empire, each ruled by a satrap.

satyagraha the Hindi term for the practice of nonviolent resistance, as advocated by Mohandas Gandhi; literally, "hold fast to the truth."

scholar-gentry in Song dynasty China, candidates who passed the civil service examinations and whose families were nonaristocratic landowners; eventually, a majority of the bureaucracy.

scholasticism the philosophical and theological system of the medieval schools, which emphasized rigorous analysis of contradictory authorities; often used to try to reconcile faith and reason.

School of Mind a philosophy espoused by Wang Yangming during the mid-Ming era of China, which argued that mind and the universe were a single unit and knowledge was therefore obtained through internal self-searching rather than through investigation of the outside world; for a while, a significant but unofficial rival to Neo-Confucianism.

scientific method a method of seeking knowledge through inductive principles; uses experiments and observations to develop generalizations.

Scientific Revolution the transition from the medieval worldview to a largely secular, rational, and materialistic perspective; began in the seventeenth century and was popularized in the eighteenth.

secularization the process of becoming more concerned with material, worldly, temporal things and less with spiritual and religious things.

self-determination the doctrine that the people of a given territory or a particular nationality should have the right to determine their own government and political future.

self-strengthening a late-nineteenth-century Chinese policy under which Western technology would be adopted while Confucian principles and institutions were maintained intact.

senate the leading council of the Roman Republic; composed of about three hundred men (senators) who served for life and dominated much of the political life of the Republic.

separation of powers a doctrine enunciated by Montesquieu in the eighteenth century that separate executive, legislative, and judicial powers serve to limit and control each other.

sepoys local troops who formed the basis of the British Indian Army; hired by the East India Company to protect British interests in South Asia.

serf a peasant who is bound to the land and obliged to provide labor services and pay various rents and fees to the lord; considered unfree but not a slave because serfs could not be bought and sold.

Shari'a a law code, originally drawn up by Muslim scholars shortly after the death of Muhammad, that provides believers with a set of prescriptions to regulate their daily lives.

sheikh originally, the ruler of a Bedouin tribe; later, also used as a more general honorific.

Shi'ite the second largest tradition of Islam, which split from the majority Sunni soon after the death of Muhammad in a disagreement over his succession; especially significant in Iran and Iraq.

Shinto a kind of state religion in Japan, derived from beliefs in nature spirits and until recently linked with belief in the divinity of the emperor and the sacredness of the Japanese nation.

shogun a powerful Japanese leader, originally military, who ruled under the titular authority of the emperor.

shogunate system the system of government in Japan in which the emperor exercised only titular authority while the shoguns (regional military dictators) exercised actual political power.

Sikhism a religion, founded in the early sixteenth century in the Punjab, that began as an attempt to reconcile the Hindu and Muslim traditions and developed into a significant alternative to both.

sipahis in the Ottoman Empire, local cavalry elites who held fiefdoms and collected taxes.

Slavophiles in the nineteenth century, Russian intellectuals who believed that Russia's tsarist system, peasant villages, and Orthodox religious faith were superior to any Western ideals.

social Darwinism the application of Darwin's principle of organic evolution to the social order; led to the belief that progress comes from the struggle for survival as the fittest advance and the weak decline.

socialism an ideology that calls for collective or government ownership of the means of production and the distribution of goods.

socialized medicine health services for all citizens provided by government assistance.

social security government programs that provide social welfare measures such as old-age pensions and sickness, accident, and disability insurance.

Socratic method a form of teaching that uses a question-and-answer format to enable students to reach conclusions by using their own reasoning.

Sophists wandering scholars and professional teachers in ancient Greece who stressed the importance of rhetoric and tended toward skepticism and relativism.

soviets councils of workers' and soldiers' deputies formed throughout Russia in 1917; played an important role in the Bolshevik Revolution.

sphere of influence a territory or region over which an outside nation exercises political or economic influence.

squadristi in Italy in the 1920s, bands of armed Fascists used to create disorder by attacking socialist offices and newspapers.

Star Wars nickname of the Strategic Defense Initiative, proposed by President Reagan, which was intended to provide a shield that would destroy any incoming missiles; named after a popular science-fiction movie series.

State Confucianism the integration of Confucian doctrine with Legalist practice under the Han dynasty in China; became the basis of Chinese political thought until the modern era.

stateless societies the pre-Columbian communities in much of the Americas that developed substantial cultures without formal nation-states.

Stoicism a philosophy founded by Zeno in the fourth century B.C.E. that taught that happiness could be obtained by accepting one's lot and living in harmony with the will of God, thereby achieving inner peace.

stupa originally, a stone tower holding relics of the Buddha; more generally, a place for devotion, often architecturally impressive and surmounted with a spire.

subinfeudation the practice in which a lord's greatest vassals subdivided their fiefs and had vassals of their own, and those vassals in turn subdivided their fiefs and so on down to simple knights, whose fiefs were too small to subdivide.

Sublime Porte the office of the grand vizier in the Ottoman Empire.

sudras the classes that represented the great bulk of the Indian population from ancient times, mostly peasants, artisans, or manual laborers; ranked below *brahmins, kshatriyas,* and *vaisyas* but above the pariahs.

suffrage the right to vote.

suffragists those who advocate the extension of the right to vote (suffrage), especially to women.

Sufism a mystical school of Islam, noted for its music, dance, and poetry, which became prominent in about the thirteenth century.

sultan "holder of power"; a title commonly used by Muslim rulers in the Ottoman Empire, Egypt, and elsewhere; still in use in parts of Asia, sometimes for regional authorities.

Sunni the largest tradition of Islam, from which the Shi'ites split soon after the death of Muhammad in a disagreement over his succession.

Supreme Ultimate according to Neo-Confucianists, a transcendent world distinct from the material world in which humans live but to which humans may aspire; a set of abstract principles, roughly equivalent to the Dao.

Surrealism an artistic movement that arose between World War I and World War II. Surrealists portrayed recognizable objects in unrecognizable relationships in order to reveal the world of the unconscious.

Swahili a mixed African-Arabian culture that developed by the twelfth century along the east coast of Africa; also, the national language of Kenya and Tanzania.

syncretism the combining of different forms of belief or practice, as when two gods are regarded as different forms of the same underlying divine force and are fused together.

Taika reforms the seventh-century "great change" reforms that established the centralized Japanese state.

taille a French tax on land or property, developed by King Louis XI in the fifteenth century as the financial basis of the monarchy. It was largely paid by the peasantry; the nobility and the clergy were exempt.

Taisho democracy the era of the 1920s in Japan when universal (male) suffrage was instituted, political parties expanded, and other democratic institutions appeared to flourish. The process of democratization proved fragile, however, and failed to continue into the 1930s.

Tantrism a mystical Buddhist sect that emphasized the importance of magical symbols and ritual in seeking a path to enlightenment.

tariffs duties (taxes) imposed on imported goods; usually imposed both to raise revenue and to discourage imports and protect domestic industries.

theocracy a government based on a divine authority.

Theravada a school of Buddhism that stresses personal behavior and the quest for understanding as a means of release from the wheel of life, rather than the intercession of bodhisattvas; predominant in Sri Lanka and Southeast Asia.

three-field system in medieval agriculture, the practice of dividing the arable land into three fields so that one could lie fallow while the other two were planted in winter grains and spring crops.

three kingdoms Koguryo, Paekche, and Silla, rivals but all under varying degrees of Chinese influence, which together controlled virtually all of Korea from the fourth to the seventh centuries.

three obediences the traditional duties of Japanese women, in permanent subservience: child to father, wife to husband, and widow to son.

three people's principles the three principles on which the program of Sun Yat-sen's Revolutionary Alliance (Tongmenghui) was based: nationalism (meaning primarily the elimination of Manchu rule over China), democracy, and people's livelihood.

tithe a tenth of one's harvest or income; paid by medieval peasants to the village church.

Tongmenghui the political organization—Revolutionary Alliance—formed by Sun Yat-sen in 1905, which united various revolutionary factions and ultimately toppled the Manchu dynasty.

totalitarian state a state characterized by government control over all aspects of economic, social, political, cultural, and intellectual life; subordination of the individual to the state; and insistence that the masses be actively involved in the regime's goals.

total war warfare in which all of a nation's resources, including civilians at home and soldiers in the field, are mobilized for the war effort.

tozama **daimyo** during the Tokugawa shogunate in Japan, the larger, more independent lords who were usually more distant from the center of shogunate power in Edo; literally, "outside daimyo."

trade union an association of workers in the same trade, formed to help members secure better wages, benefits, and working conditions.

transnational corporation another term for a "multinational corporation," or a company with divisions in more than two countries.

trench warfare warfare in which the opposing forces attack and counterattack from a relatively permanent system of trenches protected by barbed wire; characteristic of World War I.

tribunes of the plebs beginning in 494 B.C.E., Roman officials who were given the power to protect plebeians against arrest by patrician magistrates.

tribute system an important element of Chinese foreign policy under which neighboring states paid for the privilege of access to Chinese markets, received legitimation, and agreed not to harbor enemies of the Chinese Empire.

Truman Doctrine the doctrine, enunciated by Harry Truman in 1947, that the United States would provide economic aid to countries that were threatened by Communist expansion.

twice-born the males of the higher castes in traditional Indian society, who underwent an initiation ceremony at puberty.

tyranny rule by a tyrant.

tyrant in an ancient Greek *polis* (or an Italian city-state during the Renaissance), a ruler who came to power in an unconstitutional way and ruled without being subject to the law.

uhuru "freedom" in Swahili, a key slogan in African independence movements, especially in Kenya.

uji a clan in early Japanese tribal society.

ulama a convocation of leading Muslim scholars, the earliest of which shortly after the death of Muhammad drew up the *Shari'a*, a law code based largely on the Qur'an and the sayings of the Prophet, to provide believers with a set of prescriptions to regulate their daily lives.

umma the Muslim community as a whole.

uncertainty principle a principle in quantum mechanics, posited by Heisenberg, that holds that one cannot determine the path of an electron because the very act of observing the electron would affect its location.

unconditional surrender complete, unqualified surrender of a nation.

uninterrupted revolution the goal of the Great Proletarian Cultural Revolution launched by Mao Zedong in 1966.

utopian socialists intellectuals and theorists in the early nineteenth century who favored equality in social and economic conditions and wished to replace private property and competition with collective ownership and cooperation; deemed impractical and "utopian" by later socialists.

vaisya the third-ranked class in traditional Indian society, usually merchants.

varna Indian classes or castes. *See also* caste system.

vassal a person granted a fief, or landed estate, in exchange for providing military services to the lord and fulfilling certain other obligations such as appearing at the lord's court when summoned and making a payment on the knighting of the lord's eldest son.

veneration of ancestors the extension of filial piety to include care for the deceased, for instance, by burning replicas of useful objects to accompany them on their journey to the next world.

vernacular the everyday language of a region, as distinguished from a language used for special purposes. For example, in medieval Paris, French was the vernacular, but Latin was used for academic writing and for classes at the University of Paris.

vezir *see* vizier.

viceroy the administrative head of the provinces of New Spain and Peru in the Americas.

Vietnam syndrome the presumption, from the 1970s on, that the U.S. public would object to a protracted military entanglement abroad, such as another Vietnam-type conflict.

vizier the prime minister in the Abbasid caliphate and elsewhere, a chief minister.

war communism Lenin's policy of nationalizing industrial and other facilities and requisitioning the peasants' produce during the civil war in Russia.

War Guilt Clause the clause in the Treaty of Versailles that declared Germany (and Austria) responsible for starting World War I and ordered Germany to pay reparations for the damage the Allies had suffered as a result of the war.

Warsaw Pact a military alliance, formed in 1955, in which Albania, Bulgaria, Czechoslovakia, East Germany, Hungary, Poland, Romania, and the Soviet Union agreed to provide mutual assistance. After it was dissolved in 1991, most former members eventually joined NATO.

welfare state   a social and political system in which the government assumes primary responsibility for the social welfare of its citizens by providing such things as social security, unemployment benefits, and health care.

well-field system   the theoretical pattern of land ownership in early China, named for the appearance of the Chinese character for "well," in which farmland was divided into nine segments and a peasant family would cultivate one for its own use and cooperate with seven others to cultivate the ninth for the landlord.

wergeld   "money for a man"; in early Germanic law, a person's value in monetary terms, which was paid by a wrongdoer to the family of the person who had been injured or killed.

White Lotus   a Chinese Buddhist sect, founded in 1133 C.E., that sought political reform; in 1796–1804, a Chinese peasant revolt.

Westernizers   in the nineteenth century, Russian intellectuals who believed that Western ways were the solution to Russia's problems.

women's liberation movement   the struggle for equal rights for women, which has deep roots in history but achieved new prominence under this name in the 1960s, building on the work of, among others, Simone de Beauvoir and Betty Friedan.

world-machine   Newton's conception of the universe as one huge, regulated, and uniform machine that operated according to natural laws in absolute time, space, and motion.

yangban   the aristocratic class in Korea. During the Yi dynasty, entry into the bureaucracy was limited to members of this class.

Yangshao   a Neolithic society from near the Yellow River in China, sometimes identified by its painted pottery.

Young Turks   a successful Turkish reformist group in the late nineteenth and early twentieth centuries.

zaibatsu   powerful business cartels formed in Japan during the Meiji era and outlawed following World War II.

zamindars   Indian tax collectors who were assigned land from which they kept part of the revenue. The British revived the system in a misguided attempt to create a landed gentry.

Zen   (in Chinese, Chan or Ch'an) a school of Buddhism particularly important in Japan, some of whose adherents stress that enlightenment (*satori*) can be achieved suddenly, though others emphasize lengthy meditation.

ziggurat   a massive stepped tower on which a temple dedicated to the chief god or goddess of a Sumerian city was built.

Zionism   an international movement that called for the establishment of a Jewish state or a refuge for Jews in Palestine.

Zoroastrianism   a religion founded by the Persian Zoroaster in the seventh century B.C.E., characterized by worship of a supreme god, Ahuramazda, who represents the good against the evil spirit, Ahriman.

MAP CREDITS

The authors wish to acknowledge their use of the following books as reference in preparing the maps listed here:

MAP 14.1 Geoffrey Barraclough, ed., *Times Atlas of World History* (Maplewood, N.J.: Hammond Inc., 1978), p. 160.

MAP 16.3 Geoffrey Barraclough, ed., *Times Atlas of World History* (Maplewood, N.J.: Hammond, Inc., 1978), p. 173.

MAP 17.1 Jonathan Spence, *The Search for Modern China* (New York: W. W. Norton, 1990), p. 19.

MAP 17.2 Conrad Schirokauer, *A Brief History of Chinese and Japanese Civilizations,* 2nd ed. (San Diego: Harcourt Brace Jovanovich, 1989), p. 330.

MAP 17.3 John K. Fairbank, Edwin O. Reischauer, and Albert M. Craig, *East Asia: Tradition and Transformation* (Boston: Houghton Mifflin, 1973), pp. 402–403.

MAP 18.1 *Atlas of World History* (New York: Harper & Row Publishers, 1987), p. 187.

MAP 21.1 Geoffrey Barraclough, ed., *Times Atlas of World History* (Maplewood, N.J.: Hammond, Inc., 1978), p. 235.

MAP 22.2 John K. Fairbank, Edwin O. Reischauer, and Albert M. Craig, *East Asia: Tradition and Transformation* (Boston: Houghton Mifflin, 1973), p. 451.

MAP 22.4 Geoffrey Barraclough, ed., *Times Atlas of World History* (Maplewood, N.J.: Hammond, Inc., 1978), p. 243.

CHAPTER NOTES

CHAPTER 14

1. From *A Journal of the First Voyage of Vasco da Gama* (London, 1898), cited in J. H. Parry, *The European Reconnaissance: Selected Documents* (New York, 1968), p. 82.
2. H. J. Benda and J. A. Larkin, eds., *The World of Southeast Asia: Selected Historical Readings* (New York, 1967), p. 13.
3. Parry, *European Reconnaissance*, quoting from A. Cortesão, *The Summa Oriental of Tomé Pires* (London, 1944), vol. 2, pp. 283, 287.
4. Quoted in J. H. Parry, *The Age of Reconnaissance: Discovery, Exploration, and Settlement, 1450 to 1650* (New York, 1963), p. 33.
5. Quoted in R. B. Reed, "The Expansion of Europe," in R. DeMolen, ed., *The Meaning of the Renaissance and Reformation* (Boston, 1974), p. 308.
6. K. N. Chaudhuri, *Trade and Civilization in the Indian Ocean: An Economic History from the Rise of Islam to 1750* (Cambridge, 1985), p. 65.
7. Quoted in Parry, *Age of Reconnaissance*, pp. 176–177.
8. Quoted in M. Leon-Portilla, ed., *The Broken Spears: The Aztec Account of the Conquest of Mexico* (Boston, 1969), p. 51.

CHAPTER 15

1. N. Machiavelli, *The Prince*, trans. D. Wootton (Indianapolis, Ind., 1995), p. 48.
2. Quoted in R. Bainton, *Here I Stand: A Life of Martin Luther* (New York, 1950), p. 144.
3. J. Calvin, *Institutes of the Christian Religion*, trans. J. Allen (Philadelphia, 1936), vol. 1, p. 228; vol. 2, p. 181.
4. Quoted in B. S. Anderson and J. P. Zinsser, *A History of Their Own: Women in Europe from Prehistory to the Present* (New York, 1988), vol. 1, p. 259.
5. Quoted in J. O'Malley, *The First Jesuits* (Cambridge, Mass., 1993), p. 76.
6. Quoted in J. Klaits, *Servants of Satan: The Age of Witch Hunts* (Bloomington, Ind., 1985), p. 68.

CHAPTER 16

1. Cited in Christophe Courau, "Turquie: Sublime Porte de l'Europe," in *Historia* (October 2005), p. 15.
2. Quoted in V. A. Smith, *The Oxford History of India* (Oxford, 1967), p. 341.
3. Quoted in M. Edwardes, *A History of India: From the Earliest Times to the Present Day* (London, 1961), p. 188.
4. Quoted in ibid., p. 220.
5. Quoted in R. C. Craven, *Indian Art: A Concise History* (New York, 1976), p. 205.

CHAPTER 17

1. J. D. Spence, *Emperor of China: Self-Portrait of K'ang Hsi* (New York, 1974), pp. 143–144.
2. Quoted in R. Strassberg, *The World of K'ang Shang-jen: A Man of Letters in Early Ch'ing China* (New York, 1983), p. 275.

3. Quoted in F. Wakeman Jr., *The Great Enterprise: The Manchu Reconstruction of Imperial Order in Seventeenth-Century China* (Berkeley, Calif., 1985), p. 16.
4. L. Struve, *The Southern Ming, 1644–1662* (New Haven, Conn., 1984), p. 61.
5. J. L. Cranmer-Byng, *An Embassy to China: Lord Macartney's Journal, 1793–1794* (London, 1912), p. 340.
6. Quoted in D. J. Boorstin, *The Discoverers: A History of Man's Search to Know His World and Himself* (New York, 1983), p. 63.
7. Quoted in C. R. Boxer, ed., *South China in the Sixteenth Century* (London, 1953), p. 265.
8. Quoted in C. Nakane and S. Oishi, eds., *Tokugawa Japan* (Tokyo, 1990), p. 14.
9. Quoted in J. Elisonas, "Christianity and the Daimyo," in J. W. Hall, ed., *The Cambridge History of Japan*, vol. 4 (Cambridge, 1991), p. 360.
10. E. Kaempfer, *The History of Japan: Together with a Description of the Kingdom of Siam, 1690–1692*, vol. 2 (Glasgow, 1906), pp. 173–174.
11. Quoted in J. H. Parry, *European Reconnaissance: Selected Documents* (New York, 1968), p. 144.
12. Quoted in D. Keene, *The Japanese Discovery of Europe, 1720–1830*, rev. ed. (Stanford, Calif., 1969), p. 114.

CHAPTER 18

1. R. Descartes, *Philosophical Writing*, ed. and trans. N. K. Smith (New York, 1958), pp. 118–119.
2. J. Locke, *An Essay Concerning Human Understanding* (New York, 1964), pp. 89–90.
3. Quoted in P. Burke, *Popular Culture in Early Modern Europe*, rev. ed. (New York, 1994), p. 186.
4. Quoted in W. Doyle, *The Oxford History of the French Revolution* (Oxford, 1989), p. 184.
5. Quoted in L. Gershoy, *The Era of the French Revolution* (Princeton, N.J., 1957), p. 157.
6. Quoted in Doyle, *Oxford History*, p. 254.

CHAPTER 19

1. Quotations in E. R. Pike, *Human Documents of the Industrial Revolution in Britain* (London, 1966), pp. 314, 343.
2. Ibid., p. 315.
3. C. Dickens, *The Old Curiosity Shop* (New York, 2000), p. 340. Originally published in 1840–1841.
4. K. Marx and F. Engels, *The Communist Manifesto* (Harmondsworth, England, 1967), p. 80. Originally published in 1848.
5. Ibid., pp. 91, 94.
6. Quoted in L. L. Snyder, ed., *Documents of German History* (New Brunswick, N.J., 1958), p. 202.
7. Quoted in S. Galai, *The Liberation Movement in Russia, 1900–1905* (Cambridge, 1973), p. 26.

CHAPTER 20

1. Quoted in J. C. Chasteen, *Americanos: Latin America's Struggle for Independence* (Oxford, 2008), p. 122.
2. Quoted in H. Herring, *A History of Latin America* (New York, 1961), p. 255.
3. Quoted in P. Bakewell, *A History of Latin America* (Oxford, 1997), p. 367.
4. Quoted in M. C. Eakin, *The History of Latin America: Collision of Cultures* (New York, 2007), p. 188.
5. Quoted in Bakewell, *History of Latin America*, p. 372.
6. Quoted in E. B. Burns, *Latin America: A Concise Interpretive History*, 4th ed. (Englewood Cliffs, N.J., 1986), p. 116.
7. Quoted in N. Bullock and J. Read, *The Movement for Housing Reform in Germany and France, 1840–1914* (Cambridge, 1985), p. 42.
8. W. Wordsworth, "The Tables Turned," *Poems of Wordsworth*, ed. M. Arnold (London, 1963), p. 138.
9. Quoted in A. E. E. McKenzie, *The Major Achievements of Science* (New York, 1960), vol. 1, p. 310.
10. F. von Bernhardi, *Germany and the Next War*, trans. A. H. Powles (New York, 1914), pp. 18–19.
11. Quoted in J. Rewald, *History of Impressionism* (New York, 1961), pp. 456–458.
12. Quoted in A. Higonnet, *Berthe Morisot's Images of Women* (Cambridge, Mass., 1992), p. 19.

CHAPTER 21

1. Quoted in J. G. Lockhart and C. M. Wodehouse, *Rhodes* (London, 1963), pp. 69–70.
2. K. Pearson, *National Life from the Standpoint of Science* (London, 1905), p. 184.
3. Quoted in H. Braunschwig, *French Colonialism, 1871–1914* (London, 1961), p. 80.
4. Quoted in G. Garros, *Forceries Humaines* (Paris, 1926), p. 21.
5. Cited in B. Schwartz's review of D. Cannadine's *Ornamentalism: How the British Saw Their Empire,* in *The Atlantic,* November 2001, p. 135.
6. Quoted in R. Bartlett, ed., *The Record of American Diplomacy: Documents and Readings in the History of American Foreign Relations* (New York, 1952), p. 385.
7. Quoted in L. Roubaud, *Vietnam: La Tragédie Indochinoise* (Paris, 1926), p. 80.
8. Quoted in J. Iliffe, *Africans: The History of a Continent* (Cambridge, 1995), p. 124.
9. Quoted in T. Pakenham, *The Scramble for Africa* (New York, 1991), p. 13.
10. Quoted in ibid., p. 182, citing a letter to Queen Victoria dated August 7, 1879.
11. Quoted in P. C. W. Gutkind and I. Wallerstein, eds., *The Political Economy of Contemporary Africa* (Beverly Hills, Calif., 1976), p. 14.

CHAPTER 22

1. H. B. Morse, *The International Relations of the Chinese Empire* (London, 1910–1918), vol. 2, p. 622.
2. Quoted in S. Teng and J. K. Fairbank, eds., *China's Response to the West: A Documentary Survey, 1839–1923* (New York, 1970), p. 140.
3. Ibid., p. 167.
4. J. K. Fairbank, A. M. Craig, and E. O. Reischauer, *East Asia: Tradition and Transformation* (Boston, 1973), p. 514.

5. Quoted in J. W. Dower, ed., *The Origins of the Modern Japanese State: Selected Writings of E. H. Norman* (New York, 1975), p. 13.
6. C. Brinton, *The Anatomy of Revolution* (New York, 1965), quoted in W. G. Beasley, *The Meiji Restoration* (Stanford, Calif., 1972), p. 423.

CHAPTER 23

1. A. Toynbee, *Surviving the Future* (New York, 1971), pp. 106–107.
2. Quoted in J. Remak, "1914–The Third Balkan War: Origin Reconsidered," *Journal of Modern History* 43 (1971): 364–365.
3. Quoted in J. M. Winter, *The Experience of World War I* (New York, 1989), p. 142.
4. Quoted in Hew Strachan, *The First World War* (New York, 2004), pp. 94–95.
5. Quoted in ibid., p. 72.
6. Quoted in C. W. Reilly, ed., *Scars upon My Heart: Women's Poetry and Verse of the First World War* (London, 1981), p. 90.
7. Quoted in W. M. Mandel, *Soviet Women* (Garden City, N.Y., 1975), p. 43.
8. Quoted in M. D. Steinberg, *Voices of Revolution, 1917* (New Haven, Conn., 2001), p. 55.
9. Quoted in S. Audoin-Rouzeau and A. Becker, *14–18: Understanding the Great War*, trans. C. Temerson (New York, 2002), p. 212.
10. Quoted in ibid., p. 213.
11. Quoted in ibid., p. 41.
12. Quoted in R. Paxton, *Europe in the Twentieth Century,* 2nd ed. (San Diego, Calif., 1985), p. 237.
13. Quoted in I. Howe, ed., *The Basic Writings of Trotsky* (London, 1963), p. 162.

CHAPTER 24

1. Speech delivered in London, September 1931, while attending the first Roundtable Conference.
2. V. I. Lenin, "The Awakening of Asia," in *The Awakening of Asia: Selected Essays* (New York, 1963–1968), p. 22.
3. Ts'ai Yüan-p'ei, "Ta Lin Ch'in-nan Han," in *Ts'ai Yüan-p'ei Hsiensheng Ch'uan-chi* [Collected Works of Mr. Cai Yuanpei] (Taipei, 1968), pp. 1057–1058.
4. Quoted in N. R. Clifford, *Spoilt Children of Empire: Westerners in Shanghai and the Chinese Revolution of the 1920s* (Hanover, N.H., 1991), p. 93.
5. Quoted in W. T. de Bary et al., eds., *Sources of Chinese Tradition* (New York, 1963), p. 783.
6. Lu Xun, "Diary of a Madman," in *Selected Works of Lu Hsun* (Beijing, 1957), vol. 1, p. 20.

CHAPTER 25

1. B. Mussolini, "The Doctrine of Fascism," in A. Lyttleton, ed., *Italian Fascisms from Pareto to Gentile* (London, 1973), p. 42.
2. Quoted in A. De Grand, "Women Under Italian Fascism," *Historical Journal* 19 (1976): 958–959.
3. Quoted in J. J. Spielvogel and D. Redles, *Hitler and Nazi Germany: A History*, 6th ed. (Upper Saddle River, N.J., 2010), p. 60.
4. Quoted in J. Fest, *Hitler*, trans. R. Winston and C. Winston (New York, 1974), p. 418.
5. Quoted in S. Fitzpatrick, *Everyday Stalinism—Ordinary Life in Extraordinary Times: Soviet Russia in the 1930s* (New York, 1999), p. 87.
6. A. Hitler, *Mein Kampf*, trans. R. Manheim (Boston, 1971), p. 654.
7. *Documents on German Foreign Policy* (London, 1956), Series D, vol. 7, p. 204.

8. Memorandum by John Van Antwerp MacMurray, quoted in A. Waldron, *How the Peace Was Lost: The 1935 Memorandum* (Stanford, Calif., 1992), p. 5.

9. Quoted in W. Murray and A. R. Millett, *A War to Be Won: Fighting the Second World War* (Cambridge, Mass., 2000), p. 137.

10. Quoted in A. Speer, *Spandau*, trans. R. Winston and C. Winston (New York, 1976), p. 50.

11. *Nazi Conspiracy and Aggression* (Washington, D.C., 1946), vol. 6, p. 262.

12. International Military Tribunal, *Trial of the Major War Criminals* (Nuremberg, 1947–1949), vol. 22, p. 480.

13. Quoted in R. Hilberg, *The Destruction of the European Jews*, rev. ed. (New York, 1985), vol. 1, pp. 332–333.

14. *Nazi Conspiracy and Aggression*, vol. 6, p. 789.

15. Quoted in J. Campbell, *The Experience of World War II* (New York, 1989), p. 170.

16. Quoted in C. Koonz, "Mothers in the Fatherland: Women in Nazi Germany," in R. Bridenthal and C. Koonz, eds., *Becoming Visible: Women in European History* (Boston, 1977), p. 466.

17. Quoted in Campbell, *Experience of World War II*, p. 143.

18. Quoted in N. Graebner, *Cold War Diplomacy, 1945–1960* (Princeton, N.J., 1962), p. 117.

19. Ibid.

20. Quoted in W. Loth, *The Division of the World, 1941–1955* (New York, 1988), p. 81.

CHAPTER 26

1. Quoted in *Department of State Bulletin*, February 11, 1945, pp. 213–216.

2. Quoted in J. M. Jones, *The Fifteen Weeks (February 21–June 5, 1947)*, 2nd ed. (New York, 1964), pp. 140–141.

3. Quoted in W. Laqueur, *Europe in Our Time* (New York, 1992), p. 111.

4. Quoted in W. Loth, *The Division of the World, 1941–1955* (New York, 1988), pp. 160–161.

CHAPTER 27

1. Quoted in V. Zubok and C. Pleshakov, *Inside the Kremlin's Cold War: From Stalin to Khrushchev* (Cambridge, Mass., 1996), p. 166.

2. N. Khrushchev, *Khrushchev Remembers*, trans. S. Talbott (Boston, 1970), p. 77.

3. Quoted in H. Smith, *The New Russians* (New York, 1990), p. 30.

4. Quoted in F. B. Tipton and R. Aldrich, *An Economic and Social History of Europe from 1939 to the Present* (Baltimore, 1987), p. 193.

5. Quoted in Smith, *New Russians*, p. 74.

6. "Report on an Investigation of the Peasant Movement in Hunan (March 1927)," in *Quotations from Chairman Mao Tse-tung* (Beijing, 1976), p. 12.

7. Quoted in S. Karnow, *Mao and China: Inside China's Cultural Revolution* (New York, 1972), p. 95.

8. Quoted from an article by Mao in the journal *Red Flag* (June 1, 1958), in S. R. Schram, *The Political Thought of Mao Tse-tung* (New York, 1963), p. 253.

9. Liang Heng and J. Shapiro, *Son of the Revolution* (New York, 1983).

10. Quoted in J. Spence, *Chinese Roundabout: Essays in History and Culture* (New York, 1992), p. 285.

CHAPTER 28

1. Quoted in W. I. Hitchcock, *The Struggle for Europe: The Turbulent History of a Divided Continent, 1945–2002* (New York, 2003), pp. 399–400.

2. D. D. Eisenhower, *The White House Years: Waging Peace, 1956–1961* (Garden City, N.Y., 1965), p. 533.

3. Quoted in T. Judt, *Postwar: A History of Europe Since 1945* (New York, 2005), p. 390.

4. Quoted in H. Scott, *Sweden's "Right to Be Human"—Sex-Role Equality: The Goal and the Reality* (London, 1982), p. 125.

5. Quoted in M. Rowe et al., *Spare Rib Reader* (Harmondsworth, England, 1982), p. 574.

6. Quoted in R. Bridenthal, "Women in the New Europe," in R. Bridenthal, S. M. Stuard, and M. E. Wiesner, eds., *Becoming Visible: Women in European History*, 3rd ed. (Boston, 1998), pp. 564–565.

7. Quoted in Joan W. Scott, *The Politics of the Veil* (Princeton, N.J., 2009), p. 1.

8. Quoted in H. Grosshans, *The Search for Modern Europe* (Boston, 1970), p. 421.

9. Quoted in R. Maltby, ed., *Passing Parade: A History of Popular Culture in the Twentieth Century* (New York, 1989), p. 11.

CHAPTER 29

1. Quoted in G.-C. M. Mutiso, *Socio-Political Thought in African Literature* (New York, 1974), p. 117.

2. A. Ojuka, "Pedestrian, to Passing Benz-Man," quoted in A. Roscoe, *Uhuru's Fire: African Literature East to South* (Cambridge, 1977), p. 103.

3. Cited in M. Meredith, *The Fate of Africa* (New York, 2004), p. 168.

4. A. Nicol, *"A Truly Married Woman" and Other Stories* (London, 1965), p. 12.

5. A. Ata Aidoo, *No Sweetness Here* (New York, 1995), p. 136.

6. G. Médioni, "Stand Up, Africa!" *World Press Review*, July 2002, p. 34.

7. Ngugi Wa Thiong'o, *Decolonising the Mind: The Politics of Language in African Literature* (Portsmouth, N.H., 1986), p. 103.

8. Quoted in R. R. Andersen, R. F. Seibert, and J. G. Wagner, *Politics and Change in the Middle East: Sources of Conflict and Accommodation*, 4th ed. (Englewood Cliffs, N.J., 1982), p. 51.

9. S. Sachs, "Assad Looks at Syria's Economy in Inaugural Talk," *New York Times*, July 18, 2000.

10. S. Azadi, with A. Ferrante, *Out of Iran* (London, 1987), p. 223.

CHAPTER 30

1. Quoted in W. I. Hitchcock, *The Struggle for Europe: The Turbulent History of a Divided Continent, 1945–2002* (New York, 2003), pp. 399–400.

2. Quoted in L. Collins and D. Lapierre, *Freedom at Midnight* (New York, 1975), p. 252.

3. Quoted in Somini Sengupta, "In World's Largest Democracy, Tolerance Is a Weak Pillar," *New York Times*, October 29, 2008.

4. From Pankaj Mishra, "Impasse in India," *New York Review of Books*, June 28, 2007, p. 51.

5. Quoted in N. Onishi, "Crime Rattles Japanese Calm, Attracting Politicians' Notice," *New York Times*, September 6, 2003.

6. Y. Mishima and G. Bownas, eds., *New Writing in Japan* (Harmondsworth, England, 1972), p. 16.

EPILOGUE

1. Quoted in J. N. Pieterse, *Globalization and Culture* (Lanham, Md., 2004), p. 49.

2. E. Boulding, *Women in the Twentieth Century World* (New York, 1977), pp. 187–188.

Deficit spending, 688
Degas, Edgar, 660
De Gaulle, Charles, 822, 858
De Gouges, Olympe, 528, 529
Dei-Anang, Michael Francis, 856
Deism, 513
"De-Khrushchevization," 794
De Klerk, Frederik W., 863
Delacroix, Eugène, 596, 598
Delft pottery, 492
Delhi, 461, 464, 614; Persian sack of, 470
Demian (Hesse), 693, 694
Democracy, 595; in Brazil, 838; in China, 807;
    Great Depression and, 697; in India, 893,
    895; in Japan, 715–716, 718; in Middle
    East, 881; in Southeast Asia, 617, 903–904;
    in South Korea, 919; in western Europe,
    568–569; after World War I, 697; before
    World War II, 726
Democracy Wall (China), 807
Democratic National Headquarters, break-in
    at, 832
Democratic Party (U.S.), 584, 585, 830
Democratic Progressive Party (DPP), in
    Taiwan, 919
Democratic Republic of the Congo, 858, 867
Democratic Republic of Vietnam. *See*
    North Vietnam
Democratic socialism, in India, 892–893
Demography, in Japan, 916
Demoiselles d'Avignon, Les (Picasso), 605, 692
Denazification policy, 754, 766
Deng Xiaoping (China), 783, 805, 806–807, 809,
    812, 923
Denmark, 737, 743–744, 766; European
    unification and, 828; German unification
    and, 564
Department stores, 554, 555
Dependency theory, 761
Depression. *See* Great Depression
Der Herz (Schwitters), 692
Derrida, Jacques, 849
Desai, Anita, 902
Desai, Kiran, 902
Descamisados (shirtless ones), 720
Descartes, René, 510–511
Descent of Man, The (Darwin), 598
Description of a Starry Raft (Ma Huan), 392
Desert. *See* Gobi Desert region; Sahara
    Desert region
Desertification, in Africa, 862
Deshima Island, Japan, Dutch in, 496
Destalinization policy, of Khrushchev, 793,
    794, 797
Détente, in Cold War, 785
Developed nations, 930
Developing nations, 930
Devil on the Cross (Ngugi), 871
Devshirme system, 456, 456, 458
Dewey, George, 616
Dewey, John, 708
Dhahran, 704
Dharmashastra, 466
Dias, Bartolomeu, 395, 396
Diayou Island, Japan, China, and, 810, 810
Dickens, Charles, 549, 599
Dictators and dictatorships: in Latin
    America, 583, 721, 836; in Middle East,
    881–882; in Soviet Union, 690–691.
    See also Authoritarianism
Dictatorship of the proletariat, 556–557
Diderot, Denis, 513–514, 523–524
Diem, Ngo Dinh, 780
Dien Bien Phu, Battle of, 773
Diet (food), 518. *See also* Food
Diet (assembly), in Japan, 654, 660–661, 732
Diet of Worms, 422

Digital age, 928–929
Ding Ling (China), 817
Diplomacy: in China, 485; Shidehara,
    717, 732
Directory (France), 533
Direct rule, 611; in French Africa, 628–629
Discourse on Method (Descartes), 510–511
*Discourse on the Origins of the Inequality of
    Mankind* (Rousseau), 515
Discrimination, against women in India, 901
Diseases: of African slaves, 408; in Americas,
    398–399, 403; in Columbian Exchange, 405.
    See also specific diseases
Displaced persons, 754
Disraeli, Benjamin, 566
Dissidents and dissent: in China, 807–808, 808,
    808–810; in Soviet Union, 775, 795, 800; in
    World War I, 666, 676
Diversity, in India, 903
Divine Faith (Mughal Empire), 465–466
Divine-right monarchy, 440, 443
Divinity, of Japanese emperor, 911
Divorce: in China, 814, 815; in France, 534;
    in Islam, 886; in Japan, 916; in Ottoman
    Empire, 458; in postwar West, 840;
    women's rights to, 592
Djibouti, 626
Doctor Zhivago (Pasternak), 797
Doll's House, A (Ibsen), 593–594, 713
Domains, in Japan, 496
Dome of the Rock, 878
Dominican Republic, U.S. military in, 583
Dominicans, 430, 483
Dominion of Canada, 588
Dona Barbara (Gallegos), 721
Donnersmarck, Florian Henckel von, 824
Don Segundo Sombra (Guiraldes), 721
Douhet, Giulio, 752
Douwes Dekker, Eduard, 618
Dowry, in India, 901, 902
Draft (military). *See* Conscription
Drama: in Japan, 500; Shakespeare and, 447
Dream of the Red Chamber, The, 491
Dresden, Germany, firebombing of, 753
Dreyfus, Alfred, 604
Dreyman, Georg, 824, 824
Drought, 929
Drugs: drug culture and, 840; Mexican cartels
    and, 839; Romantics and, 596
Dualism, Cartesian, 511
Dual Monarchy (Austria-Hungary), 568, 570
Dubai, 884
Dubcek, Alexander, 784
Du Bois, W. E. B., 684
Duchamp, Marcel, 692
Duma (Russia), 571, 678
Dunkirk, 737
Duong Thu Huong, 910
Dupleix, Joseph François, 471
Dutch: in Africa, 624; in China, 481; colonies
    of, 403–404, 617, 651, 903; exploration by,
    397–398; India and, 470, 471; Japan and,
    496, 502, 650; in North America, 520;
    realistic art by, 446; in South Africa, 406;
    Southeast Asia and, 413, 616; trade and, 518;
    and United Provinces of the Netherlands,
    434. *See also* Netherlands
Dutch East India Company (VOC), 398, 413,
    437, 617
Dutch East Indies, 616, 619; environment in, 651;
    independence in, 903; Japan and, 739, 749;
    nationalism in, 611, 697–698, 706; in World
    War II, 739. *See also* Indonesia
Dutch Republic, Belgium and, 560
Dutch West India Company, 403
Dyarchy, 483
Dylan, Bob, 841

Early modern era, 388
Earth: global unity and, 930. *See also*
    Astronomy; Universe
Earthquakes, in Japan, 717, 915
East Africa: Chinese voyages to, 388; Europeans
    in, 396, 412–413; German, 673, 674;
    Portugal in, 406; slavery and, 410, 620,
    623–624
East Asia: Australia, New Zealand, and, 922–923;
    in Cold War, 769; cultural factors in miracle
    in, 923; Japan and, 674, 912. *See also* New
    Order, in East Asia
East Berlin, 775. *See also* Berlin; East Germany
Eastern Europe: absolutism in, 441–442;
    Calvinism in, 430; Cold War and, 774–776,
    786; COMECON in, 766; after communism,
    786, 802–803, 825–828; culture in, 797–798;
    democracy in, 825–828; dissent in, 774;
    education in, 798; environment in, 846;
    independent states in, 802; industrialization
    in, 548; Jews in, 602, 745, 745–747; in 1948,
    763; old order in, 569–570; Postmodernism
    in, 849–850, 850; religion in, 775; serfs in,
    520; Slavic peoples of, 733, 744, 747–748;
    social changes in, 798–799; Soviet Union
    and, 760, 763, 786, 791–792, 792; after
    World War II, 763, 763, 791
"Eastern Question," 562, 563
"East for Essence, West for Practical Use," 641
East Germany, 766, 798, 824, 846; Communist
    control in, 766, 776, 785; industry
    in, 766; reunification and, 803, 823.
    See also Germany
East India Company. *See* British East India
    Company; Dutch East India Company
East Indies. *See* Dutch East Indies
Eastman, George, 602
East Pakistan, 894, 895. *See also* Bangladesh
East Timor, independence of, 907
Eber, Nandor, 565
Ebert, Friedrich, 682
Echeverría, Luis (Mexico), 839
Ecology. *See* Environment
Economics: as motive for expansion, 609; Smith
    on, 514–515
Economy: in Africa, 761, 868; in Australia,
    922–923; in Brazil, 837–838; in Chile, 836;
    in China, 481, 486–489, 648–649, 812–813;
    colonialism and, 651; in East Asia, 923; in
    Eastern Europe, 826; in England, 566, 688,
    824–825; in Europe (17th century), 437;
    in Europe (18th century), 518; European
    expansion and, 393–394; in France, 526,
    688–689; in Germany, 687, 823; global,
    927–928; of Hong Kong, 921; in India,
    472–473, 474, 896–900; in Italy, 564; in
    Japan, 497, 716–717, 910–911, 912, 913,
    914–915; in Korea, 503; in Latin America,
    581, 582–583, 718–719, 833–834, 836,
    837–838; in Malacca, 391; in Mughal
    Empire, 466; in New Zealand, 922–923;
    in Russia after Soviet Union, 690; Safavid,
    462; in Singapore, 920; in Southeast Asia,
    418–419, 908; in South Korea, 918; in Soviet
    Union, 790, 791, 795–797; in Taiwan, 919;
    in United States, 690, 751, 829, 831; World
    War I and, 687; worldwide, 388, 554–555.
    See also Capitalism; Great Depression;
    Industrial Revolution
Ecstasy of Saint Theresa (Bernini), 446, 446
Ecuador, 578
Edict of Nantes, 434
Edirne (Adrianople), 459
Edison, Thomas, 553
Edo. *See* Tokyo
Education: in Africa, 868–869, 869; Buddhist, 415;
    in China, 649, 805, 812; in Cuba, 835;

and, 525; Napoleon and, 535; in New
World, 398–399, *399*; Philippines and,
609, 615; Roman Catholic Church in, 434;
Southeast Asia and, *616*. *See also* Americas;
Colonies and colonization
Spanish-American War, 583, 588
Spanish Civil War, 733
Spanish Empire, 400–403, *401*. *See also*
Americas; Spain
Spanish Netherlands, 434
Speech to the Constitutional Convention of
1856–1857 (Arriaga), 582
Speer, Albert, 751
Spengler, Oswald, 686
Spheres of influence: in Asia, 643, *643, 656,
656–657*; in Iran, 702
Spice Islands (Moluccas), 396, *397*, 437; Jesuits
in, 432
Spices and spice trade: European commerce and,
437; Islam and, 391; Portugal and, 396–397;
Southeast Asia and, 413–419, 618
Spinning jenny, 543
Spirit of the Laws, The (Montesquieu), 512
Spiritual life. *See* Religion
Sports, 596, 795, 798, 886
Spratly Islands, China and, 810, *810*
Sputnik, 851
Squadristi (Fascist bands), 727
Squadrons, 438
Square with White Border (Kandinsky), 605
Srebrenica, 826
Sri Lanka (Ceylon), *651*; British rule in, *614*; India
and, 894; political refugees from, 846
SS (Nazi guard squadrons), 729
Stalin, Joseph: China and, 770, *772*; Cold
War and, 766, 767; Iron Curtain and,
763; Khrushchev and, 793, 794, 797; mass
murder by, 731–732; at Potsdam, 755;
statues of, *775*; at Tehran, 754; Trotsky and,
691; after World War II, 763, 764; World
War II and, 749–750, 754–755, 768; at Yalta,
755, *755*, 762, *762*, 768
Stalingrad, battle at, 740, 741, 742, *742*
Stamp Act (1765), 521
Standard of living: industrialization and, 551–553;
in Southeast Asia, 418–419; in Taiwan, 919;
in West, 589
Standard Oil, in Middle East, 704
Standing army, 438–439. *See also* Military
Starry Messenger, The (Galileo), 509–510
Starry Night, The (van Gogh), *603*
Starvation, 930
Star Wars (Strategic Defense Initiative), 786, 803
Stasi (secret police), 785, 823
State (nation): church and, 430, 581; in Europe,
524–525, 568–572
State (U.S.), social conditions and, 587–588
State Peace and Development Council
(SPDC), 907
Steamboats, 547
Steam engine, 543–544, 616, 657
Steel and steel industry, 553, 688; in Latin
America, 720, 834; in United States, 587
Steppenwolf (Hesse), 693
Sterilization, in India, 896
Stock market, in United States (1929), 687
Stonebreakers, The (Courbet), 599, *599*
Stowe, Harriet Beecher, 618
Strait of Magellan, *397*
Strategic Arms Limitation Talks. *See* SALT I
and II
Strategic Defense Initiative (SDI). *See* Star Wars
Stream of consciousness technique, in arts, 693
Streltsy revolt, 443
Stresemann, Gustav, 687
Streusand, Douglas, 473
Struggle for the Banner (Siqueiros), 722

Strutt, Jedediah, 549
Stuart dynasty, in England, 442–444
Student protests: in France, 841; over Vietnam
War, 840, 841
Sturmabteilung (Storm Troops), 728
Sublime Porte (grand vizier), 458
Submarine warfare, in World War I, 674
Sub-Saharan Africa. *See* Africa
Subsistence farming, in Africa, 858
Sudan, 862, 930; European imperialism and, *621,
623, 626*; religious tensions in, 866
Sudetenland, 733–734, 754
Suez Canal, 621, *622, 623, 625*, 705, 738, 873, 874
Suffrage. *See* Universal male suffrage; Voting and
voting rights
Suffragists, 592
Sufism, 391, 457, 461
Sugar and sugar industry, 402, 407, *407, 521*,
622–623, 719, 834
Suharto (Indonesia), 905, 906–907
Suitable Boy, A (Seth), 900
Sukarno (Indonesia), 777, 903, 904–905, 908
Sukarnoputri, Megawati, 907
Sulawesi, 391, *907*
Suleyman I the Magnificent (Ottoman Turks),
450, 454, 455, 456, 458
Suleymaniye Mosque (Istanbul), 459, *460*
Sullivan, Louis H., 604–605
Sultan and sultanate, 451, 701; in Malay
peninsula, 415–418; Ottoman, 455–456, 458
Sumatra, 391, 413, 907
Sunday Battle, *625*
Sun Kings, in France and China, *441*
Sunni Muslims, 878; in Iraq, 704, *880*; Ottomans
as, 457
Sun Shines over the Sangan River, The (Ding
Ling), 817
Sun Tzu, *Art of War, The*, 453
Sun Yat-sen, 645–646, 648, 706, 707, 709, *710*
Suol Sleng prison, *909*
Superpowers, 791, 875; United States as,
829–832. *See also* Cold War; Soviet Union;
United States
Supreme Court (U.S.), 584; on election of
2000, 832
Surat, India, 398, 470
Surrealism, 660, 693, *693*, 722
Survival of the fittest, 598, 600
Suttner, Bertha von, 592
Suzuki Haranobu, *500*
Swahili coast, 620
Swahili culture, 412–413
Swan, Joseph, 553
Swaziland, 628
Sweden, *738*, 828, 840, 842, 846, 848; military
in, 438; Napoleon and, 535; Russian war
with, 442
Swiss Republic, 535
Switzerland, 846; Calvinism in, 430; Reformation
in, 427–429
Symbolists, 602, 660
Syncretism, in Mughal India, 473
Syria: France and, 686, *686*, 874; government
of, 881; Iraq and, 704; protests in, 881; in
United Arab Republic, 874–875

Tabriz, 461, 702
Tabula rasa (blank mind), Locke on, 511
Taille (French tax), 526
Taipei, 891, 919
Taiping Rebellion (China), 528, 622, 623, 640–641,
641, 650, 658
Taisho democracy, 715, 718
Taiwan, 482, 911, *919*; after Chiang Kai-shek,
783; Chinese reunification with, 919–920;
in Cold War, 768–771, 773, 778, 782;

Democracy Memorial Hall in, *920*; Japan
and, 656, *656*, 658, 912; as Little Tiger,
919–920; mainland China and, 919–920.
See also Nationalists (China)
Taj Mahal, 459, 469, 475, *476*
Taliban, in Afghanistan, 845, 852, 880–881, 895
Tamerlane, 451
Tamil languages, 476
Tamil rebels, 894
Tanganyika (Zanzibar, Tanzania), 626, 858
Tango, 720
Tanizaki, Junichiro, 716
Tanks, 675, 737, 742
Tannenberg, Battle of, 670, *671*
Tanzania, 412, 858, 859, 862–863
Tapioca, 412
Tariffs, 437; Japan and, 725–726
Taxation: of American colonies, 521; in China,
481, 483; in England, 825; in Japan, 654;
Ottoman, 457; by Turks, 455
Tea, 618; in China, *489*, 639, 712; in Japan,
651, 654
Teachers, 594
Team sports, 596
Technocratic society, 839
Technology: in China, 489, 648, 807; exploration
and, 388–389; in India, 894, 897;
industrialization and, 543–547; leisure
and, 596; in Ottoman Empire, 458;
Technological Revolution and, 852; Third
Wave, 852; urban, 589; after World War II,
850–851. *See also* Science(s)
Tehran, 702
Tehran Conference, 754, *792*
Telecommunications, 929
Telegraph, 614
Telephone, 553
Telescope, 512, *512*
Television, 798, 853
Temple Mount (Jerusalem), 877
Tenant farming, in Japan, 914
Tennyson, Alfred (Lord), 591
Tenochtitlán, 398, *417*
Territories, in Japan, 496
Terrorism: in Bali, 907; coalition against, 844; in
Europe, 844; in India, 894; Islamic, 844–845,
845, 875, 885; in Israel, 844, 875, 877;
Pakistan and, 895; in United States, 786,
787, 825, 832, 844–845, *845*, 852, 880–881
Textbooks, on Japan in World War II, 914
Textiles and textile industry: in Britain, 543–544,
545, 688; child labor in, 552; in China, 712,
813; in Europe, 518; in India, 473, 474,
548–549, 614, 615; industrialization and,
543–544, *545*; in Japan, 497, *545*, 655; in
Ottoman Empire, 459–460, *460*; Safavid,
462–463; workers in, 655. *See also* Cotton
and cotton industry; Silk and silk industry
Thailand, 415, 908; in ASEAN, 908; Ayuthaya
in, 391; borders of, 908; development in,
616; government in, 906; imperialism and,
610, *616*
Thakin, in Burma, 697, 698
Thatcher, Margaret, 825, *825*
Theater. *See* Drama
Theater of the Absurd, 848
Thein Sein (Burma), 907
Theravada Buddhism, 415
Thien Mu Pagoda (Hué), *505*
Things Fall Apart (Achebe), 861
Third Coalition, Napoleonic wars and, 535
Third Estate, 423–424, 526, 527, 528
Third Republic (France), 569
Third Wave, 852
Third World, 777, 786
Thirteenth Amendment (U.S.), 587
Thirty-Six Views of Mount Fuji (Hokusai), 502